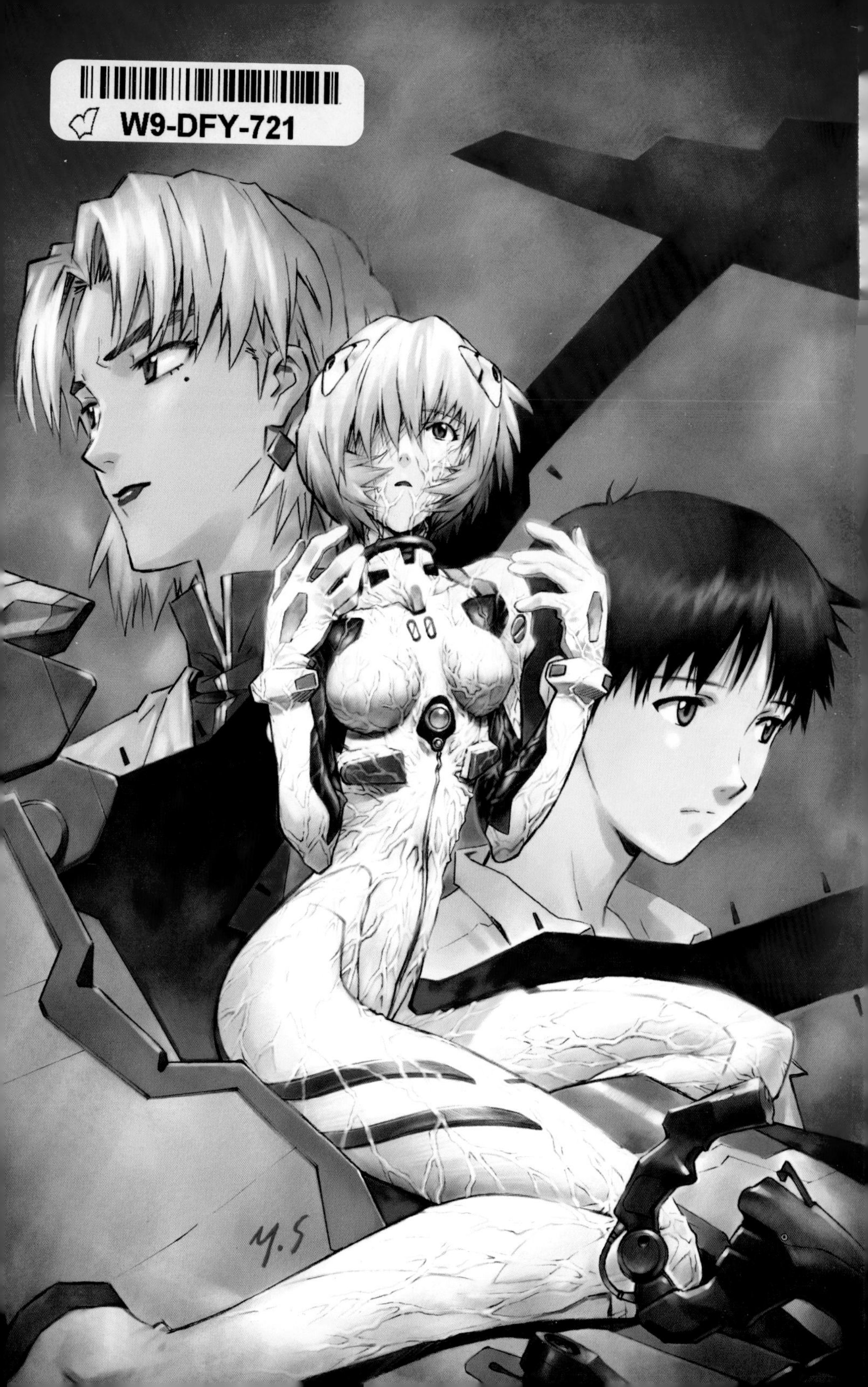
M.S

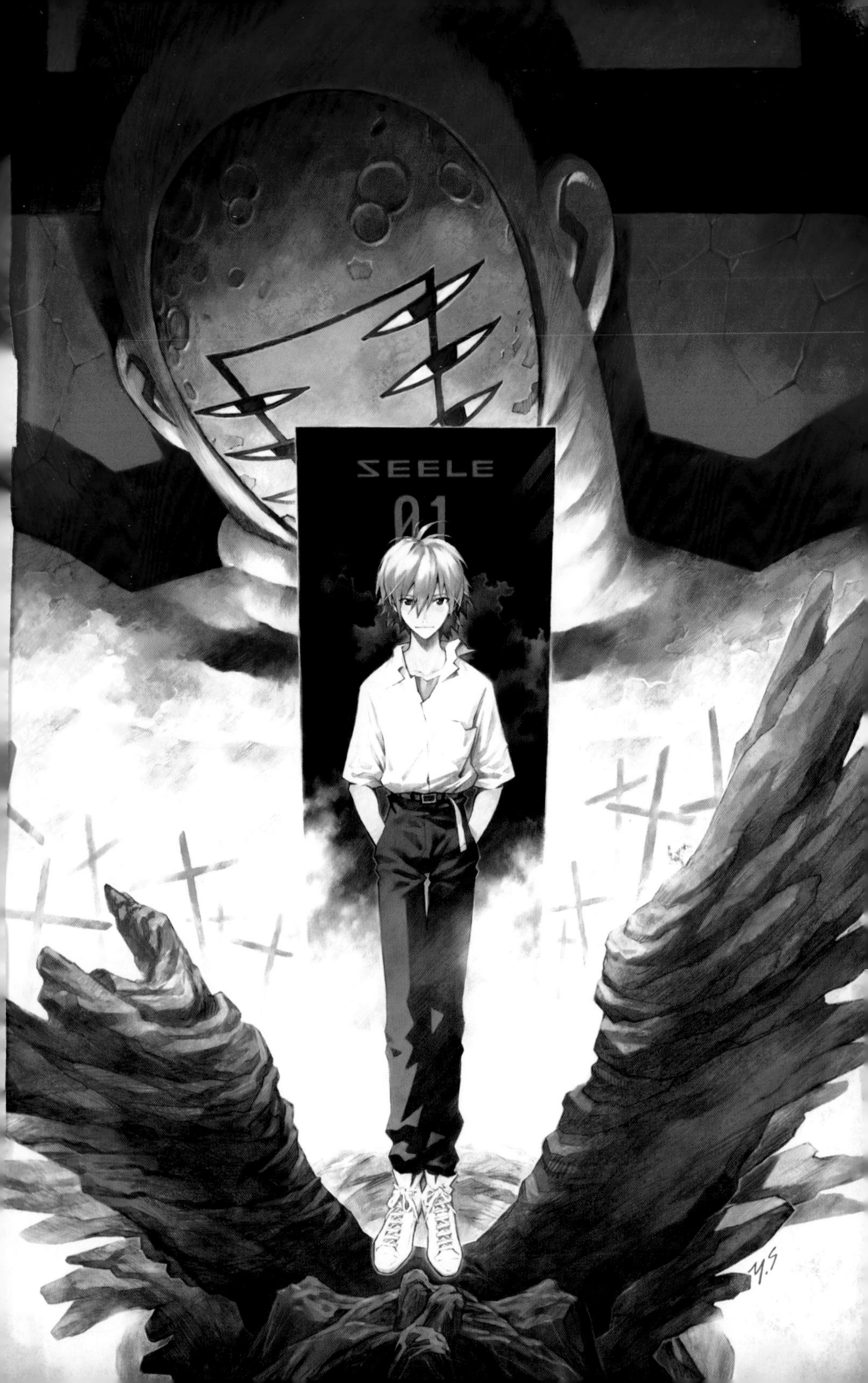
SEELE
01
Y.S

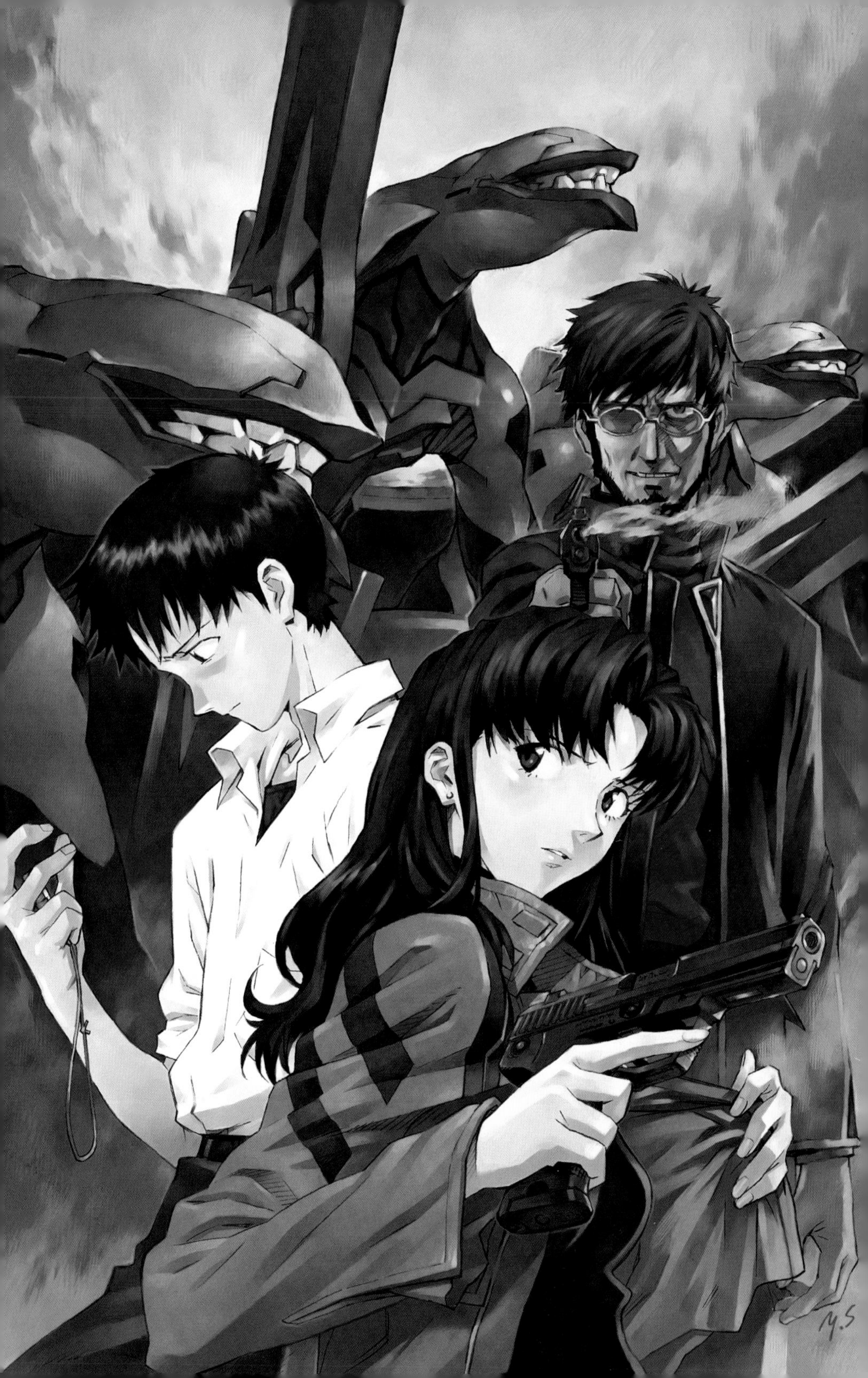
M.S

NEON GENESIS EVANGELION
3-in-1 Edition • Volume 4

STORY AND ART BY
YOSHIYUKI SADAMOTO

ORIGINAL CONCEPT BY
khara

TRANSLATION // Lillian Olsen
ENGLISH ADAPTATION AND ADDITIONAL MATERIAL // Fred Burke, Carl Gustav Horn
ADDITIONAL TRANSLATION // William Flanagan, David Ury
VIZ MEDIA EDITION LETTERING // Wayne Truman
VIZ MEDIA EDITION DESIGN // Ronnie Casson
VIZ MEDIA EDITION EDITORS // Megan Bates, Carl Gustav Horn
3-IN-1 EDITION DESIGNER // Fawn Lau
3-IN-1 EDITION EDITOR // Mike Montesa

NEON GENESIS EVANGELION Volume 10, 11 & 12
Illustration by YOSHIYUKI SADAMOTO © khara
Edited by KADOKAWA SHOTEN
First published in Japan in 2006, 2007, 2010 by KADOKAWA
CORPORATION, Tokyo. English translation rights arranged
with KADOKAWA CORPORATION, Tokyo.

The stories, characters and incidents mentioned in this
publication are entirely fictional.

Printed in China

Published by VIZ Media, LLC
P.O. Box 77010
San Francisco, CA 94107

10 9 8 7 6 5 4
First printing, August 2013
Fourth printing, December 2017

PARENTAL ADVISORY
NEON GENESIS EVANGELION is rated T+
for Older Teen and is recommended for ages
16 and up. It contains violence and mild nudity.
ratings.viz.com

www.viz.com

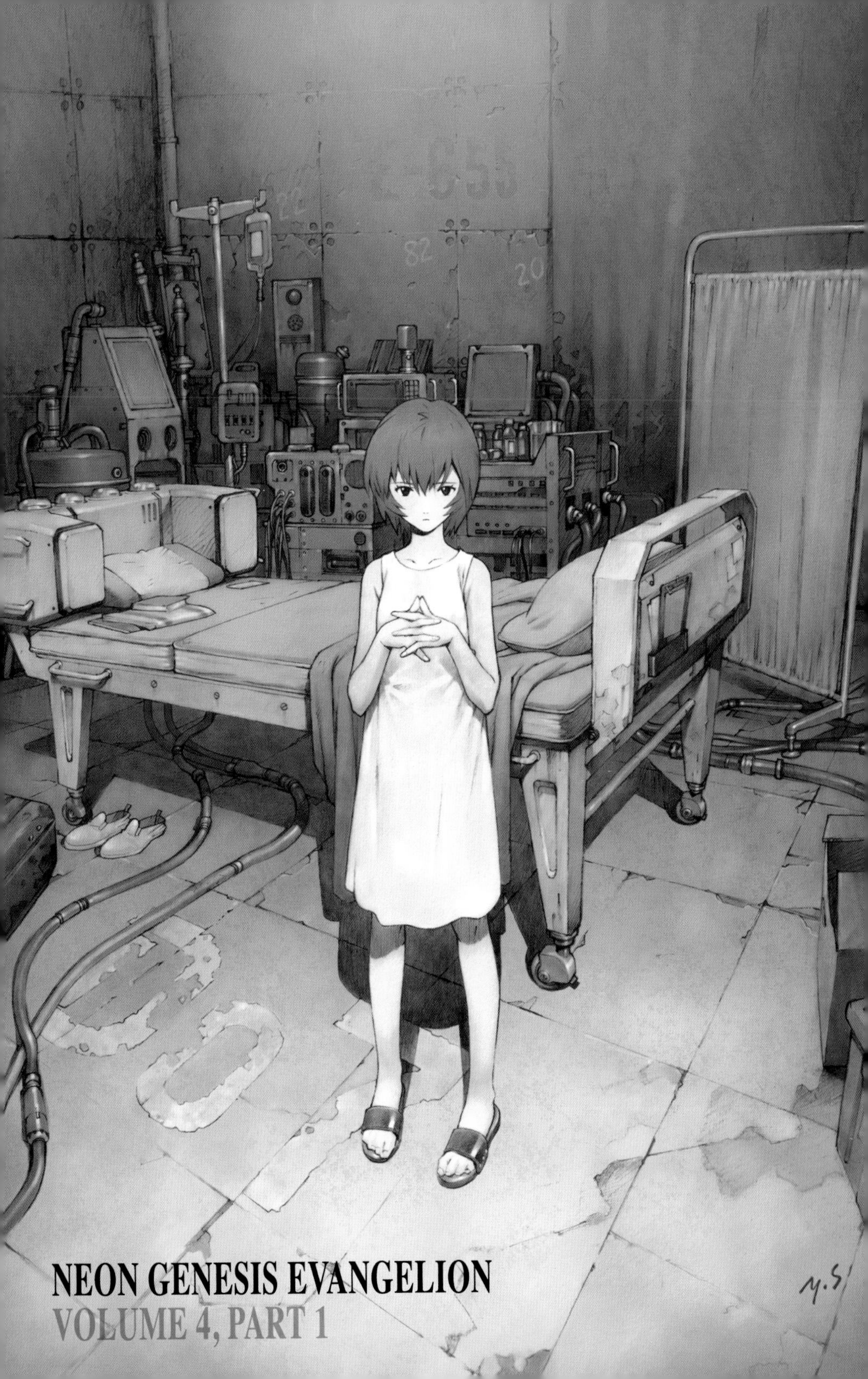
M.S

NEON GENESIS EVANGELION
VOLUME 4, PART 1

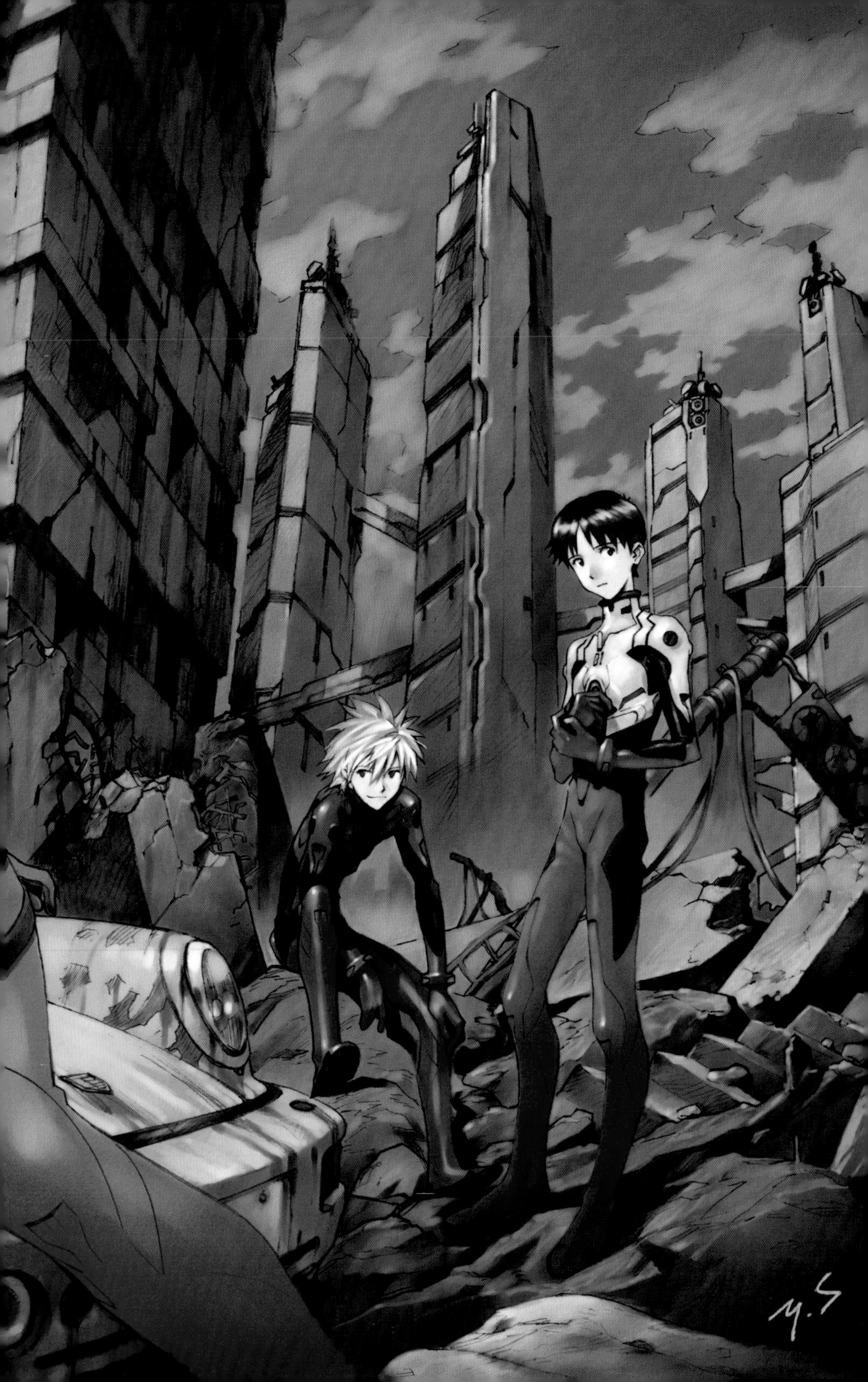

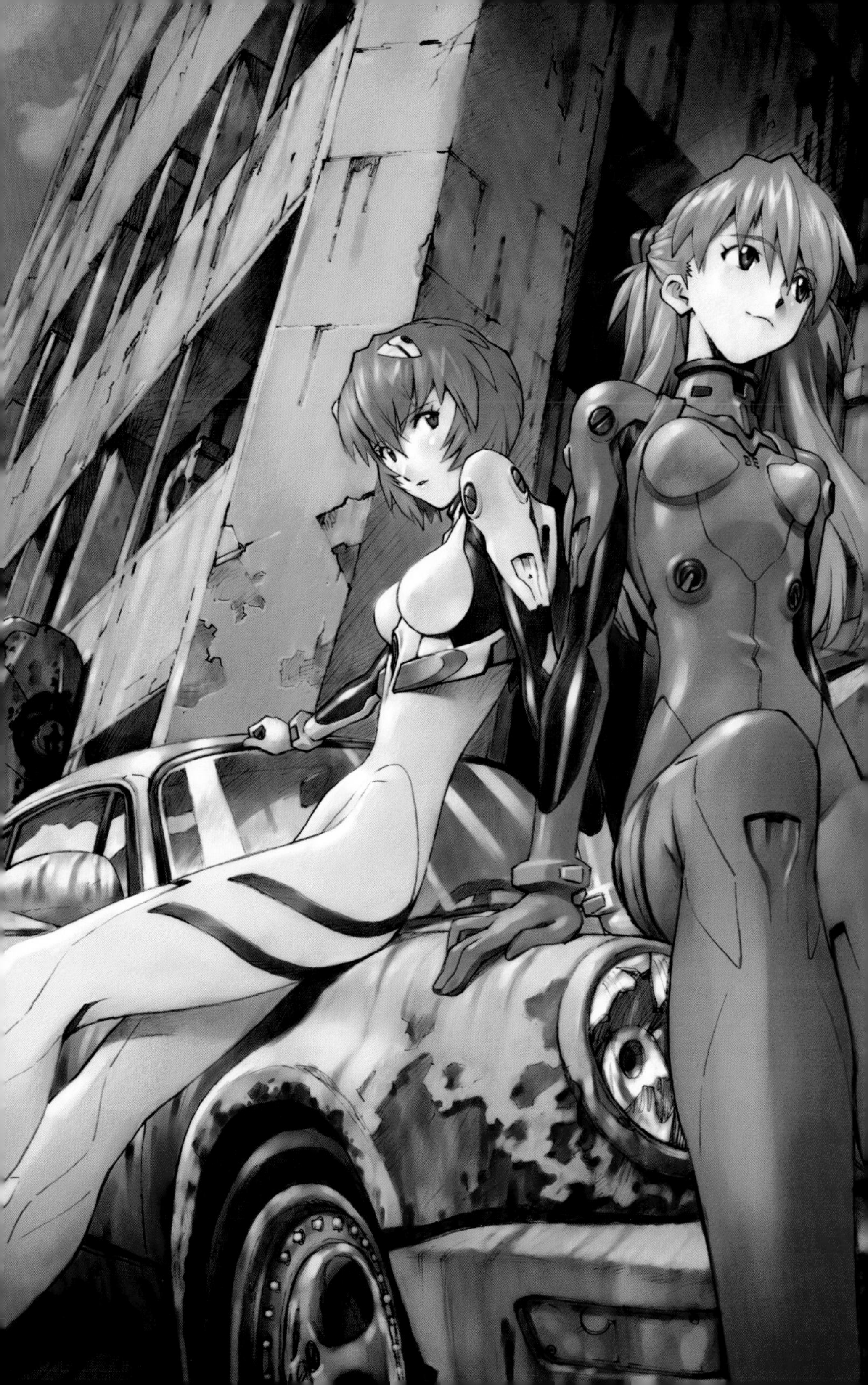

CONTENTS

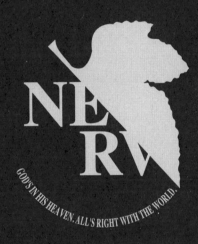

NE
RV

GOD'S IN HIS HEAVEN. ALL'S RIGHT WITH THE WORLD.

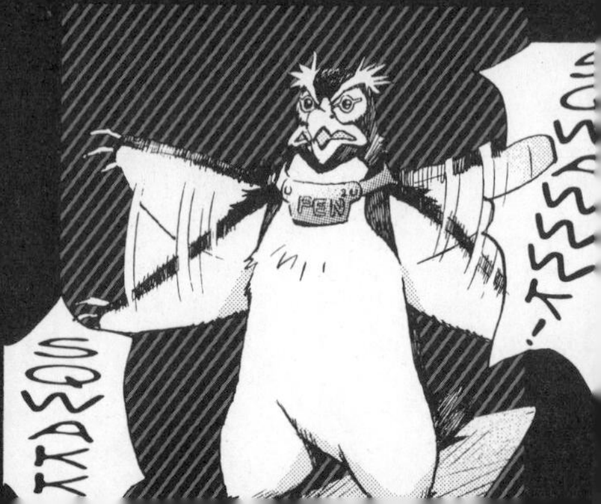
PEN
SQWAKK

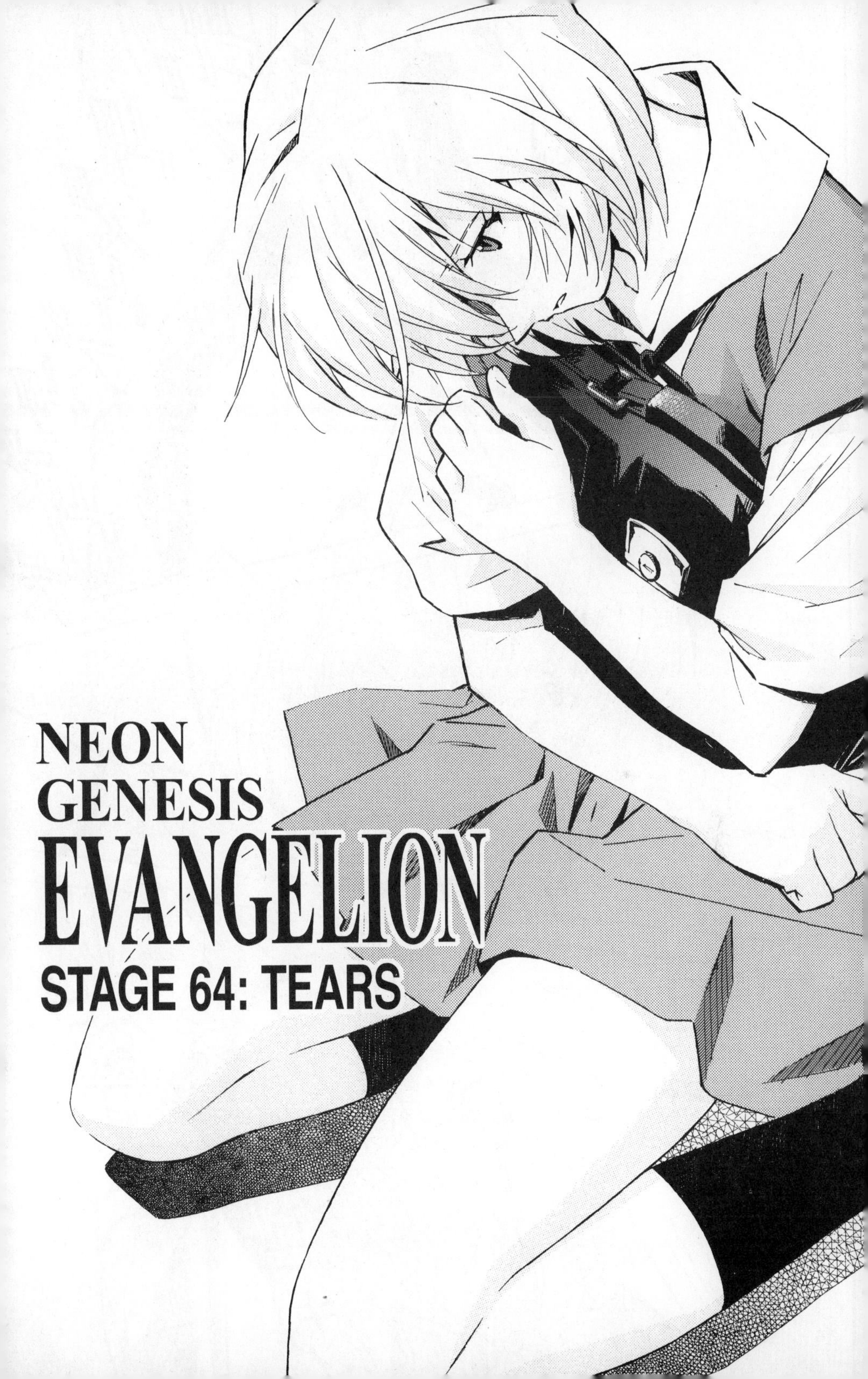
NEON
GENESIS
EVANGELION
STAGE 64: TEARS

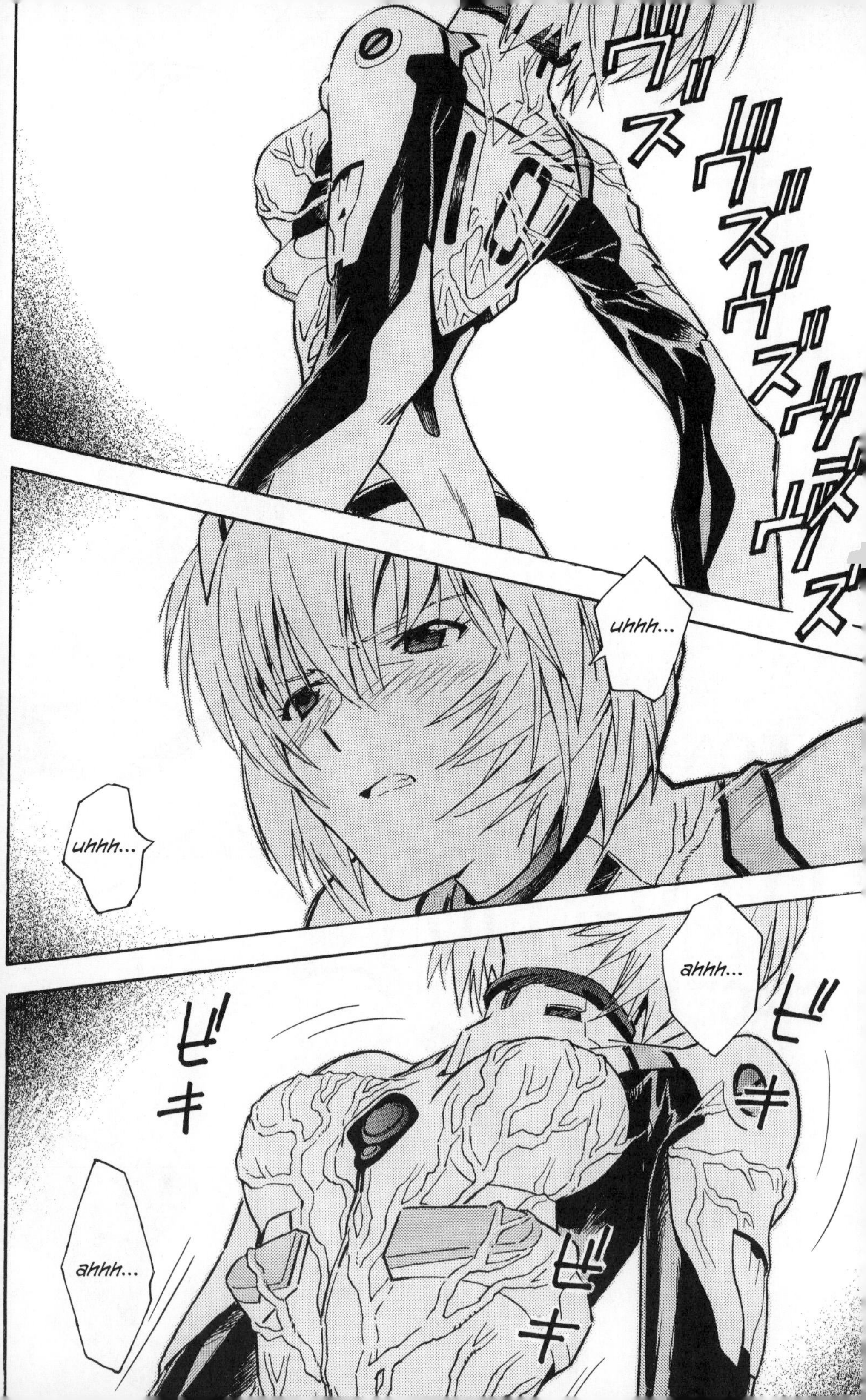
uhhh...
uhhh...
ahhh...
ビキ
ビキ
ビキ
ahhh...

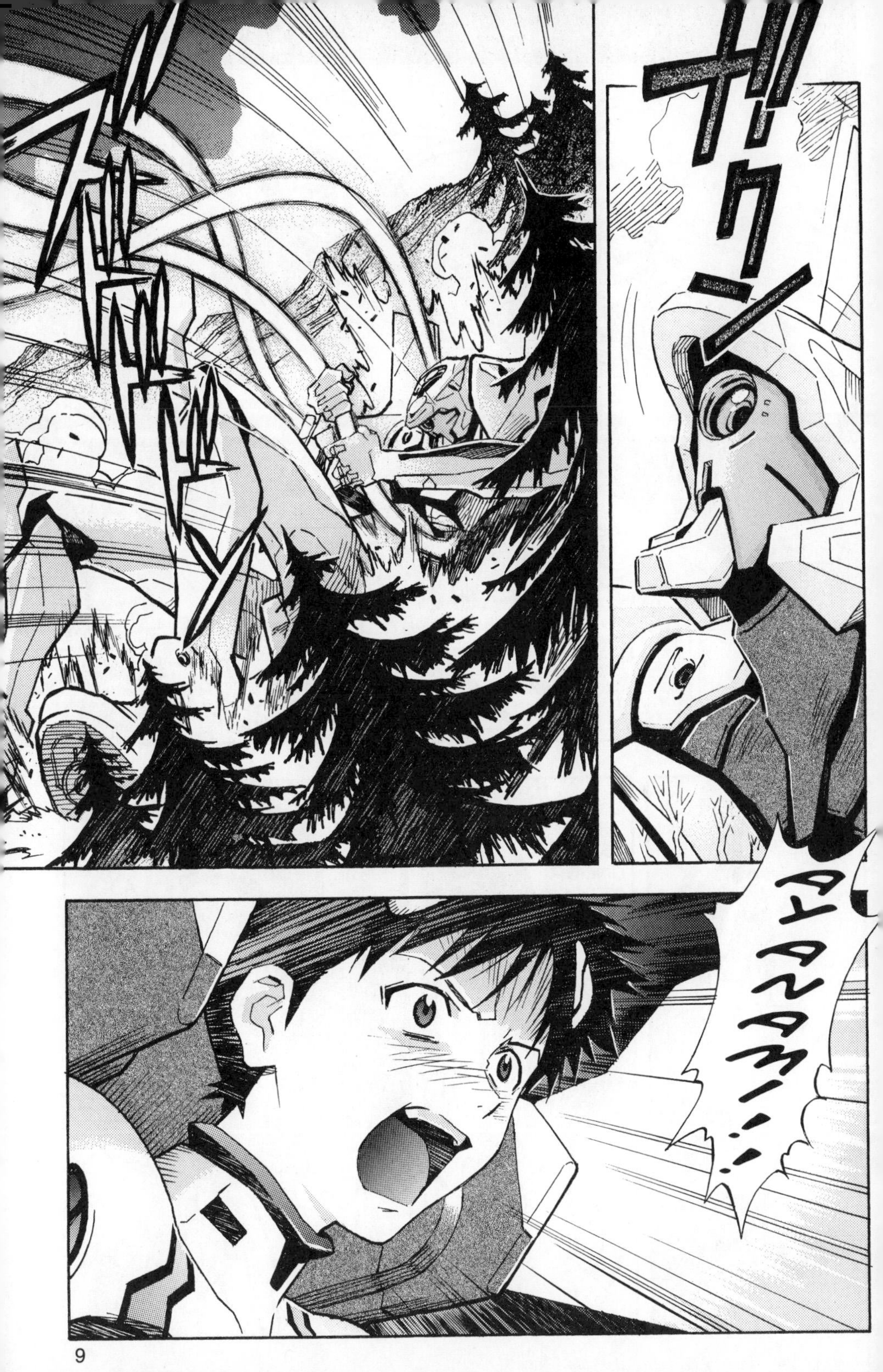
AYANAMI!!!

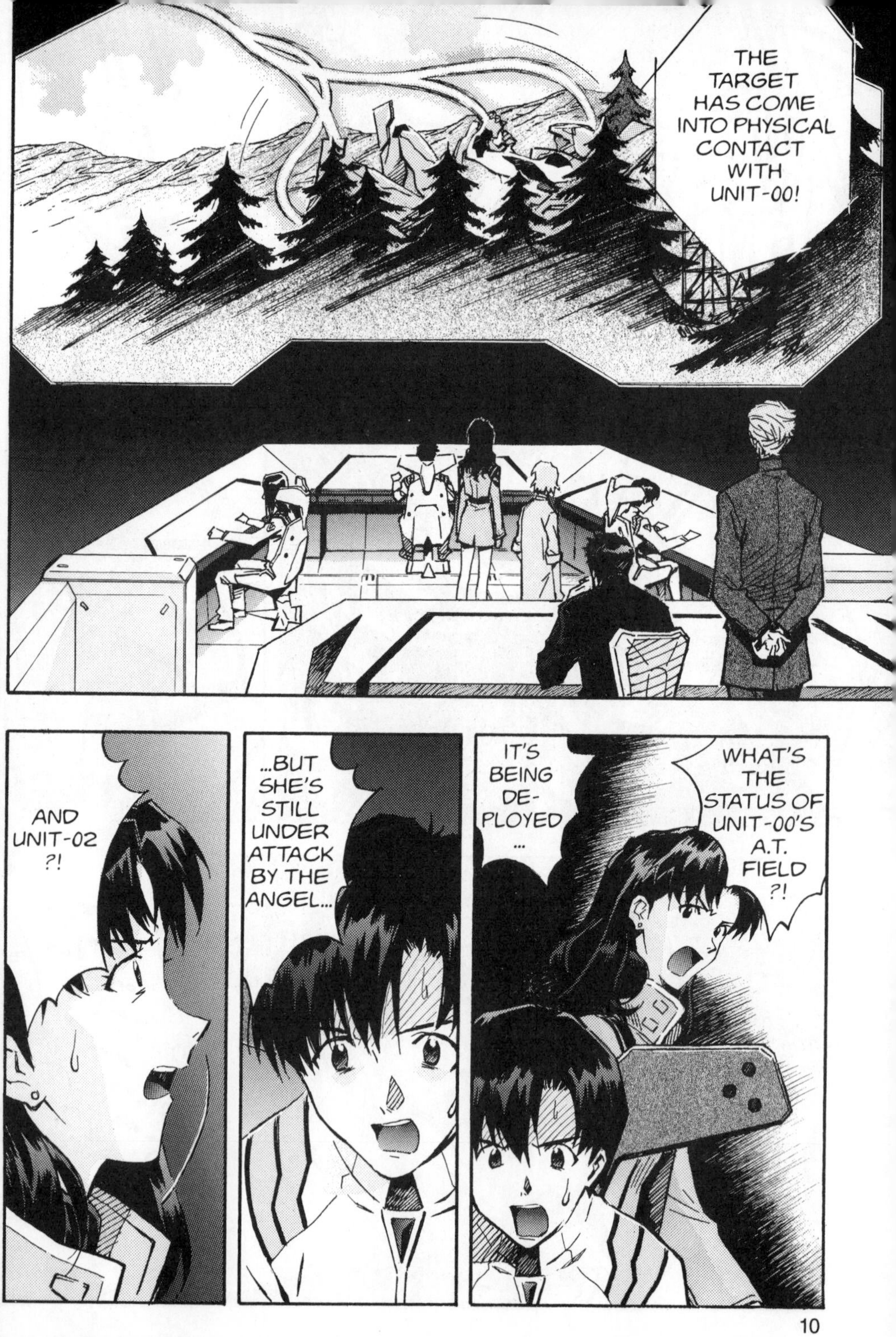
THE TARGET HAS COME INTO PHYSICAL CONTACT WITH UNIT-00!
WHAT'S THE STATUS OF UNIT-00'S A.T. FIELD ?!
IT'S BEING DE-PLOYED ...
...BUT SHE'S STILL UNDER ATTACK BY THE ANGEL...
AND UNIT-02 ?!

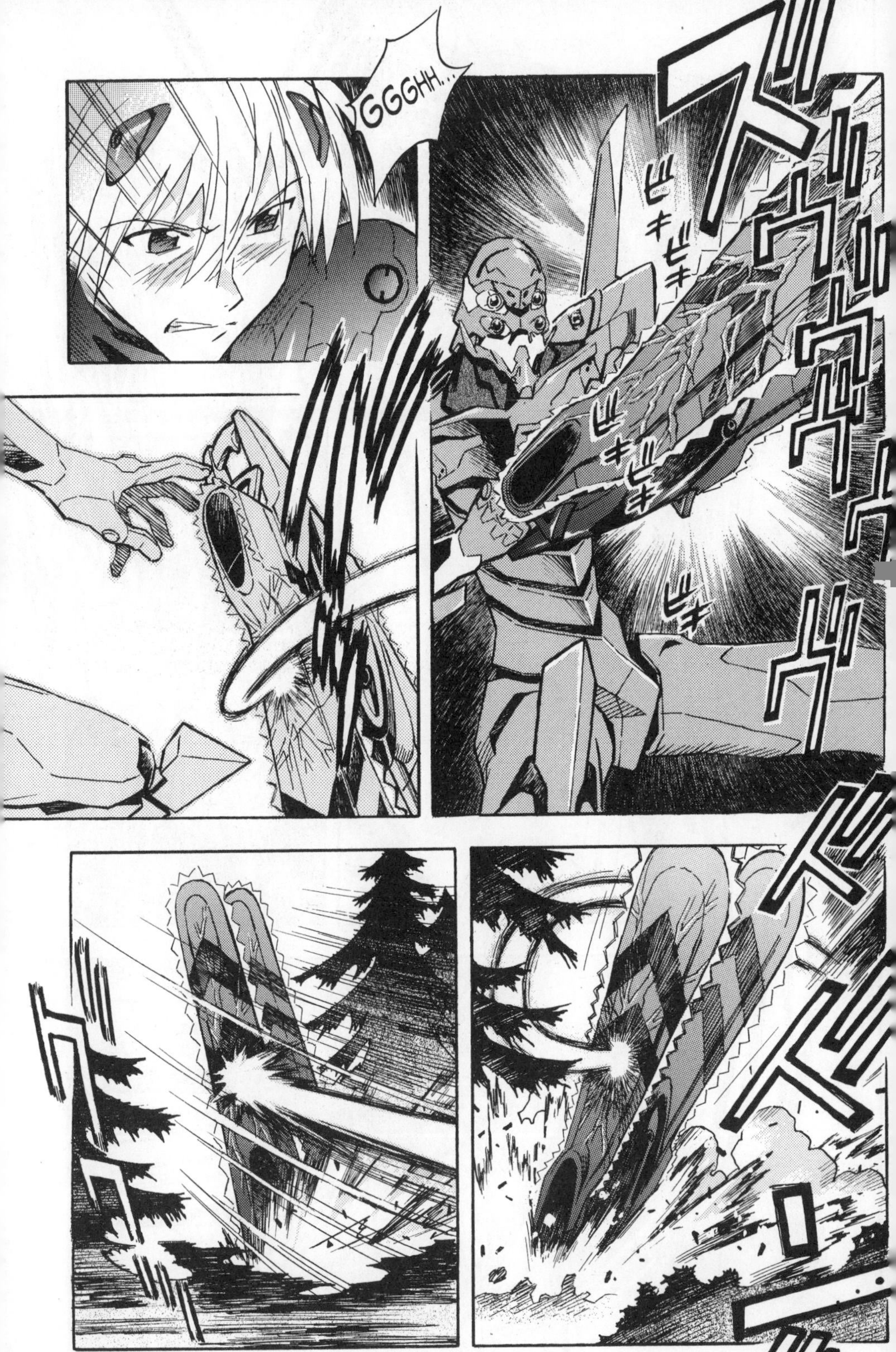
ビキビキ
ビキビキ
GGGHH...

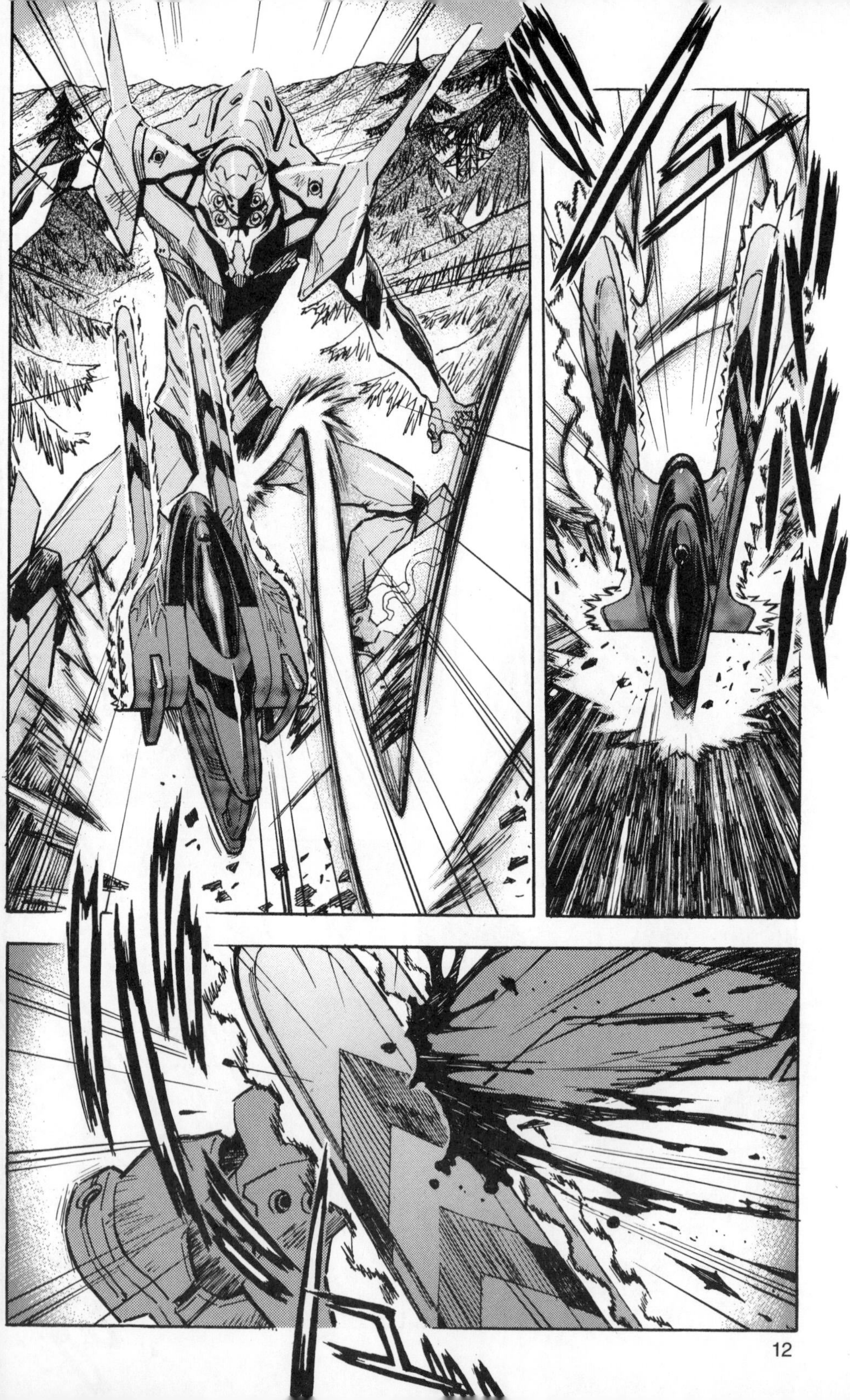

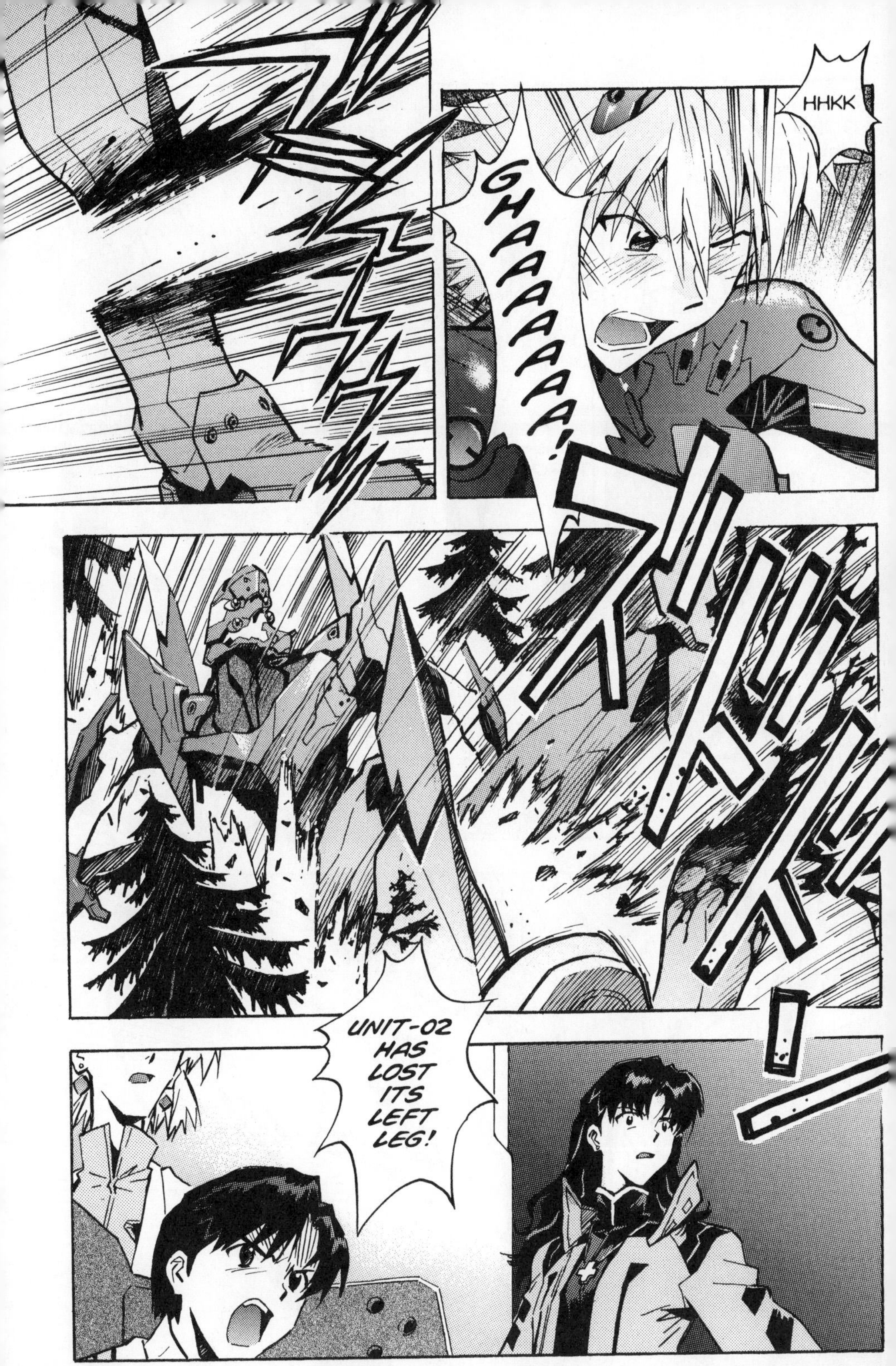
HHKK
GHAAAAAAAA!
UNIT-02 HAS LOST ITS LEFT LEG!

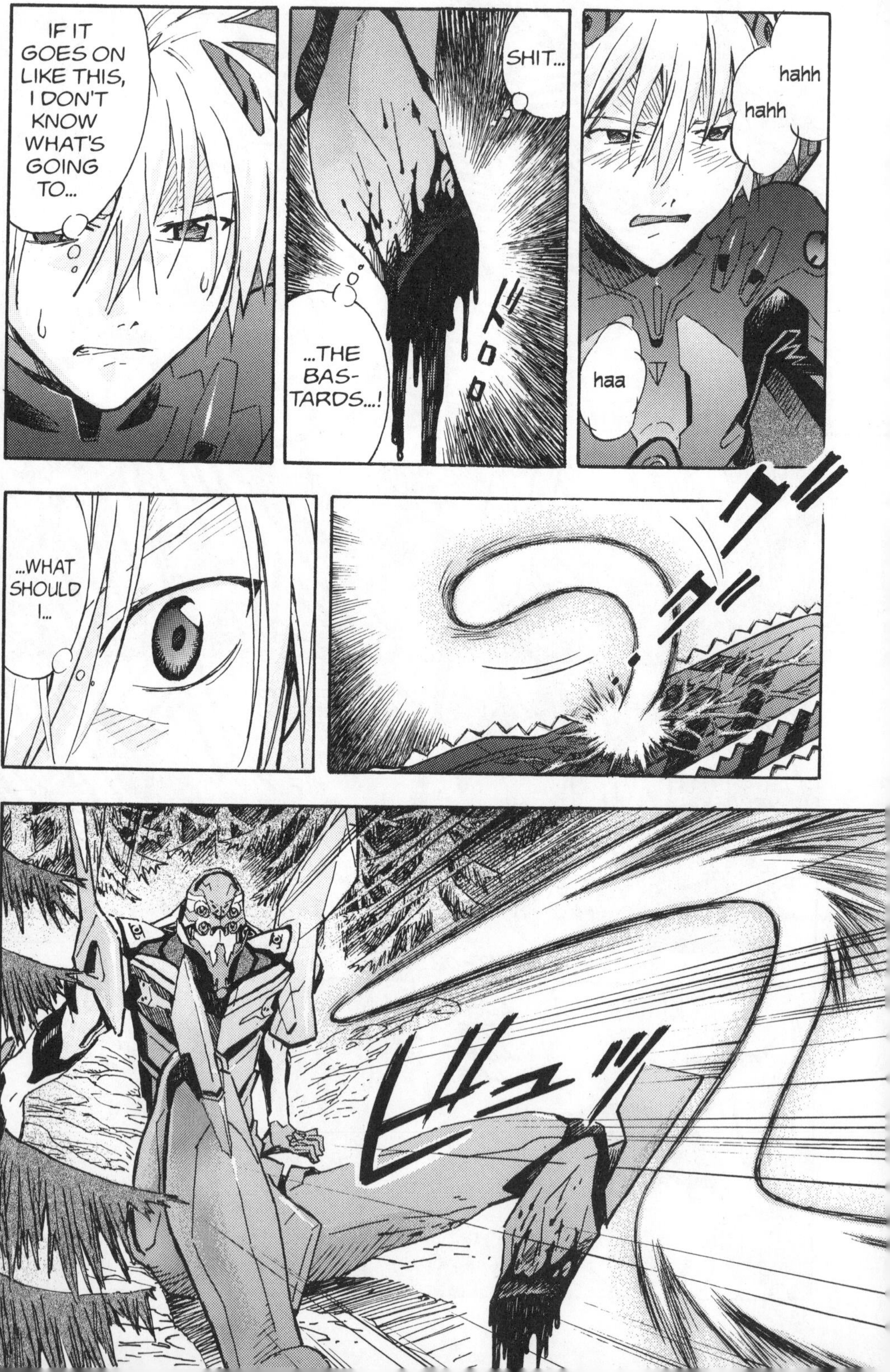
hahh
hahh
haa
SHIT...
...THE BAS-TARDS...!
ドロロ
IF IT GOES ON LIKE THIS, I DON'T KNOW WHAT'S GOING TO...
ググ
...WHAT SHOULD I...
ビュッ

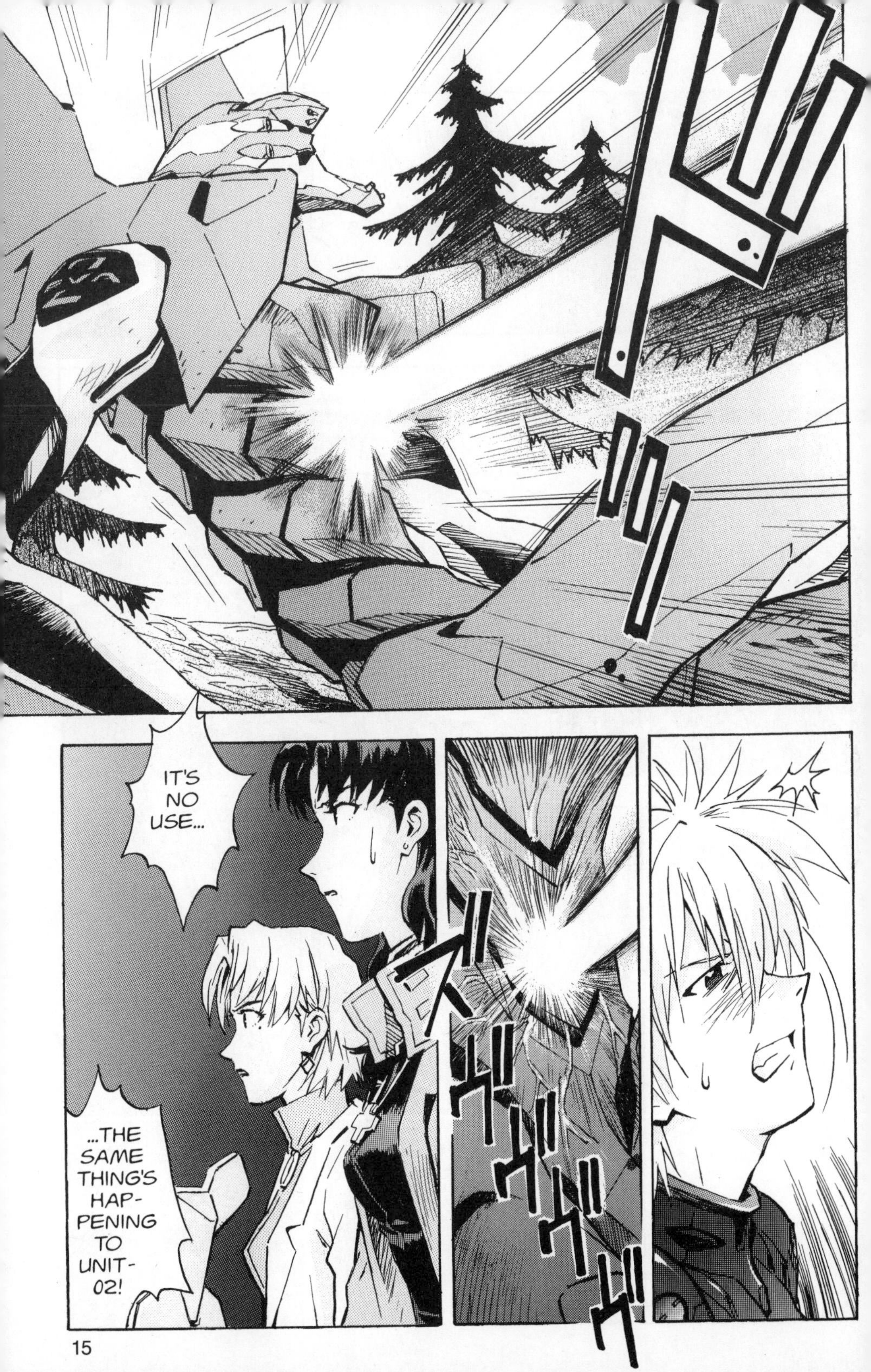
IT'S NO USE...
...THE SAME THING'S HAP-PENING TO UNIT-02!

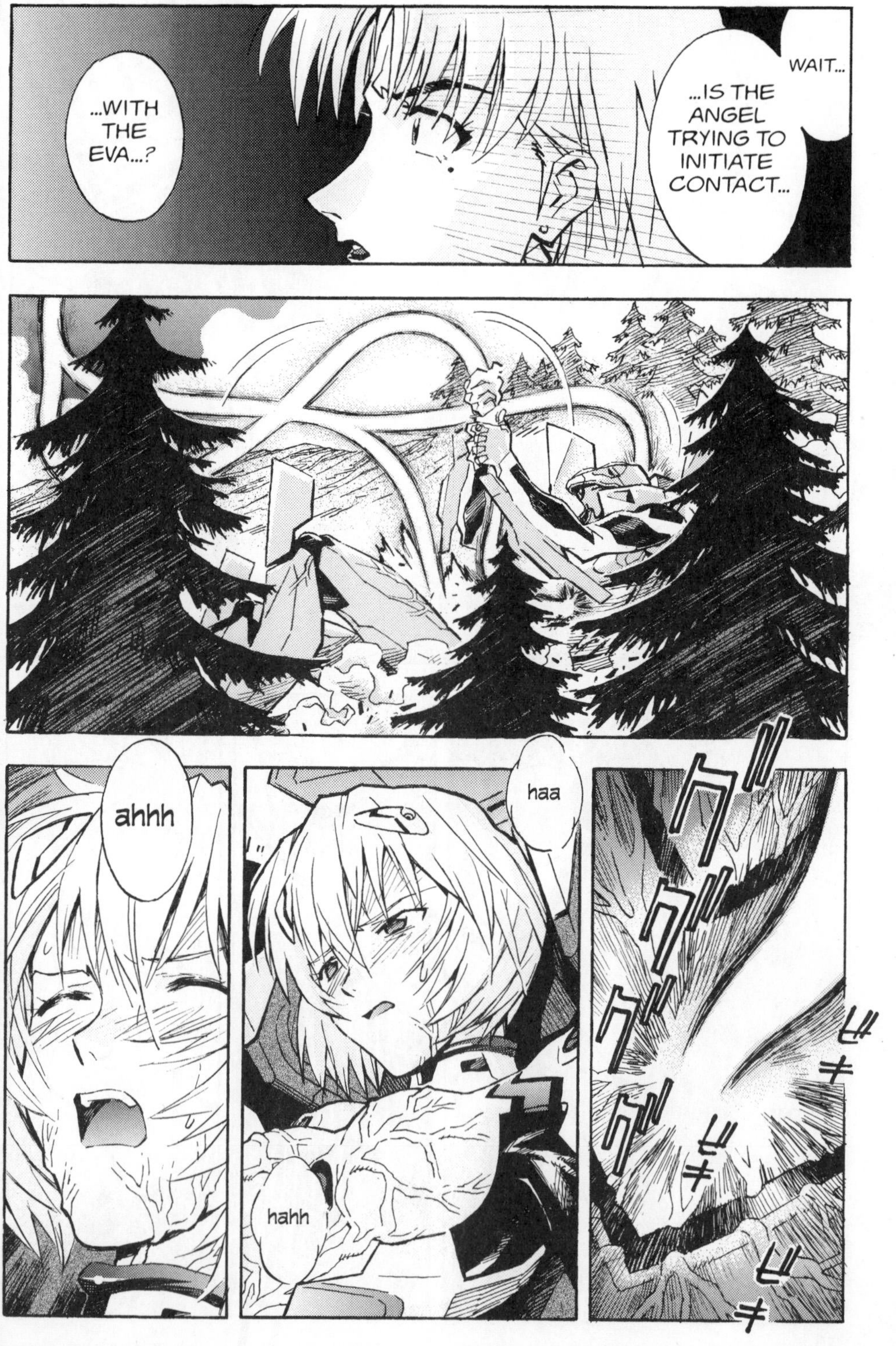
WAIT...
...IS THE ANGEL TRYING TO INITIATE CONTACT...
...WITH THE EVA...?
ビキ
ビキ
ビキ
haa
hahh
ahhh

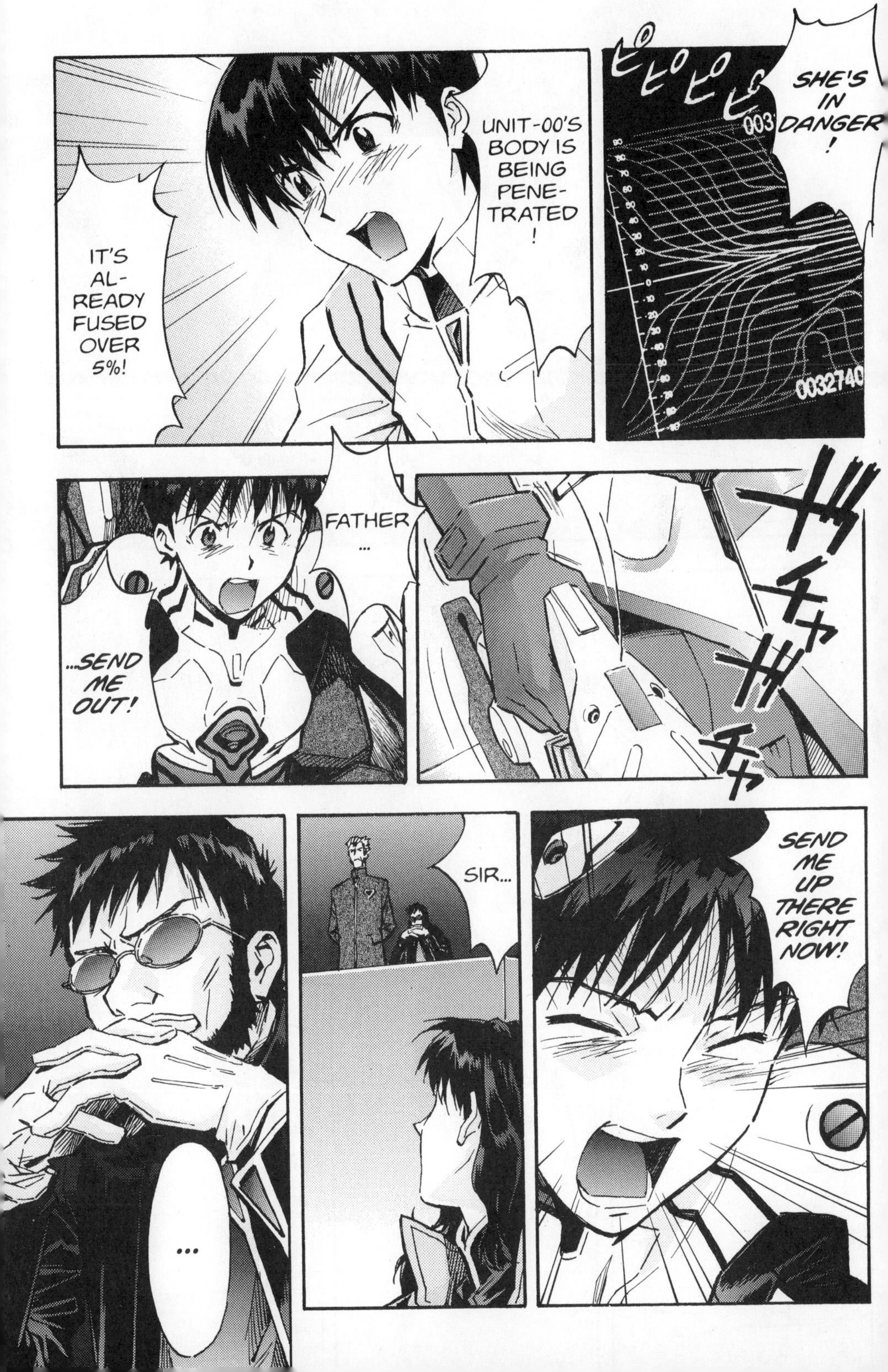
ピピピピ
003
SHE'S IN DANGER!
0032740
UNIT-00'S BODY IS BEING PENE-TRATED!
IT'S AL-READY FUSED OVER 5%!
ガチャガチャ
FATHER...
...SEND ME OUT!
SEND ME UP THERE RIGHT NOW!
SIR...
...

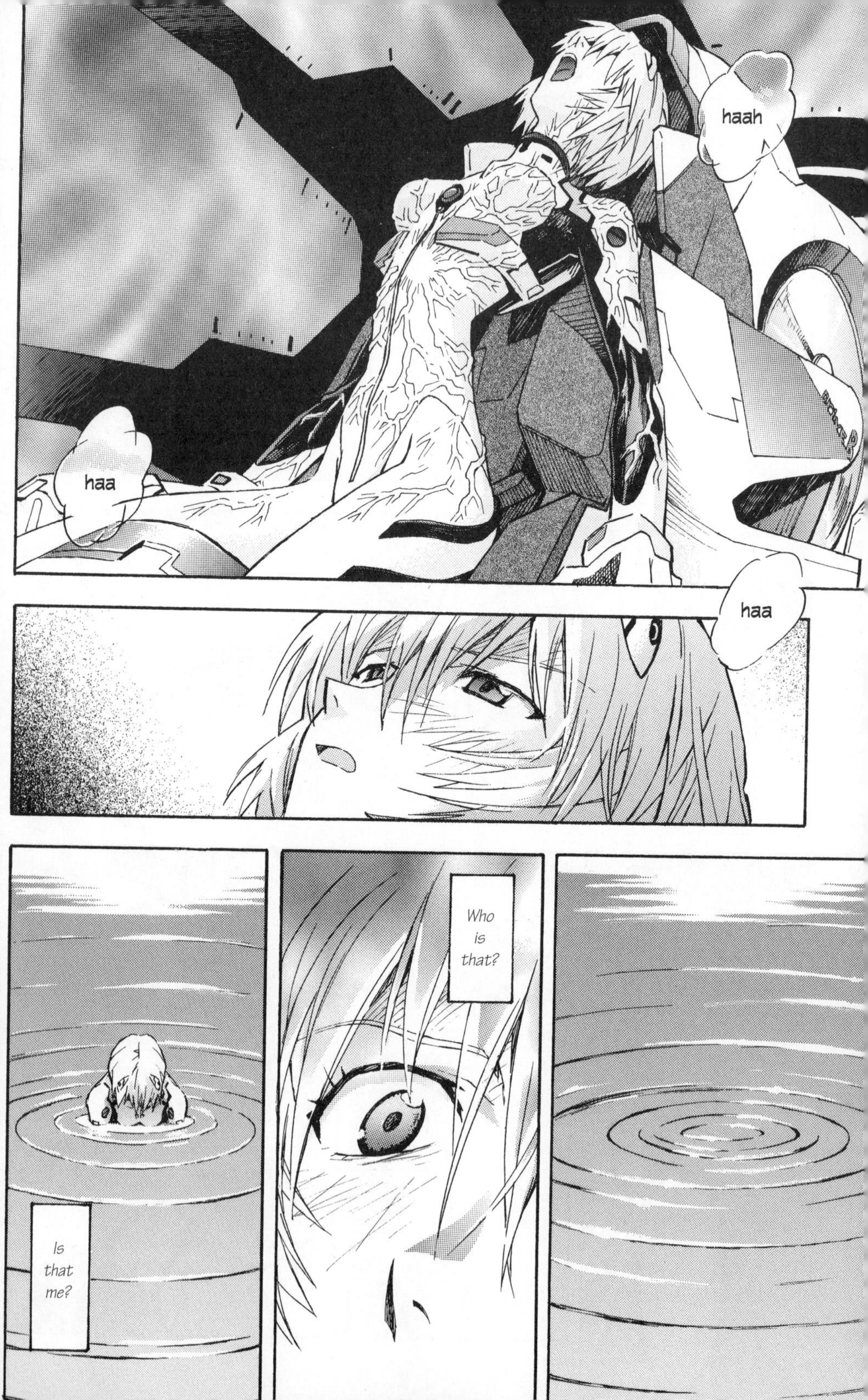
haah
haa
haa
Who is that?
Is that me?

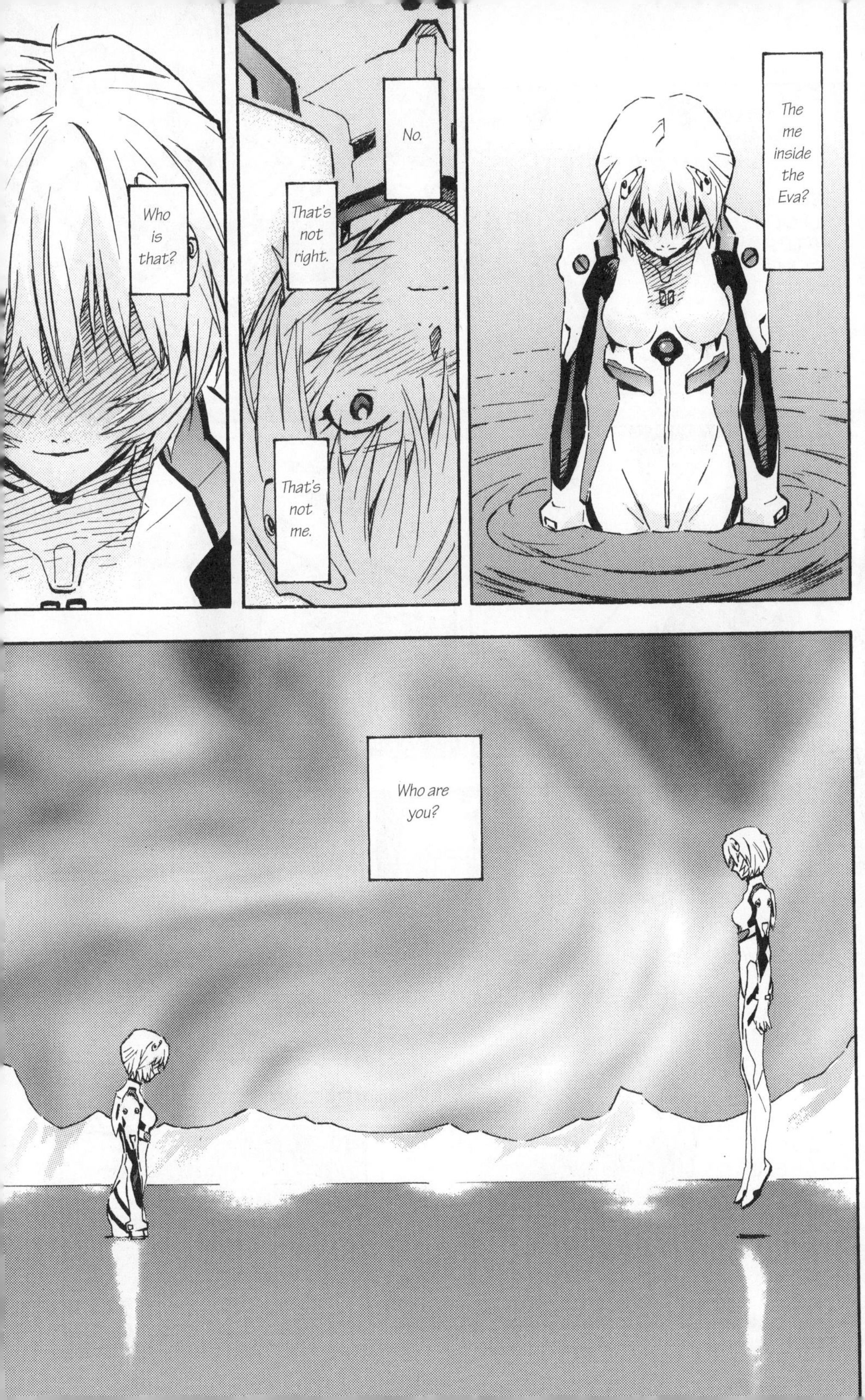
The me inside the Eva?
No.
That's not right.
That's not me.
Who is that?
Who are you?

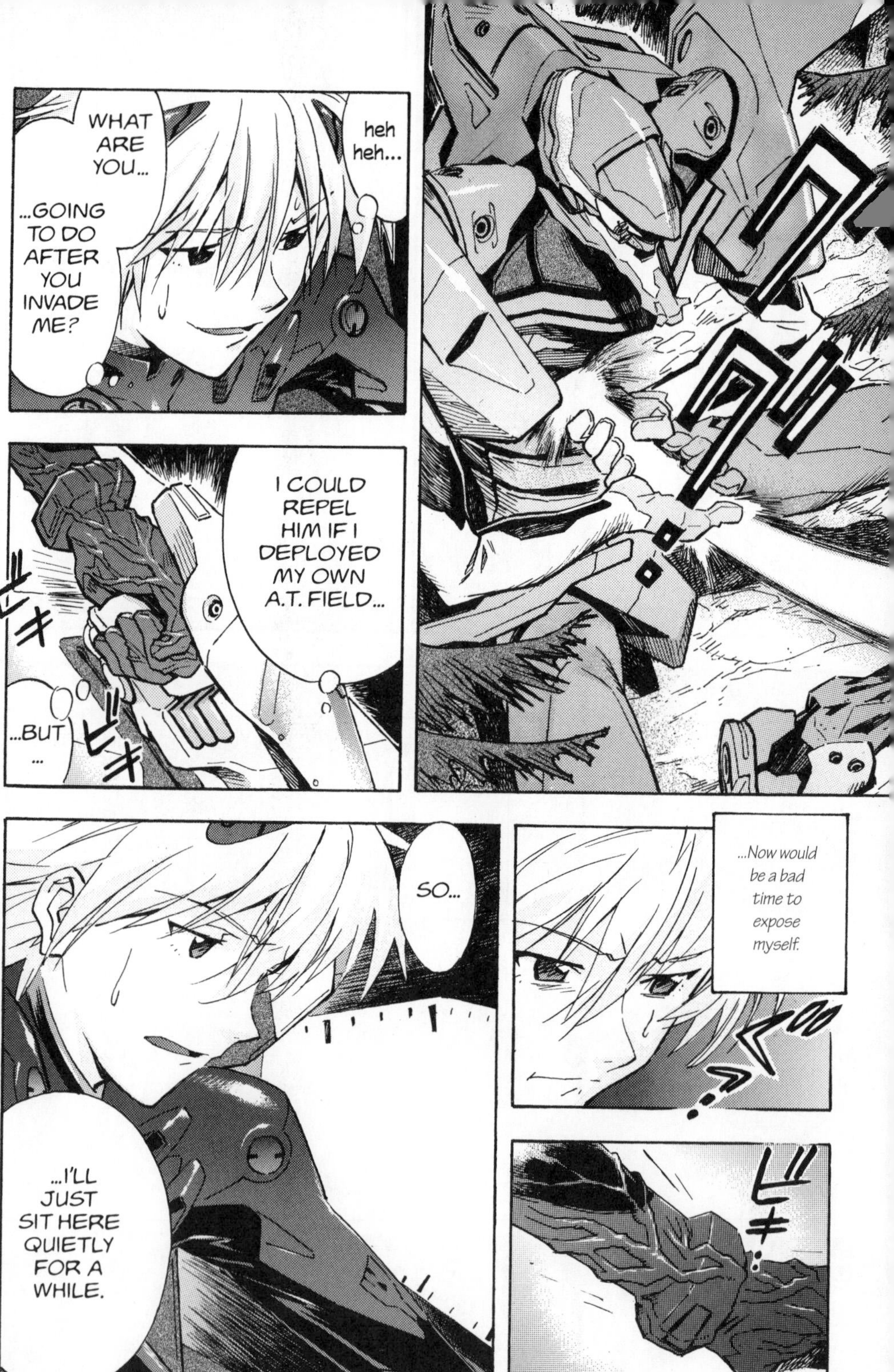
heh heh...
WHAT ARE YOU...
...GOING TO DO AFTER YOU INVADE ME?
I COULD REPEL HIM IF I DEPLOYED MY OWN A.T. FIELD...
ビキ
ビキ
...BUT ...
...Now would be a bad time to expose myself.
ビキ
SO...
...I'LL JUST SIT HERE QUIETLY FOR A WHILE.

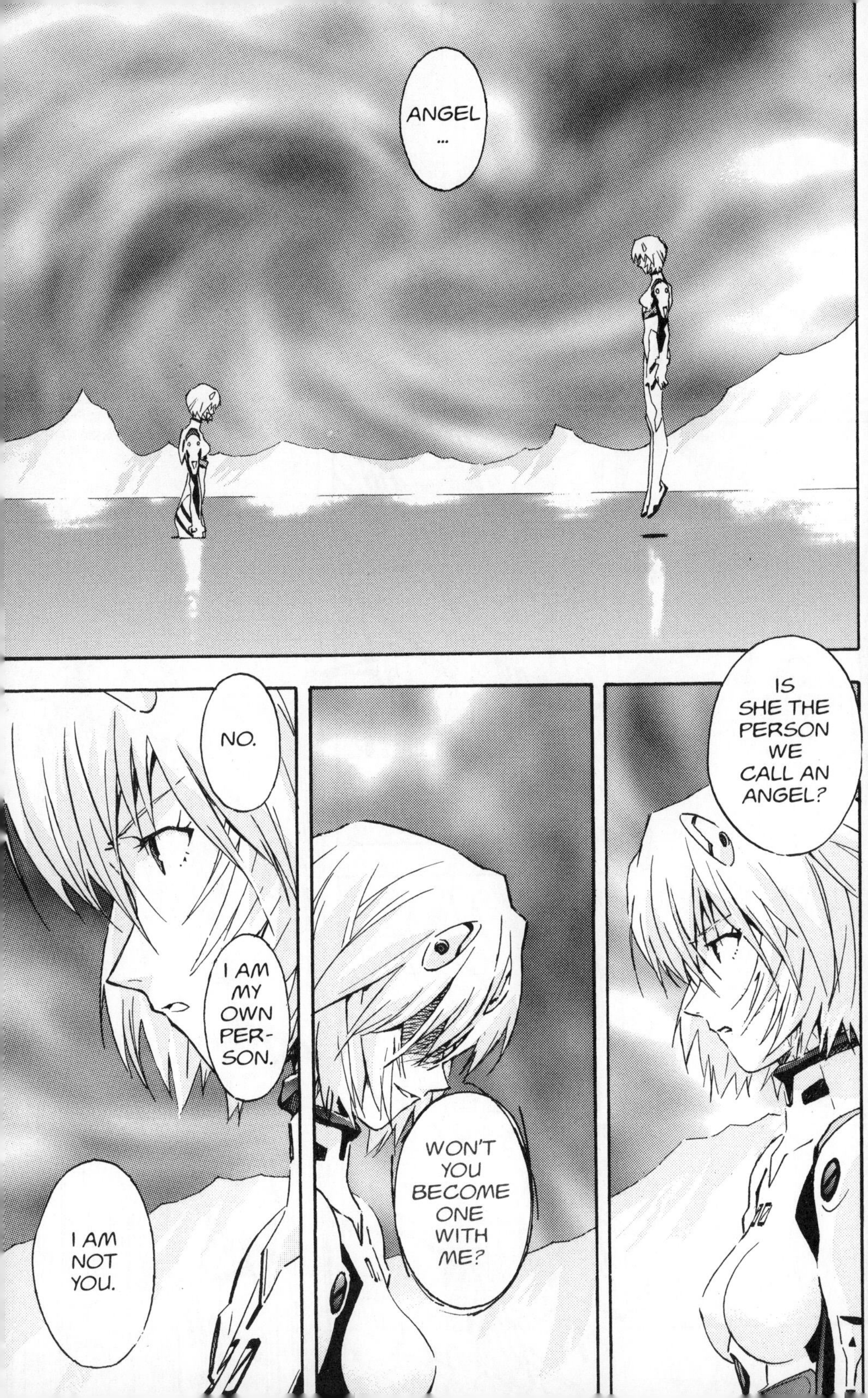
ANGEL ...
IS SHE THE PERSON WE CALL AN ANGEL?
WON'T YOU BECOME ONE WITH ME?
NO.
I AM MY OWN PERSON.
I AM NOT YOU.

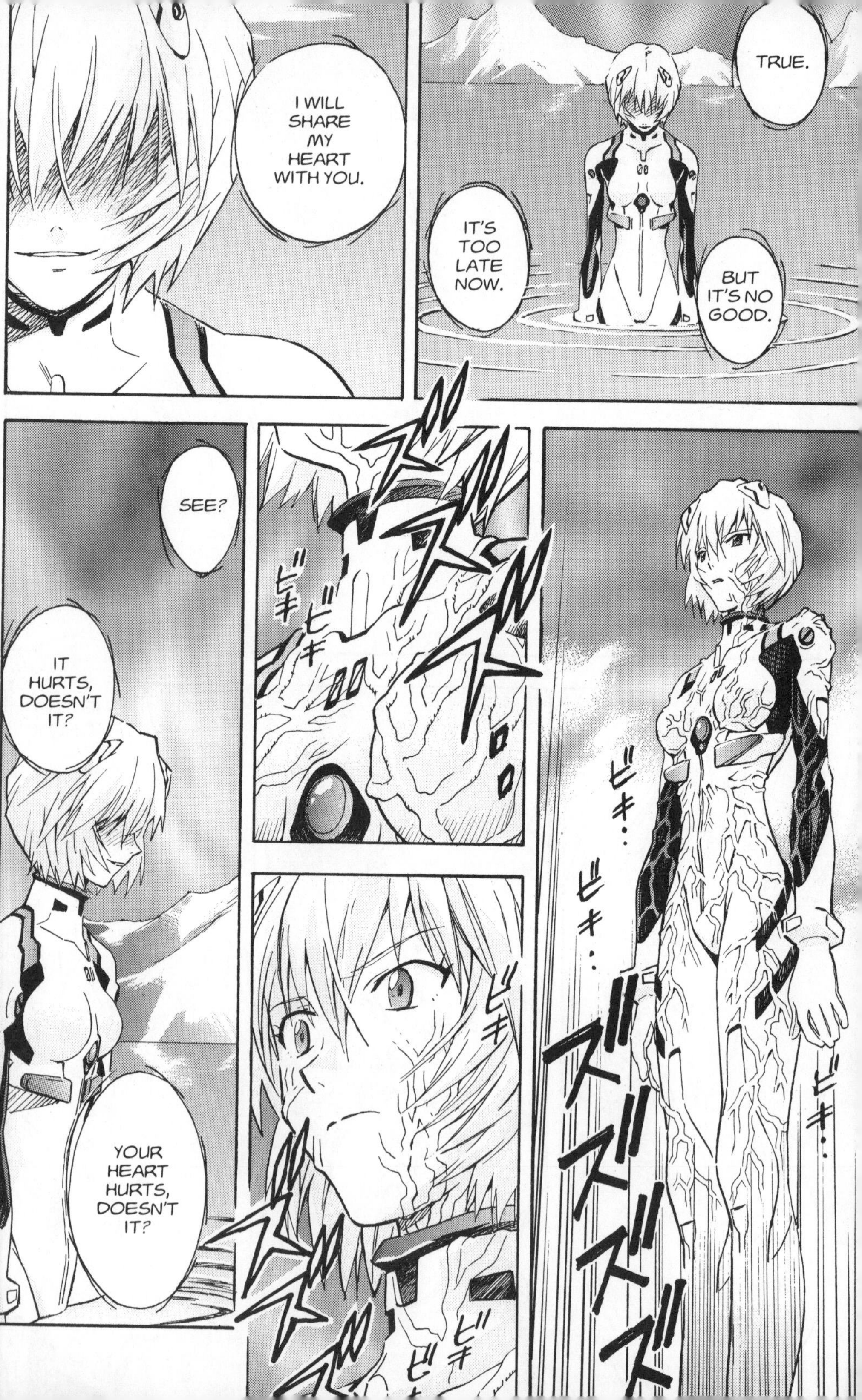
TRUE.
BUT IT'S NO GOOD.
IT'S TOO LATE NOW.
I WILL SHARE MY HEART WITH YOU.
ビキ‥
ビキ‥
ビキ‥
ズズズズ
ズズズ
ビキ
ビキ
ビキ
ビキ
ビキ
SEE?
IT HURTS, DOESN'T IT?
YOUR HEART HURTS, DOESN'T IT?

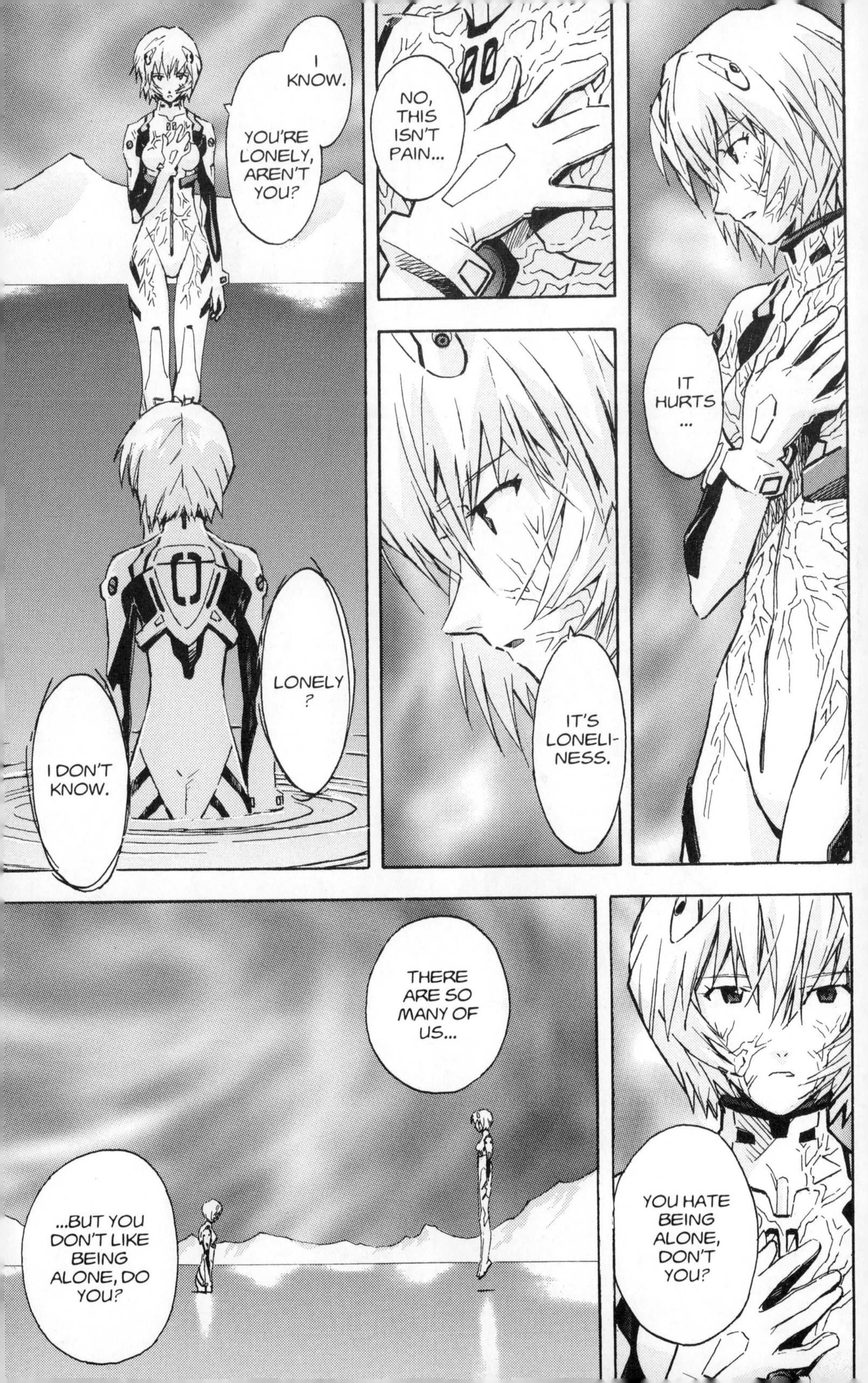
IT HURTS ...
NO, THIS ISN'T PAIN...
IT'S LONELINESS.
I KNOW.
YOU'RE LONELY, AREN'T YOU?
LONELY?
I DON'T KNOW.
YOU HATE BEING ALONE, DON'T YOU?
THERE ARE SO MANY OF US...
...BUT YOU DON'T LIKE BEING ALONE, DO YOU?

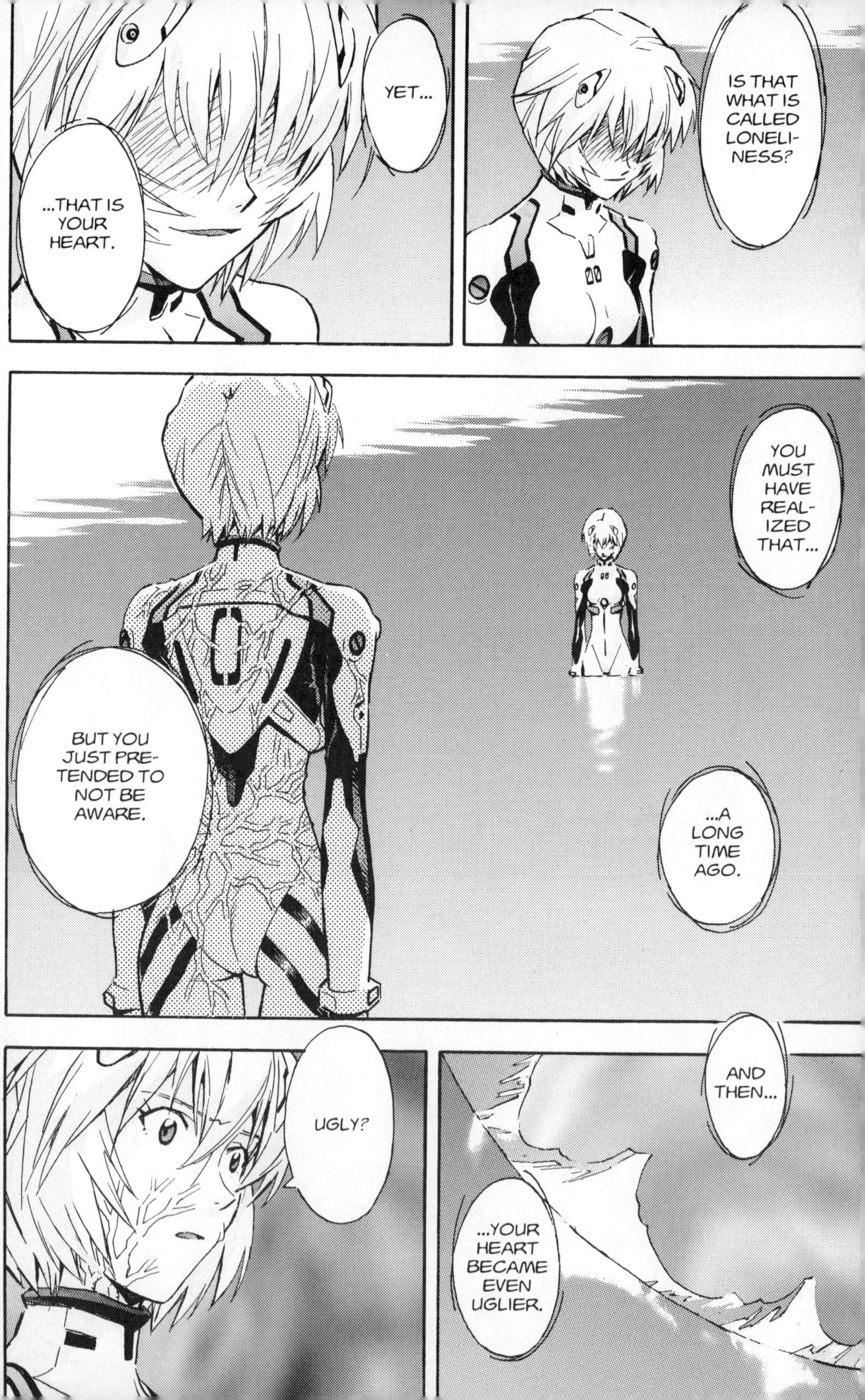
IS THAT WHAT IS CALLED LONELI-NESS?
YET...
...THAT IS YOUR HEART.
YOU MUST HAVE REAL-IZED THAT...
...A LONG TIME AGO.
BUT YOU JUST PRE-TENDED TO NOT BE AWARE.
AND THEN...
...YOUR HEART BECAME EVEN UGLIER.
UGLY?

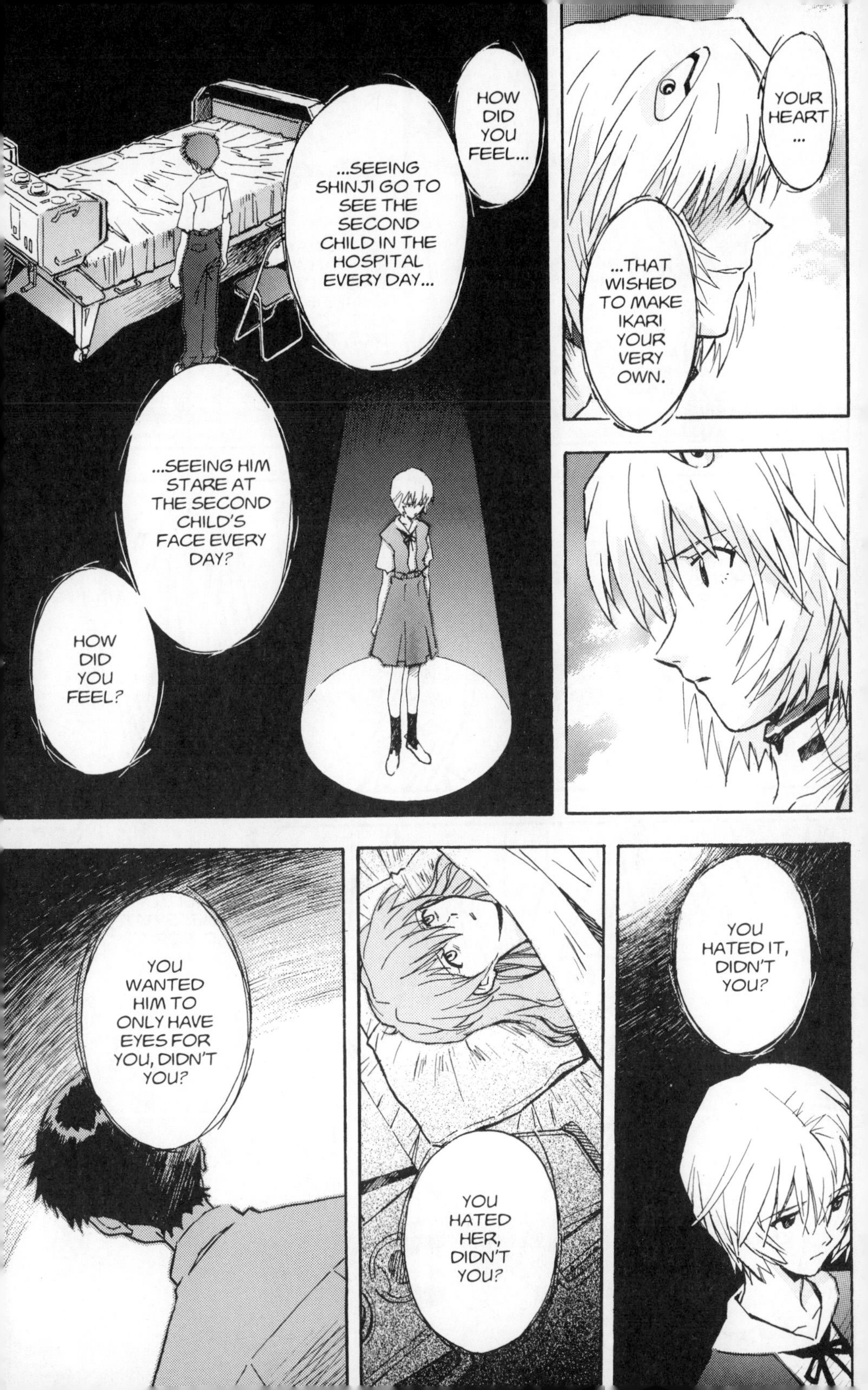
YOUR HEART ...
...THAT WISHED TO MAKE IKARI YOUR VERY OWN.
HOW DID YOU FEEL...
...SEEING SHINJI GO TO SEE THE SECOND CHILD IN THE HOSPITAL EVERY DAY...
...SEEING HIM STARE AT THE SECOND CHILD'S FACE EVERY DAY?
HOW DID YOU FEEL?
YOU HATED IT, DIDN'T YOU?
YOU HATED HER, DIDN'T YOU?
YOU WANTED HIM TO ONLY HAVE EYES FOR YOU, DIDN'T YOU?

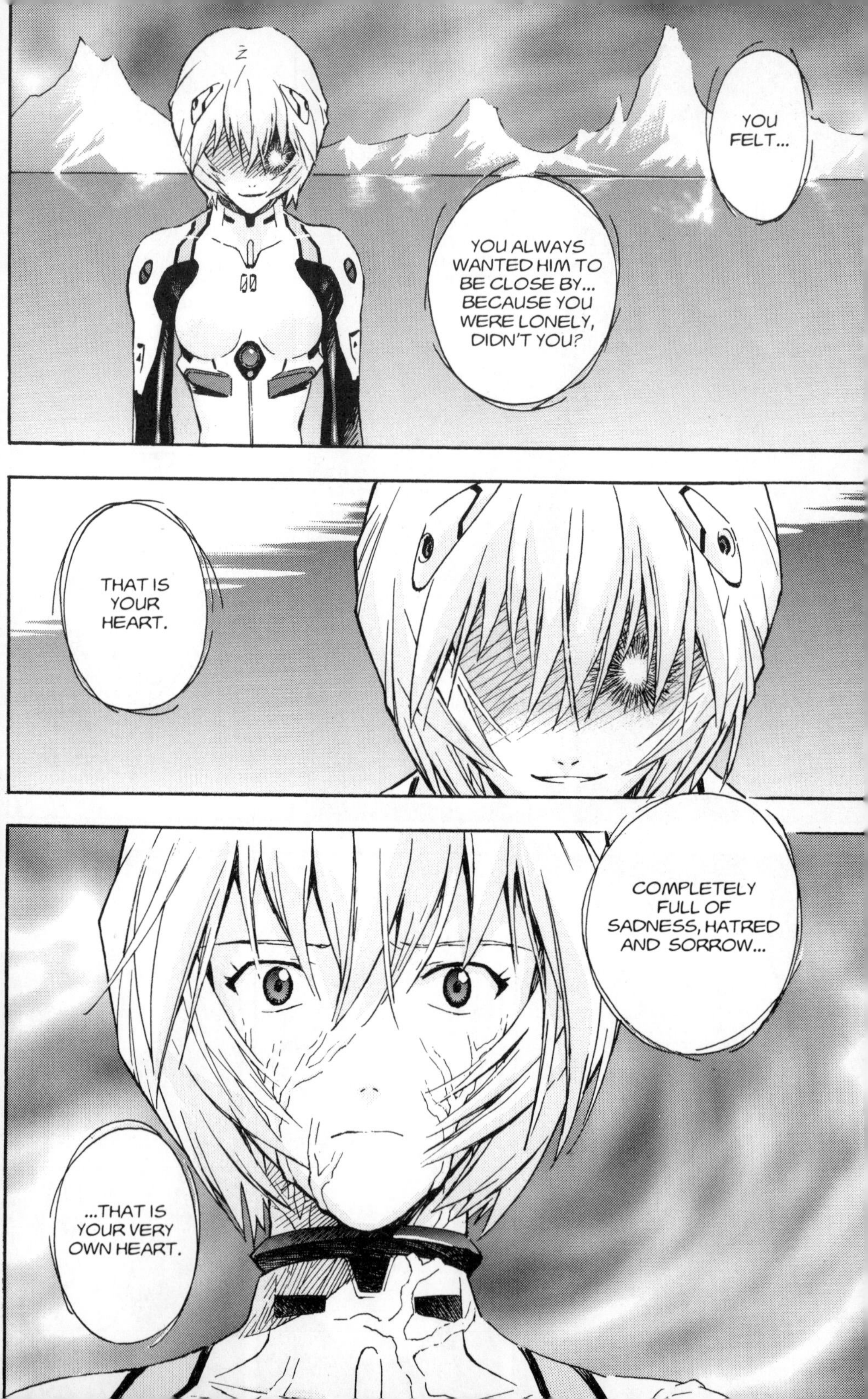
YOU FELT...
YOU ALWAYS WANTED HIM TO BE CLOSE BY... BECAUSE YOU WERE LONELY, DIDN'T YOU?
THAT IS YOUR HEART.
COMPLETELY FULL OF SADNESS, HATRED AND SORROW...
...THAT IS YOUR VERY OWN HEART.

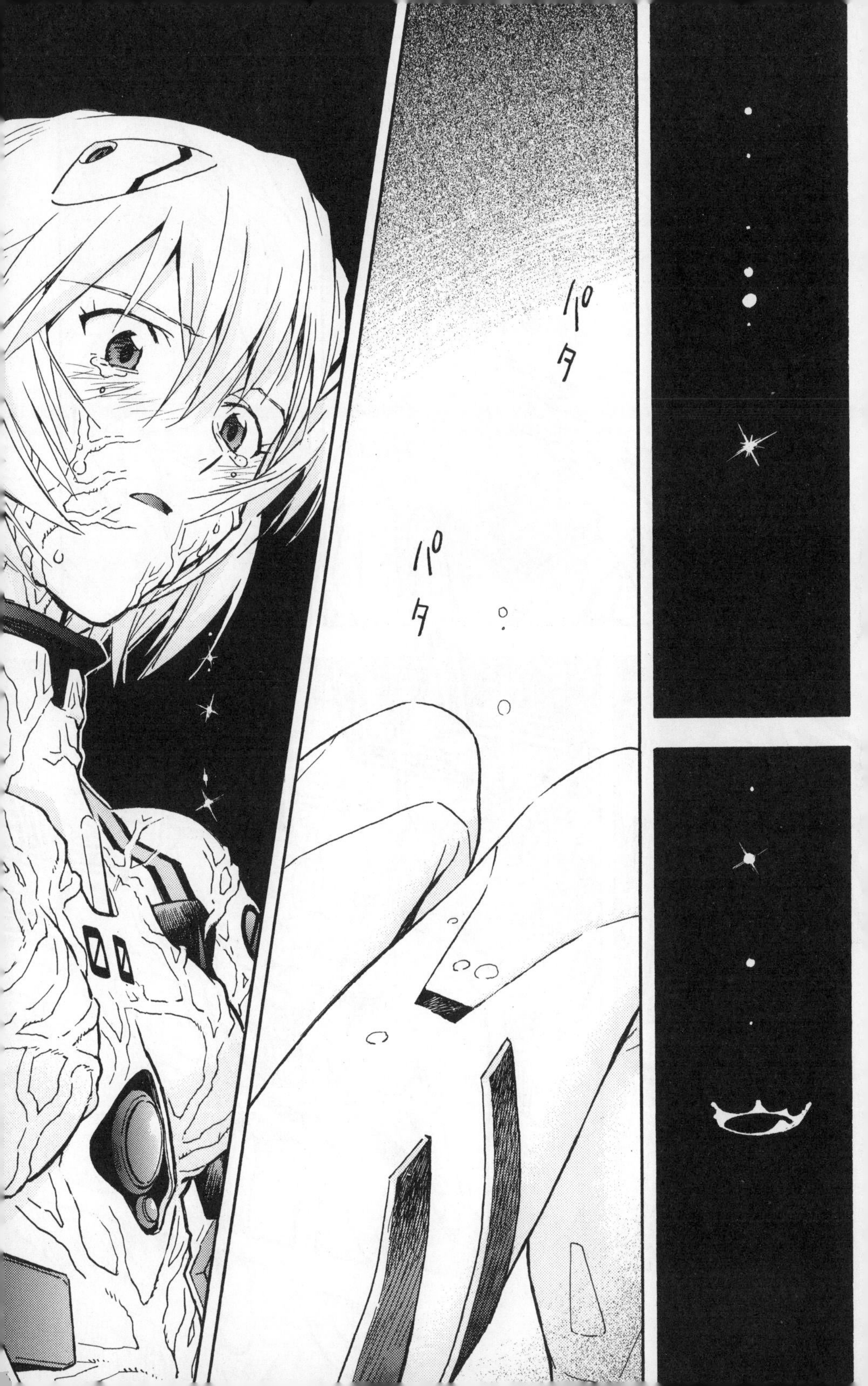
パタ
パタ

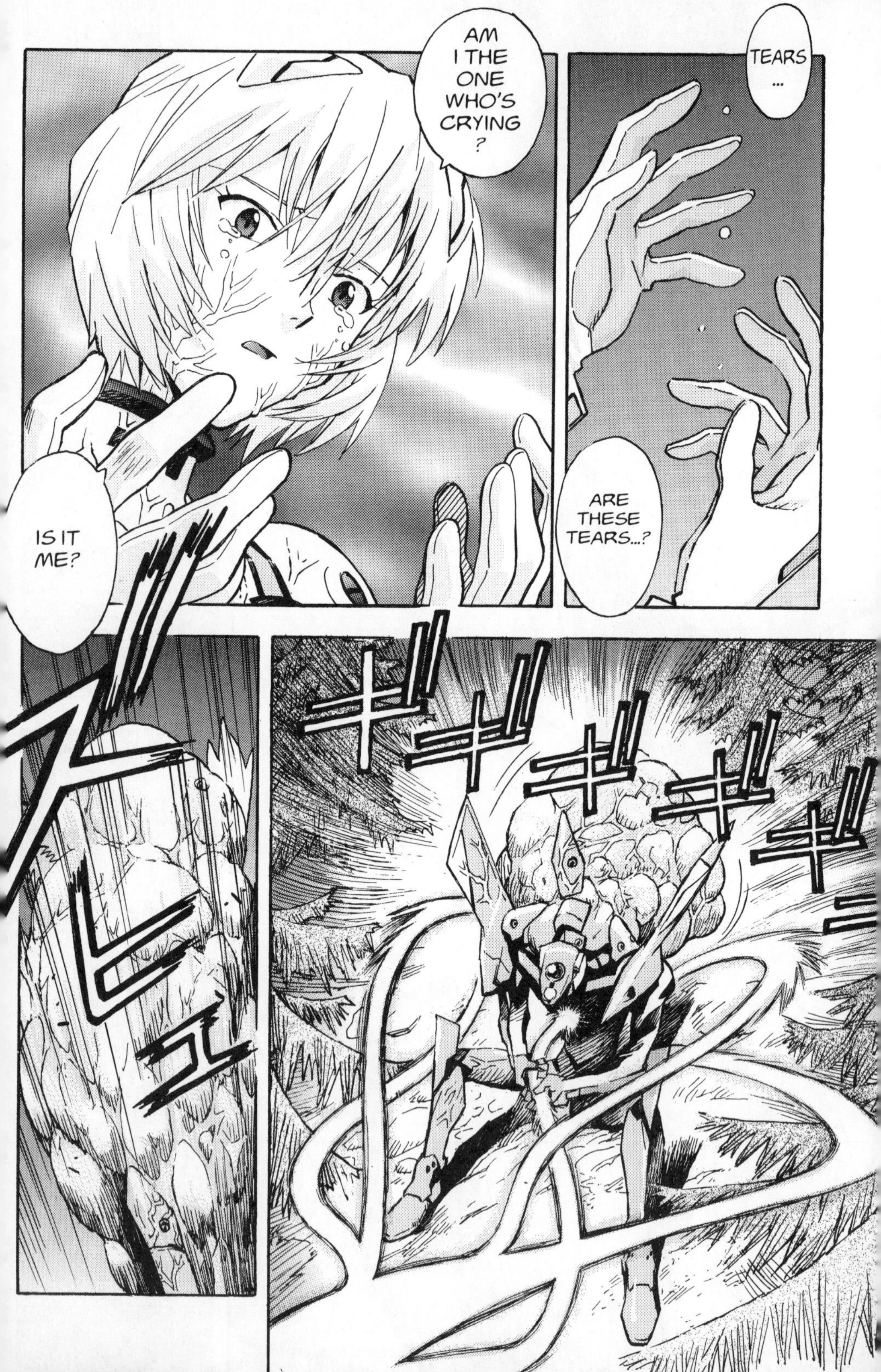
TEARS ...
ARE THESE TEARS...?
AM I THE ONE WHO'S CRYING ?
IS IT ME?

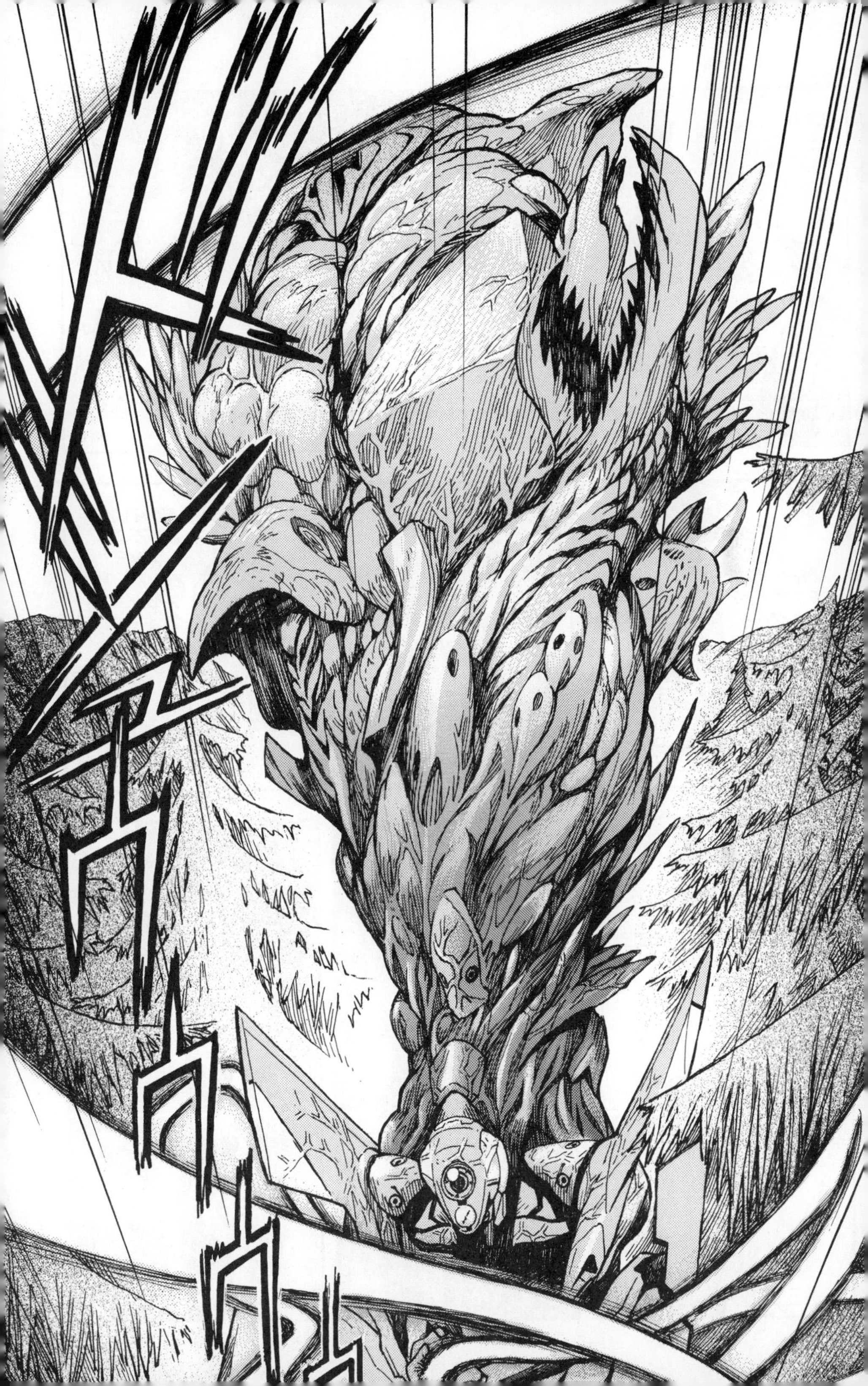

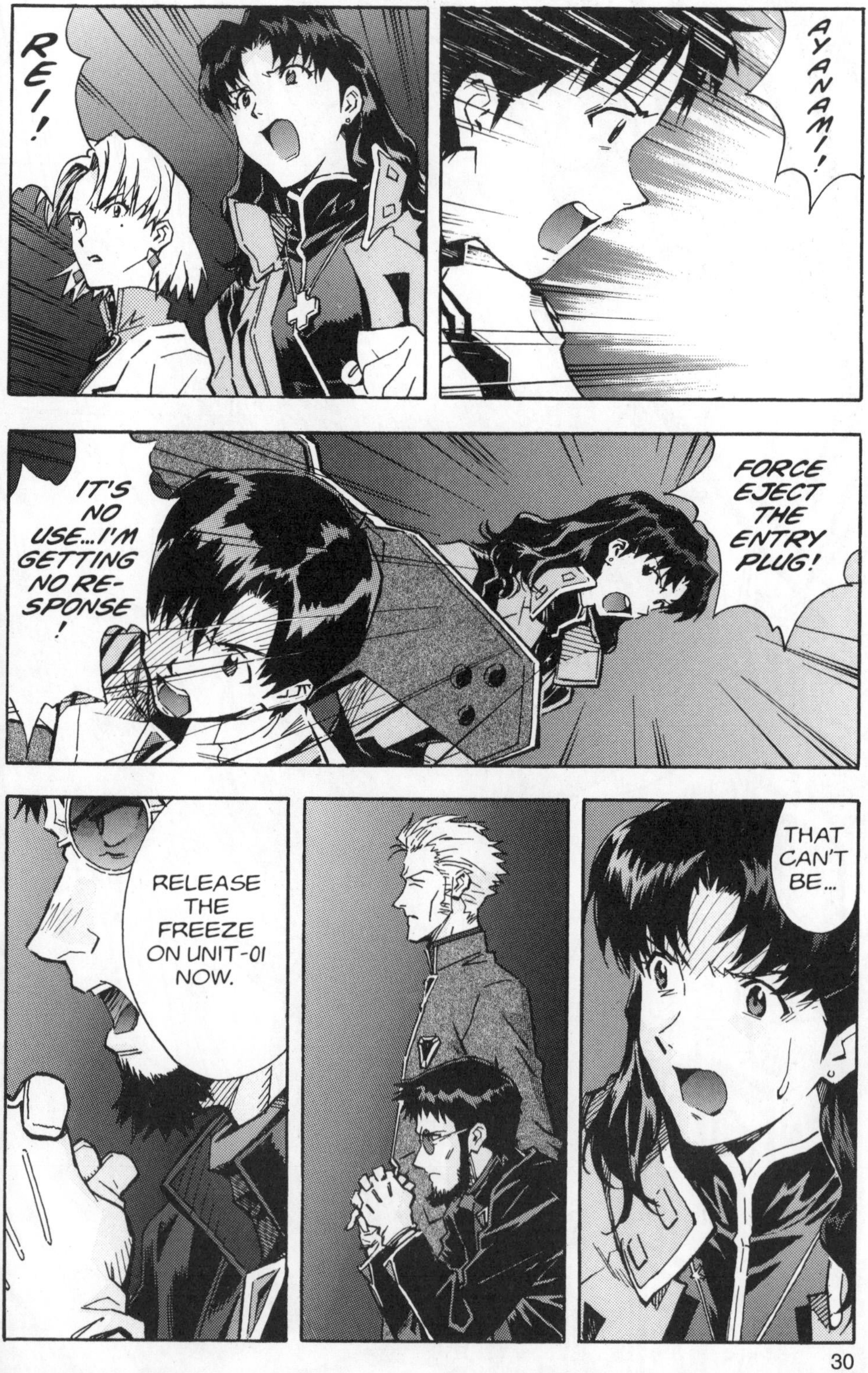
AYANAMI!
REI!
FORCE EJECT THE ENTRY PLUG!
IT'S NO USE...I'M GETTING NO RESPONSE!
THAT CAN'T BE...
RELEASE THE FREEZE ON UNIT-01 NOW.

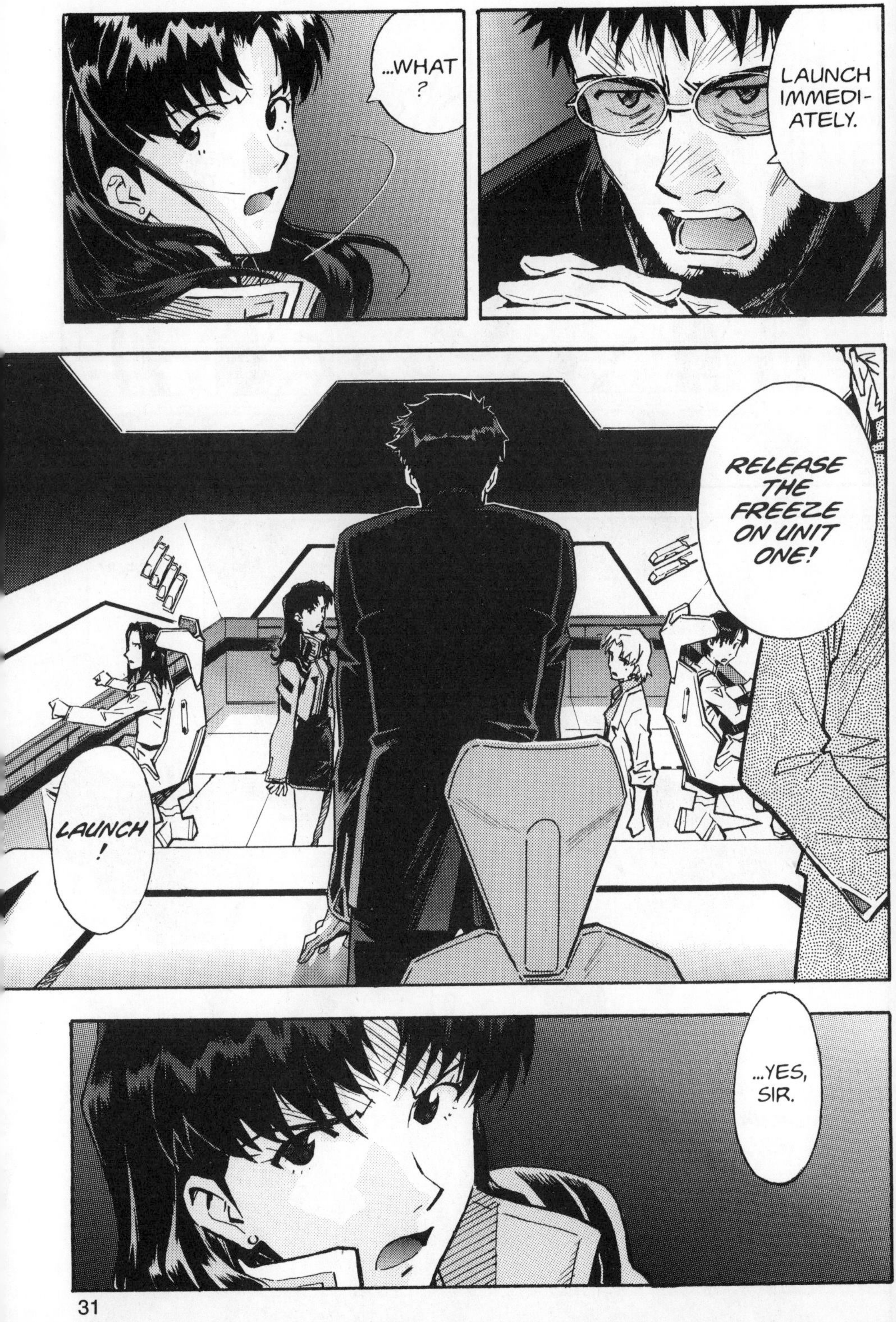
LAUNCH IMMEDI-ATELY.
...WHAT?
RELEASE THE FREEZE ON UNIT ONE!
LAUNCH!
...YES, SIR.

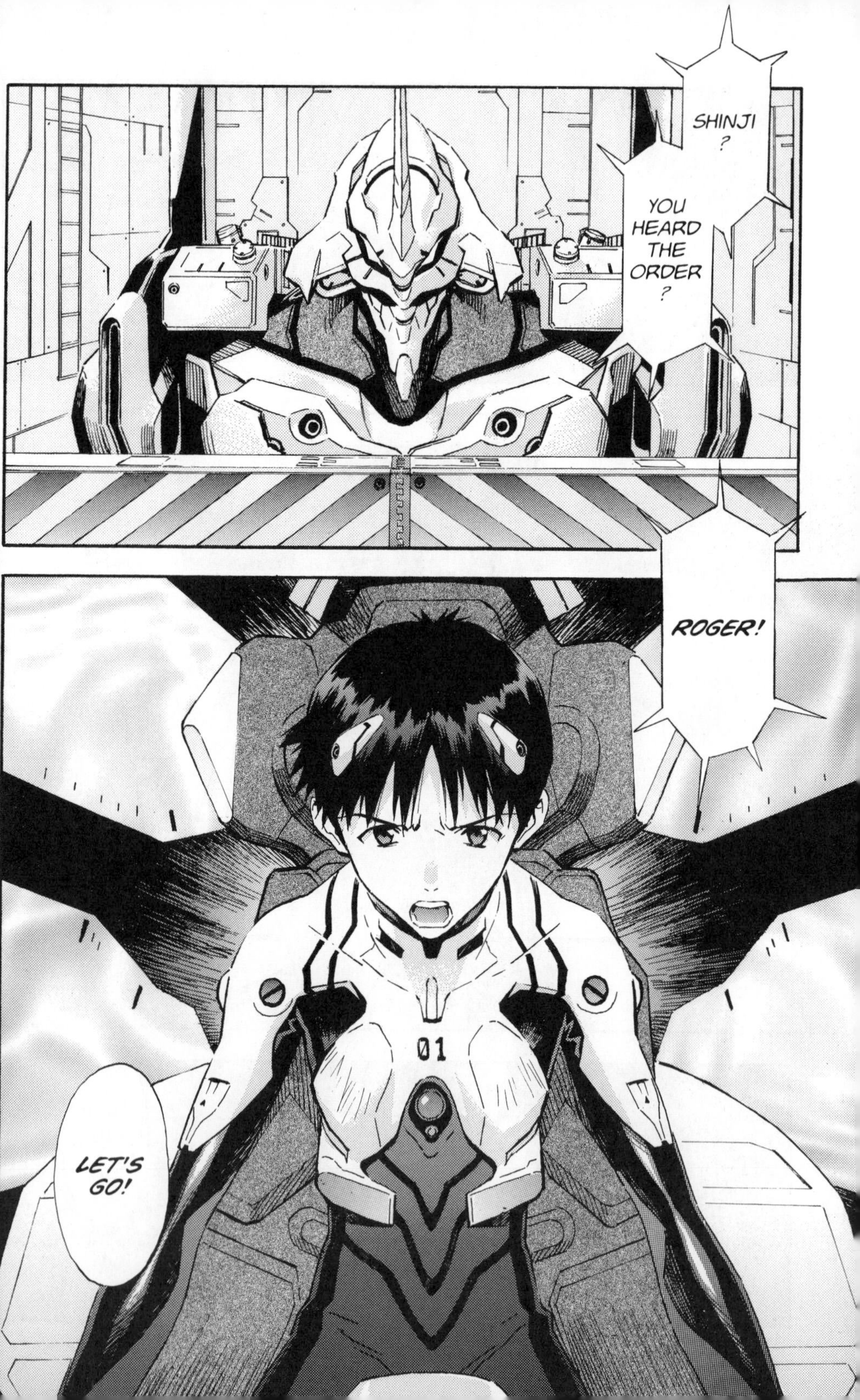
SHINJI
?
YOU HEARD THE ORDER
?
ROGER!
LET'S GO!

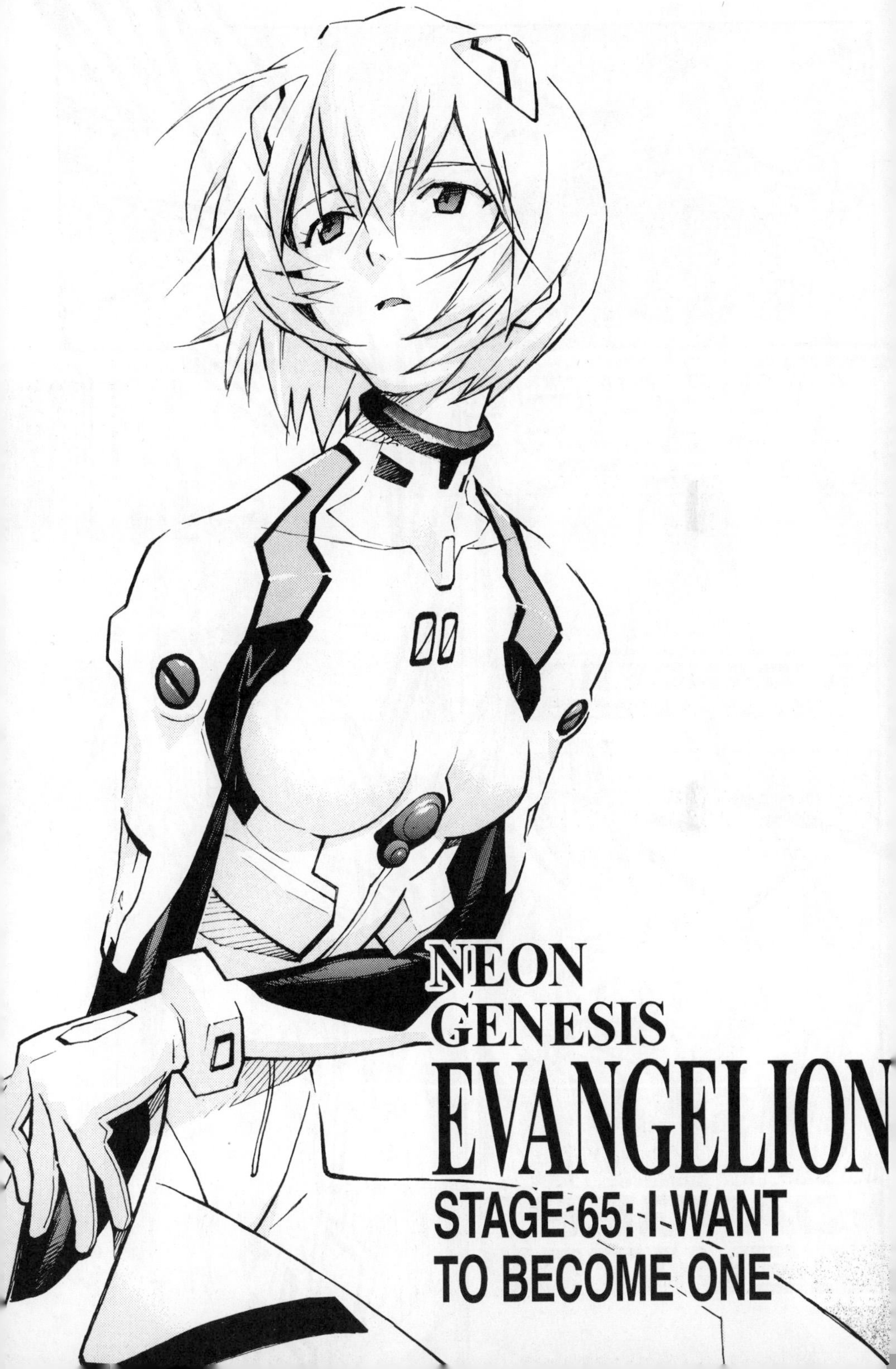

NEON GENESIS
EVANGELION
STAGE 65: I WANT TO BECOME ONE

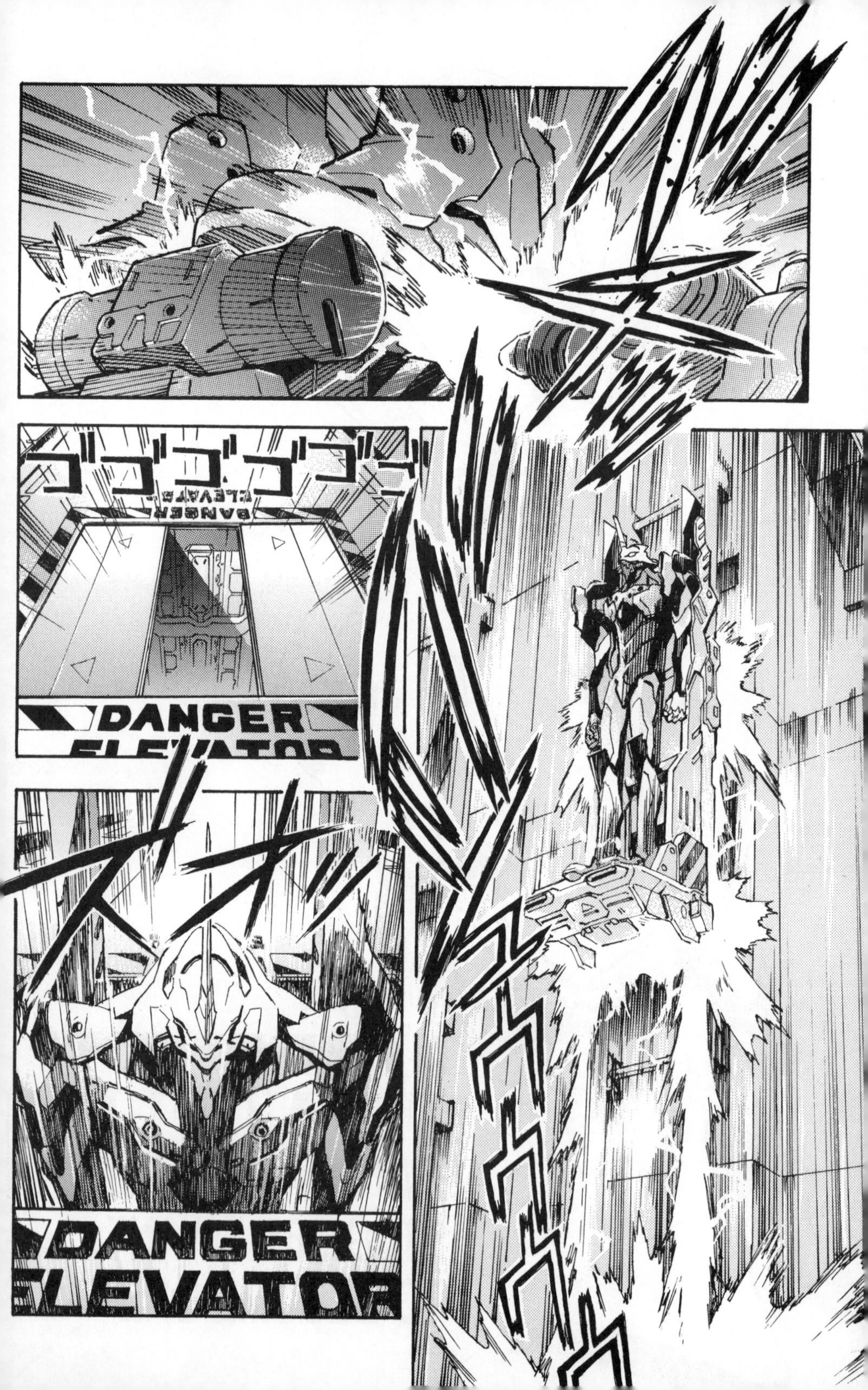
ゴゴゴゴゴ
DANGER
ズオッ
DANGER
ELEVATOR

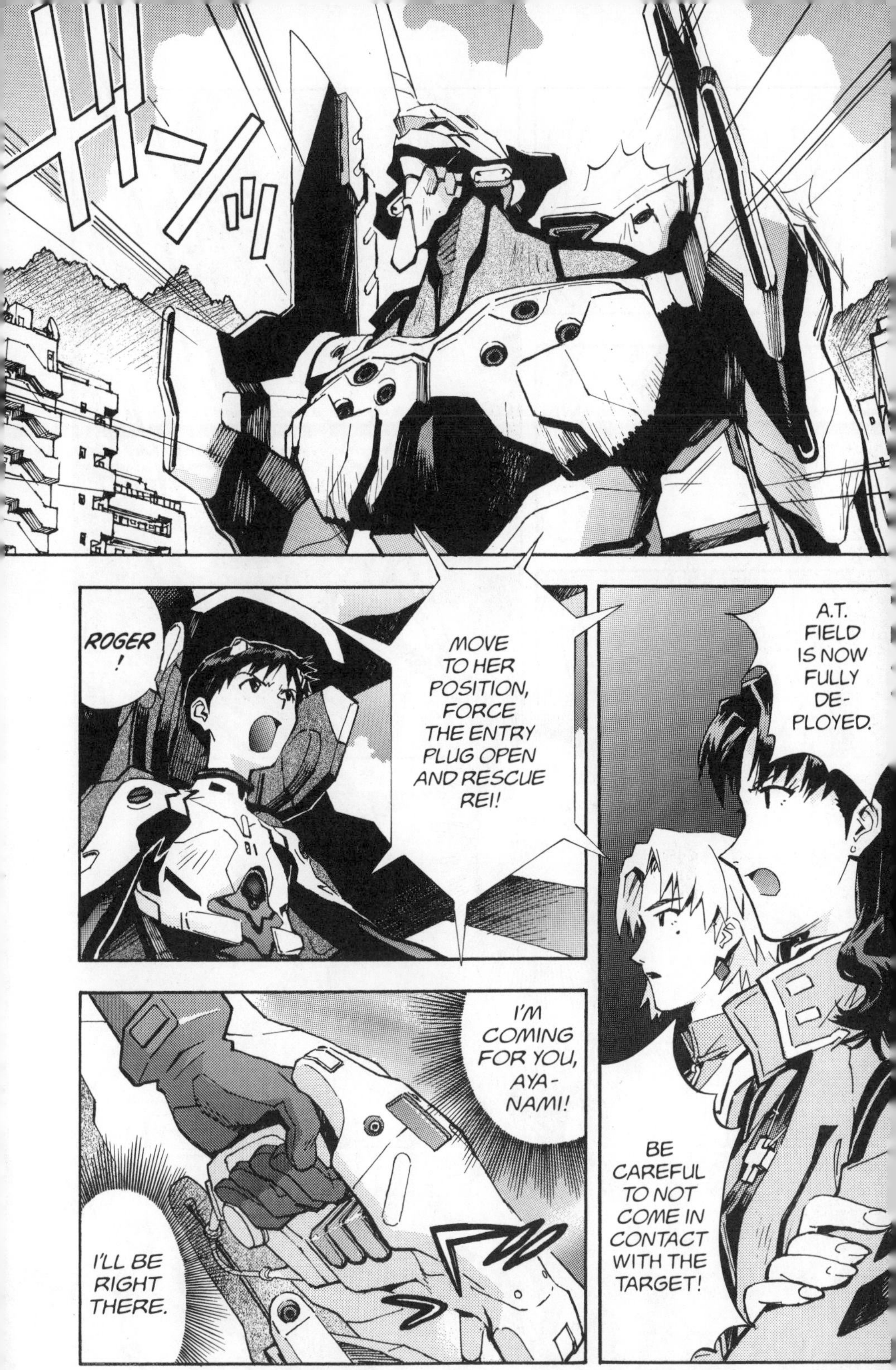
A.T. FIELD IS NOW FULLY DE-PLOYED.
BE CAREFUL TO NOT COME IN CONTACT WITH THE TARGET!
MOVE TO HER POSITION, FORCE THE ENTRY PLUG OPEN AND RESCUE REI!
ROGER!
I'M COMING FOR YOU, AYA-NAMI!
I'LL BE RIGHT THERE.

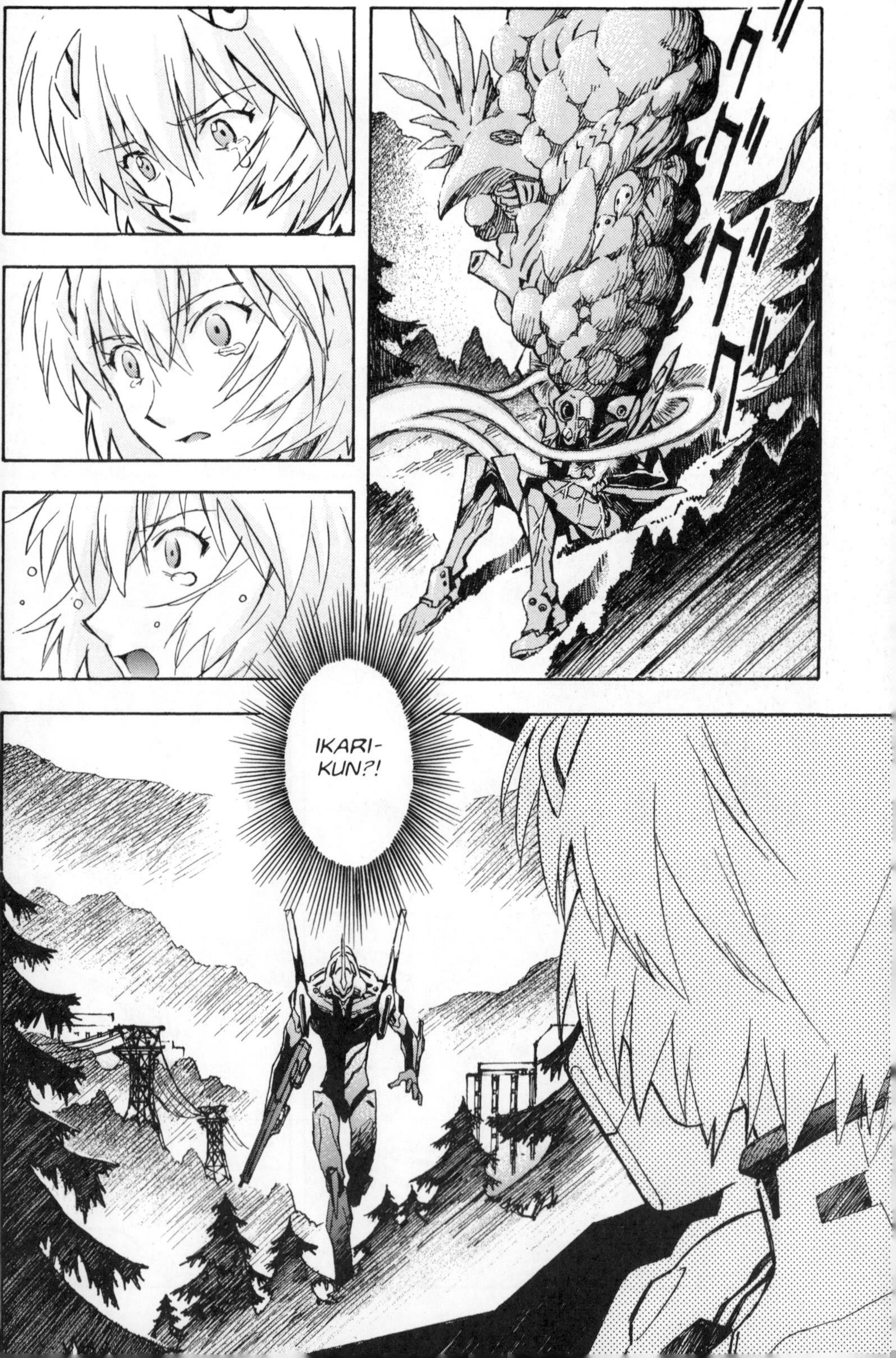
IKARI-KUN?!

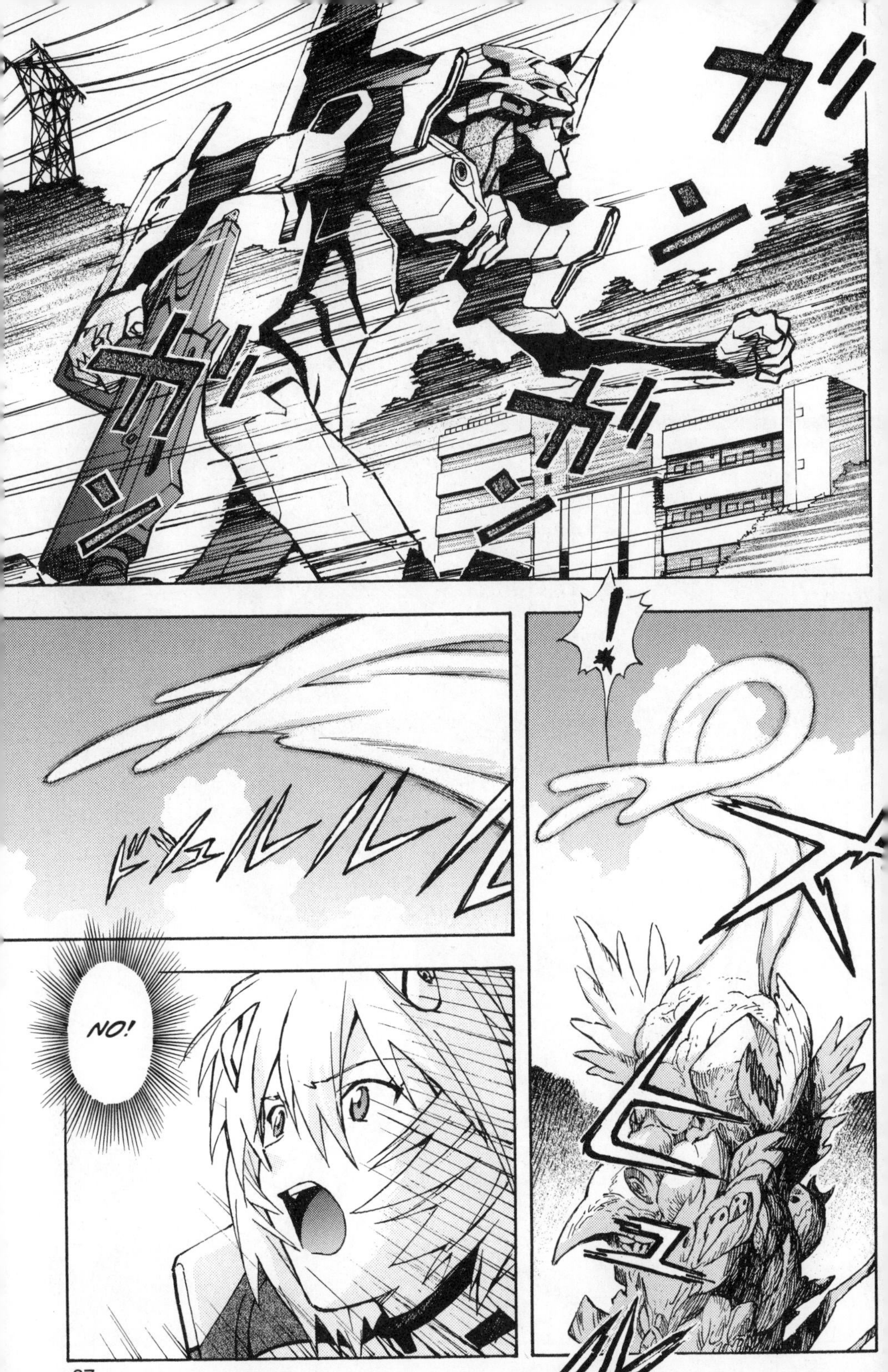

ガン
ガッ
ガッ
ドシュルルル
!
NO!

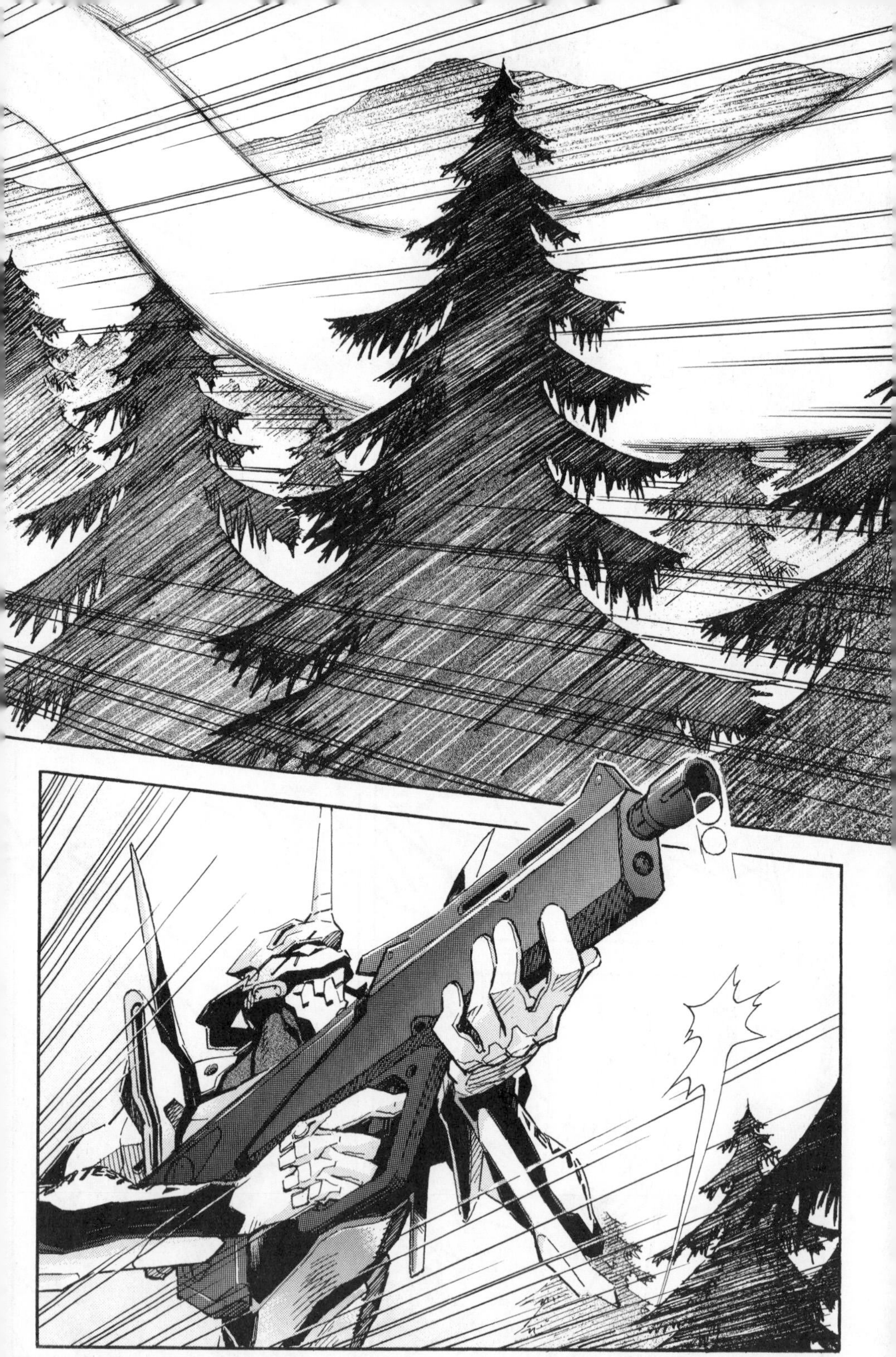

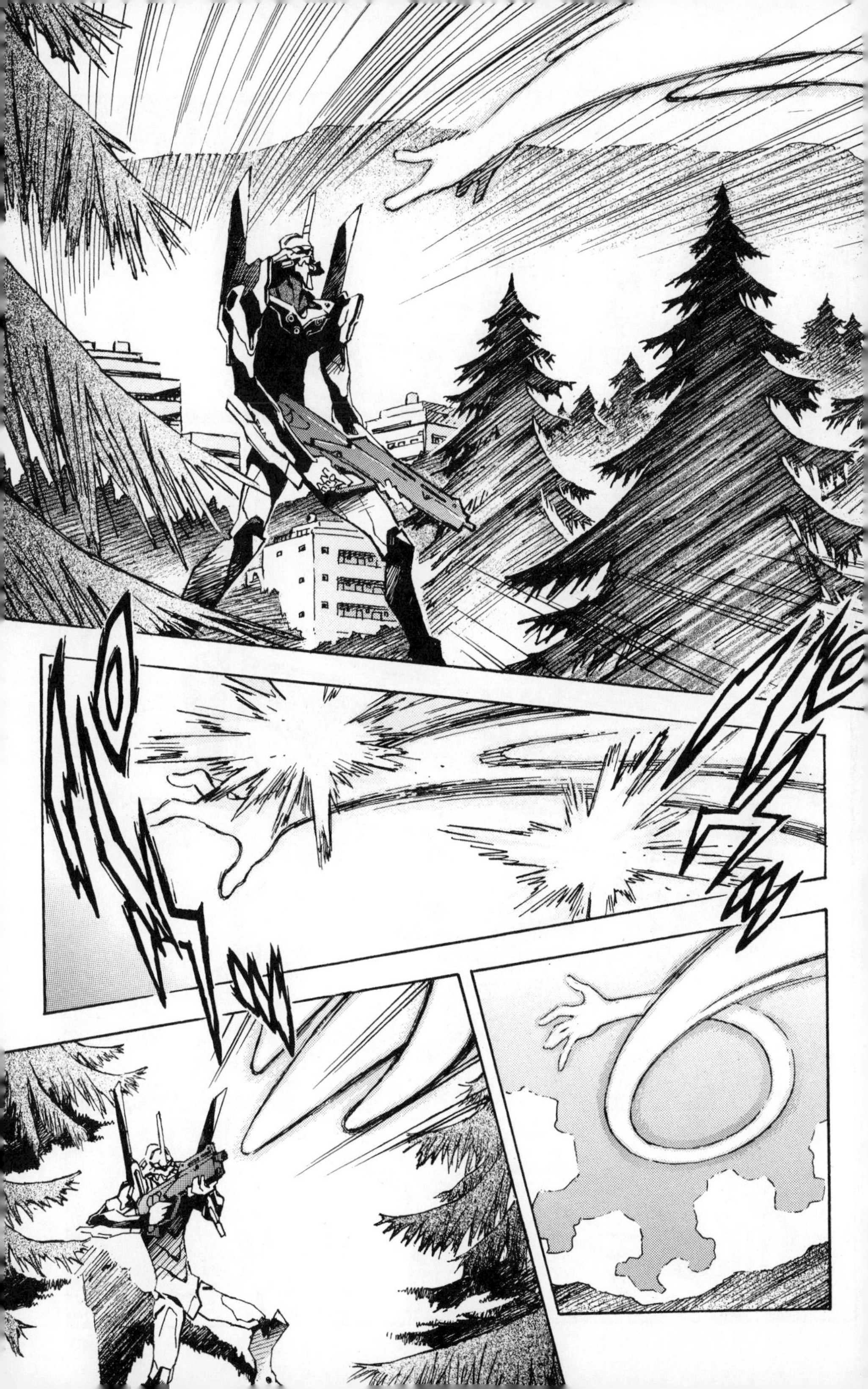

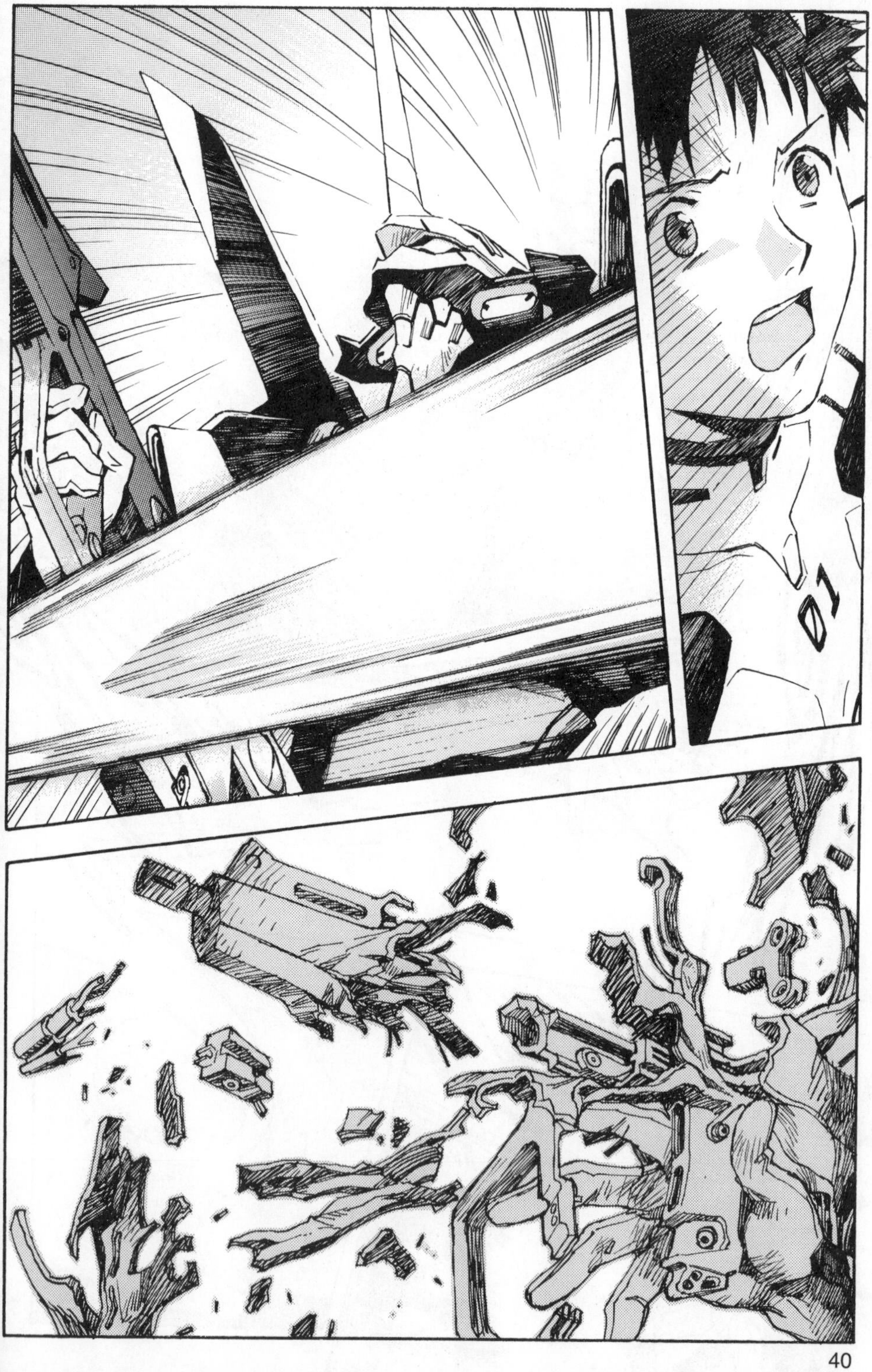

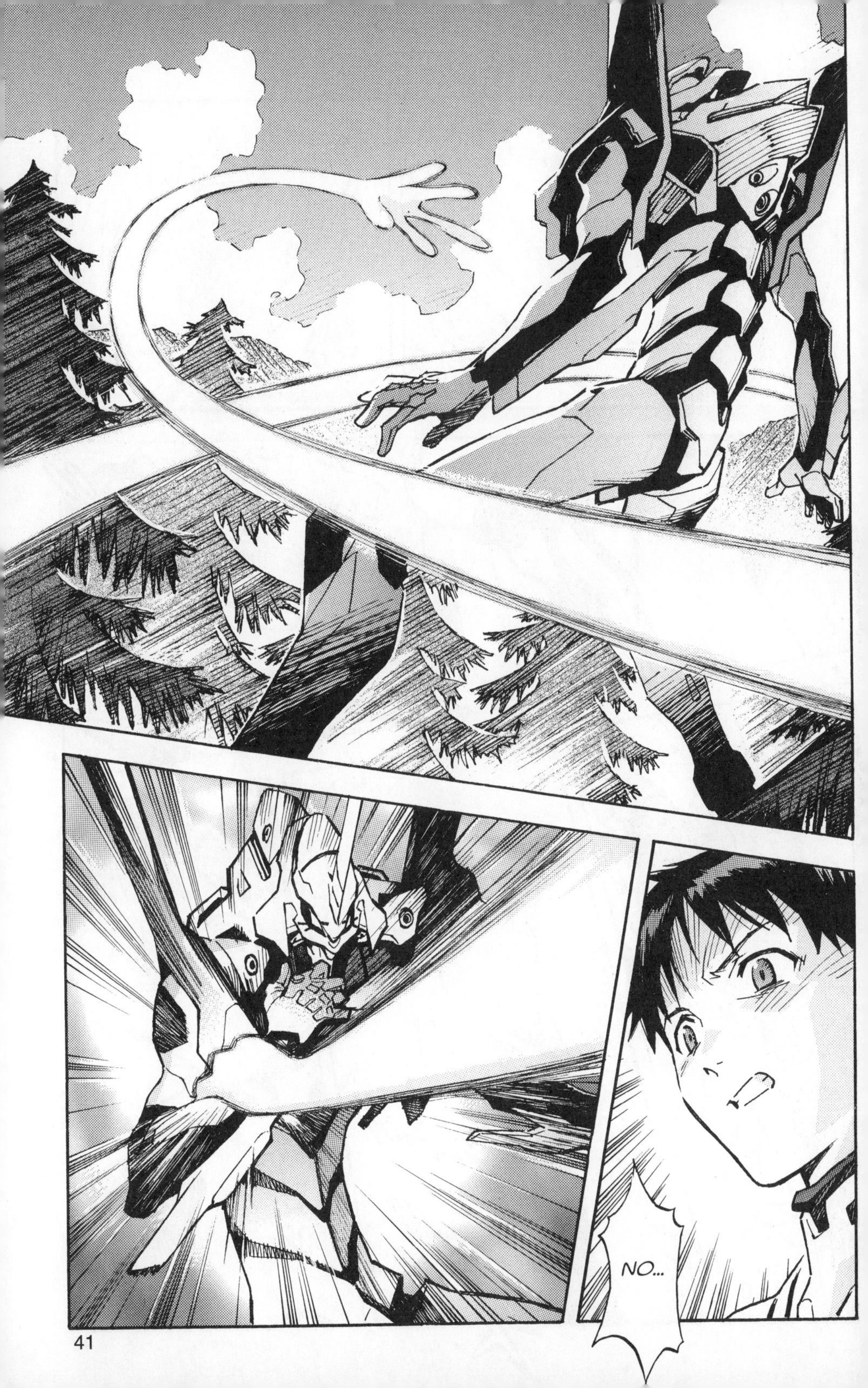
NO...

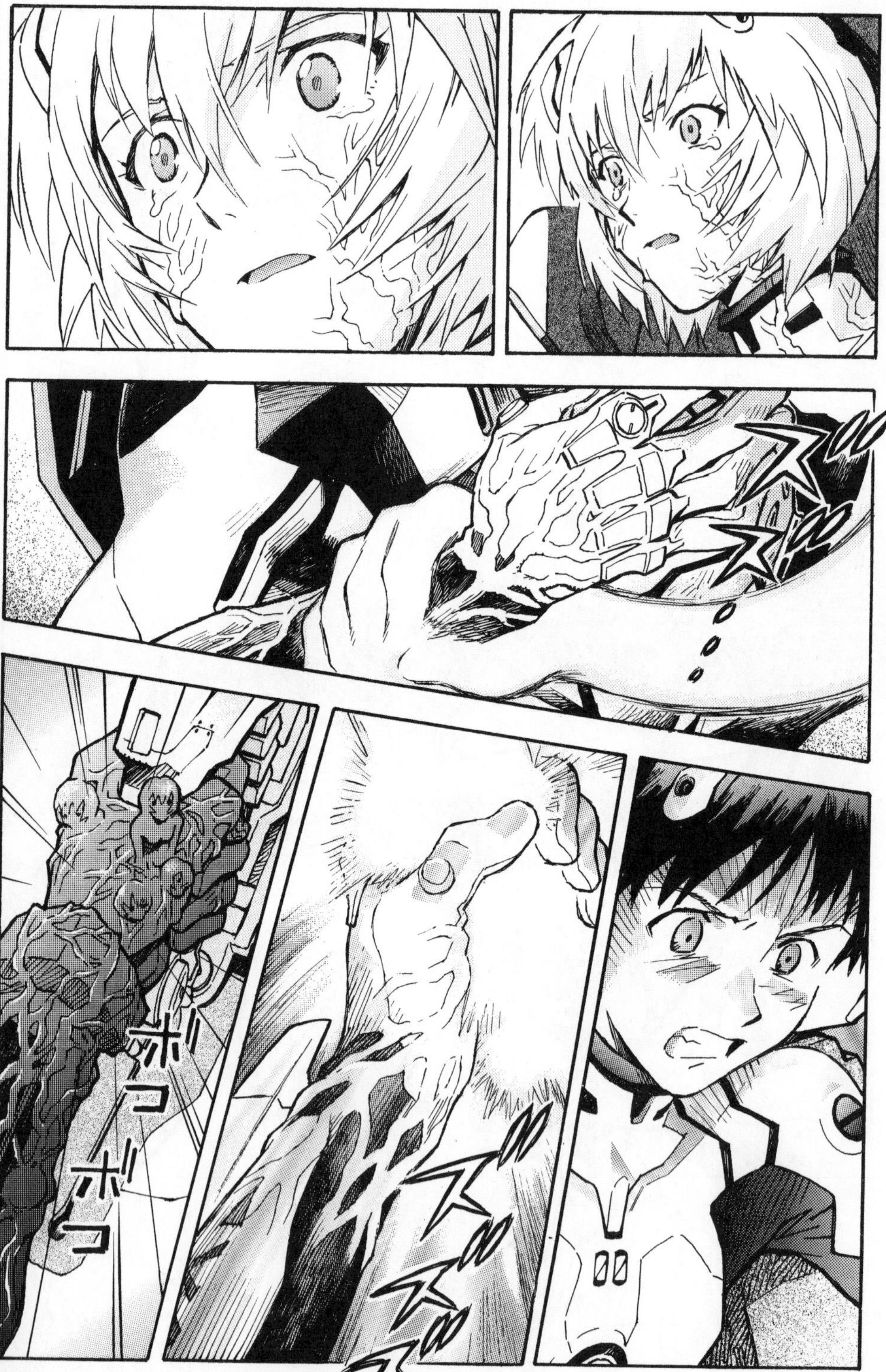
ボコ
ボコ

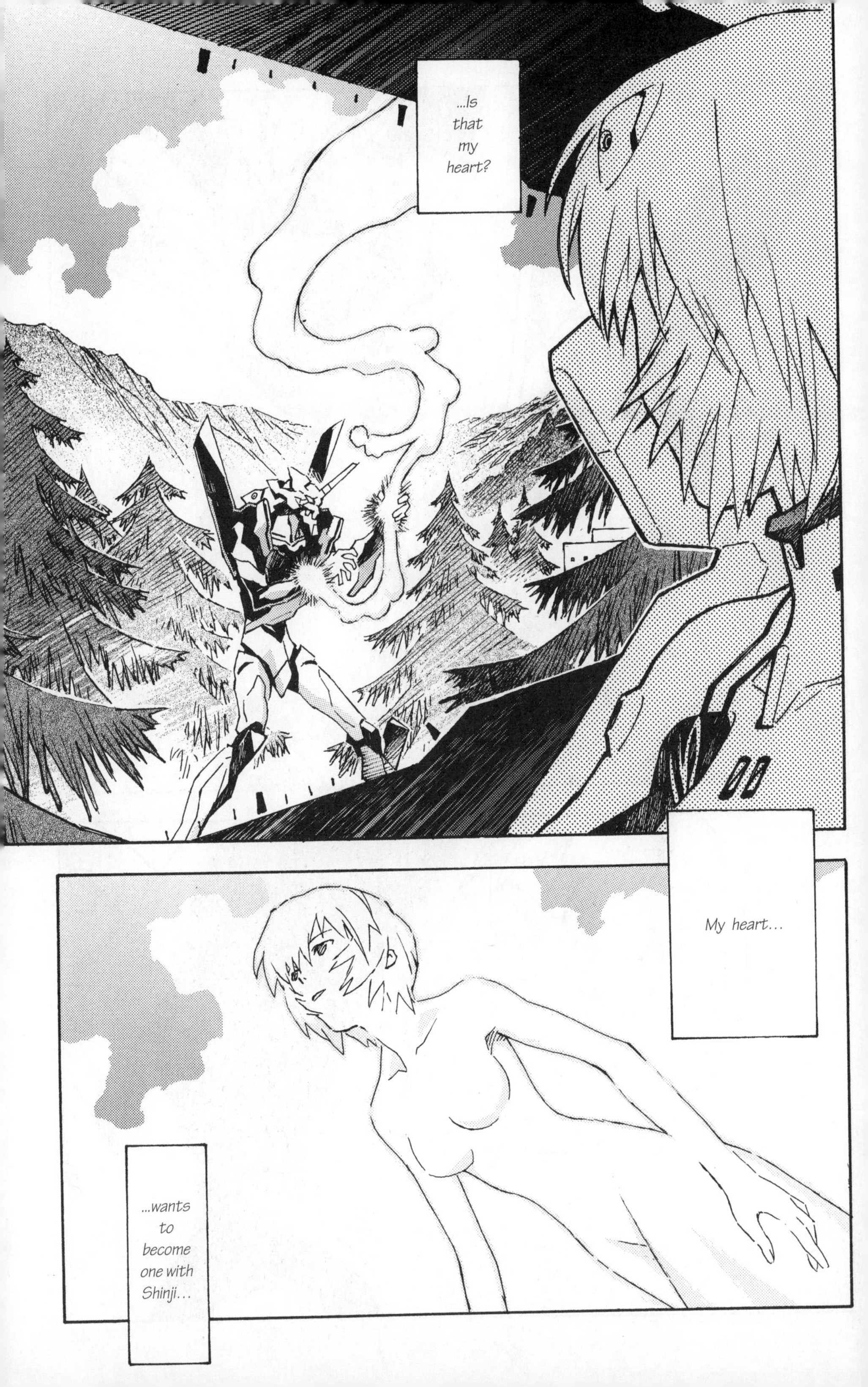
...Is that my heart?
My heart...
...wants to become one with Shinji...

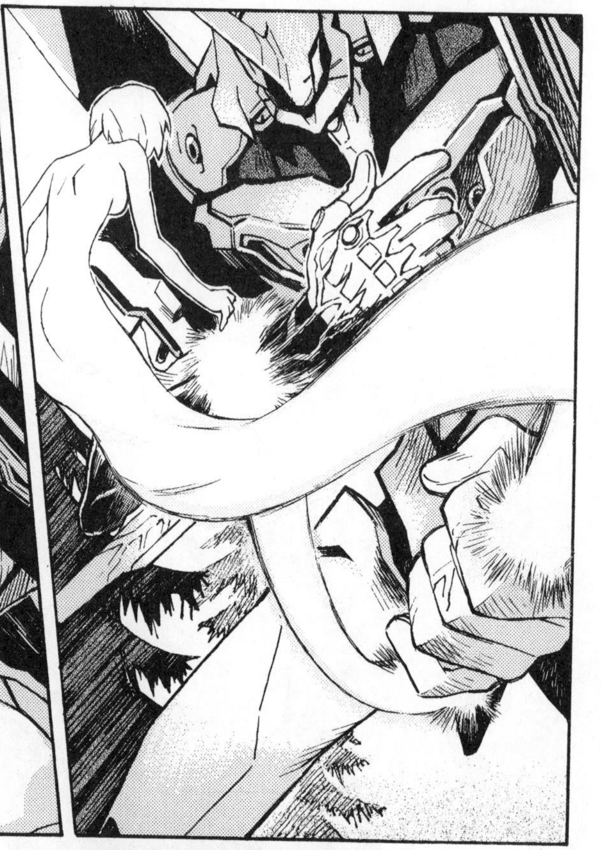

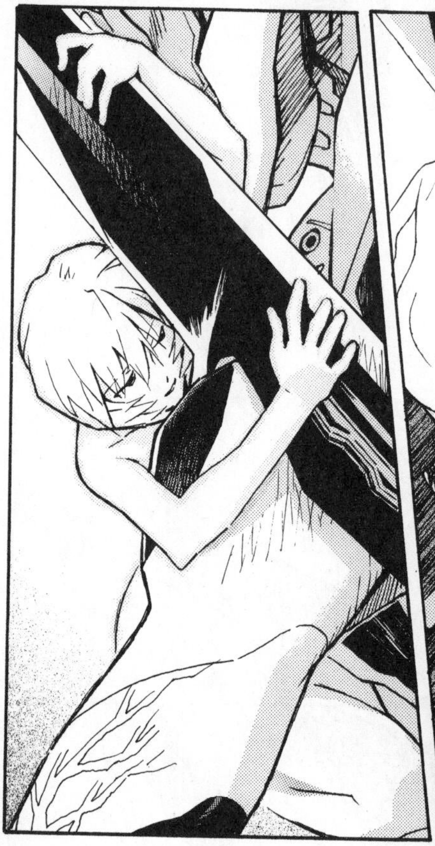

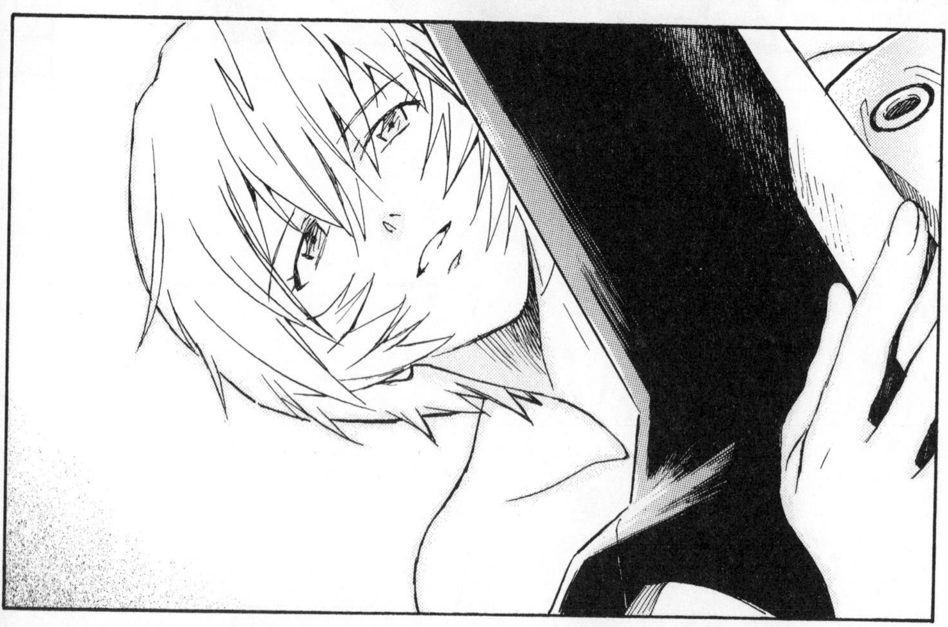

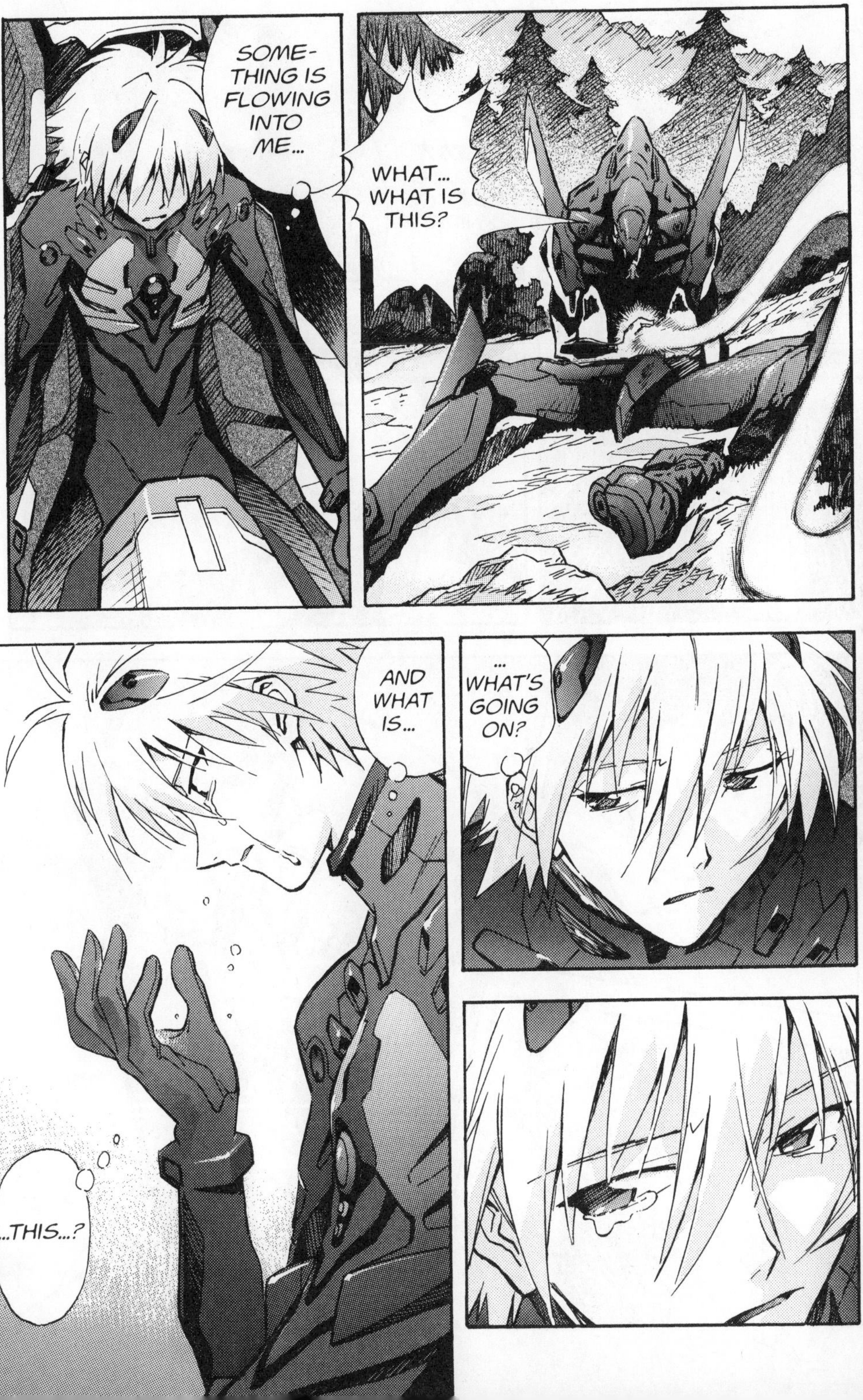
WHAT... WHAT IS THIS?
SOME-THING IS FLOWING INTO ME...
... WHAT'S GOING ON?
AND WHAT IS...
...THIS...?

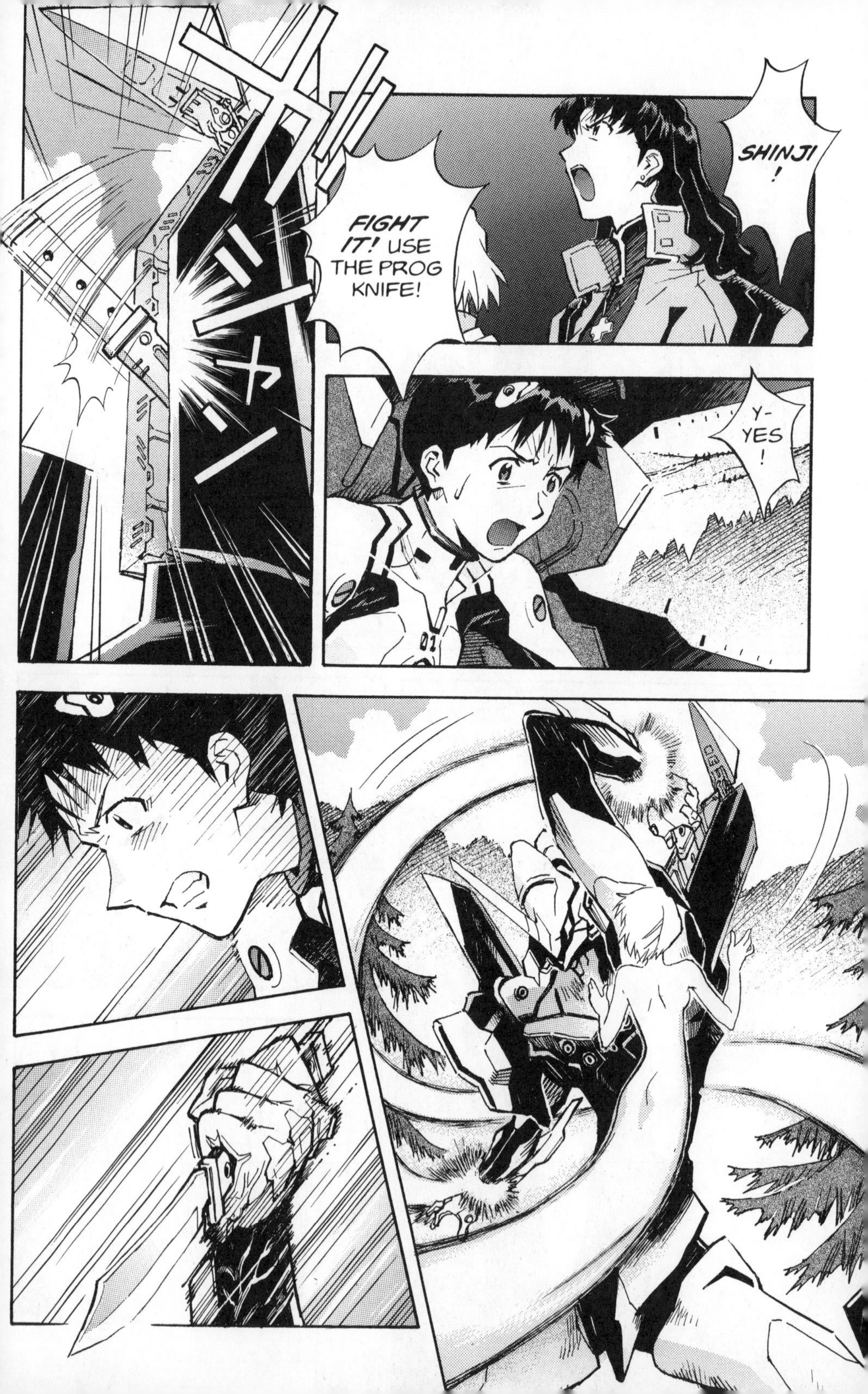
SHINJI!
FIGHT IT! USE THE PROG KNIFE!
Y-YES!

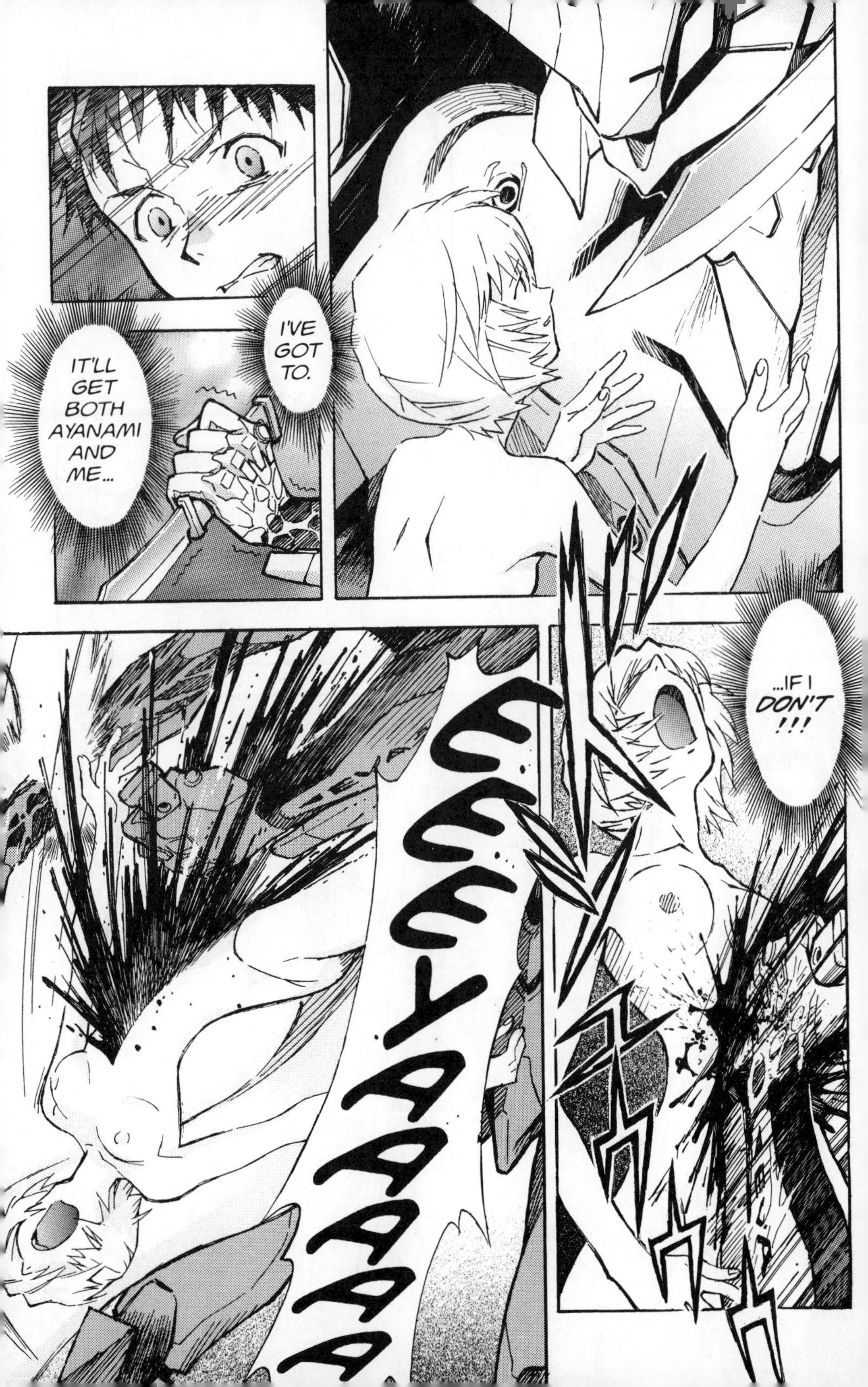
I'VE GOT TO.
IT'LL GET BOTH AYANAMI AND ME...
...IF I DON'T!!!
EEEEYAAAAAAA

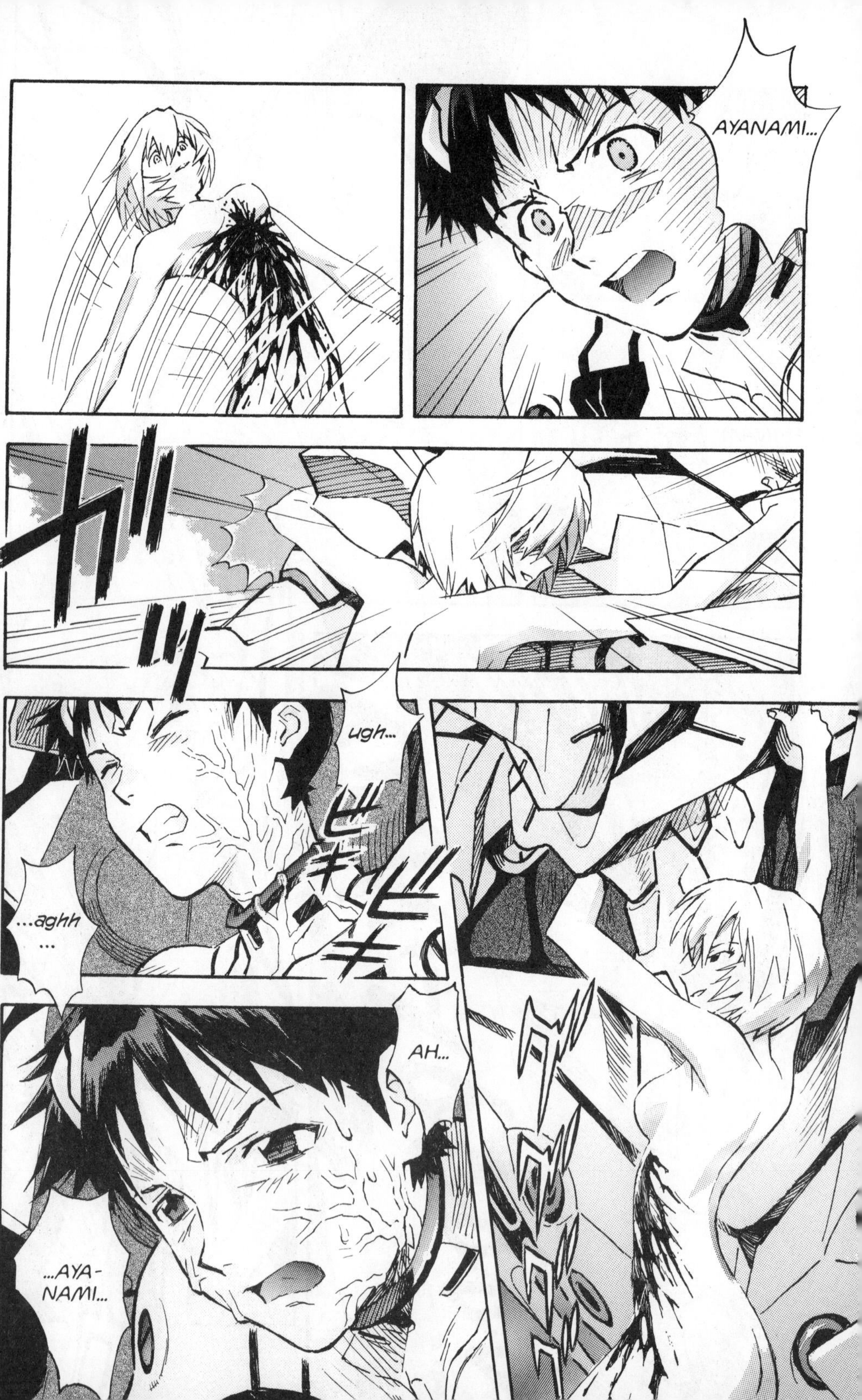
AYANAMI...
ugh...
...aghh ...
AH...
...AYA-NAMI...

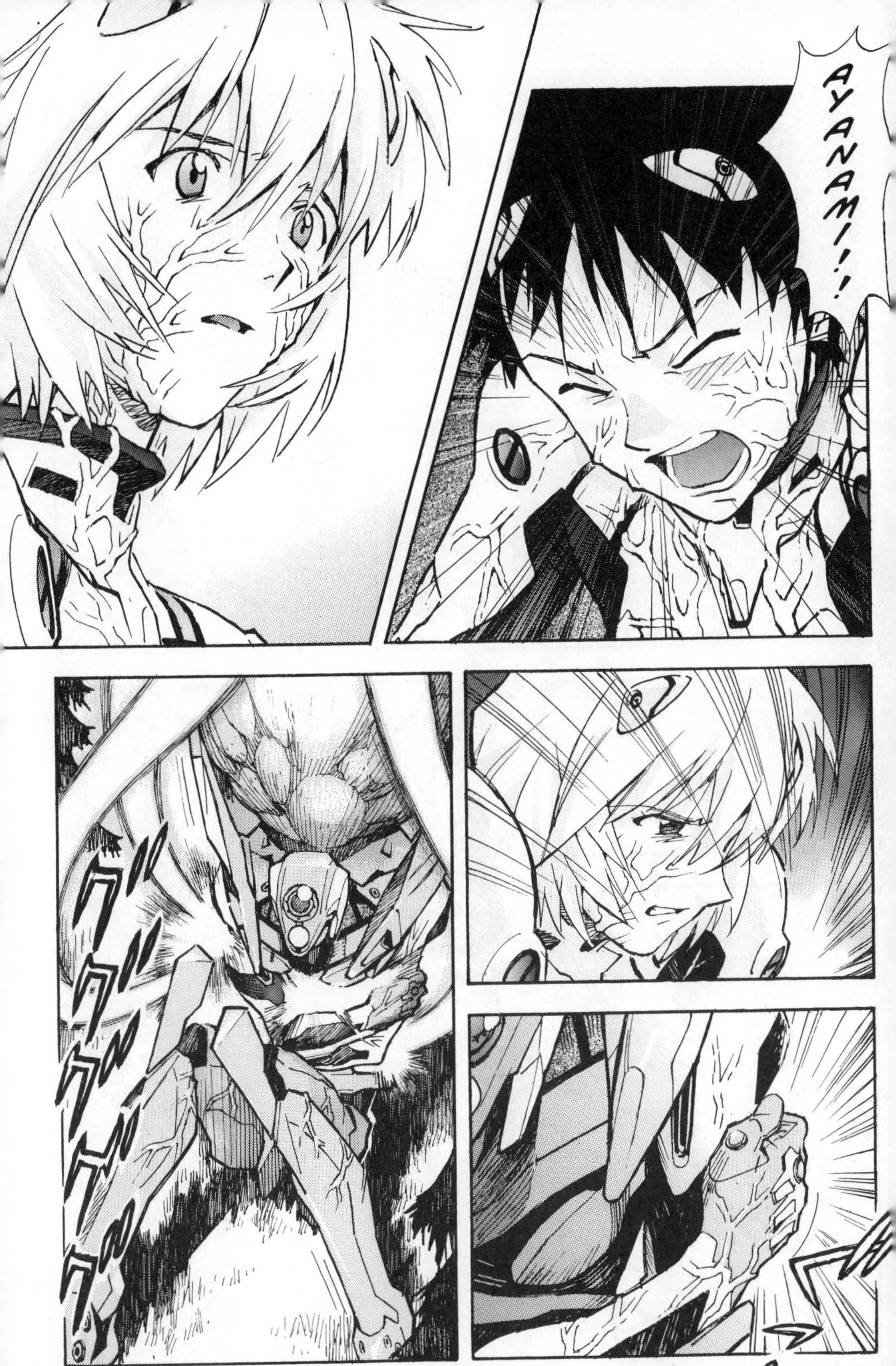
AYANAMI!!!

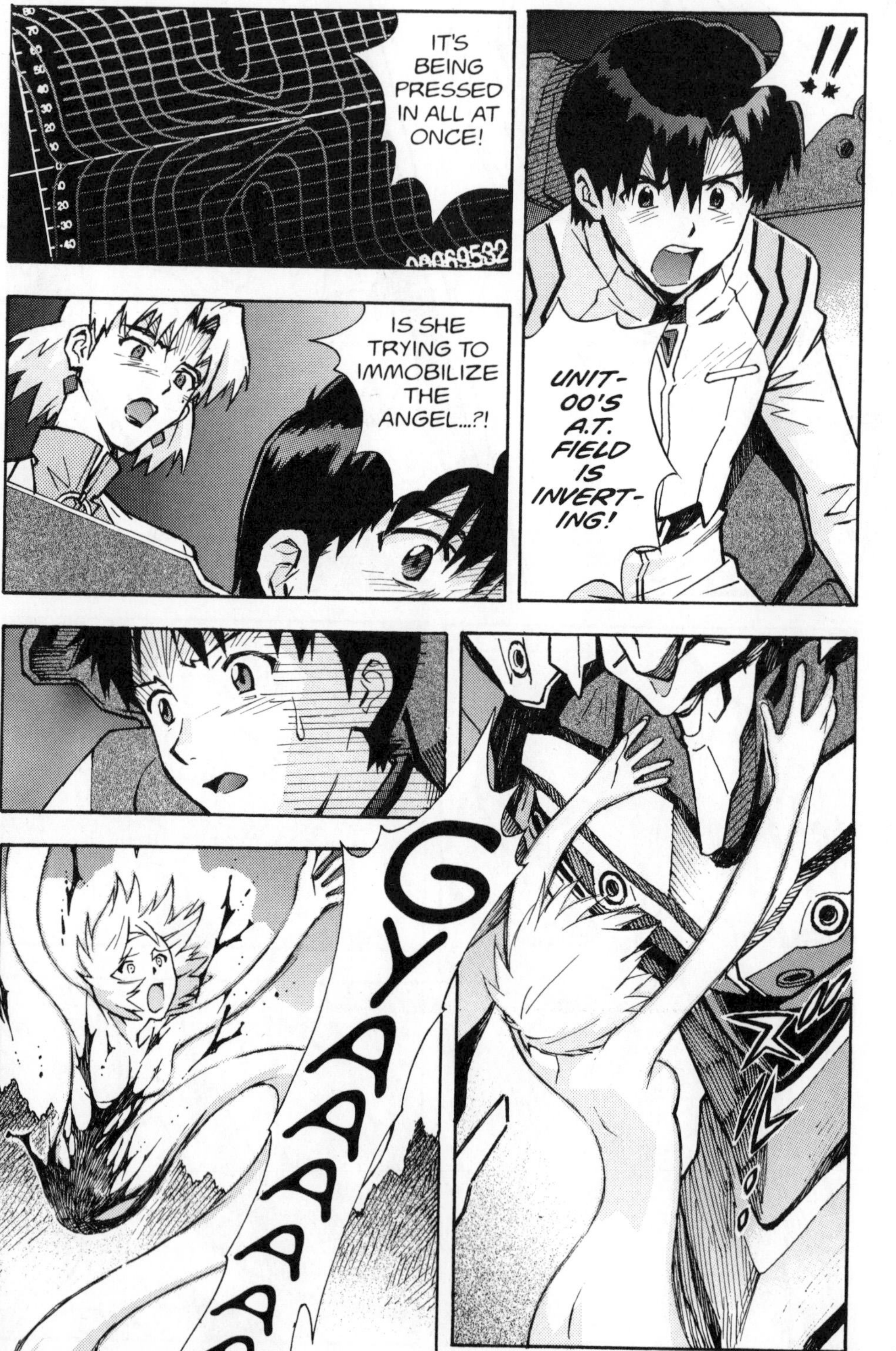
!!
UNIT-00'S A.T. FIELD IS INVERTING!
IT'S BEING PRESSED IN ALL AT ONCE!
IS SHE TRYING TO IMMOBILIZE THE ANGEL...?!
GYAAAAAAA

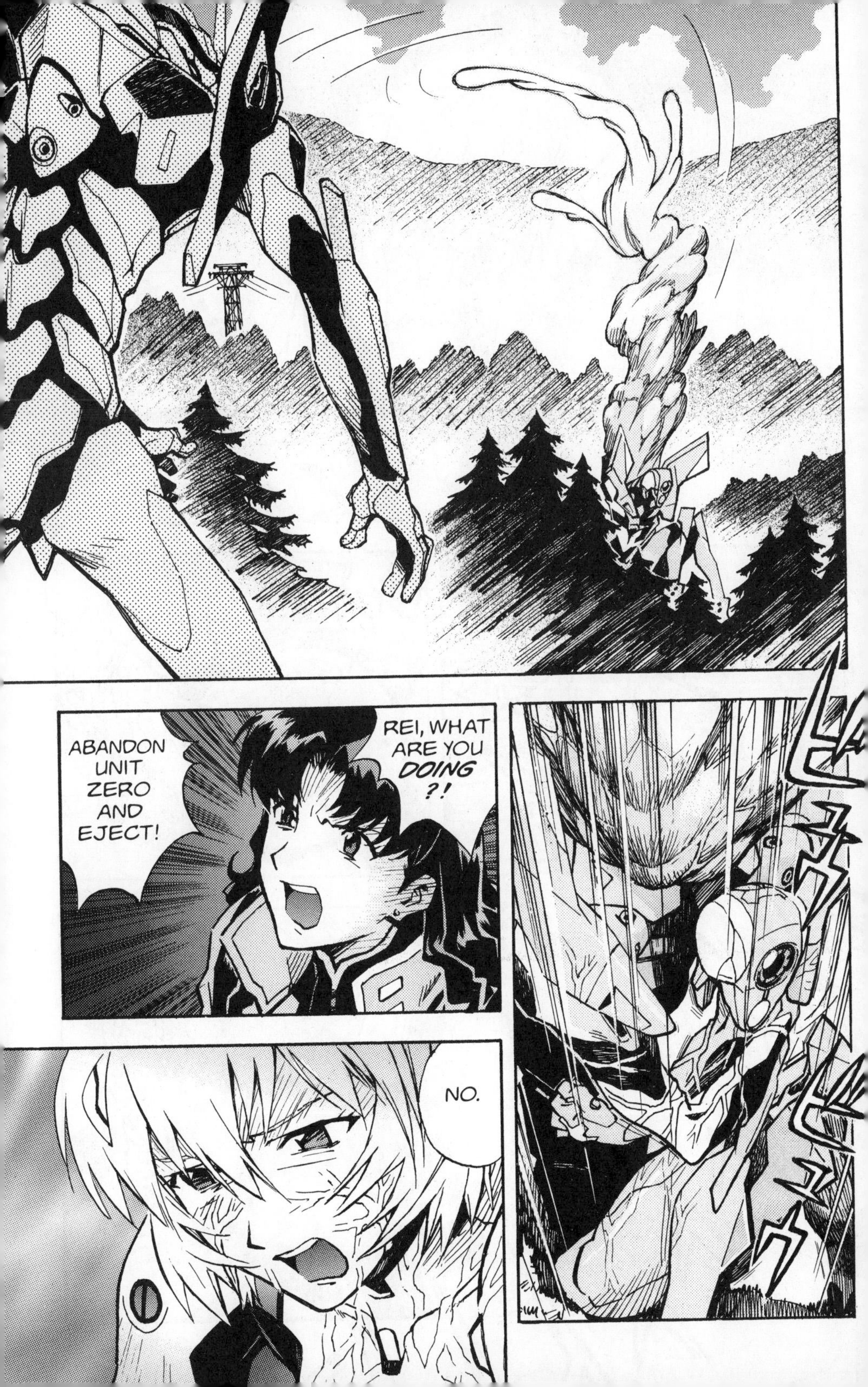
REI, WHAT ARE YOU *DOING* ?!
ABANDON UNIT ZERO AND EJECT!
NO.

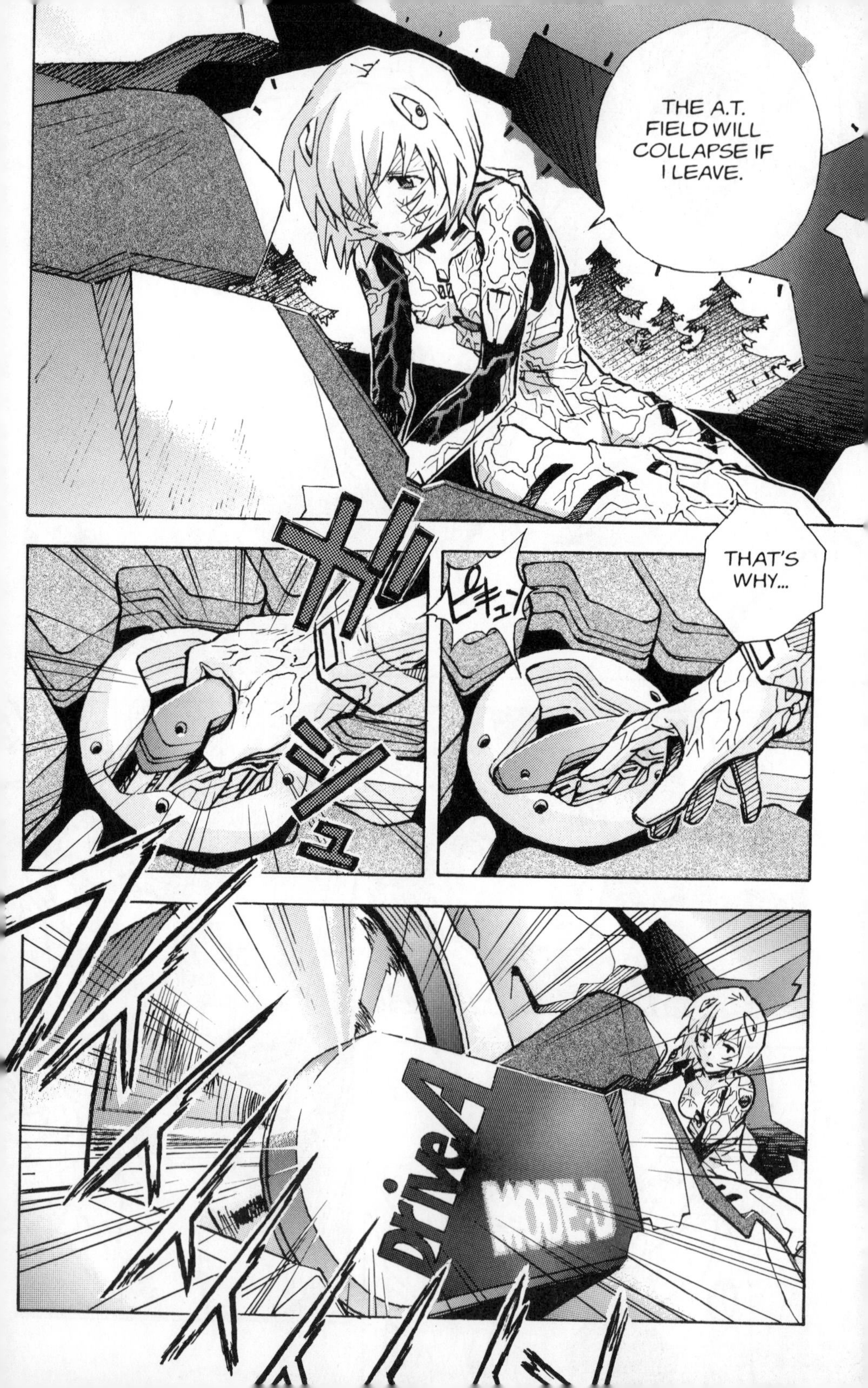
THE A.T. FIELD WILL COLLAPSE IF I LEAVE.
THAT'S WHY...
ピキュン
MODE:D

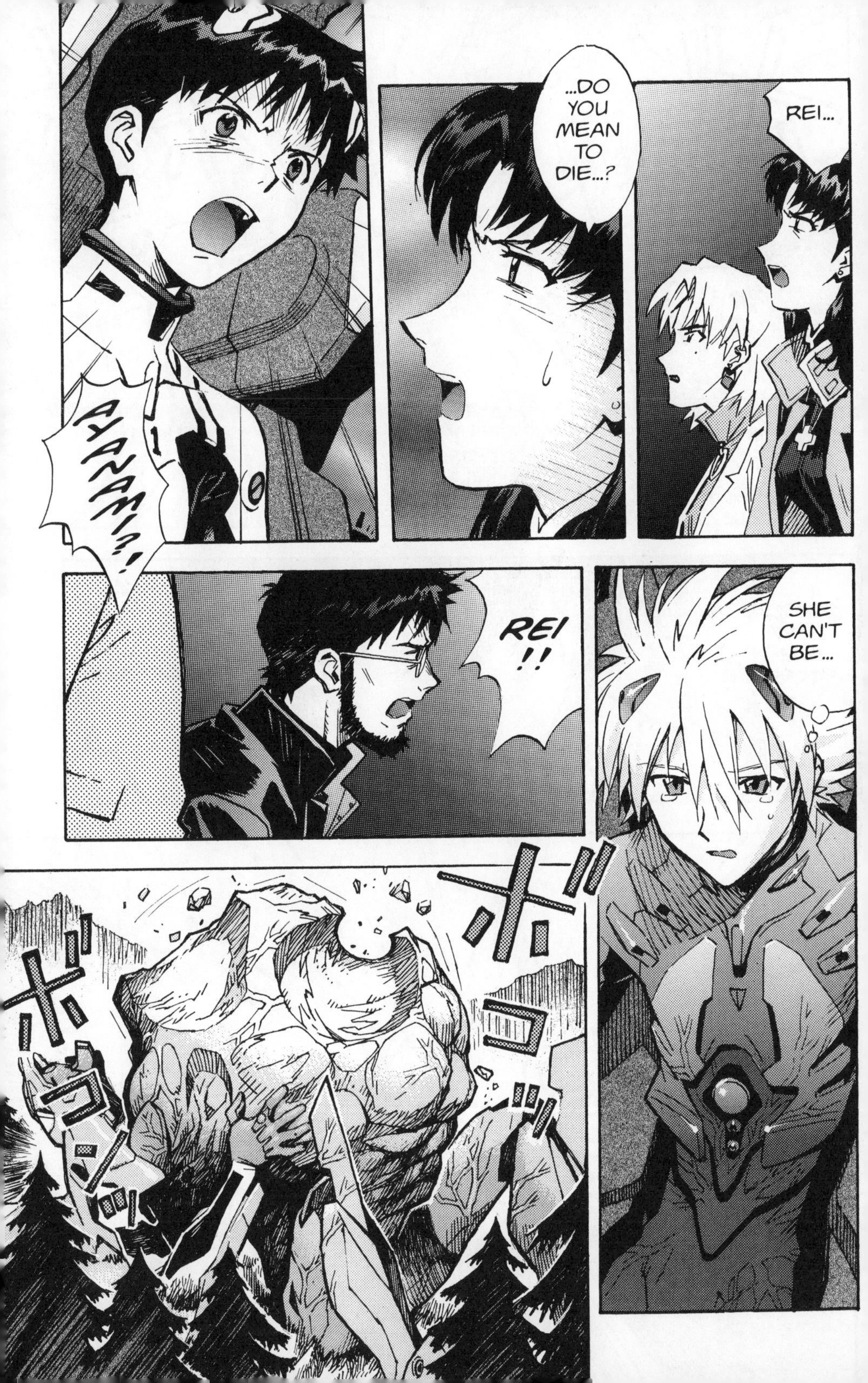
REI...
...DO YOU MEAN TO DIE...?
AYANAMI?!
SHE CAN'T BE...
REI!!

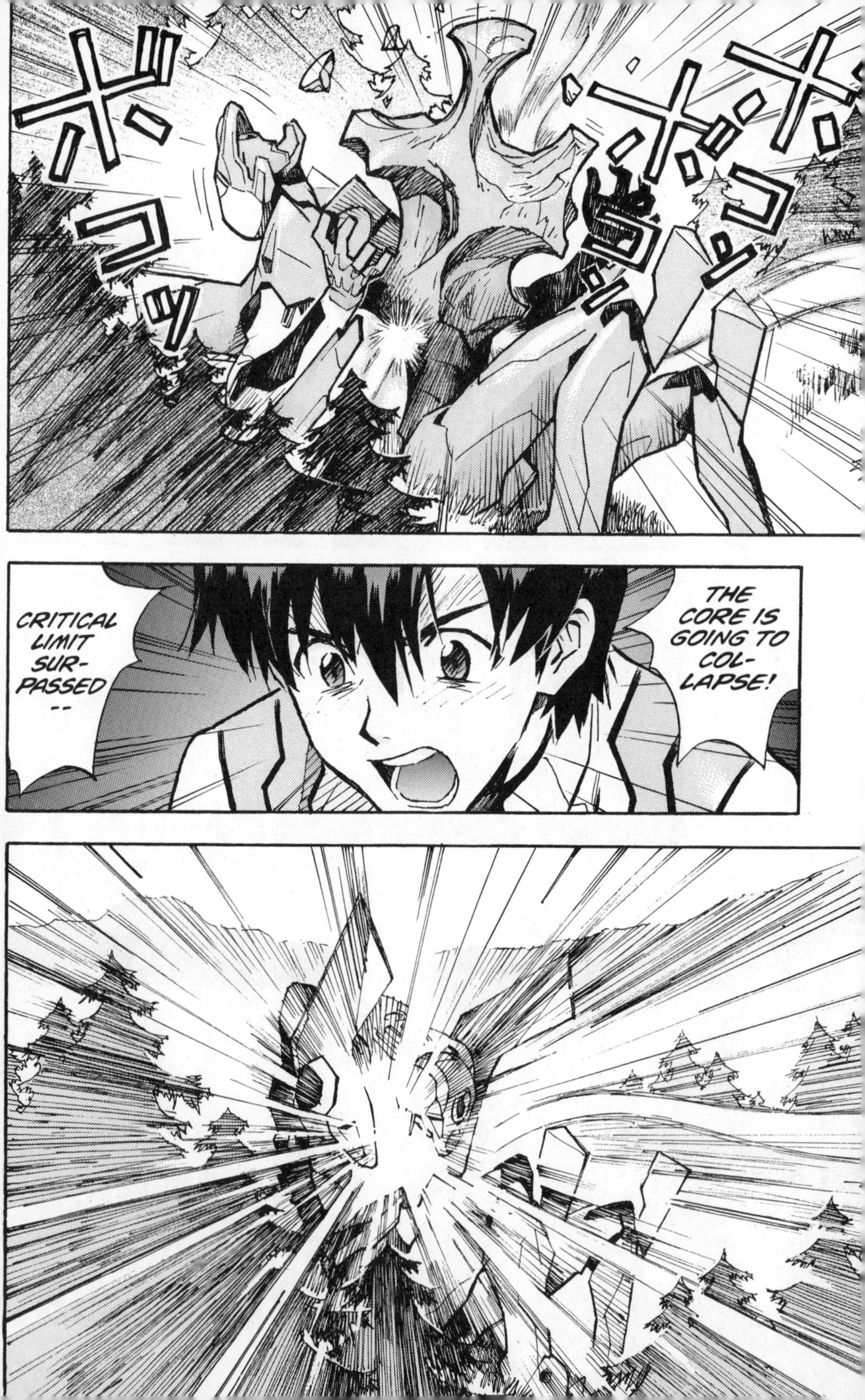
THE CORE IS GOING TO COL-LAPSE!
CRITICAL LIMIT SUR-PASSED --

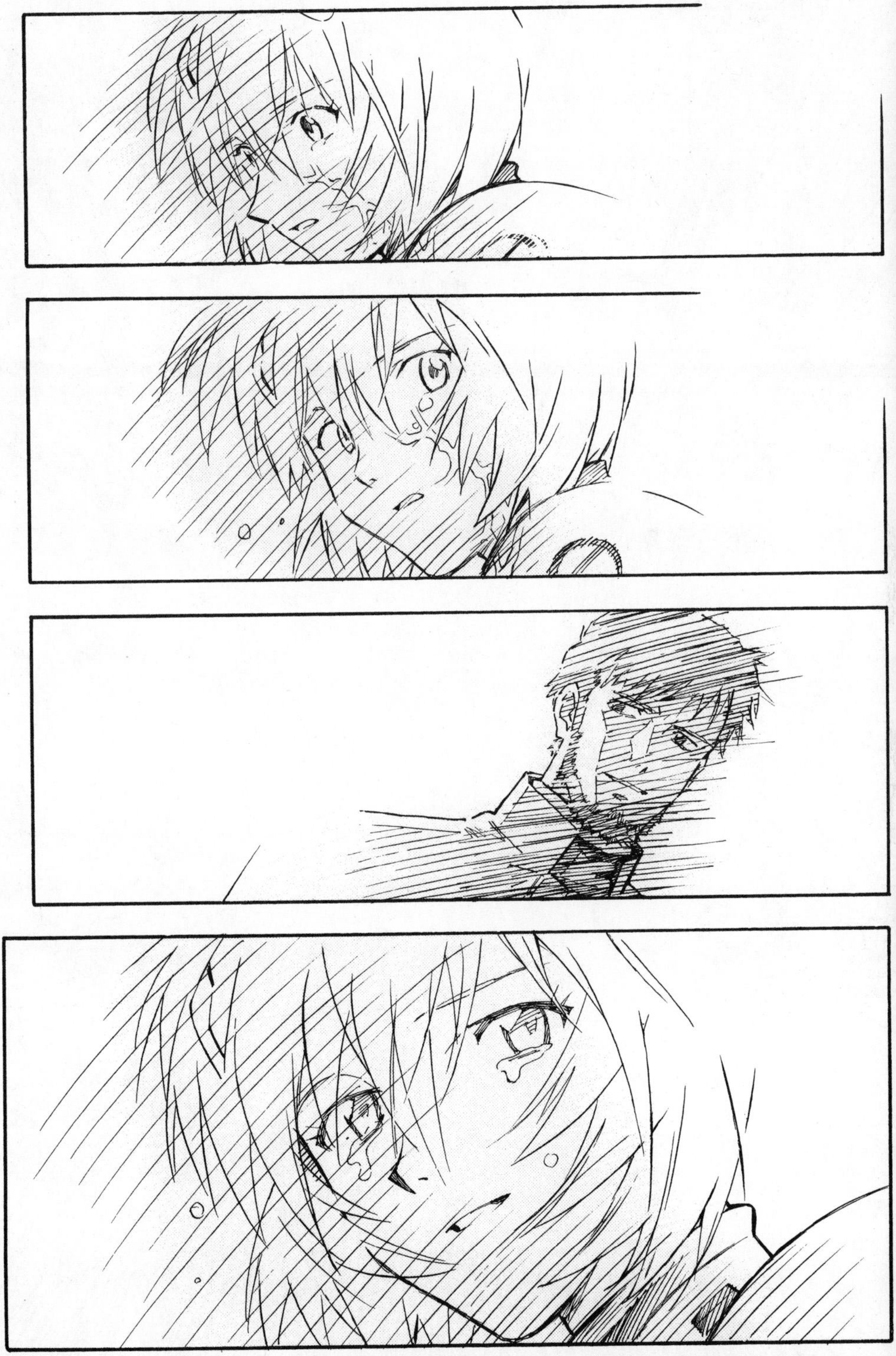

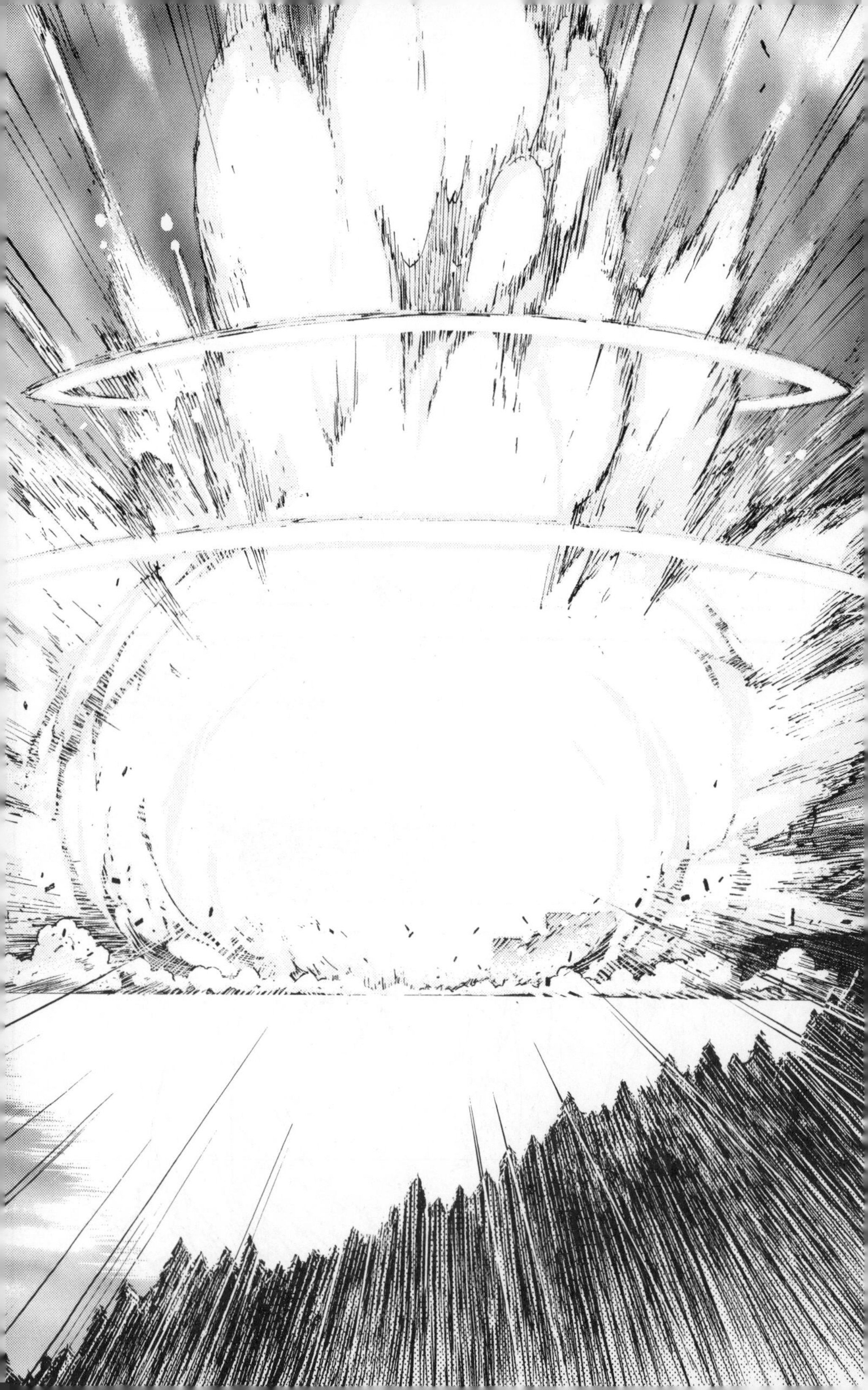

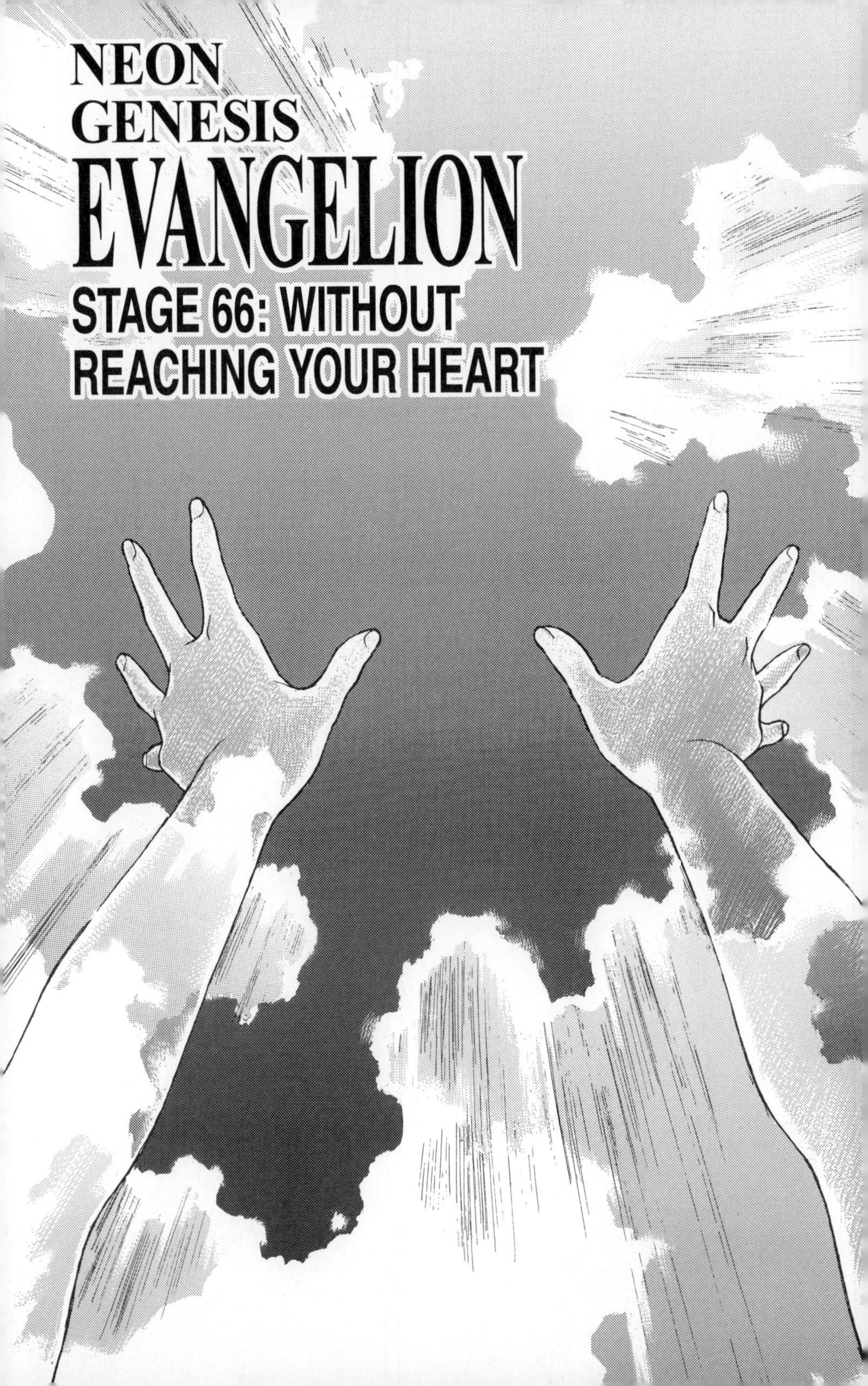
NEON
GENESIS
EVANGELION
STAGE 66: WITHOUT
REACHING YOUR HEART

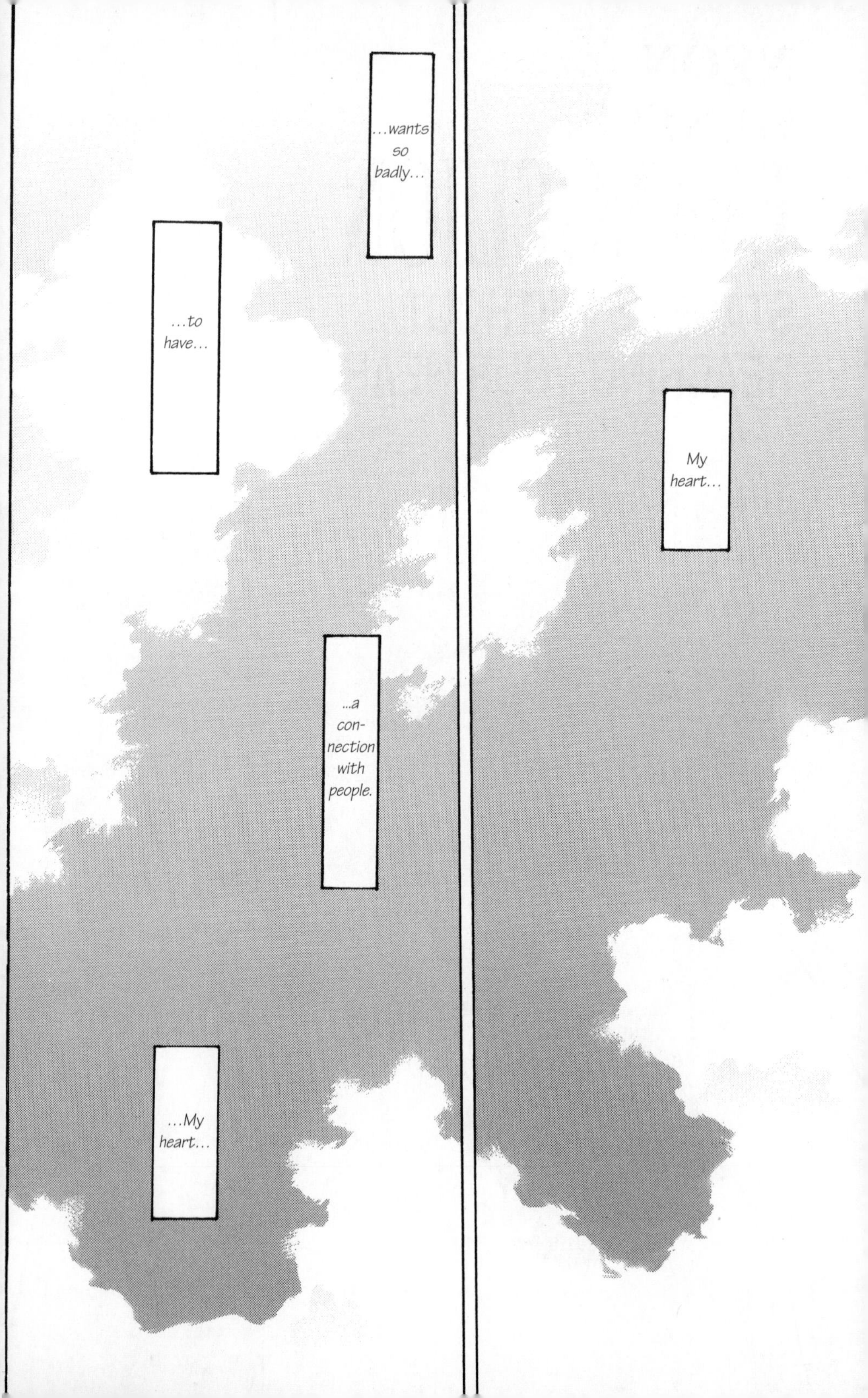
My heart…
…wants so badly…
…to have…
...a con-nection with people.
…My heart…

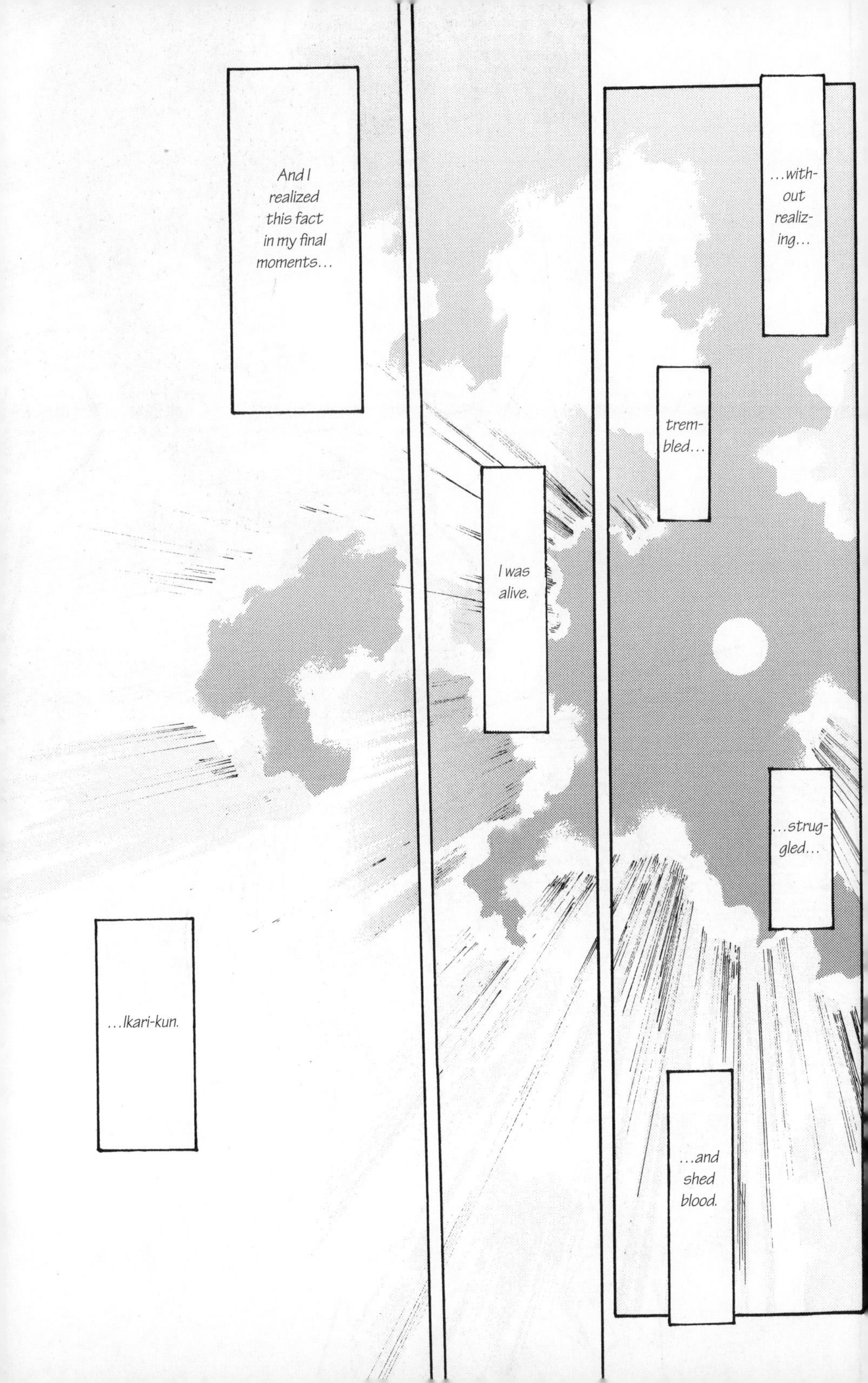
...with-out realiz-ing...
trem-bled...
...strug-gled...
...and shed blood.
I was alive.
And I realized this fact in my final moments...
...Ikari-kun.

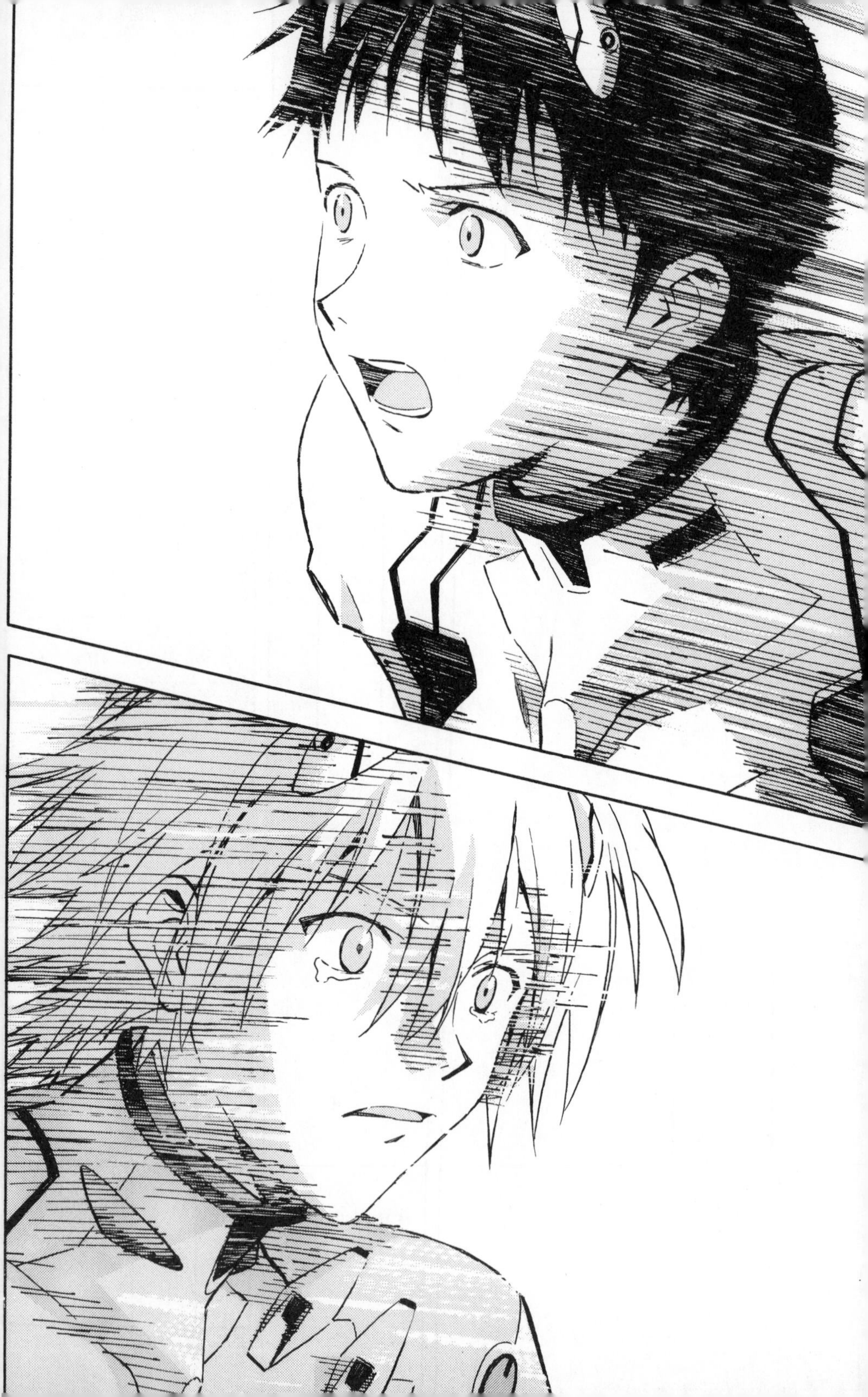

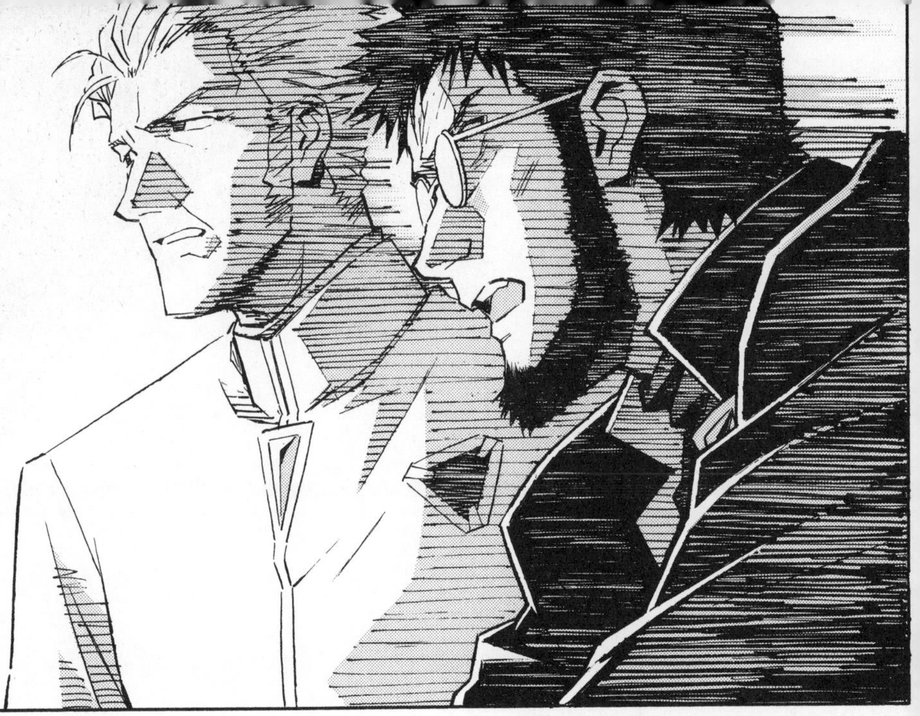
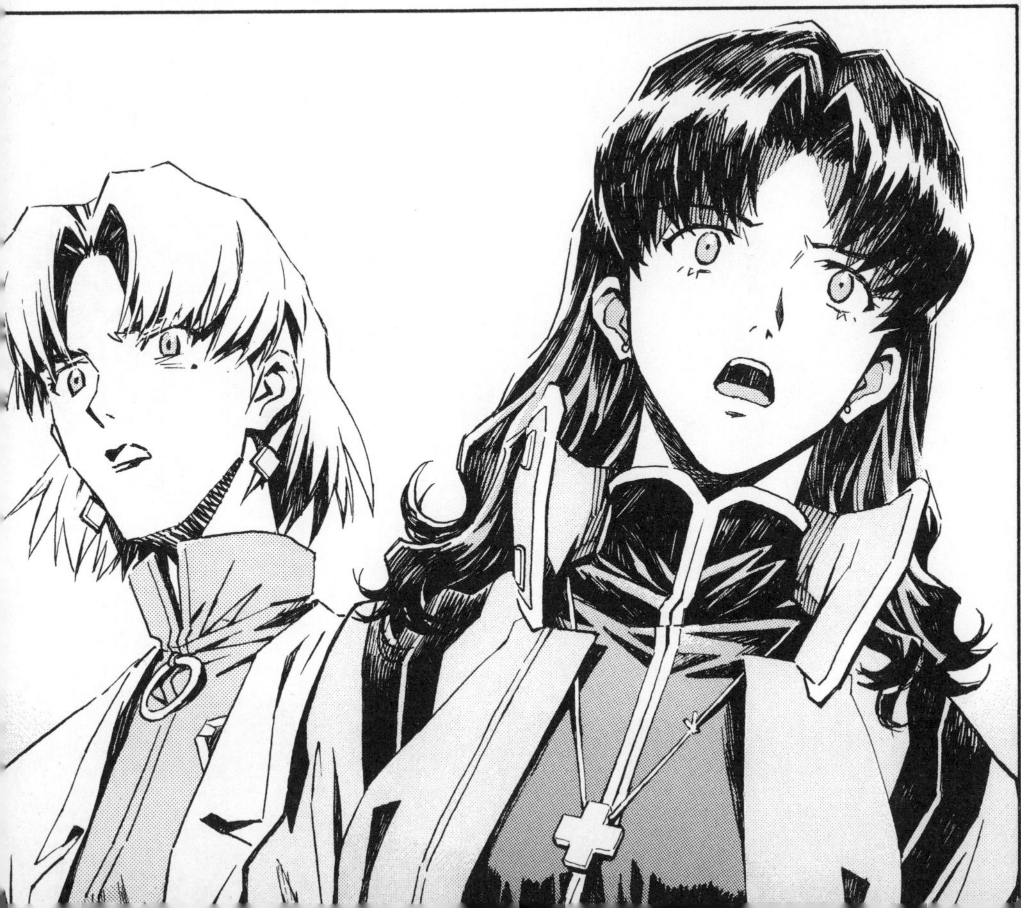

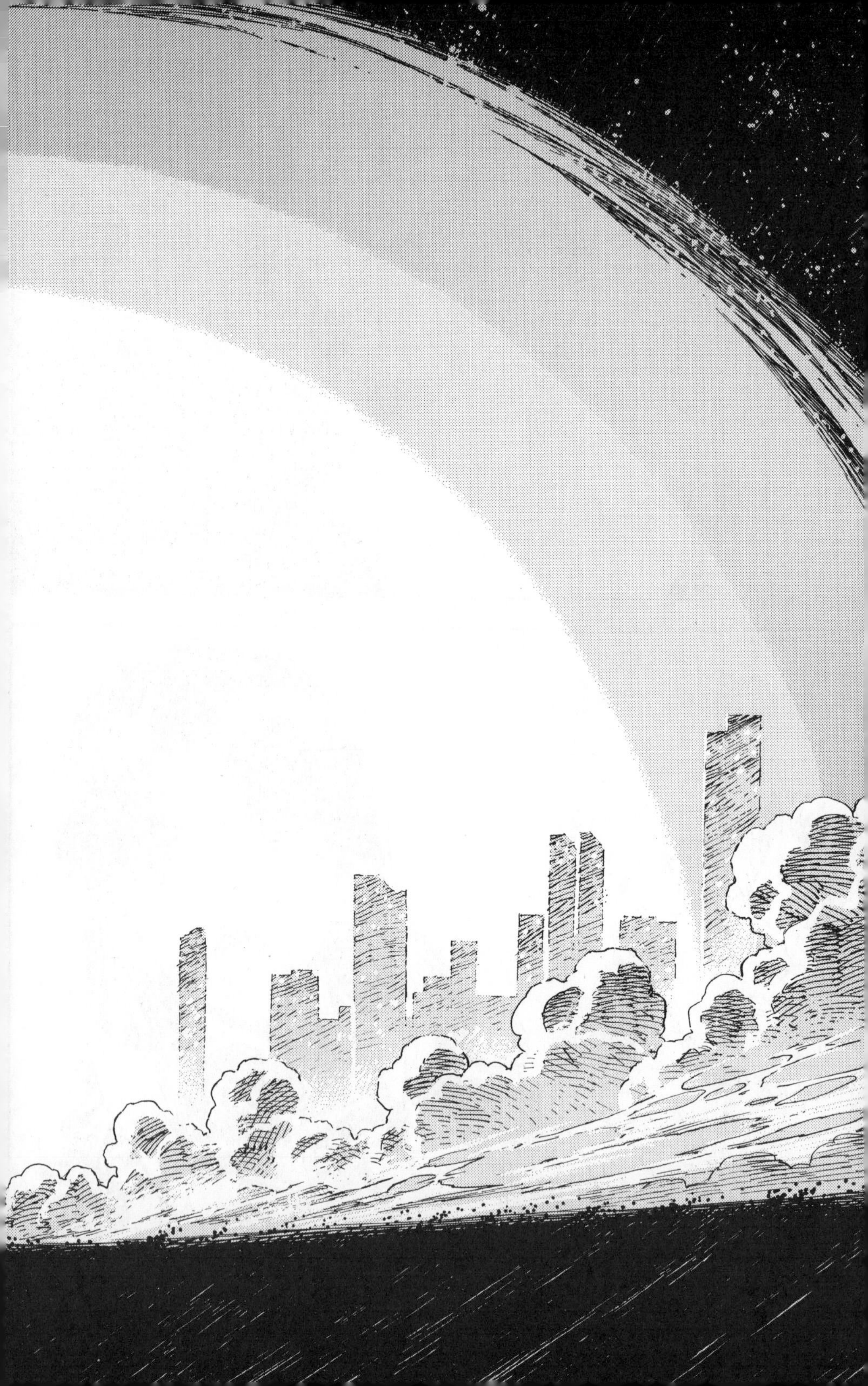

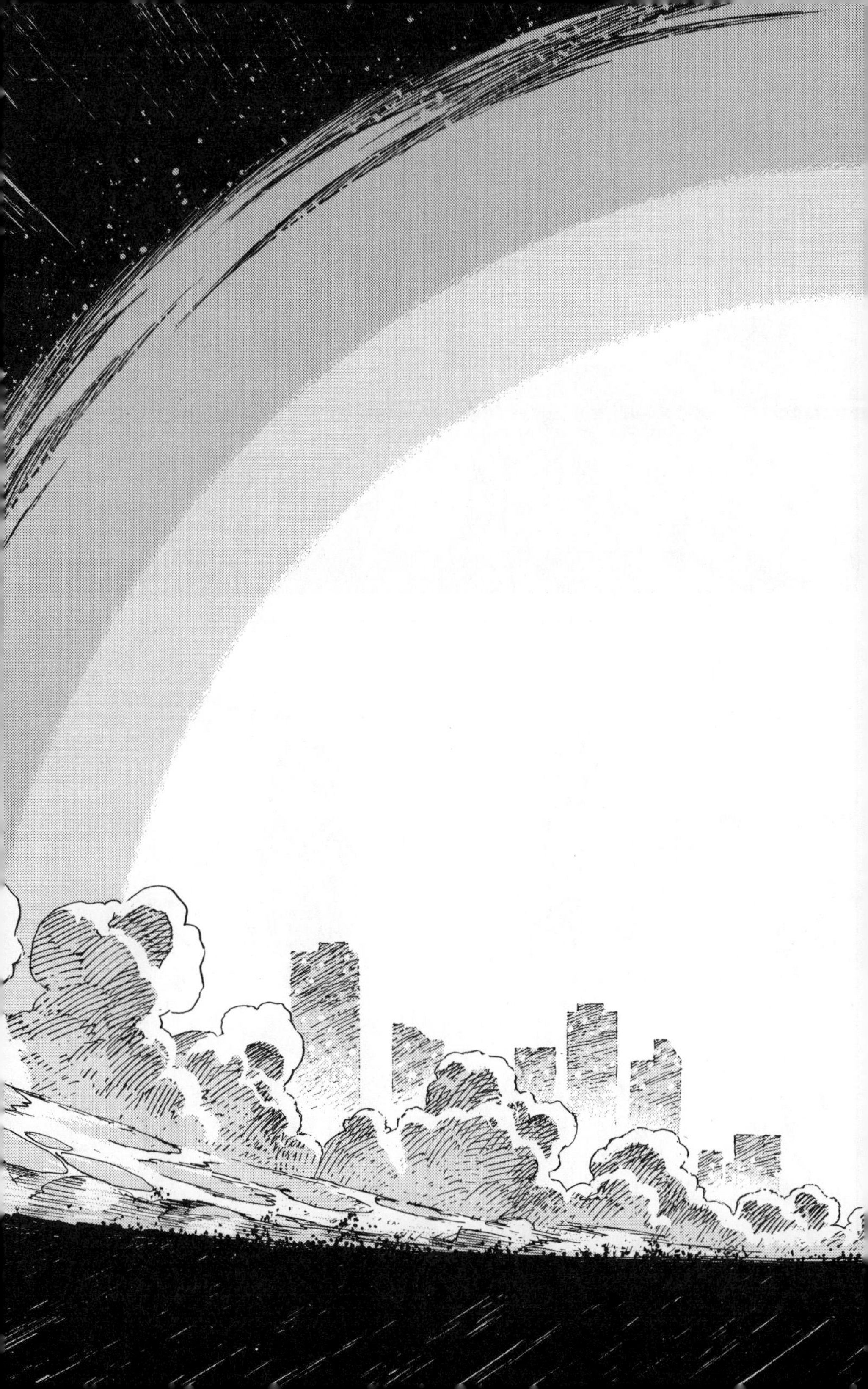

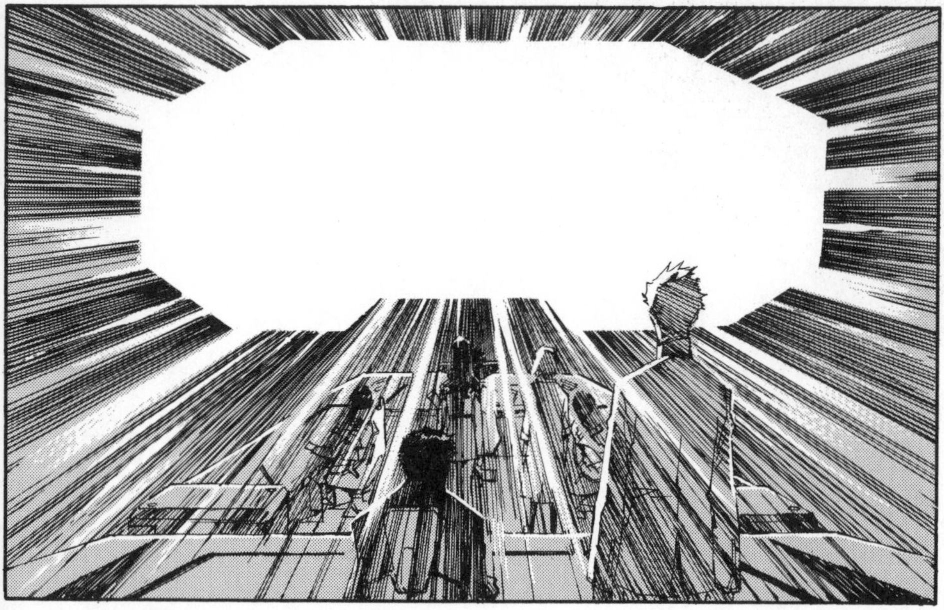
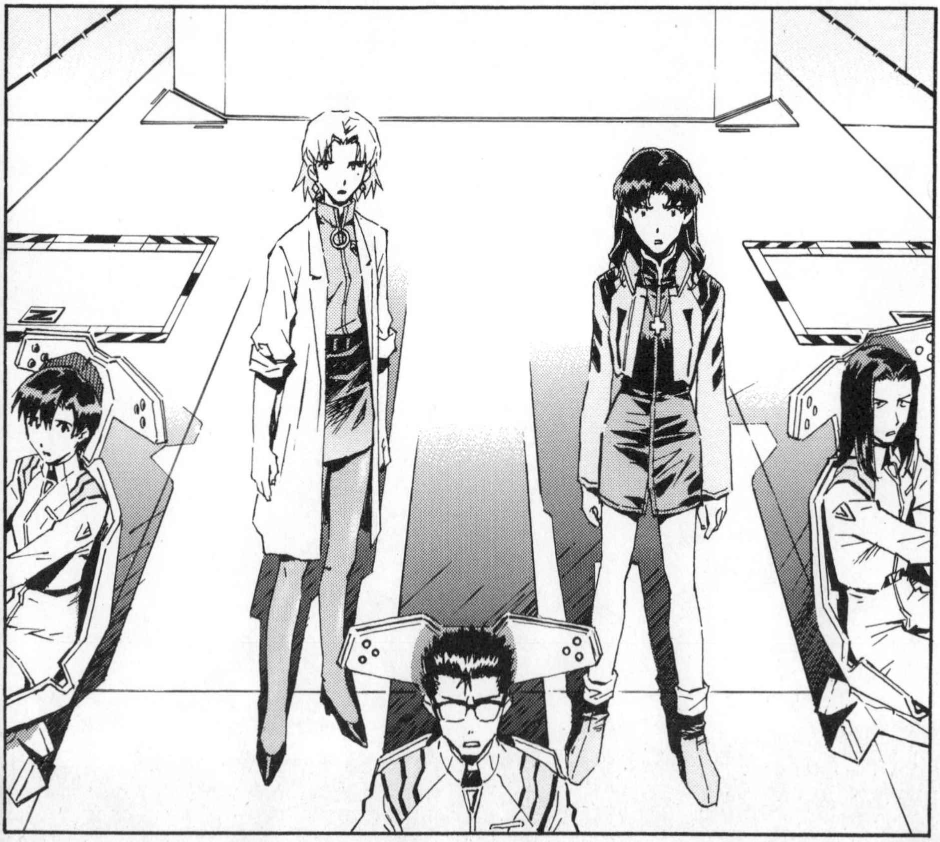

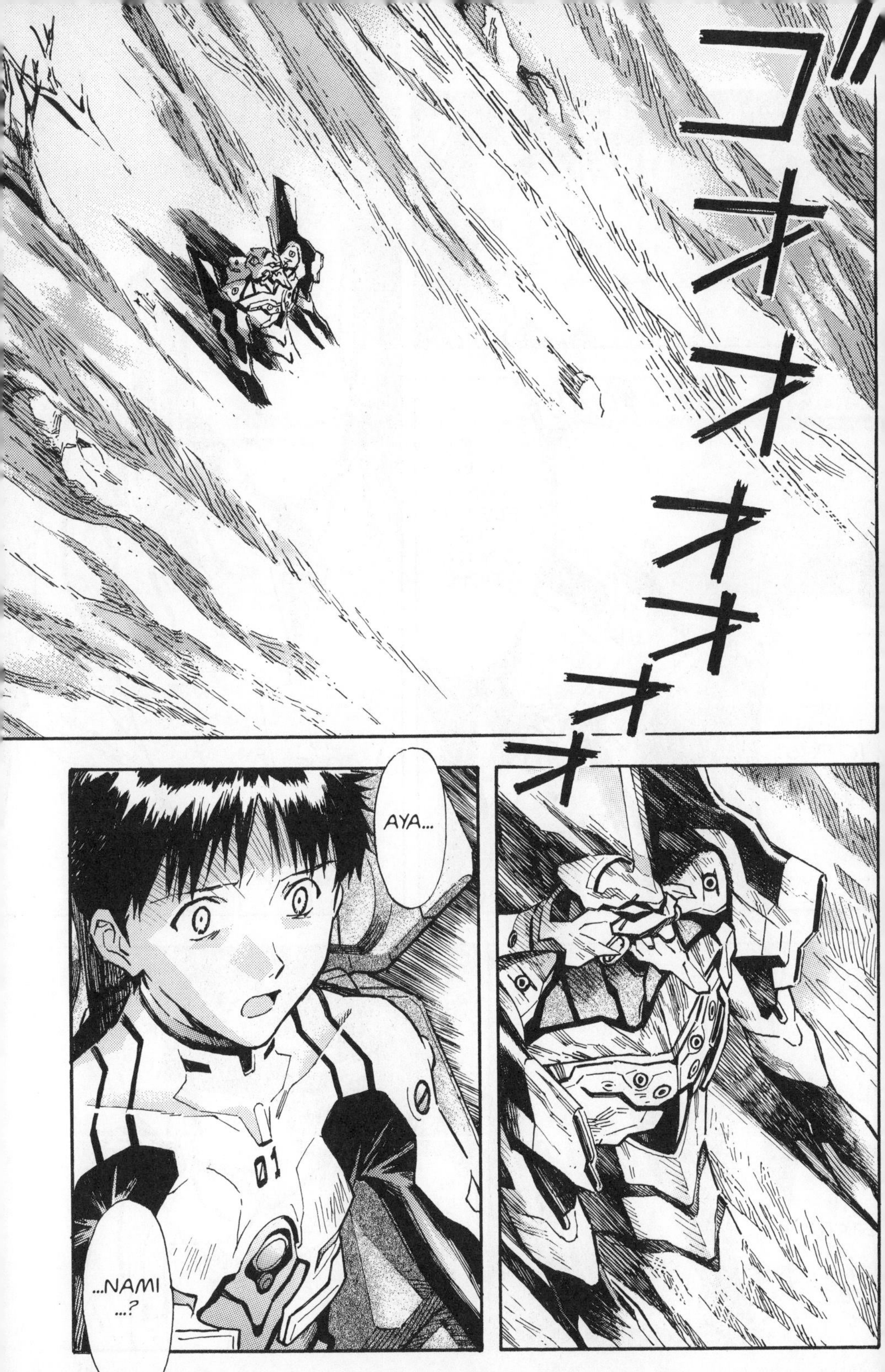
ゴオオオオオオ
AYA...
...NAMI ...?

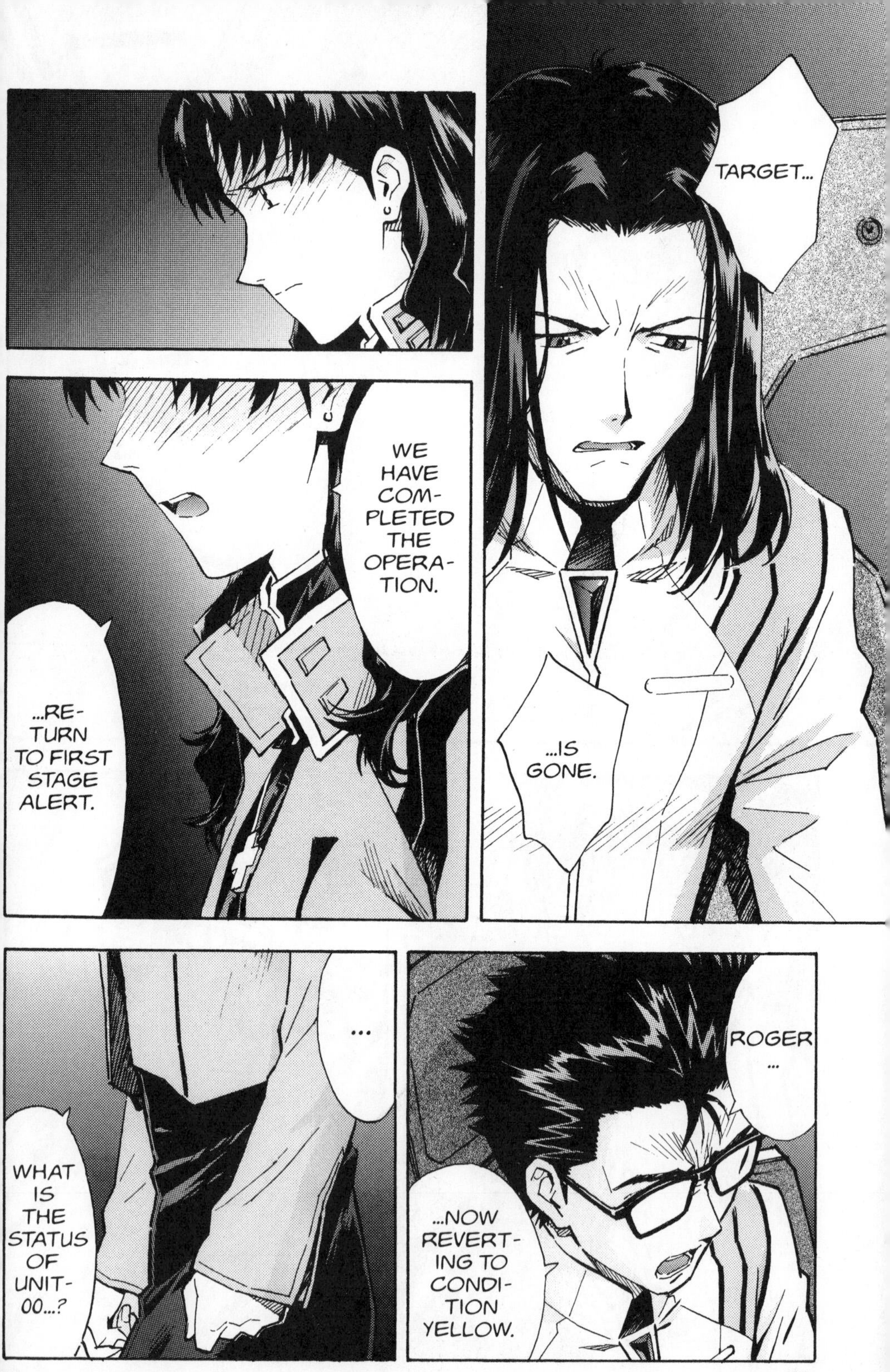
TARGET...
...IS GONE.
WE HAVE COMPLETED THE OPERATION.
...RETURN TO FIRST STAGE ALERT.
ROGER...
...NOW REVERTING TO CONDITION YELLOW.
...
WHAT IS THE STATUS OF UNIT-00...?

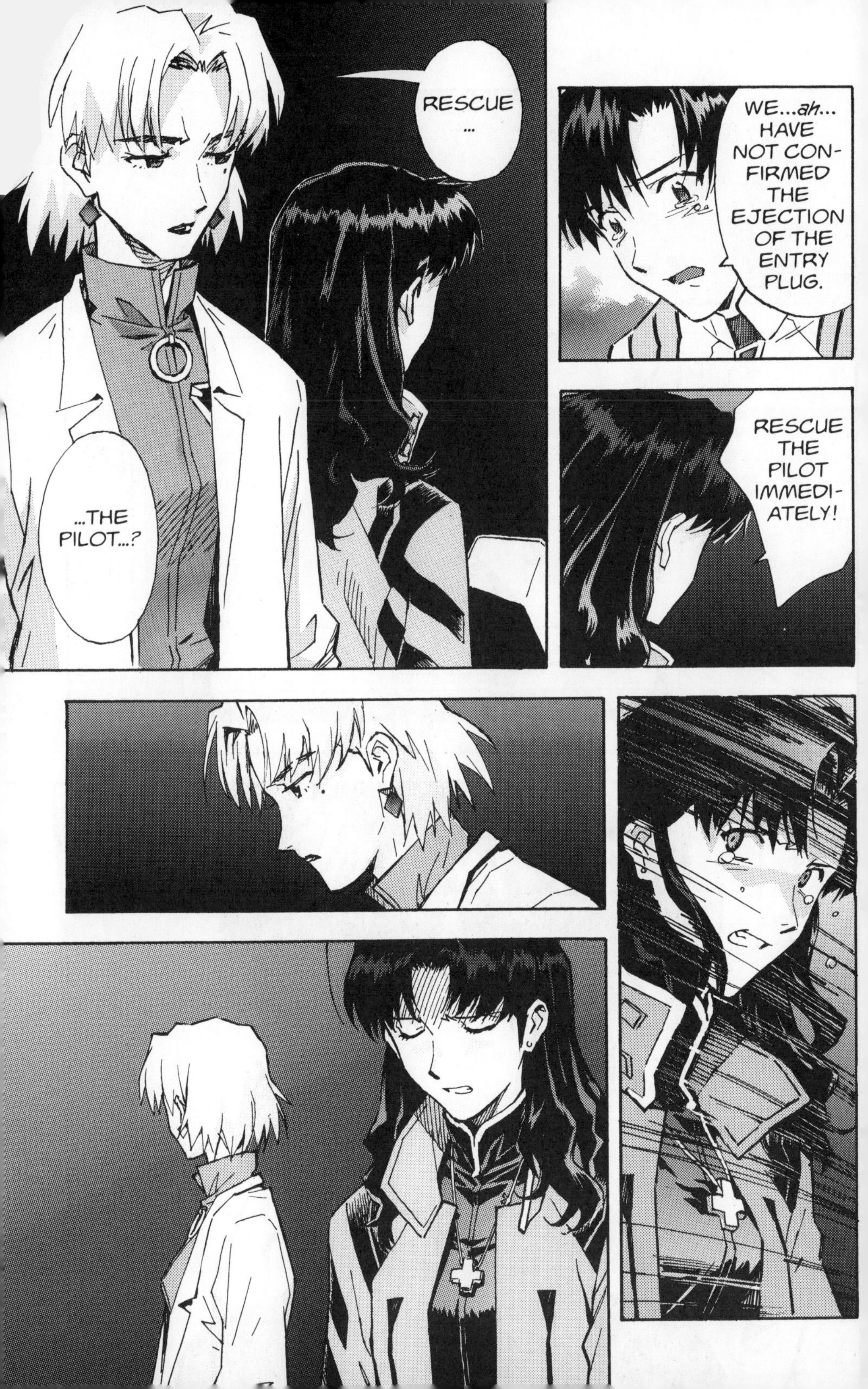
WE...*ah*... HAVE NOT CONFIRMED THE EJECTION OF THE ENTRY PLUG.
RESCUE THE PILOT IMMEDIATELY!
RESCUE...
...THE PILOT...?

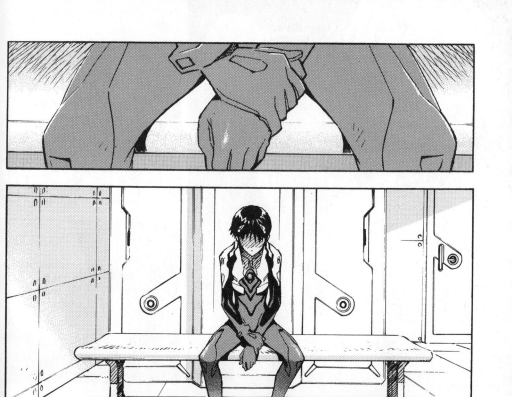

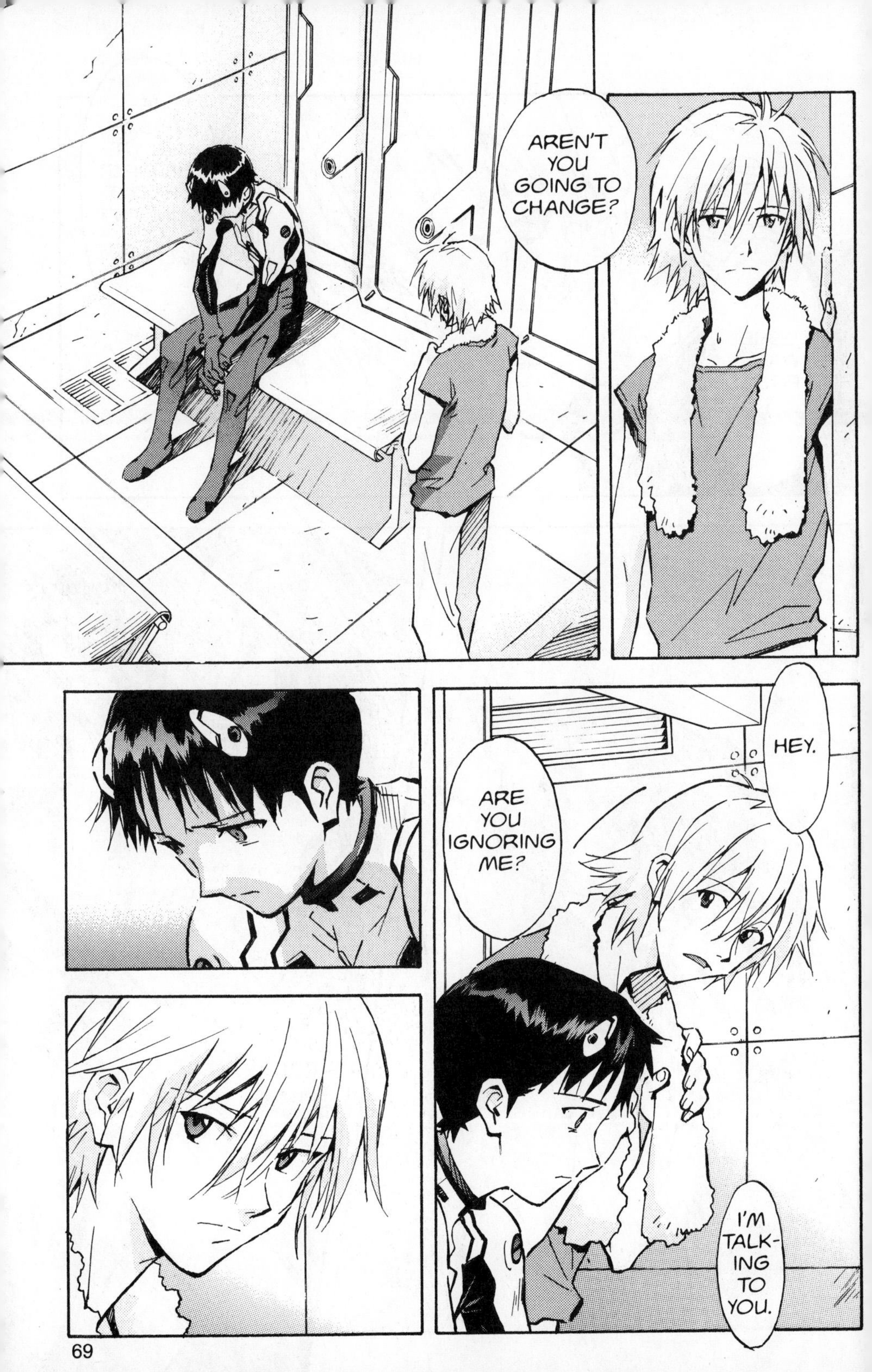
AREN'T YOU GOING TO CHANGE?
HEY.
ARE YOU IGNORING ME?
I'M TALKING TO YOU.

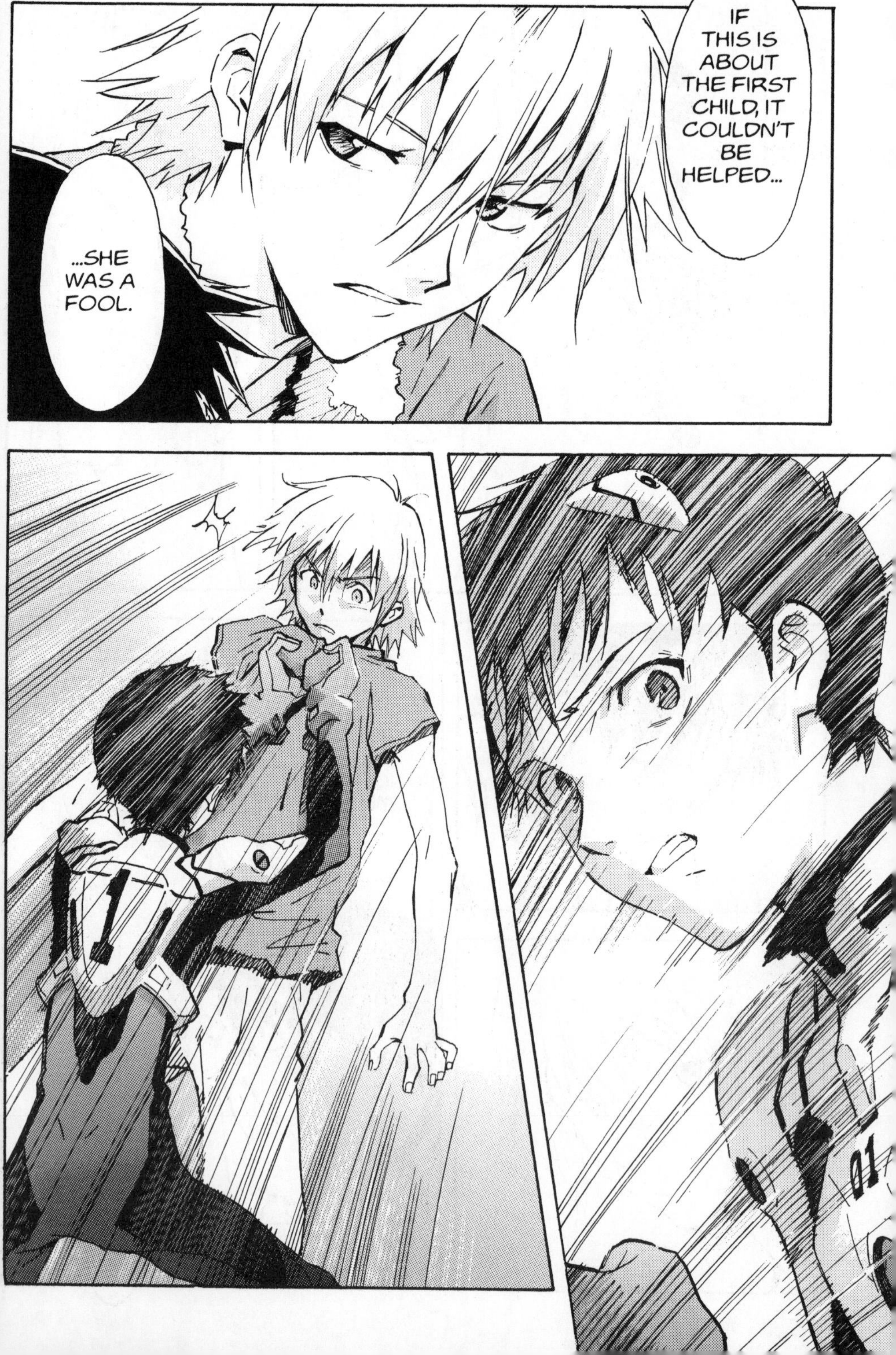
IF THIS IS ABOUT THE FIRST CHILD, IT COULDN'T BE HELPED...
...SHE WAS A FOOL.

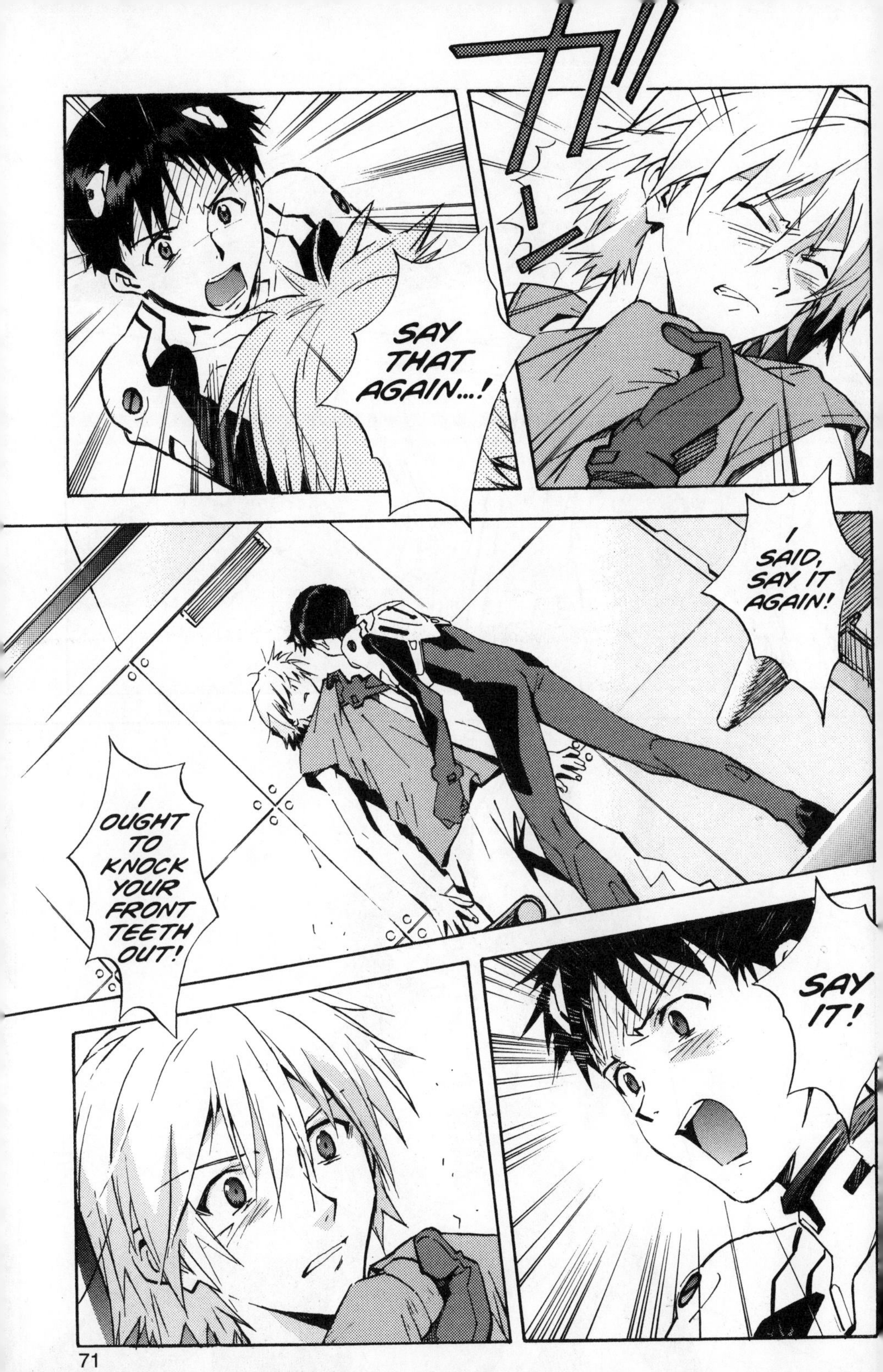
SAY THAT AGAIN...!
I SAID, SAY IT AGAIN!
I OUGHT TO KNOCK YOUR FRONT TEETH OUT!
SAY IT!

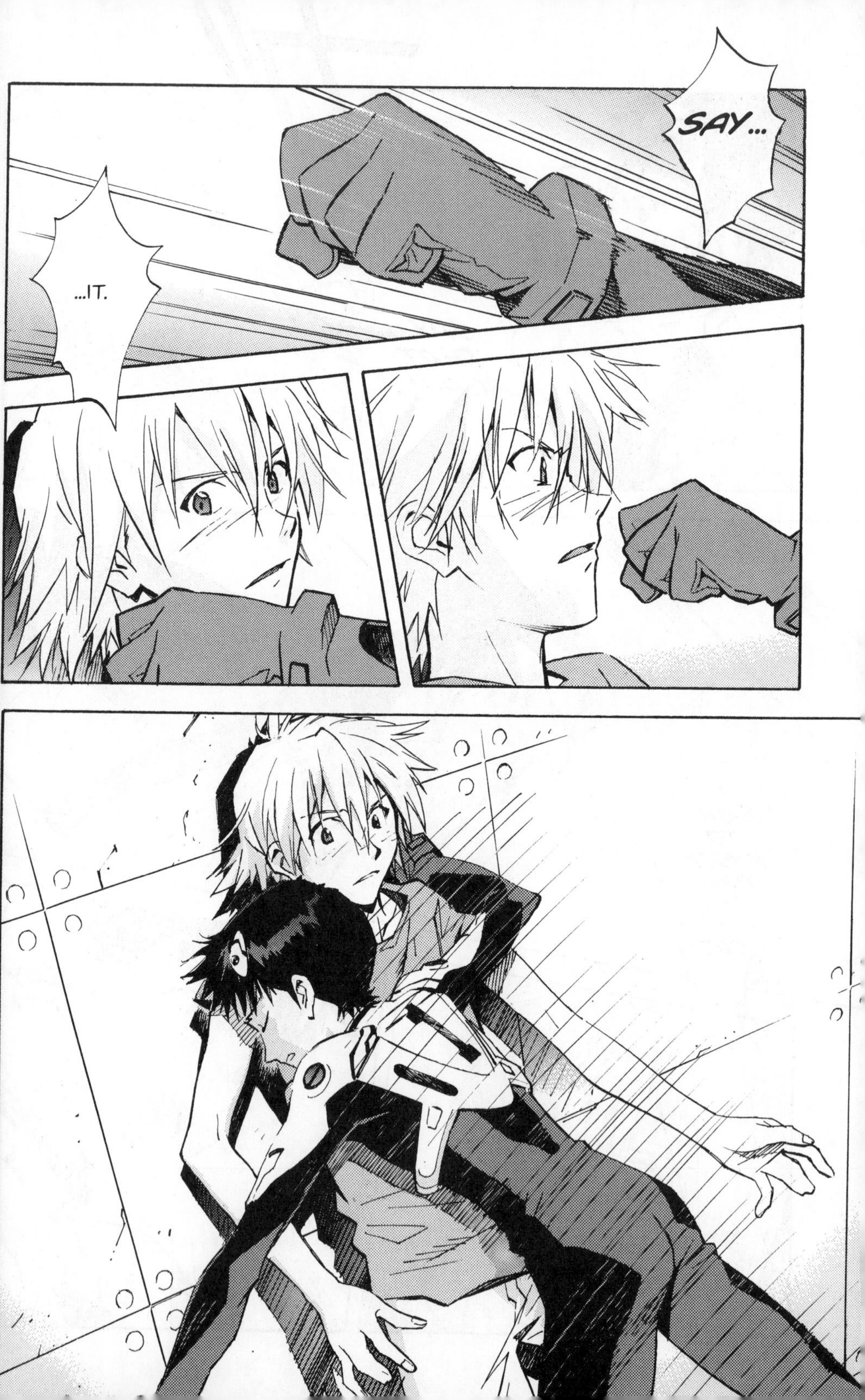
SAY...
...IT.

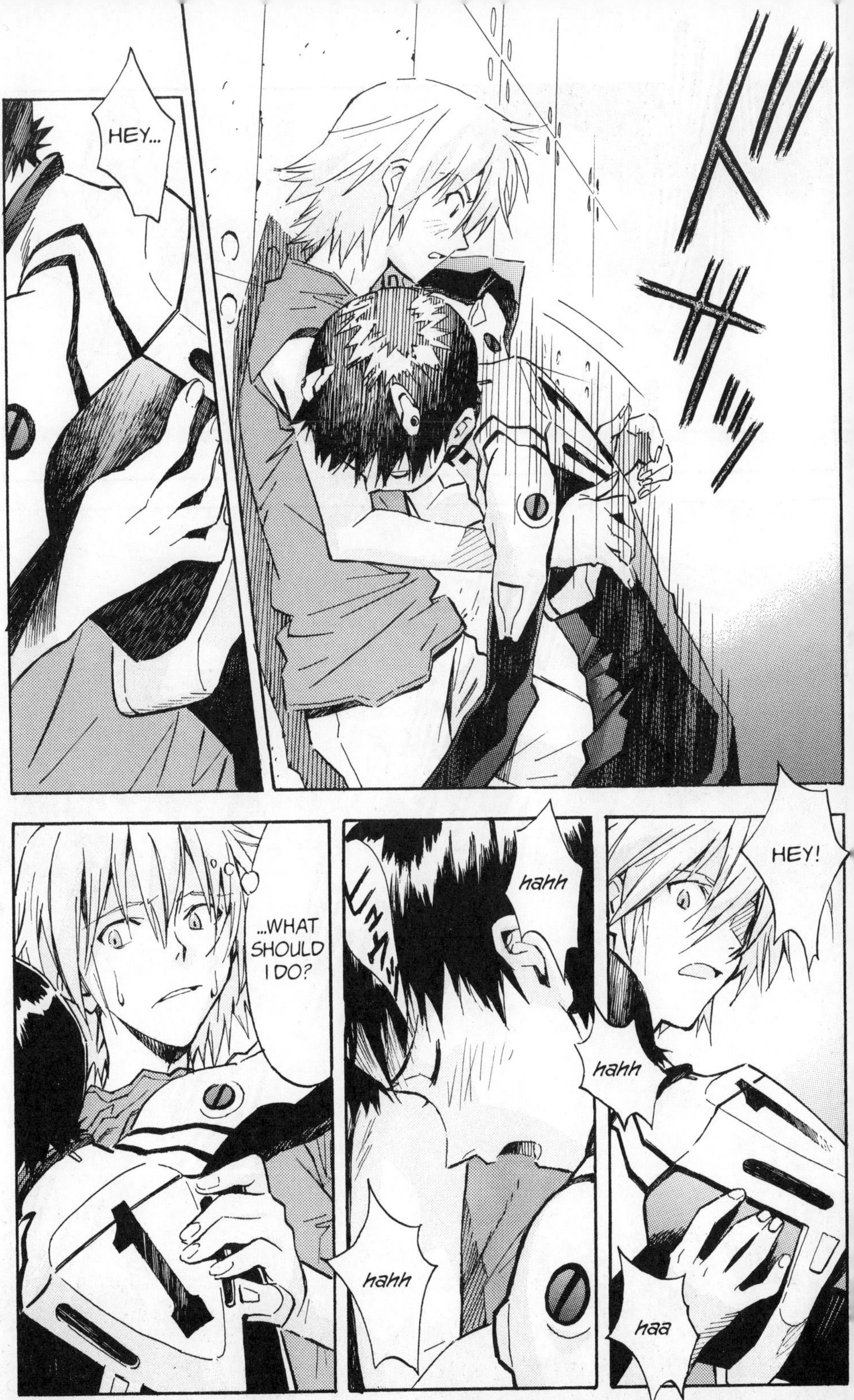
HEY...
HEY!
haa
hahh
hahh
hahh
...WHAT SHOULD I DO?

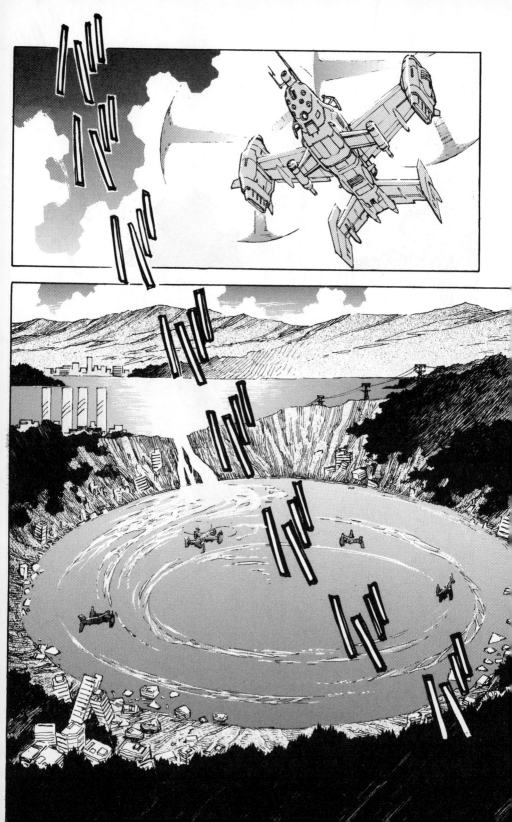

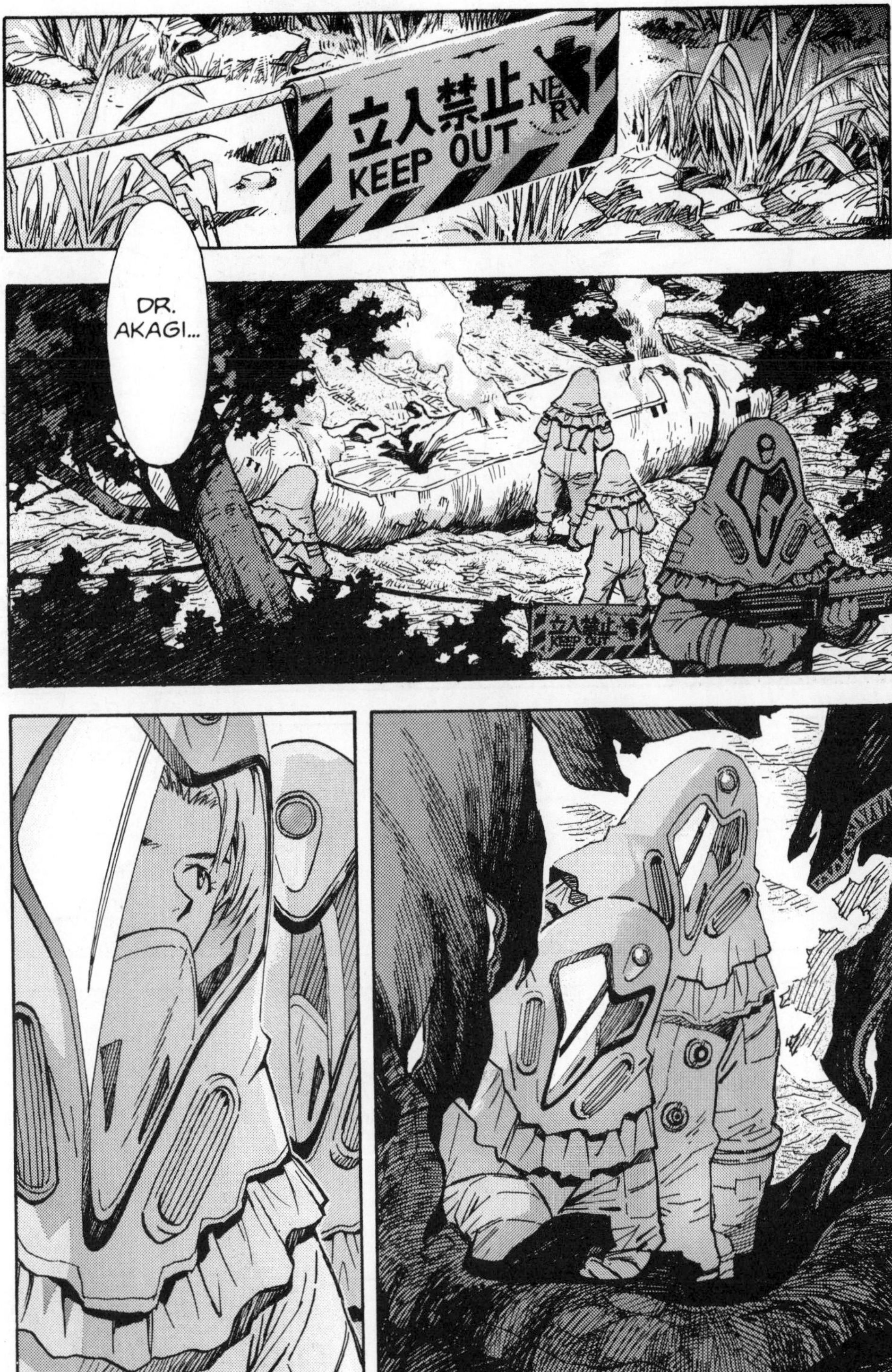
立入禁止
NERV
KEEP OUT
DR. AKAGI...

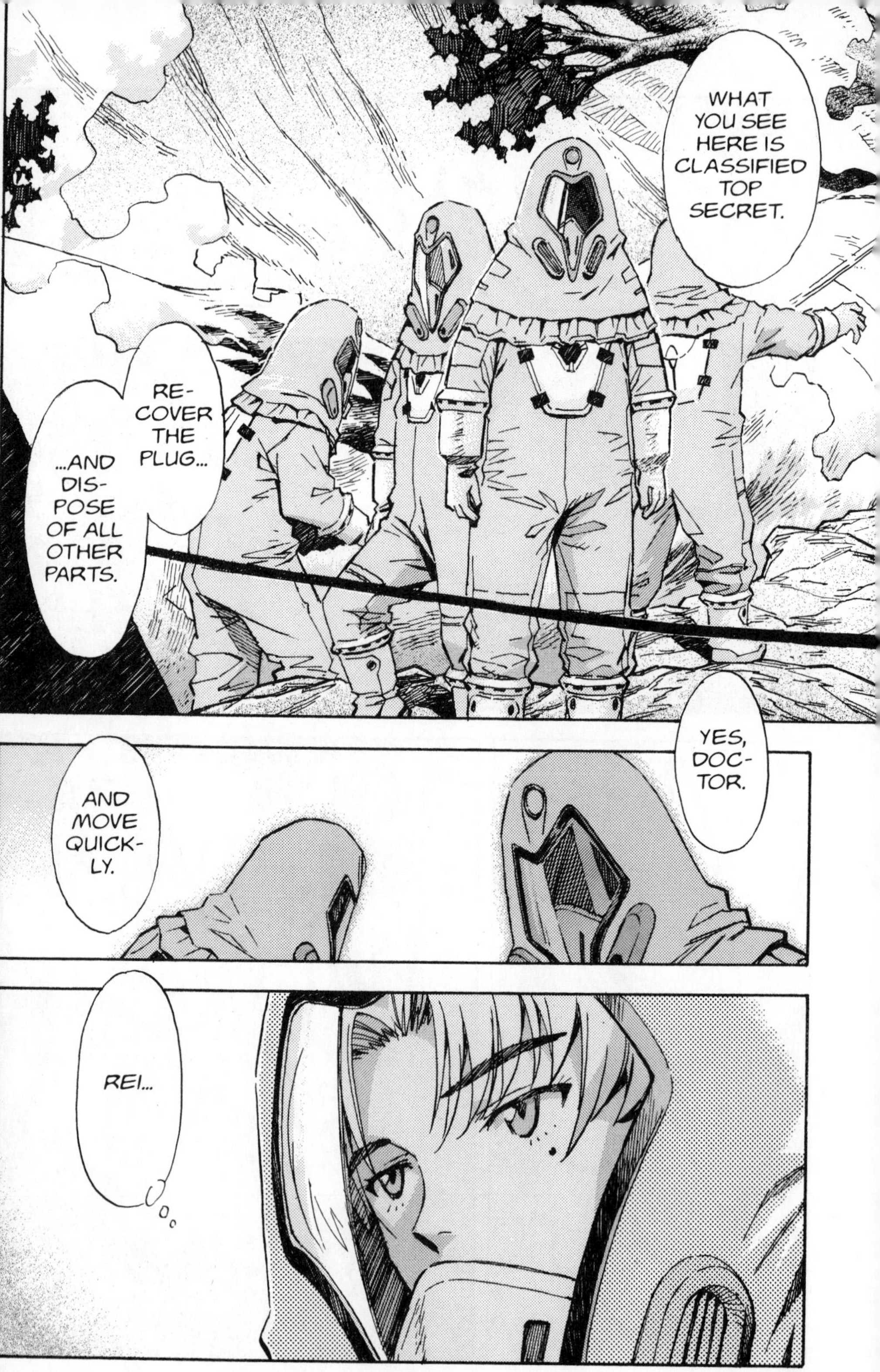
WHAT YOU SEE HERE IS CLASSIFIED TOP SECRET.
RE-COVER THE PLUG...
...AND DIS-POSE OF ALL OTHER PARTS.
YES, DOC-TOR.
AND MOVE QUICK-LY.
REI...

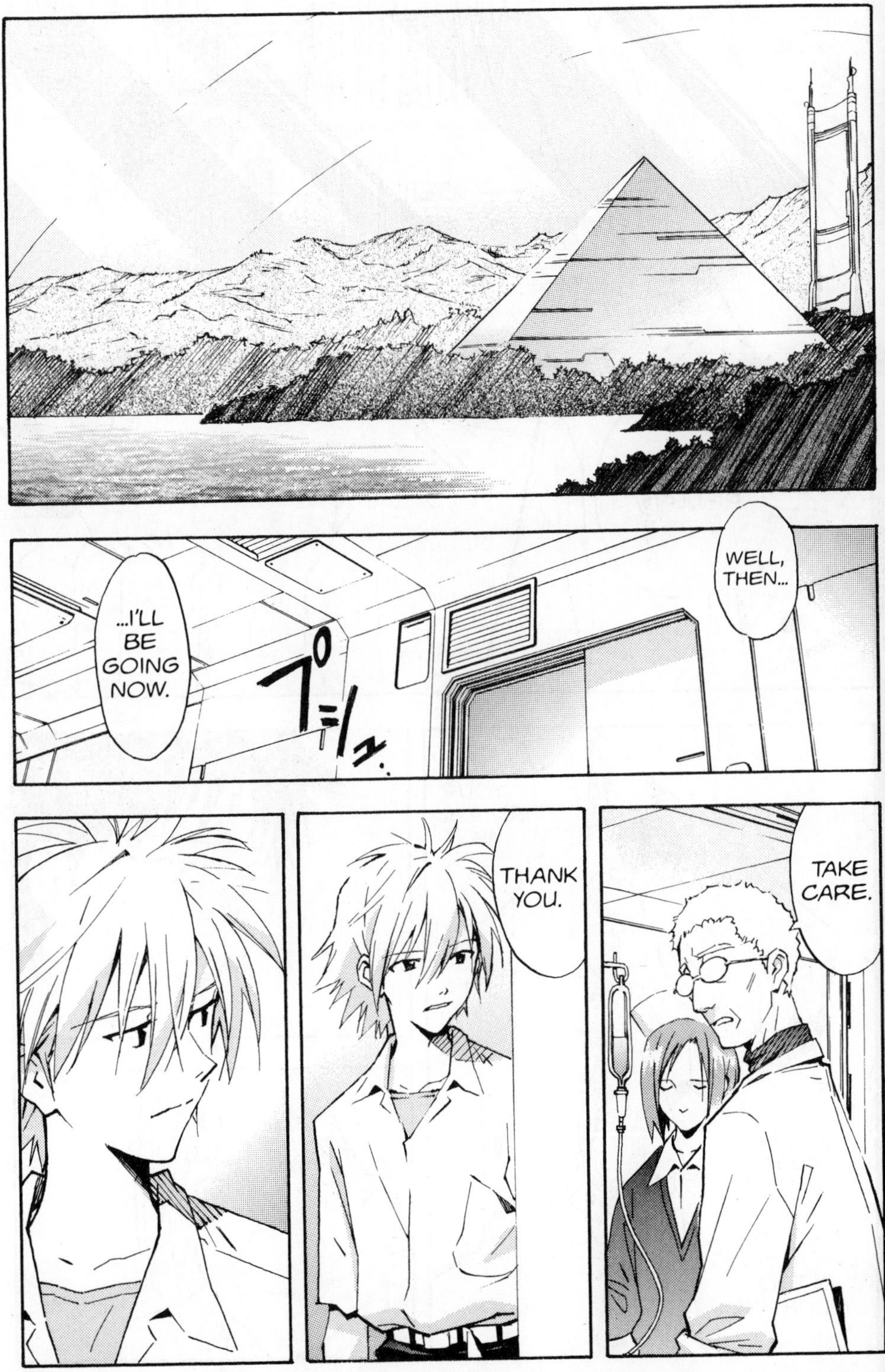
WELL, THEN...
...I'LL BE GOING NOW.
プシュ..
TAKE CARE.
THANK YOU.

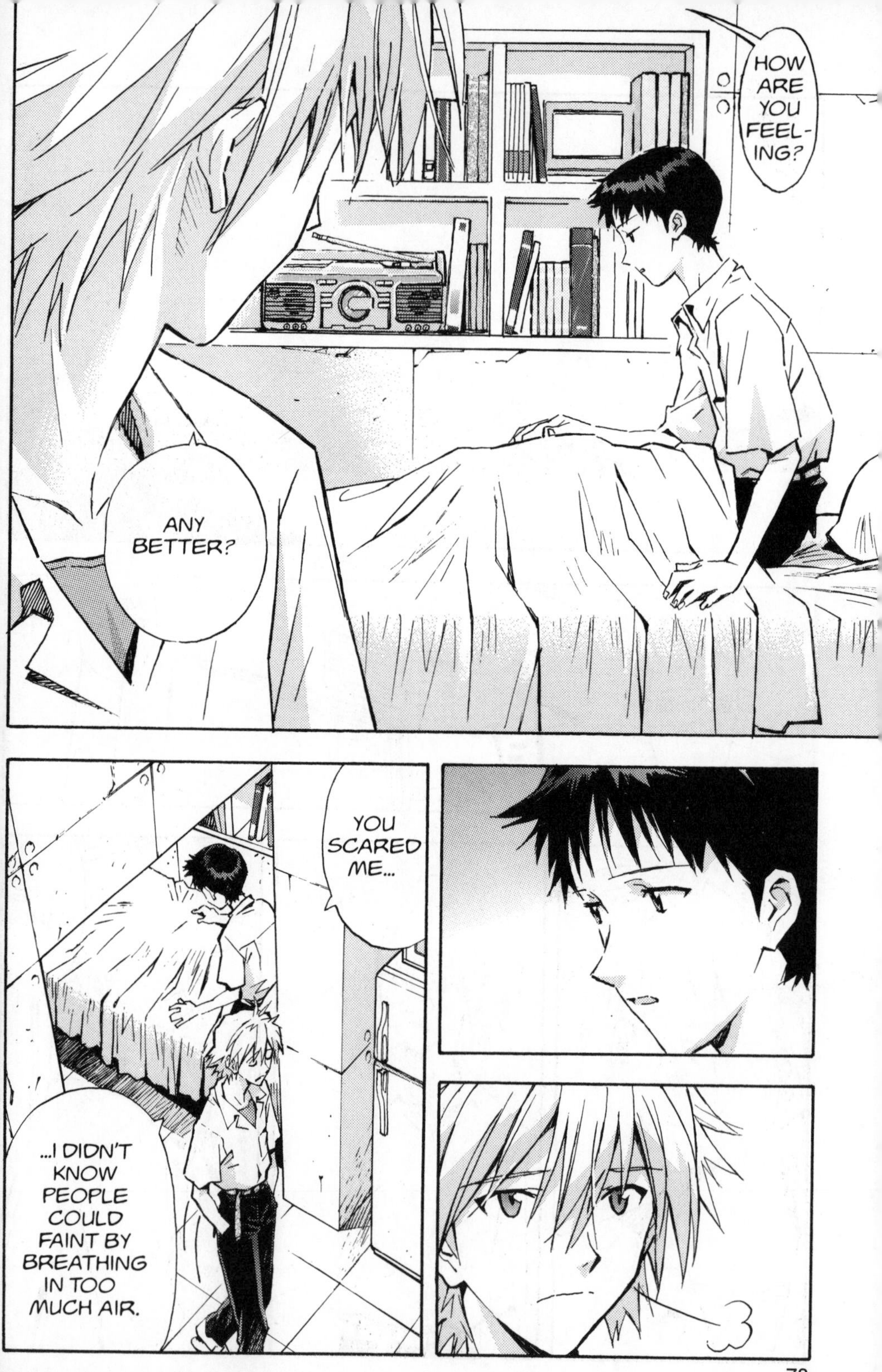
HOW ARE YOU FEEL-ING?
ANY BETTER?
YOU SCARED ME...
...I DIDN'T KNOW PEOPLE COULD FAINT BY BREATHING IN TOO MUCH AIR.

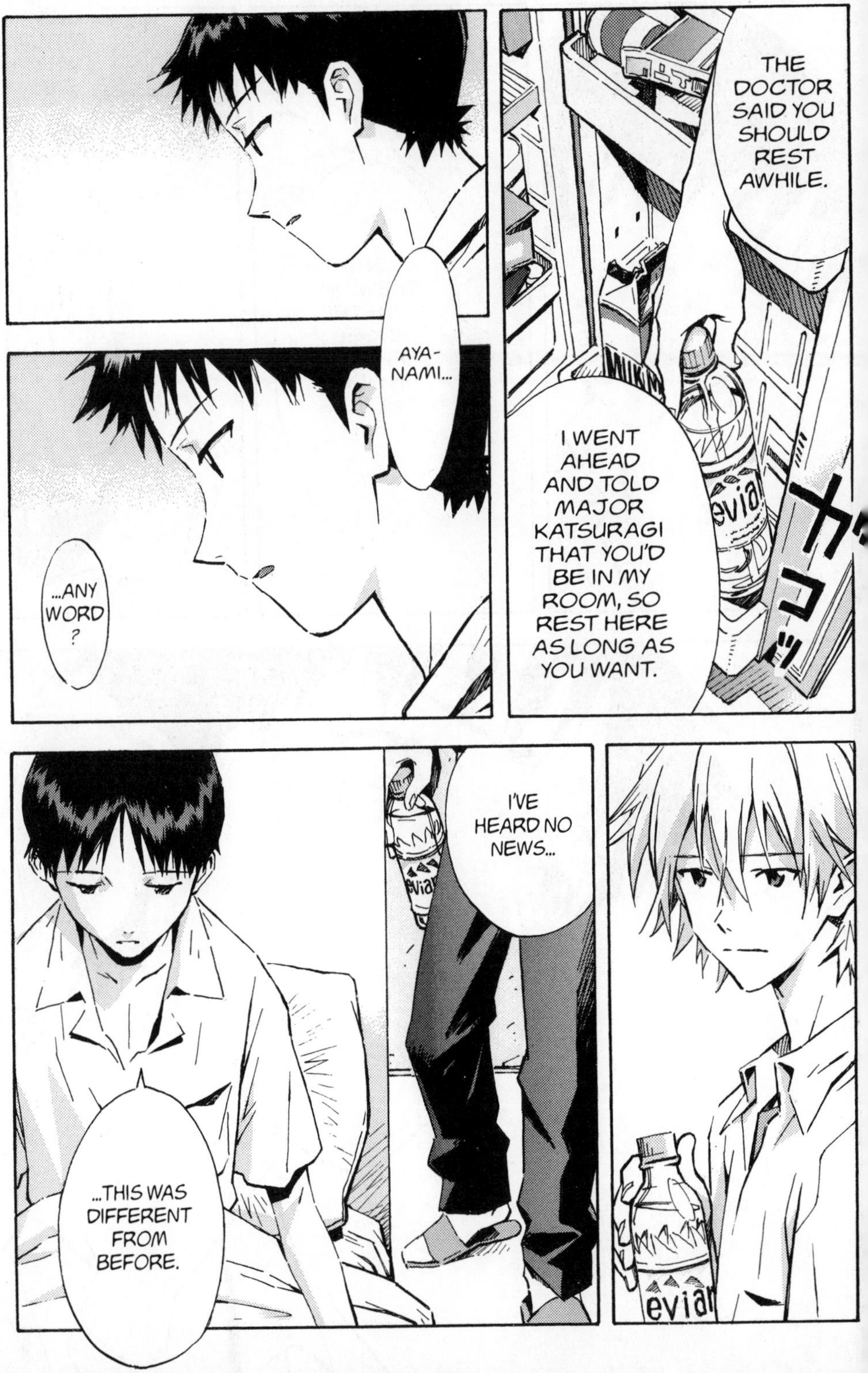
THE DOCTOR SAID YOU SHOULD REST AWHILE.
I WENT AHEAD AND TOLD MAJOR KATSURAGI THAT YOU'D BE IN MY ROOM, SO REST HERE AS LONG AS YOU WANT.
ガコッ
AYA-NAMI...
...ANY WORD?
I'VE HEARD NO NEWS...
...THIS WAS DIFFERENT FROM BEFORE.

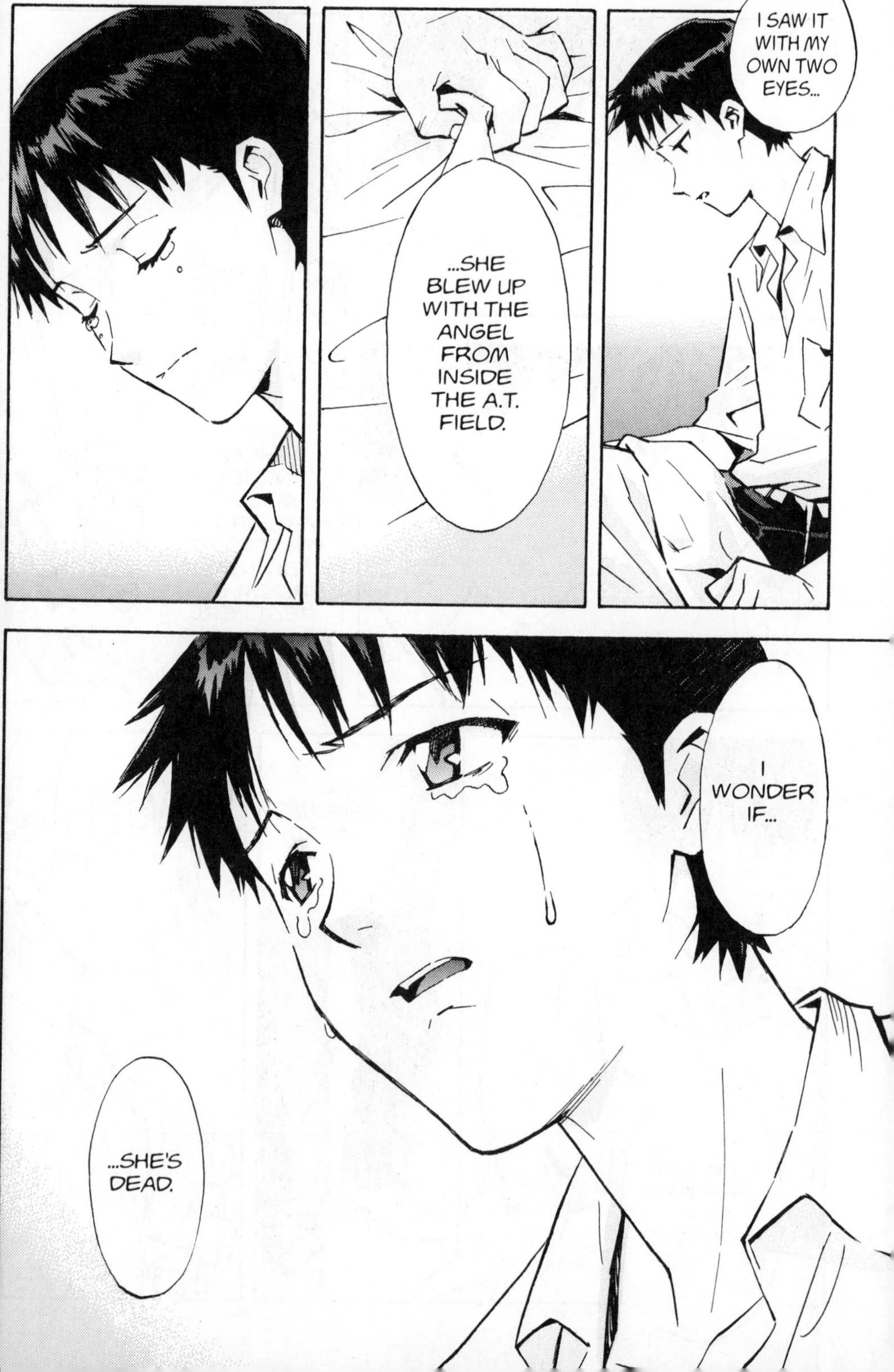
I SAW IT WITH MY OWN TWO EYES...
...SHE BLEW UP WITH THE ANGEL FROM INSIDE THE A.T. FIELD.
I WONDER IF...
...SHE'S DEAD.

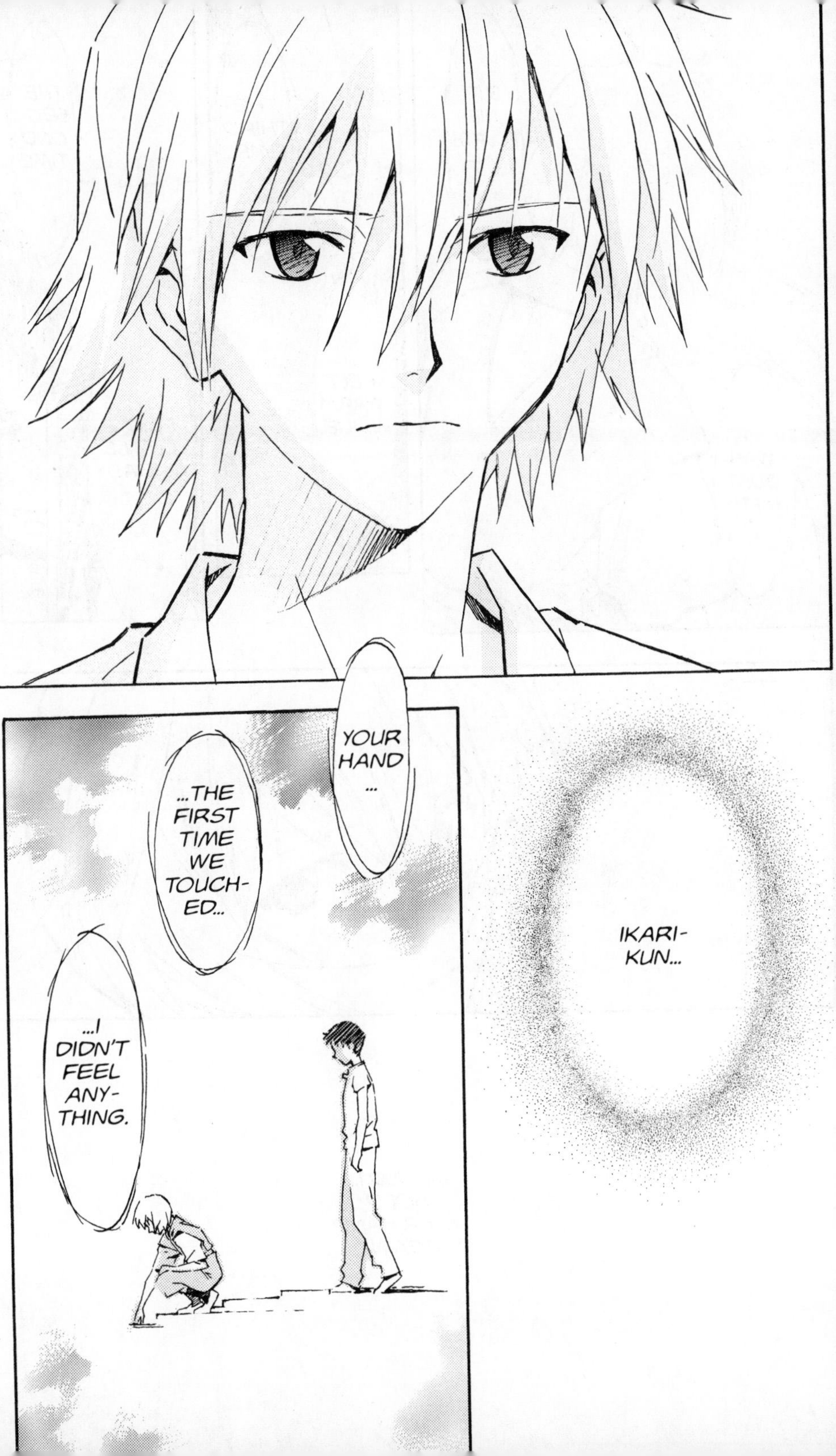
IKARI-KUN...
YOUR HAND...
...THE FIRST TIME WE TOUCHED...
...I DIDN'T FEEL ANYTHING.

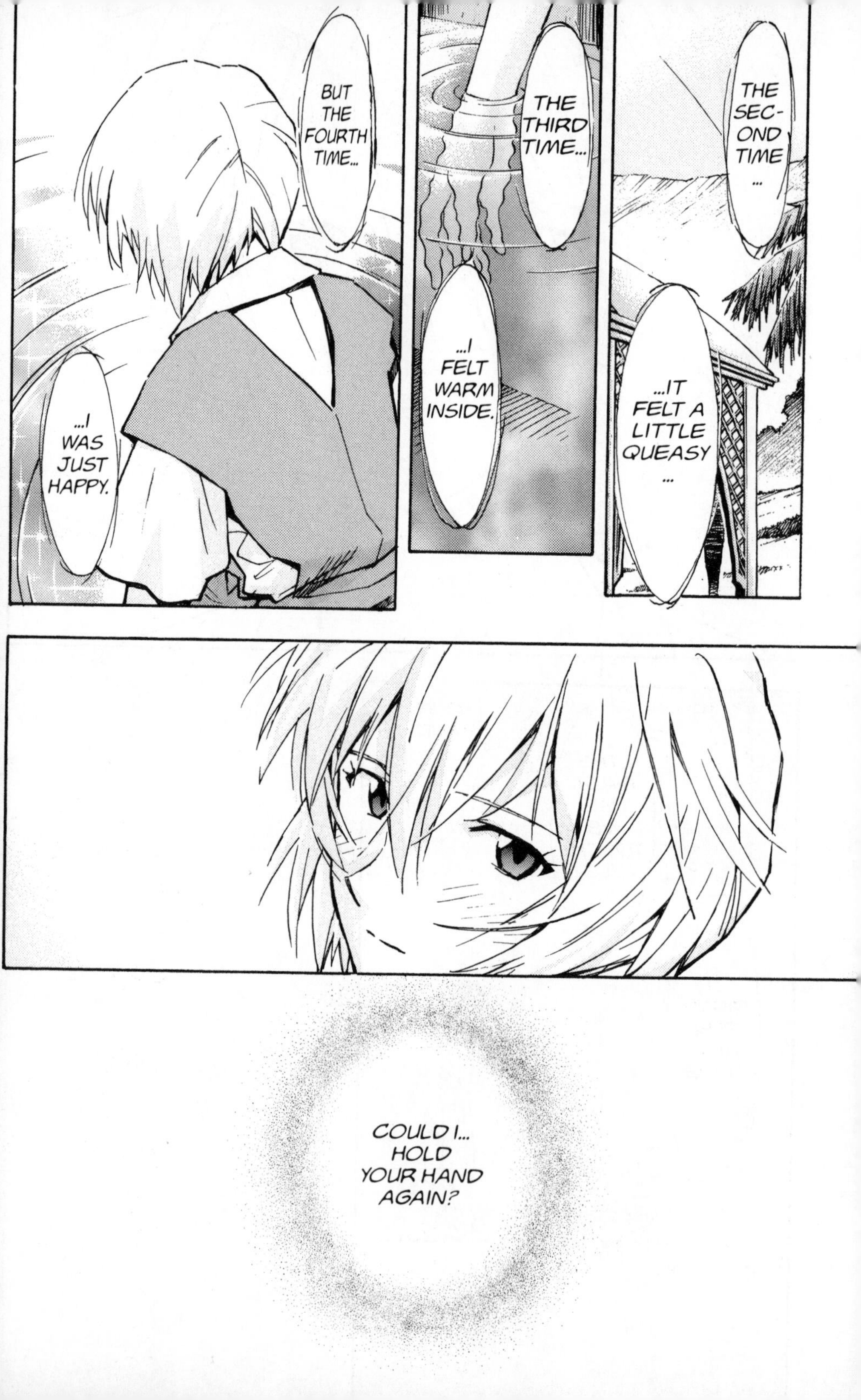
THE SECOND TIME...
...IT FELT A LITTLE QUEASY...
THE THIRD TIME...
...I FELT WARM INSIDE.
BUT THE FOURTH TIME...
...I WAS JUST HAPPY.
COULD I... HOLD YOUR HAND AGAIN?

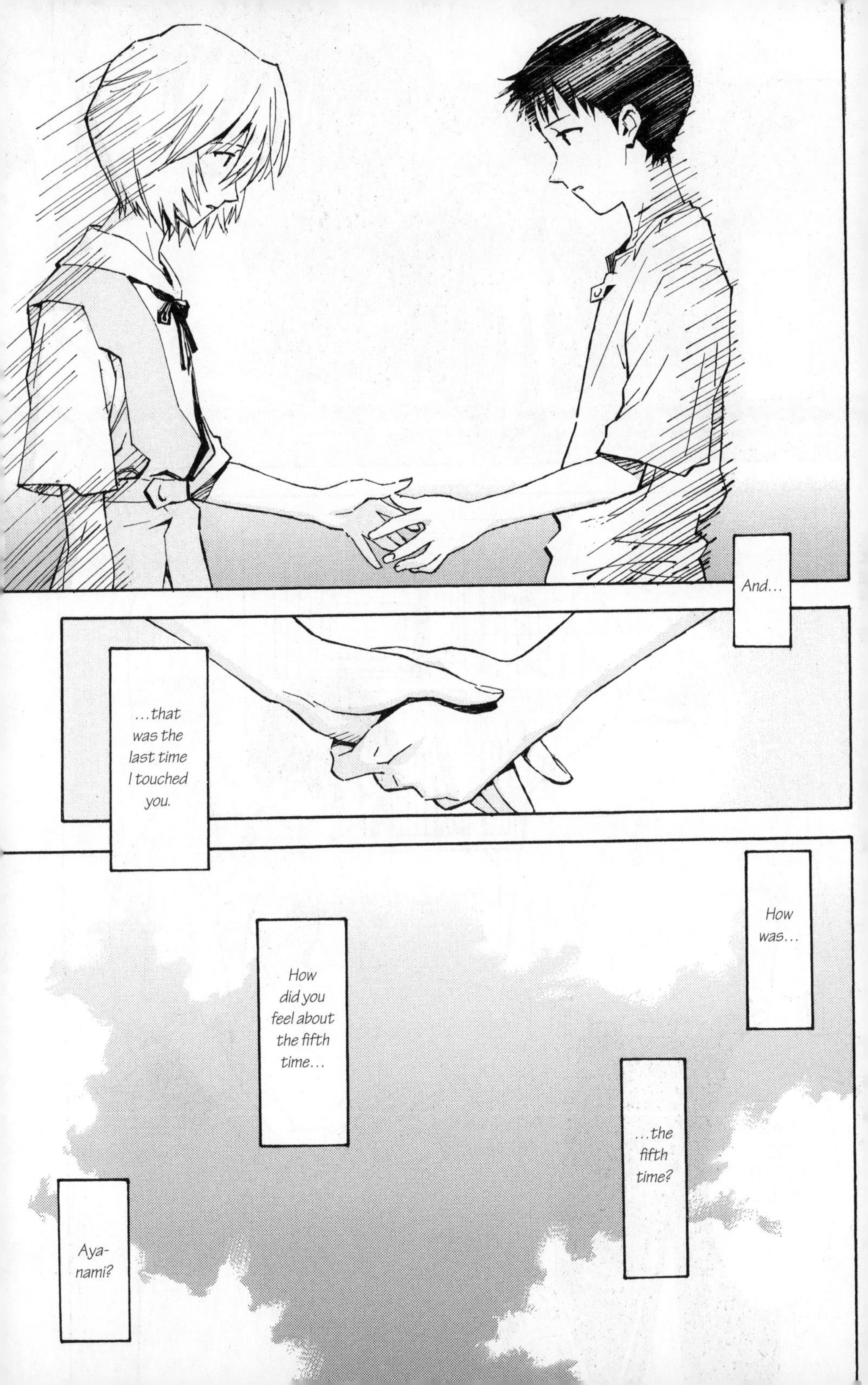
And...
...that was the last time I touched you.
How was...
...the fifth time?
How did you feel about the fifth time...
Aya-nami?

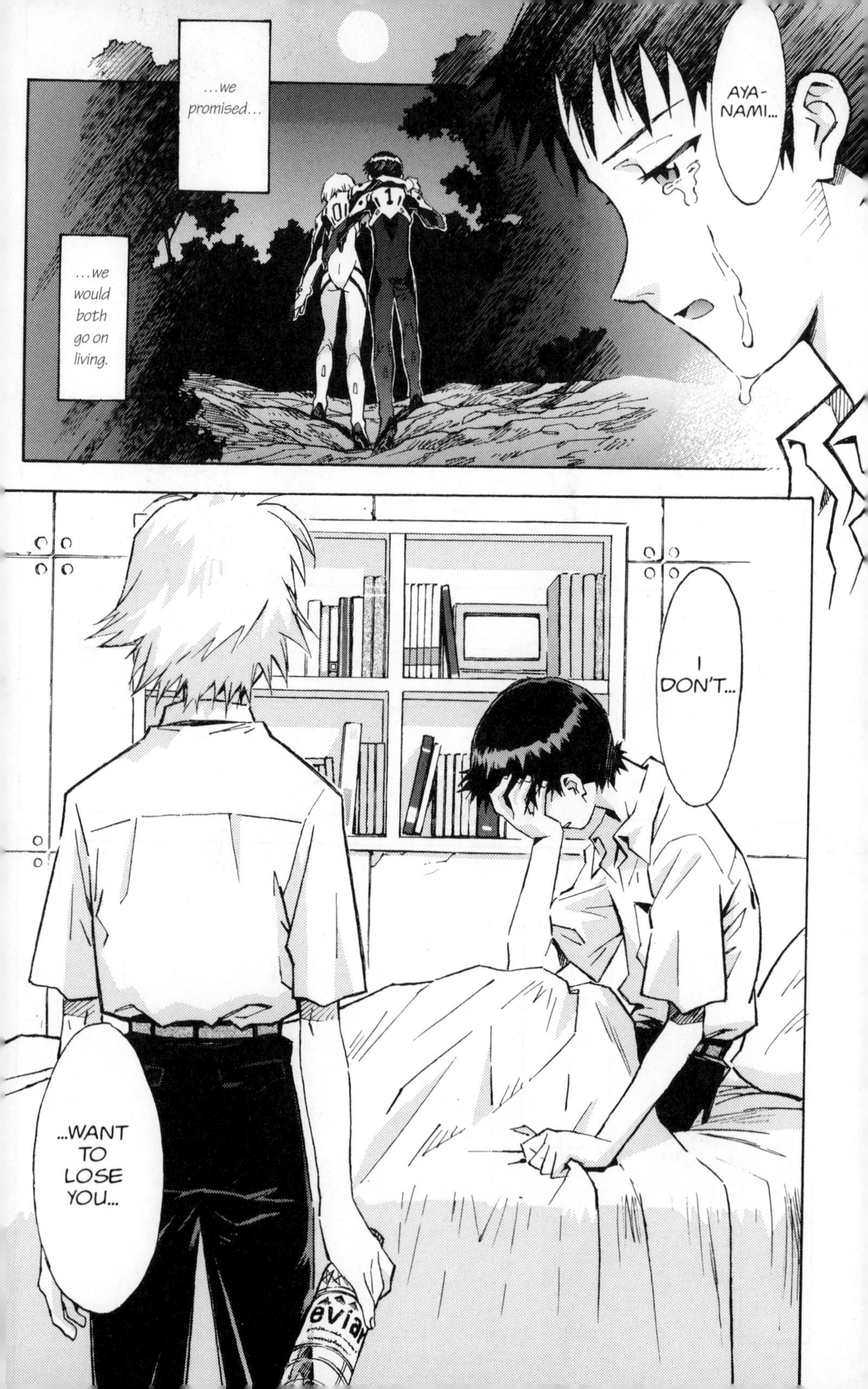
AYA-NAMI...
...we promised...
...we would both go on living.
I DON'T...
...WANT TO LOSE YOU...

NEON GENESIS EVANGELION

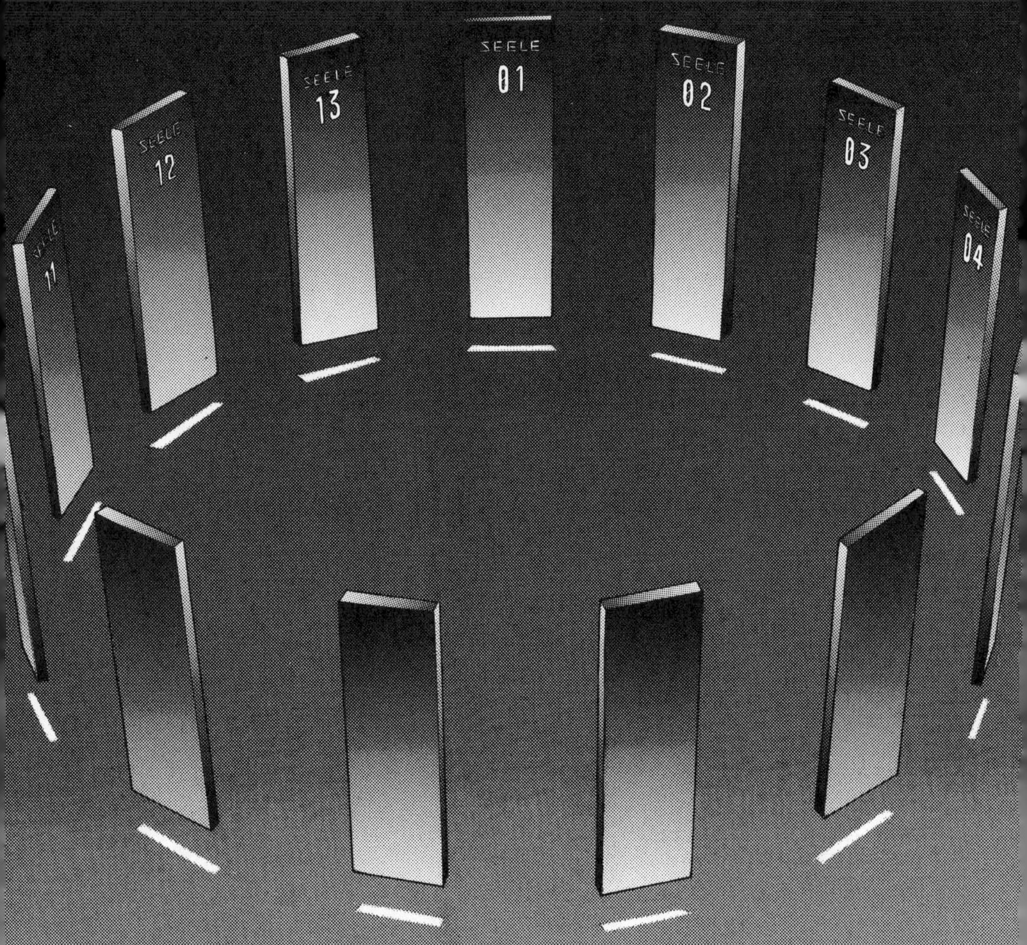
SEELE 01
SEELE 02
SEELE 03
SEELE 04
SEELE 11
SEELE 12
SEELE 13

STAGE 67: TWISTED NIGHT

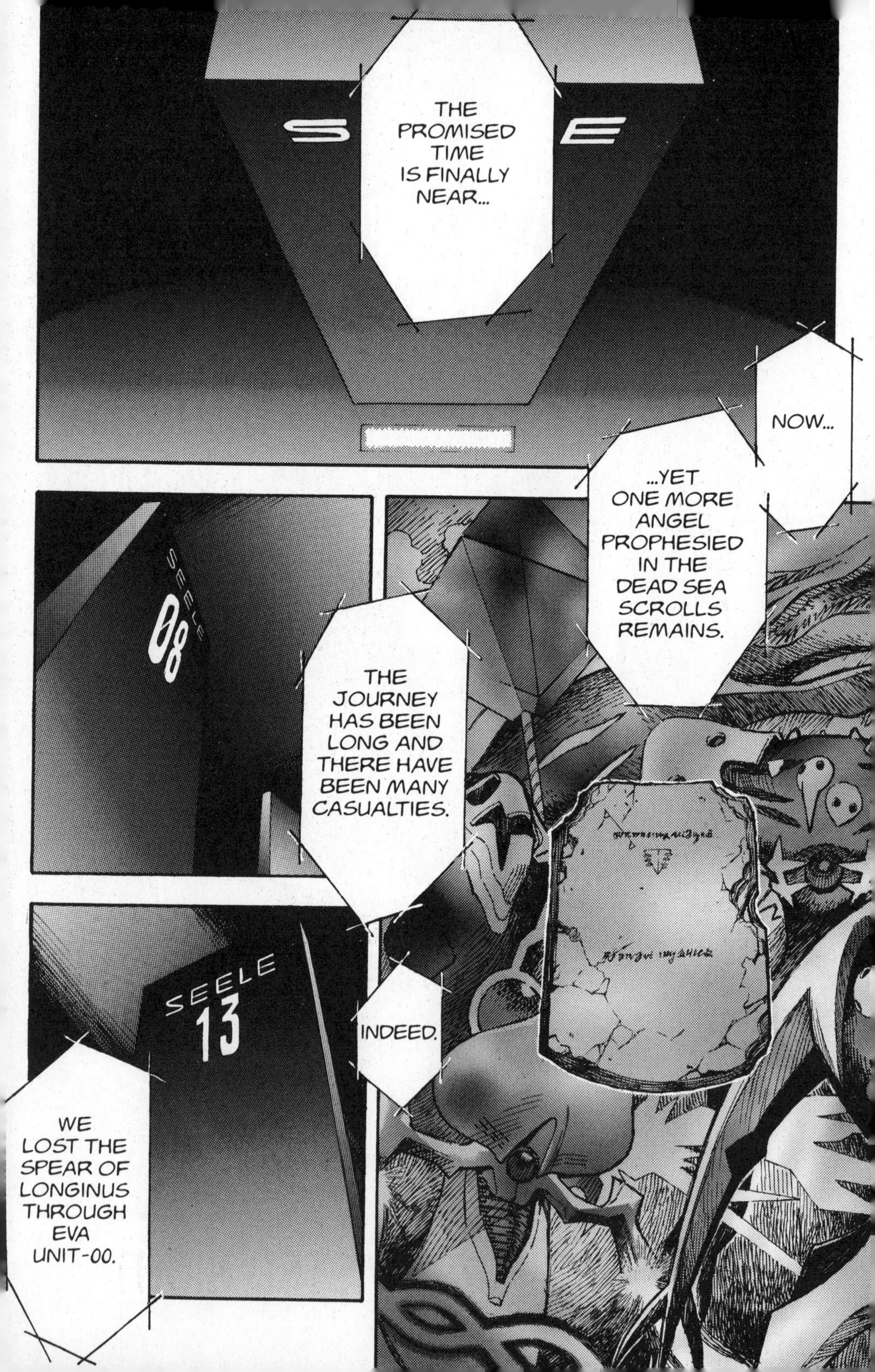
THE PROMISED TIME IS FINALLY NEAR...
NOW...
...YET ONE MORE ANGEL PROPHESIED IN THE DEAD SEA SCROLLS REMAINS.
SEELE 08
THE JOURNEY HAS BEEN LONG AND THERE HAVE BEEN MANY CASUALTIES.
INDEED.
SEELE 13
WE LOST THE SPEAR OF LONGINUS THROUGH EVA UNIT-00.

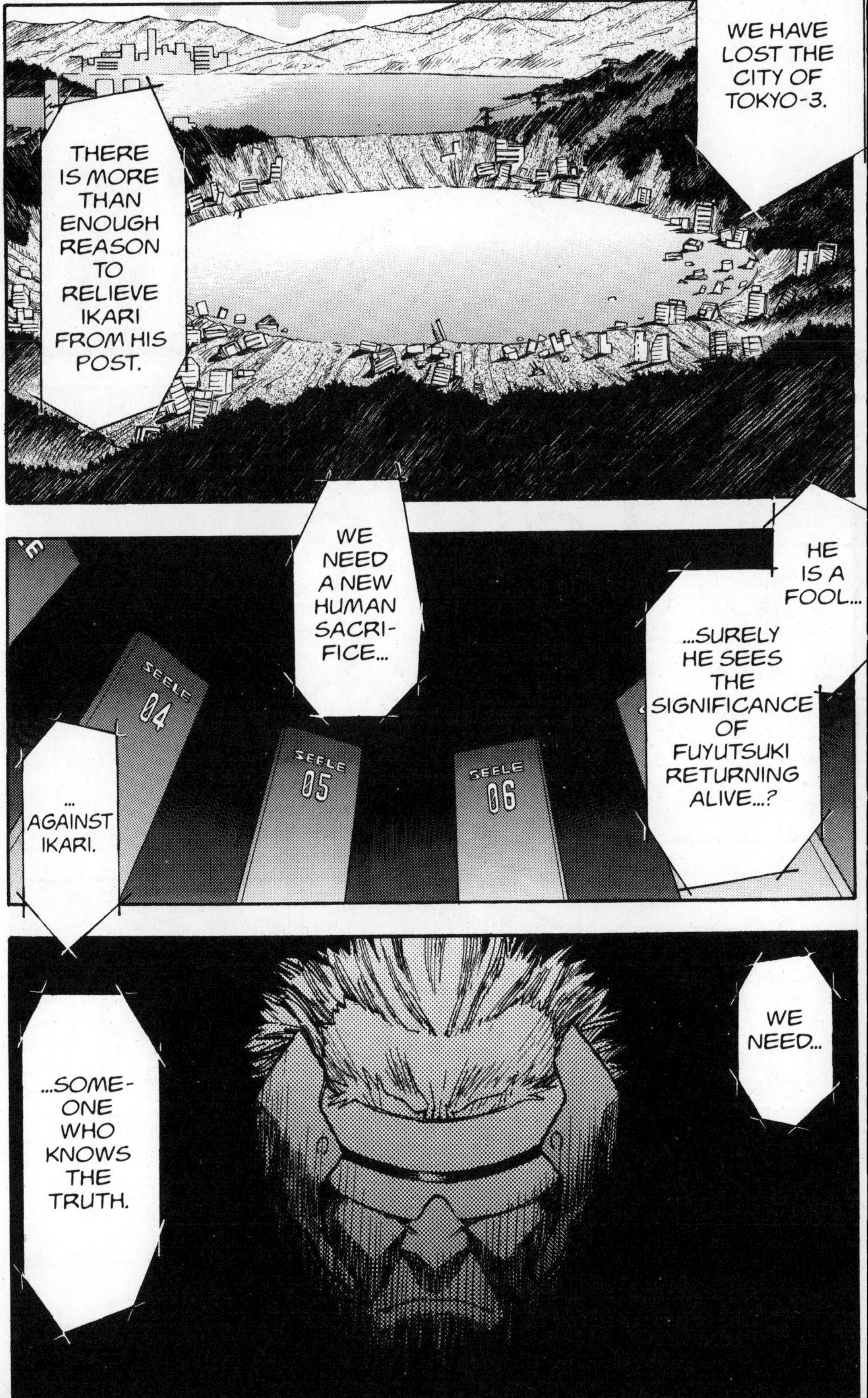
WE HAVE LOST THE CITY OF TOKYO-3.
THERE IS MORE THAN ENOUGH REASON TO RELIEVE IKARI FROM HIS POST.
HE IS A FOOL...
...SURELY HE SEES THE SIGNIFICANCE OF FUYUTSUKI RETURNING ALIVE...?
WE NEED A NEW HUMAN SACRI-FICE...
SEELE 06
SEELE 05
SEELE 04
... AGAINST IKARI.
WE NEED...
...SOME-ONE WHO KNOWS THE TRUTH.

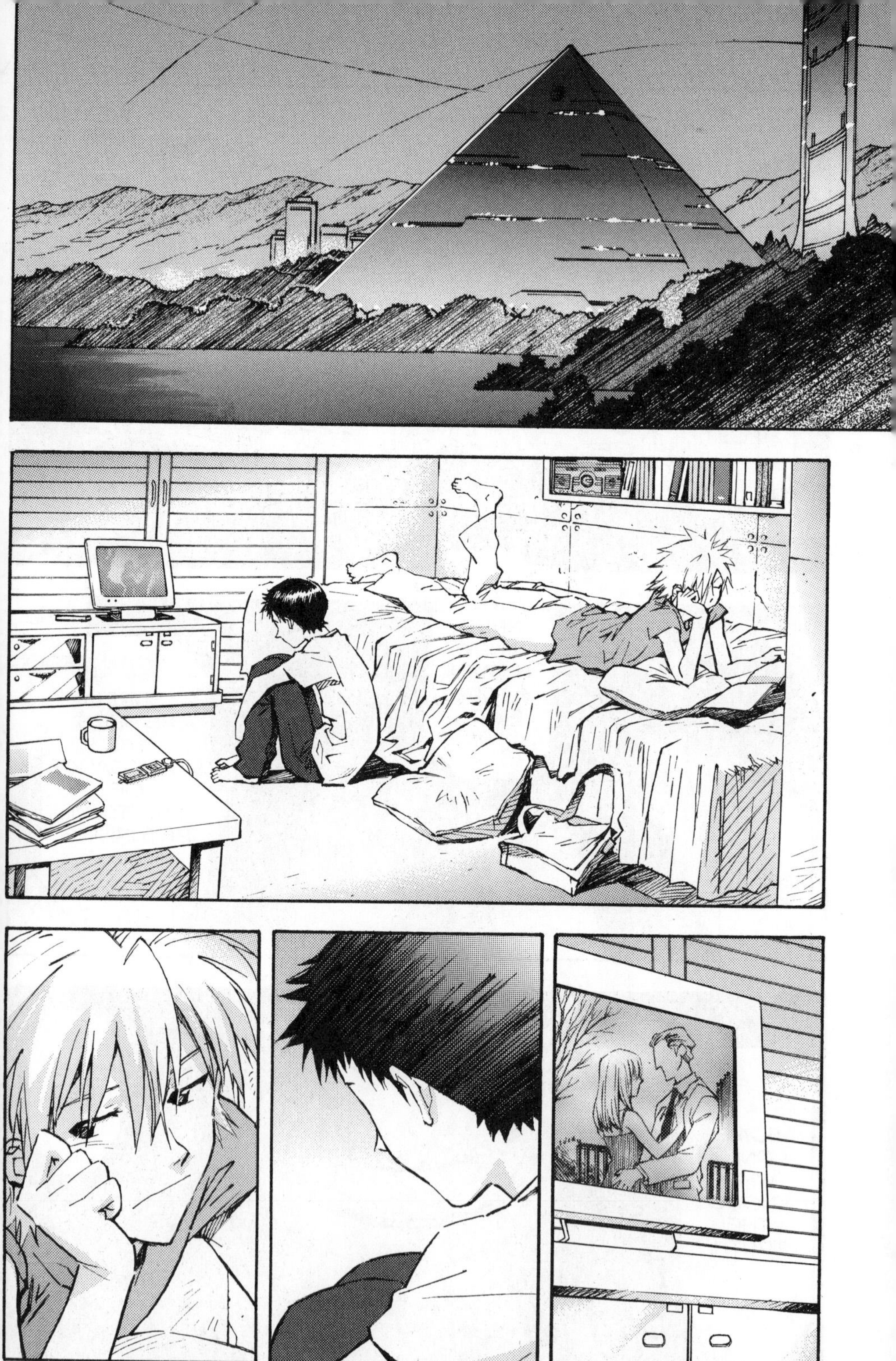

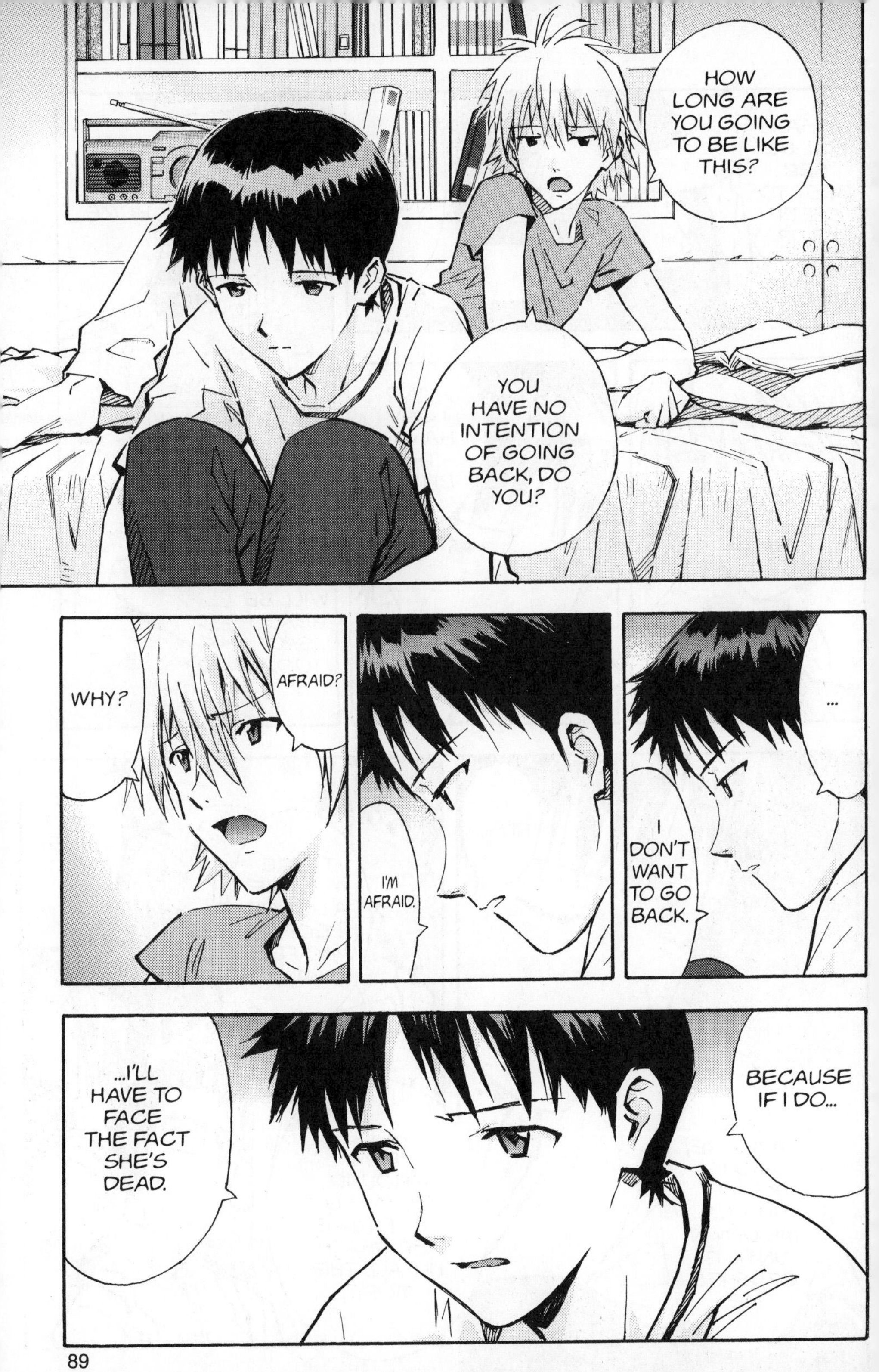
HOW LONG ARE YOU GOING TO BE LIKE THIS?
YOU HAVE NO INTENTION OF GOING BACK, DO YOU?
...
I DON'T WANT TO GO BACK.
I'M AFRAID.
AFRAID?
WHY?
BECAUSE IF I DO...
...I'LL HAVE TO FACE THE FACT SHE'S DEAD.

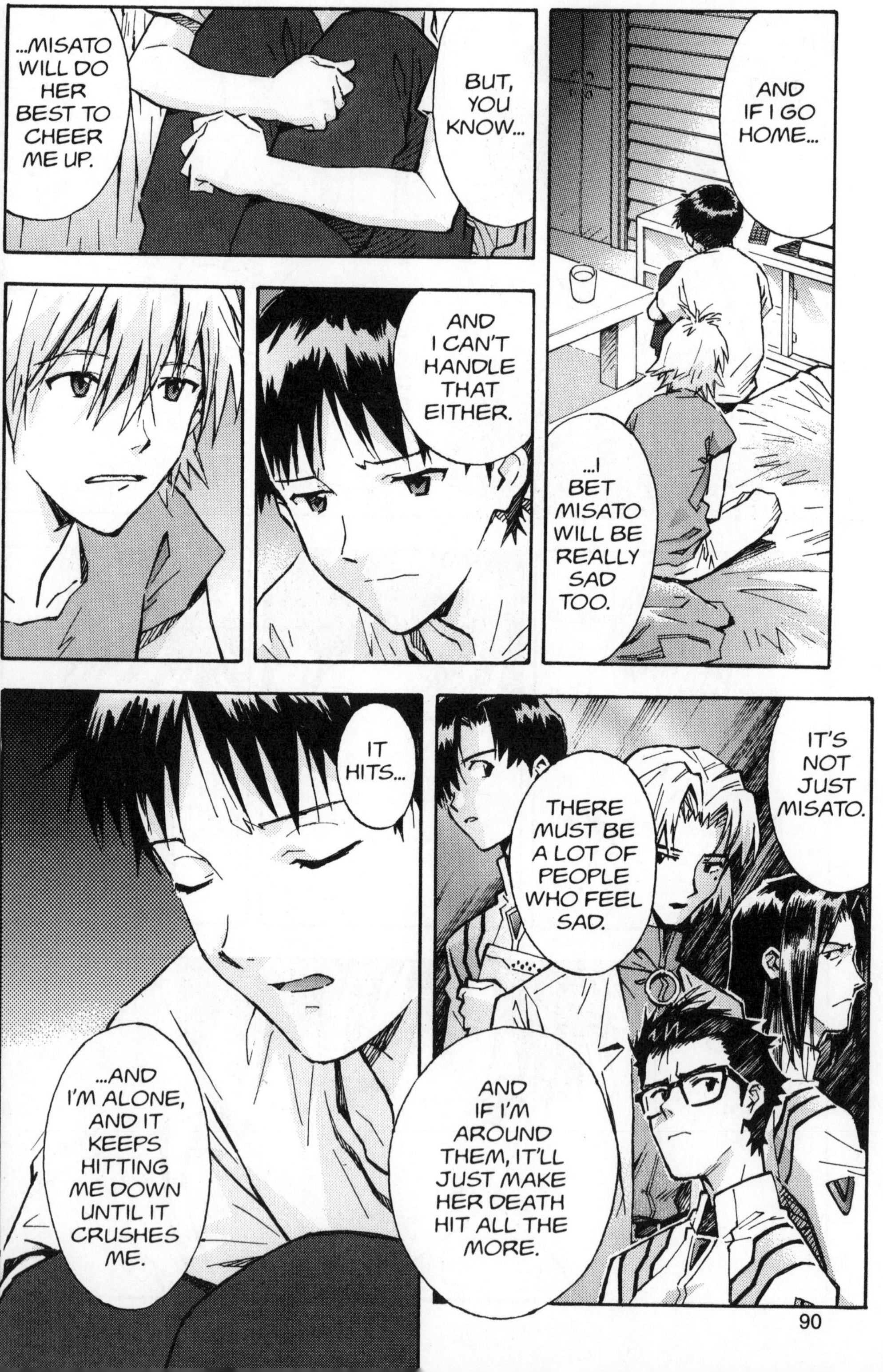
AND IF I GO HOME...
...I BET MISATO WILL BE REALLY SAD TOO.
BUT, YOU KNOW...
...MISATO WILL DO HER BEST TO CHEER ME UP.
AND I CAN'T HANDLE THAT EITHER.
IT'S NOT JUST MISATO.
THERE MUST BE A LOT OF PEOPLE WHO FEEL SAD.
AND IF I'M AROUND THEM, IT'LL JUST MAKE HER DEATH HIT ALL THE MORE.
IT HITS...
...AND I'M ALONE, AND IT KEEPS HITTING ME DOWN UNTIL IT CRUSHES ME.

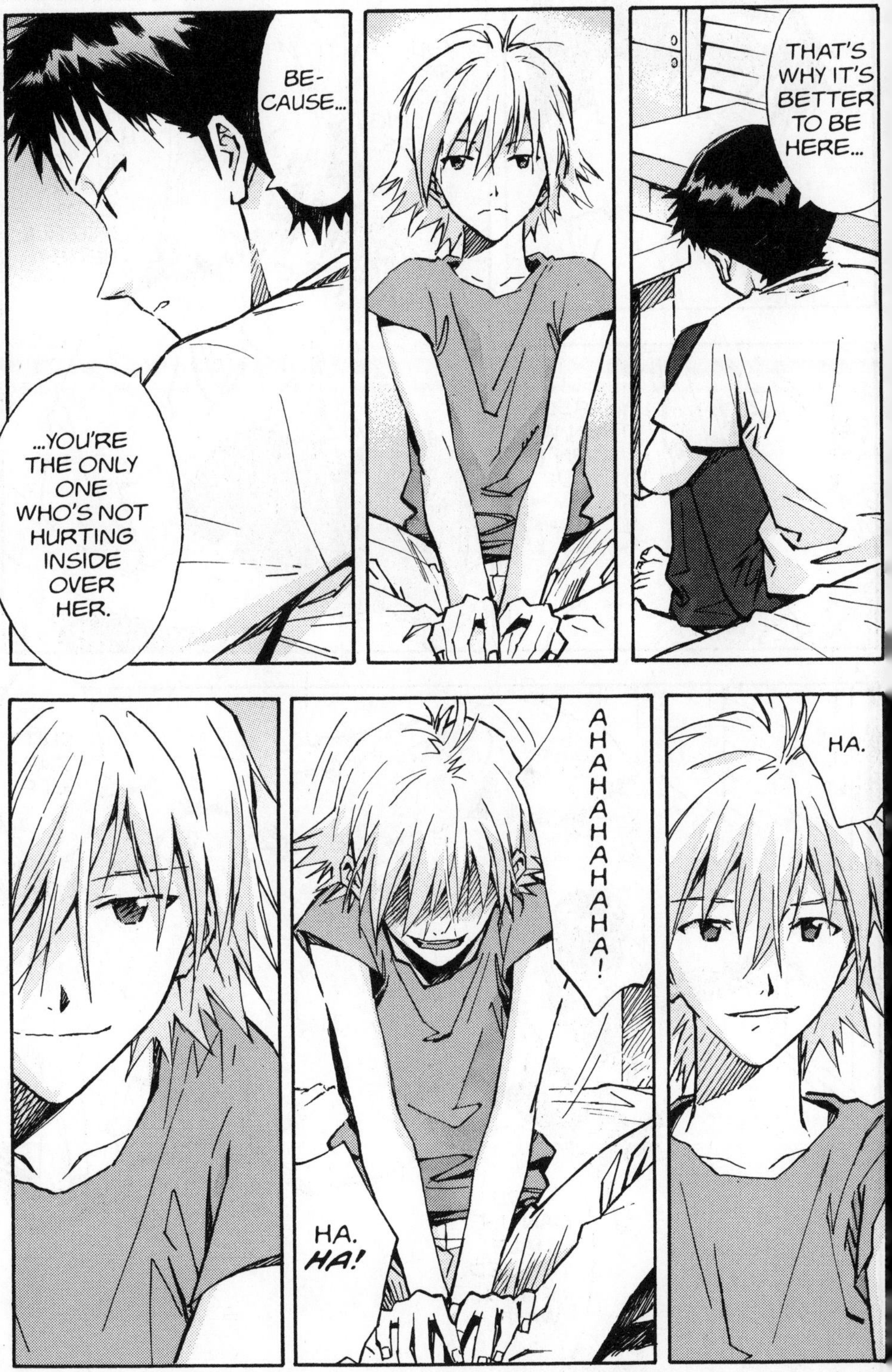
THAT'S WHY IT'S BETTER TO BE HERE...
BE-CAUSE...
...YOU'RE THE ONLY ONE WHO'S NOT HURTING INSIDE OVER HER.
HA.
AHAHAHAHAHAHA!
HA. HA!

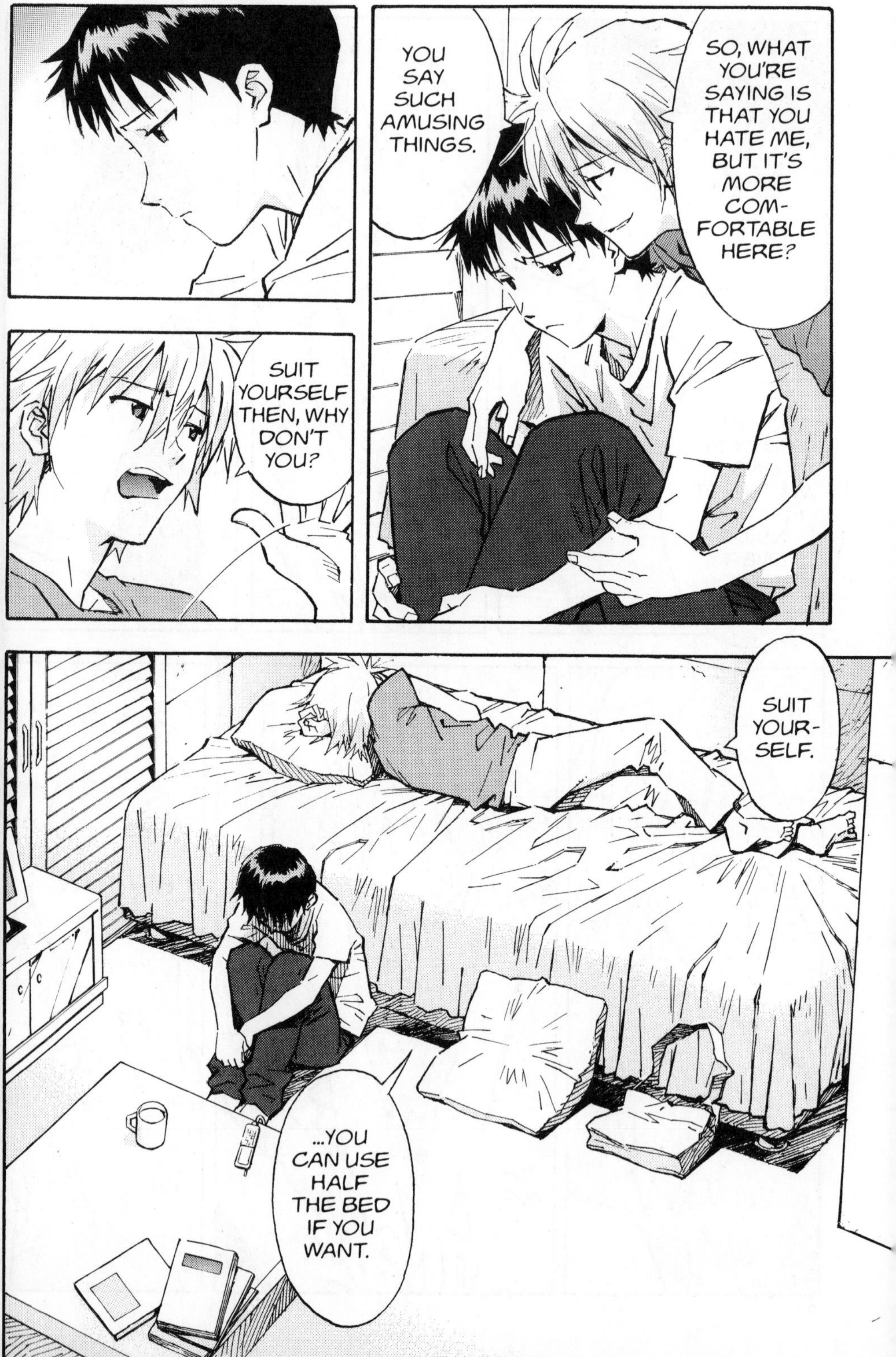
SO, WHAT YOU'RE SAYING IS THAT YOU HATE ME, BUT IT'S MORE COM-FORTABLE HERE?
YOU SAY SUCH AMUSING THINGS.
SUIT YOURSELF THEN, WHY DON'T YOU?
SUIT YOUR-SELF.
...YOU CAN USE HALF THE BED IF YOU WANT.

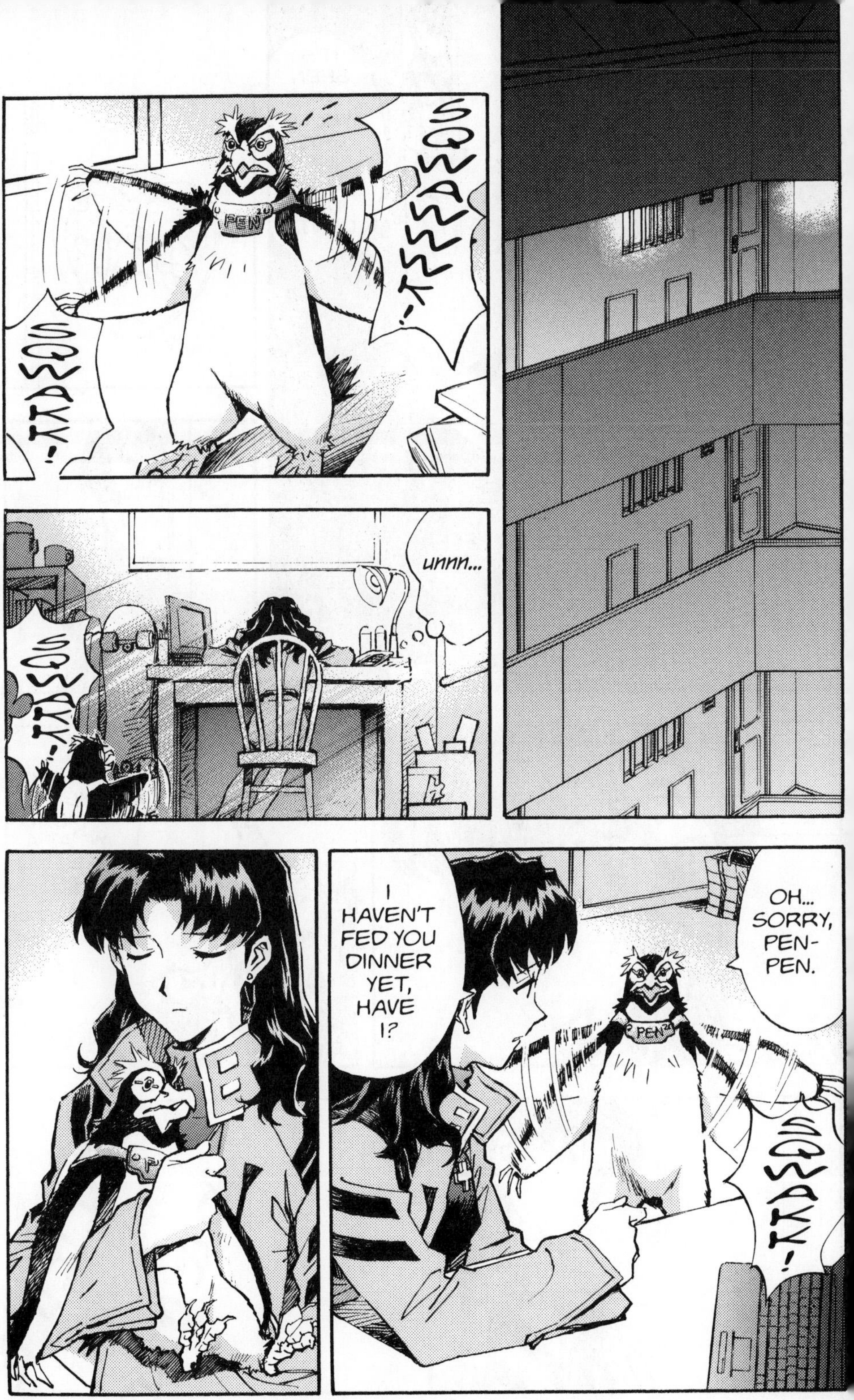
SQWAWWWK!
SQWAKK!
unnn...
SQWAKK!
OH... SORRY, PEN-PEN.
I HAVEN'T FED YOU DINNER YET, HAVE I?
SQWAKK!

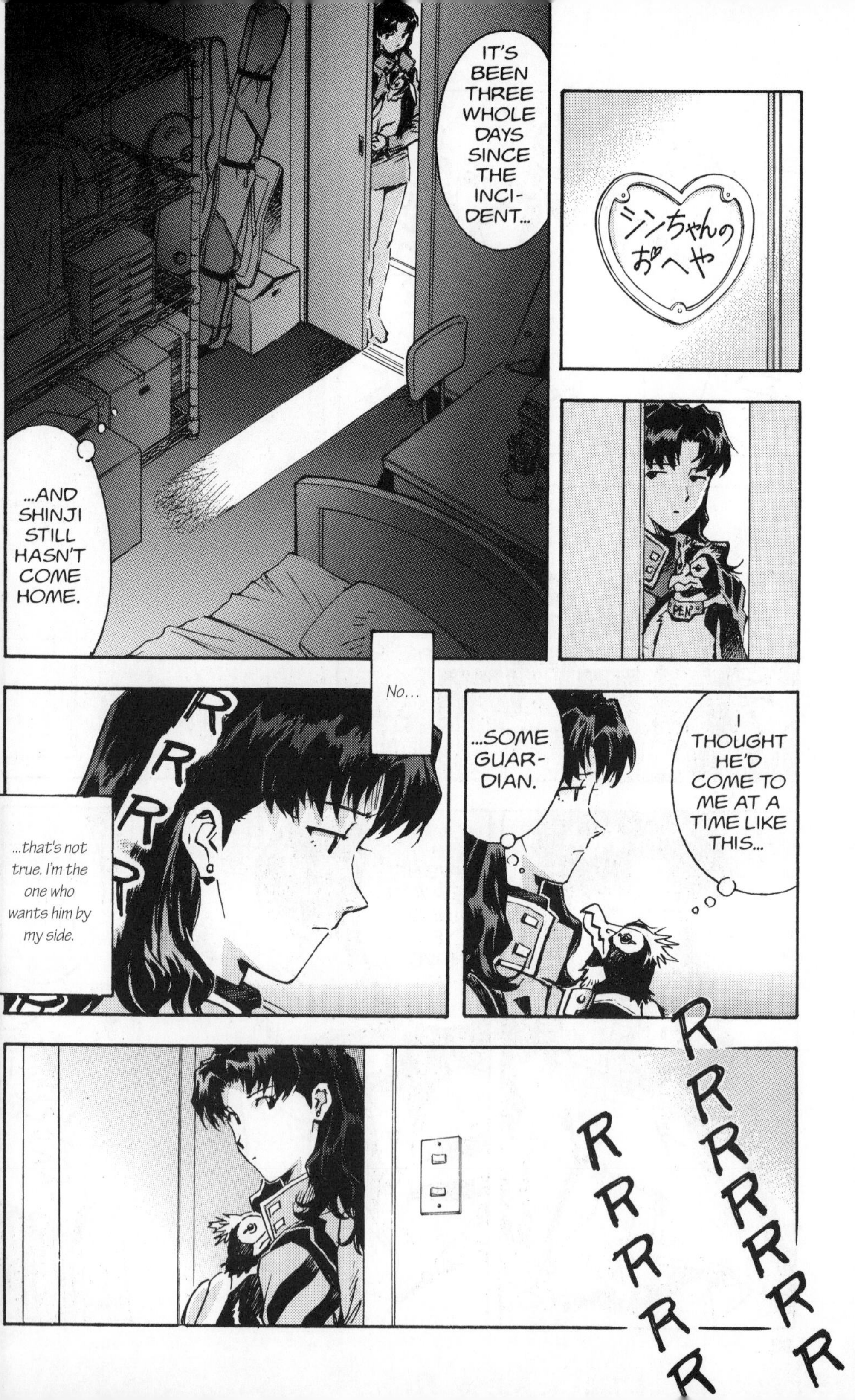
シンちゃんのお♥へや
IT'S BEEN THREE WHOLE DAYS SINCE THE INCI-DENT...
...AND SHINJI STILL HASN'T COME HOME.
I THOUGHT HE'D COME TO ME AT A TIME LIKE THIS...
...SOME GUAR-DIAN.
No...
...that's not true. I'm the one who wants him by my side.
RRRRRRR
RRRRRRRRRRR

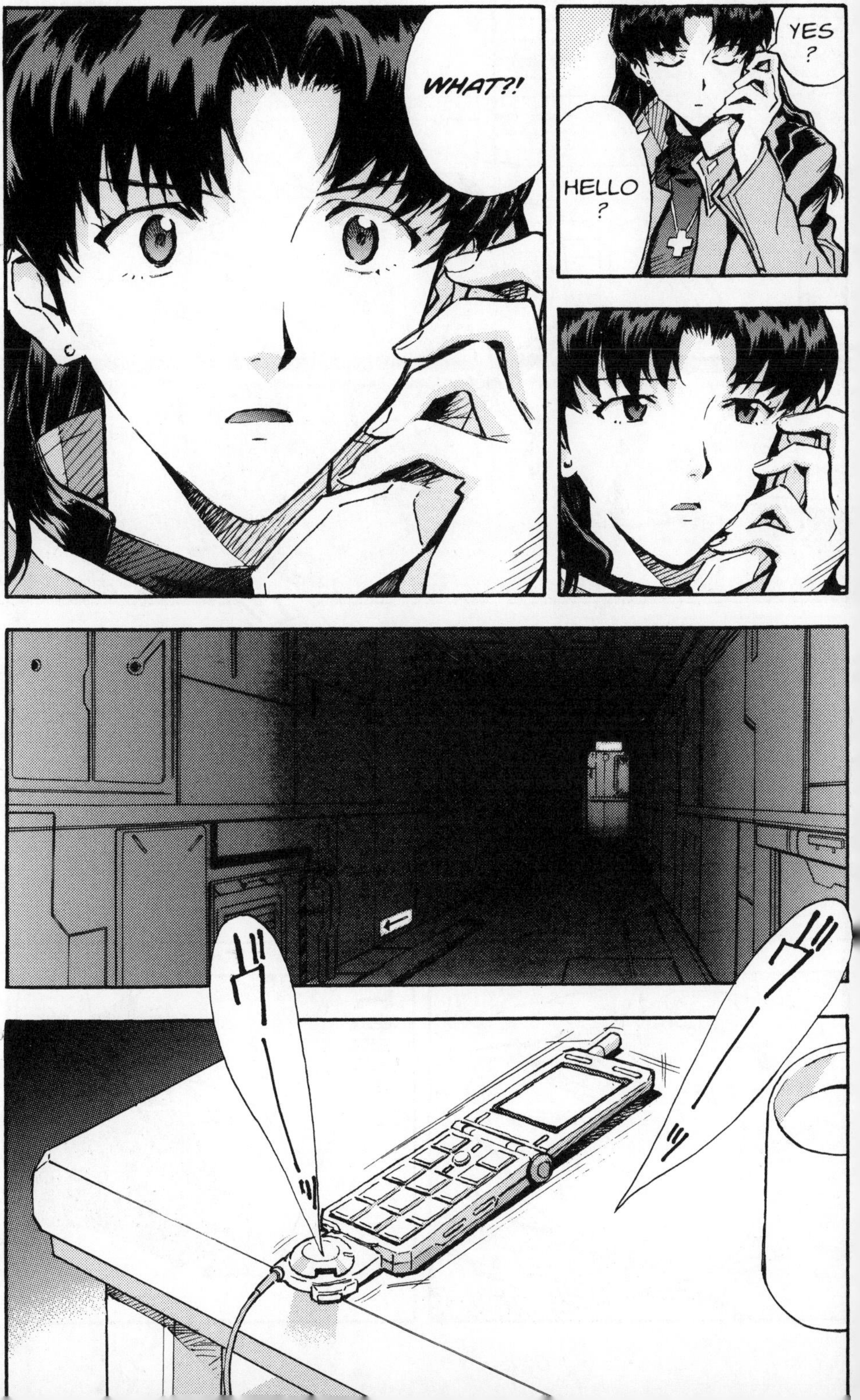
YES ?
HELLO ?
WHAT?!

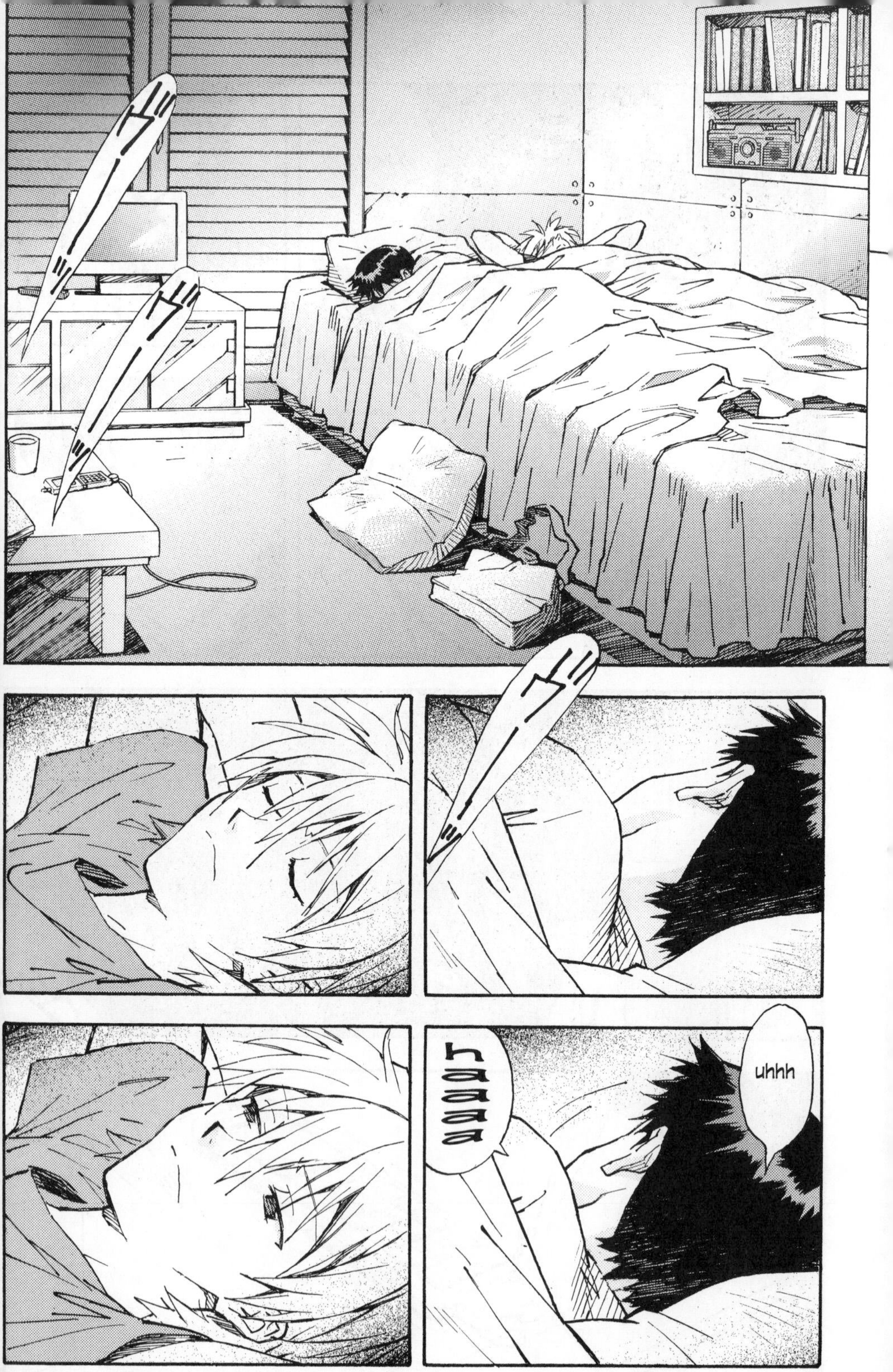
uhhh
haaaa

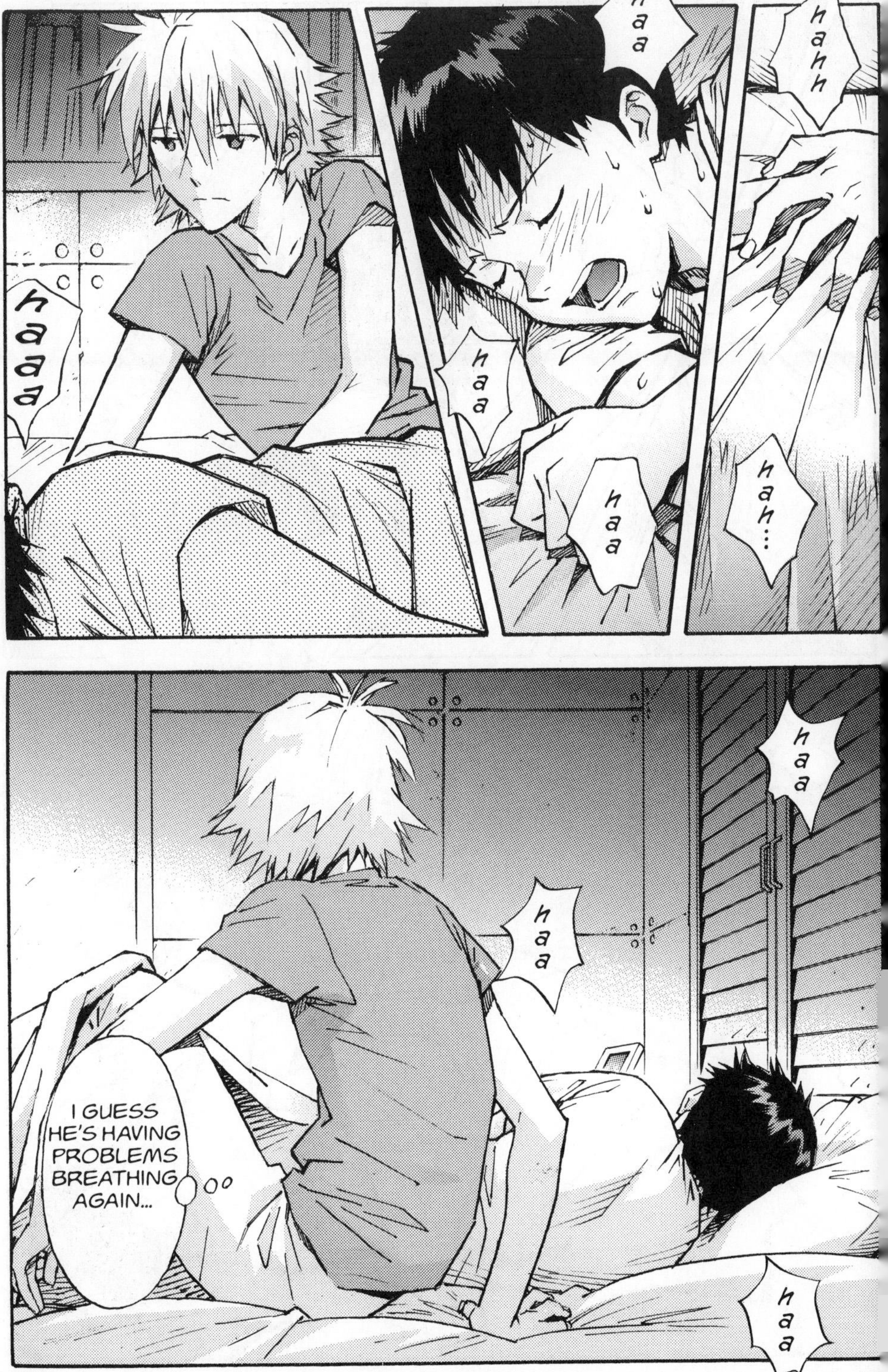
hahh
hah...
haa
haa
haa
haaaa
haa
haa
I GUESS HE'S HAVING PROBLEMS BREATHING AGAIN...
haa

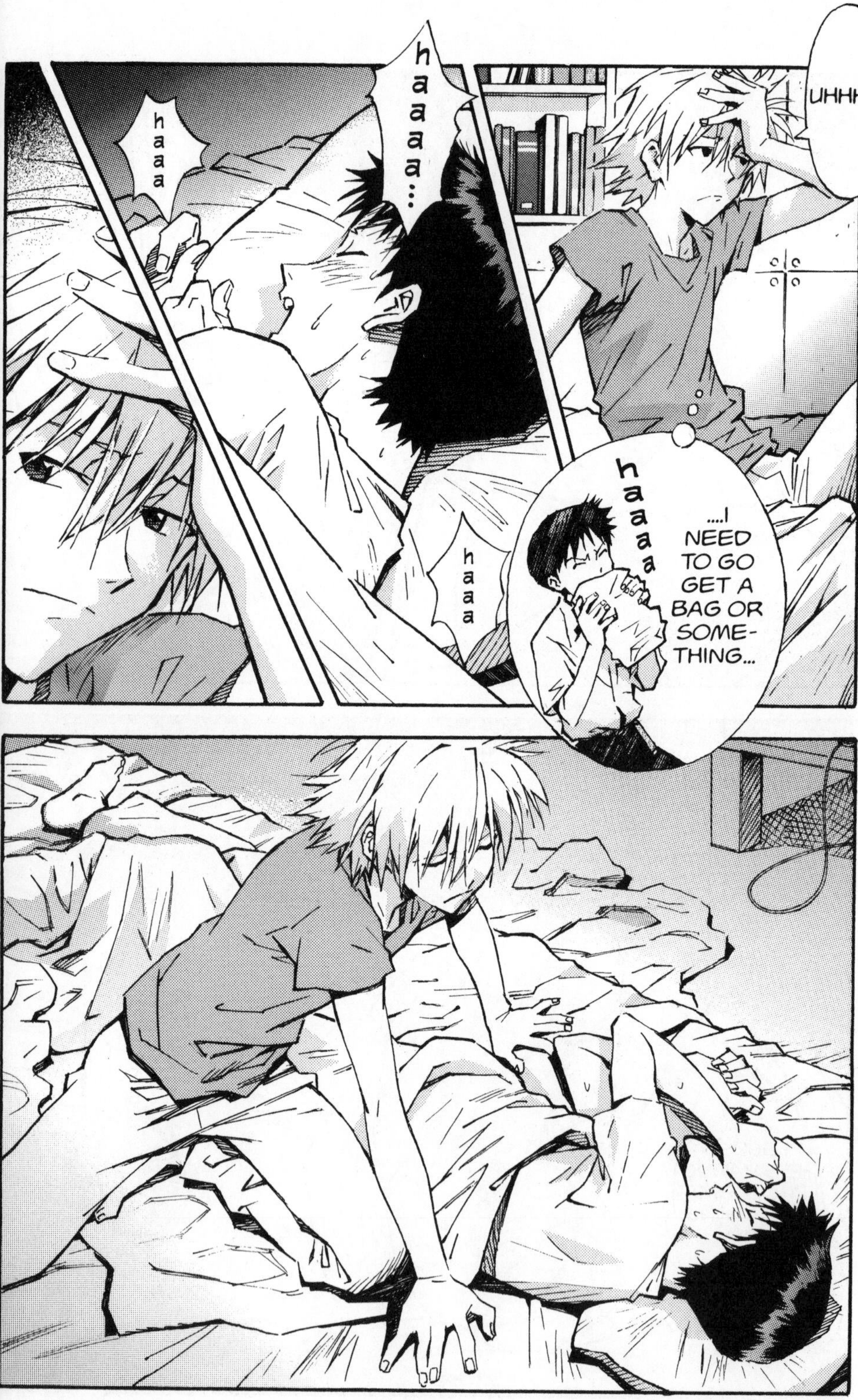
UHHH...
....I NEED TO GO GET A BAG OR SOME-THING...
haaaaa
haaaa...
haaa
haaa

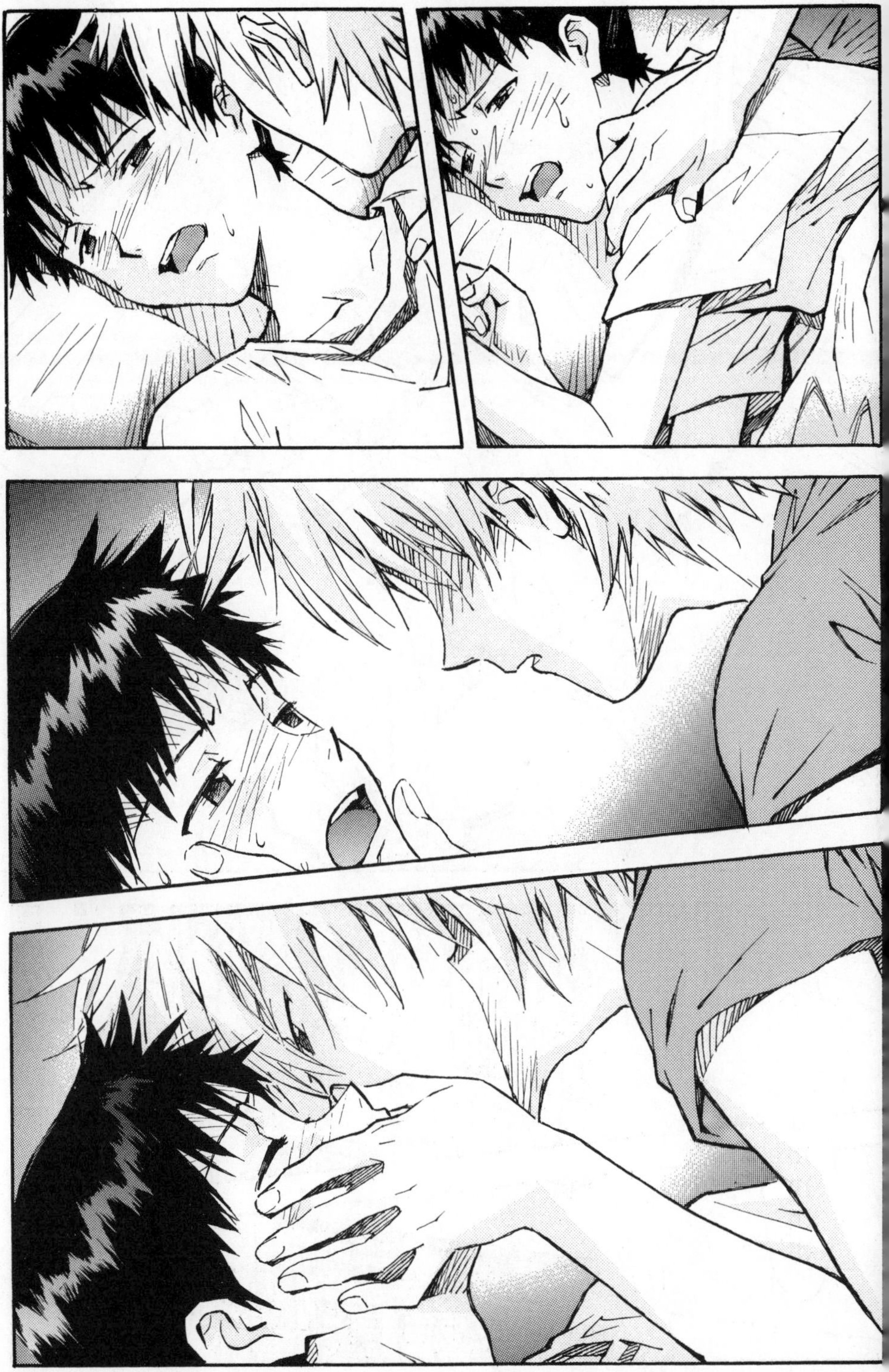

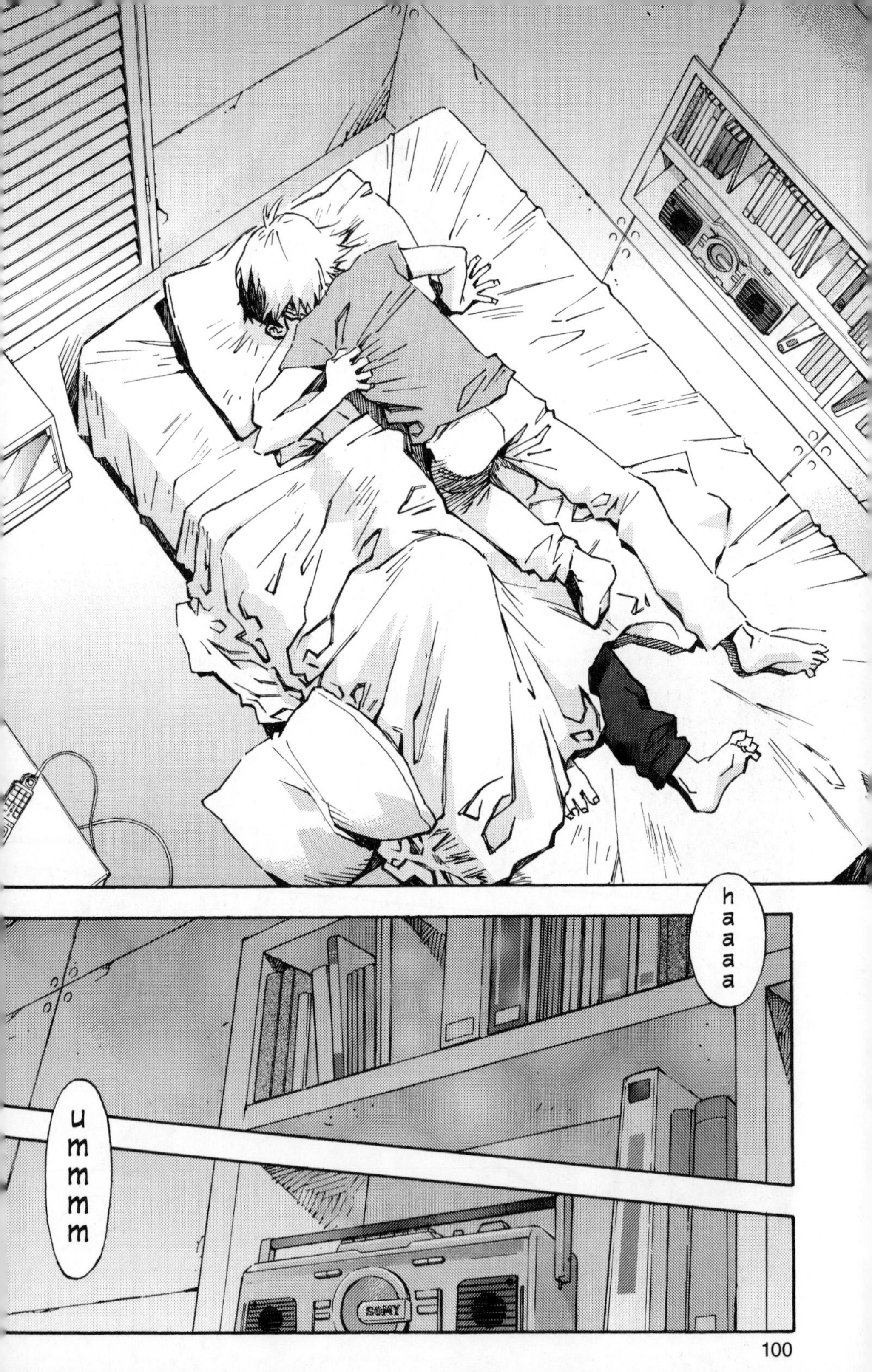
haaaa
ummmm

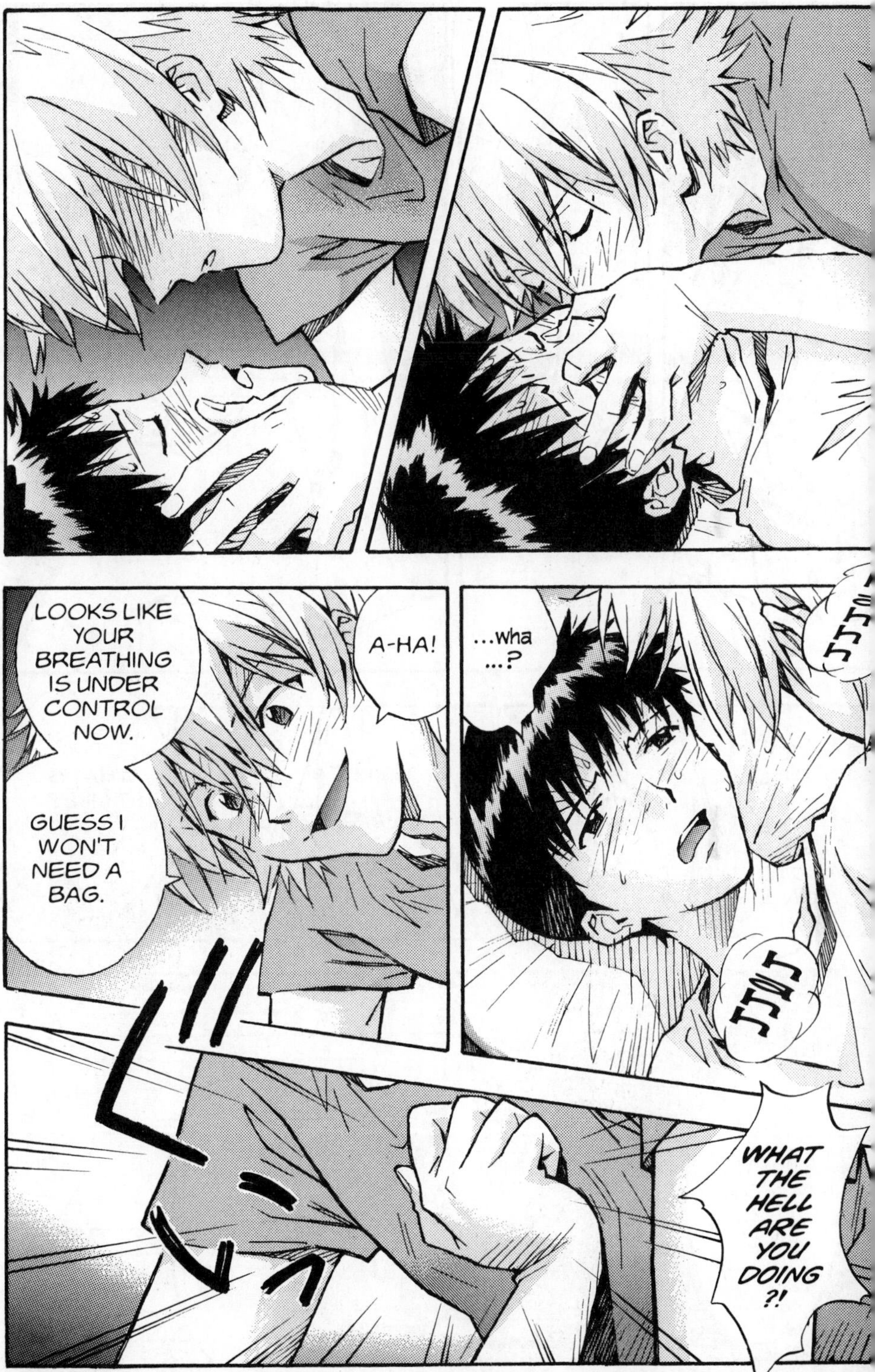
...wha ...?
A-HA!
LOOKS LIKE YOUR BREATHING IS UNDER CONTROL NOW.
GUESS I WON'T NEED A BAG.
WHAT THE HELL ARE YOU DOING?!

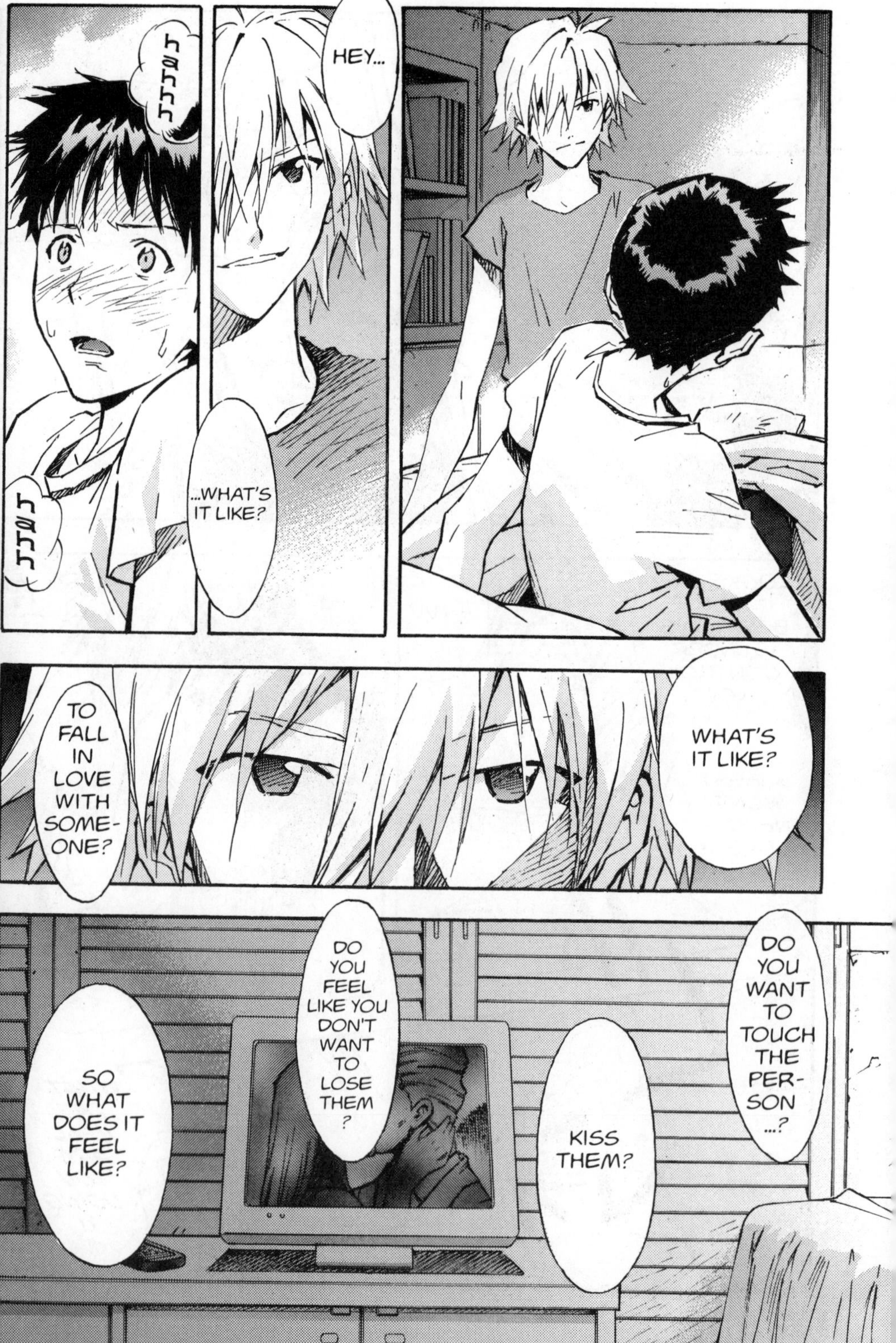
HEY...
...WHAT'S IT LIKE?
hahhh
hahh
WHAT'S IT LIKE?
TO FALL IN LOVE WITH SOME-ONE?
DO YOU WANT TO TOUCH THE PER-SON ...?
KISS THEM?
DO YOU FEEL LIKE YOU DON'T WANT TO LOSE THEM ?
SO WHAT DOES IT FEEL LIKE?

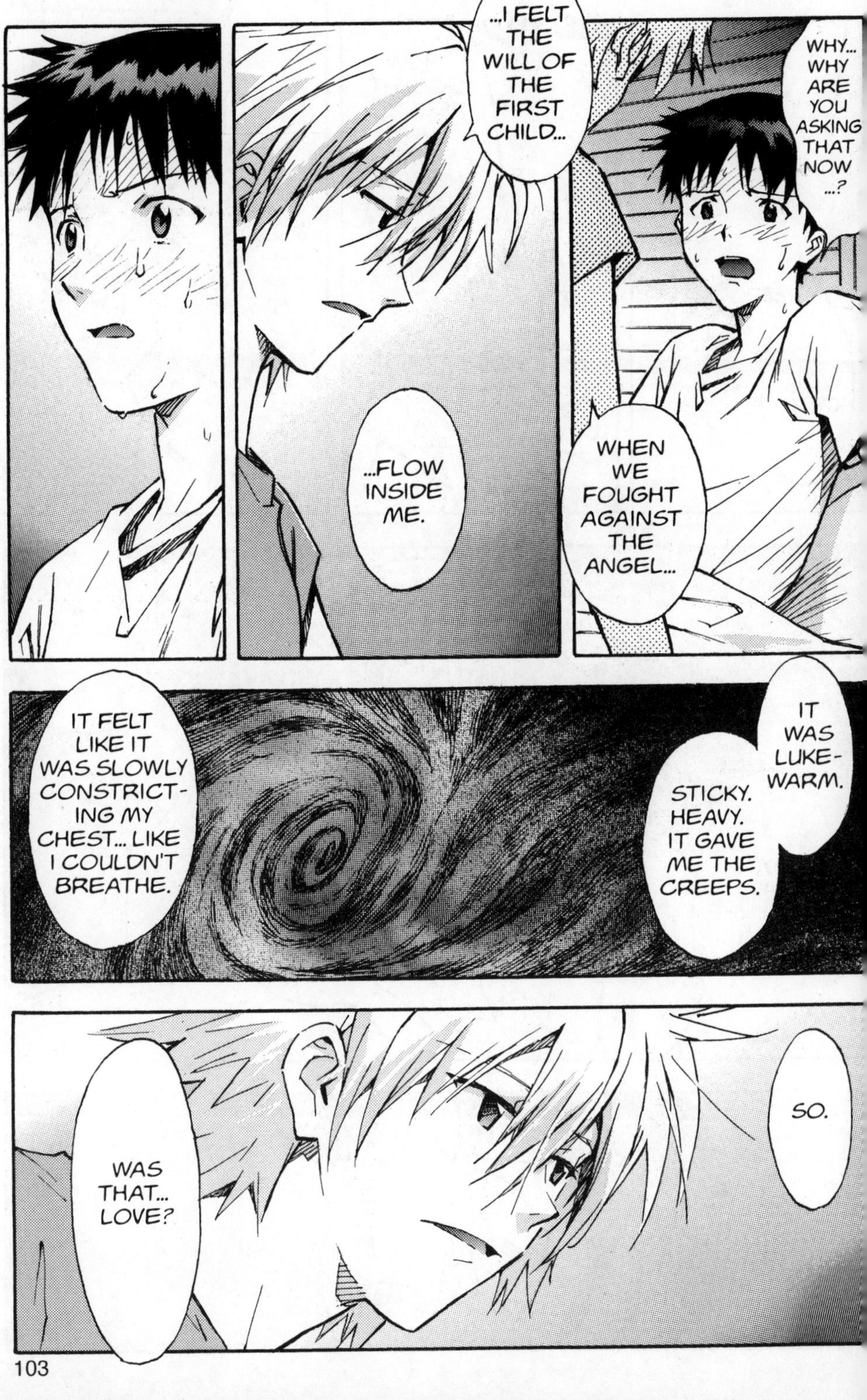
WHY... WHY ARE YOU ASKING THAT NOW ...?
WHEN WE FOUGHT AGAINST THE ANGEL...
...I FELT THE WILL OF THE FIRST CHILD...
...FLOW INSIDE ME.
IT WAS LUKE-WARM.
STICKY. HEAVY. IT GAVE ME THE CREEPS.
IT FELT LIKE IT WAS SLOWLY CONSTRICT-ING MY CHEST... LIKE I COULDN'T BREATHE.
SO.
WAS THAT... LOVE?

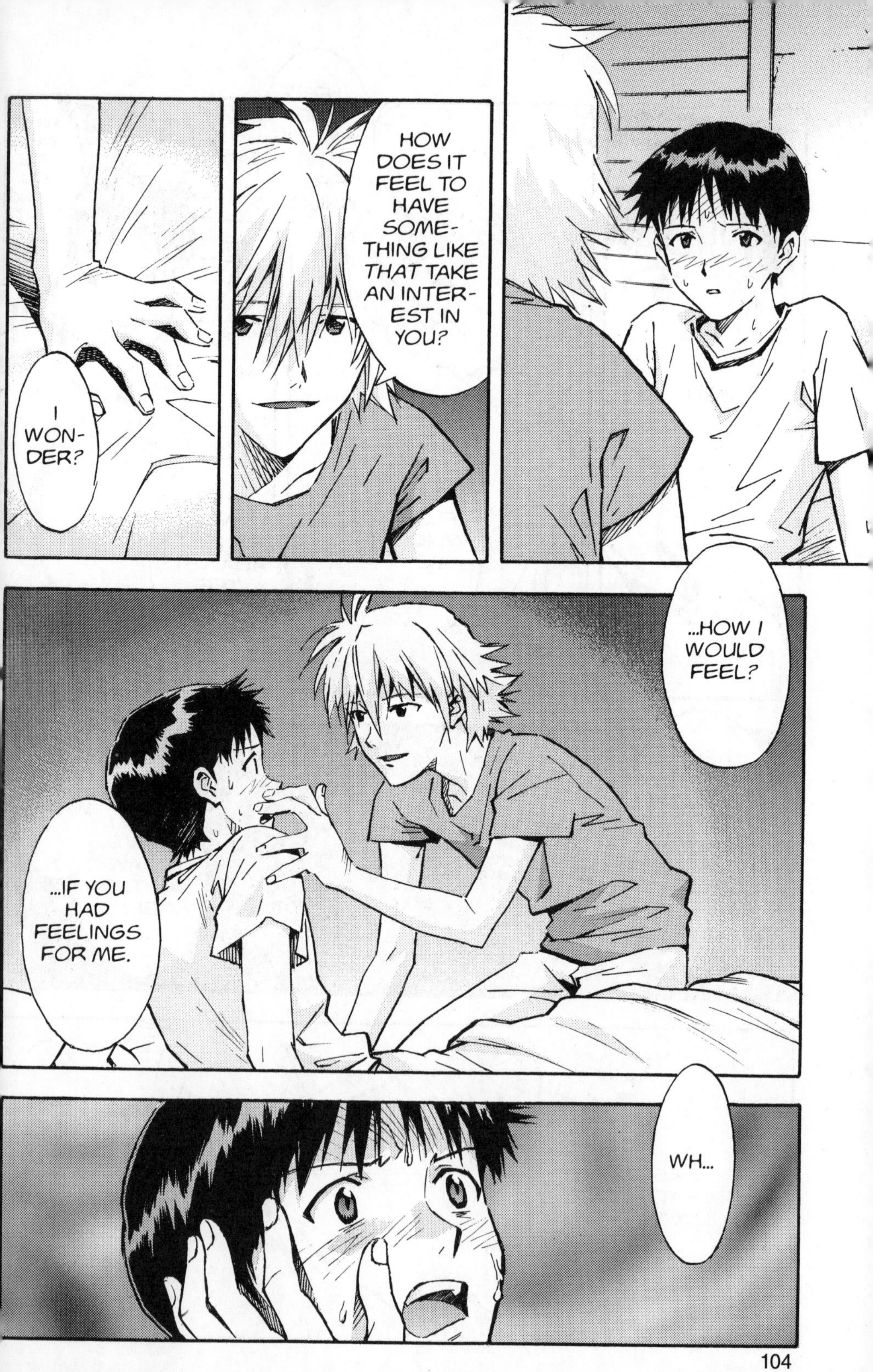
HOW DOES IT FEEL TO HAVE SOMETHING LIKE THAT TAKE AN INTEREST IN YOU?
I WONDER?
...HOW I WOULD FEEL?
...IF YOU HAD FEELINGS FOR ME.
WH...

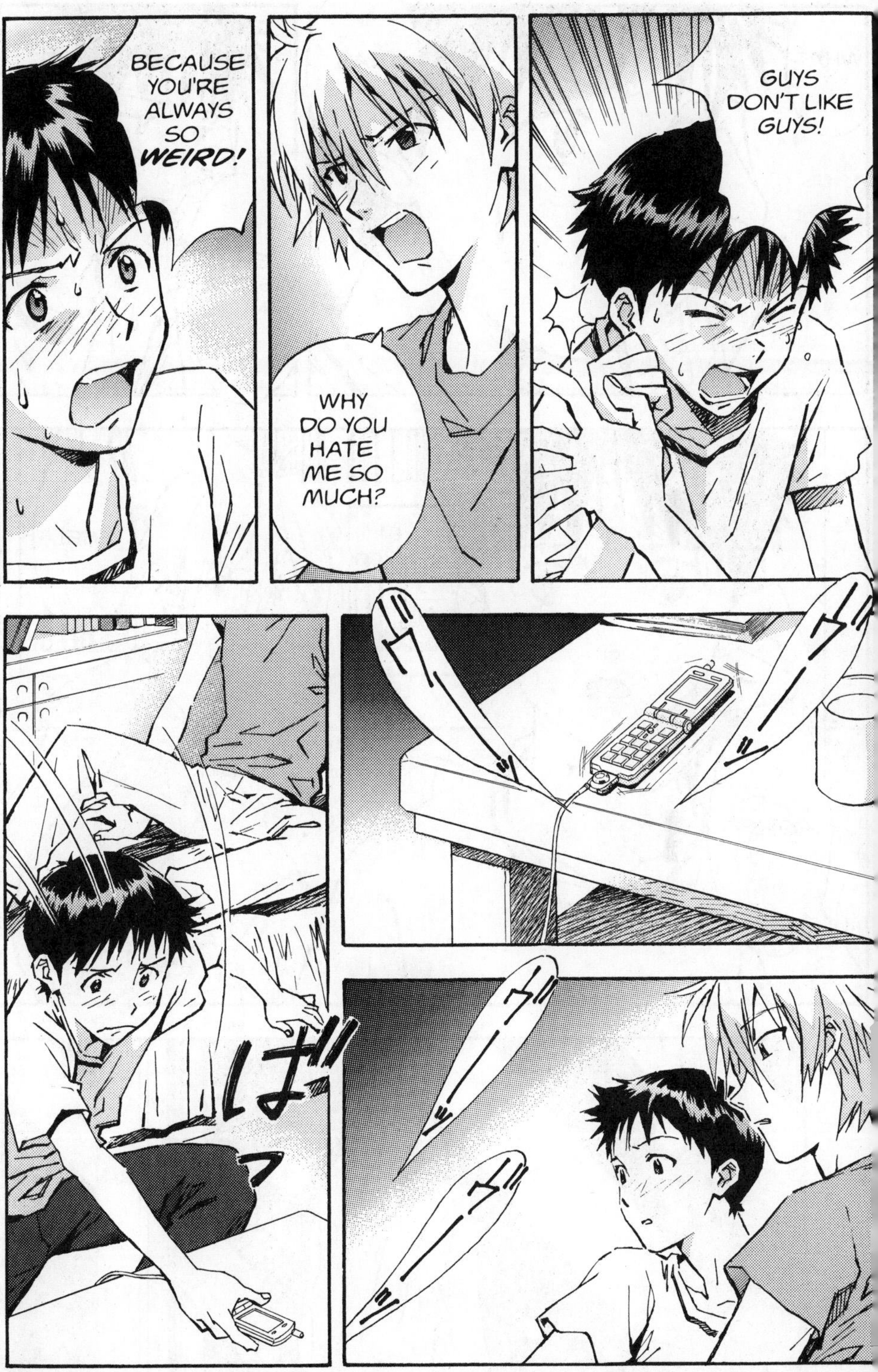
GUYS DON'T LIKE GUYS!
WHY DO YOU HATE ME SO MUCH?
BECAUSE YOU'RE ALWAYS SO *WEIRD!*
ば

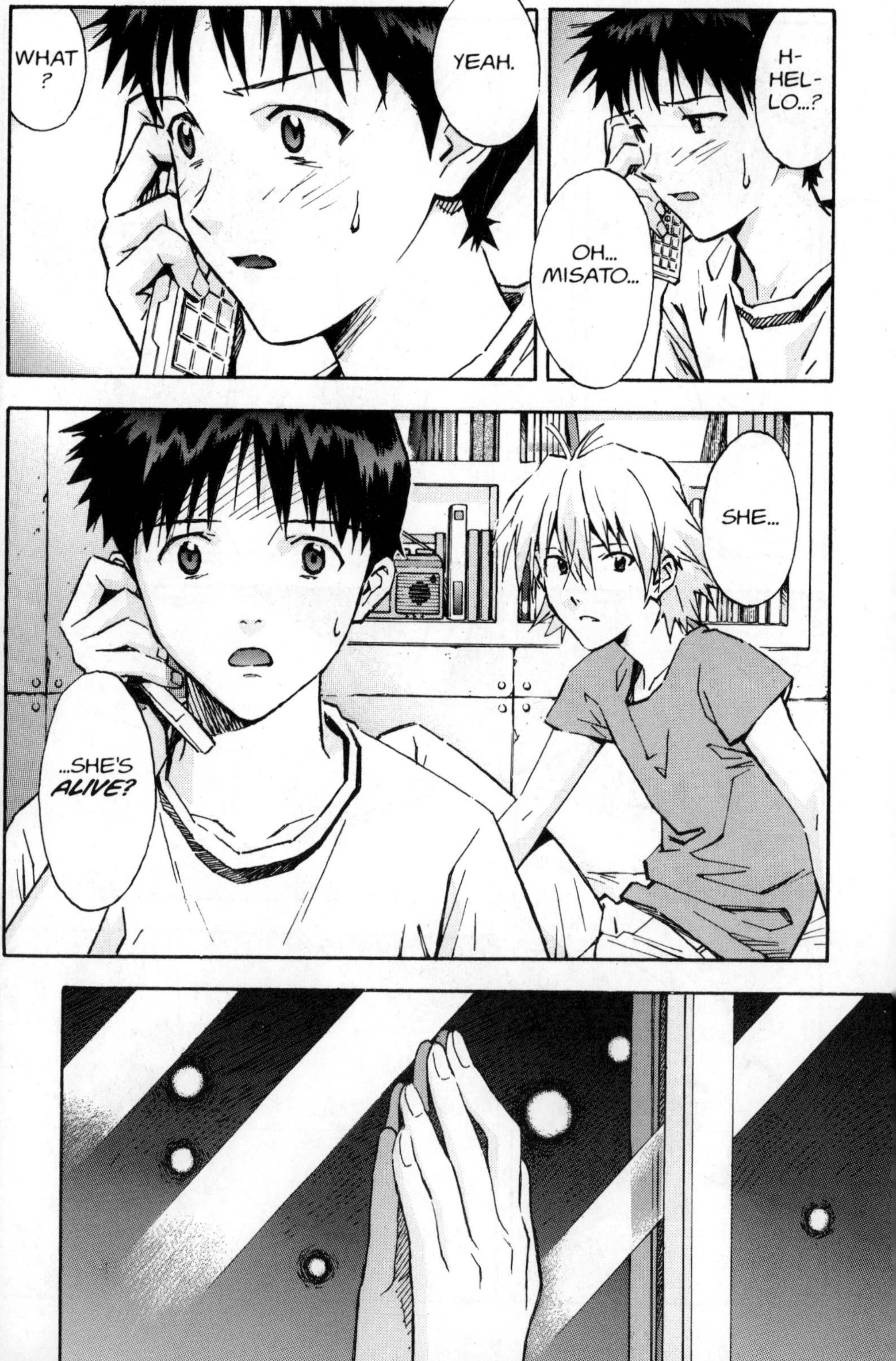
H- HEL- LO...?
OH... MISATO...
YEAH.
WHAT ?
SHE...
...SHE'S *ALIVE?*

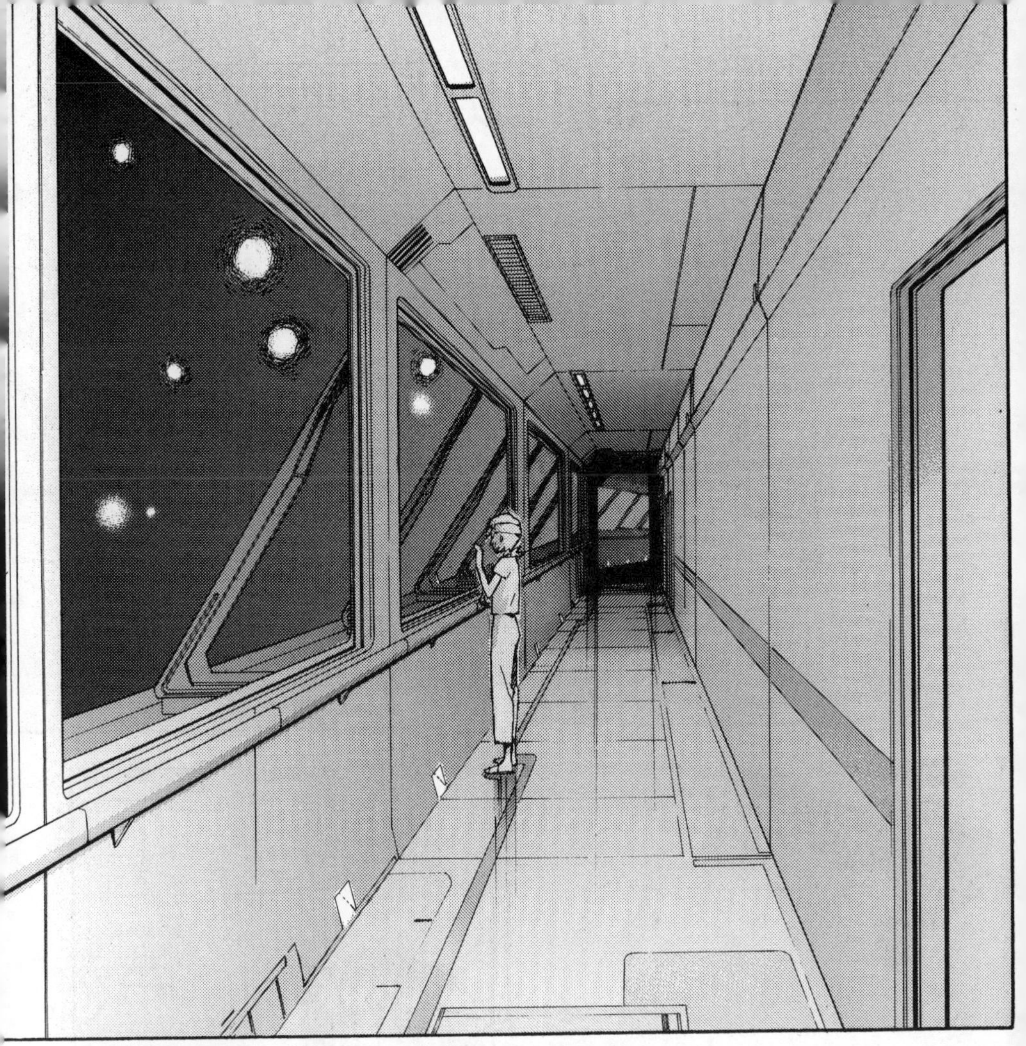
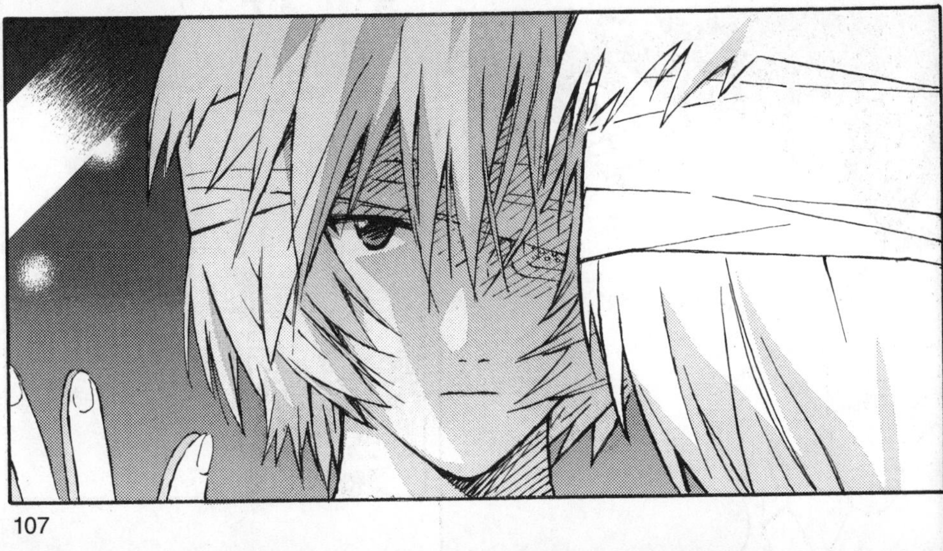

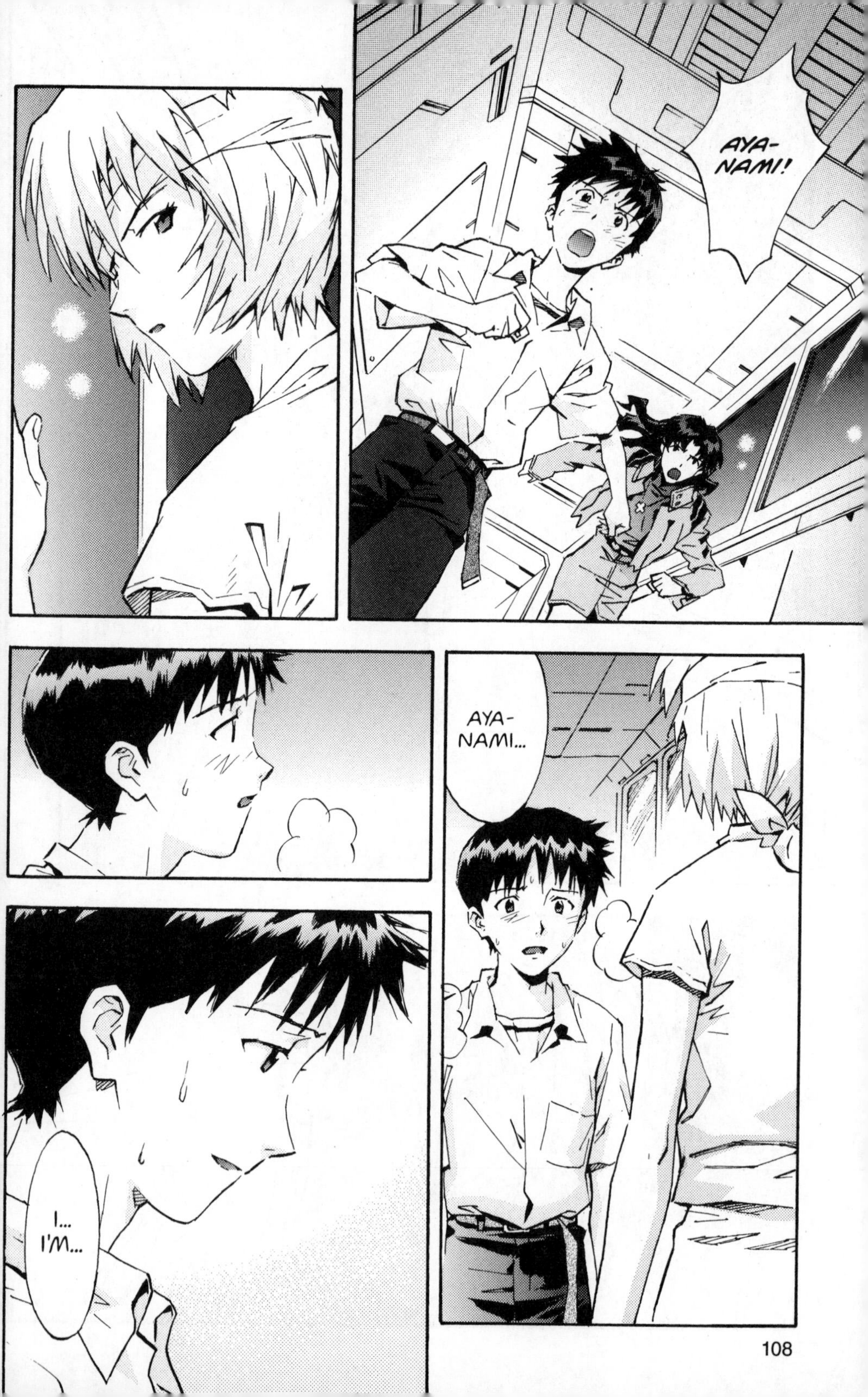
AYA-NAMI!
AYA-NAMI...
I... I'M...

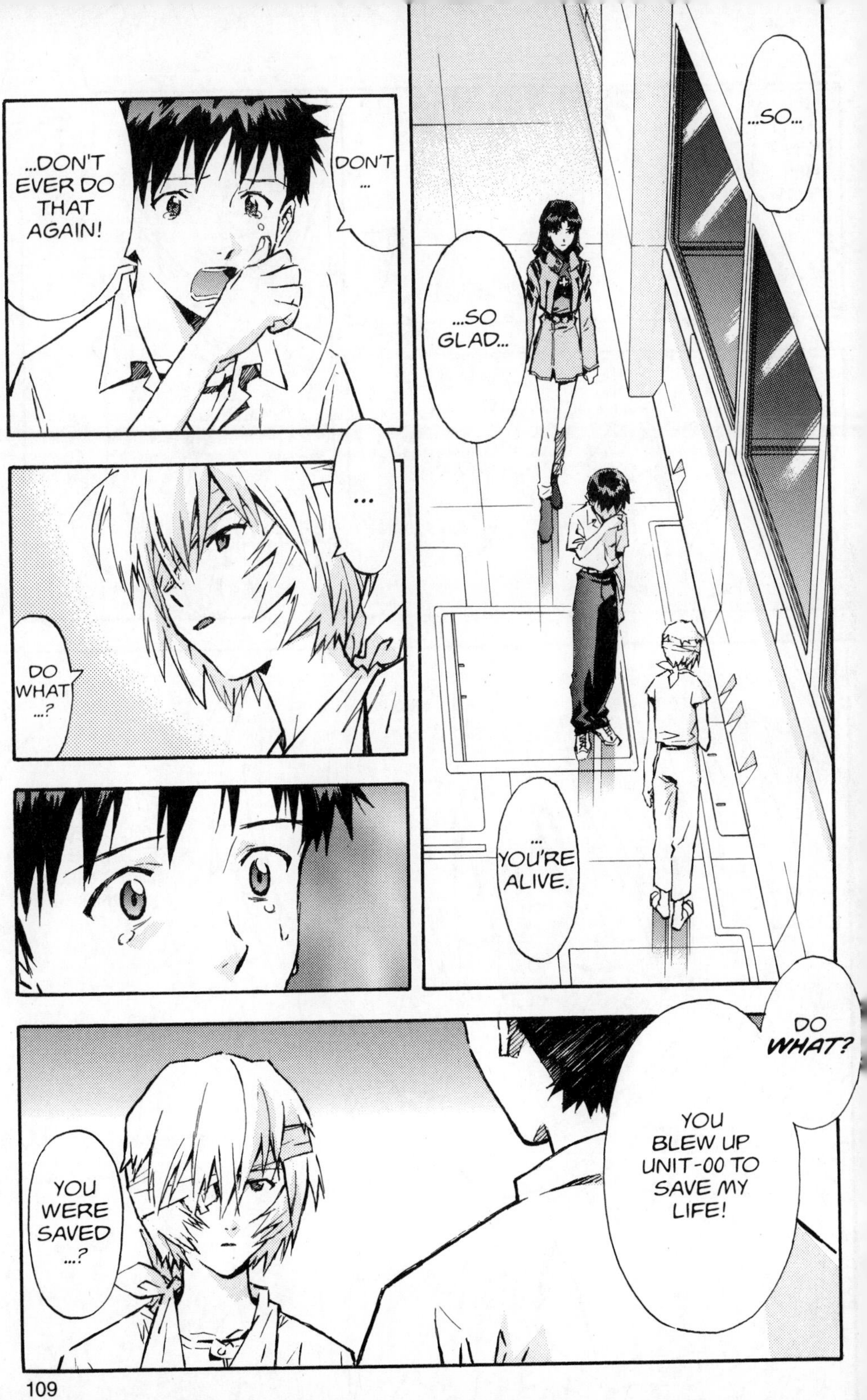
...SO...
...SO GLAD...
... YOU'RE ALIVE.
DON'T ...
...DON'T EVER DO THAT AGAIN!
...
DO WHAT ...?
DO *WHAT?*
YOU BLEW UP UNIT-00 TO SAVE MY LIFE!
YOU WERE SAVED ...?

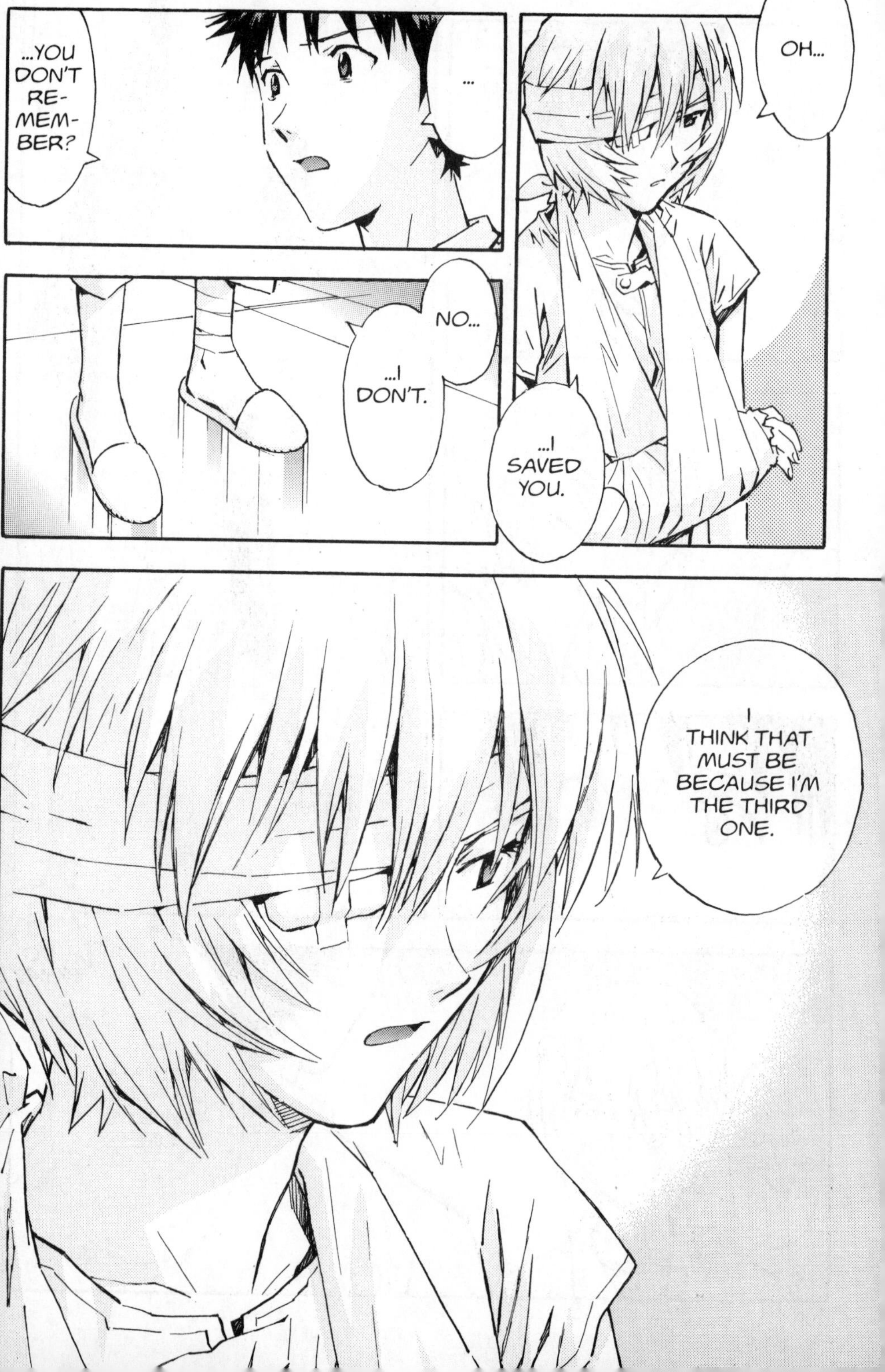
OH...
...I SAVED YOU.
...
...YOU DON'T RE-MEM-BER?
NO...
...I DON'T.
I THINK THAT MUST BE BECAUSE I'M THE THIRD ONE.

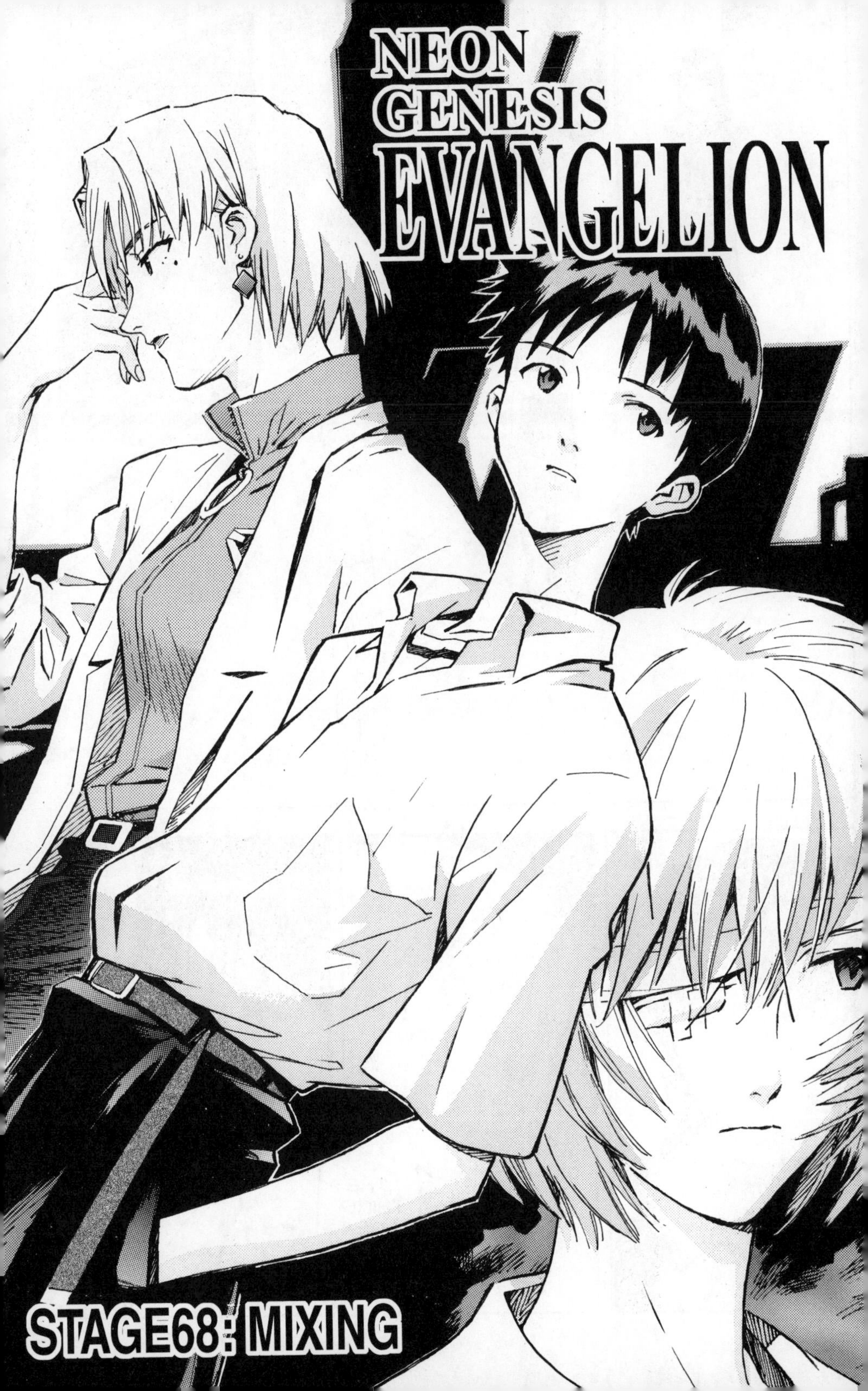
NEON GENESIS EVANGELION
STAGE68: MIXING

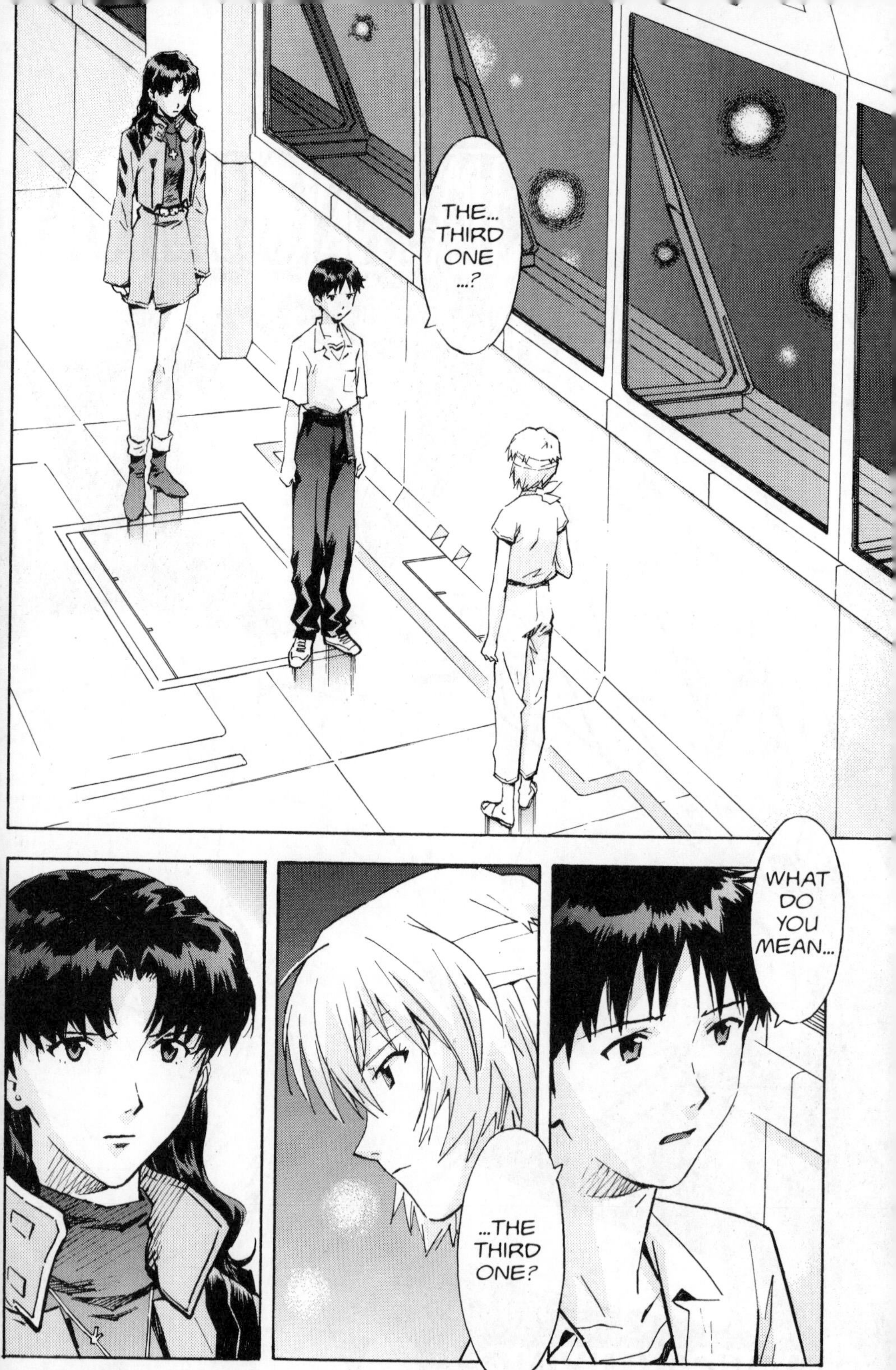
THE... THIRD ONE ...?
WHAT DO YOU MEAN...
...THE THIRD ONE?

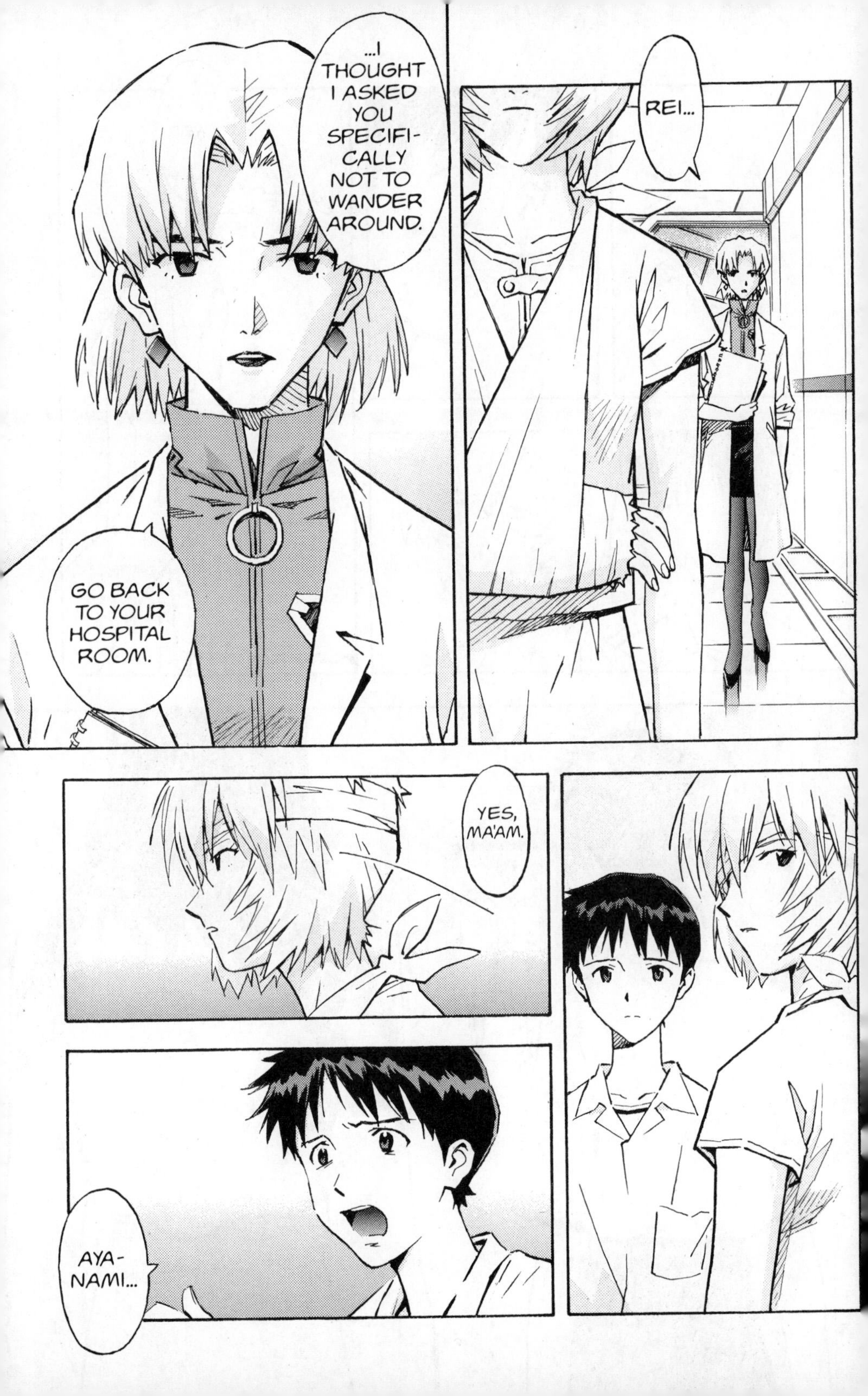
REI...
...I THOUGHT I ASKED YOU SPECIFICALLY NOT TO WANDER AROUND.
GO BACK TO YOUR HOSPITAL ROOM.
YES, MA'AM.
AYA-NAMI...

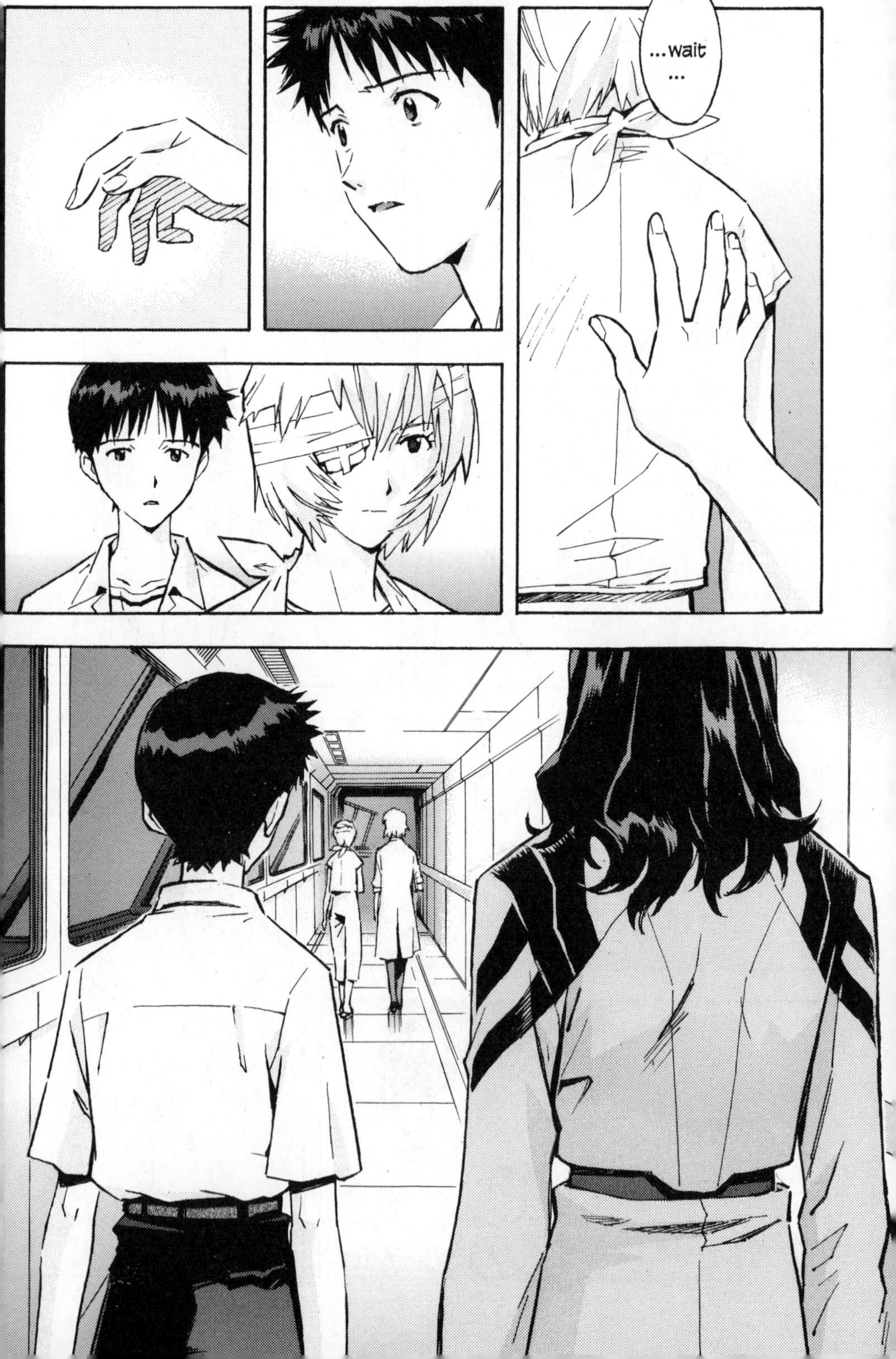
...wait
...

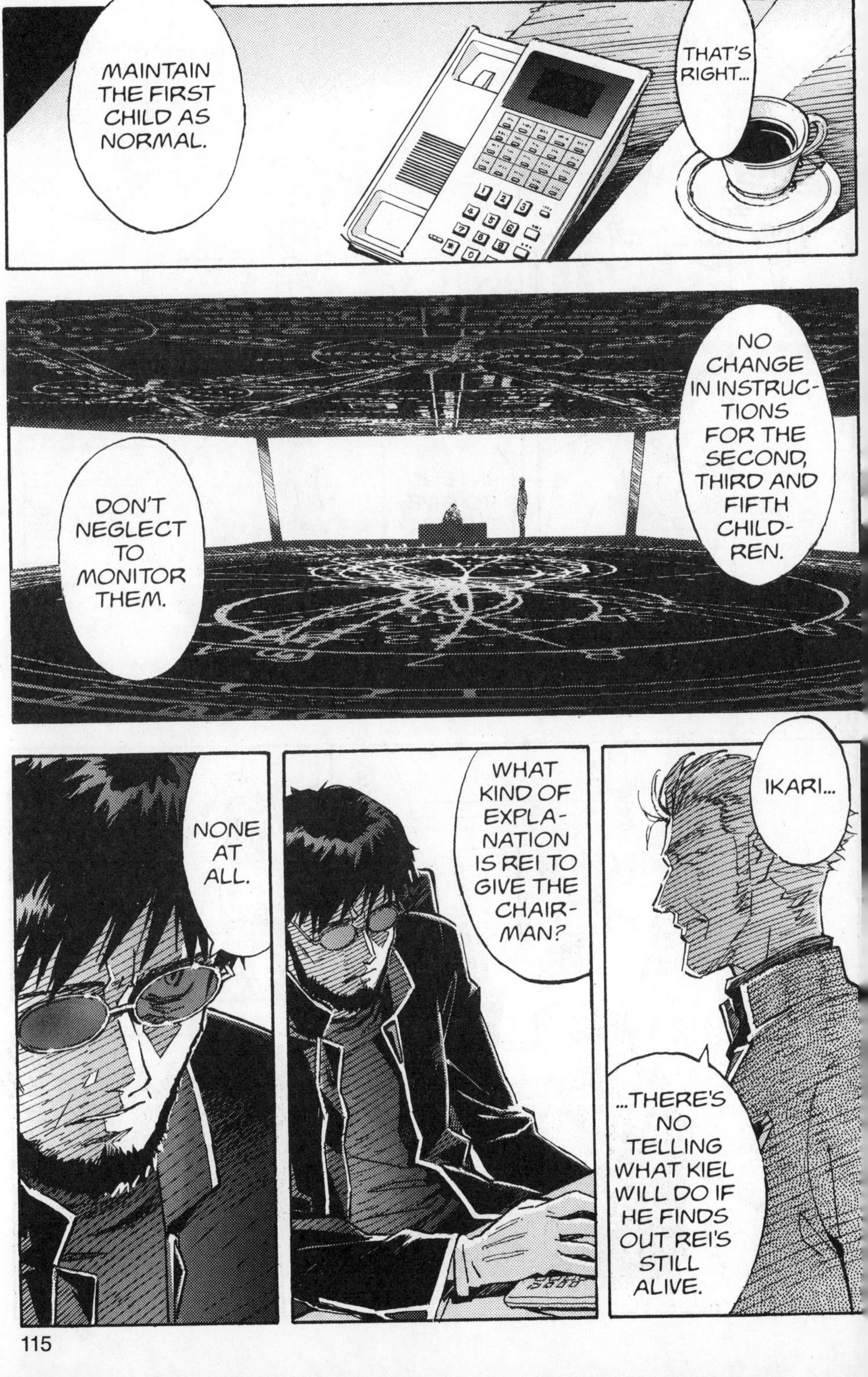
THAT'S RIGHT...
MAINTAIN THE FIRST CHILD AS NORMAL.
NO CHANGE IN INSTRUC-TIONS FOR THE SECOND, THIRD AND FIFTH CHILD-REN.
DON'T NEGLECT TO MONITOR THEM.
IKARI...
...THERE'S NO TELLING WHAT KIEL WILL DO IF HE FINDS OUT REI'S STILL ALIVE.
WHAT KIND OF EXPLA-NATION IS REI TO GIVE THE CHAIR-MAN?
NONE AT ALL.

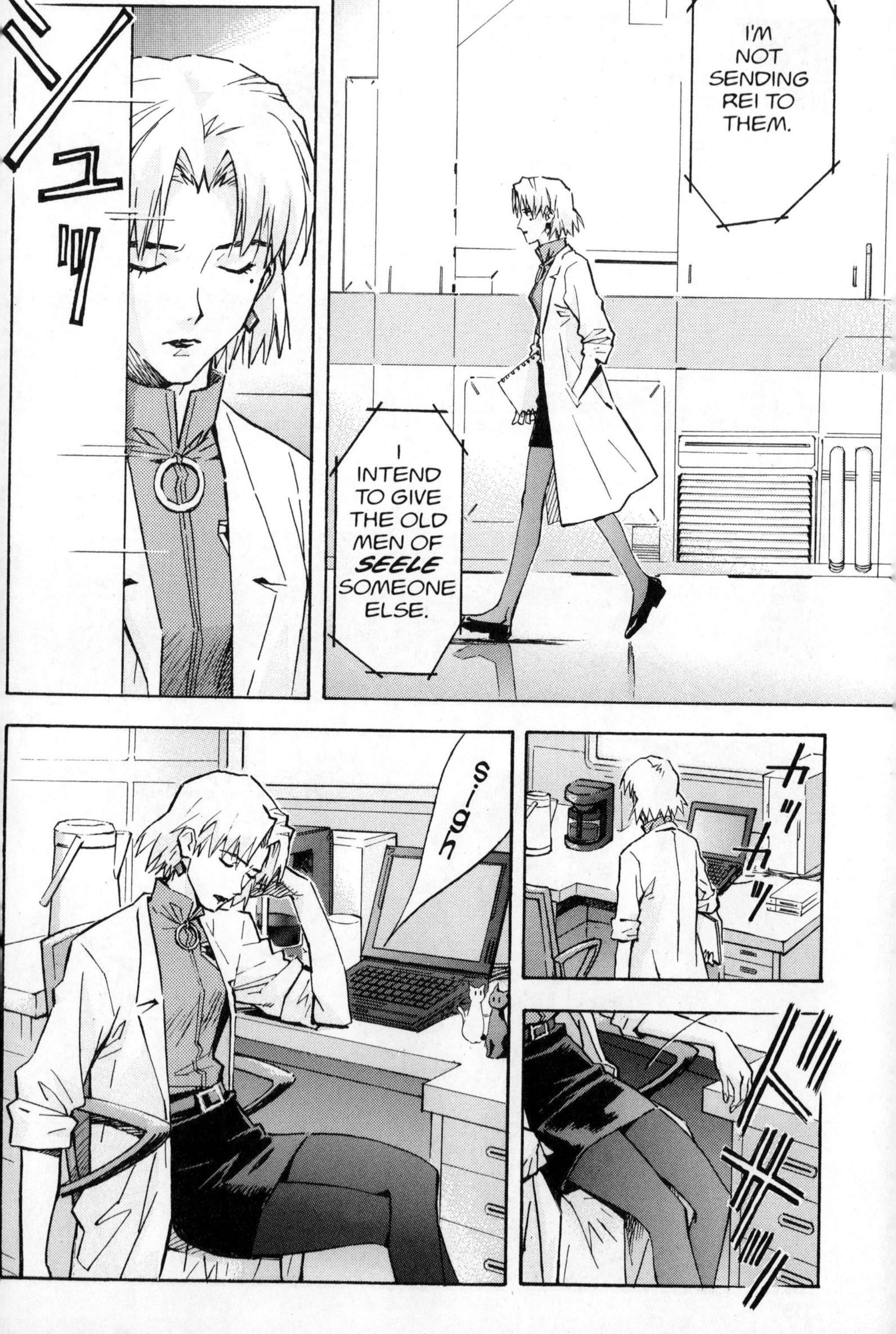
I'M NOT SENDING REI TO THEM.
I INTEND TO GIVE THE OLD MEN OF ***SEELE*** SOMEONE ELSE.
シュッ
カッカッ
sigh

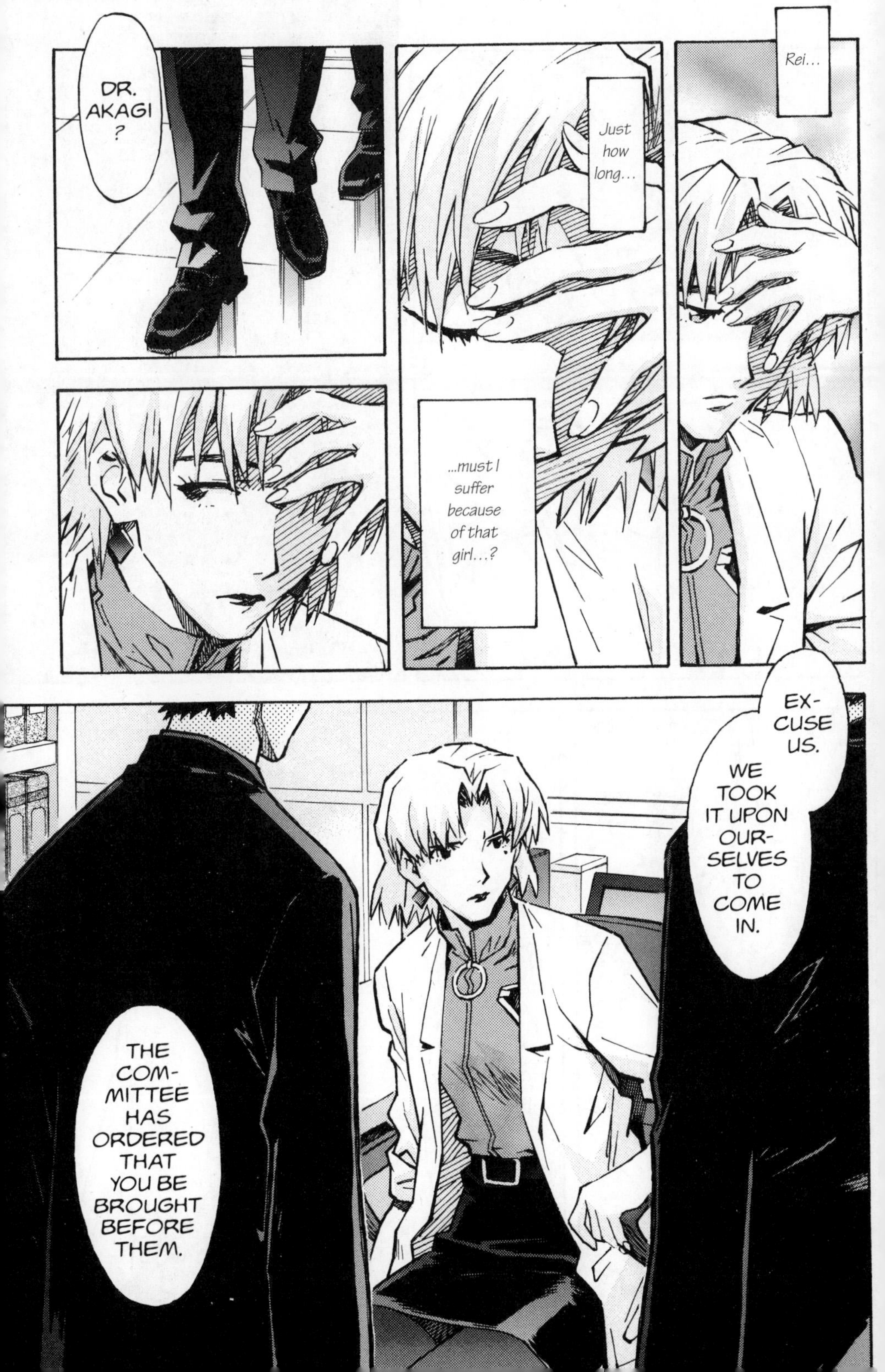
Rei…
Just how long…
...must I suffer because of that girl…?
DR. AKAGI?
EXCUSE US. WE TOOK IT UPON OURSELVES TO COME IN.
THE COMMITTEE HAS ORDERED THAT YOU BE BROUGHT BEFORE THEM.

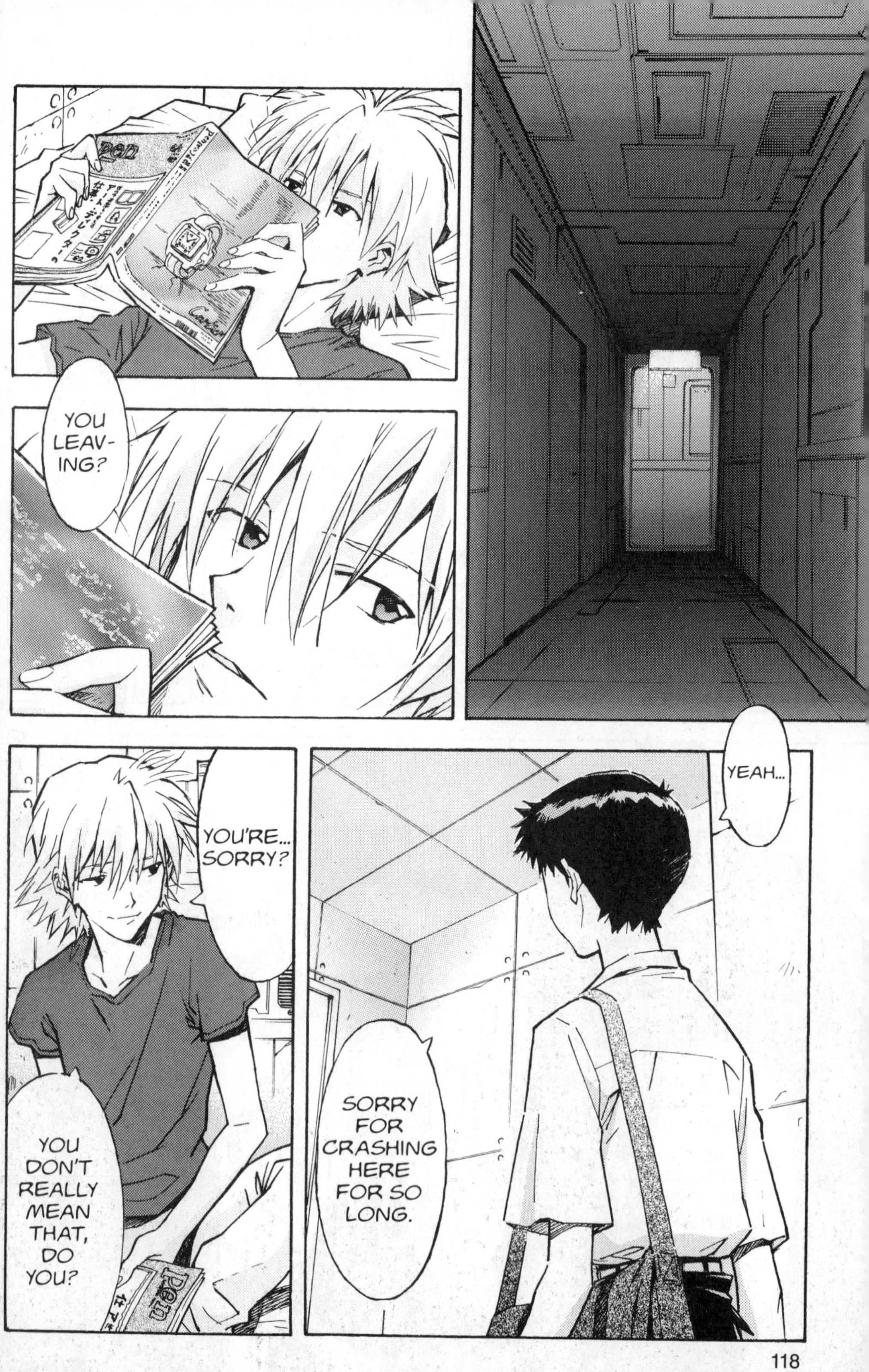
YOU LEAVING?
YEAH...
SORRY FOR CRASHING HERE FOR SO LONG.
YOU'RE... SORRY?
YOU DON'T REALLY MEAN THAT, DO YOU?

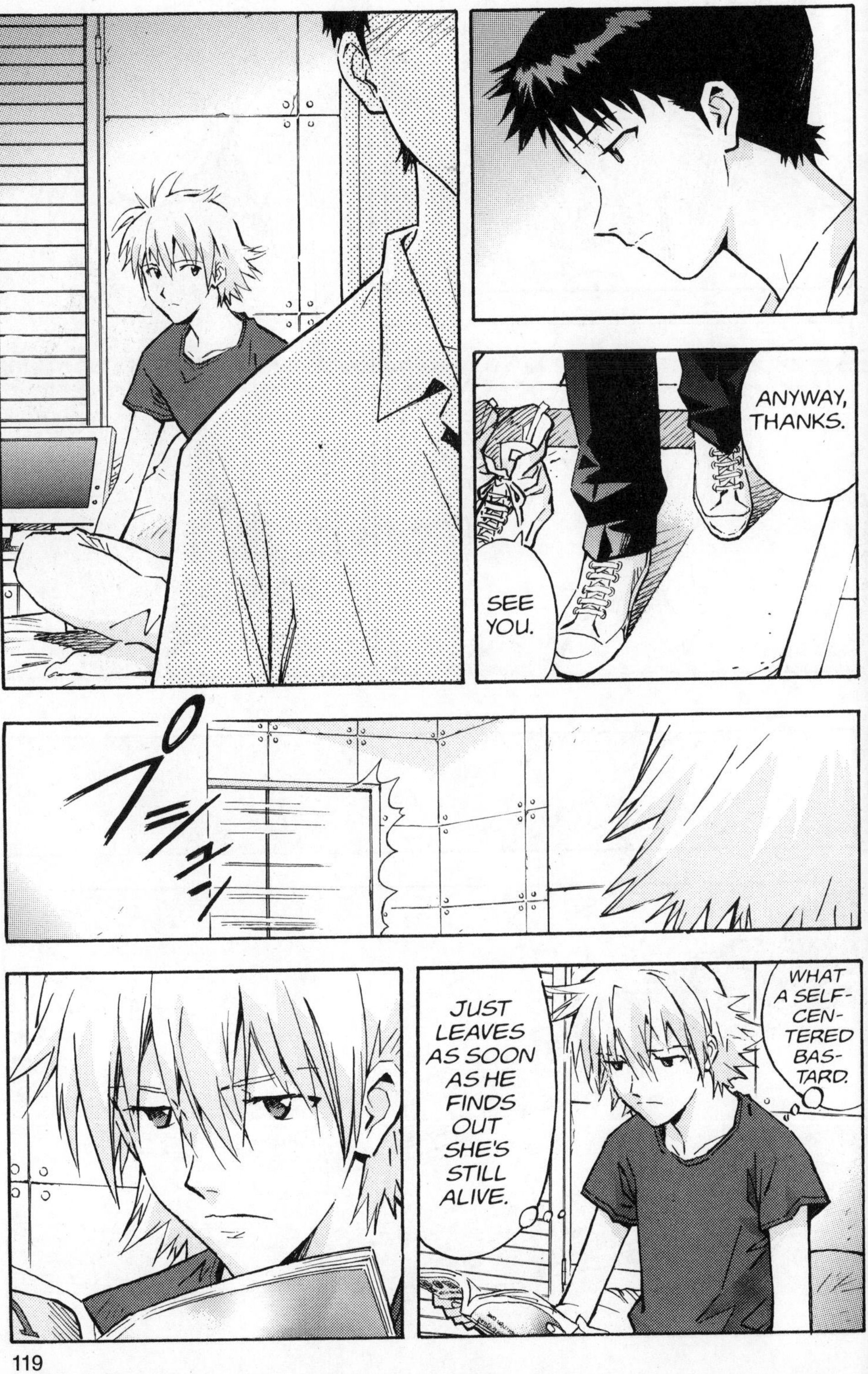
ANYWAY, THANKS.
SEE YOU.
プシュッ
WHAT A SELF-CENTERED BASTARD.
JUST LEAVES AS SOON AS HE FINDS OUT SHE'S STILL ALIVE.

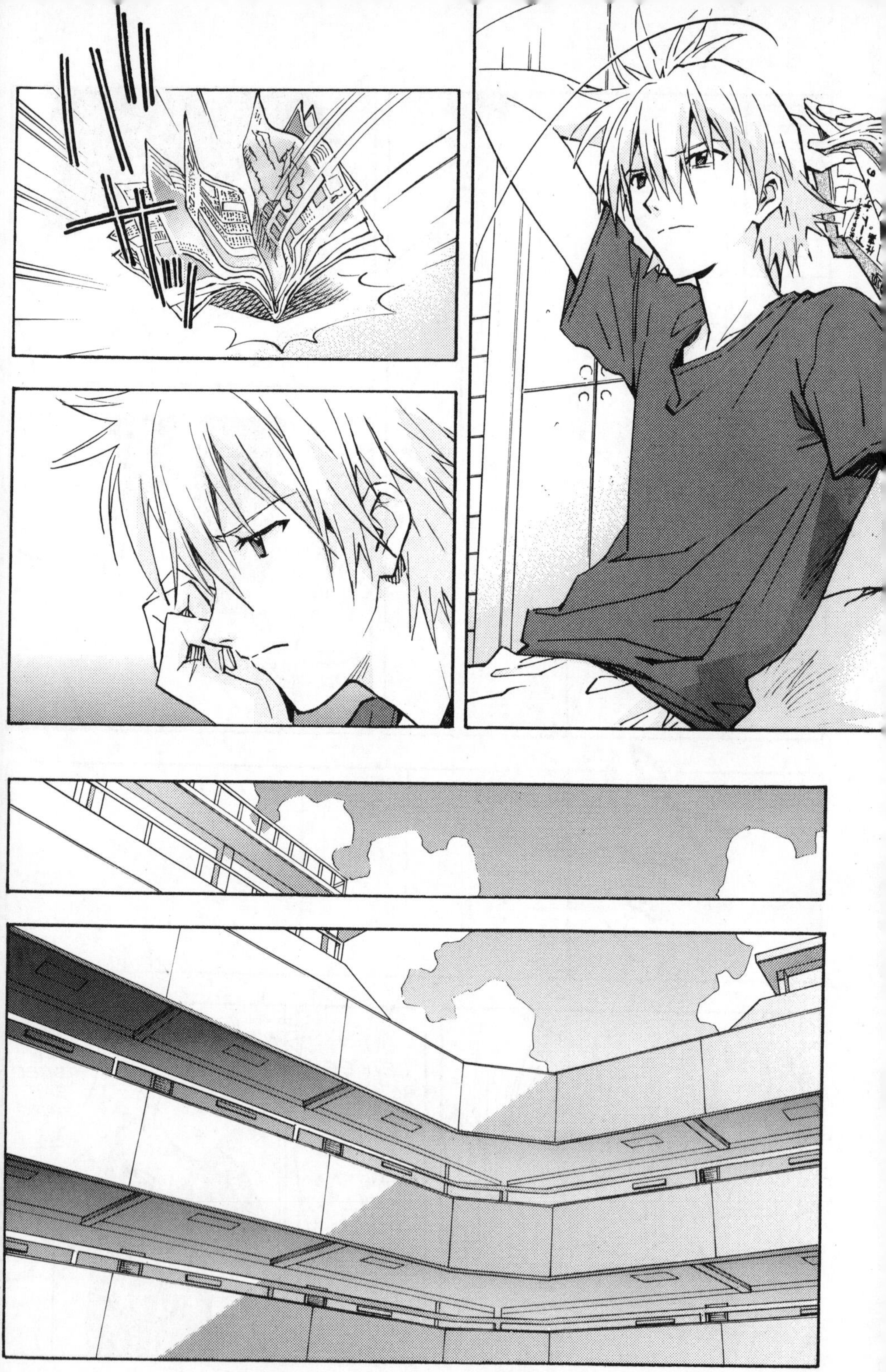

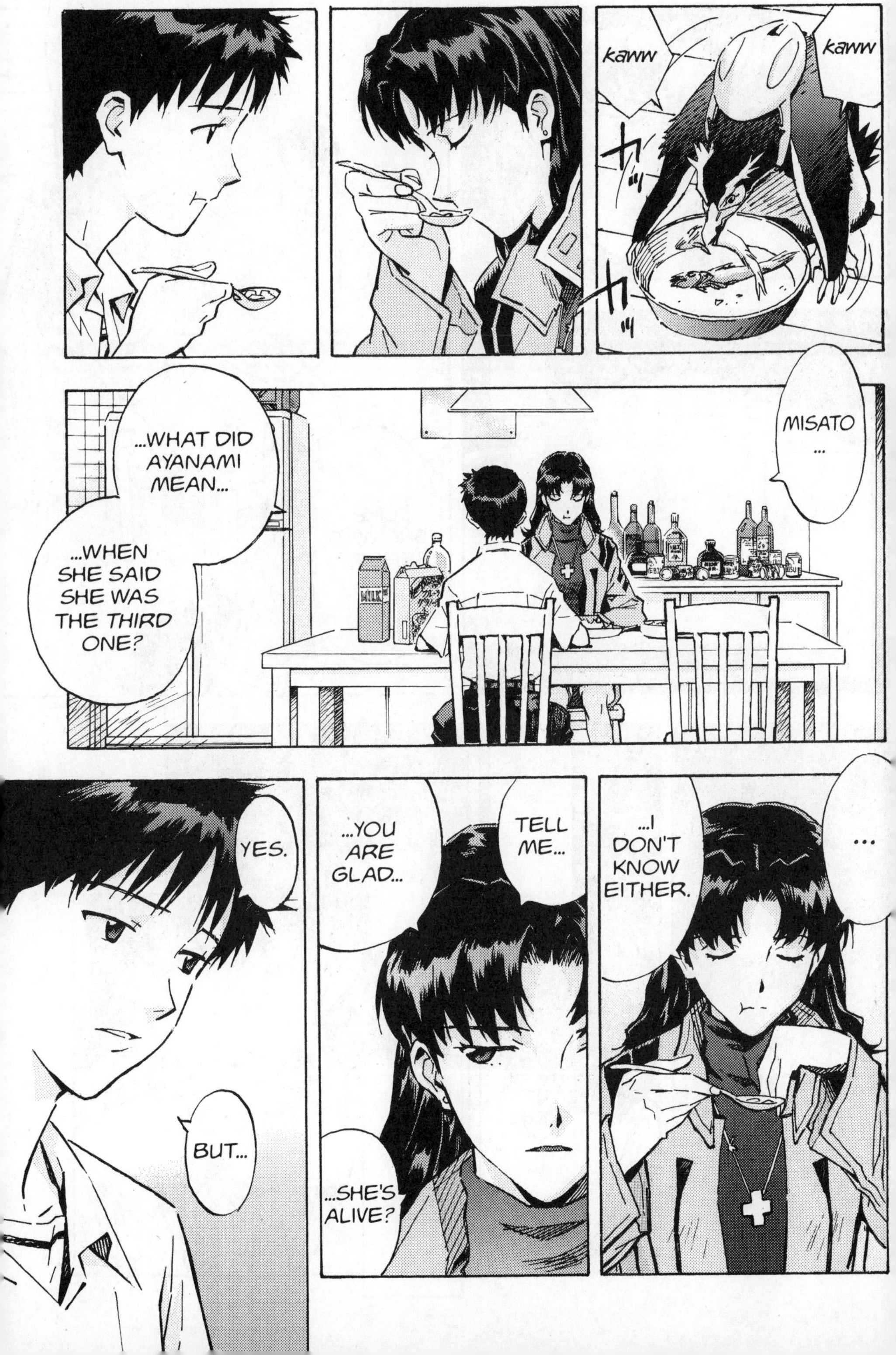
kaww
kaww
MISATO...
...WHAT DID AYANAMI MEAN...
...WHEN SHE SAID SHE WAS THE THIRD ONE?
...
...I DON'T KNOW EITHER.
TELL ME...
...YOU ARE GLAD...
...SHE'S ALIVE?
YES.
BUT...

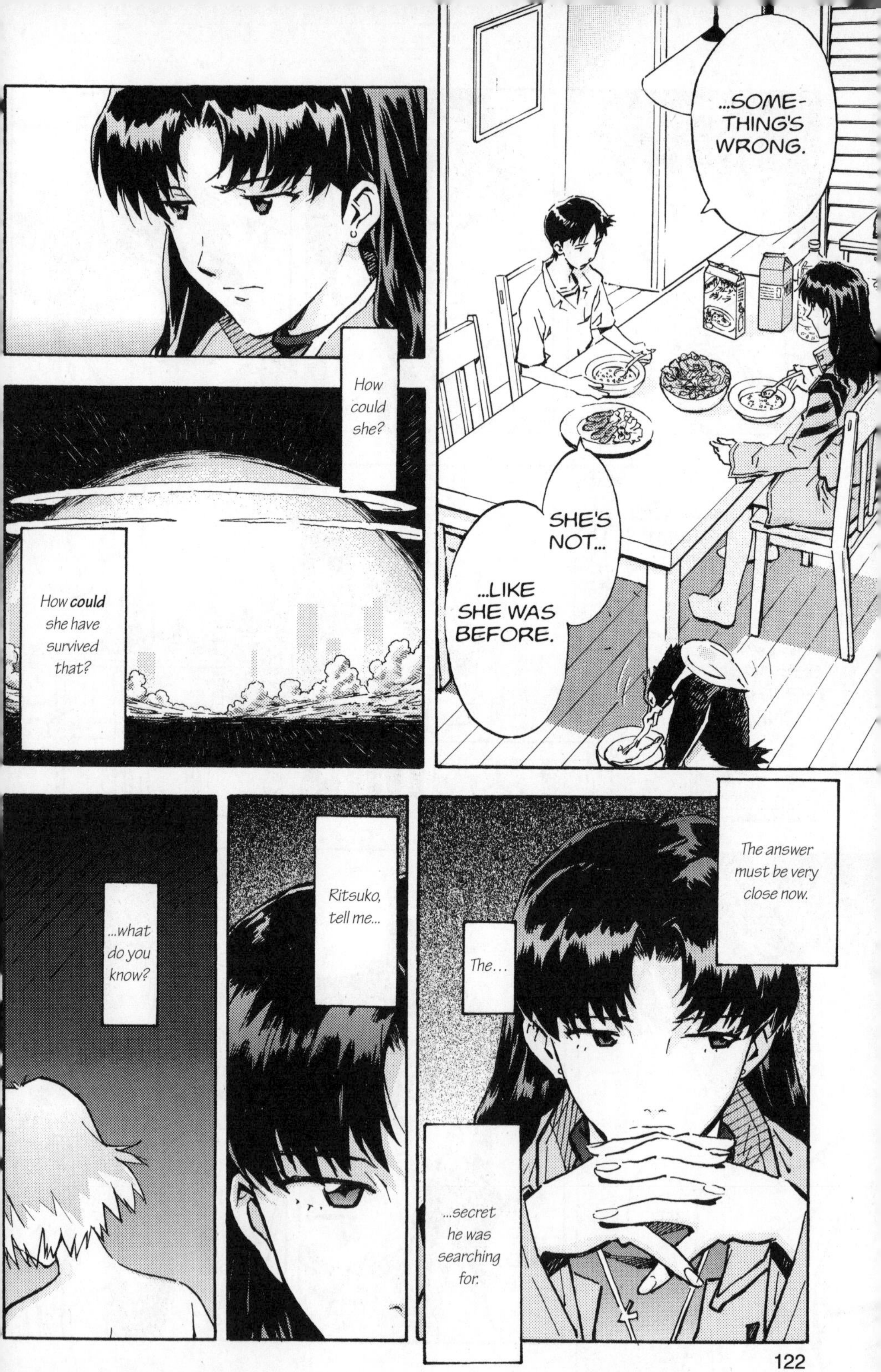

...SOME-THING'S WRONG.
SHE'S NOT...
...LIKE SHE WAS BEFORE.
How could she?
How **could** she have survived that?
The answer must be very close now.
The...
...secret he was searching for.
Ritsuko, tell me...
...what do you know?

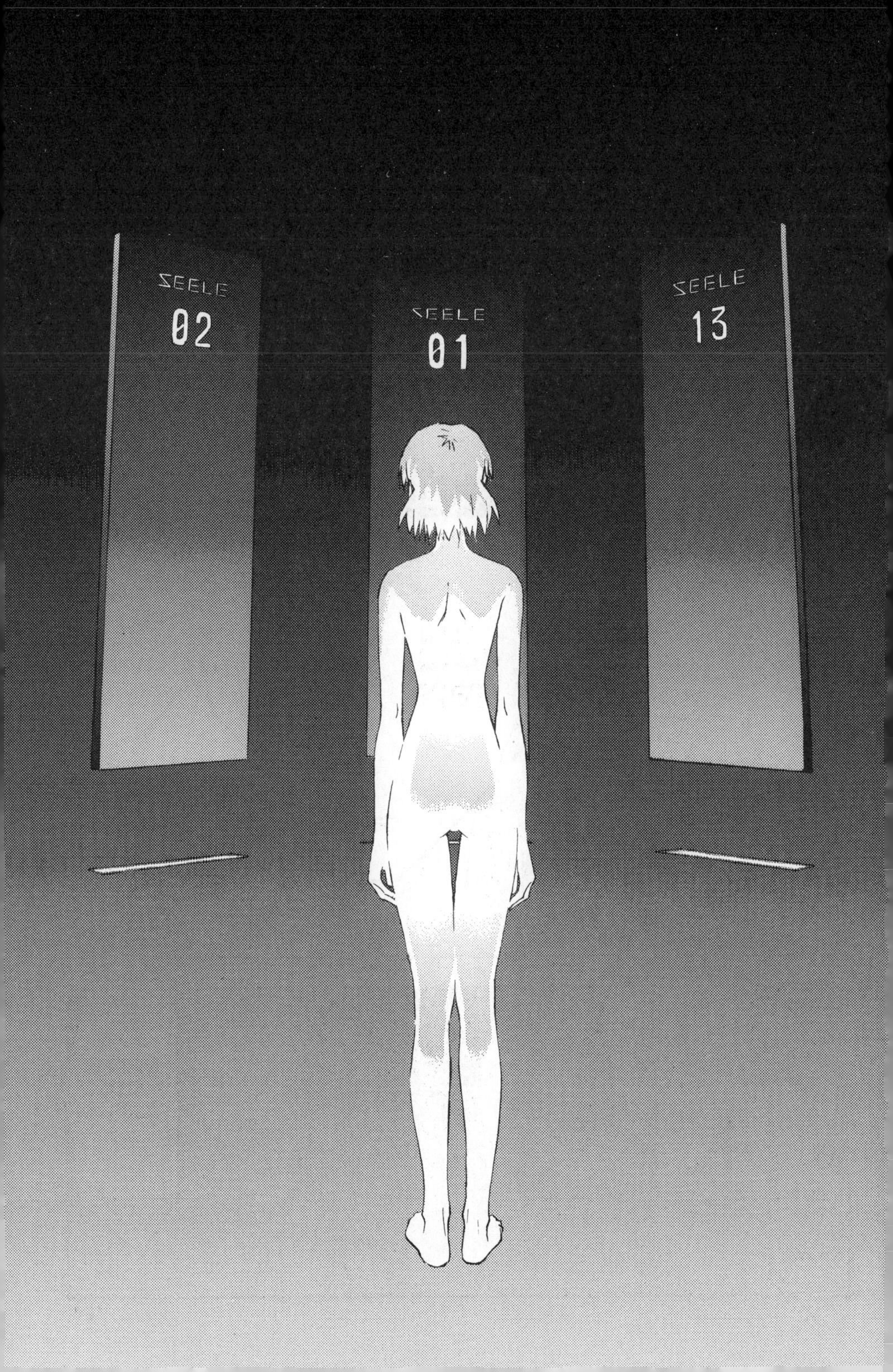
SEELE 13
SEELE 01
SEELE 02

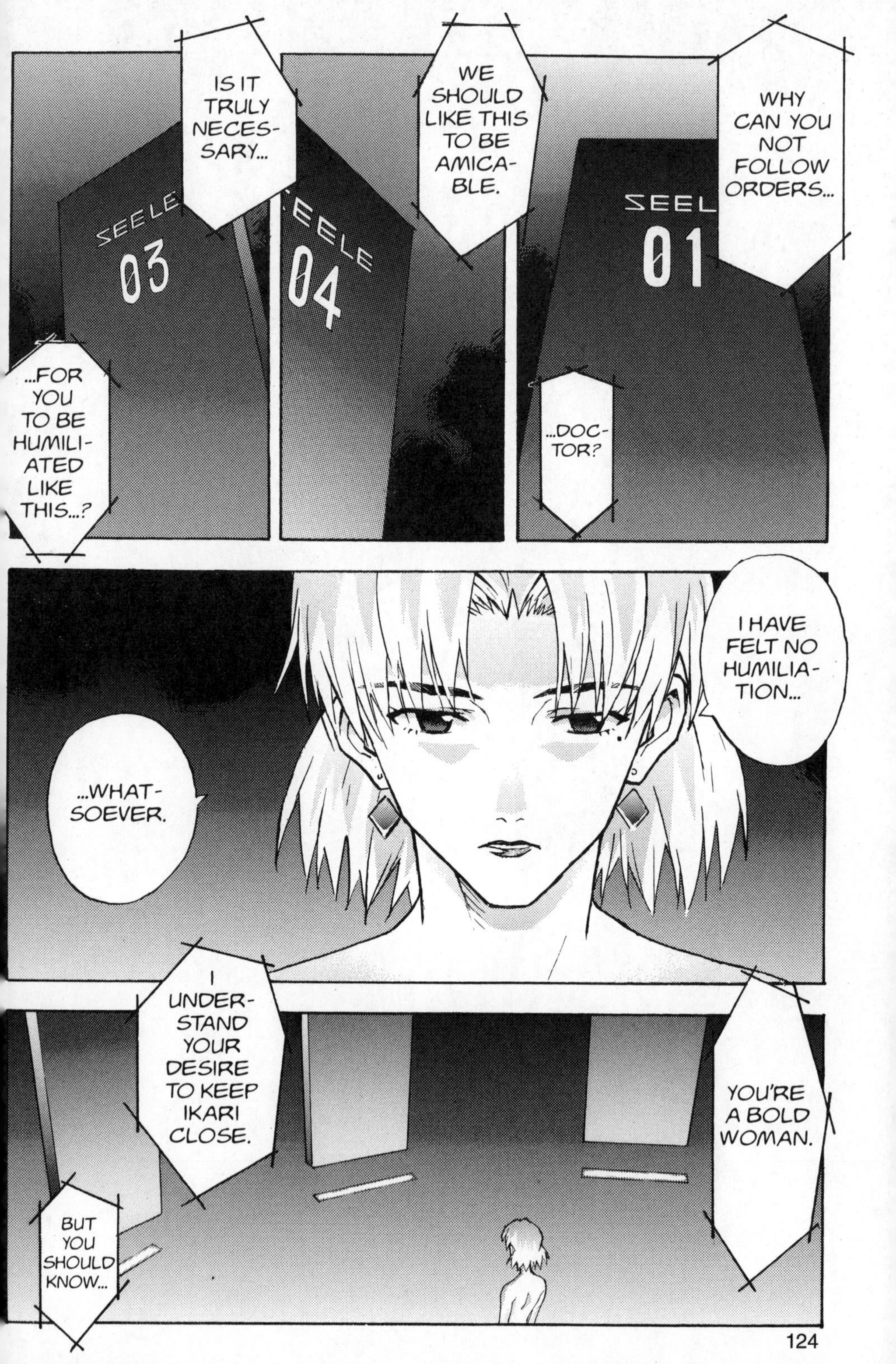
WHY CAN YOU NOT FOLLOW ORDERS...
...DOCTOR?
WE SHOULD LIKE THIS TO BE AMICA-BLE.
IS IT TRULY NECES-SARY...
...FOR YOU TO BE HUMILI-ATED LIKE THIS...?
I HAVE FELT NO HUMILIA-TION...
...WHAT-SOEVER.
YOU'RE A BOLD WOMAN.
I UNDER-STAND YOUR DESIRE TO KEEP IKARI CLOSE.
BUT YOU SHOULD KNOW...

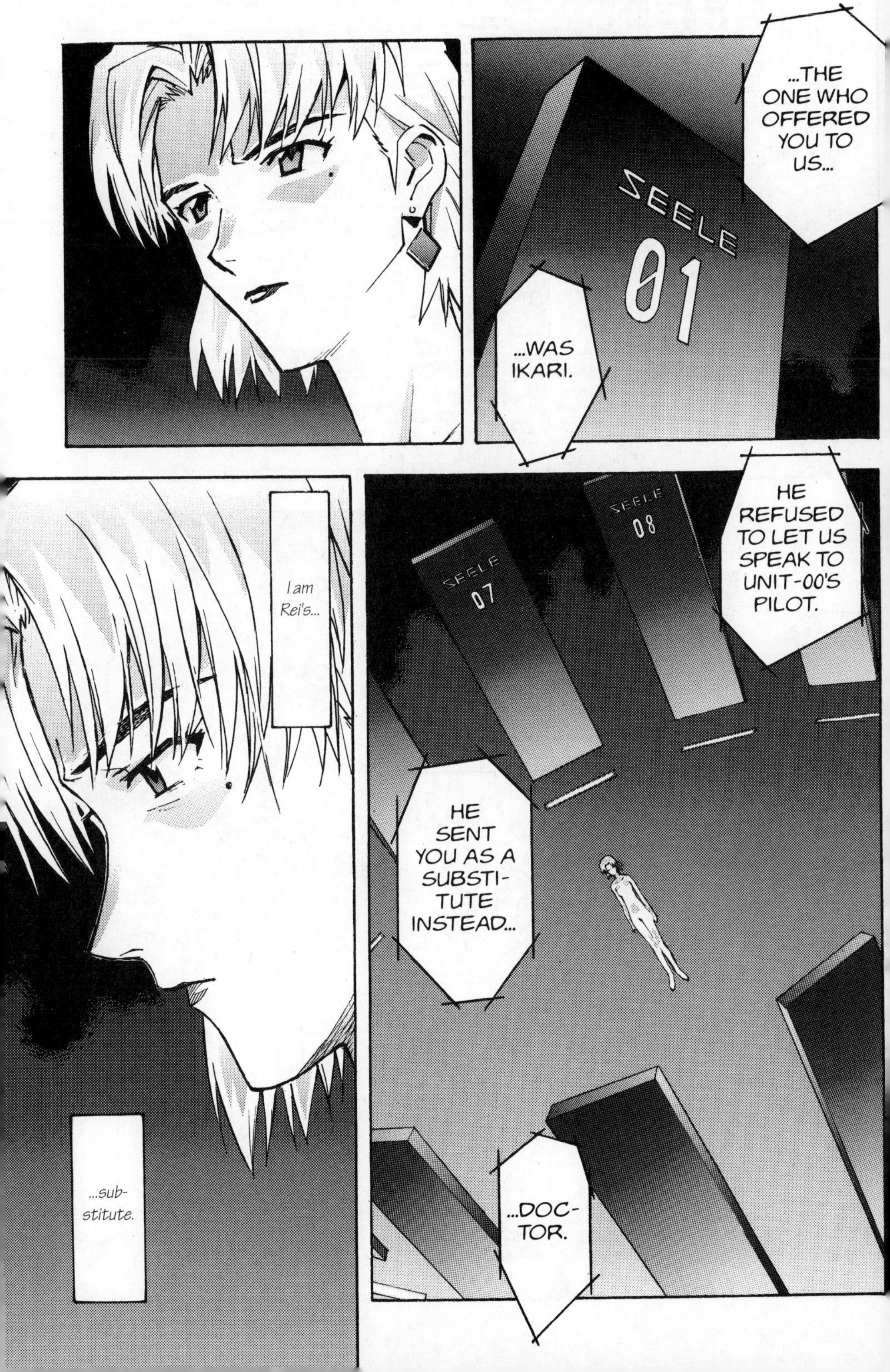

...THE ONE WHO OFFERED YOU TO US...
SEELE 01
...WAS IKARI.
HE REFUSED TO LET US SPEAK TO UNIT-00'S PILOT.
SEELE 08
SEELE 07
HE SENT YOU AS A SUBSTI- TUTE INSTEAD...
...DOC- TOR.
I am Rei's...
...sub- stitute.

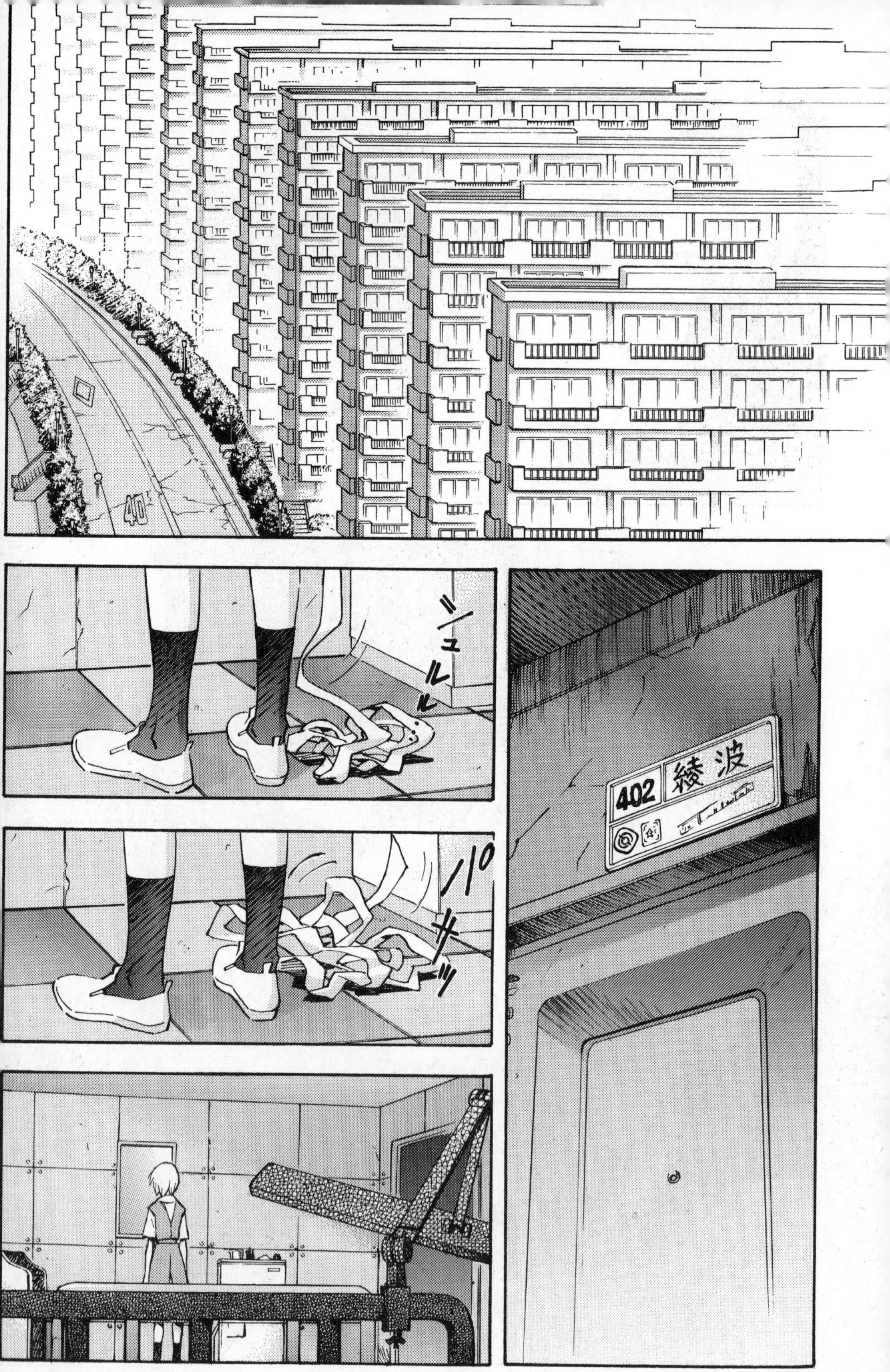
40
402 綾波
シュルル
パサッ

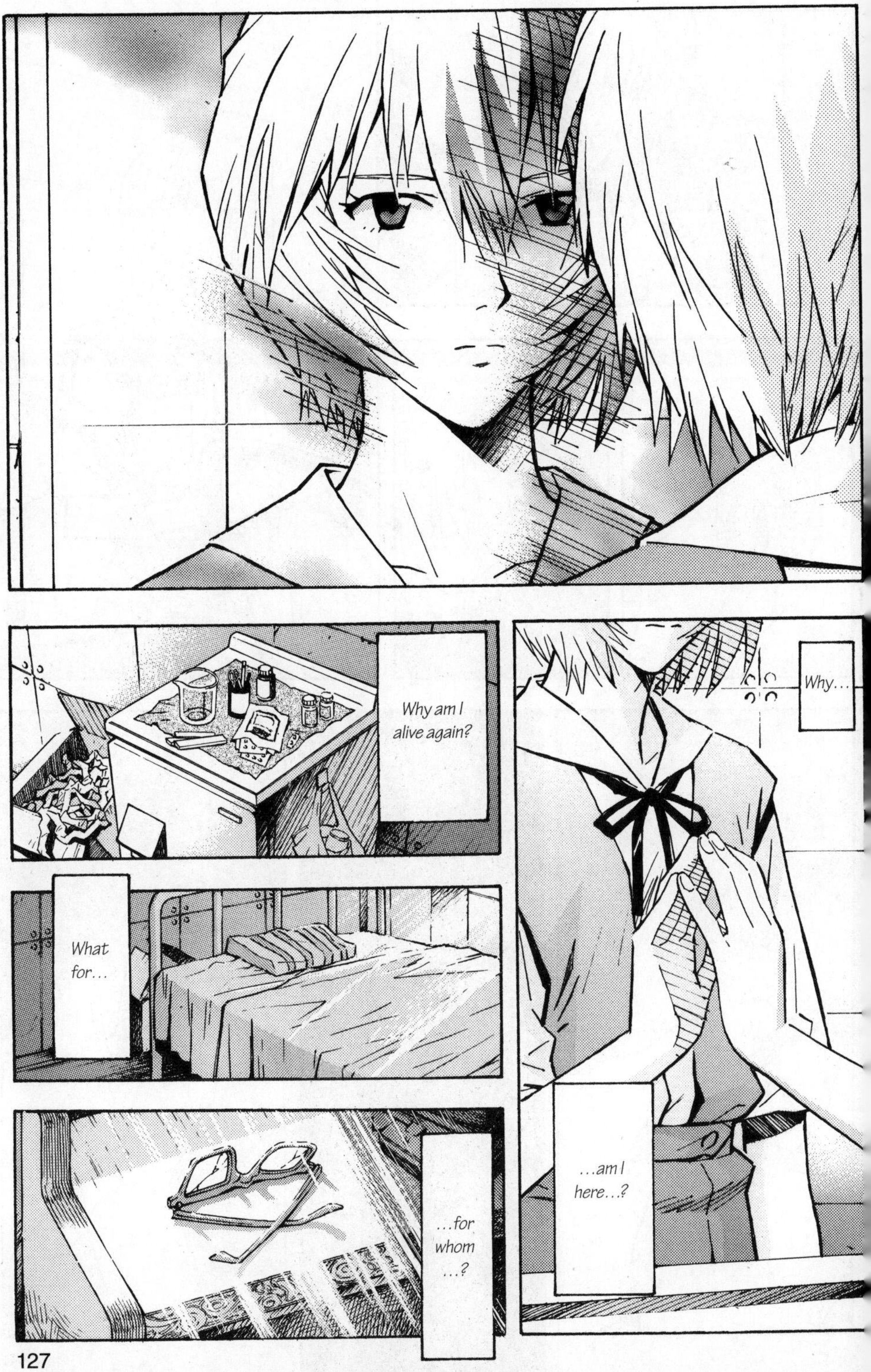
Why…
…am I here…?
Why am I alive again?
What for…
…for whom …?

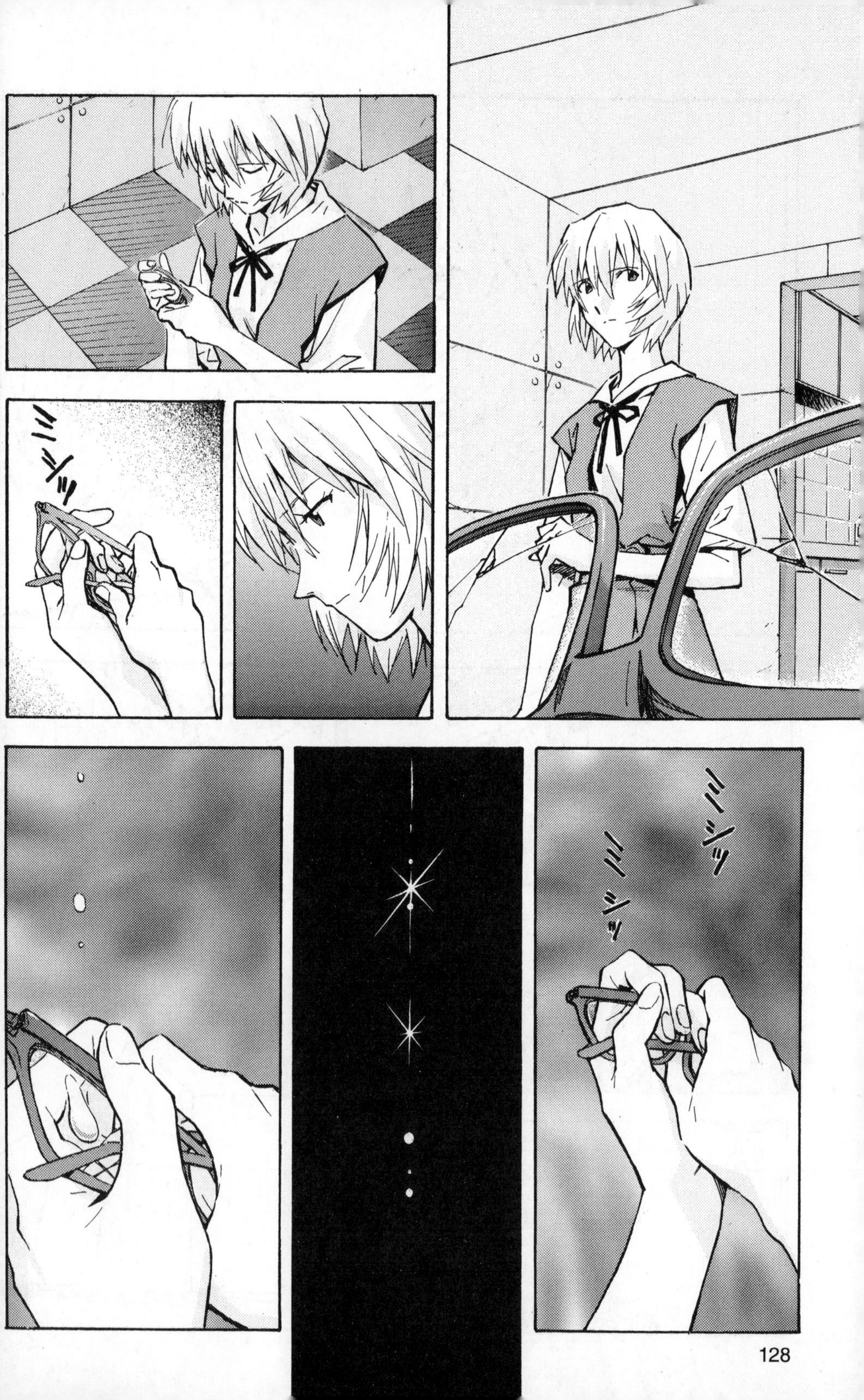
ミシッ
ミシッ
ミシッ

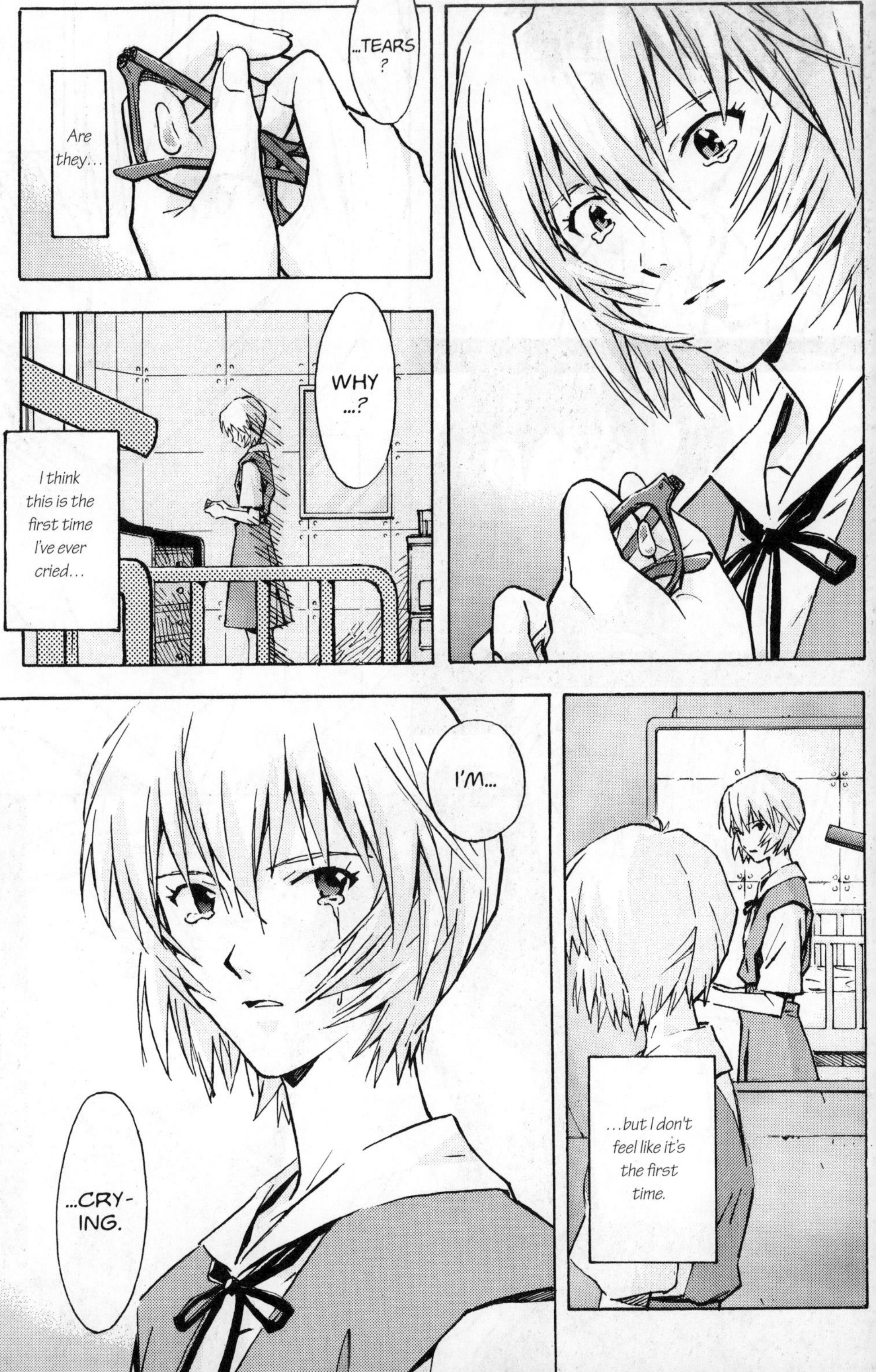
Are they…
…TEARS?
WHY…?
I think this is the first time I've ever cried…
I'M…
…CRY-ING.
…but I don't feel like it's the first time.

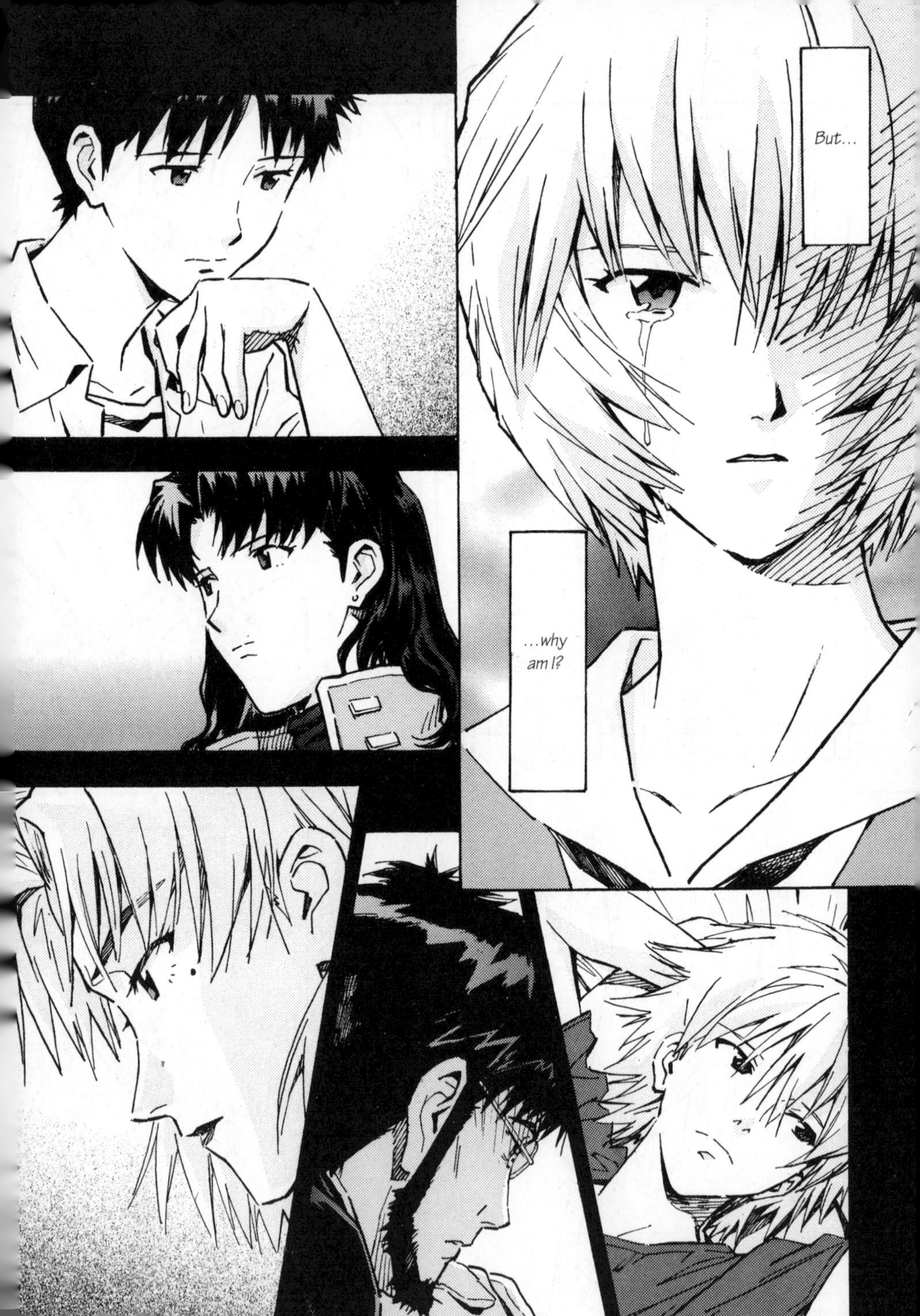
But...
...why am I?

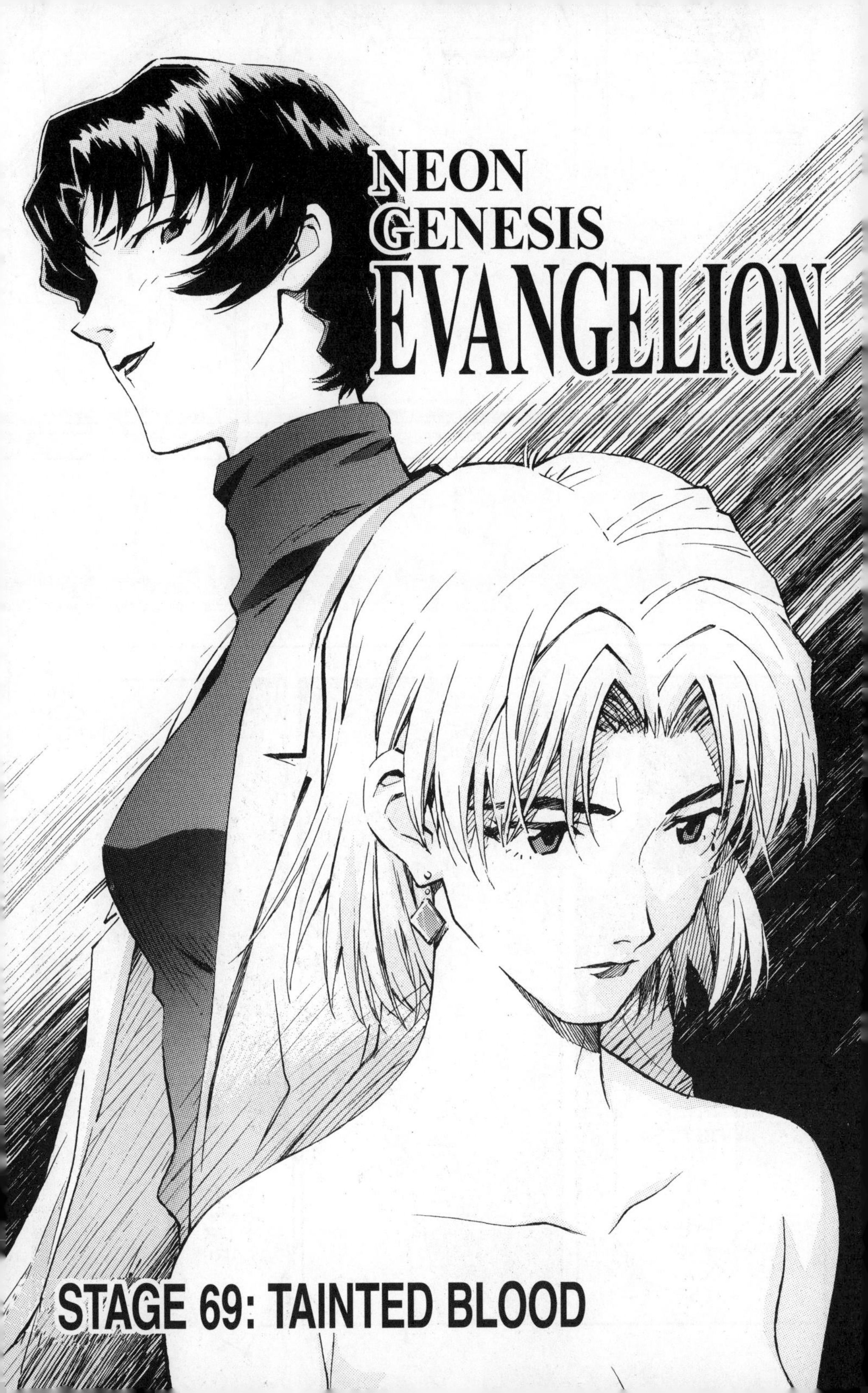
NEON GENESIS EVANGELION
STAGE 69: TAINTED BLOOD

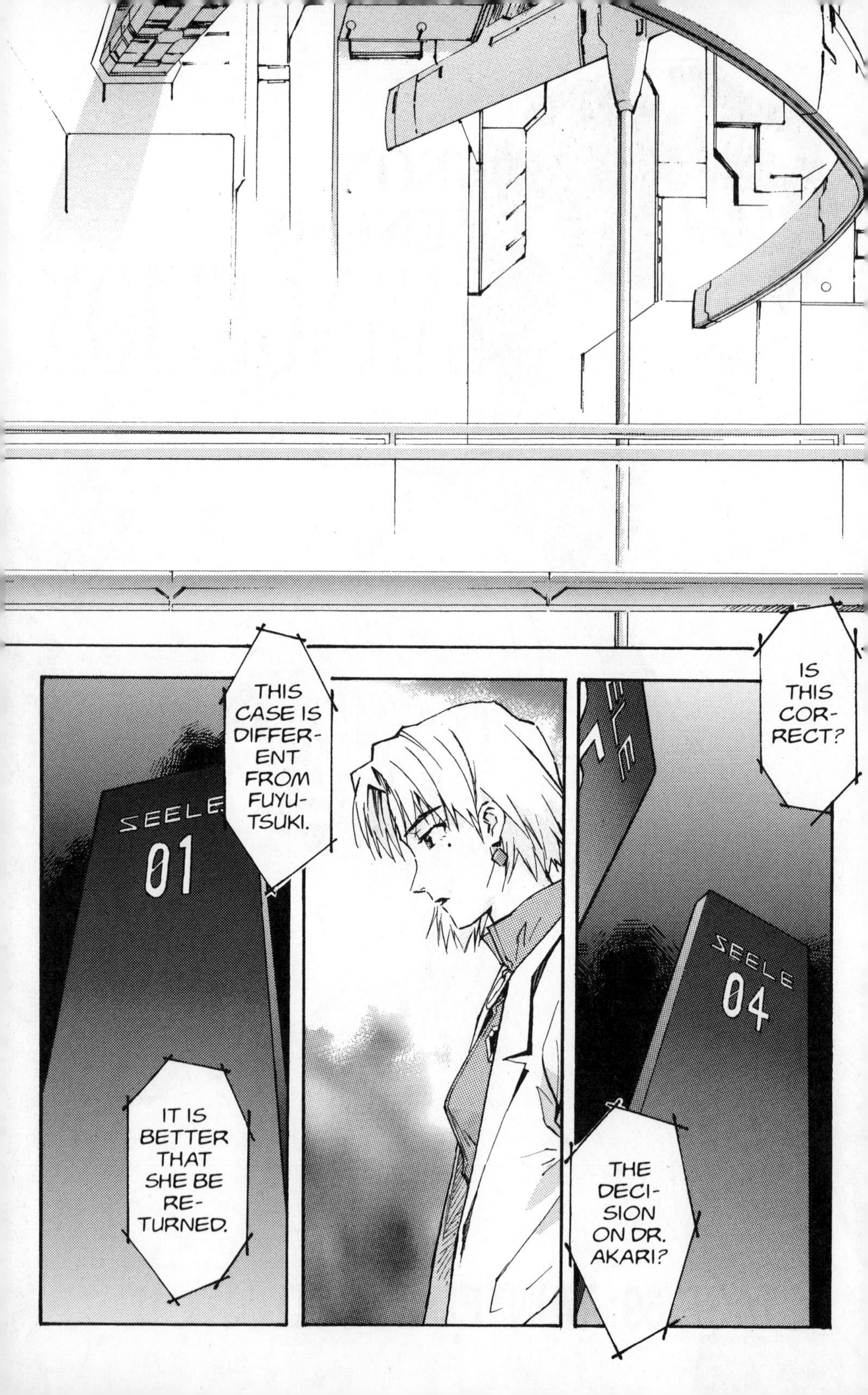

IS THIS CORRECT?
SEELE 04
THE DECISION ON DR. AKARI?
THIS CASE IS DIFFERENT FROM FUYUTSUKI.
SEELE 01
IT IS BETTER THAT SHE BE RETURNED.

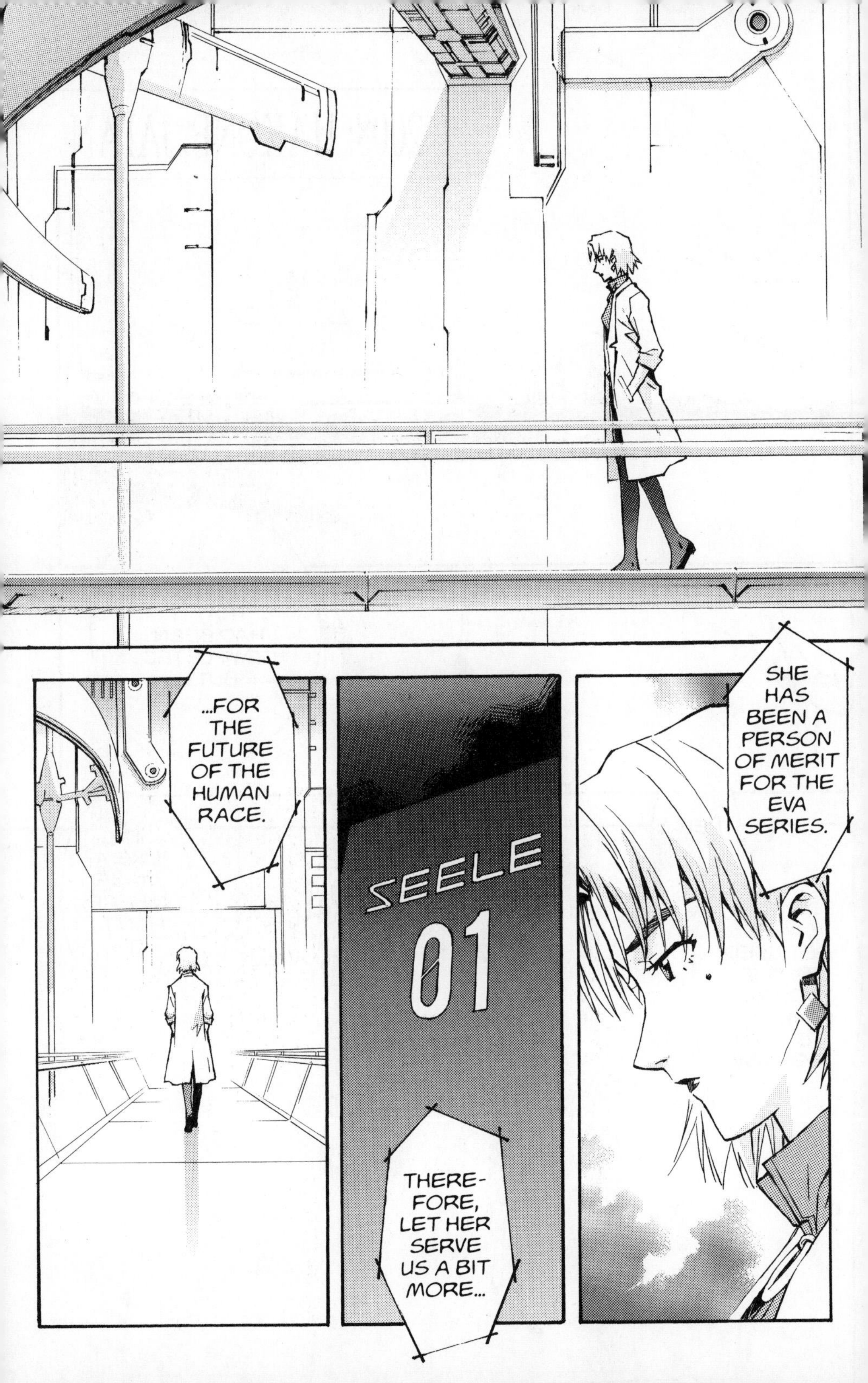
SHE HAS BEEN A PERSON OF MERIT FOR THE EVA SERIES.
SEELE 01
THERE-FORE, LET HER SERVE US A BIT MORE...
...FOR THE FUTURE OF THE HUMAN RACE.

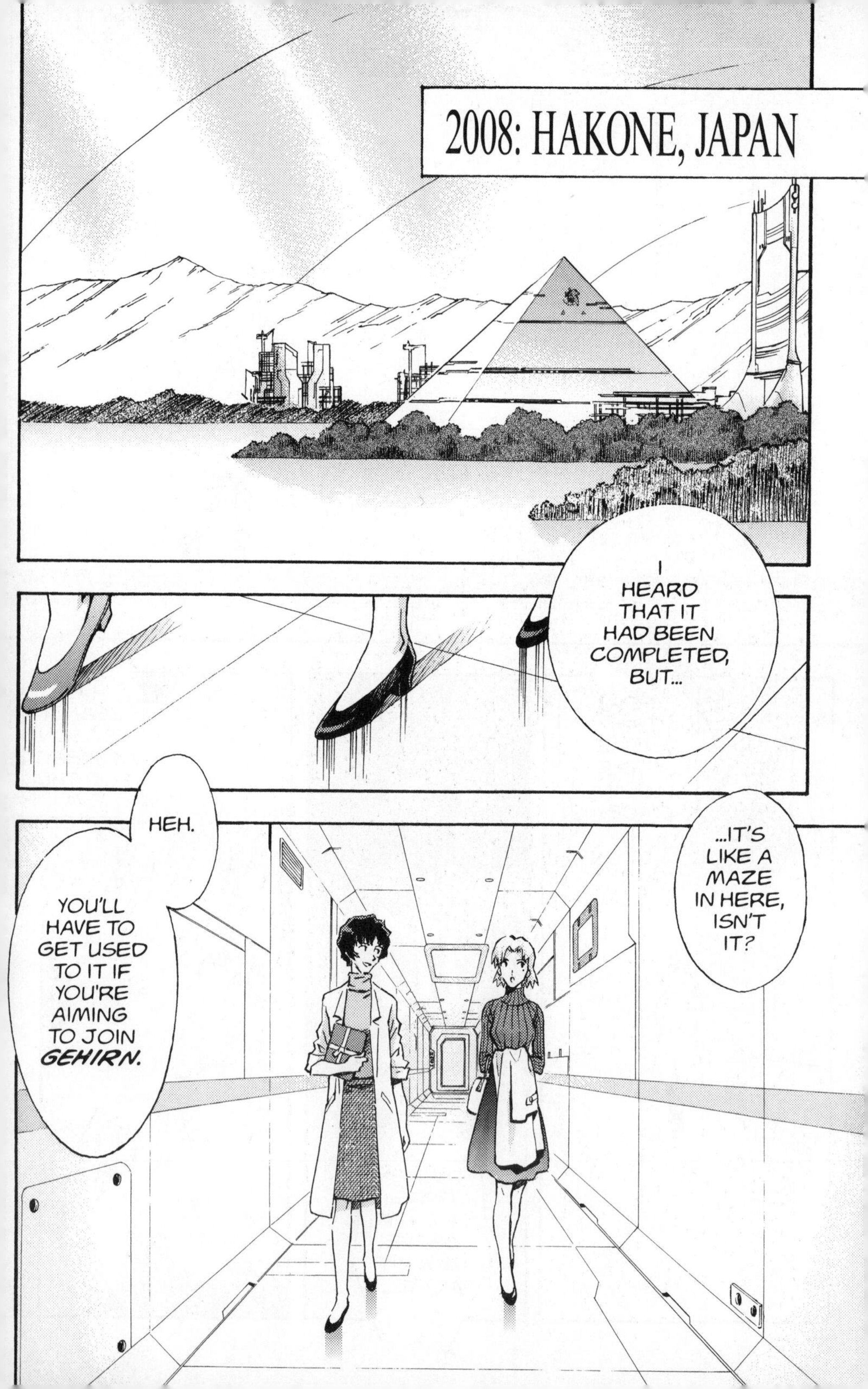
2008: HAKONE, JAPAN
I HEARD THAT IT HAD BEEN COMPLETED, BUT...
...IT'S LIKE A MAZE IN HERE, ISN'T IT?
HEH.
YOU'LL HAVE TO GET USED TO IT IF YOU'RE AIMING TO JOIN GEHIRN.

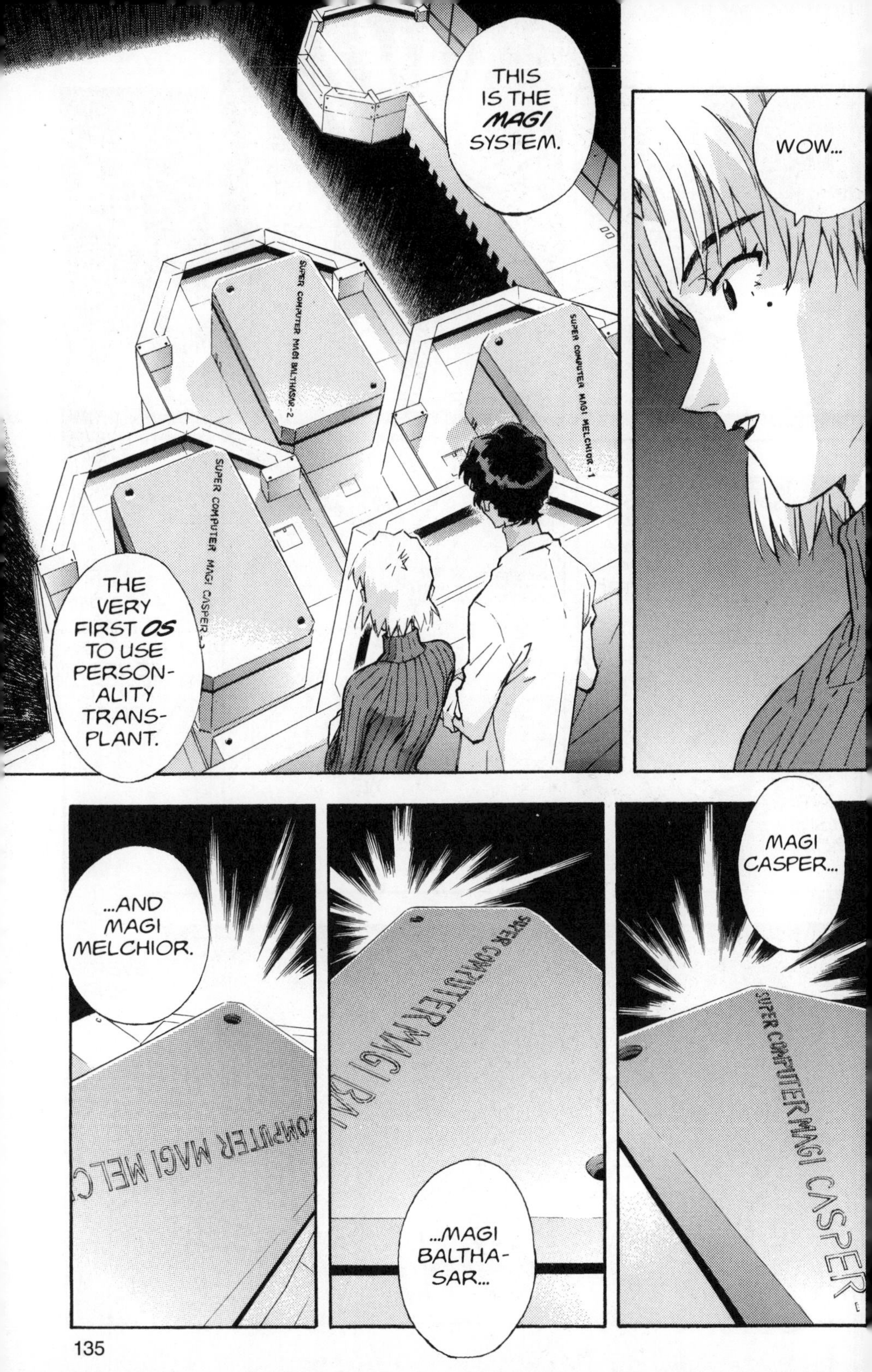
WOW...
THIS IS THE MAGI SYSTEM.
SUPER COMPUTER MAGI MELCHIOR-1
SUPER COMPUTER MAGI BALTHASAR-2
THE VERY FIRST OS TO USE PERSONALITY TRANSPLANT.
MAGI CASPER...
SUPER COMPUTER MAGI CASPER
...MAGI BALTHASAR...
...AND MAGI MELCHIOR.

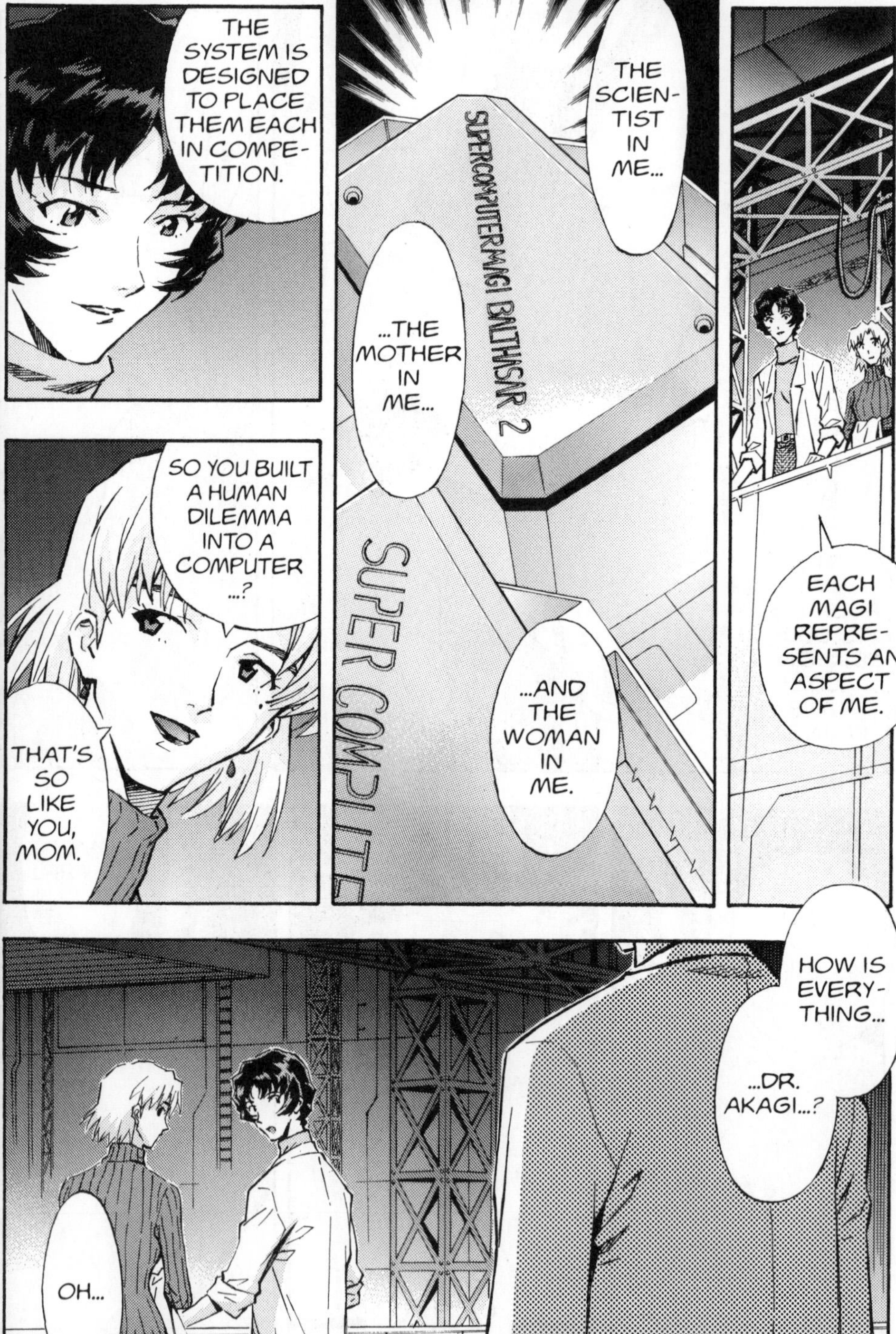
EACH MAGI REPRESENTS AN ASPECT OF ME.
THE SCIENTIST IN ME...
SUPERCOMPUTER MAGI BALTHASAR 2
...THE MOTHER IN ME...
...AND THE WOMAN IN ME.
THE SYSTEM IS DESIGNED TO PLACE THEM EACH IN COMPETITION.
SO YOU BUILT A HUMAN DILEMMA INTO A COMPUTER ...?
THAT'S SO LIKE YOU, MOM.
HOW IS EVERYTHING...
...DR. AKAGI...?
OH...

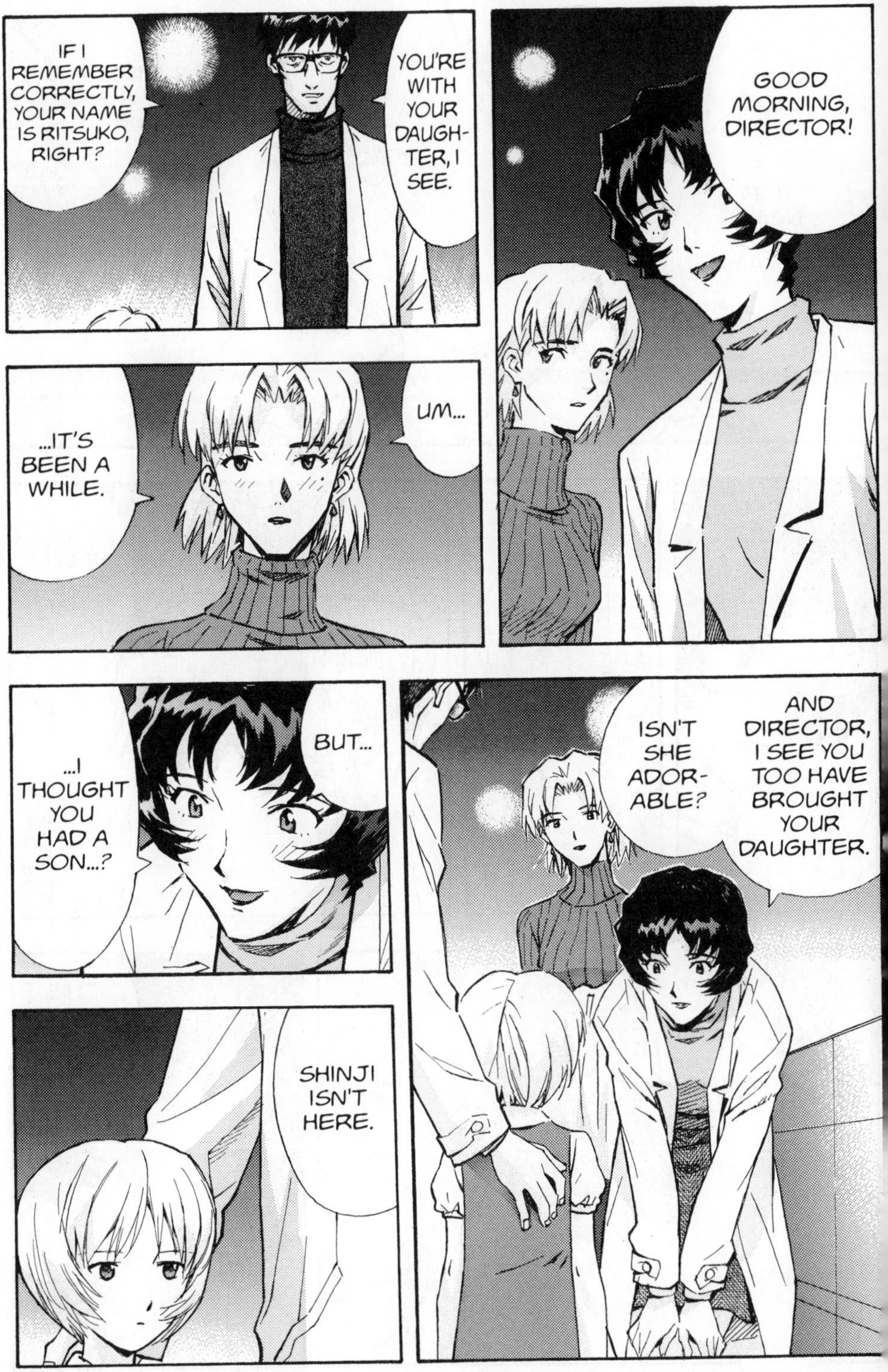
GOOD MORNING, DIRECTOR!
YOU'RE WITH YOUR DAUGHTER, I SEE.
IF I REMEMBER CORRECTLY, YOUR NAME IS RITSUKO, RIGHT?
UM...
...IT'S BEEN A WHILE.
AND DIRECTOR, I SEE YOU TOO HAVE BROUGHT YOUR DAUGHTER.
ISN'T SHE ADORABLE?
BUT...
...I THOUGHT YOU HAD A SON...?
SHINJI ISN'T HERE.

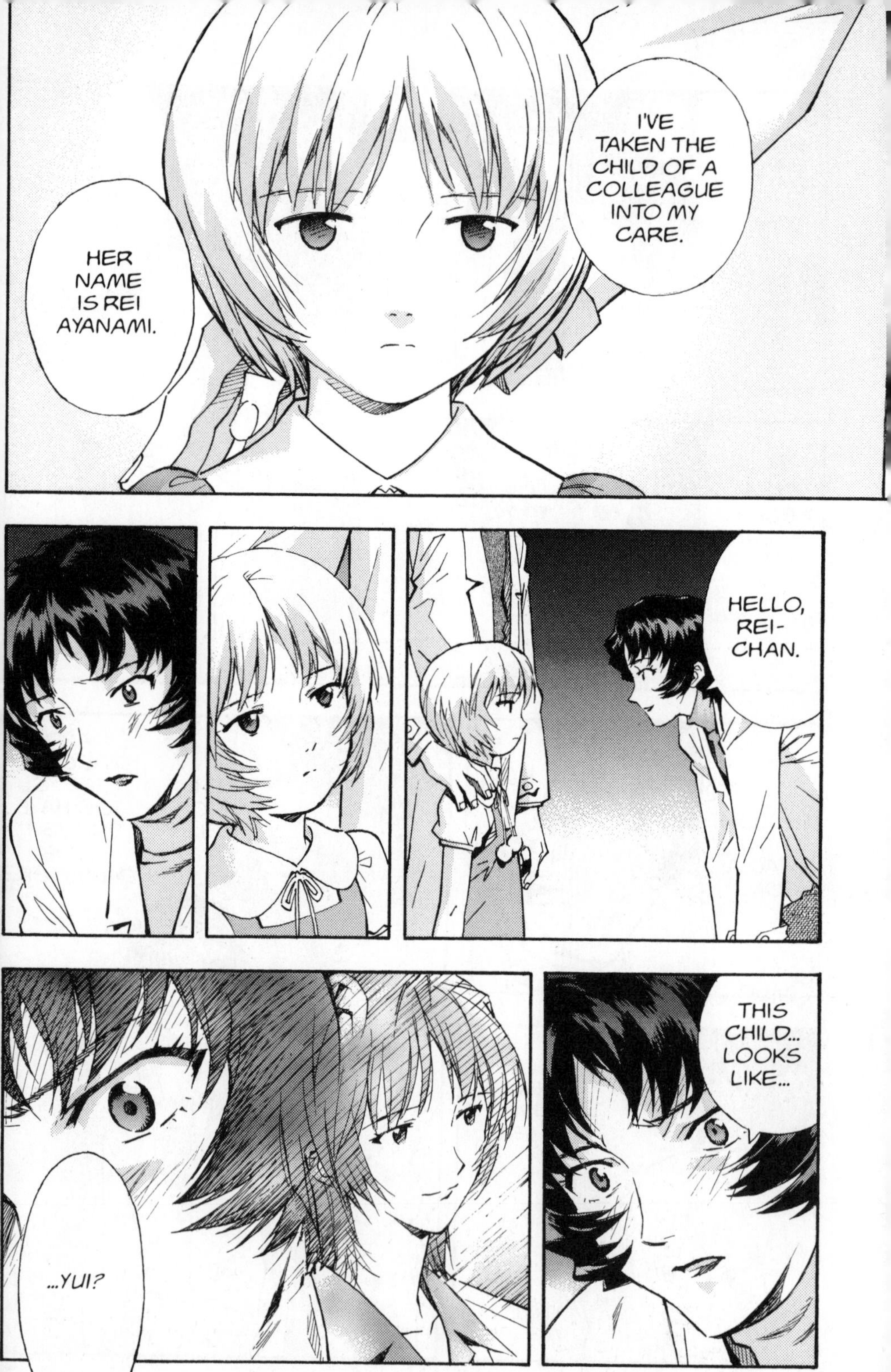
I'VE TAKEN THE CHILD OF A COLLEAGUE INTO MY CARE.
HER NAME IS REI AYANAMI.
HELLO, REI-CHAN.
THIS CHILD... LOOKS LIKE...
...YUI?

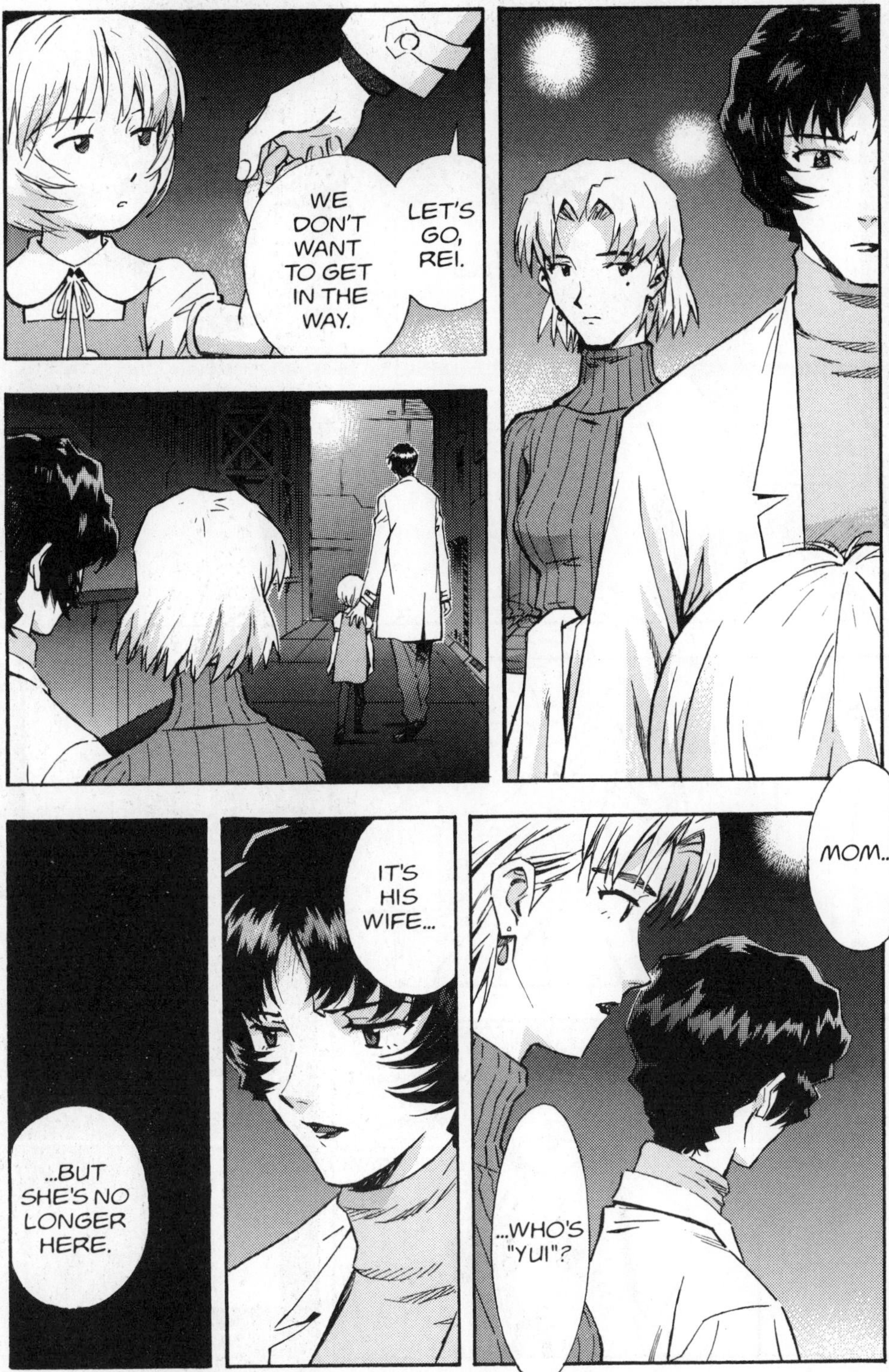
LET'S GO, REI.
WE DON'T WANT TO GET IN THE WAY.
MOM...
...WHO'S "YUI"?
IT'S HIS WIFE...
...BUT SHE'S NO LONGER HERE.

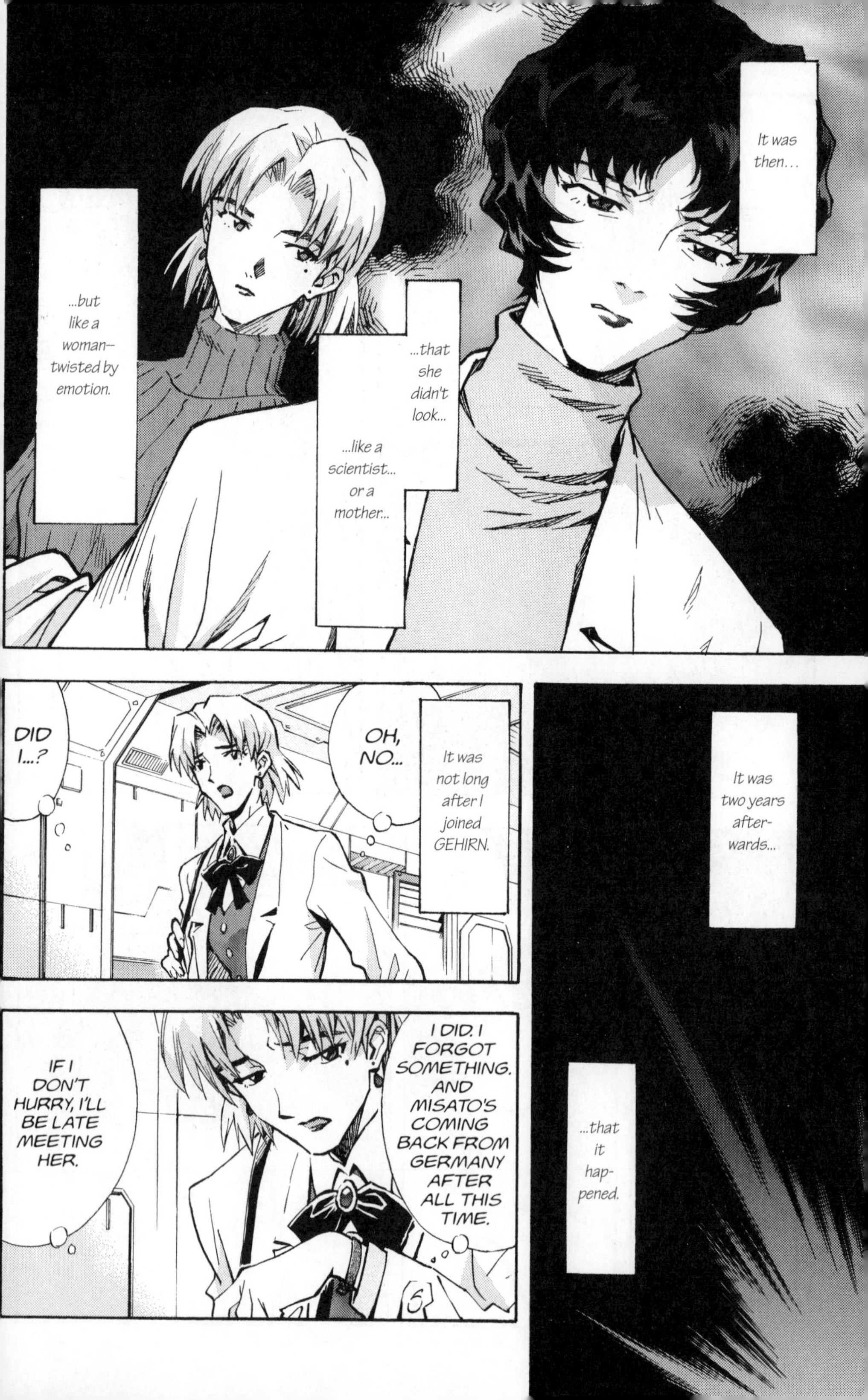
It was then...
...that she didn't look...
...like a scientist... or a mother...
...but like a woman— twisted by emotion.
It was two years afterwards...
...that it happened.
It was not long after I joined GEHIRN.
OH, NO...
DID I...?
I DID. I FORGOT SOMETHING. AND MISATO'S COMING BACK FROM GERMANY AFTER ALL THIS TIME.
IF I DON'T HURRY, I'LL BE LATE MEETING HER.

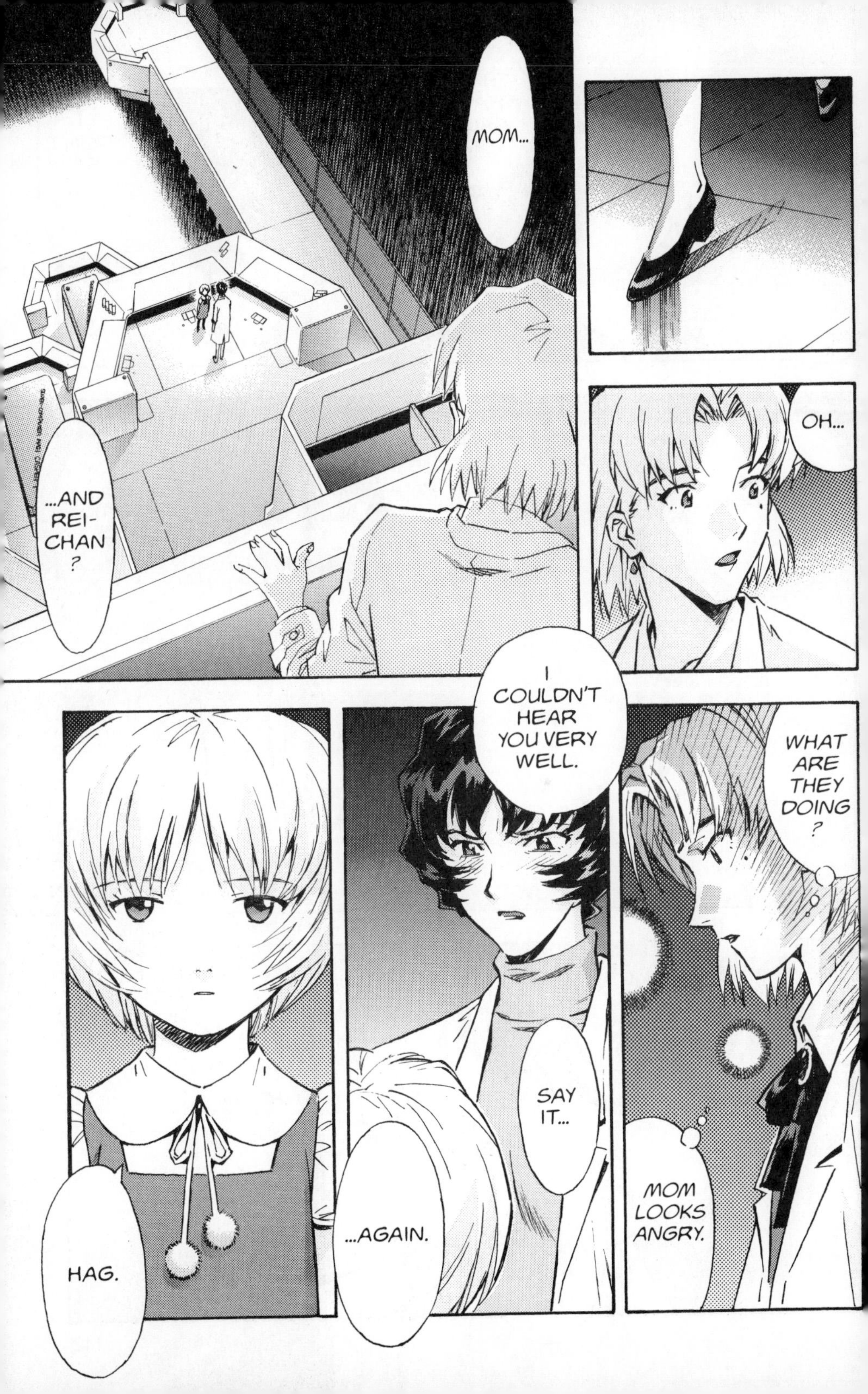
MOM...
...AND REI-CHAN?
OH...
WHAT ARE THEY DOING?
MOM LOOKS ANGRY.
I COULDN'T HEAR YOU VERY WELL.
SAY IT...
...AGAIN.
HAG.

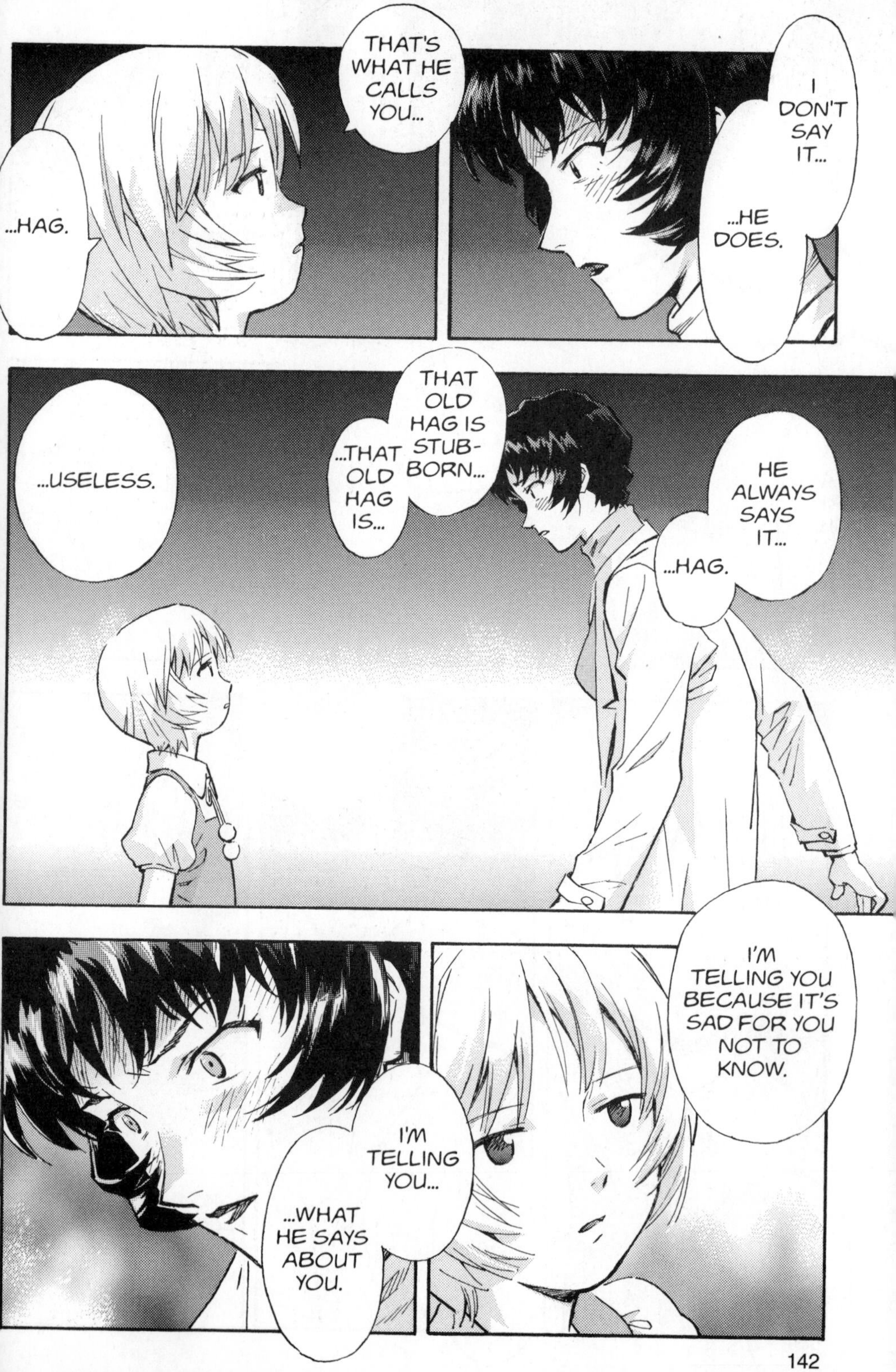
I DON'T SAY IT...
...HE DOES.
THAT'S WHAT HE CALLS YOU...
...HAG.
HE ALWAYS SAYS IT...
...HAG.
THAT OLD HAG IS STUBBORN...
...THAT OLD HAG IS...
...USELESS.
I'M TELLING YOU BECAUSE IT'S SAD FOR YOU NOT TO KNOW.
I'M TELLING YOU...
...WHAT HE SAYS ABOUT YOU.

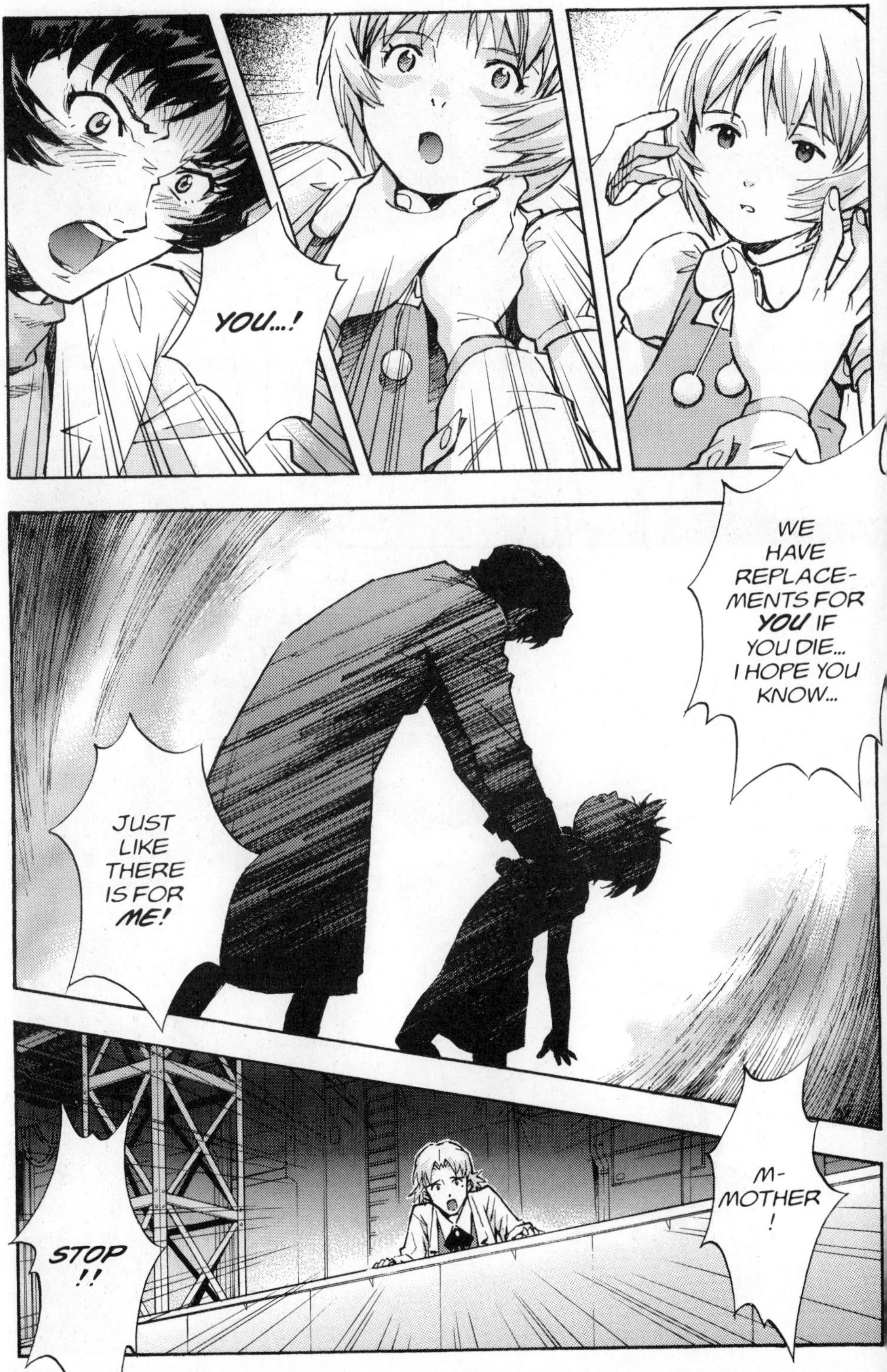
YOU...!
WE HAVE REPLACEMENTS FOR YOU IF YOU DIE... I HOPE YOU KNOW...
JUST LIKE THERE IS FOR ME!
M-MOTHER!
STOP!!

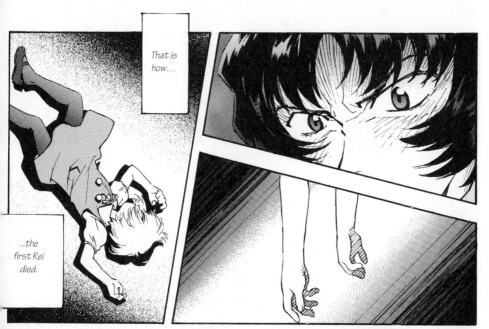

That is how…

…the first Rei died.

And my mother ran…

…and threw herself off…

…the top of MAGI Melchior.

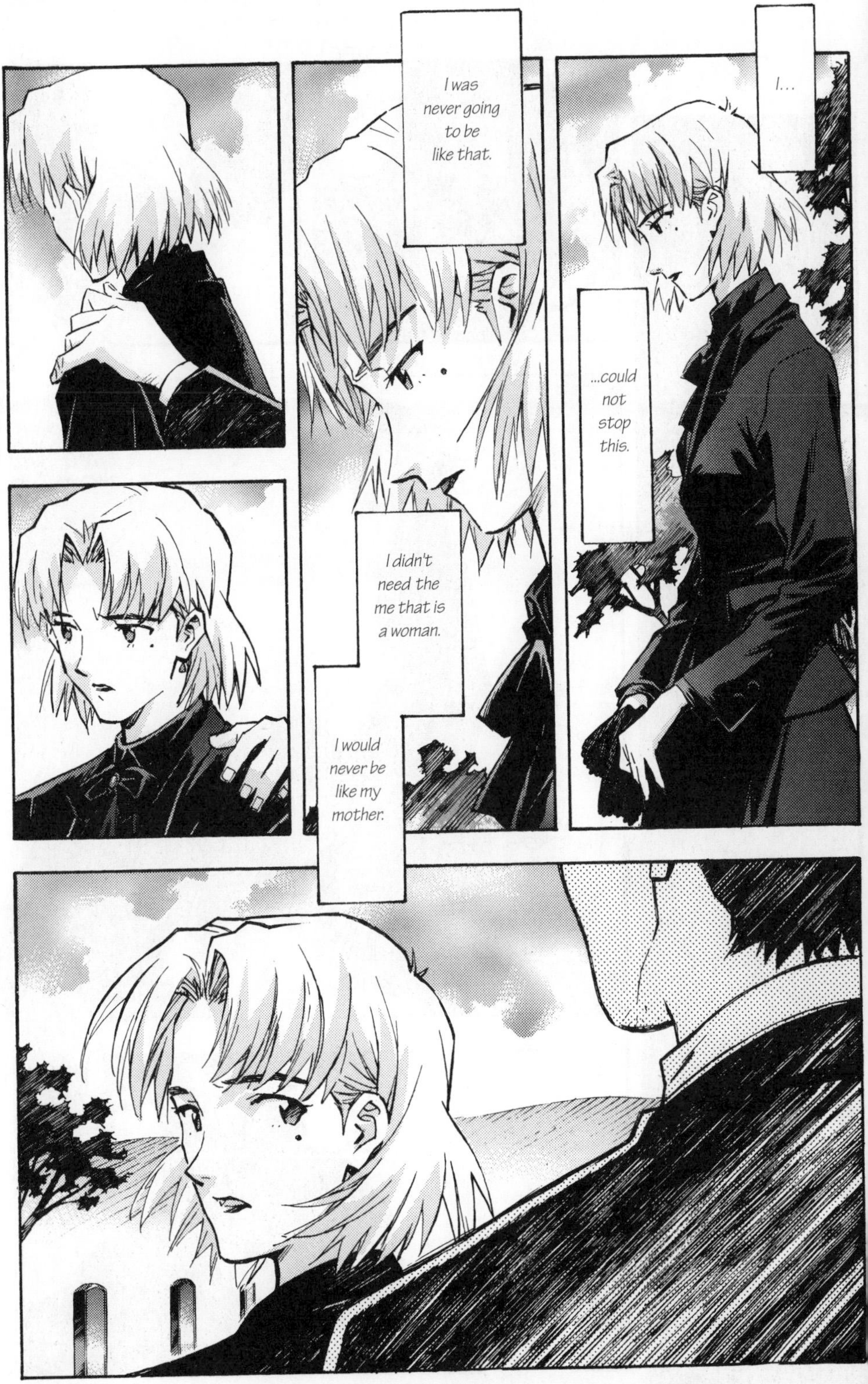
I...
...could not stop this.
I was never going to be like that.
I didn't need the me that is a woman.
I would never be like my mother.

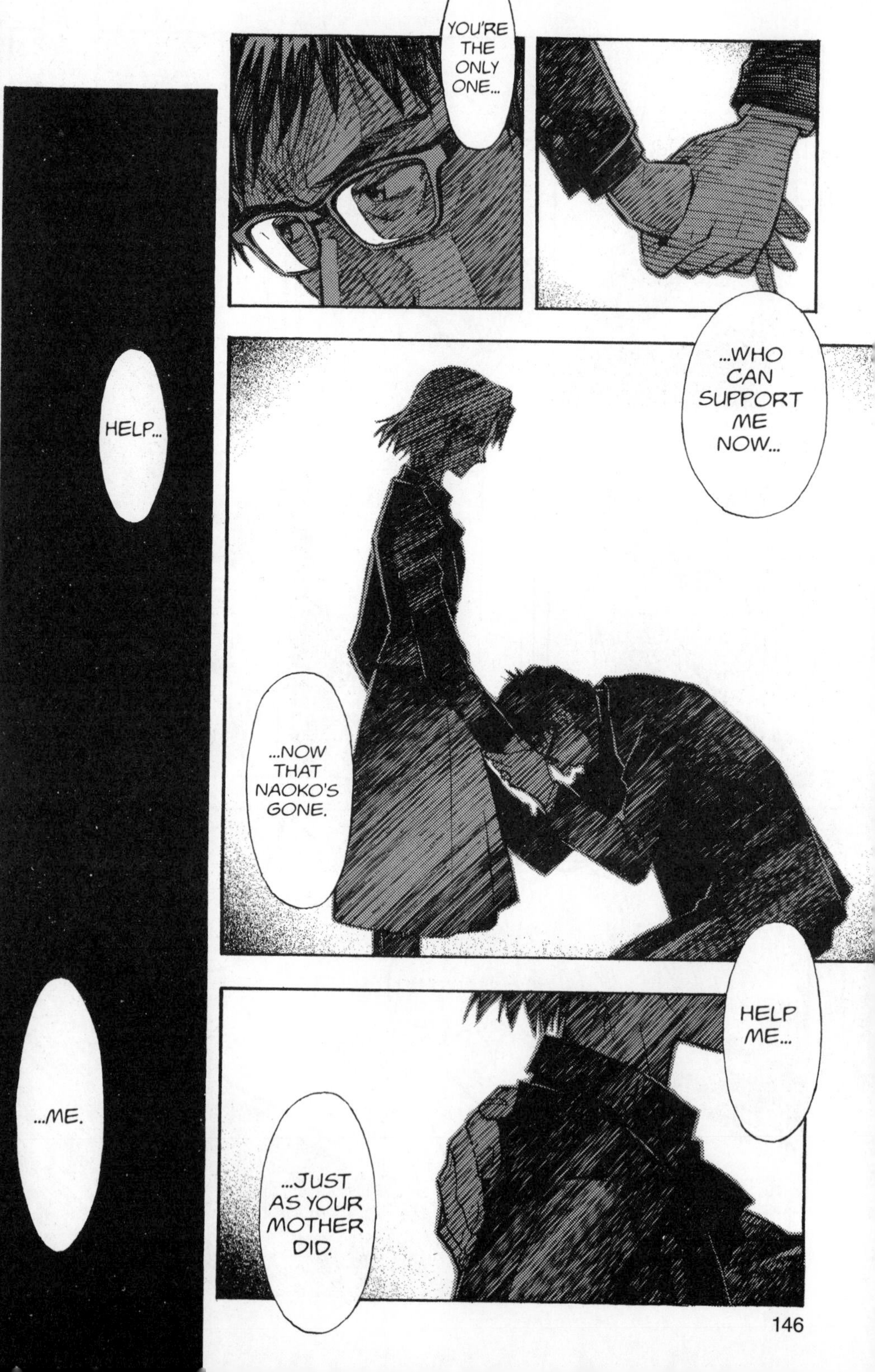
YOU'RE THE ONLY ONE...
...WHO CAN SUPPORT ME NOW...
...NOW THAT NAOKO'S GONE.
HELP ME...
...JUST AS YOUR MOTHER DID.
HELP...
...ME.

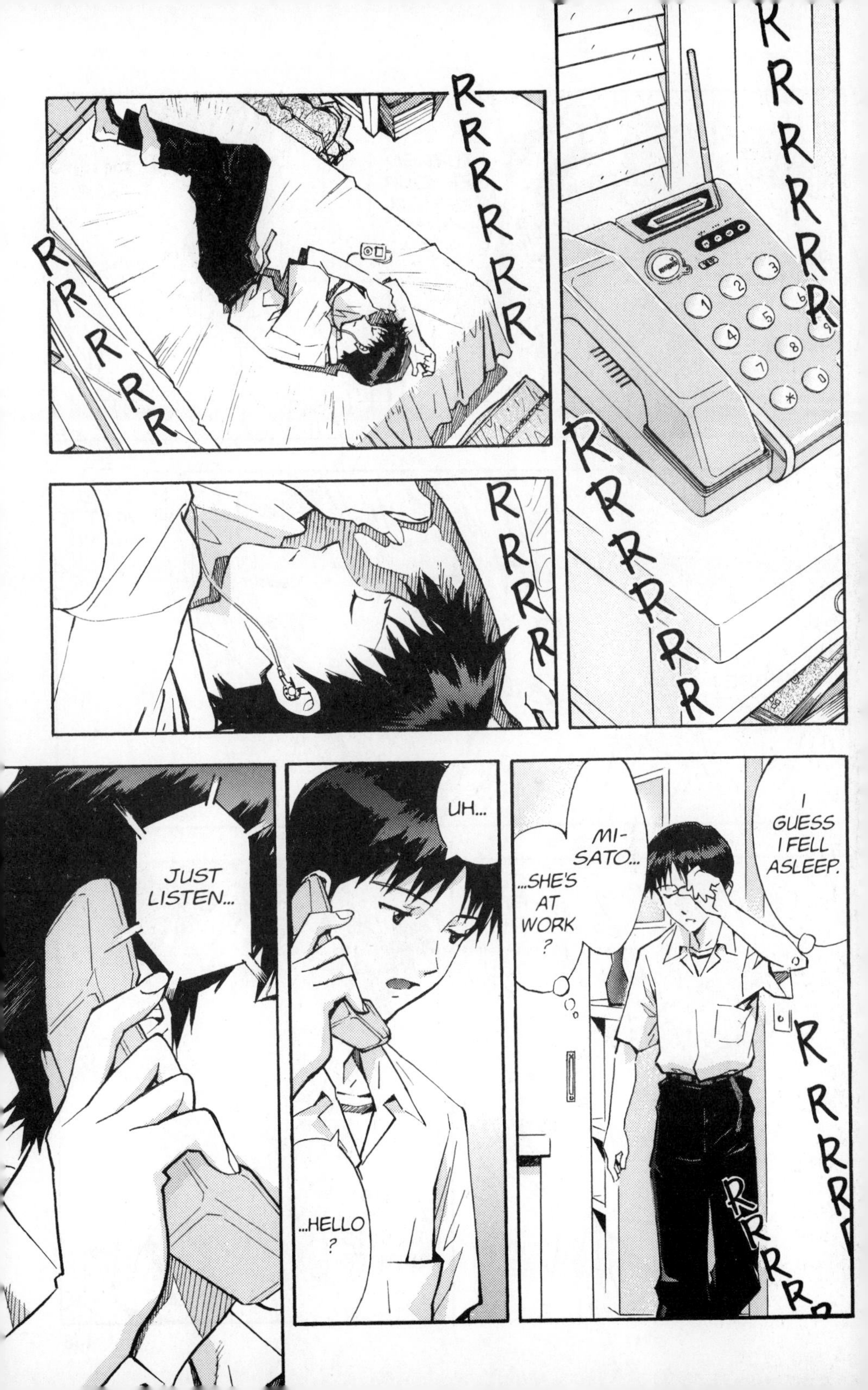
RRRRRRRRR
RRRRRRRRR
RRRRRR
RRRRR
RRRRRR
I GUESS I FELL ASLEEP.
MI-SATO...
...SHE'S AT WORK?
RRRRRRRR
UH...
...HELLO?
JUST LISTEN...

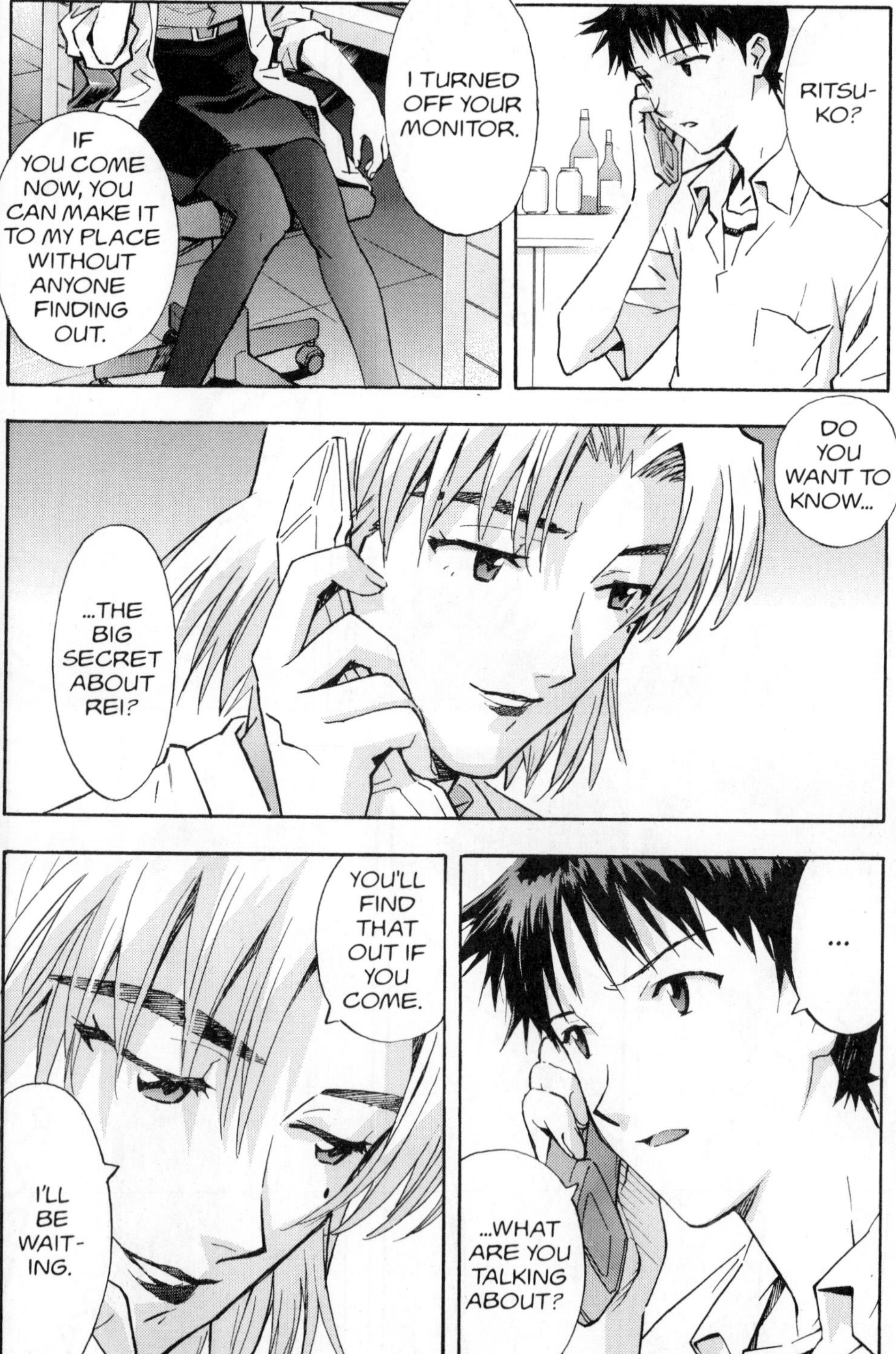
RITSU-KO?
I TURNED OFF YOUR MONITOR.
IF YOU COME NOW, YOU CAN MAKE IT TO MY PLACE WITHOUT ANYONE FINDING OUT.
DO YOU WANT TO KNOW...
...THE BIG SECRET ABOUT REI?
...
...WHAT ARE YOU TALKING ABOUT?
YOU'LL FIND THAT OUT IF YOU COME.
I'LL BE WAIT-ING.

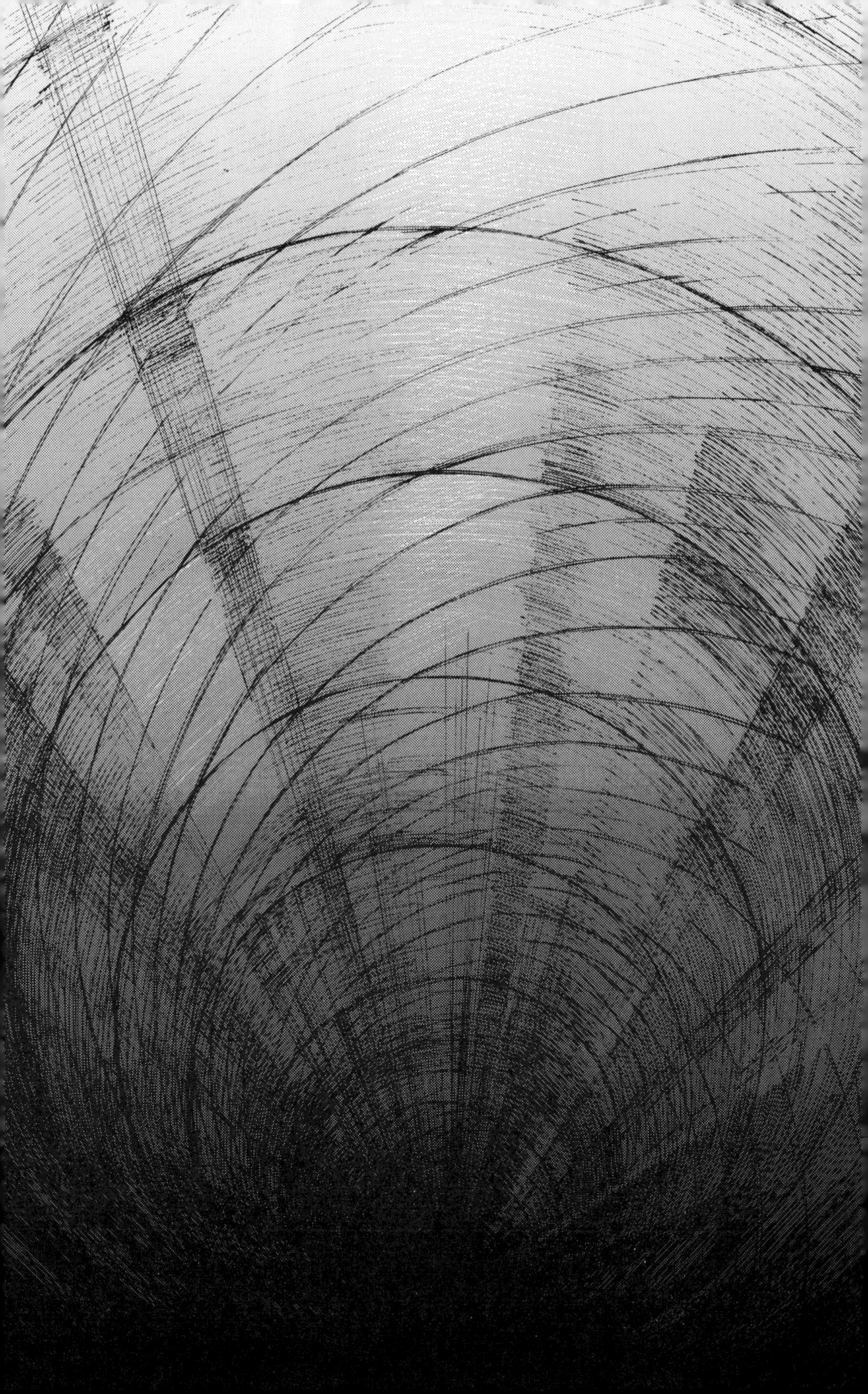

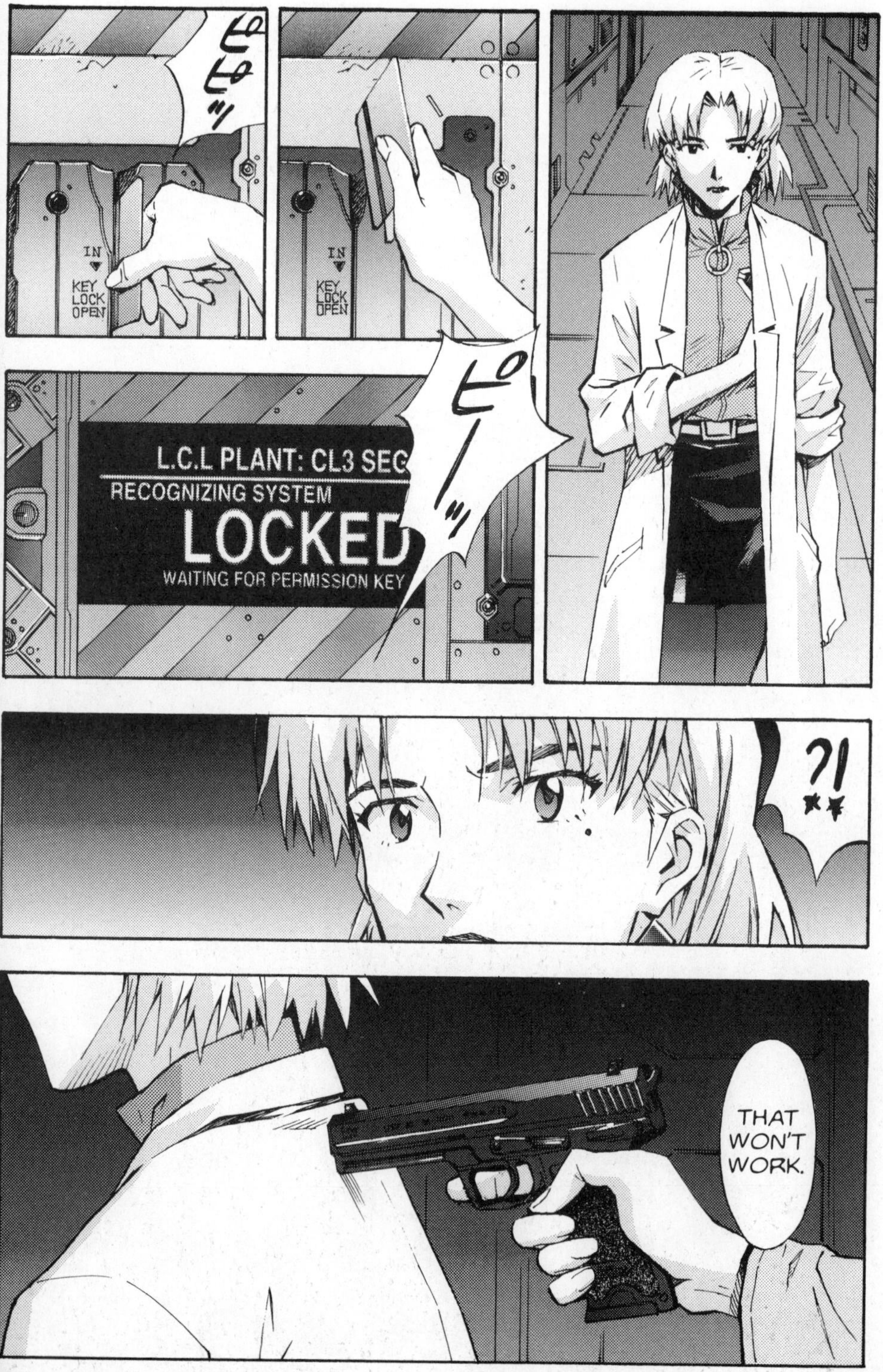
IN
KEY LOCK OPEN
IN
KEY LOCK OPEN
ピロピッ
L.C.L PLANT: CL3 SEG
RECOGNIZING SYSTEM
LOCKED
WAITING FOR PERMISSION KEY
ピーーッ
?!
THAT WON'T WORK.

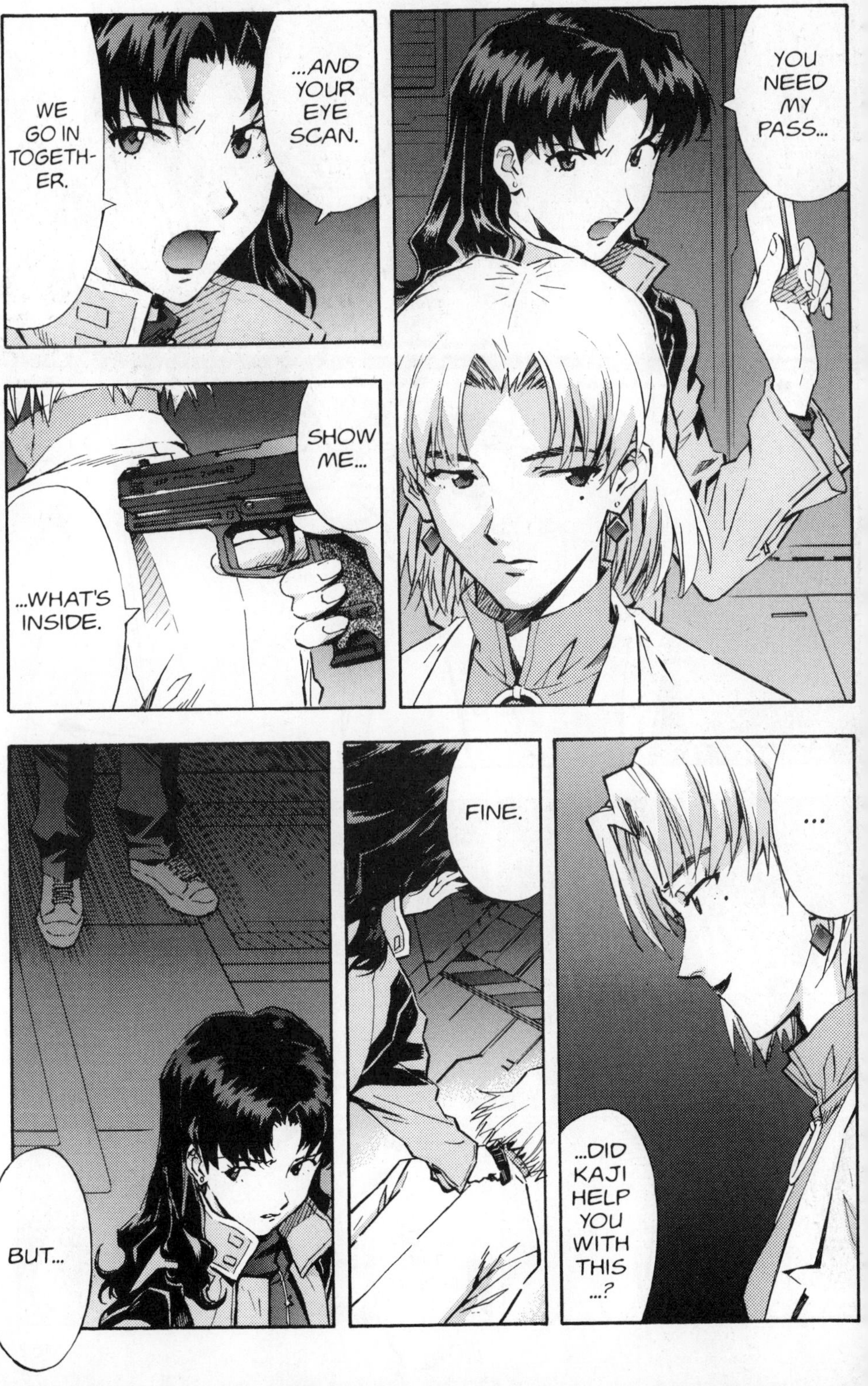
YOU NEED MY PASS...
...AND YOUR EYE SCAN.
WE GO IN TOGETH-ER.
SHOW ME...
...WHAT'S INSIDE.
...
...DID KAJI HELP YOU WITH THIS ...?
FINE.
BUT...

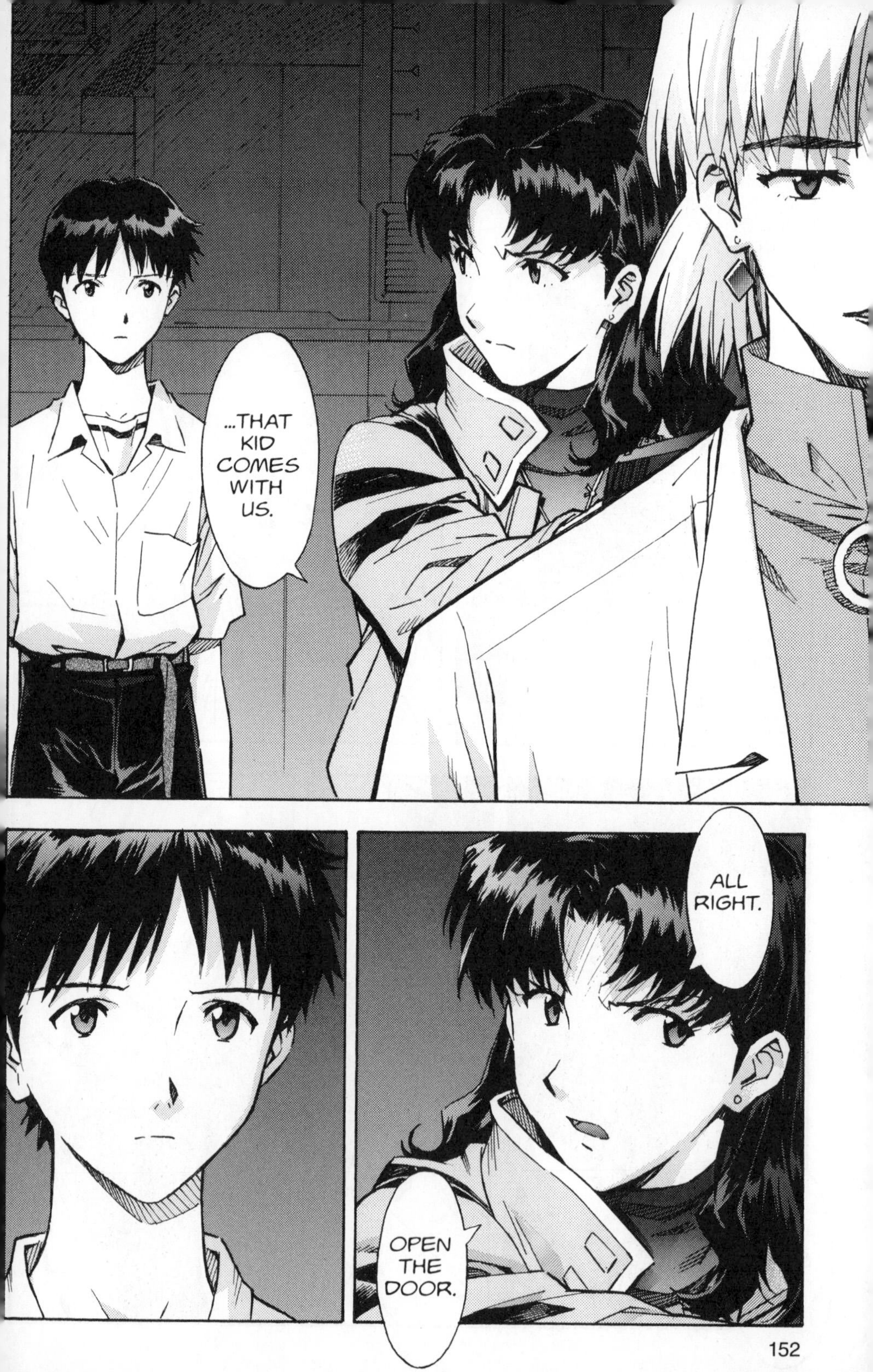
...THAT KID COMES WITH US.
ALL RIGHT.
OPEN THE DOOR.

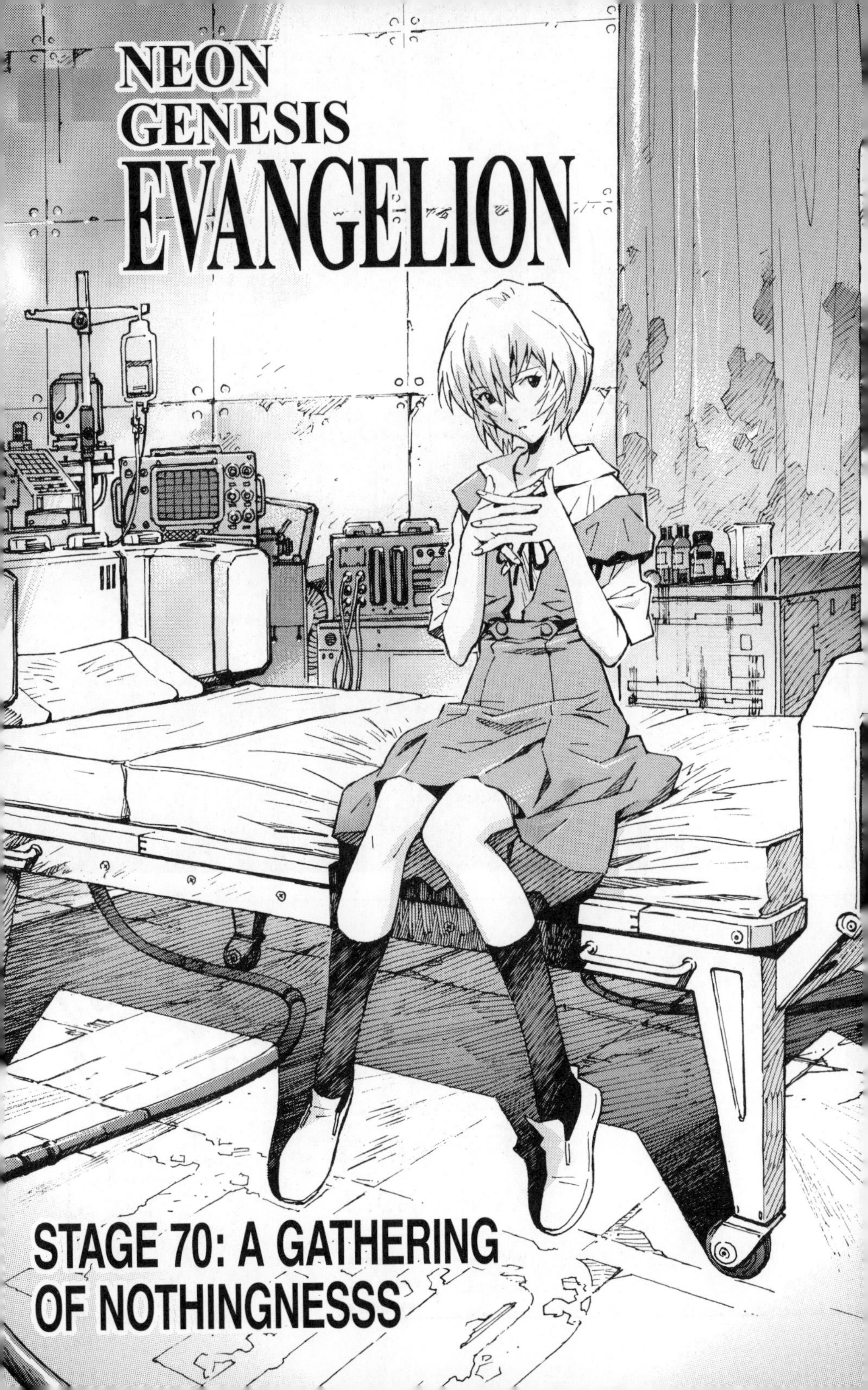
NEON GENESIS EVANGELION
STAGE 70: A GATHERING OF NOTHINGNESSS

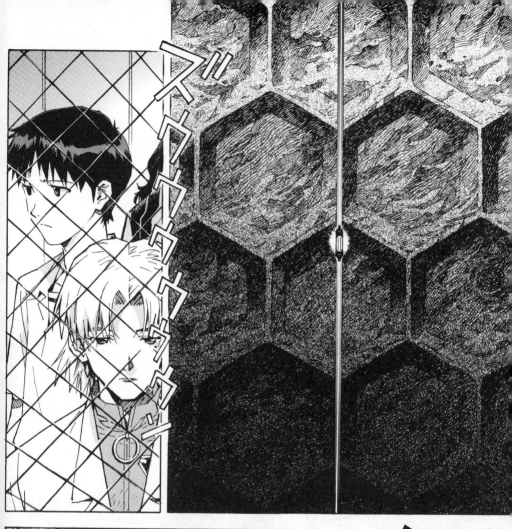

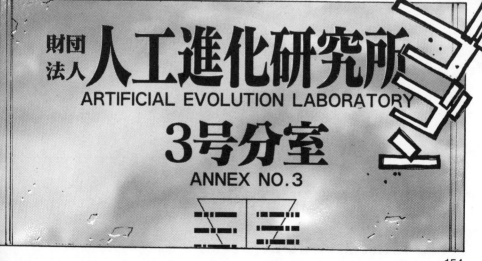

財団
法人 **人工進化研究所**
ARTIFICIAL EVOLUTION LABORATORY

3号分室
ANNEX NO.3

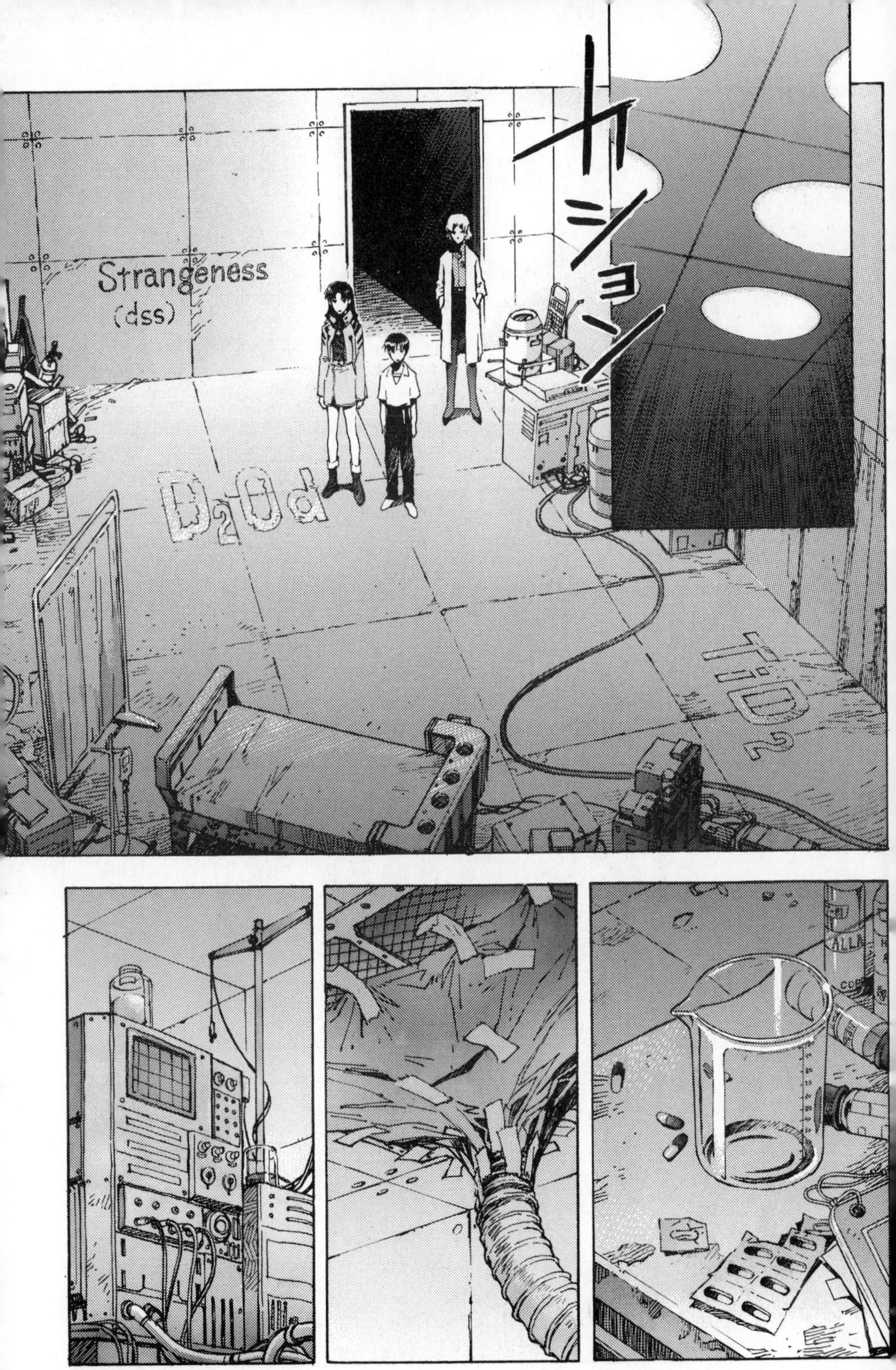
ガショーン
Strangeness
(dss)

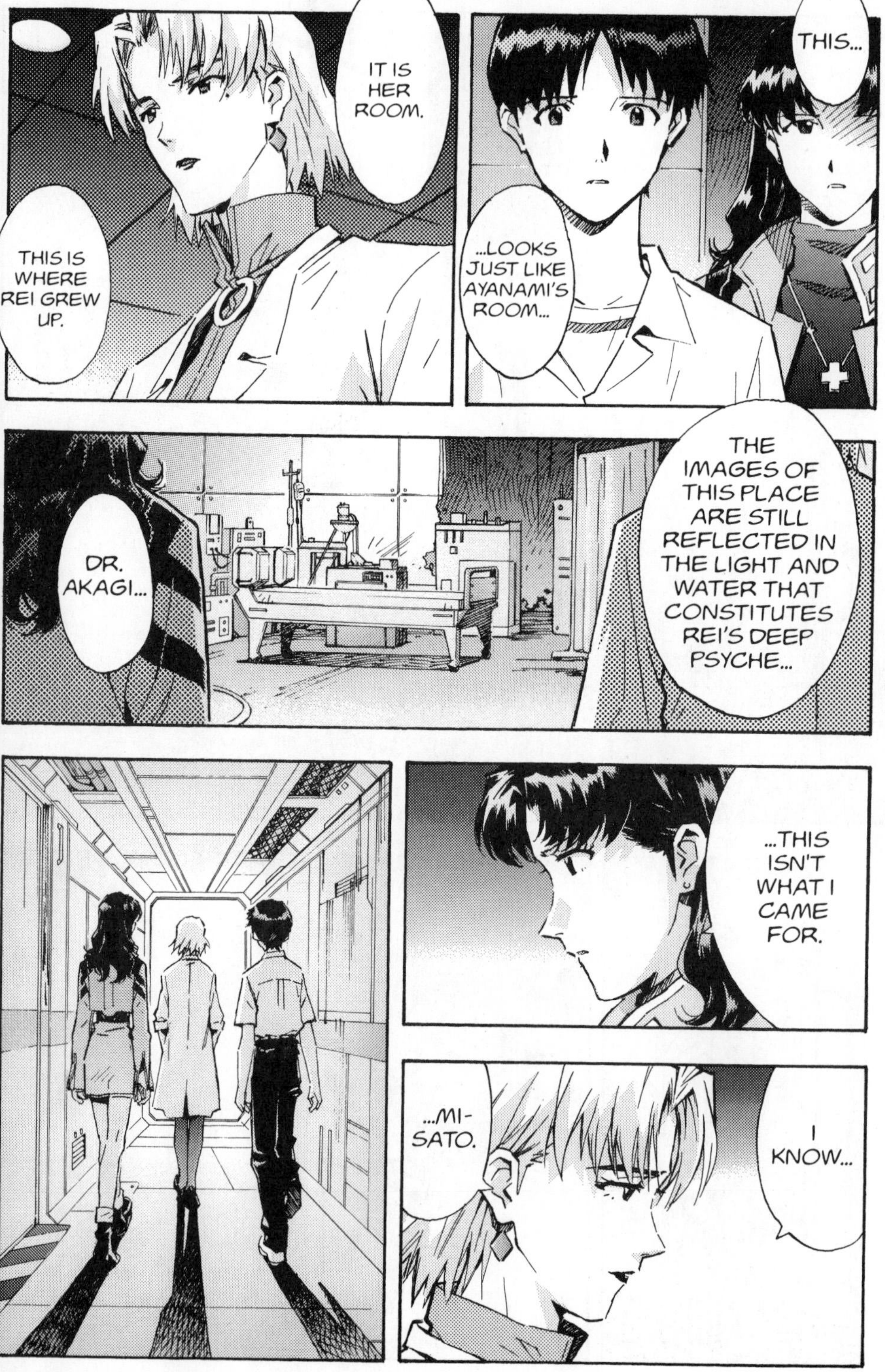
THIS...
...LOOKS JUST LIKE AYANAMI'S ROOM...
IT IS HER ROOM.
THIS IS WHERE REI GREW UP.
THE IMAGES OF THIS PLACE ARE STILL REFLECTED IN THE LIGHT AND WATER THAT CONSTITUTES REI'S DEEP PSYCHE...
DR. AKAGI...
...THIS ISN'T WHAT I CAME FOR.
I KNOW...
...MI-SATO.

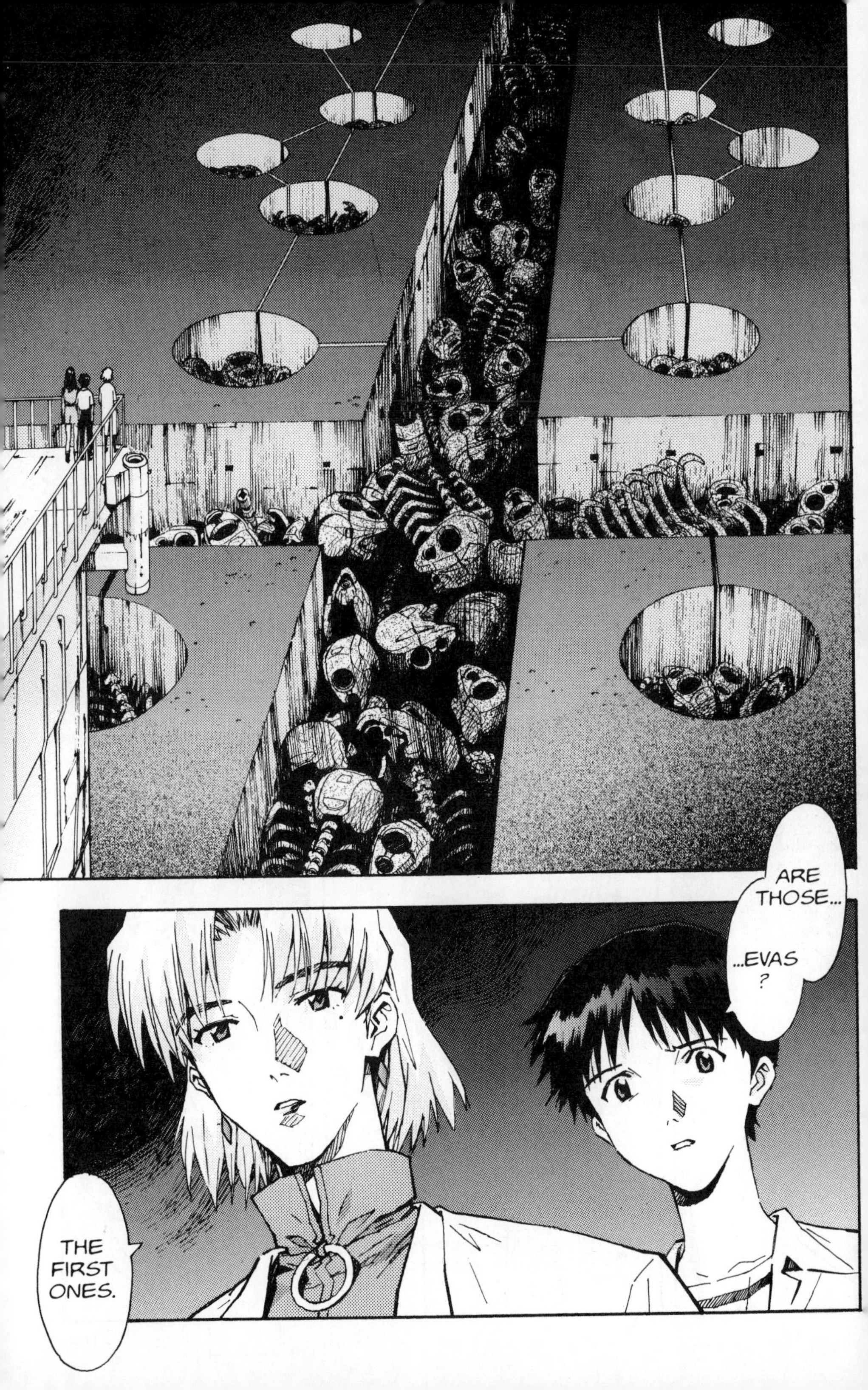
ARE THOSE...
...EVAS?
THE FIRST ONES.

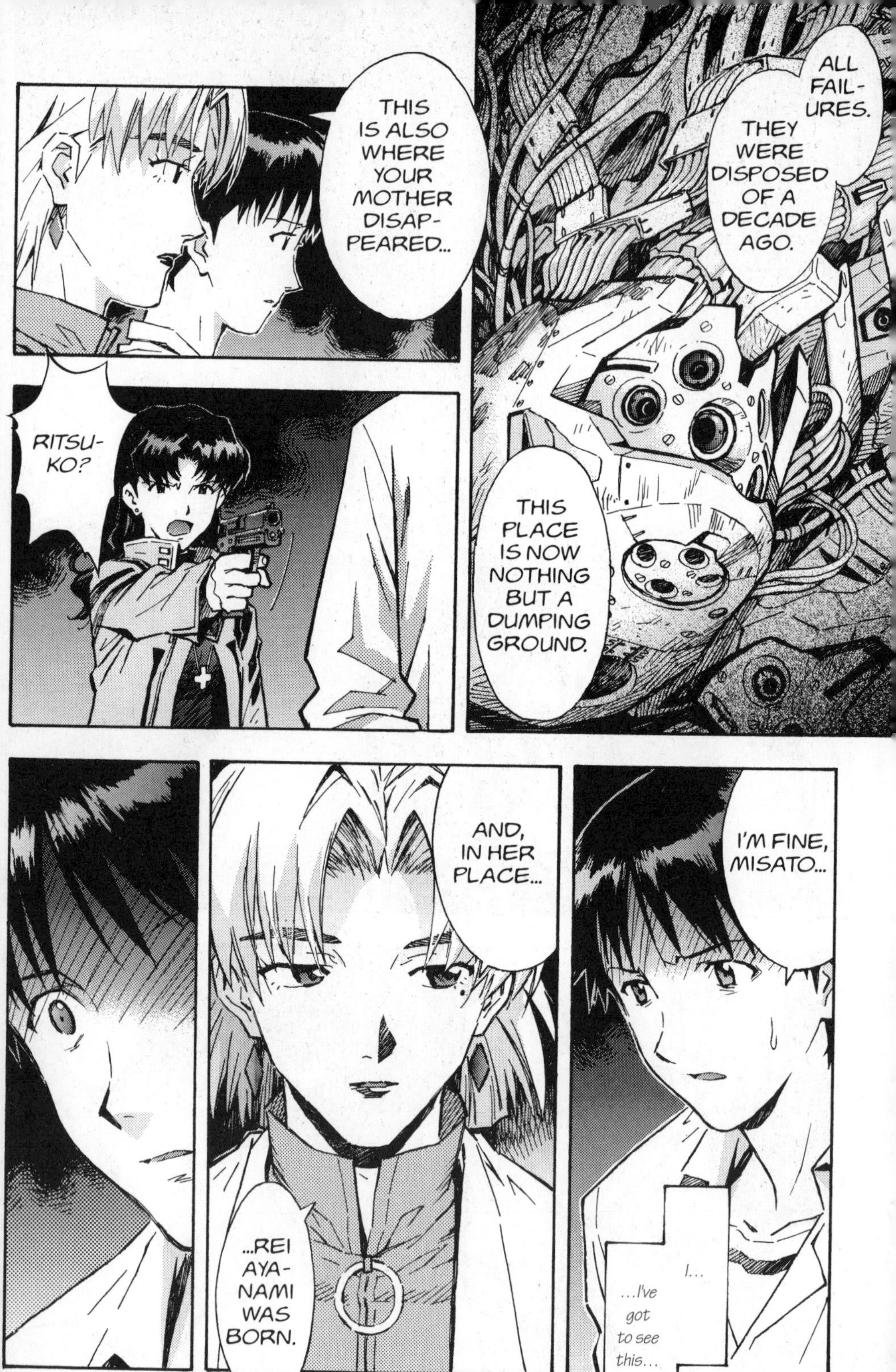
ALL FAILURES. THEY WERE DISPOSED OF A DECADE AGO.
THIS PLACE IS NOW NOTHING BUT A DUMPING GROUND.
THIS IS ALSO WHERE YOUR MOTHER DISAPPEARED...
RITSUKO?
I'M FINE, MISATO...
I... ...I've got to see this...
AND, IN HER PLACE...
...REI AYANAMI WAS BORN.

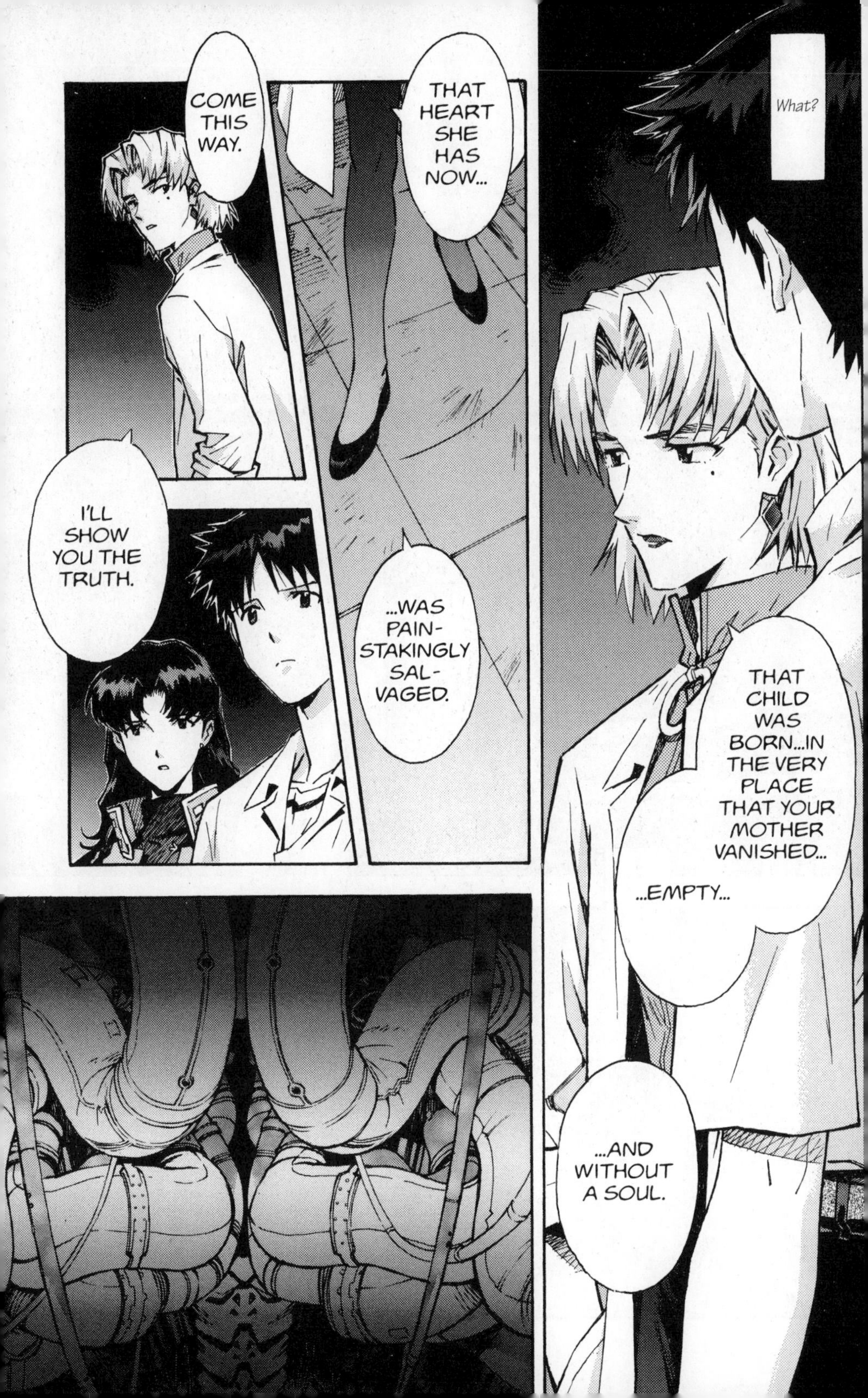
What?
THAT CHILD WAS BORN...IN THE VERY PLACE THAT YOUR MOTHER VANISHED...
...EMPTY...
...AND WITHOUT A SOUL.
THAT HEART SHE HAS NOW...
...WAS PAIN-STAKINGLY SAL-VAGED.
COME THIS WAY.
I'LL SHOW YOU THE TRUTH.

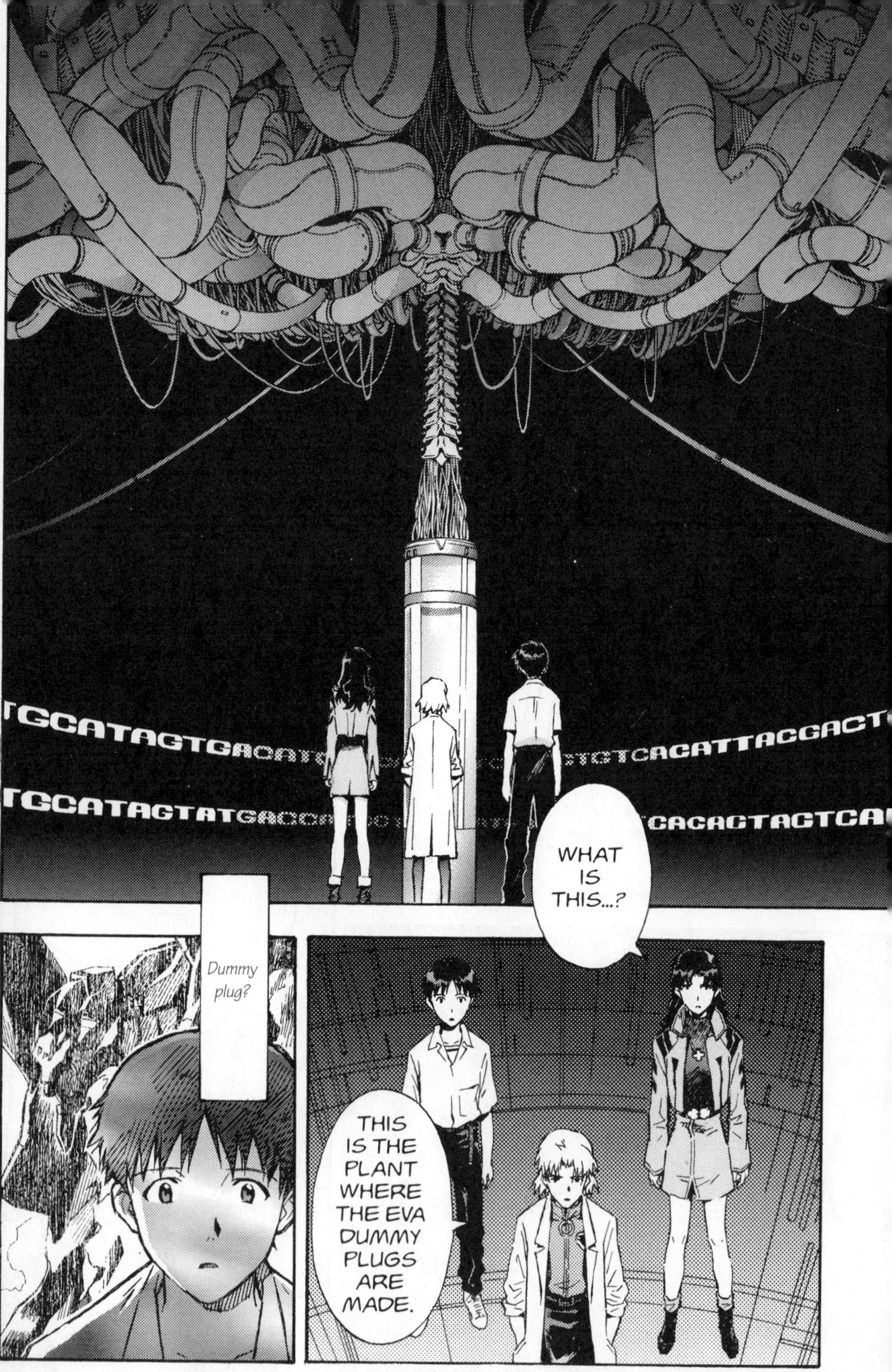
WHAT IS THIS...?
THIS IS THE PLANT WHERE THE EVA DUMMY PLUGS ARE MADE.
Dummy plug?

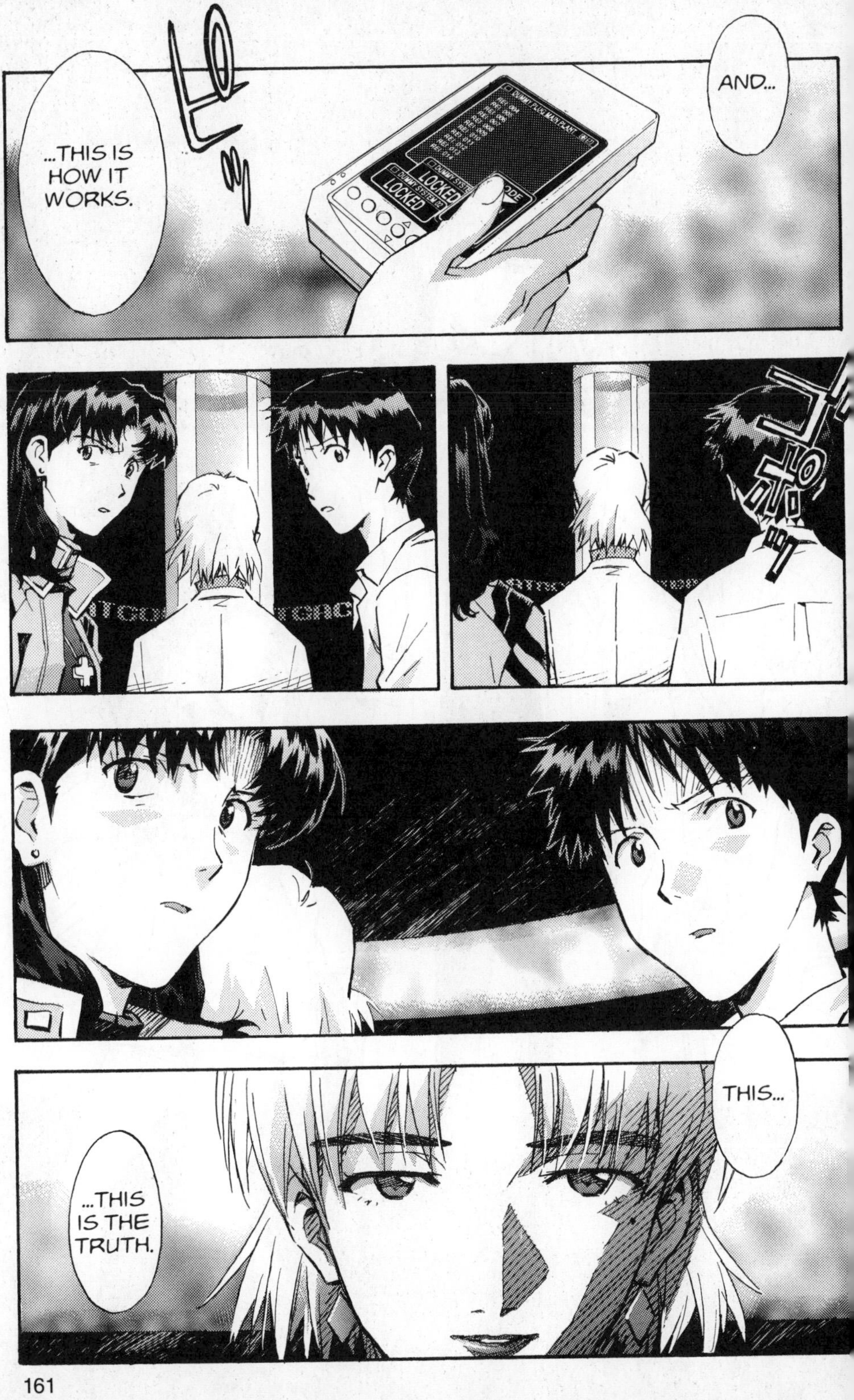
AND...
...THIS IS HOW IT WORKS.
LOCKED
LOCKED
THIS...
...THIS IS THE TRUTH.

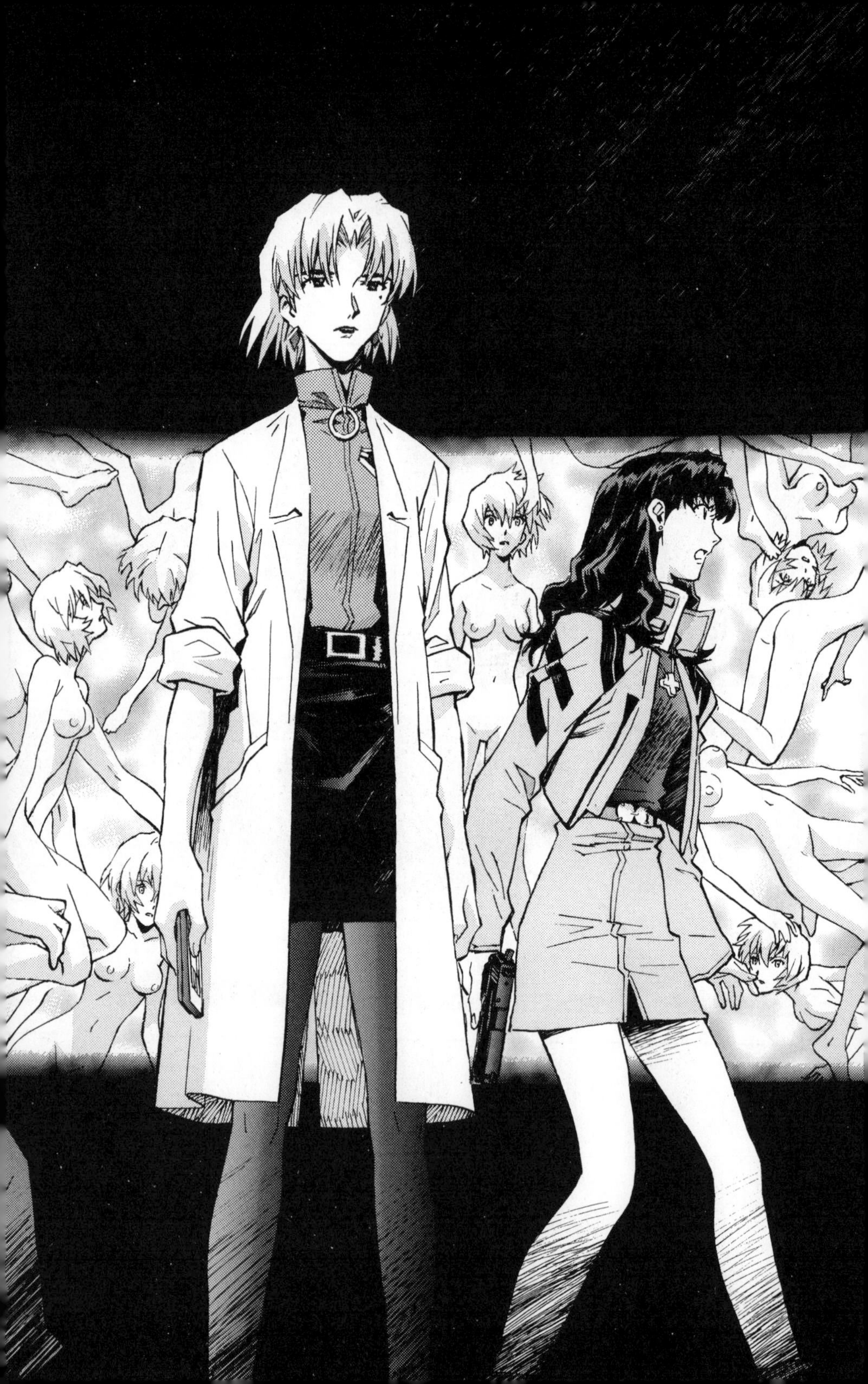

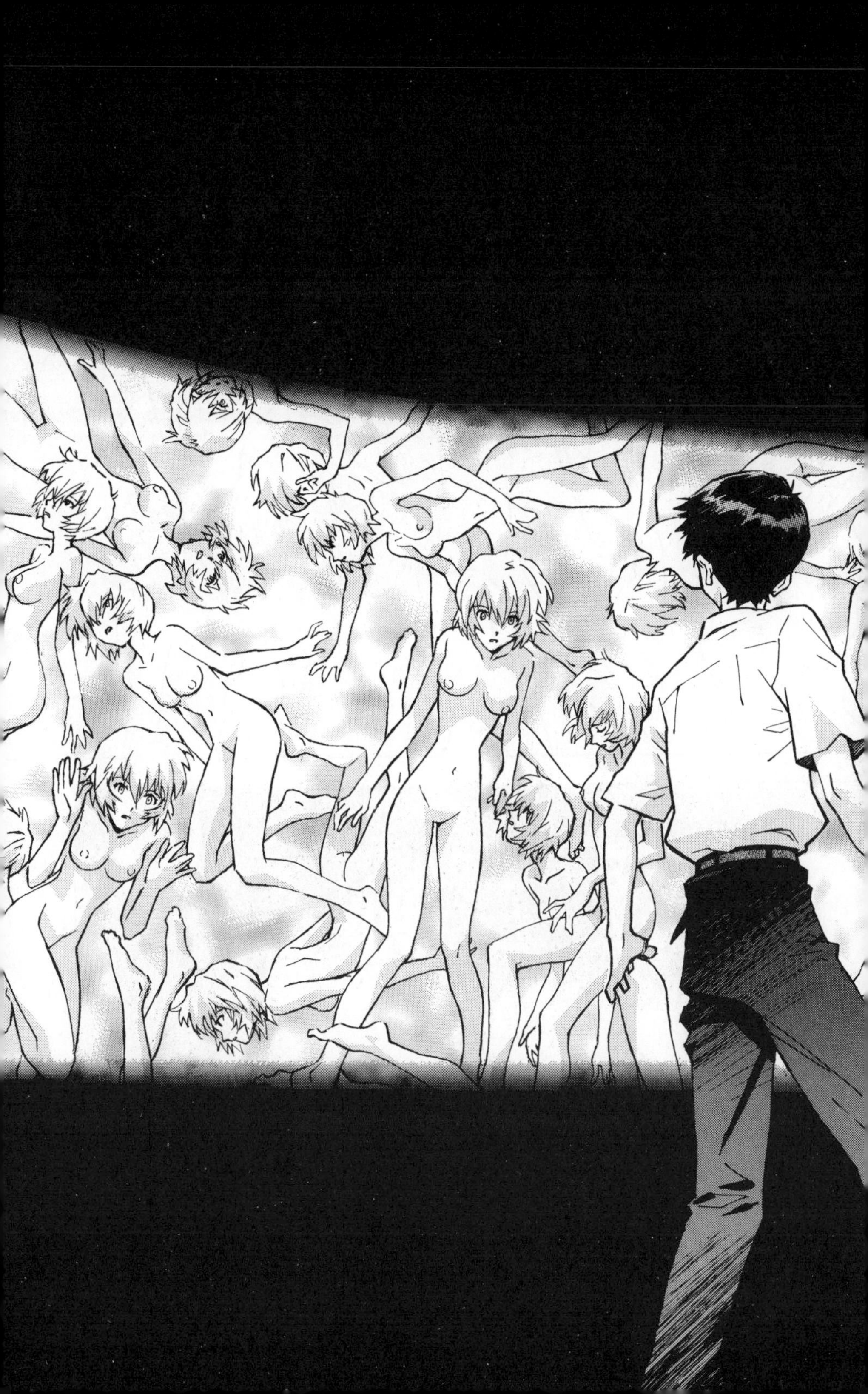

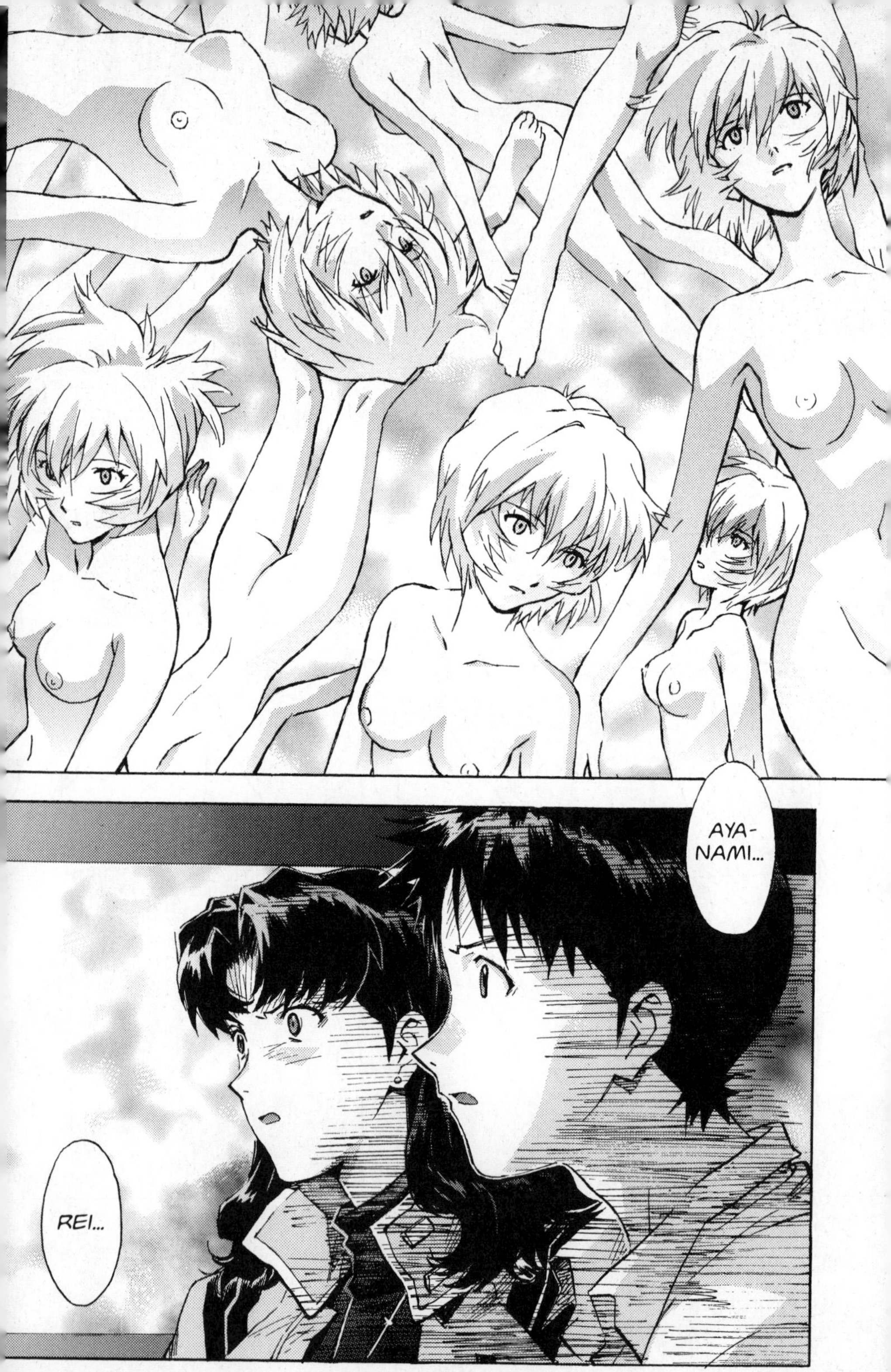
AYA-NAMI...
REI...

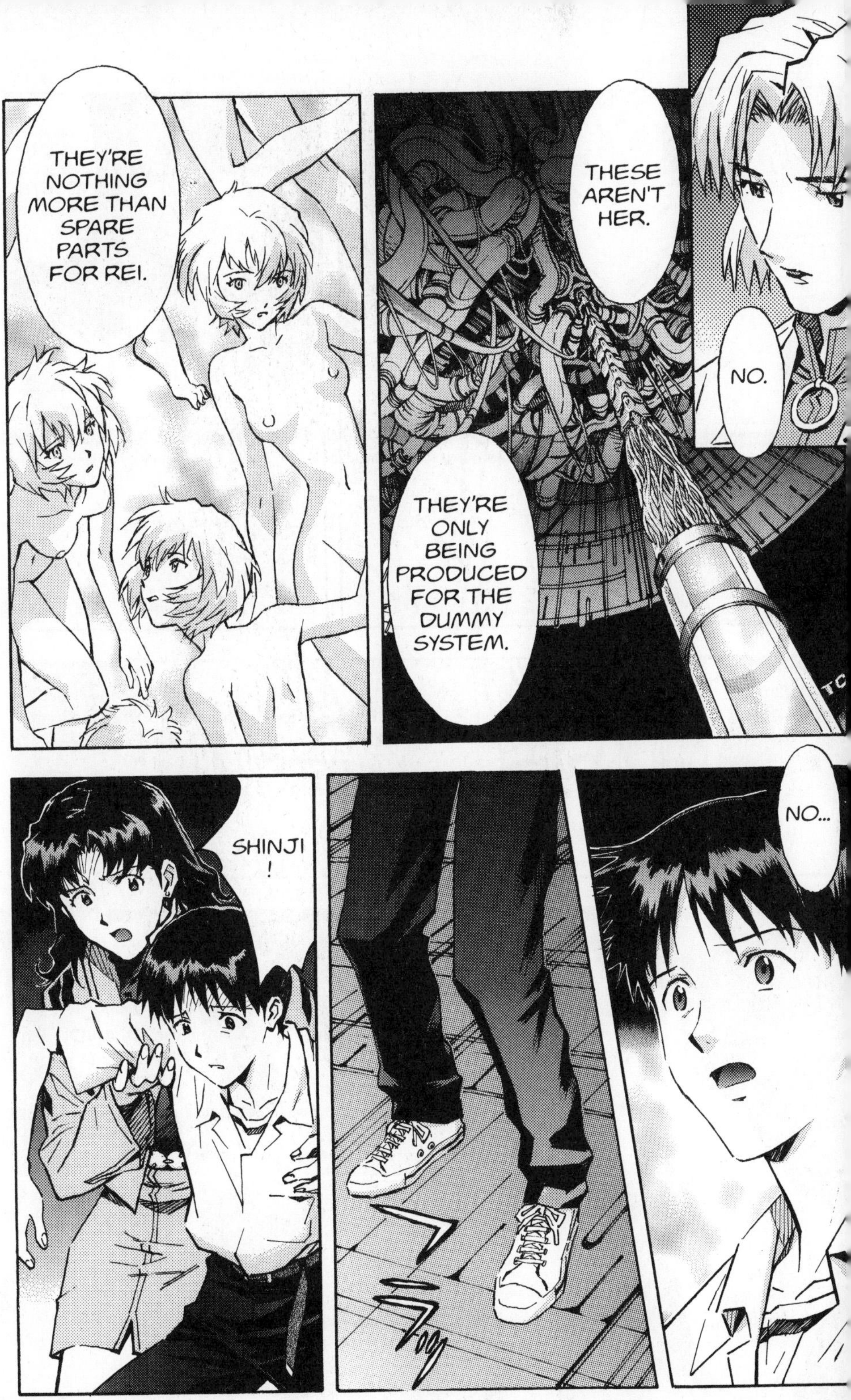
NO.
THESE AREN'T HER.
THEY'RE ONLY BEING PRODUCED FOR THE DUMMY SYSTEM.
THEY'RE NOTHING MORE THAN SPARE PARTS FOR REI.
NO...
SHINJI!

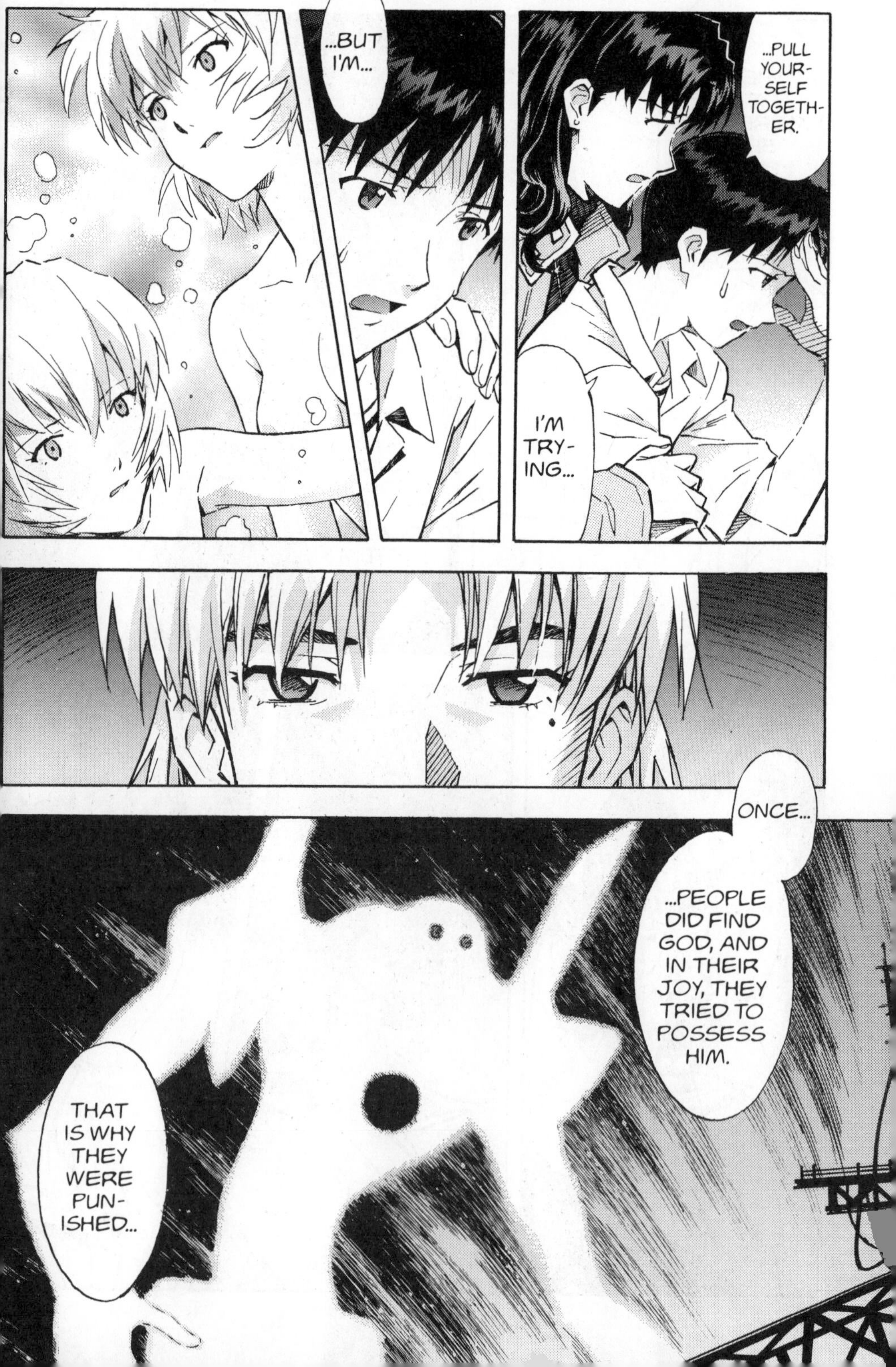
...PULL YOURSELF TOGETHER.
I'M TRYING...
...BUT I'M...
ONCE...
...PEOPLE DID FIND GOD, AND IN THEIR JOY, THEY TRIED TO POSSESS HIM.
THAT IS WHY THEY WERE PUNISHED...

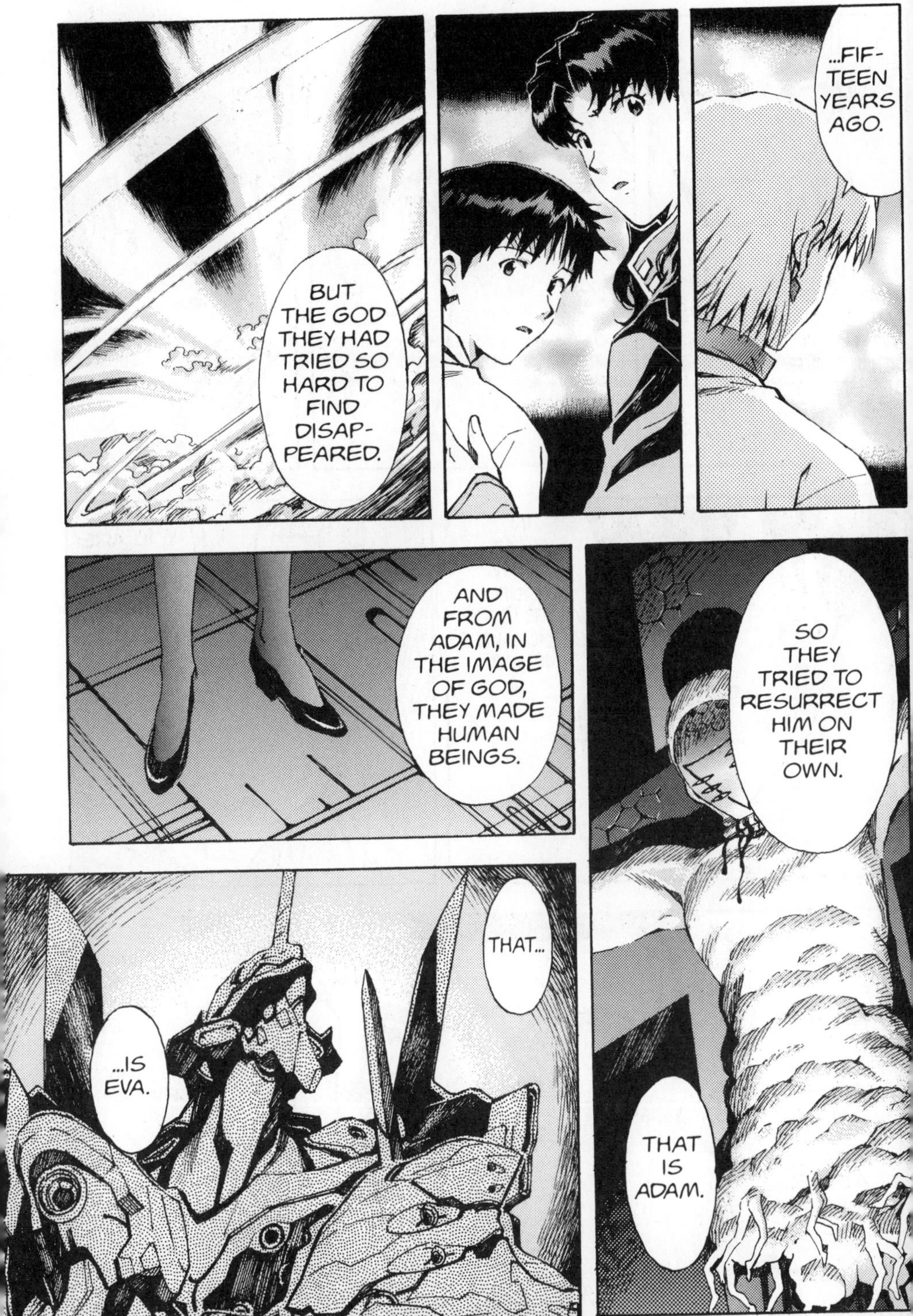
...FIFTEEN YEARS AGO.
BUT THE GOD THEY HAD TRIED SO HARD TO FIND DISAPPEARED.
SO THEY TRIED TO RESURRECT HIM ON THEIR OWN.
THAT IS ADAM.
AND FROM ADAM, IN THE IMAGE OF GOD, THEY MADE HUMAN BEINGS.
THAT...
...IS EVA.

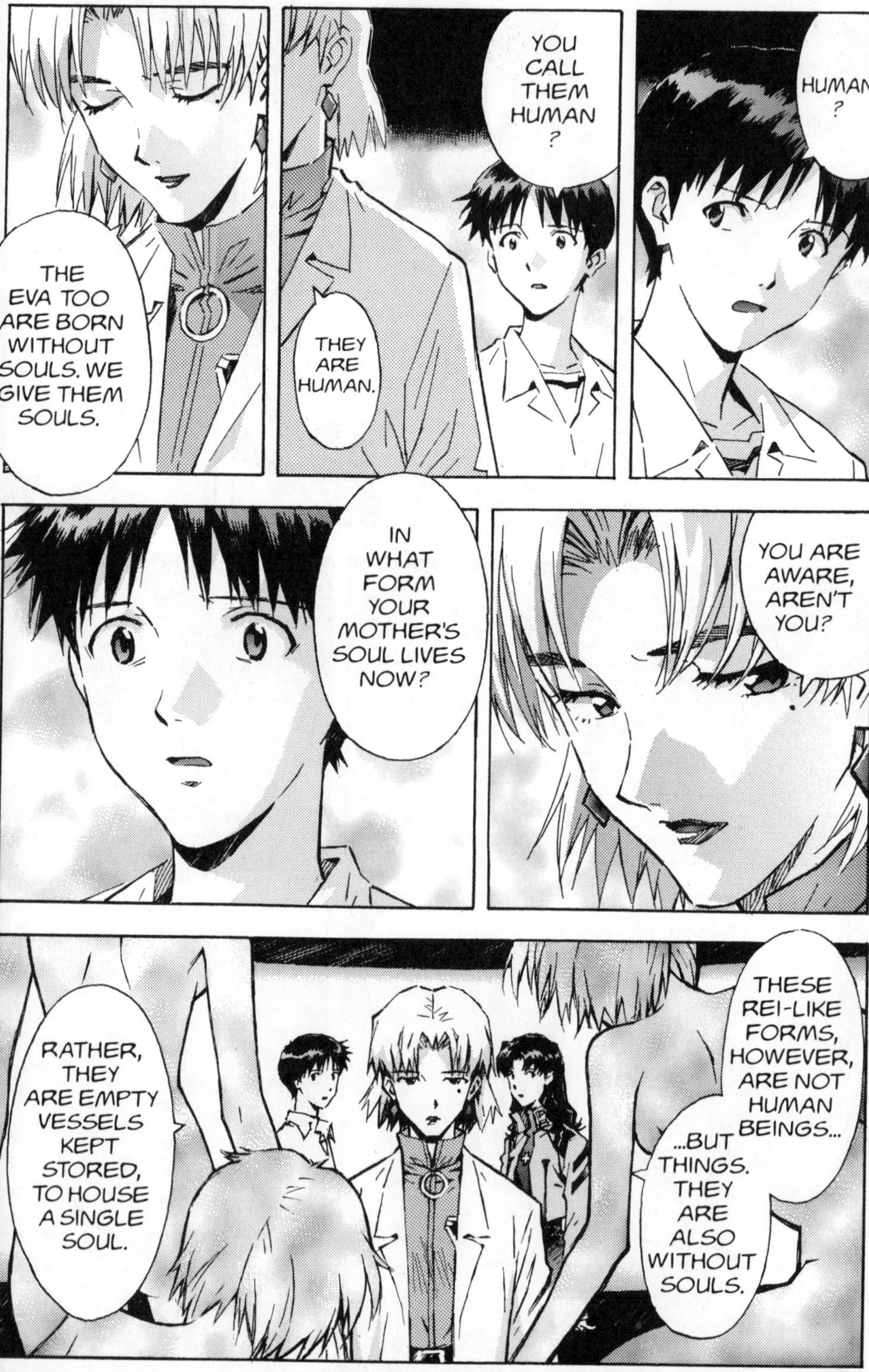
HUMAN?
YOU CALL THEM HUMAN?
THEY ARE HUMAN.
THE EVA TOO ARE BORN WITHOUT SOULS. WE GIVE THEM SOULS.
YOU ARE AWARE, AREN'T YOU?
IN WHAT FORM YOUR MOTHER'S SOUL LIVES NOW?
THESE REI-LIKE FORMS, HOWEVER, ARE NOT HUMAN BEINGS...
...BUT THINGS. THEY ARE ALSO WITHOUT SOULS.
RATHER, THEY ARE EMPTY VESSELS KEPT STORED, TO HOUSE A SINGLE SOUL.

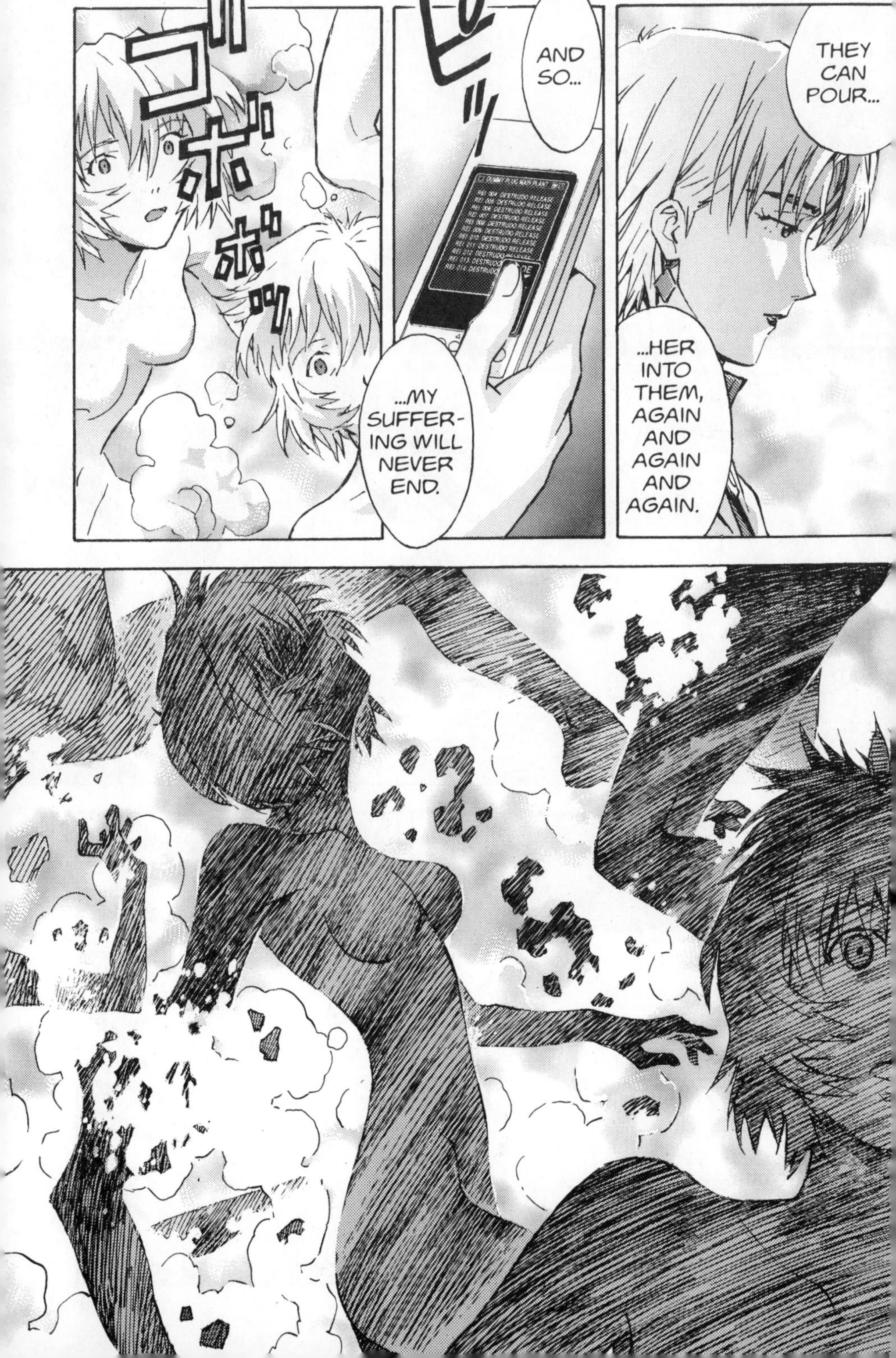
THEY CAN POUR...
...HER INTO THEM, AGAIN AND AGAIN AND AGAIN.
ピッ
AND SO...
...MY SUFFERING WILL NEVER END.
ゴポポポ

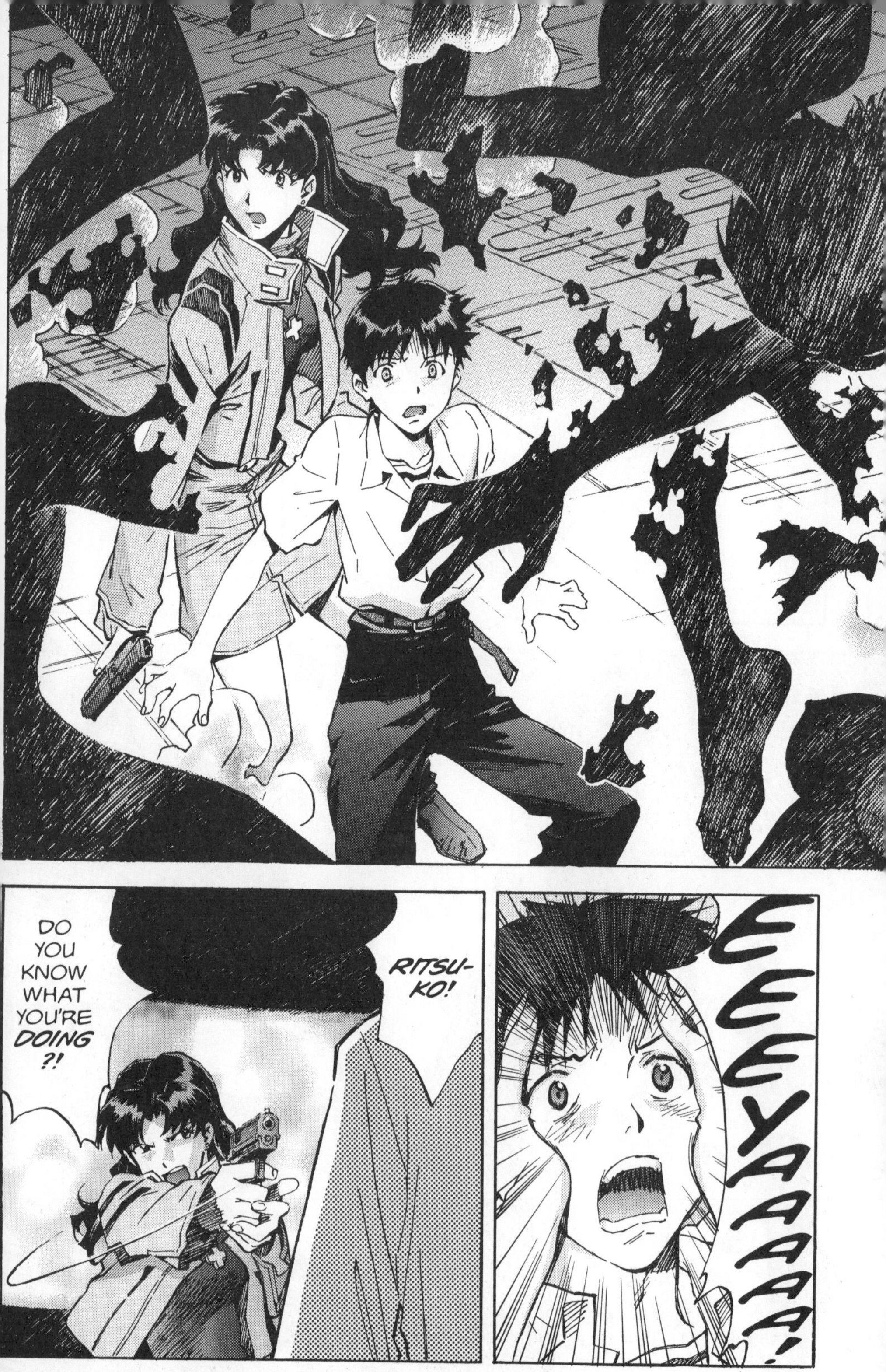
EEEYAAAAAA!
RITSU-KO!
DO YOU KNOW WHAT YOU'RE *DOING* ?!

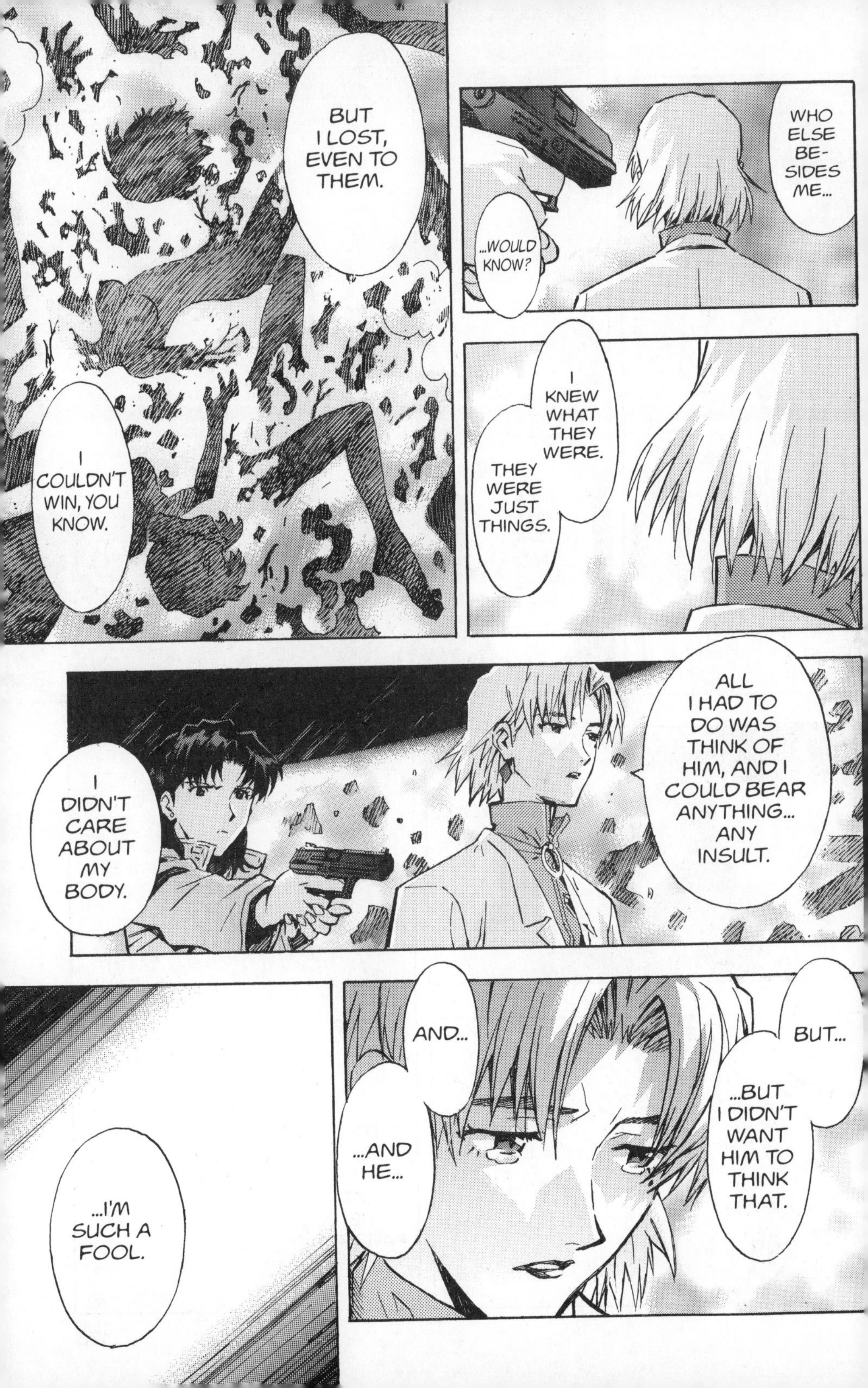
WHO ELSE BE- SIDES ME...
...WOULD KNOW?
I KNEW WHAT THEY WERE.
THEY WERE JUST THINGS.
BUT I LOST, EVEN TO THEM.
I COULDN'T WIN, YOU KNOW.
ALL I HAD TO DO WAS THINK OF HIM, AND I COULD BEAR ANYTHING... ANY INSULT.
I DIDN'T CARE ABOUT MY BODY.
BUT...
...BUT I DIDN'T WANT HIM TO THINK THAT.
AND...
...AND HE...
...I'M SUCH A FOOL.

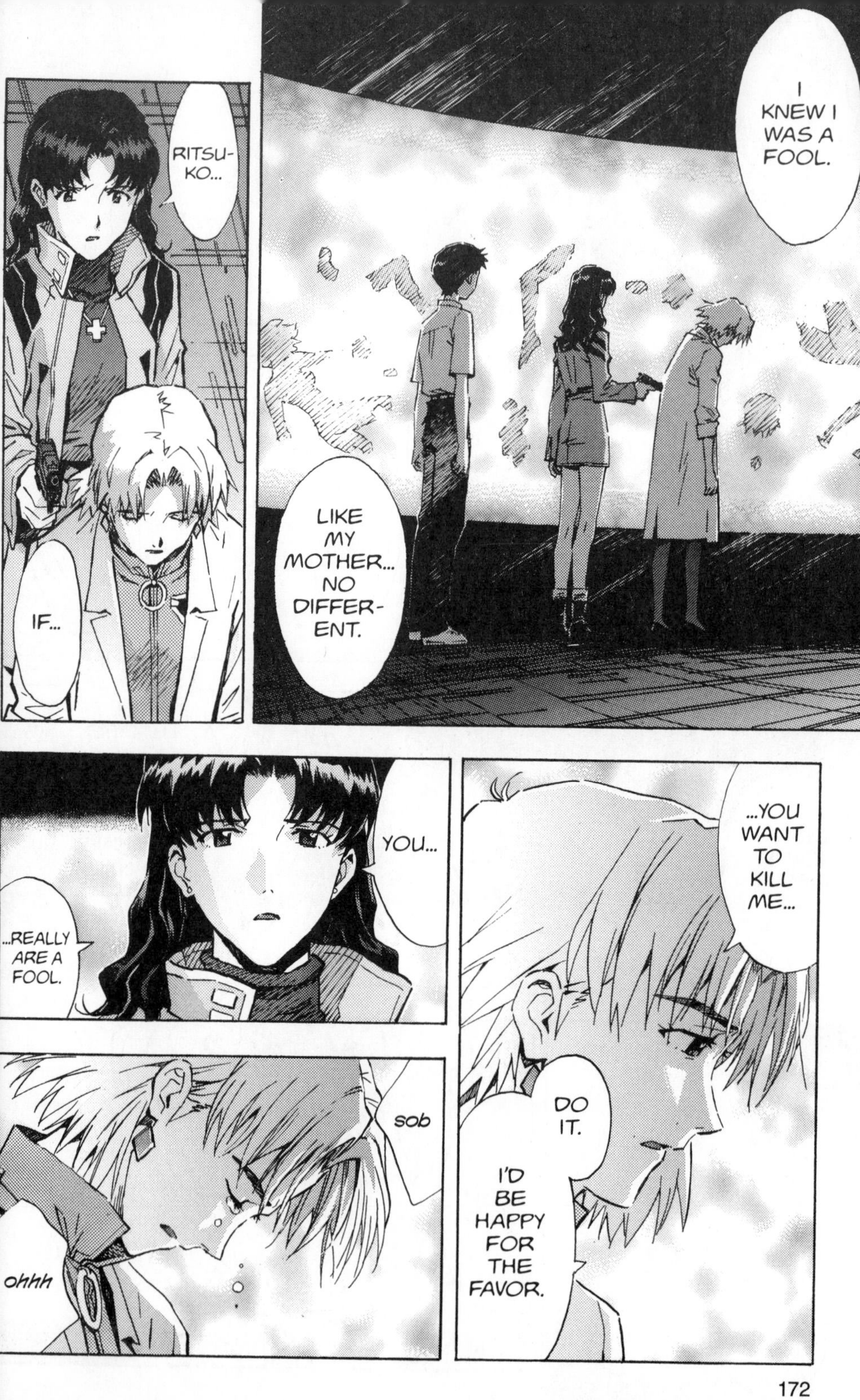
I KNEW I WAS A FOOL.
LIKE MY MOTHER... NO DIFFERENT.
RITSU-KO...
IF...
...YOU WANT TO KILL ME...
DO IT.
I'D BE HAPPY FOR THE FAVOR.
YOU...
...REALLY ARE A FOOL.
sob
ohhh

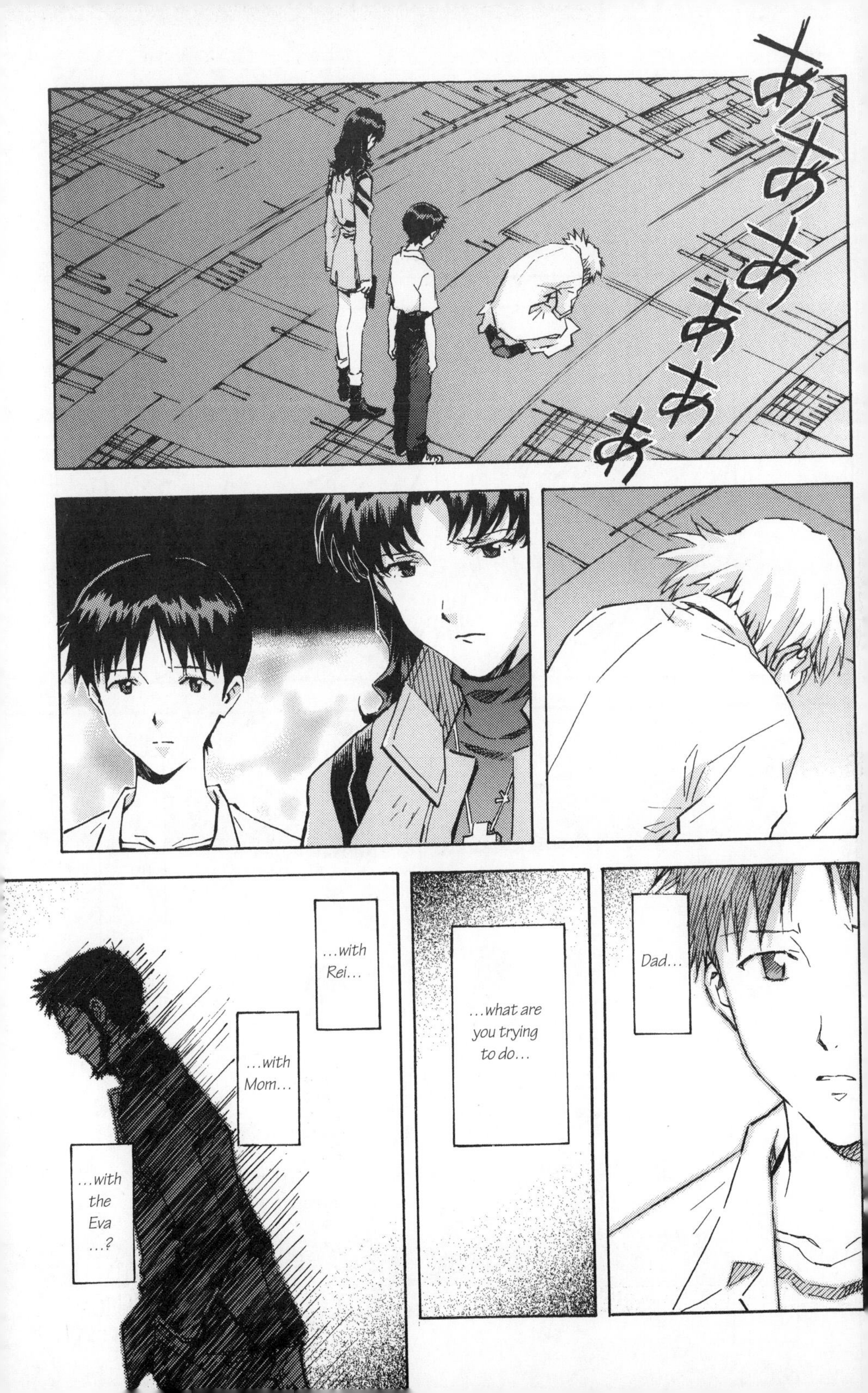
ああああああ
Dad…
…what are you trying to do…
…with Rei…
…with Mom…
…with the Eva …?

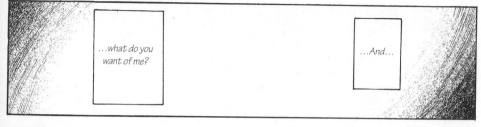

...what do you want of me?

...And...

Mom...

Rei...

what...

...do I do now ...?

TO BE CONTINUED IN EVANGELION VOLUME ELEVEN

YOSHIYUKI SADAMOTO

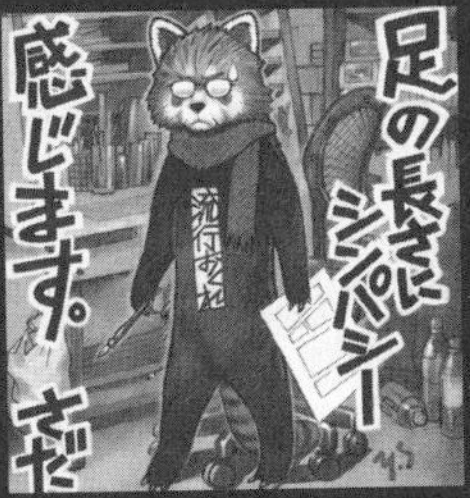
足の長さにシンパシー
感じます。
さだ

THE AUTHOR IN HIS STUDIO IS LABELED OUT OF FASHION, WHILE A MESSAGE FROM A MYSTERIOUS "SADA" EXPRESSES SYMPATHY OVER THE LENGTH OF HIS LEGS.

WRITER AND ARTIST

I've thought at great length about how nice it is to be young, especially when it comes to love. As long as you have feelings of love towards one another, you can overcome obstacles, but those obstacles become more difficult the older you get. Work, income, domestic life, health, the future—especially the future—which, even as you contemplate it, sees your pure unadulterated love go stale.

Although the world that Shinji, Rei, and Asuka are experiencing is, of course, a two-dimensional, imaginary one, I believe there is a place like this somewhere out there. I am writing this and reliving my youth, even if only emotionally, while eating CoQ10 gelatin.

THE MYSTERIOUS STRANGER

THE ANIME, THE MANGA, AND THE MARK TWAIN NOVELLA

"GOD WILL PROVIDE FOR THIS KITTEN."
"WHAT MAKES YOU THINK SO?"
URSULA'S EYES SNAPPED WITH ANGER.
"BECAUSE I KNOW IT!" SHE SAID. "NOT A SPARROW
FALLS TO THE GROUND WITHOUT HIS SEEING IT."
"BUT IT FALLS, JUST THE SAME.
WHAT GOOD IS SEEING IT FALL?"

—FROM *THE MYSTERIOUS STRANGER*

There is a short novel by Mark Twain, written near the end of his life and published posthumously, entitled *The Mysterious Stranger*. The tale is set in a small village in 16th century Austria, where three boys one day meet a young man different from themselves: "He had new and good clothes on, and was handsome and had a winning face and a pleasant voice, and was easy and graceful and unembarrassed, not slouchy and awkward and diffident, like other boys."

The mysterious stranger starts to do small but amazing tricks for them—causing water to turn to ice, conjuring grapes and bread out of thin air, even making birds out of clay that can fly. At last one boy, the story's narrator, works up the courage to ask the stranger who he is:

"An angel," he said, quite simply, and set another bird free and clapped his hands and made it fly away.

The angel then proceeds to really impress them by making an entire toy castle, complete with five hundred miniature soldiers and workmen that move around by themselves. Naturally the boys get involved with this ultimate playset, making their own knights and cannon and cavalry, and although they get rather nervous again when the angel reveals his name is Satan, he assures them he is not that Satan, but only named after the fallen one.

"We others are still ignorant of sin; we are not able to commit it; we are without blemish, and we shall abide in that estate always." Distracted by two of the miniature workmen, "Satan reached out his hand and crushed the life out of them with his fingers...and went on talking where he had left off: 'We cannot do wrong; neither have we any disposition to do it, for we do not know what it is.'"

Horrified as the other boys are, "he made us drunk with the joy of being with him and of looking into the heaven of his eyes, and of feeling the ecstasy that thrilled along our veins from the touch of his hand."

Yes, Kaworu Nagisa made quite an impression on the fans of *Neon Genesis Evangelion*, despite the fact that, in the original broadcast version of the TV show (before it got all director's-cutted, box-setted, special-editioned, and platinum-lined) he shows up for only slightly less than thirteen minutes of total screen time, the climax of which being an entire minute where nothing happens at all.

That's what being a beautiful angel will do for you, especially when you make the most of your thirteen minutes on Earth by having a whirlwind romance with the main character that ends in a lover's quarrel with Prog Knives and finally a voluntary martyrdom at the hand of your boy here. Relationships don't come any more tragic than that of Kaworu Nagisa and Shinji Ikari, and when fans (including this one) first saw it on TV, the affair was so brief and shocking the story logic of it didn't click in until much later.

In the anime, Kaworu is acknowledged as the Final Messenger, and, of all the Angels Shinji has to fight, this is the most ruthless battle, won at the highest possible cost to himself. It took even longer for me to realize that the showdown in episode 24 had also taken us full circle from Shinji's first fight in episodes 1 and 2, which emphasized his personal helplessness against the looming Angel Sachiel. Against Kaworu, it is the Angel who becomes the small, helpless figure, while Shinji is represented only by the gargantuan, frightful helm and arm of his Eva Unit-01. We never see Shinji's human face once throughout the whole final minute of decision.

So as Col. Trautman would have said instead of Major Katsuragi, "It's over, Shinji! IT'S OVER!" Kaworu v. Shinji (or Kaworu x Shinji, in the doujinshi) was the big final showdown between humanity and the Angels. And with the outcome leaving Shinji at his most wretched ever, wouldn't it be nice if everyone just died—your wish being Eva's command, as it turns out that fortunately humanity hardly ever needed the Angels to slaughter itself.

///

"I AM PERISHING ALREADY—I AM FAILING— I AM PASSING AWAY. IN A LITTLE WHILE YOU WILL BE ALONE IN SHORELESS SPACE, TO WANDER ITS LIMITLESS SOLITUDES WITHOUT FRIEND OR COMRADE FOREVER...BUT I, YOUR POOR SERVANT, HAVE REVEALED YOU TO YOURSELF AND SET YOU FREE. DREAM OTHER DREAMS, AND BETTER!"

—FROM *THE MYSTERIOUS STRANGER*

Satan's words near the end of Mark Twain's story also uncannily prefigure the end of the world and the Instrumentality, both of which follow his death in the TV show in such quick order you picture Anno as a hairnetted fry cook dinging the counter bell. By now you see Sadamoto's handling of Kaworu, and perhaps nothing illustrates the different experiences of the manga and the anime better than his handling of this critical character.

No longer the last Angel to be fought, Kaworu actually becomes an active Eva pilot and fights an Angel—the dude even has the nerve to observe the fight is fixed, based on his knowledge of SEELE's prophecies. Sadamoto of course introduces him at an earlier point in the narrative—at the equivalent of episode 19's end—and then sends him to NERV near the equivalent of episode 22's beginning—before certain important events, to put it mildly, can occur.

When one notes this kind of thing, of course, it's important to restate that the *Evangelion* manga has always been a separate but equal "official" version of Eva, with no particular obligation to align itself with the anime, and indeed it was with Book Five, the first released after *The End of Evangelion*, that Sadamoto began to truly seem free to go in his own direction.

Nevertheless, as the "other" official version of the Eva story, it is reasonable for fans to view it as an "alternate history" relative to the anime, and the way Kaworu has been introduced makes us realize the manga may end very differently indeed. Despite the fact we know here that Kaworu is an Angel from the very beginning, he appears destined to at least hang around long enough to pick up a few paychecks. It's not clear when your health benefits kick in at NERV, although if Ritsuko is your primary caregiver it might be best to forego them.

///

"AN ANGEL'S LOVE IS SUBLIME, ADORABLE, DIVINE, BEYOND THE IMAGINATION OF MAN— INFINITELY BEYOND IT! BUT IT IS LIMITED TO HIS OWN AUGUST ORDER. IF IT FELL UPON ONE OF YOUR RACE FOR ONLY AN INSTANT, IT WOULD CONSUME ITS OBJECT TO ASHES. NO, WE CANNOT LOVE MEN BUT WE CAN BE HARMLESSLY INDIFFERENT TO THEM; WE CAN ALSO LIKE THEM, SOMETIMES."

—FROM *THE MYSTERIOUS STRANGER*

In volume 9 we see the most staggering difference thus far between the manga and the anime; Sadamoto's Shinji doesn't even like Kaworu, much less love him. Of course, you could say the less-ethereal Kaworu of the manga is harder to love. I can't believe Sadamoto had him tell Rei he thought she'd be "heftier." And yet he did.

I don't think any A.T. fields actually got penetrated in the anime. While I do think Shinji felt sexually attracted to Kaworu, and that you the audience are supposed to feel that he felt it, what Kaworu himself thought was a very different matter. Like Rei, I believe Kaworu to be innocent—coyly, he appears not to be so, because while Rei needed to be reached out to, Kaworu has come to reach out; whereas Rei has spent her existence being observed, Kaworu has come to observe.

Indeed, in the manga, Shinji's irritation about Kaworu's invasion of his personal space seems almost a parody of his attitude in the anime. In the TV show, when Kaworu put his hand on Shinji's, he flinched but did not pull away; whereas in the manga it's easy to imagine Shinji slugging him. Instead he goes to run after Rei, hoping to get closer to her again.

I hardly think the change reflects any phobia on Sadamoto's part (after all, we even get to see Shinji's "Unit One" in the manga), but the fact is the manga Shinji is less emotionally bleak and empty, and hence less vulnerable. Shinji's just as negative in the manga, of course, but it's an active variety, rather than the passive negative creep (in the best Nirvana song sense) we know from the anime. We don't have to imagine him slugging Gendo; from the look of surprise on Dad's face in Book Seven he would have smacked the beard off his face if Kaji hadn't stopped him.

Neither is Shinji in a positive emotional situation where we leave him here, either; indeed at this point in the manga there's arguably no one he can turn to—the more brutal fate that befell Toji has cut him off from his school friends, Rei has become hesitant, Kaji is dead, and his perennial self-esteem booster Asuka is going to need to rebuild her internal supply before she can even get back to calling him a loser and idiot.

So, like Misato trying to put her own hand on Shinji's, all I can do for now while we wait for Sadamoto Sensei is to recommend for your winter vacation reading list *The Mysterious Stranger*, which I can almost guarantee will give you new angles to think about Kaworu, and may even earn you class credit besides. A quick look at the novel's comments on Amazon list a teacher who says fundamentalist students walked out of his class when he taught it; another compares it to *The Matrix*; those who dislike it call it "sick," "bitter," and "twisted." Sounds like good old *Evangelion* to me!

—Carl Gustav Horn

Although The Mysterious Stranger *can also be found in a number of print editions, including* The Portable Mark Twain *from Penguin Books (haw haw) the story is legally available online at* **http://etext.lib.virginia.edu/toc/modeng/public/TwaMyst.html.**

The same site has a book called The Holy Bible, King James Version, *which fans of Evangelion might also enjoy, although it's technically "Editor's Choice."*

NERV

GOD'S IN HIS HEAVEN. ALL'S RIGHT WITH THE WORLD.

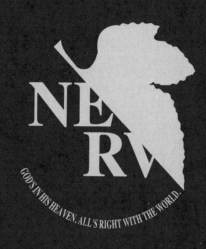

NEON GENESIS EVANGELION
VOLUME 4, PART 2

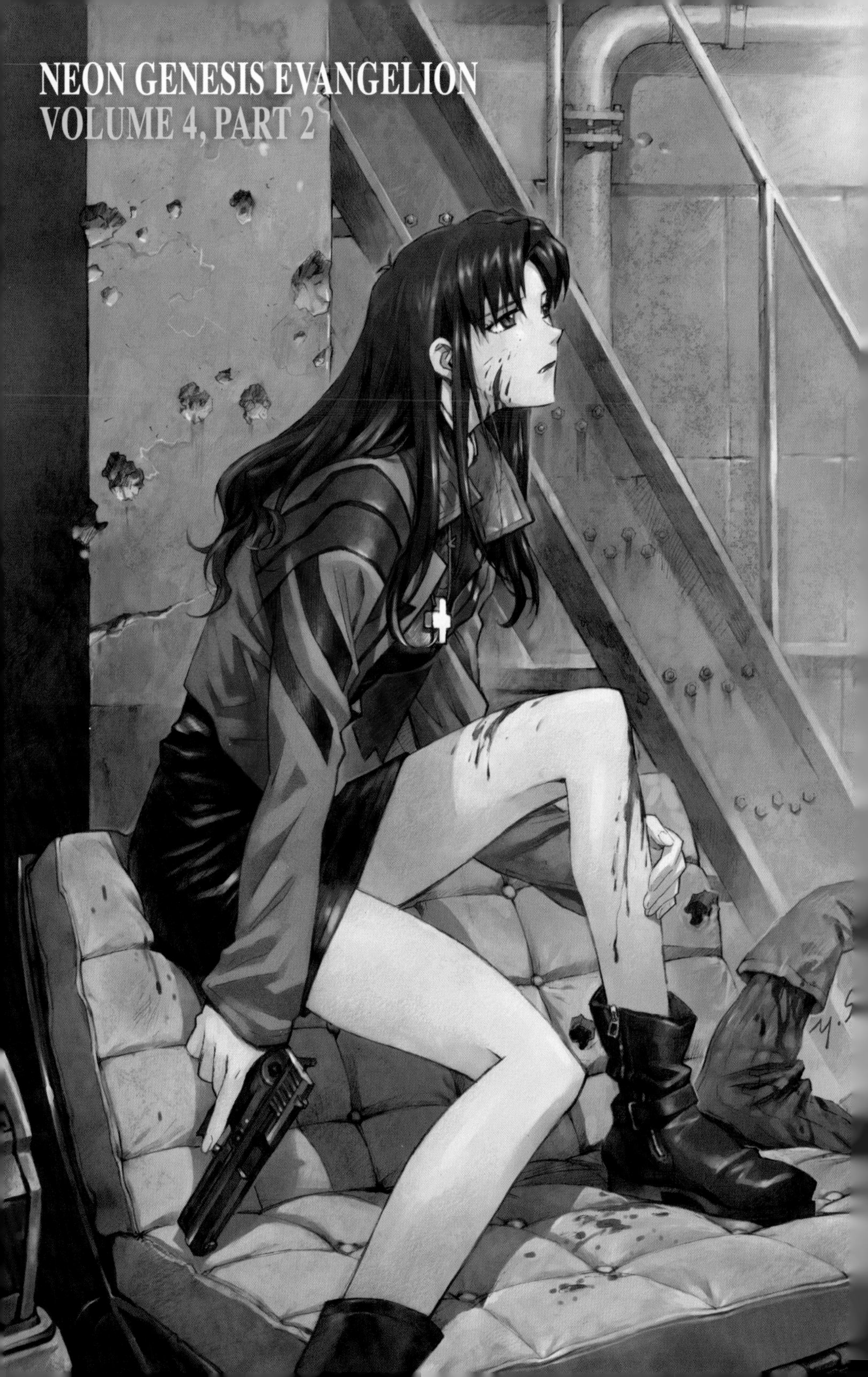

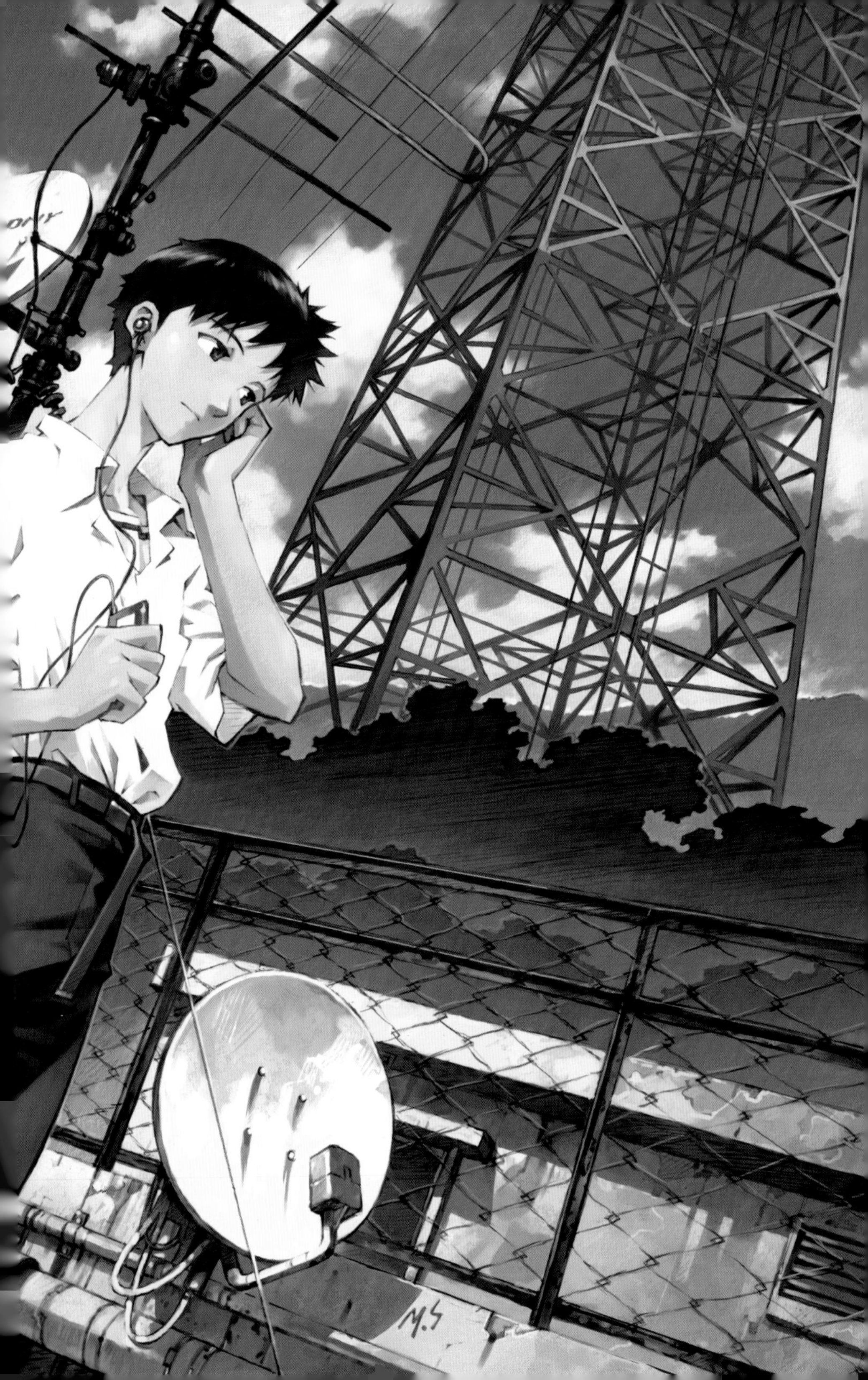

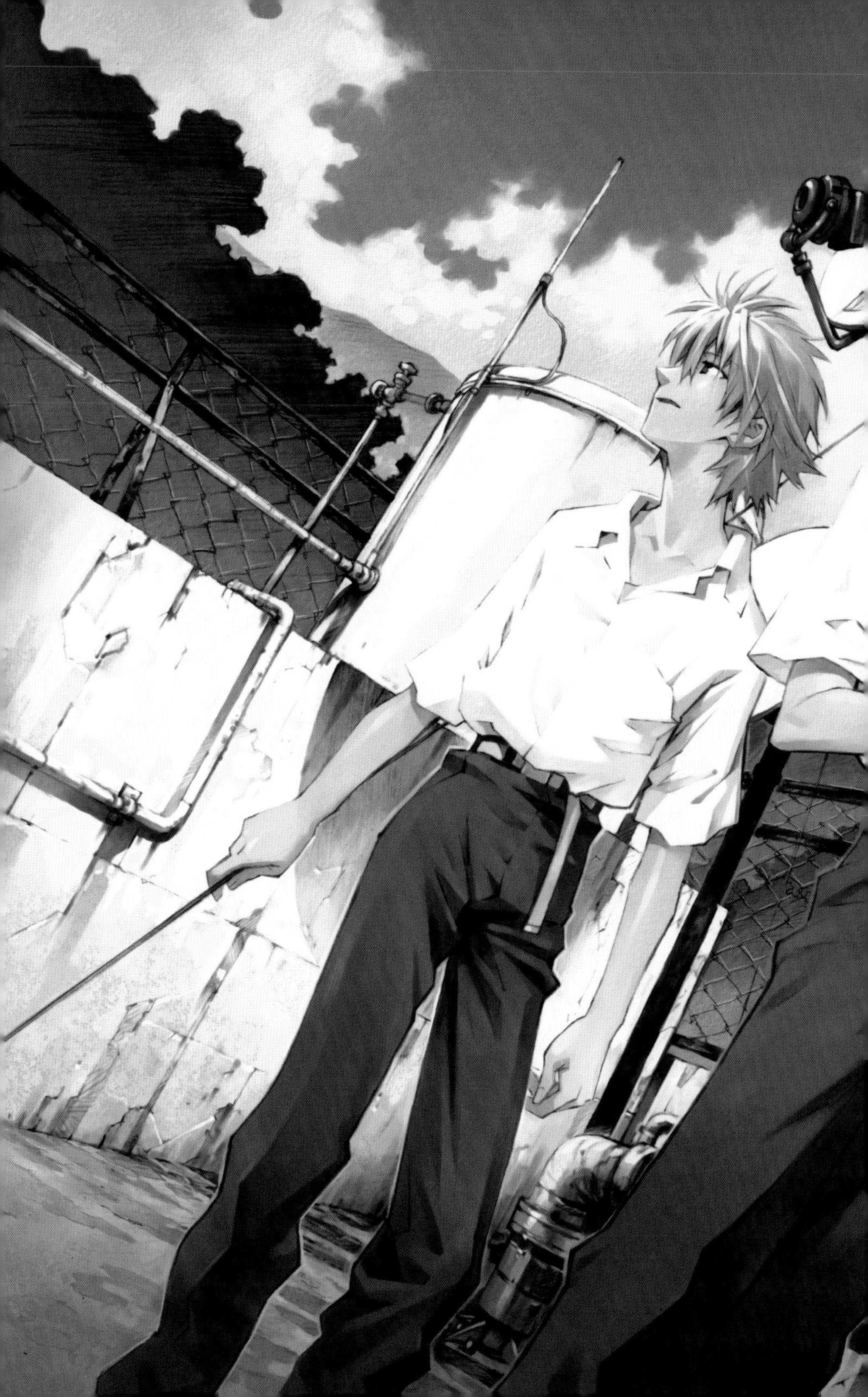

CONTENTS

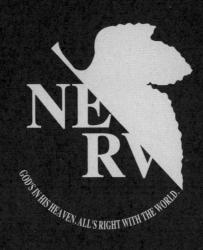
GOD'S IN HIS HEAVEN. ALL'S RIGHT WITH THE WORLD.

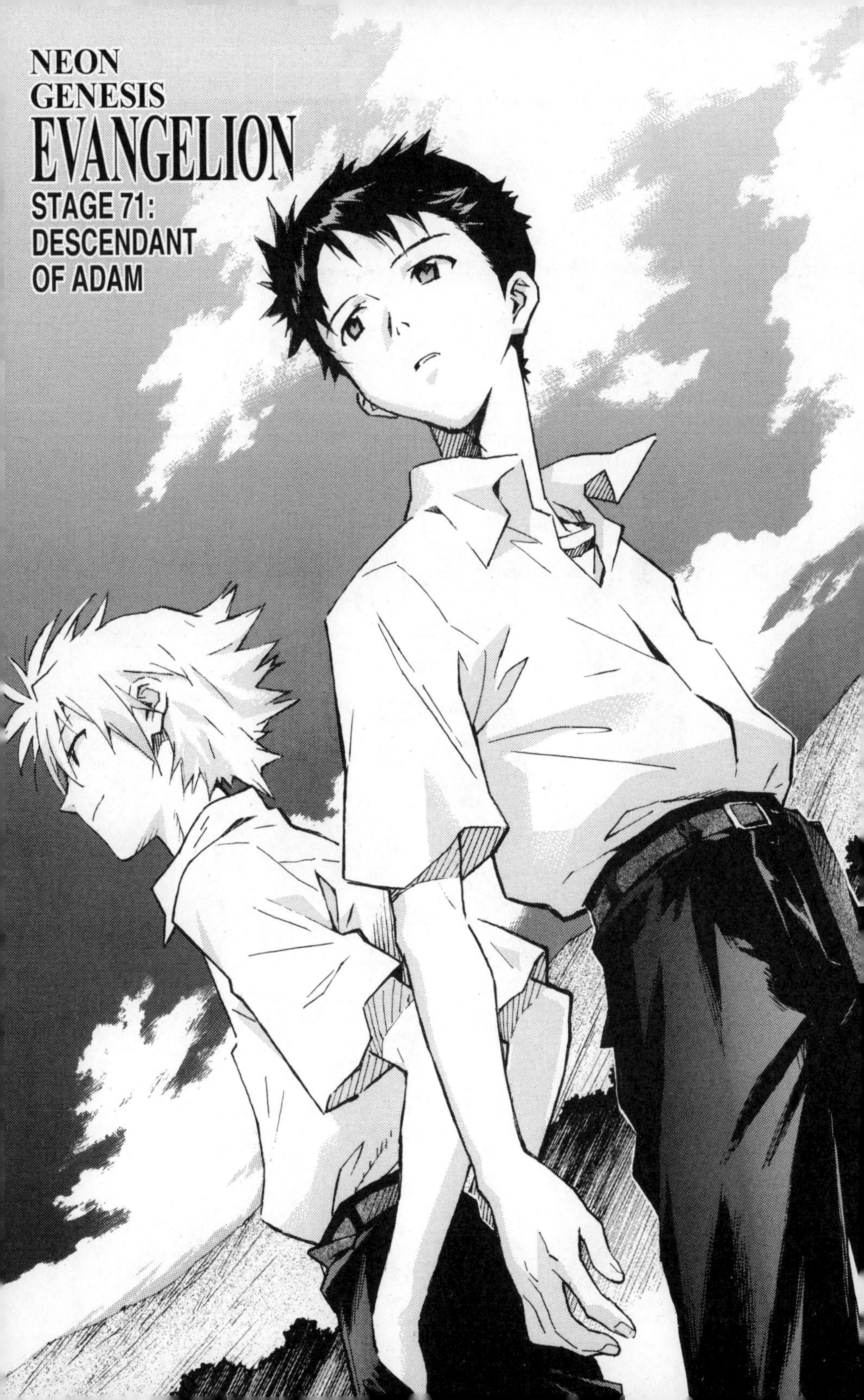
NEON GENESIS EVANGELION
STAGE 71:
DESCENDANT OF ADAM

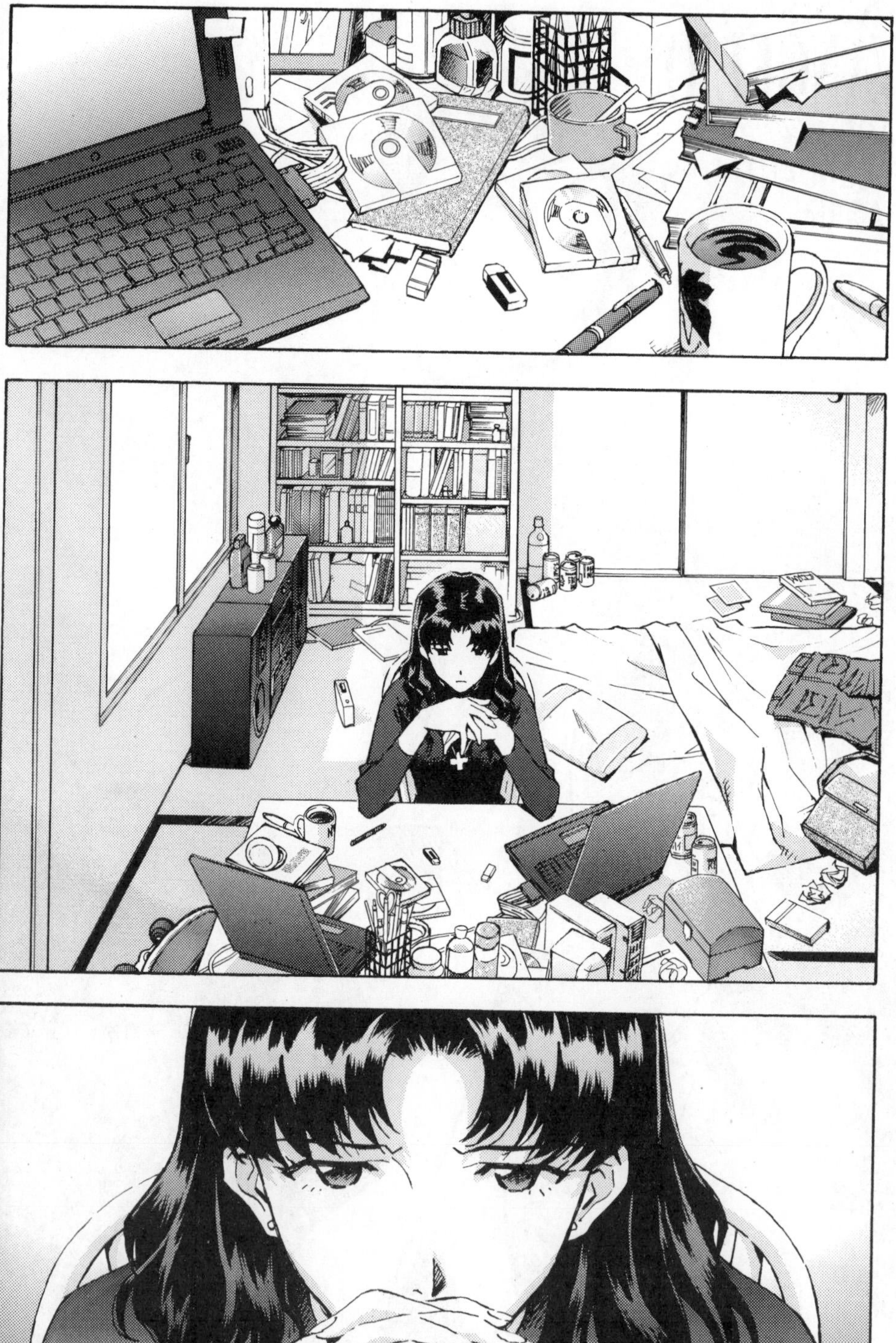

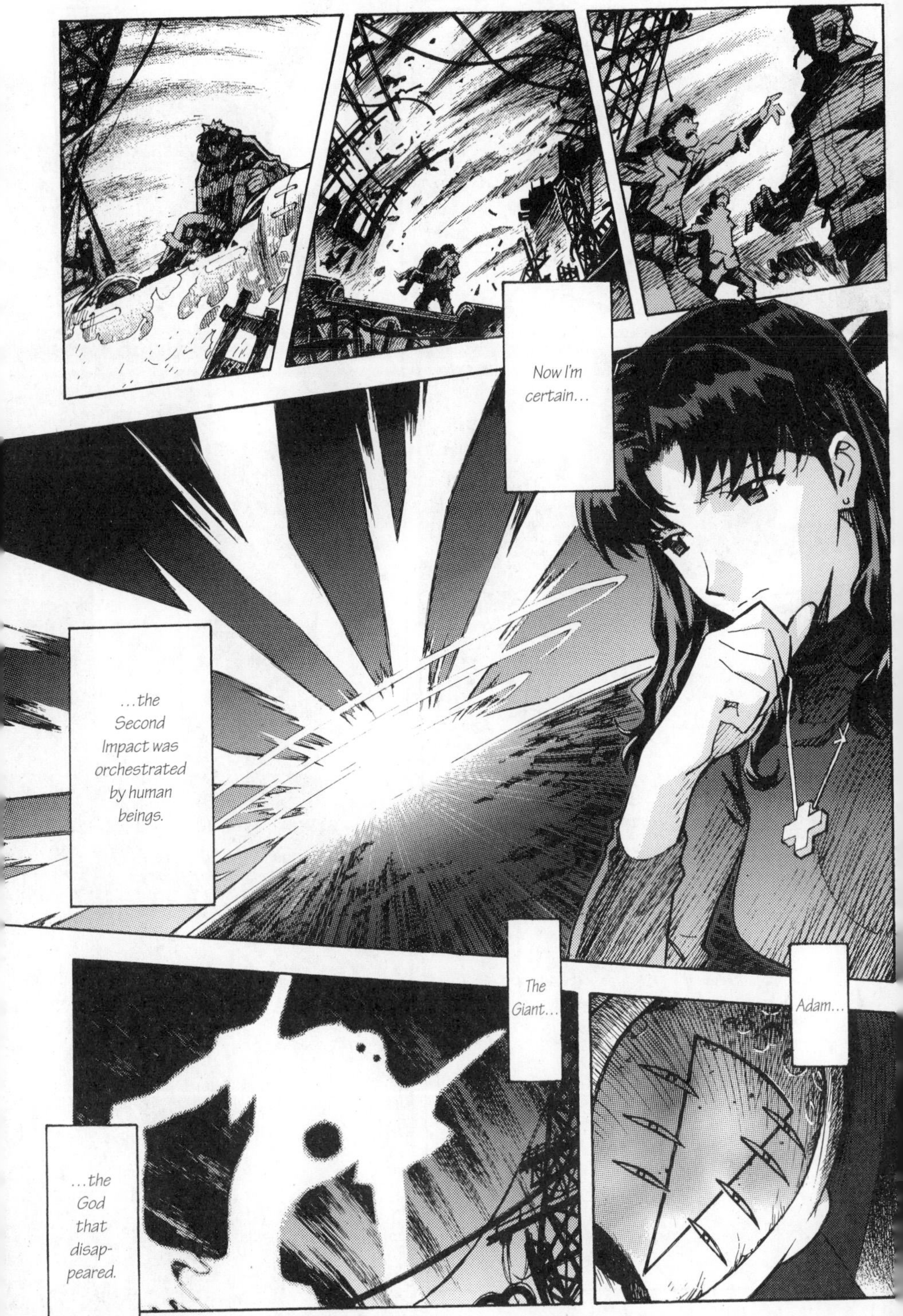
Now I'm certain...
...the Second Impact was orchestrated by human beings.
Adam...
The Giant...
...the God that disappeared.

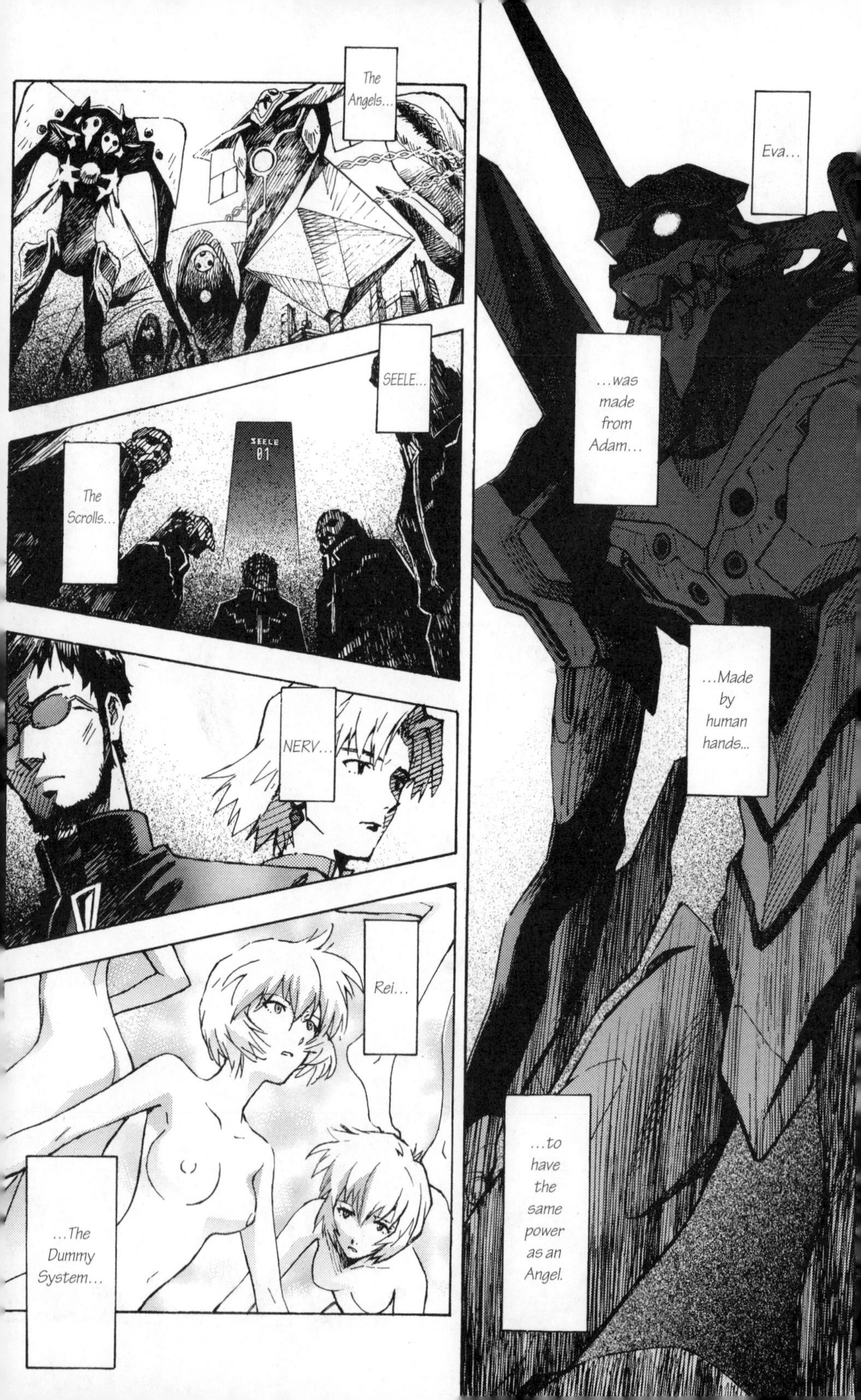
Eva…
…was made from Adam…
…Made by human hands…
…to have the same power as an Angel.
The Angels…
SEELE…
SEELE 01
The Scrolls…
NERV…
Rei…
…The Dummy System…

EVEN I'M START-ING TO SEE IT...

...THE AWFUL THING...

...THAT'S GOING TO HAPPEN.

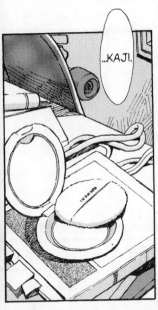

...KAJI.

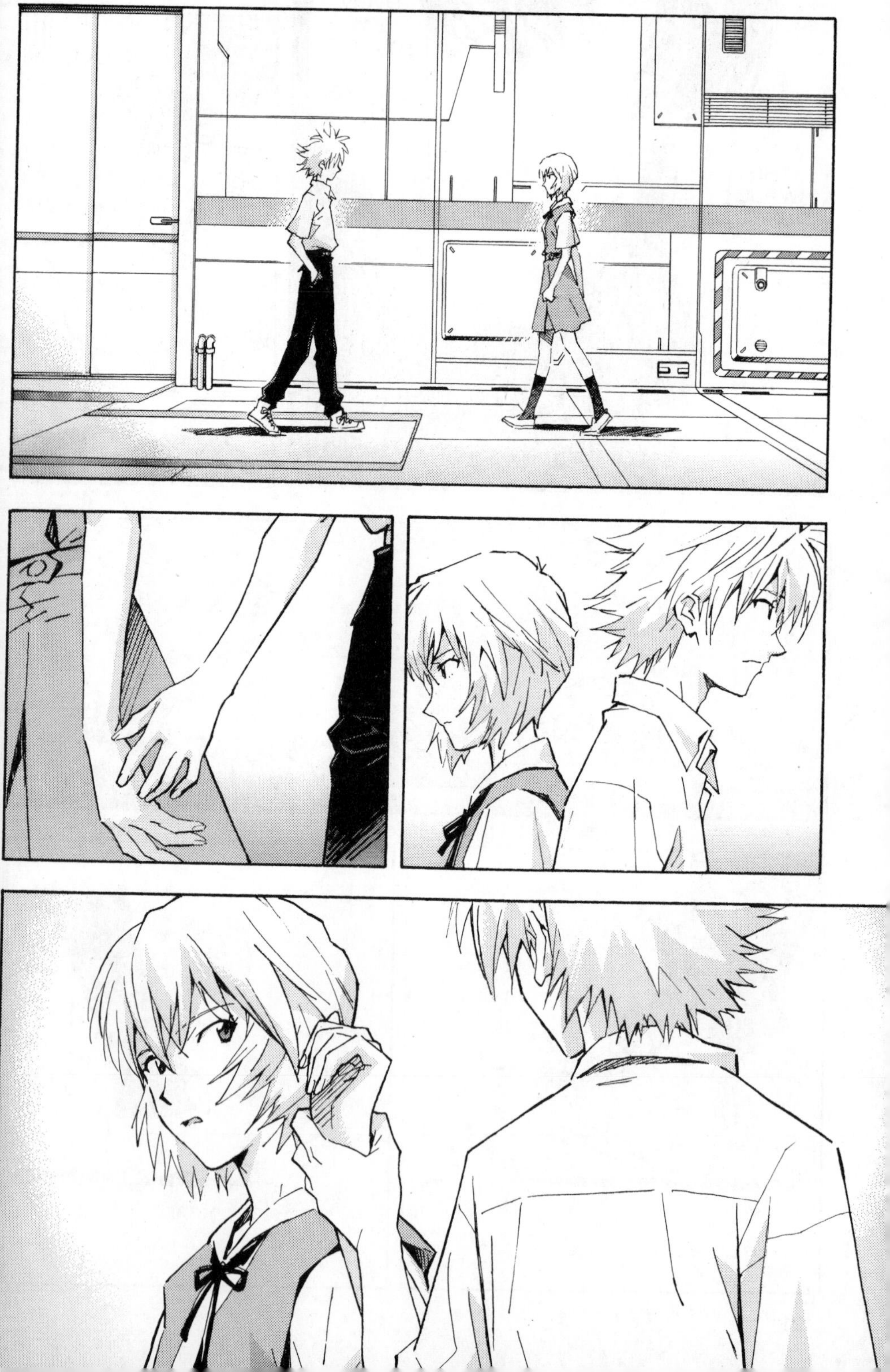

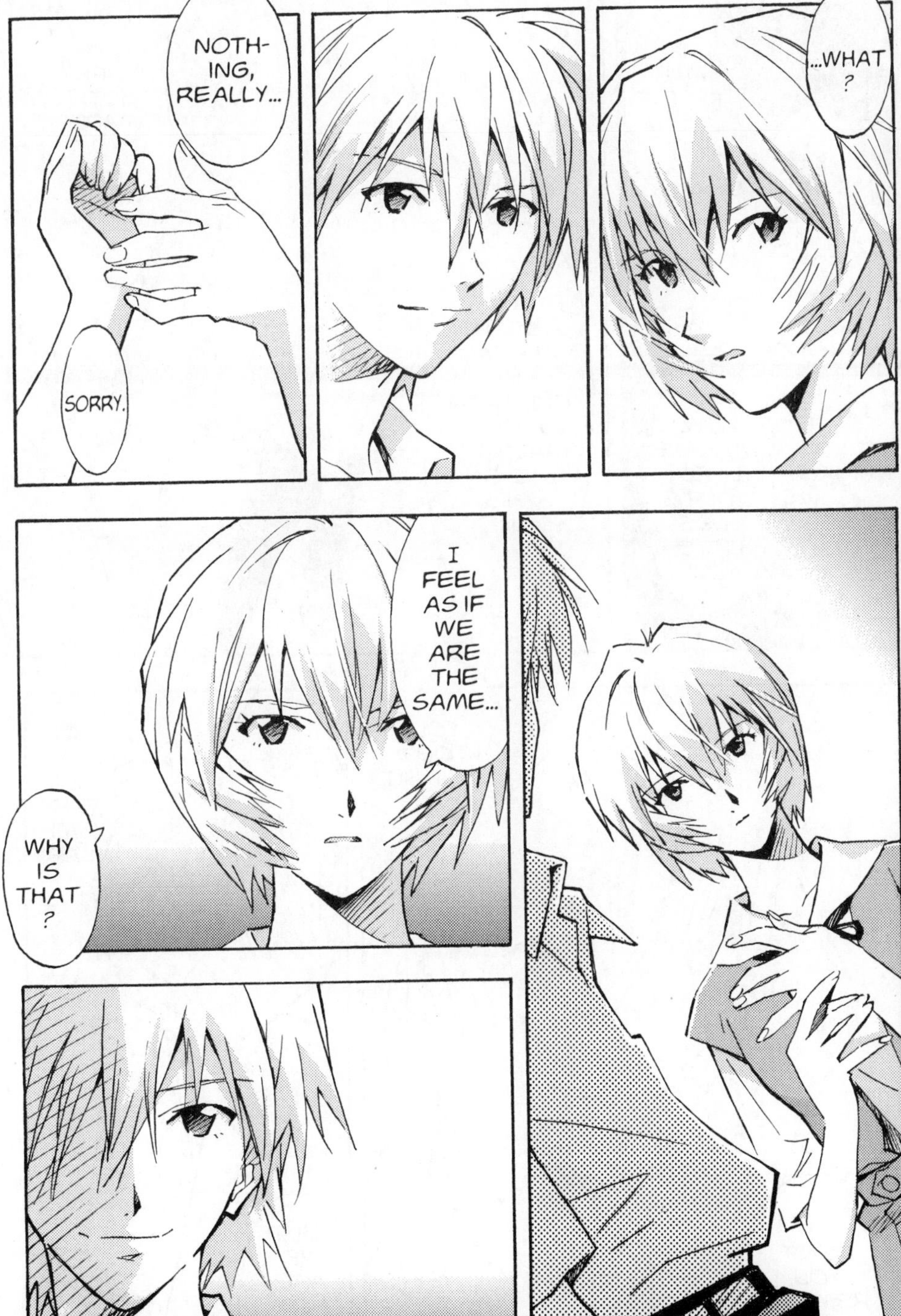
NOTH-ING, REALLY...
SORRY.
...WHAT?
I FEEL AS IF WE ARE THE SAME...
WHY IS THAT?

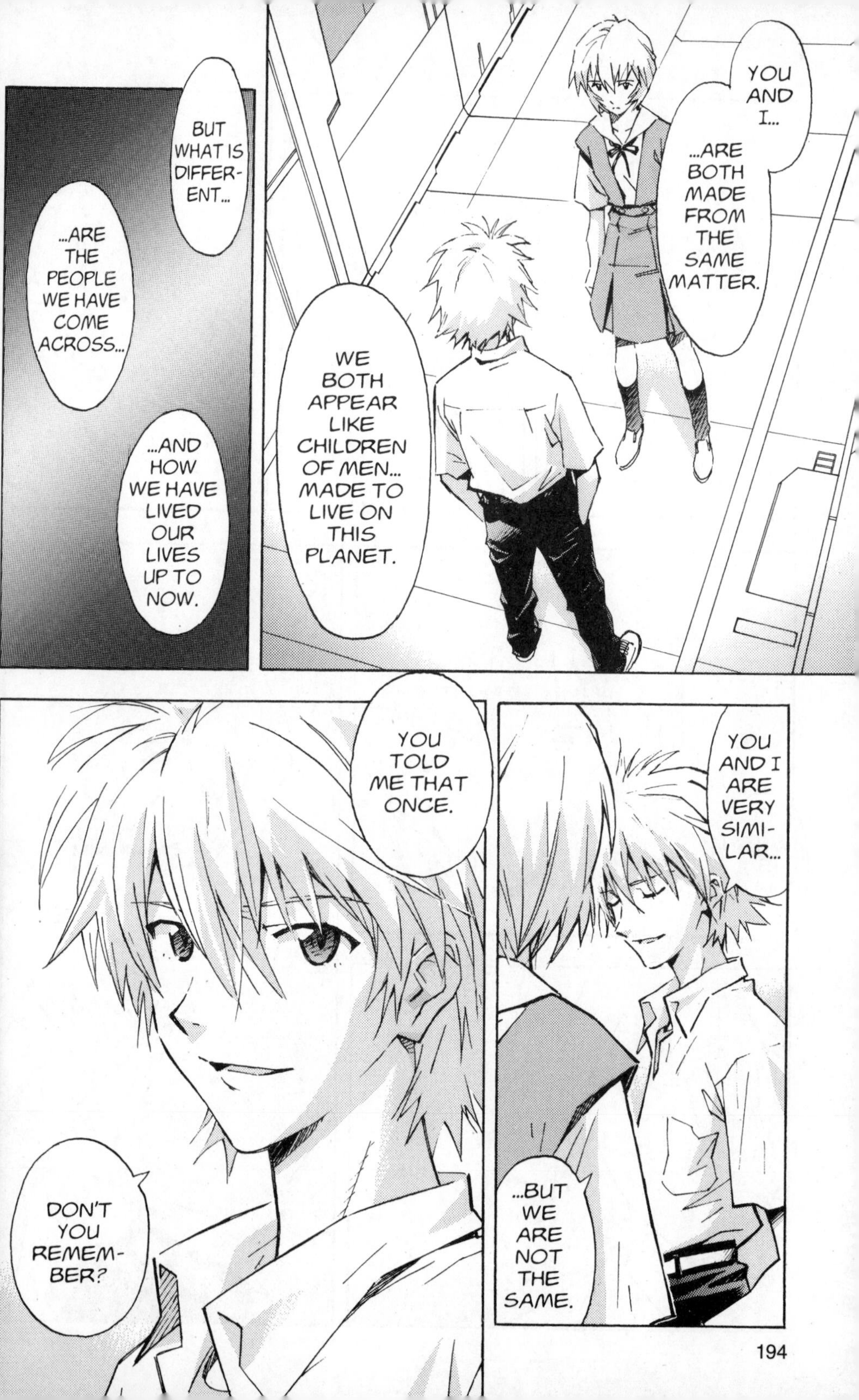
YOU AND I...
...ARE BOTH MADE FROM THE SAME MATTER.
WE BOTH APPEAR LIKE CHILDREN OF MEN... MADE TO LIVE ON THIS PLANET.
BUT WHAT IS DIFFER-ENT...
...ARE THE PEOPLE WE HAVE COME ACROSS...
...AND HOW WE HAVE LIVED OUR LIVES UP TO NOW.
YOU AND I ARE VERY SIMI-LAR...
...BUT WE ARE NOT THE SAME.
YOU TOLD ME THAT ONCE.
DON'T YOU REMEM-BER?

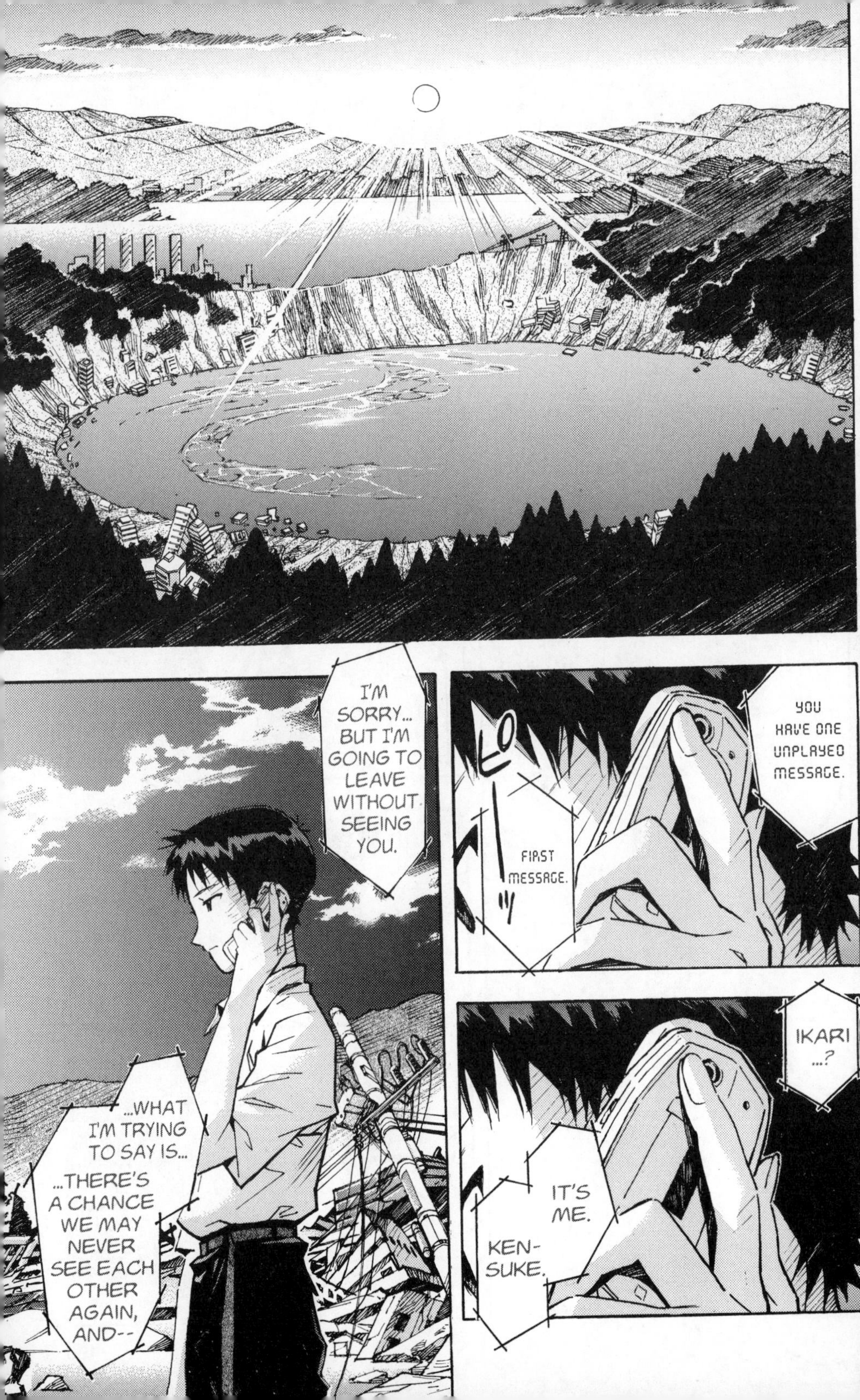
YOU HAVE ONE UNPLAYED MESSAGE.
FIRST MESSAGE.
IKARI ...?
IT'S ME.
KEN-SUKE.
I'M SORRY... BUT I'M GOING TO LEAVE WITHOUT SEEING YOU.
...WHAT I'M TRYING TO SAY IS...
...THERE'S A CHANCE WE MAY NEVER SEE EACH OTHER AGAIN, AND--

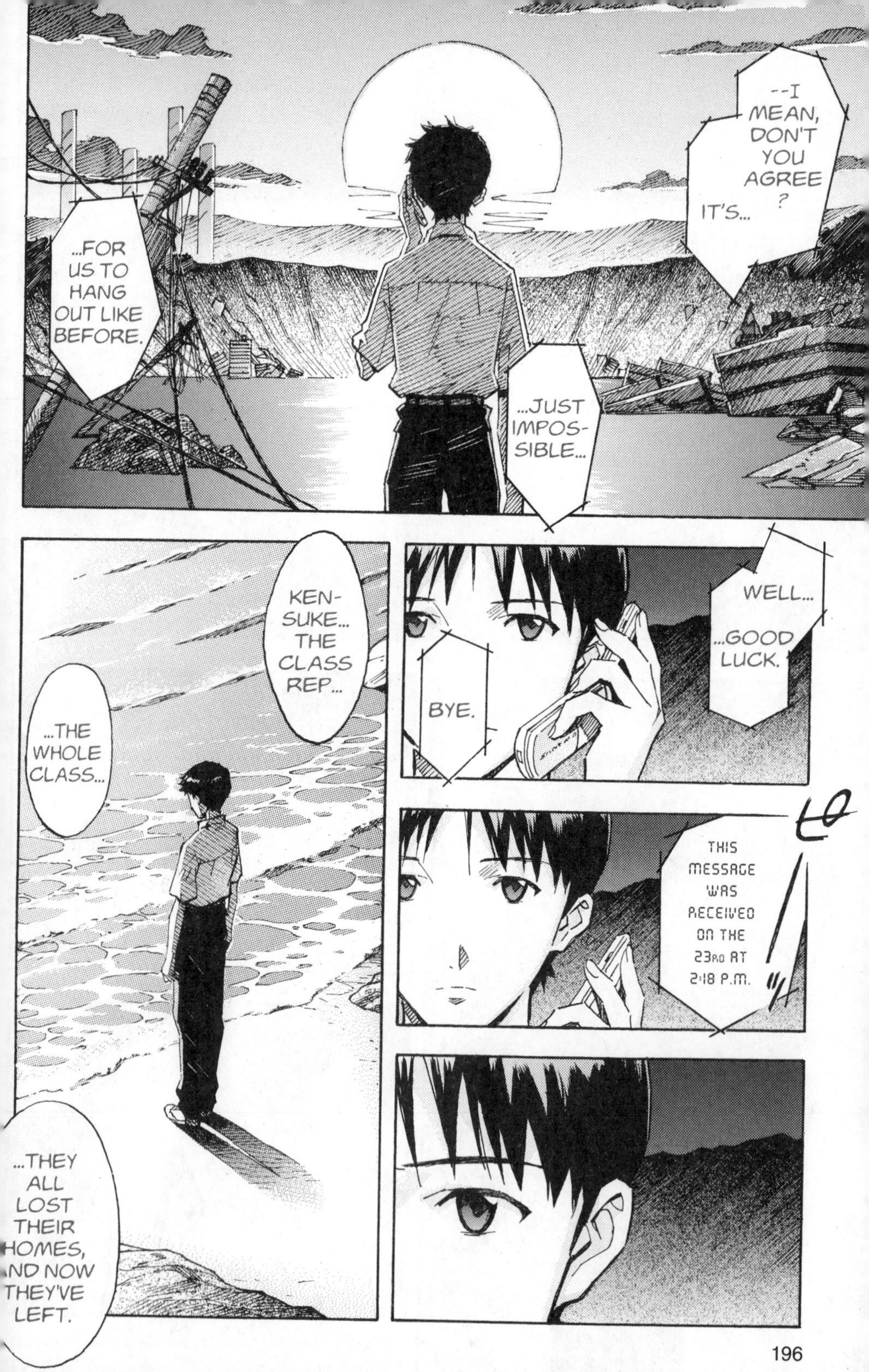
--I MEAN, DON'T YOU AGREE?
IT'S...
...JUST IMPOSSIBLE...
...FOR US TO HANG OUT LIKE BEFORE.
WELL...
...GOOD LUCK.
BYE.
THIS MESSAGE WAS RECEIVED ON THE 23RD AT 2:18 P.M.
KEN-SUKE... THE CLASS REP...
...THE WHOLE CLASS...
...THEY ALL LOST THEIR HOMES, ND NOW THEY'VE LEFT.

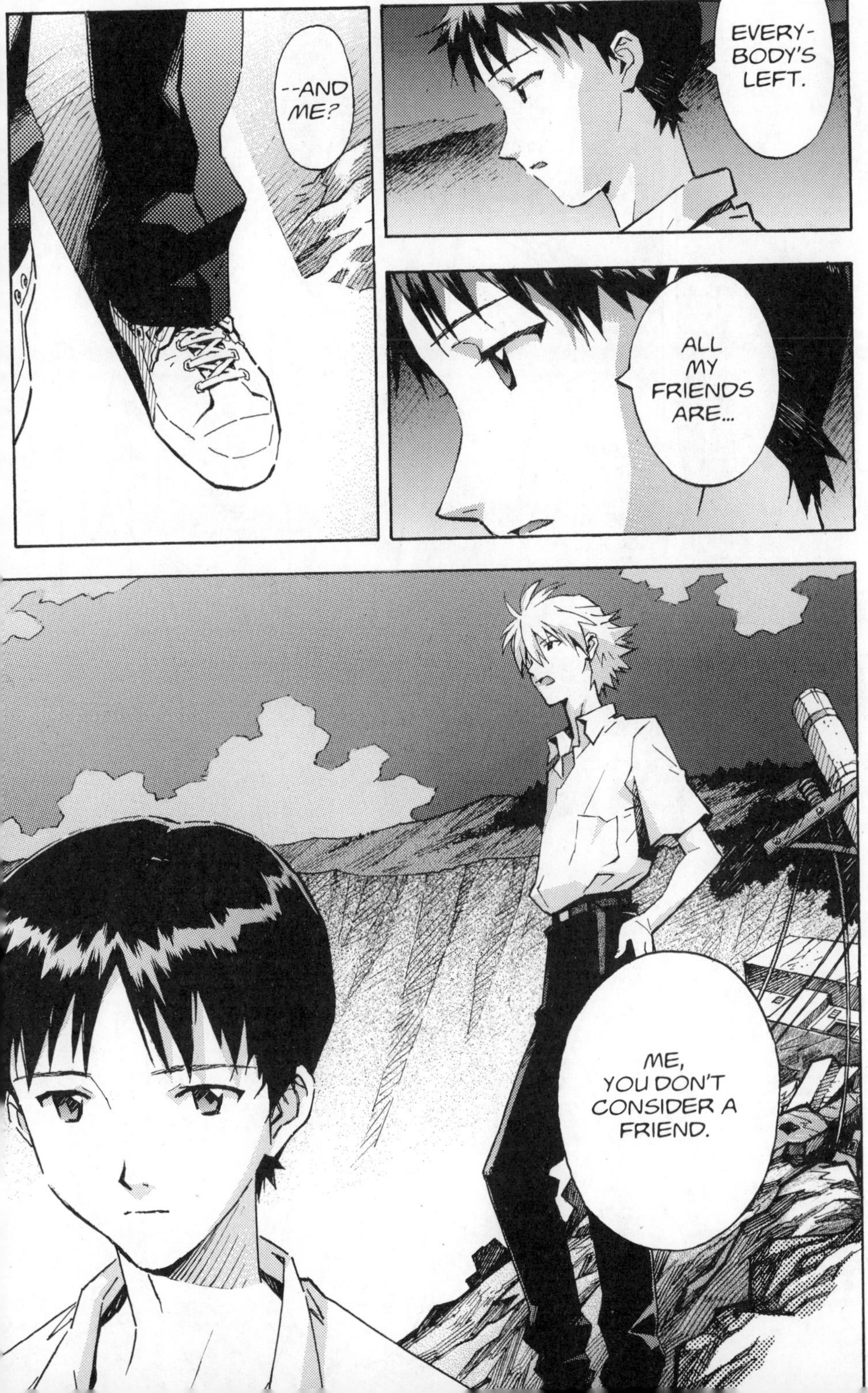
EVERY-BODY'S LEFT.
ALL MY FRIENDS ARE...
--AND ME?
ME, YOU DON'T CONSIDER A FRIEND.

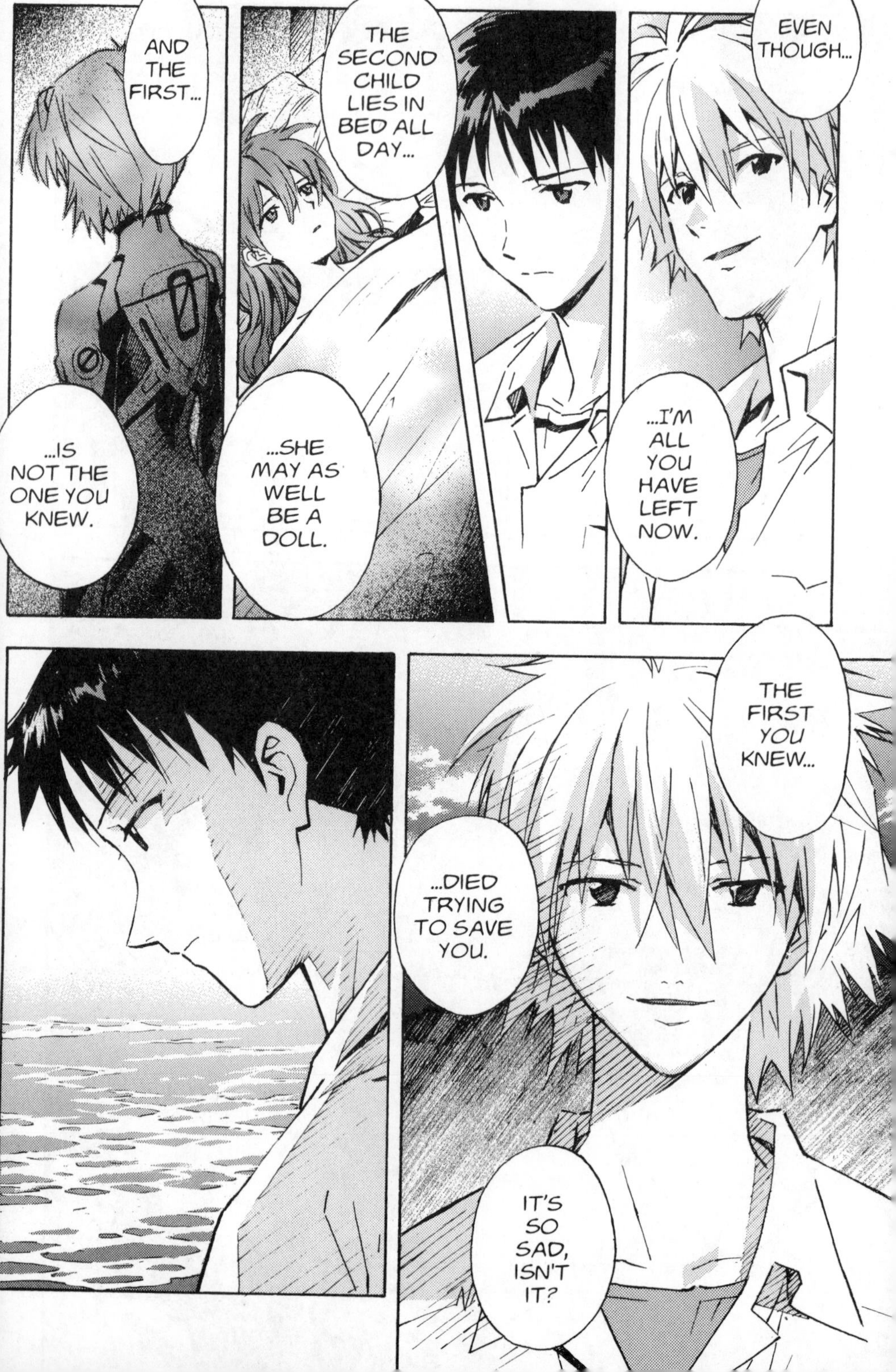
EVEN THOUGH...
...I'M ALL YOU HAVE LEFT NOW.
THE SECOND CHILD LIES IN BED ALL DAY...
...SHE MAY AS WELL BE A DOLL.
AND THE FIRST...
...IS NOT THE ONE YOU KNEW.
THE FIRST YOU KNEW...
...DIED TRYING TO SAVE YOU.
IT'S SO SAD, ISN'T IT?

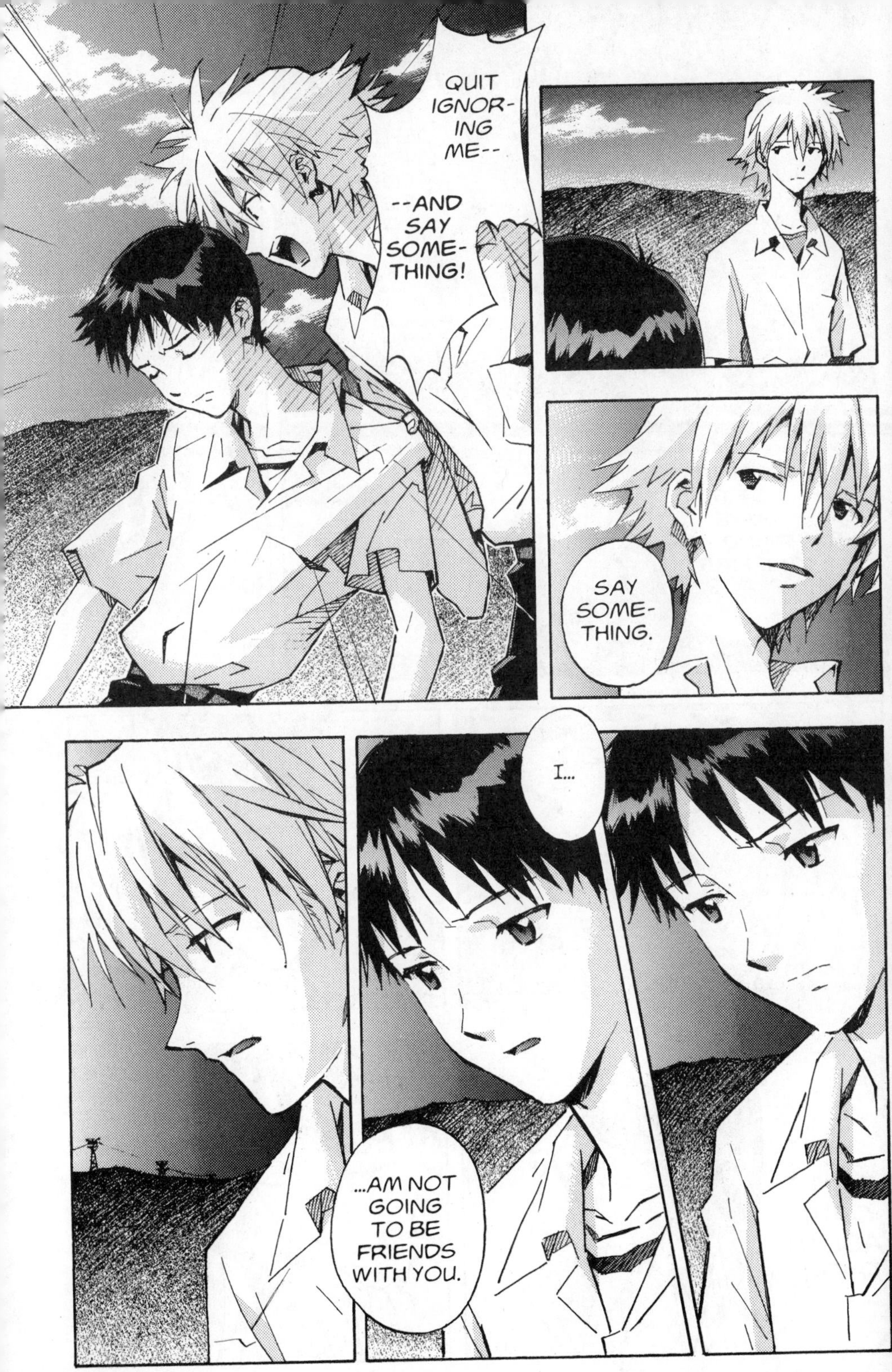
SAY SOMETHING.
QUIT IGNORING ME--
--AND SAY SOMETHING!
I...
...AM NOT GOING TO BE FRIENDS WITH YOU.

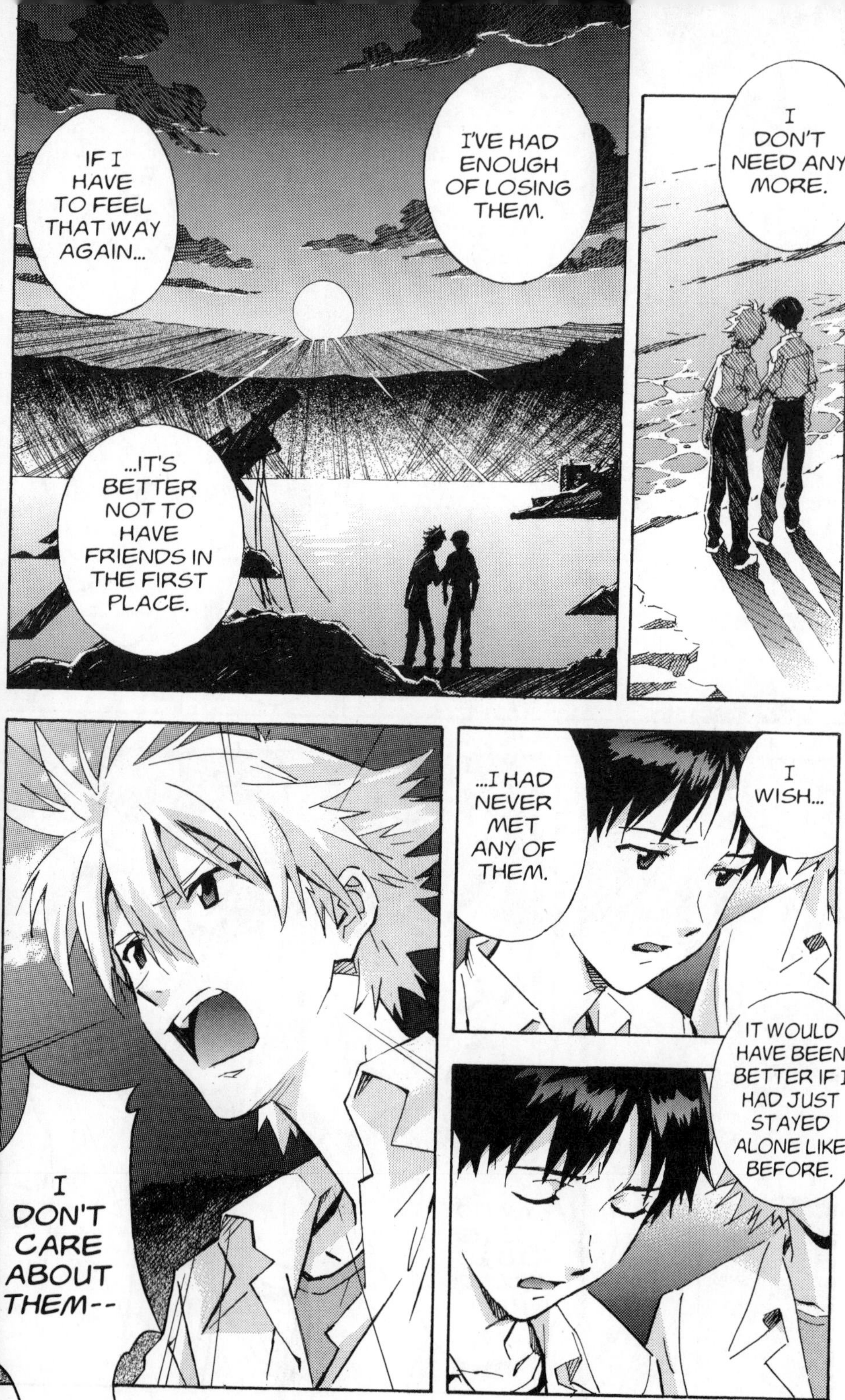
I DON'T NEED ANY MORE.
I'VE HAD ENOUGH OF LOSING THEM.
IF I HAVE TO FEEL THAT WAY AGAIN...
...IT'S BETTER NOT TO HAVE FRIENDS IN THE FIRST PLACE.
I WISH...
...I HAD NEVER MET ANY OF THEM.
IT WOULD HAVE BEEN BETTER IF I HAD JUST STAYED ALONE LIKE BEFORE.
I DON'T CARE ABOUT THEM--

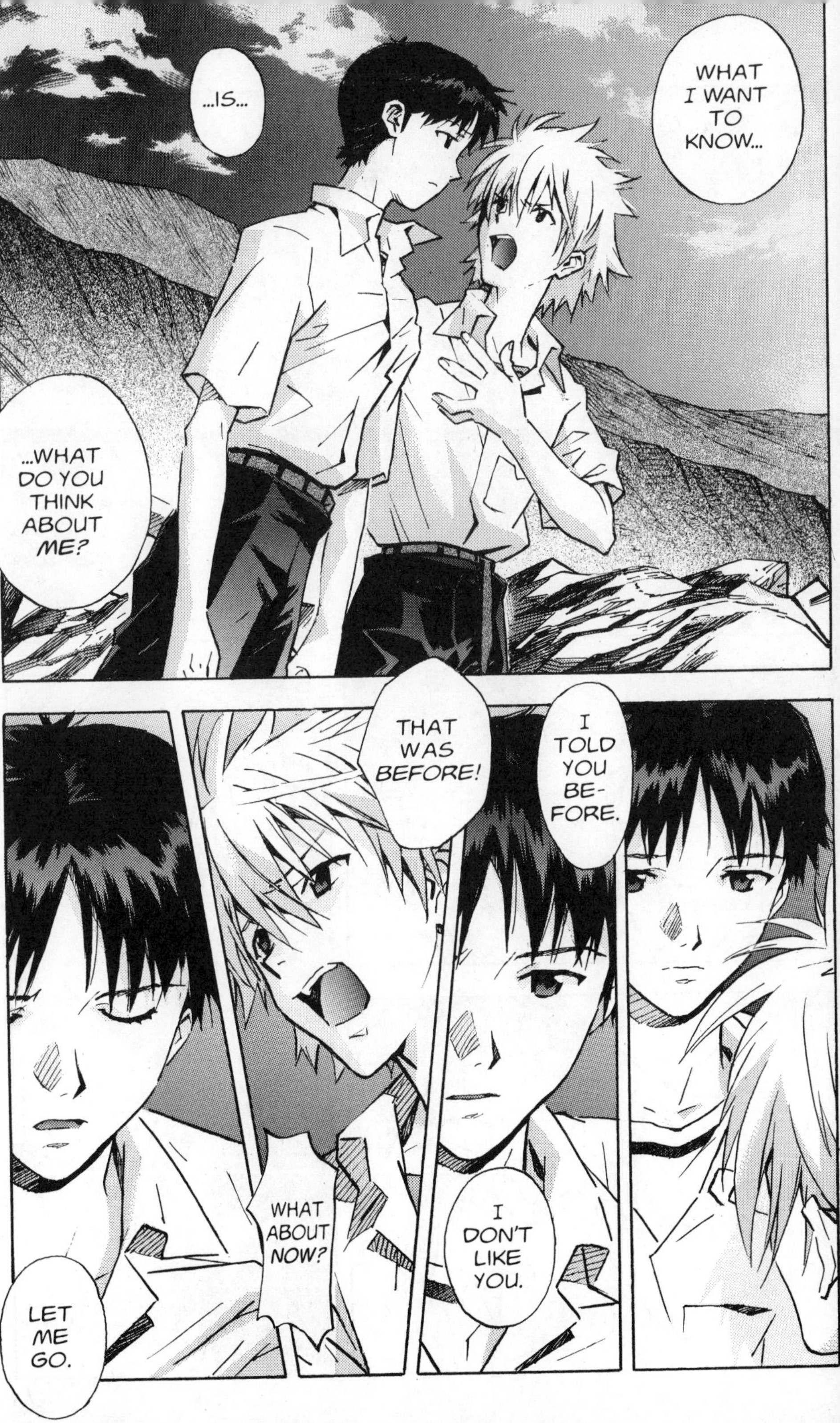
WHAT I WANT TO KNOW...
...IS...
...WHAT DO YOU THINK ABOUT *ME?*
I TOLD YOU BE-FORE.
THAT WAS *BEFORE!*
WHAT ABOUT *NOW?*
I DON'T LIKE YOU.
LET ME GO.

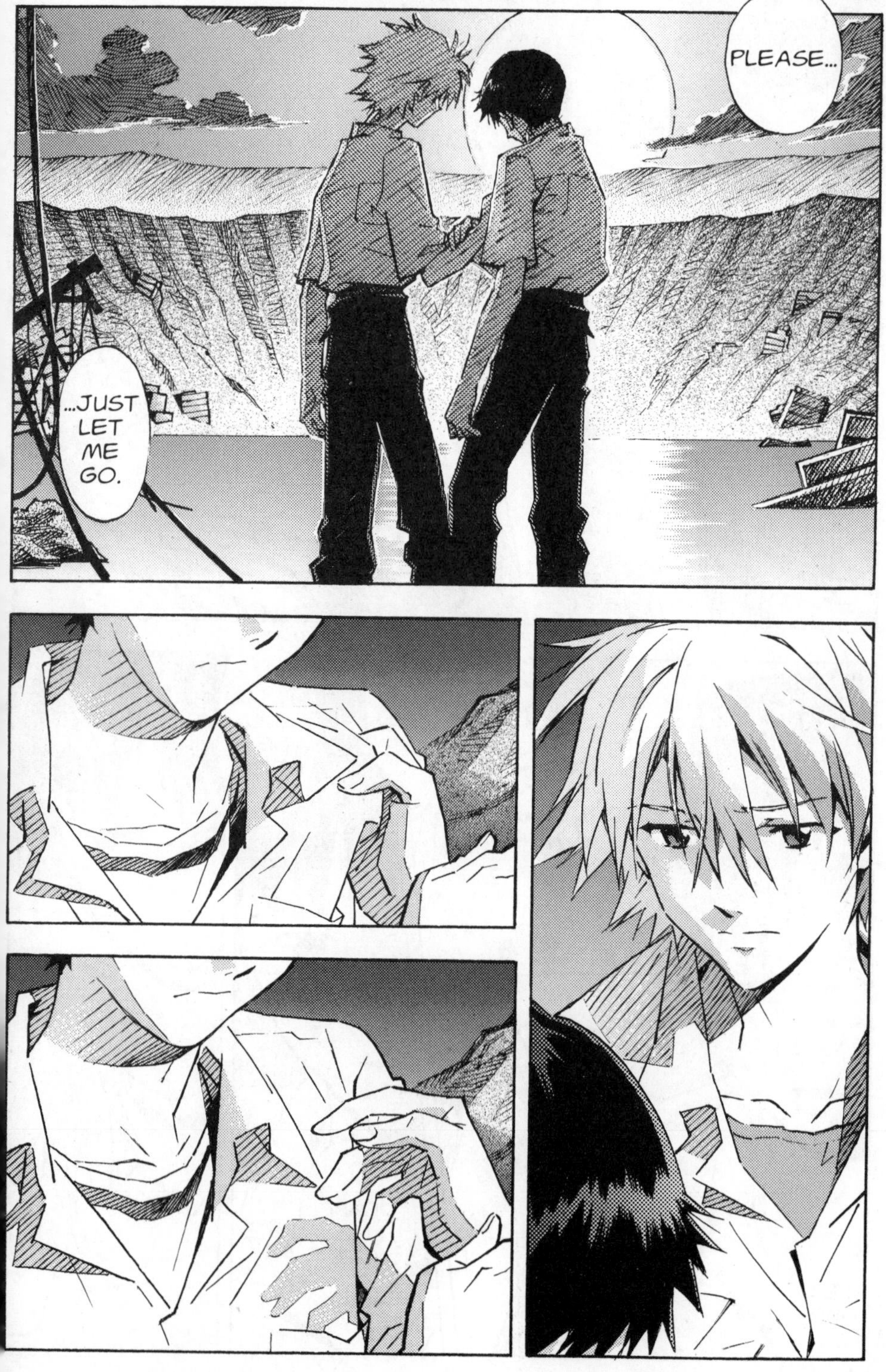
PLEASE...
...JUST LET ME GO.

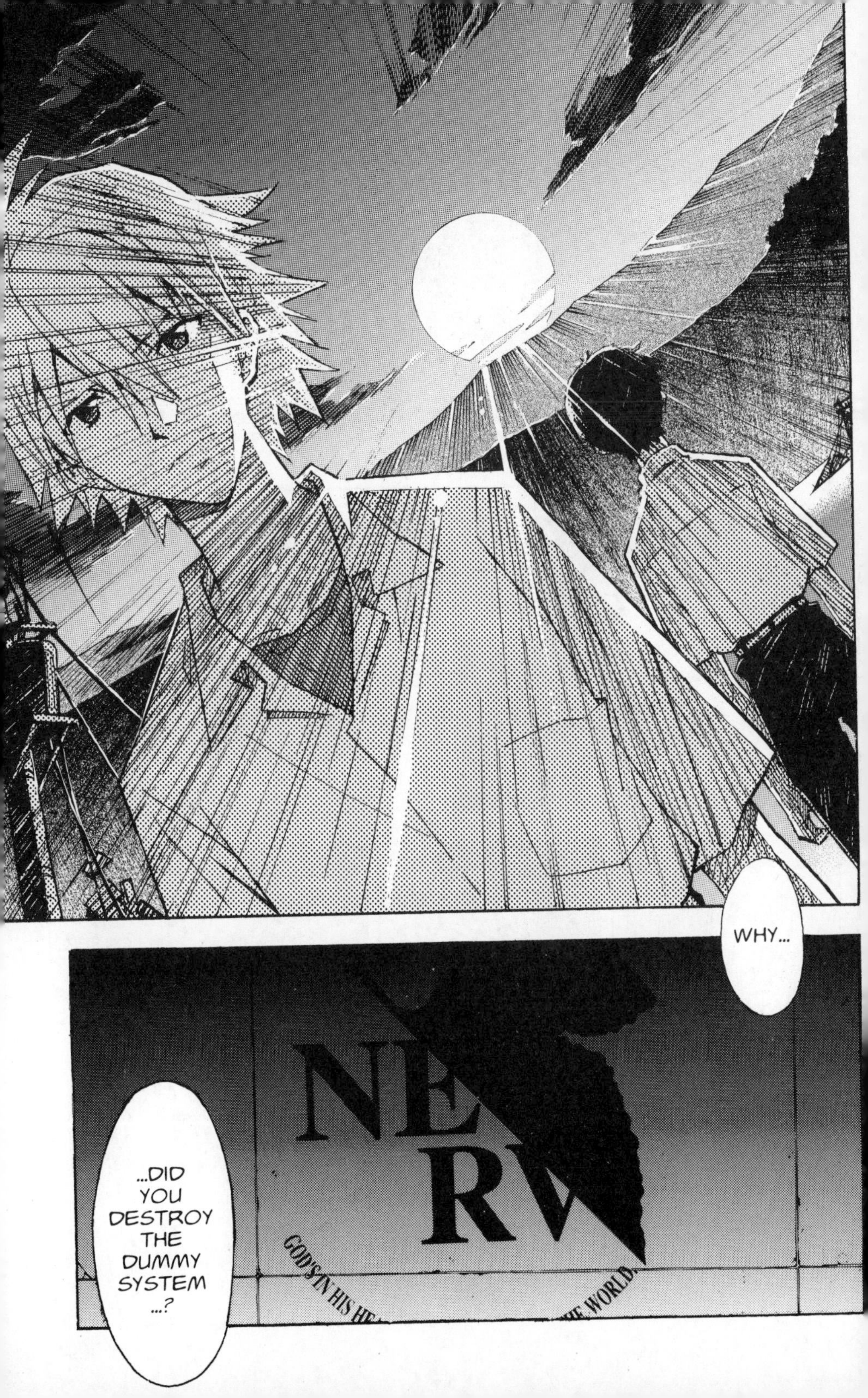
WHY...
NERV
GOD'S IN HIS HE... THE WORLD
...DID YOU DESTROY THE DUMMY SYSTEM ...?

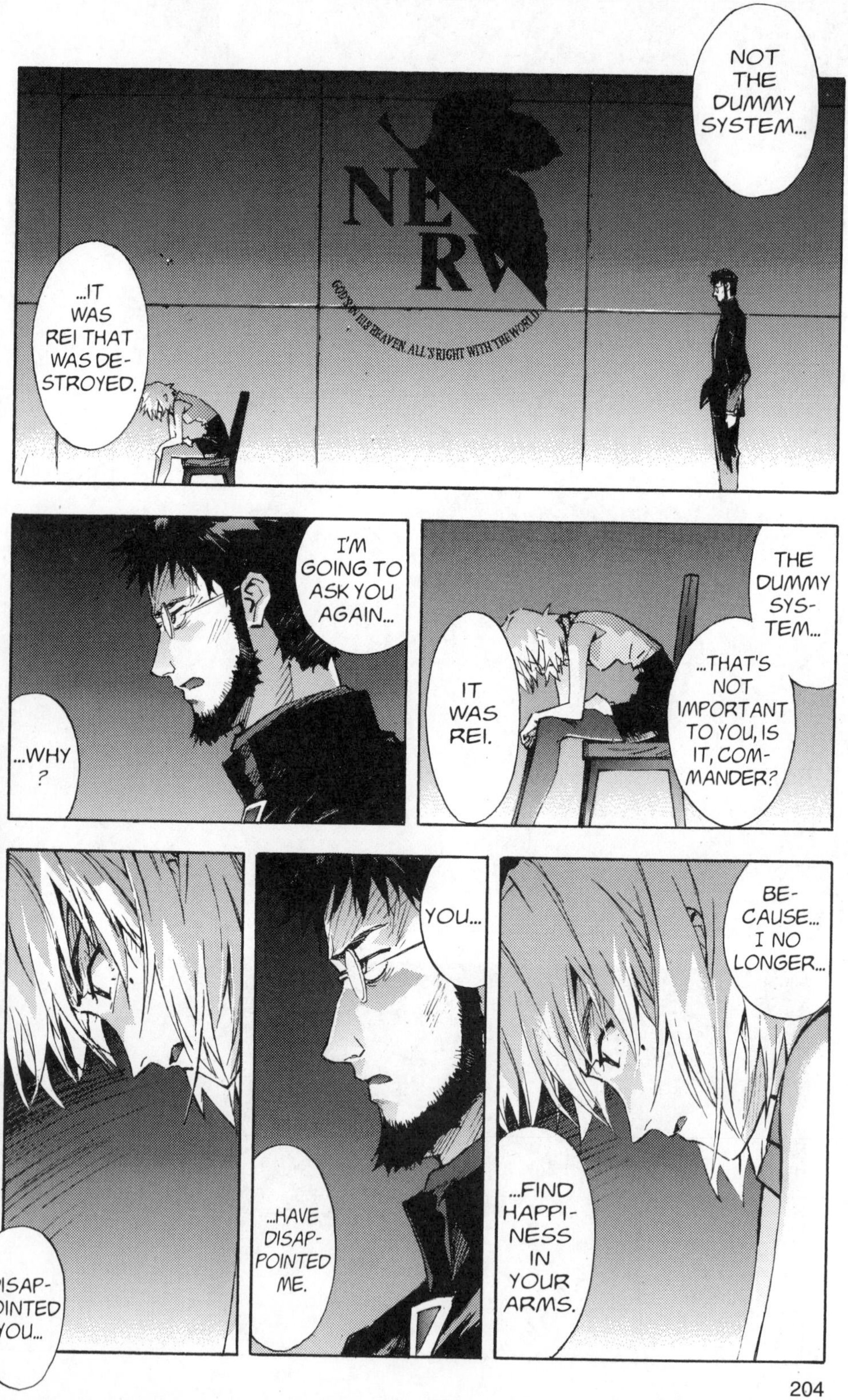
NOT THE DUMMY SYSTEM...
NERV
GOD'S IN HIS HEAVEN. ALL'S RIGHT WITH THE WORLD
...IT WAS REI THAT WAS DE-STROYED.
THE DUMMY SYS-TEM...
...THAT'S NOT IMPORTANT TO YOU, IS IT, COM-MANDER?
IT WAS REI.
I'M GOING TO ASK YOU AGAIN...
...WHY?
BE-CAUSE... I NO LONGER...
...FIND HAPPI-NESS IN YOUR ARMS.
YOU...
...HAVE DISAP-POINTED ME.
DISAP-POINTED YOU...

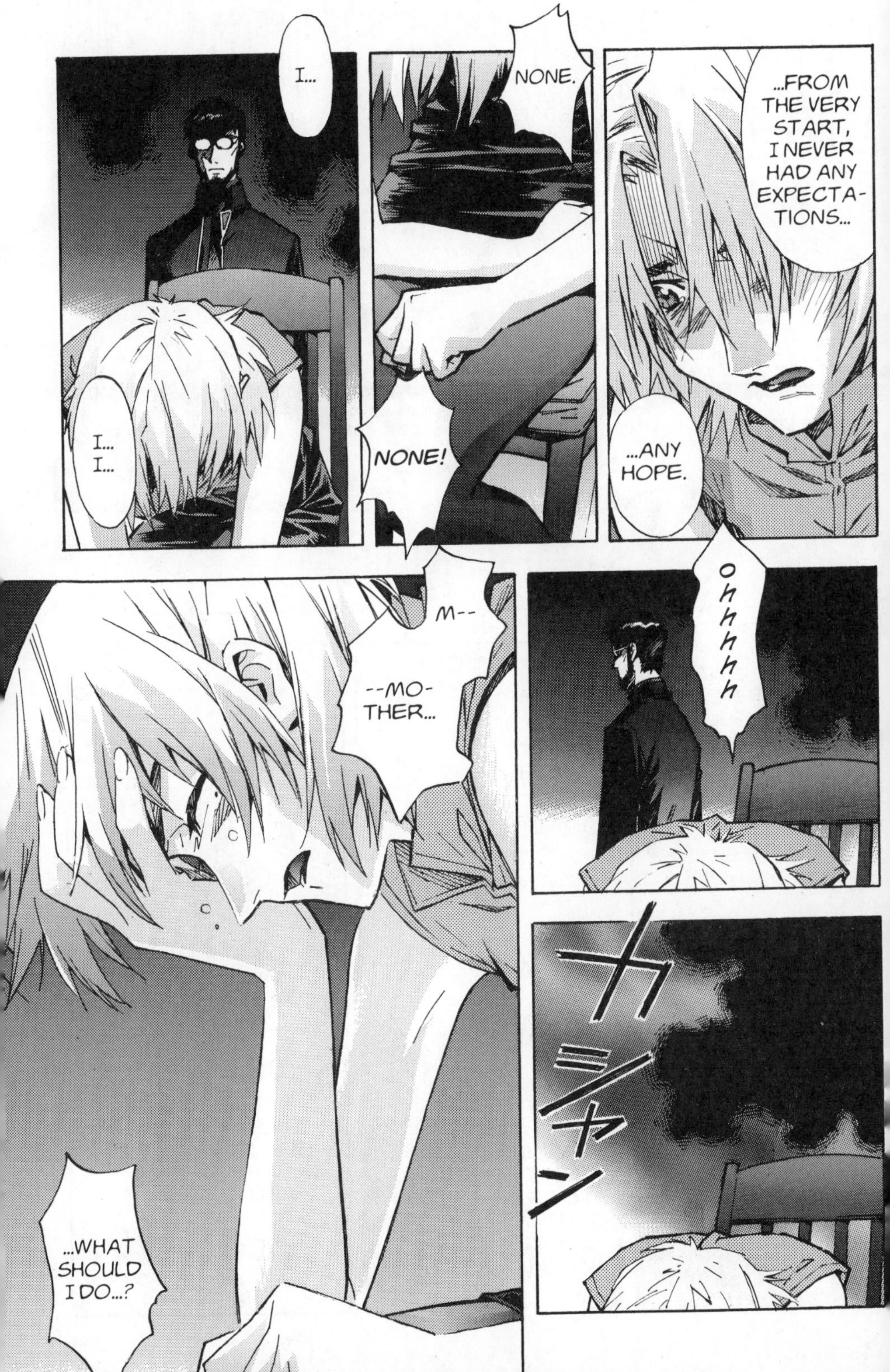
...FROM THE VERY START, I NEVER HAD ANY EXPECTATIONS...
...ANY HOPE.
NONE.
NONE!
I...
I... I...
Ohhhhh
ガシャーン
M--
--MOTHER...
...WHAT SHOULD I DO...?

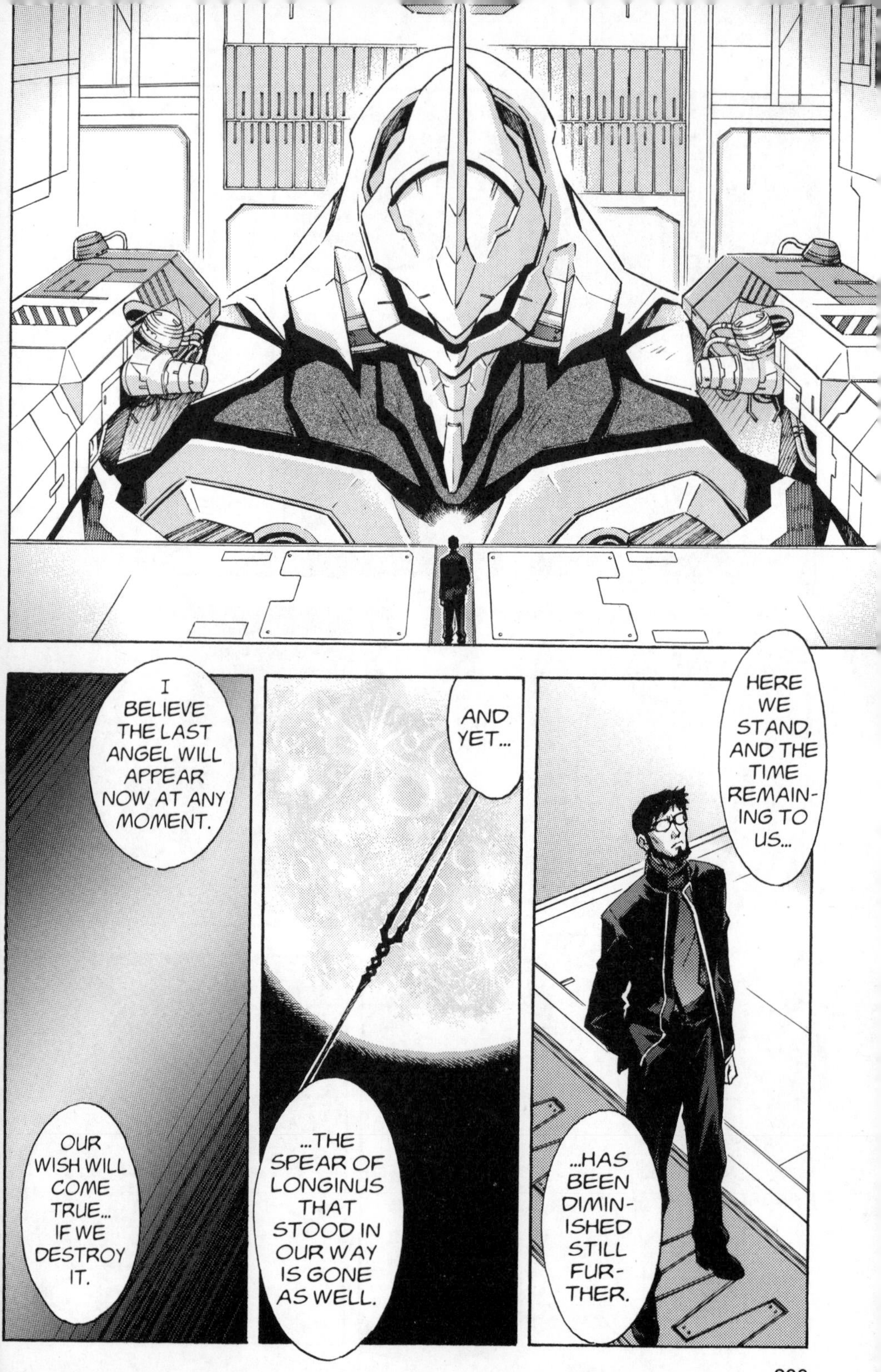
HERE WE STAND, AND THE TIME REMAINING TO US...
...HAS BEEN DIMINISHED STILL FURTHER.
AND YET...
...THE SPEAR OF LONGINUS THAT STOOD IN OUR WAY IS GONE AS WELL.
I BELIEVE THE LAST ANGEL WILL APPEAR NOW AT ANY MOMENT.
OUR WISH WILL COME TRUE... IF WE DESTROY IT.

YUI...
SOON...
...IT'S NEAR.
...THE TIME WILL COME WHEN WE CAN MEET.

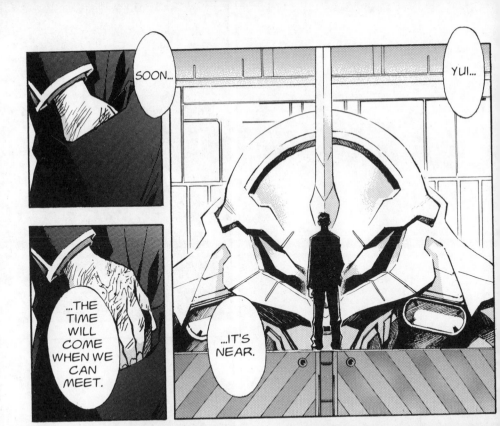

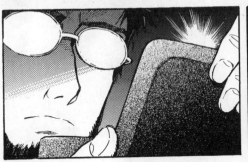

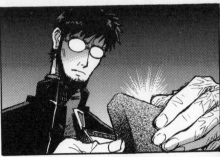

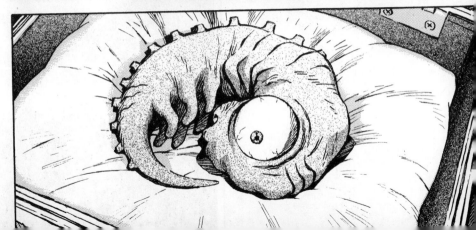

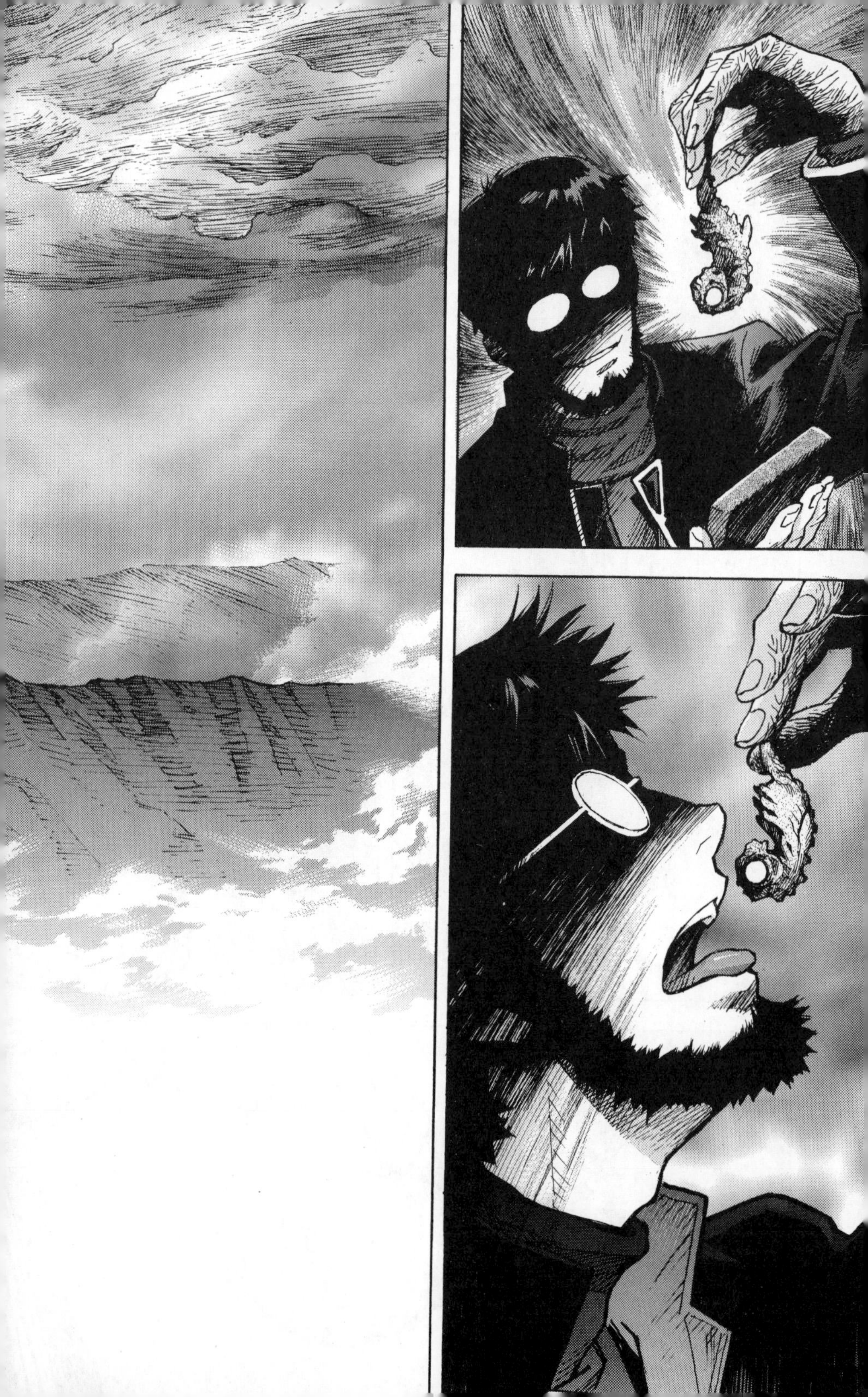

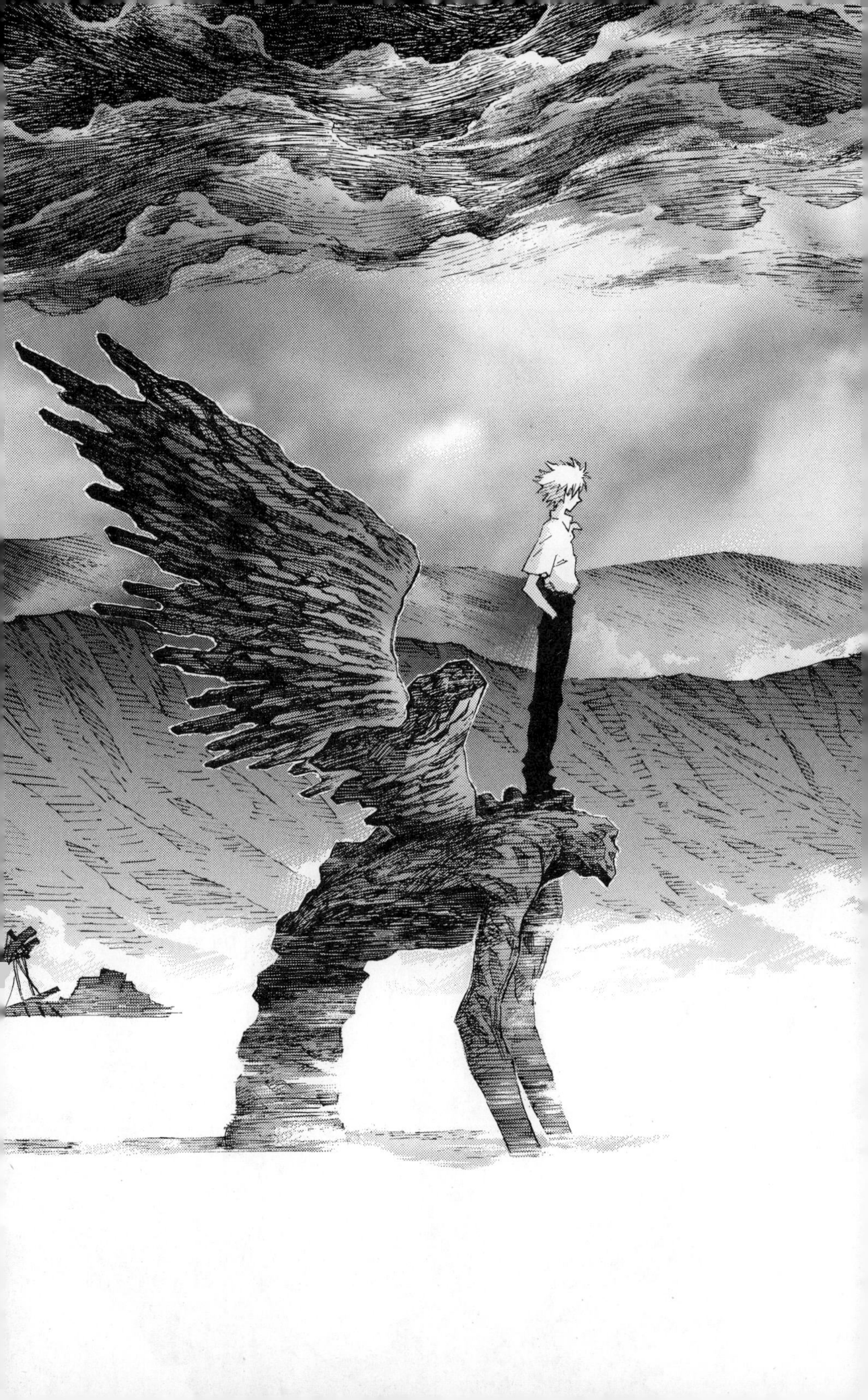

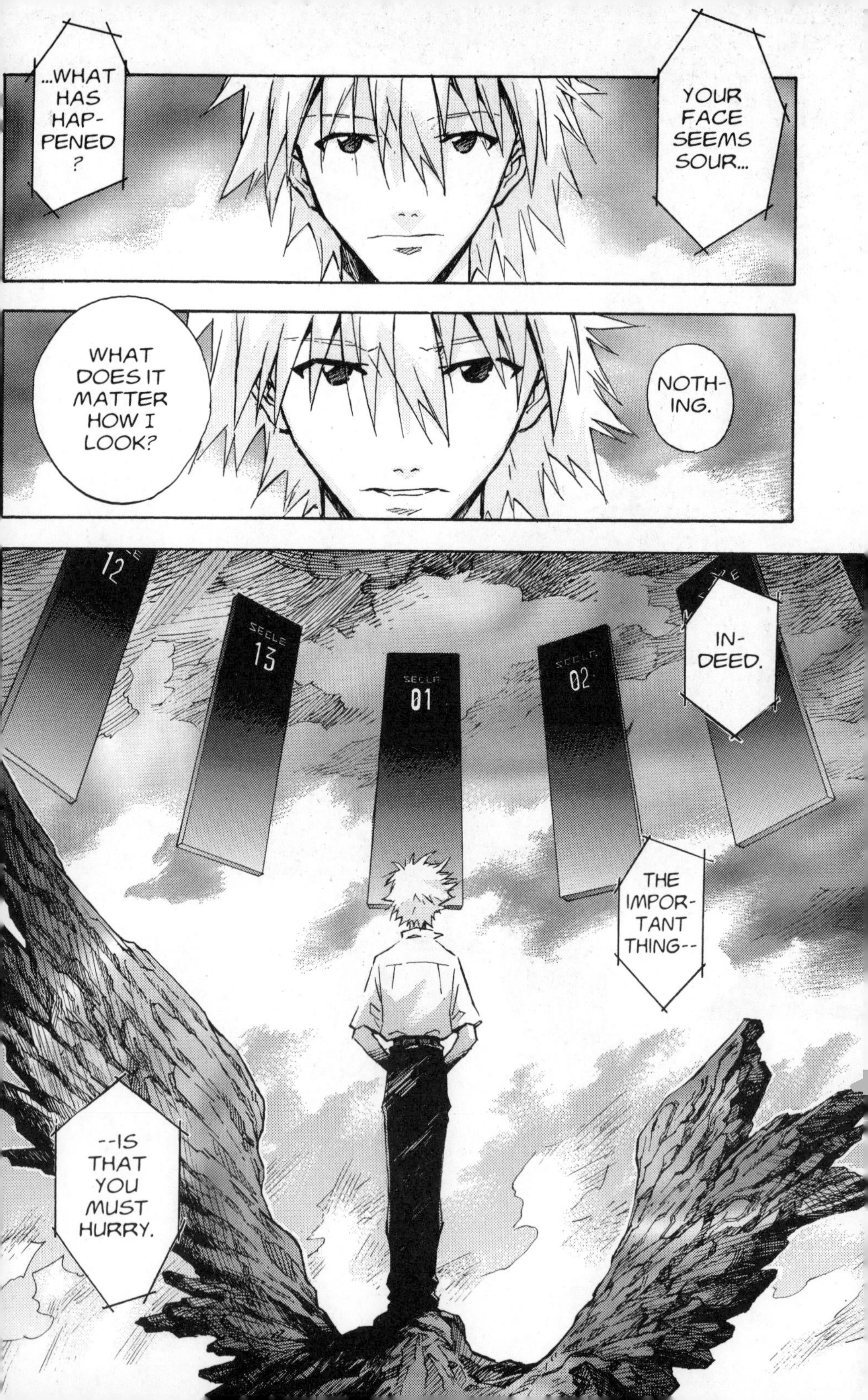
YOUR FACE SEEMS SOUR...
...WHAT HAS HAPPENED?
NOTHING.
WHAT DOES IT MATTER HOW I LOOK?
INDEED.
THE IMPORTANT THING--
--IS THAT YOU MUST HURRY.

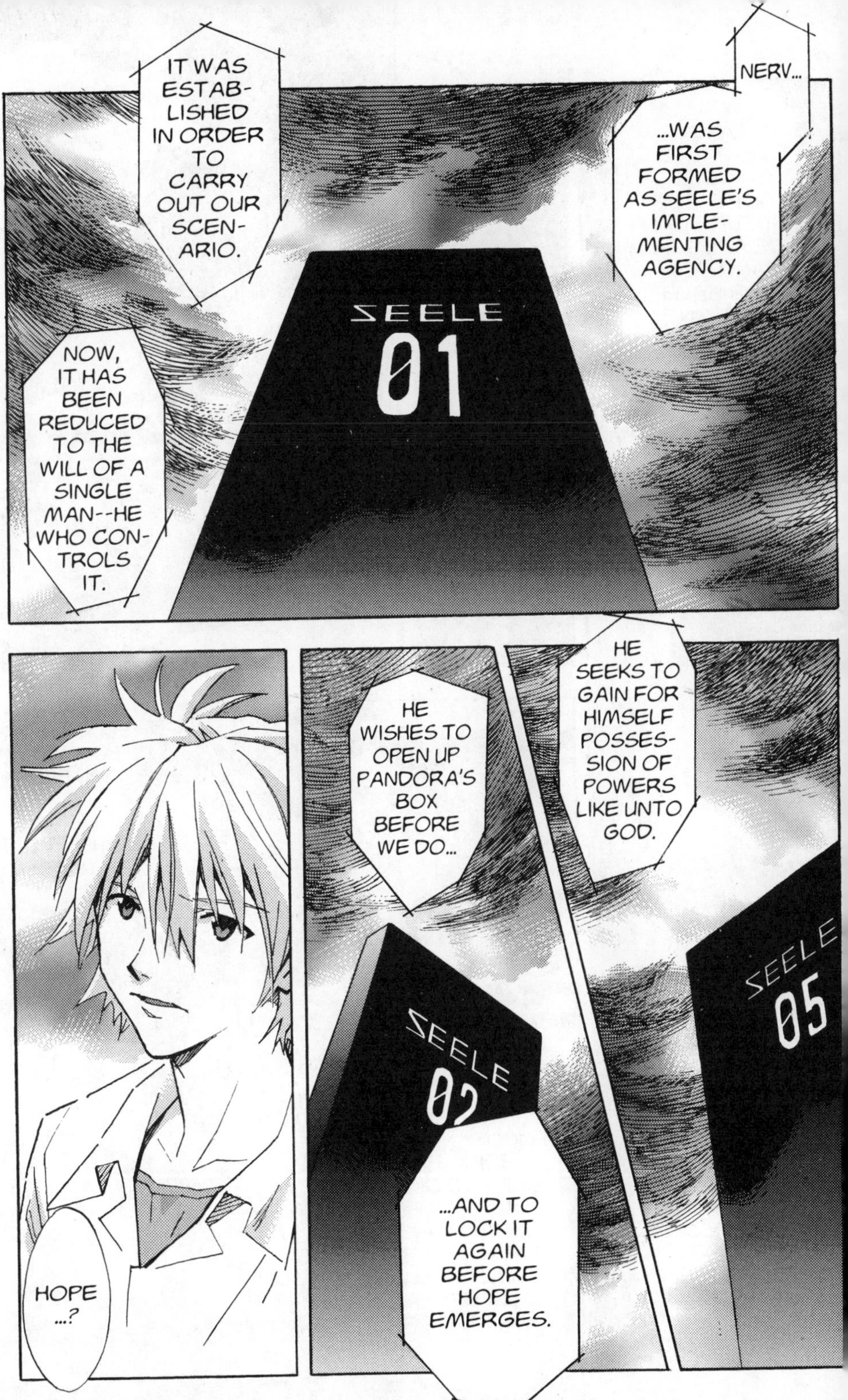
NERV...
...WAS FIRST FORMED AS SEELE'S IMPLEMENTING AGENCY.
IT WAS ESTABLISHED IN ORDER TO CARRY OUT OUR SCENARIO.
SEELE 01
NOW, IT HAS BEEN REDUCED TO THE WILL OF A SINGLE MAN--HE WHO CONTROLS IT.
HE SEEKS TO GAIN FOR HIMSELF POSSESSION OF POWERS LIKE UNTO GOD.
SEELE 05
HE WISHES TO OPEN UP PANDORA'S BOX BEFORE WE DO...
SEELE 02
...AND TO LOCK IT AGAIN BEFORE HOPE EMERGES.
HOPE ...?

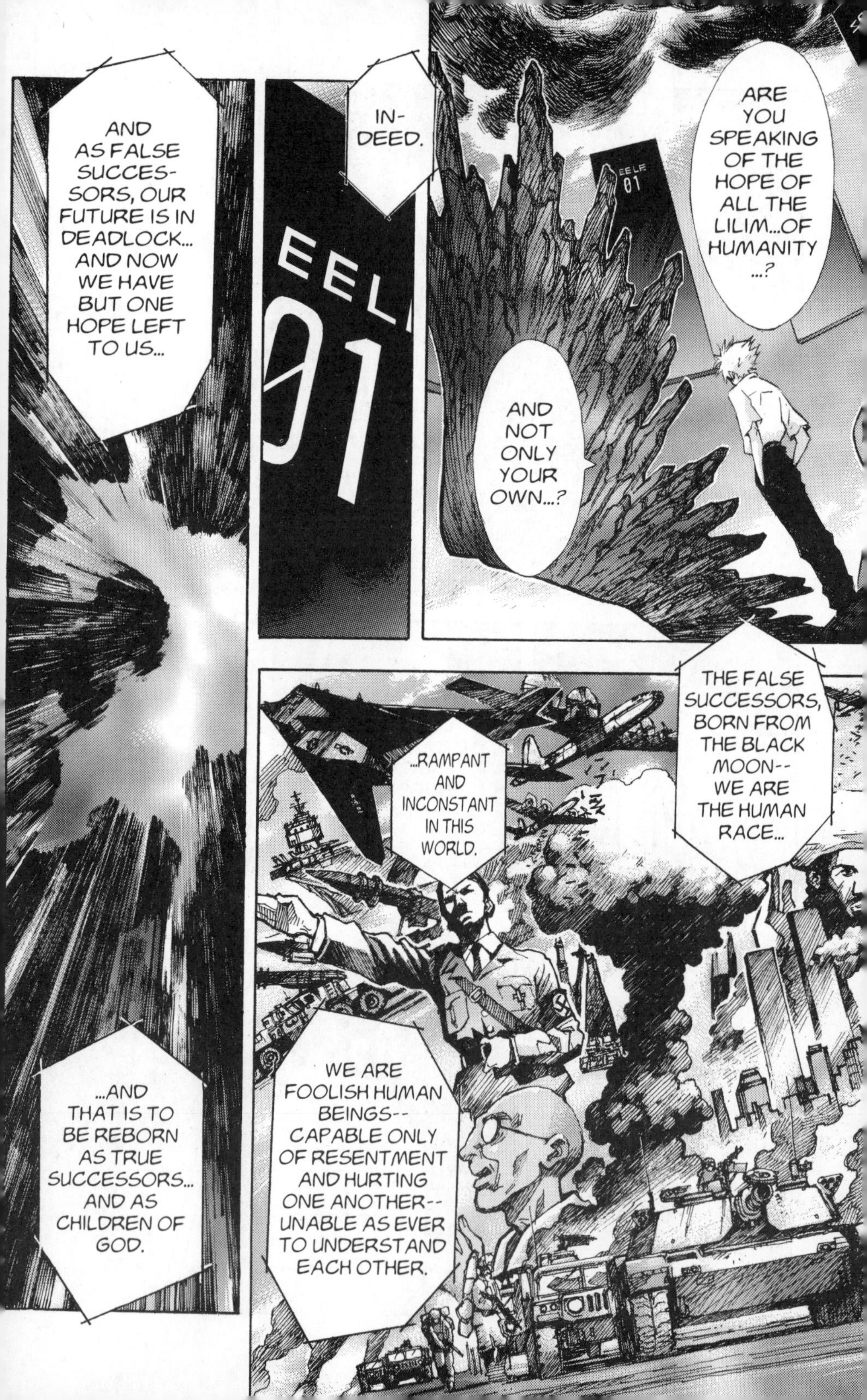
ARE YOU SPEAKING OF THE HOPE OF ALL THE LILIM...OF HUMANITY...?
AND NOT ONLY YOUR OWN...?
IN-DEED.
THE FALSE SUCCESSORS, BORN FROM THE BLACK MOON--WE ARE THE HUMAN RACE...
...RAMPANT AND INCONSTANT IN THIS WORLD.
WE ARE FOOLISH HUMAN BEINGS--CAPABLE ONLY OF RESENTMENT AND HURTING ONE ANOTHER--UNABLE AS EVER TO UNDERSTAND EACH OTHER.
AND AS FALSE SUCCES-SORS, OUR FUTURE IS IN DEADLOCK... AND NOW WE HAVE BUT ONE HOPE LEFT TO US...
...AND THAT IS TO BE REBORN AS TRUE SUCCESSORS... AND AS CHILDREN OF GOD.

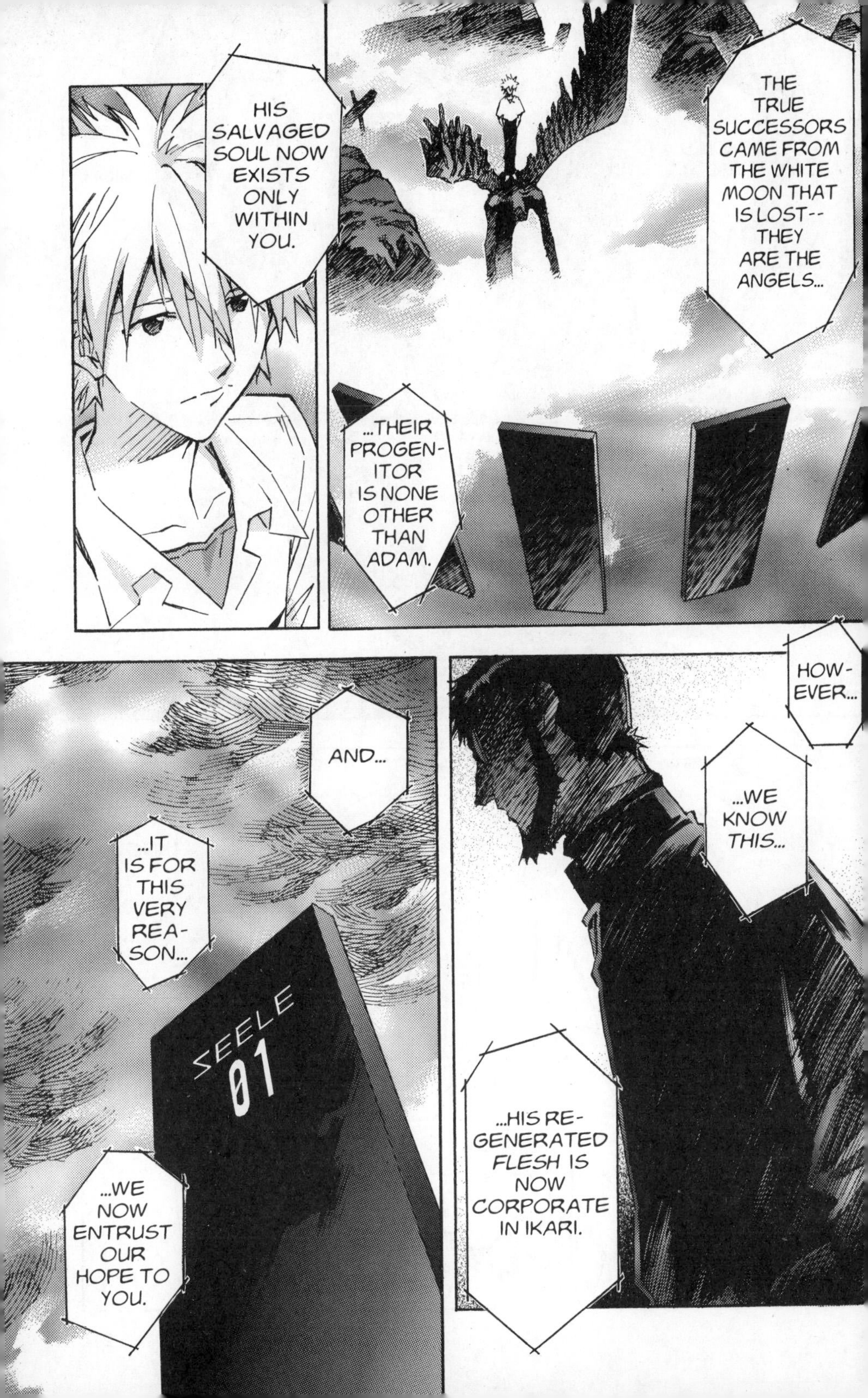
THE TRUE SUCCESSORS CAME FROM THE WHITE MOON THAT IS LOST-- THEY ARE THE ANGELS...
...THEIR PROGENITOR IS NONE OTHER THAN ADAM.
HIS SALVAGED SOUL NOW EXISTS ONLY WITHIN YOU.
HOWEVER...
...WE KNOW THIS...
...HIS REGENERATED FLESH IS NOW CORPORATE IN IKARI.
AND...
...IT IS FOR THIS VERY REASON...
SEELE 01
...WE NOW ENTRUST OUR HOPE TO YOU.

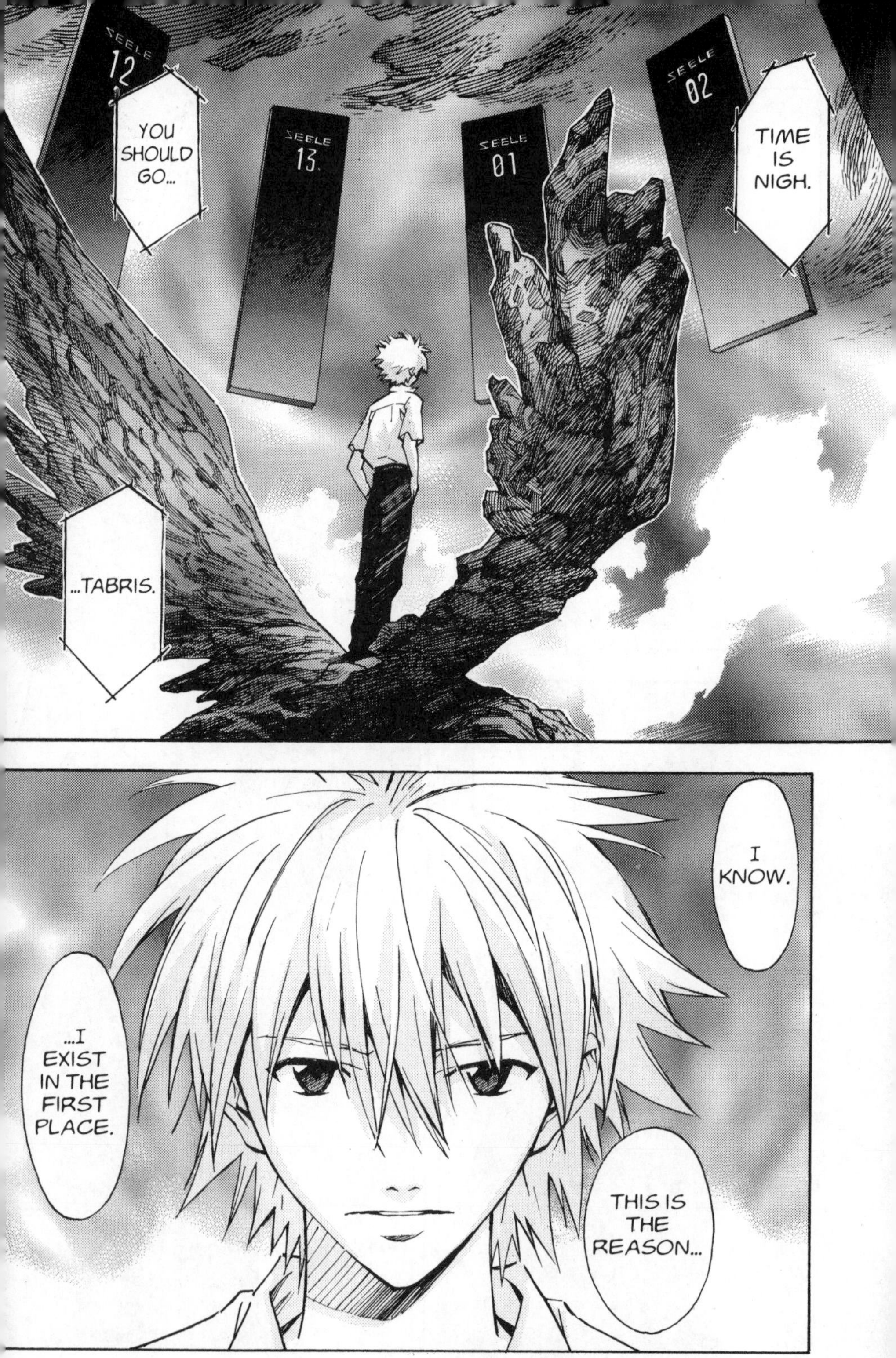
SEELE 02
SEELE 01
SEELE 13
SEELE 12
TIME IS NIGH.
YOU SHOULD GO...
...TABRIS.
I KNOW.
THIS IS THE REASON...
...I EXIST IN THE FIRST PLACE.

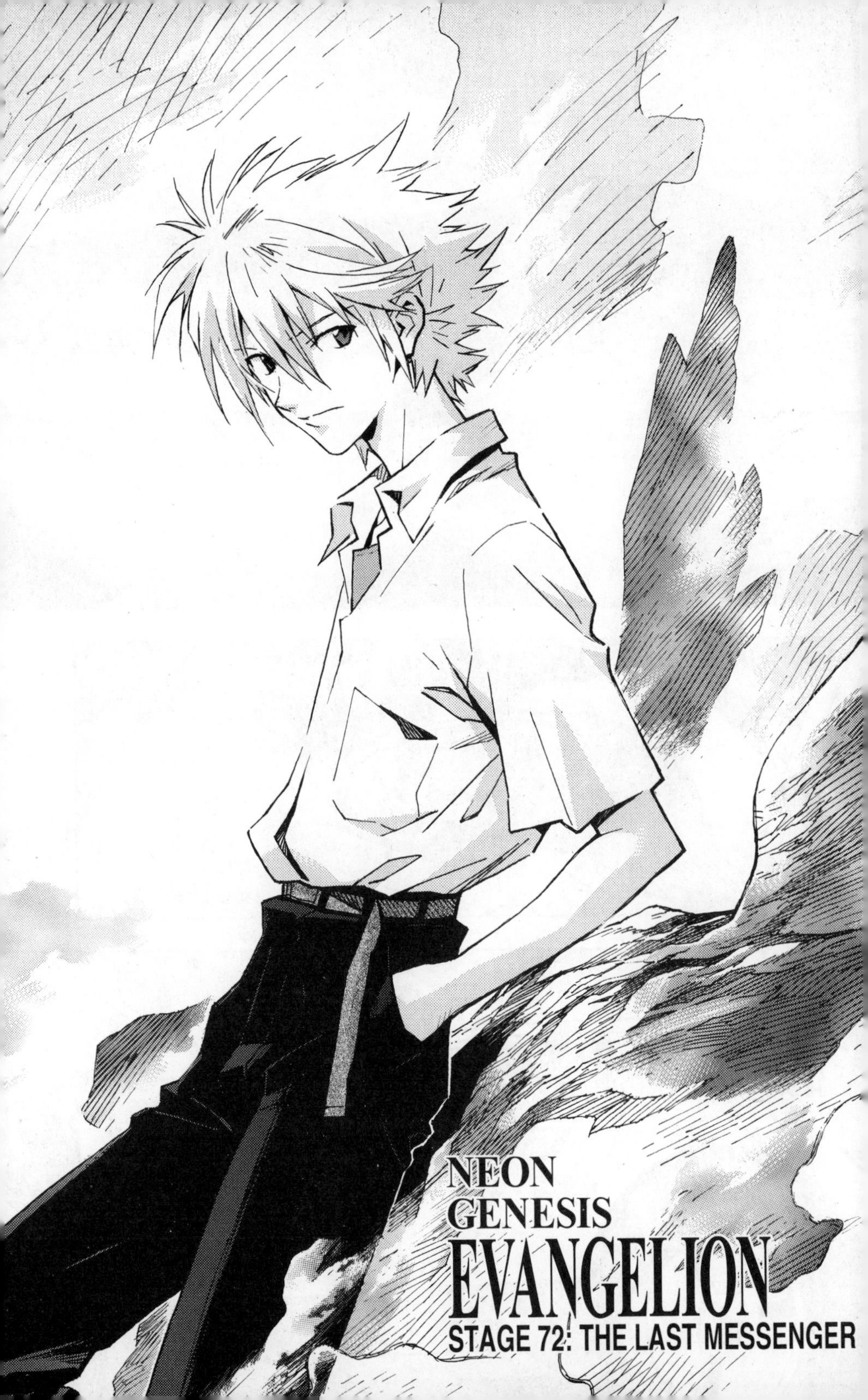
NEON
GENESIS
EVANGELION
STAGE 72: THE LAST MESSENGER

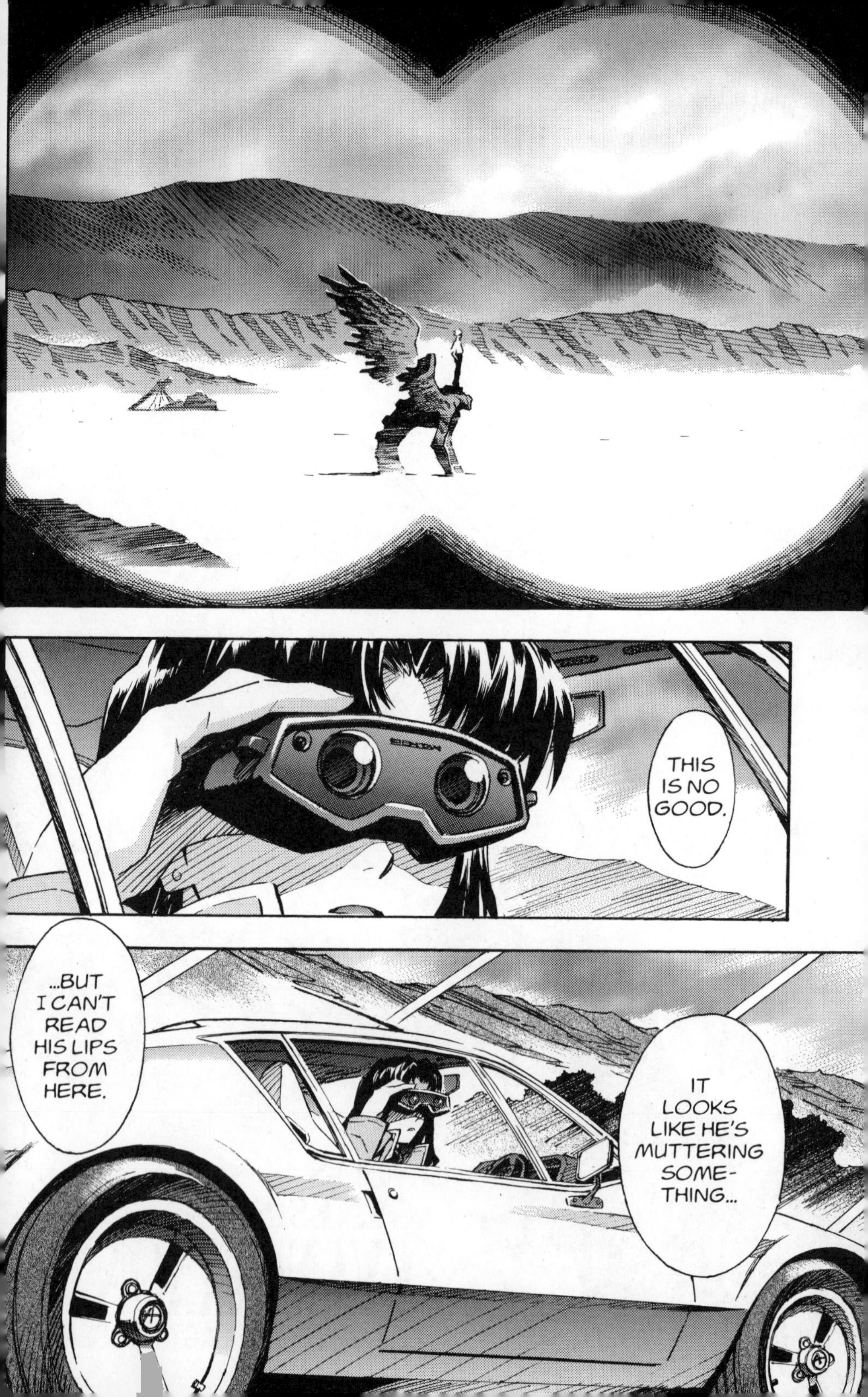
THIS IS NO GOOD.
IT LOOKS LIKE HE'S MUTTERING SOME-THING...
...BUT I CAN'T READ HIS LIPS FROM HERE.

I BOR-
ROWED
IT FROM
LT. IBUKI
WITHOUT
ASKING.

YEAH.

SO, WERE
YOU ABLE
TO GET
HIS DATA
...?

...I DON'T
BELIEVE
HE'D GET UP
SO EARLY IN
THE MORNING
JUST TO
TALK TO
HIMSELF.

HE'S
DAN-
GER-
OUS.

...FOR
ALWAYS
MAKING
YOU BE THE
BAD GUY...
AND
STEALING
FOR ME.

I'M
SORRY...

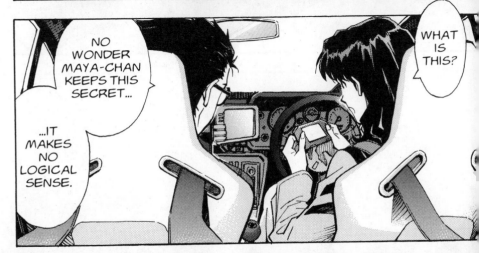

NO
WONDER
MAYA-CHAN
KEEPS THIS
SECRET...

...IT
MAKES
NO
LOGICAL
SENSE.

WHAT
IS
THIS?

217

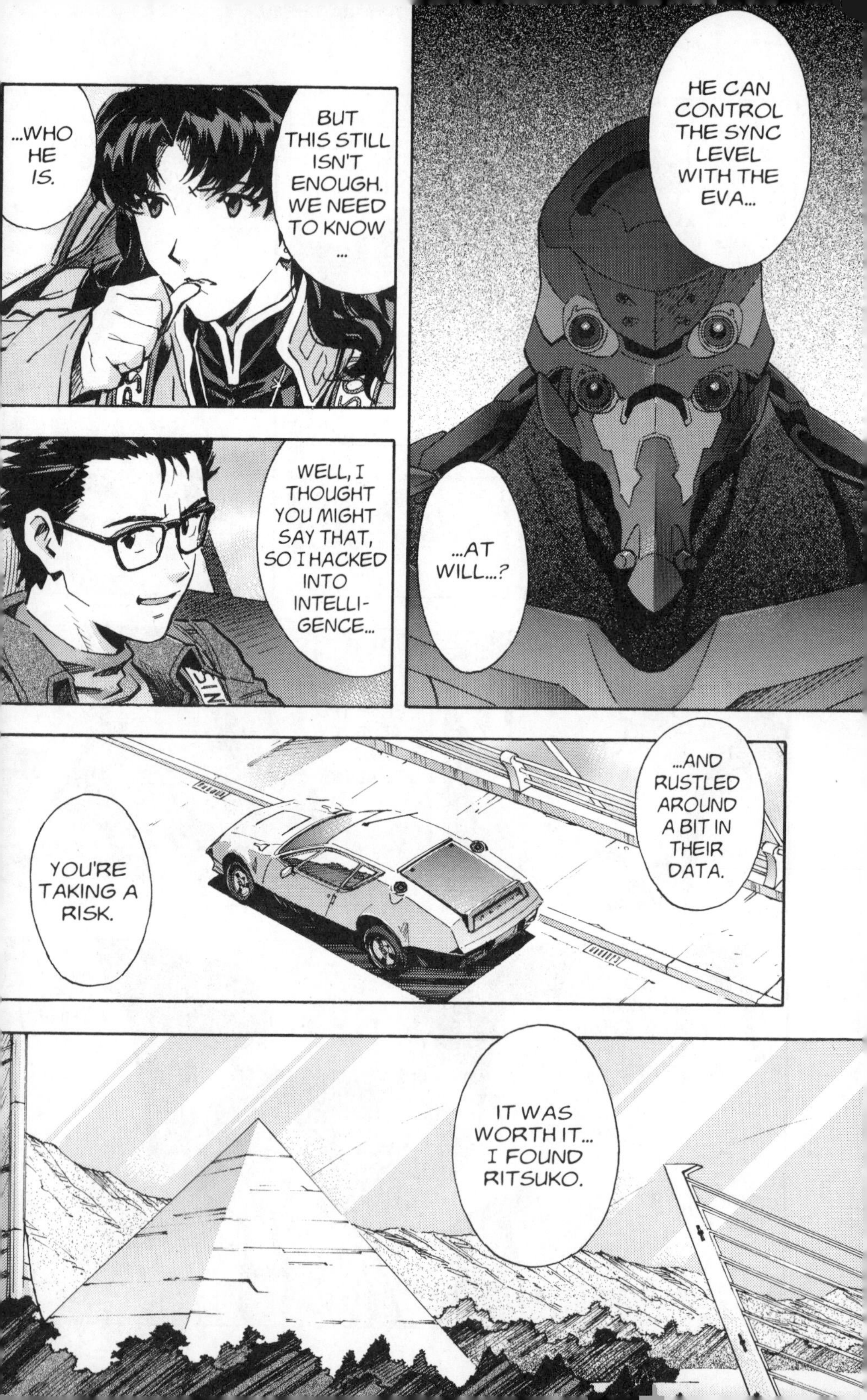
HE CAN CONTROL THE SYNC LEVEL WITH THE EVA...
...AT WILL...?
BUT THIS STILL ISN'T ENOUGH. WE NEED TO KNOW ...
...WHO HE IS.
WELL, I THOUGHT YOU MIGHT SAY THAT, SO I HACKED INTO INTELLI-GENCE...
...AND RUSTLED AROUND A BIT IN THEIR DATA.
YOU'RE TAKING A RISK.
IT WAS WORTH IT... I FOUND RITSUKO.

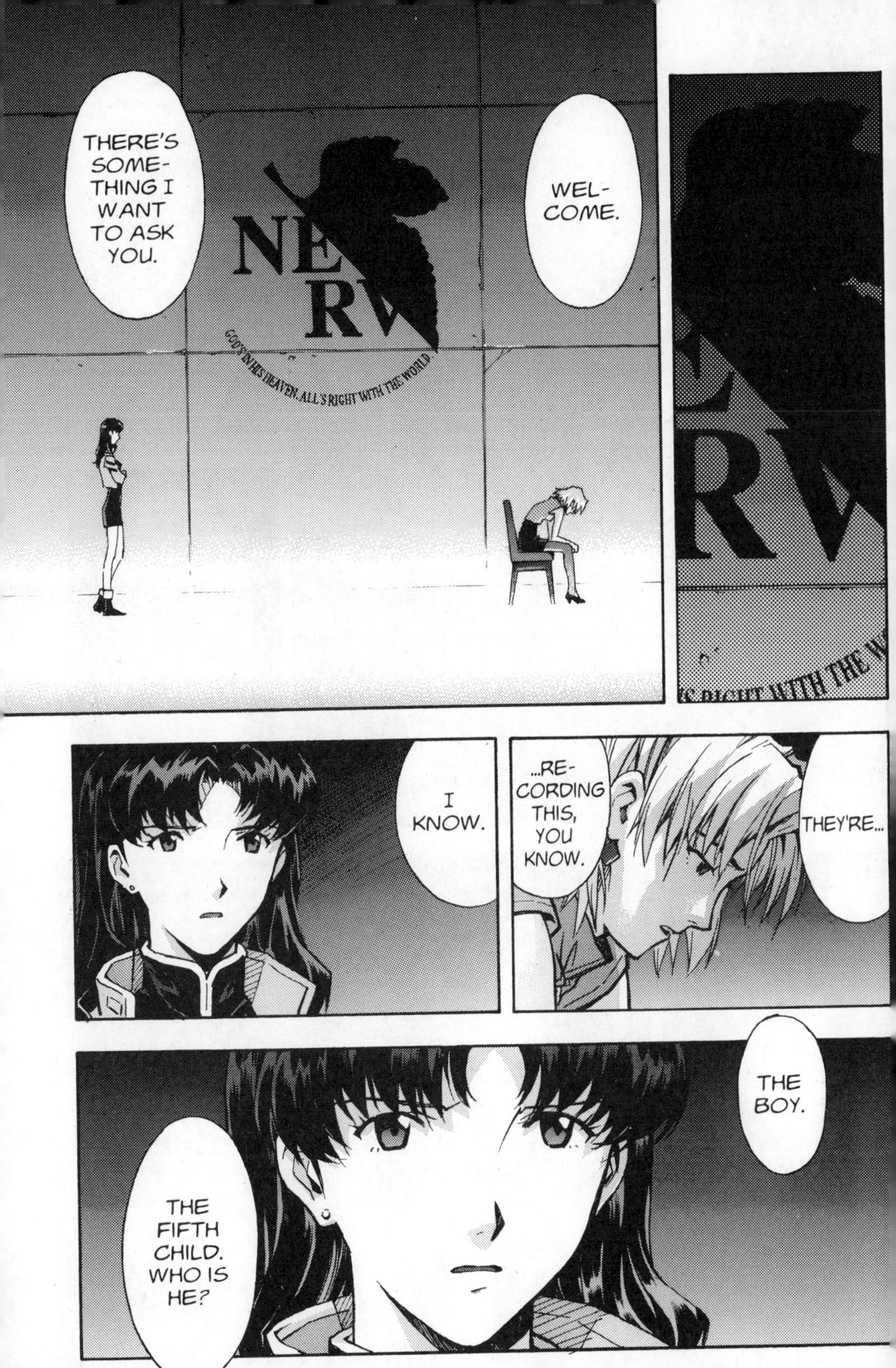
WEL-
COME.
THERE'S SOME-THING I WANT TO ASK YOU.
NERV
GOD'S IN HIS HEAVEN. ALL'S RIGHT WITH THE WORLD
THEY'RE...
...RE-CORDING THIS, YOU KNOW.
I KNOW.
THE BOY.
THE FIFTH CHILD. WHO IS HE?

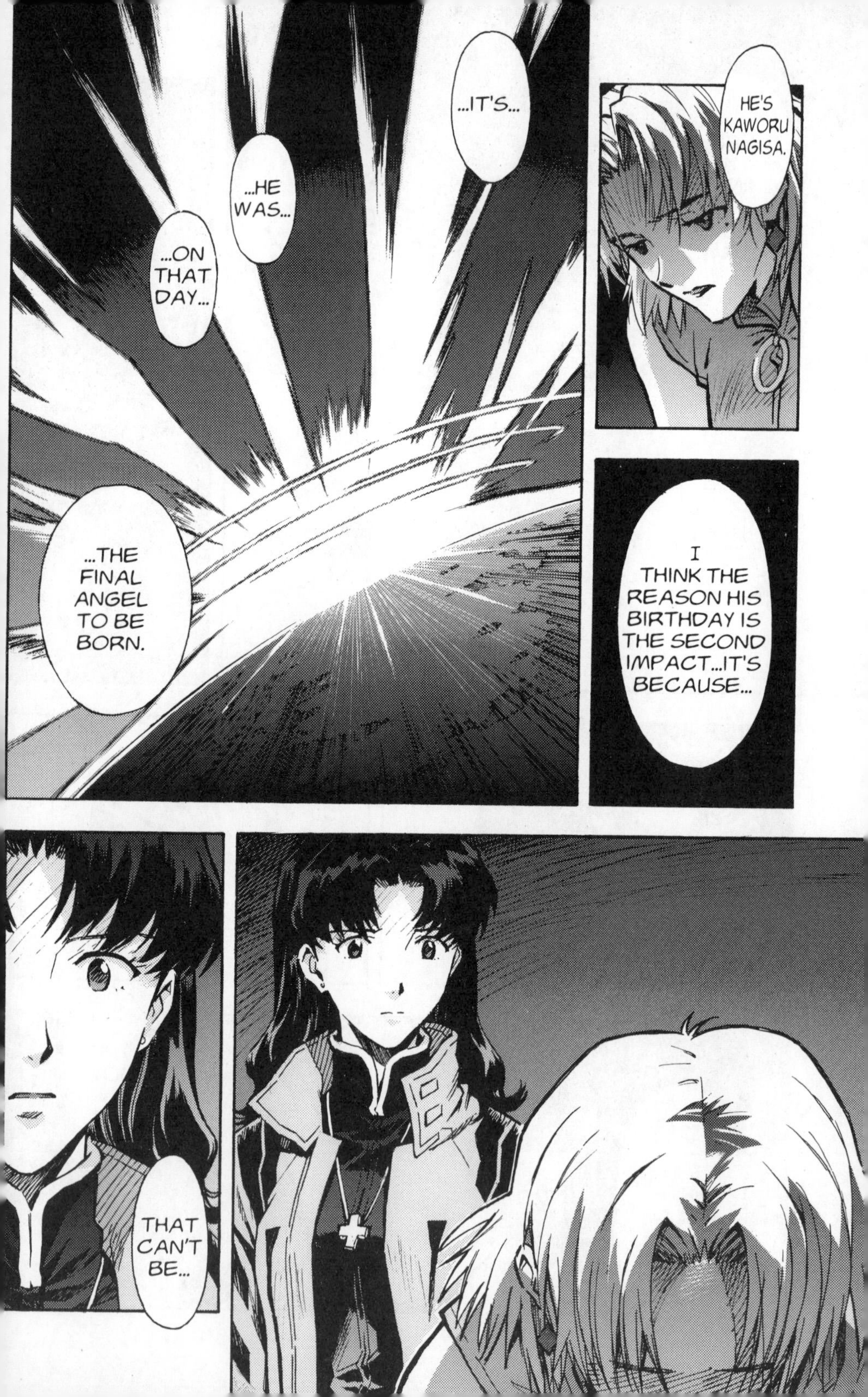
HE'S KAWORU NAGISA.
I THINK THE REASON HIS BIRTHDAY IS THE SECOND IMPACT...IT'S BECAUSE...
...IT'S...
...HE WAS...
...ON THAT DAY...
...THE FINAL ANGEL TO BE BORN.
THAT CAN'T BE...

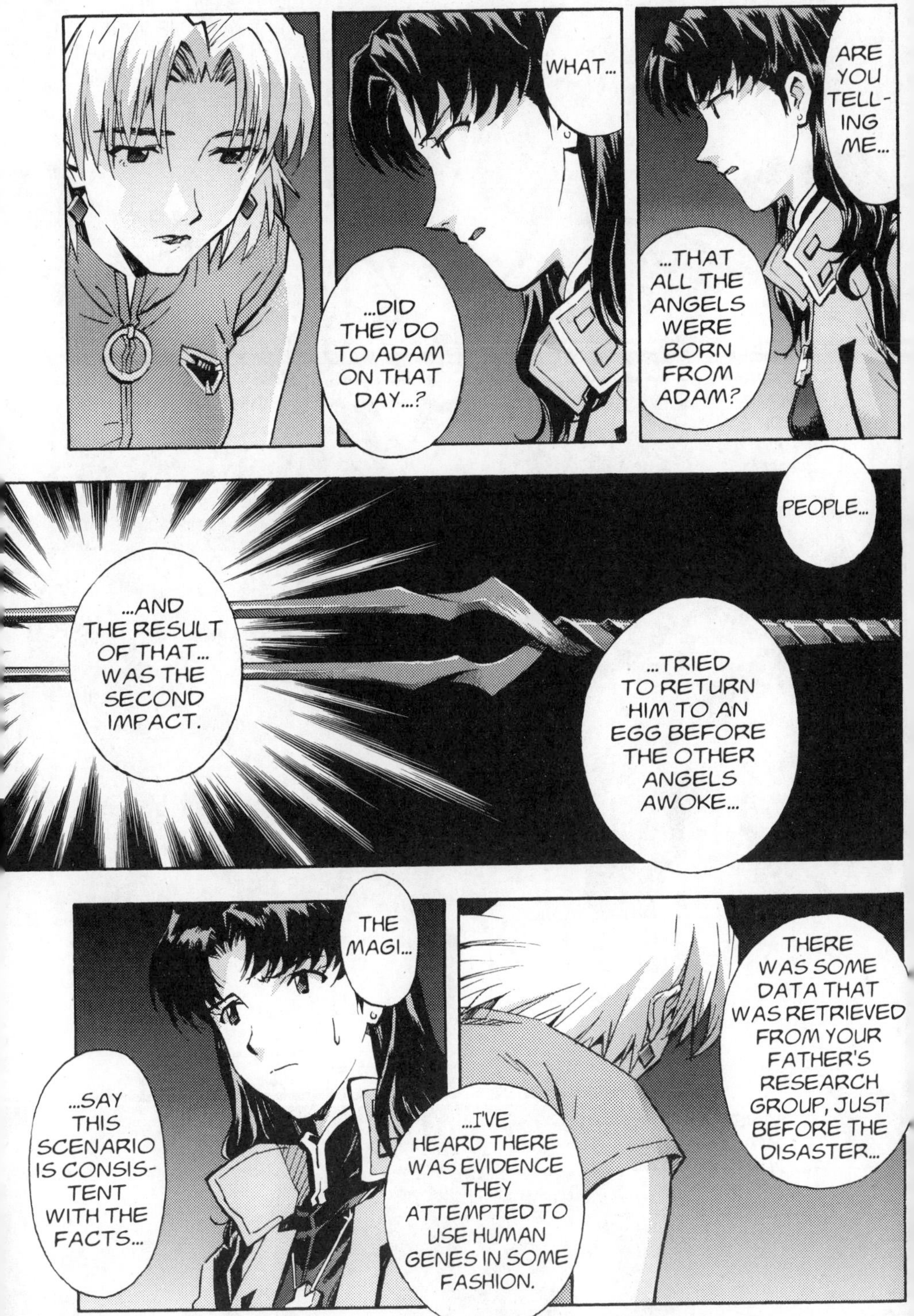
ARE YOU TELL-ING ME...
...THAT ALL THE ANGELS WERE BORN FROM ADAM?
WHAT...
...DID THEY DO TO ADAM ON THAT DAY...?
PEOPLE...
...TRIED TO RETURN HIM TO AN EGG BEFORE THE OTHER ANGELS AWOKE...
...AND THE RESULT OF THAT... WAS THE SECOND IMPACT.
THERE WAS SOME DATA THAT WAS RETRIEVED FROM YOUR FATHER'S RESEARCH GROUP, JUST BEFORE THE DISASTER...
...I'VE HEARD THERE WAS EVIDENCE THEY ATTEMPTED TO USE HUMAN GENES IN SOME FASHION.
THE MAGI...
...SAY THIS SCENARIO IS CONSIS-TENT WITH THE FACTS...

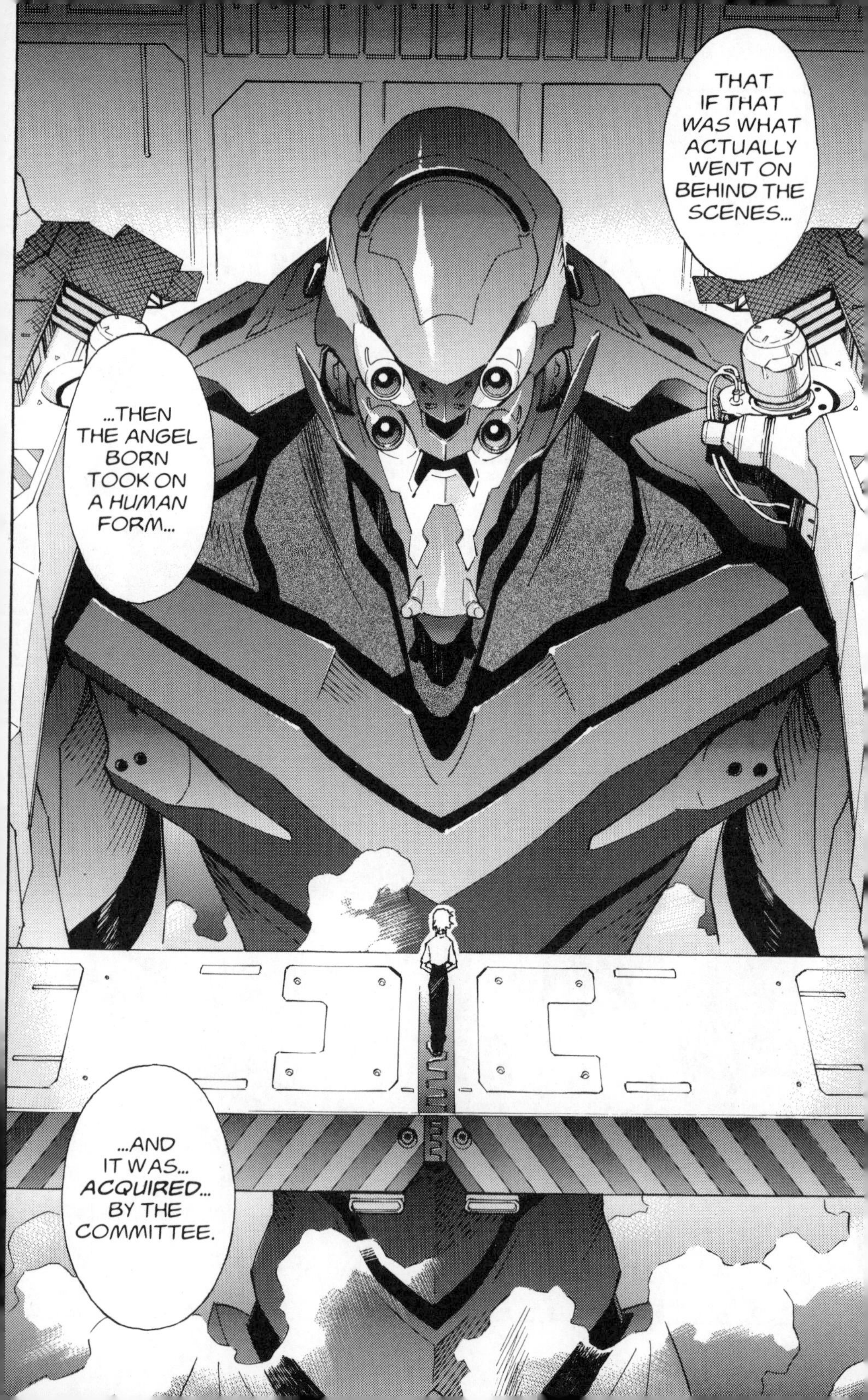
THAT IF THAT WAS WHAT ACTUALLY WENT ON BEHIND THE SCENES...
...THEN THE ANGEL BORN TOOK ON A HUMAN FORM...
...AND IT WAS... ACQUIRED... BY THE COMMITTEE.

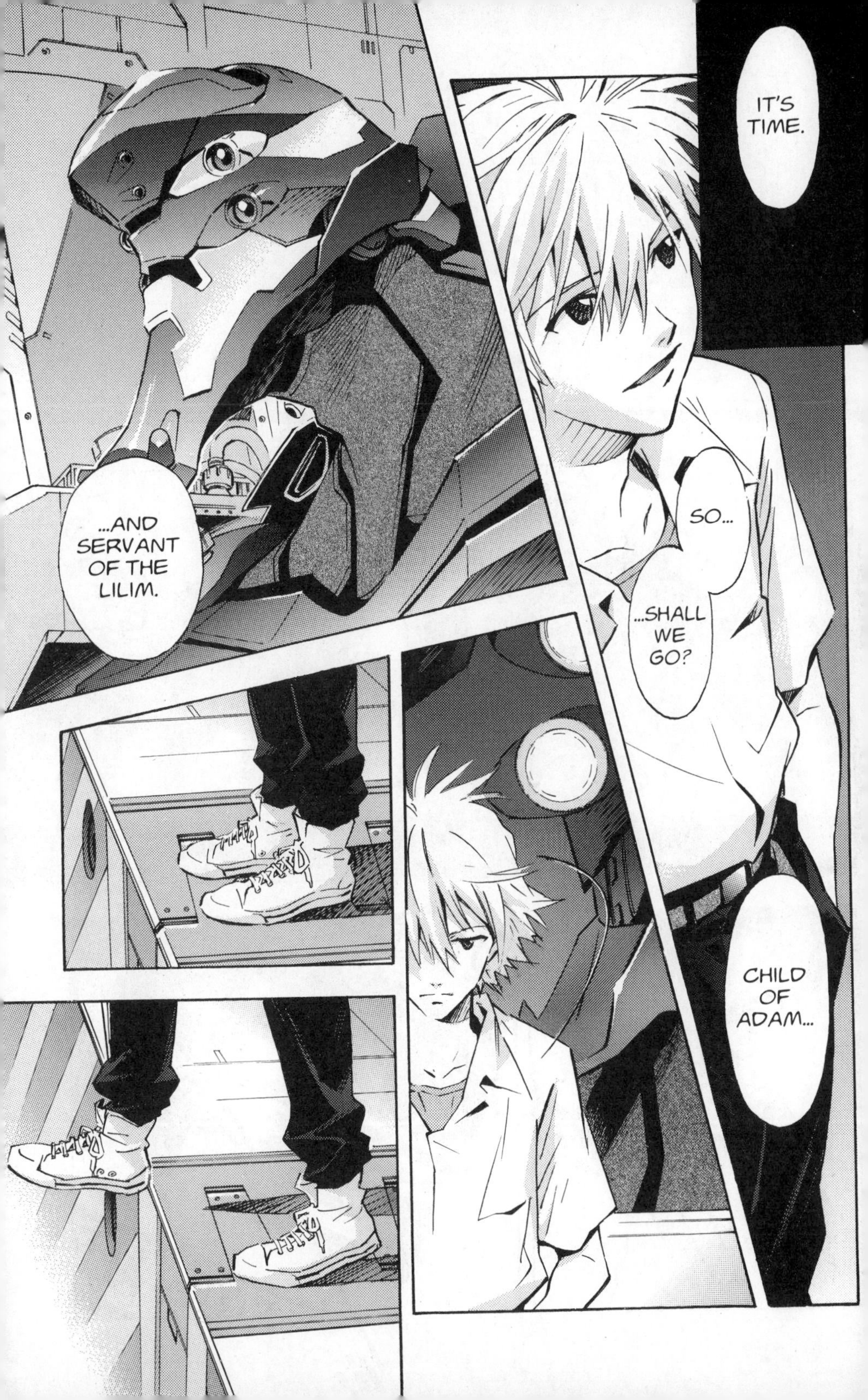
IT'S TIME.
SO...
...SHALL WE GO?
CHILD OF ADAM...
...AND SERVANT OF THE LILIM.

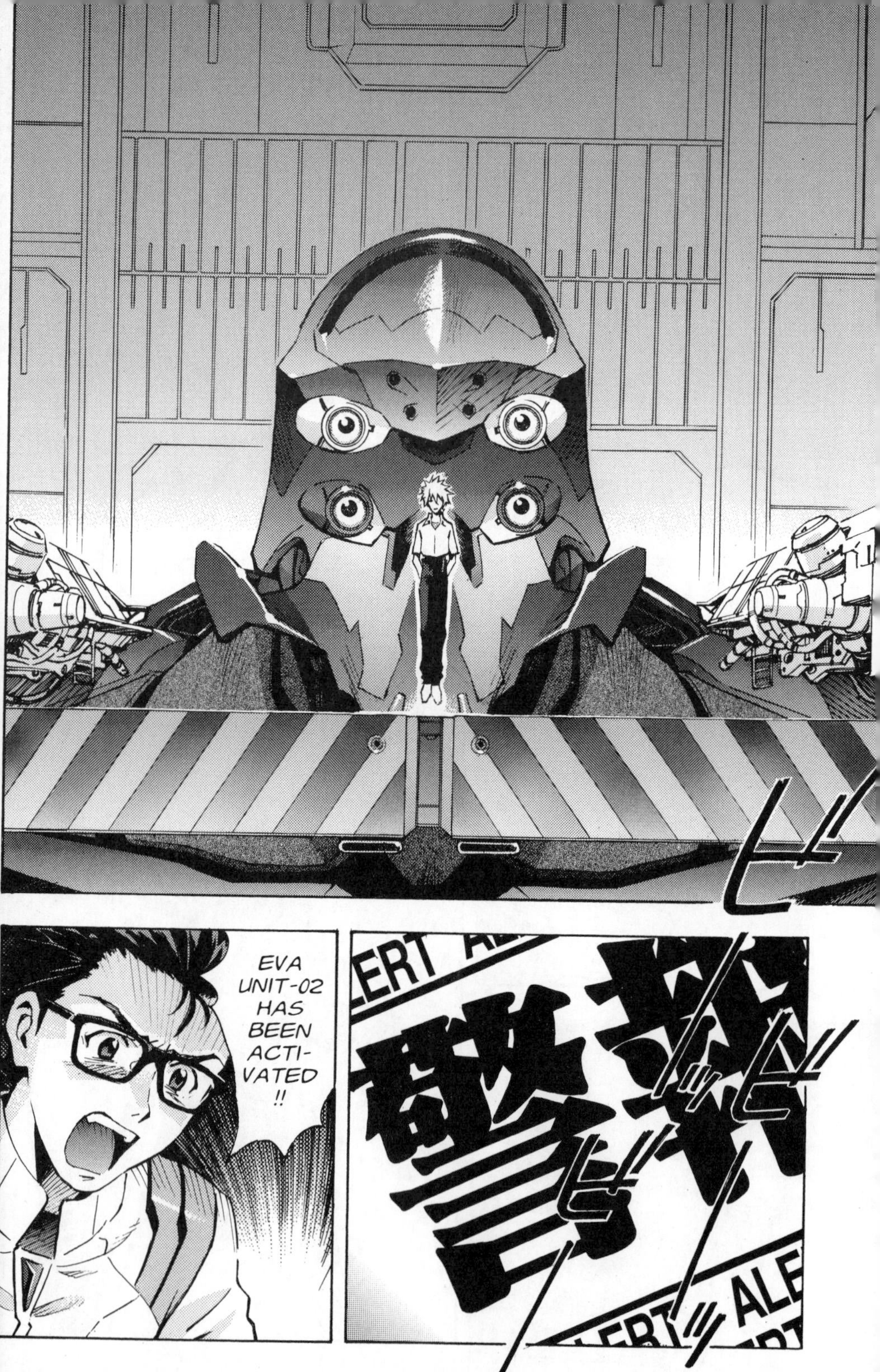
ALERT
警報
EVA UNIT-02 HAS BEEN ACTIVATED !!

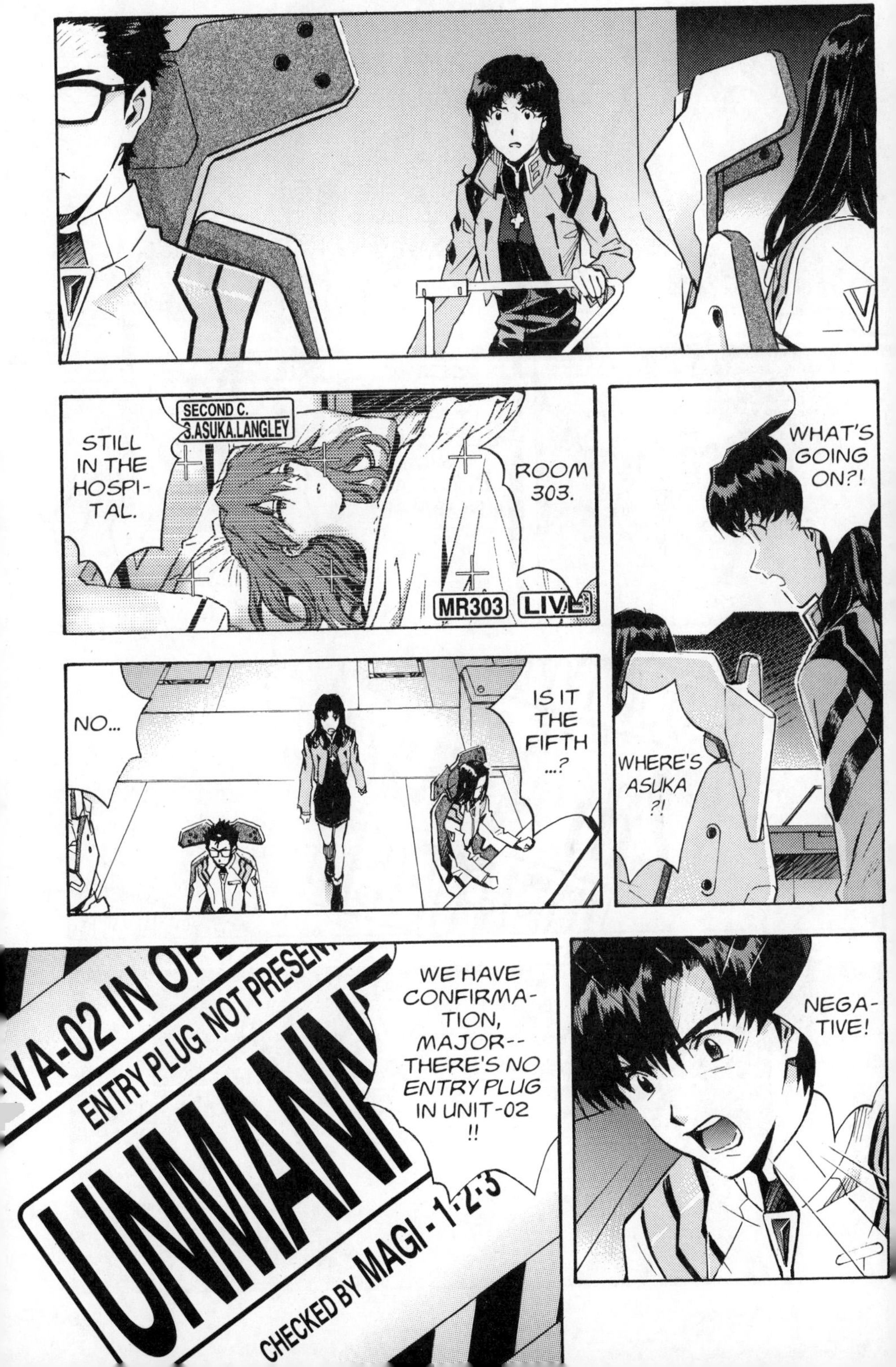
WHAT'S GOING ON?!
WHERE'S ASUKA ?!
SECOND C.
3.ASUKA.LANGLEY
STILL IN THE HOSPITAL.
ROOM 303.
MR303
LIVE
IS IT THE FIFTH ...?
NO...
NEGA-TIVE!
WE HAVE CONFIRMATION, MAJOR-- THERE'S NO ENTRY PLUG IN UNIT-02 !!
VA-02 IN OP
ENTRY PLUG NOT PRESEN
UNMAN
CHECKED BY MAGI - 1·2·3

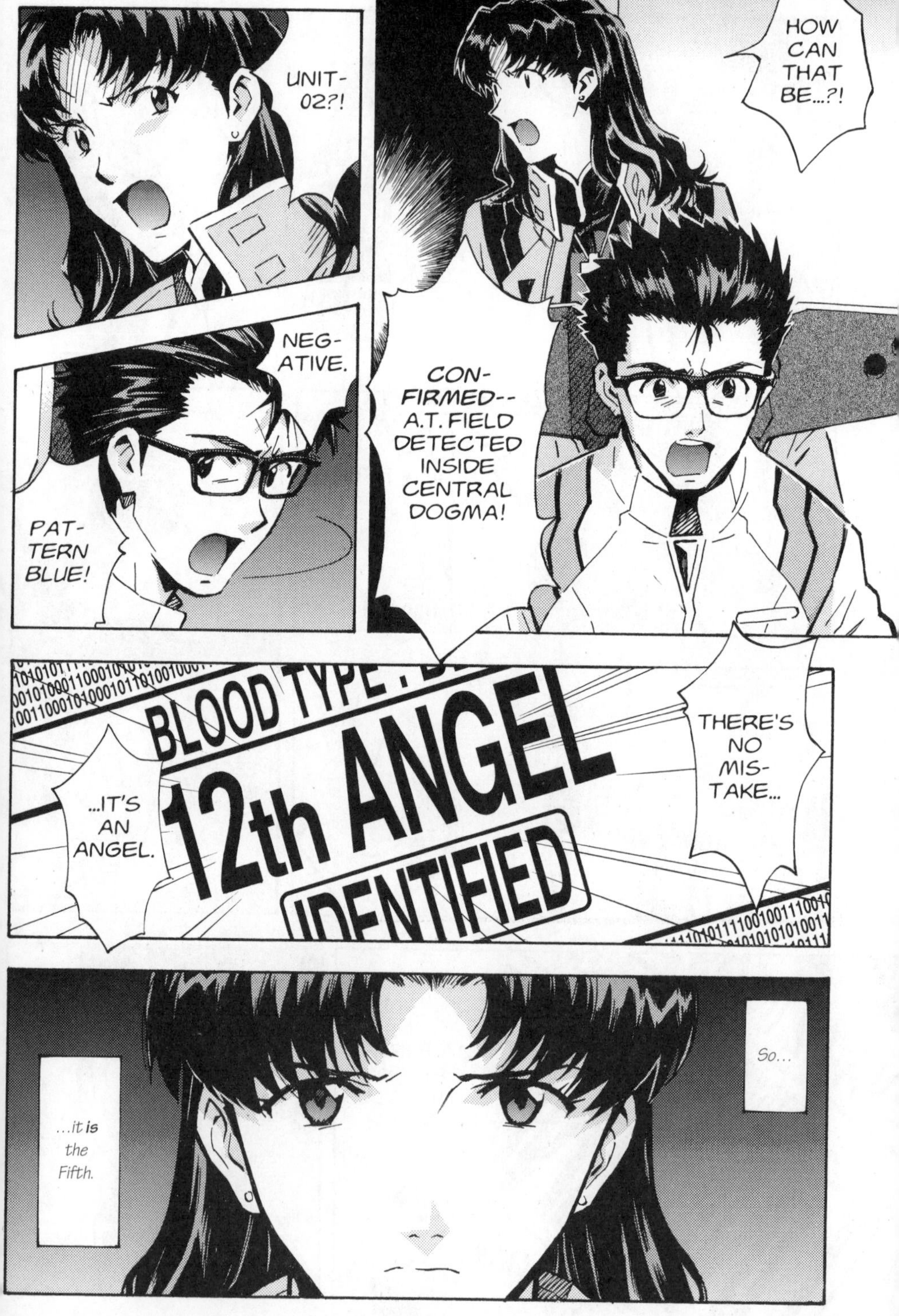
HOW CAN THAT BE...?!
CON-FIRMED-- A.T. FIELD DETECTED INSIDE CENTRAL DOGMA!
UNIT-02?!
NEG-ATIVE.
PAT-TERN BLUE!
THERE'S NO MIS-TAKE...
BLOOD TYPE: B
12th ANGEL
IDENTIFIED
...IT'S AN ANGEL.
So...
...it is the Fifth.

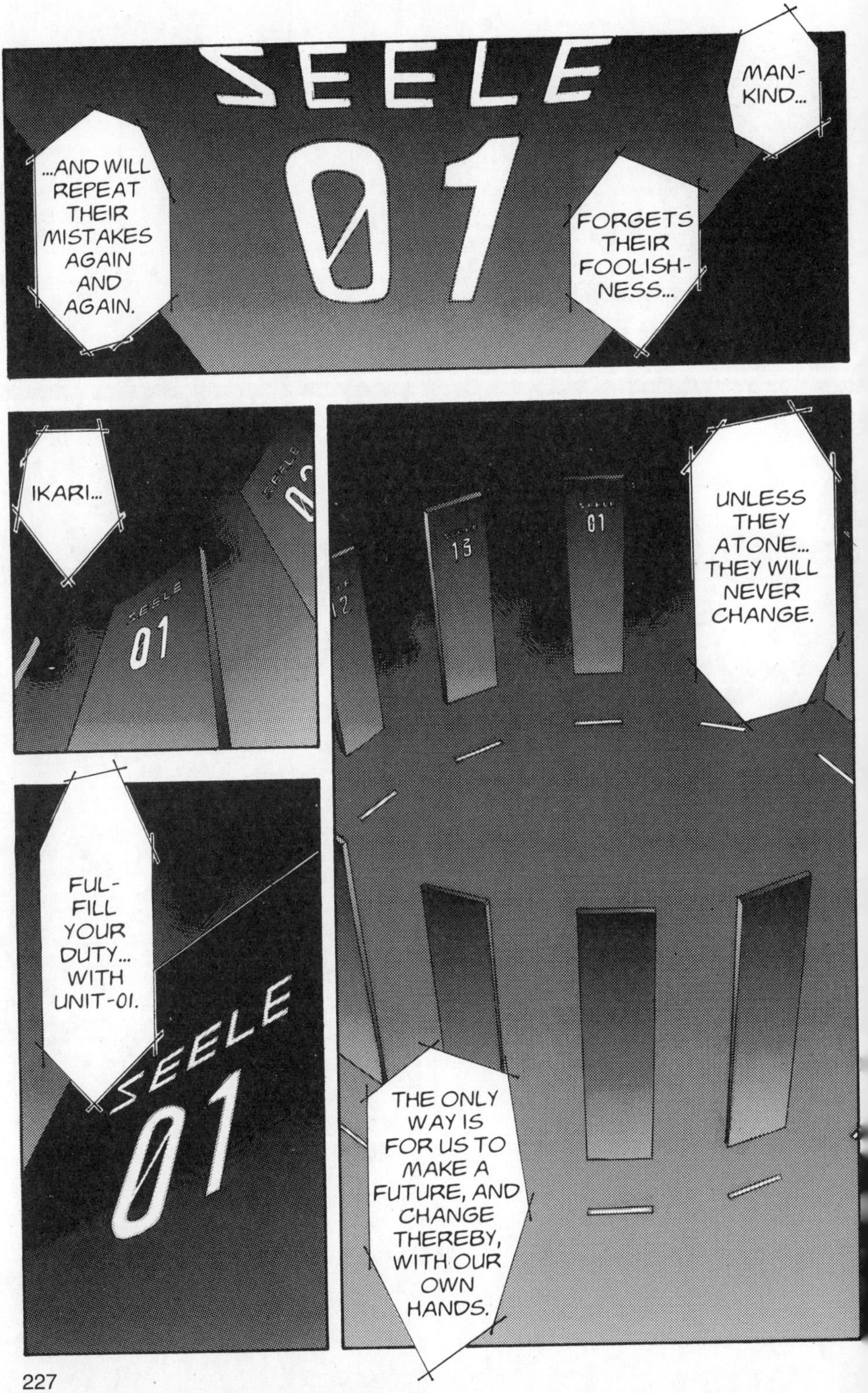
SEELE
01
MAN-KIND...
FORGETS THEIR FOOLISH-NESS...
...AND WILL REPEAT THEIR MISTAKES AGAIN AND AGAIN.
UNLESS THEY ATONE... THEY WILL NEVER CHANGE.
THE ONLY WAY IS FOR US TO MAKE A FUTURE, AND CHANGE THEREBY, WITH OUR OWN HANDS.
IKARI...
FUL-FILL YOUR DUTY... WITH UNIT-01.
SEELE
01

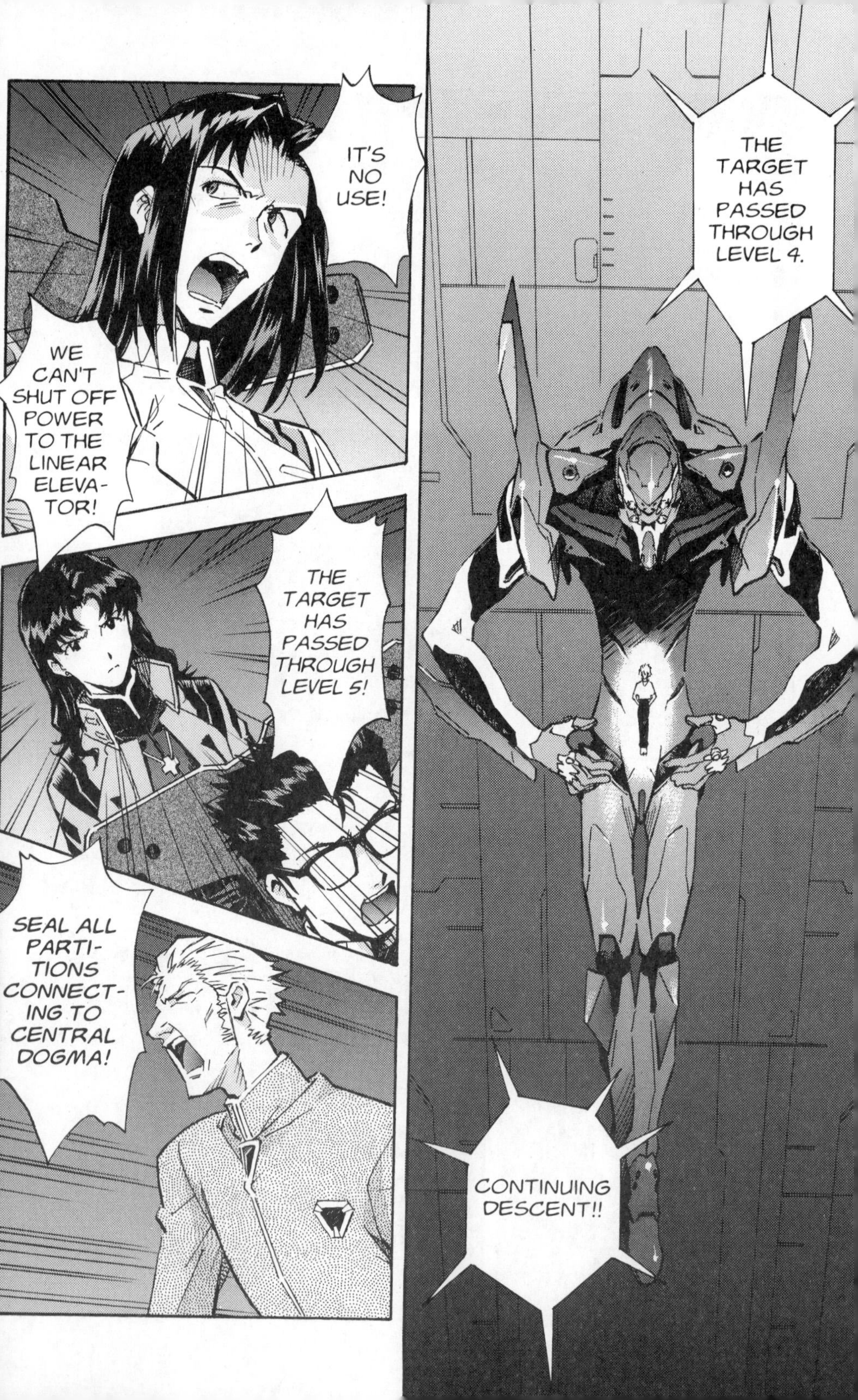
THE TARGET HAS PASSED THROUGH LEVEL 4.
CONTINUING DESCENT!!
IT'S NO USE!
WE CAN'T SHUT OFF POWER TO THE LINEAR ELEVA-TOR!
THE TARGET HAS PASSED THROUGH LEVEL 5!
SEAL ALL PARTI-TIONS CONNECT-ING TO CENTRAL DOGMA!

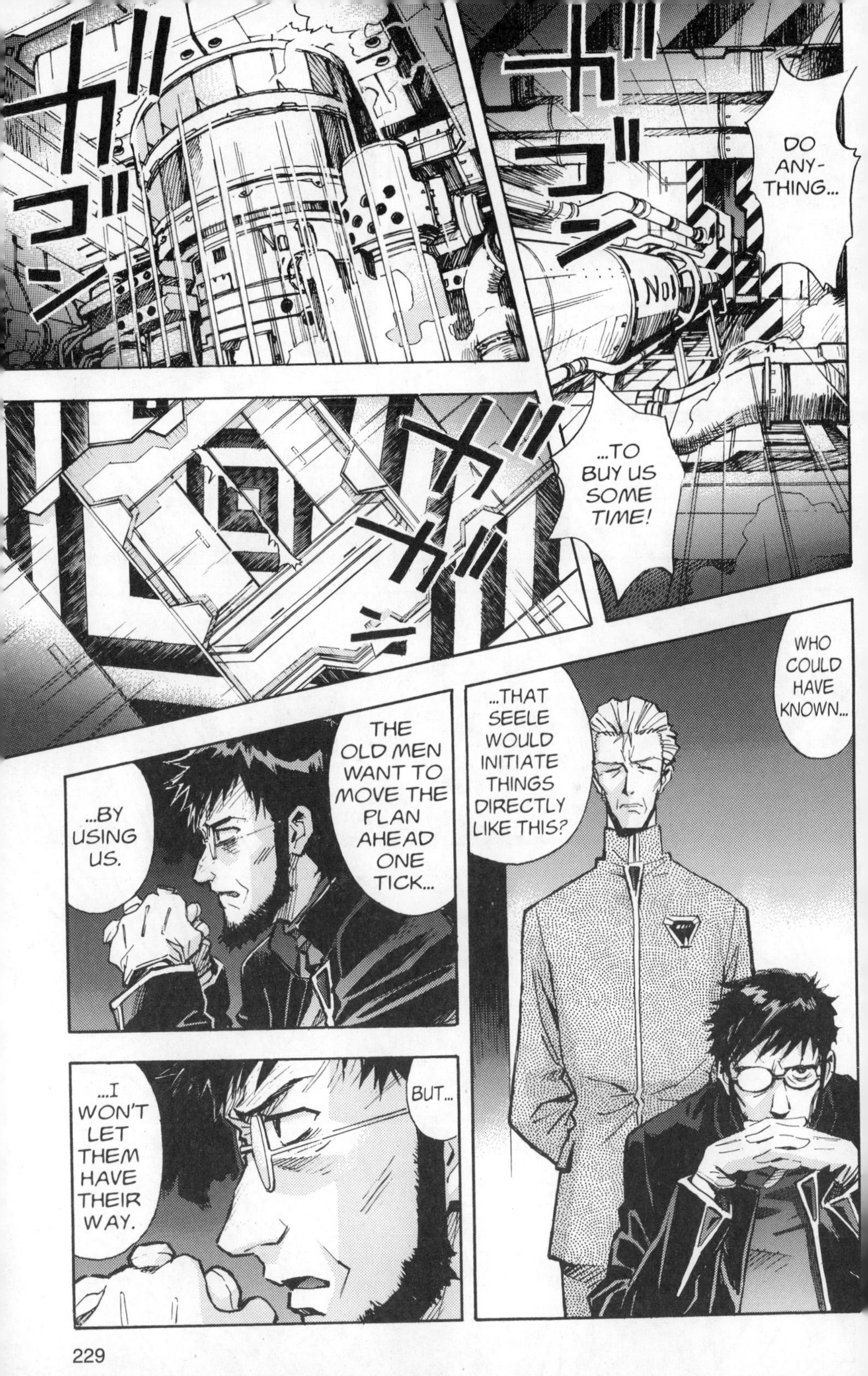
DO ANY-THING...
...TO BUY US SOME TIME!
WHO COULD HAVE KNOWN...
...THAT SEELE WOULD INITIATE THINGS DIRECTLY LIKE THIS?
THE OLD MEN WANT TO MOVE THE PLAN AHEAD ONE TICK...
...BY USING US.
BUT...
...I WON'T LET THEM HAVE THEIR WAY.

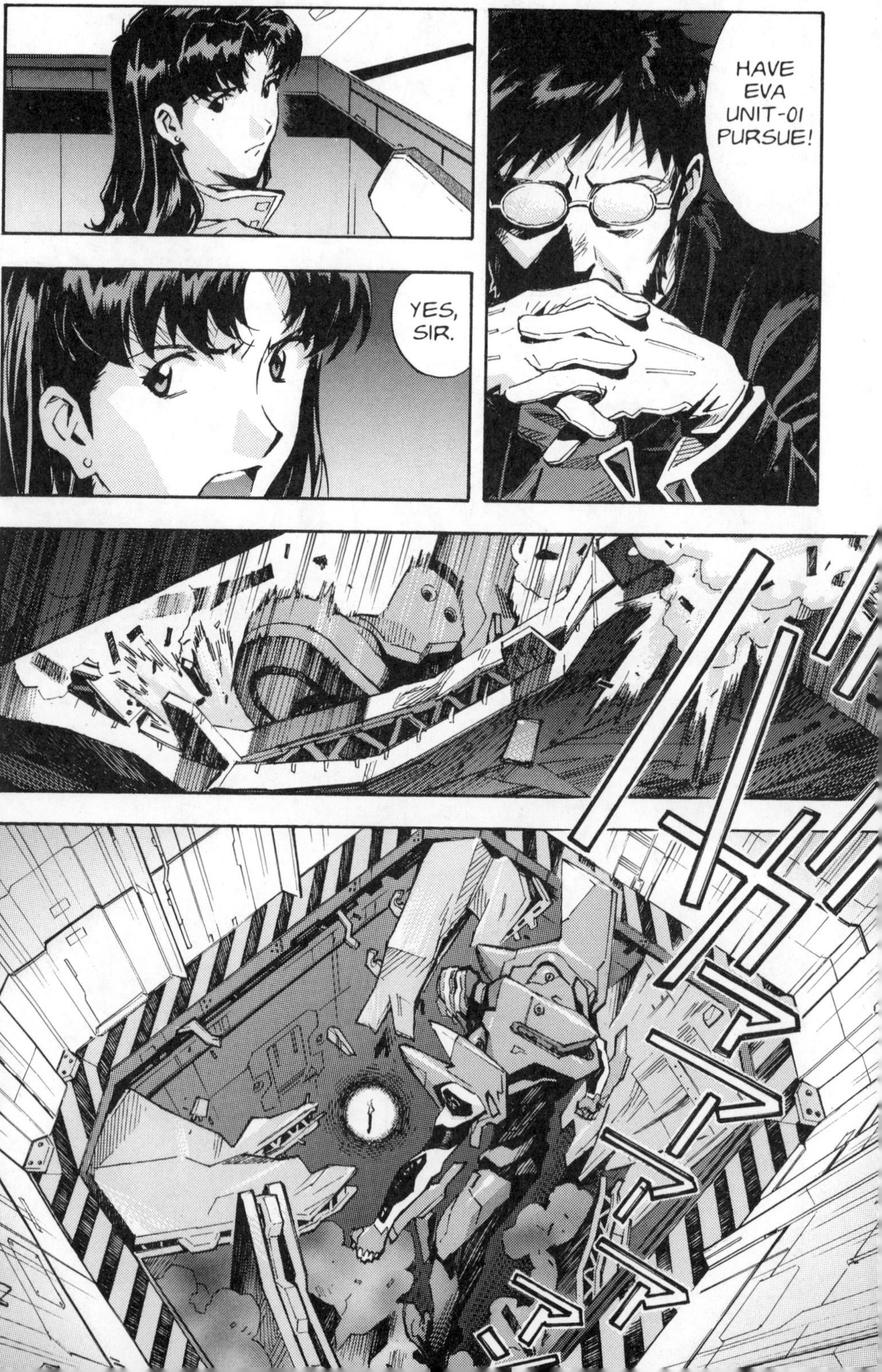
HAVE EVA UNIT-01 PURSUE!
YES, SIR.

SHINJI!

EVA UNIT-02 HAS PENE-TRATED THE ARMORED PARTITION!

PARTITION No.

17

XXXXX

Object EVA-02

Object 12th ANGEL

PARTITION N

18

XX

DAMAGED
CONDITION

PROTECTION

19

XXXXX

PARTITION No.

20

CRISIS LEV

CON-FIRMED! THE TARGET HAS PASSED THROUGH PARTITION 17!!

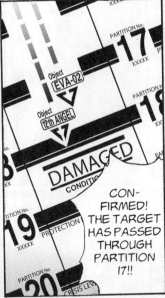

PREVENT THE TARGET FROM REACHING THE LOWEST LEVEL...

...BY ANY MEANS NECES-SARY!

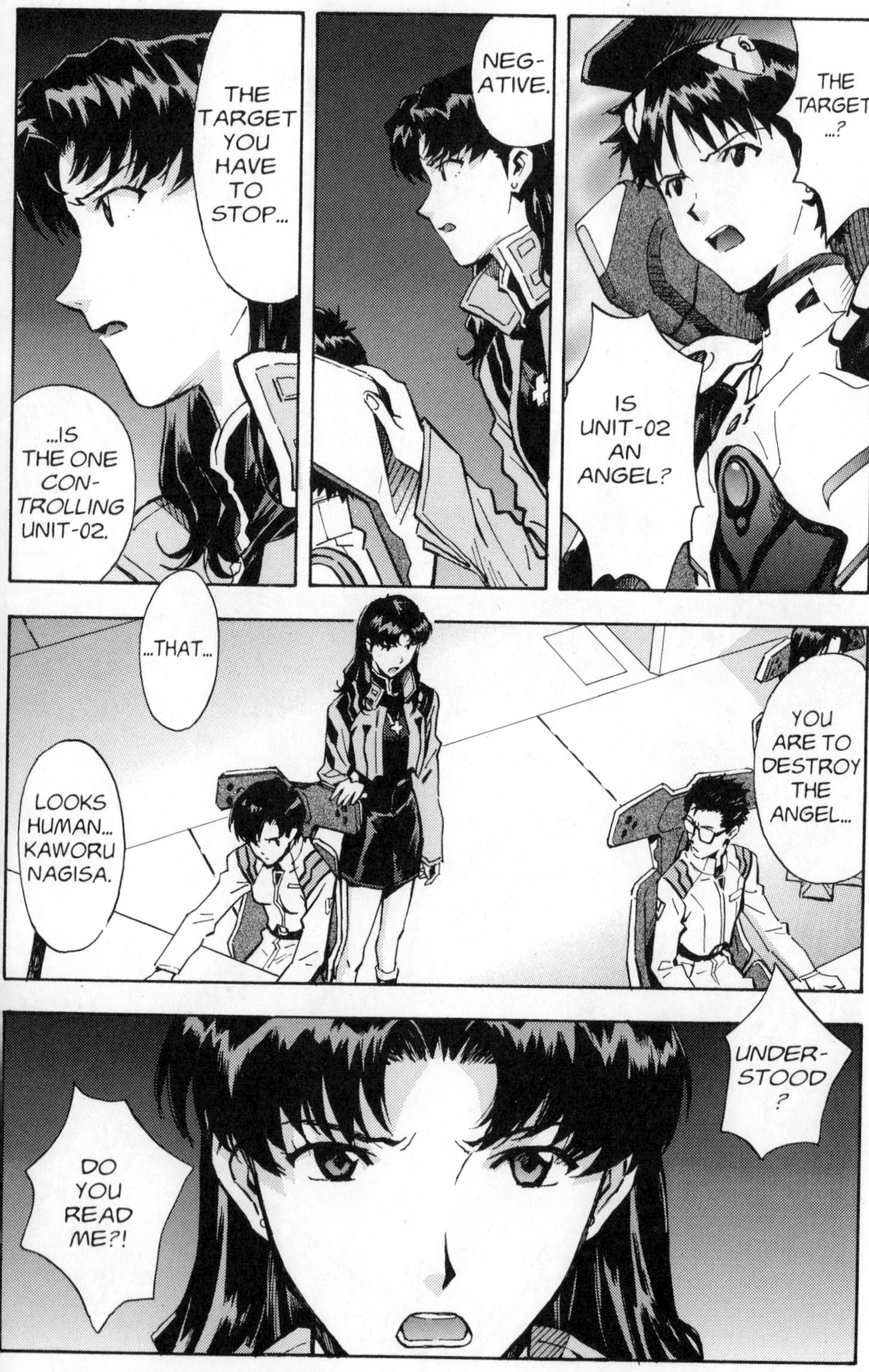
THE TARGET ...?
IS UNIT-02 AN ANGEL?
NEG-ATIVE.
THE TARGET YOU HAVE TO STOP...
...IS THE ONE CON-TROLLING UNIT-02.
YOU ARE TO DESTROY THE ANGEL...
...THAT...
LOOKS HUMAN... KAWORU NAGISA.
UNDER-STOOD ?
DO YOU READ ME?!

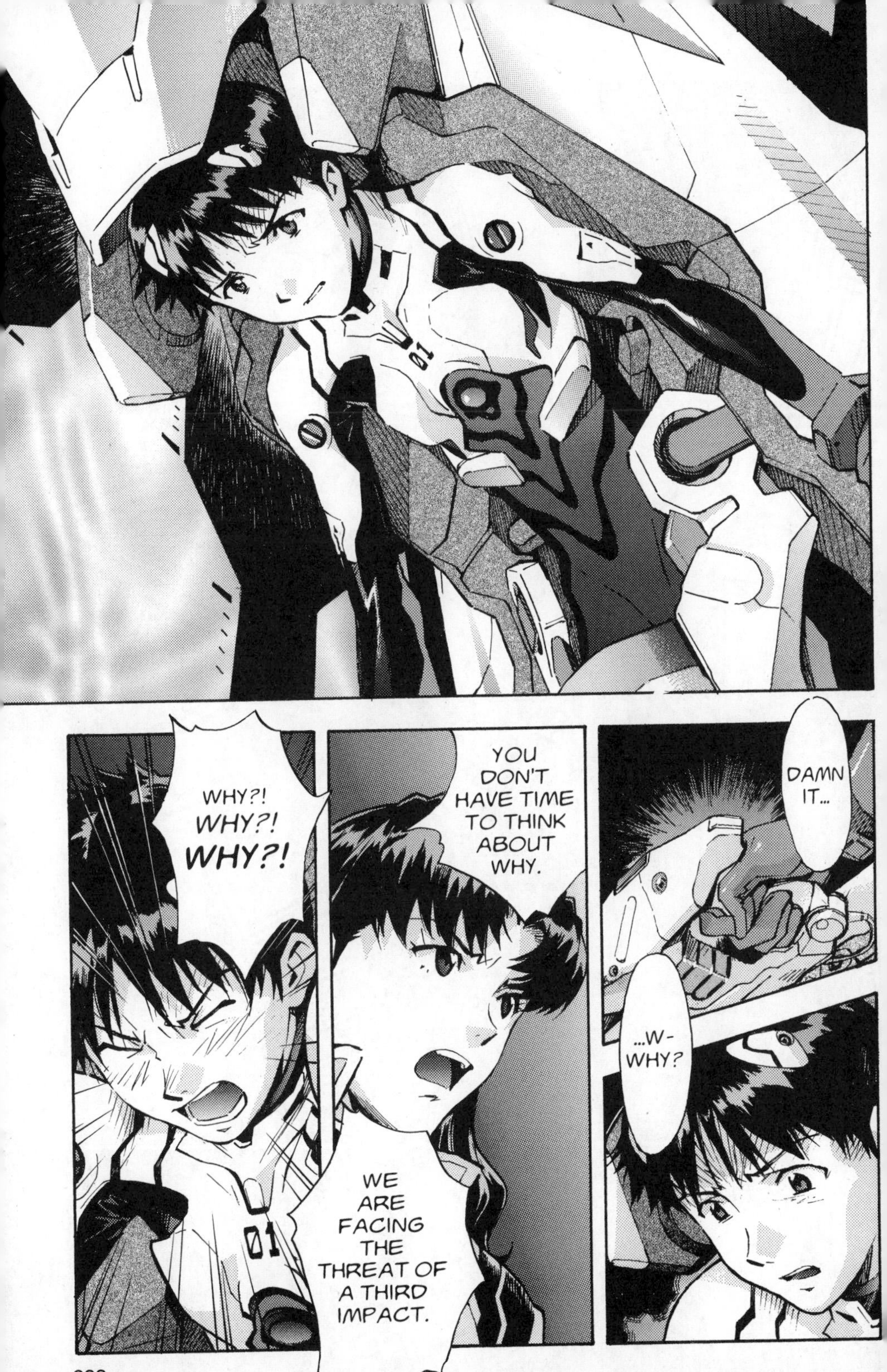
DAMN IT...
...W-WHY?
YOU DON'T HAVE TIME TO THINK ABOUT WHY.
WE ARE FACING THE THREAT OF A THIRD IMPACT.
WHY?! WHY?! WHY?!

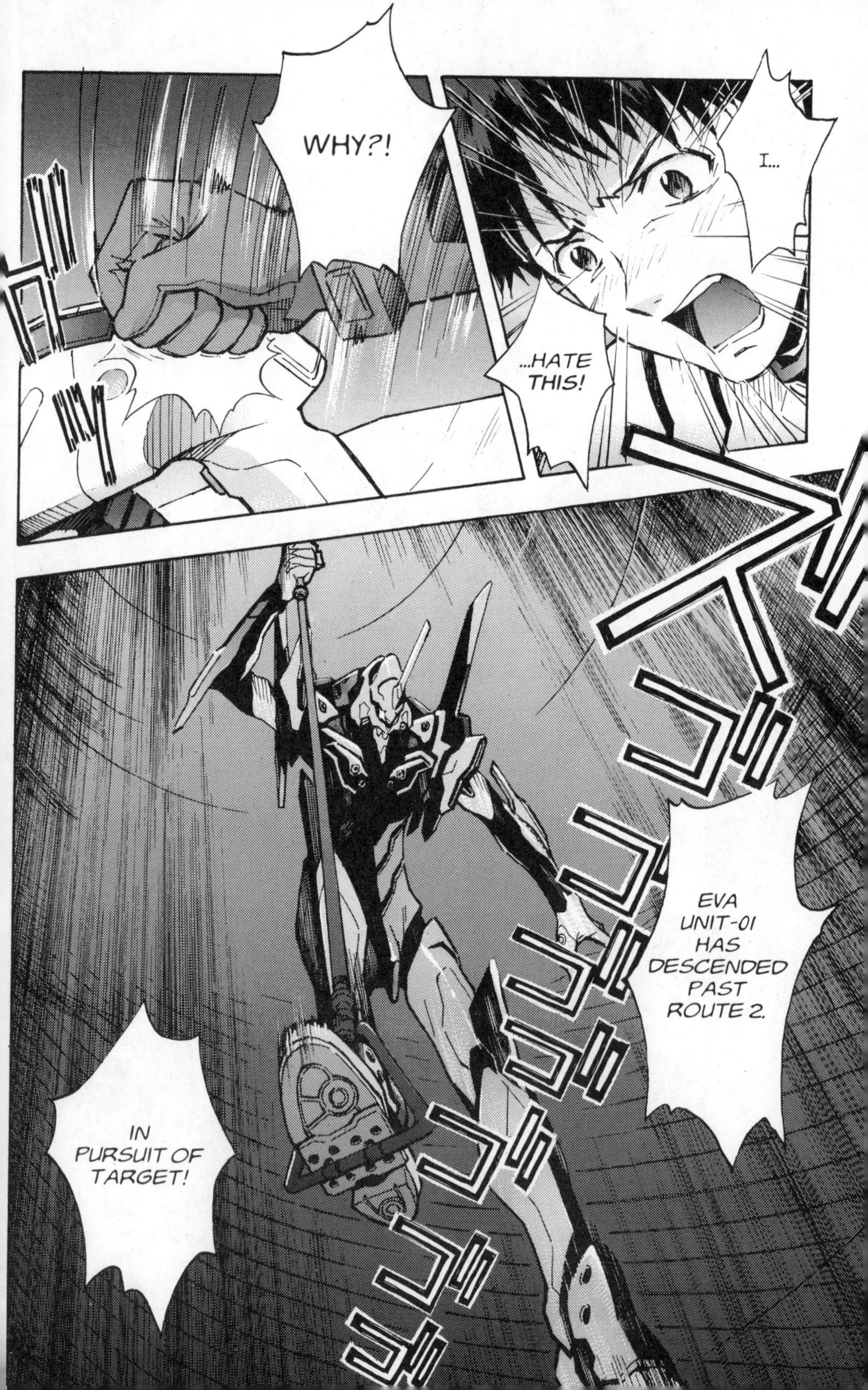
I...
...HATE THIS!
WHY?!
EVA UNIT-01 HAS DESCENDED PAST ROUTE 2.
IN PURSUIT OF TARGET!

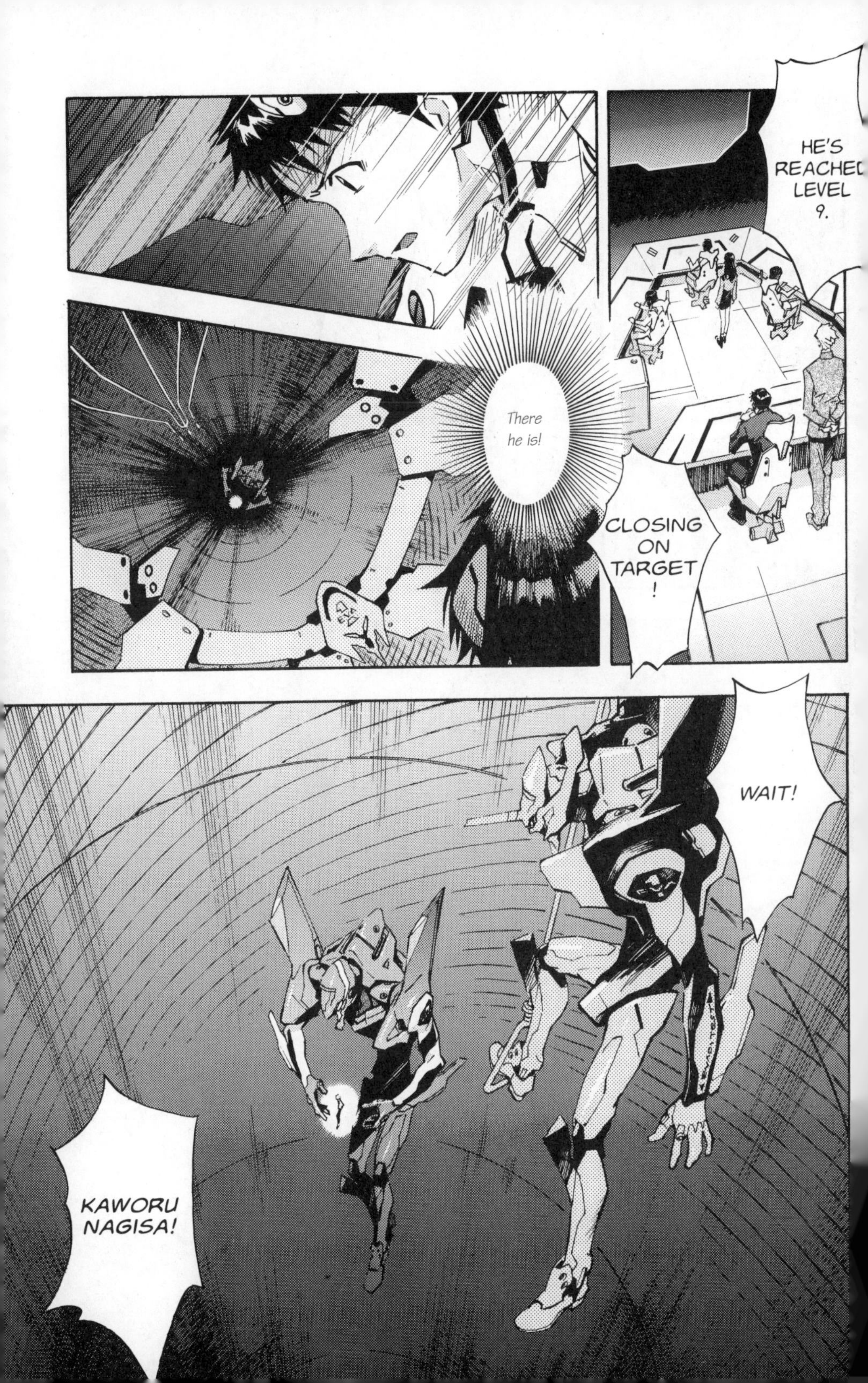
HE'S REACHED LEVEL 9.
CLOSING ON TARGET!
There he is!
WAIT!
KAWORU NAGISA!

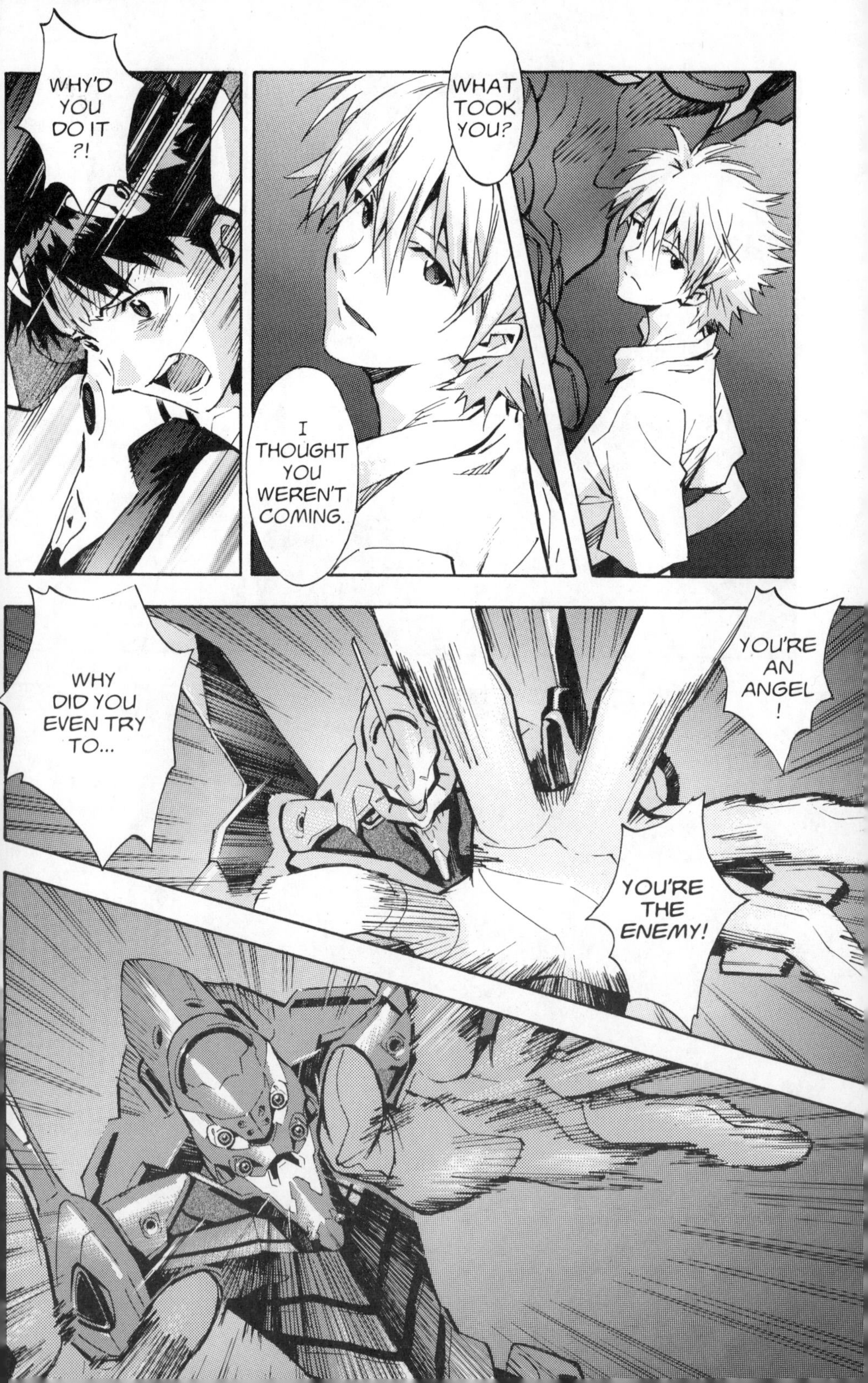
WHAT TOOK YOU?
I THOUGHT YOU WEREN'T COMING.
WHY'D YOU DO IT ?!
YOU'RE AN ANGEL !
WHY DID YOU EVEN TRY TO...
YOU'RE THE ENEMY!

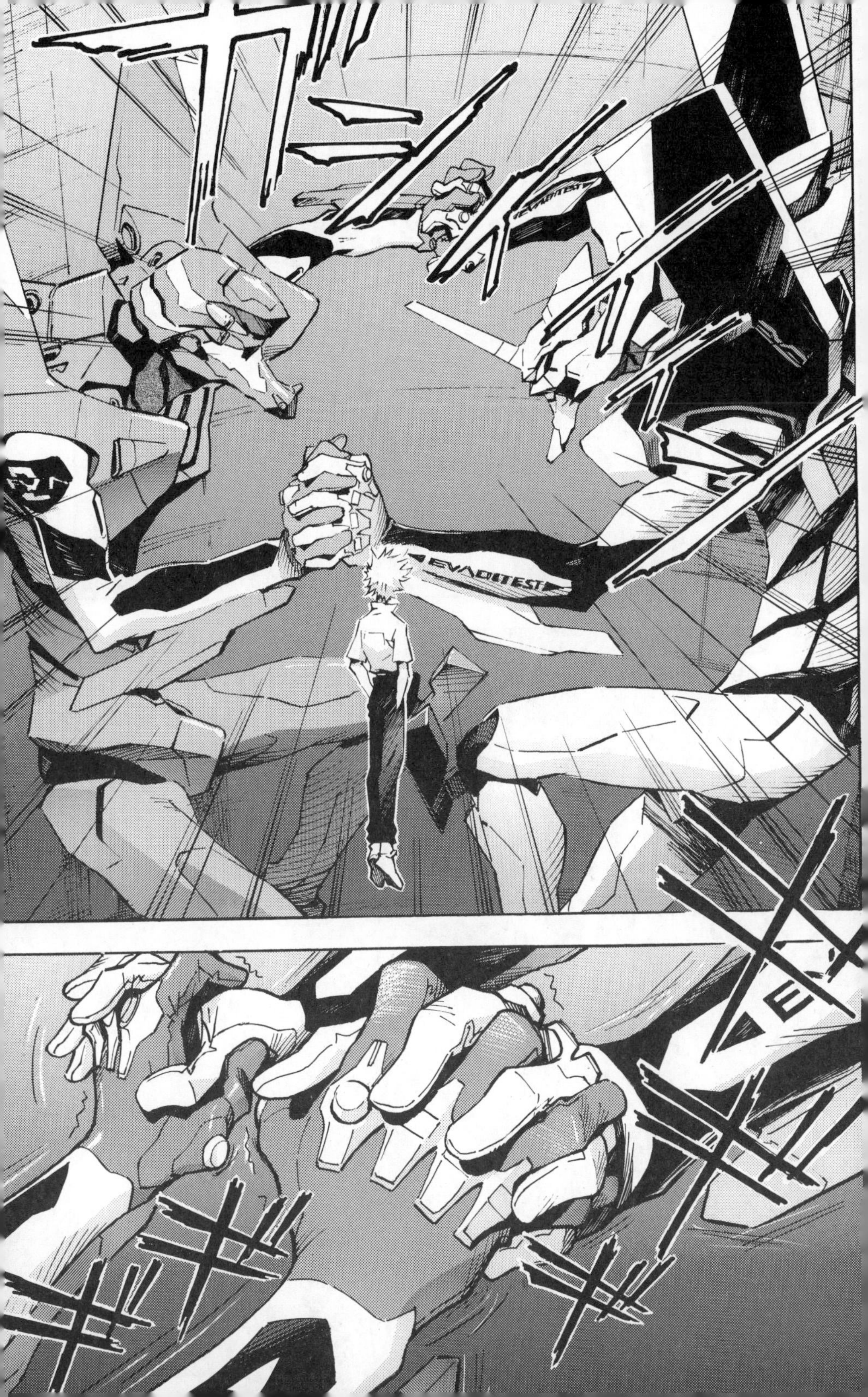
EVA01TEST
EVA01TEST

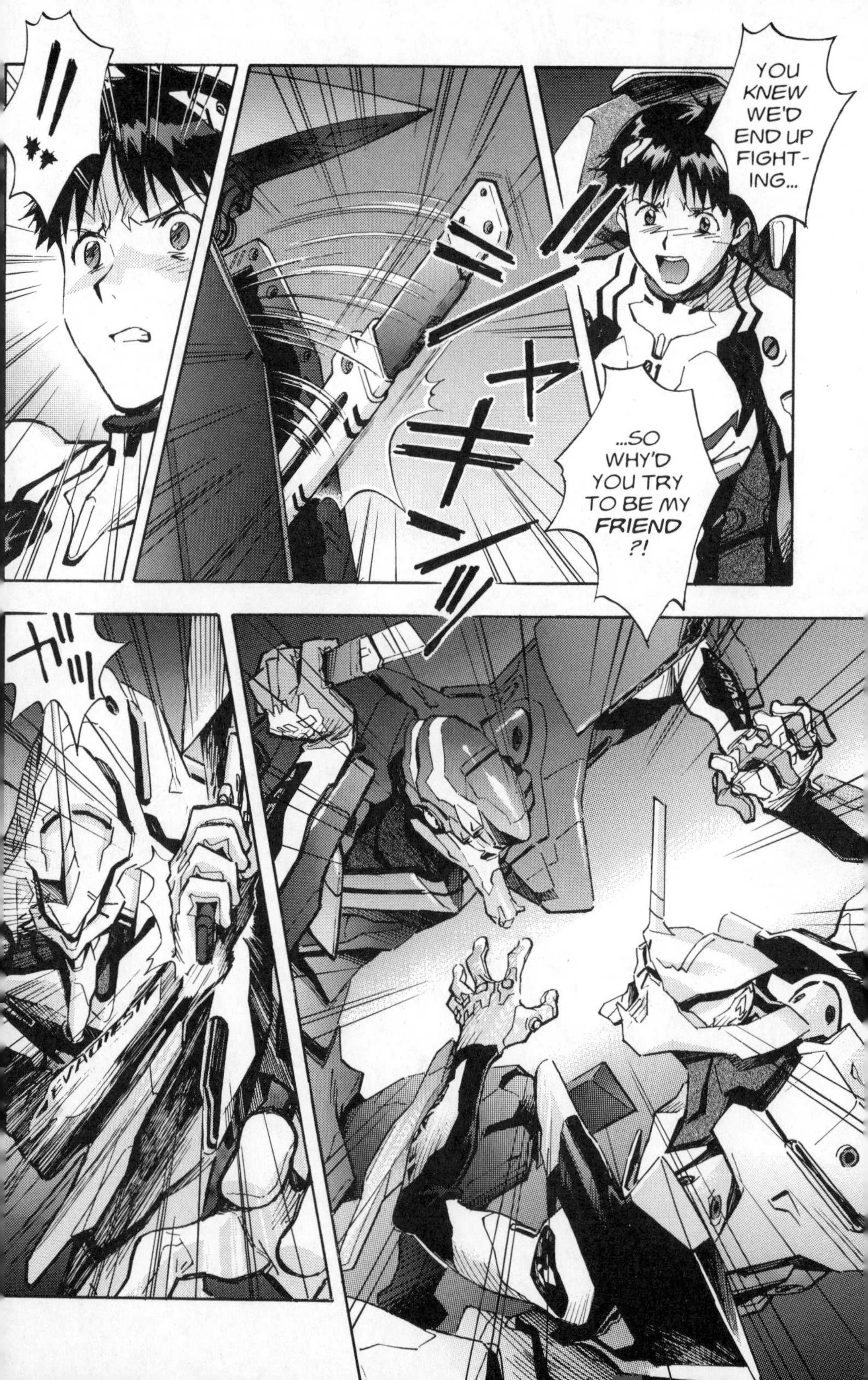
YOU KNEW WE'D END UP FIGHT-ING...
...SO WHY'D YOU TRY TO BE MY **FRIEND** ?!

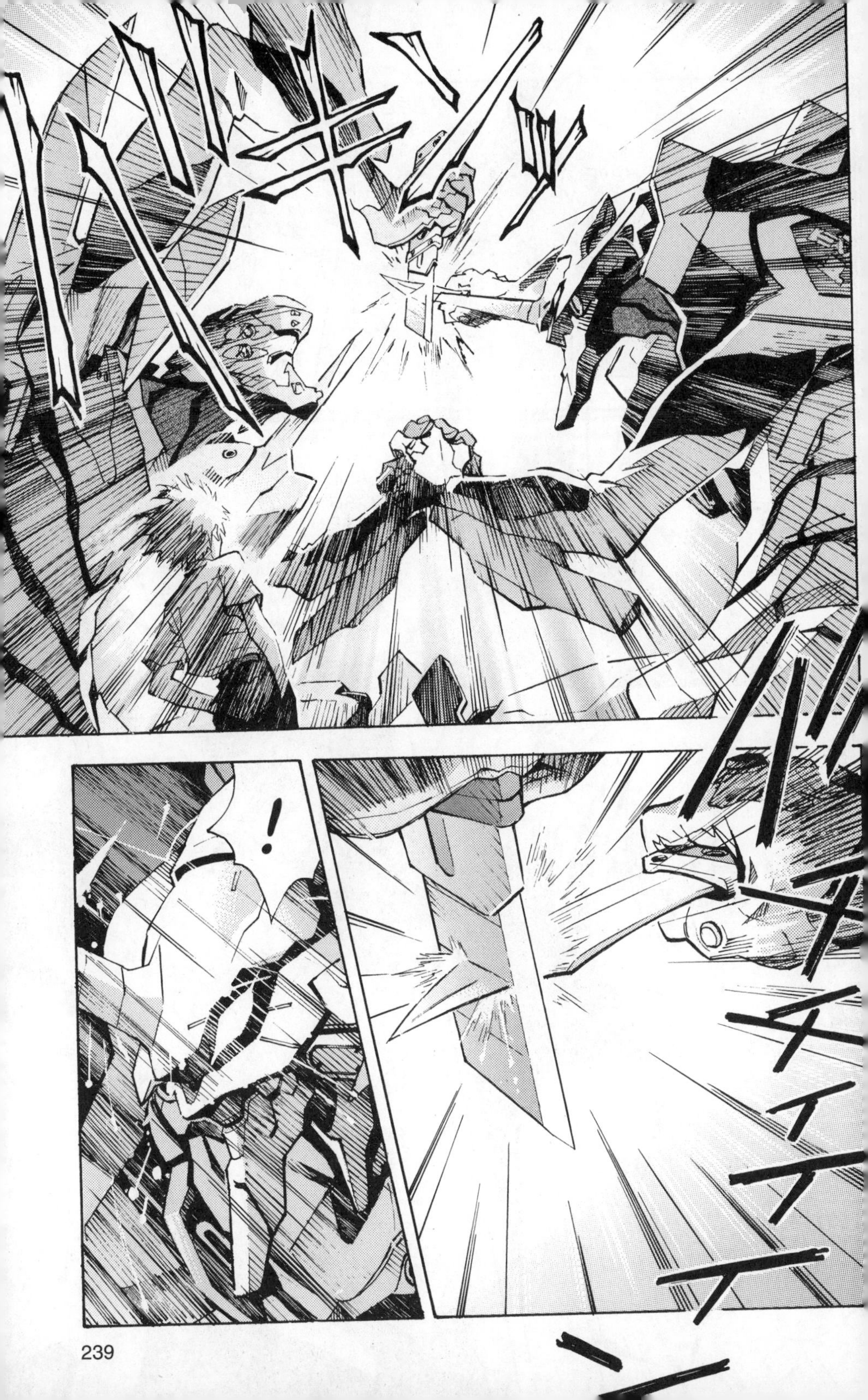
!

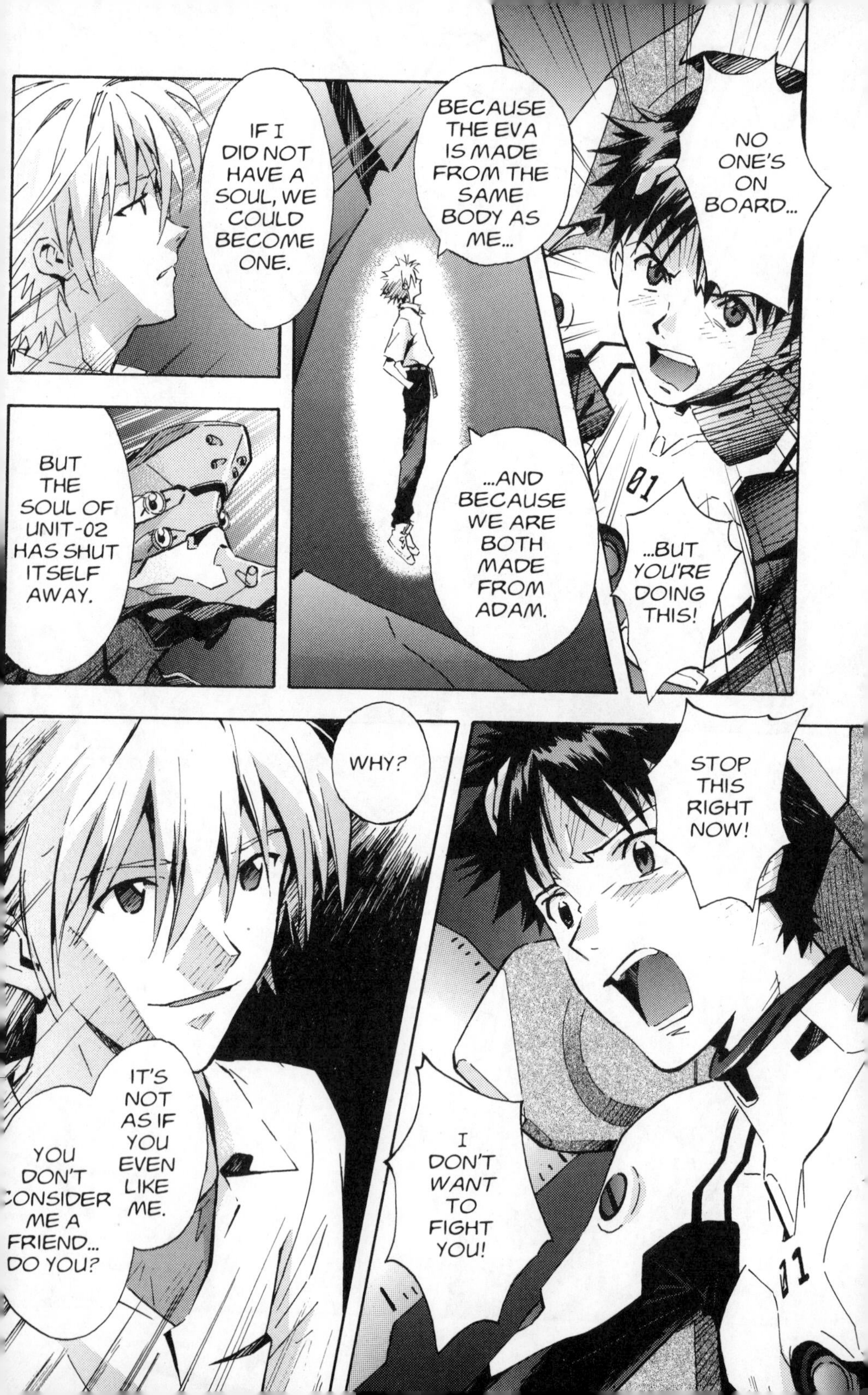
NO ONE'S ON BOARD...
...BUT YOU'RE DOING THIS!
BECAUSE THE EVA IS MADE FROM THE SAME BODY AS ME...
...AND BECAUSE WE ARE BOTH MADE FROM ADAM.
IF I DID NOT HAVE A SOUL, WE COULD BECOME ONE.
BUT THE SOUL OF UNIT-02 HAS SHUT ITSELF AWAY.
STOP THIS RIGHT NOW!
I DON'T WANT TO FIGHT YOU!
WHY?
IT'S NOT AS IF YOU EVEN LIKE ME.
YOU DON'T CONSIDER ME A FRIEND... DO YOU?

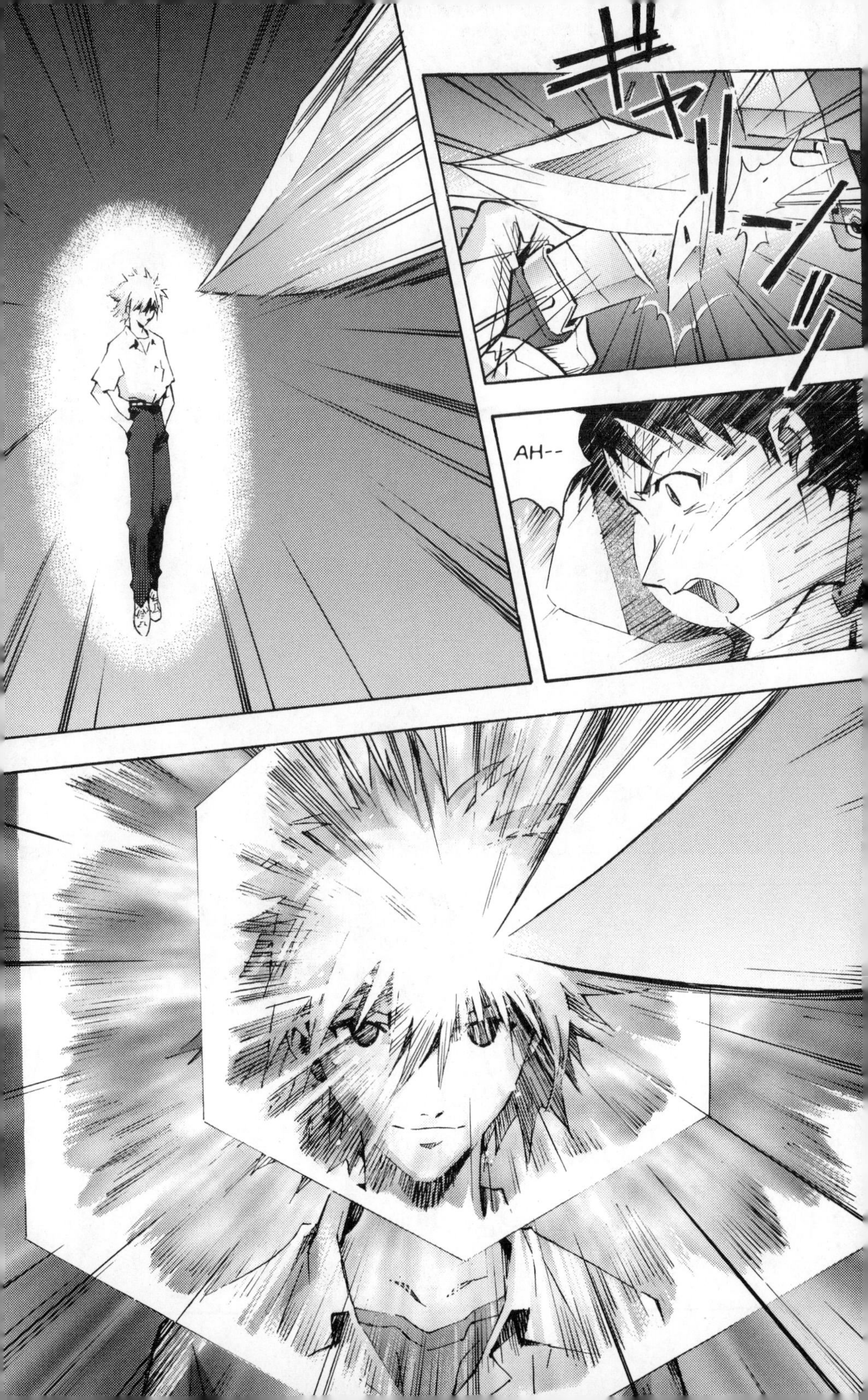
ギャリーン
AH--

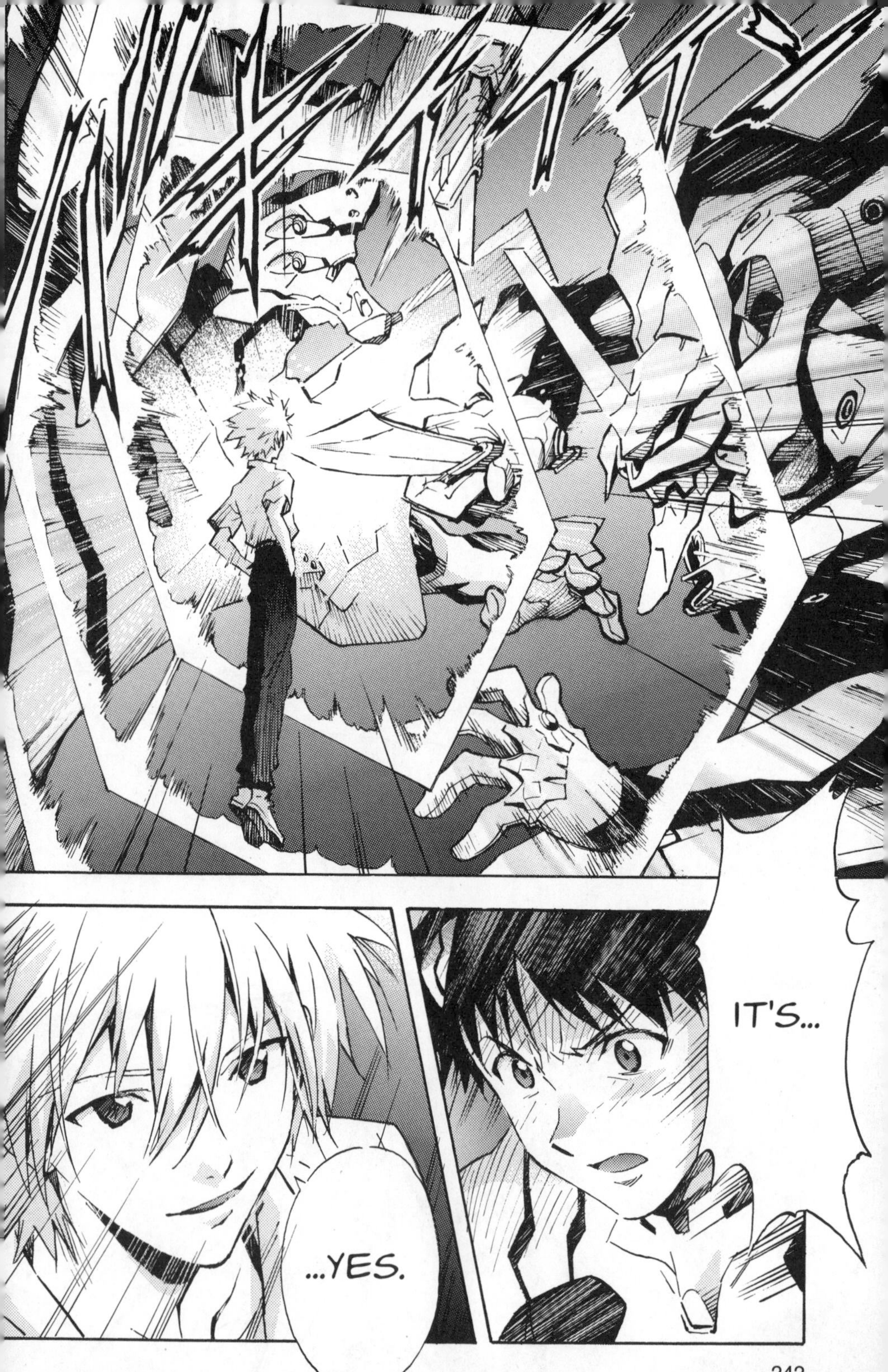
IT'S...
...YES.

NEON GENESIS EVANGELION

STAGE 73: REACHING THE BOUNDARY

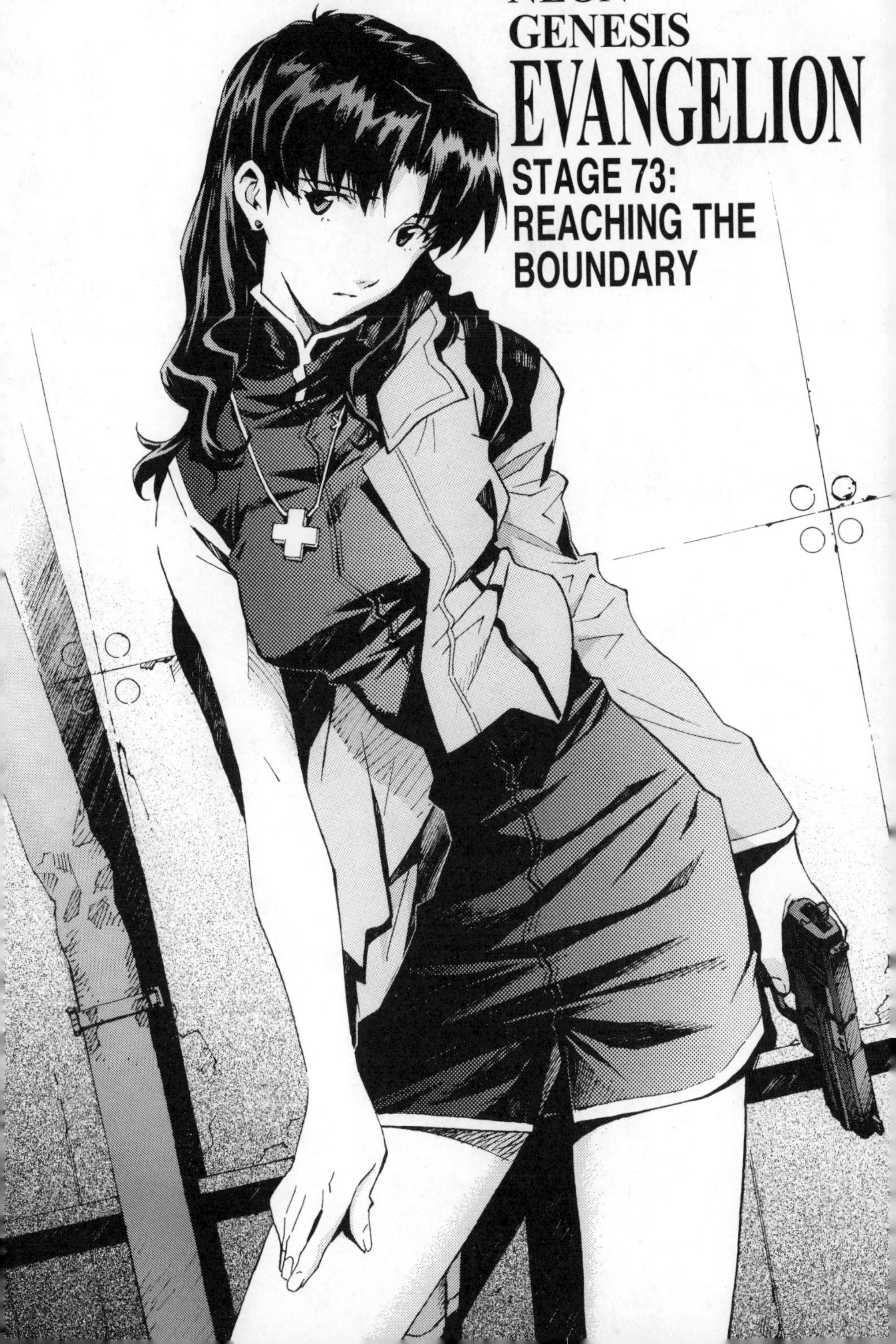

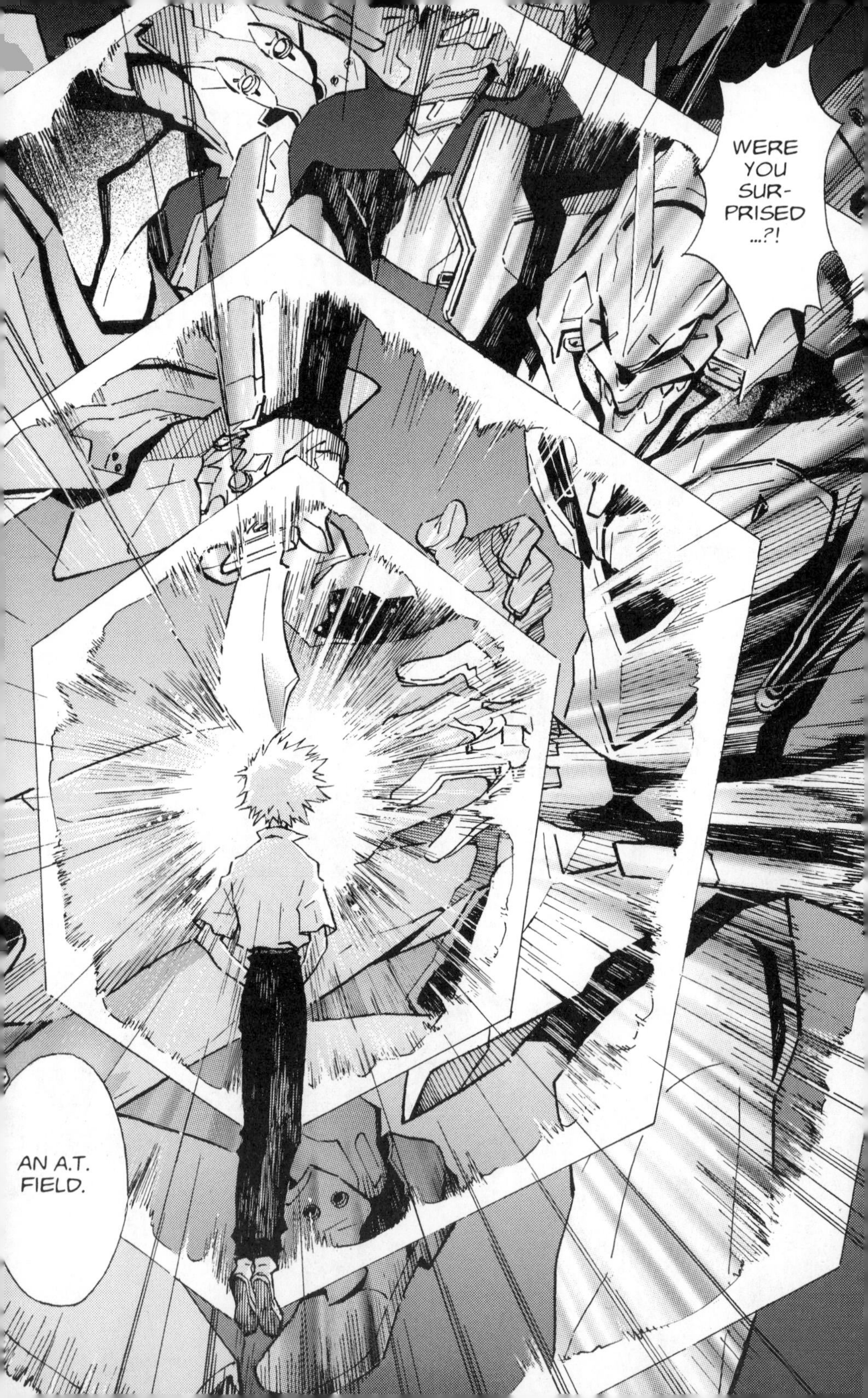
WERE YOU SUR- PRISED ...?!
AN A.T. FIELD.

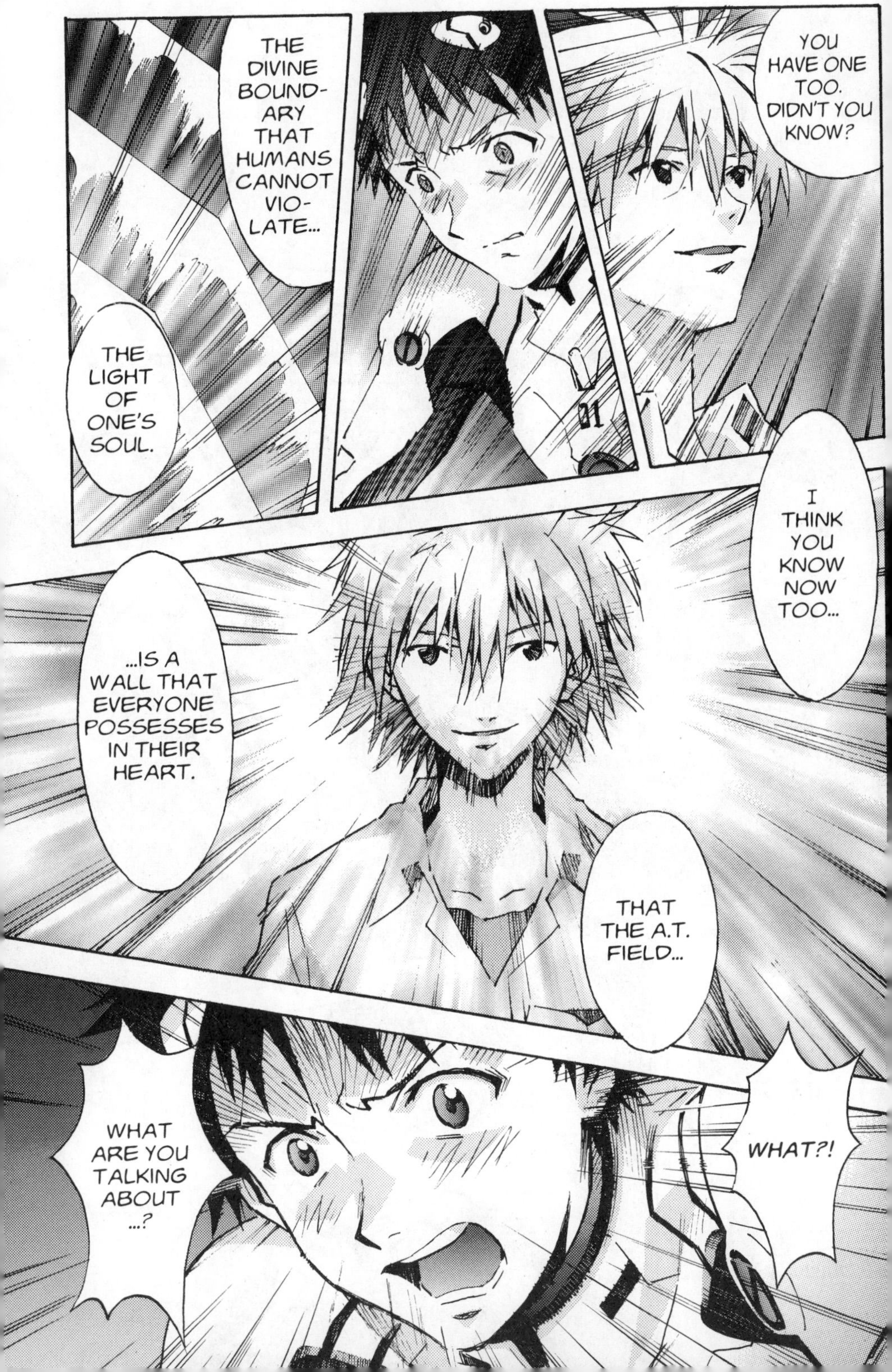
YOU HAVE ONE TOO. DIDN'T YOU KNOW?
THE DIVINE BOUNDARY THAT HUMANS CANNOT VIOLATE...
THE LIGHT OF ONE'S SOUL.
I THINK YOU KNOW NOW TOO...
THAT THE A.T. FIELD...
...IS A WALL THAT EVERYONE POSSESSES IN THEIR HEART.
WHAT?!
WHAT ARE YOU TALKING ABOUT ...?

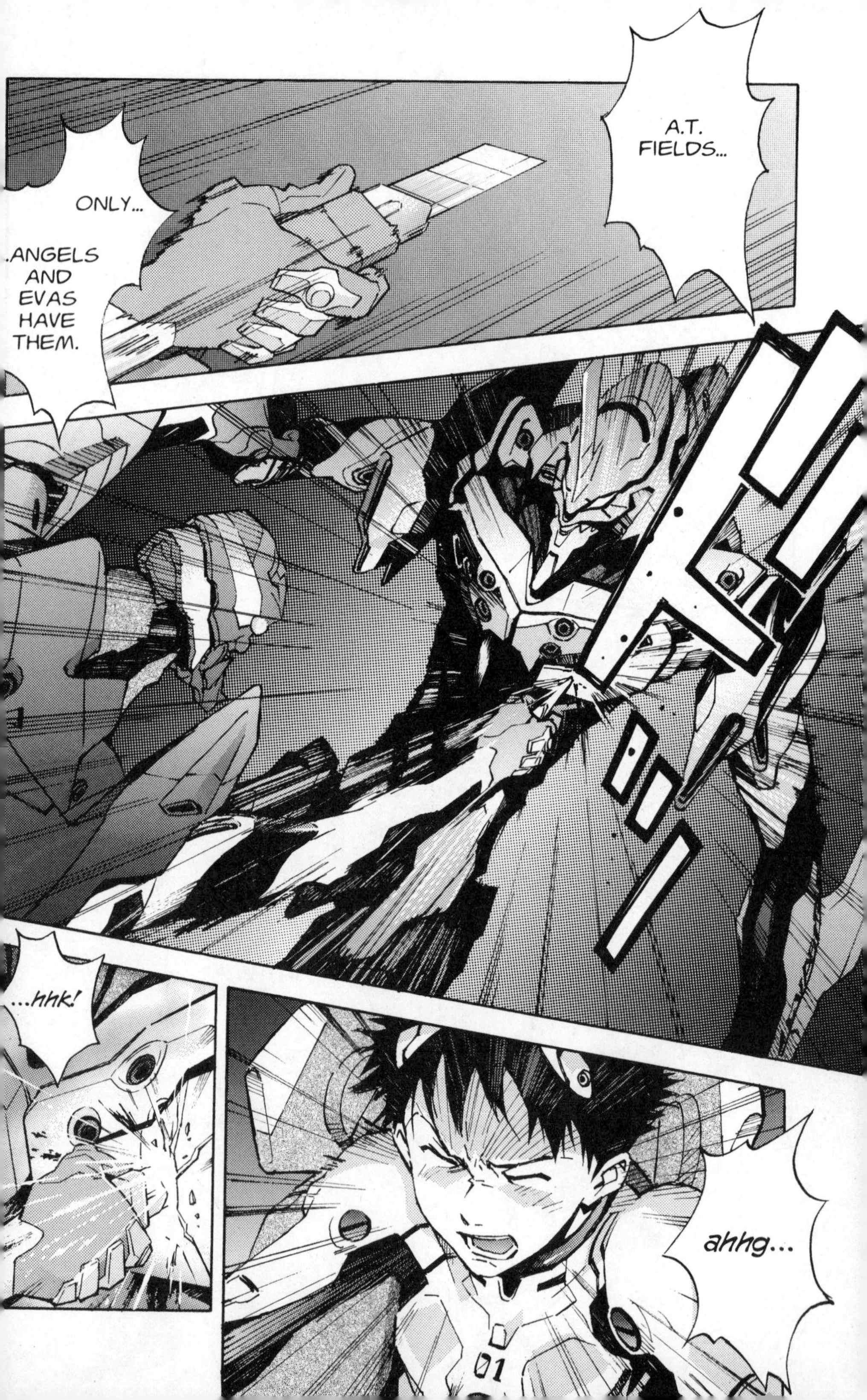
A.T. FIELDS...
ONLY...
.ANGELS AND EVAS HAVE THEM.
ahhg...
...hhk!

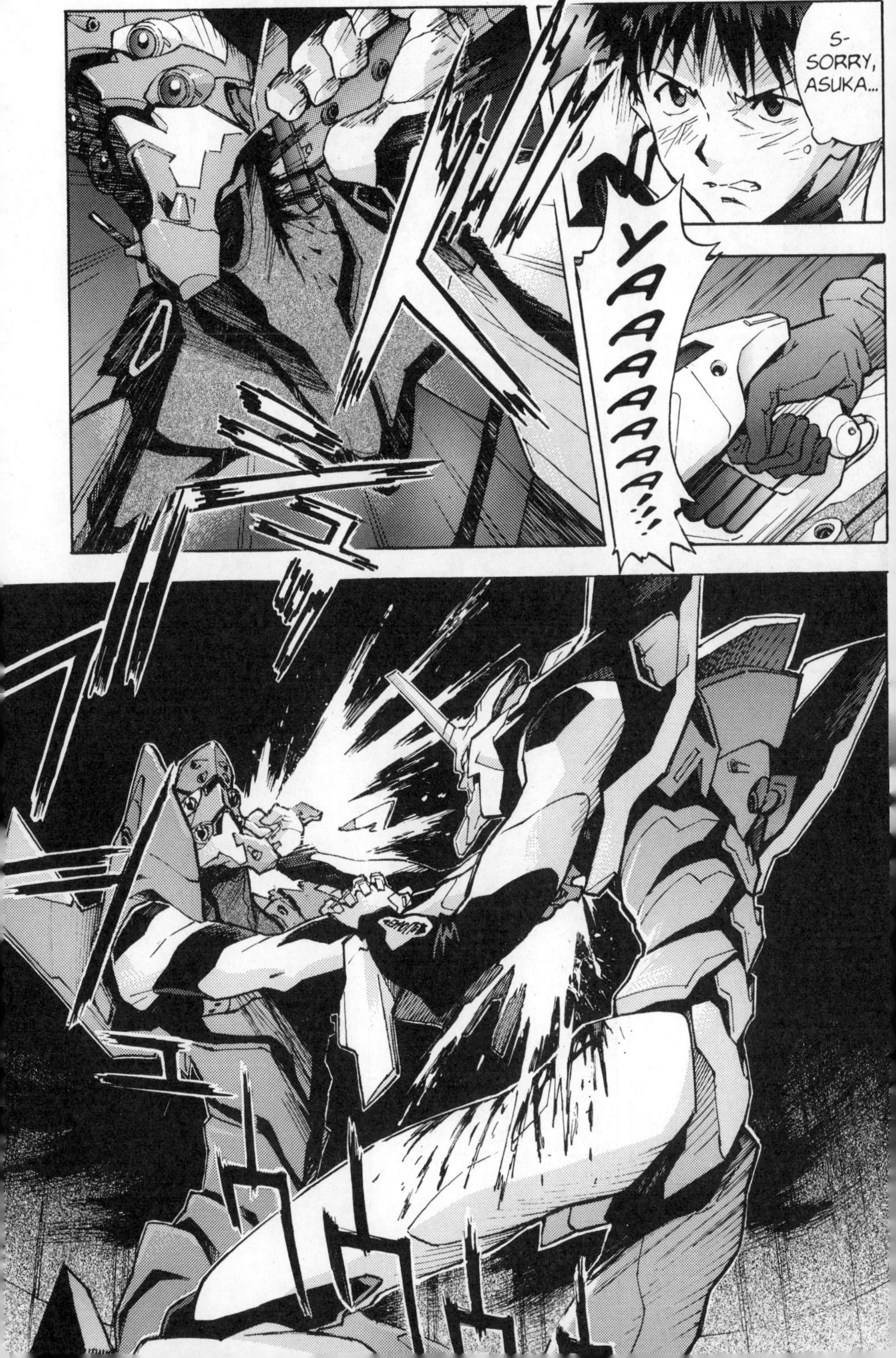
S-SORRY, ASUKA...
YAAAAAAAA!!!

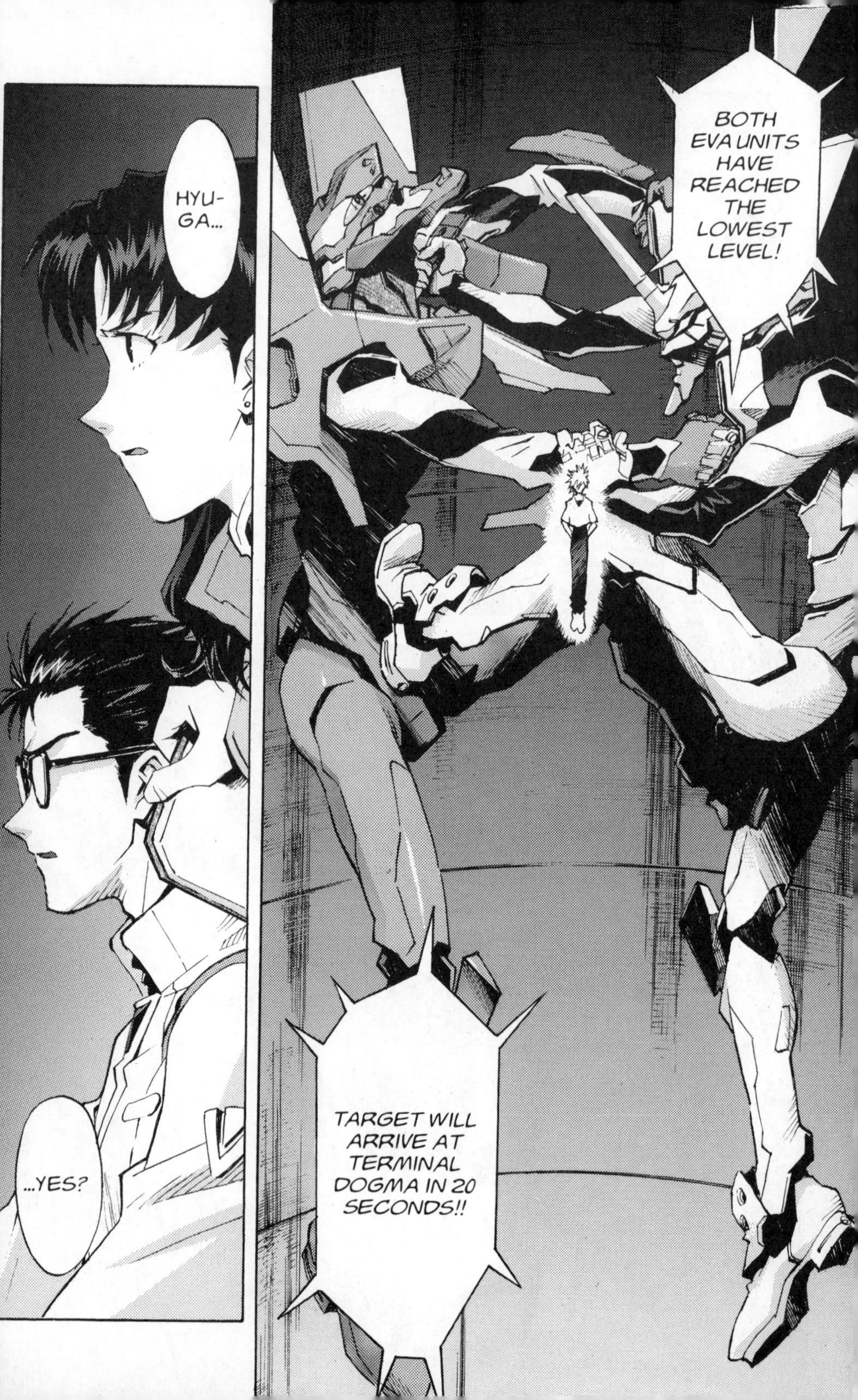
BOTH EVA UNITS HAVE REACHED THE LOWEST LEVEL!
TARGET WILL ARRIVE AT TERMINAL DOGMA IN 20 SECONDS!!
HYU-GA...
...YES?

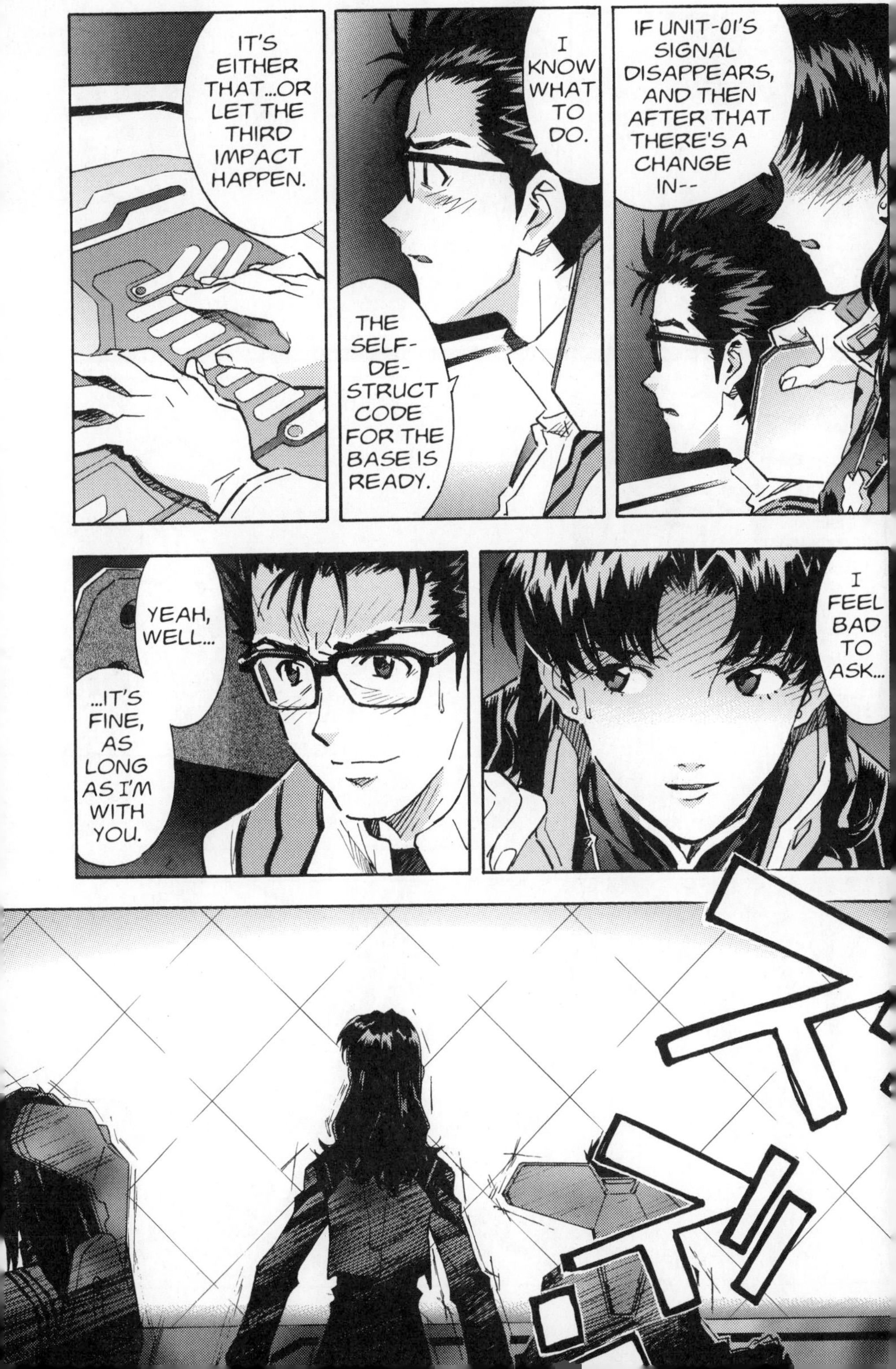
IF UNIT-01'S SIGNAL DISAPPEARS, AND THEN AFTER THAT THERE'S A CHANGE IN--
I KNOW WHAT TO DO.
THE SELF-DESTRUCT CODE FOR THE BASE IS READY.
IT'S EITHER THAT...OR LET THE THIRD IMPACT HAPPEN.
I FEEL BAD TO ASK...
YEAH, WELL...
...IT'S FINE, AS LONG AS I'M WITH YOU.

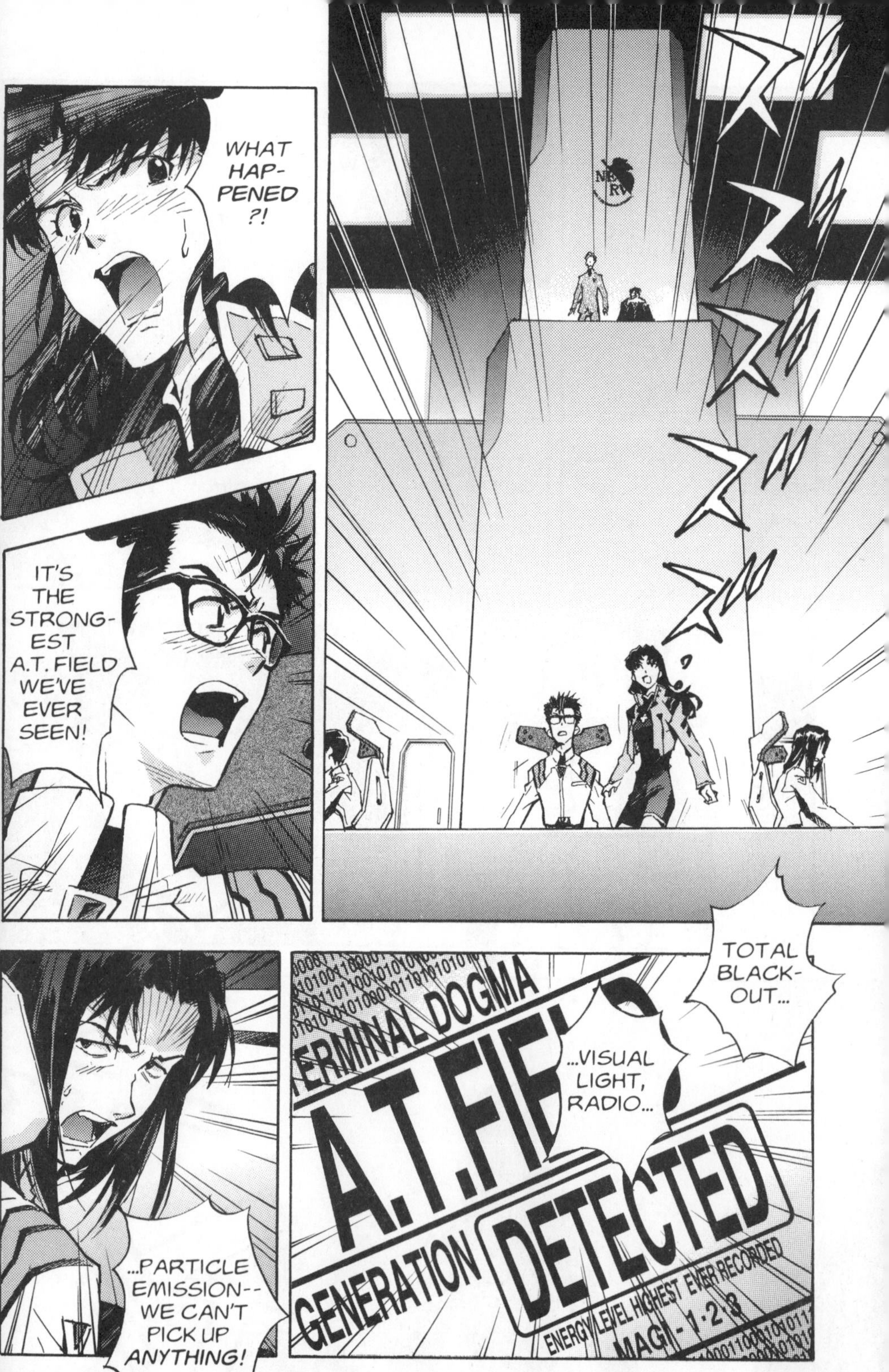
WHAT HAP-PENED?!
IT'S THE STRONGEST A.T. FIELD WE'VE EVER SEEN!
TOTAL BLACK-OUT...
TERMINAL DOGMA
A.T.FIE
GENERATION
DETECTED
ENERGY LEVEL HIGHEST EVER RECORDED
MAGI-1·2·3
...VISUAL LIGHT, RADIO...
...PARTICLE EMISSION-- WE CAN'T PICK UP ANYTHING!

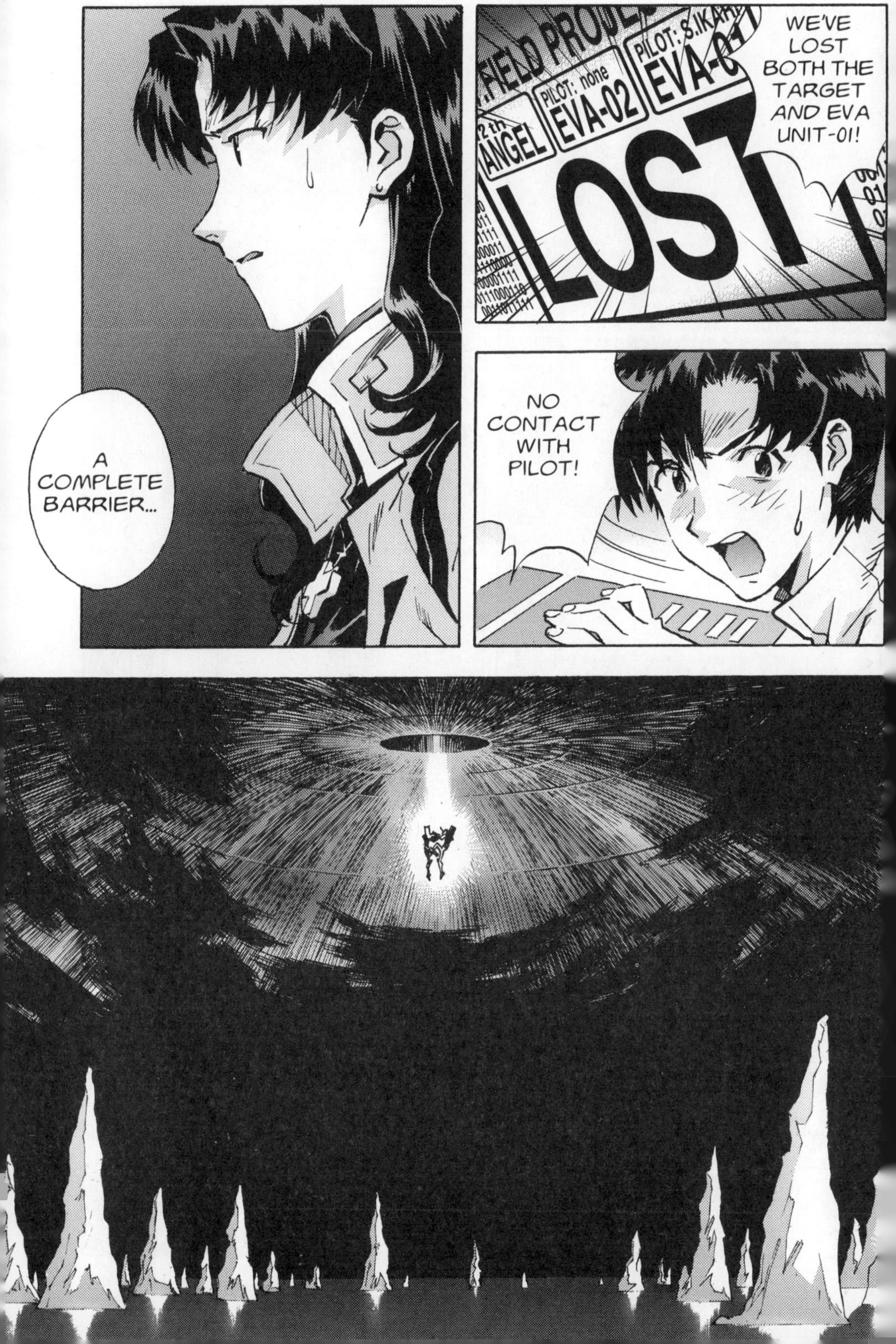
PILOT: none
EVA-02
ANGEL
LOST
WE'VE LOST BOTH THE TARGET AND EVA UNIT-01!
NO CONTACT WITH PILOT!
A COMPLETE BARRIER...

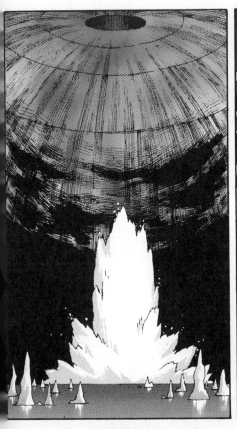

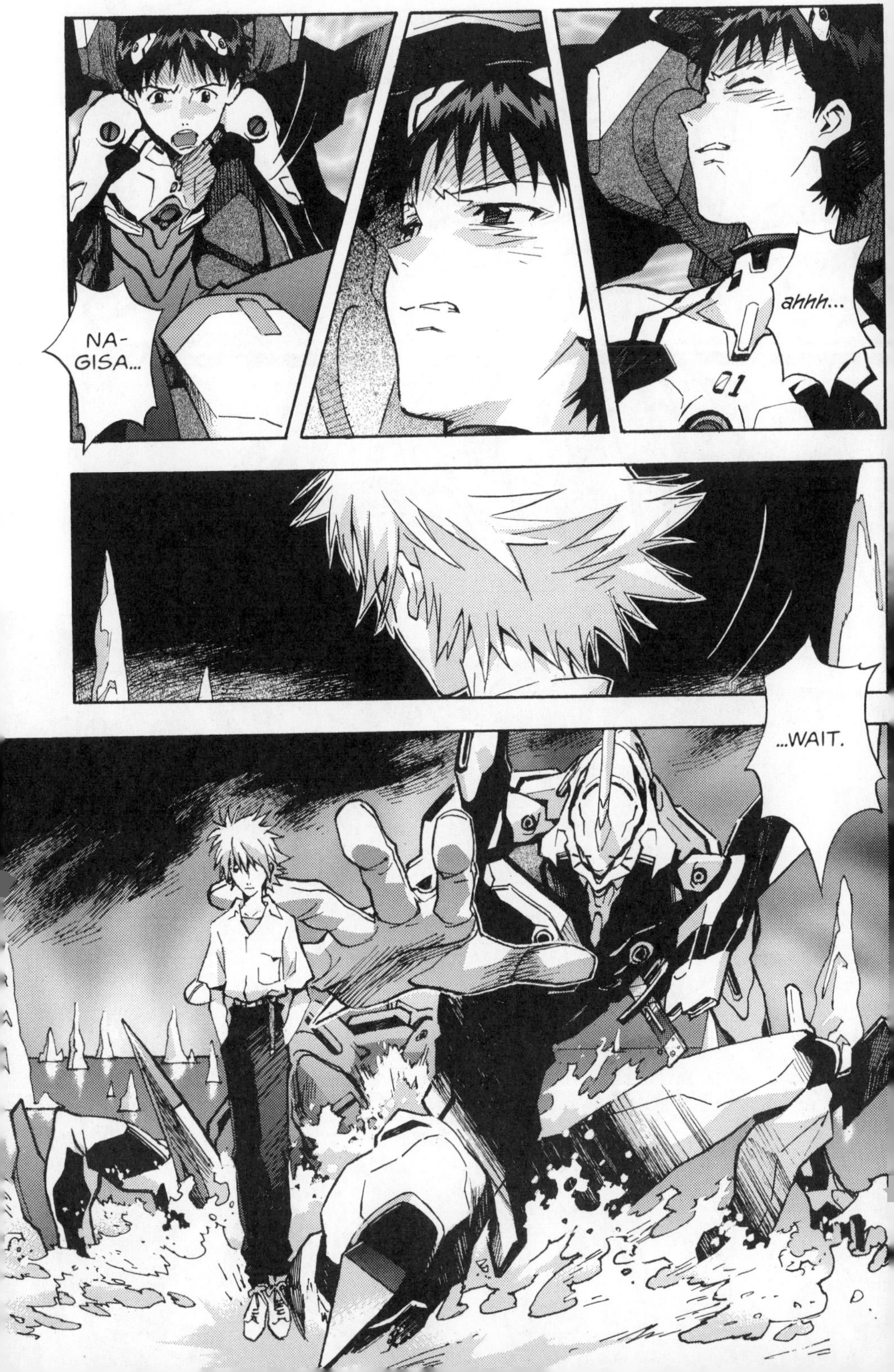
ahhh...
NA-GISA...
...WAIT.

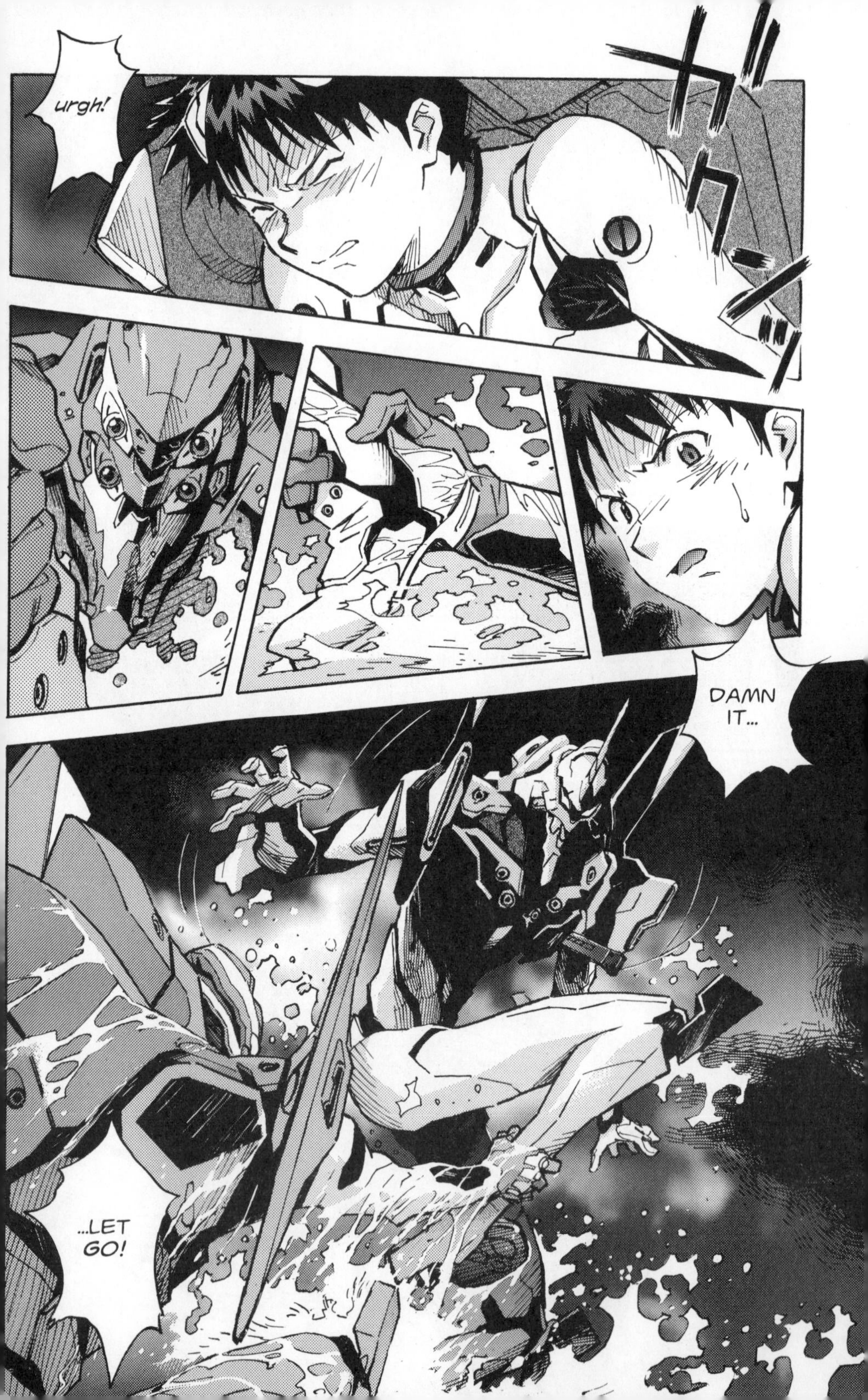
urgh!
DAMN IT...
...LET GO!

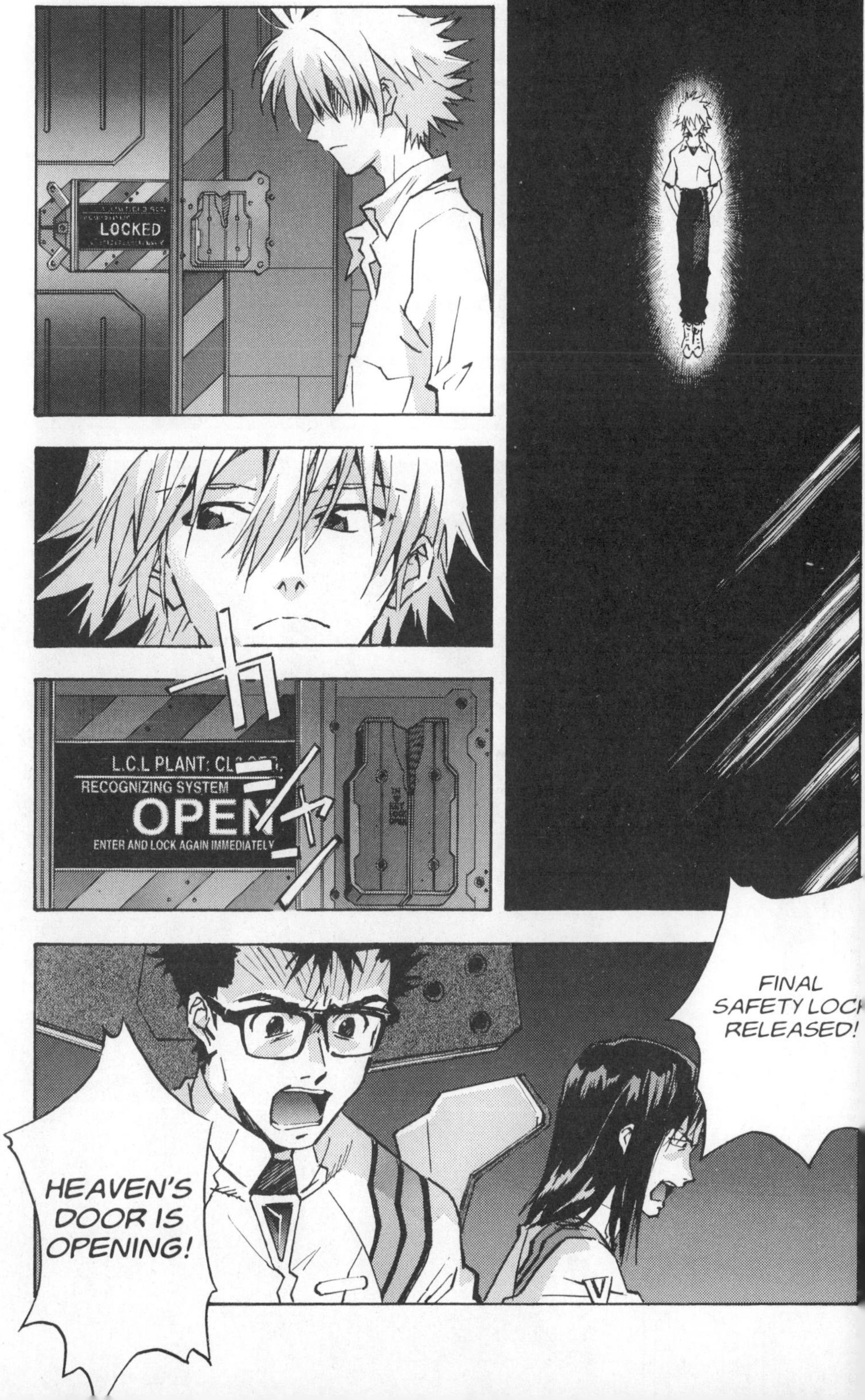
LOCKED
L.C.L PLANT: CL
RECOGNIZING SYSTEM
OPEN
ENTER AND LOCK AGAIN IMMEDIATELY
FINAL SAFETY LOCK RELEASED!
HEAVEN'S DOOR IS OPENING!

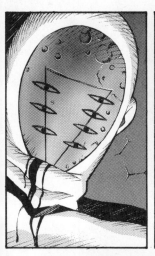

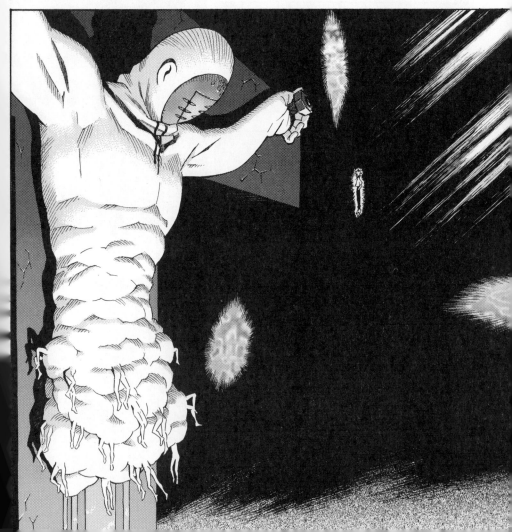

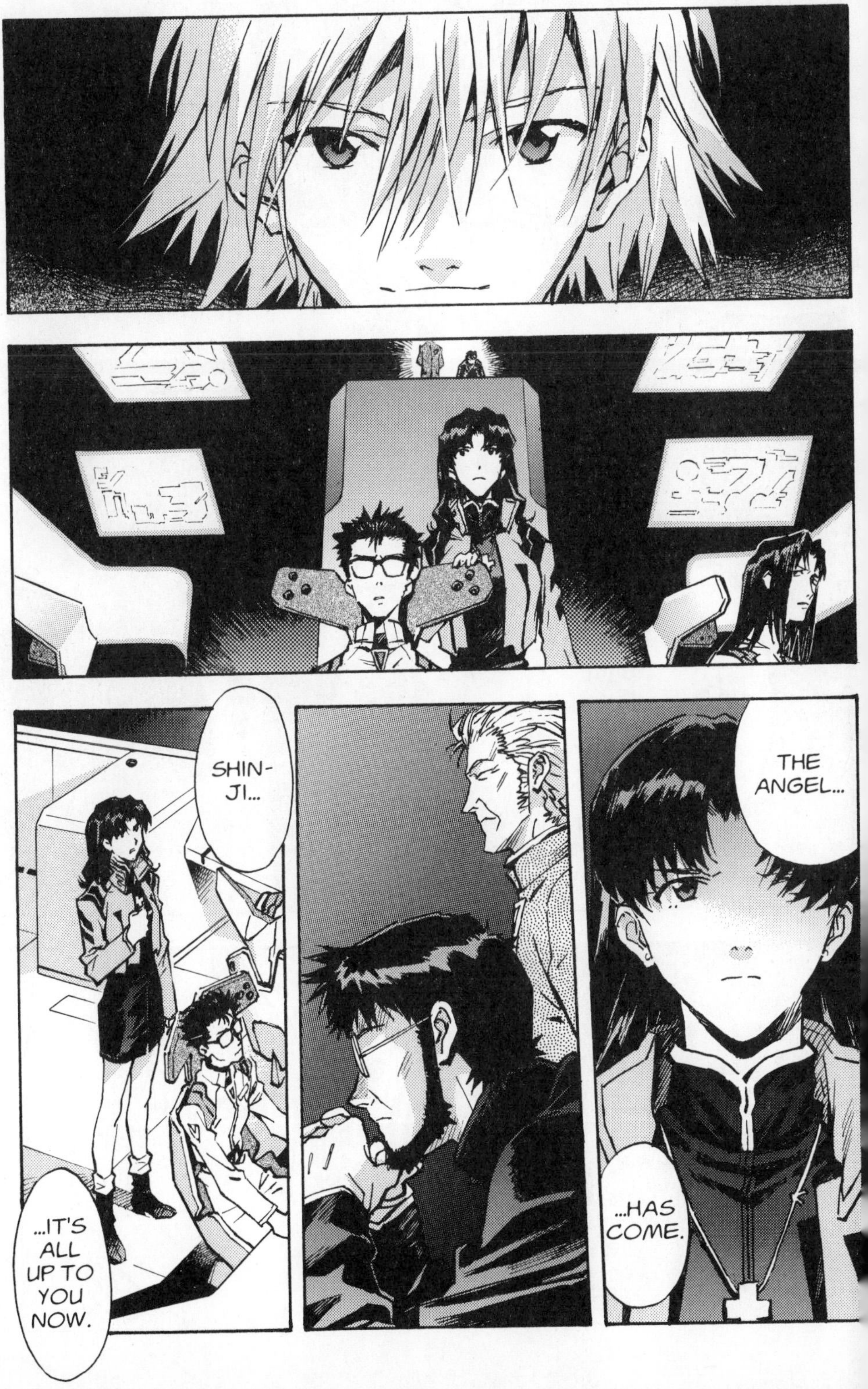
THE ANGEL...
...HAS COME.
SHIN-JI...
...IT'S ALL UP TO YOU NOW.

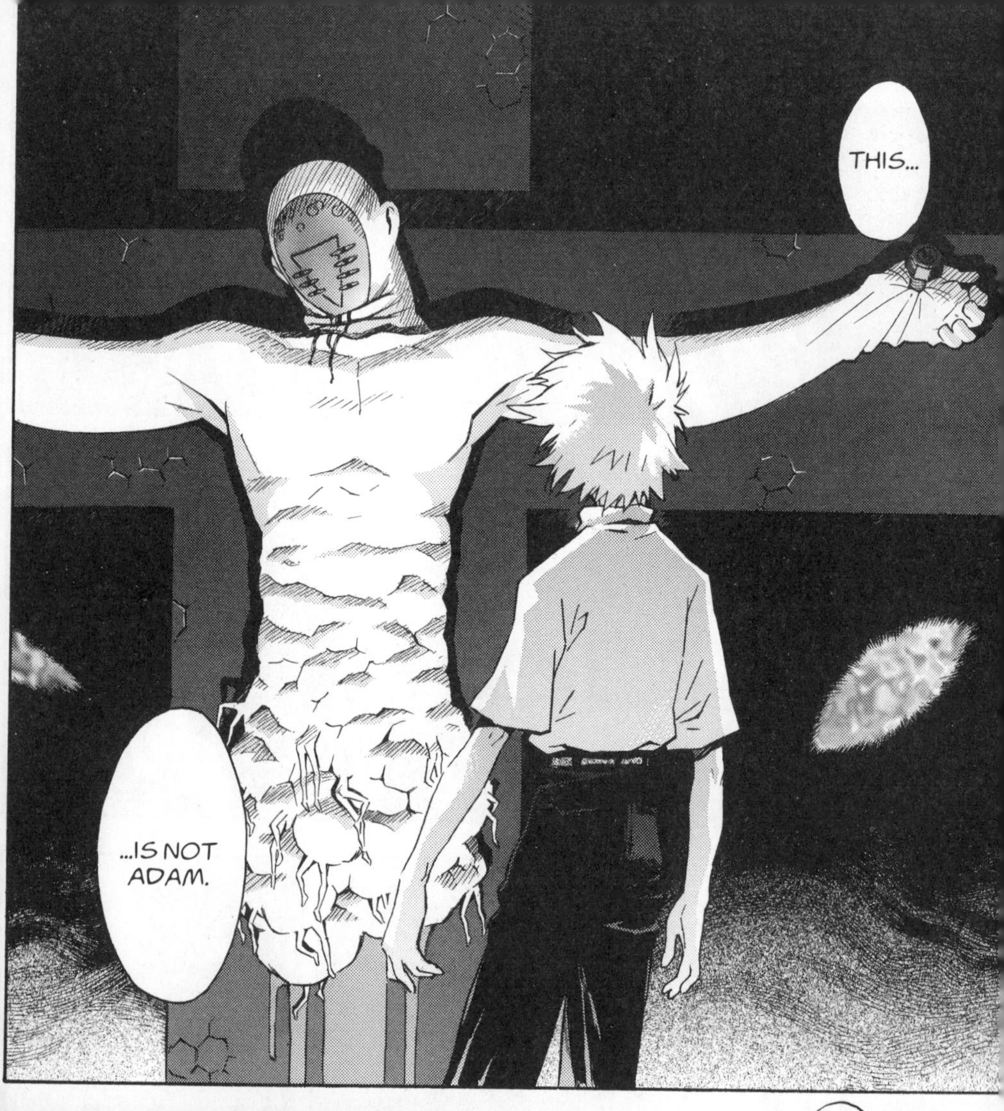
THIS...
...IS NOT ADAM.

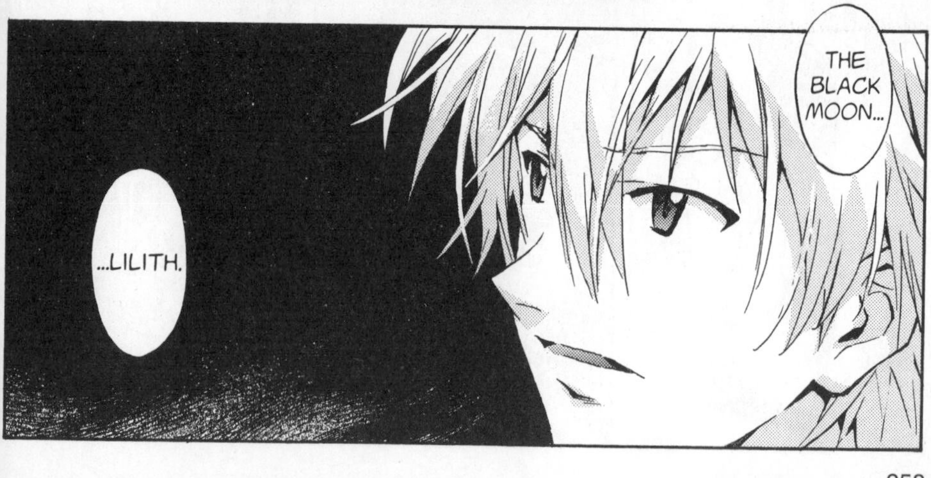
THE BLACK MOON...
...LILITH.

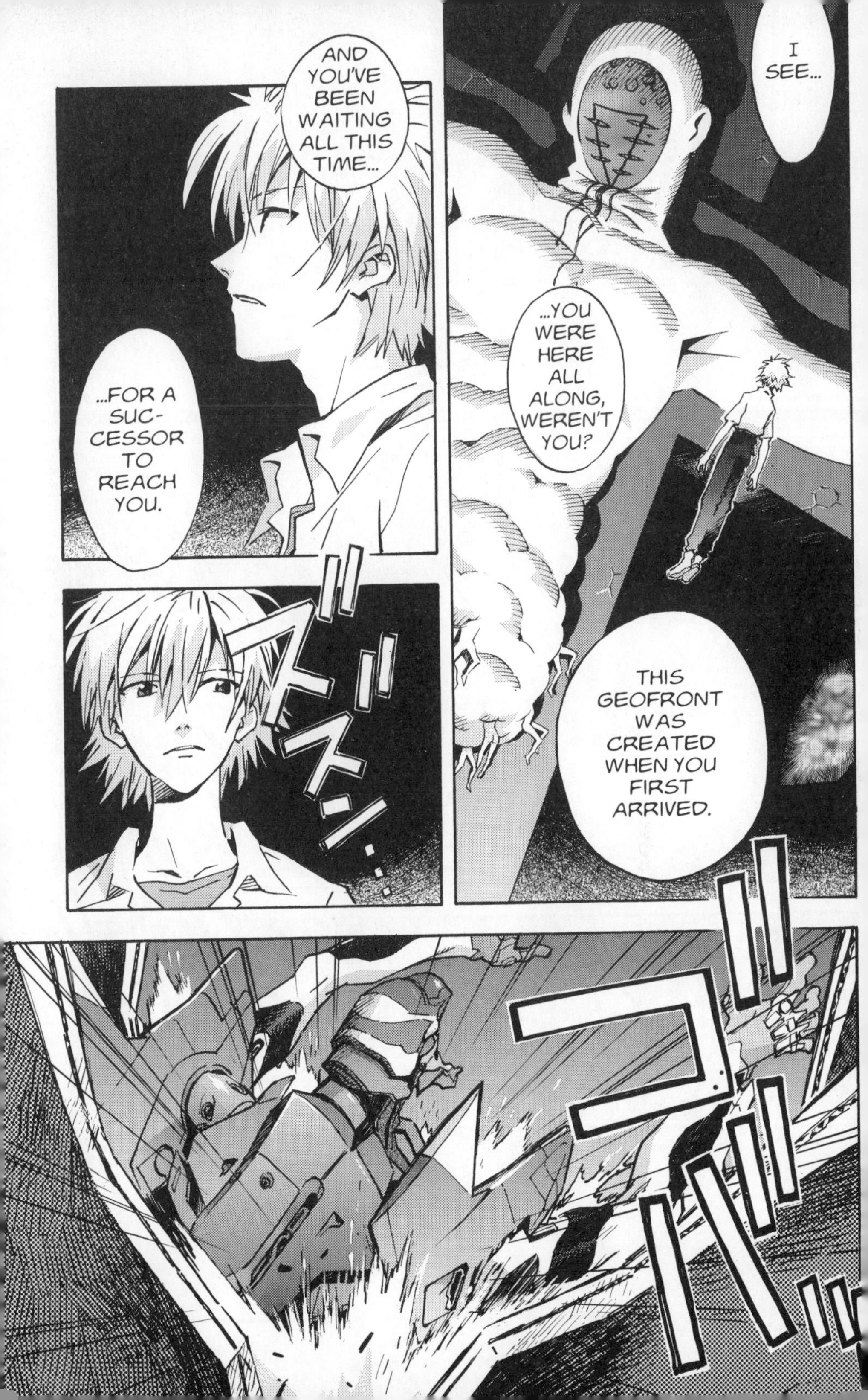
I SEE...
...YOU WERE HERE ALL ALONG, WEREN'T YOU?
THIS GEOFRONT WAS CREATED WHEN YOU FIRST ARRIVED.
AND YOU'VE BEEN WAITING ALL THIS TIME...
...FOR A SUC-CESSOR TO REACH YOU.

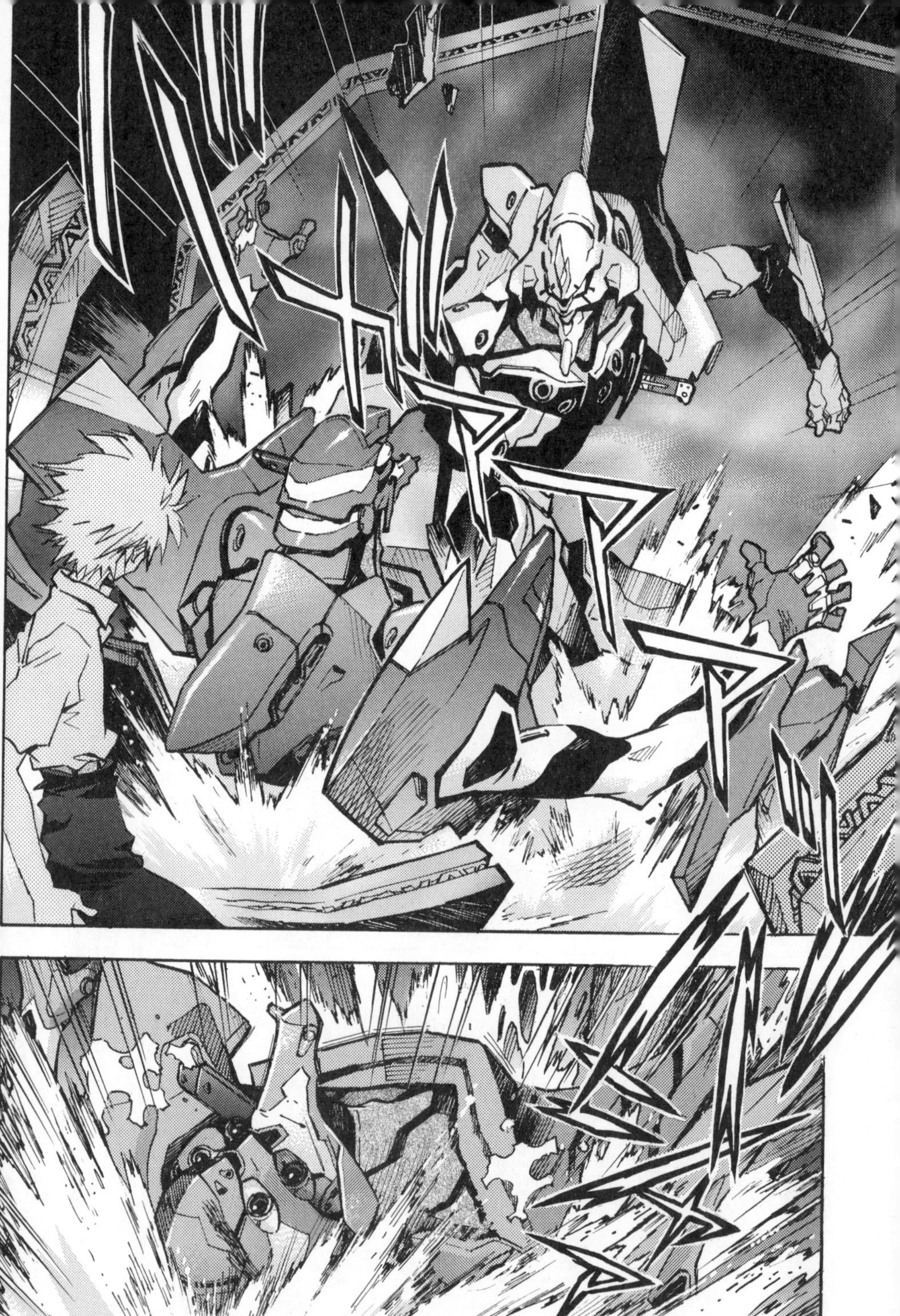

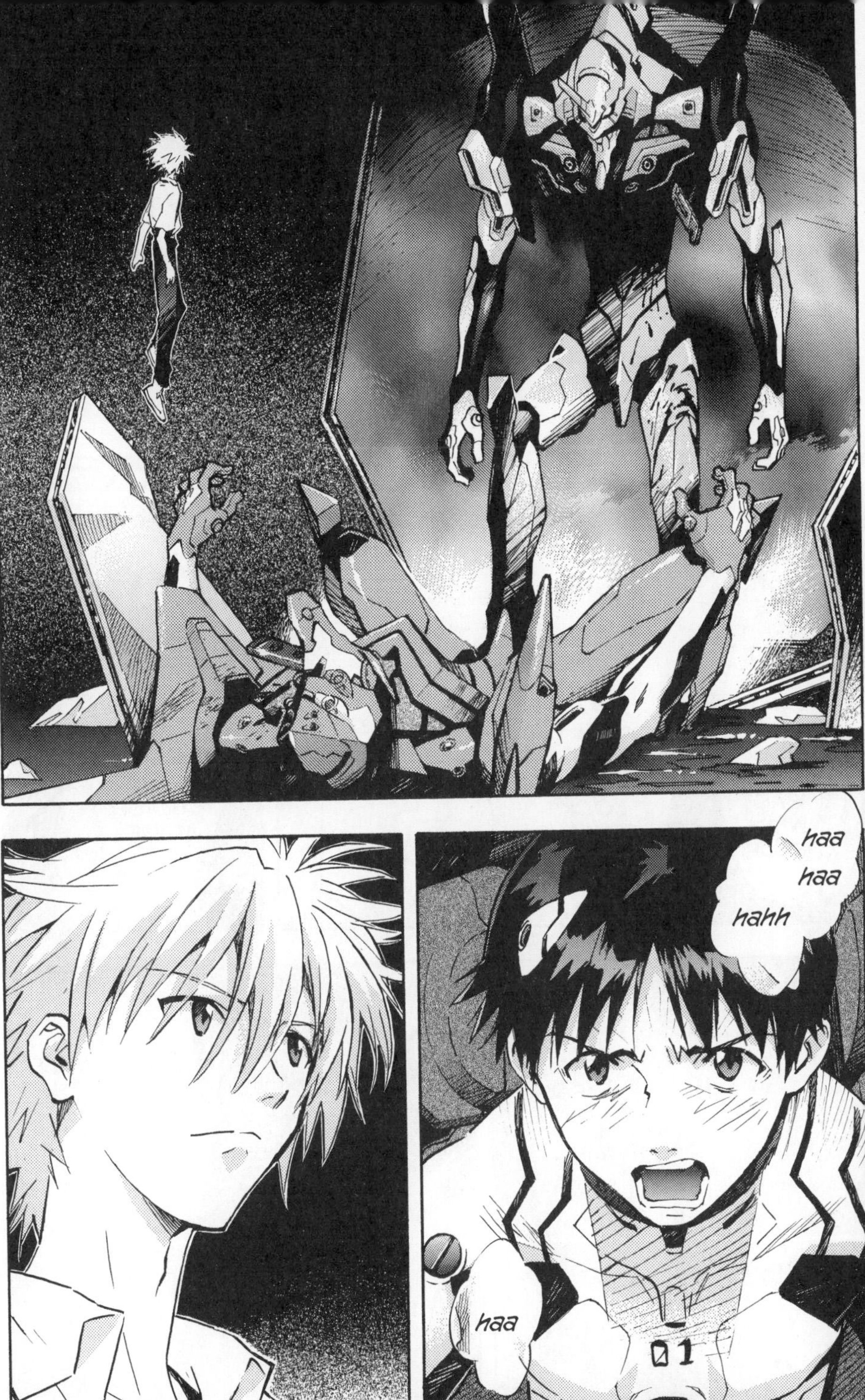
haa
haa
hahh
haa

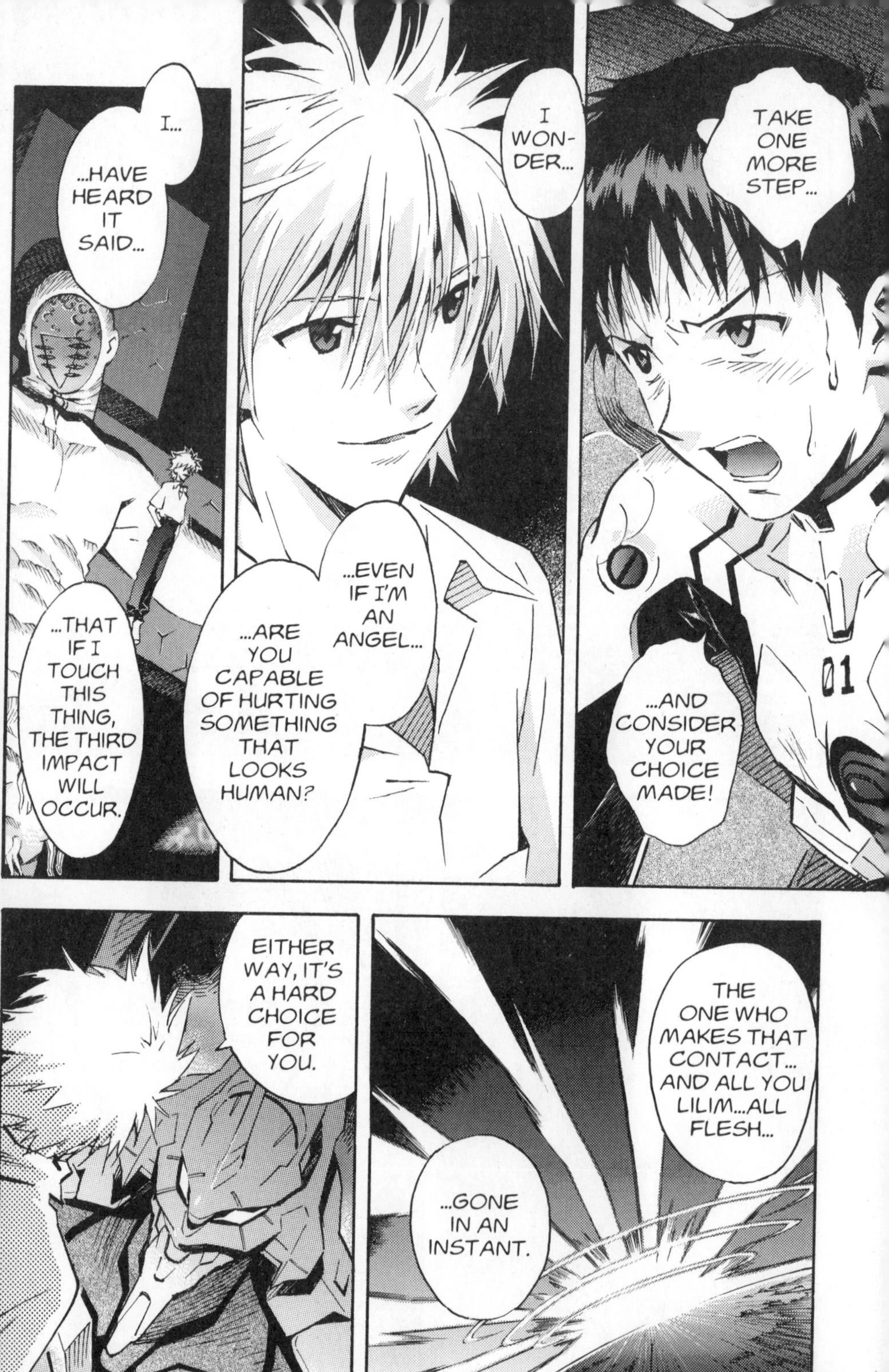
TAKE ONE MORE STEP...
...AND CONSIDER YOUR CHOICE MADE!
I WONDER...
...EVEN IF I'M AN ANGEL...
...ARE YOU CAPABLE OF HURTING SOMETHING THAT LOOKS HUMAN?
I...
...HAVE HEARD IT SAID...
...THAT IF I TOUCH THIS THING, THE THIRD IMPACT WILL OCCUR.
THE ONE WHO MAKES THAT CONTACT... AND ALL YOU LILIM...ALL FLESH...
...GONE IN AN INSTANT.
EITHER WAY, IT'S A HARD CHOICE FOR YOU.

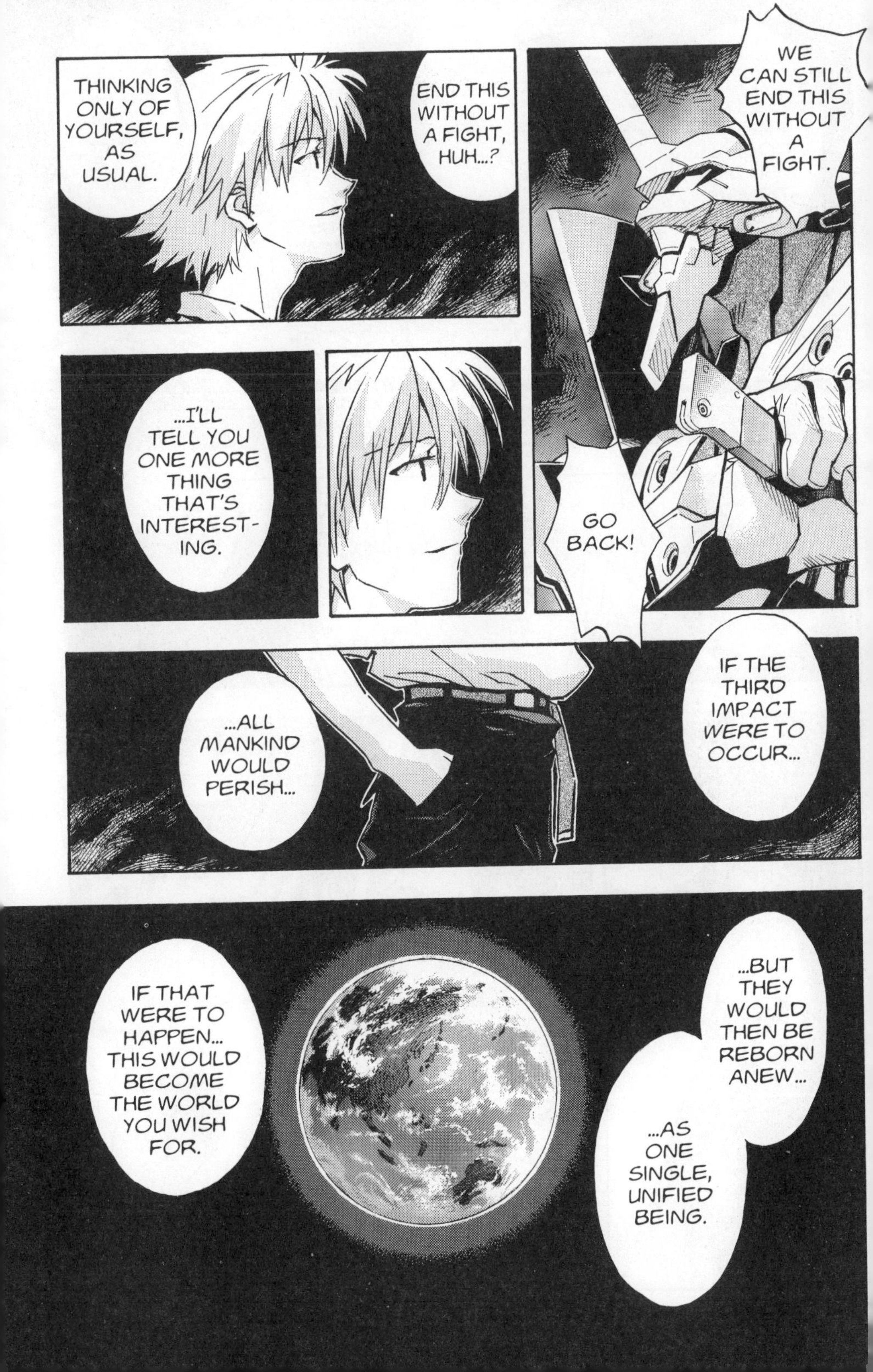
WE CAN STILL END THIS WITHOUT A FIGHT.
GO BACK!
END THIS WITHOUT A FIGHT, HUH...?
THINKING ONLY OF YOURSELF, AS USUAL.
...I'LL TELL YOU ONE MORE THING THAT'S INTEREST-ING.
IF THE THIRD IMPACT WERE TO OCCUR...
...ALL MANKIND WOULD PERISH...
...BUT THEY WOULD THEN BE REBORN ANEW...
...AS ONE SINGLE, UNIFIED BEING.
IF THAT WERE TO HAPPEN... THIS WOULD BECOME THE WORLD YOU WISH FOR.

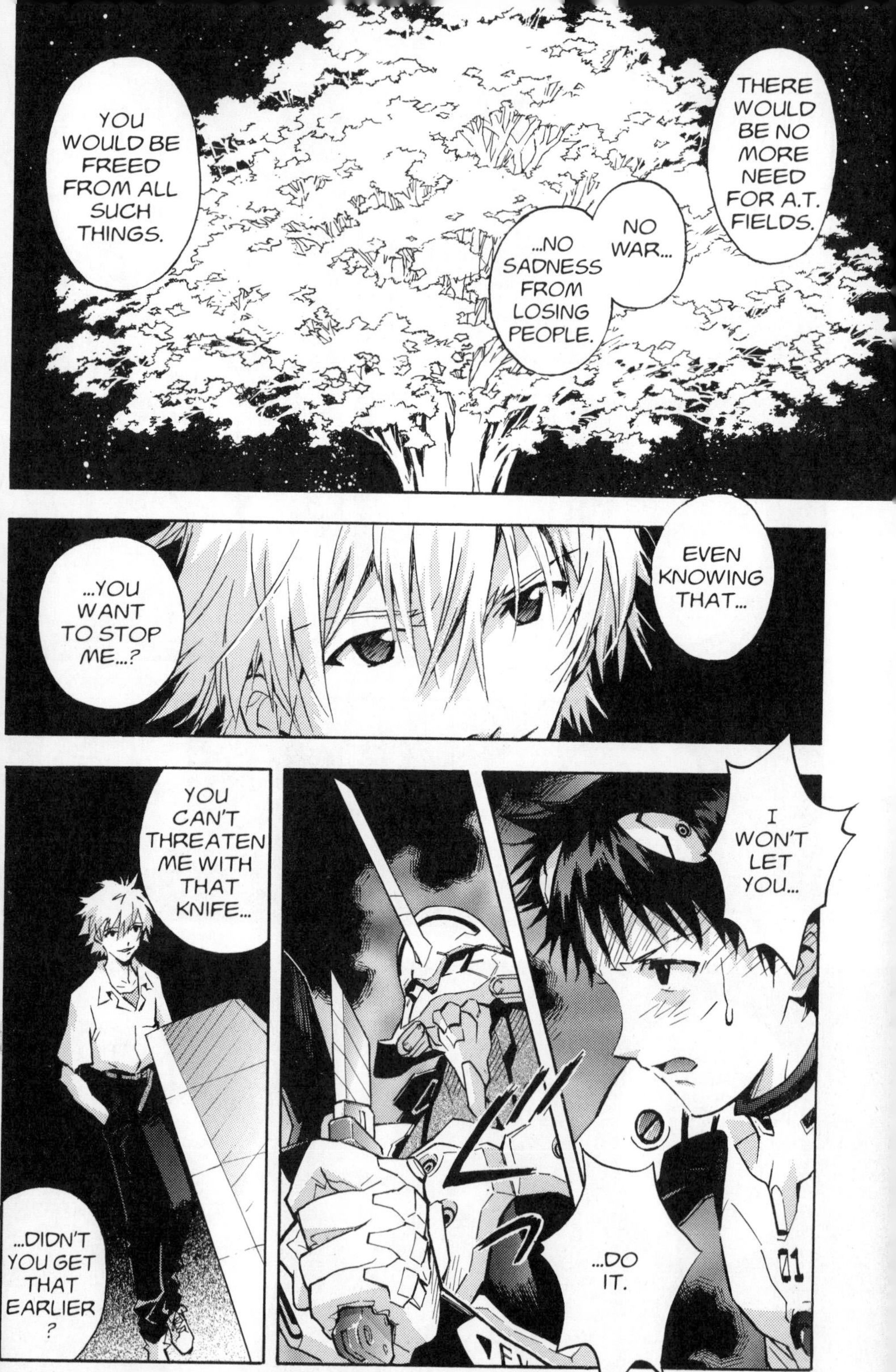
THERE WOULD BE NO MORE NEED FOR A.T. FIELDS.
NO WAR...
...NO SADNESS FROM LOSING PEOPLE.
YOU WOULD BE FREED FROM ALL SUCH THINGS.
EVEN KNOWING THAT...
...YOU WANT TO STOP ME...?
I WON'T LET YOU...
...DO IT.
YOU CAN'T THREATEN ME WITH THAT KNIFE...
...DIDN'T YOU GET THAT EARLIER?

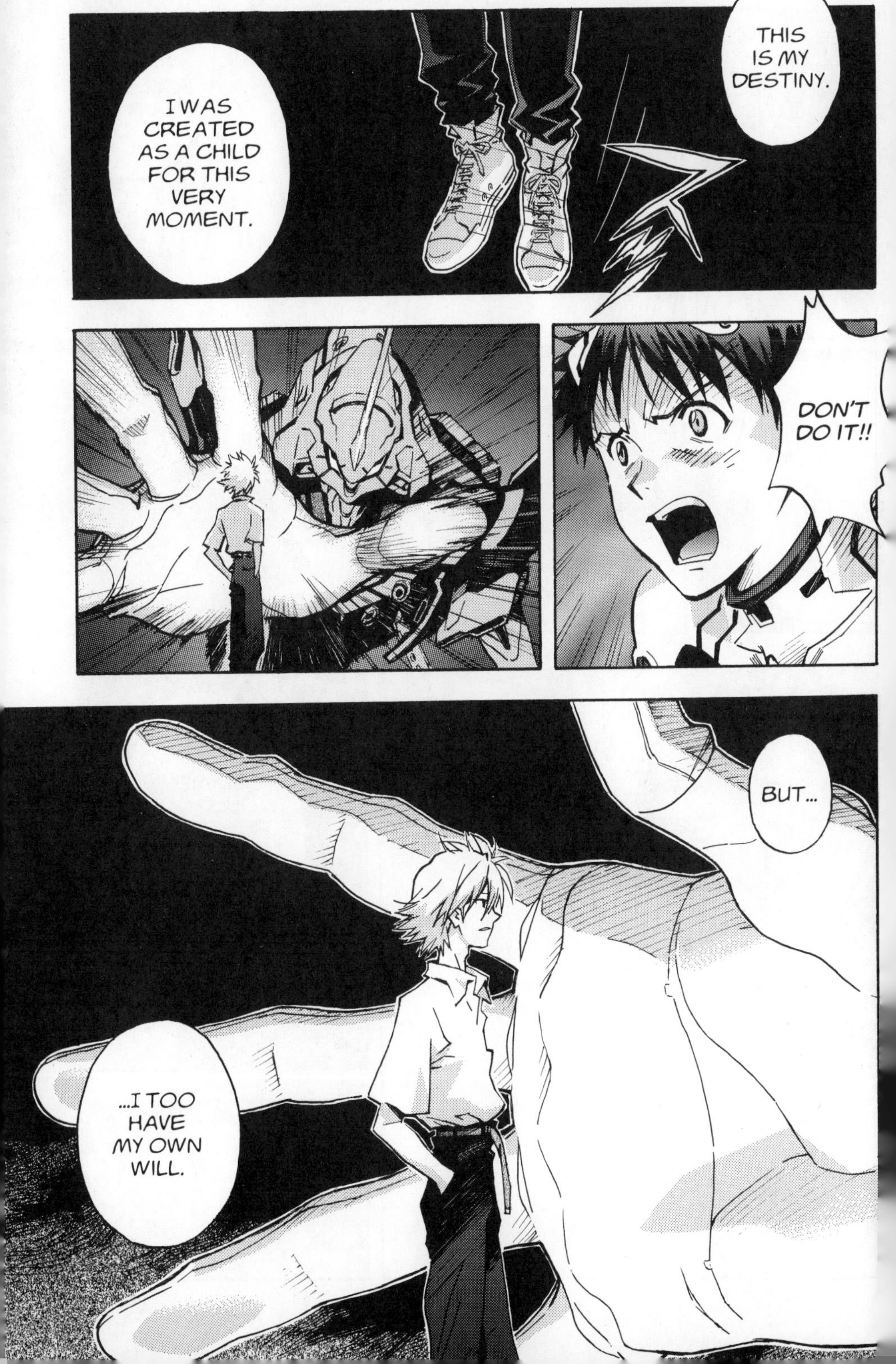
THIS IS MY DESTINY.
I WAS CREATED AS A CHILD FOR THIS VERY MOMENT.
DON'T DO IT!!
BUT...
...I TOO HAVE MY OWN WILL.

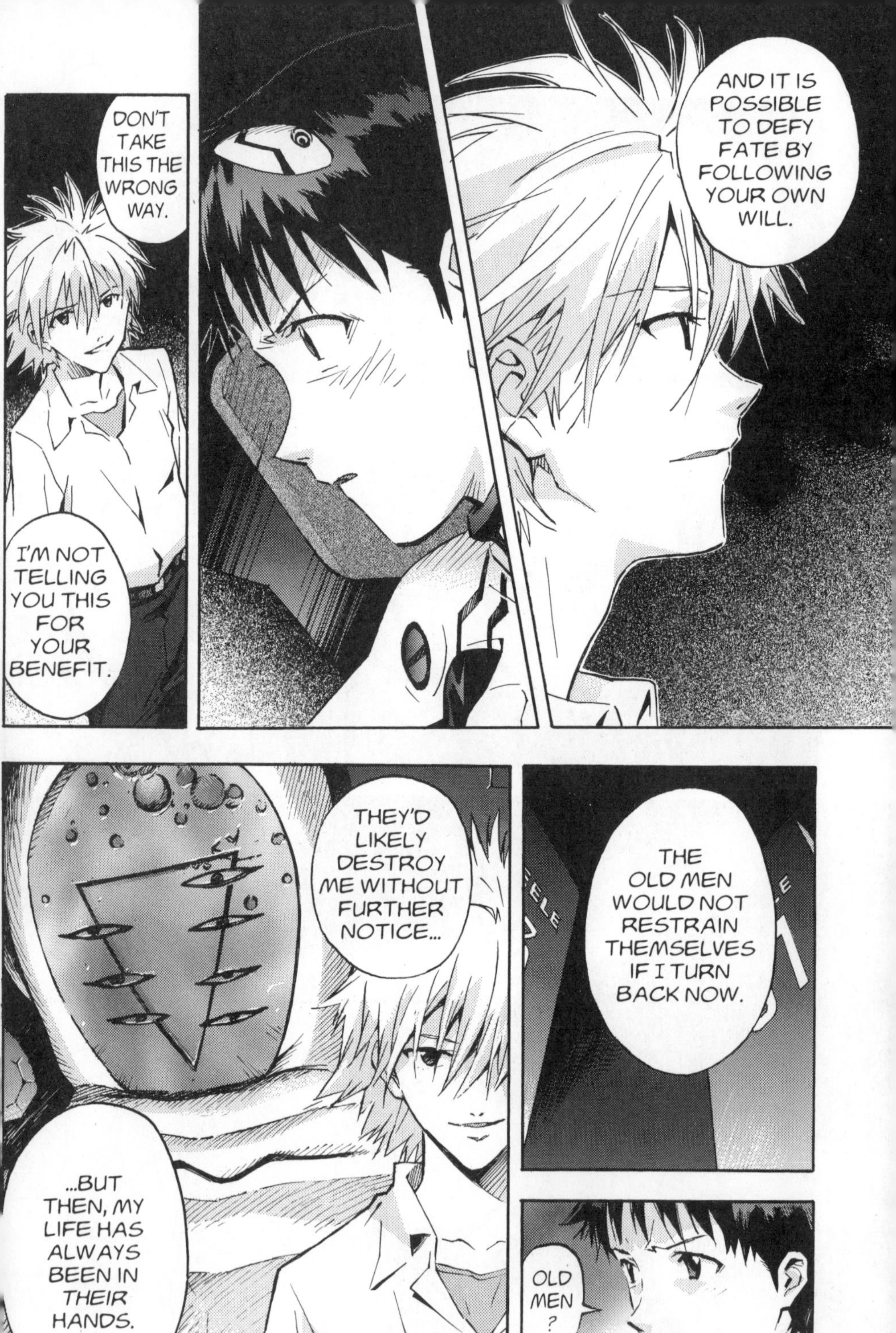
AND IT IS POSSIBLE TO DEFY FATE BY FOLLOWING YOUR OWN WILL.
DON'T TAKE THIS THE WRONG WAY.
I'M NOT TELLING YOU THIS FOR YOUR BENEFIT.
THE OLD MEN WOULD NOT RESTRAIN THEMSELVES IF I TURN BACK NOW.
OLD MEN?
THEY'D LIKELY DESTROY ME WITHOUT FURTHER NOTICE...
...BUT THEN, MY LIFE HAS ALWAYS BEEN IN THEIR HANDS.

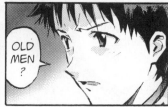

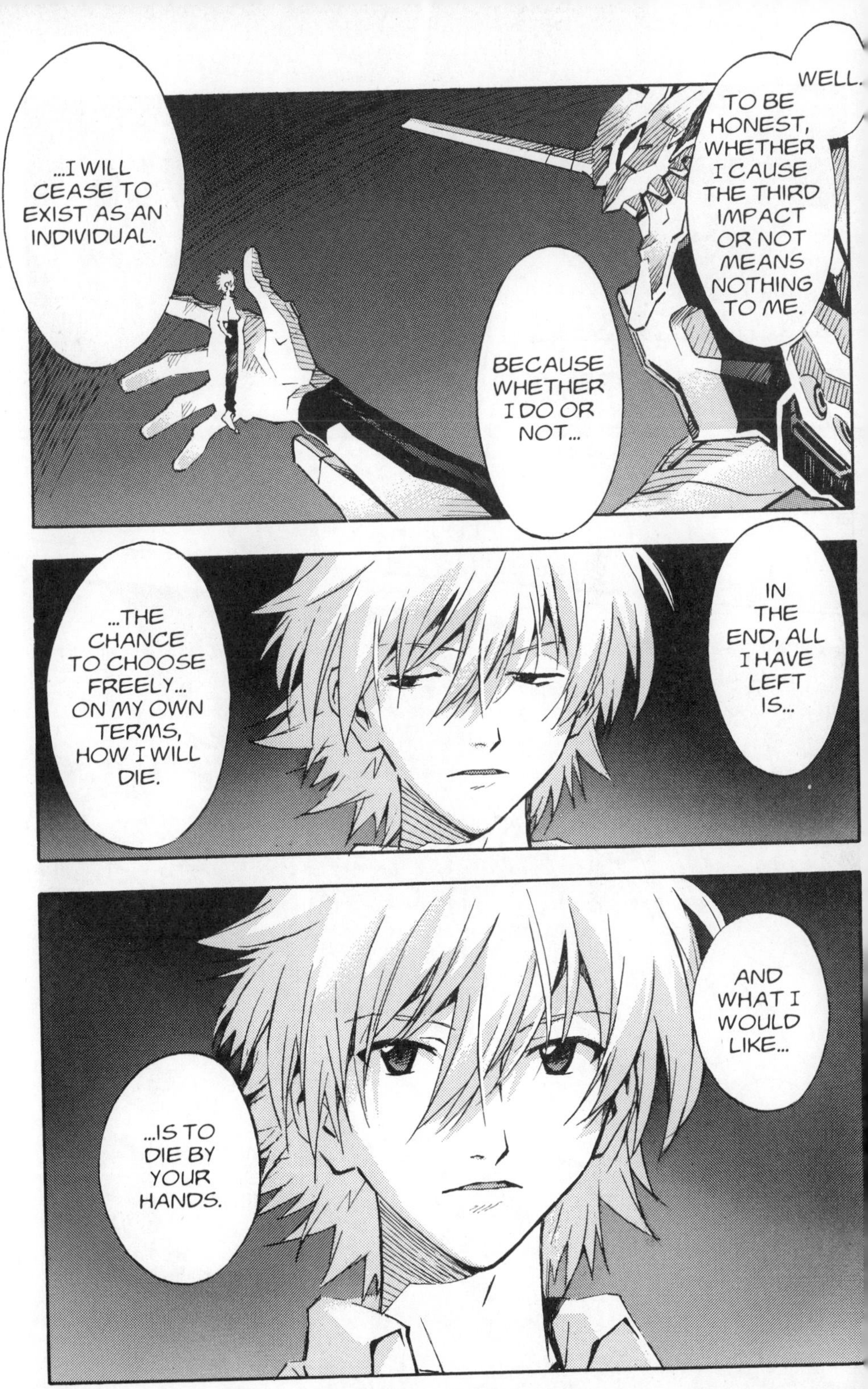
WELL. TO BE HONEST, WHETHER I CAUSE THE THIRD IMPACT OR NOT MEANS NOTHING TO ME.
BECAUSE WHETHER I DO OR NOT...
...I WILL CEASE TO EXIST AS AN INDIVIDUAL.
IN THE END, ALL I HAVE LEFT IS...
...THE CHANCE TO CHOOSE FREELY... ON MY OWN TERMS, HOW I WILL DIE.
AND WHAT I WOULD LIKE...
...IS TO DIE BY YOUR HANDS.

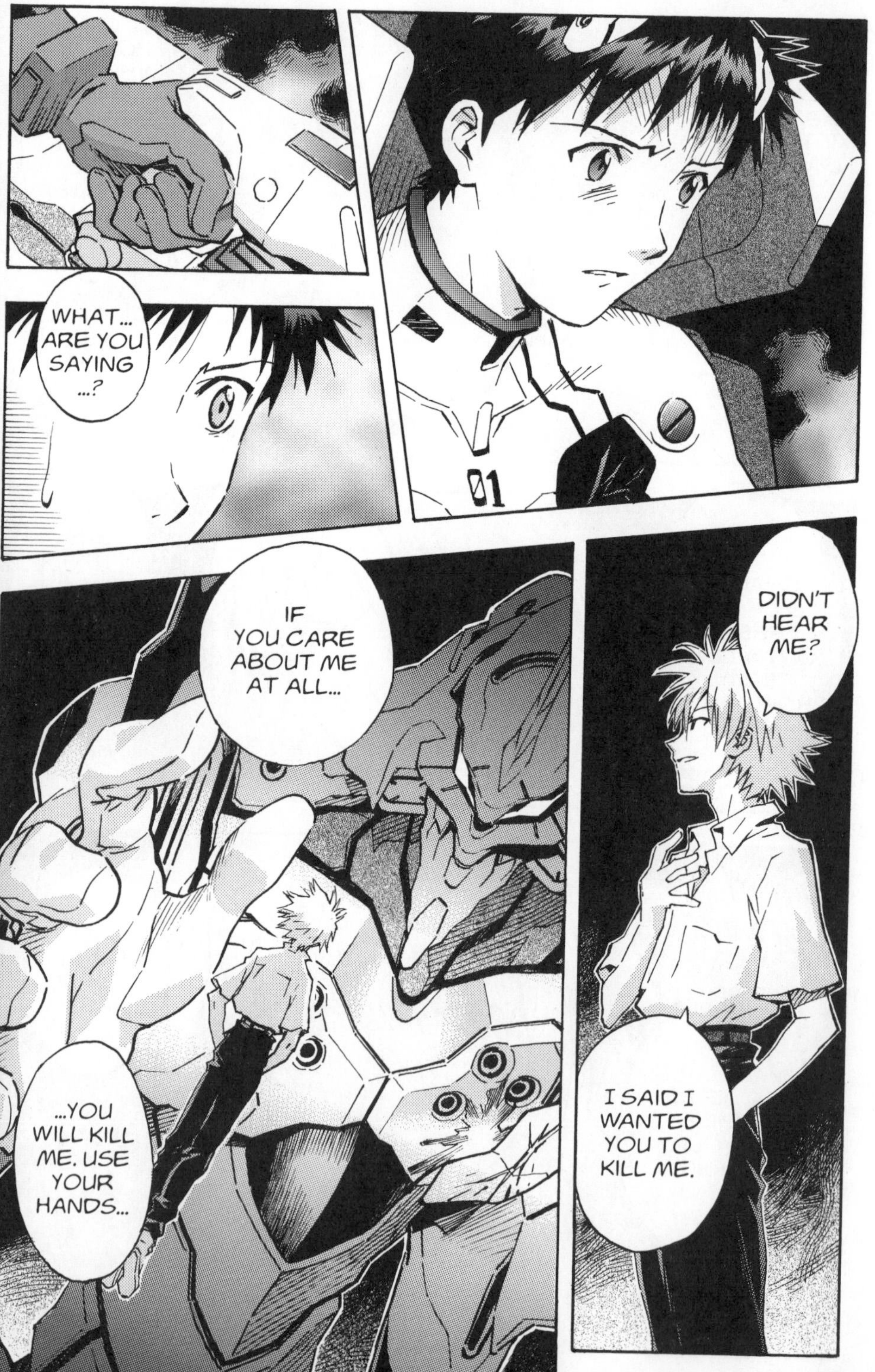
WHAT... ARE YOU SAYING ...?
DIDN'T HEAR ME?
I SAID I WANTED YOU TO KILL ME.
IF YOU CARE ABOUT ME AT ALL...
...YOU WILL KILL ME. USE YOUR HANDS...

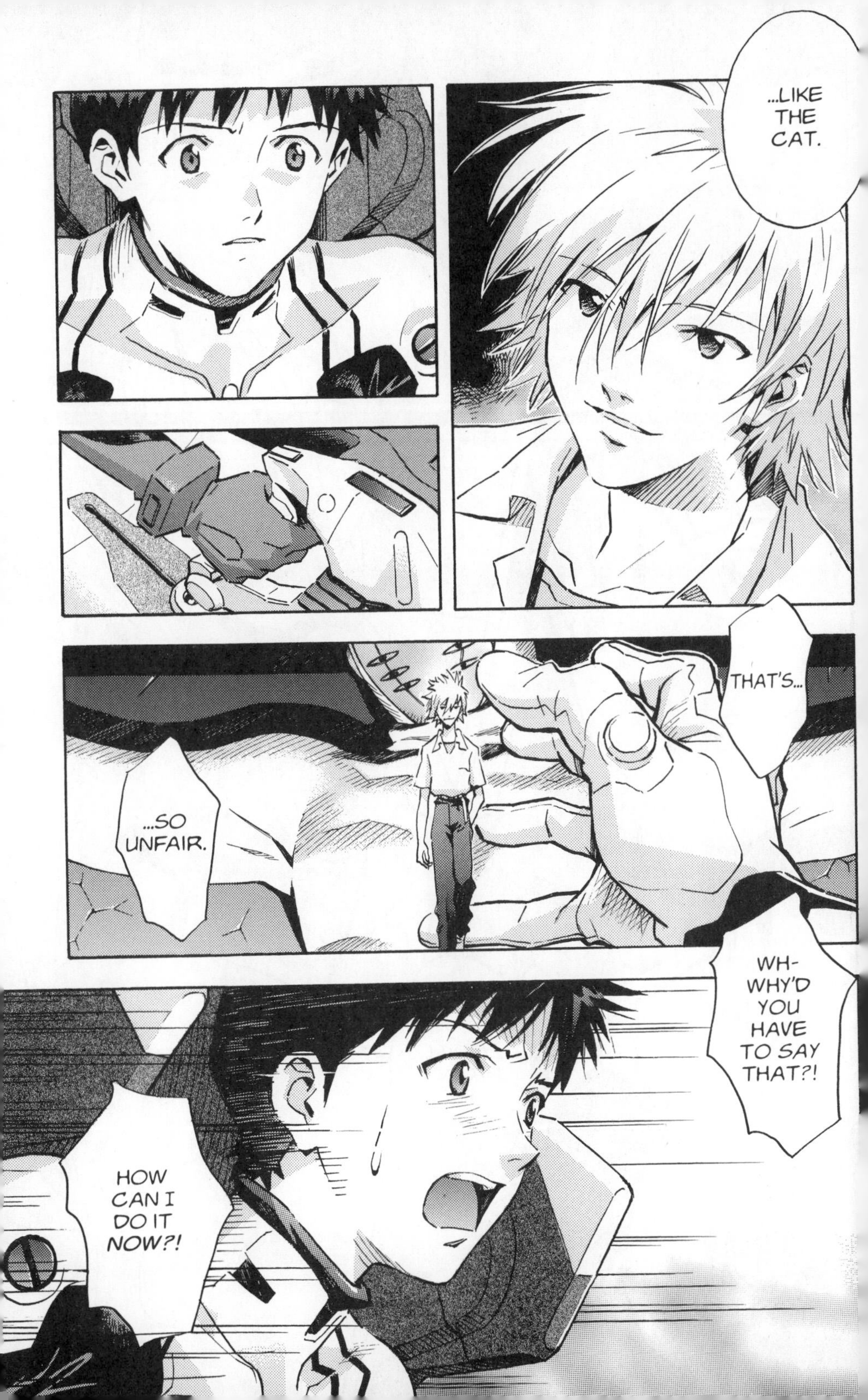
...LIKE THE CAT.
THAT'S...
...SO UNFAIR.
WH- WHY'D YOU HAVE TO SAY THAT?!
HOW CAN I DO IT NOW?!

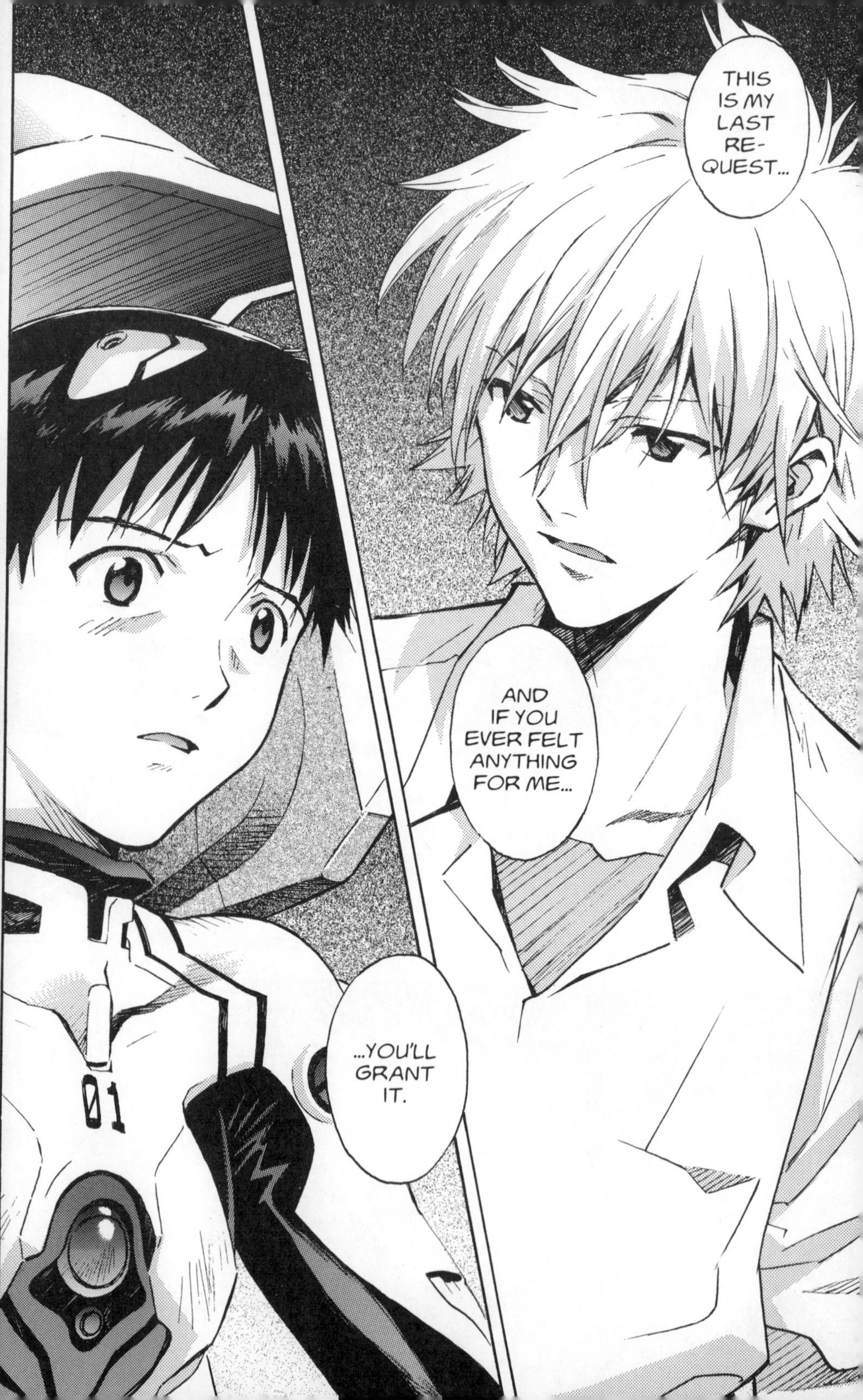
THIS IS MY LAST RE-QUEST...
AND IF YOU EVER FELT ANYTHING FOR ME...
...YOU'LL GRANT IT.
01

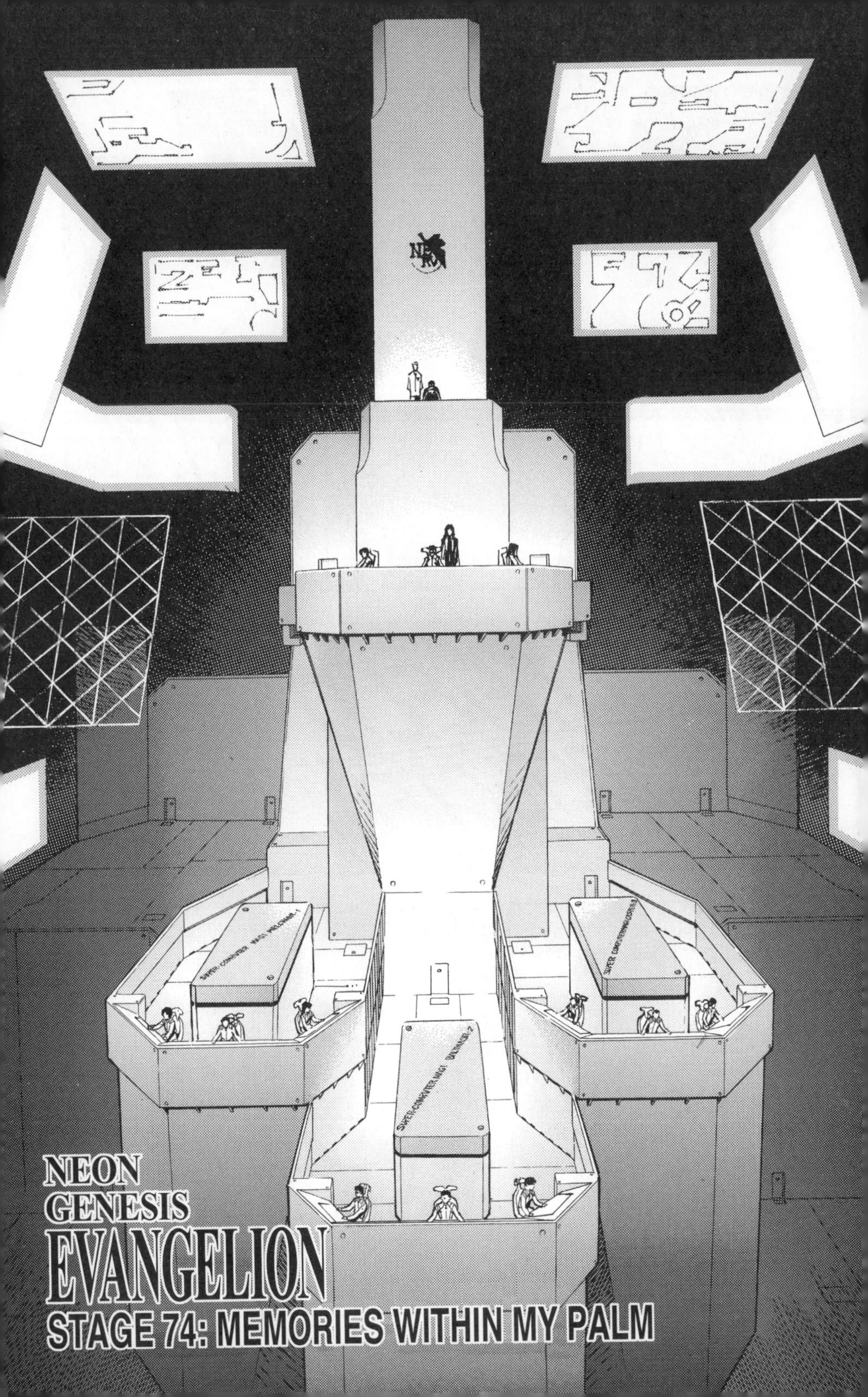
SUPER-COMPUTER MAGI MELCHIOR-1
SUPER-COMPUTER MAGI BALTHASAR-2
NEON GENESIS EVANGELION
STAGE 74: MEMORIES WITHIN MY PALM

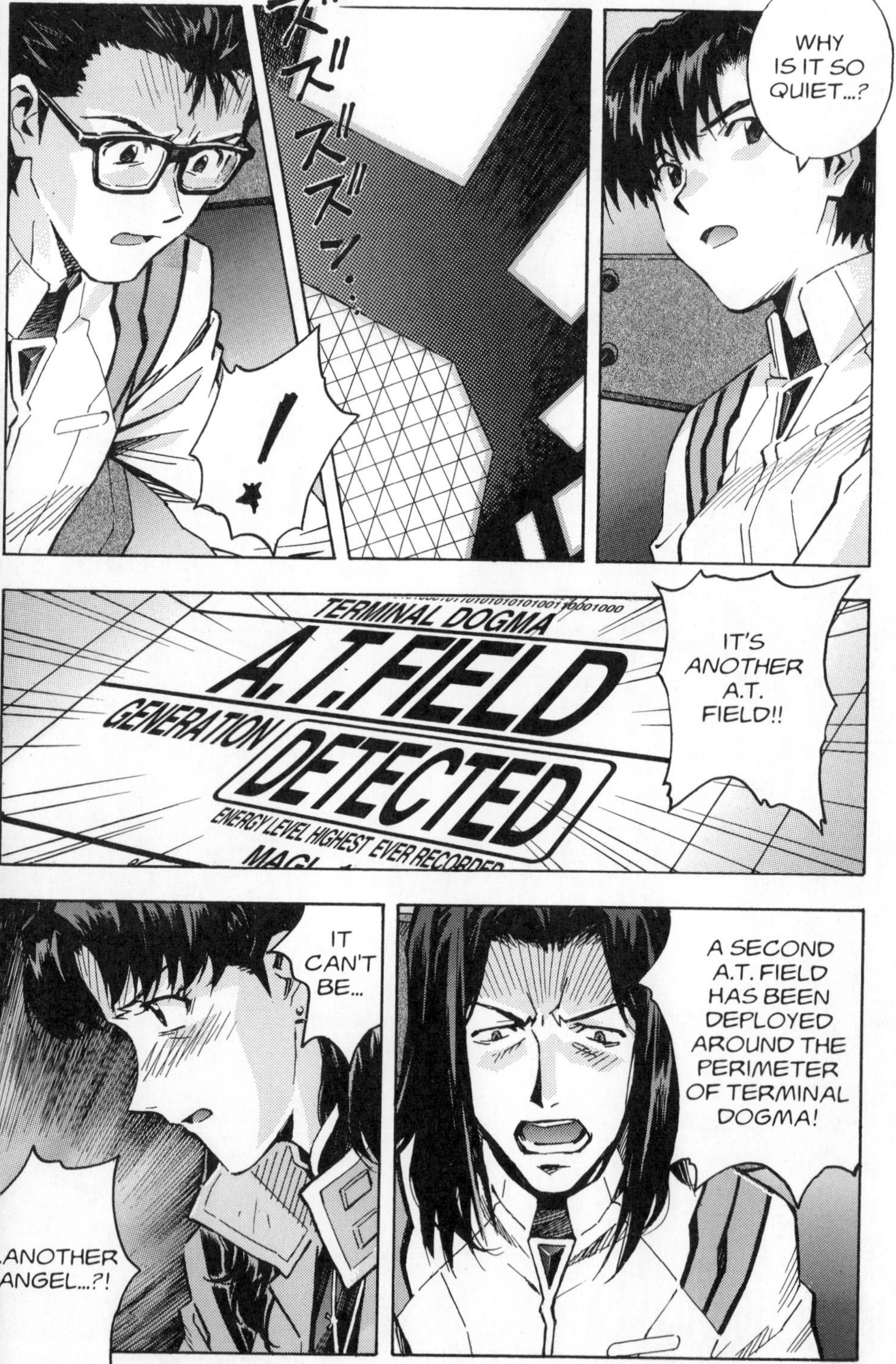
WHY IS IT SO QUIET...?
!
IT'S ANOTHER A.T. FIELD!!
TERMINAL DOGMA
A.T. FIELD
GENERATION
DETECTED
ENERGY LEVEL HIGHEST EVER RECORDED
A SECOND A.T. FIELD HAS BEEN DEPLOYED AROUND THE PERIMETER OF TERMINAL DOGMA!
IT CAN'T BE...
...ANOTHER ANGEL...?!

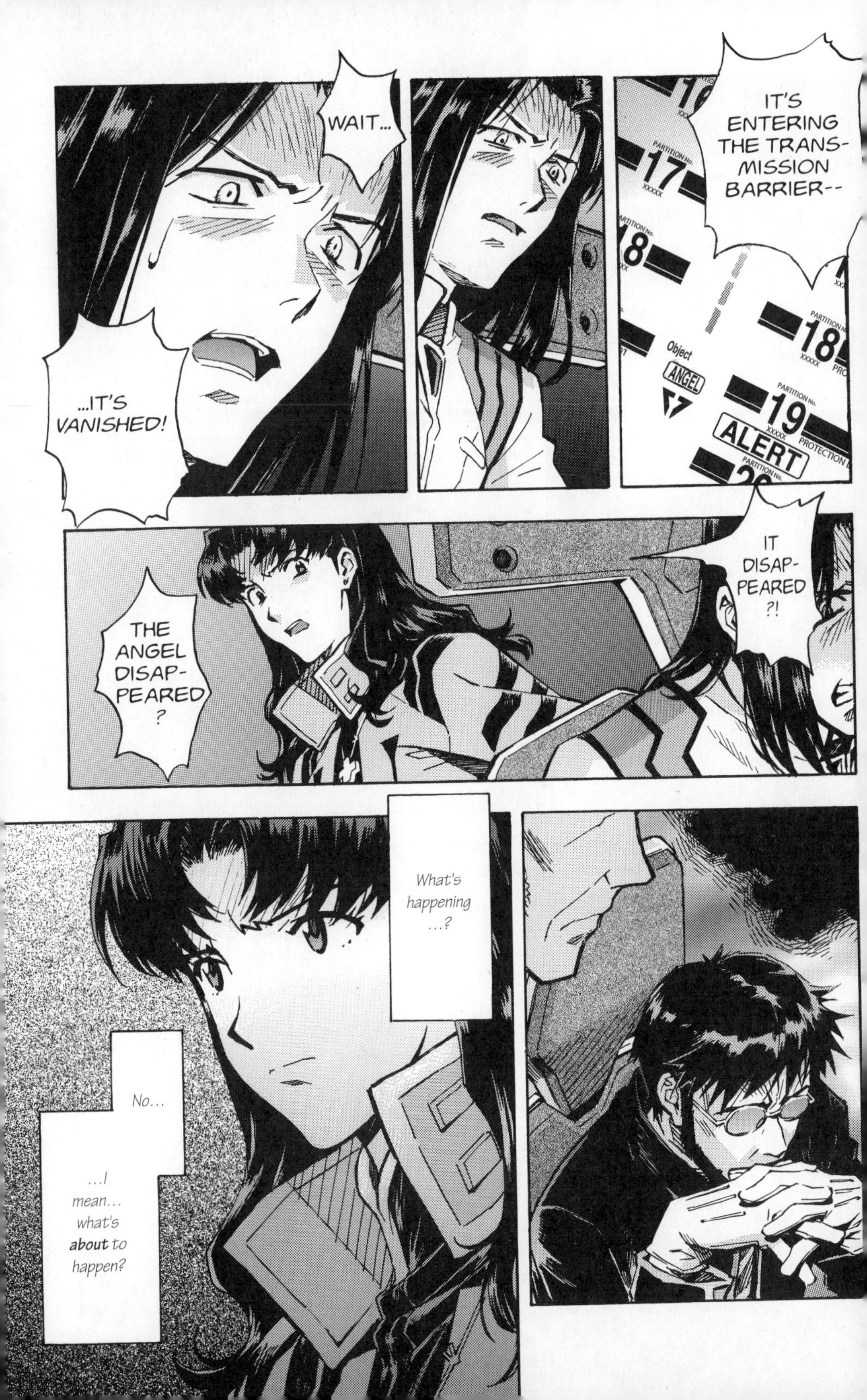

IT'S ENTERING THE TRANS-MISSION BARRIER--
PARTITION No. 17
PARTITION No. 18
Object ANGEL
PARTITION No. 19
ALERT
WAIT...
...IT'S VANISHED!
IT DISAPPEARED?!
THE ANGEL DISAPPEARED?
What's happening...?
No...
...I mean... what's **about** to happen?

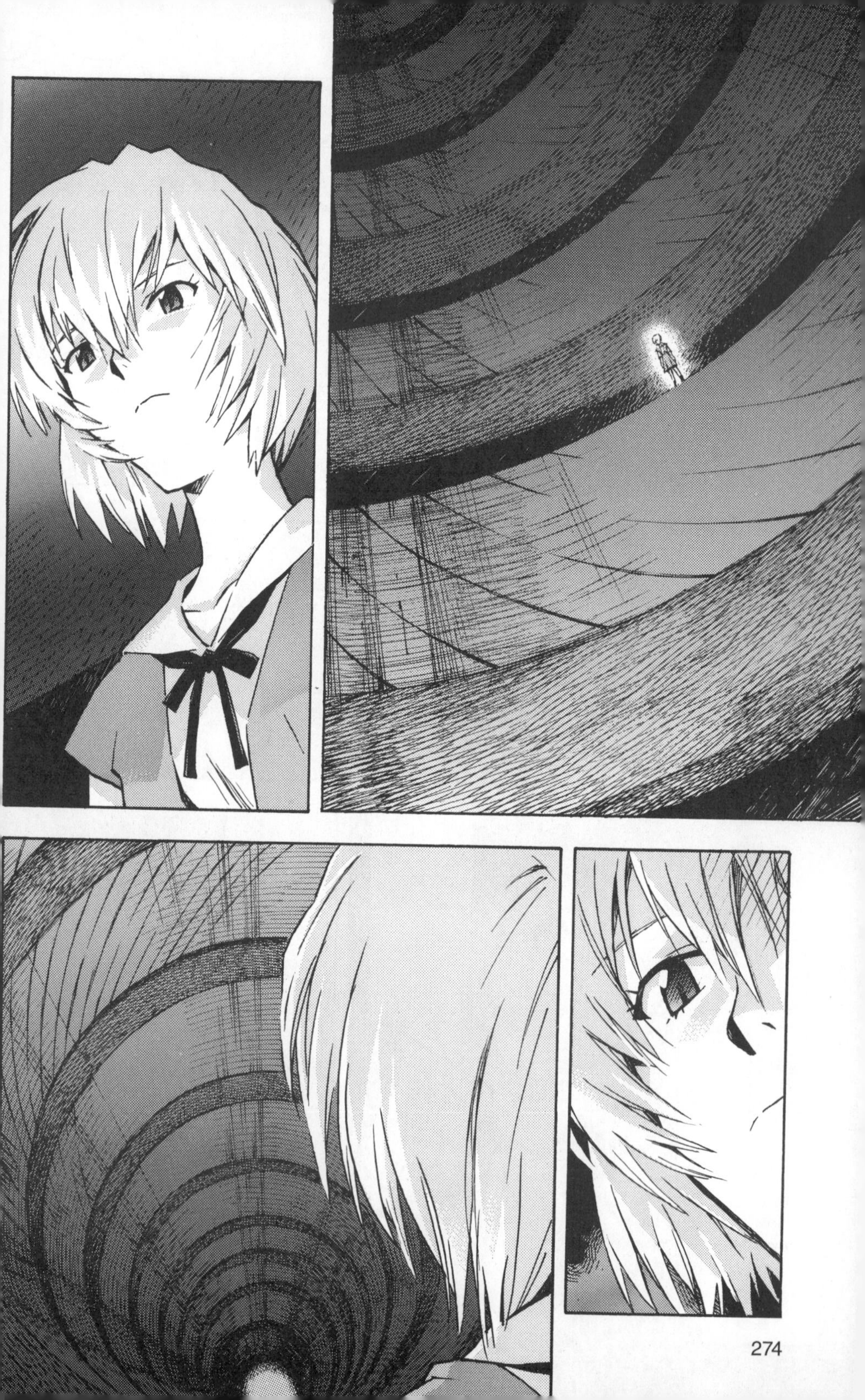

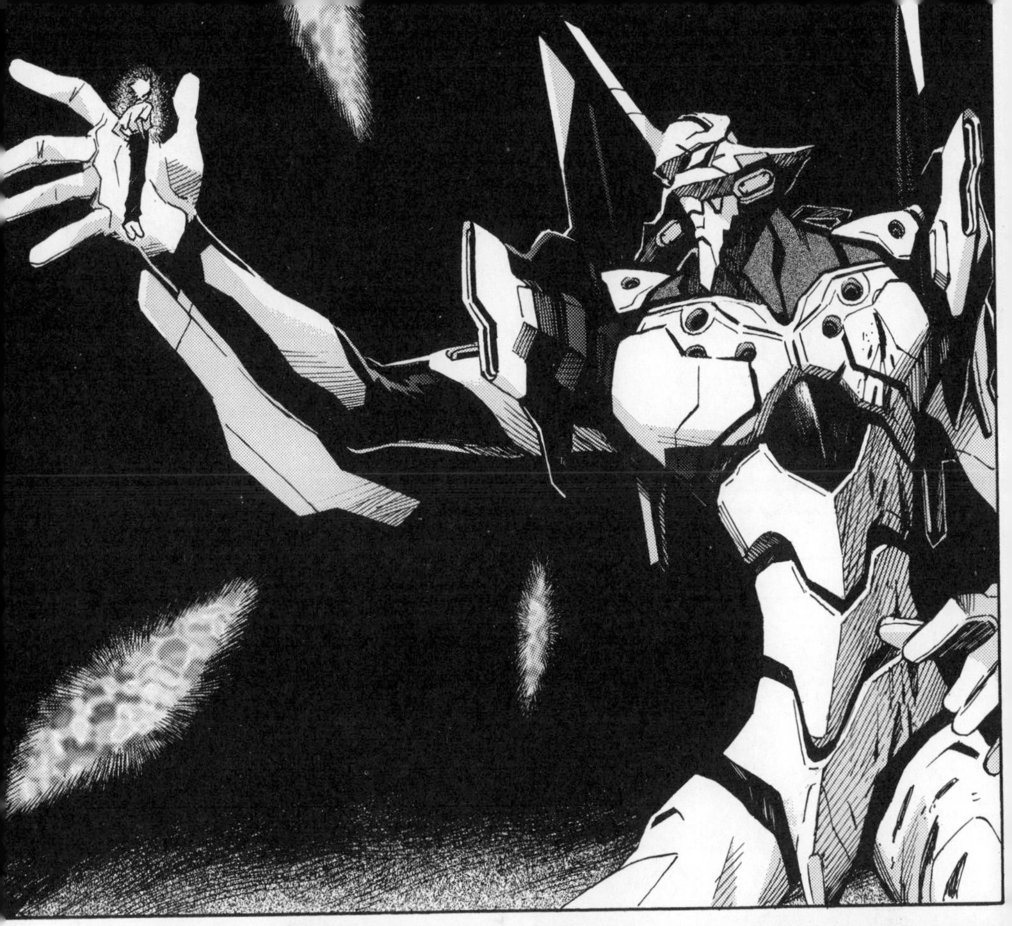

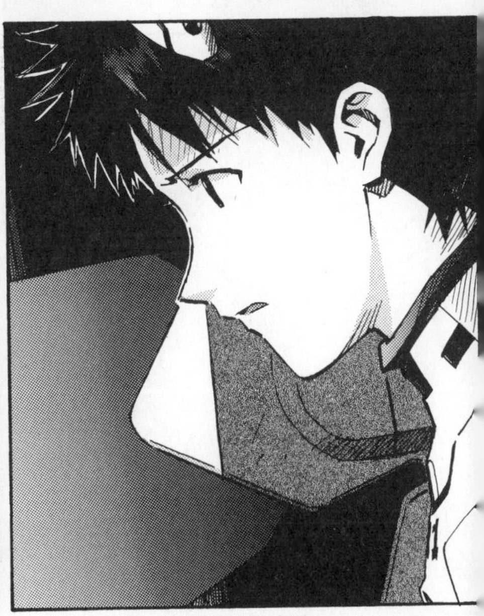

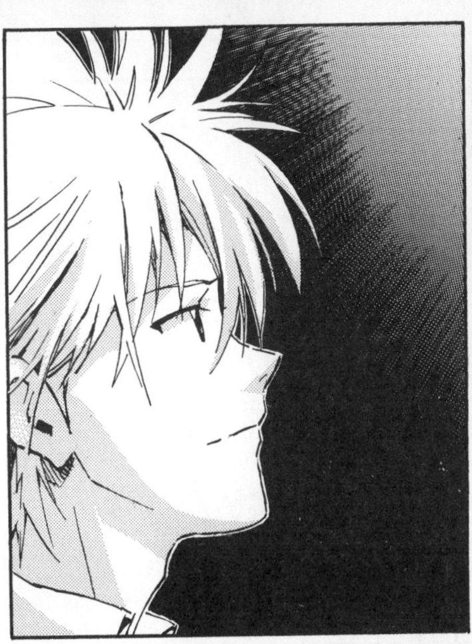

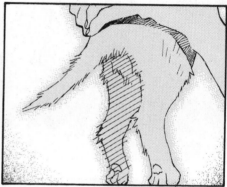

...BUT THE CAT...

...WOULD HAVE DIED.

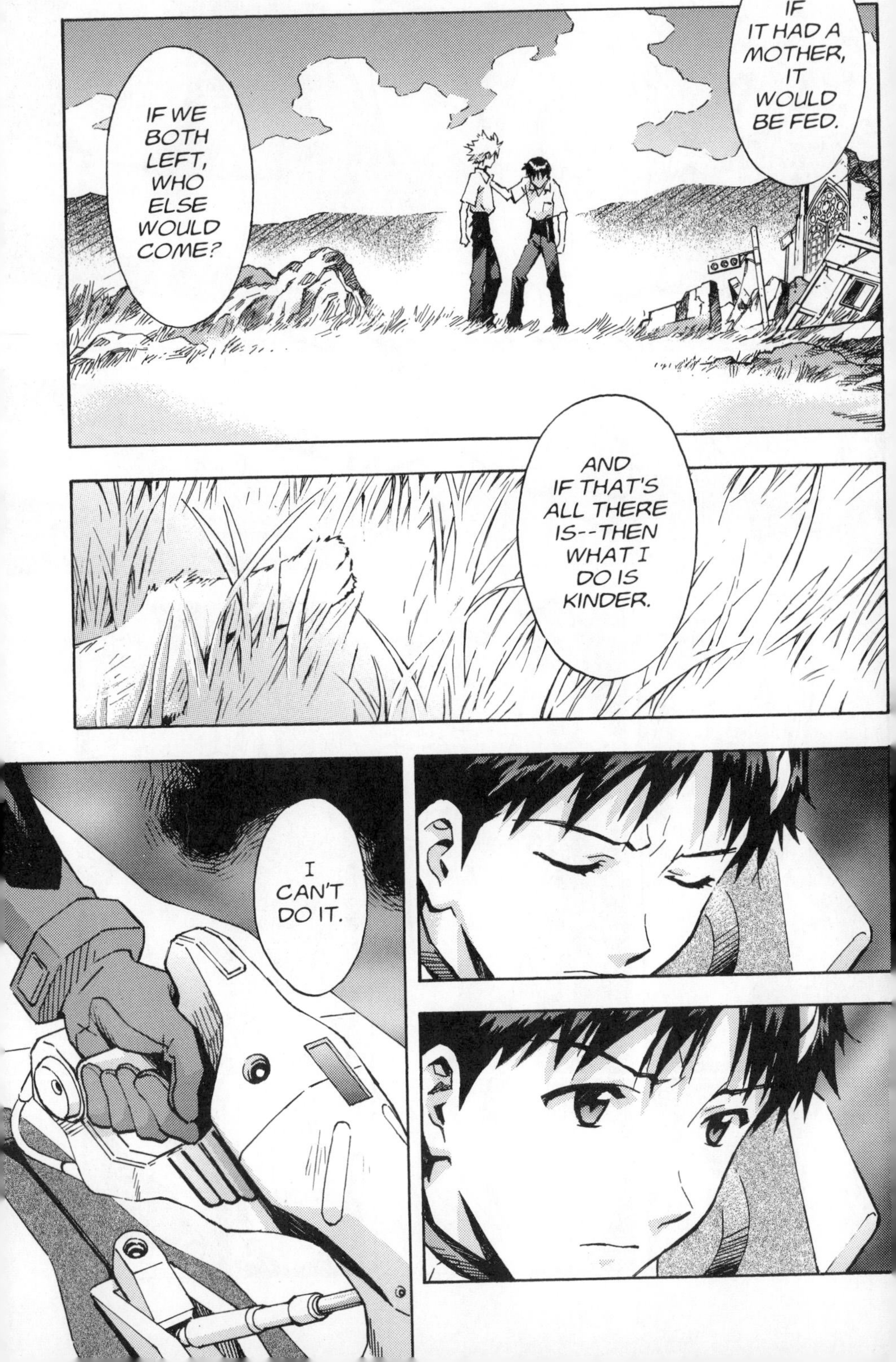
IF IT HAD A MOTHER, IT WOULD BE FED.
IF WE BOTH LEFT, WHO ELSE WOULD COME?
AND IF THAT'S ALL THERE IS--THEN WHAT I DO IS KINDER.
I CAN'T DO IT.

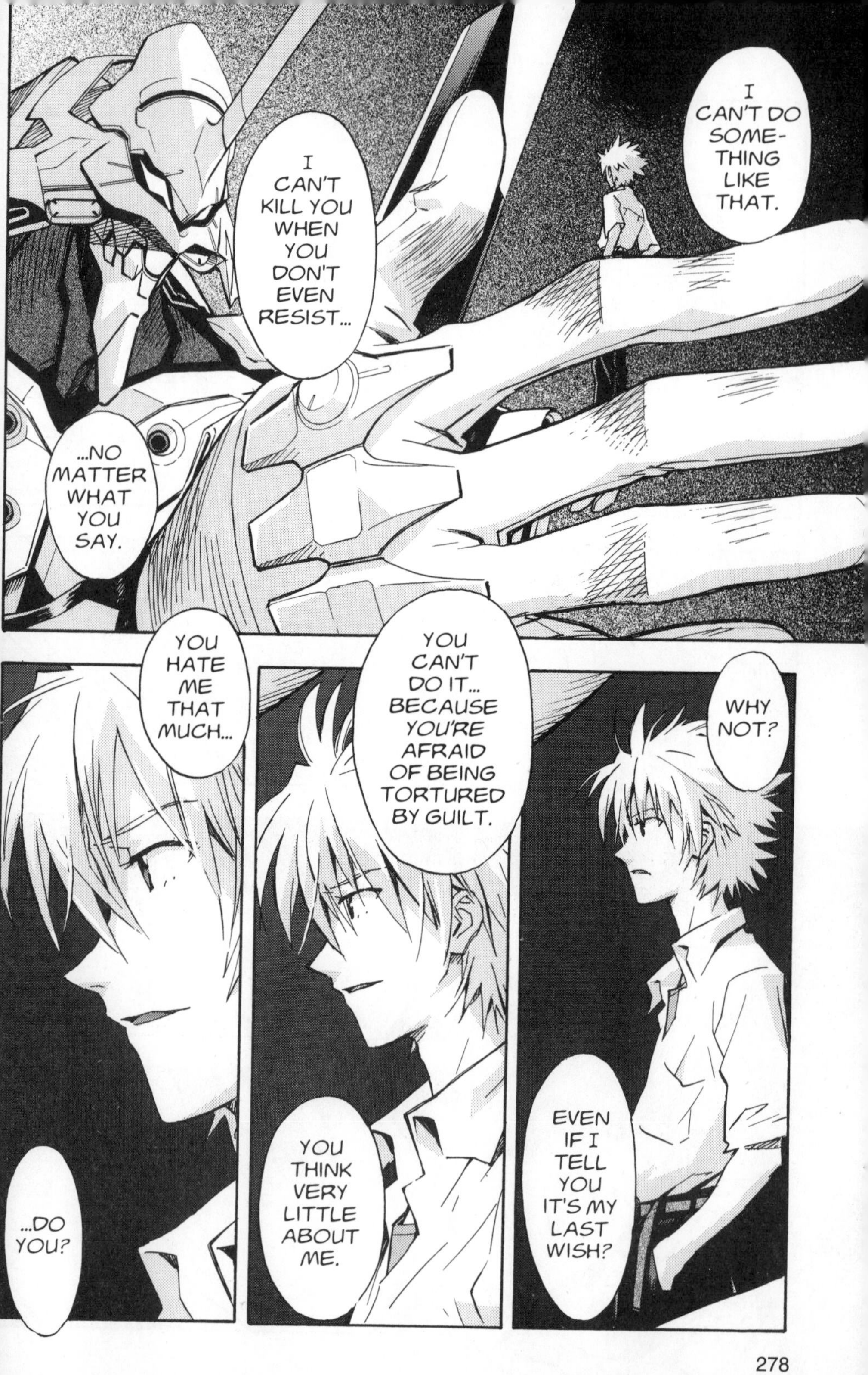
I CAN'T DO SOME-THING LIKE THAT.
I CAN'T KILL YOU WHEN YOU DON'T EVEN RESIST...
...NO MATTER WHAT YOU SAY.
WHY NOT?
EVEN IF I TELL YOU IT'S MY LAST WISH?
YOU CAN'T DO IT... BECAUSE YOU'RE AFRAID OF BEING TORTURED BY GUILT.
YOU THINK VERY LITTLE ABOUT ME.
YOU HATE ME THAT MUCH...
...DO YOU?

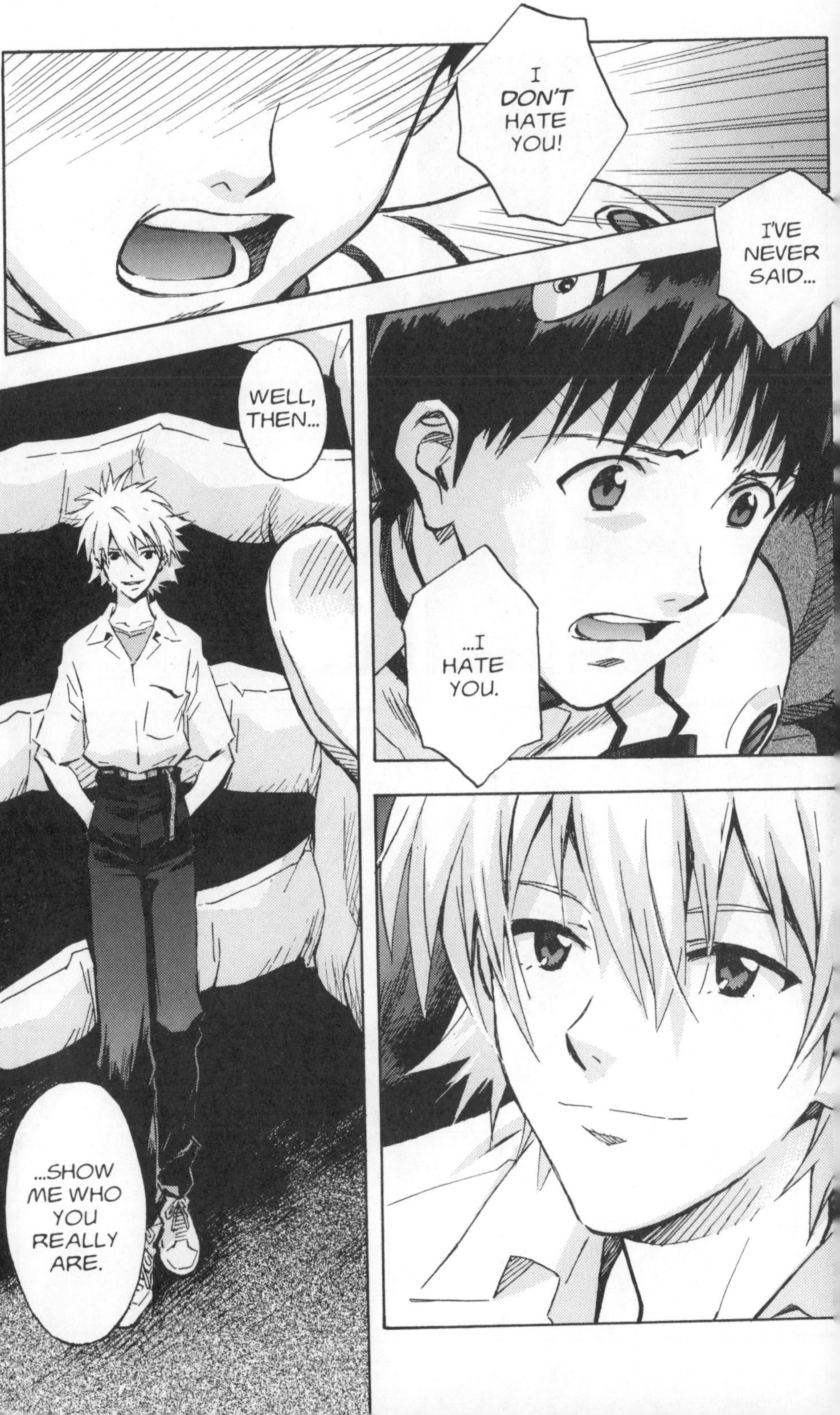
I DON'T HATE YOU!
I'VE NEVER SAID...
...I HATE YOU.
WELL, THEN...
...SHOW ME WHO YOU REALLY ARE.

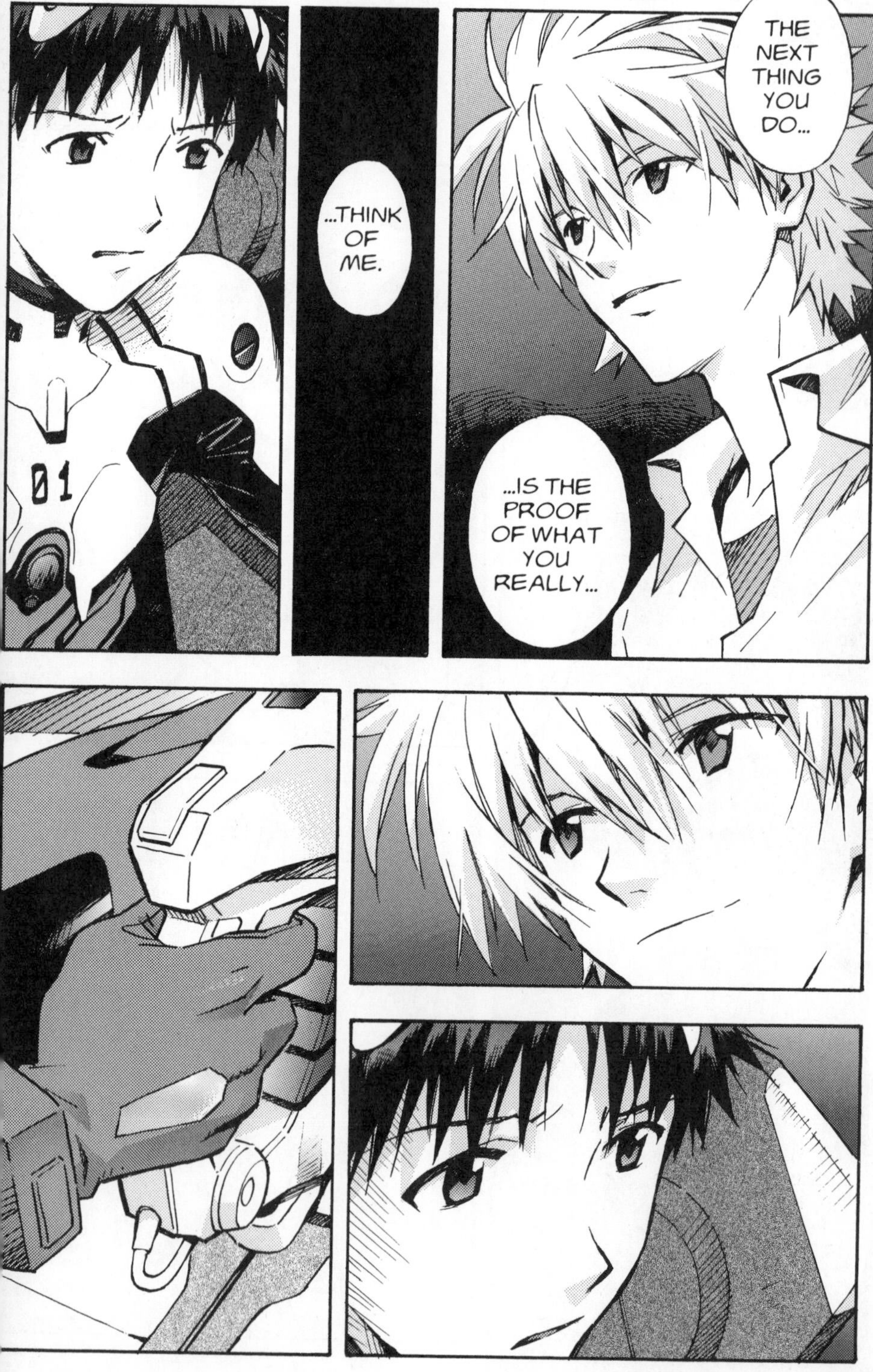
THE NEXT THING YOU DO...
...IS THE PROOF OF WHAT YOU REALLY...
...THINK OF ME.

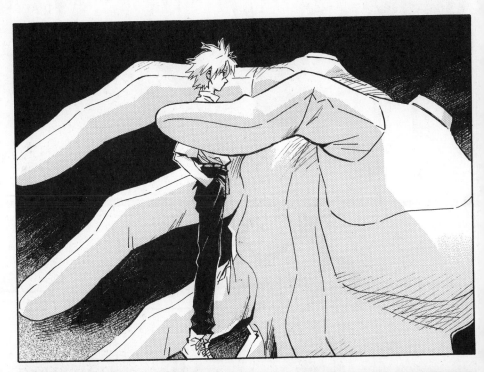

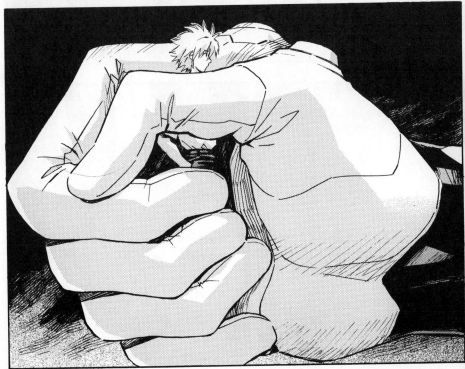

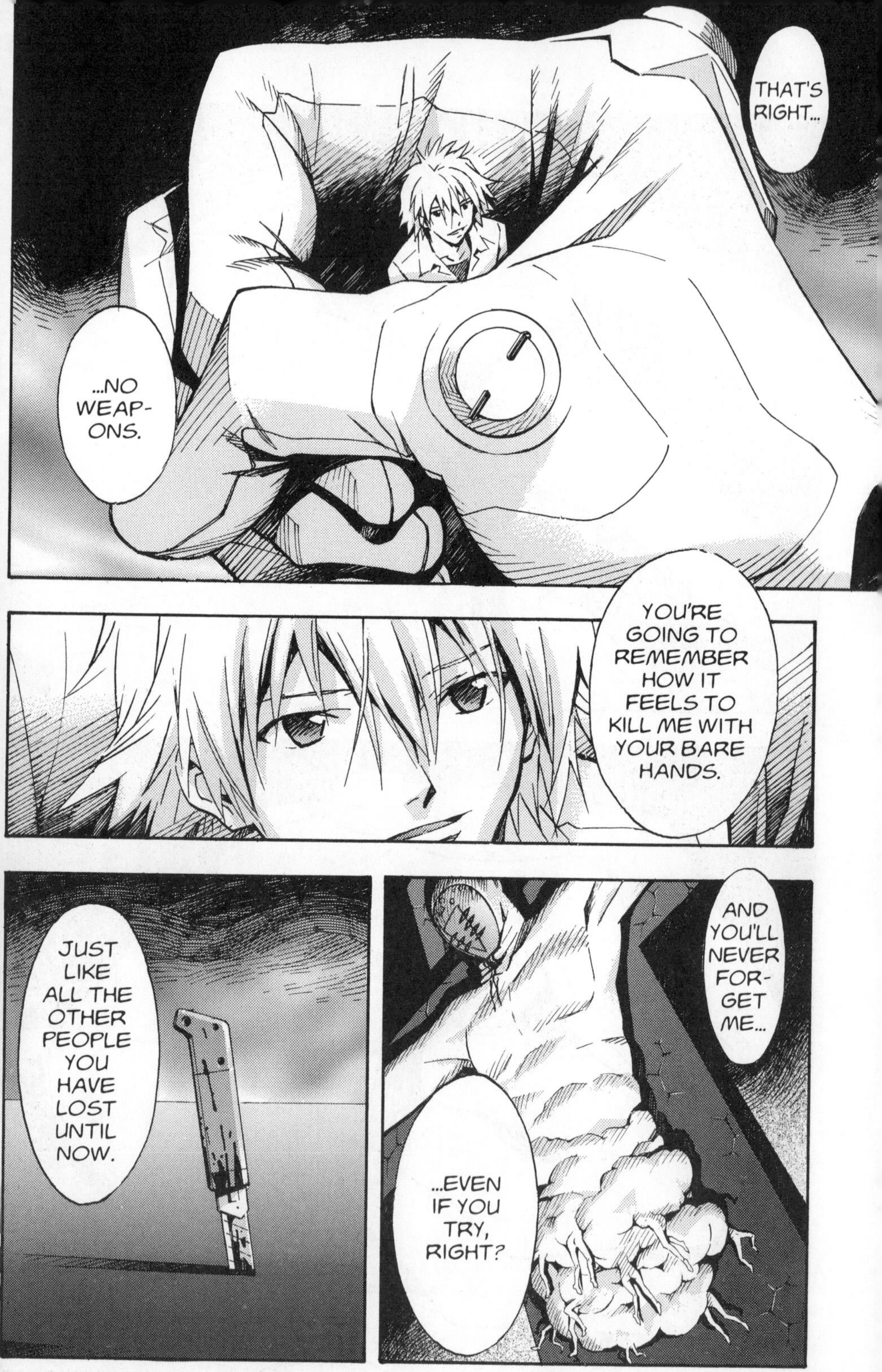
THAT'S RIGHT...
...NO WEAPONS.
YOU'RE GOING TO REMEMBER HOW IT FEELS TO KILL ME WITH YOUR BARE HANDS.
AND YOU'LL NEVER FORGET ME...
...EVEN IF YOU TRY, RIGHT?
JUST LIKE ALL THE OTHER PEOPLE YOU HAVE LOST UNTIL NOW.

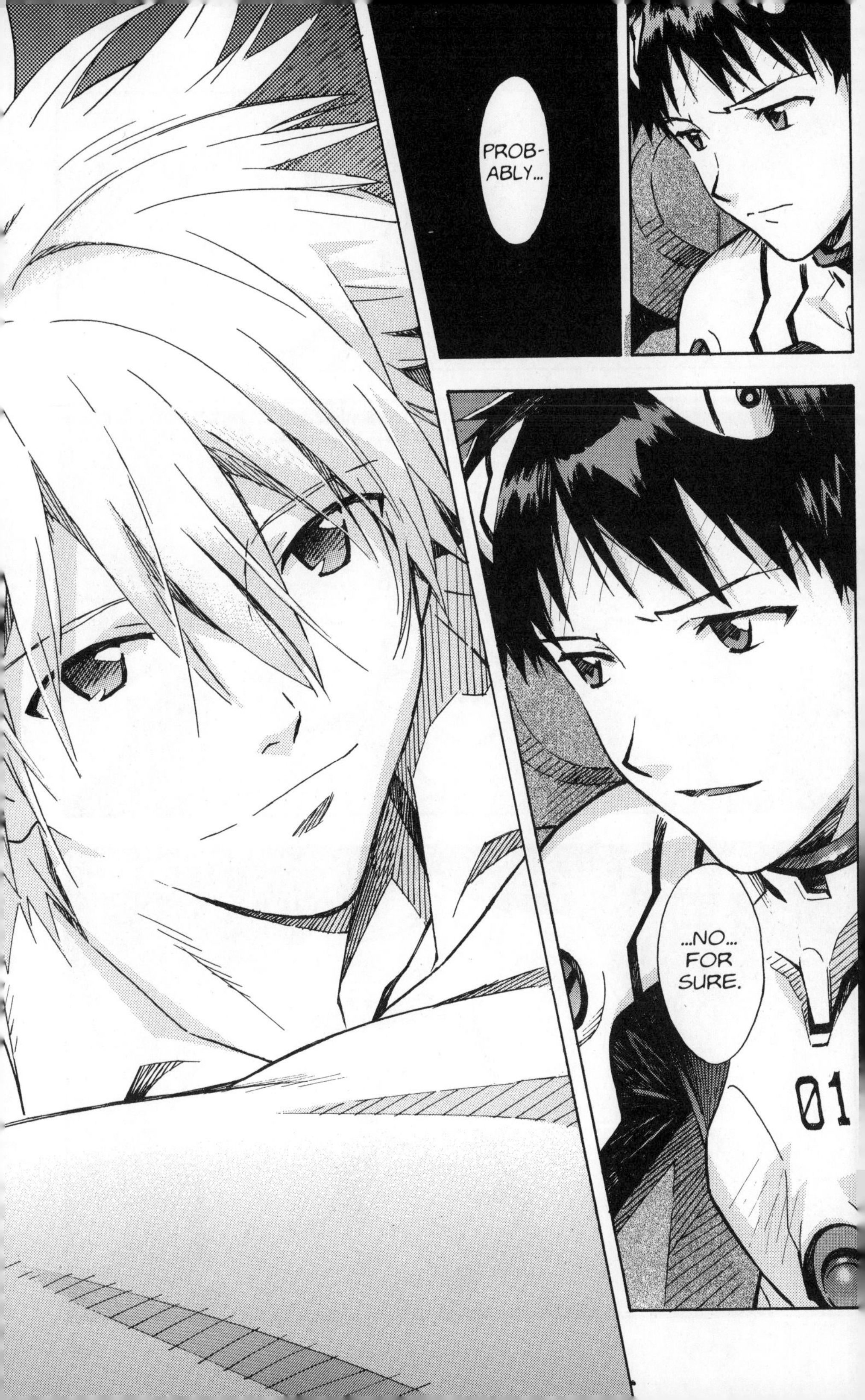
PROB-
ABLY...
...NO...
FOR
SURE.

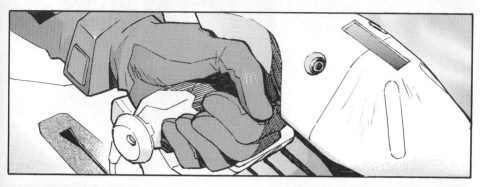

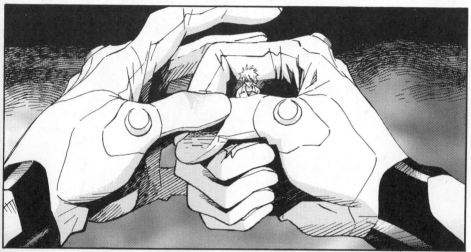

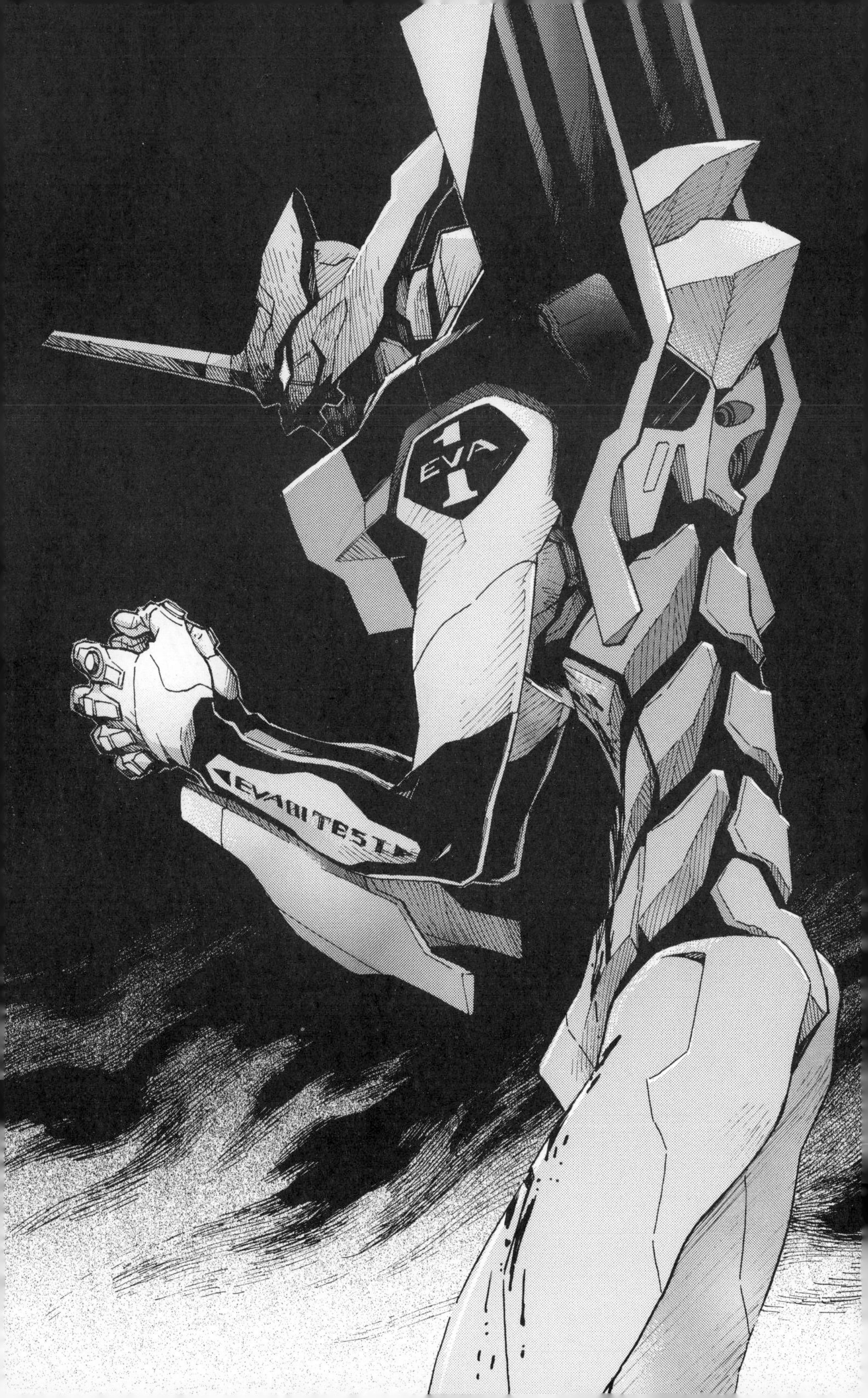
1 EVA
EVA01 TEST

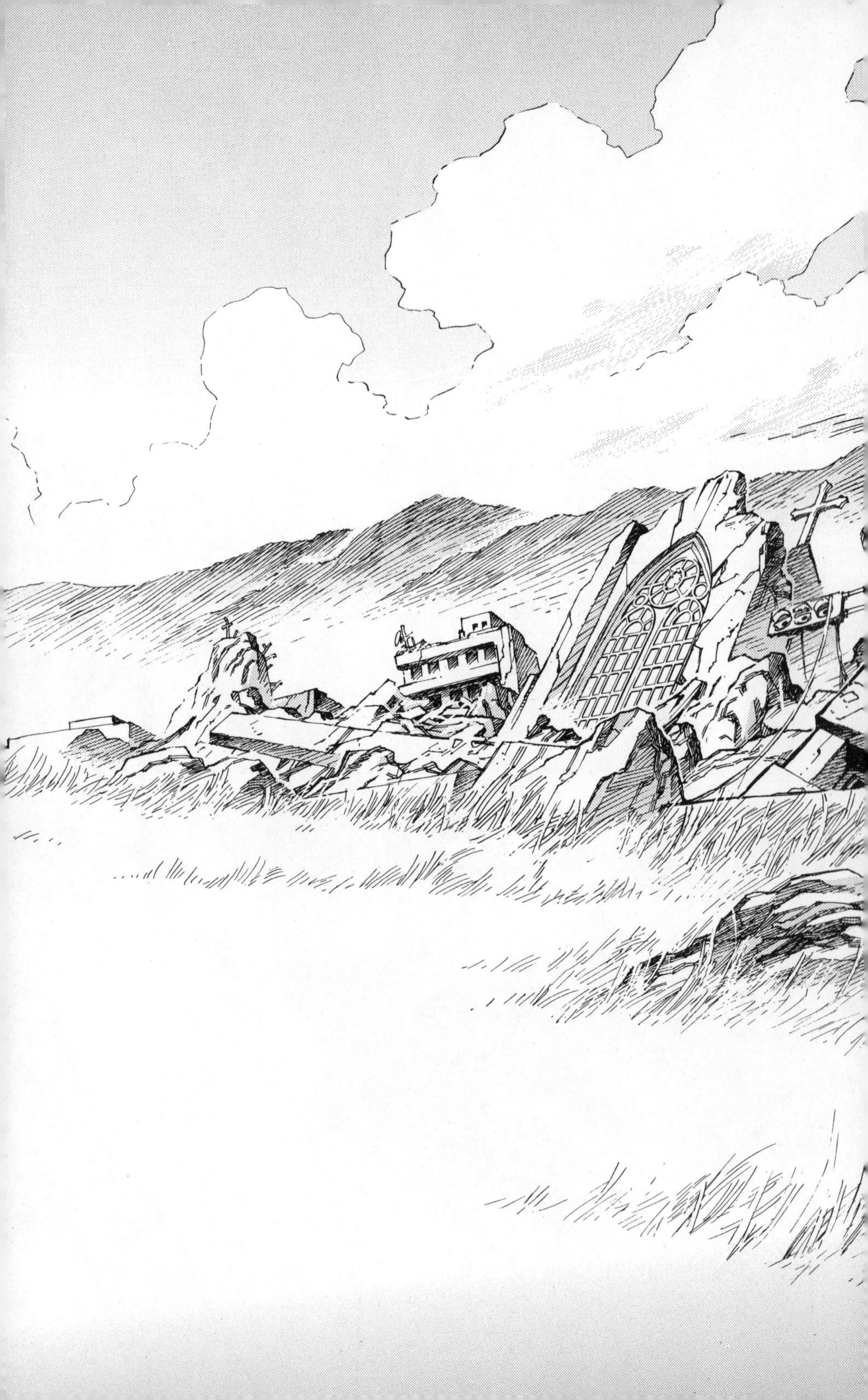

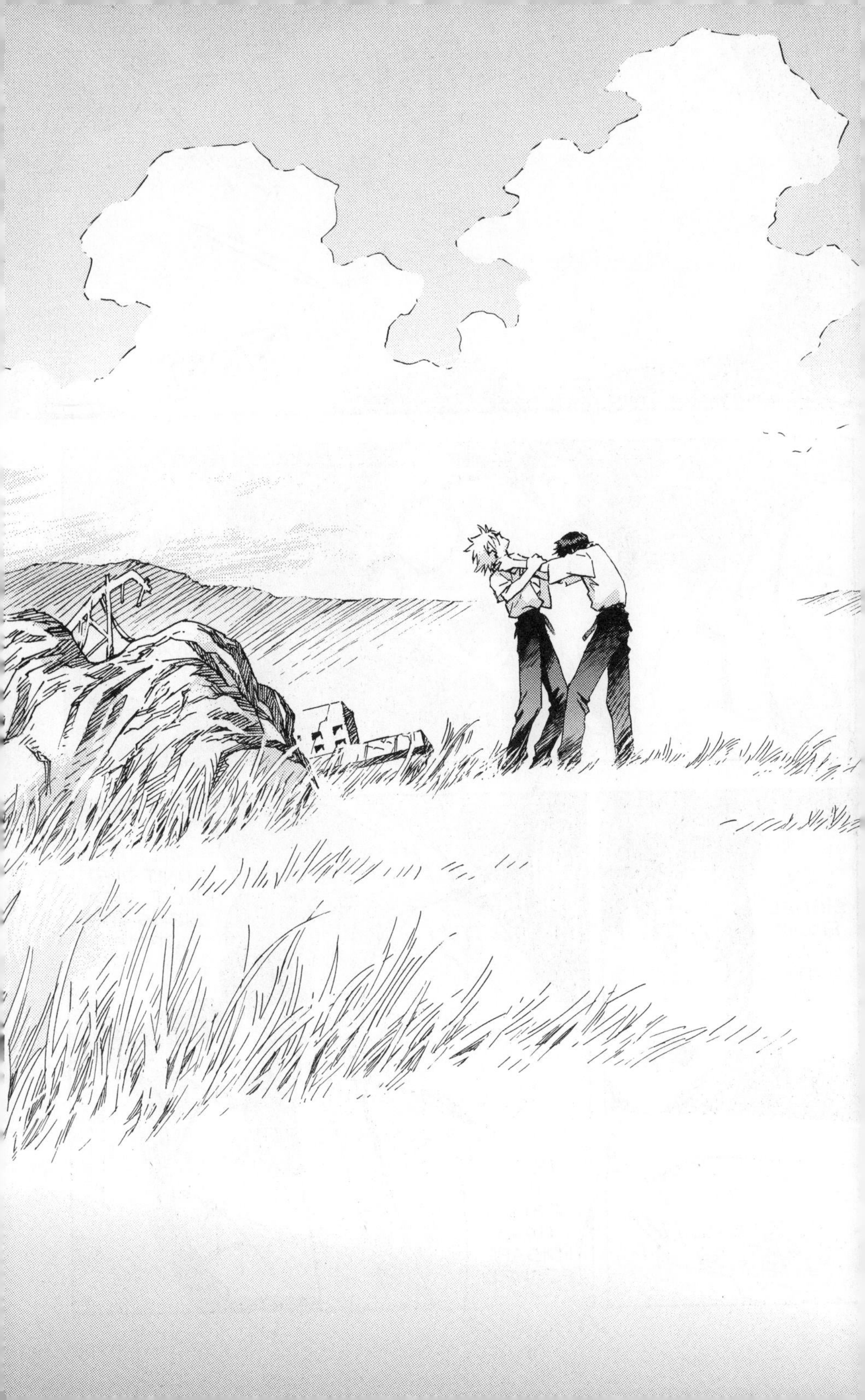

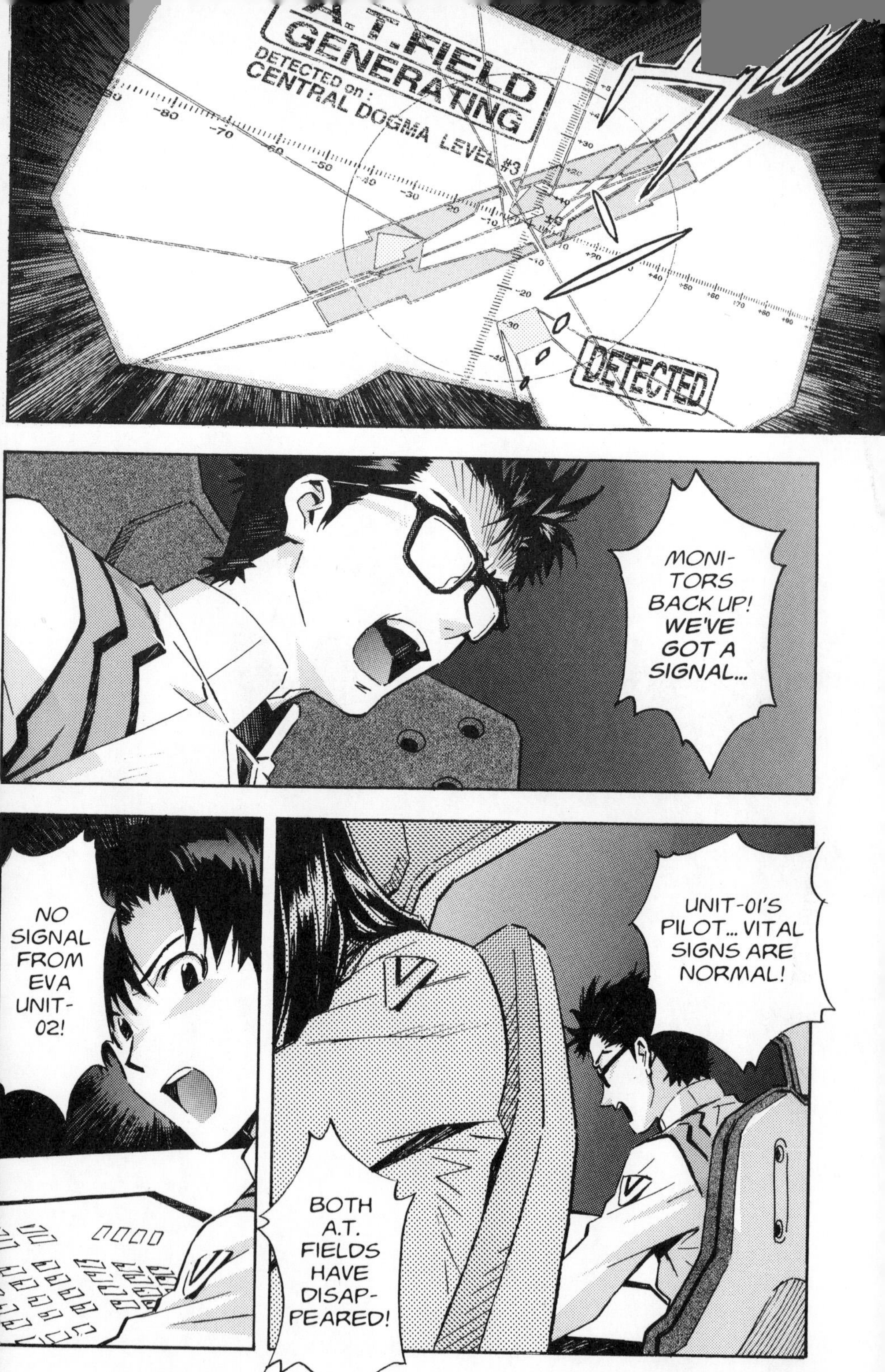
A.T.FIELD GENERATING
DETECTED on : CENTRAL DOGMA LEVEL #3
DETECTED
MONITORS BACK UP! WE'VE GOT A SIGNAL...
UNIT-01'S PILOT... VITAL SIGNS ARE NORMAL!
BOTH A.T. FIELDS HAVE DISAPPEARED!
NO SIGNAL FROM EVA UNIT-02!

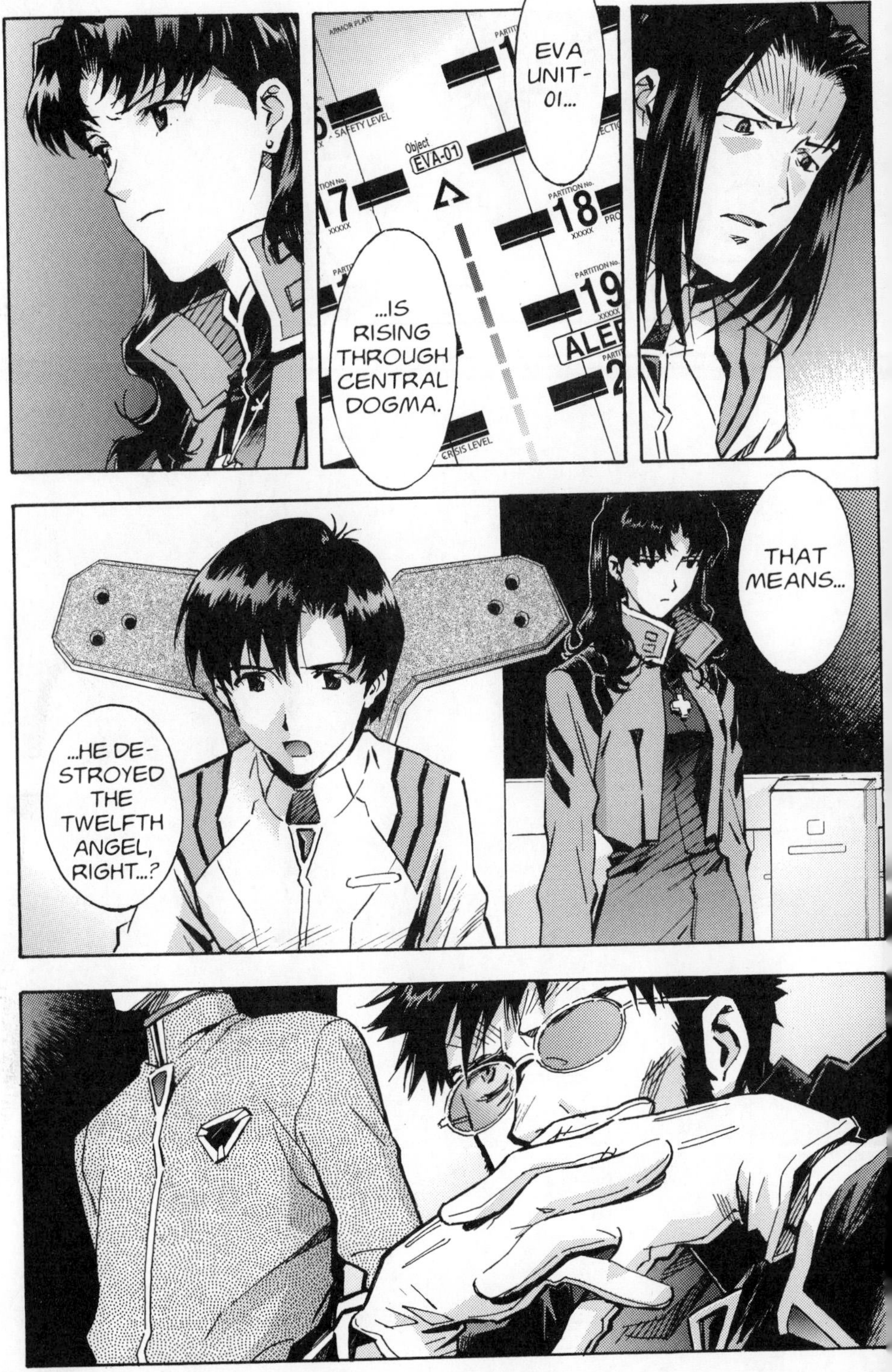
EVA UNIT-01...
...IS RISING THROUGH CENTRAL DOGMA.
ARMOR PLATE
SAFETY LEVEL
Object
EVA-01
PARTITION No.
17
PARTITION No.
18
CRISIS LEVEL
THAT MEANS...
...HE DESTROYED THE TWELFTH ANGEL, RIGHT...?

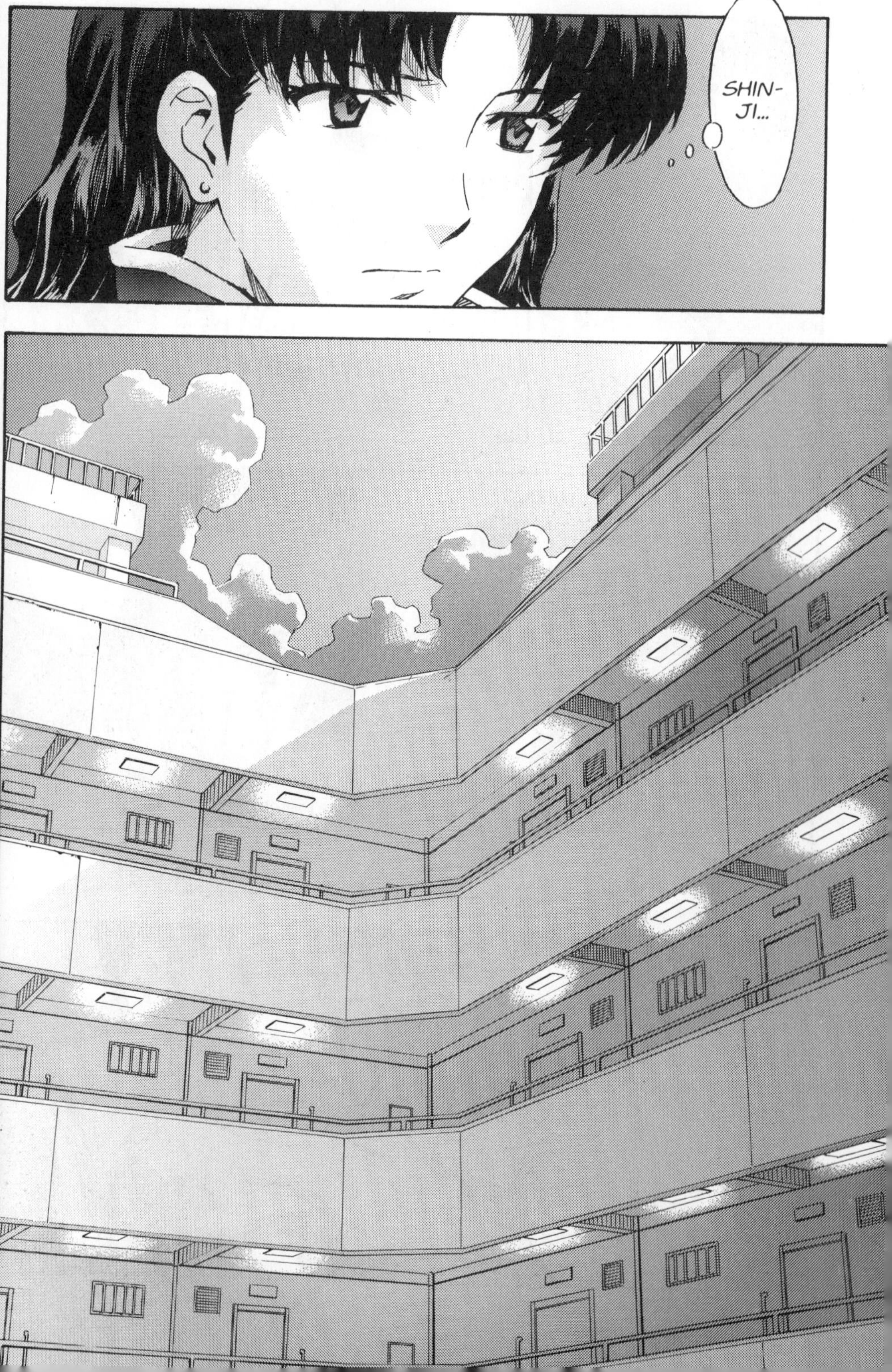
SHIN-
JI...

....I'M
COMING
IN.

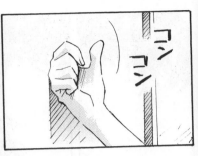

SHIN-JI...

IT'S
EVENING
ALREADY...

...WHY DON'T YOU GET UP AND HAVE SOME-THING TO EAT?

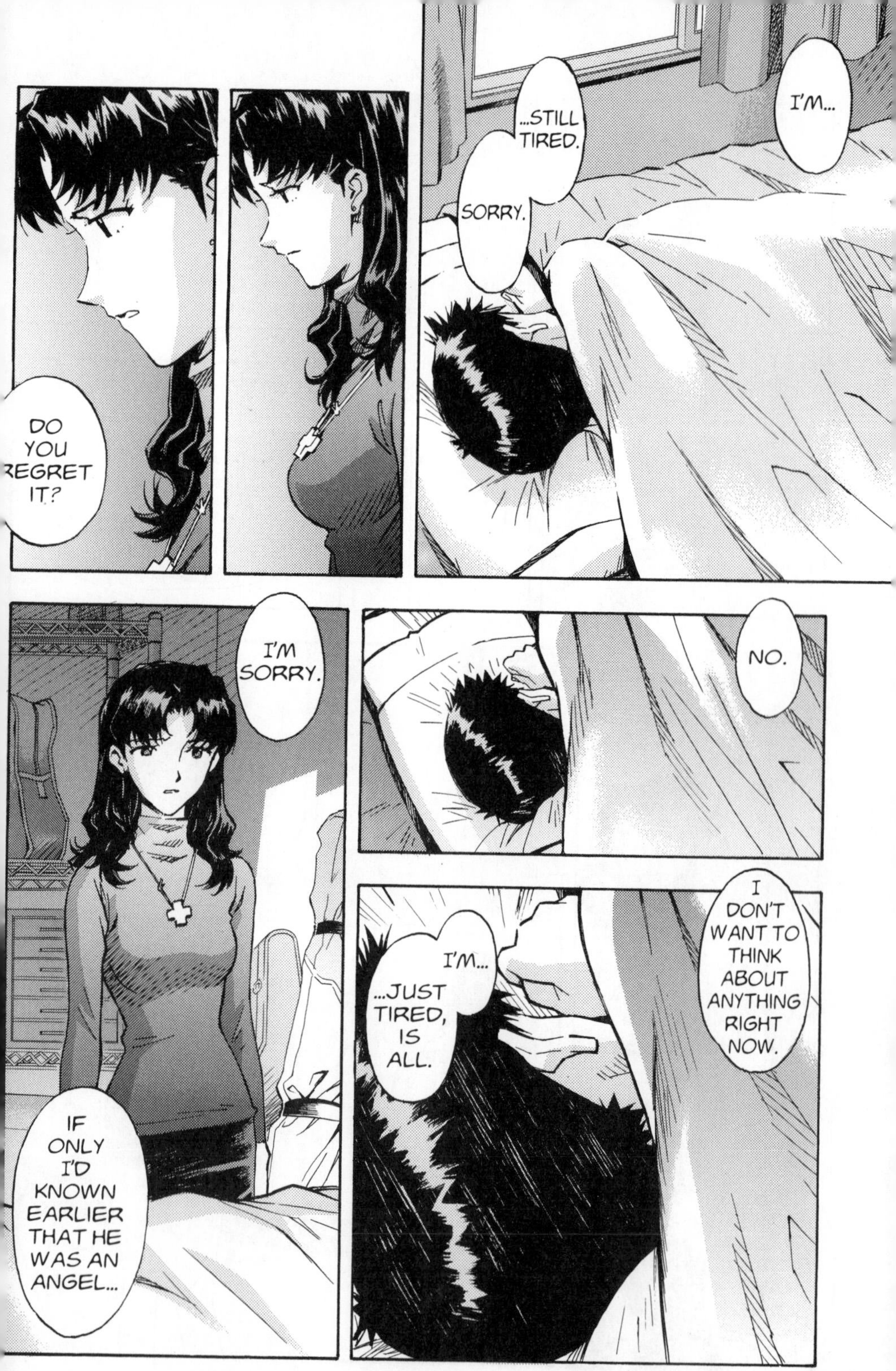
I'M...
...STILL TIRED.
SORRY.
DO YOU REGRET IT?
I'M SORRY.
NO.
I DON'T WANT TO THINK ABOUT ANYTHING RIGHT NOW.
I'M...
...JUST TIRED, IS ALL.
IF ONLY I'D KNOWN EARLIER THAT HE WAS AN ANGEL...

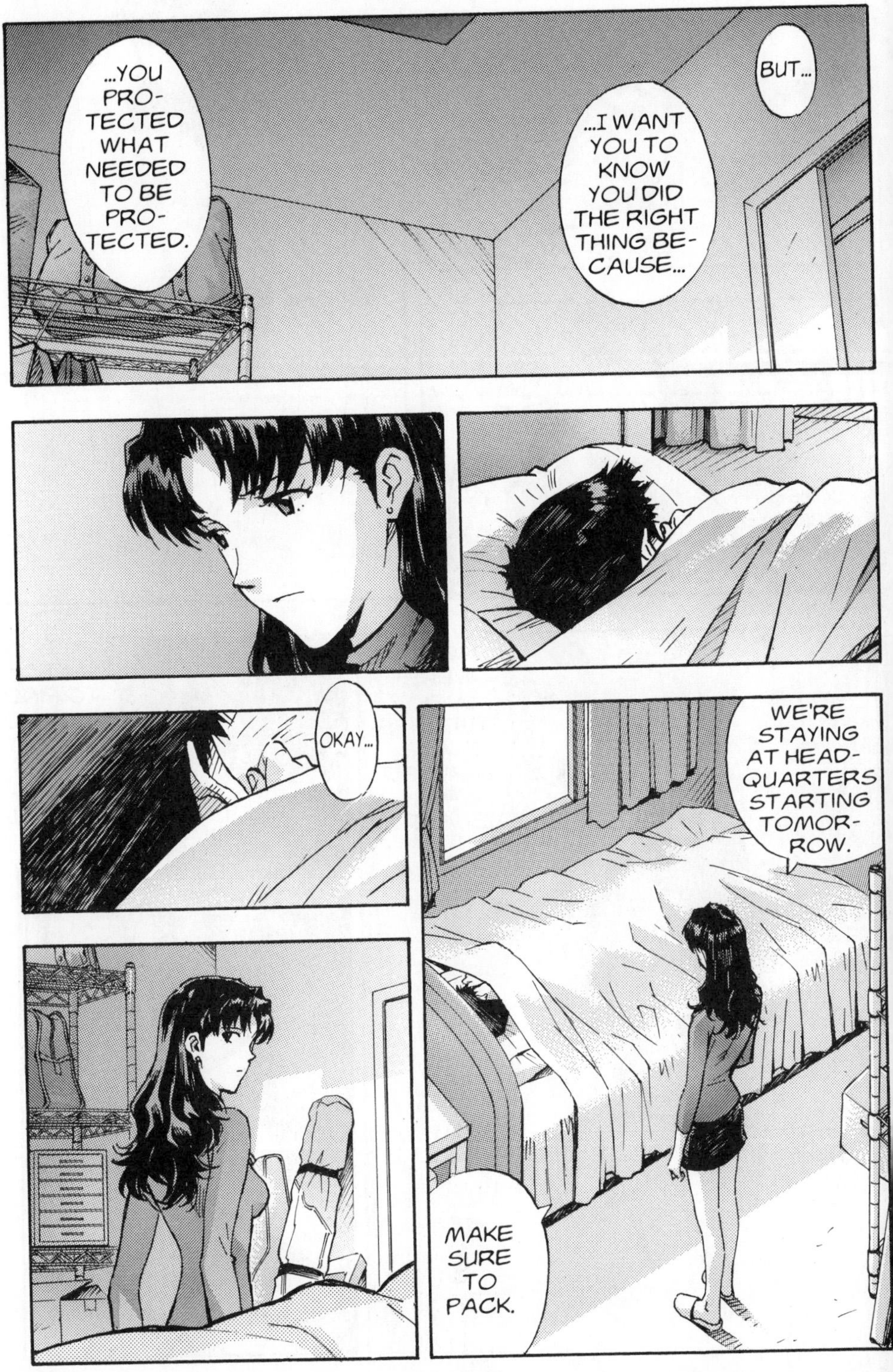
BUT...
...I WANT YOU TO KNOW YOU DID THE RIGHT THING BE-CAUSE...
...YOU PRO-TECTED WHAT NEEDED TO BE PRO-TECTED.
WE'RE STAYING AT HEAD-QUARTERS STARTING TOMOR-ROW.
MAKE SURE TO PACK.
OKAY...

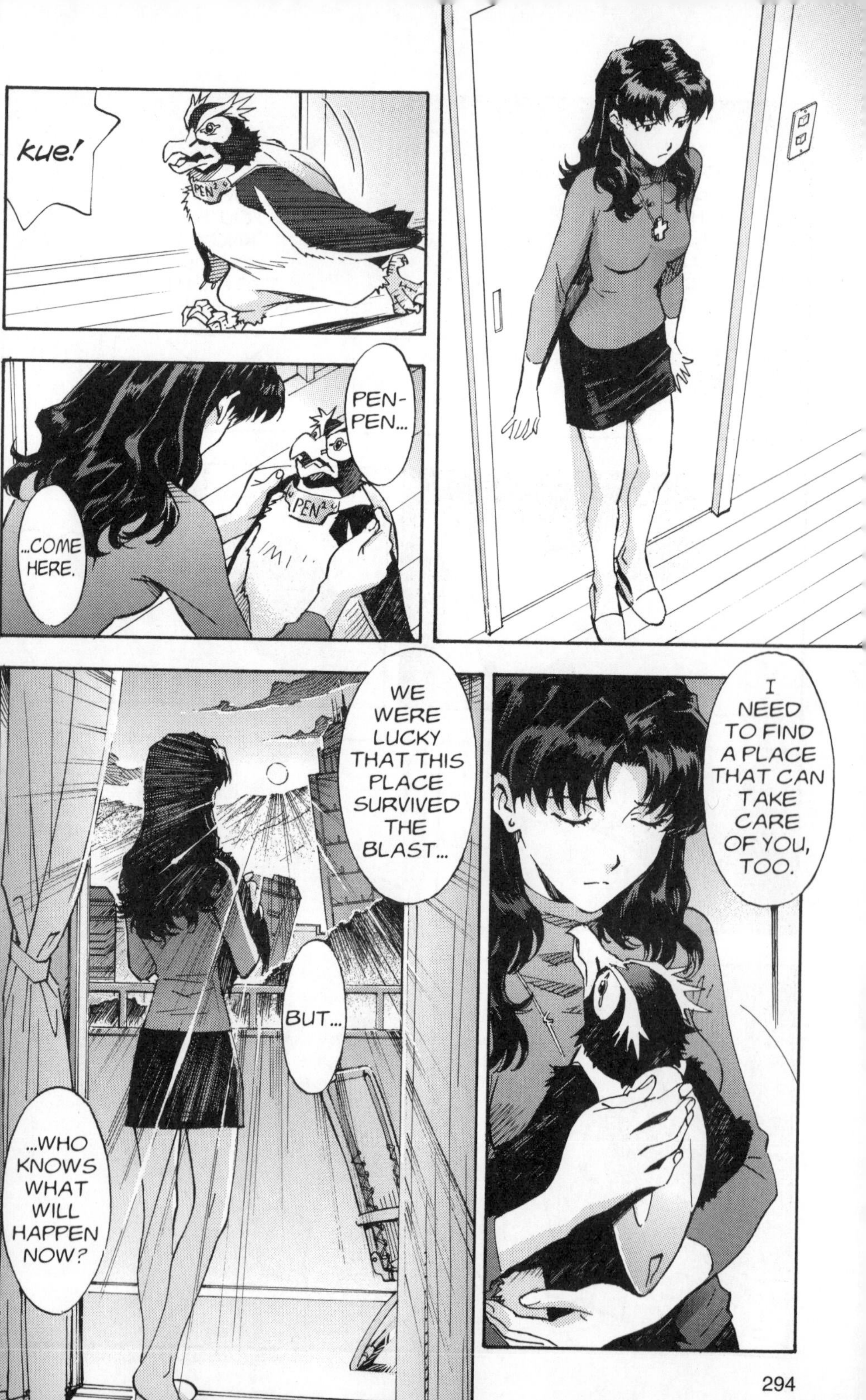
kue!
PEN-PEN...
...COME HERE.
I NEED TO FIND A PLACE THAT CAN TAKE CARE OF YOU, TOO.
WE WERE LUCKY THAT THIS PLACE SURVIVED THE BLAST...
BUT...
...WHO KNOWS WHAT WILL HAPPEN NOW?

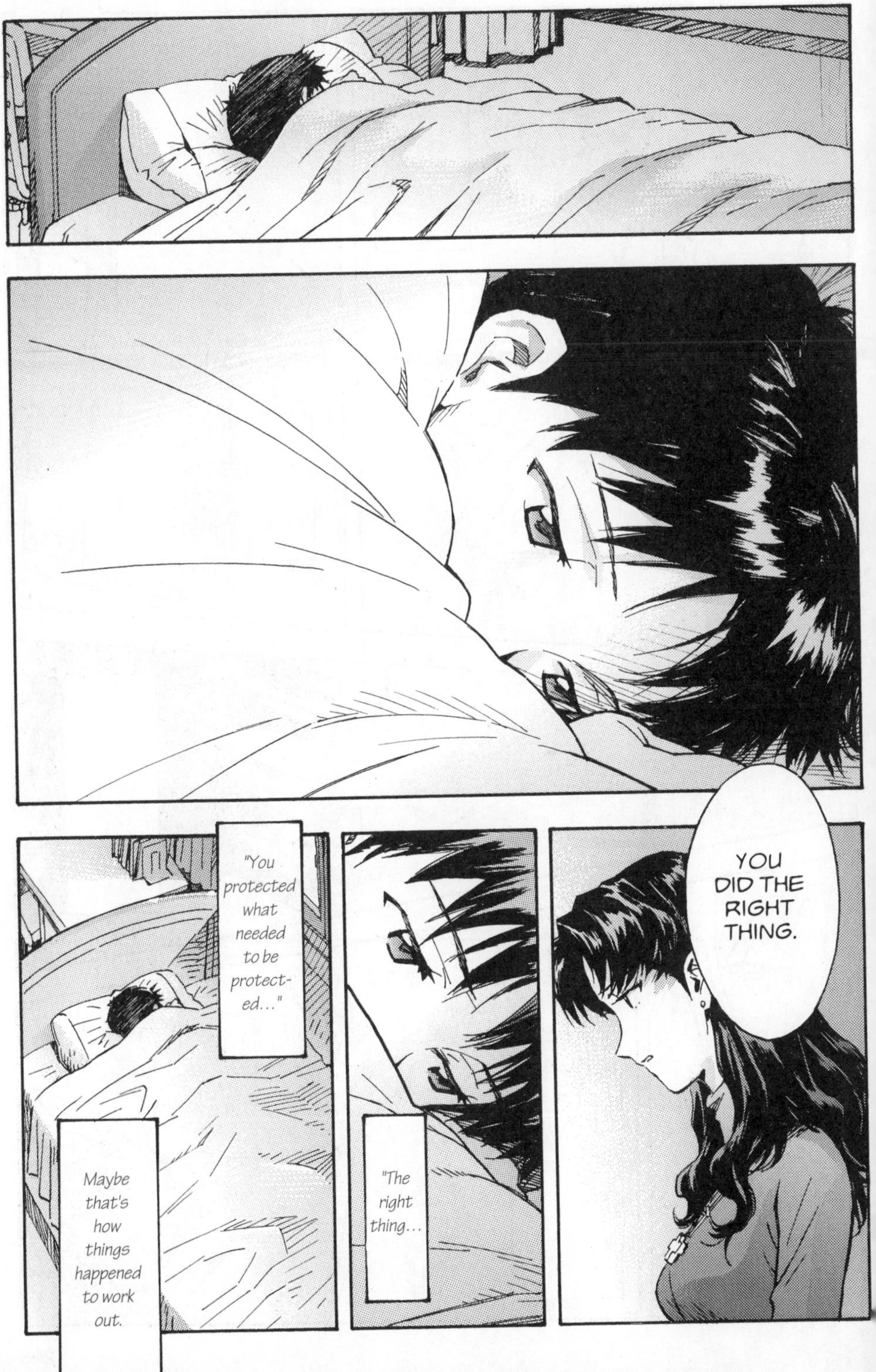
YOU DID THE RIGHT THING.
"The right thing…
"You protected what needed to be protect-ed…"
Maybe that's how things happened to work out.

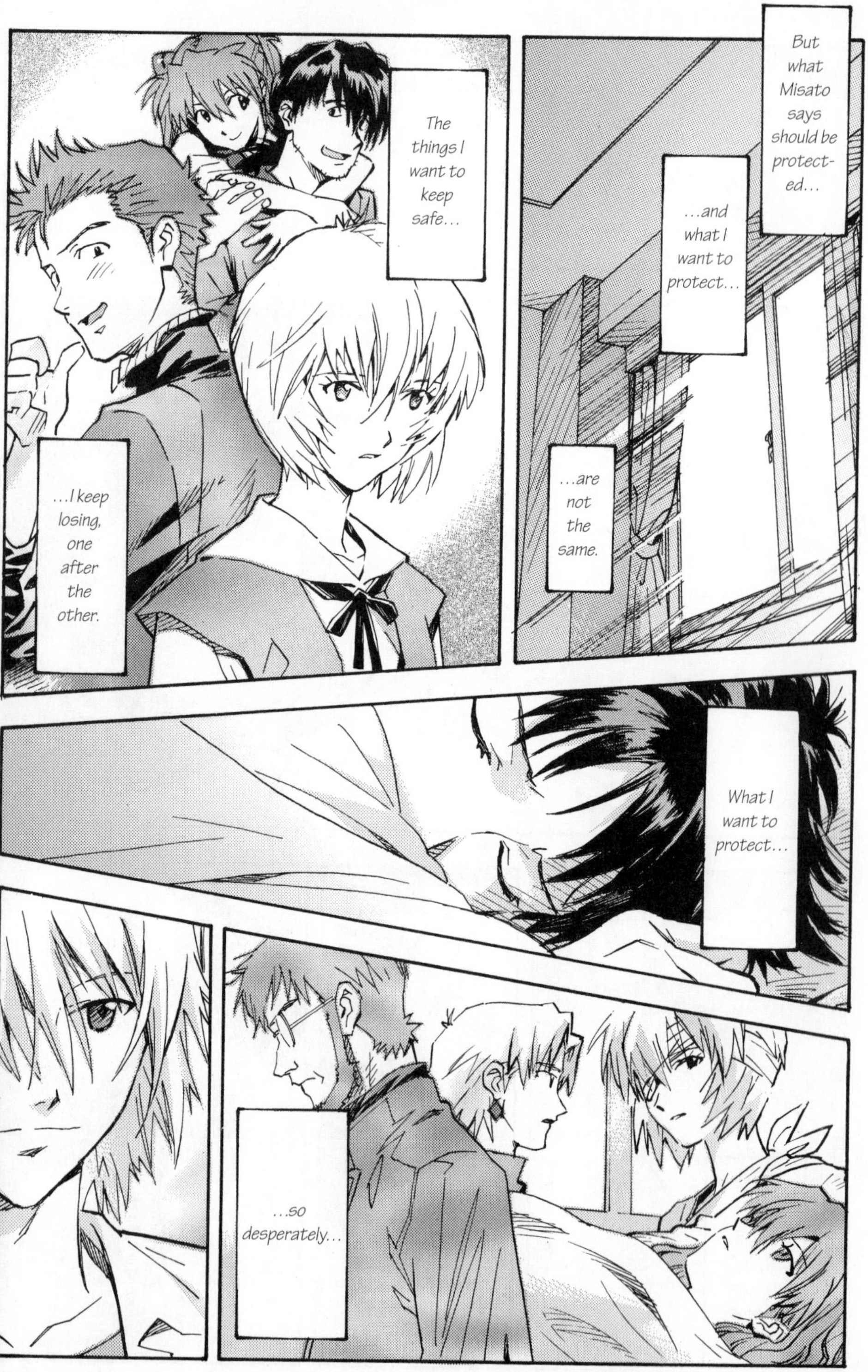
But what Misato says should be protected…
…and what I want to protect…
…are not the same.
The things I want to keep safe…
…I keep losing, one after the other.
What I want to protect…
…so desperately…

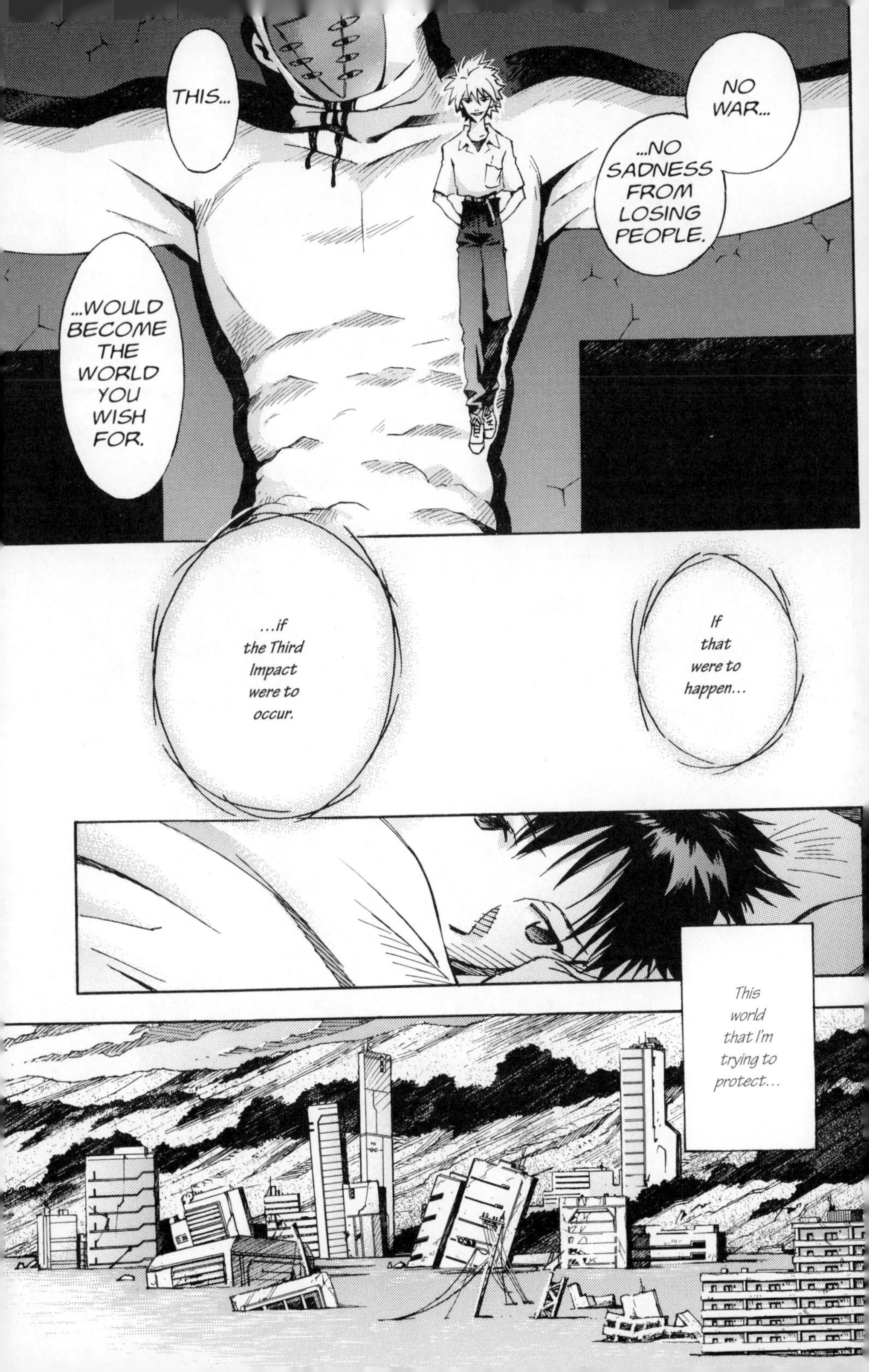
NO WAR...
...NO SADNESS FROM LOSING PEOPLE.
THIS...
...WOULD BECOME THE WORLD YOU WISH FOR.
If that were to happen...
...if the Third Impact were to occur.
This world that I'm trying to protect...

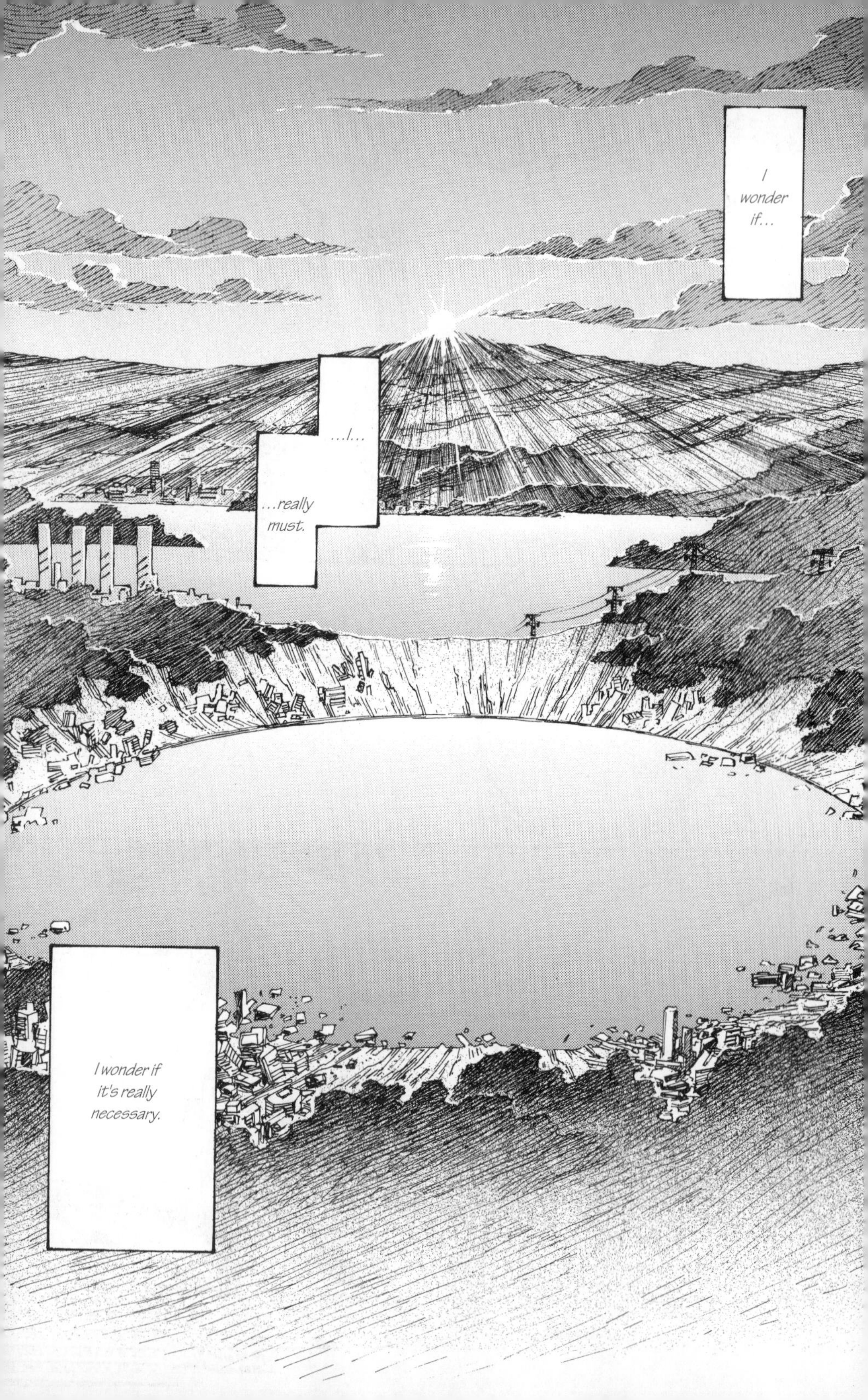
I wonder if…
…I…
…really must.
I wonder if it's really necessary.

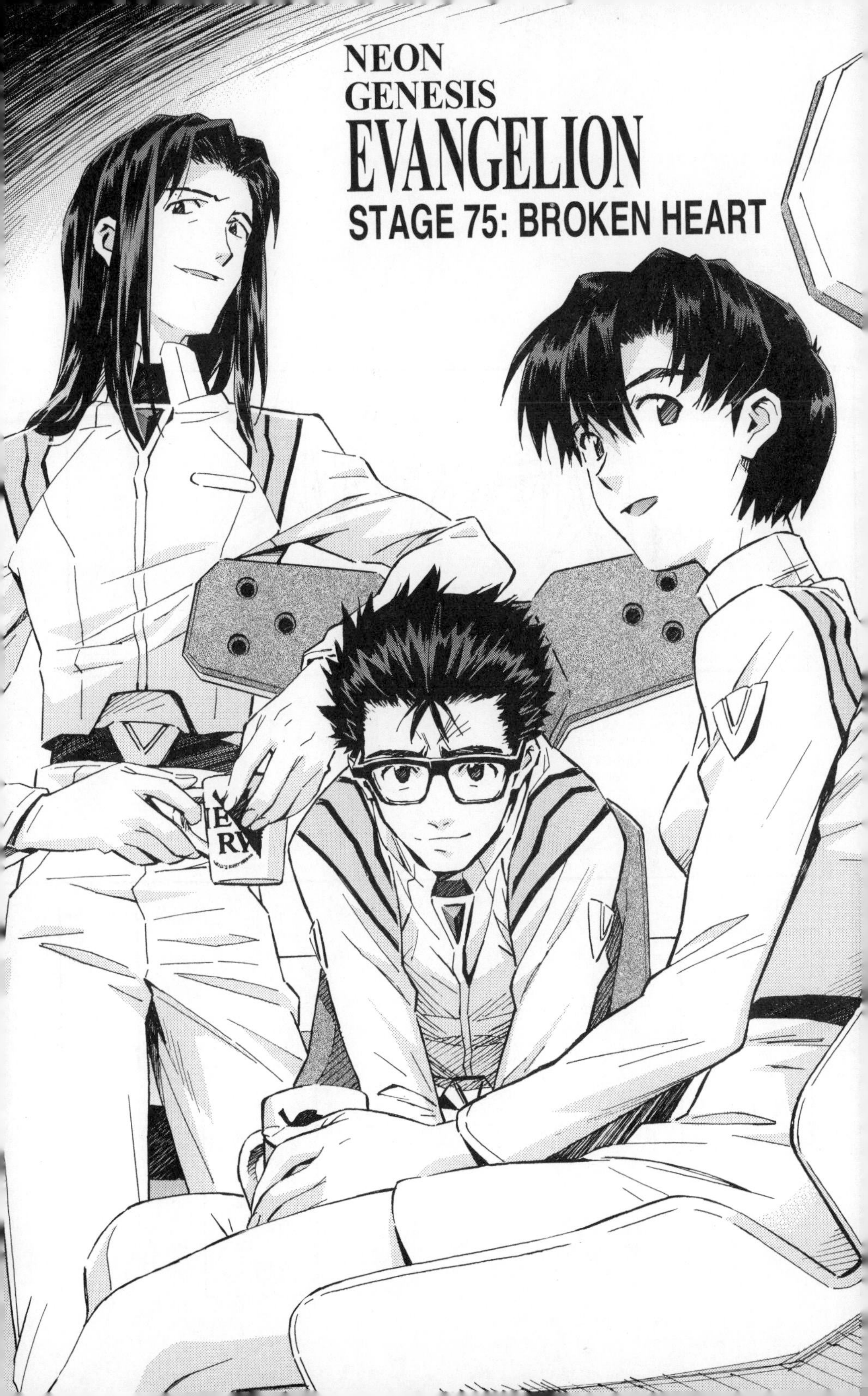
NEON
GENESIS
EVANGELION
STAGE 75: BROKEN HEART

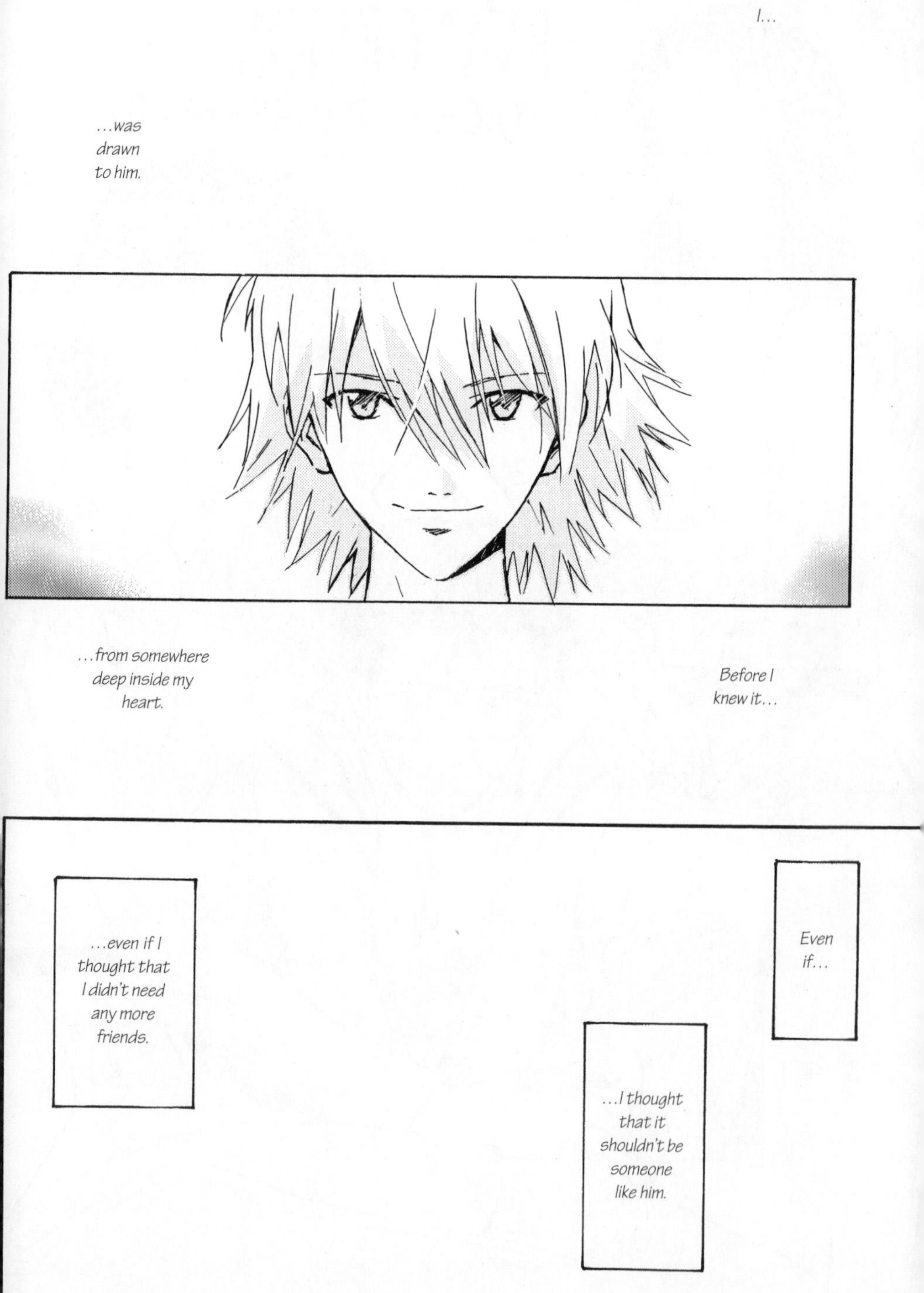
I…
…was drawn to him.
Before I knew it…
…from somewhere deep inside my heart.
Even if…
…I thought that it shouldn't be someone like him.
…even if I thought that I didn't need any more friends.

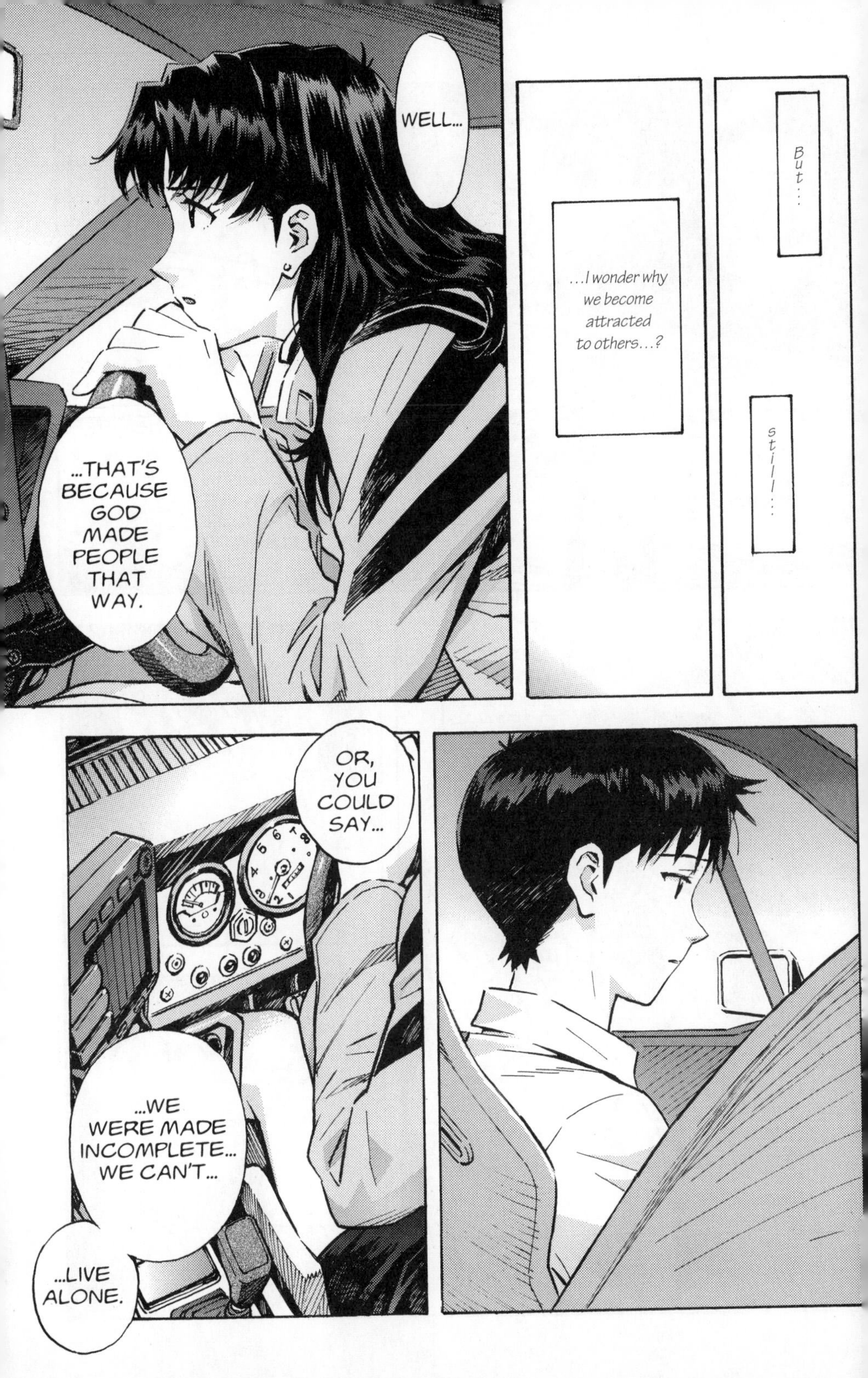
But...
still...
...I wonder why we become attracted to others...?
WELL...
...THAT'S BECAUSE GOD MADE PEOPLE THAT WAY.
OR, YOU COULD SAY...
...WE WERE MADE INCOMPLETE... WE CAN'T...
...LIVE ALONE.

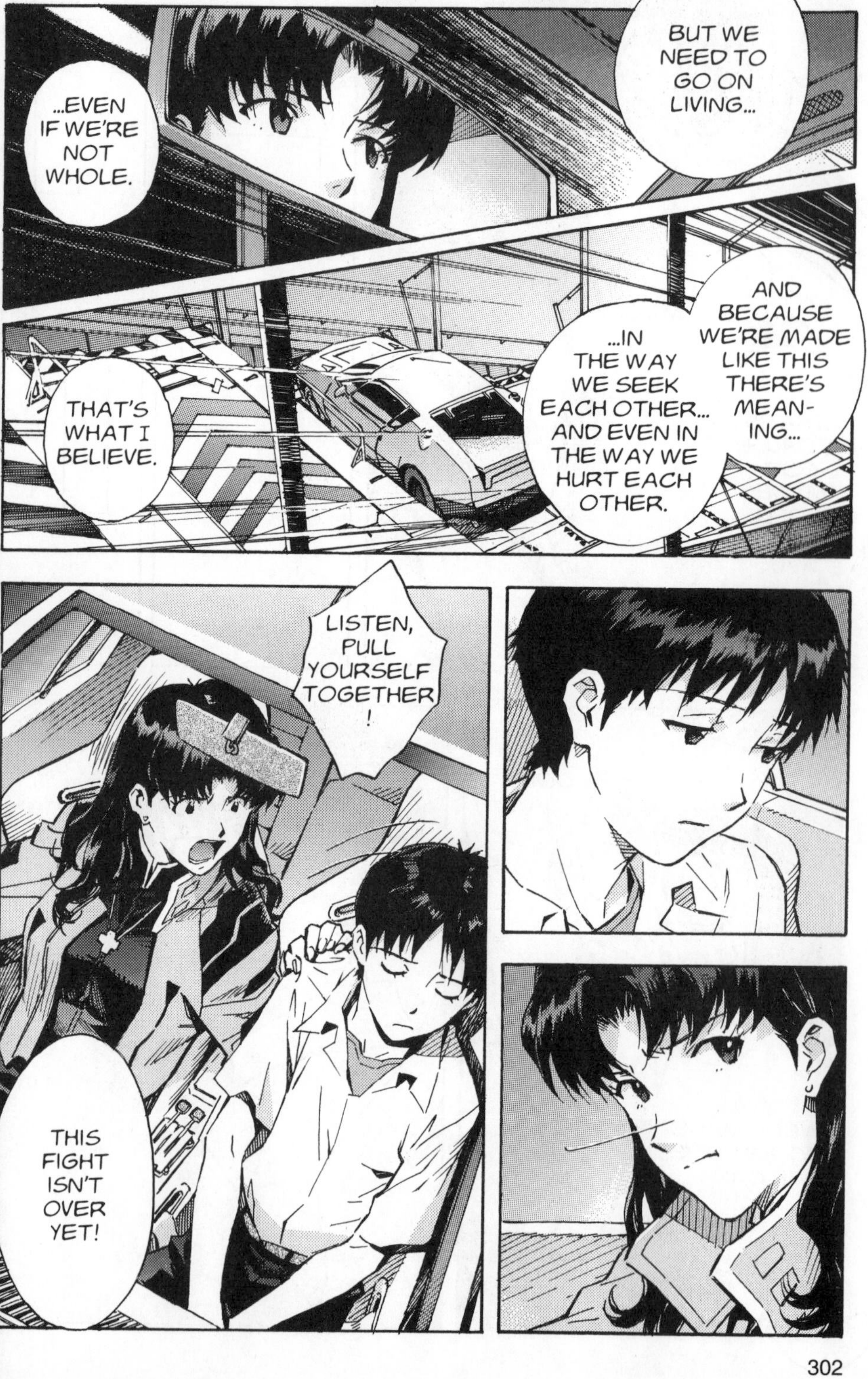
BUT WE NEED TO GO ON LIVING...
...EVEN IF WE'RE NOT WHOLE.
AND BECAUSE WE'RE MADE LIKE THIS THERE'S MEAN-ING...
...IN THE WAY WE SEEK EACH OTHER... AND EVEN IN THE WAY WE HURT EACH OTHER.
THAT'S WHAT I BELIEVE.
LISTEN, PULL YOURSELF TOGETHER!
THIS FIGHT ISN'T OVER YET!

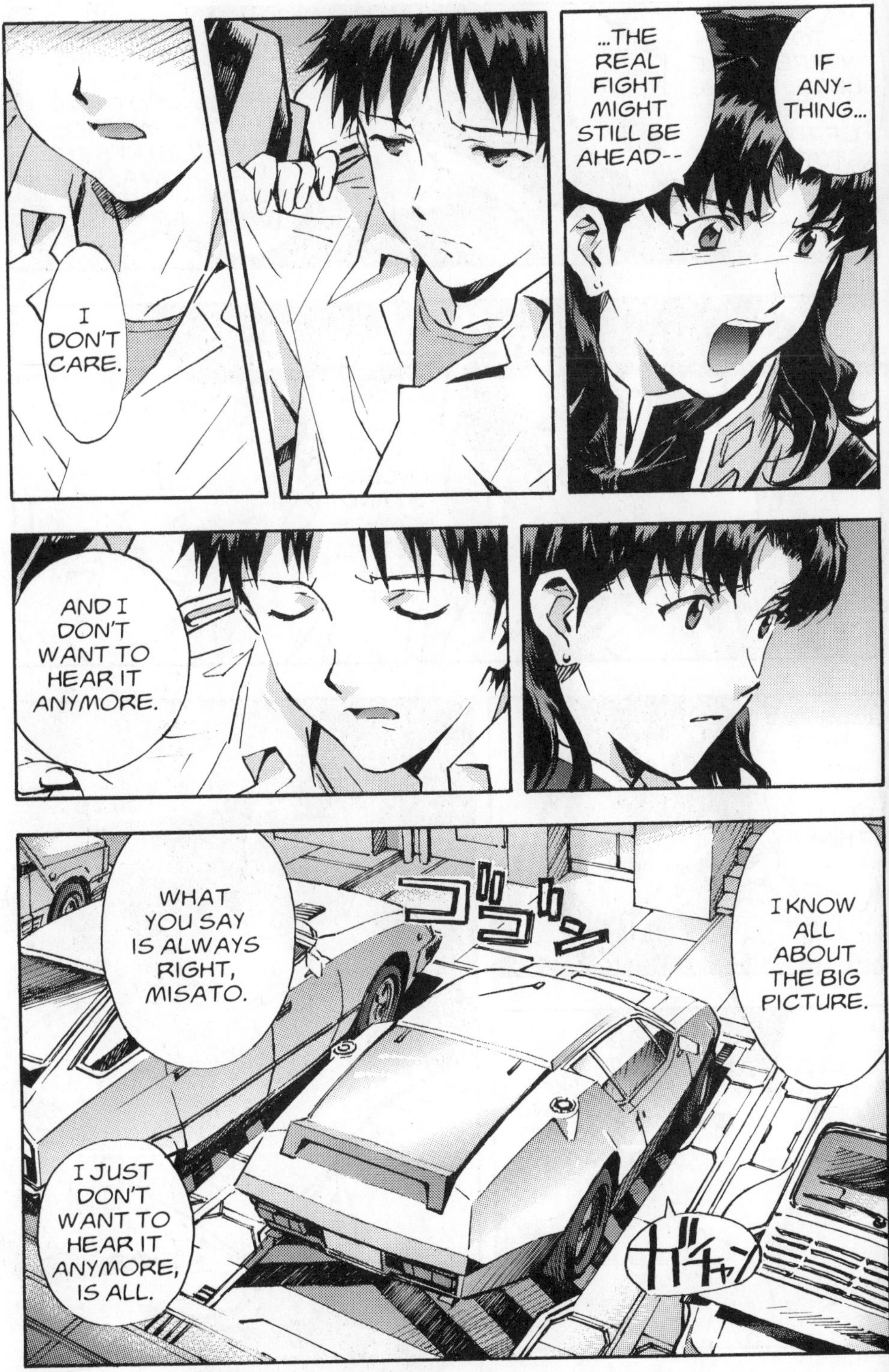
IF ANY-THING...
...THE REAL FIGHT MIGHT STILL BE AHEAD--
I DON'T CARE.
AND I DON'T WANT TO HEAR IT ANYMORE.
I KNOW ALL ABOUT THE BIG PICTURE.
WHAT YOU SAY IS ALWAYS RIGHT, MISATO.
I JUST DON'T WANT TO HEAR IT ANYMORE, IS ALL.

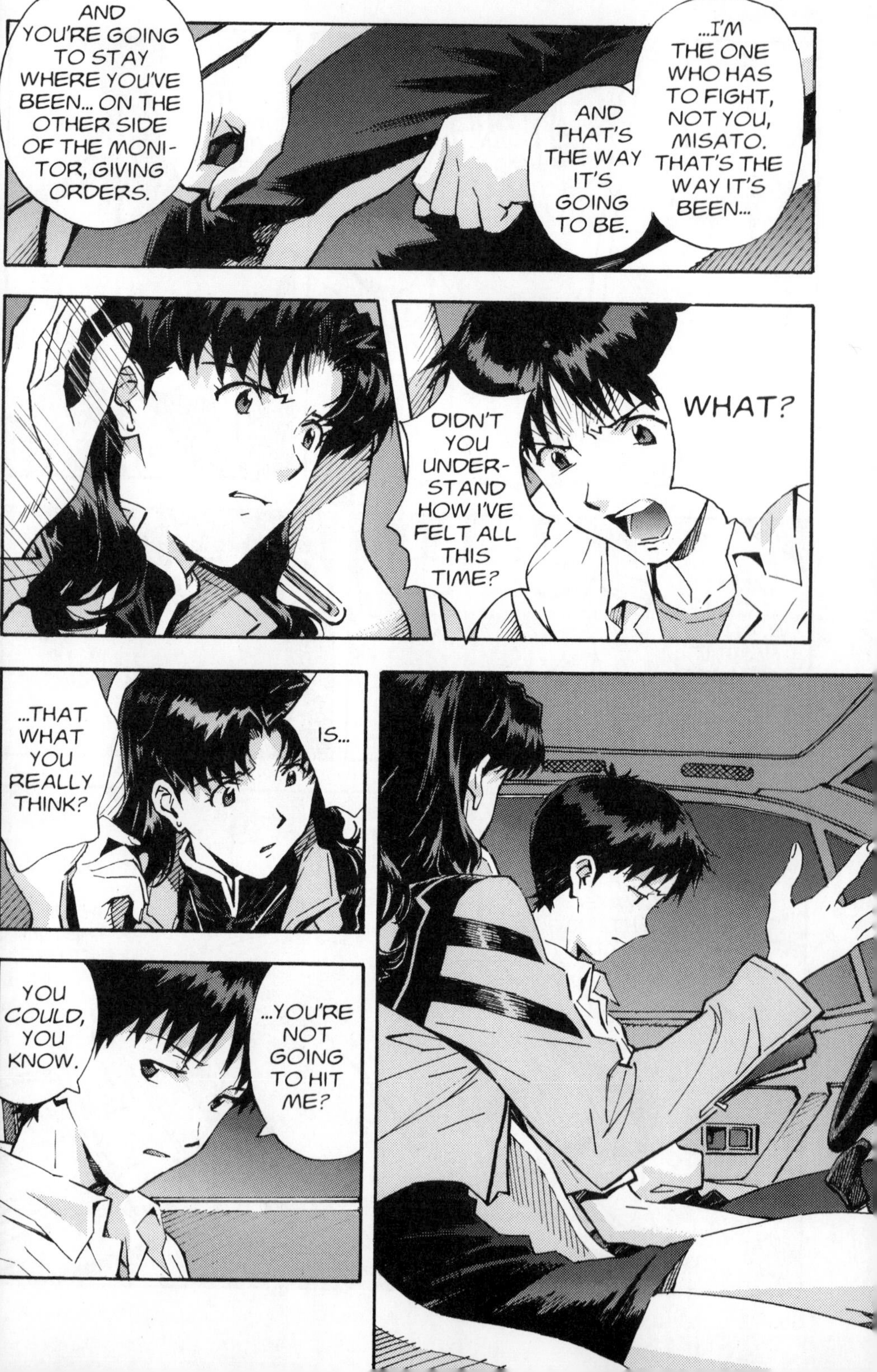
...I'M THE ONE WHO HAS TO FIGHT, NOT YOU, MISATO. THAT'S THE WAY IT'S BEEN...
AND THAT'S THE WAY IT'S GOING TO BE.
AND YOU'RE GOING TO STAY WHERE YOU'VE BEEN... ON THE OTHER SIDE OF THE MONITOR, GIVING ORDERS.
WHAT?
DIDN'T YOU UNDERSTAND HOW I'VE FELT ALL THIS TIME?
IS...
...THAT WHAT YOU REALLY THINK?
...YOU'RE NOT GOING TO HIT ME?
YOU COULD, YOU KNOW.

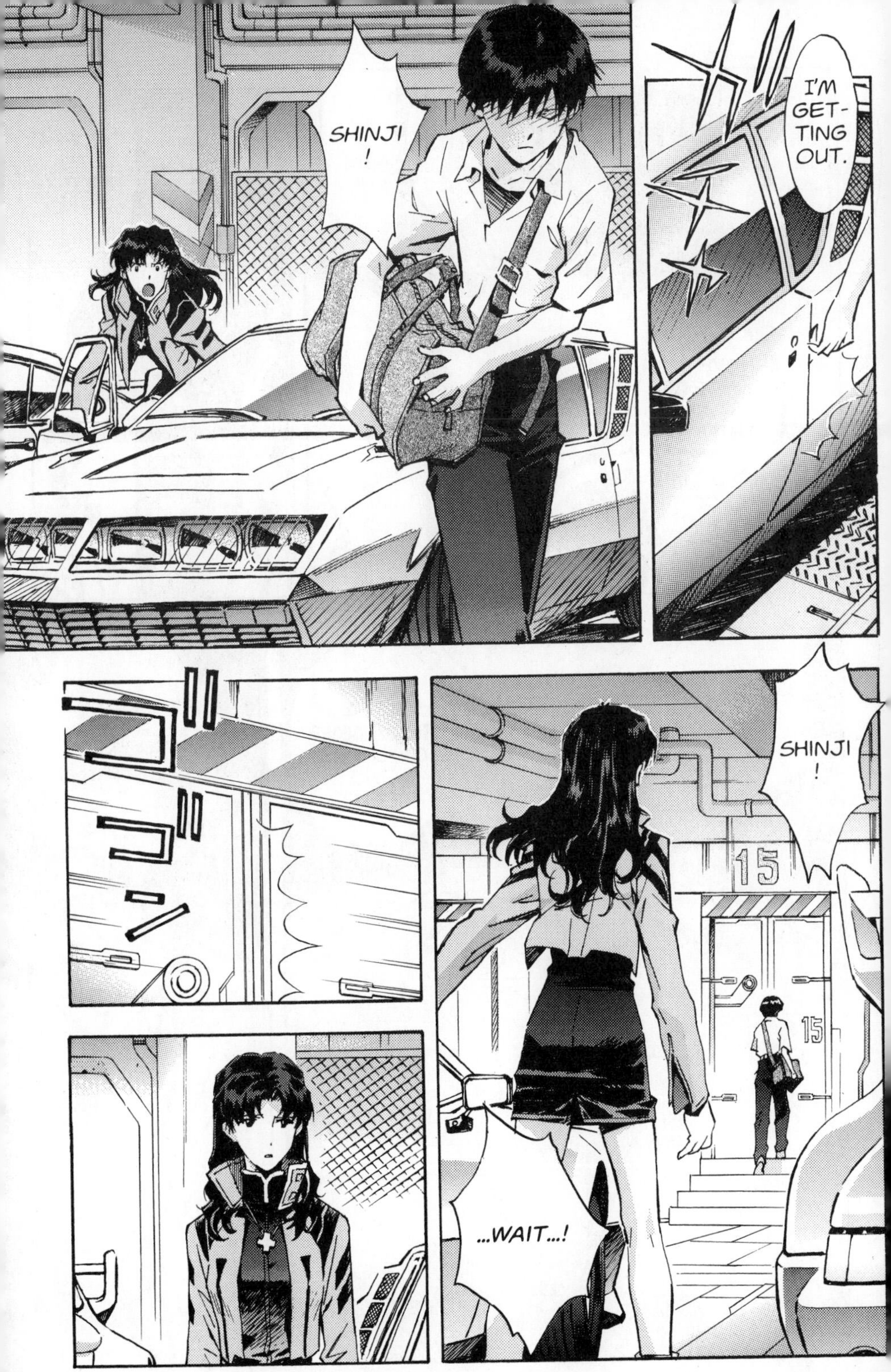
I'M GETTING OUT.
SHINJI!
SHINJI!
...WAIT...!

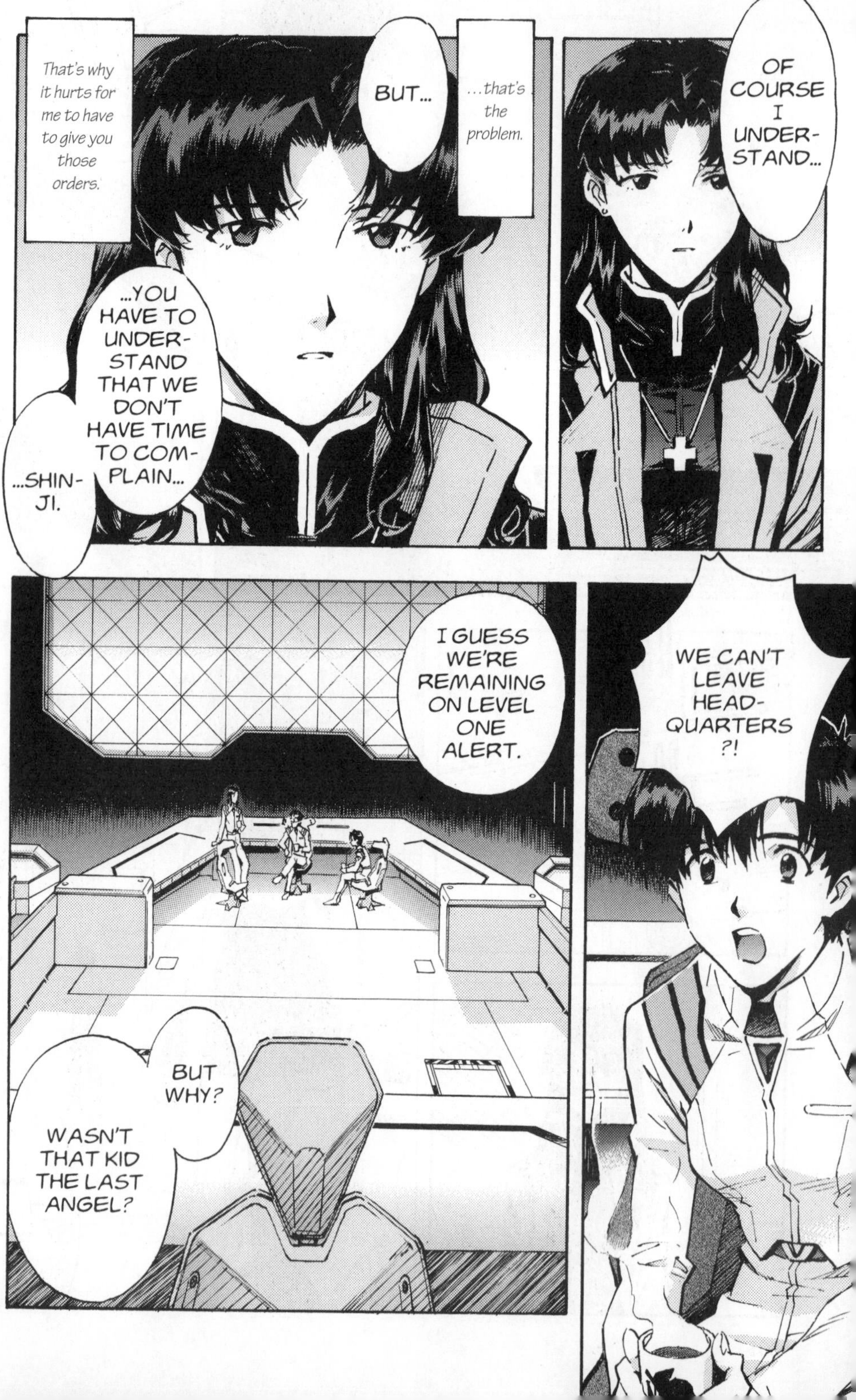
OF COURSE I UNDER-STAND...
...that's the problem.
BUT...
That's why it hurts for me to have to give you those orders.
...YOU HAVE TO UNDER-STAND THAT WE DON'T HAVE TIME TO COM-PLAIN...
...SHIN-JI.
WE CAN'T LEAVE HEAD-QUARTERS ?!
I GUESS WE'RE REMAINING ON LEVEL ONE ALERT.
BUT WHY?
WASN'T THAT KID THE LAST ANGEL?

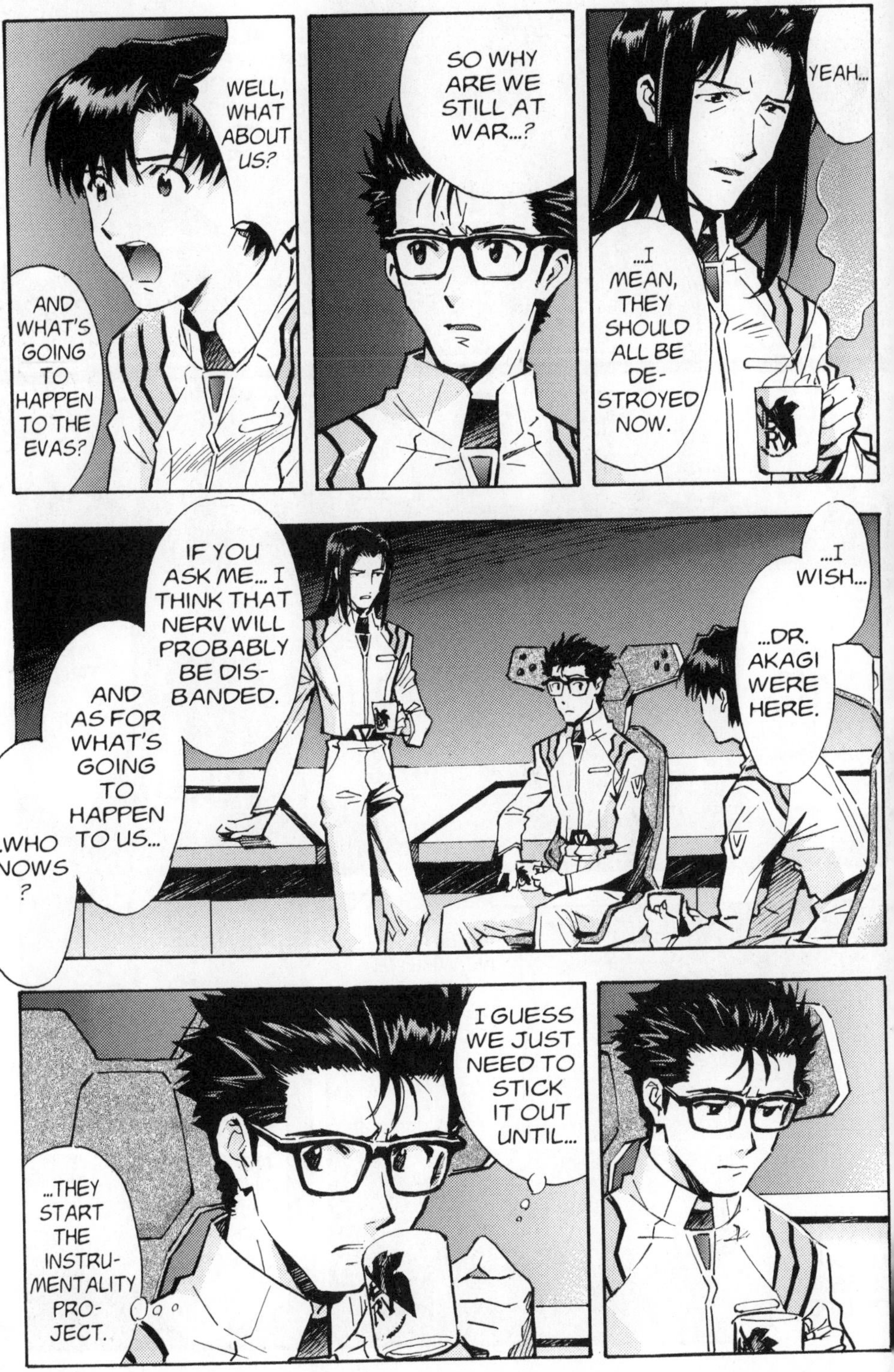
YEAH...
...I MEAN, THEY SHOULD ALL BE DESTROYED NOW.
SO WHY ARE WE STILL AT WAR...?
WELL, WHAT ABOUT US?
AND WHAT'S GOING TO HAPPEN TO THE EVAS?
...I WISH...
...DR. AKAGI WERE HERE.
IF YOU ASK ME... I THINK THAT NERV WILL PROBABLY BE DISBANDED.
AND AS FOR WHAT'S GOING TO HAPPEN TO US...
...WHO KNOWS?
I GUESS WE JUST NEED TO STICK IT OUT UNTIL...
...THEY START THE INSTRUMENTALITY PROJECT.

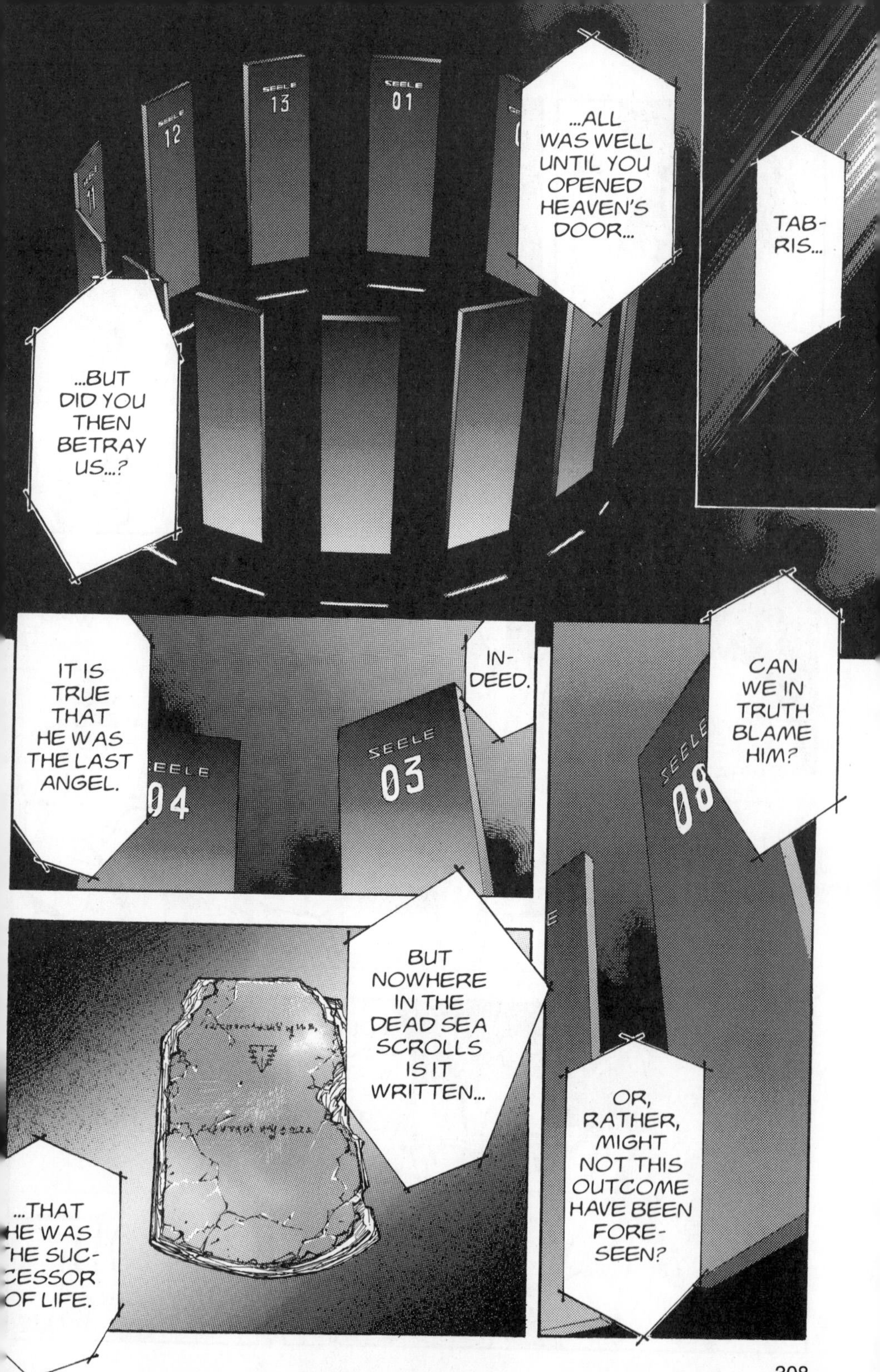
TABRIS...
...ALL WAS WELL UNTIL YOU OPENED HEAVEN'S DOOR...
...BUT DID YOU THEN BETRAY US...?
CAN WE IN TRUTH BLAME HIM?
OR, RATHER, MIGHT NOT THIS OUTCOME HAVE BEEN FORESEEN?
INDEED.
IT IS TRUE THAT HE WAS THE LAST ANGEL.
BUT NOWHERE IN THE DEAD SEA SCROLLS IS IT WRITTEN...
...THAT HE WAS THE SUCCESSOR OF LIFE.

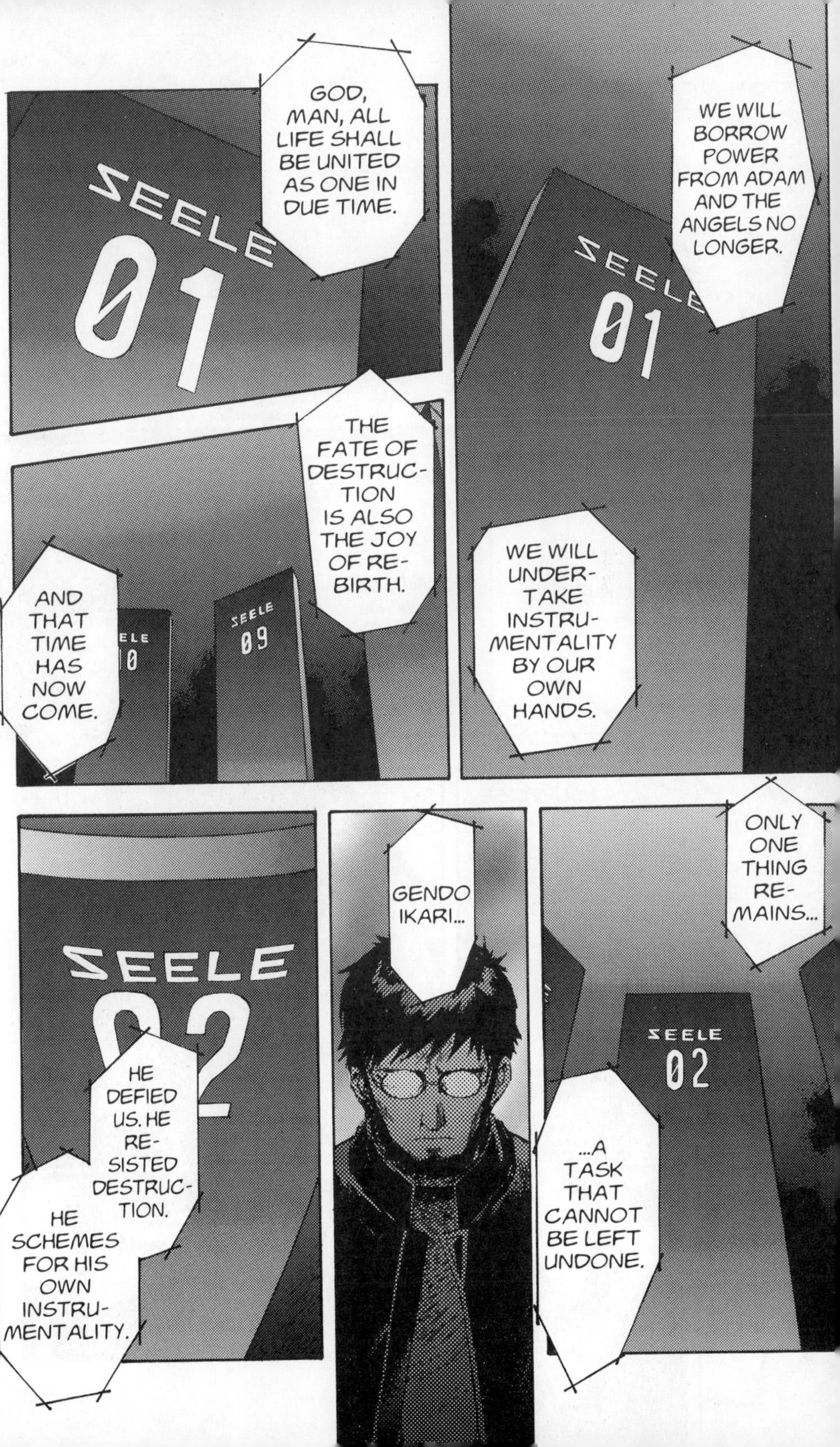
WE WILL BORROW POWER FROM ADAM AND THE ANGELS NO LONGER.
SEELE 01
WE WILL UNDER-TAKE INSTRU-MENTALITY BY OUR OWN HANDS.
GOD, MAN, ALL LIFE SHALL BE UNITED AS ONE IN DUE TIME.
SEELE 01
THE FATE OF DESTRUC-TION IS ALSO THE JOY OF RE-BIRTH.
SEELE 09
AND THAT TIME HAS NOW COME.
ONLY ONE THING RE-MAINS...
SEELE 02
...A TASK THAT CANNOT BE LEFT UNDONE.
GENDO IKARI...
SEELE
HE DEFIED US. HE RE-SISTED DESTRUC-TION.
HE SCHEMES FOR HIS OWN INSTRU-MENTALITY.

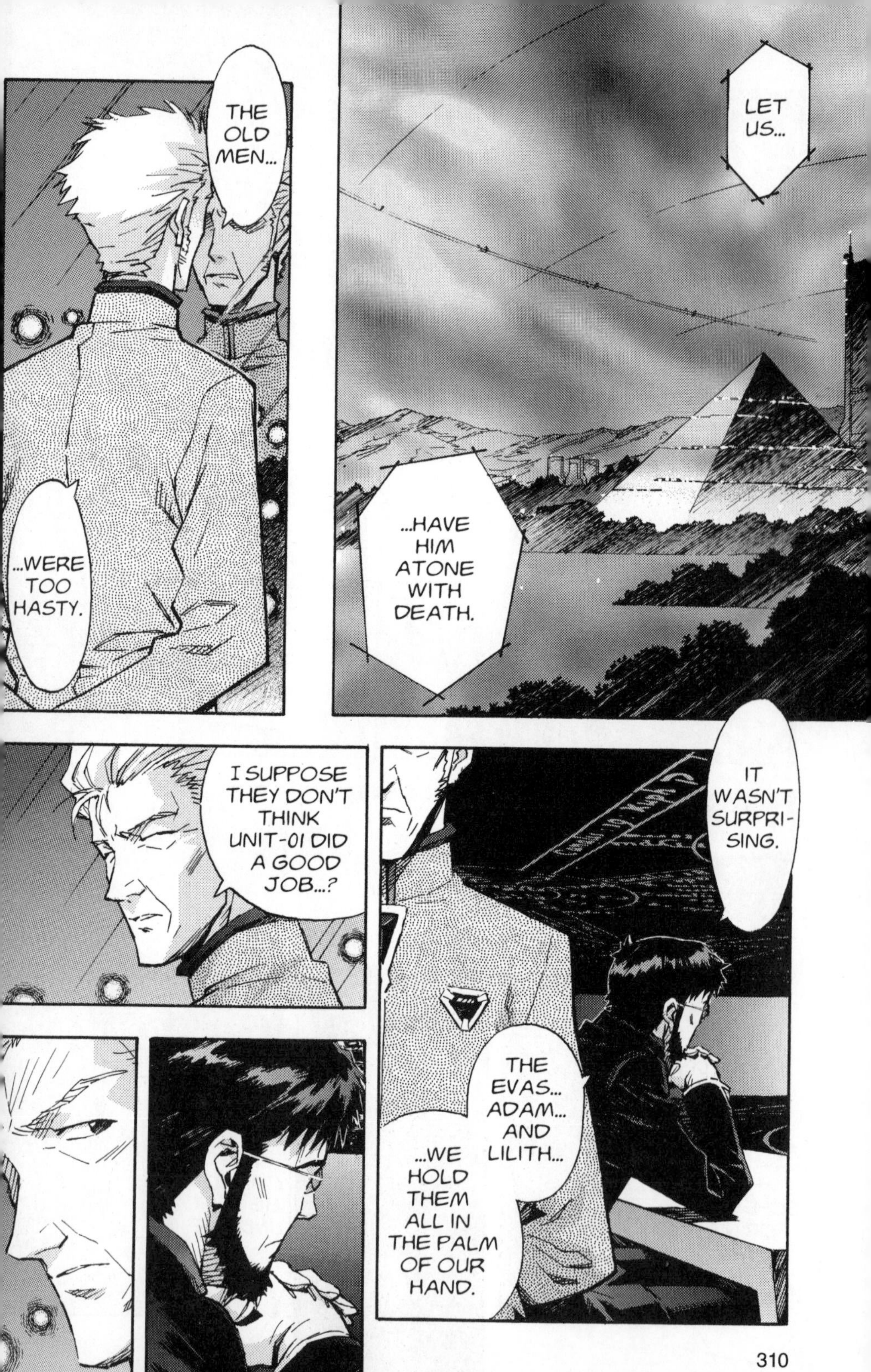
LET US...
...HAVE HIM ATONE WITH DEATH.
THE OLD MEN...
...WERE TOO HASTY.
IT WASN'T SURPRI-SING.
THE EVAS... ADAM... AND LILITH...
...WE HOLD THEM ALL IN THE PALM OF OUR HAND.
I SUPPOSE THEY DON'T THINK UNIT-01 DID A GOOD JOB...?

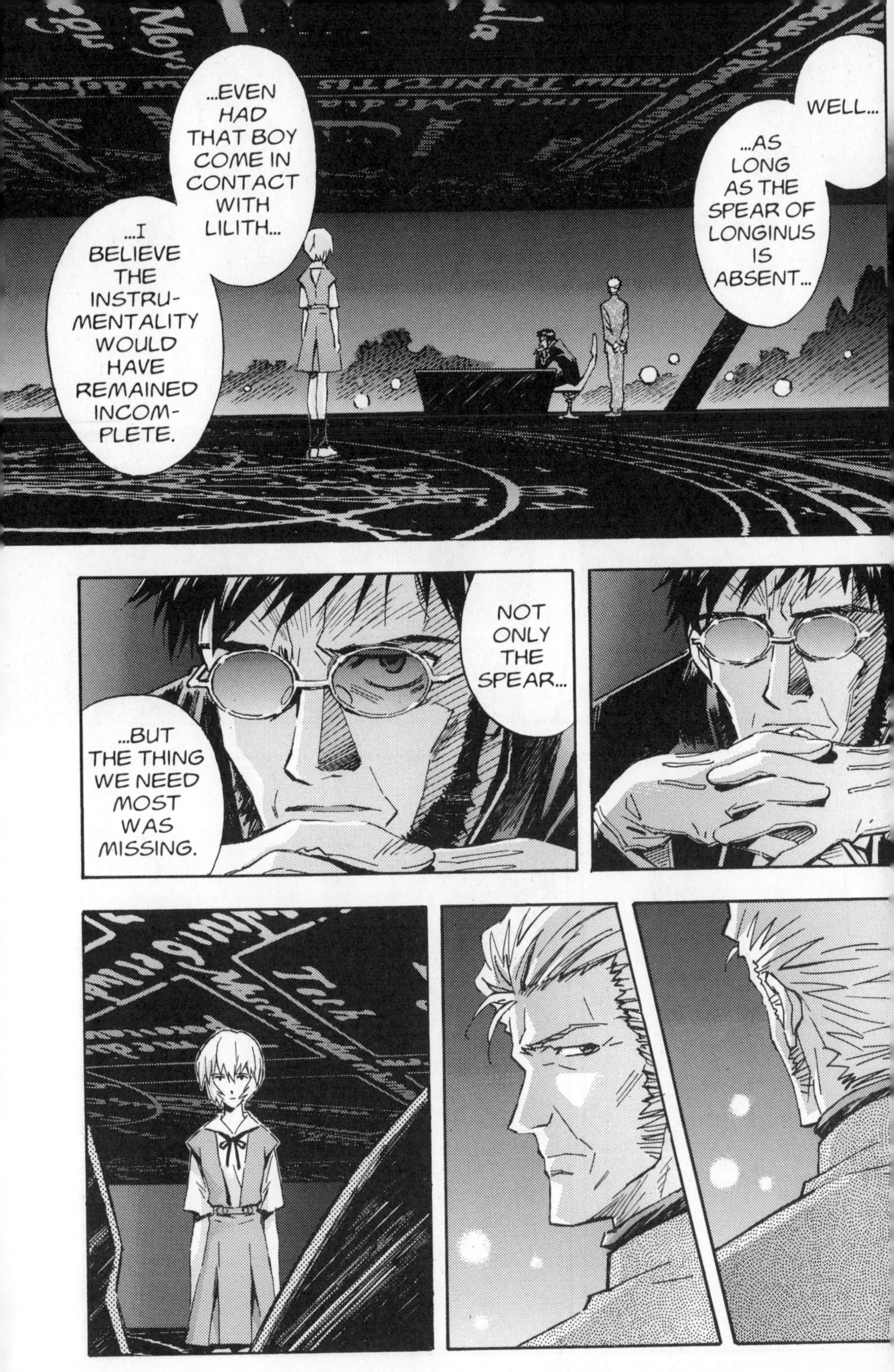
WELL...
...AS LONG AS THE SPEAR OF LONGINUS IS ABSENT...
...EVEN HAD THAT BOY COME IN CONTACT WITH LILITH...
...I BELIEVE THE INSTRUMENTALITY WOULD HAVE REMAINED INCOMPLETE.
NOT ONLY THE SPEAR...
...BUT THE THING WE NEED MOST WAS MISSING.

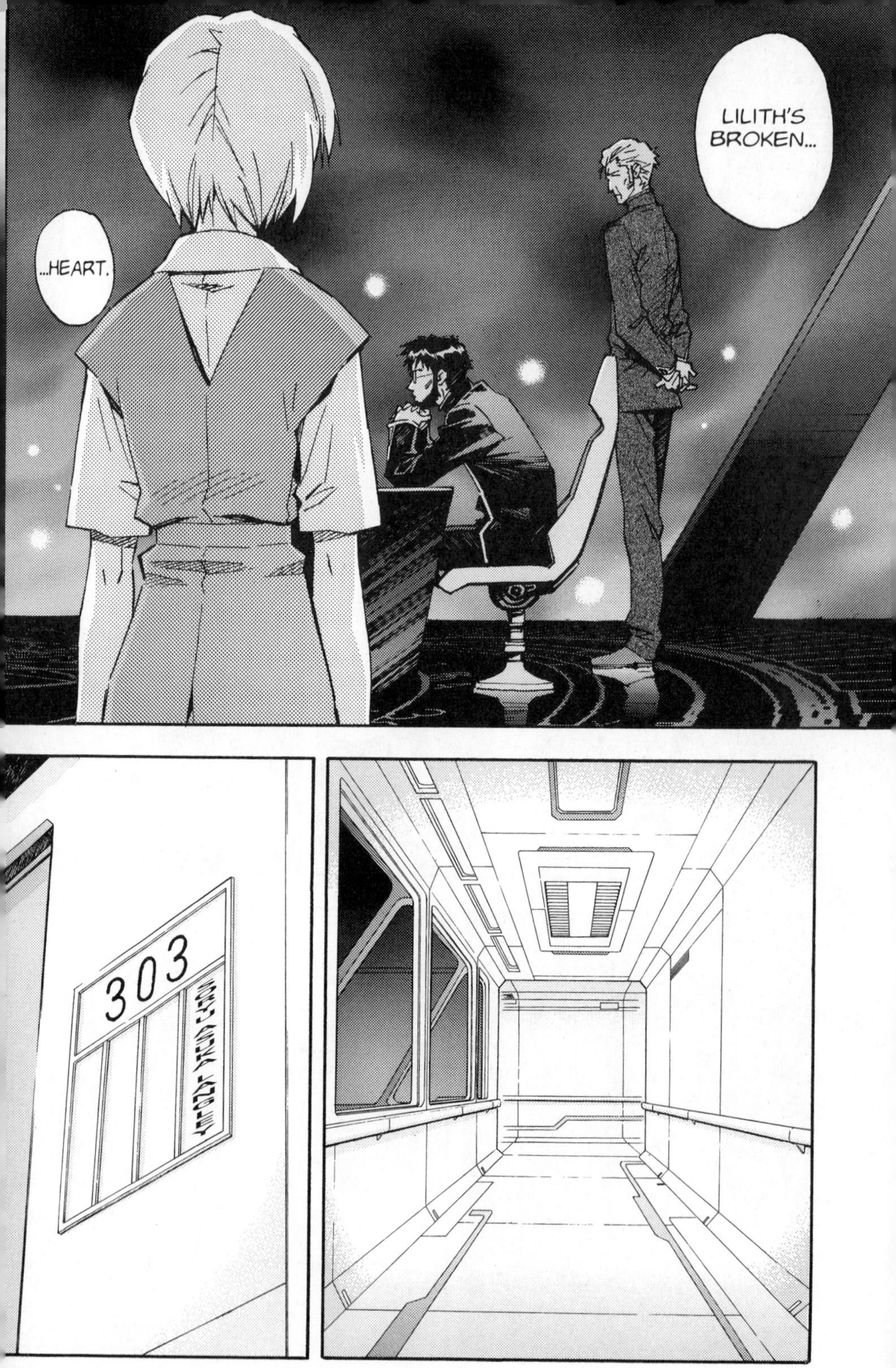
LILITH'S BROKEN...
...HEART.
303
SORYU ASUKA LANGLEY

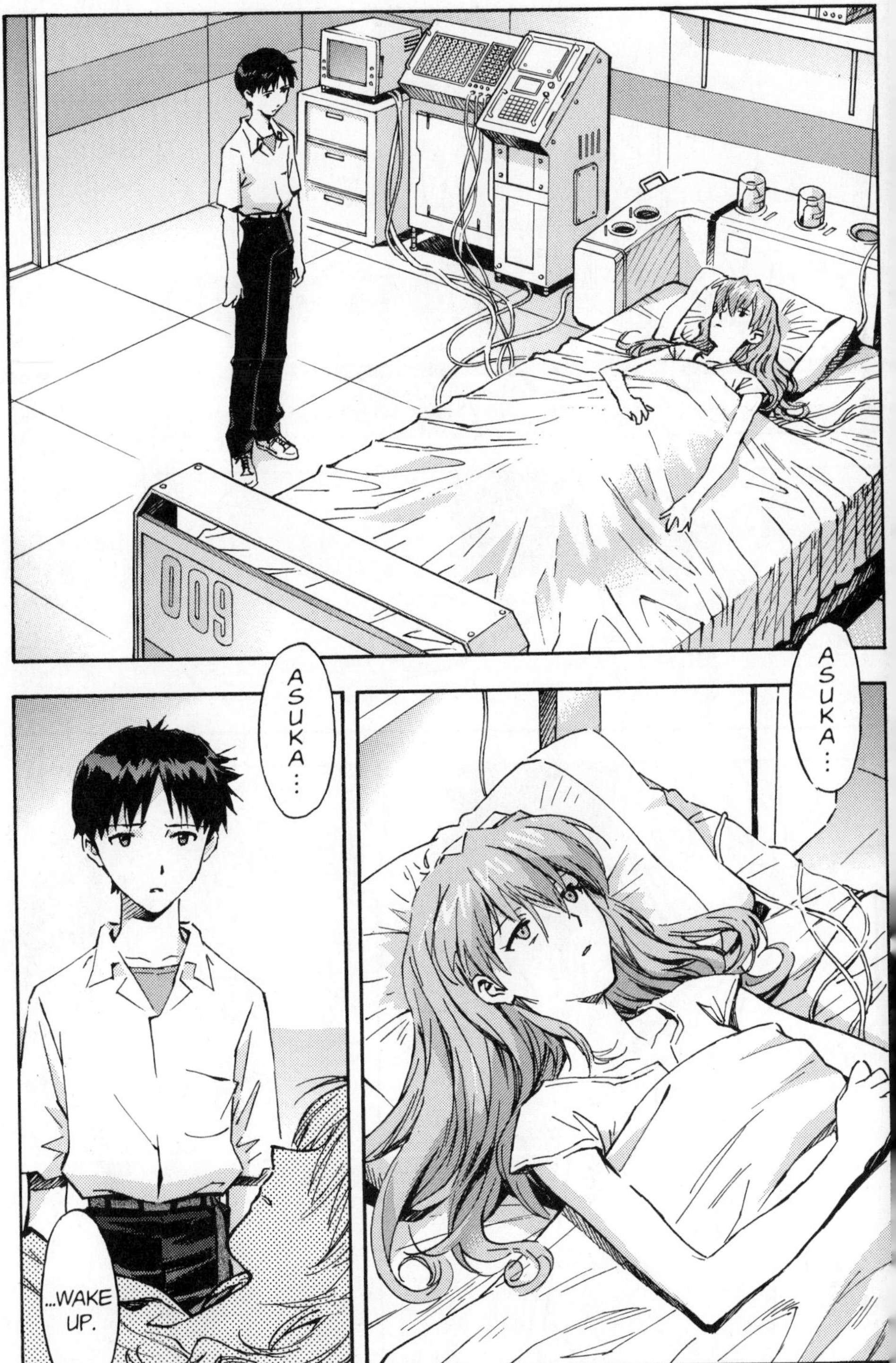

ASUKA...
ASUKA...
...WAKE UP.

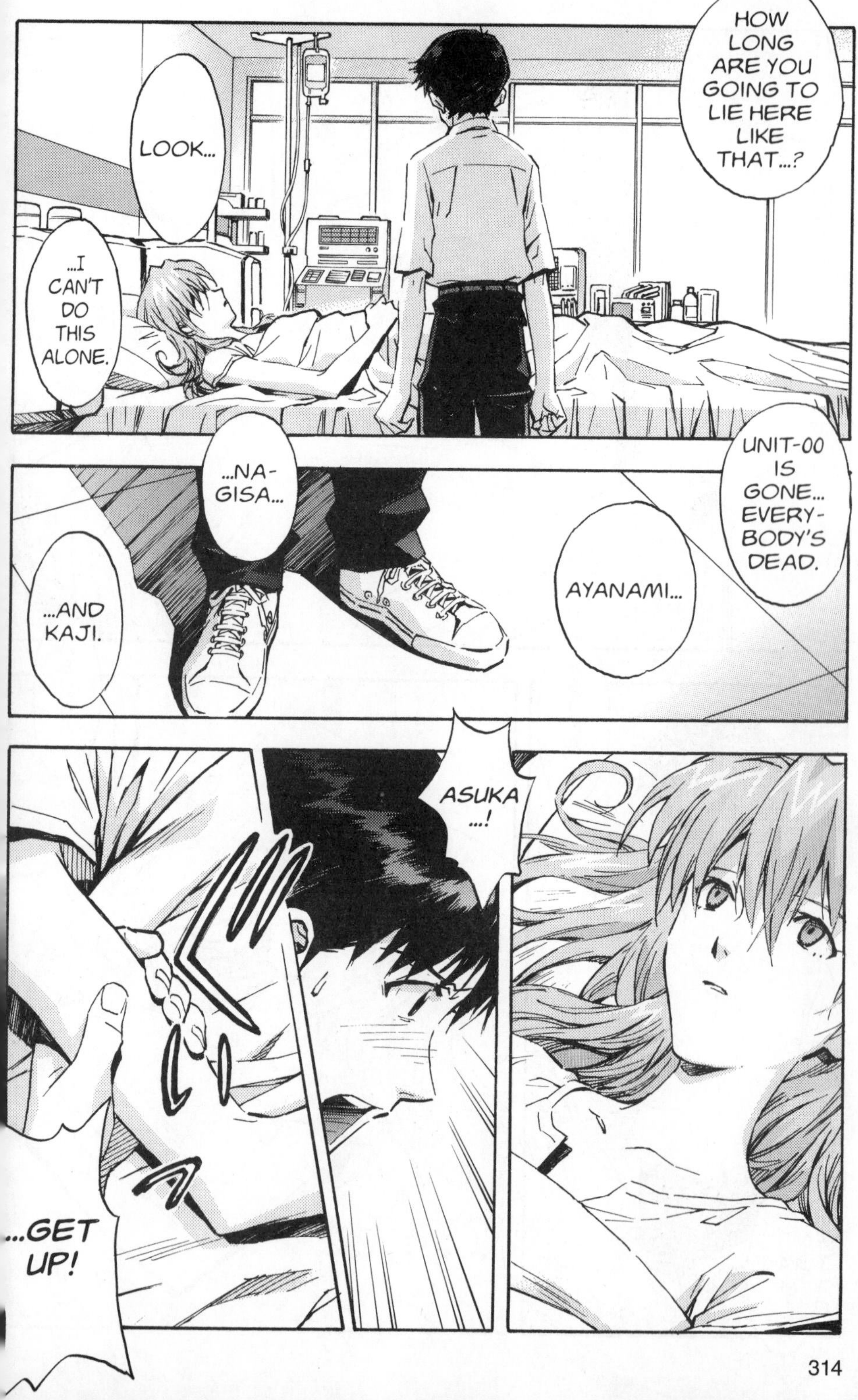
HOW LONG ARE YOU GOING TO LIE HERE LIKE THAT...?
LOOK...
...I CAN'T DO THIS ALONE.
UNIT-00 IS GONE... EVERY-BODY'S DEAD.
AYANAMI...
...NA-GISA...
...AND KAJI.
ASUKA ...!
...GET UP!

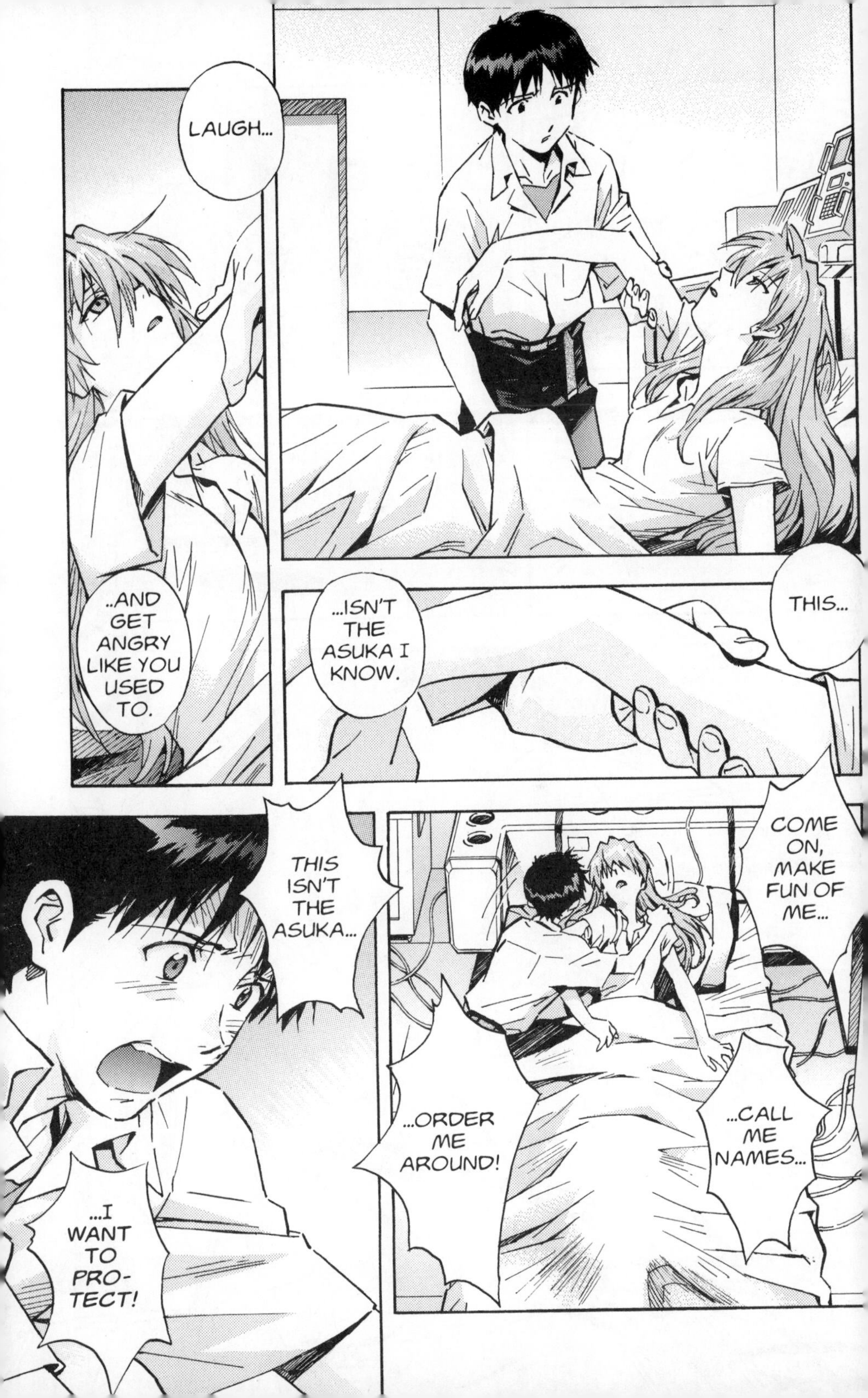
THIS...
...ISN'T THE ASUKA I KNOW.
LAUGH...
...AND GET ANGRY LIKE YOU USED TO.
COME ON, MAKE FUN OF ME...
...CALL ME NAMES...
...ORDER ME AROUND!
THIS ISN'T THE ASUKA...
...I WANT TO PRO-TECT!

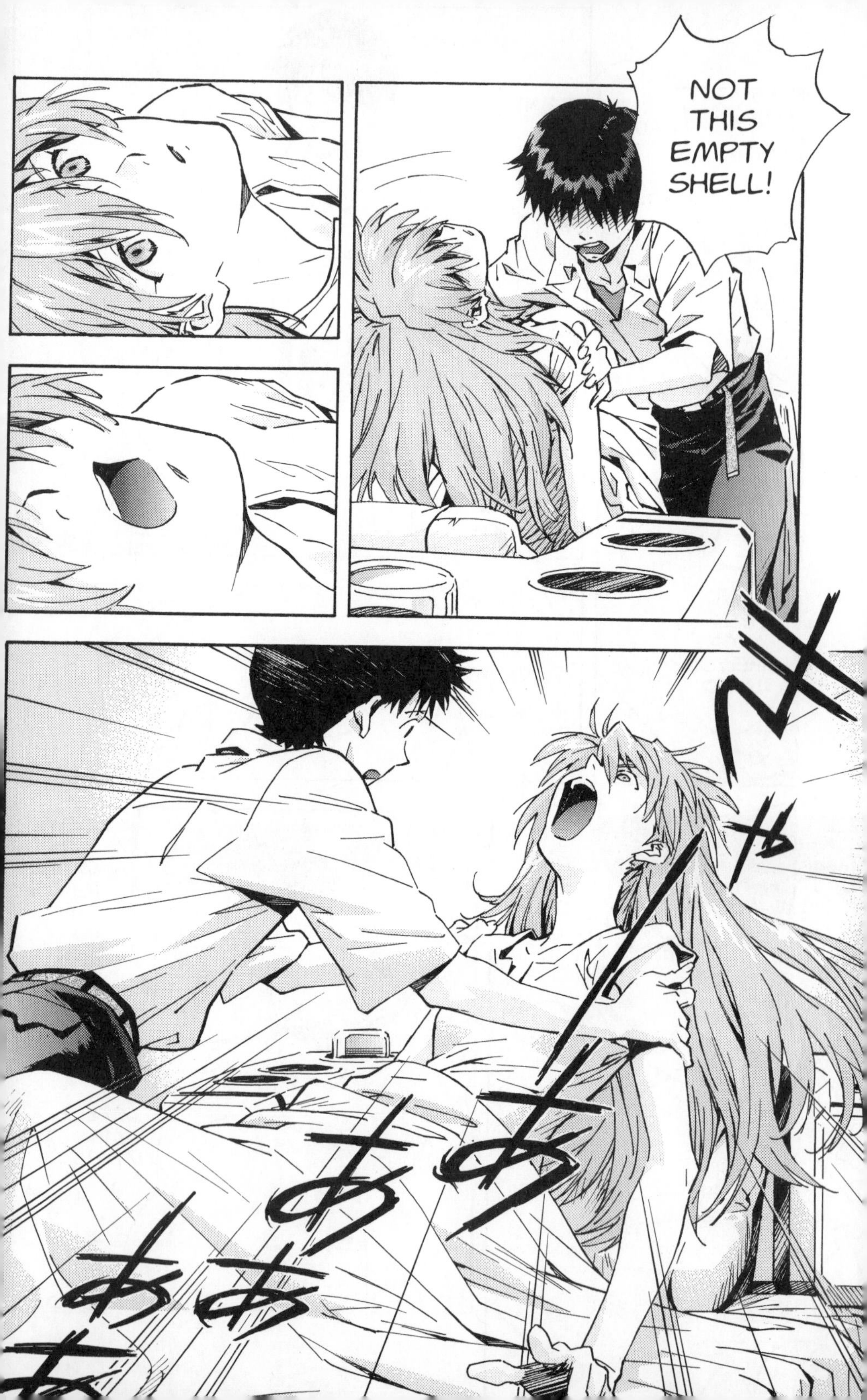
NOT THIS EMPTY SHELL!

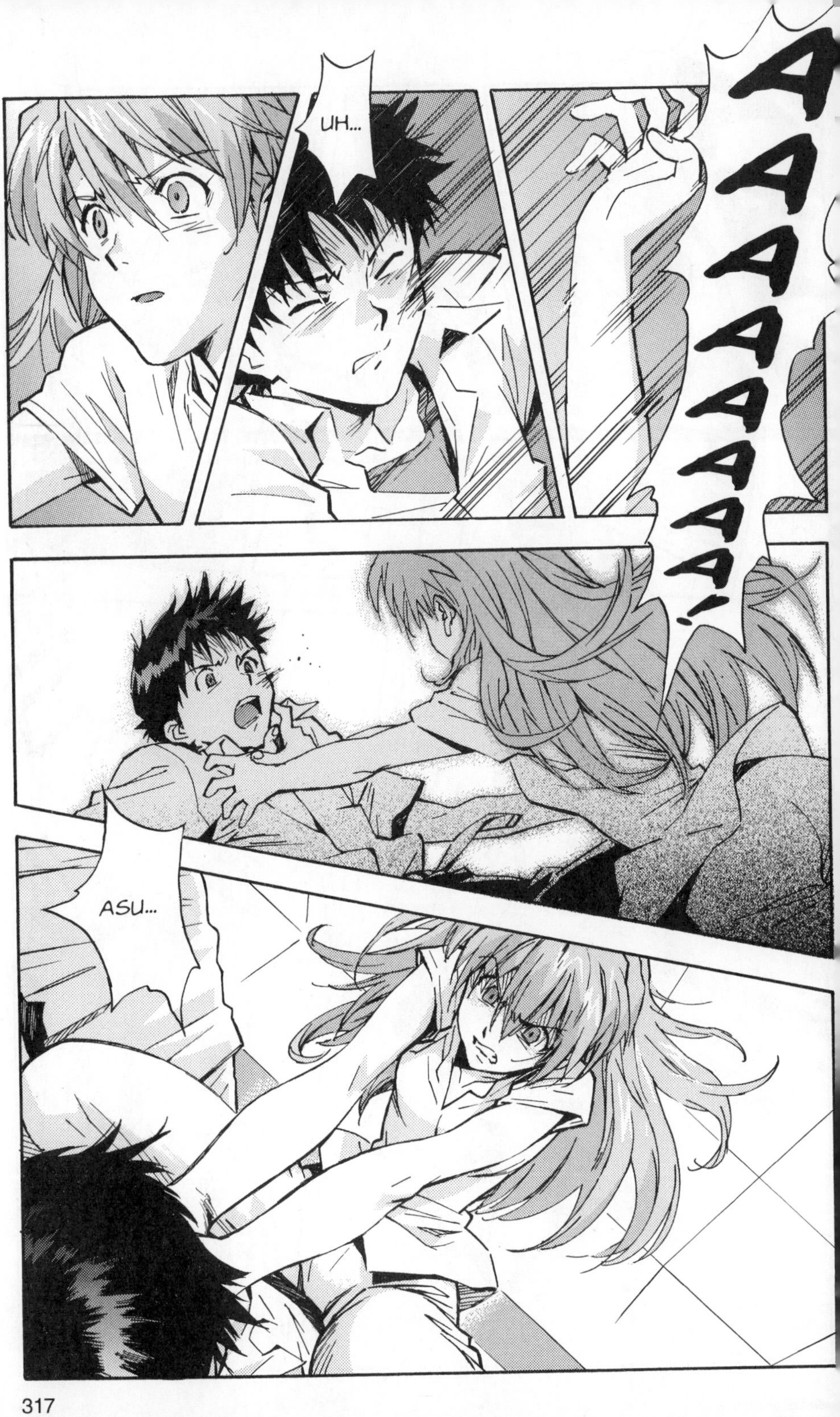
AAAAAAAA!
UH...
ASU...

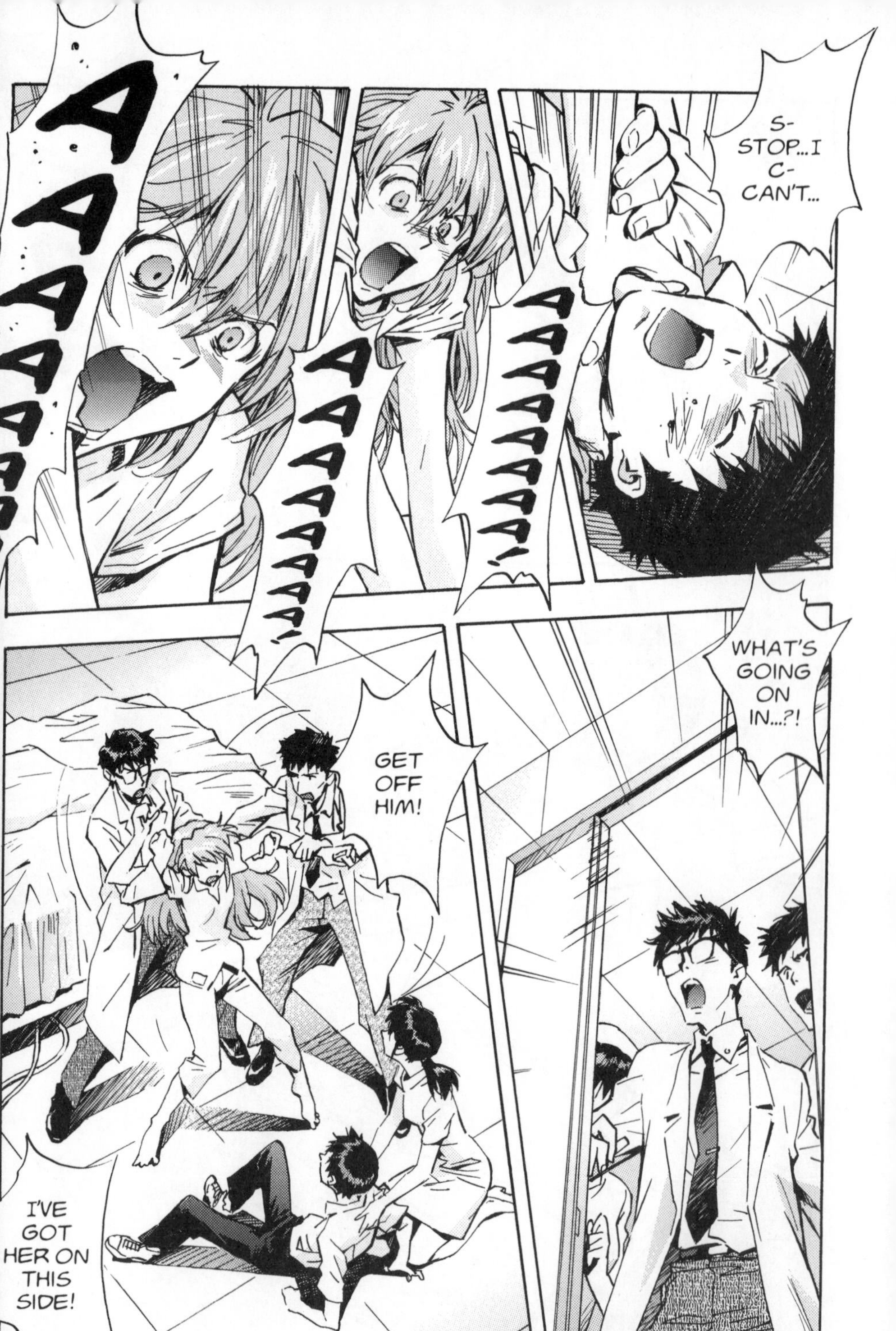
S-
STOP...I
C-
CAN'T...
AAAAAAAAA!
AAAAAAAAA!
AAAAAA
WHAT'S GOING ON IN...?!
GET OFF HIM!
I'VE GOT HER ON THIS SIDE!

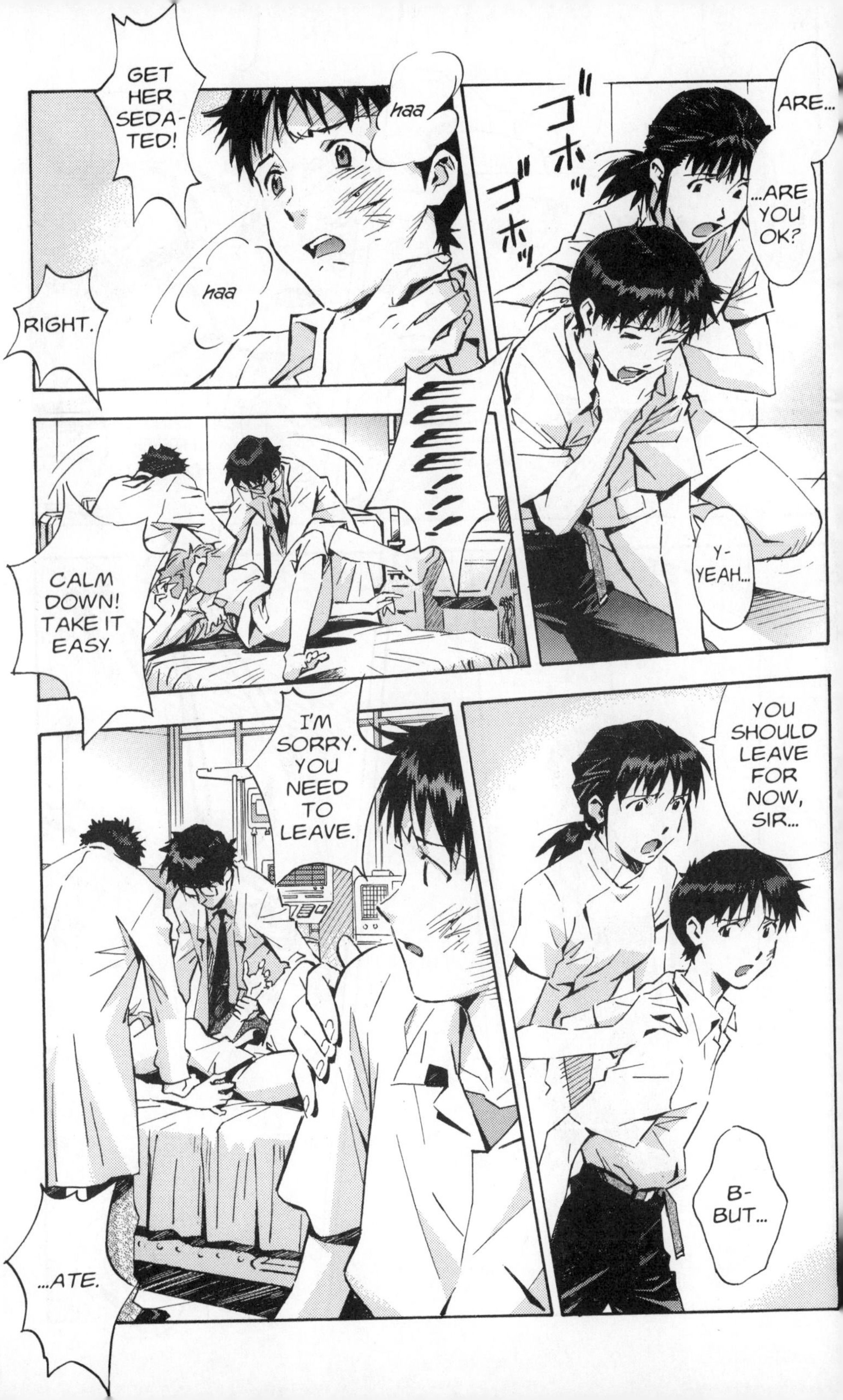
ARE...
...ARE YOU OK?
ゴホッ
ゴホッ
Y-YEAH...
haa
haa
GET HER SEDATED!
RIGHT.
EEEEEEE!!!!
CALM DOWN! TAKE IT EASY.
YOU SHOULD LEAVE FOR NOW, SIR...
B-BUT...
I'M SORRY. YOU NEED TO LEAVE.
...ATE.

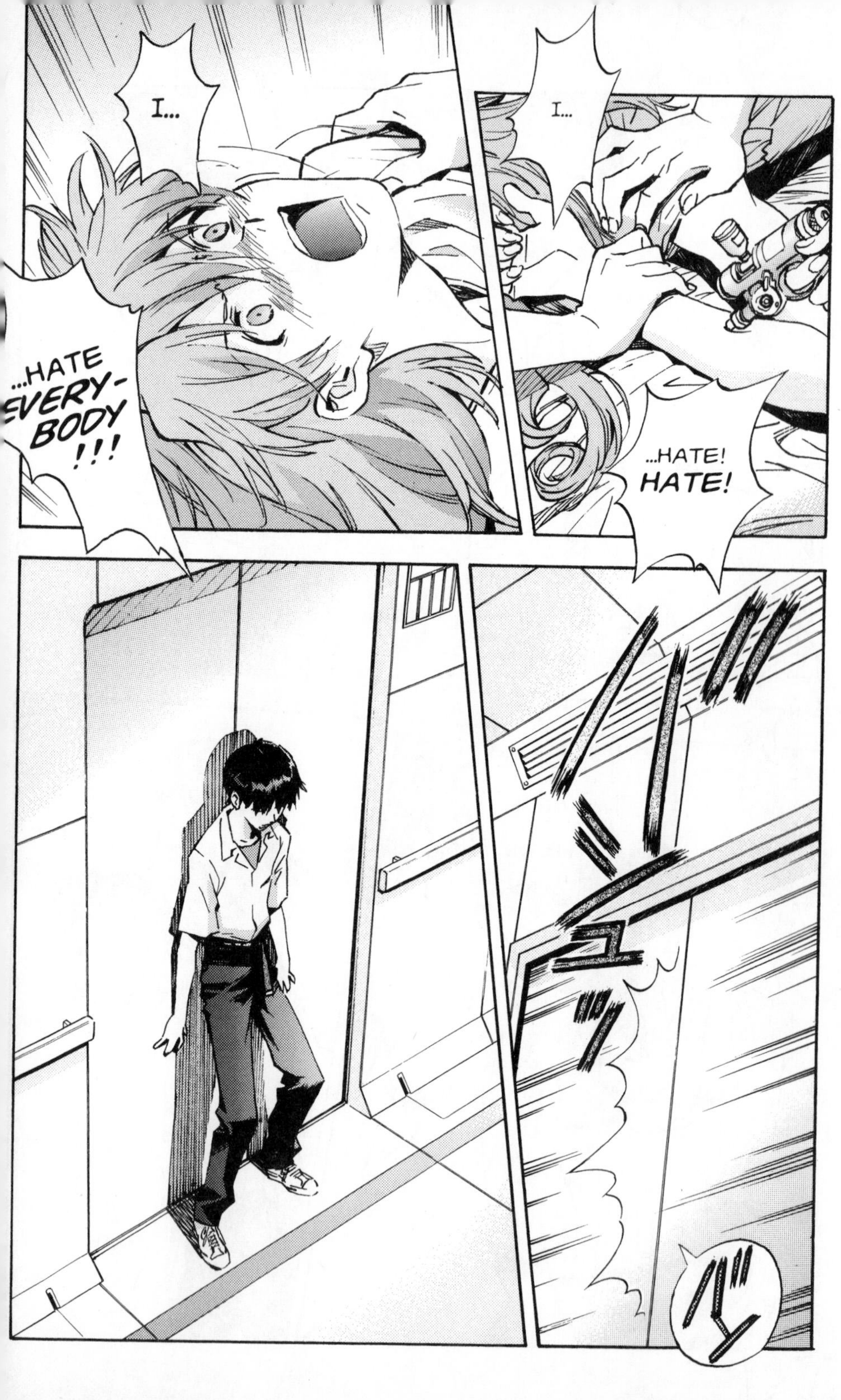
I...
...HATE! HATE!
I...
...HATE EVERY-BODY!!!

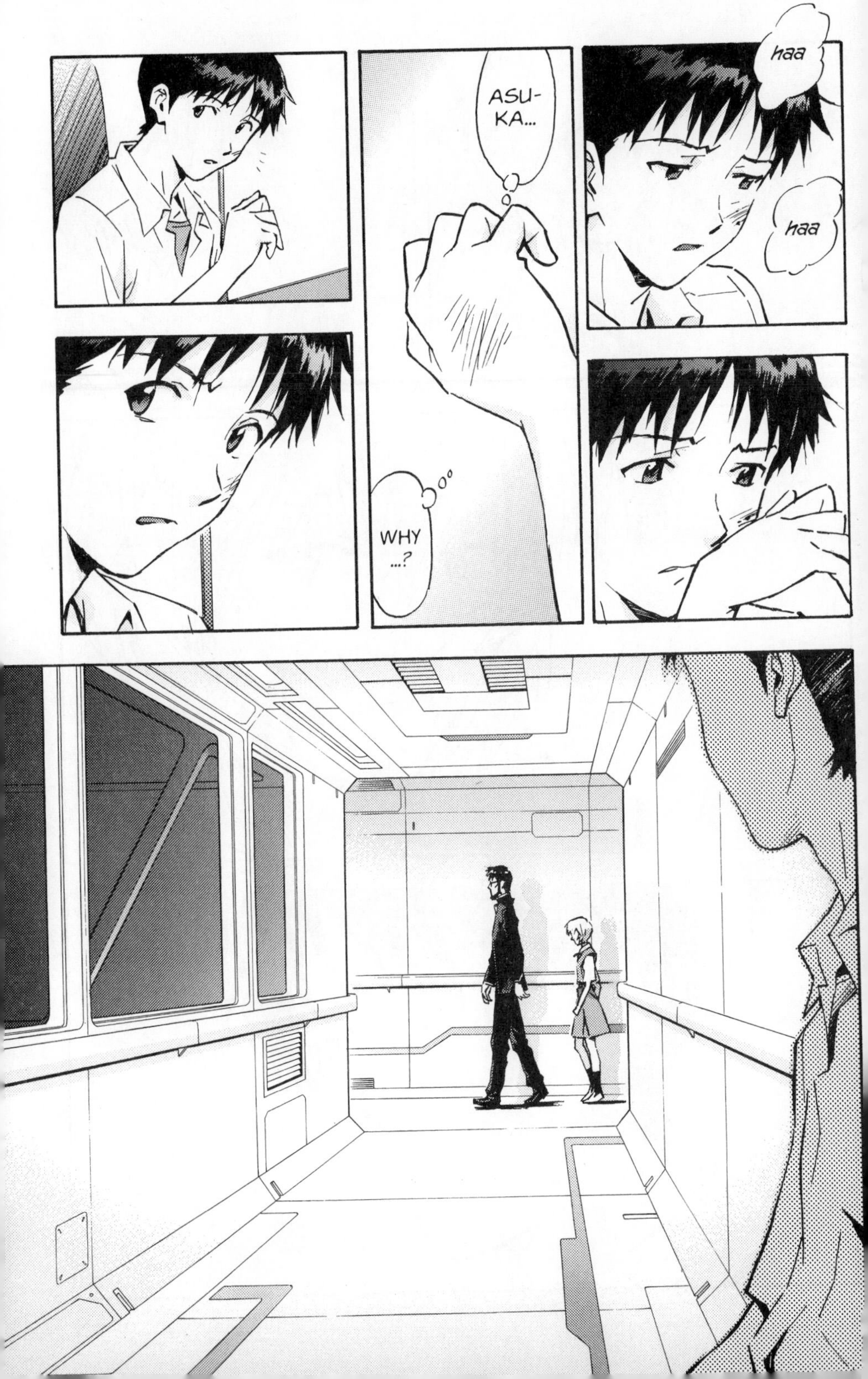
haa
haa
ASU-KA...
WHY ...?

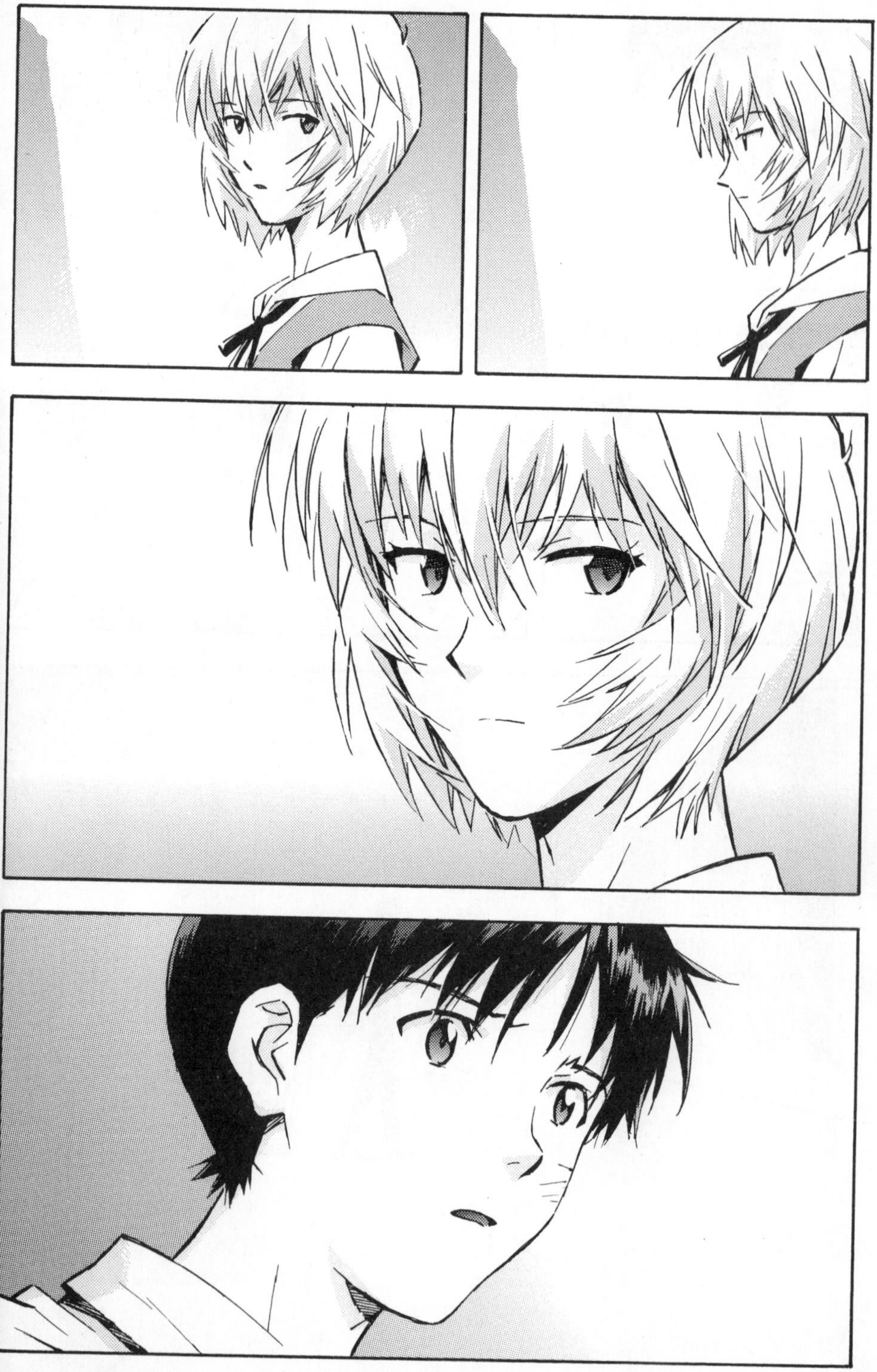

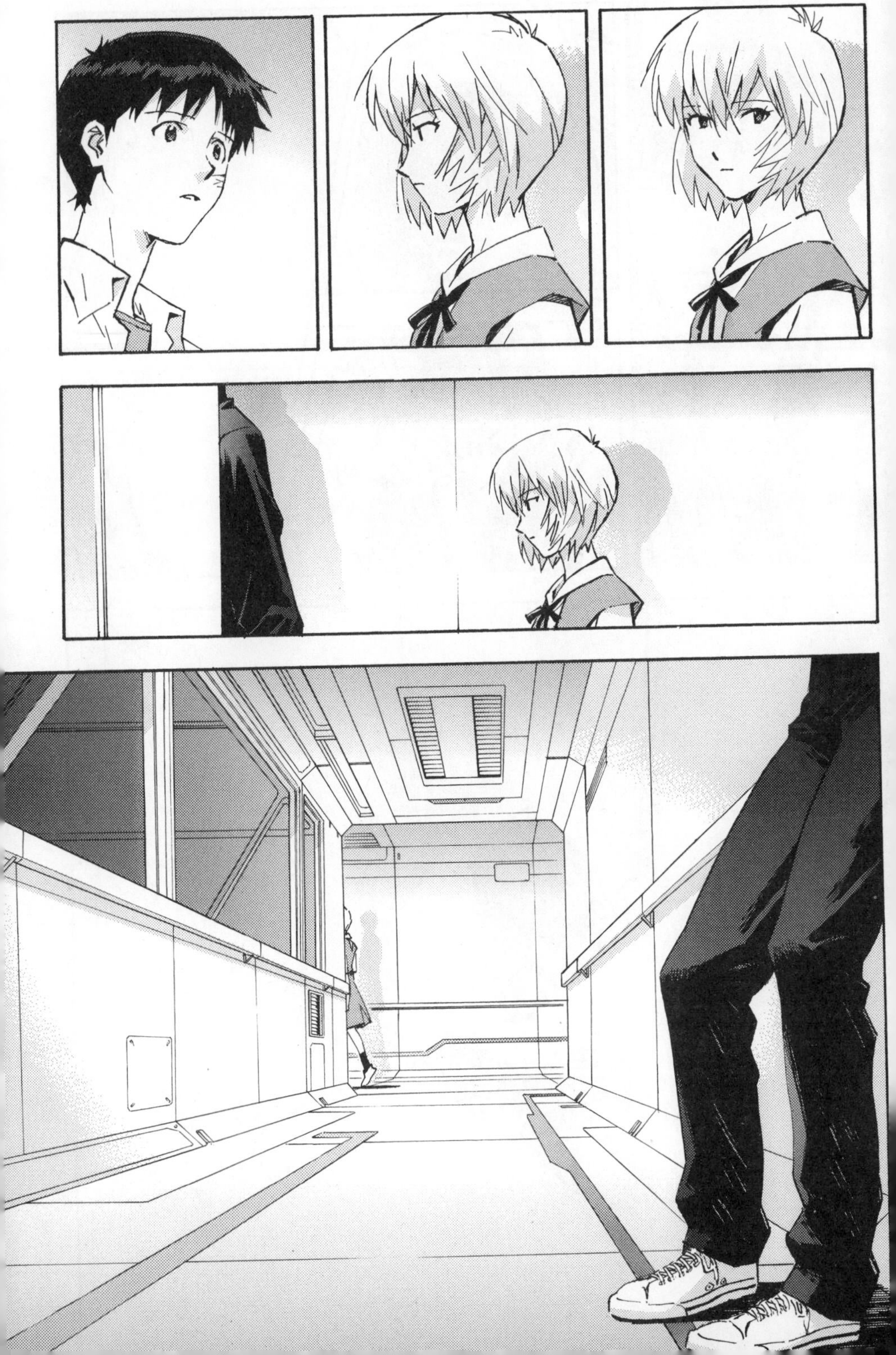

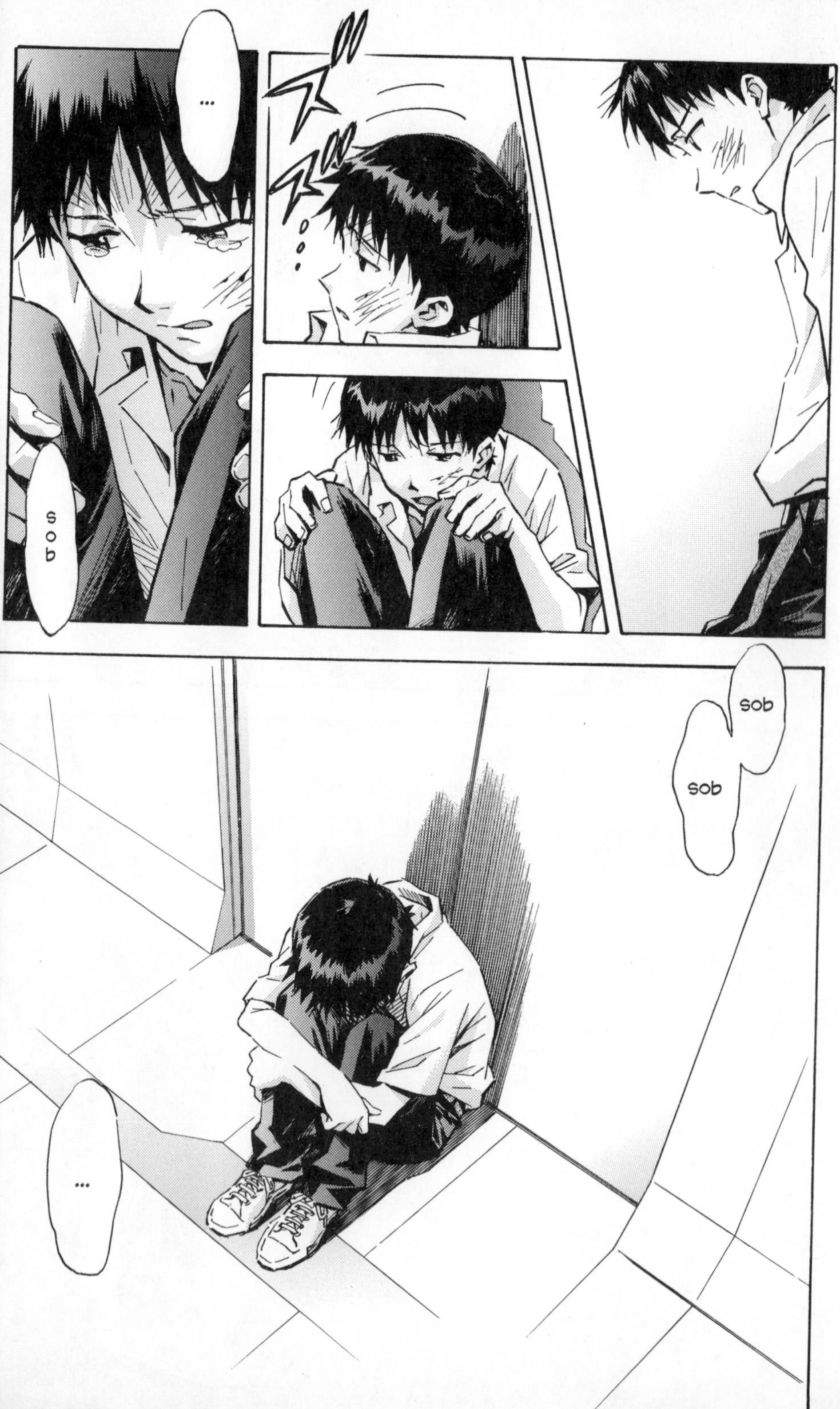
...
sob
sob
sob
...

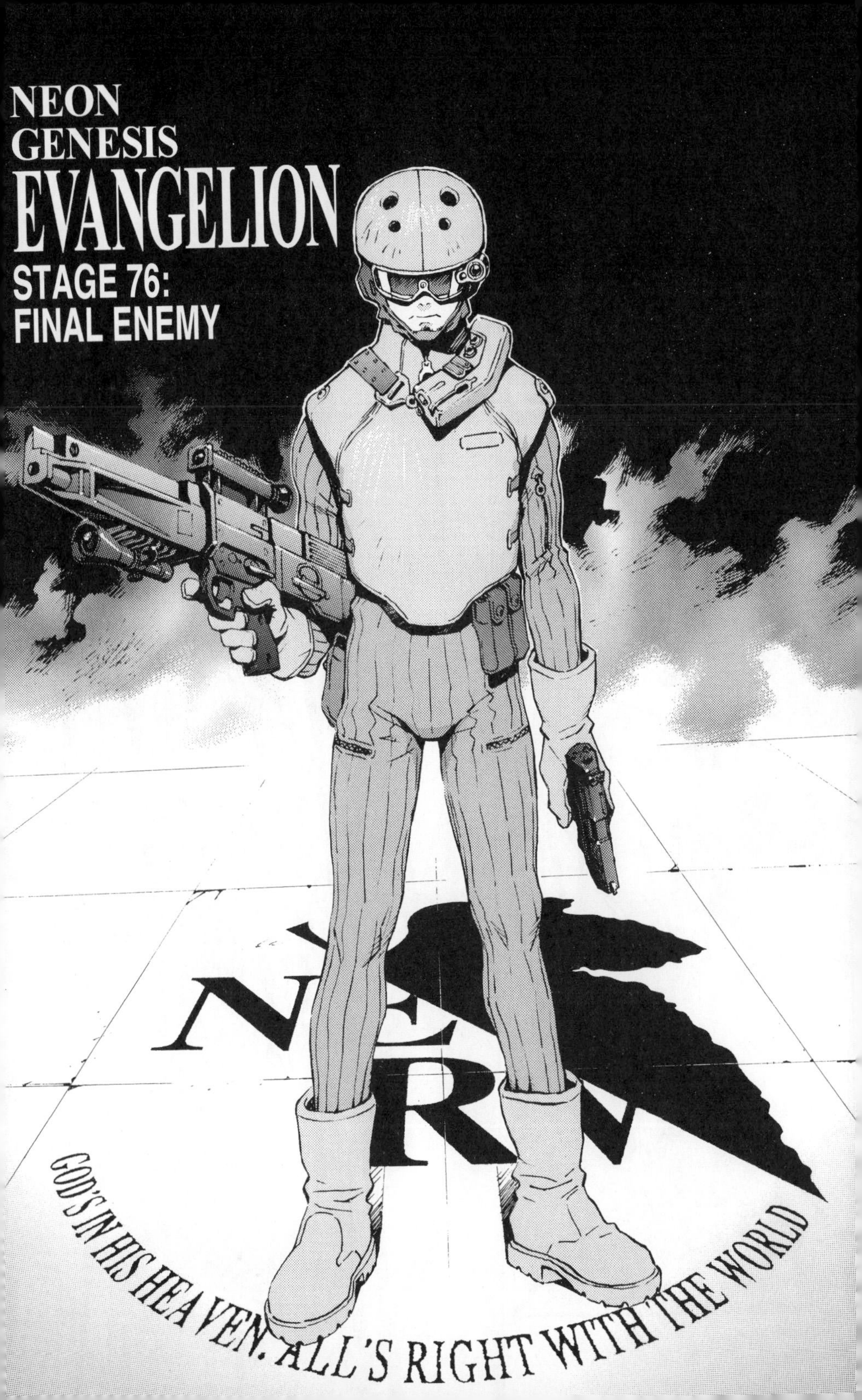
NEON
GENESIS
EVANGELION
STAGE 76:
FINAL ENEMY
NERV
GOD'S IN HIS HEAVEN. ALL'S RIGHT WITH THE WORLD

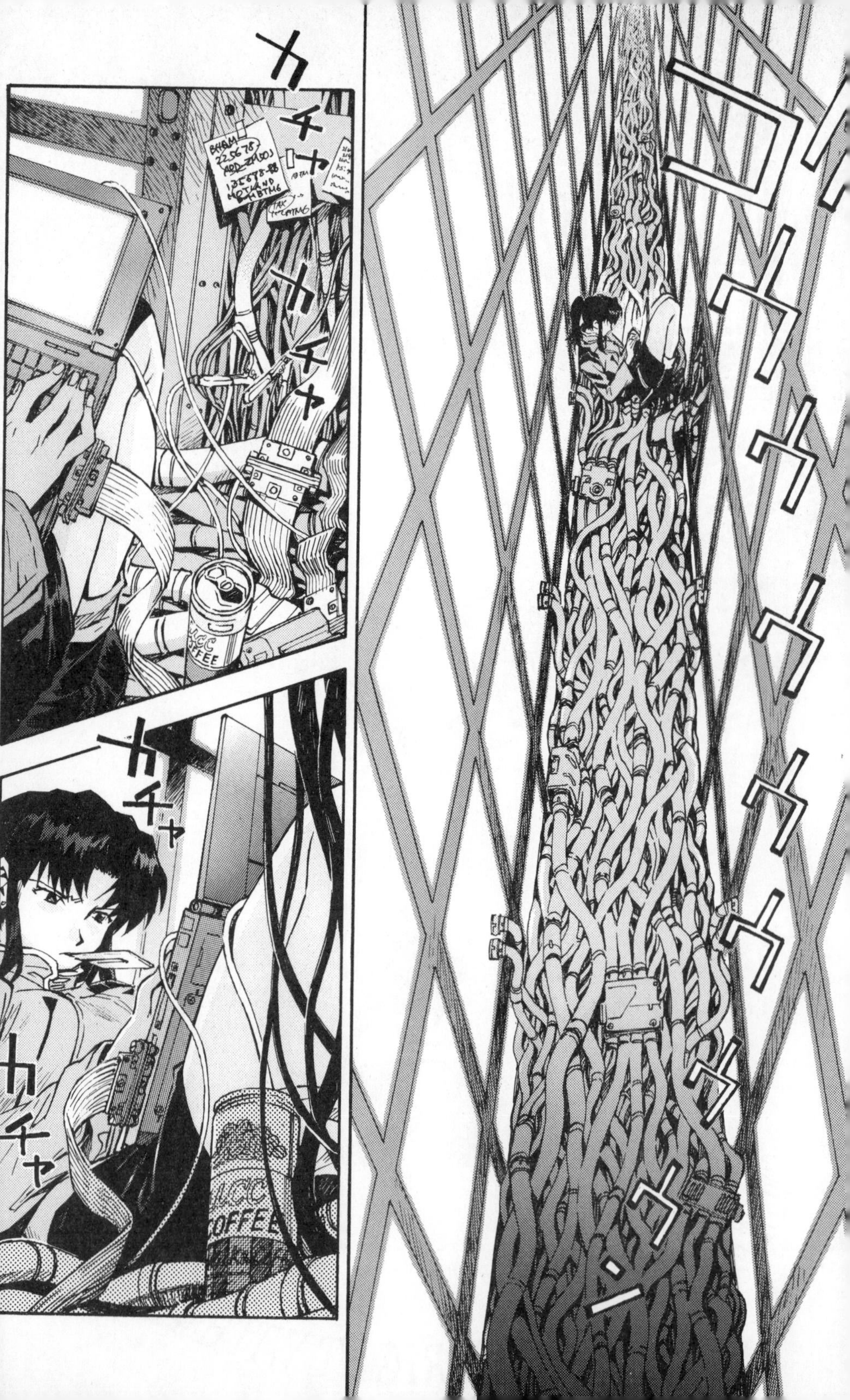
カチャ
カチャ
UCC COFFEE
カチャ
カチャ
UCC COFFEE

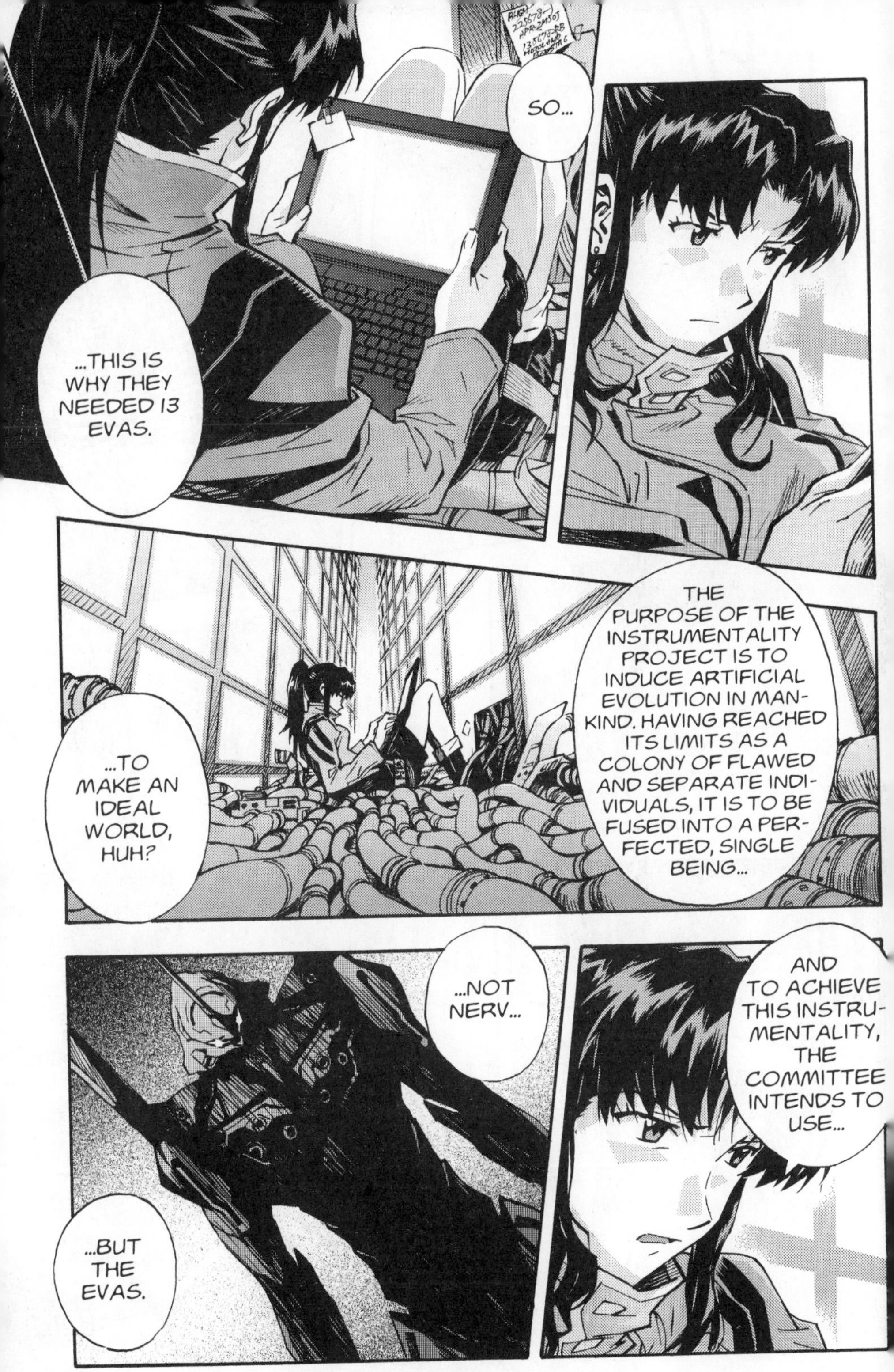
SO...
...THIS IS WHY THEY NEEDED 13 EVAS.
THE PURPOSE OF THE INSTRUMENTALITY PROJECT IS TO INDUCE ARTIFICIAL EVOLUTION IN MAN-KIND. HAVING REACHED ITS LIMITS AS A COLONY OF FLAWED AND SEPARATE INDI-VIDUALS, IT IS TO BE FUSED INTO A PER-FECTED, SINGLE BEING...
...TO MAKE AN IDEAL WORLD, HUH?
AND TO ACHIEVE THIS INSTRU-MENTALITY, THE COMMITTEE INTENDS TO USE...
...NOT NERV...
...BUT THE EVAS.

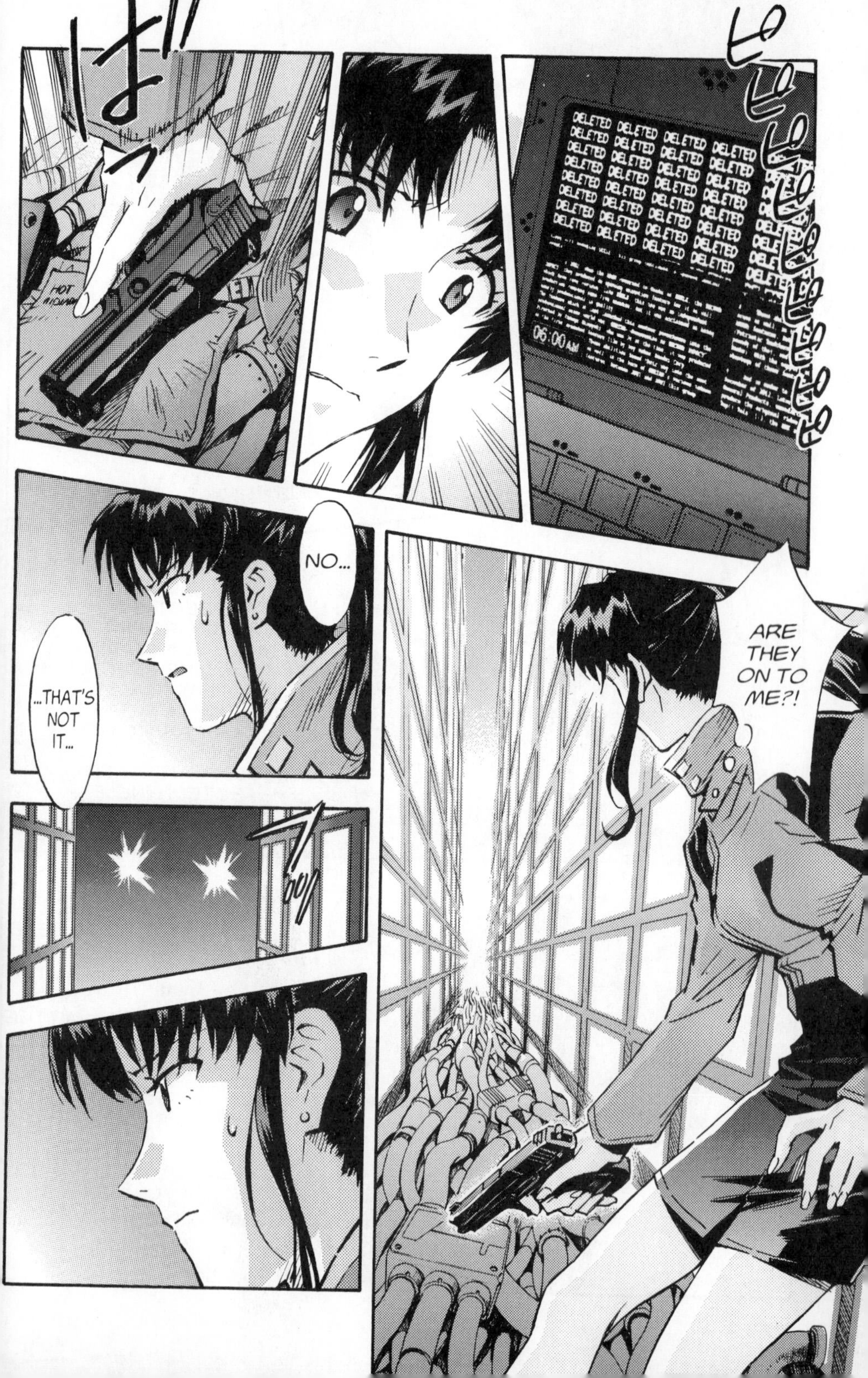
06:00 AM
はっ!!
ARE THEY ON TO ME?!
NO...
...THAT'S NOT IT...

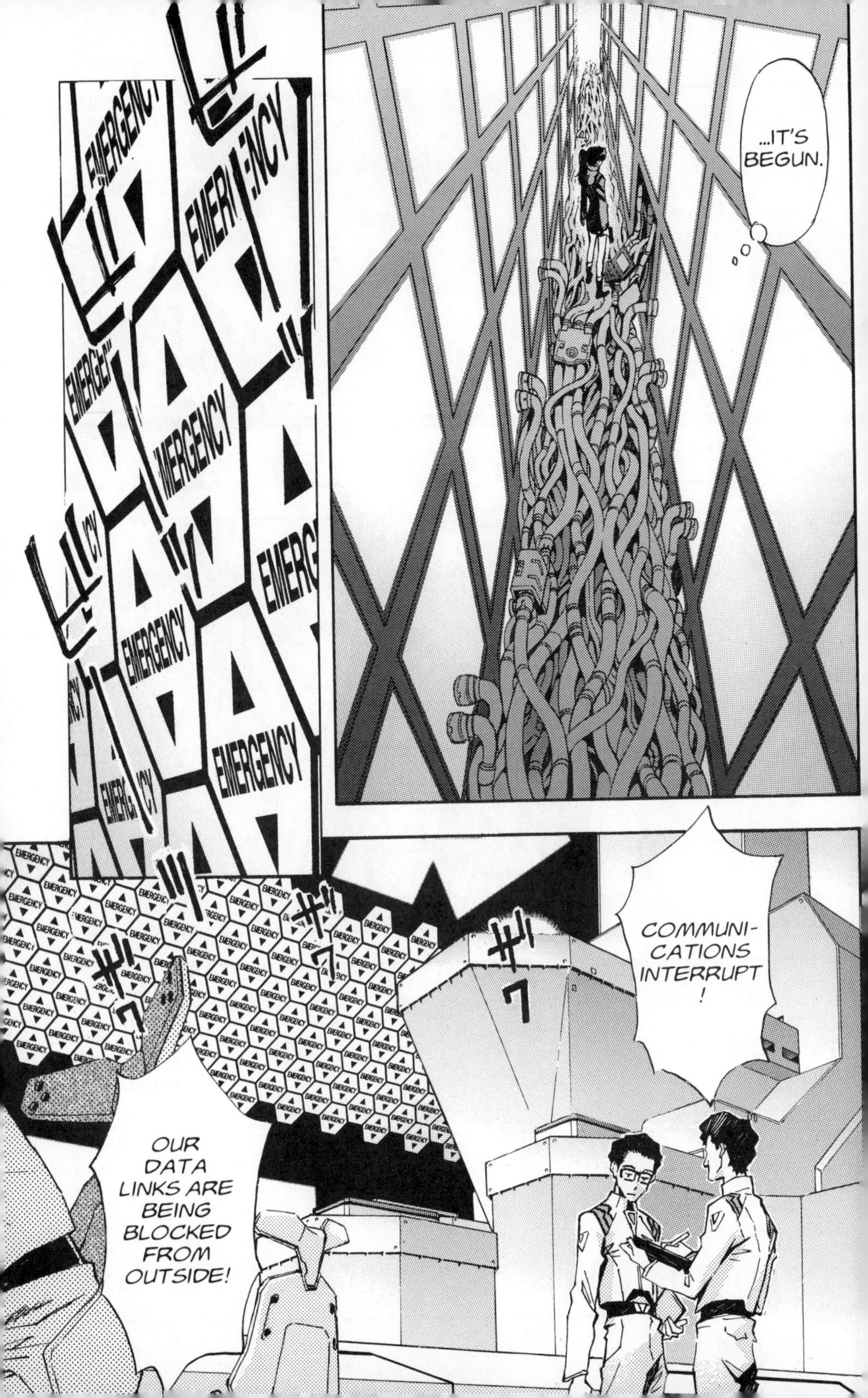
...IT'S BEGUN.
EMERGENCY
COMMUNI-CATIONS INTERRUPT!
OUR DATA LINKS ARE BEING BLOCKED FROM OUTSIDE!

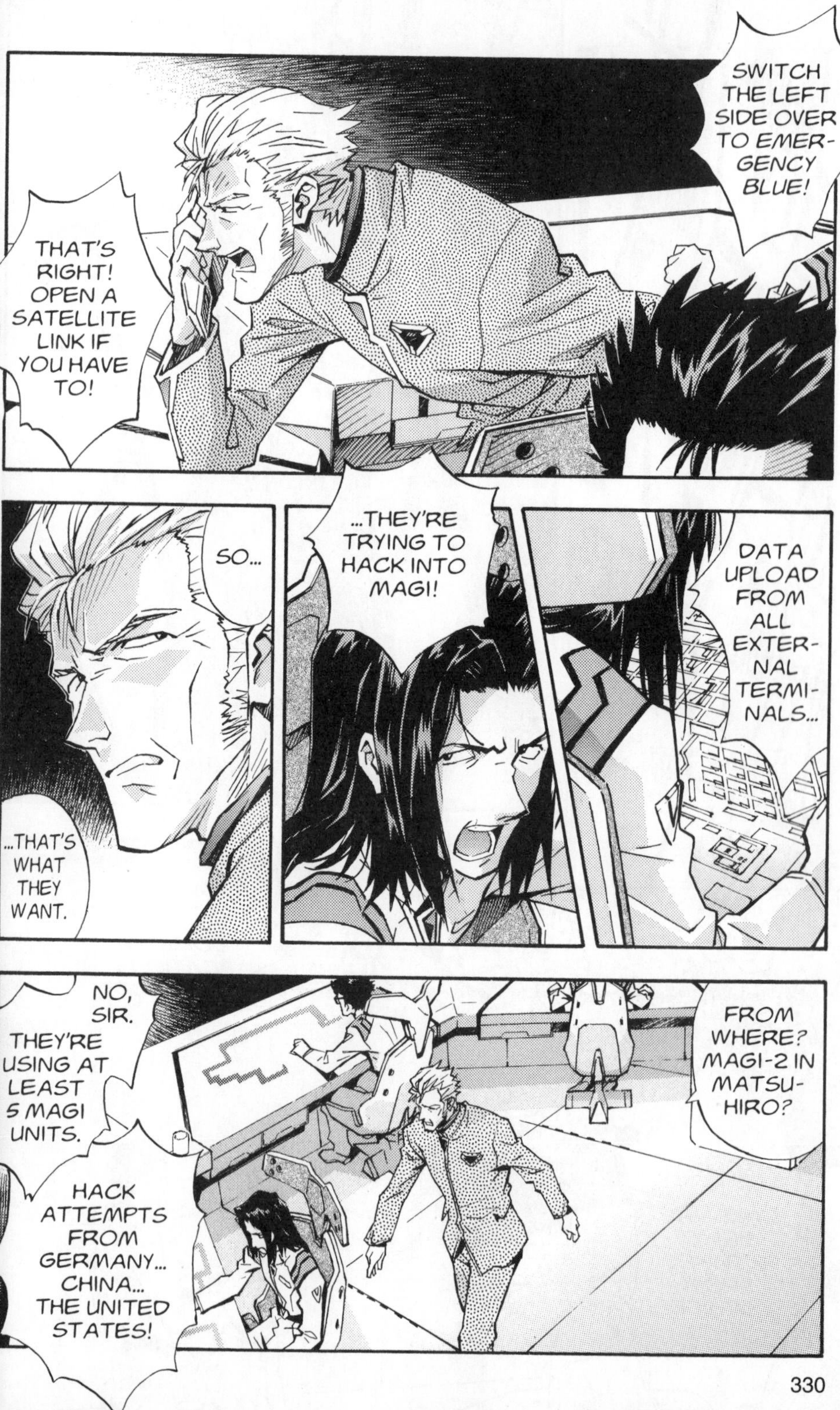
SWITCH THE LEFT SIDE OVER TO EMERGENCY BLUE!
THAT'S RIGHT! OPEN A SATELLITE LINK IF YOU HAVE TO!
DATA UPLOAD FROM ALL EXTERNAL TERMINALS...
...THEY'RE TRYING TO HACK INTO MAGI!
SO...
...THAT'S WHAT THEY WANT.
FROM WHERE? MAGI-2 IN MATSUHIRO?
NO, SIR. THEY'RE USING AT LEAST 5 MAGI UNITS.
HACK ATTEMPTS FROM GERMANY... CHINA... THE UNITED STATES!

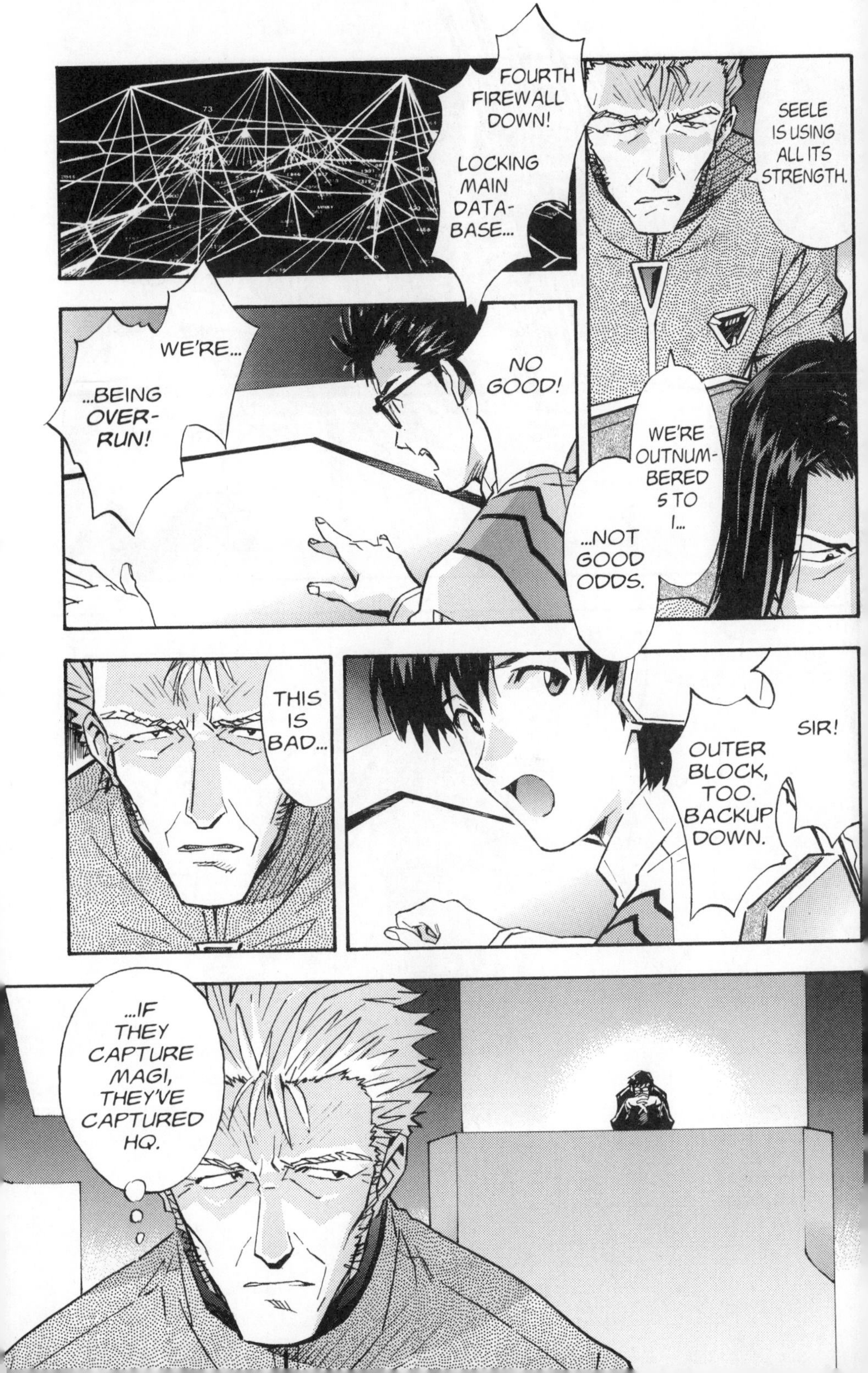
SEELE IS USING ALL ITS STRENGTH.
FOURTH FIREWALL DOWN!
LOCKING MAIN DATA-BASE...
NO GOOD!
WE'RE...
...BEING OVER-RUN!
WE'RE OUTNUM-BERED 5 TO 1...
...NOT GOOD ODDS.
SIR!
OUTER BLOCK, TOO. BACKUP DOWN.
THIS IS BAD...
...IF THEY CAPTURE MAGI, THEY'VE CAPTURED HQ.

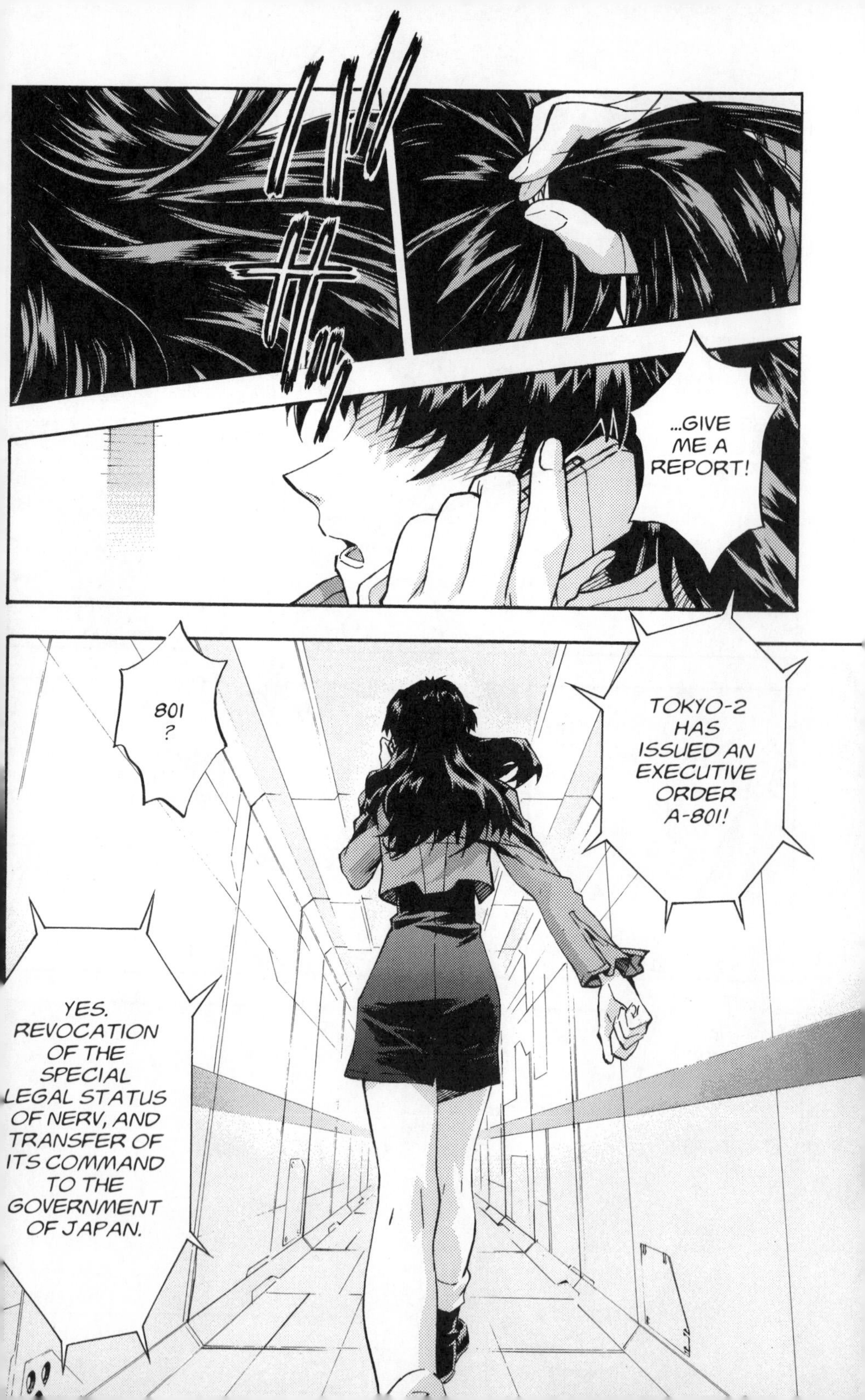
...GIVE ME A REPORT!
TOKYO-2 HAS ISSUED AN EXECUTIVE ORDER A-801!
801 ?
YES. REVOCATION OF THE SPECIAL LEGAL STATUS OF NERV, AND TRANSFER OF ITS COMMAND TO THE GOVERNMENT OF JAPAN.

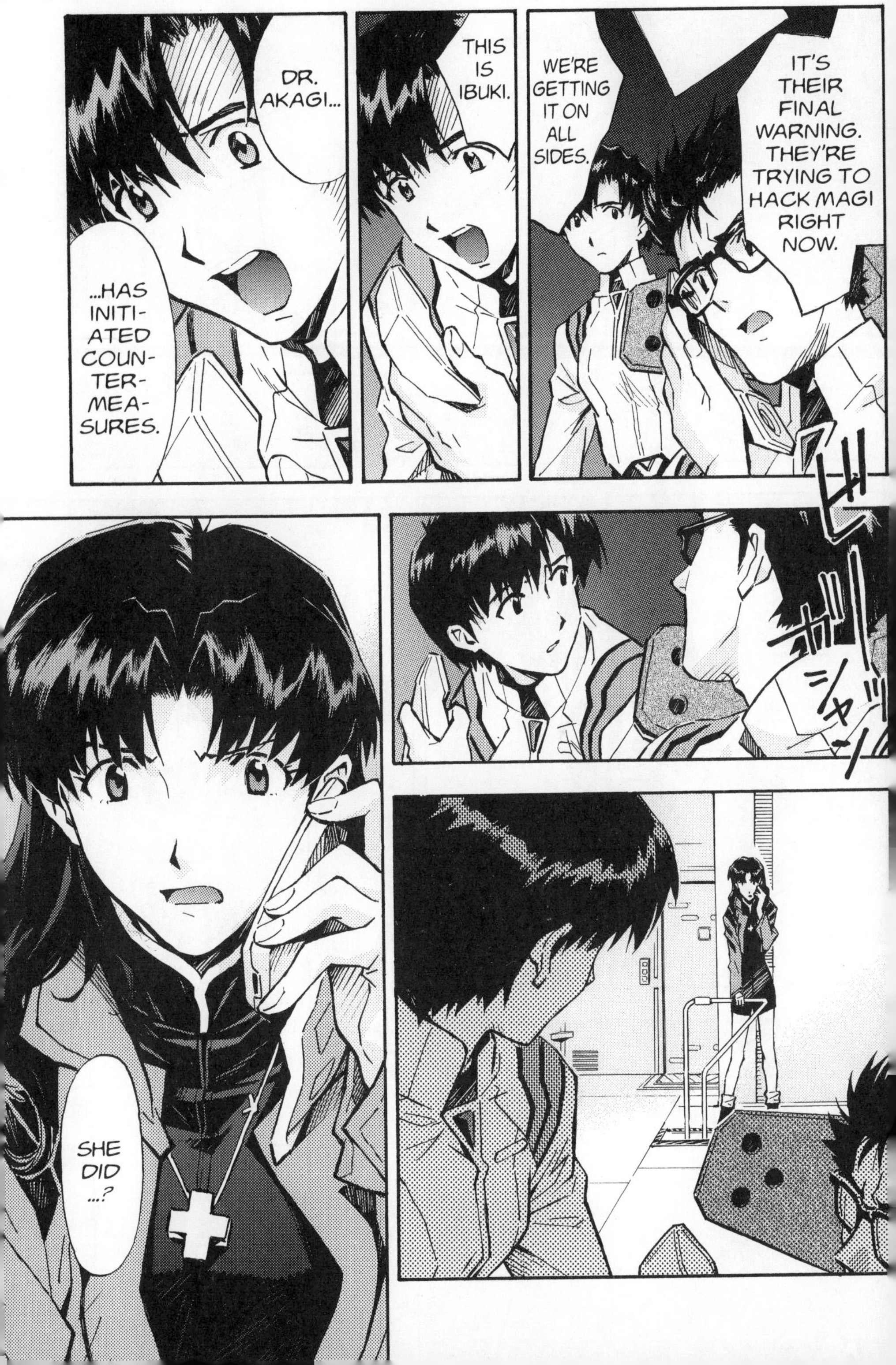
IT'S THEIR FINAL WARNING. THEY'RE TRYING TO HACK MAGI RIGHT NOW.
WE'RE GETTING IT ON ALL SIDES.
THIS IS IBUKI.
DR. AKAGI...
...HAS INITIATED COUNTER-MEA-SURES.
SHE DID ...?

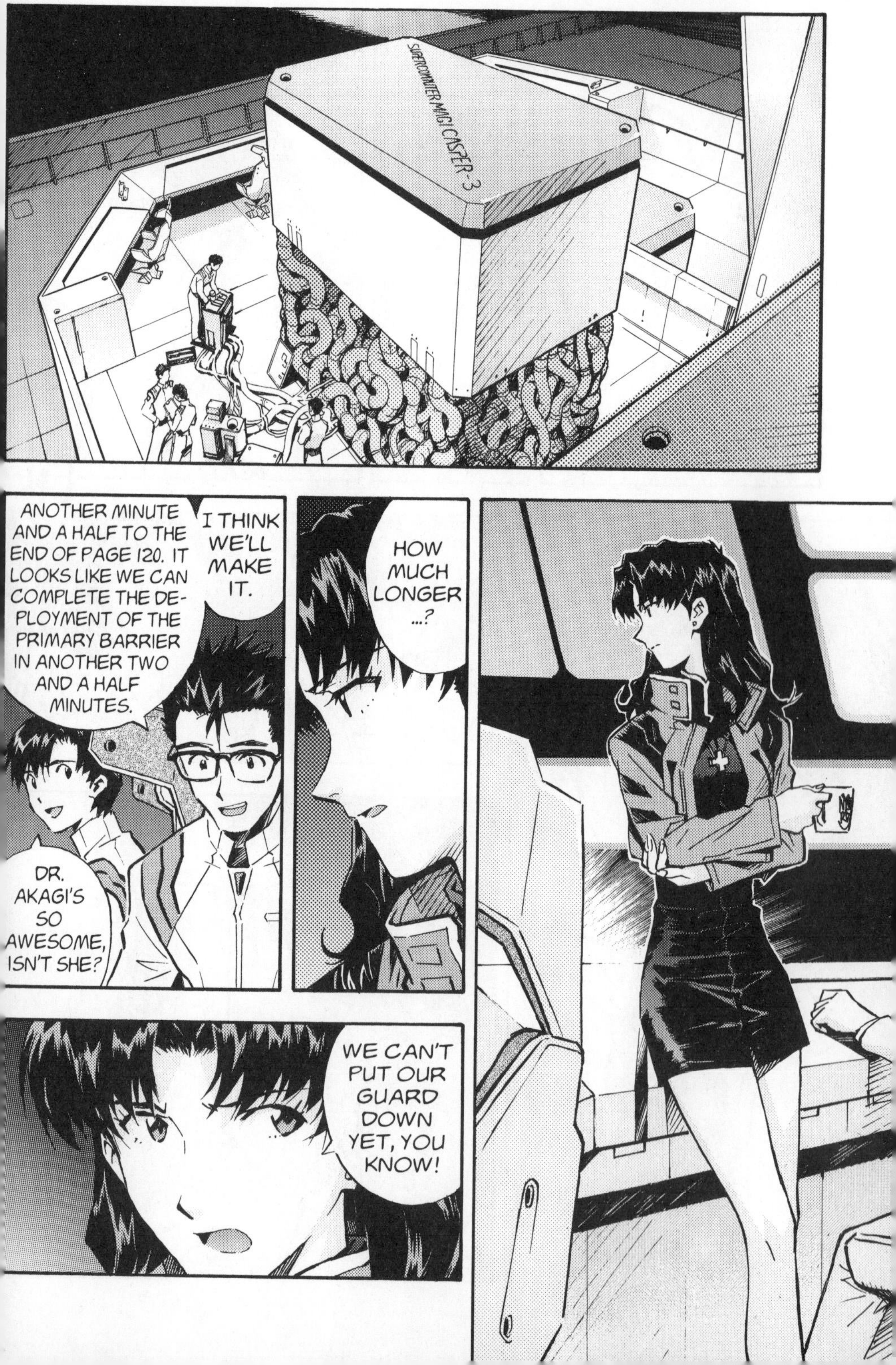

SUPERCOMPUTER MAGI CASPER-3
HOW MUCH LONGER ...?
ANOTHER MINUTE AND A HALF TO THE END OF PAGE 120. IT LOOKS LIKE WE CAN COMPLETE THE DE-PLOYMENT OF THE PRIMARY BARRIER IN ANOTHER TWO AND A HALF MINUTES.
I THINK WE'LL MAKE IT.
DR. AKAGI'S SO AWESOME, ISN'T SHE?
WE CAN'T PUT OUR GUARD DOWN YET, YOU KNOW!

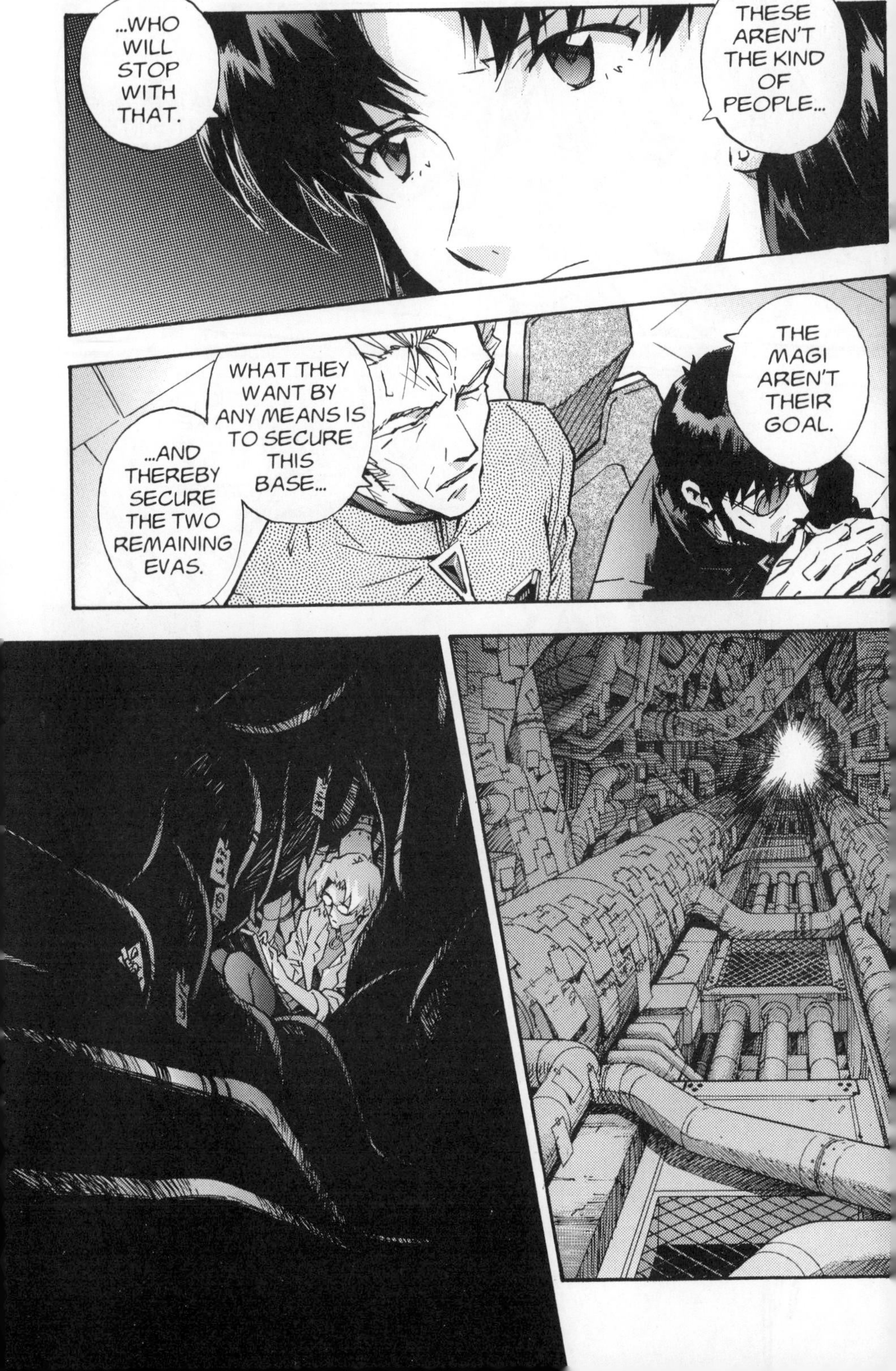
THESE AREN'T THE KIND OF PEOPLE...
...WHO WILL STOP WITH THAT.
THE MAGI AREN'T THEIR GOAL.
WHAT THEY WANT BY ANY MEANS IS TO SECURE THIS BASE...
...AND THEREBY SECURE THE TWO REMAINING EVAS.

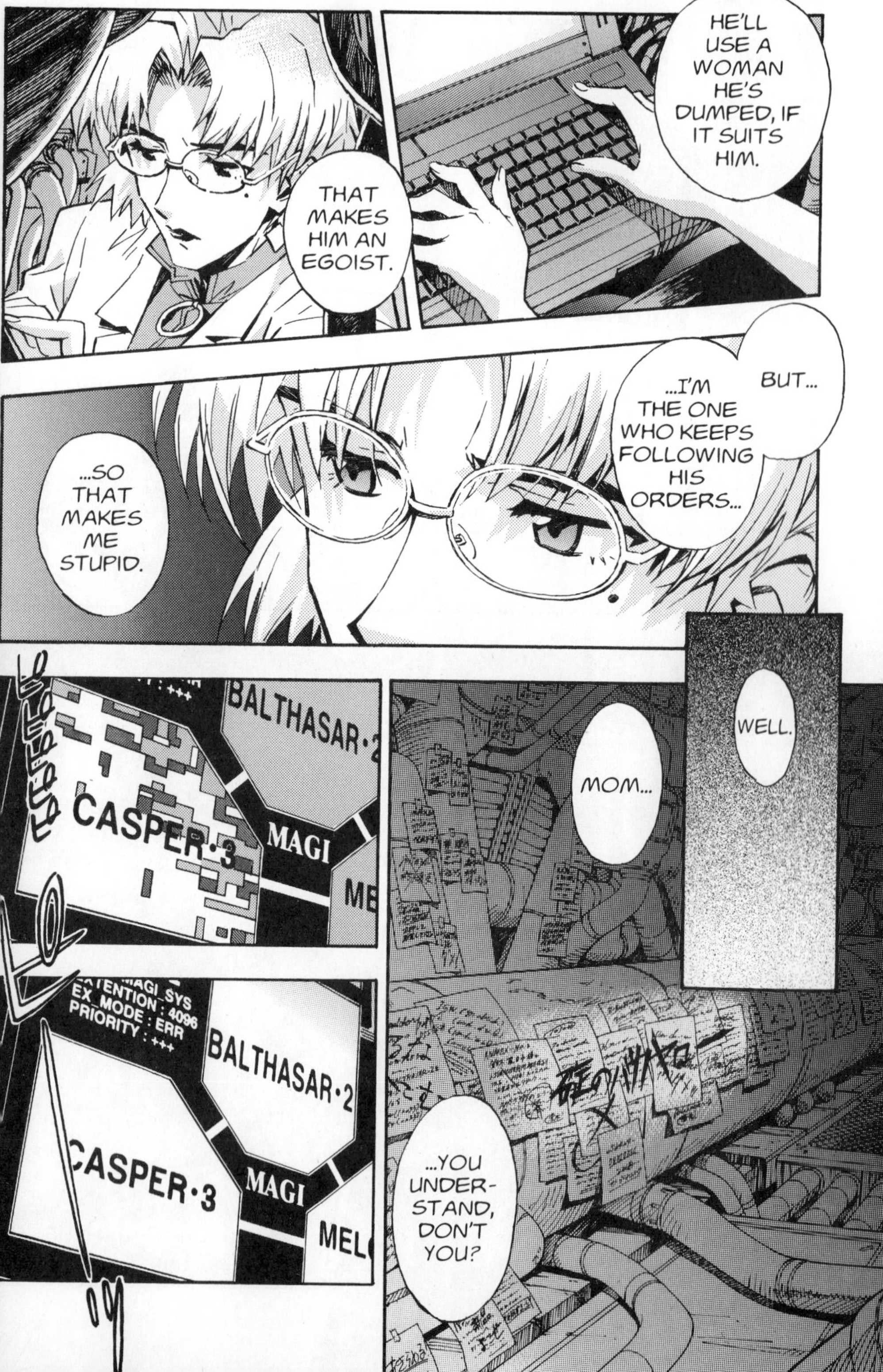
HE'LL USE A WOMAN HE'S DUMPED, IF IT SUITS HIM.
THAT MAKES HIM AN EGOIST.
BUT...
...I'M THE ONE WHO KEEPS FOLLOWING HIS ORDERS...
...SO THAT MAKES ME STUPID.
WELL.
MOM...
...YOU UNDERSTAND, DON'T YOU?
BALTHASAR·2
CASPER·3
MAGI
EX_MODE : ERR
PRIORITY : +++
BALTHASAR·2
CASPER·3
MAGI

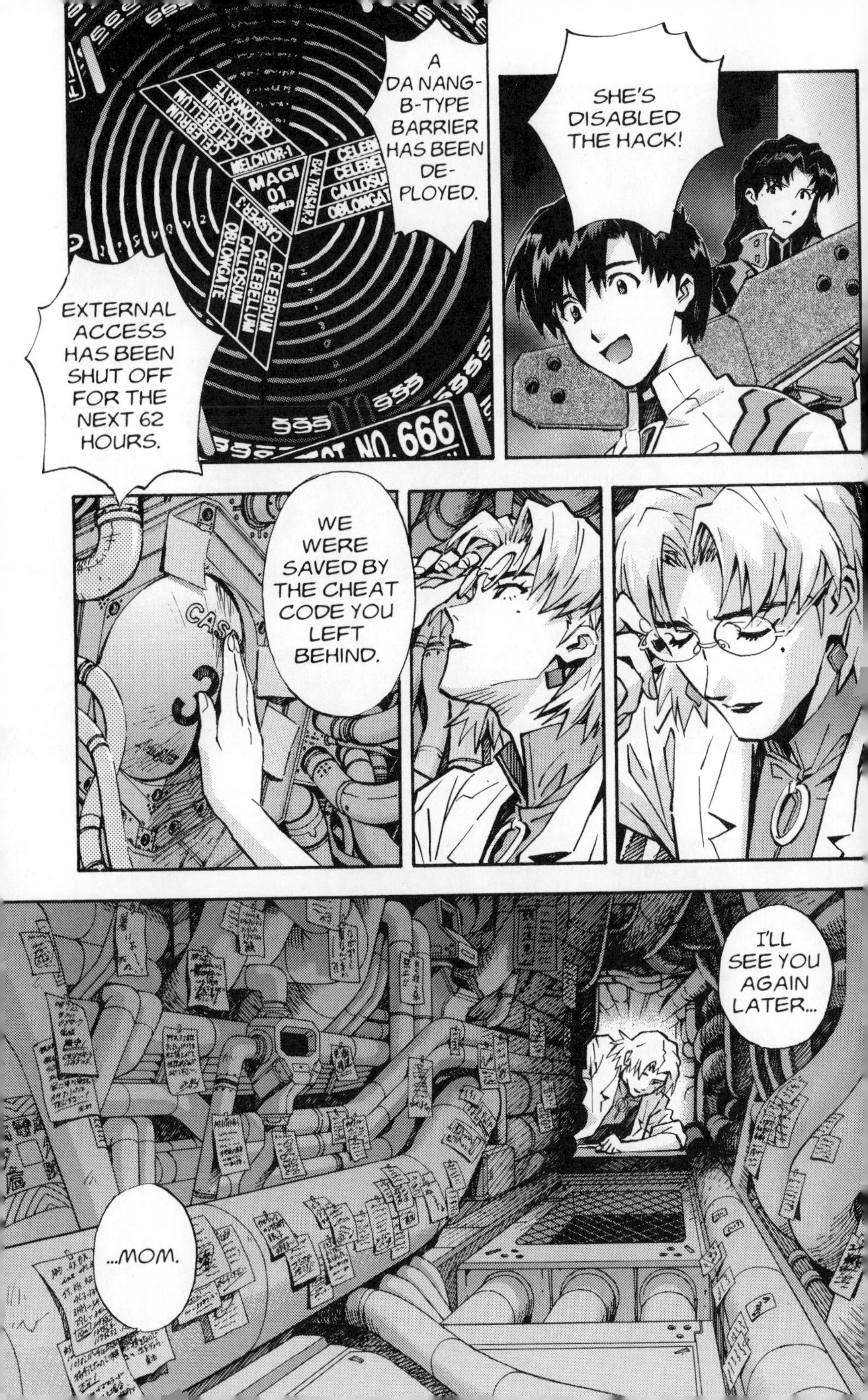
SHE'S DISABLED THE HACK!
A DA NANG-B-TYPE BARRIER HAS BEEN DE-PLOYED.
MAGI 01
MELCHIOR-1
CELEBRUM
CELEBELLUM
CALLOSUM
OBLONGATE
BALTHASAR-2
CASPER-3
EXTERNAL ACCESS HAS BEEN SHUT OFF FOR THE NEXT 62 HOURS.
WE WERE SAVED BY THE CHEAT CODE YOU LEFT BEHIND.
I'LL SEE YOU AGAIN LATER...
...MOM.

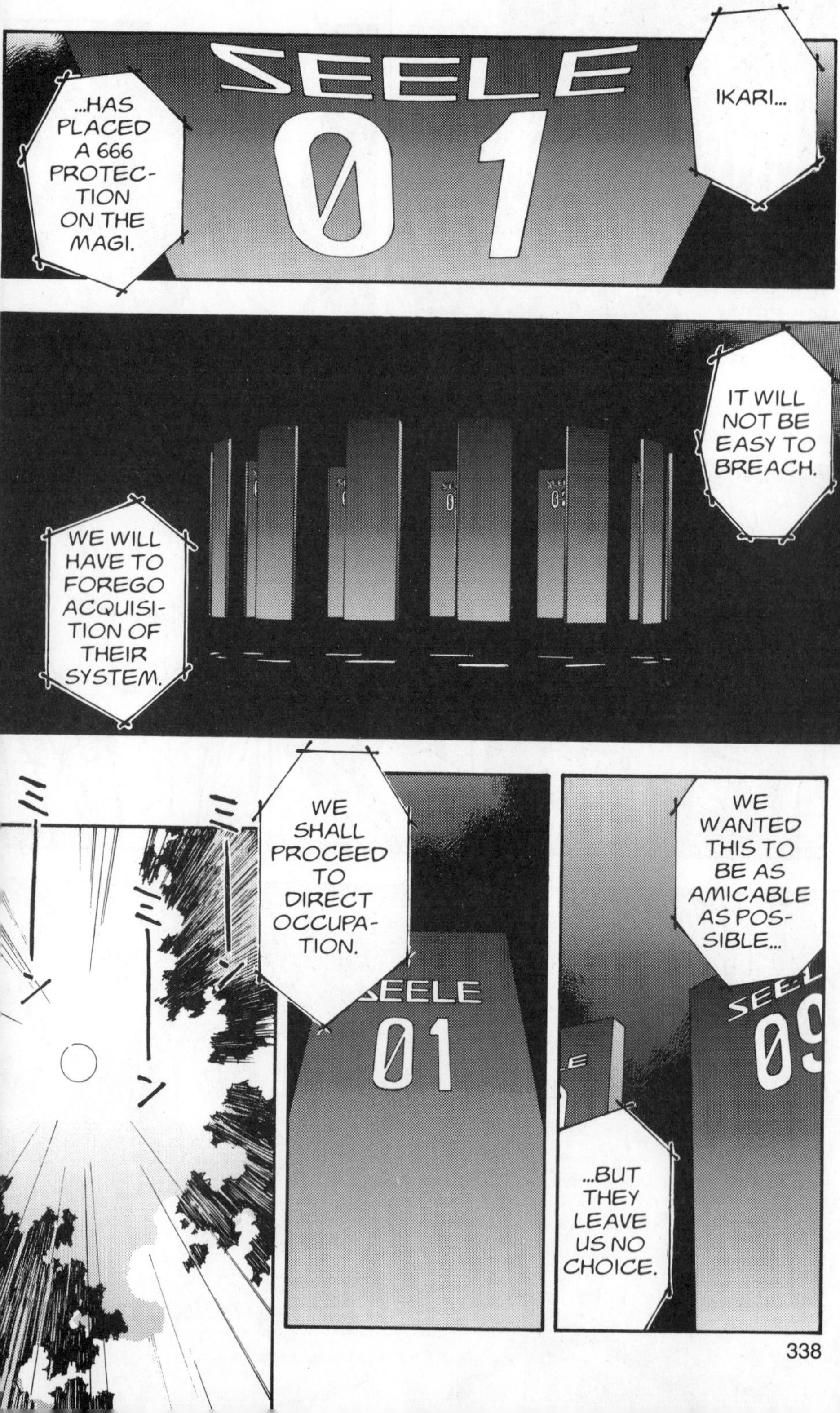
IKARI...
SEELE 01
...HAS PLACED A 666 PROTECTION ON THE MAGI.
IT WILL NOT BE EASY TO BREACH.
WE WILL HAVE TO FOREGO ACQUISITION OF THEIR SYSTEM.
WE WANTED THIS TO BE AS AMICABLE AS POSSIBLE...
SEELE 09
...BUT THEY LEAVE US NO CHOICE.
WE SHALL PROCEED TO DIRECT OCCUPATION.
SEELE 01

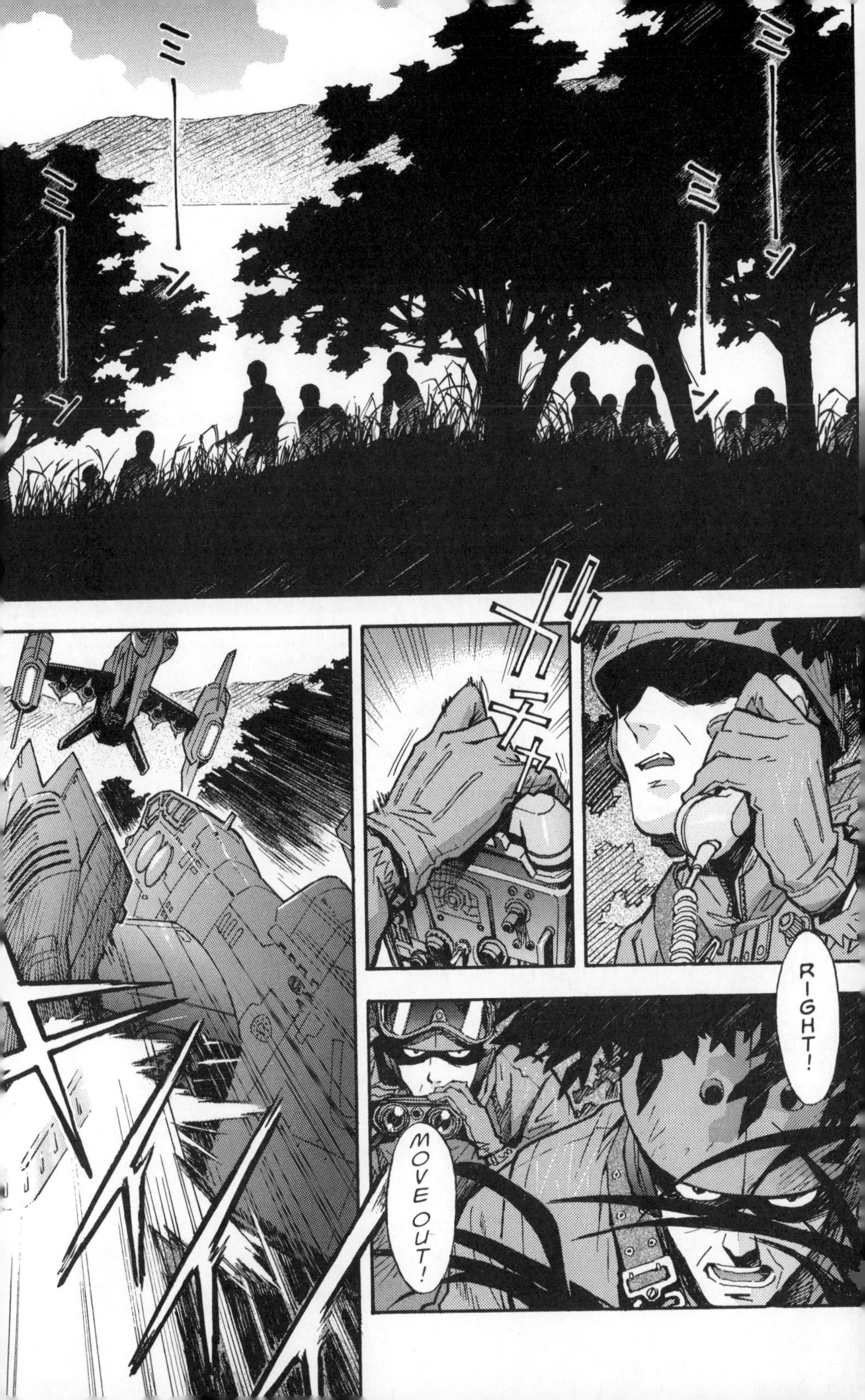
ミーン
ミーン
ミーン
ミーン
ガチャ
RIGHT!
MOVE OUT!

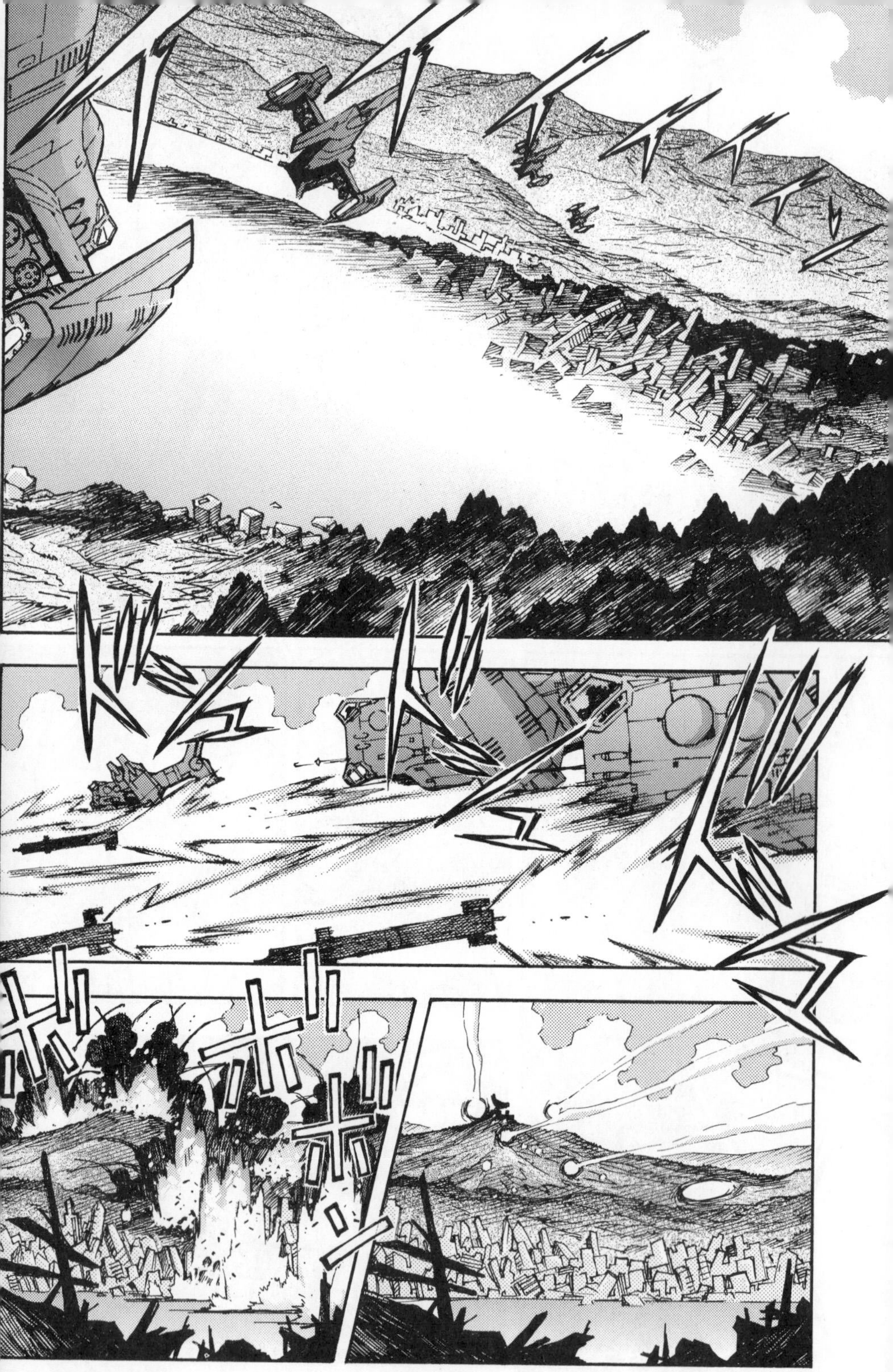

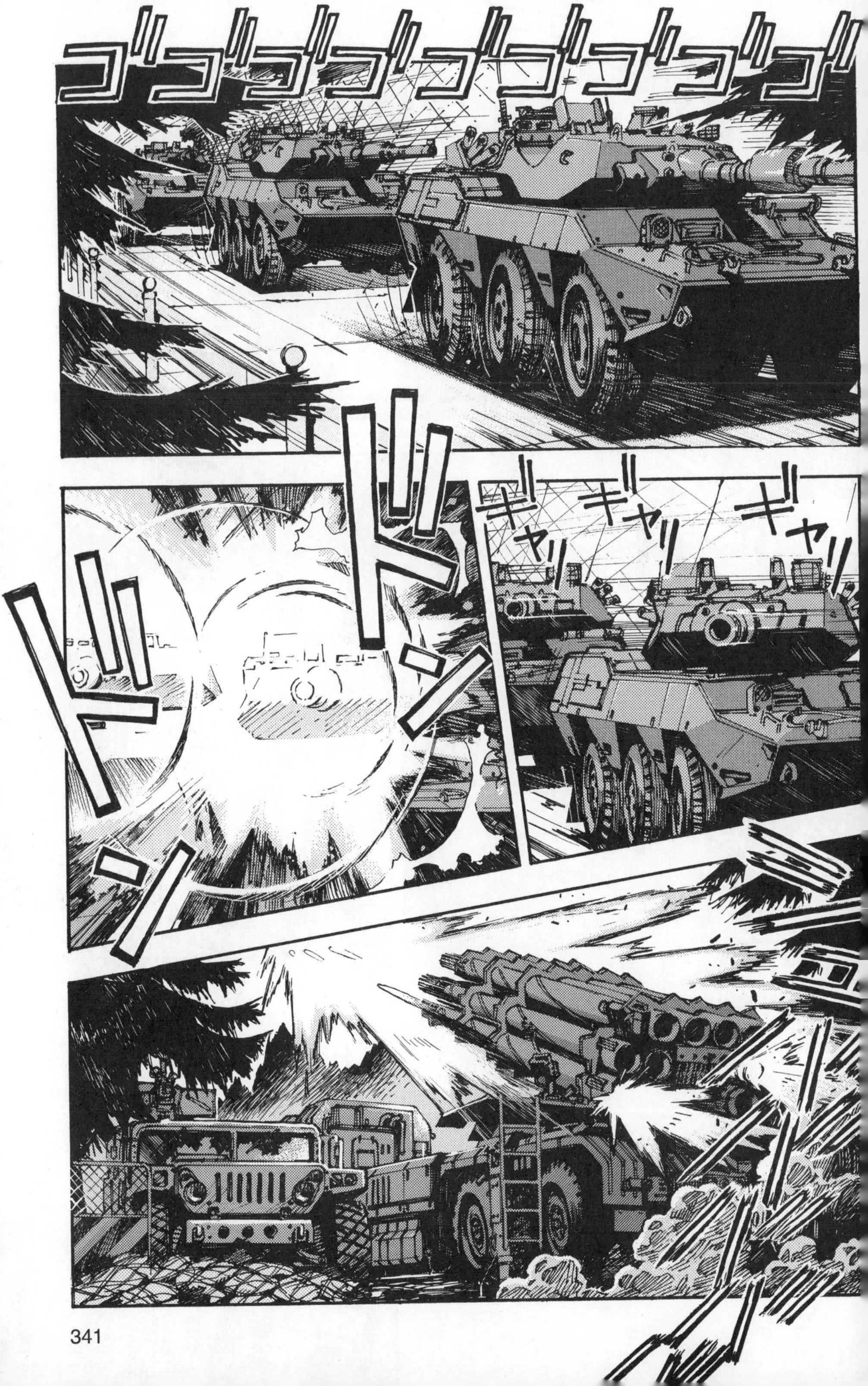
ゴゴッゴッゴッゴゴッゴッ
ギャリ
ギャリ
ギャリ
ドドン
ドドン

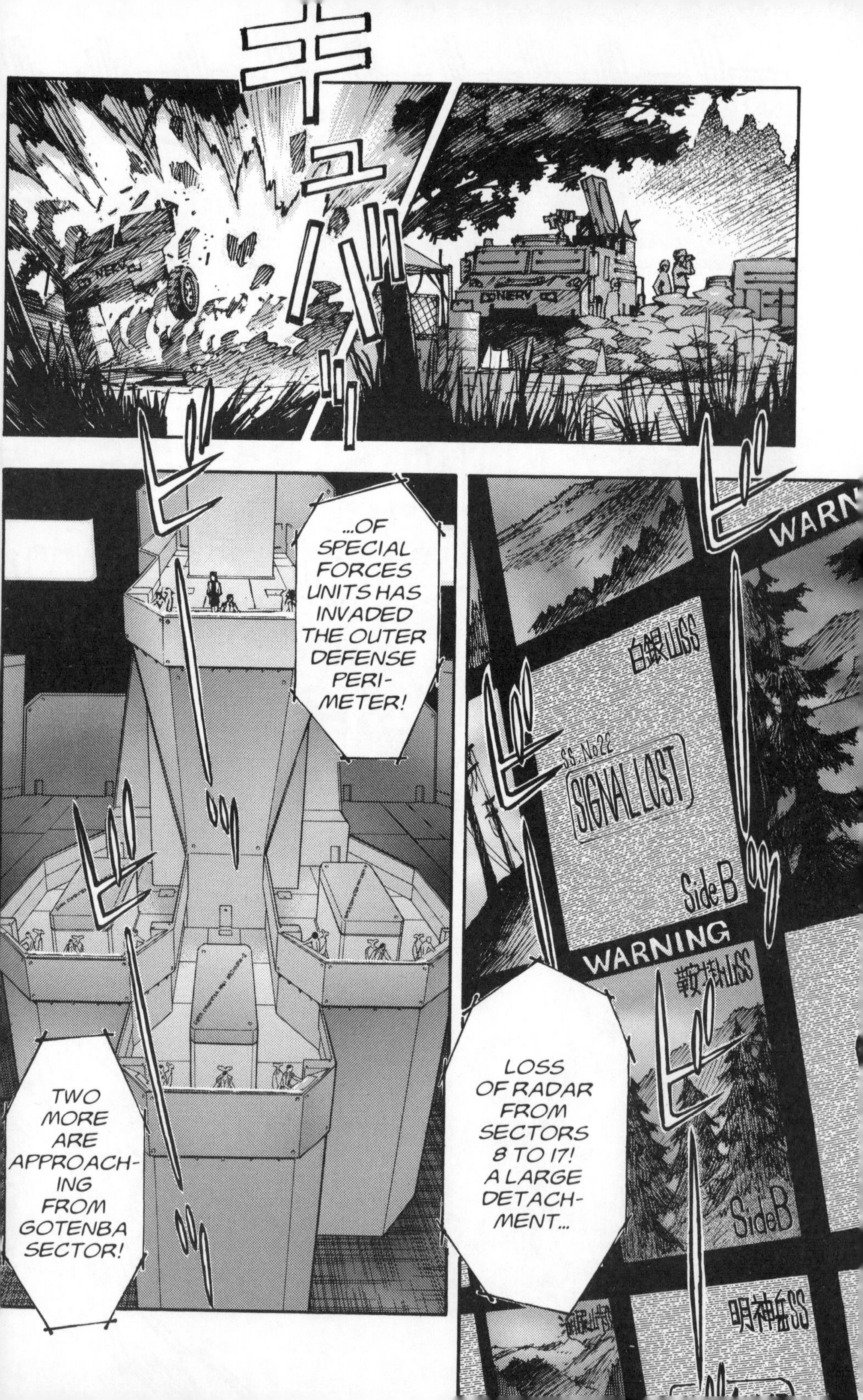
キュ
WARNING
白銀山SS
S.S. No.22
SIGNAL LOST
Side B
WARNING
Side B
明神岳SS
LOSS OF RADAR FROM SECTORS 8 TO 17! A LARGE DETACHMENT...
...OF SPECIAL FORCES UNITS HAS INVADED THE OUTER DEFENSE PERIMETER!
TWO MORE ARE APPROACHING FROM GOTENBA SECTOR!

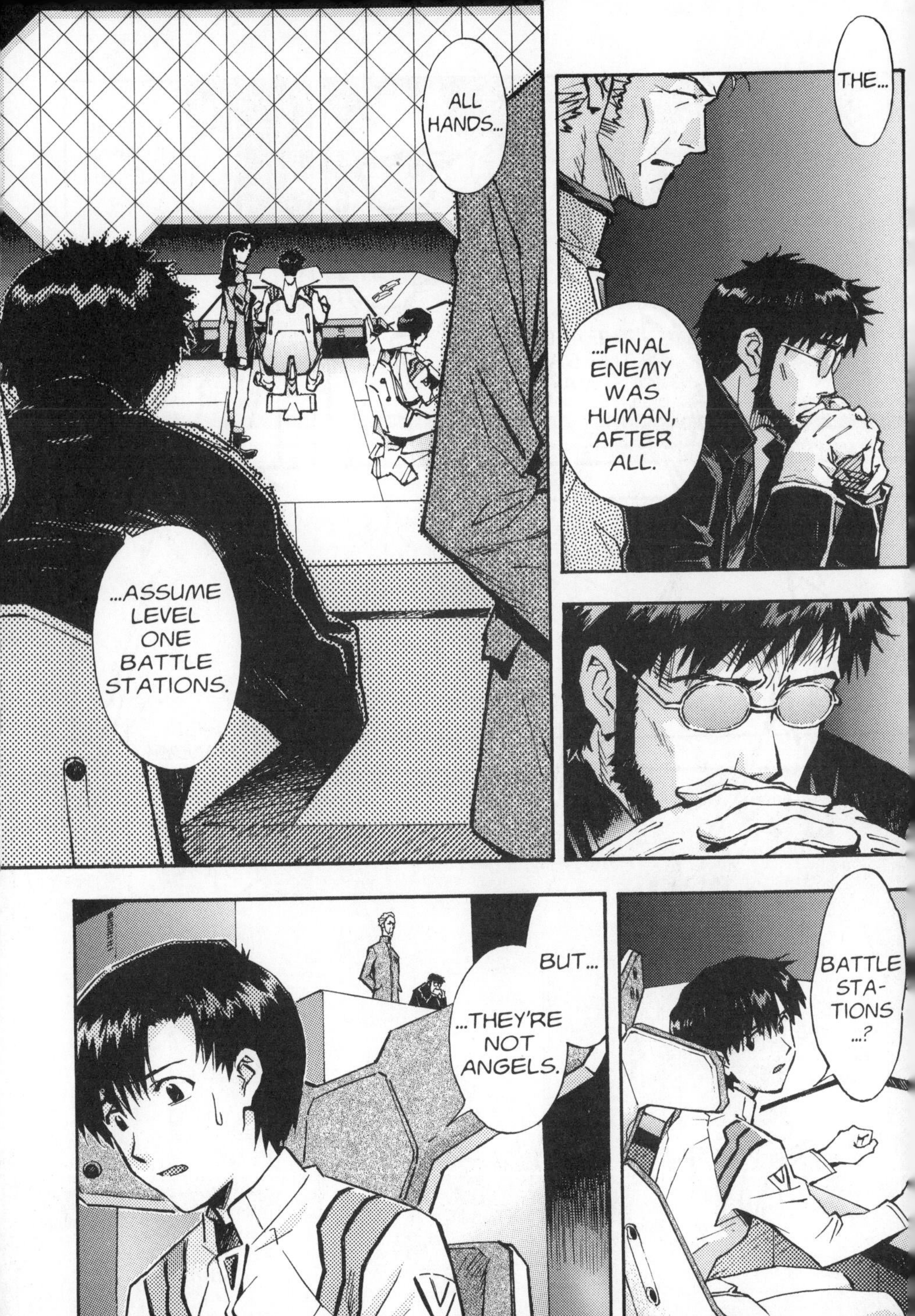
THE...
...FINAL ENEMY WAS HUMAN, AFTER ALL.
ALL HANDS...
...ASSUME LEVEL ONE BATTLE STATIONS.
BATTLE STA- TIONS ...?
BUT...
...THEY'RE NOT ANGELS.

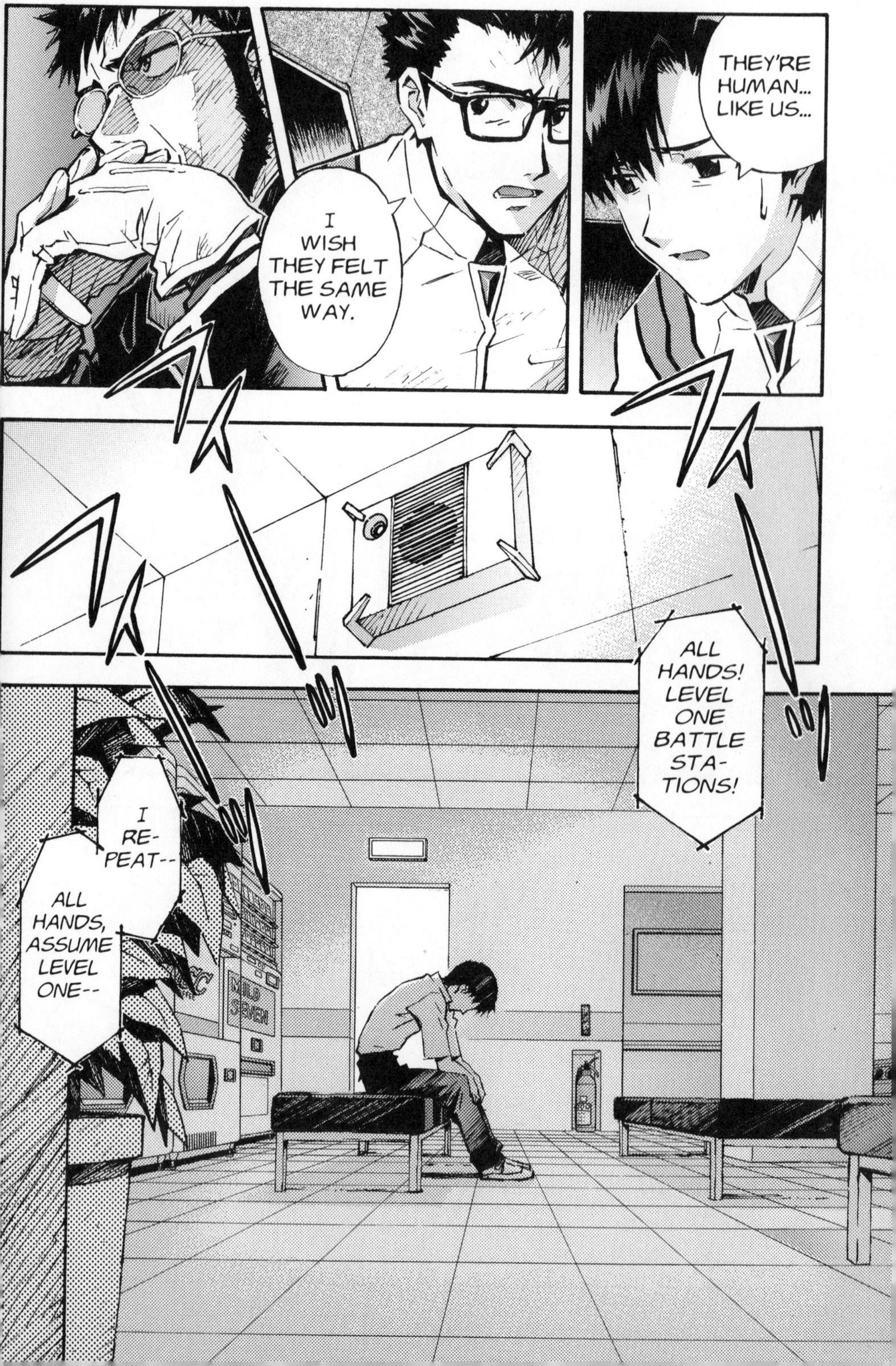
THEY'RE HUMAN... LIKE US...
I WISH THEY FELT THE SAME WAY.
ALL HANDS! LEVEL ONE BATTLE STA-TIONS!
I RE-PEAT--
ALL HANDS, ASSUME LEVEL ONE--

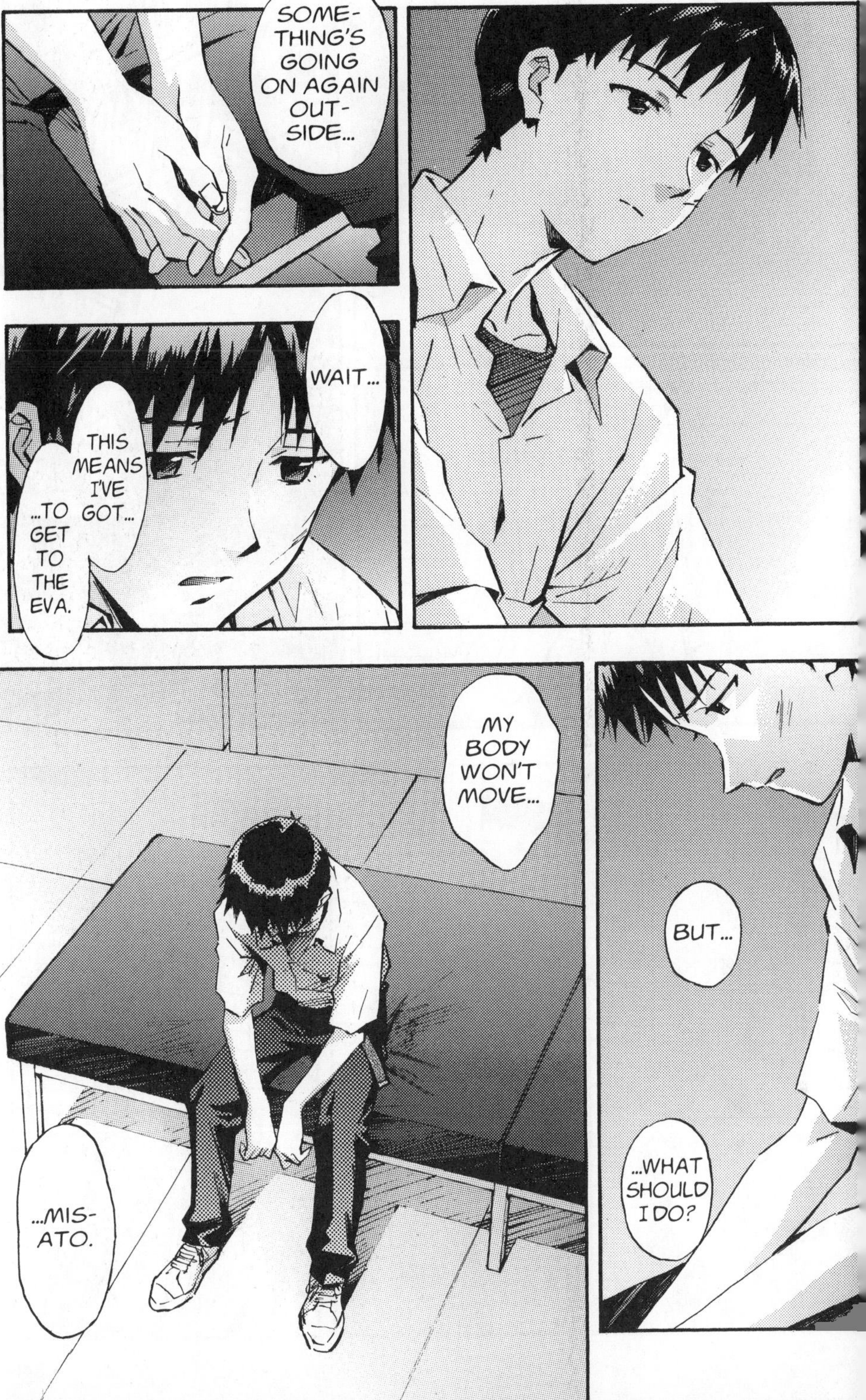
SOME-THING'S GOING ON AGAIN OUT-SIDE...
WAIT...
THIS MEANS I'VE GOT...
...TO GET TO THE EVA.
BUT...
...WHAT SHOULD I DO?
MY BODY WON'T MOVE...
...MIS-ATO.

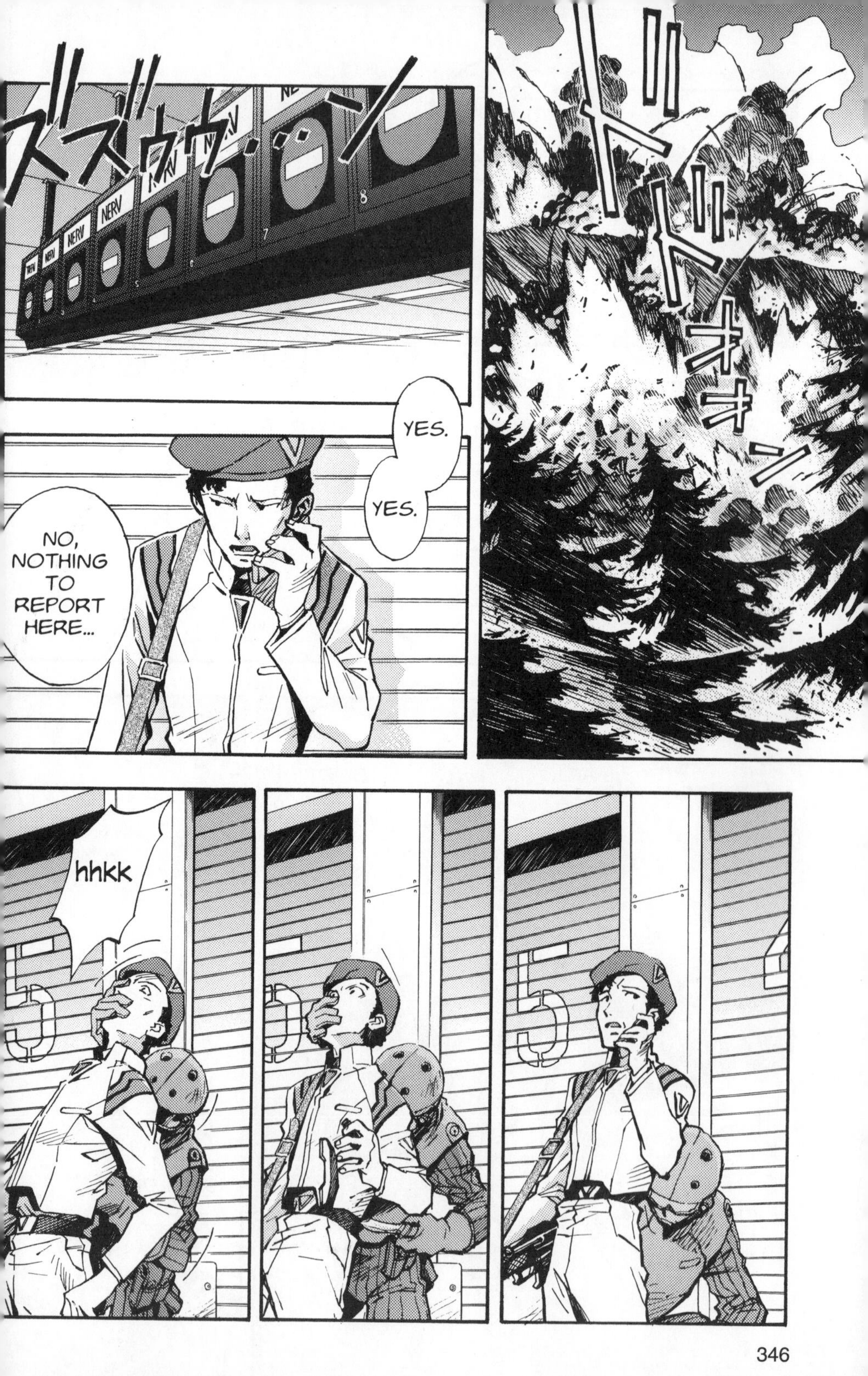
ドドオオーン
ズズウウ‥ーン
YES.
YES.
NO, NOTHING TO REPORT HERE...
hhkk

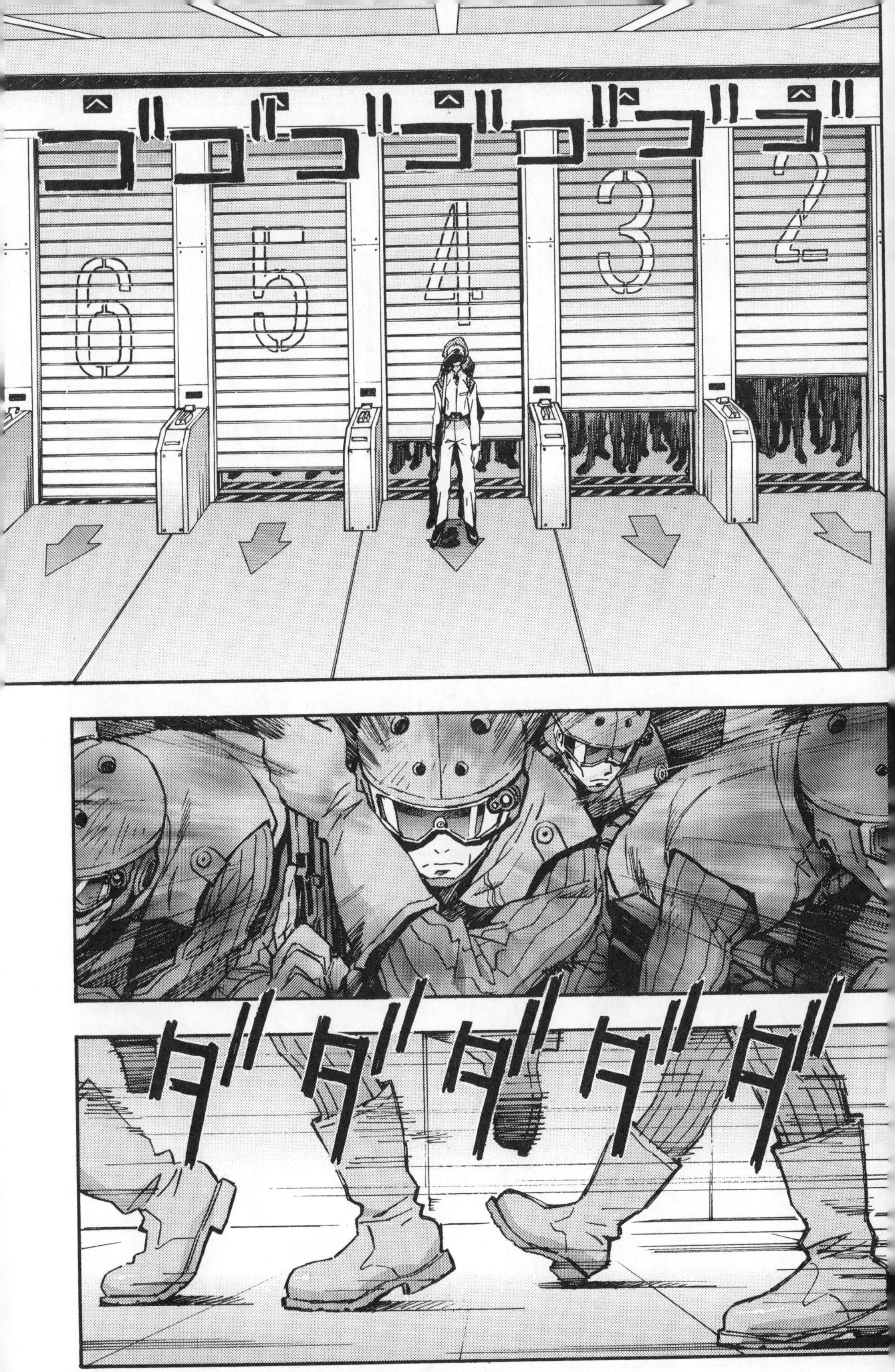
ゴゴゴゴゴゴゴ
ダダダダダ

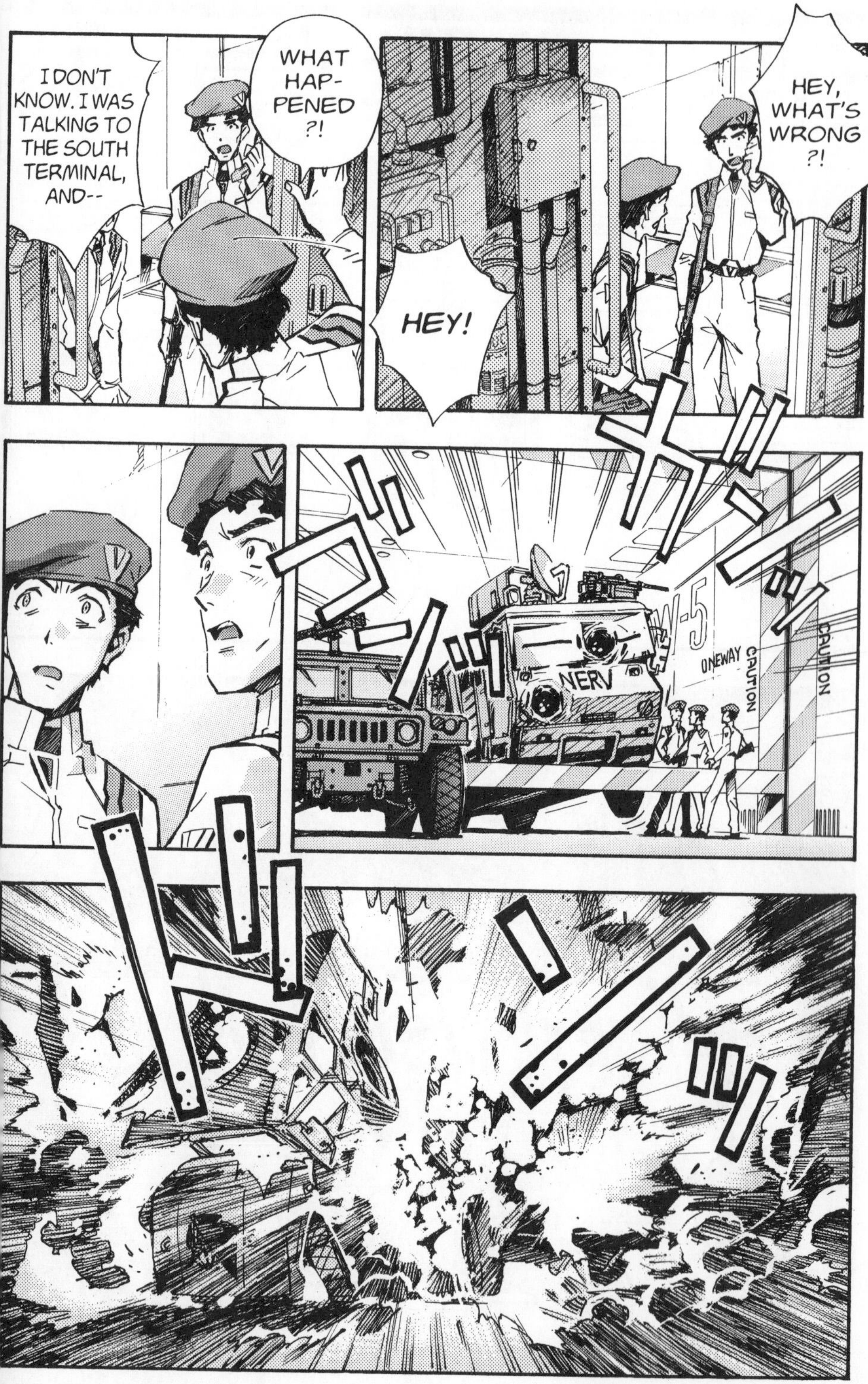
HEY, WHAT'S WRONG ?!
HEY!
WHAT HAP-PENED ?!
I DON'T KNOW. I WAS TALKING TO THE SOUTH TERMINAL, AND--
NERV
W-5
ONEWAY
CAUTION
CAUTION

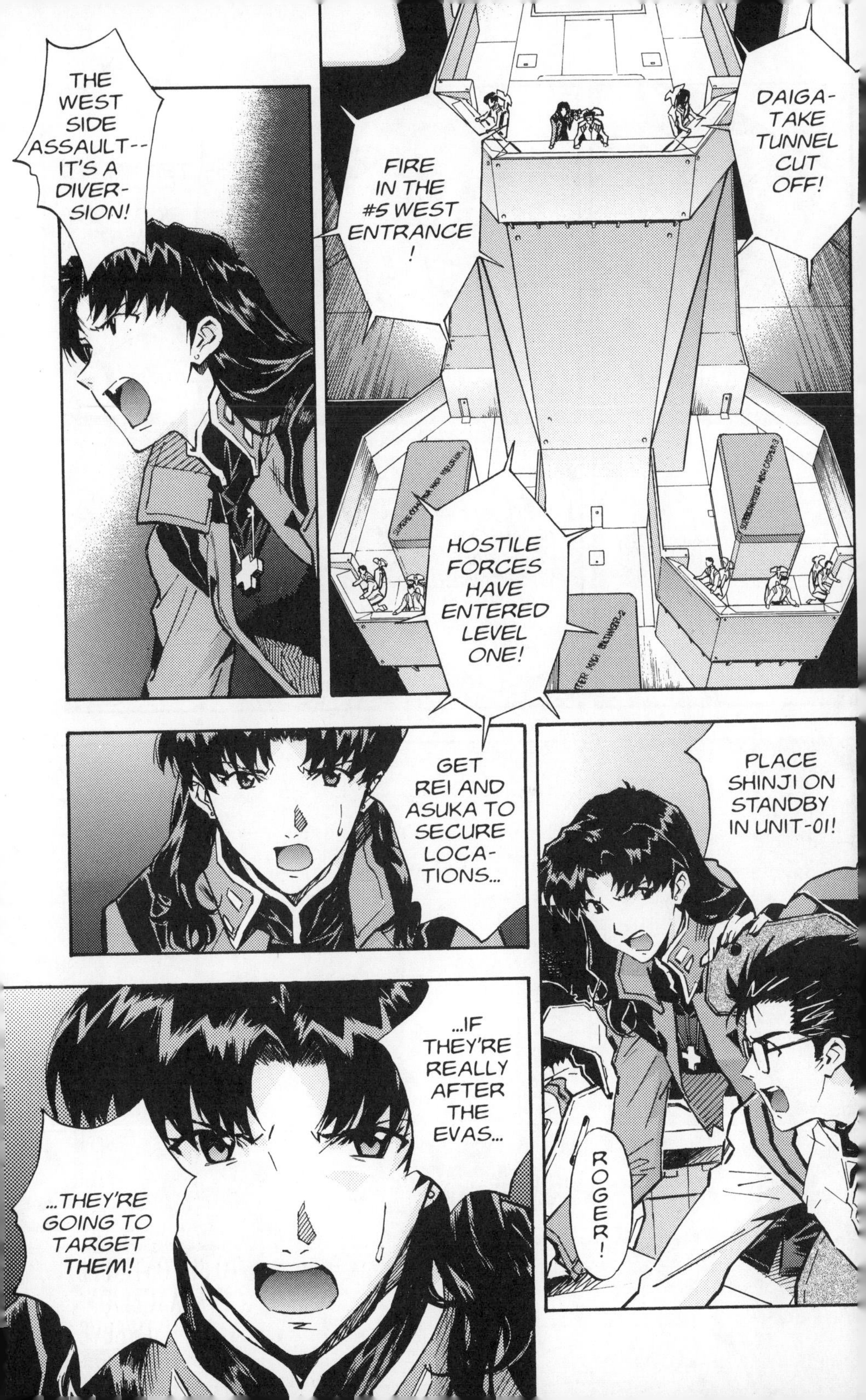
DAIGA-TAKE TUNNEL CUT OFF!
FIRE IN THE #5 WEST ENTRANCE!
HOSTILE FORCES HAVE ENTERED LEVEL ONE!
THE WEST SIDE ASSAULT--IT'S A DIVERSION!
PLACE SHINJI ON STANDBY IN UNIT-01!
ROGER!
GET REI AND ASUKA TO SECURE LOCATIONS...
...IF THEY'RE REALLY AFTER THE EVAS...
...THEY'RE GOING TO TARGET THEM!

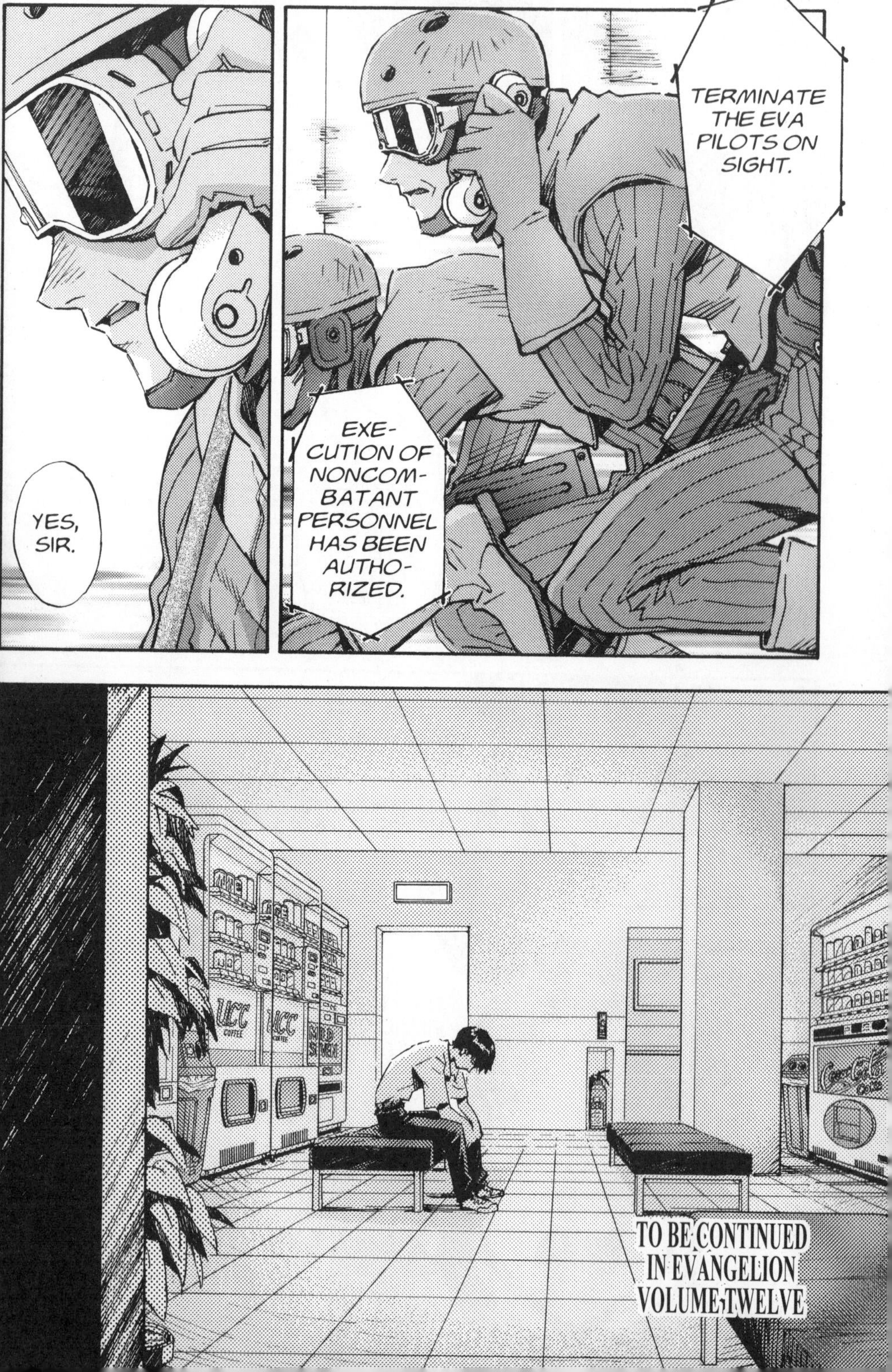
TERMINATE THE EVA PILOTS ON SIGHT.
EXECUTION OF NONCOMBATANT PERSONNEL HAS BEEN AUTHORIZED.
YES, SIR.
TO BE CONTINUED IN EVANGELION VOLUME TWELVE

YOSHIYUKI SADAMOTO

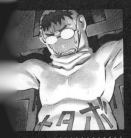

THE AUTHOR COSPLAYS AS LILITH, BUT GAZES DOWN IN CHAGRIN AT THE BRAND "METABO"-METABOLIC SYNDROME.

WRITER AND ARTIST

I have never had feelings for someone of the same sex before...or so I thought. In my childhood I was enamored with anime and superheroes. I tried imitating them a lot, and apparently there was even a time that I thought I was Obake-no-Q-taro. All of the pictures taken of me during that phase had me doing mischievous poses, so I think that there may have even been a time that I was mischievous.

Even after reaching an age of discretion, I was influenced by novels and movies that depict the way men live and die. Stories about Kamen Rider, Bruce Lee, the Seven Samurai, James Bond, Lupin III, and the like. More often than not though, they were about men. Hmm.

In Kaworu's case, through Rei's heart flowing into his own, he is held captive by feelings that would get him nowhere—because he was still unable to even comprehend the feelings.

Actually, when I was drawing this volume, I was thinking to myself, "Kaworu is a pretty good guy," and "Shinji, try and understand," and "You're actually a little interested, aren't you?"

Then, I came to the realization that I was sort of starting to develop feelings for Kaworu. Whoa! Yikes!

NERV

GOD'S IN HIS HEAVEN. ALL'S RIGHT WITH THE WORLD.

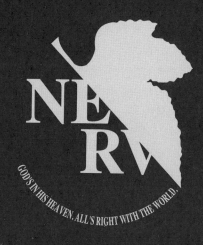

NEON GENESIS EVANGELION VOLUME 4, PART 3

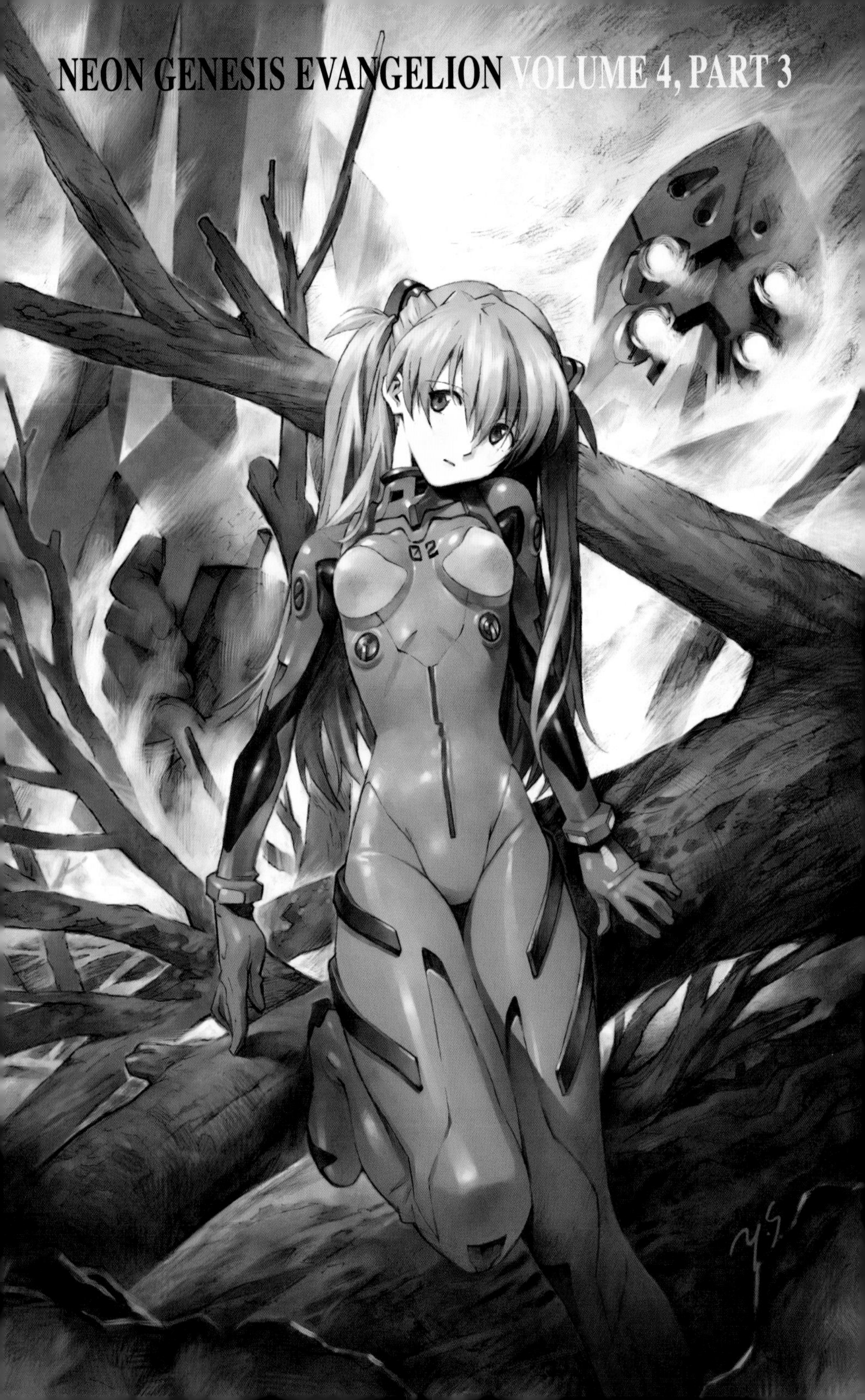

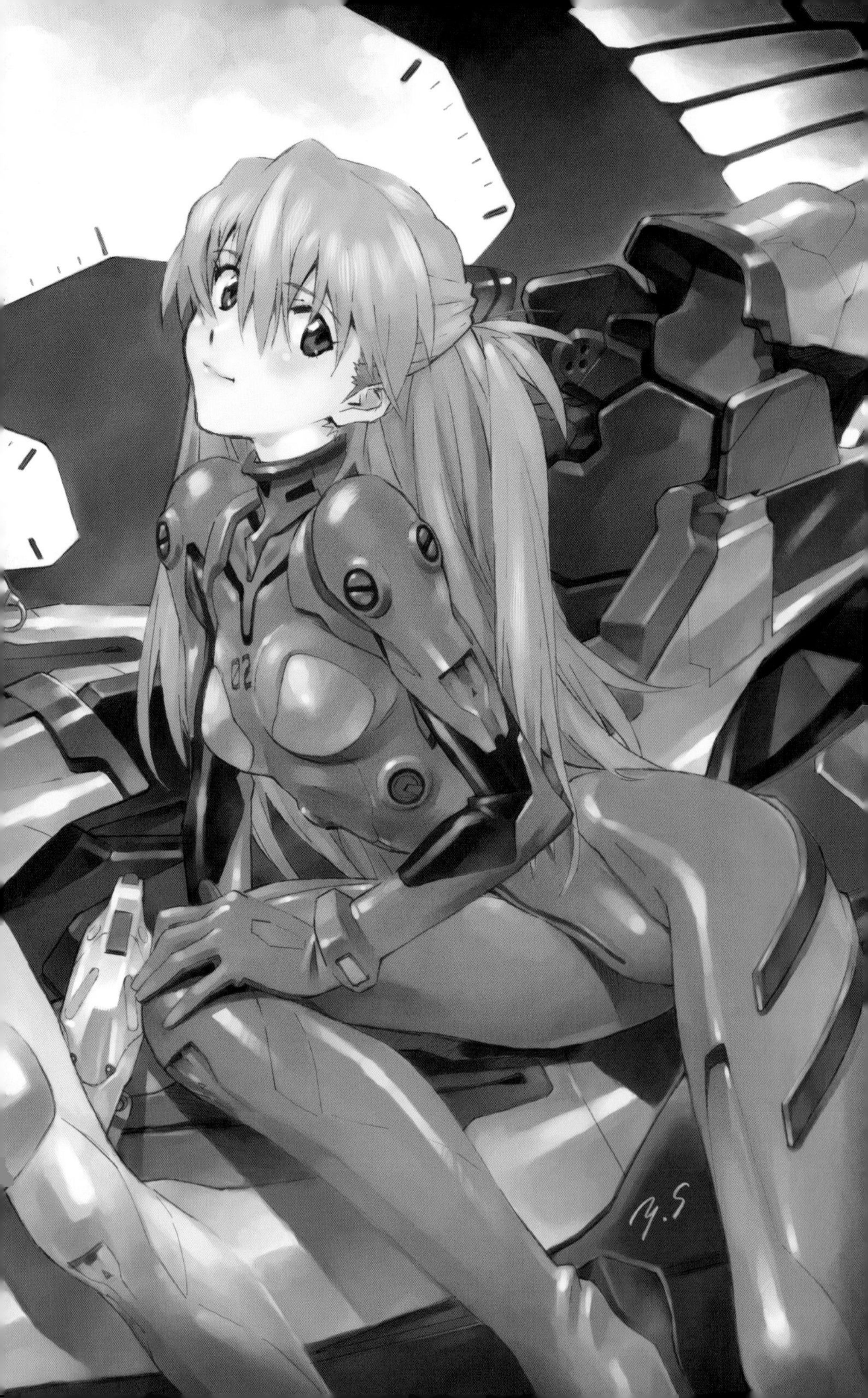
02

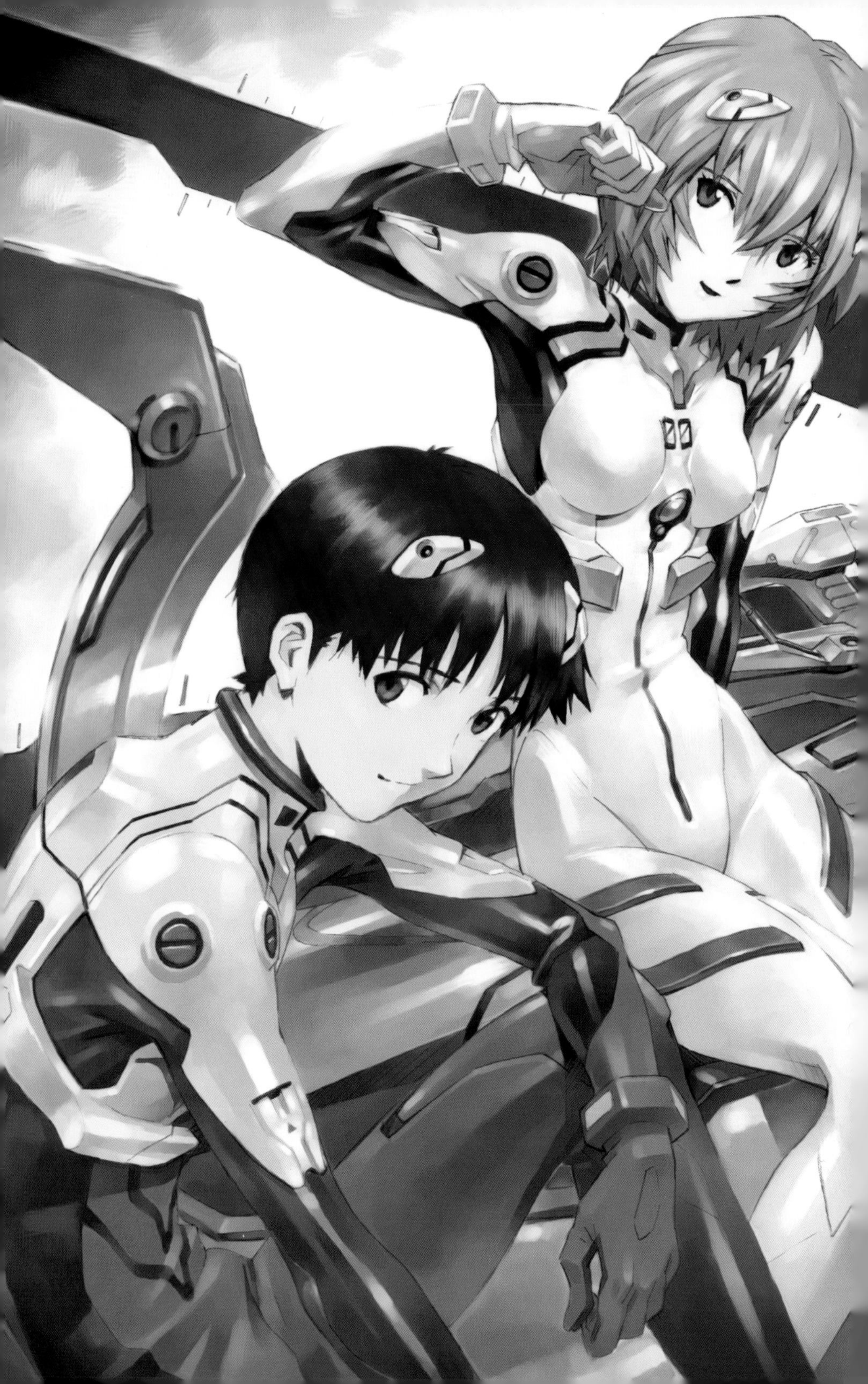

CONTENTS

NE
RV

GOD'S IN HIS HEAVEN. ALL'S RIGHT WITH THE WORLD.

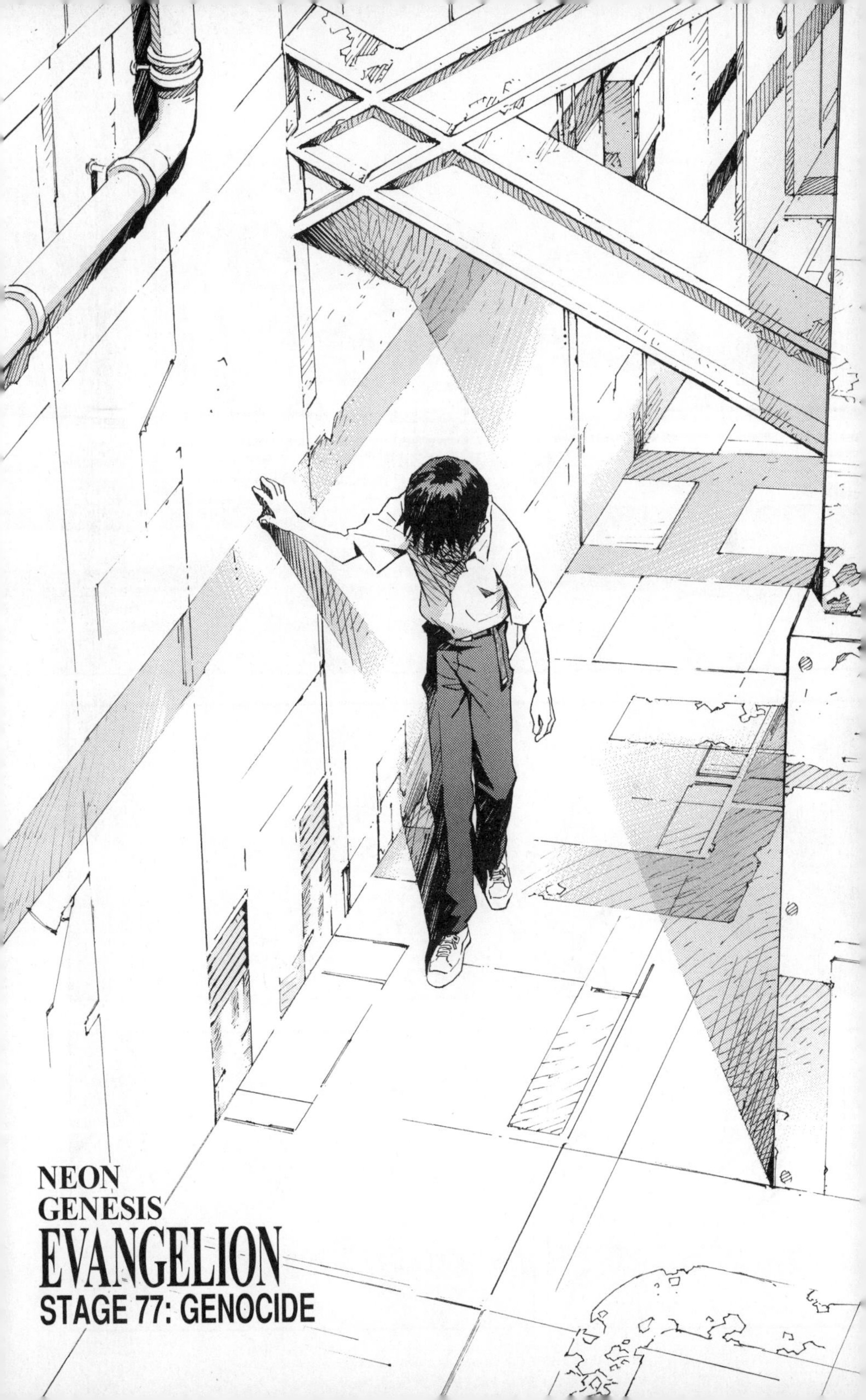
NEON
GENESIS
EVANGELION
STAGE 77: GENOCIDE

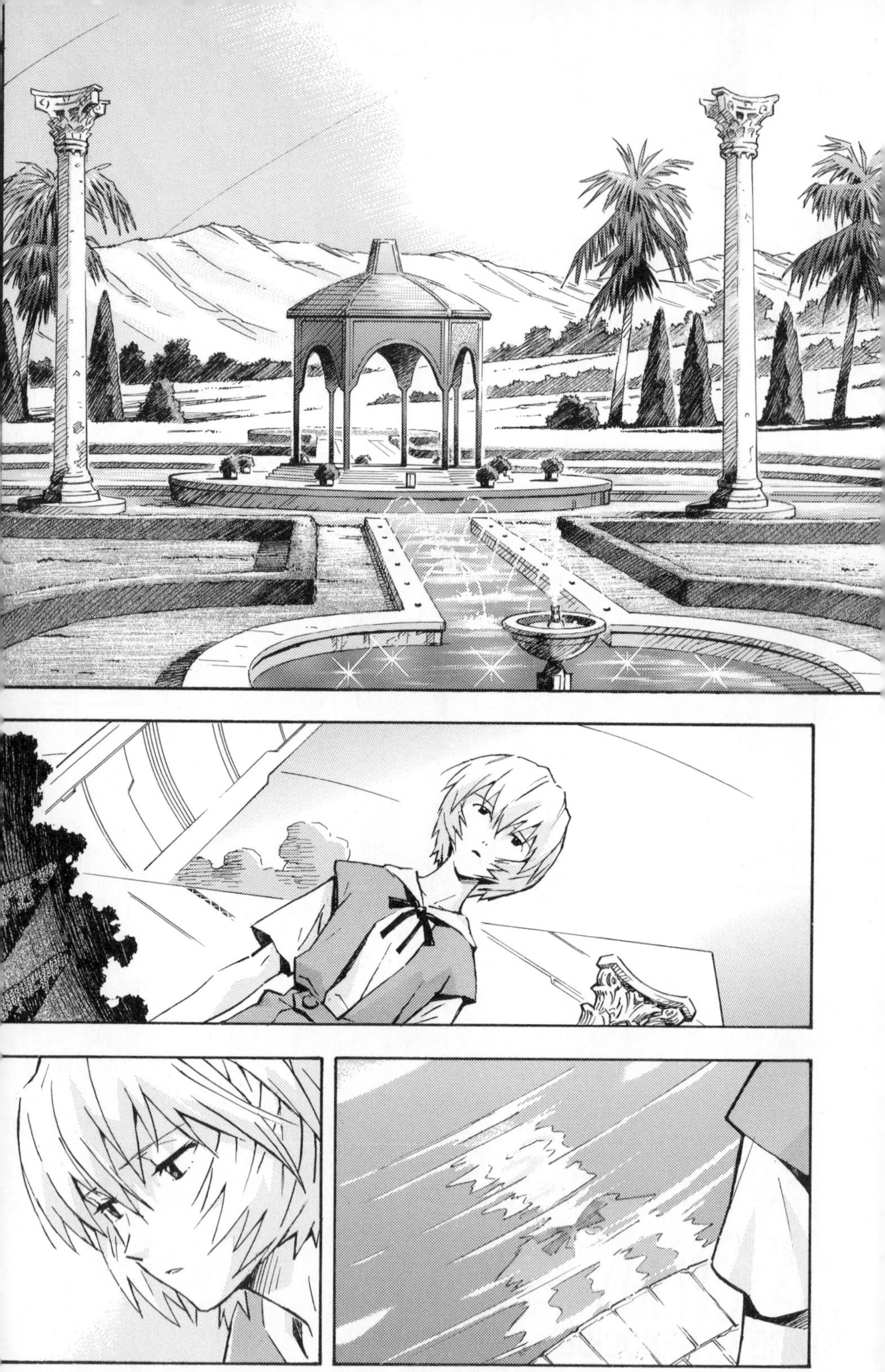

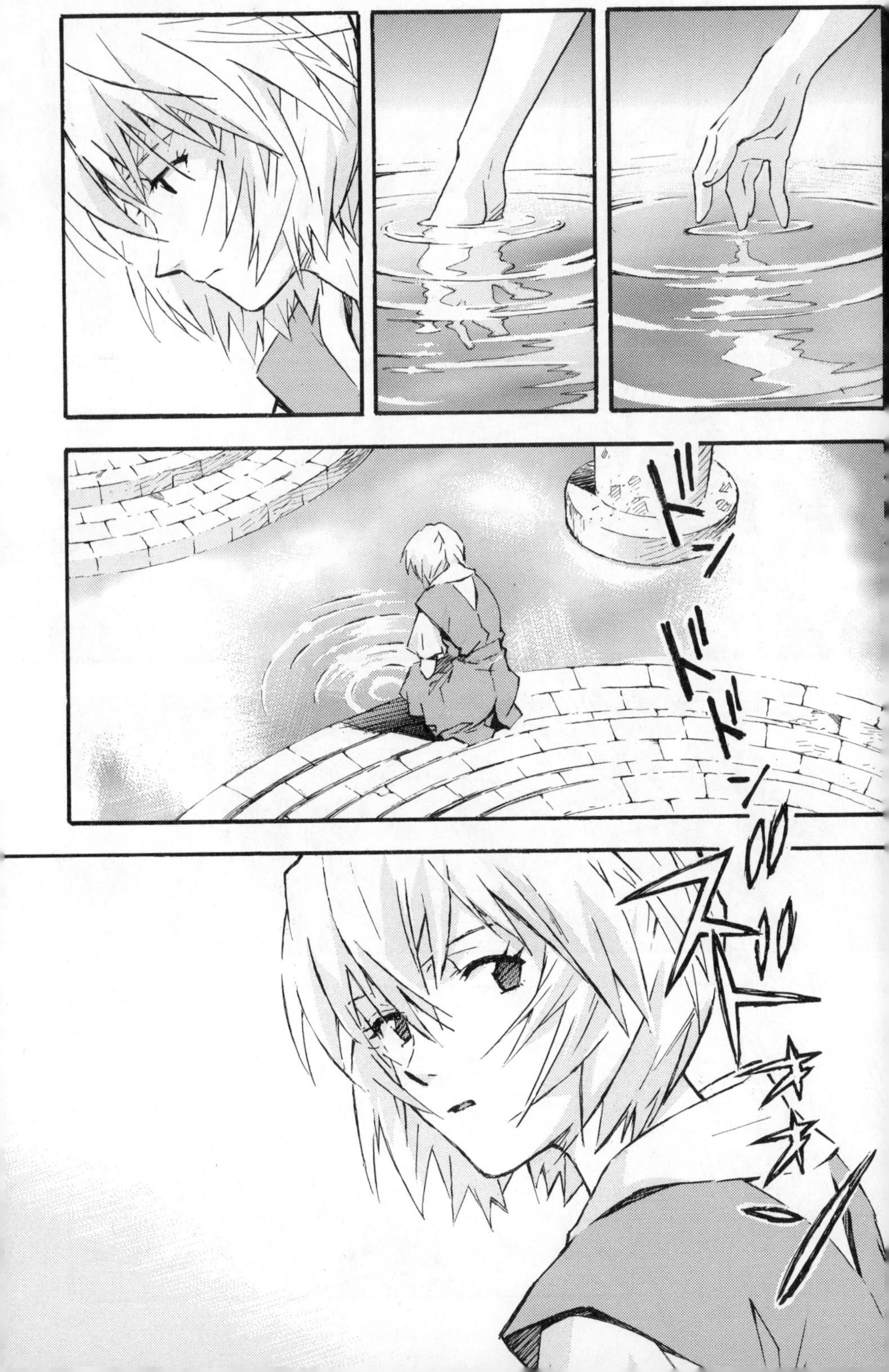
ドーン
ドドーン
ズズォォン

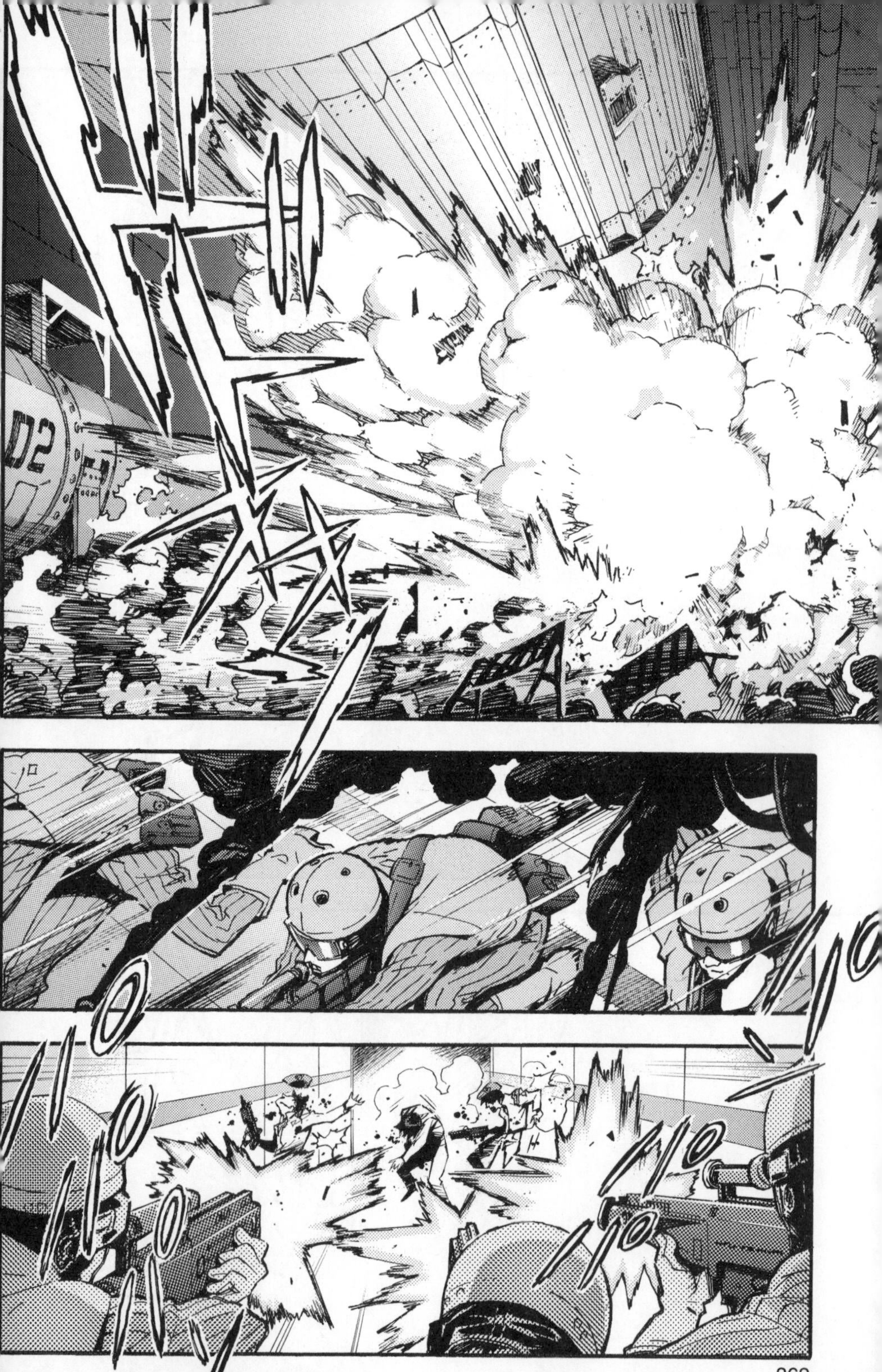

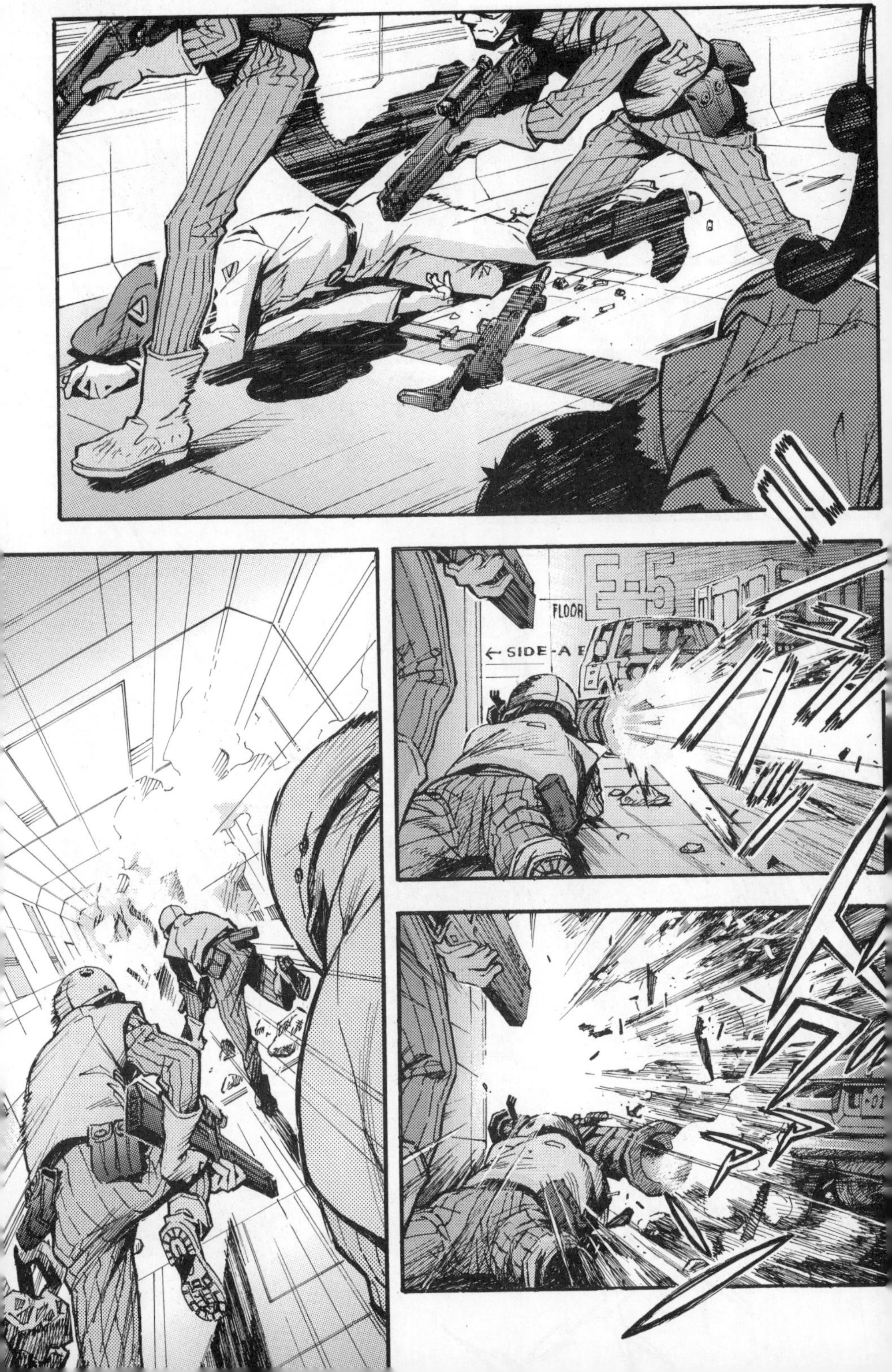
E-5
FLOOR
← SIDE-A

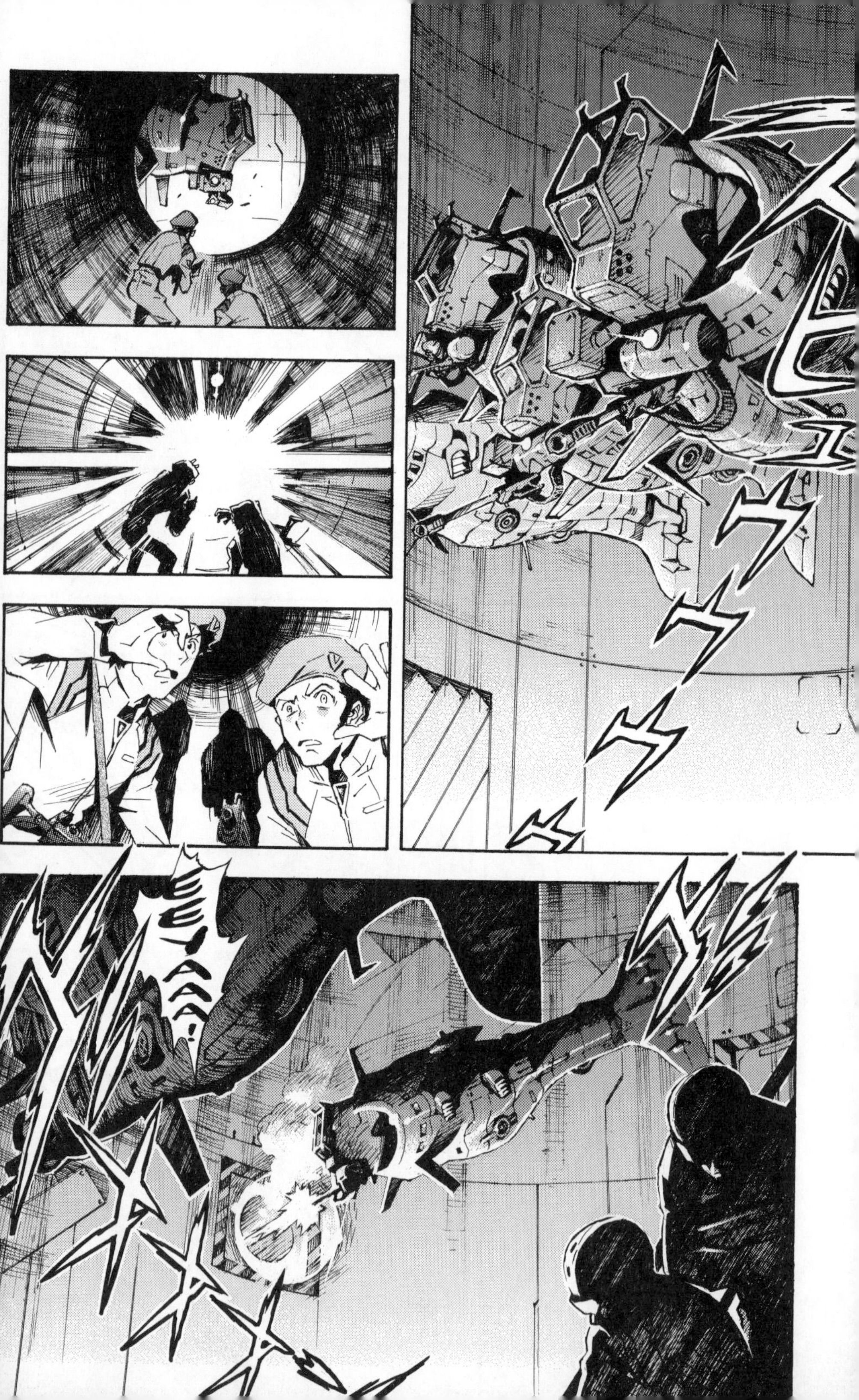
EEIAAA!

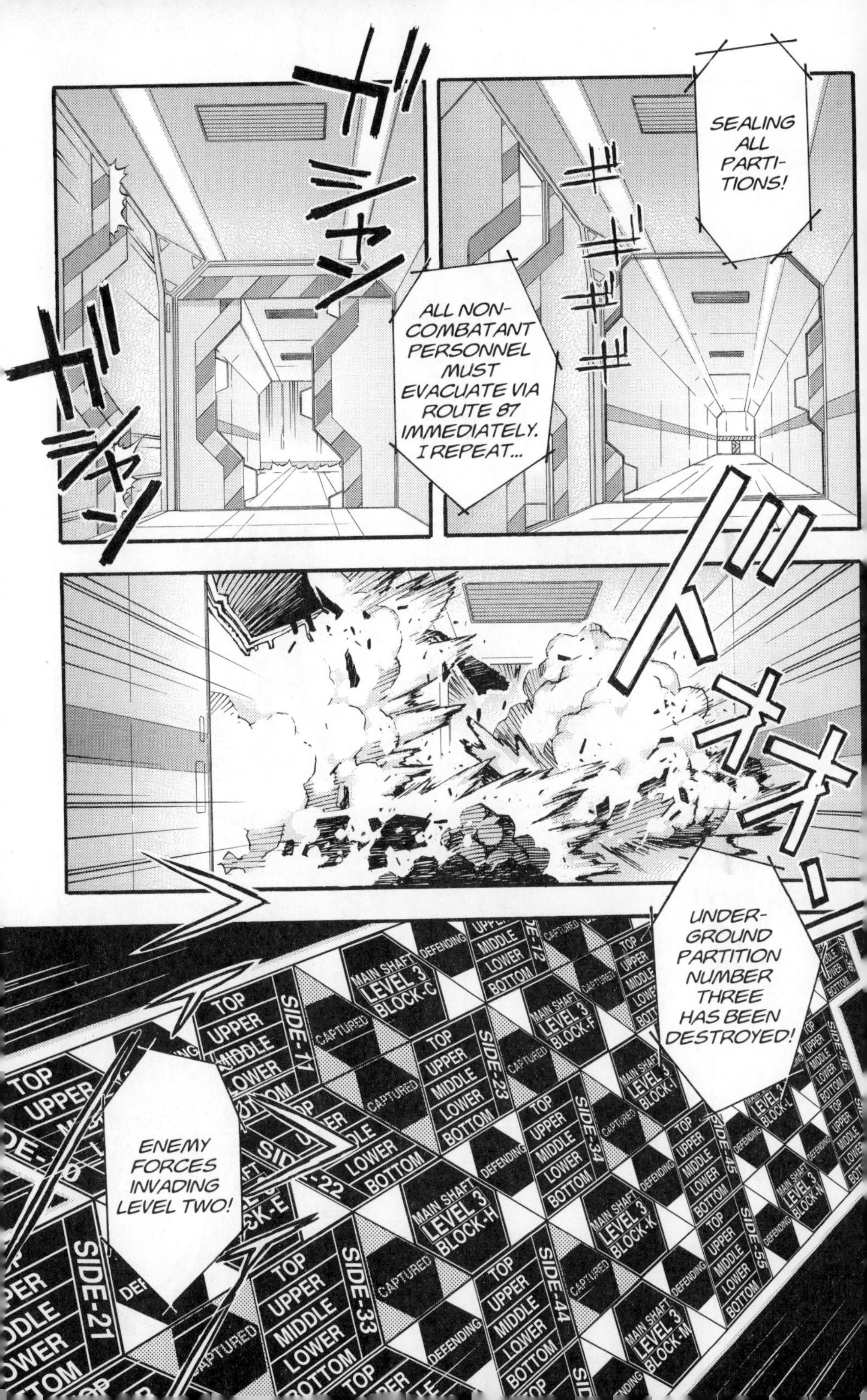
SEALING ALL PARTITIONS!
ギギギギギ
ALL NON-COMBATANT PERSONNEL MUST EVACUATE VIA ROUTE 87 IMMEDIATELY. I REPEAT...
ガシャン
ガシャン
ドオオー
UNDER-GROUND PARTITION NUMBER THREE HAS BEEN DESTROYED!
ENEMY FORCES INVADING LEVEL TWO!
MAIN SHAFT LEVEL 3 BLOCK-C
MAIN SHAFT LEVEL 3 BLOCK-F
MAIN SHAFT LEVEL 3 BLOCK-H
MAIN SHAFT LEVEL 3 BLOCK-K
MAIN SHAFT LEVEL 3 BLOCK-M
TOP UPPER MIDDLE LOWER BOTTOM
SIDE-11
SIDE-12
SIDE-21
SIDE-22
SIDE-23
SIDE-33
SIDE-34
SIDE-44
SIDE-45
SIDE-55
CAPTURED
DEFENDING

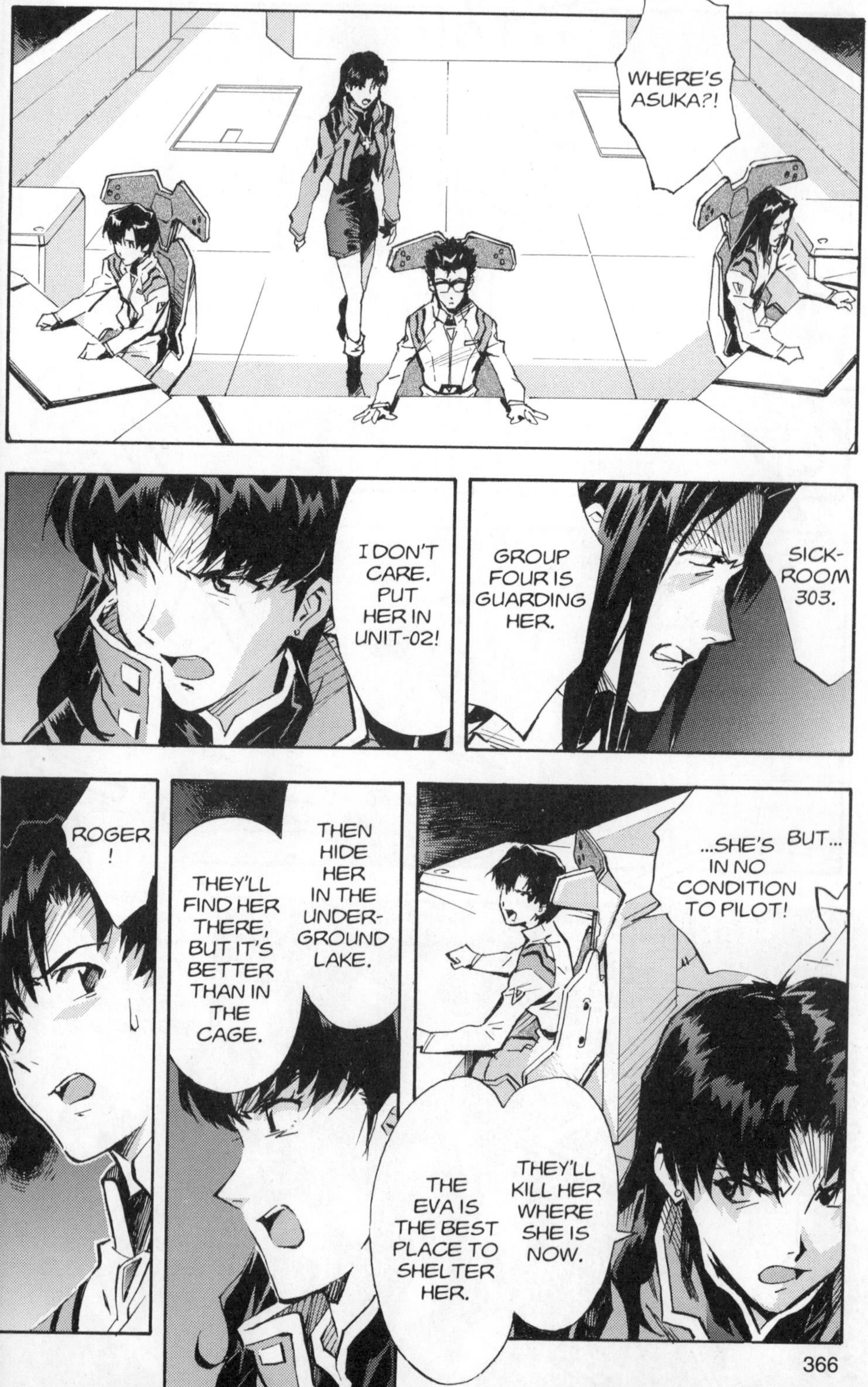
WHERE'S ASUKA?!
SICK-ROOM 303.
GROUP FOUR IS GUARDING HER.
I DON'T CARE. PUT HER IN UNIT-02!
BUT...
...SHE'S IN NO CONDITION TO PILOT!
THEY'LL KILL HER WHERE SHE IS NOW.
THE EVA IS THE BEST PLACE TO SHELTER HER.
THEN HIDE HER IN THE UNDERGROUND LAKE.
THEY'LL FIND HER THERE, BUT IT'S BETTER THAN IN THE CAGE.
ROGER!

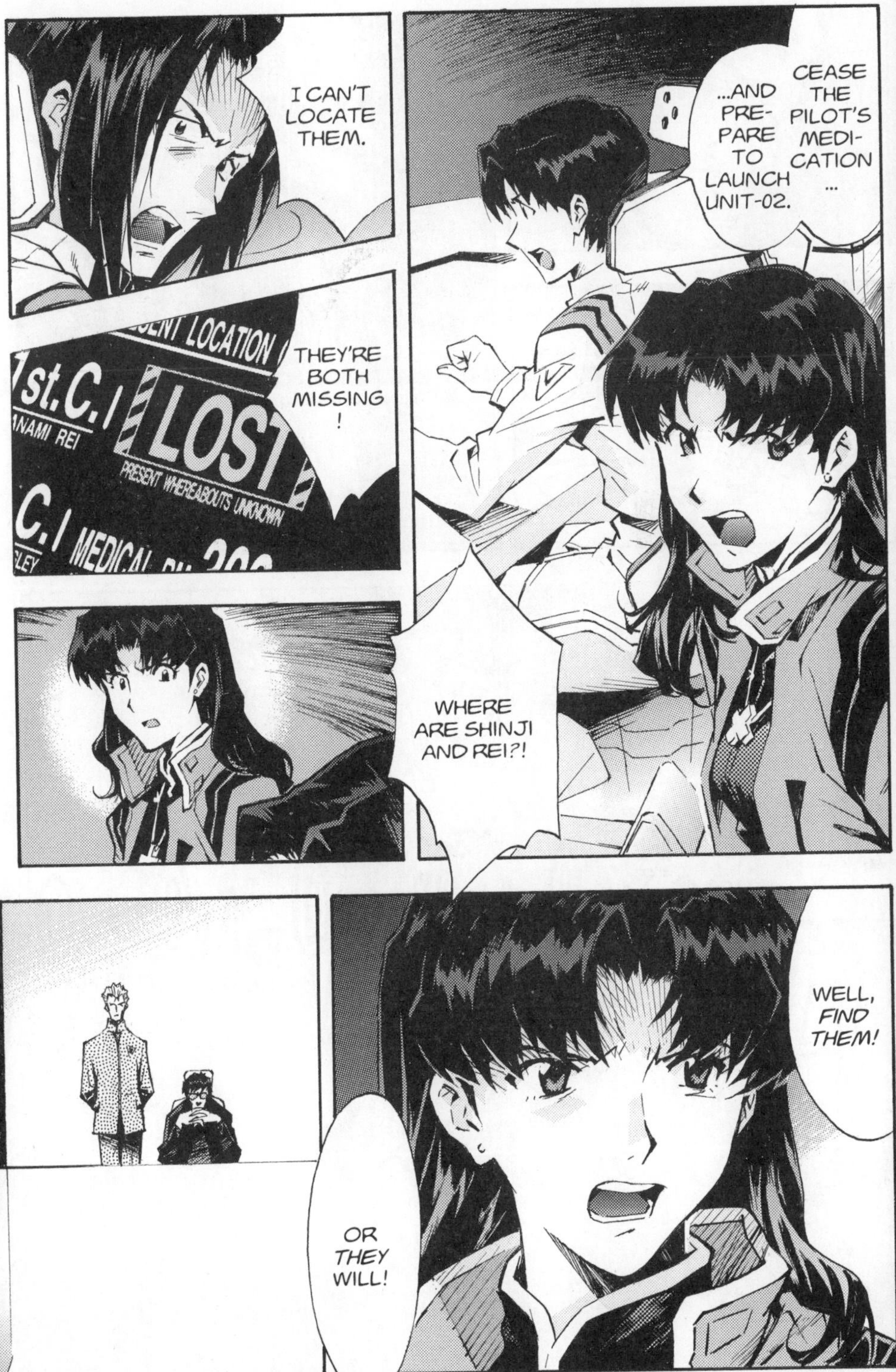
CEASE THE PILOT'S MEDICATION ...
...AND PREPARE TO LAUNCH UNIT-02.
WHERE ARE SHINJI AND REI?!
I CAN'T LOCATE THEM.
1st.C.I
LOST
PRESENT WHEREABOUTS UNKNOWN
THEY'RE BOTH MISSING!
WELL, FIND THEM!
OR THEY WILL!

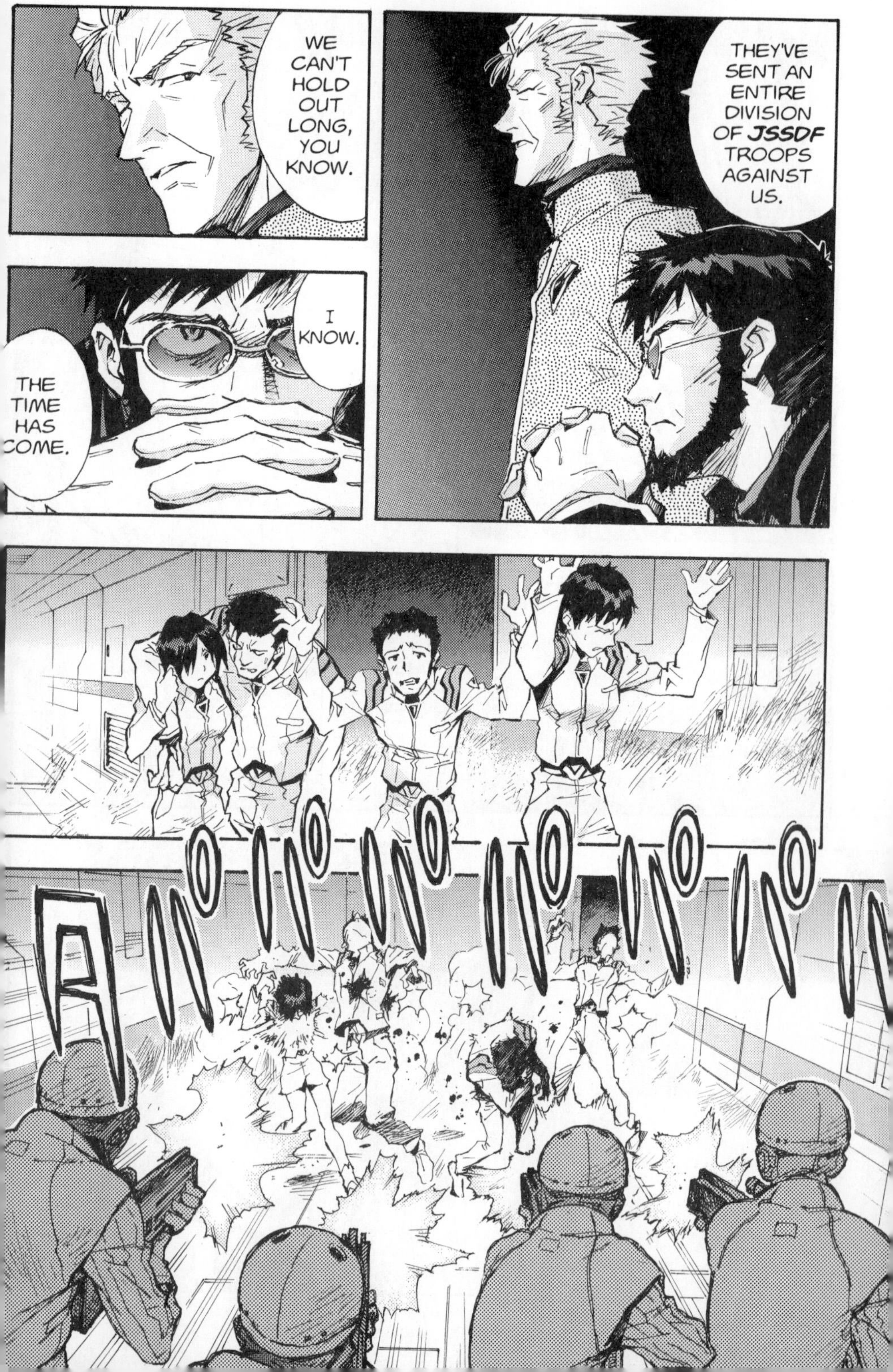
THEY'VE SENT AN ENTIRE DIVISION OF JSSDF TROOPS AGAINST US.
WE CAN'T HOLD OUT LONG, YOU KNOW.
I KNOW.
THE TIME HAS COME.

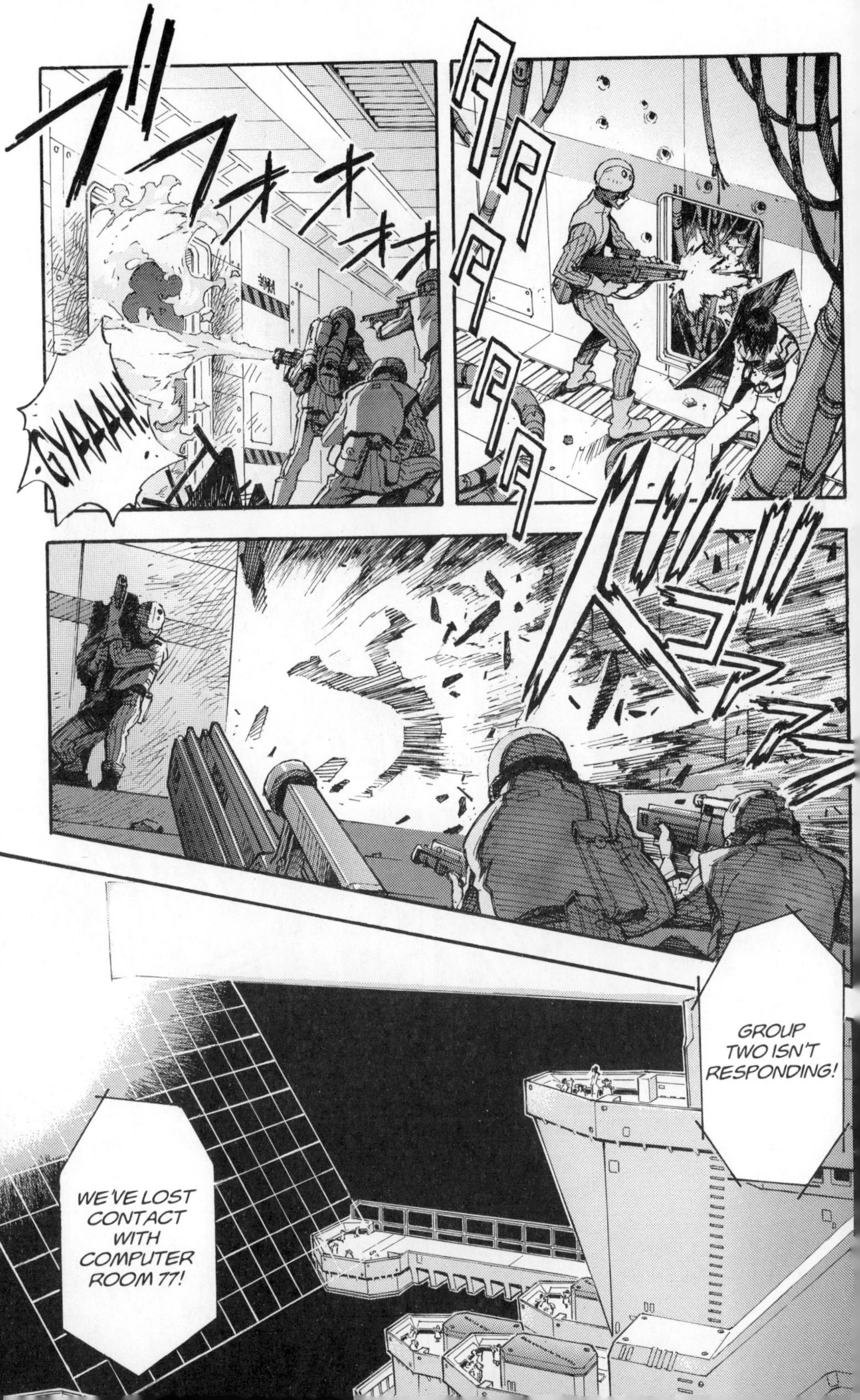
GYAAAH!
GROUP TWO ISN'T RESPONDING!
WE'VE LOST CONTACT WITH COMPUTER ROOM 77!

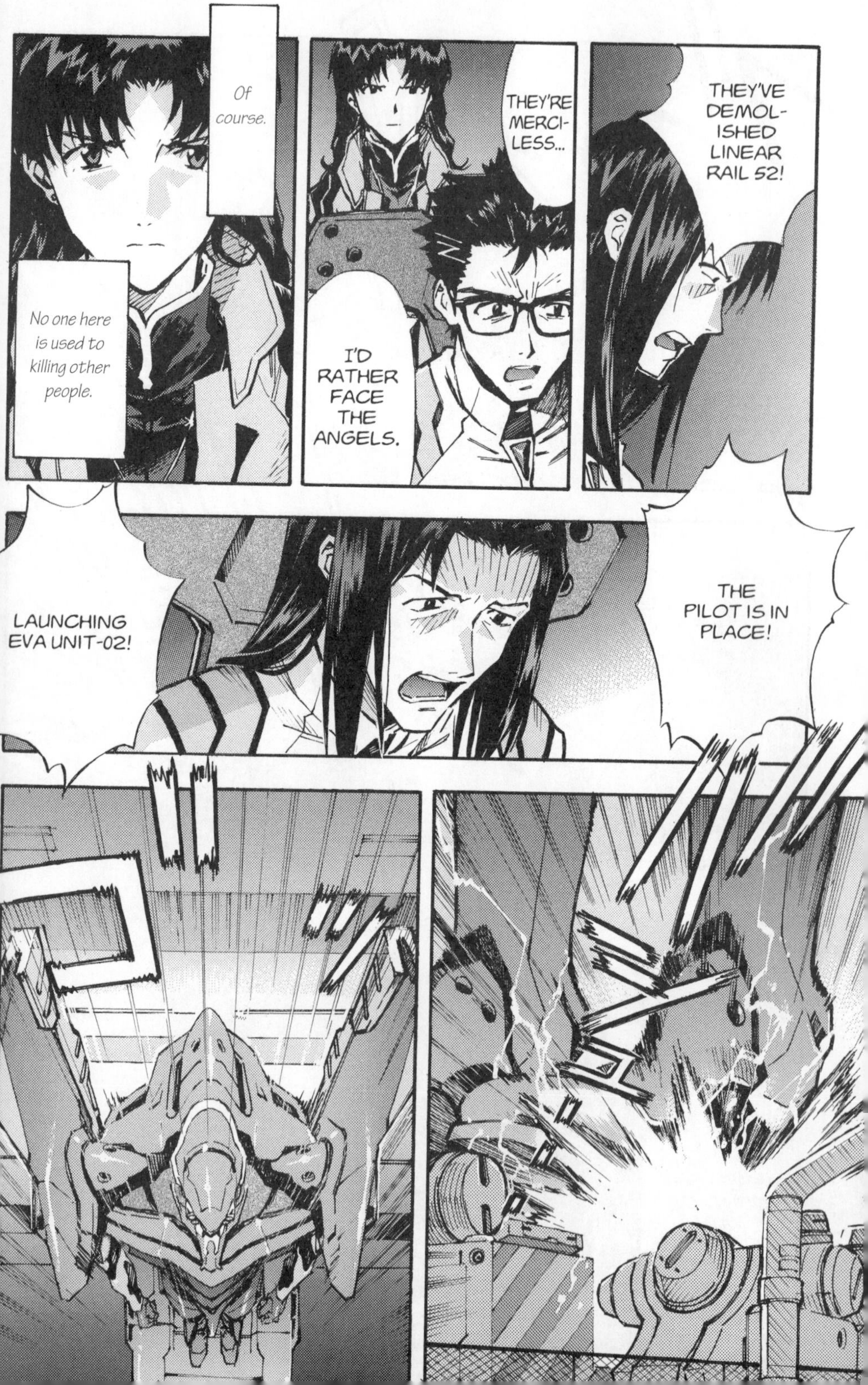
THEY'VE DEMOL-ISHED LINEAR RAIL 52!
THEY'RE MERCI-LESS...
I'D RATHER FACE THE ANGELS.
Of course.
No one here is used to killing other people.
THE PILOT IS IN PLACE!
LAUNCHING EVA UNIT-02!

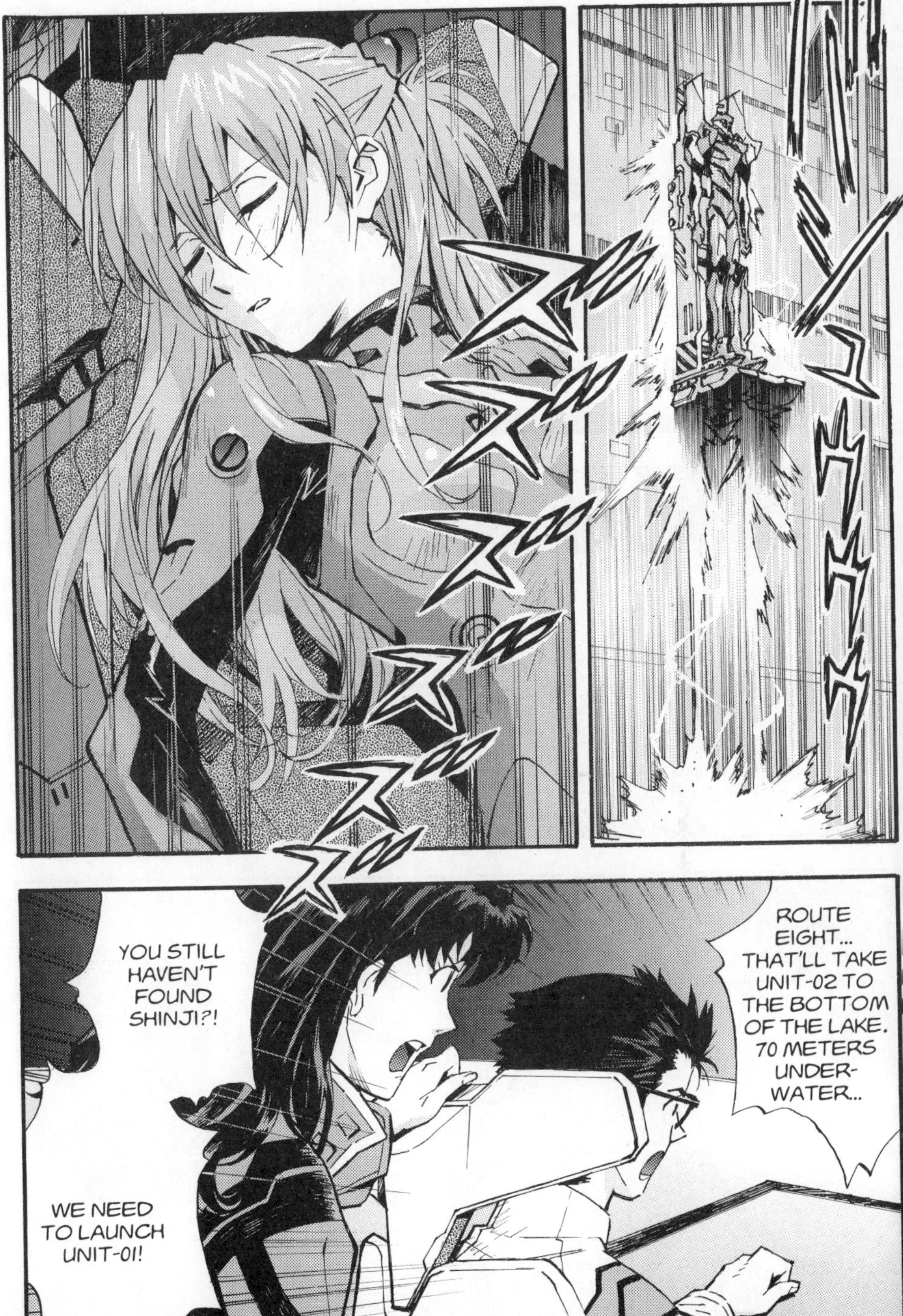
ROUTE EIGHT... THAT'LL TAKE UNIT-02 TO THE BOTTOM OF THE LAKE. 70 METERS UNDER-WATER...
YOU STILL HAVEN'T FOUND SHINJI?!
WE NEED TO LAUNCH UNIT-01!

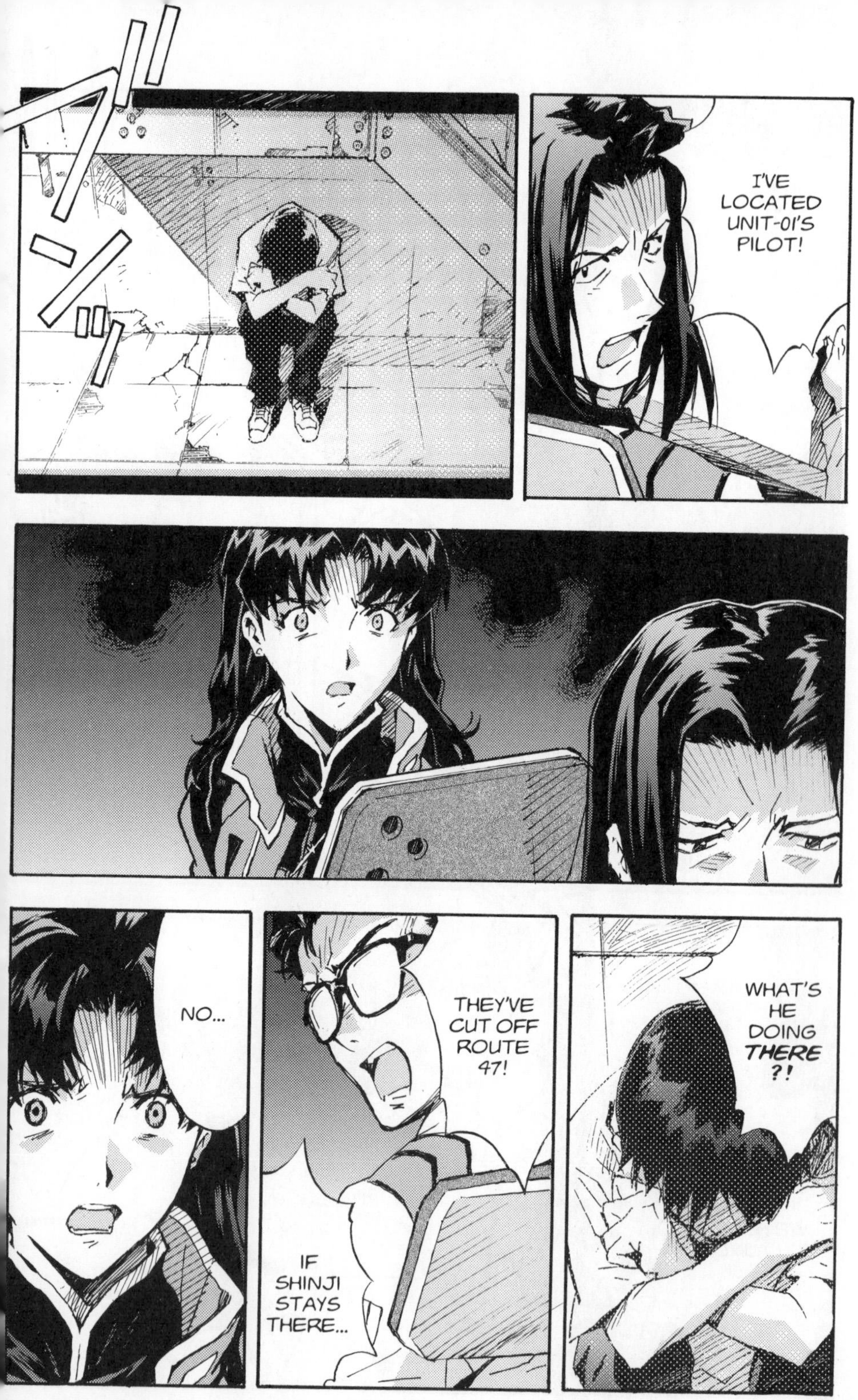
I'VE LOCATED UNIT-01'S PILOT!
WHAT'S HE DOING ***THERE***?!
THEY'VE CUT OFF ROUTE 47!
IF SHINJI STAYS THERE...
NO...

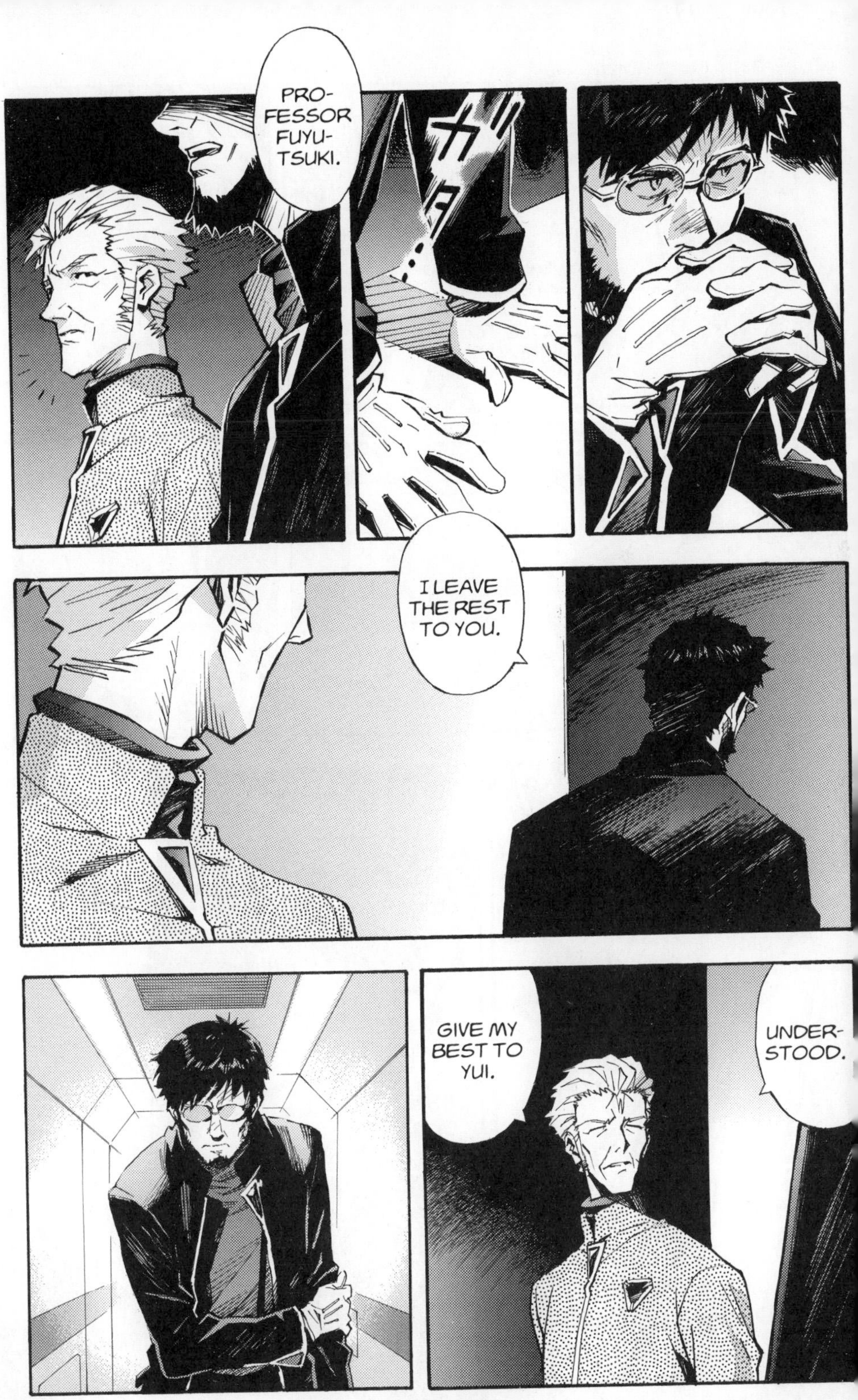
PRO-FESSOR FUYU-TSUKI.
I LEAVE THE REST TO YOU.
UNDER-STOOD.
GIVE MY BEST TO YUI.

HEH...

SO THIS IS WHERE YOU CHOSE TO APPEAR...

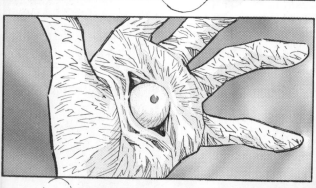

sob...

sob...

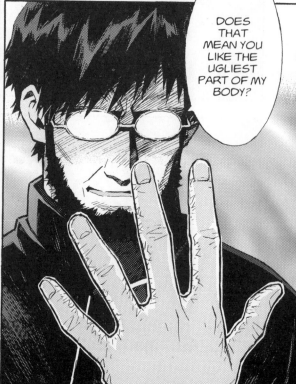

DOES THAT MEAN YOU LIKE THE UGLIEST PART OF MY BODY?

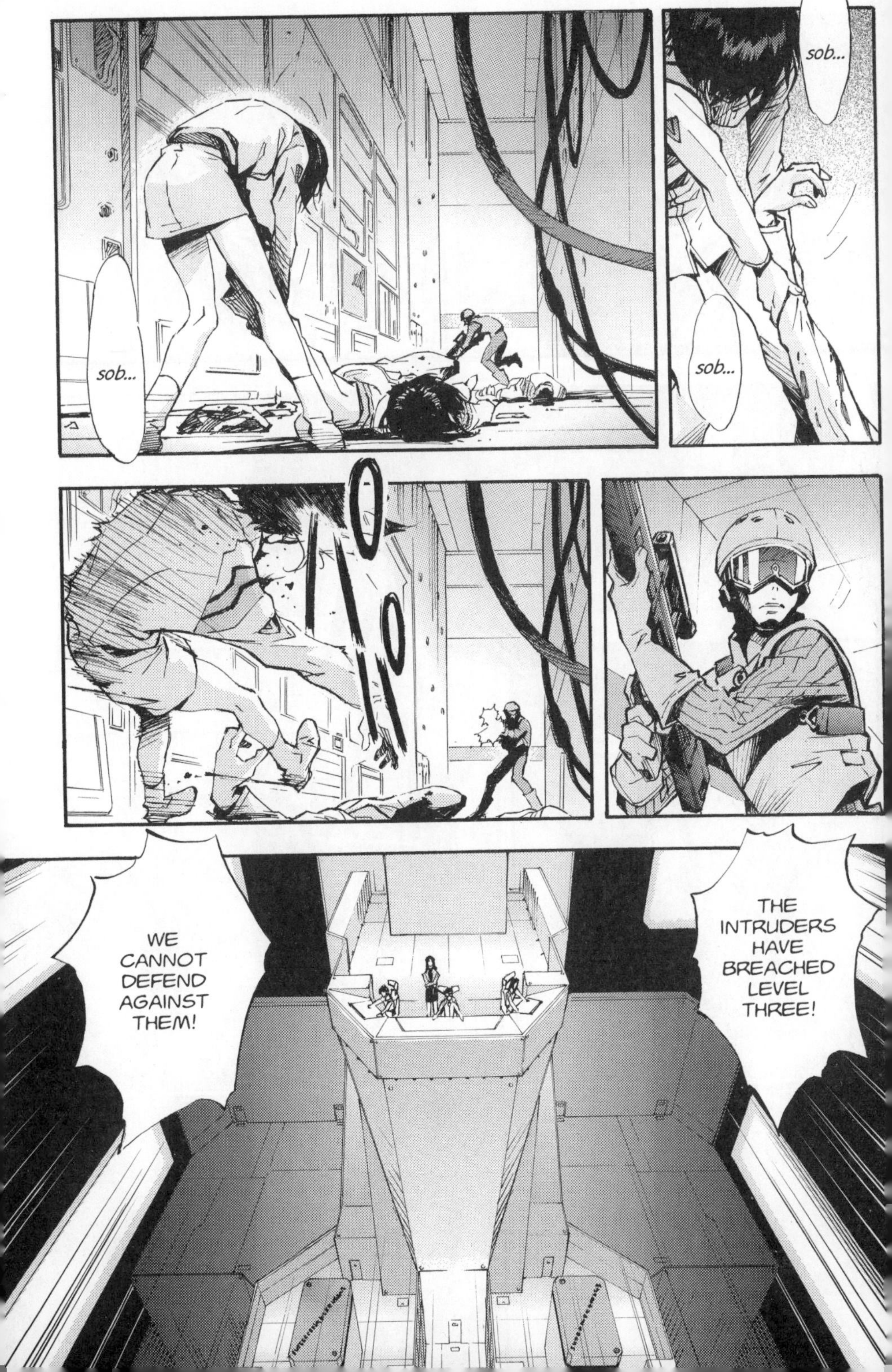
sob...
sob...
sob...
THE INTRUDERS HAVE BREACHED LEVEL THREE!
WE CANNOT DEFEND AGAINST THEM!

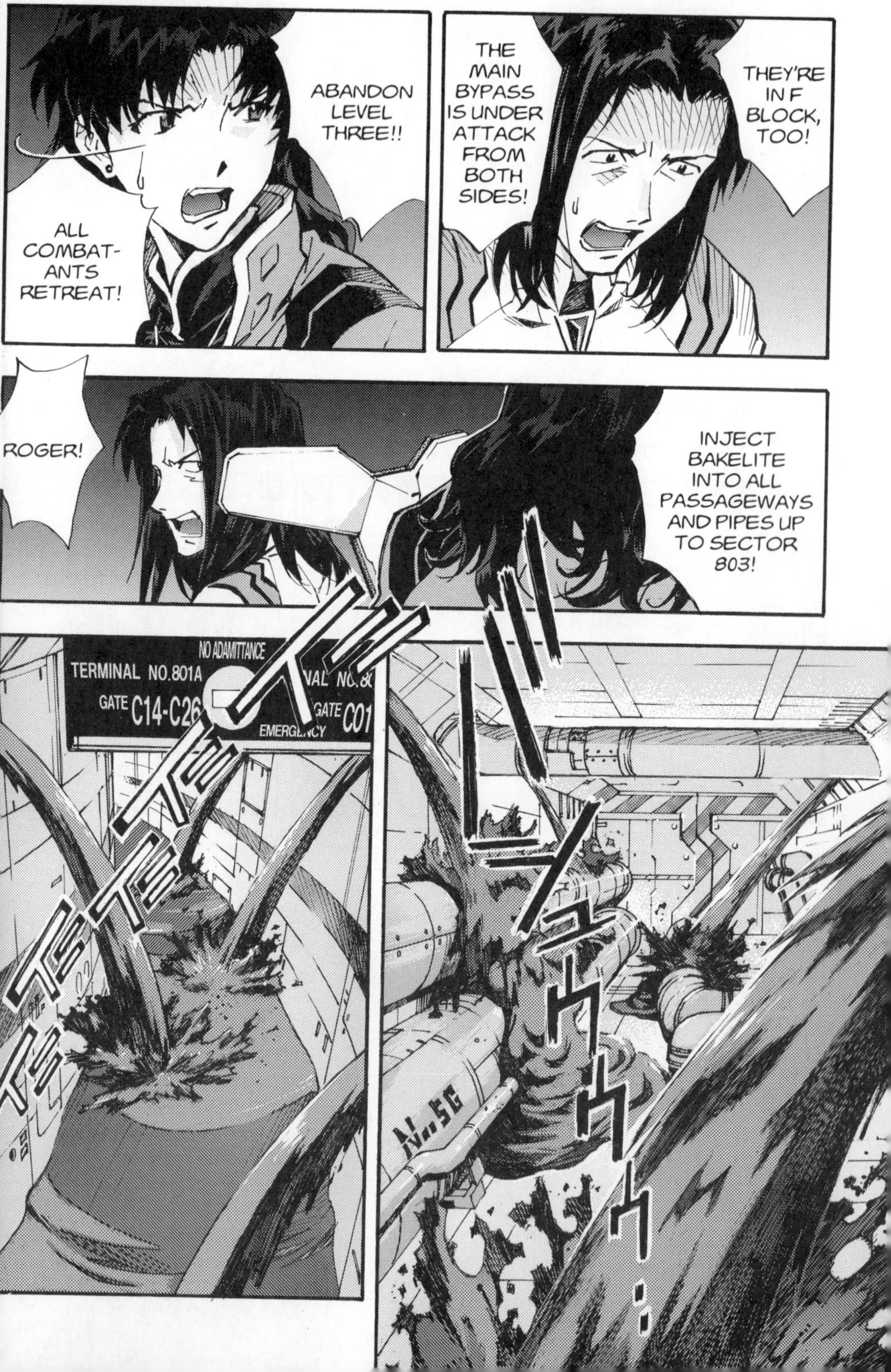
THEY'RE IN F BLOCK, TOO!
THE MAIN BYPASS IS UNDER ATTACK FROM BOTH SIDES!
ABANDON LEVEL THREE!!
ALL COMBAT-ANTS RETREAT!
INJECT BAKELITE INTO ALL PASSAGEWAYS AND PIPES UP TO SECTOR 803!
ROGER!
NO ADAMITTANCE
TERMINAL NO.801A
GATE C14-C26
GATE C01
EMERGENCY
No.5G

THAT...

...SHOULD HOLD THEM AWHILE.

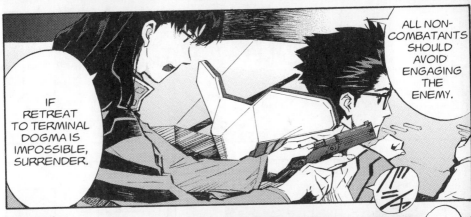

ALL NON-COMBATANTS SHOULD AVOID ENGAGING THE ENEMY.

IF RETREAT TO TERMINAL DOGMA IS IMPOSSIBLE, SURRENDER.

ROGER.

TAKE OVER FOR ME.

I'M SORRY.

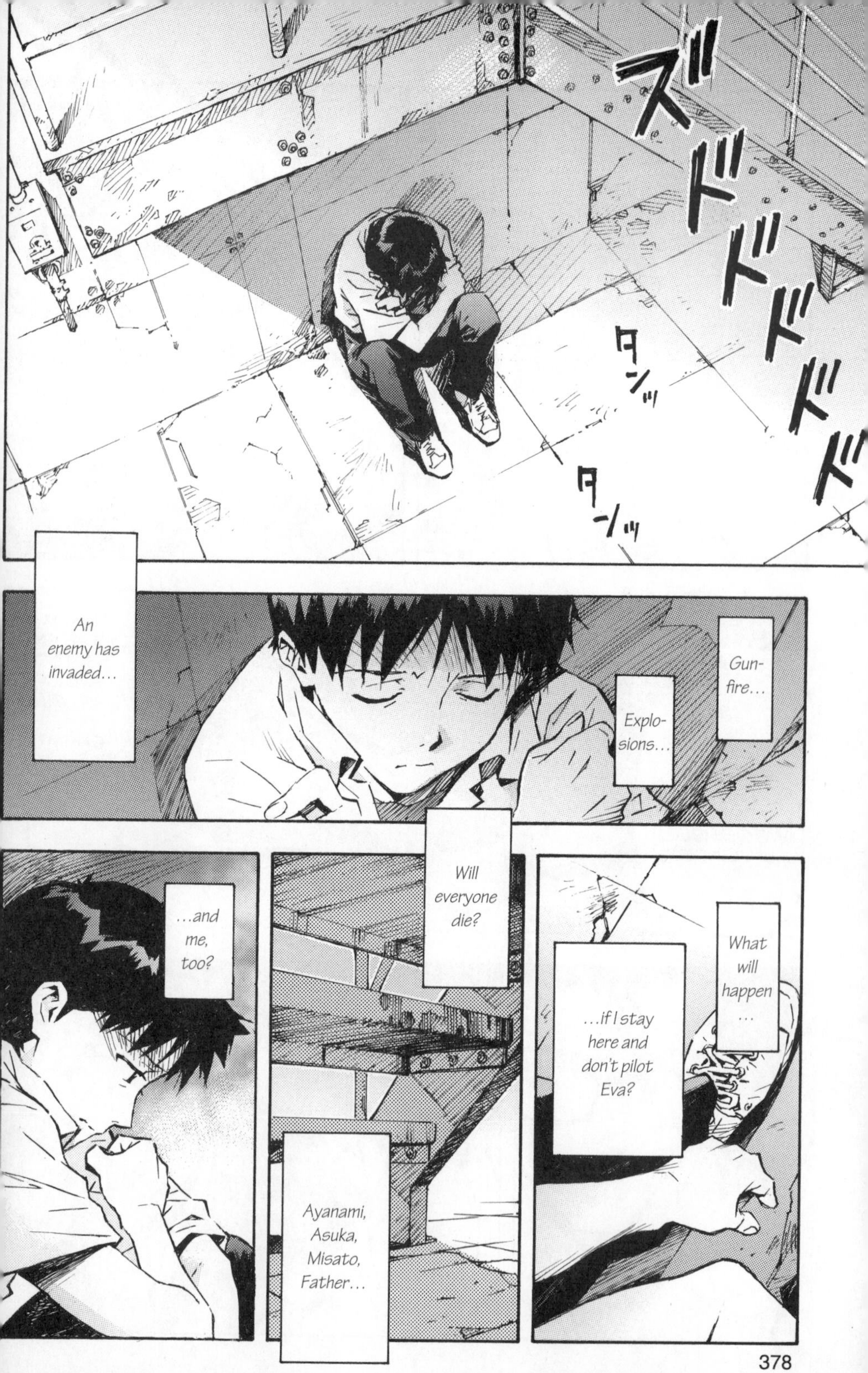
ズドドドドド
タンッ
タンッ
Gun-fire…
Explo-sions…
An enemy has invaded…
What will happen…
…if I stay here and don't pilot Eva?
Will everyone die?
Ayanami, Asuka, Misato, Father…
…and me, too?

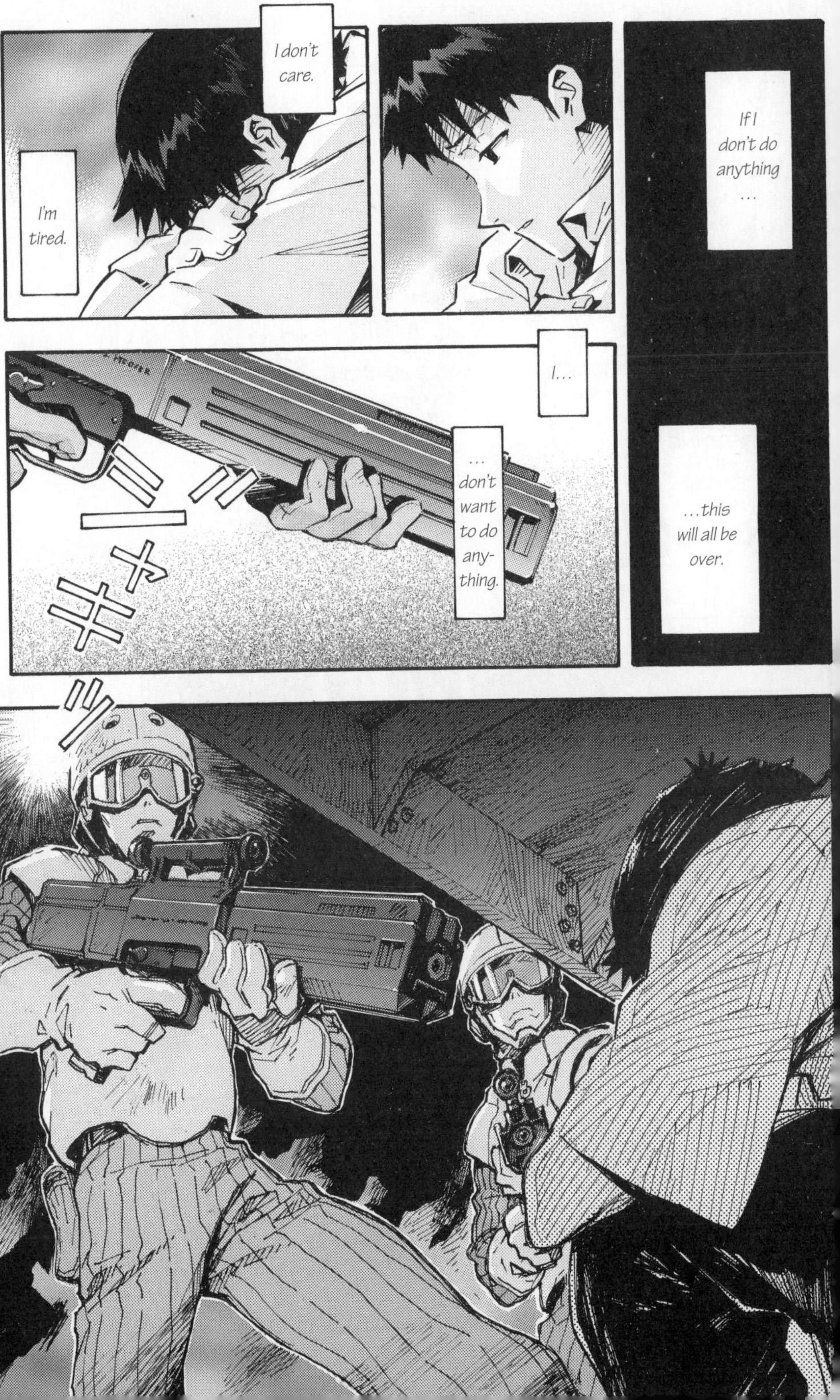
If I don't do anything …
…this will all be over.
I don't care.
I'm tired.
I…
… don't want to do any-thing.

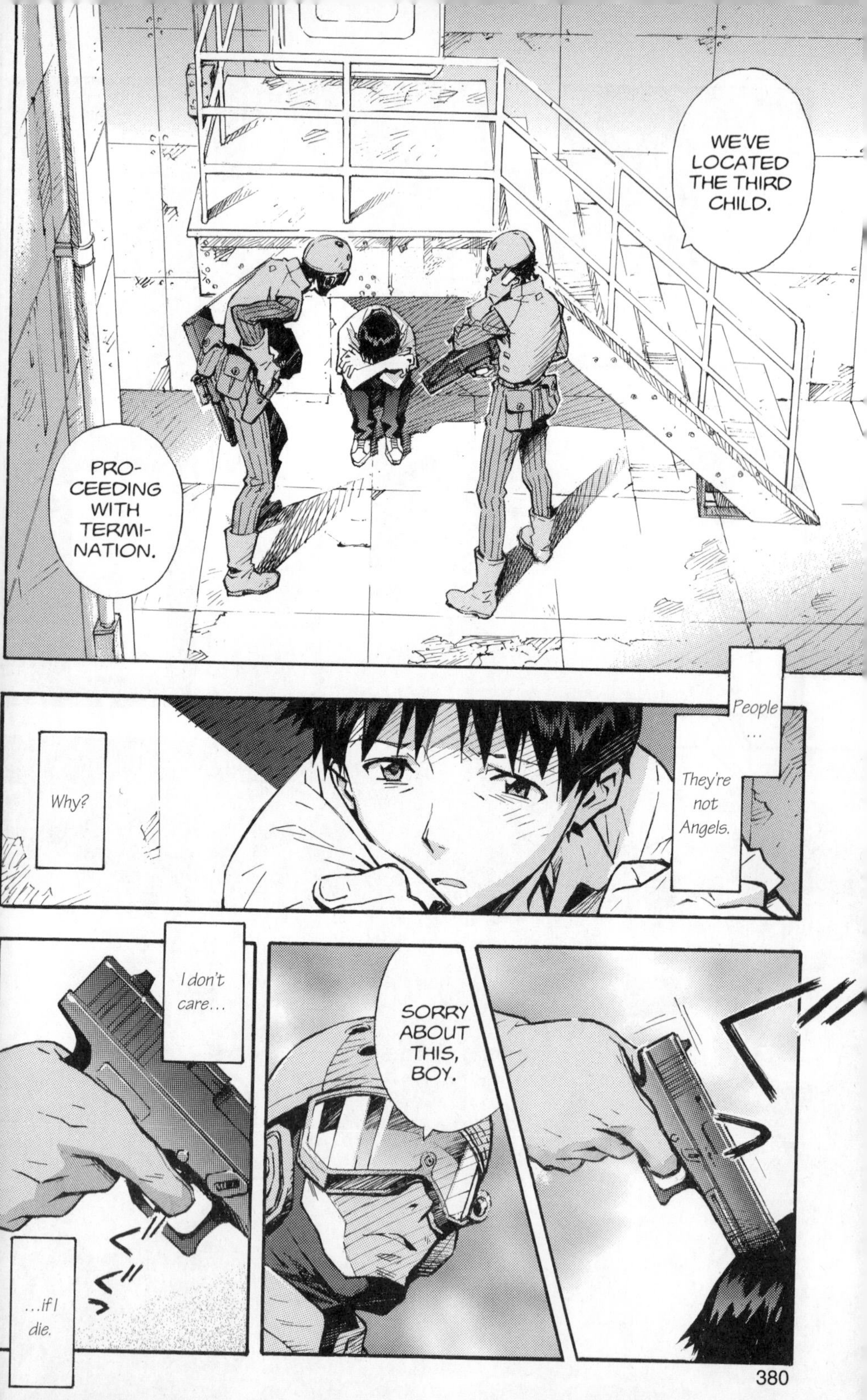

WE'VE LOCATED THE THIRD CHILD.
PRO-CEEDING WITH TERMI-NATION.
People... They're not Angels.
Why?
SORRY ABOUT THIS, BOY.
I don't care...
...if I die.

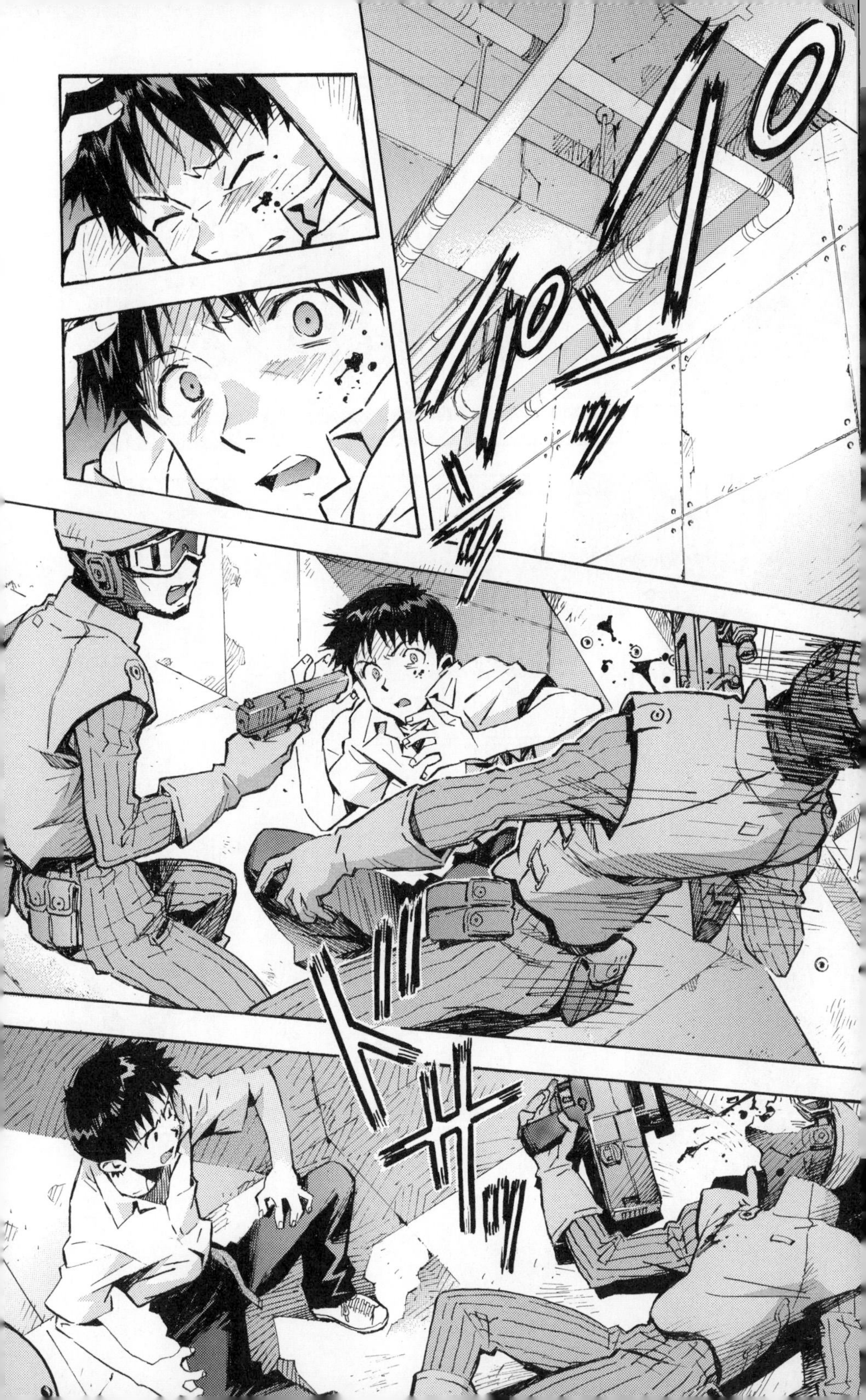
ドサッ

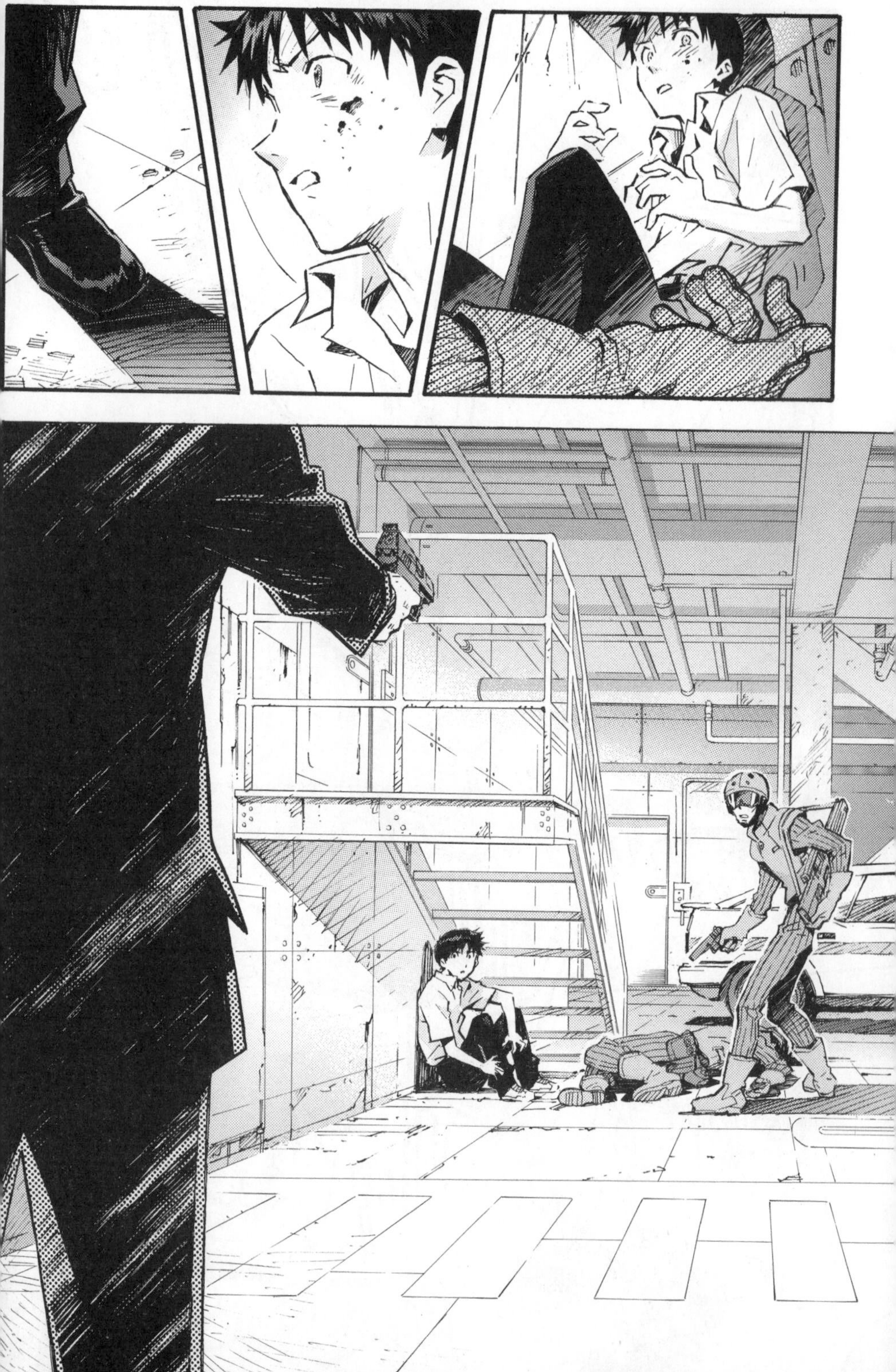

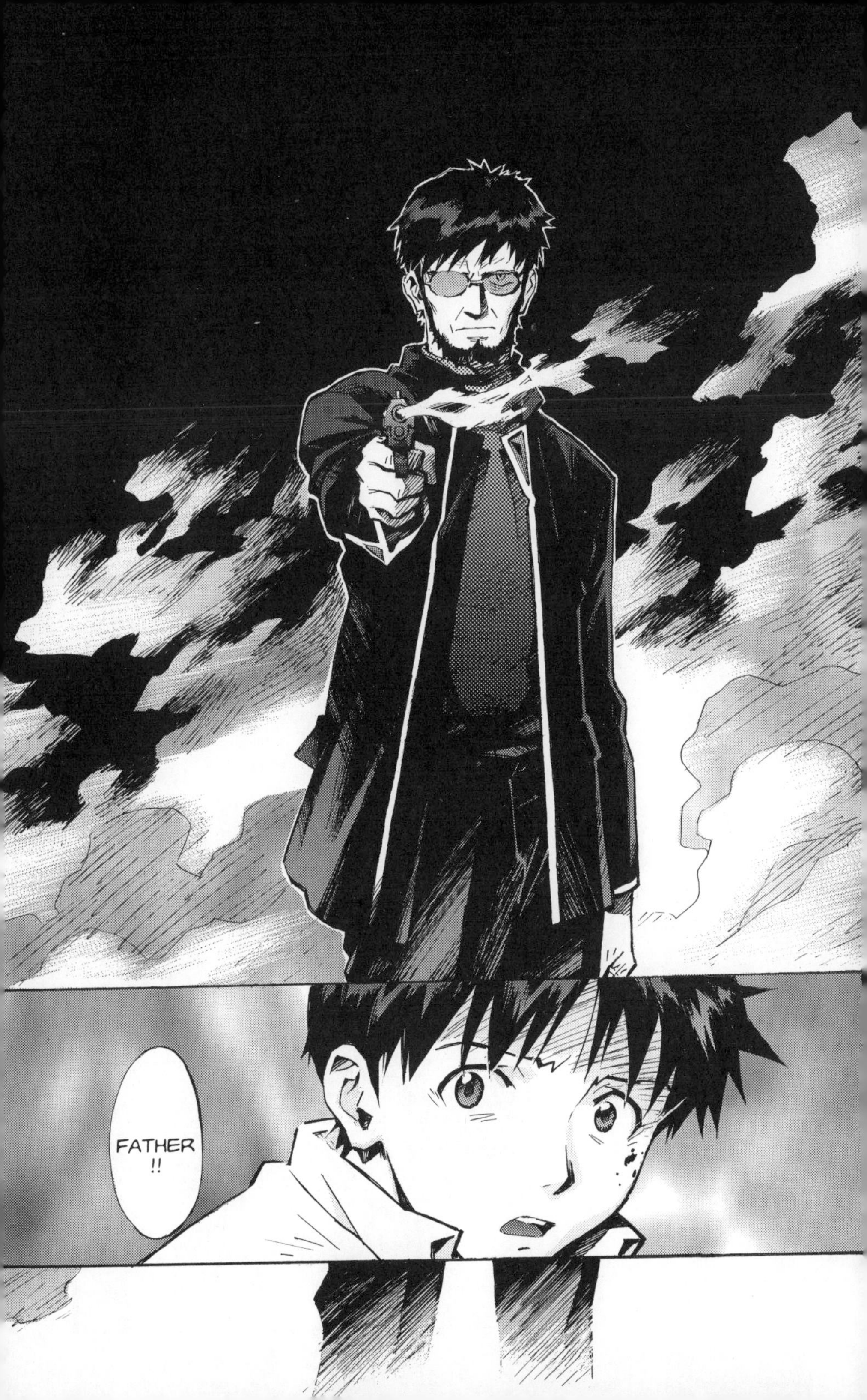
FATHER !!

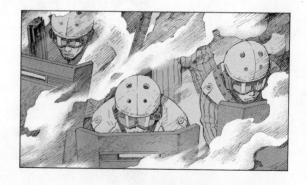

NEON GENESIS EVANGELION

STAGE 78: FATHER AND CHILD

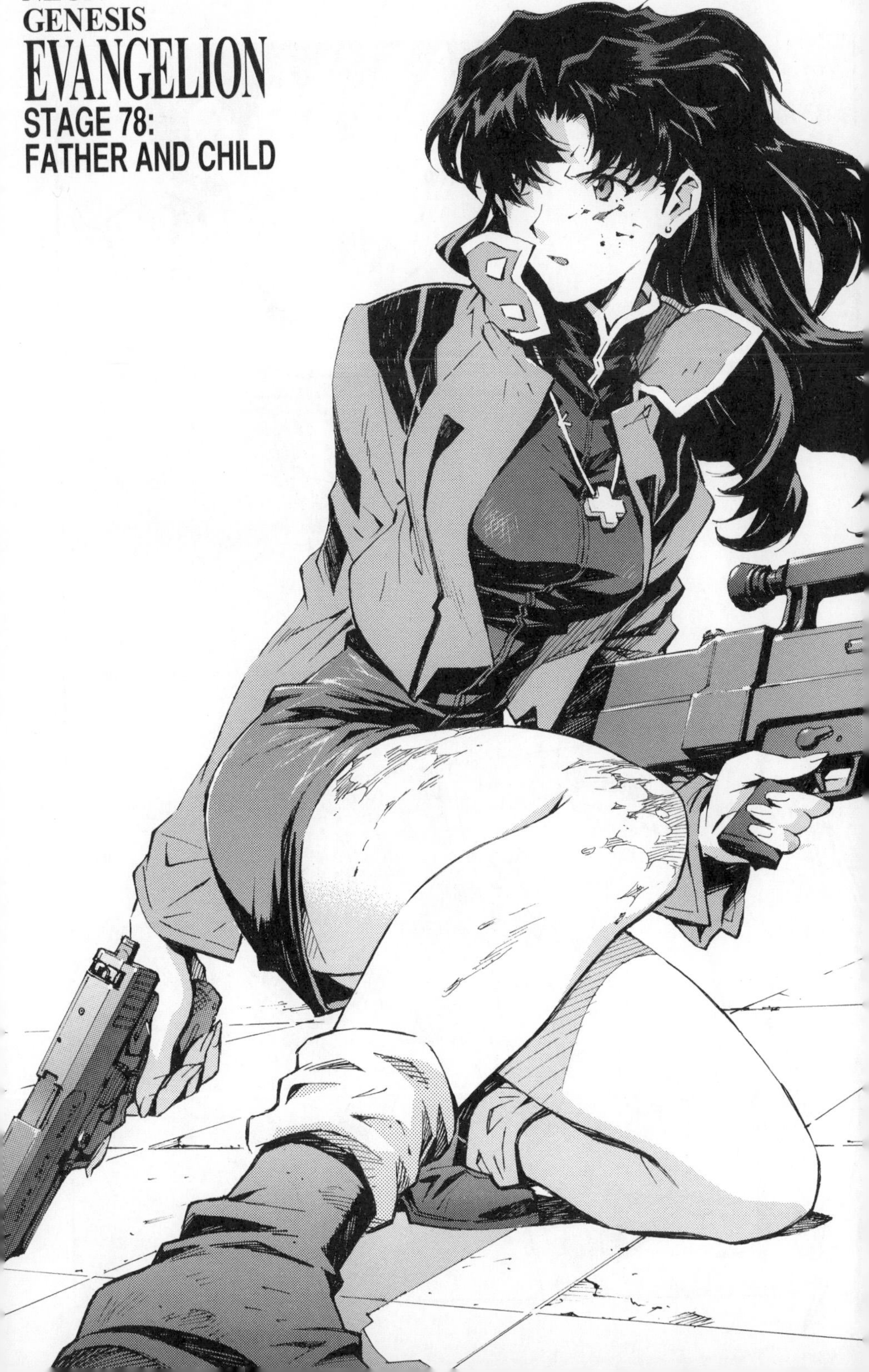

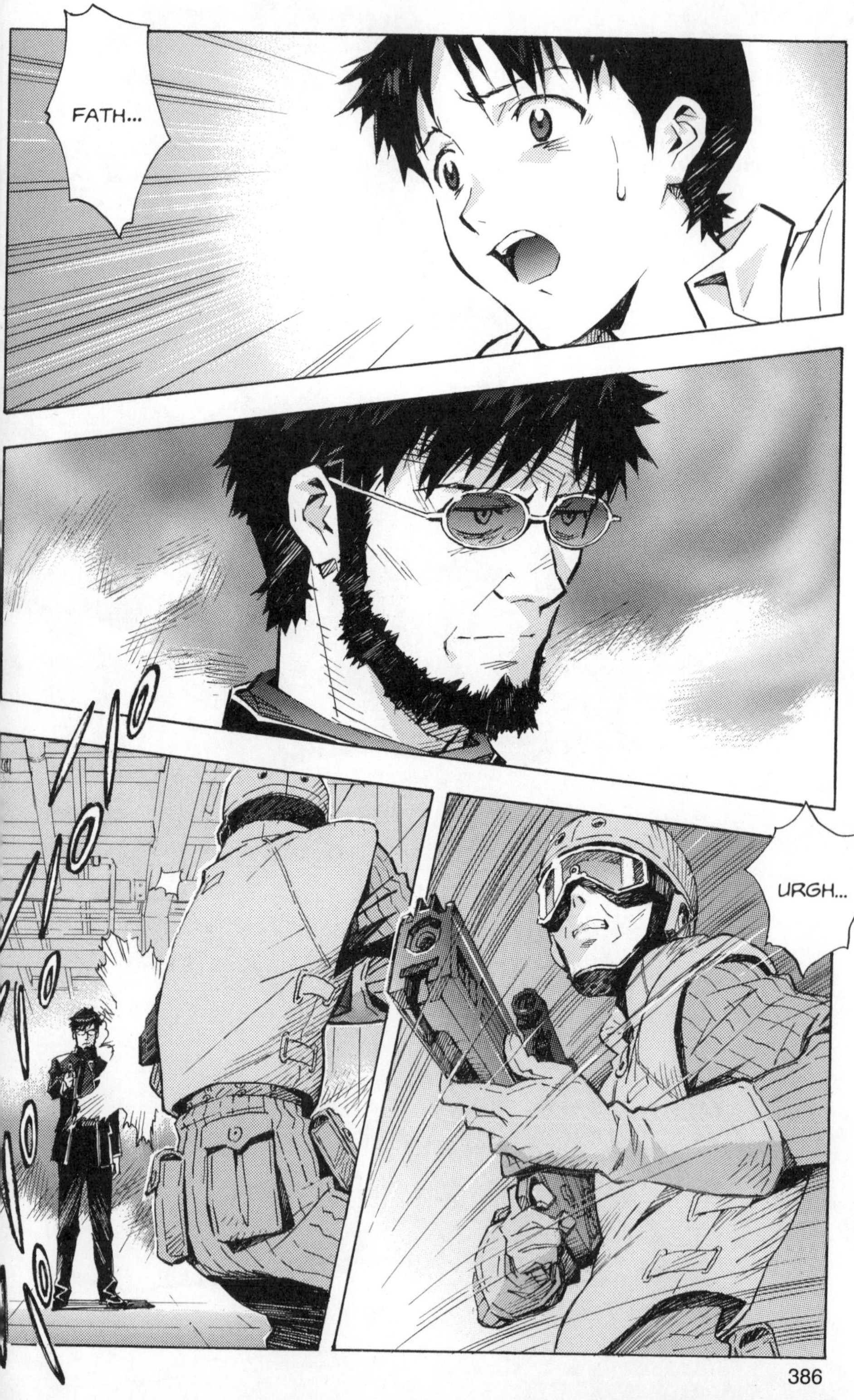
FATH...
URGH...

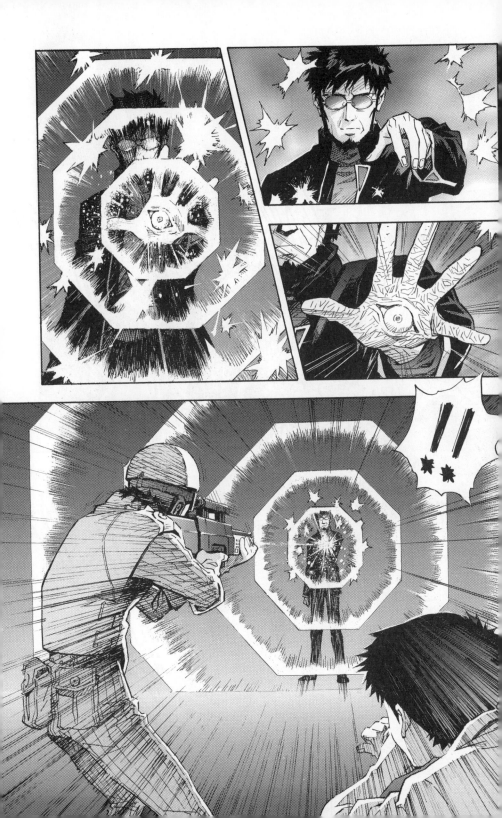

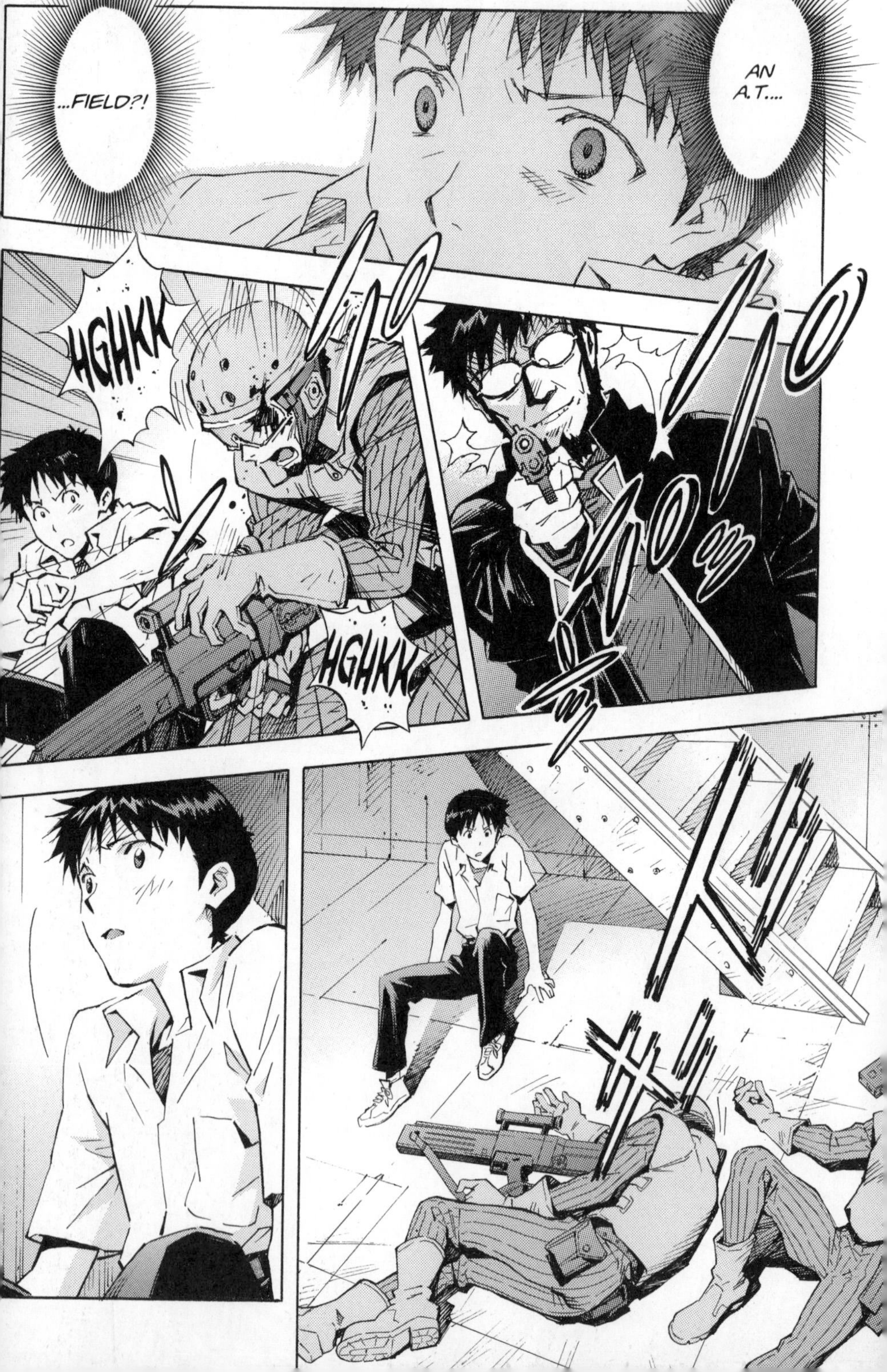
AN A.T....
...FIELD?!
HGHKK
HGHKK

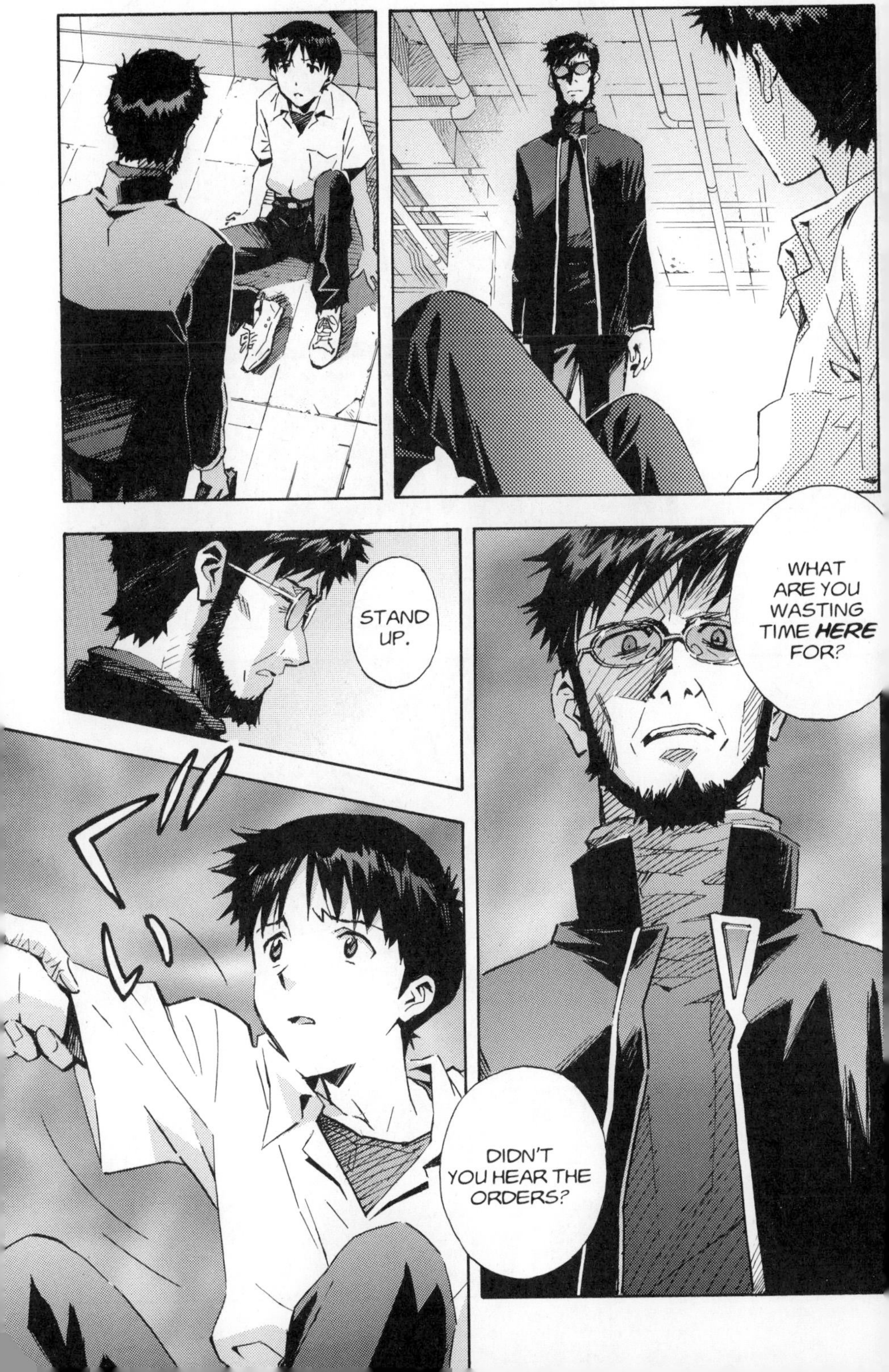
WHAT ARE YOU WASTING TIME HERE FOR?
DIDN'T YOU HEAR THE ORDERS?
STAND UP.

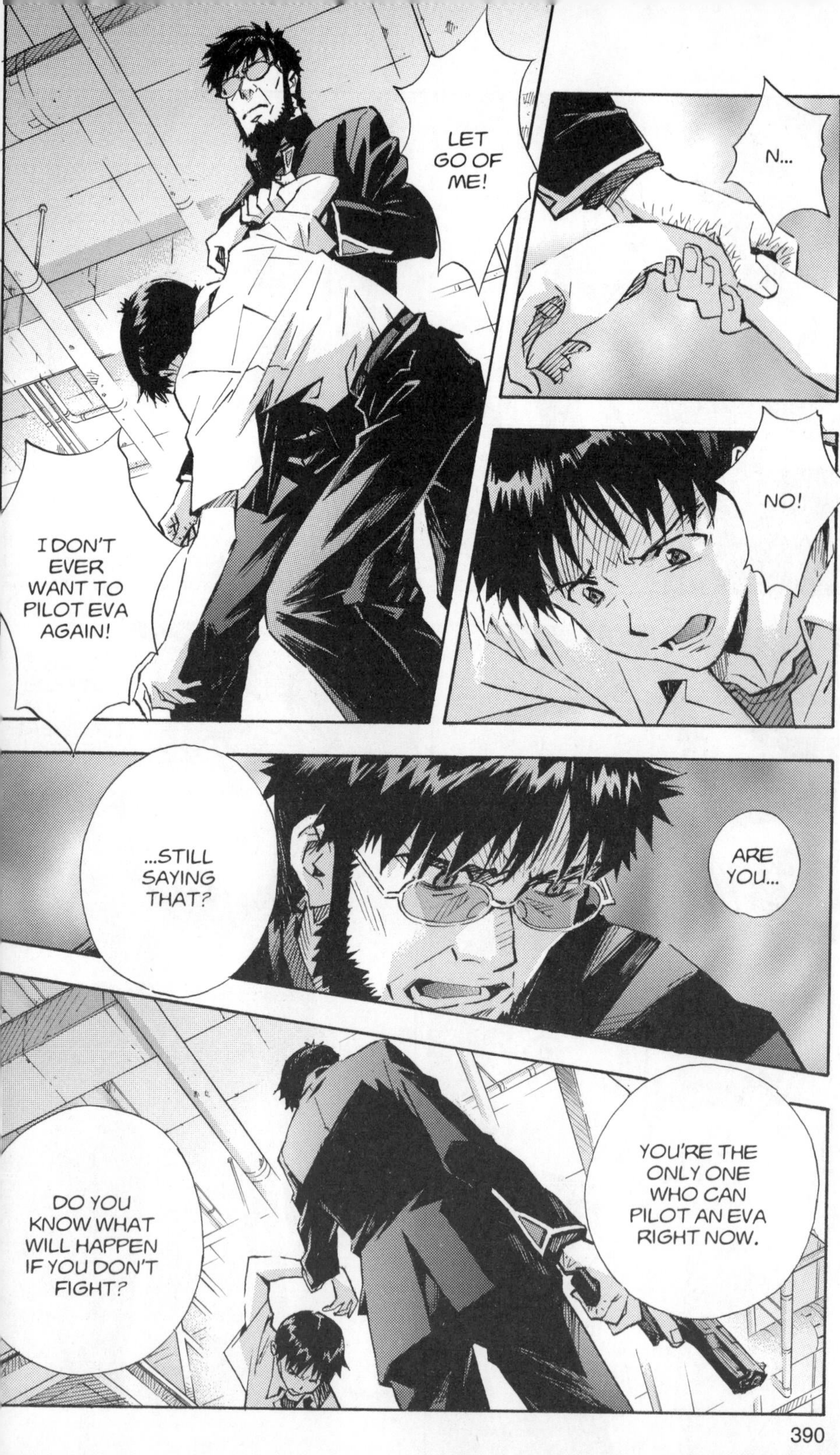
N...
NO!
LET GO OF ME!
I DON'T EVER WANT TO PILOT EVA AGAIN!
ARE YOU...
...STILL SAYING THAT?
YOU'RE THE ONLY ONE WHO CAN PILOT AN EVA RIGHT NOW.
DO YOU KNOW WHAT WILL HAPPEN IF YOU DON'T FIGHT?

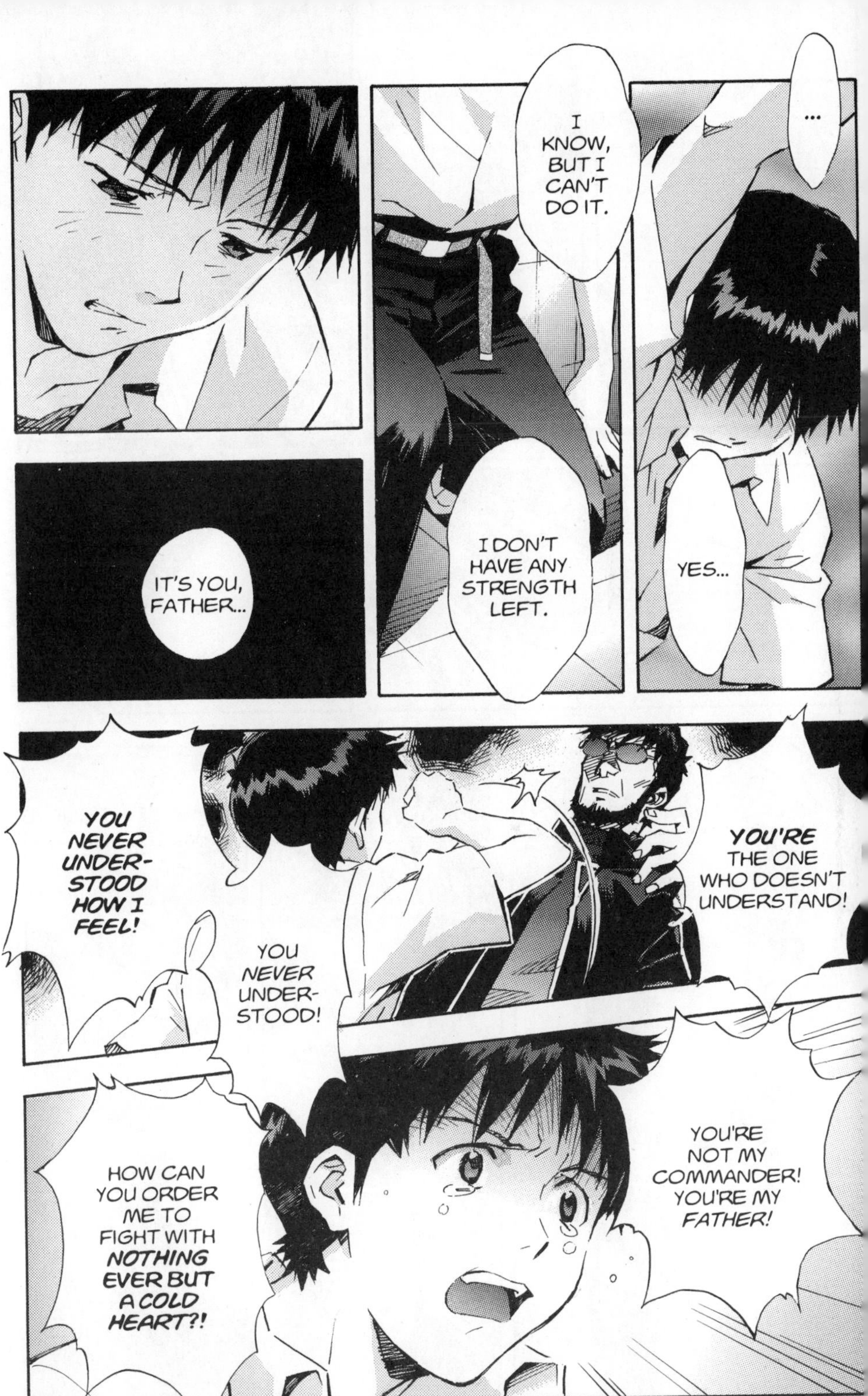
...
YES...
I KNOW, BUT I CAN'T DO IT.
I DON'T HAVE ANY STRENGTH LEFT.
IT'S YOU, FATHER...
YOU'RE THE ONE WHO DOESN'T UNDERSTAND!
YOU NEVER UNDERSTOOD!
YOU NEVER UNDERSTOOD HOW I FEEL!
YOU'RE NOT MY COMMANDER! YOU'RE MY FATHER!
HOW CAN YOU ORDER ME TO FIGHT WITH NOTHING EVER BUT A COLD HEART?!

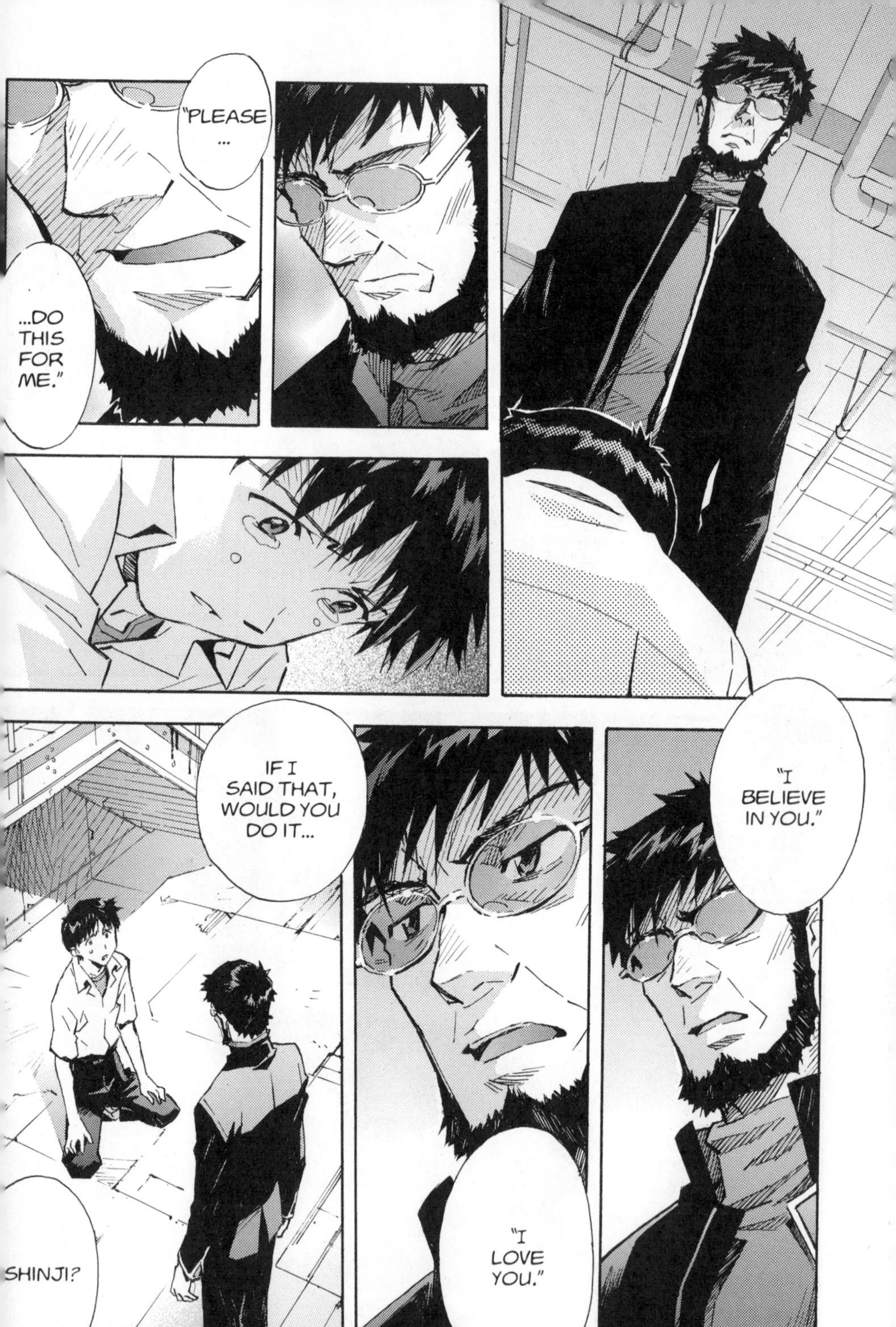
"PLEASE
...
...DO THIS FOR ME."
"I BELIEVE IN YOU."
"I LOVE YOU."
IF I SAID THAT, WOULD YOU DO IT...
SHINJI?

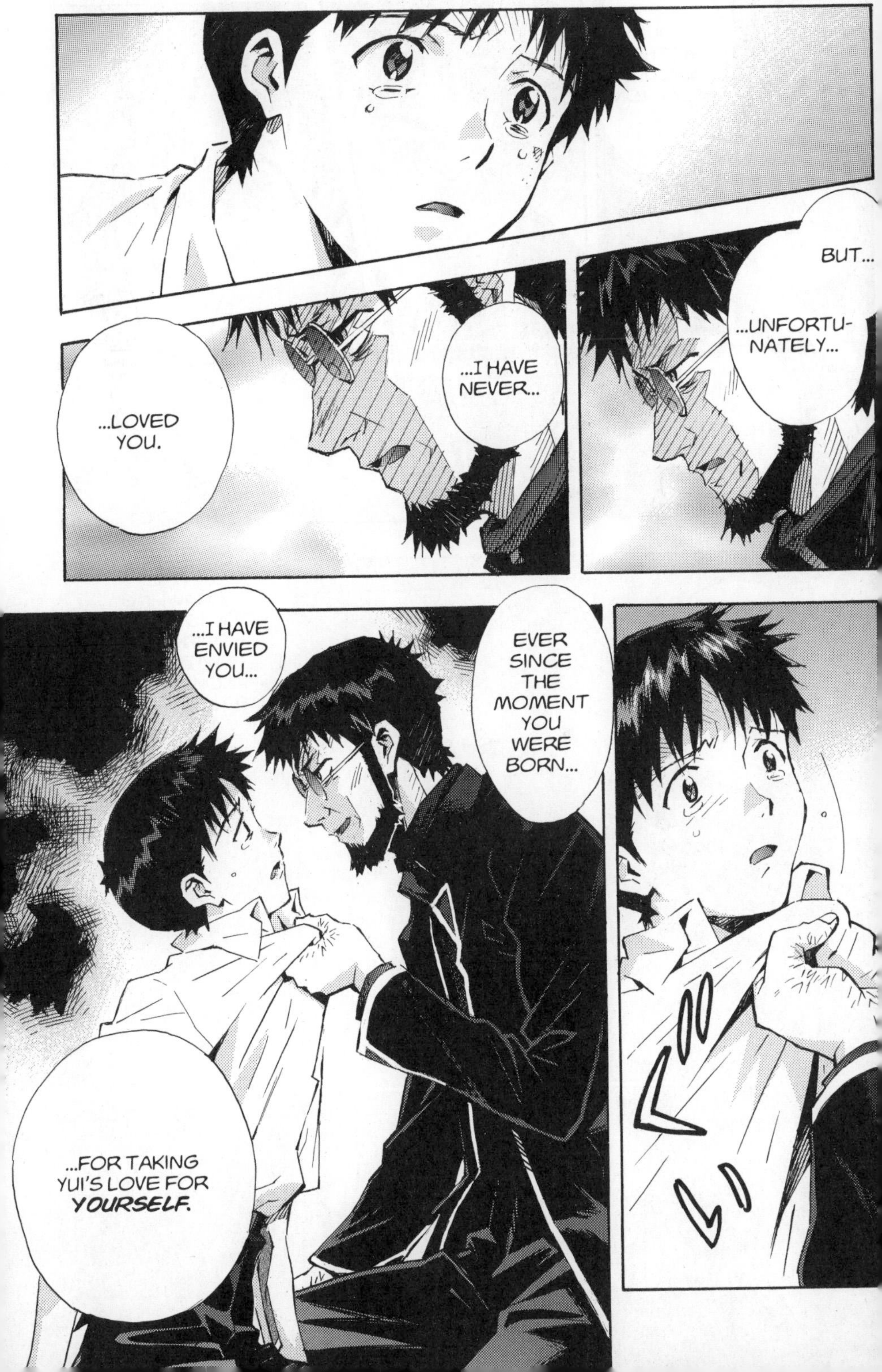
BUT...
...UNFORTU-NATELY...
...I HAVE NEVER...
...LOVED YOU.
EVER SINCE THE MOMENT YOU WERE BORN...
...I HAVE ENVIED YOU...
...FOR TAKING YUI'S LOVE FOR ***YOURSELF***.

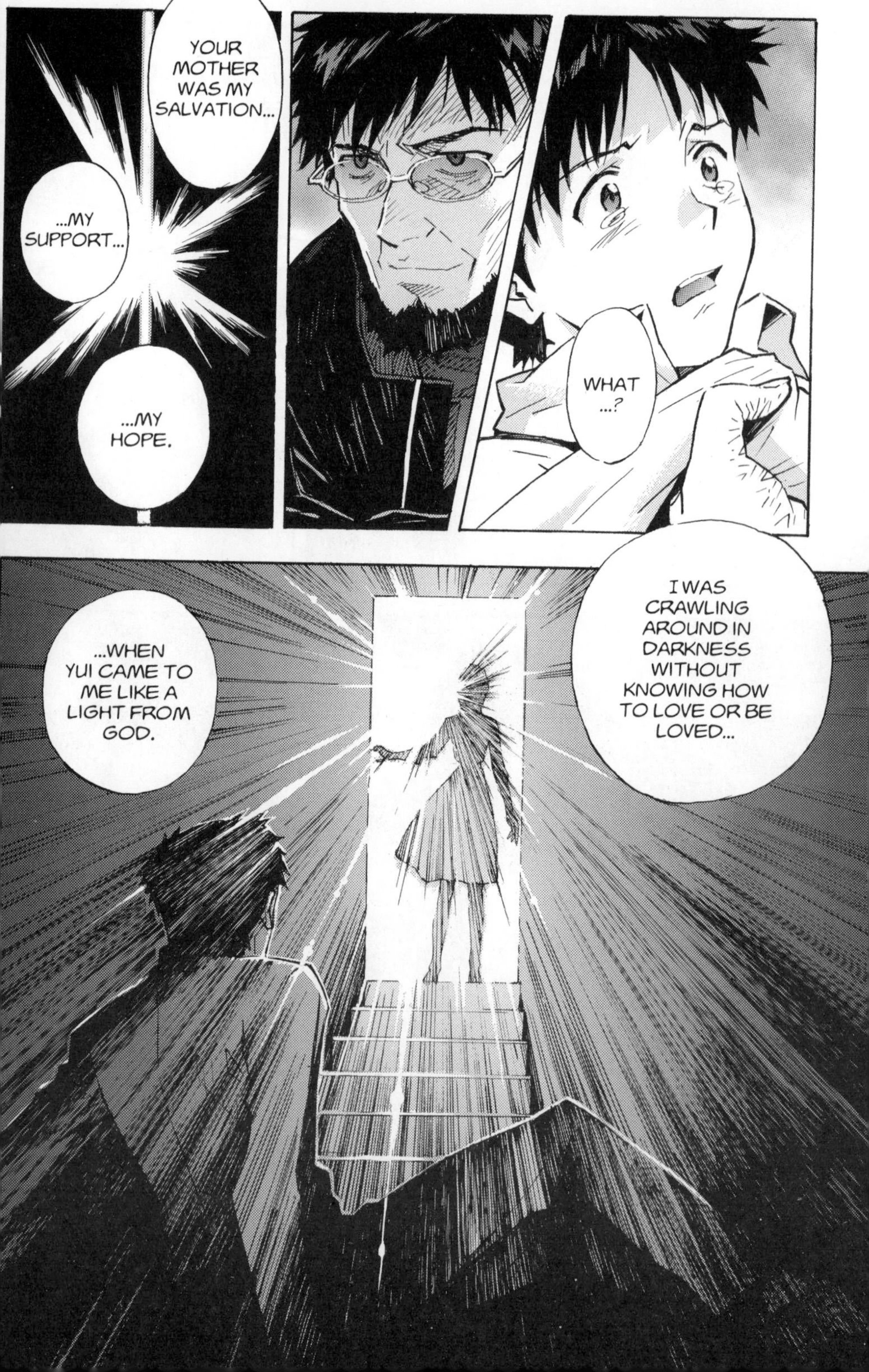
WHAT ...?
YOUR MOTHER WAS MY SALVATION...
...MY SUPPORT...
...MY HOPE.
I WAS CRAWLING AROUND IN DARKNESS WITHOUT KNOWING HOW TO LOVE OR BE LOVED...
...WHEN YUI CAME TO ME LIKE A LIGHT FROM GOD.

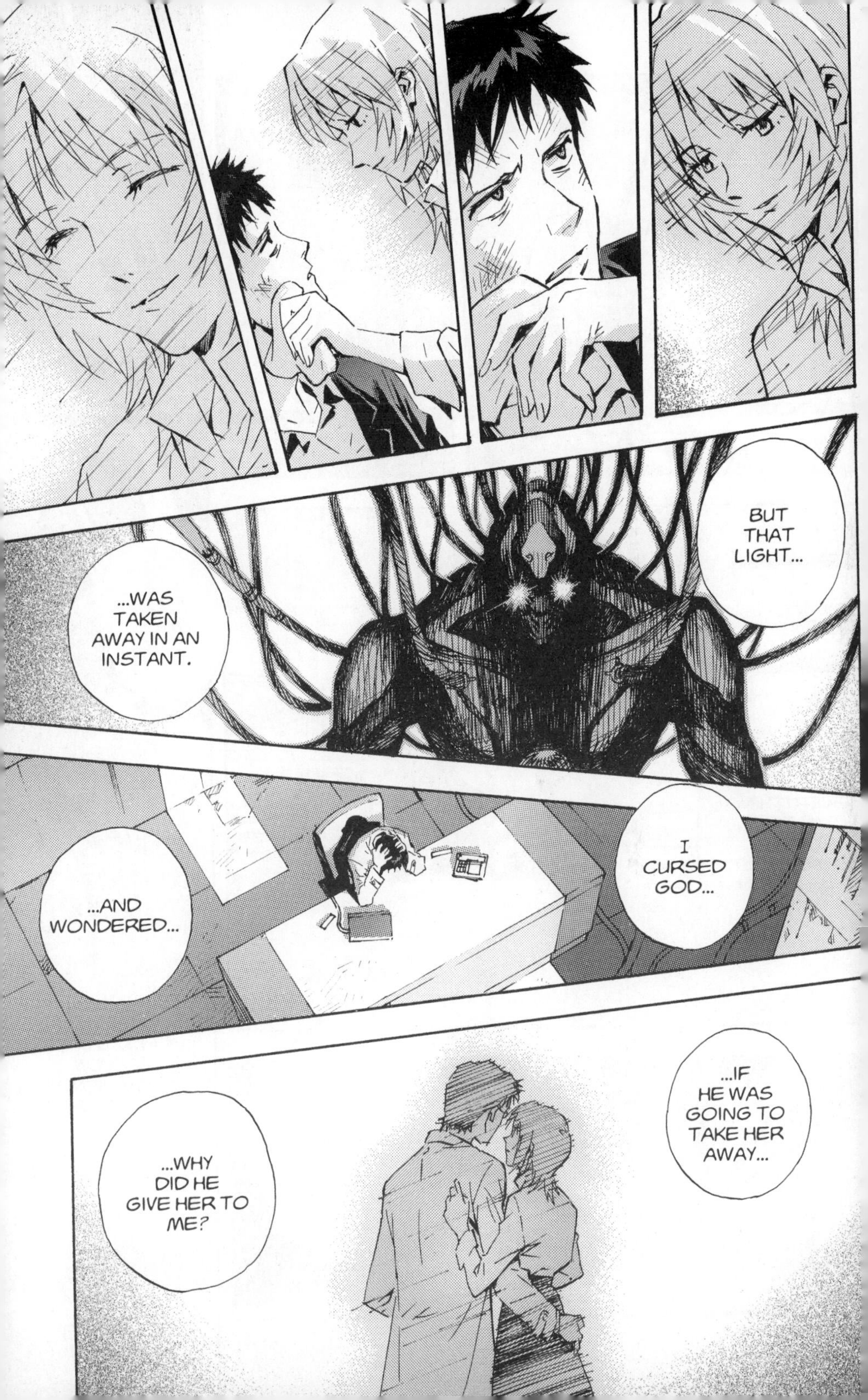
BUT THAT LIGHT...
...WAS TAKEN AWAY IN AN INSTANT.
I CURSED GOD...
...AND WONDERED...
...IF HE WAS GOING TO TAKE HER AWAY...
...WHY DID HE GIVE HER TO ME?

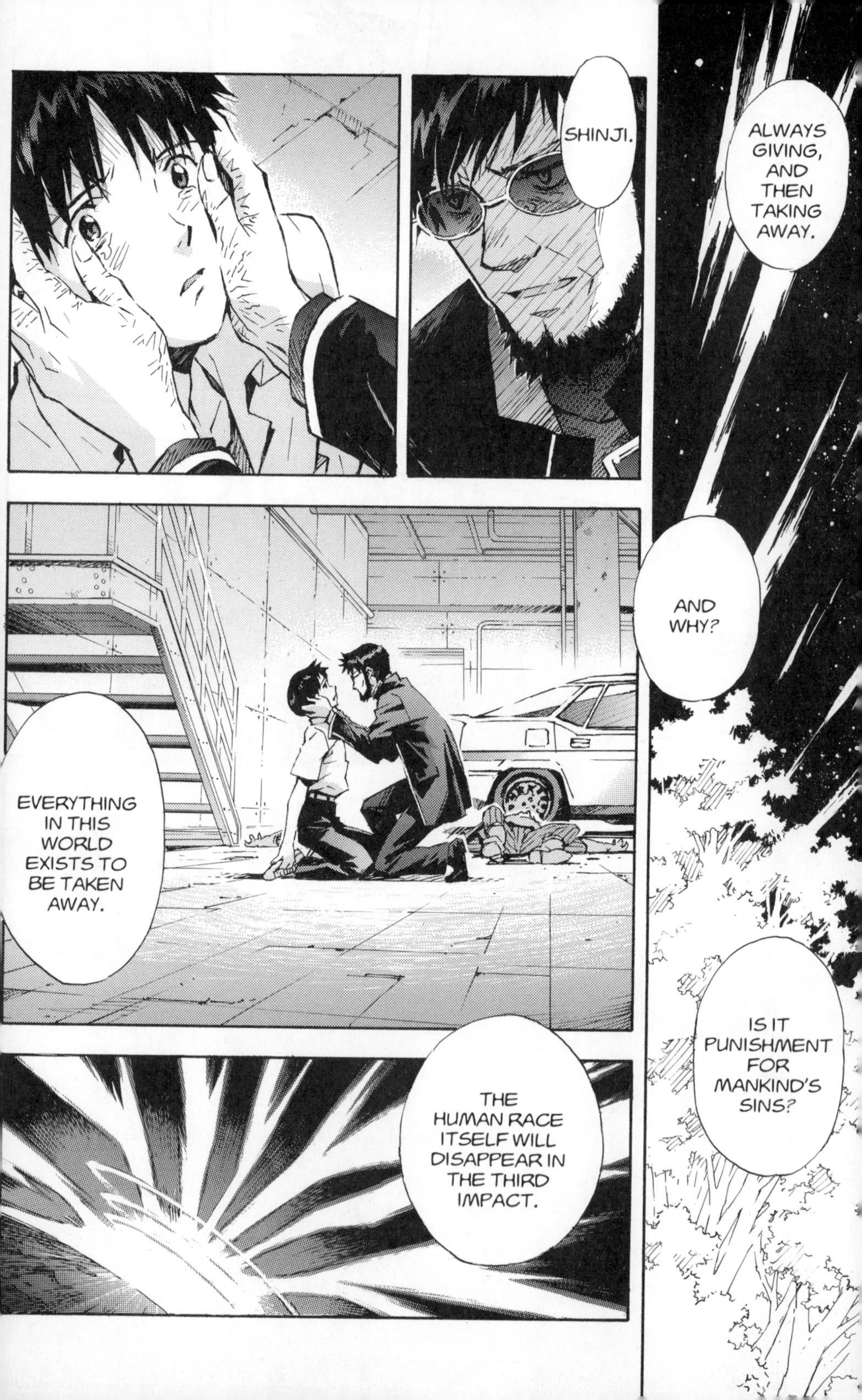
ALWAYS GIVING, AND THEN TAKING AWAY.
AND WHY?
IS IT PUNISHMENT FOR MANKIND'S SINS?
SHINJI.
EVERYTHING IN THIS WORLD EXISTS TO BE TAKEN AWAY.
THE HUMAN RACE ITSELF WILL DISAPPEAR IN THE THIRD IMPACT.

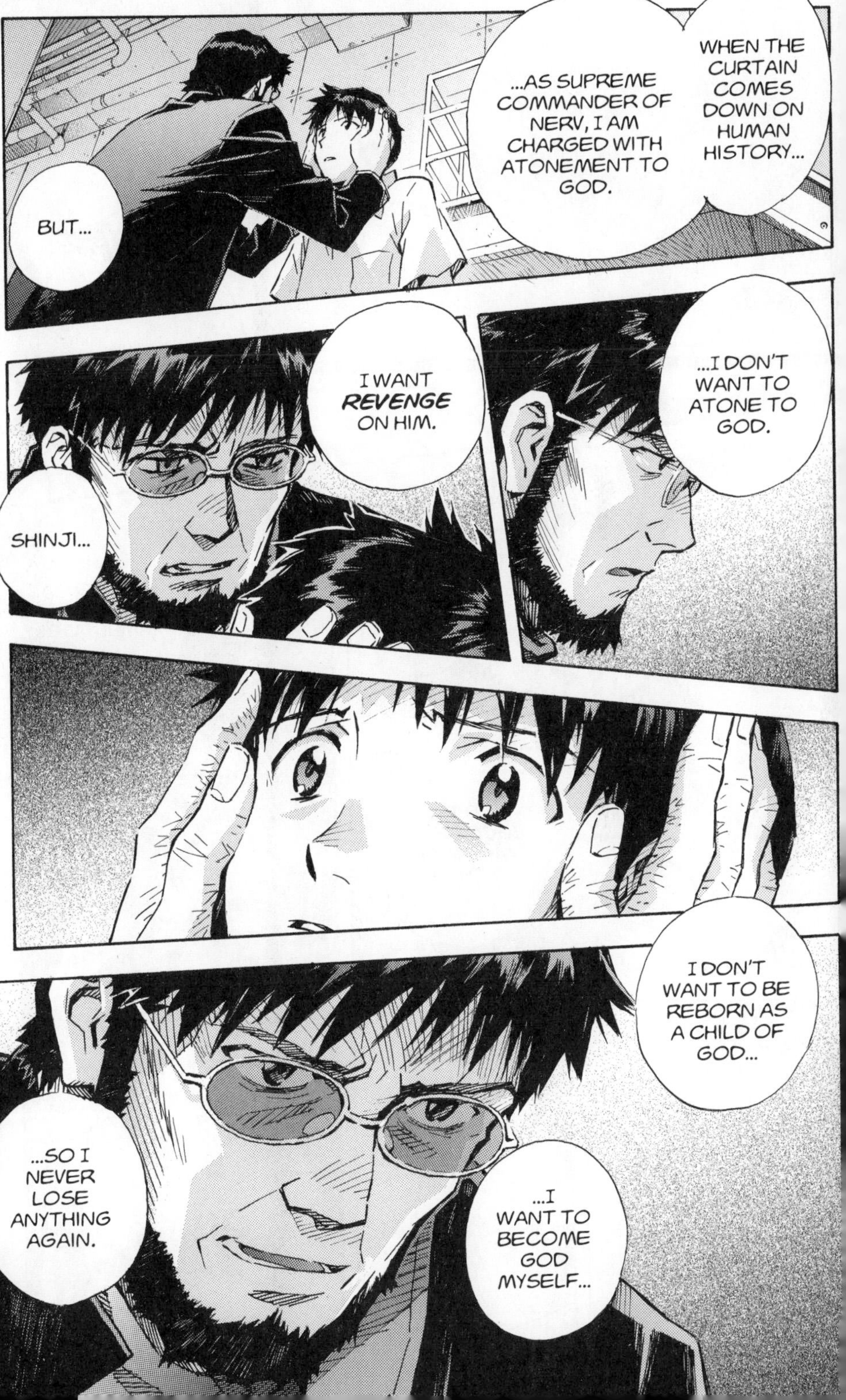
WHEN THE CURTAIN COMES DOWN ON HUMAN HISTORY...
...AS SUPREME COMMANDER OF NERV, I AM CHARGED WITH ATONEMENT TO GOD.
BUT...
...I DON'T WANT TO ATONE TO GOD.
I WANT *REVENGE* ON HIM.
SHINJI...
I DON'T WANT TO BE REBORN AS A CHILD OF GOD...
...I WANT TO BECOME GOD MYSELF...
...SO I NEVER LOSE ANYTHING AGAIN.

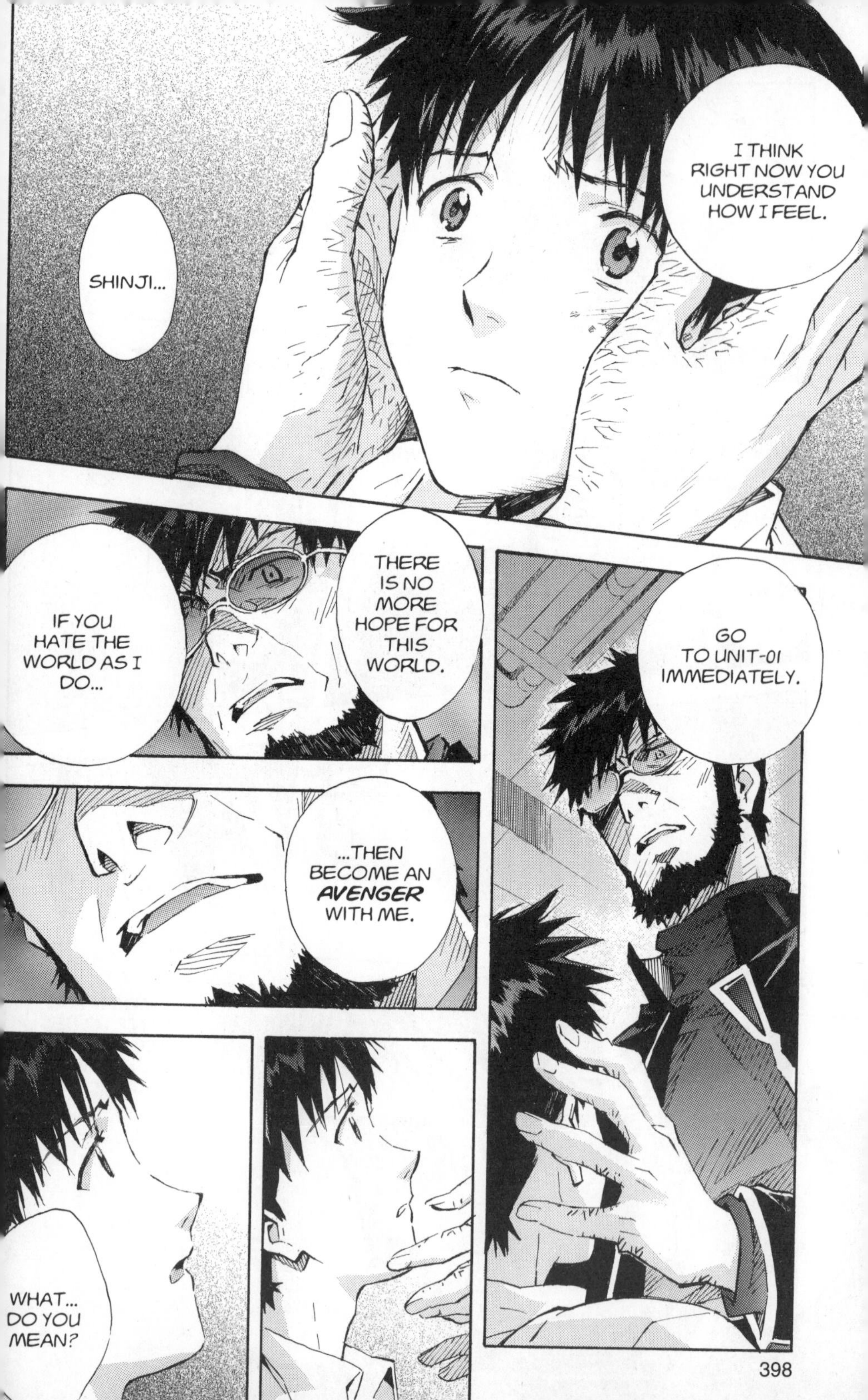
I THINK RIGHT NOW YOU UNDERSTAND HOW I FEEL.
SHINJI...
GO TO UNIT-01 IMMEDIATELY.
THERE IS NO MORE HOPE FOR THIS WORLD.
IF YOU HATE THE WORLD AS I DO...
...THEN BECOME AN *AVENGER* WITH ME.
WHAT... DO YOU MEAN?

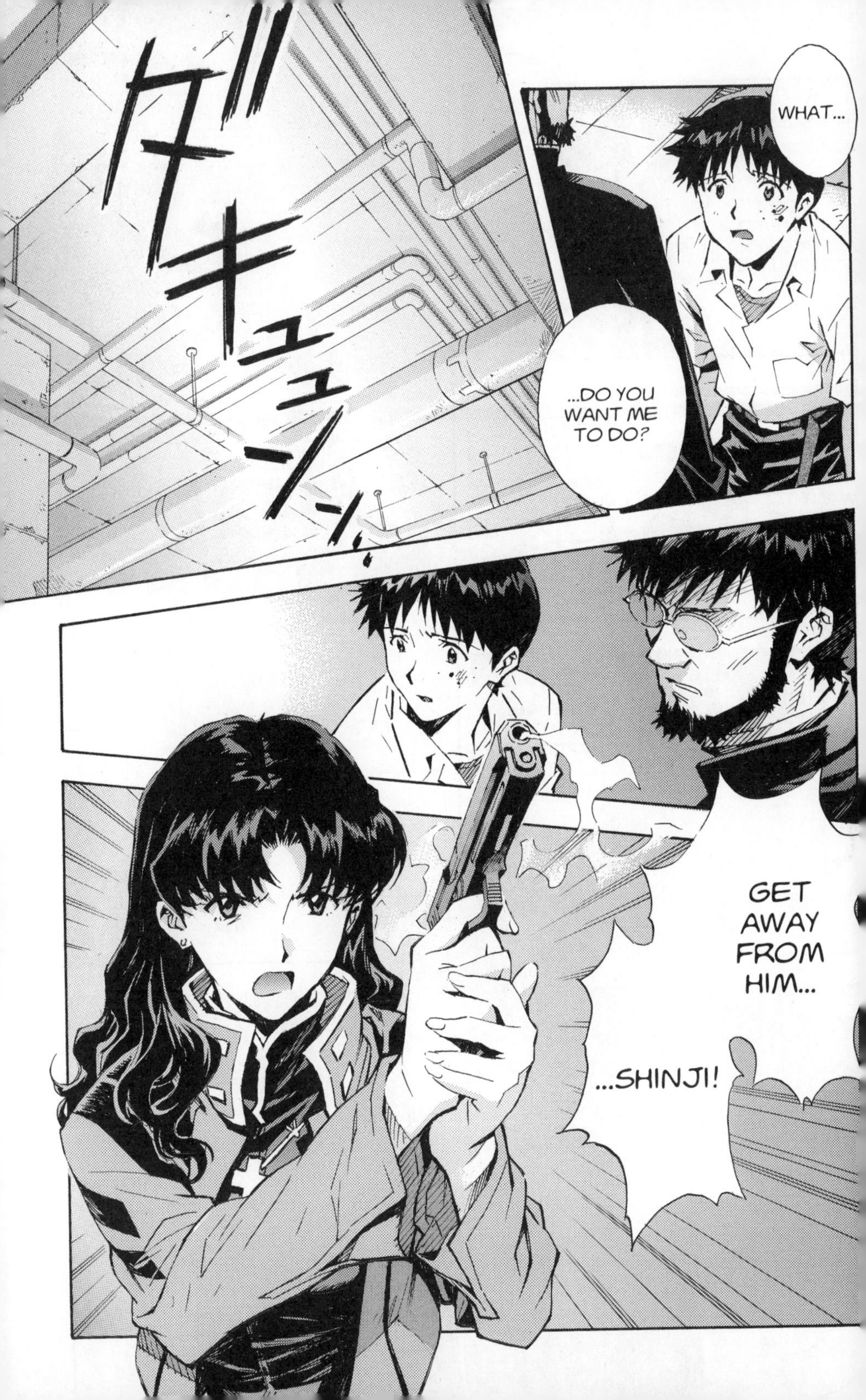

WHAT...
...DO YOU WANT ME TO DO?
ガキュューン
GET AWAY FROM HIM...
...SHINJI!

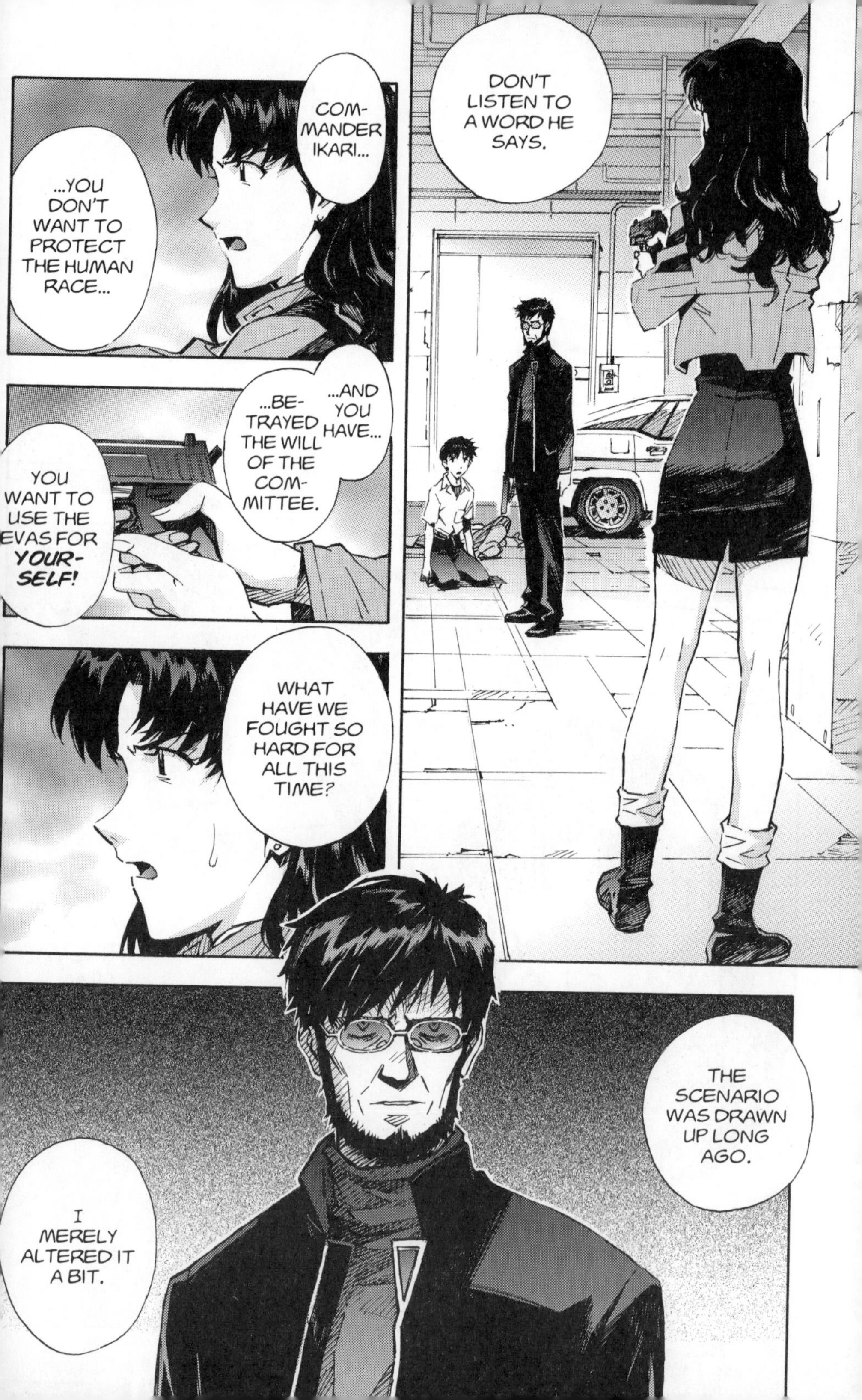
DON'T LISTEN TO A WORD HE SAYS.
COM-MANDER IKARI...
...YOU DON'T WANT TO PROTECT THE HUMAN RACE...
...AND YOU HAVE...
...BE-TRAYED THE WILL OF THE COM-MITTEE.
YOU WANT TO USE THE EVAS FOR ***YOUR-SELF!***
WHAT HAVE WE FOUGHT SO HARD FOR ALL THIS TIME?
THE SCENARIO WAS DRAWN UP LONG AGO.
I MERELY ALTERED IT A BIT.

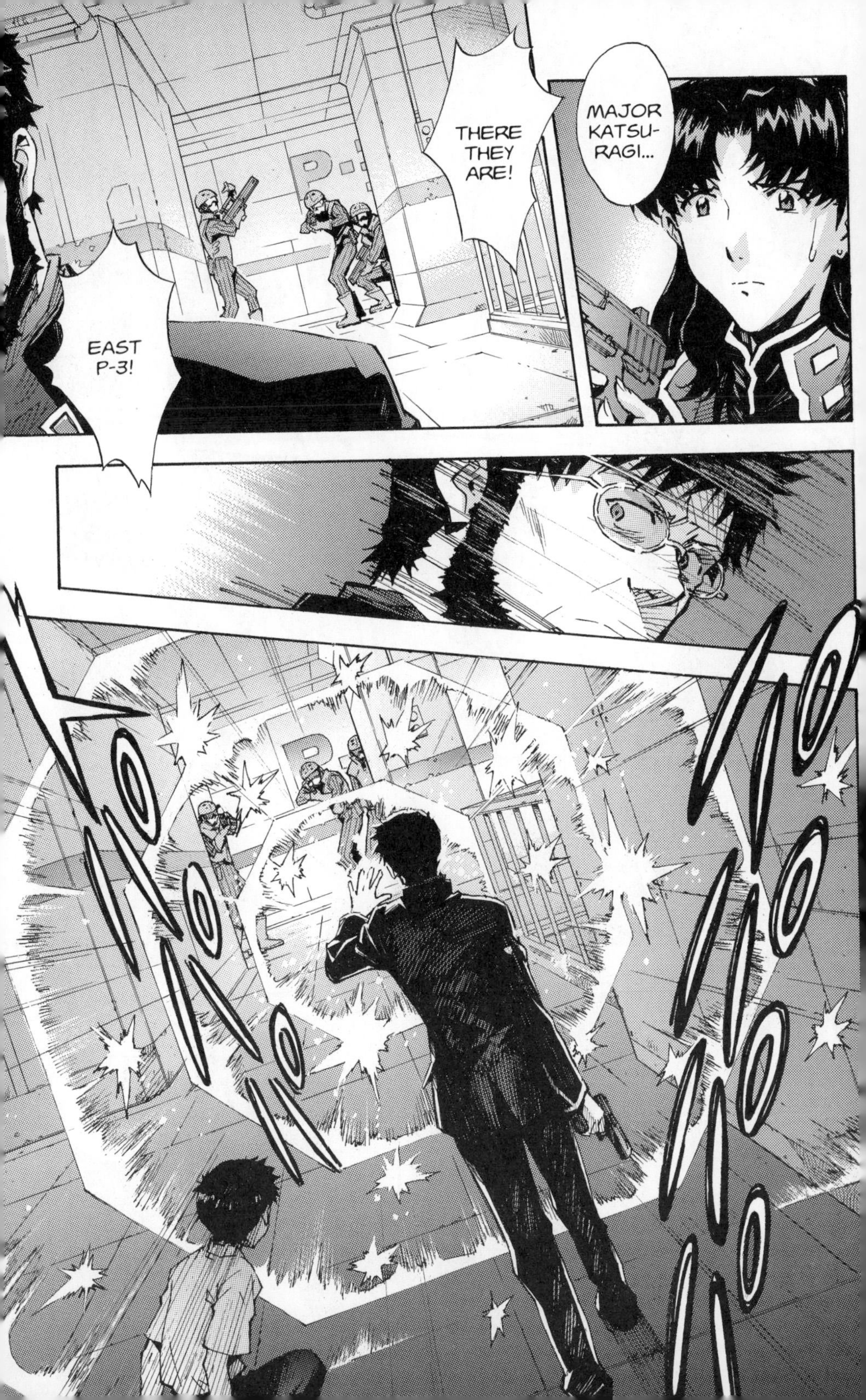
MAJOR KATSU-RAGI...
THERE THEY ARE!
EAST P-3!

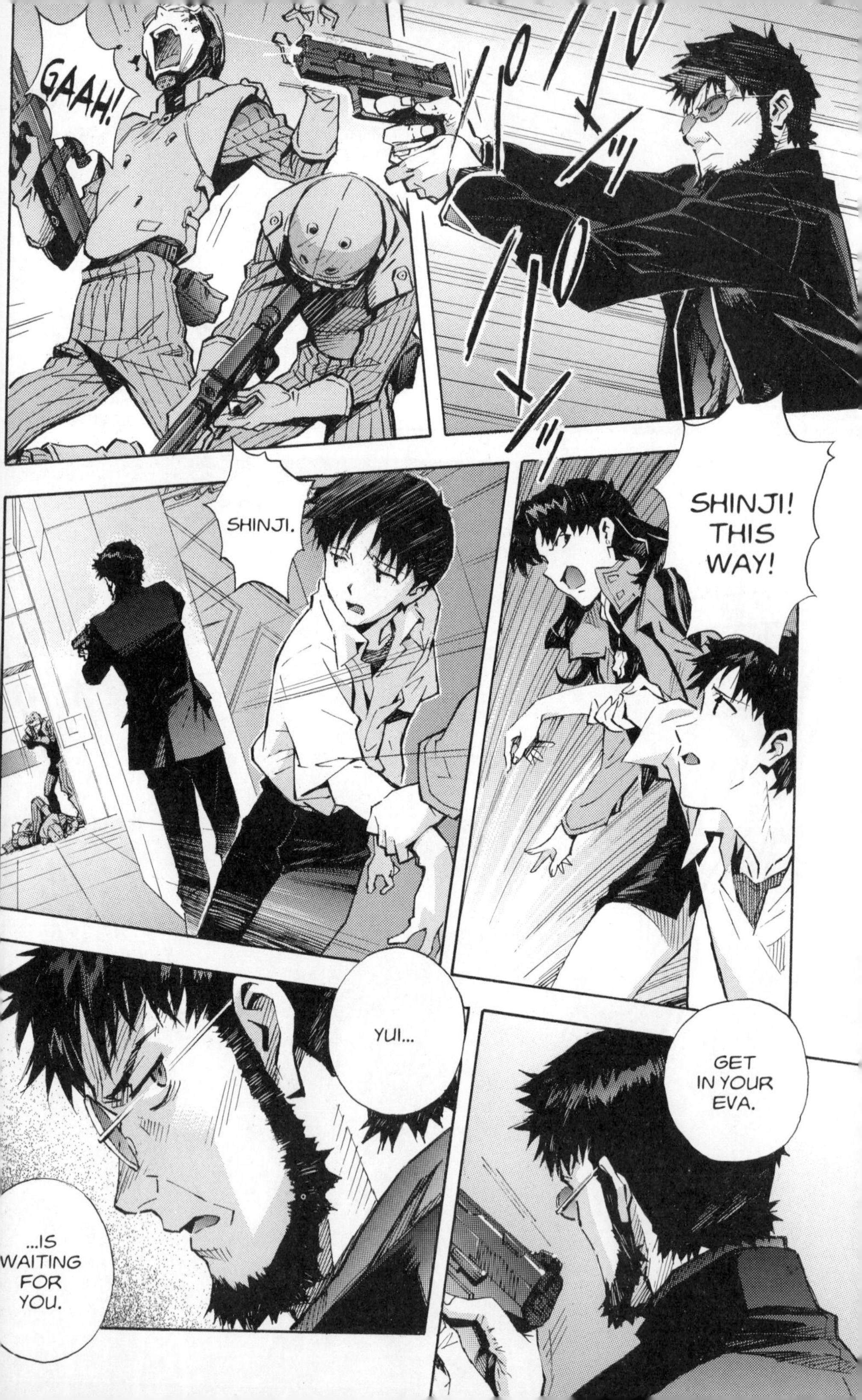
GAAH!
SHINJI! THIS WAY!
SHINJI.
GET IN YOUR EVA.
YUI...
...IS WAITING FOR YOU.

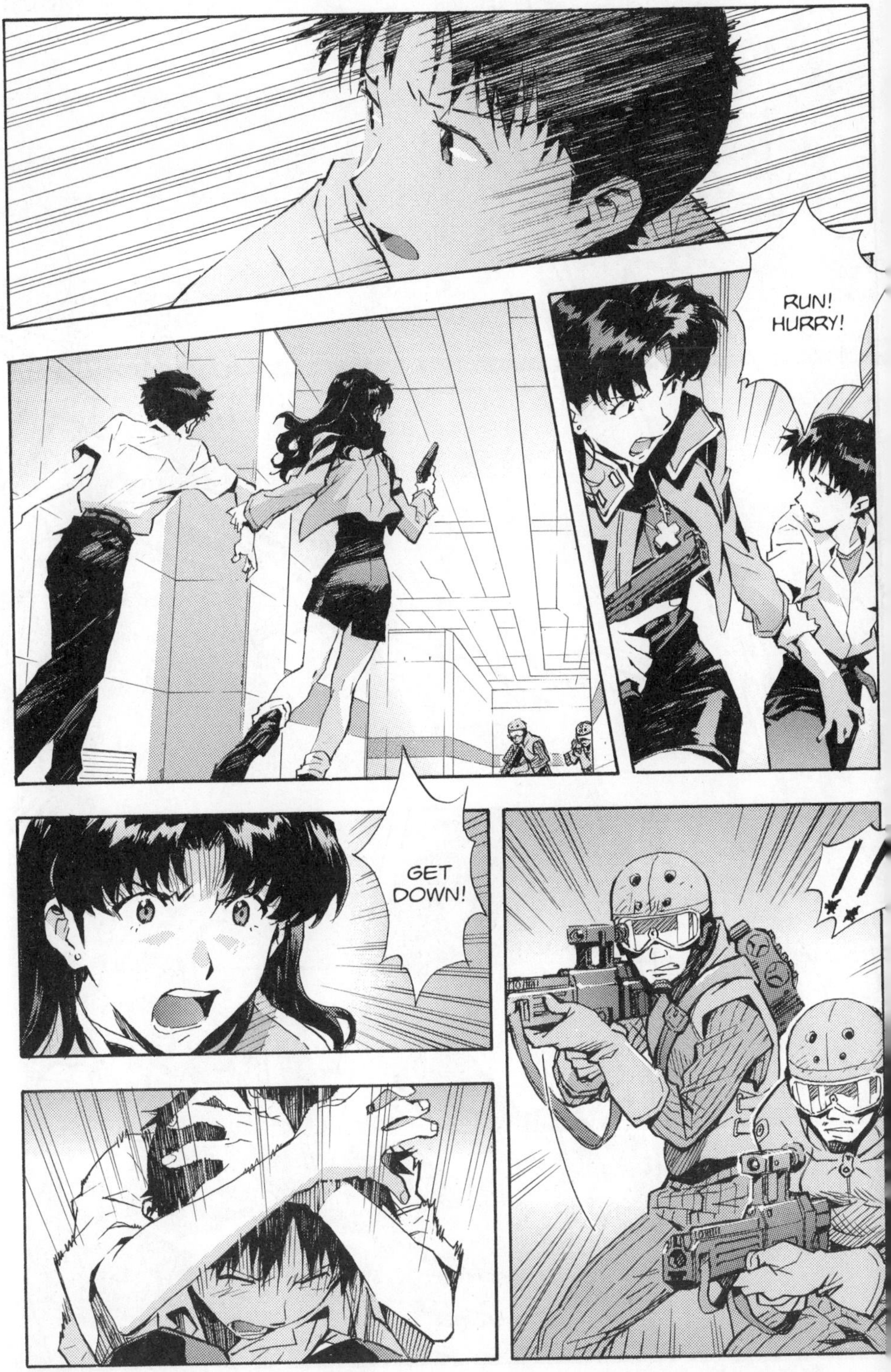
RUN! HURRY!
!!
GET DOWN!

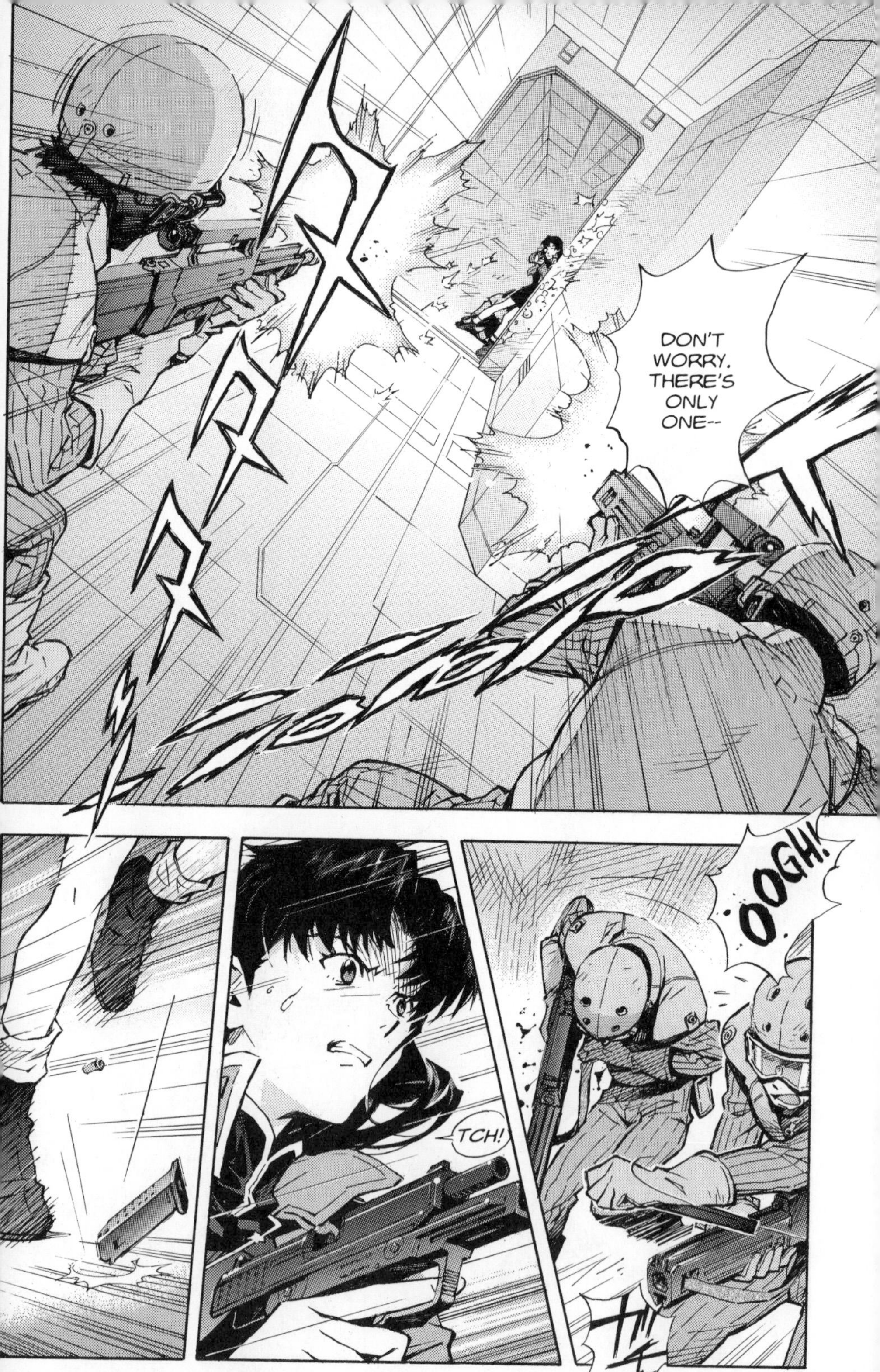
DON'T WORRY. THERE'S ONLY ONE--
OOGH!
TCH!

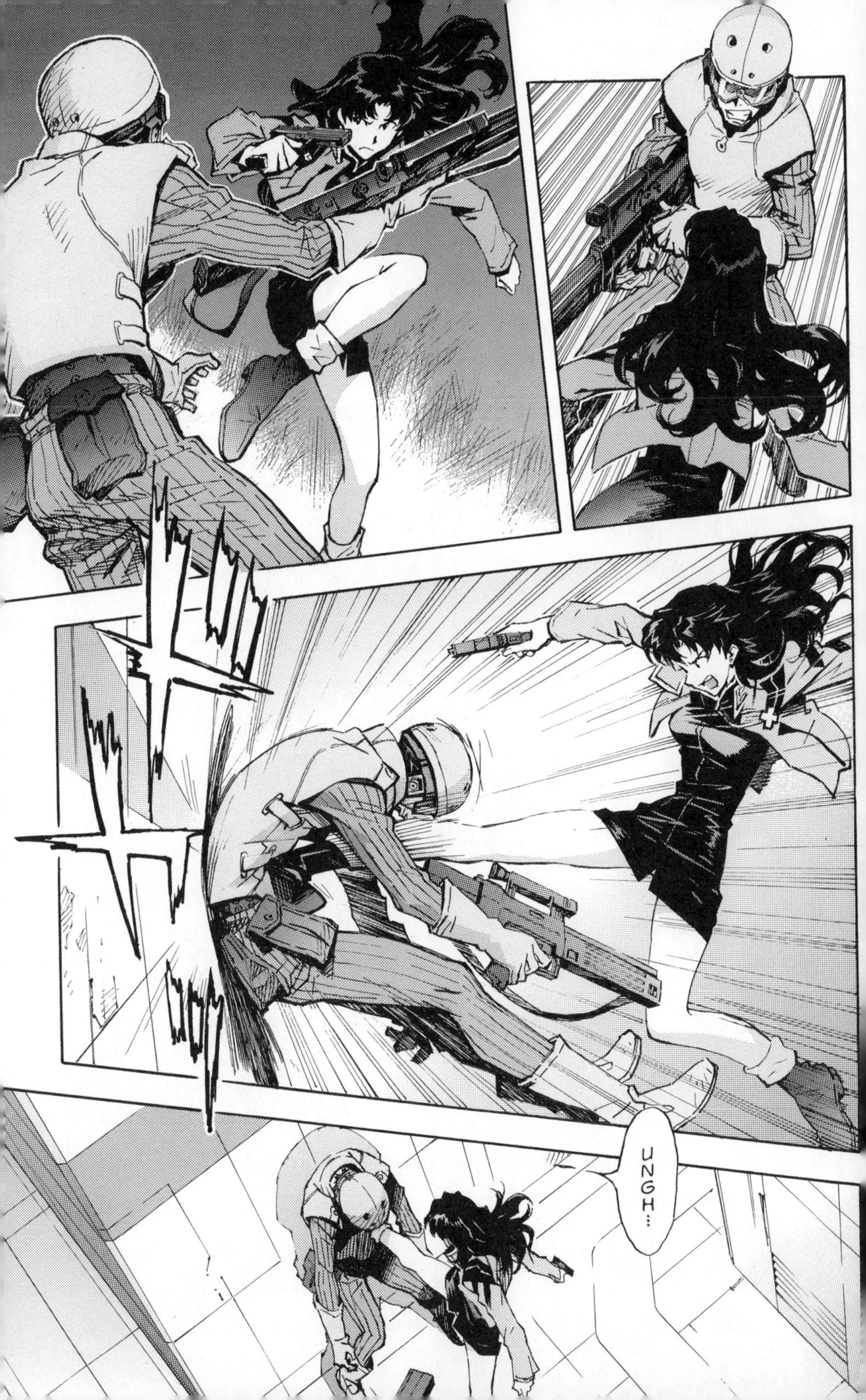
UNGH...

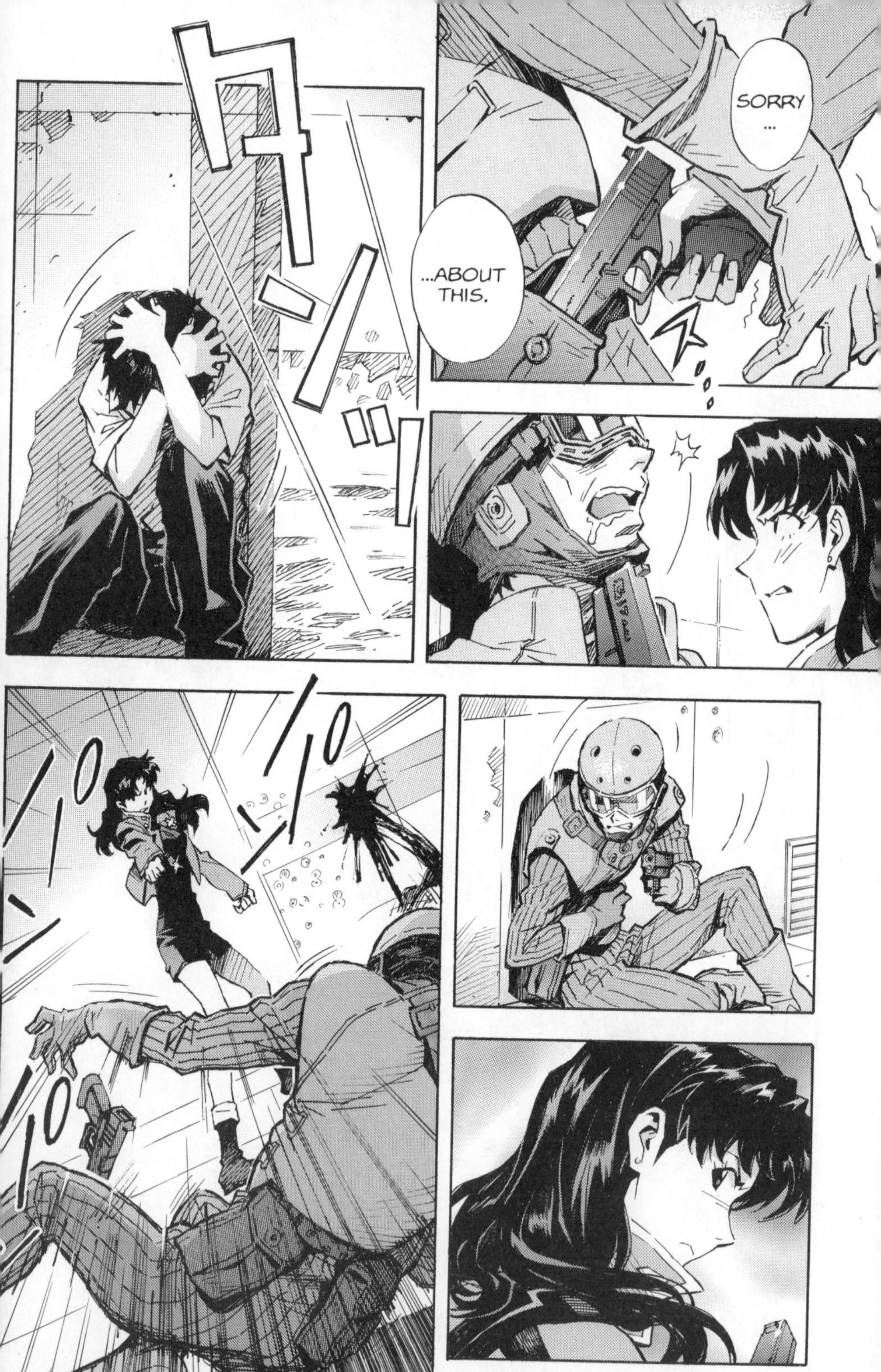
SORRY ...
...ABOUT THIS.

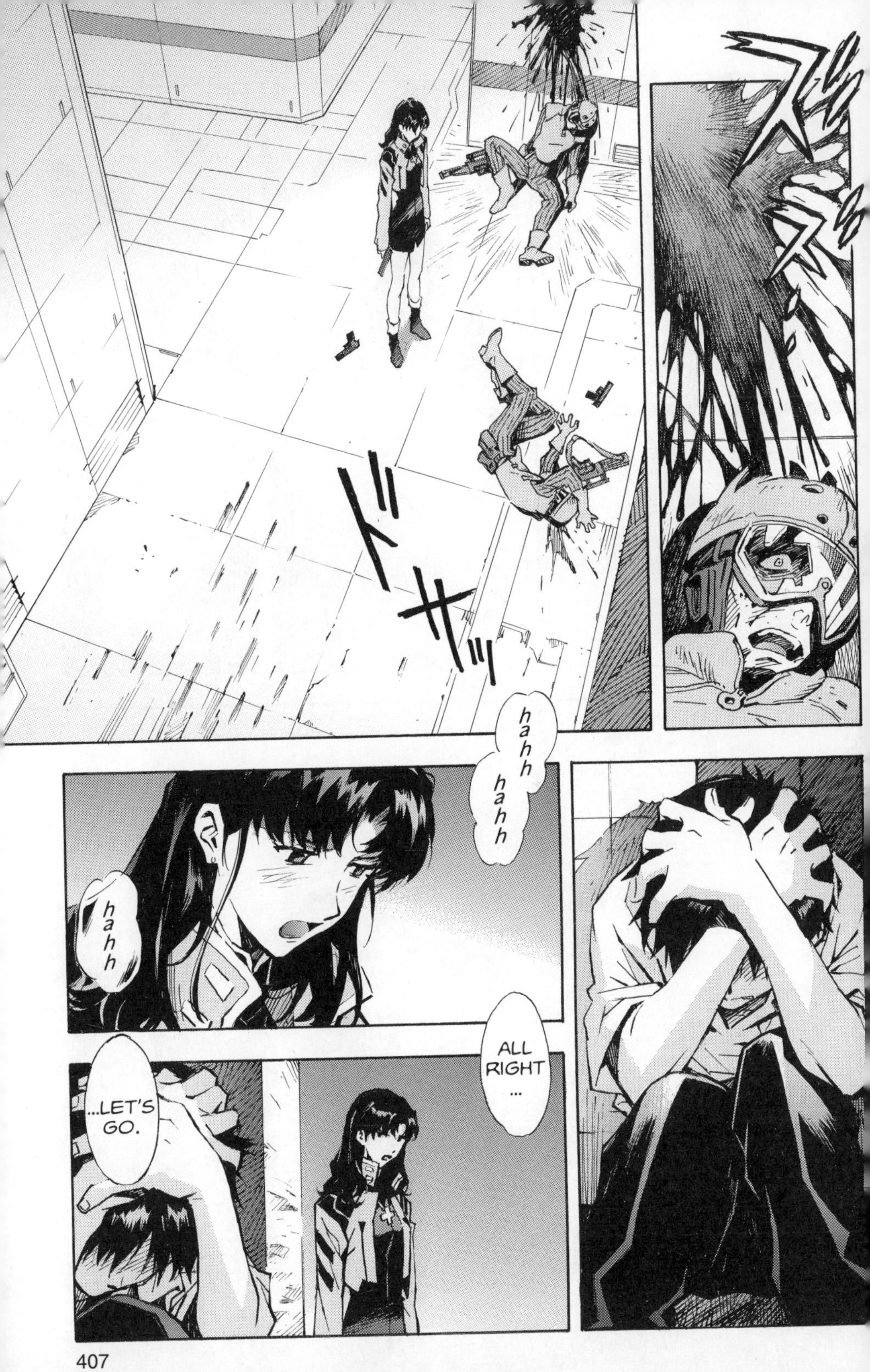
hahh
hahh
hahh
ALL RIGHT ...
...LET'S GO.

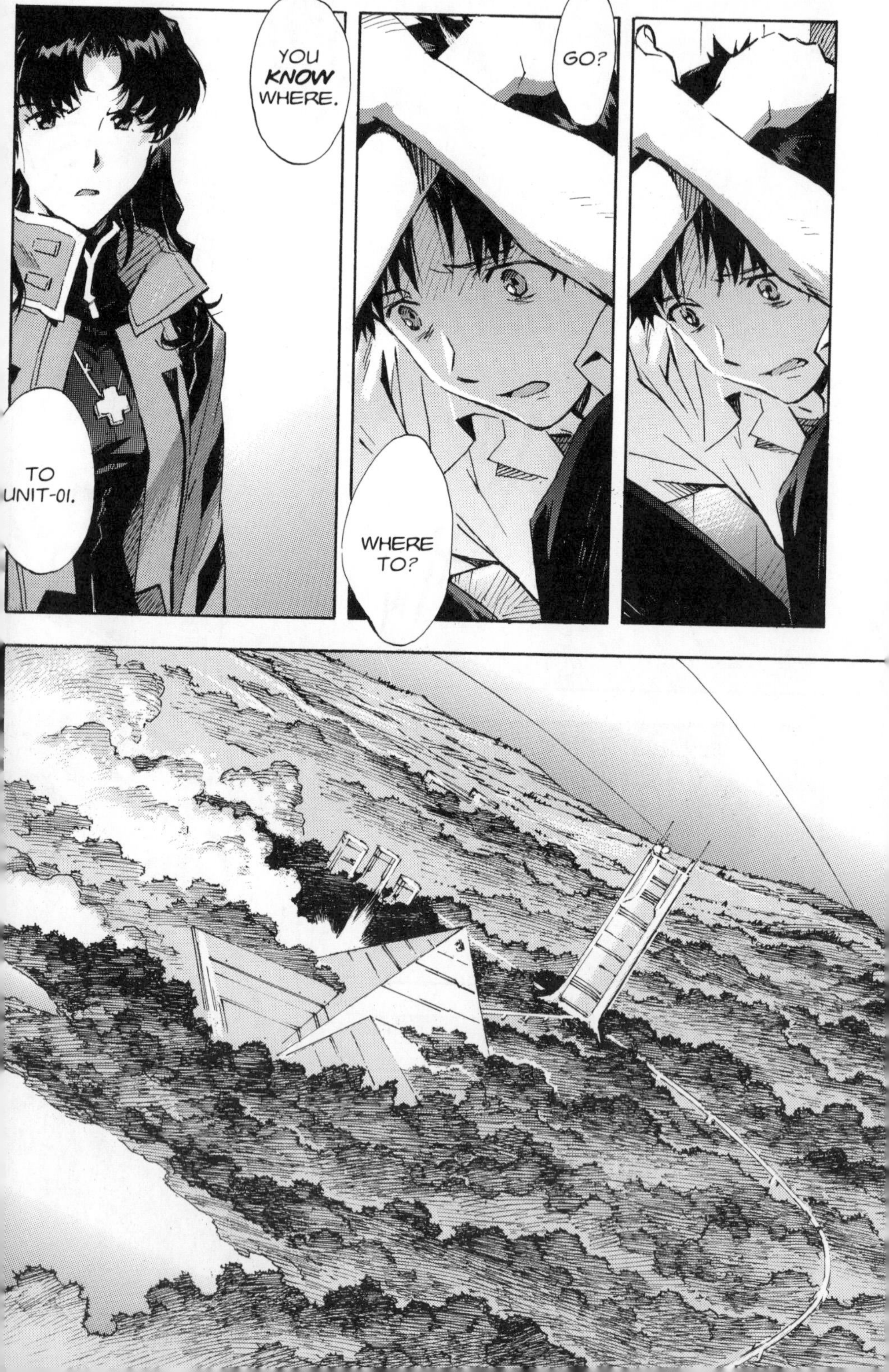
GO?
WHERE TO?
YOU KNOW WHERE.
TO UNIT-01.

NEON GENESIS

EVANGELION

STAGE 79: THE PROMISED TIME

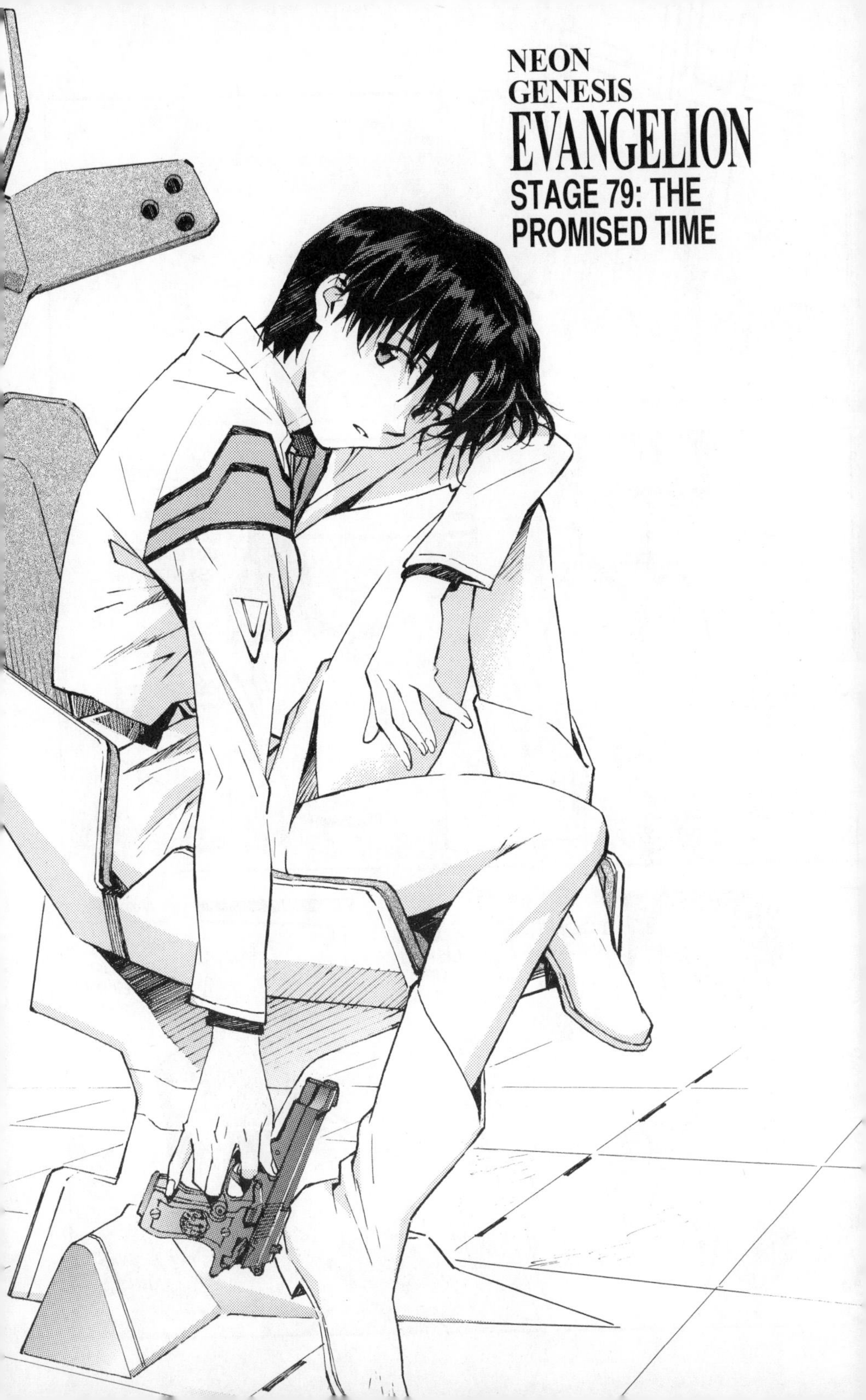

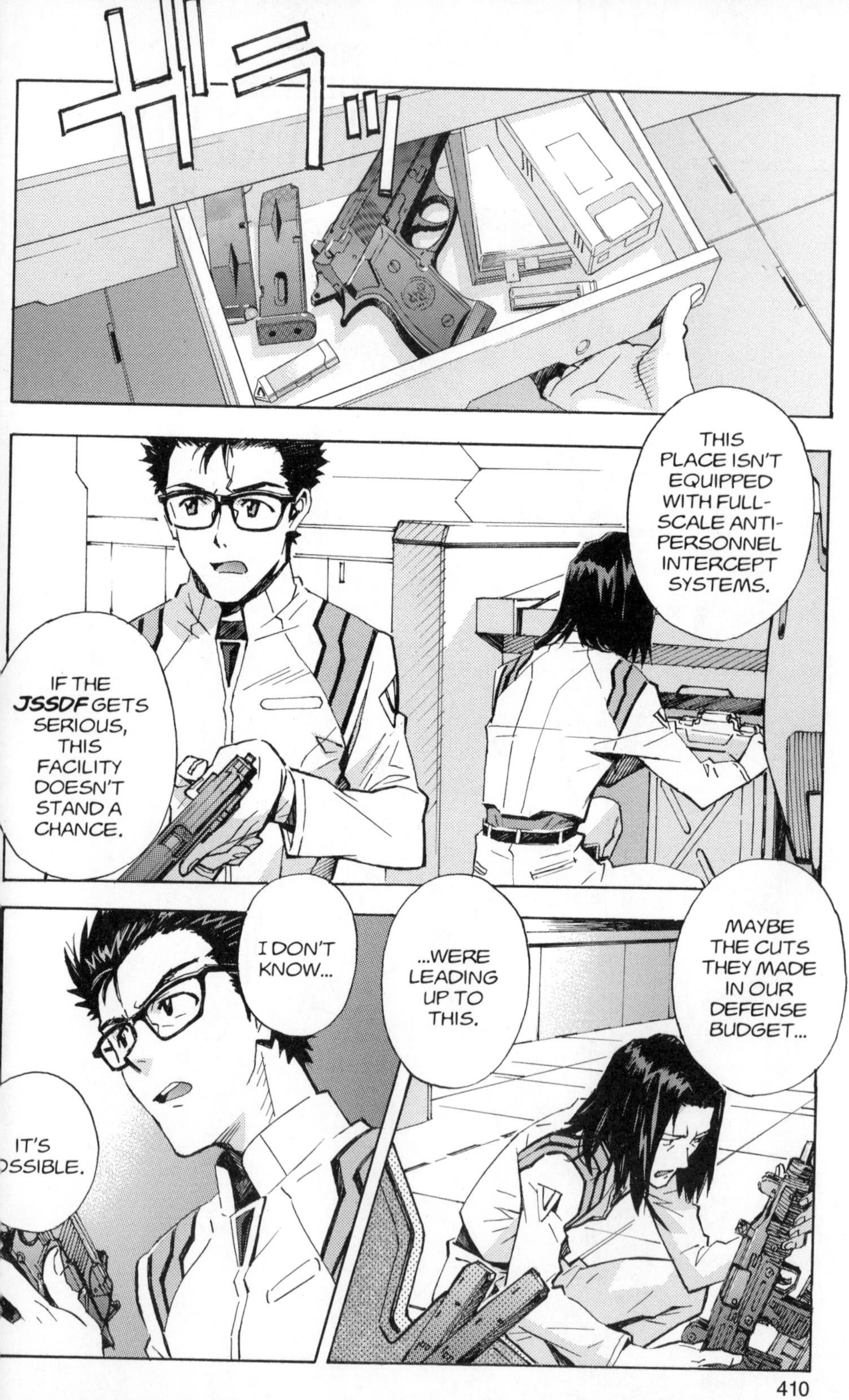
ガラッ
THIS PLACE ISN'T EQUIPPED WITH FULL-SCALE ANTI-PERSONNEL INTERCEPT SYSTEMS.
IF THE JSSDF GETS SERIOUS, THIS FACILITY DOESN'T STAND A CHANCE.
MAYBE THE CUTS THEY MADE IN OUR DEFENSE BUDGET...
...WERE LEADING UP TO THIS.
I DON'T KNOW...
IT'S SSIBLE.

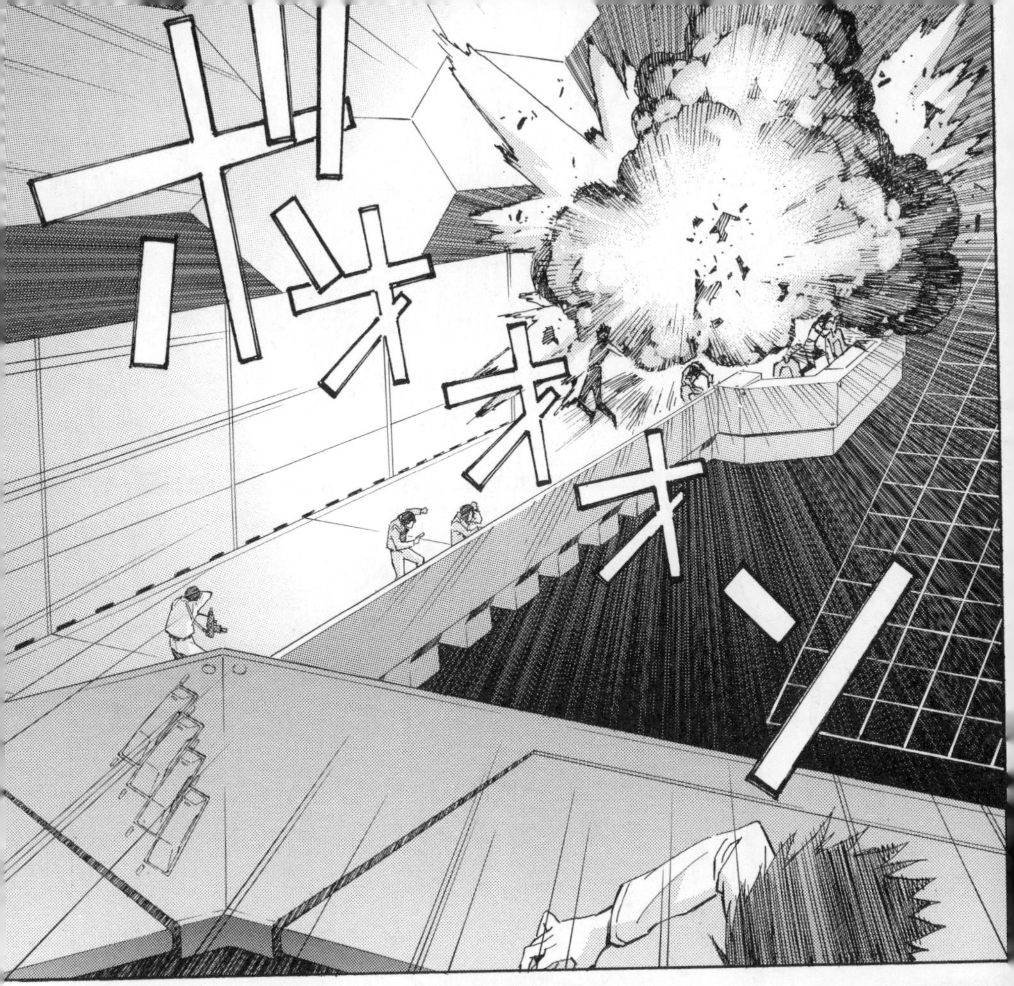
ボオオオン

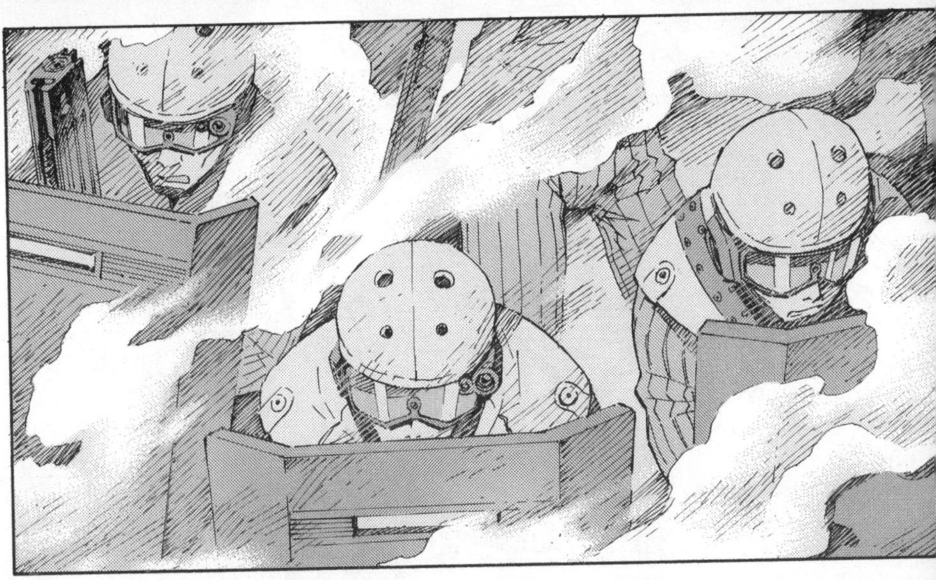

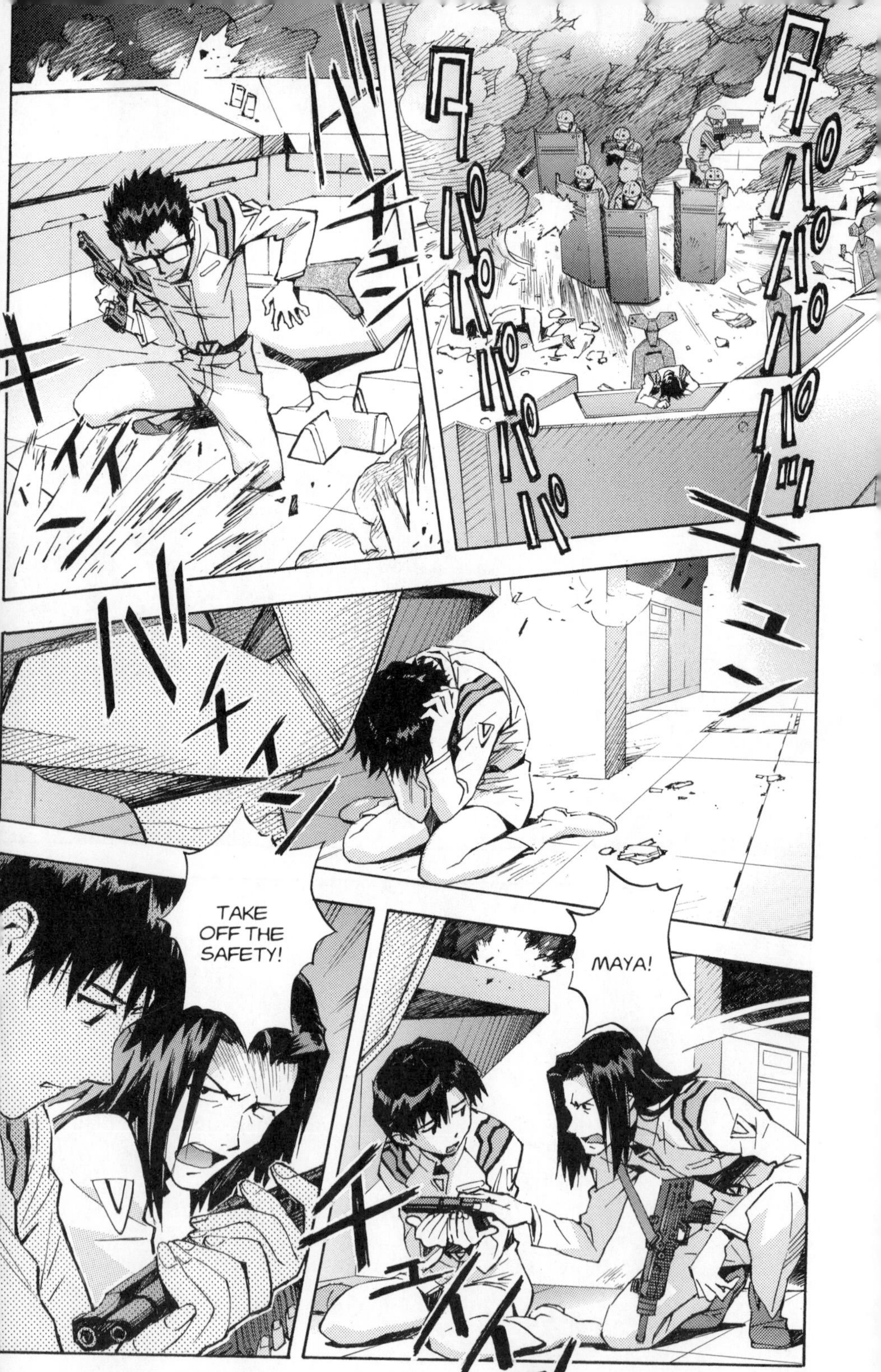
MAYA!
TAKE OFF THE SAFETY!

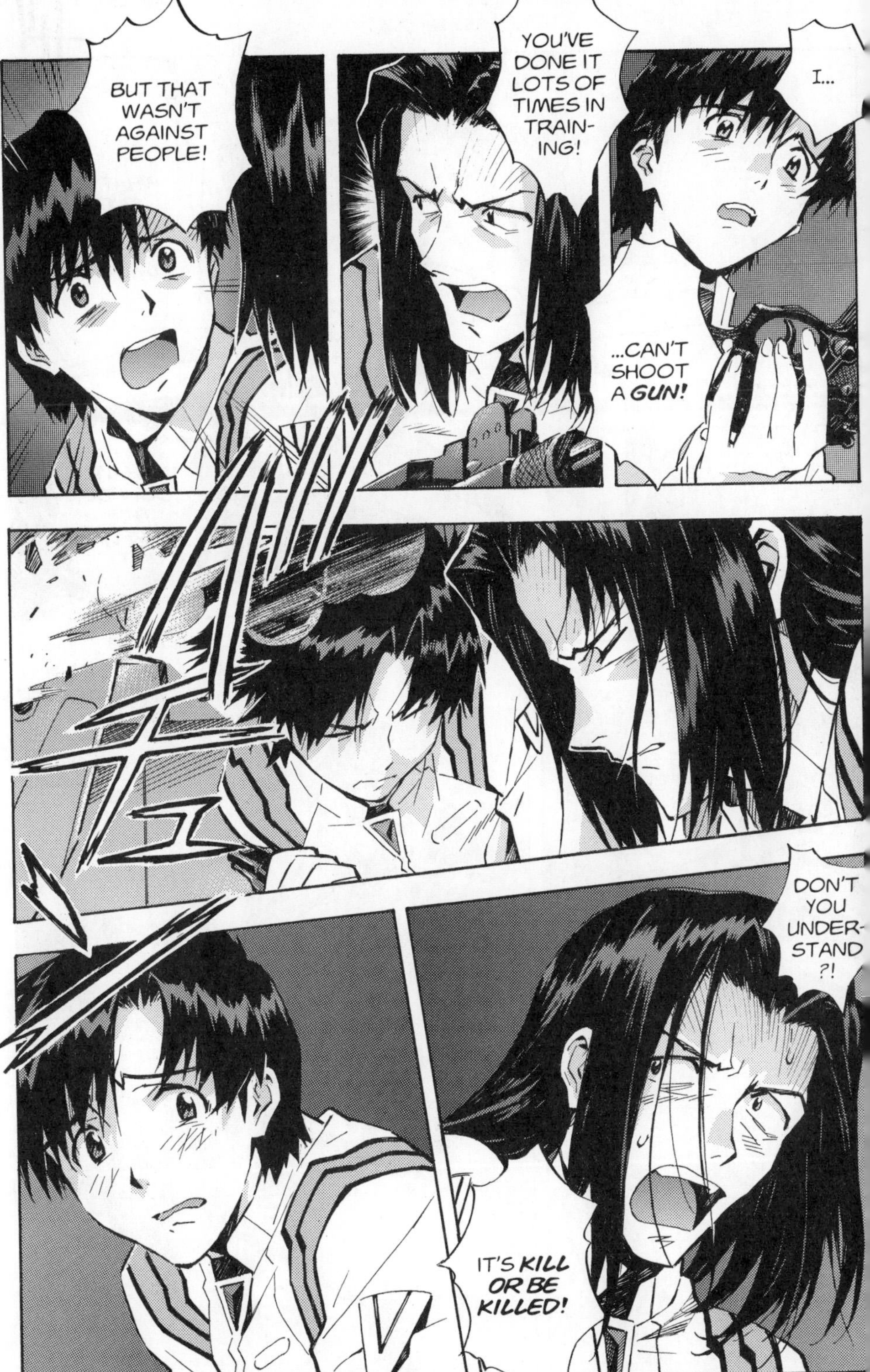
I...
...CAN'T SHOOT A GUN!
YOU'VE DONE IT LOTS OF TIMES IN TRAIN-ING!
BUT THAT WASN'T AGAINST PEOPLE!
DON'T YOU UNDER-STAND ?!
IT'S KILL OR BE KILLED!

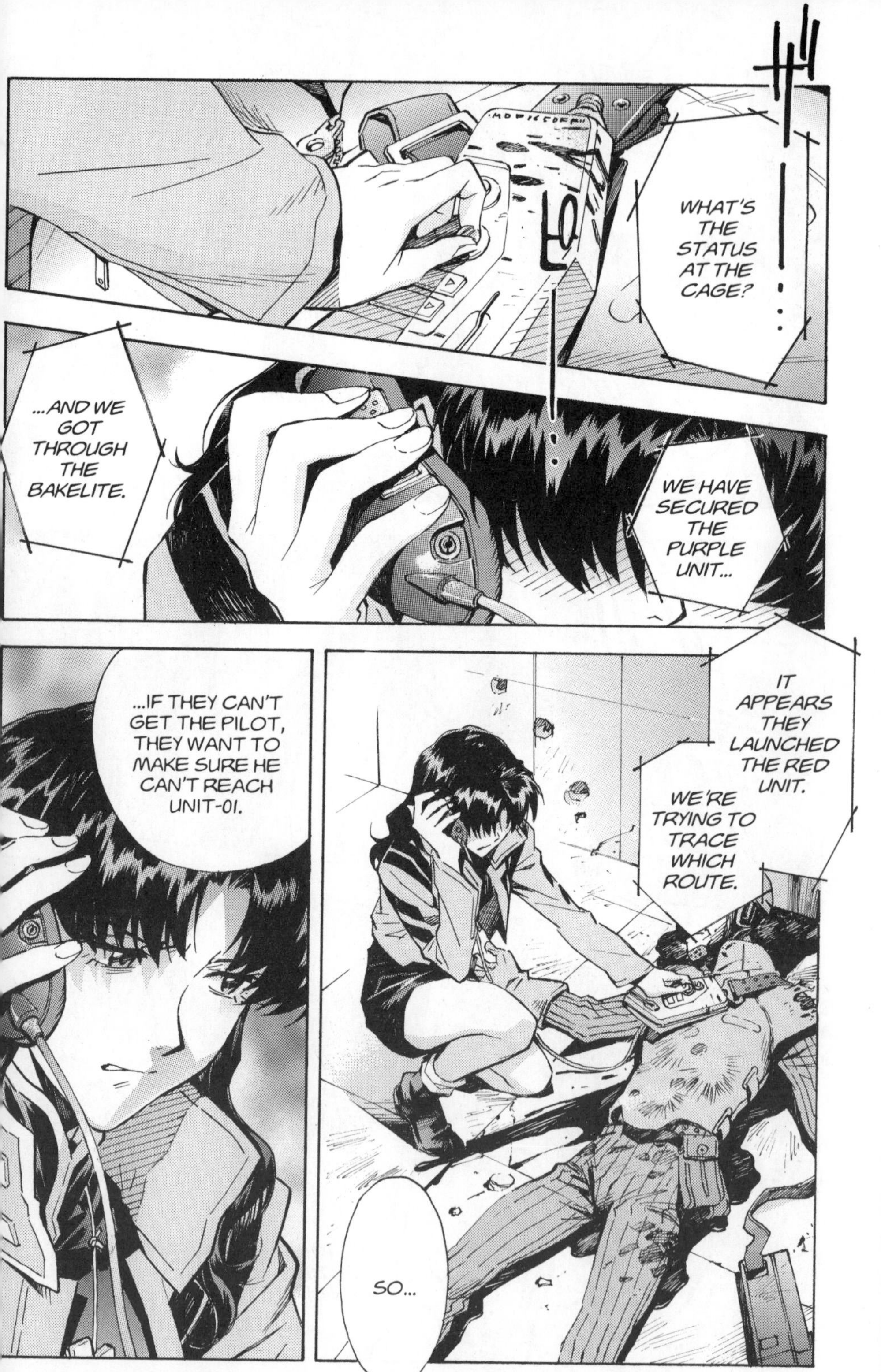
WHAT'S THE STATUS AT THE CAGE?
WE HAVE SECURED THE PURPLE UNIT...
...AND WE GOT THROUGH THE BAKELITE.
IT APPEARS THEY LAUNCHED THE RED UNIT.
WE'RE TRYING TO TRACE WHICH ROUTE.
SO...
...IF THEY CAN'T GET THE PILOT, THEY WANT TO MAKE SURE HE CAN'T REACH UNIT-01.

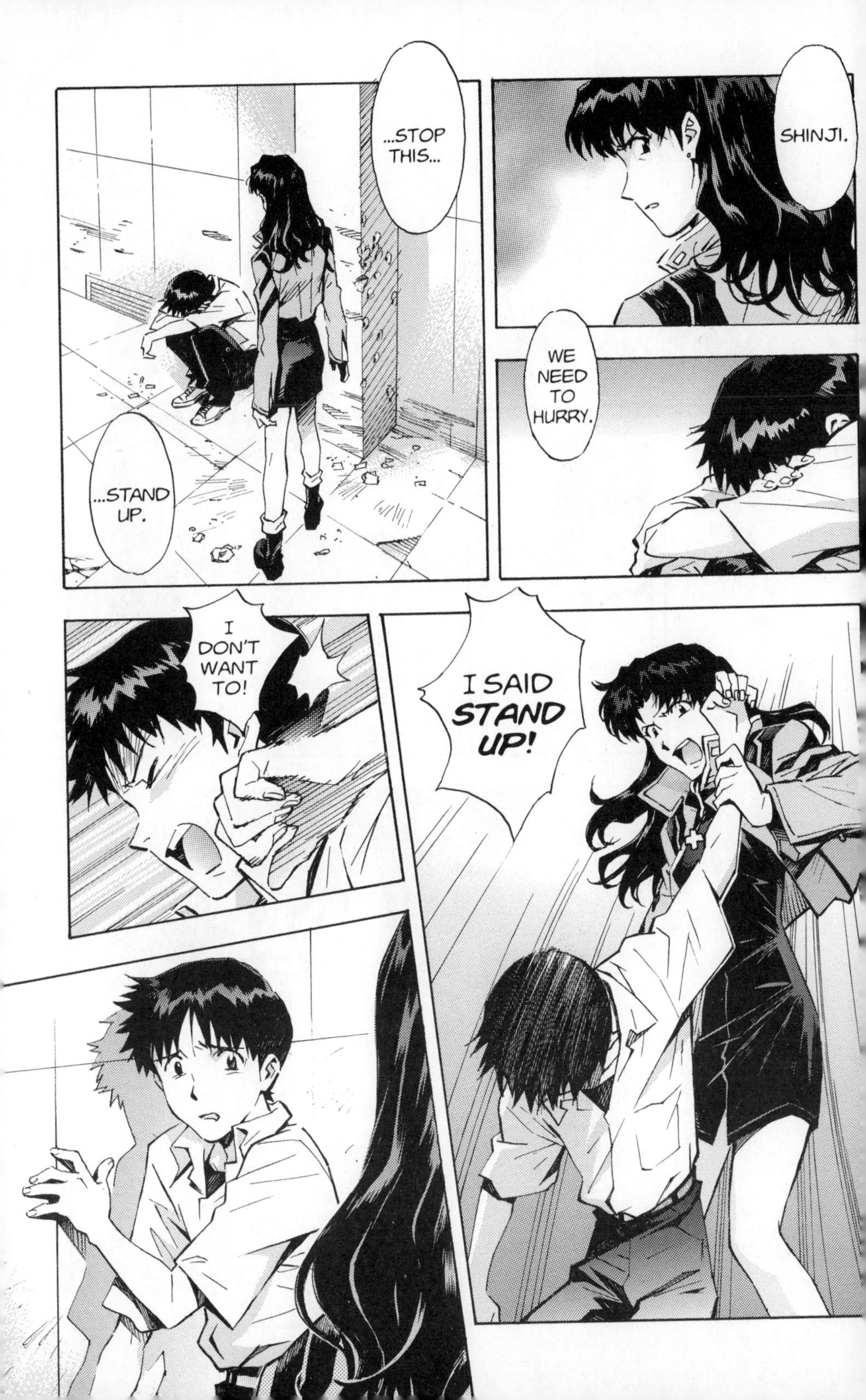

SHINJI.
WE NEED TO HURRY.
...STOP THIS...
...STAND UP.
I SAID **STAND UP!**
I DON'T WANT TO!

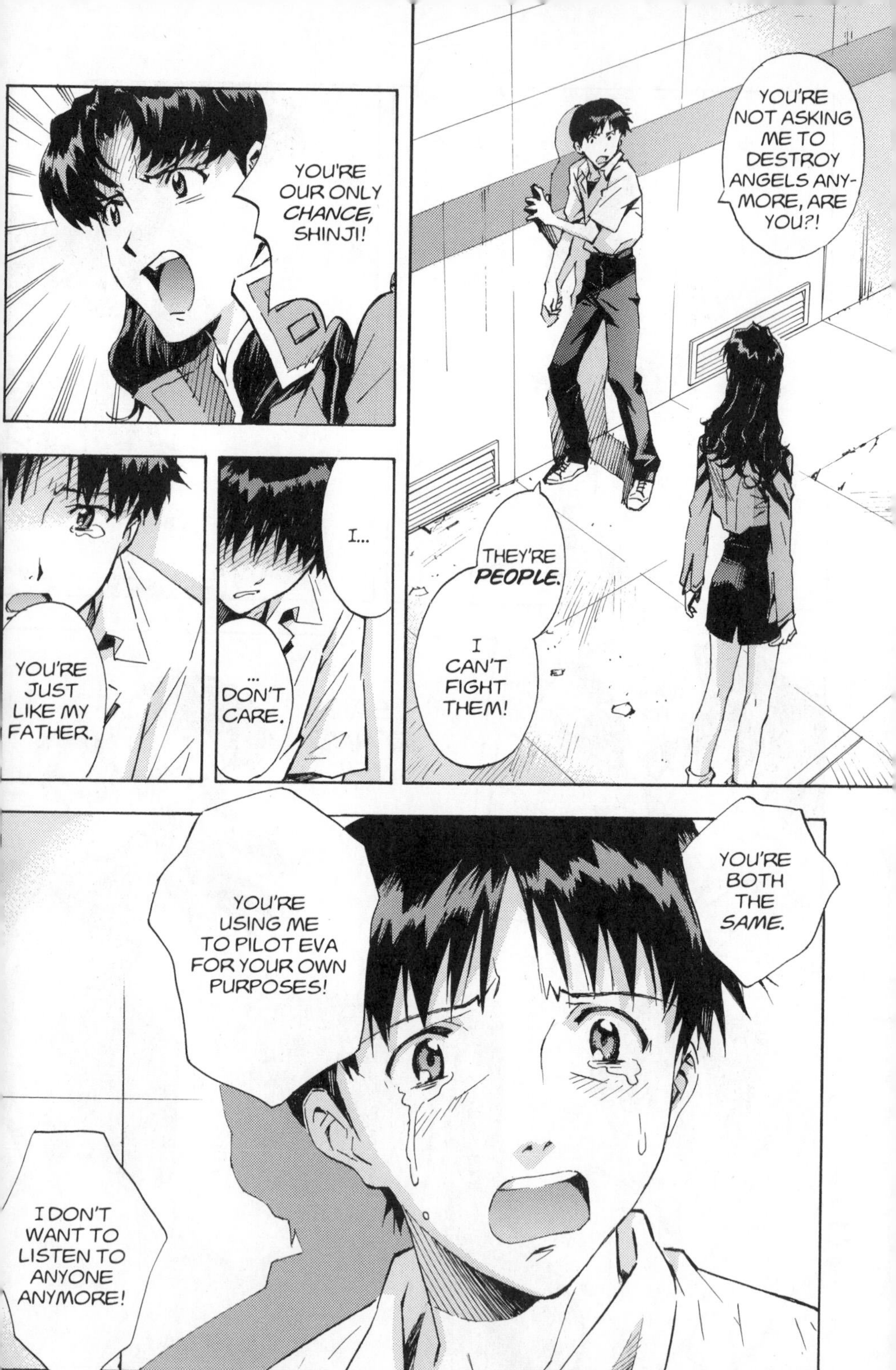
YOU'RE NOT ASKING ME TO DESTROY ANGELS ANY-MORE, ARE YOU?!
THEY'RE *PEOPLE*.
I CAN'T FIGHT THEM!
YOU'RE OUR ONLY *CHANCE*, SHINJI!
I...
...DON'T CARE.
YOU'RE JUST LIKE MY FATHER.
YOU'RE BOTH THE *SAME*.
YOU'RE USING ME TO PILOT EVA FOR YOUR OWN PURPOSES!
I DON'T WANT TO LISTEN TO ANYONE ANYMORE!

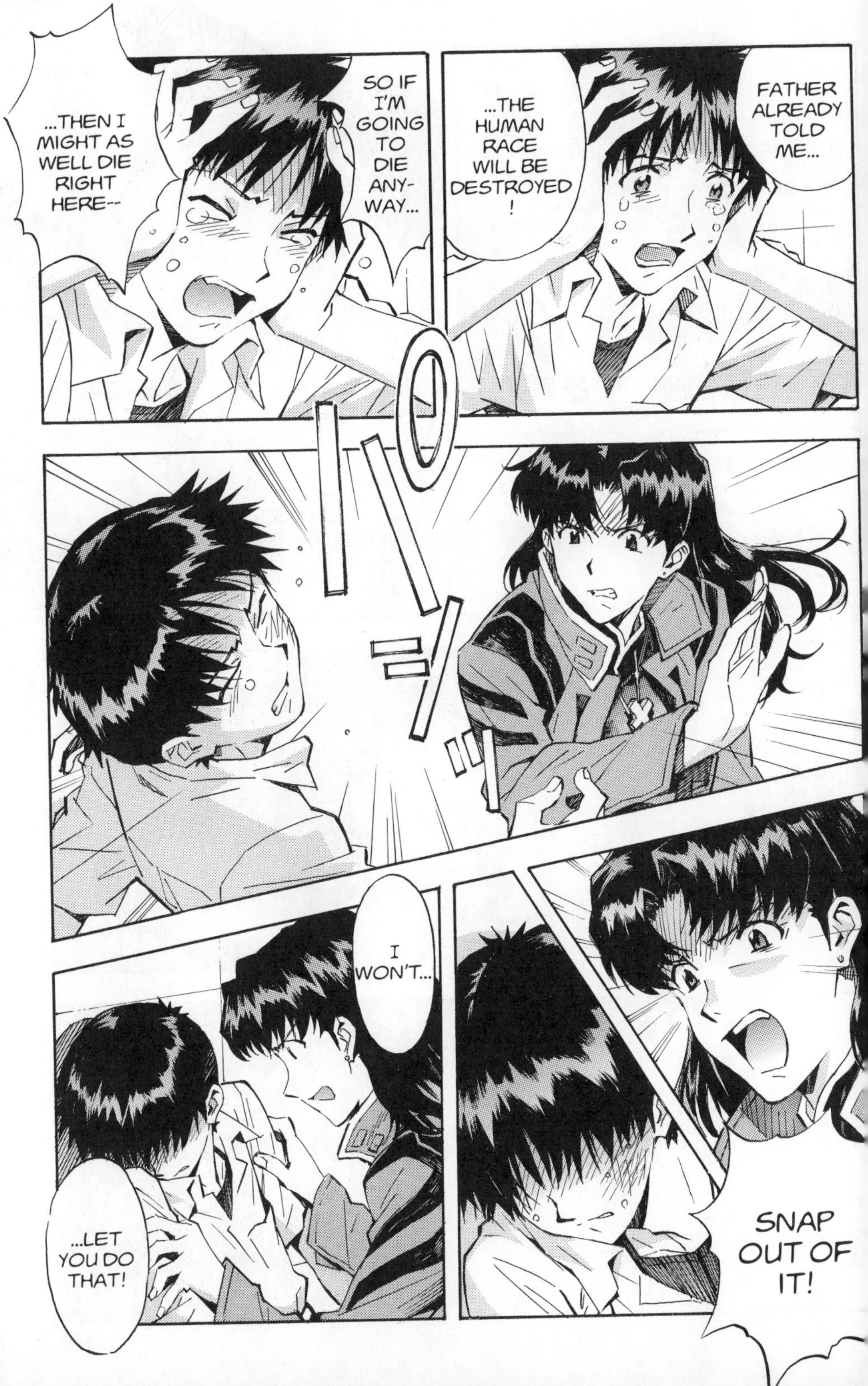
FATHER ALREADY TOLD ME...
...THE HUMAN RACE WILL BE DESTROYED!
SO IF I'M GOING TO DIE ANYWAY...
...THEN I MIGHT AS WELL DIE RIGHT HERE--
SNAP OUT OF IT!
I WON'T...
...LET YOU DO THAT!

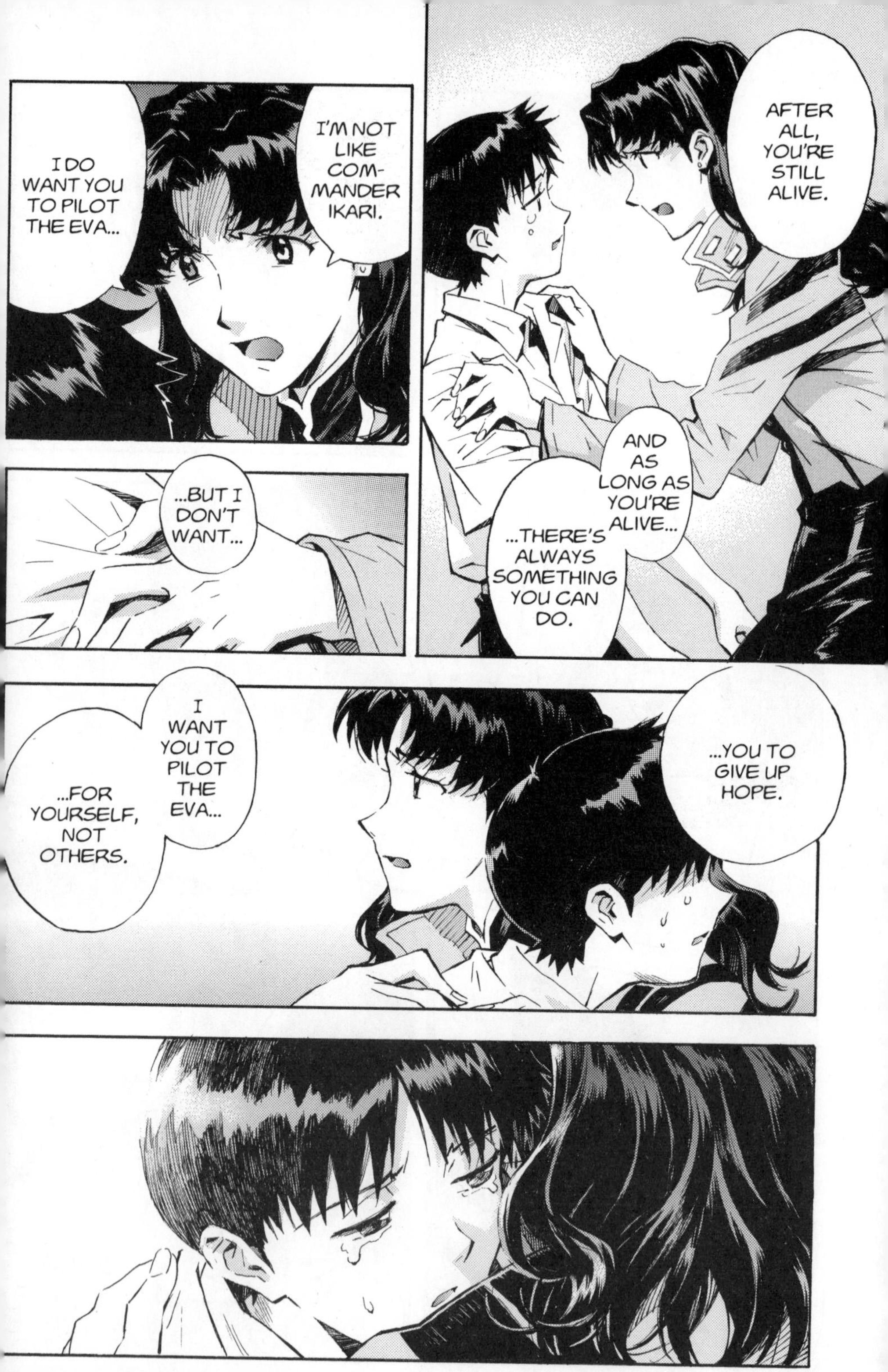
AFTER ALL, YOU'RE STILL ALIVE.
AND AS LONG AS YOU'RE ALIVE...
...THERE'S ALWAYS SOMETHING YOU CAN DO.
I'M NOT LIKE COM-MANDER IKARI.
I DO WANT YOU TO PILOT THE EVA...
...BUT I DON'T WANT...
...YOU TO GIVE UP HOPE.
I WANT YOU TO PILOT THE EVA...
...FOR YOURSELF, NOT OTHERS.

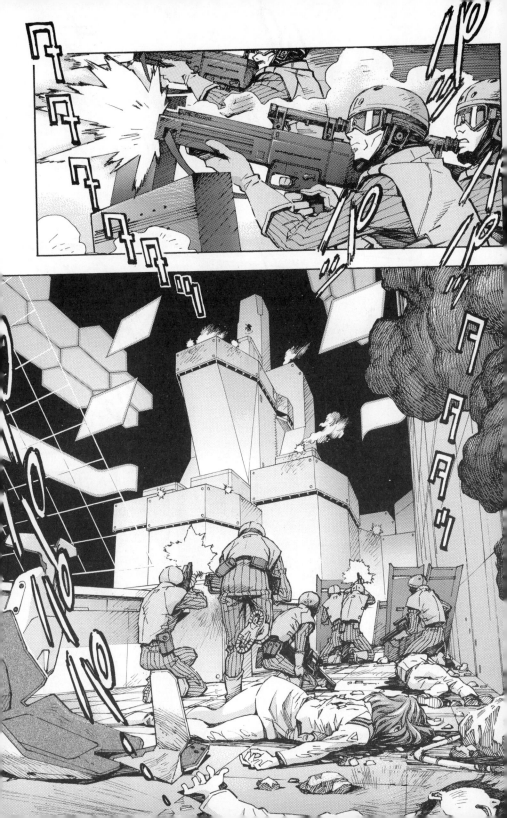

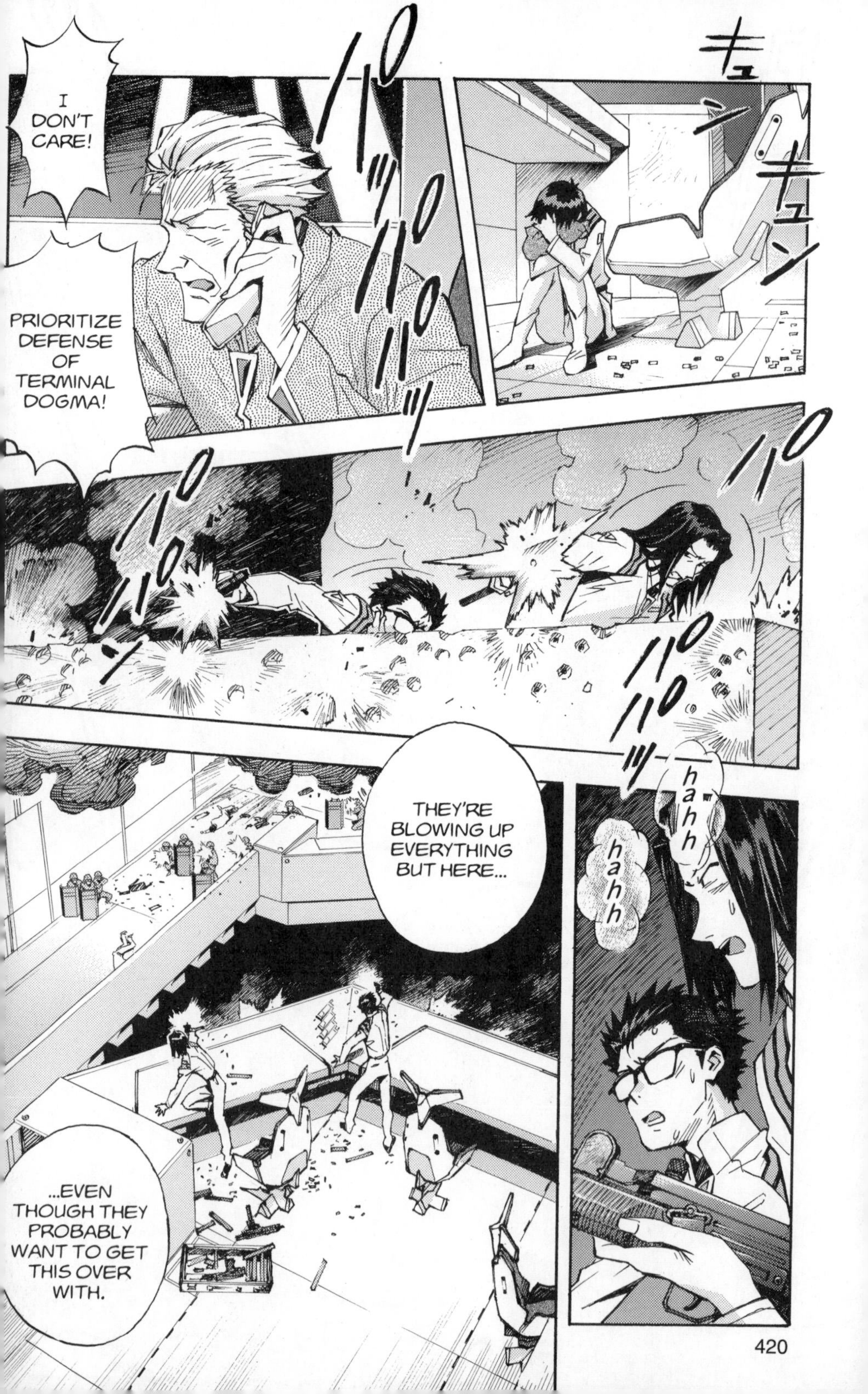
キュン
キュン
I DON'T CARE!
PRIORITIZE DEFENSE OF TERMINAL DOGMA!
hahh
hahh
THEY'RE BLOWING UP EVERYTHING BUT HERE...
...EVEN THOUGH THEY PROBABLY WANT TO GET THIS OVER WITH.

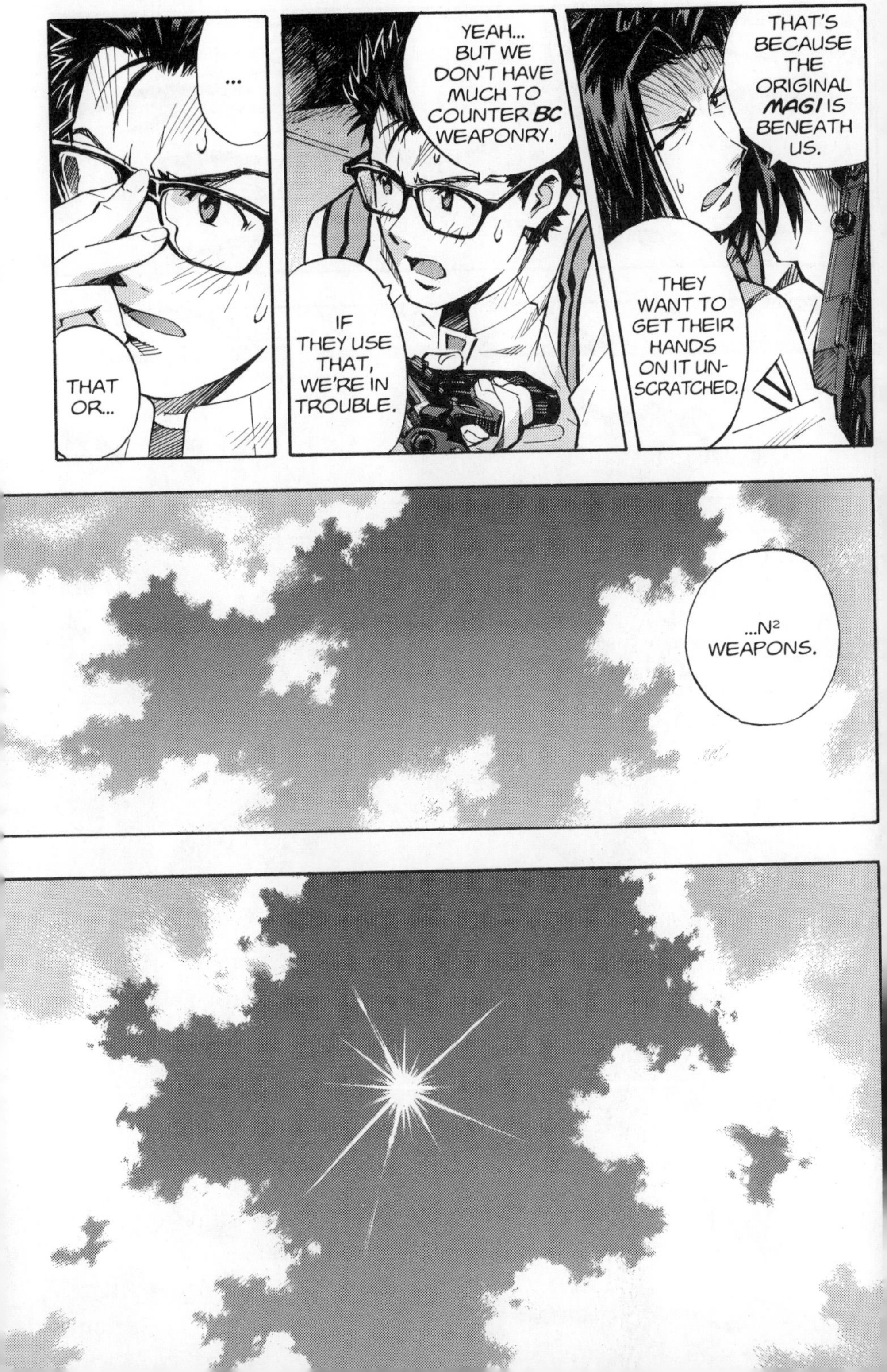
THAT'S BECAUSE THE ORIGINAL MAGI IS BENEATH US.
THEY WANT TO GET THEIR HANDS ON IT UN-SCRATCHED.
YEAH... BUT WE DON'T HAVE MUCH TO COUNTER BC WEAPONRY.
IF THEY USE THAT, WE'RE IN TROUBLE.
...
THAT OR...
...N^2 WEAPONS.

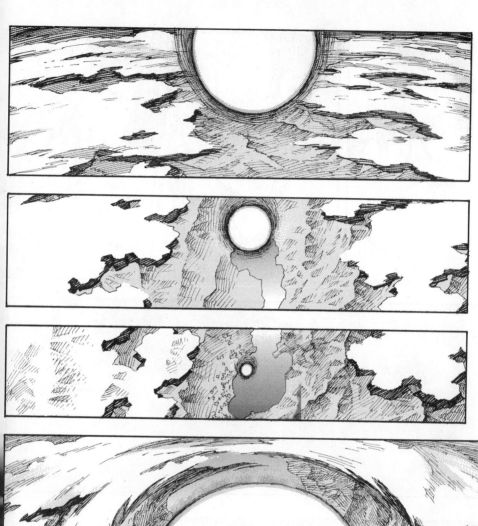

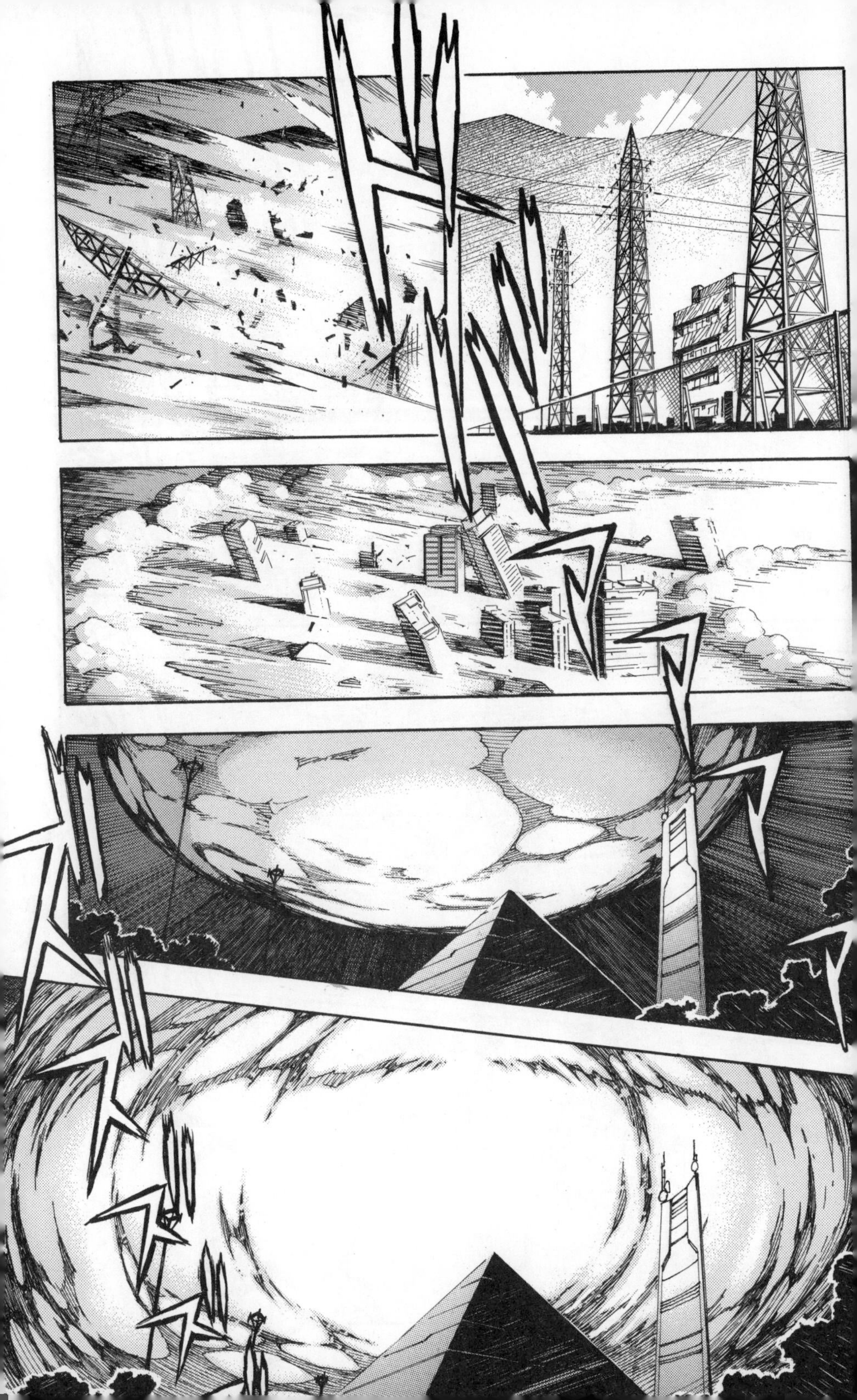

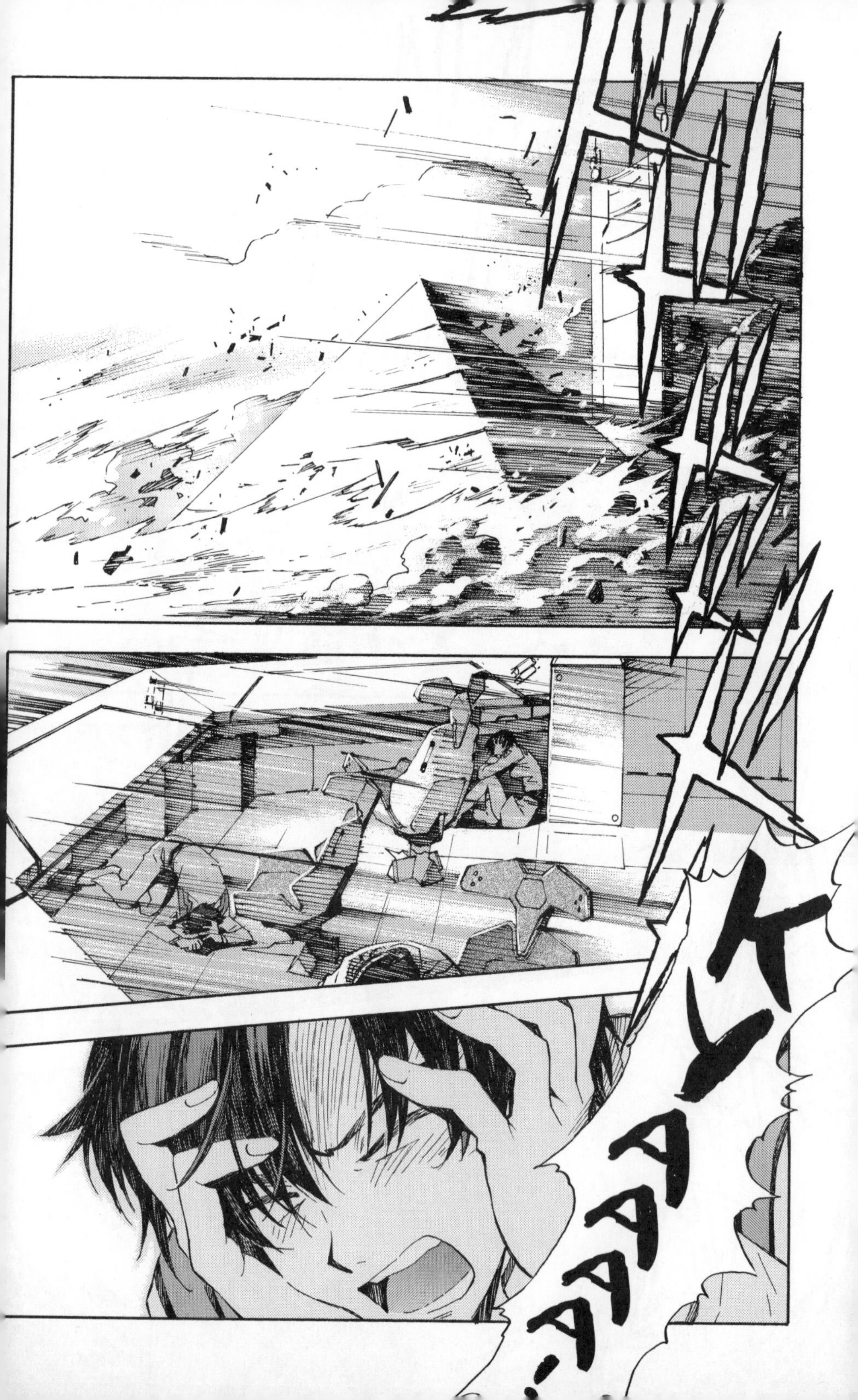
KYAAAA!

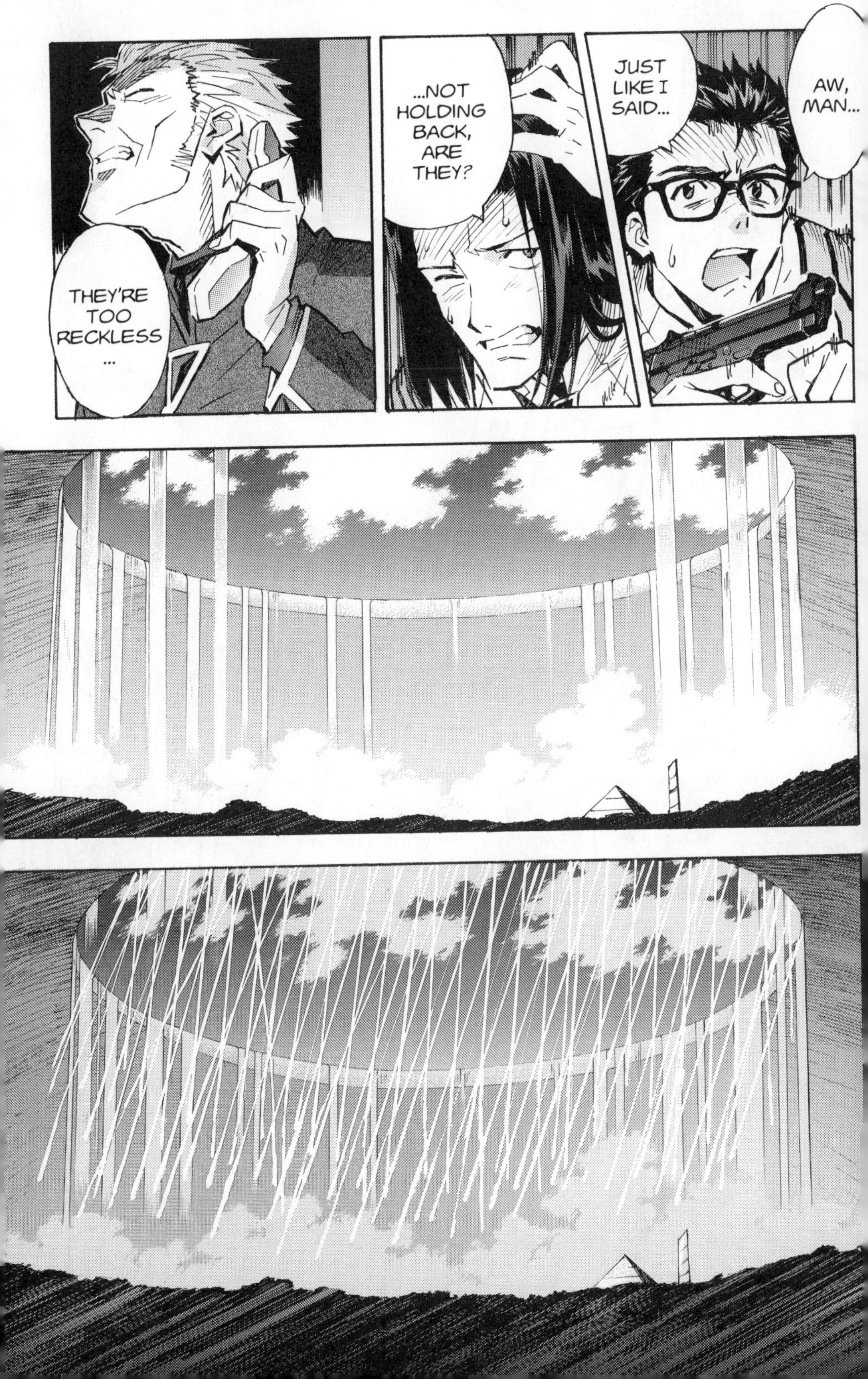
AW, MAN...
JUST LIKE I SAID...
...NOT HOLDING BACK, ARE THEY?
THEY'RE TOO RECKLESS ...

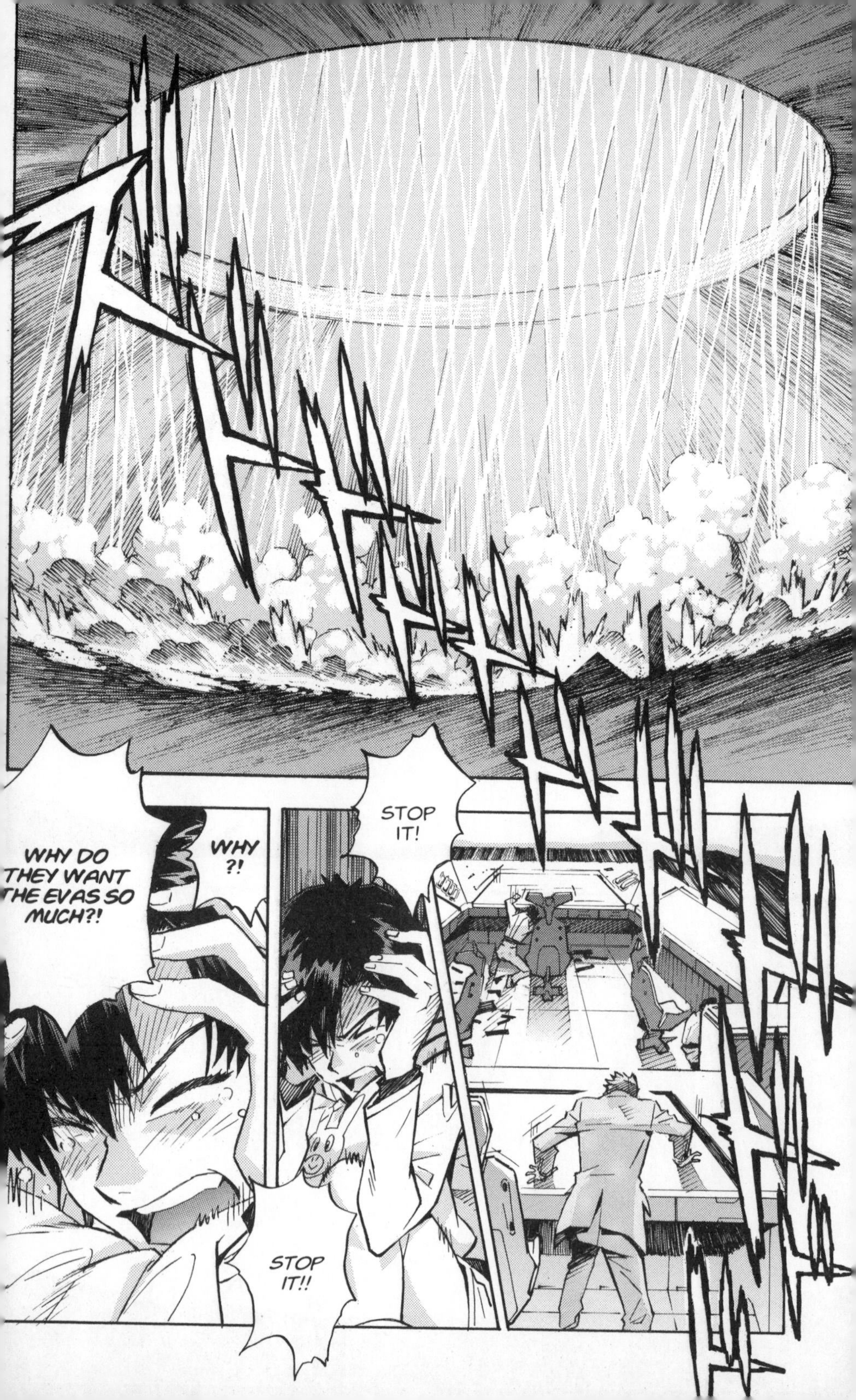
STOP IT!
STOP IT!!
WHY ?!
WHY DO THEY WANT THE EVAS SO MUCH?!

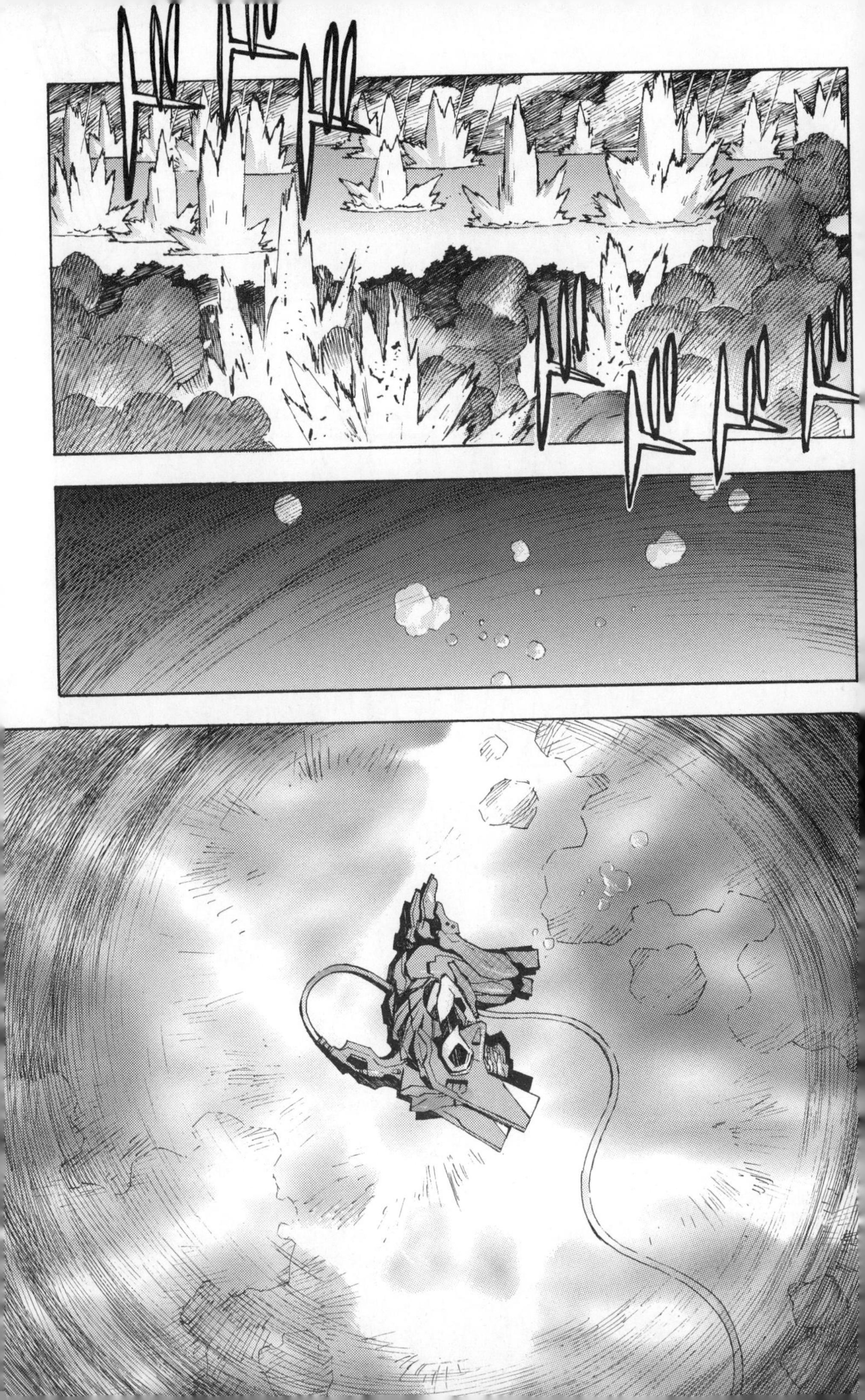

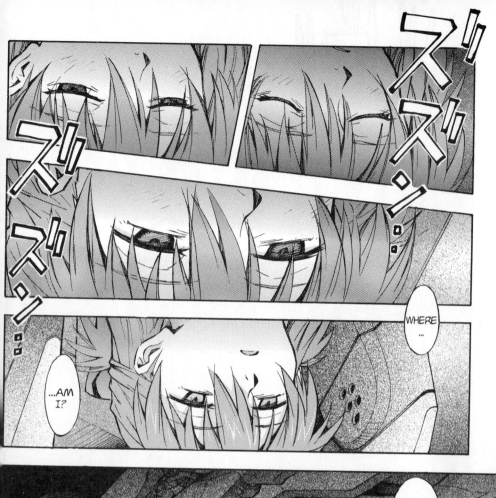

WHERE
...

...AM
I?

AN
ENTRY
PLUG...

...INSIDE
UNIT-02?

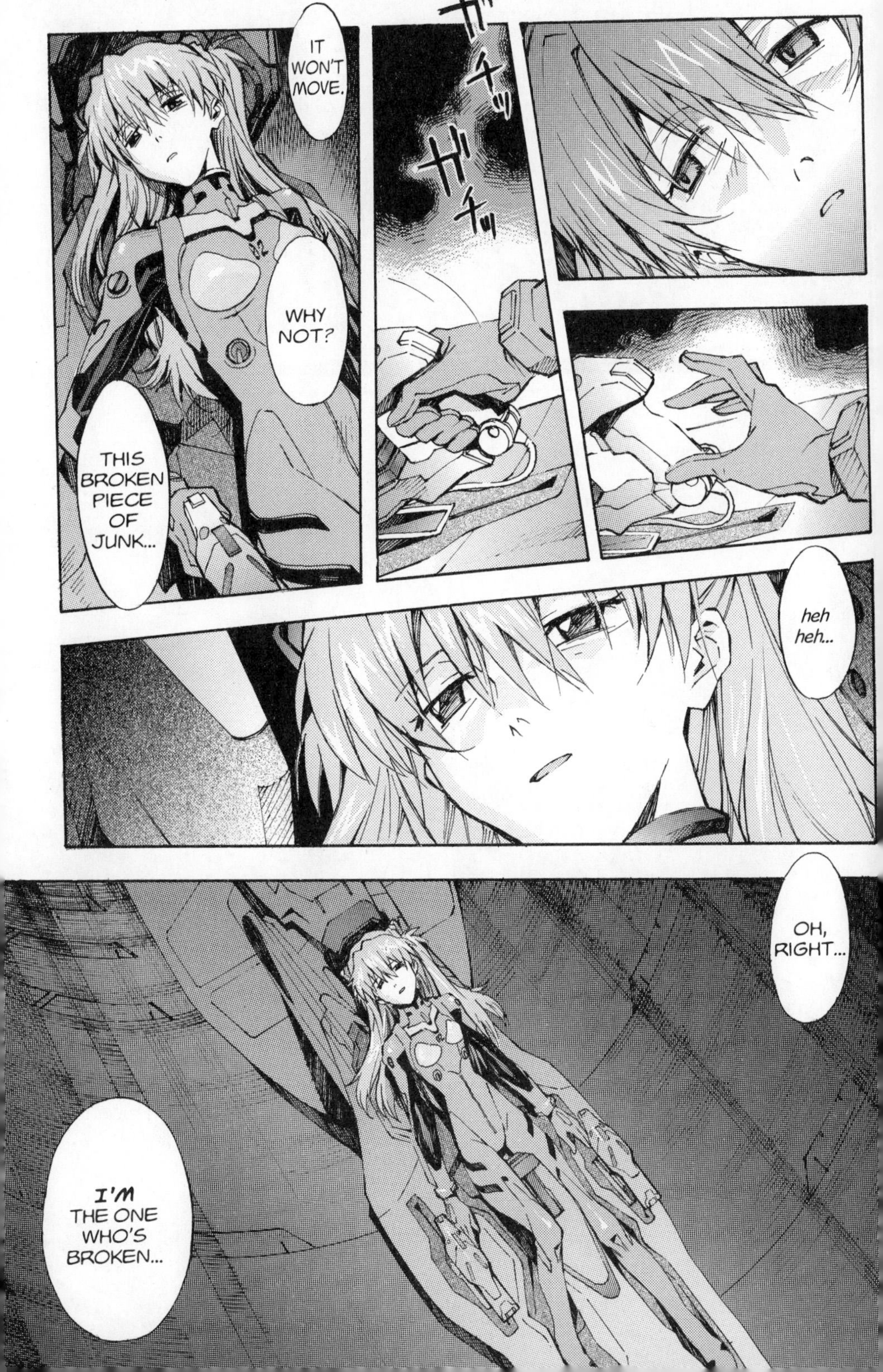
ガチッ
ガチッ
IT WON'T MOVE.
WHY NOT?
THIS BROKEN PIECE OF JUNK...
heh heh...
OH, RIGHT...
I'M THE ONE WHO'S BROKEN...

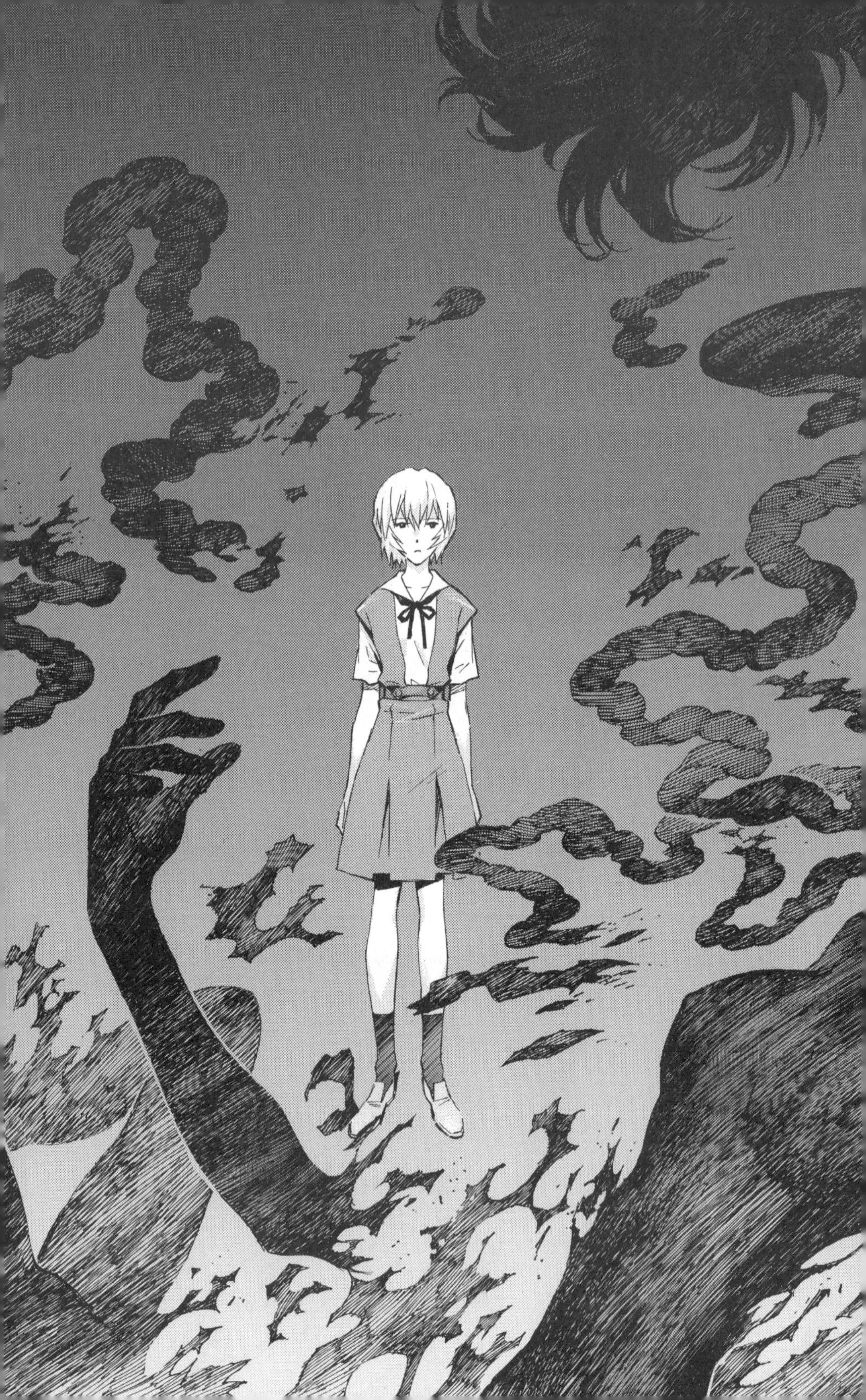

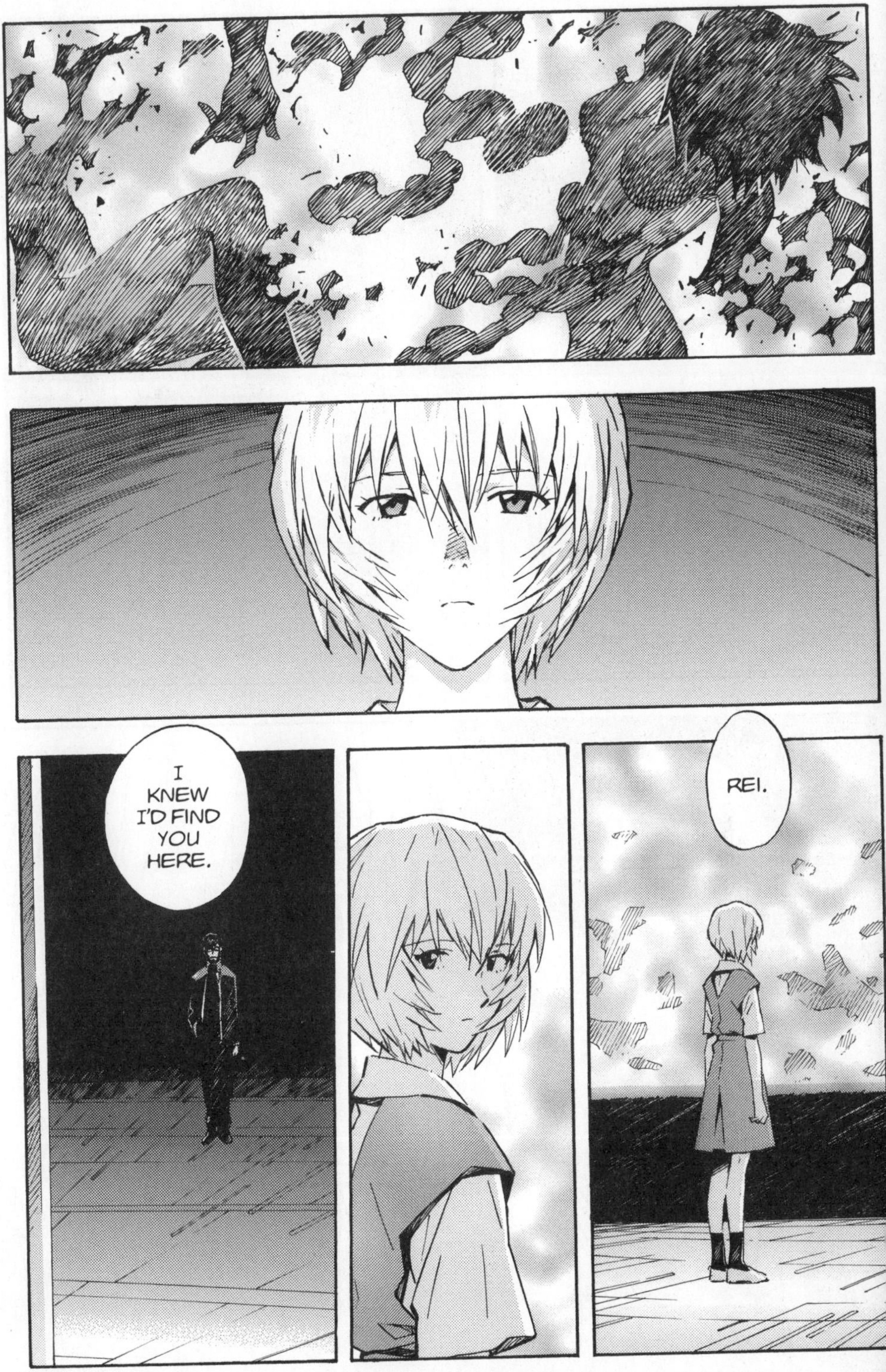
REI.
I KNEW I'D FIND YOU HERE.

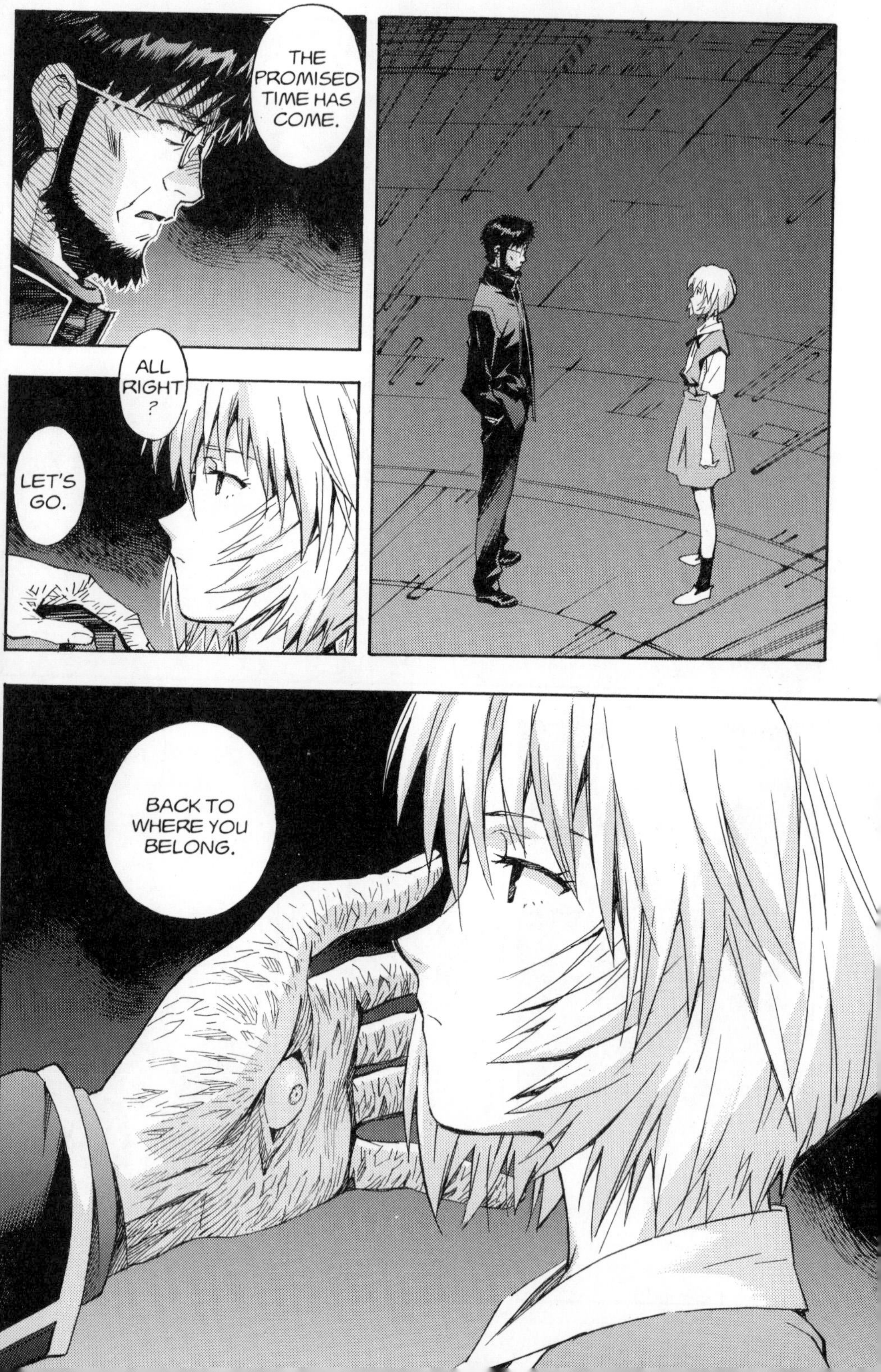
THE PROMISED TIME HAS COME.
ALL RIGHT?
LET'S GO.
BACK TO WHERE YOU BELONG.

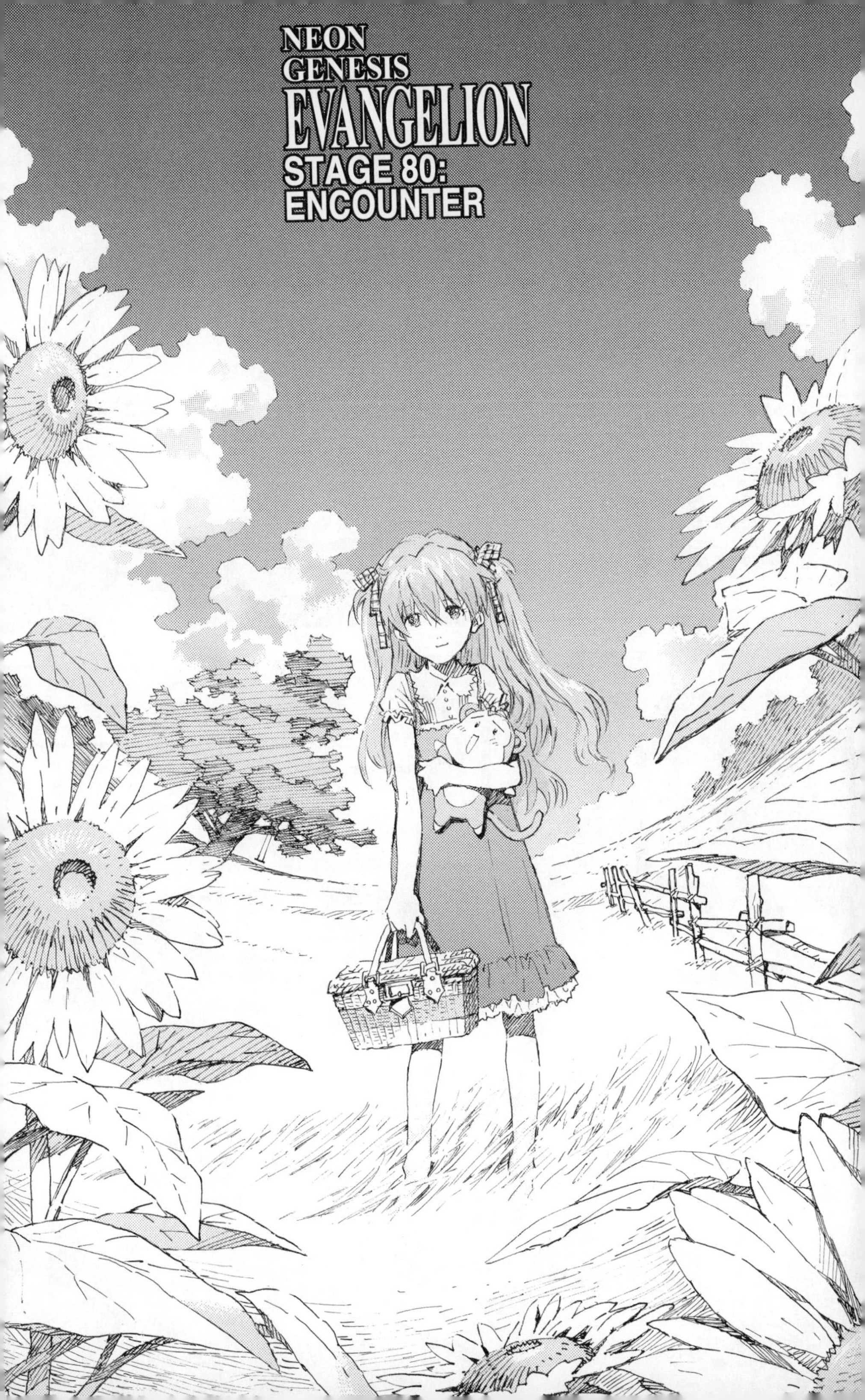
NEON
GENESIS
EVANGELION
STAGE 80:
ENCOUNTER

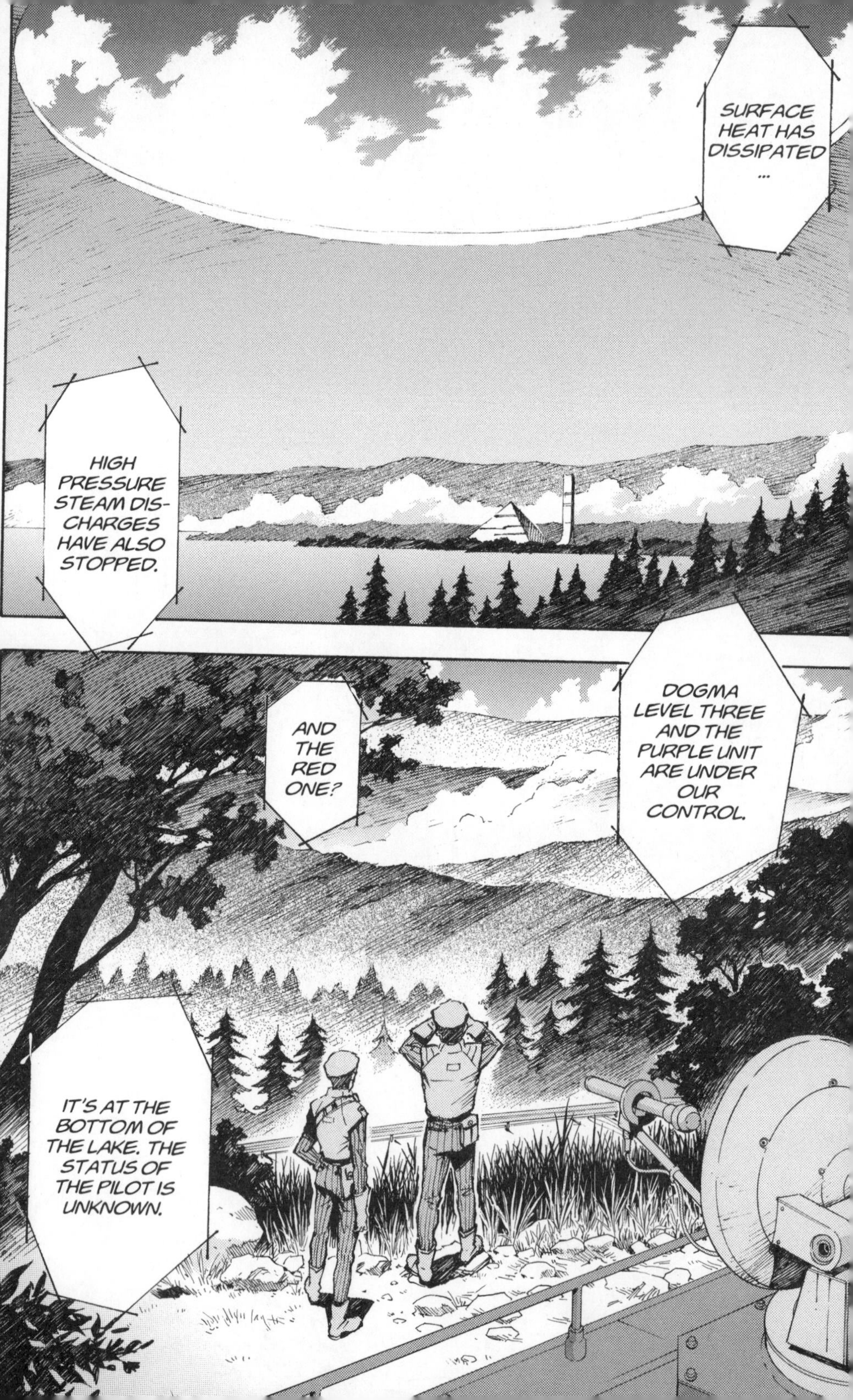
SURFACE HEAT HAS DISSIPATED ...
HIGH PRESSURE STEAM DIS- CHARGES HAVE ALSO STOPPED.
DOGMA LEVEL THREE AND THE PURPLE UNIT ARE UNDER OUR CONTROL.
AND THE RED ONE?
IT'S AT THE BOTTOM OF THE LAKE. THE STATUS OF THE PILOT IS UNKNOWN.

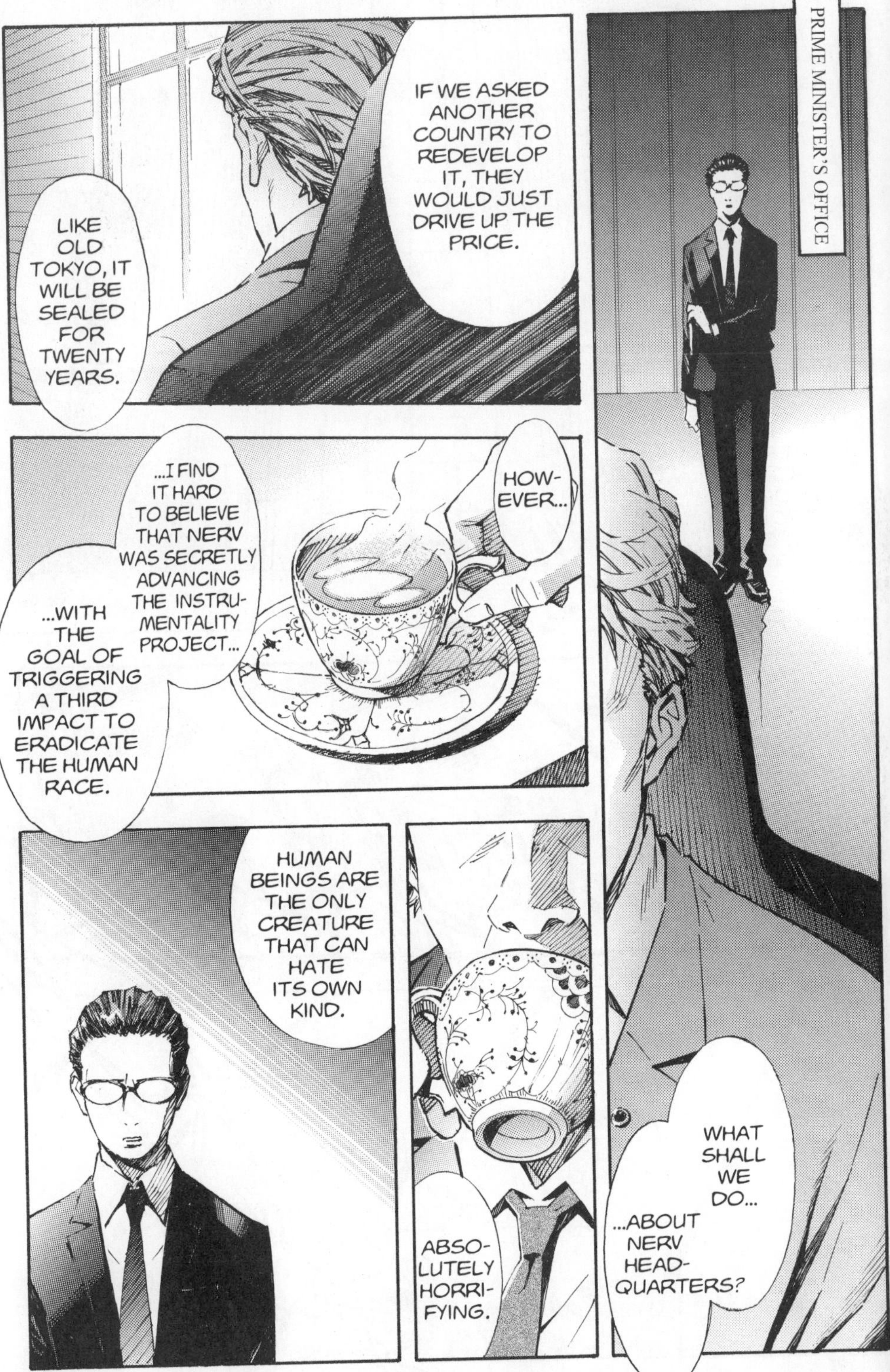
PRIME MINISTER'S OFFICE
WHAT SHALL WE DO...
...ABOUT NERV HEADQUARTERS?
IF WE ASKED ANOTHER COUNTRY TO REDEVELOP IT, THEY WOULD JUST DRIVE UP THE PRICE.
LIKE OLD TOKYO, IT WILL BE SEALED FOR TWENTY YEARS.
HOW-EVER...
...I FIND IT HARD TO BELIEVE THAT NERV WAS SECRETLY ADVANCING THE INSTRUMENTALITY PROJECT...
...WITH THE GOAL OF TRIGGERING A THIRD IMPACT TO ERADICATE THE HUMAN RACE.
ABSO-LUTELY HORRI-FYING.
HUMAN BEINGS ARE THE ONLY CREATURE THAT CAN HATE ITS OWN KIND.

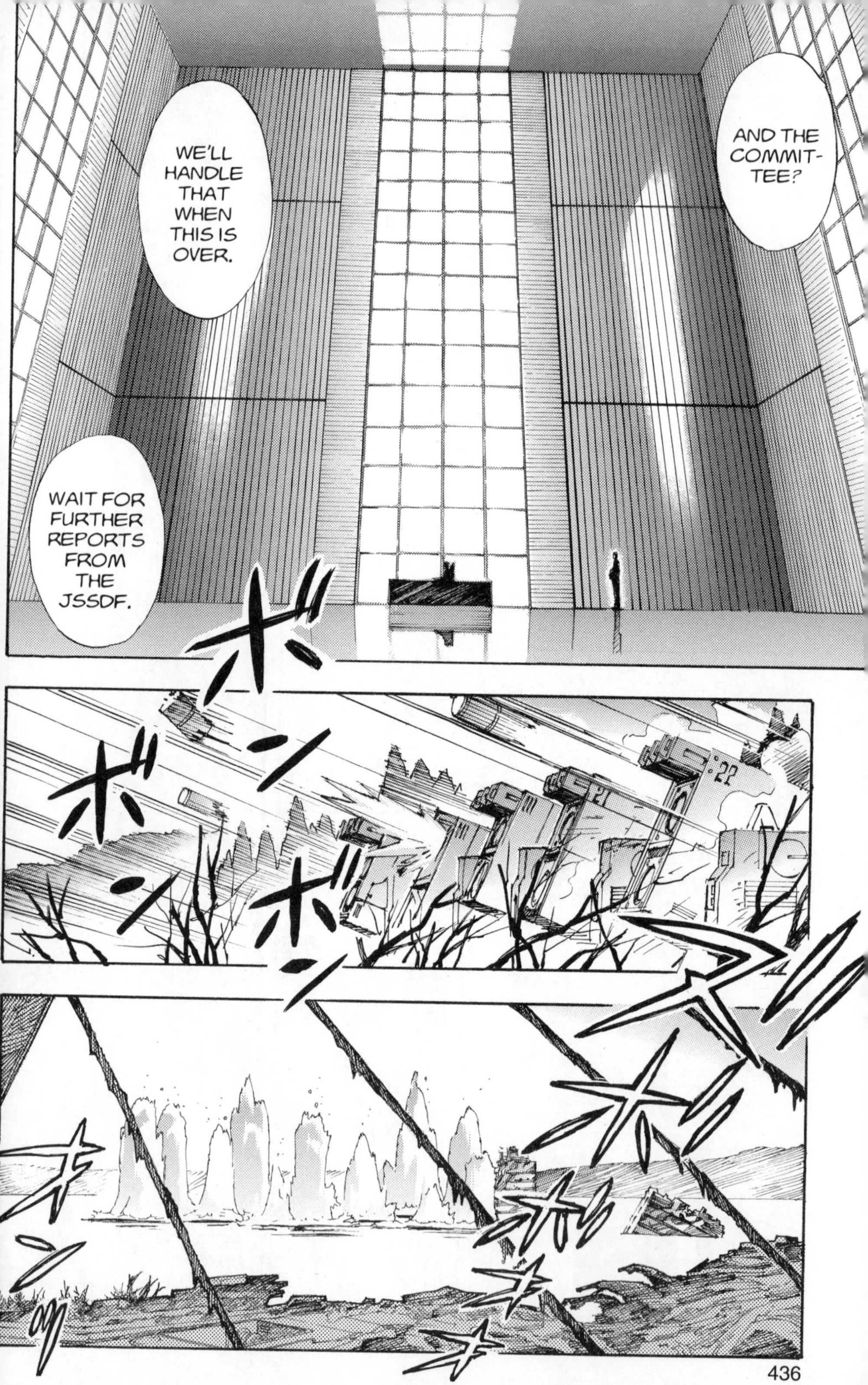
AND THE COMMIT-TEE?
WE'LL HANDLE THAT WHEN THIS IS OVER.
WAIT FOR FURTHER REPORTS FROM THE JSSDF.

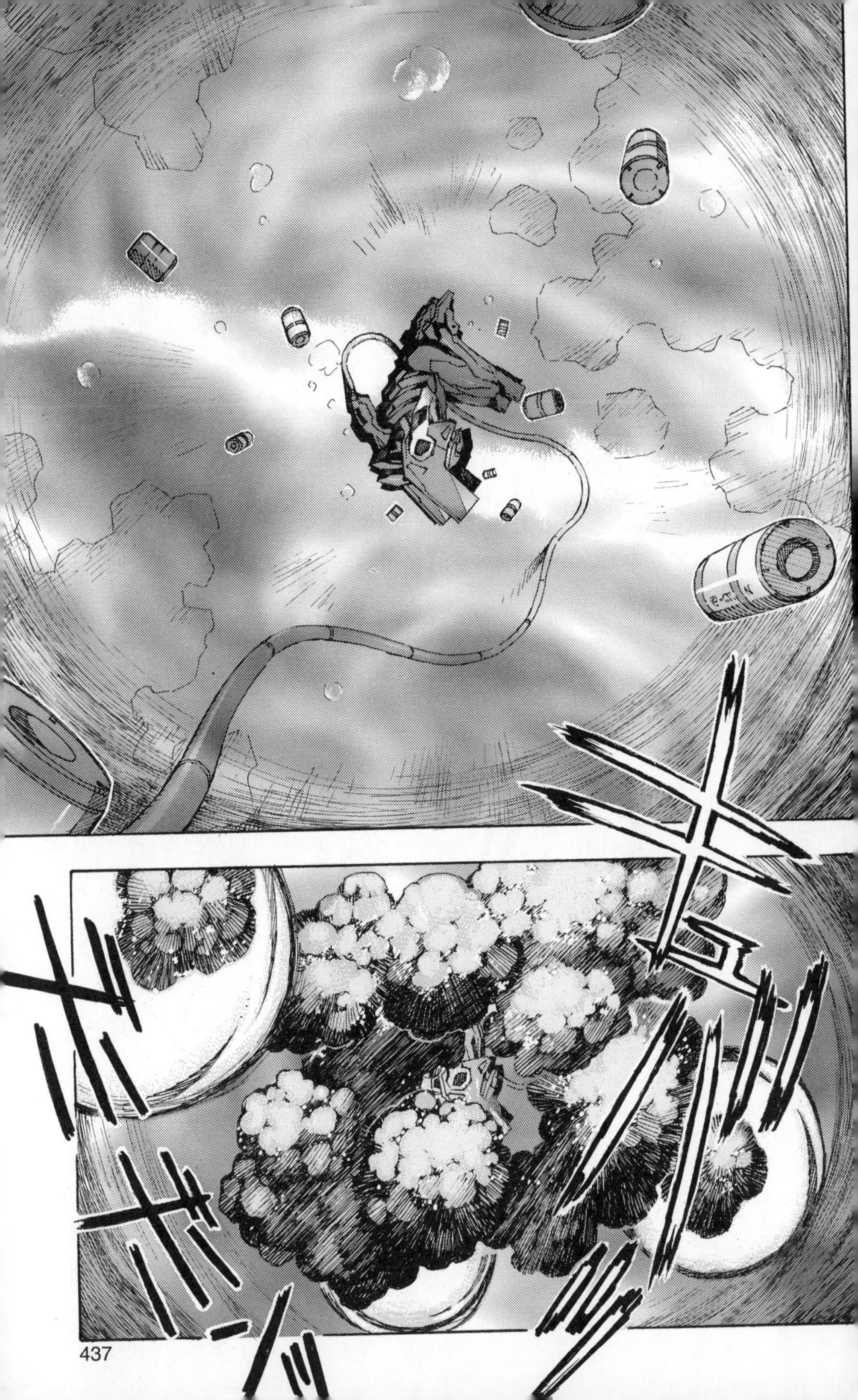

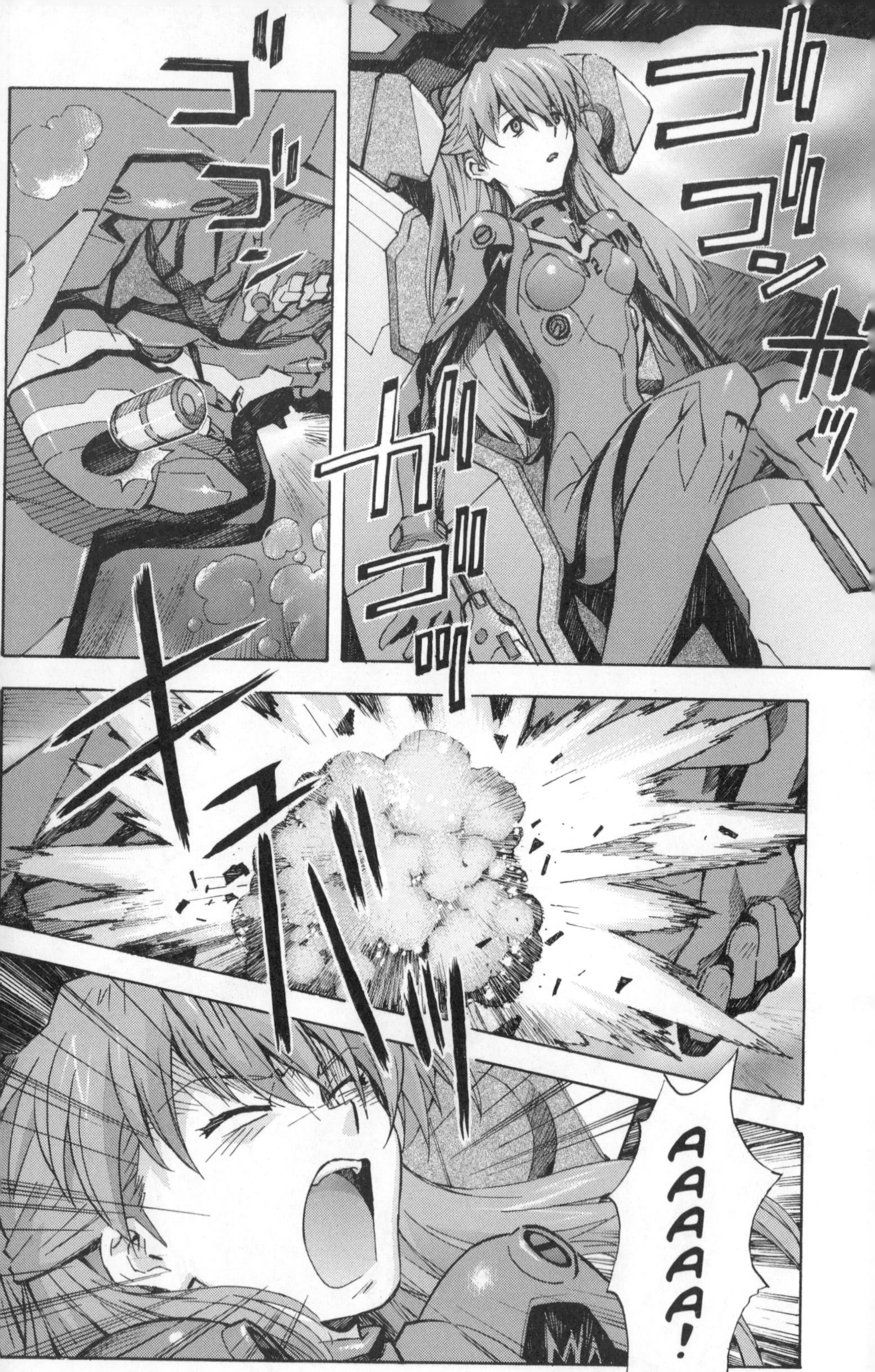
AAAAA!

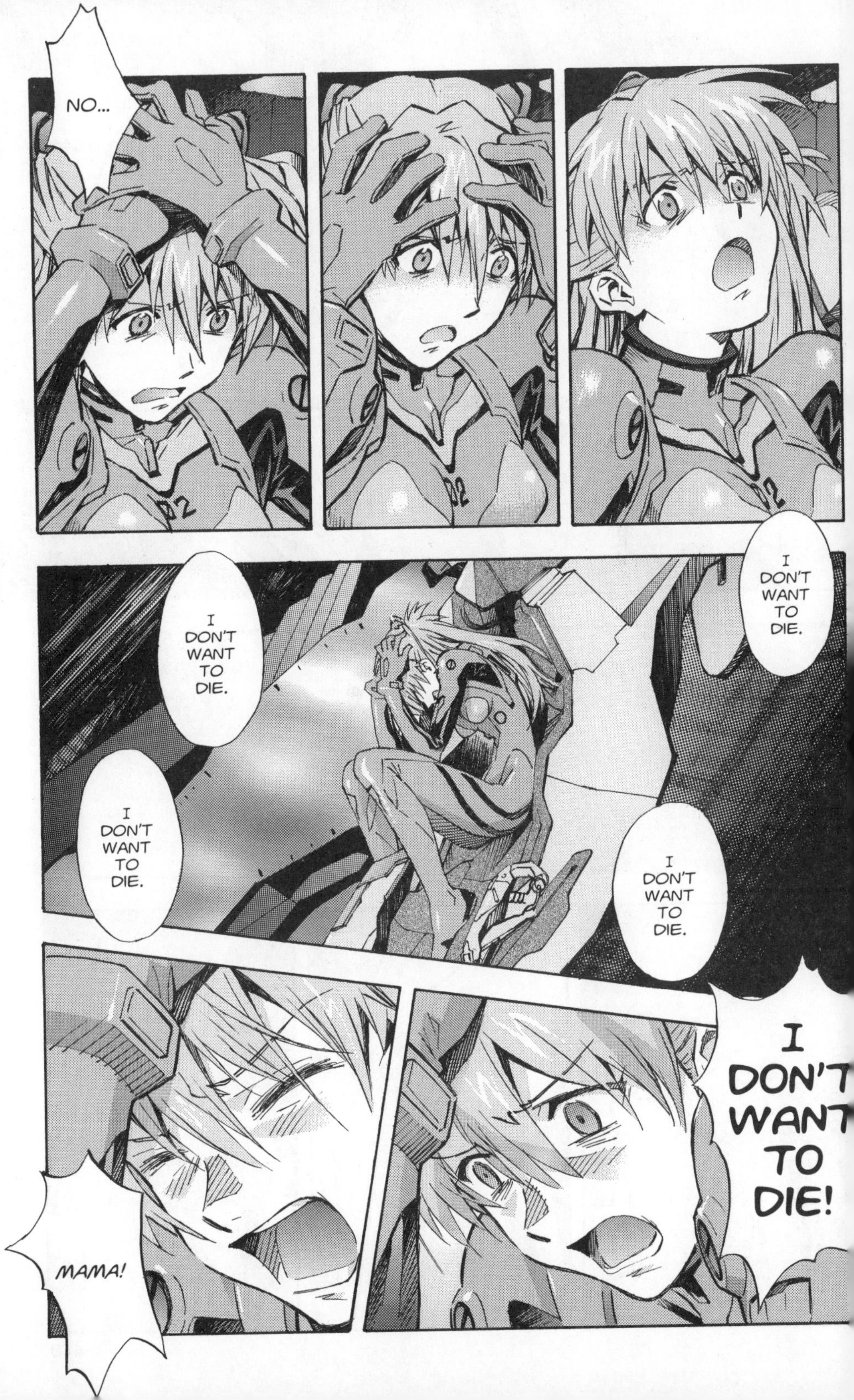
NO...
I DON'T WANT TO DIE.
I DON'T WANT TO DIE.
I DON'T WANT TO DIE.
I DON'T WANT TO DIE.
I DON'T WANT TO DIE!
MAMA!

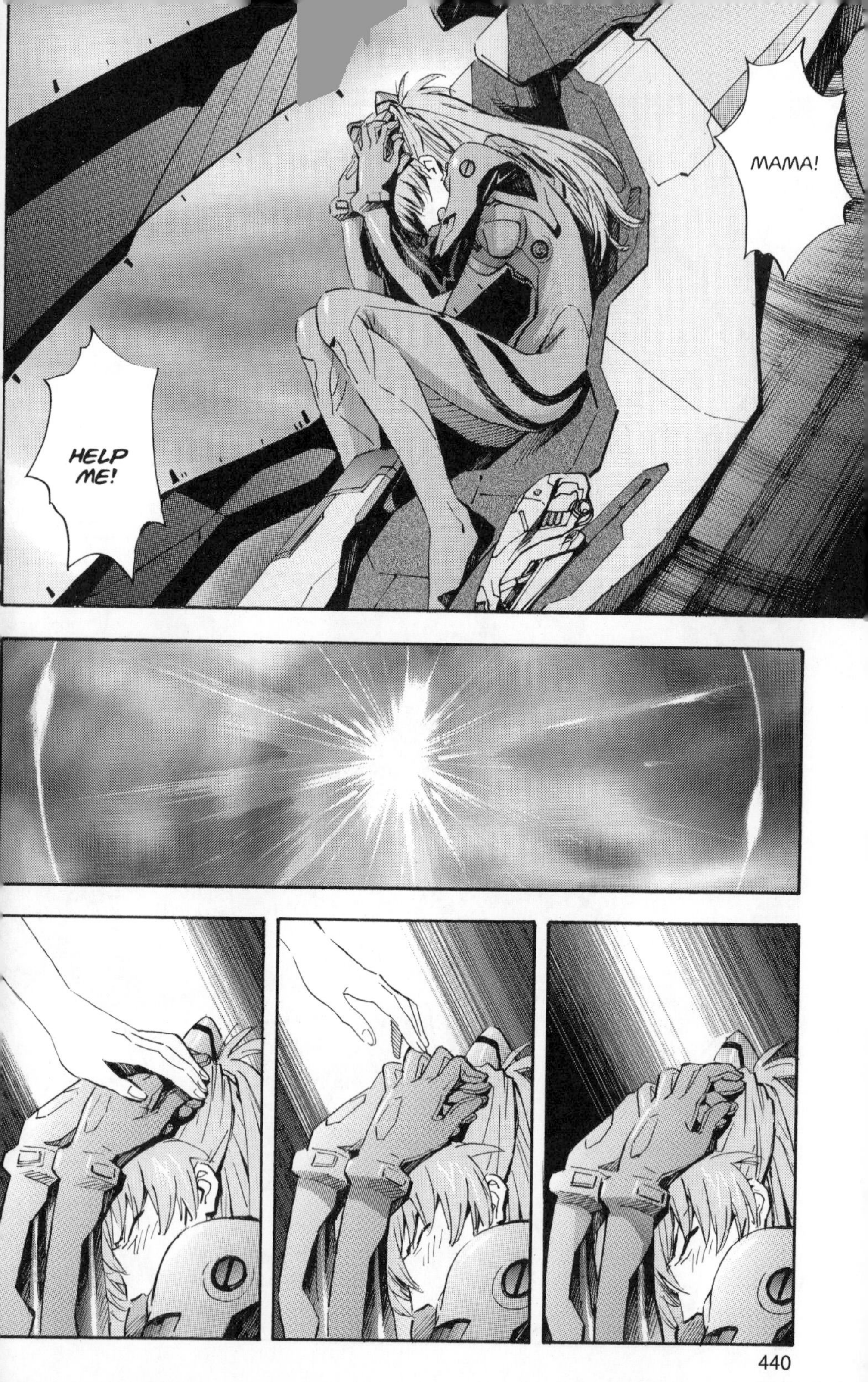
MAMA!
HELP ME!

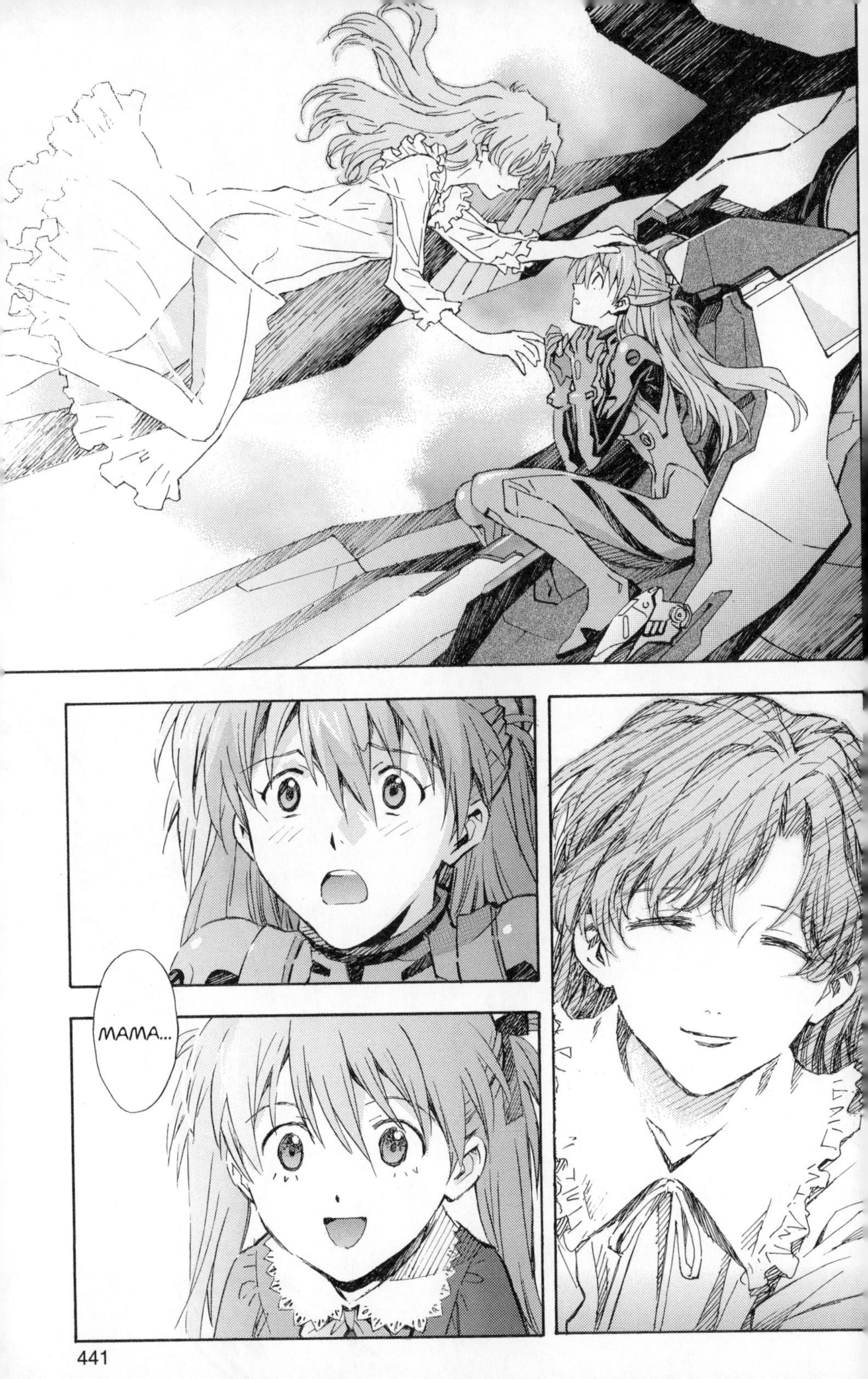
MAMA...

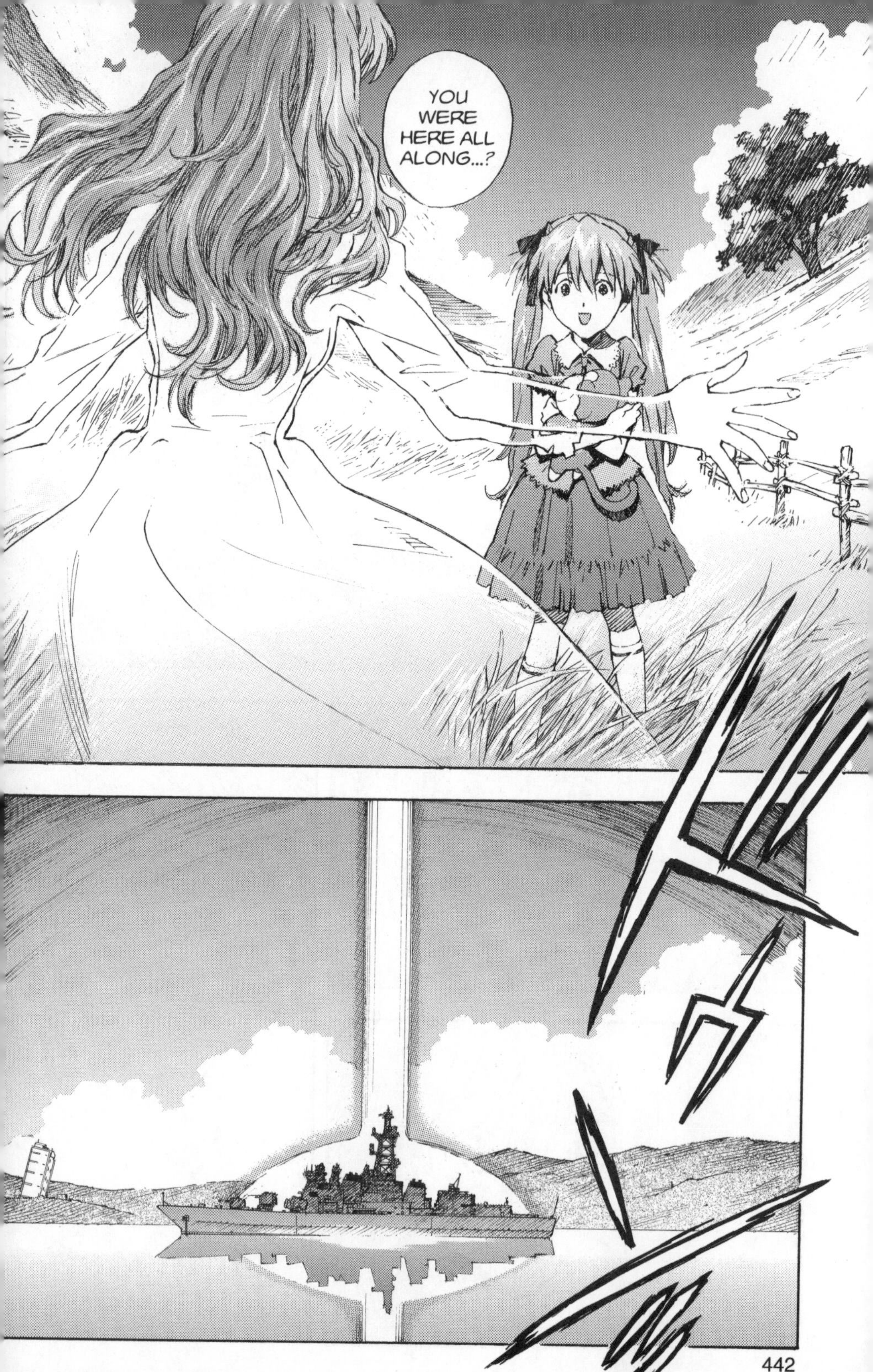
YOU WERE HERE ALL ALONG...?

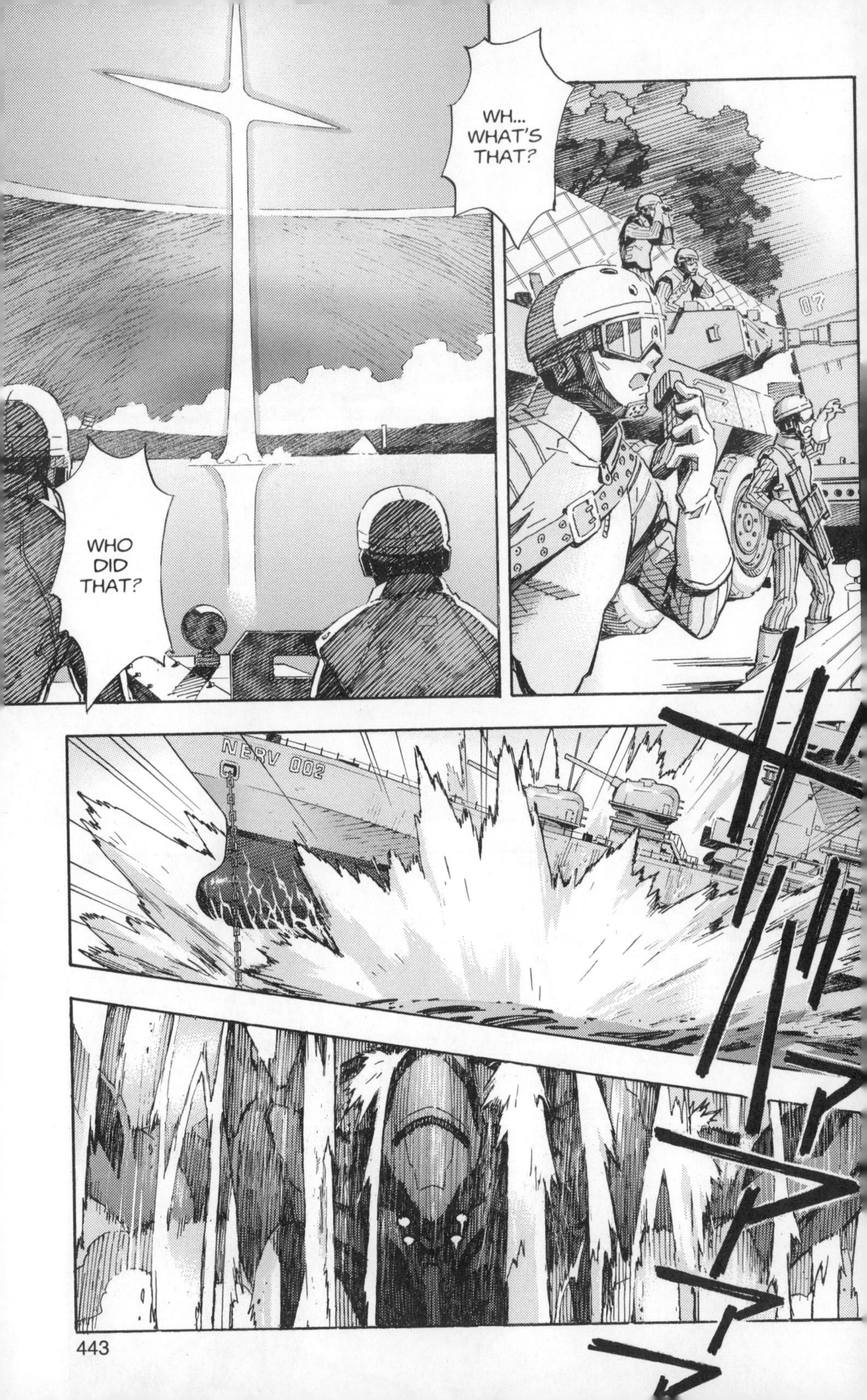
WH... WHAT'S THAT?
WHO DID THAT?
NERV 002

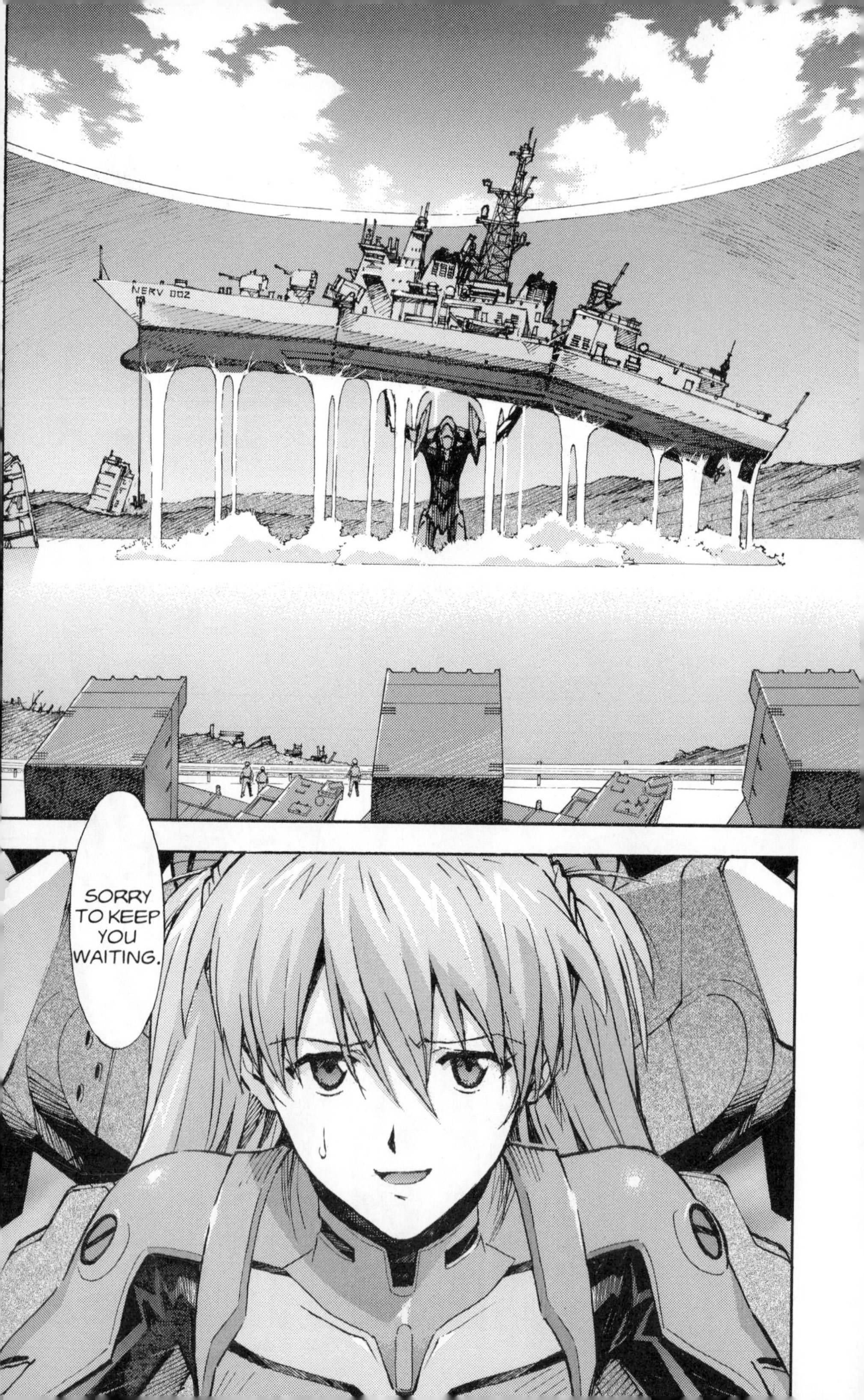
NERV 002
SORRY TO KEEP YOU WAITING.

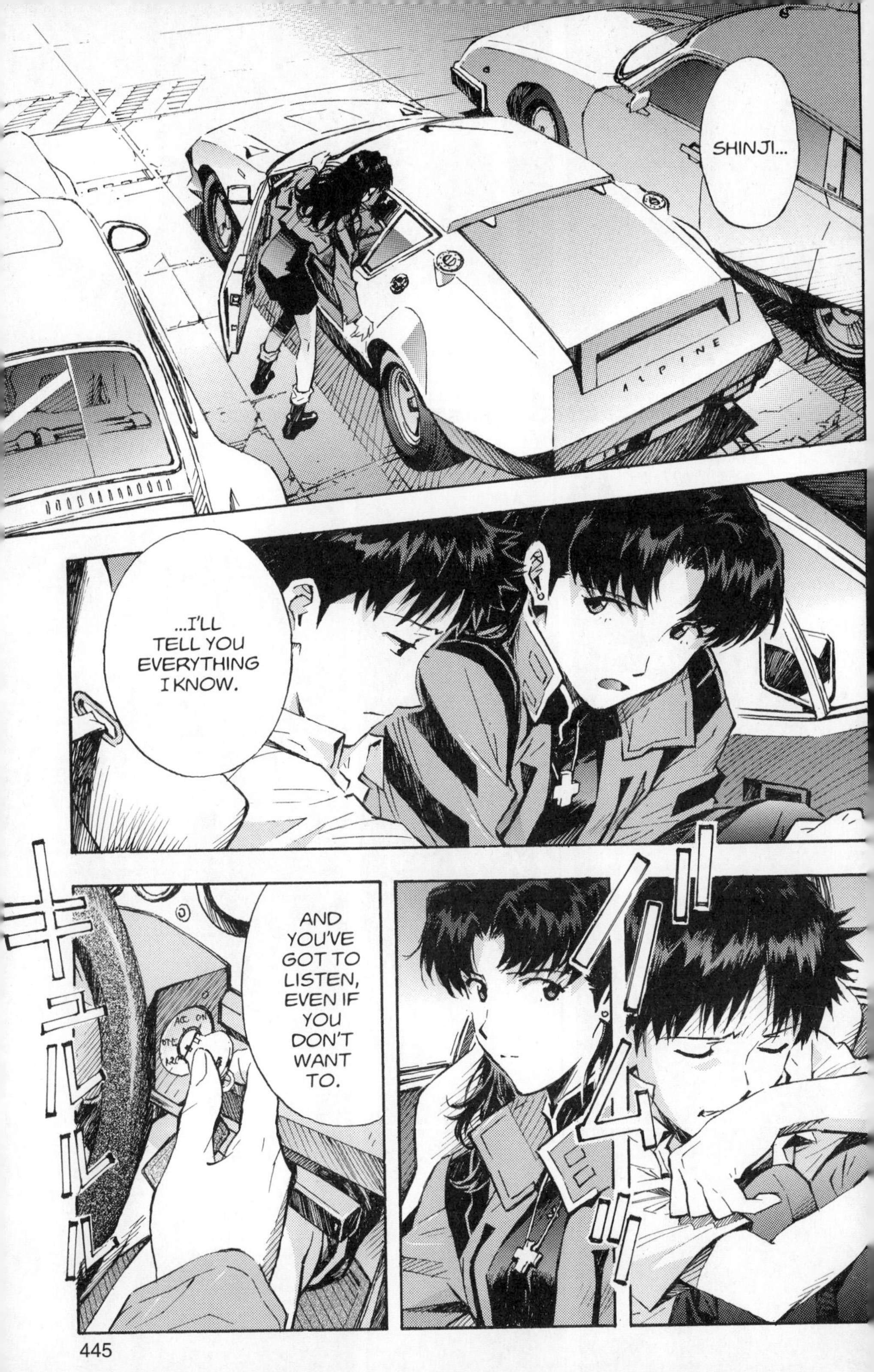
SHINJI...
...I'LL TELL YOU EVERYTHING I KNOW.
AND YOU'VE GOT TO LISTEN, EVEN IF YOU DON'T WANT TO.

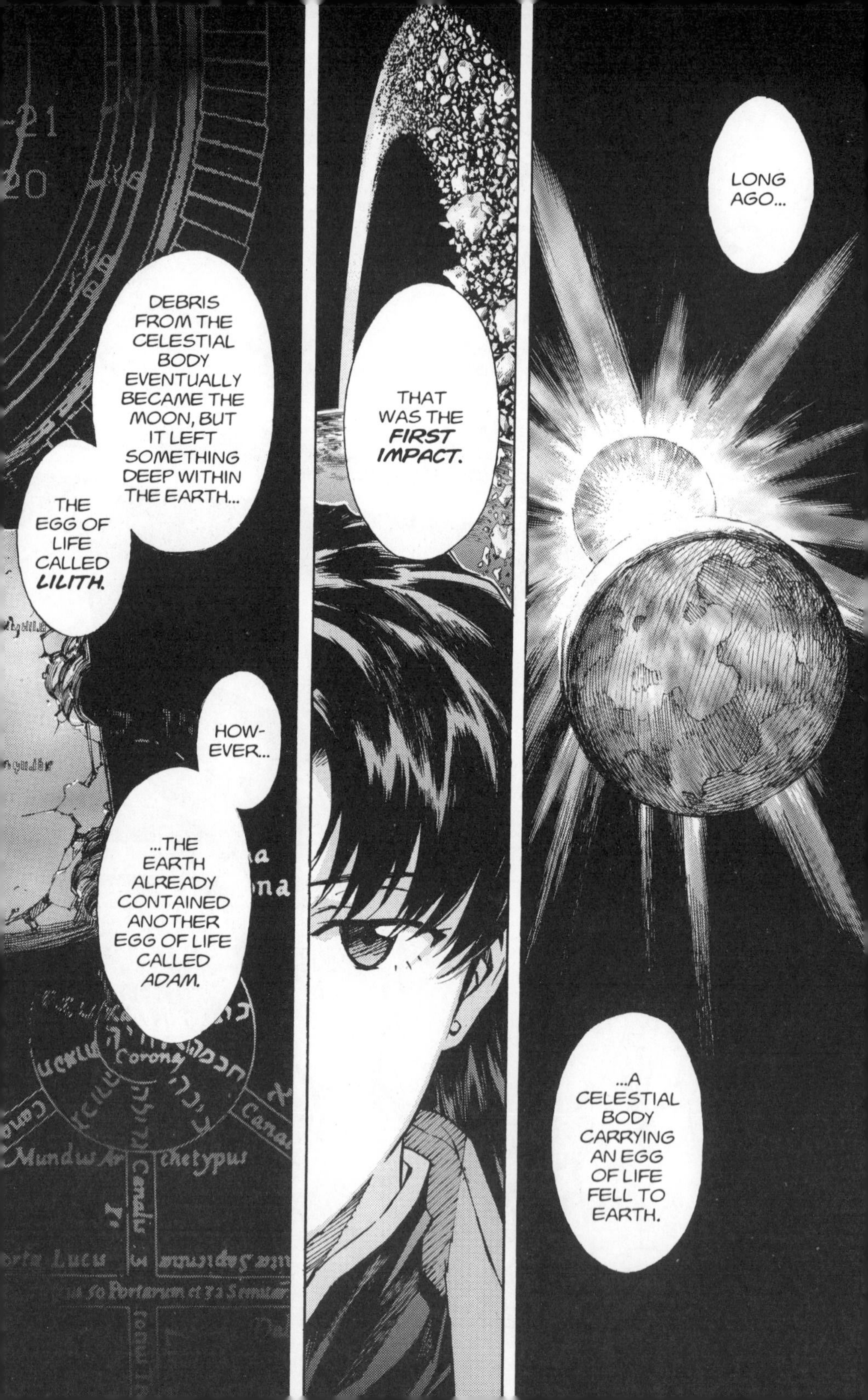
LONG AGO...
...A CELESTIAL BODY CARRYING AN EGG OF LIFE FELL TO EARTH.
THAT WAS THE *FIRST IMPACT*.
DEBRIS FROM THE CELESTIAL BODY EVENTUALLY BECAME THE MOON, BUT IT LEFT SOMETHING DEEP WITHIN THE EARTH...
THE EGG OF LIFE CALLED *LILITH*.
HOW-EVER...
...THE EARTH ALREADY CONTAINED ANOTHER EGG OF LIFE CALLED *ADAM*.

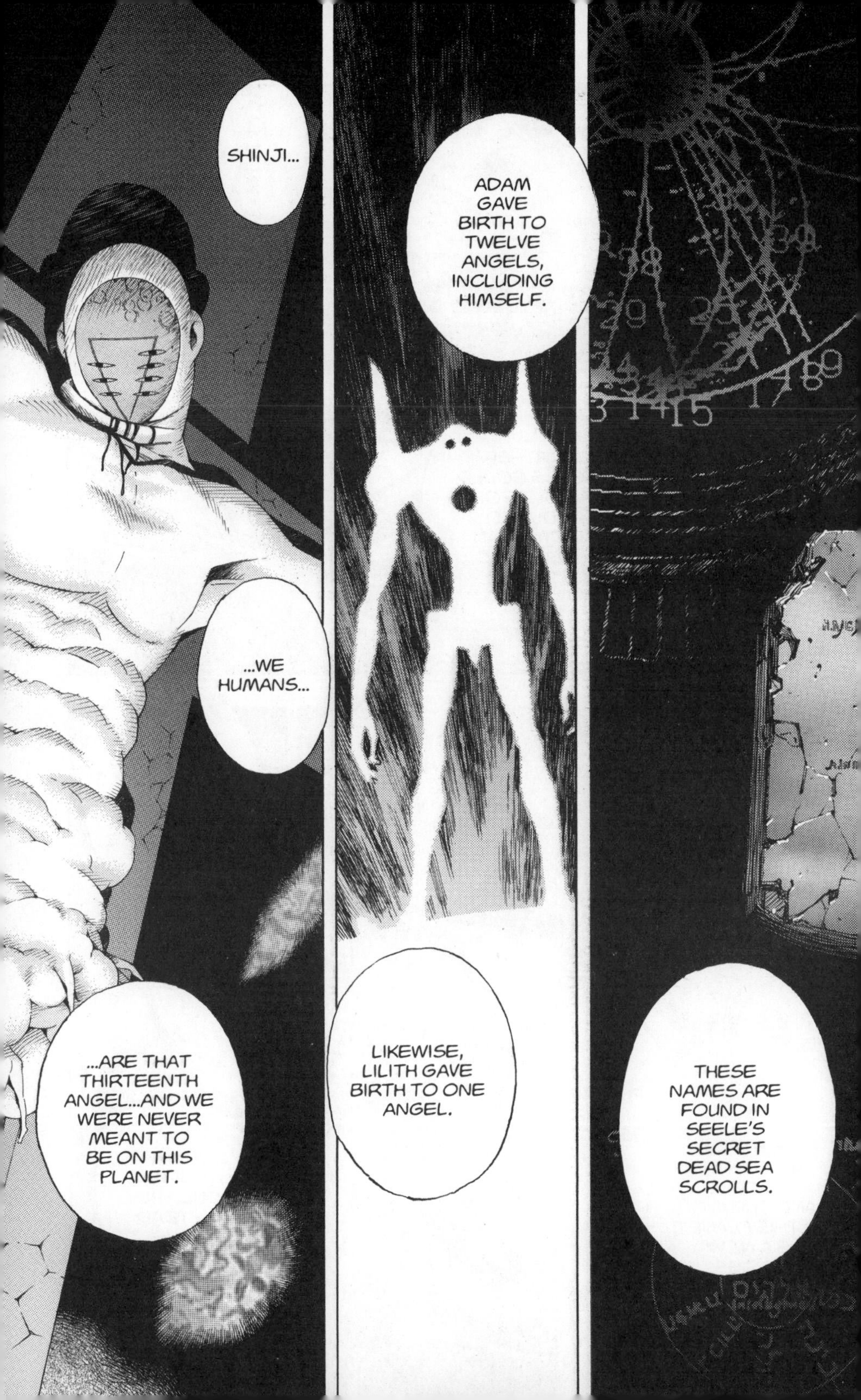
THESE NAMES ARE FOUND IN SEELE'S SECRET DEAD SEA SCROLLS.
ADAM GAVE BIRTH TO TWELVE ANGELS, INCLUDING HIMSELF.
LIKEWISE, LILITH GAVE BIRTH TO ONE ANGEL.
SHINJI...
...WE HUMANS...
...ARE THAT THIRTEENTH ANGEL...AND WE WERE NEVER MEANT TO BE ON THIS PLANET.

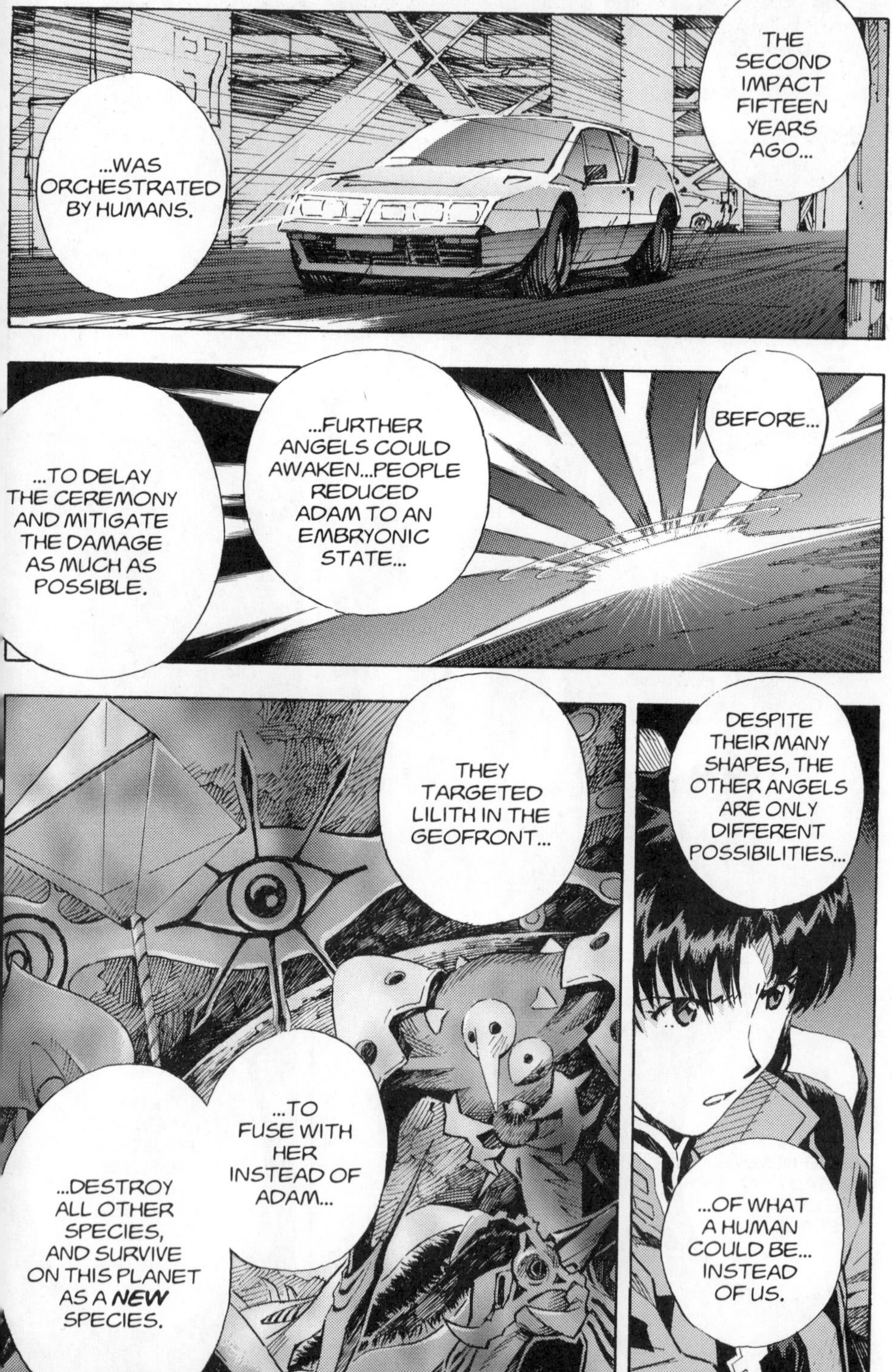
THE SECOND IMPACT FIFTEEN YEARS AGO...
...WAS ORCHESTRATED BY HUMANS.
BEFORE...
...FURTHER ANGELS COULD AWAKEN...PEOPLE REDUCED ADAM TO AN EMBRYONIC STATE...
...TO DELAY THE CEREMONY AND MITIGATE THE DAMAGE AS MUCH AS POSSIBLE.
DESPITE THEIR MANY SHAPES, THE OTHER ANGELS ARE ONLY DIFFERENT POSSIBILITIES...
...OF WHAT A HUMAN COULD BE... INSTEAD OF US.
THEY TARGETED LILITH IN THE GEOFRONT...
...TO FUSE WITH HER INSTEAD OF ADAM...
...DESTROY ALL OTHER SPECIES, AND SURVIVE ON THIS PLANET AS A ***NEW*** SPECIES.

HOW-
EVER...

...SEELE AND YOUR FATHER STILL HOPE FOR THE THIRD IMPACT.

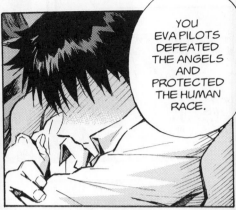

YOU EVA PILOTS DEFEATED THE ANGELS AND PROTECTED THE HUMAN RACE.

THEY WISH TO DESTROY HUMANKIND, THE LAST ANGEL...

...AND EVOLVE INTO A NEW FORM OF LIFE.

THAT IS THE INSTRUMEN-TALITY PROJECT.

BUT IT SEEMS...

THE EVAS HOLD THE KEY TO THE INSTRUMEN-TALITY PROJECT.

SHINJI...

...SEELE AND YOUR FATHER HAVE DIFFERENT GOALS.

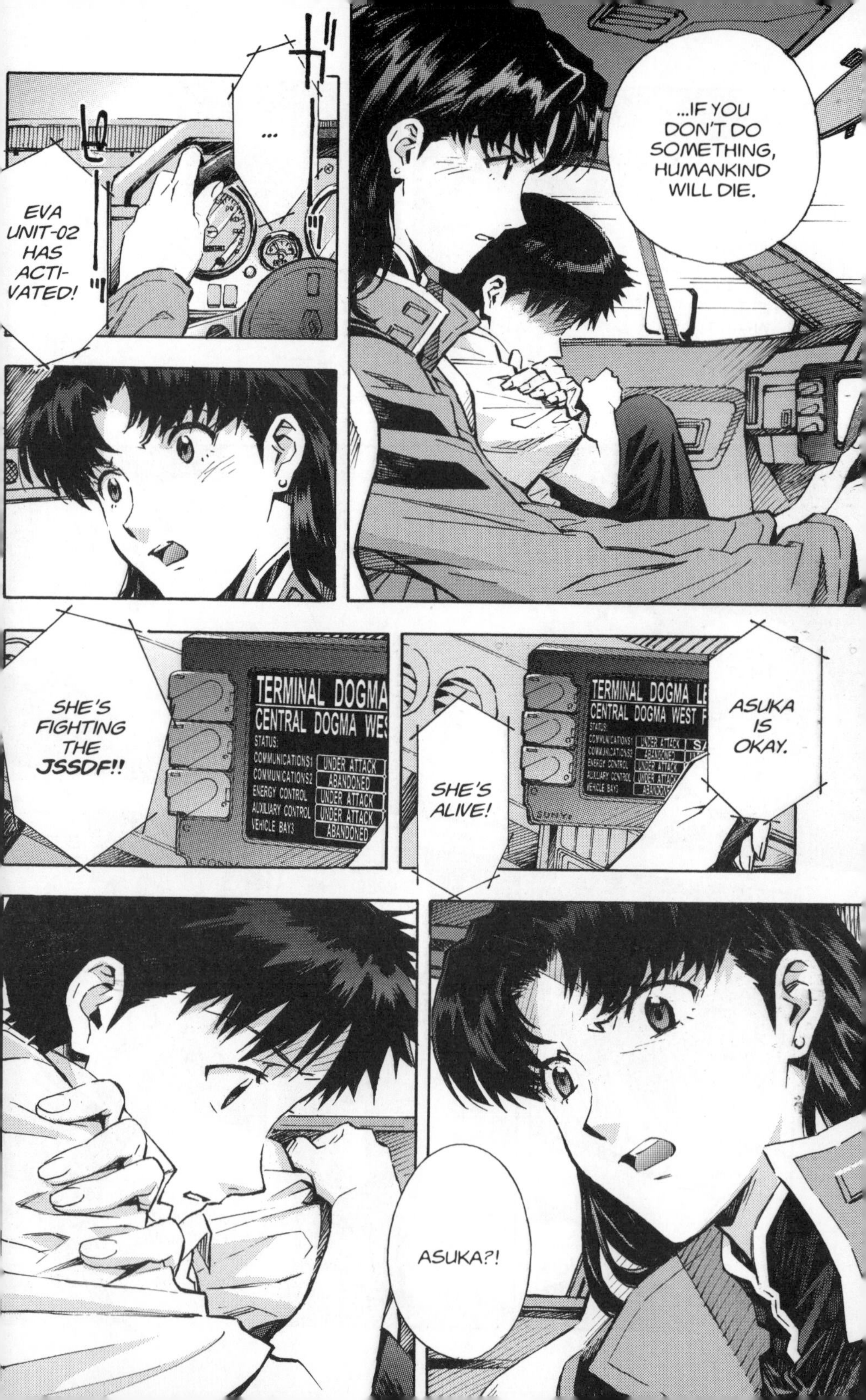
...IF YOU DON'T DO SOMETHING, HUMANKIND WILL DIE.
...
EVA UNIT-02 HAS ACTIVATED!
ASUKA IS OKAY.
SHE'S ALIVE!
SHE'S FIGHTING THE **JSSDF!!**
TERMINAL DOGMA
CENTRAL DOGMA WES
STATUS:
COMMUNICATIONS1 UNDER ATTACK
COMMUNICATIONS2 ABANDONED
ENERGY CONTROL UNDER ATTACK
AUXILIARY CONTROL UNDER ATTACK
VEHICLE BAY3 ABANDONED
ASUKA?!

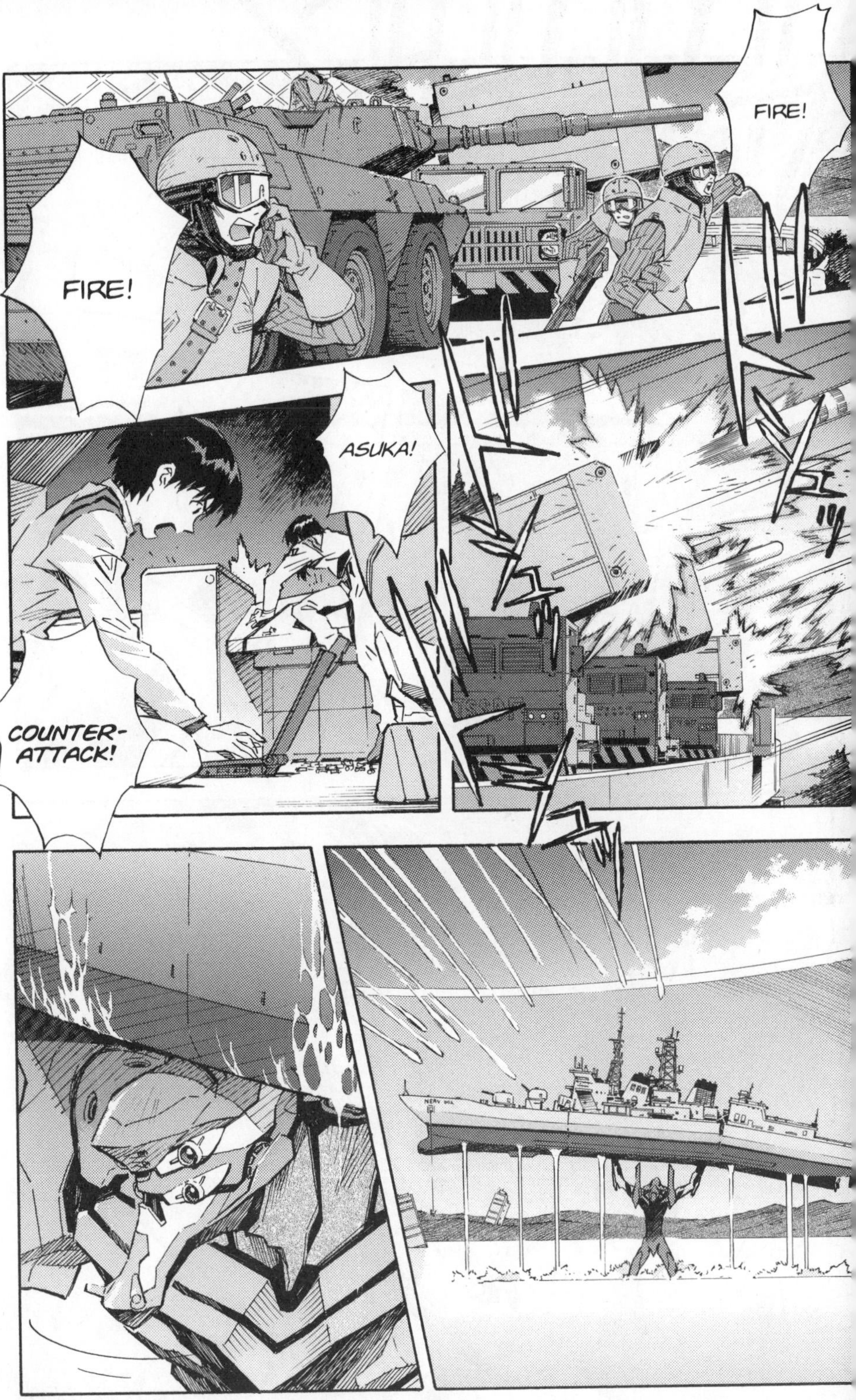
FIRE!
FIRE!
ASUKA!
COUNTER-ATTACK!

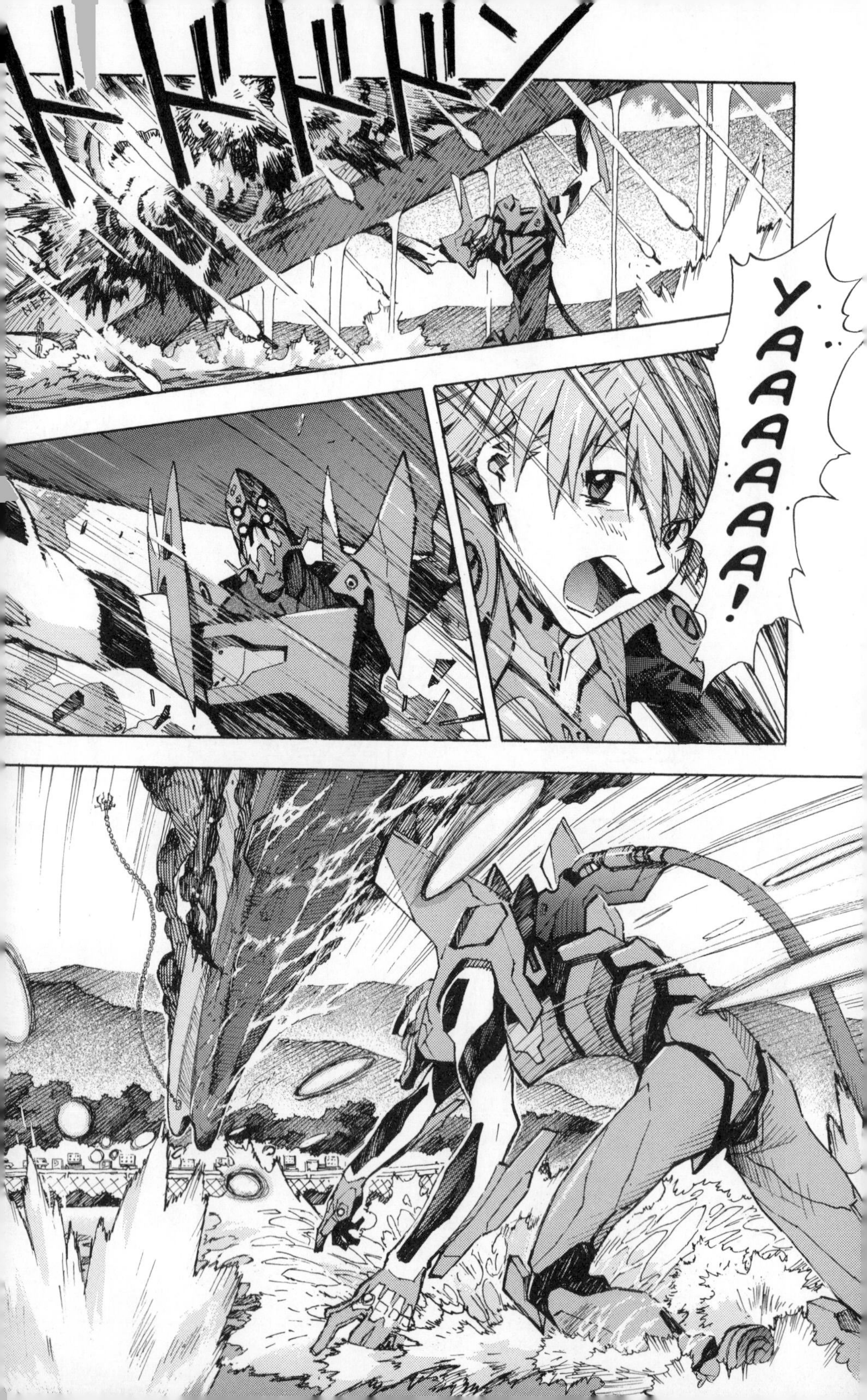

YAAAAAAA!
NERV

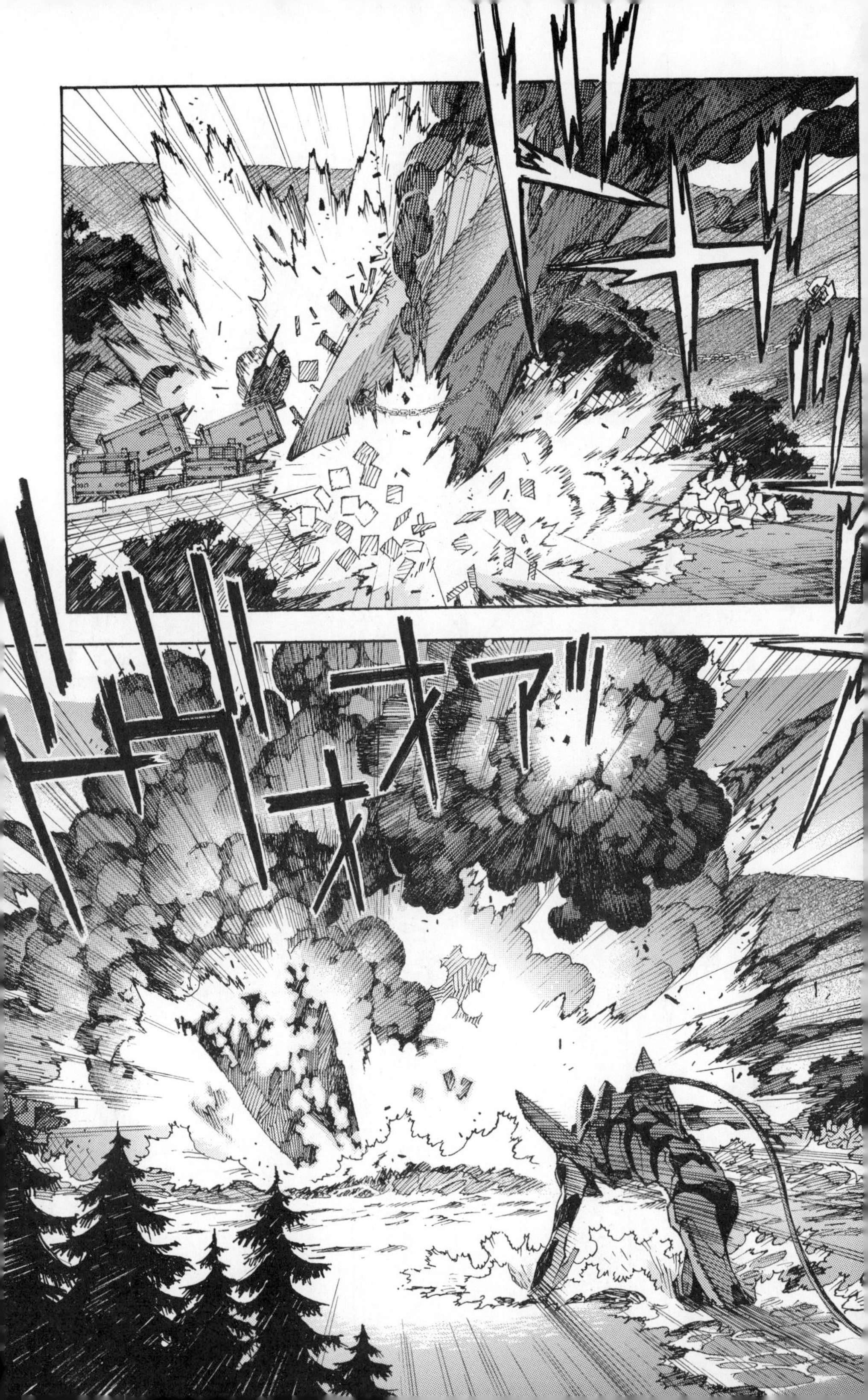
ドガオォア゛

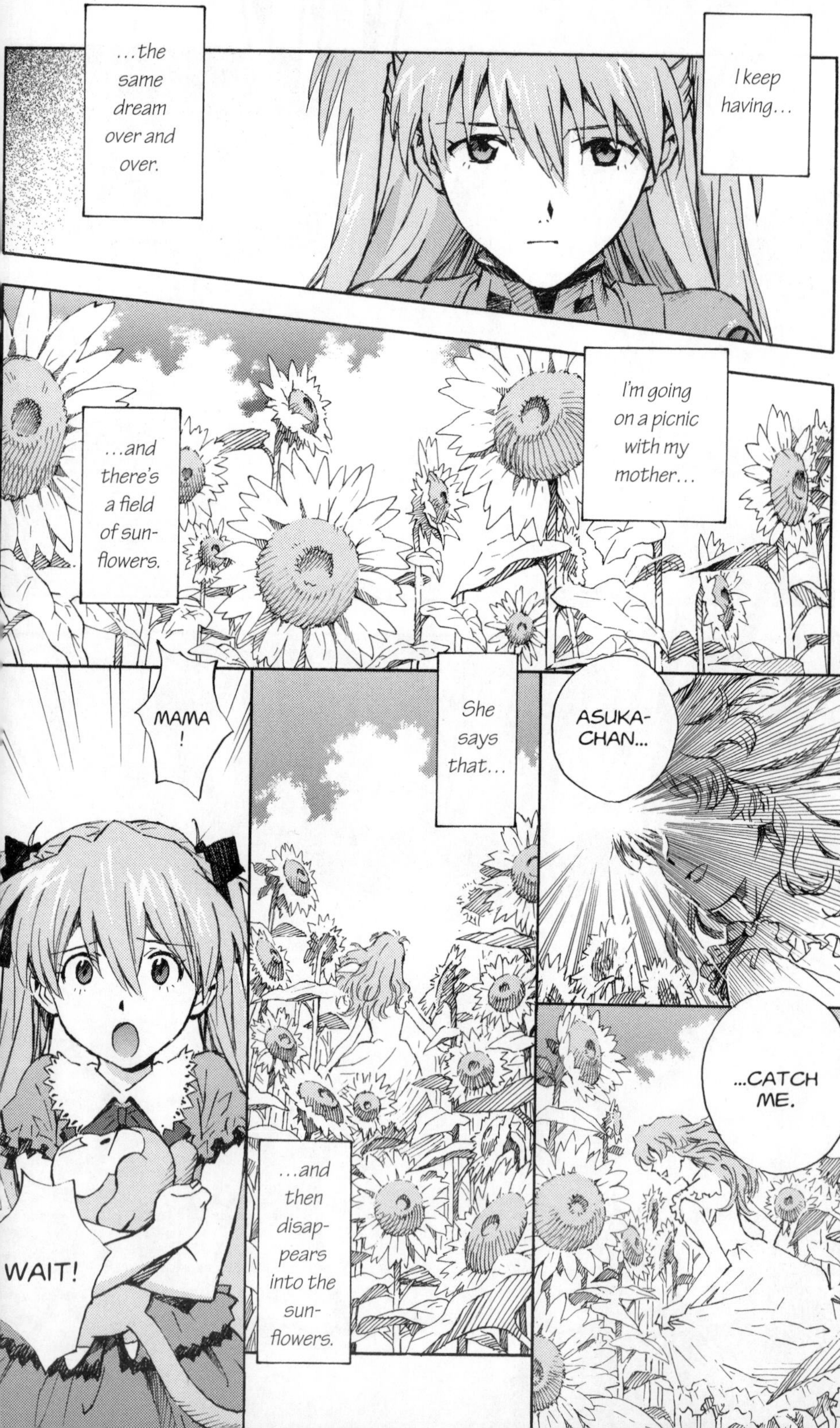
I keep having…
…the same dream over and over.
I'm going on a picnic with my mother…
…and there's a field of sunflowers.
ASUKA-CHAN...
...CATCH ME.
She says that…
…and then disappears into the sunflowers.
MAMA!
WAIT!

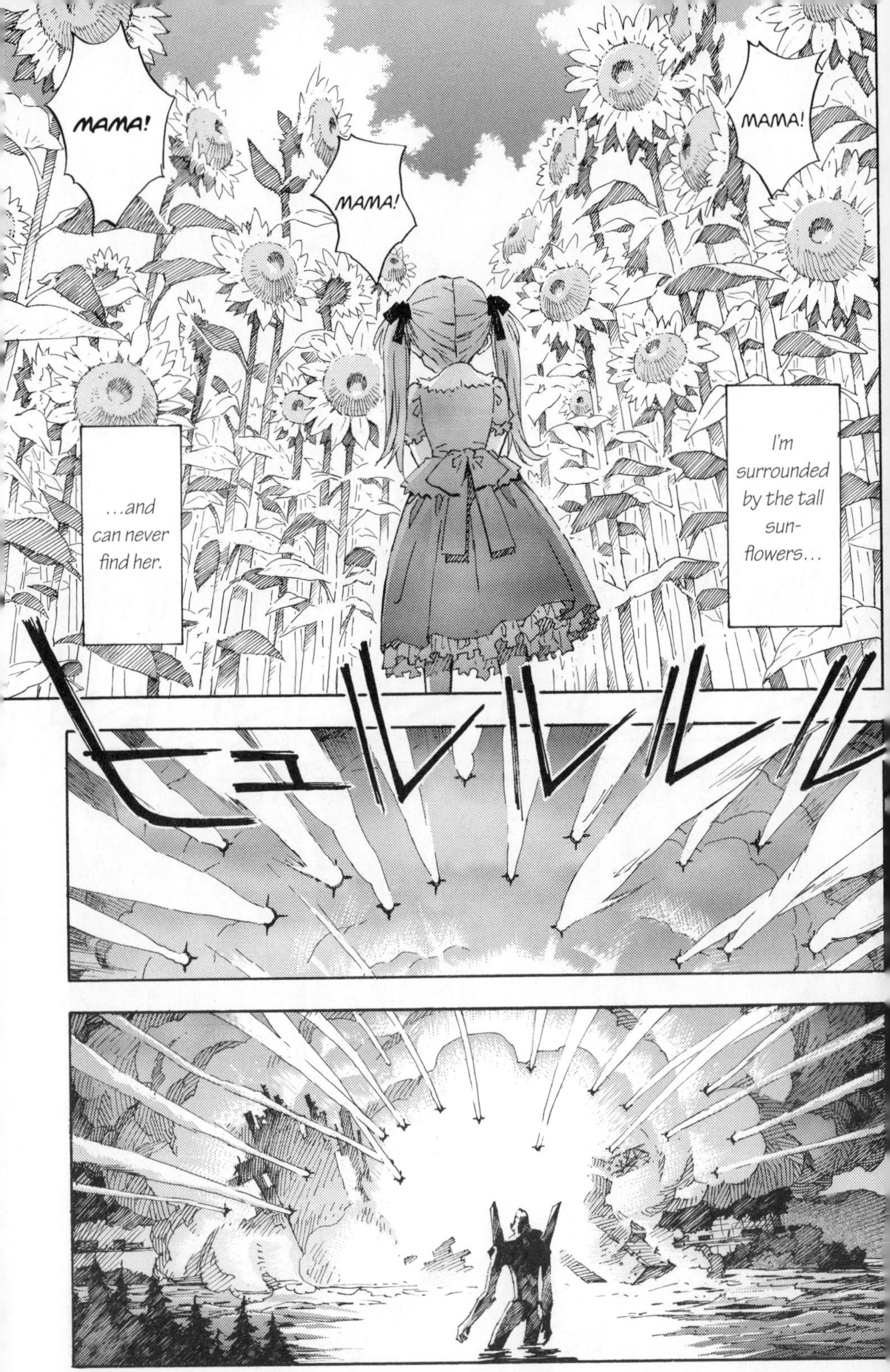
MAMA!
MAMA!
MAMA!
I'm surrounded by the tall sun-flowers...
...and can never find her.

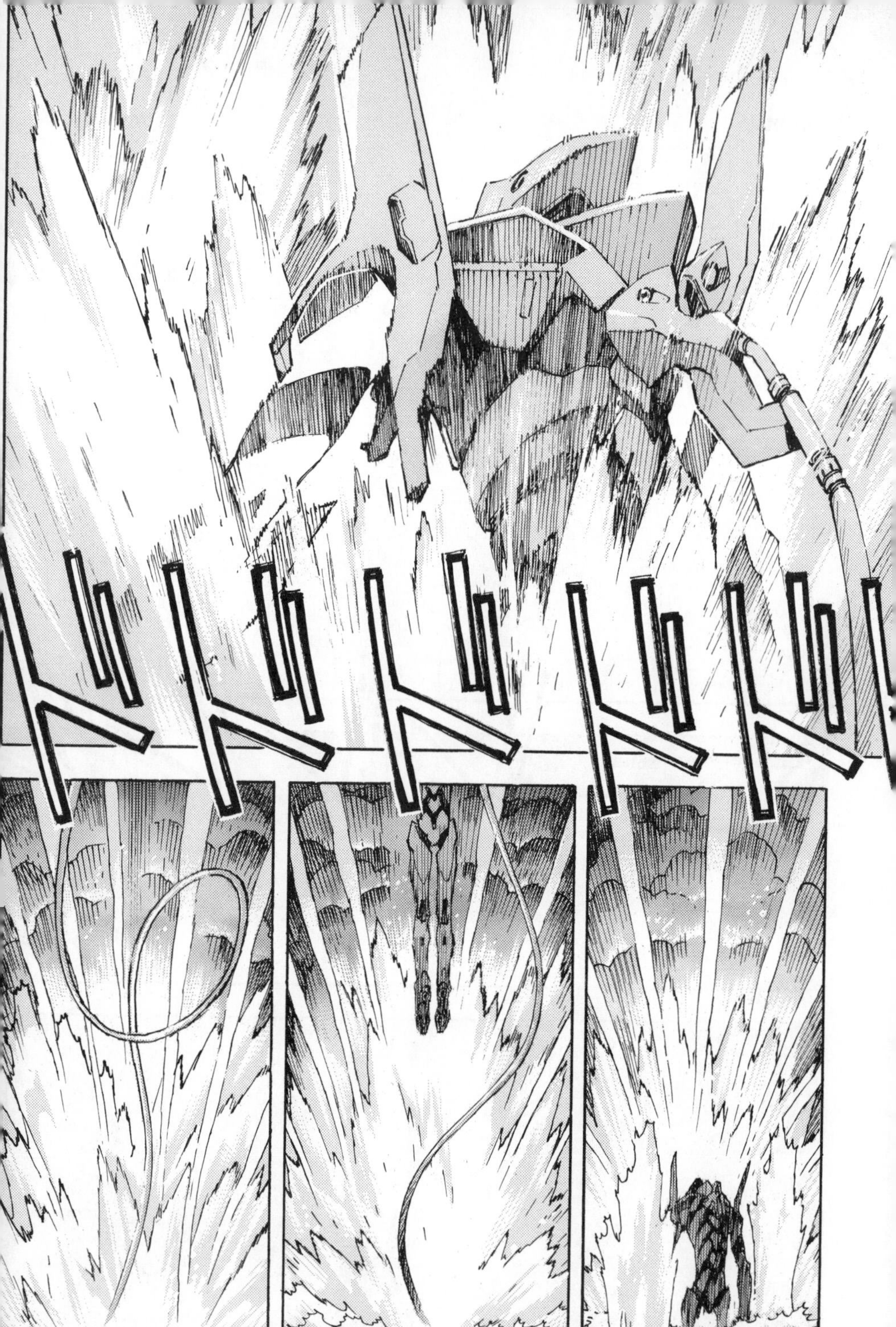
ドドドドド

I'm sorry...

I couldn't find you...

...even though you...

...were always right here...

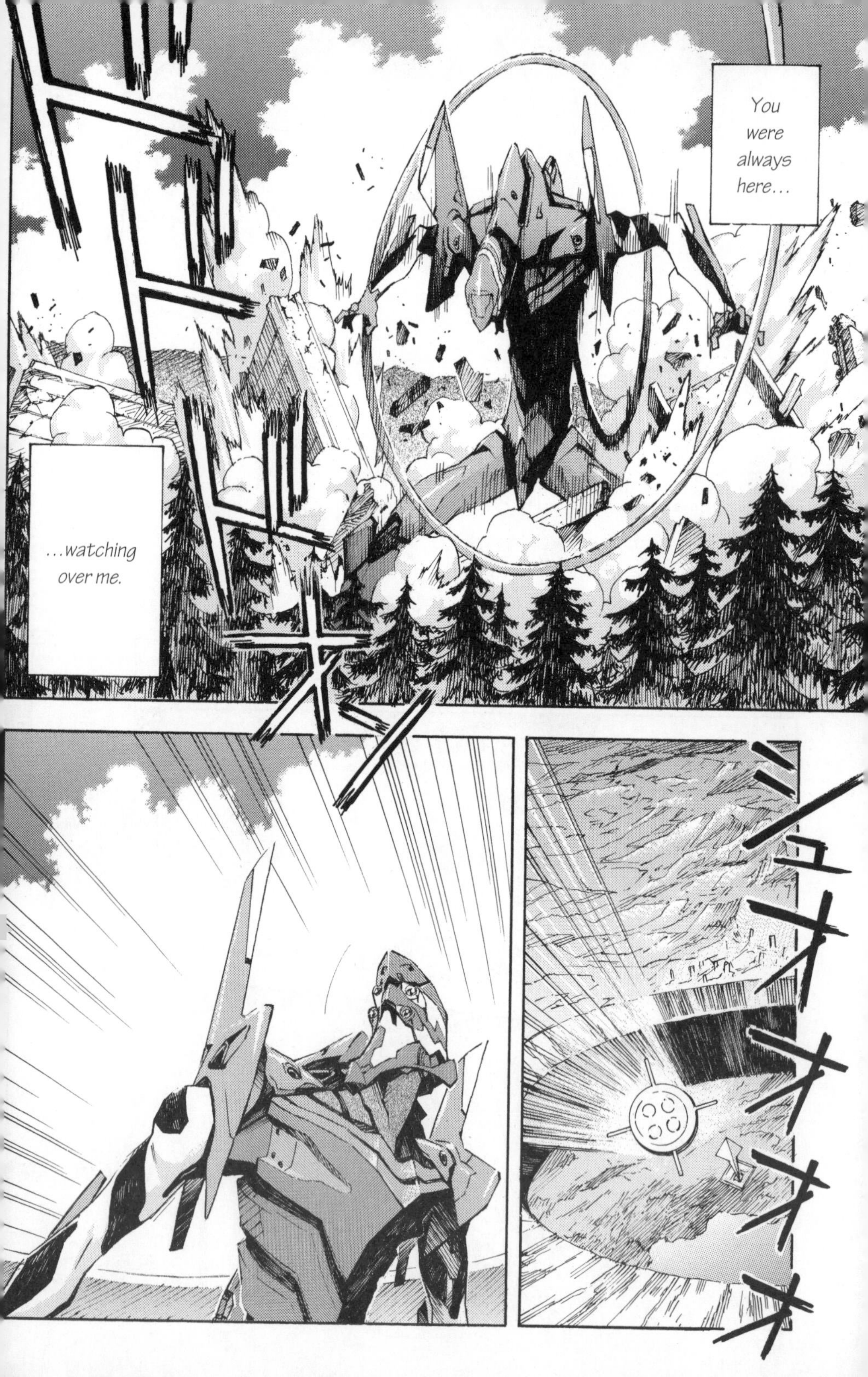
You were always here…
…watching over me.

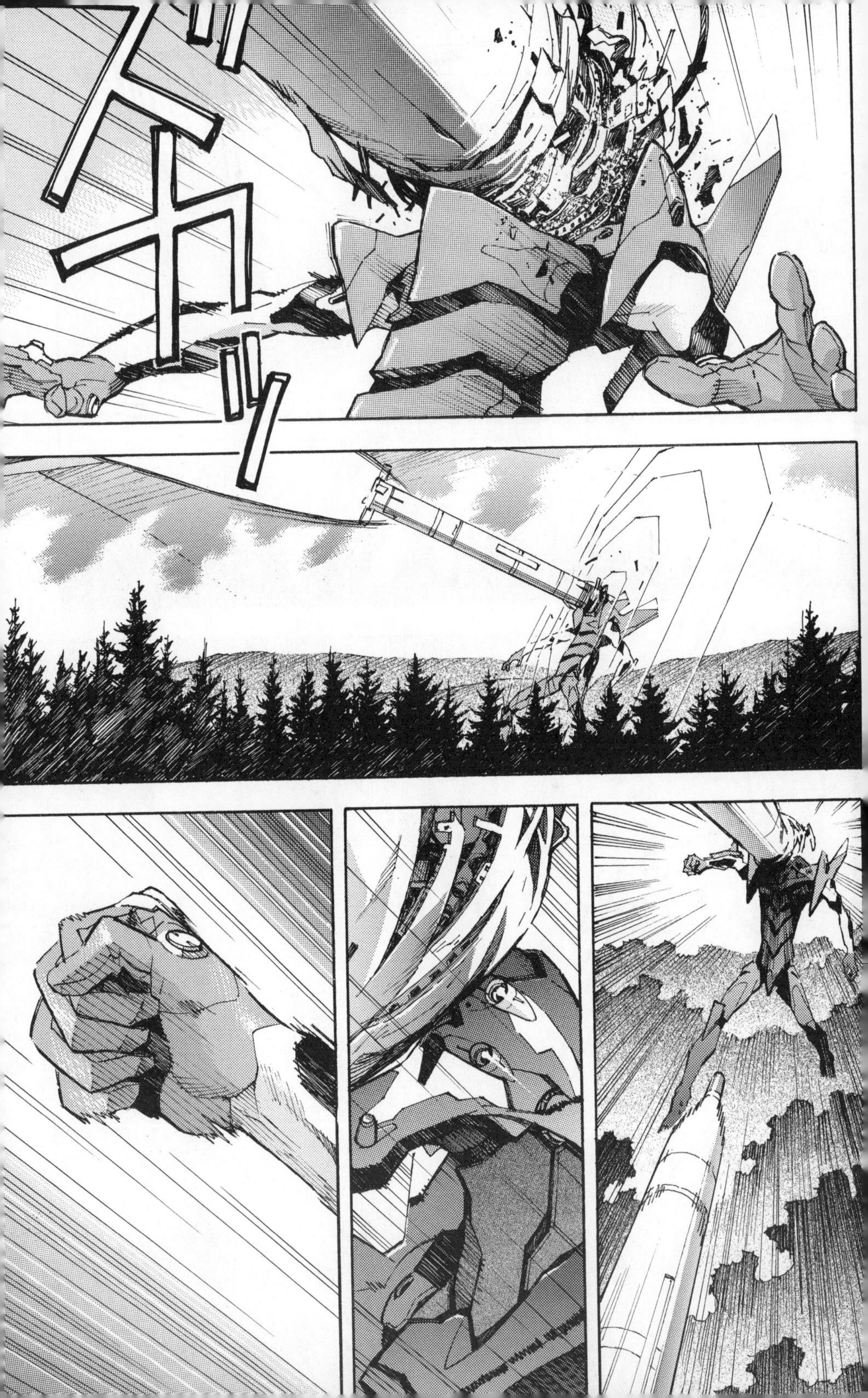

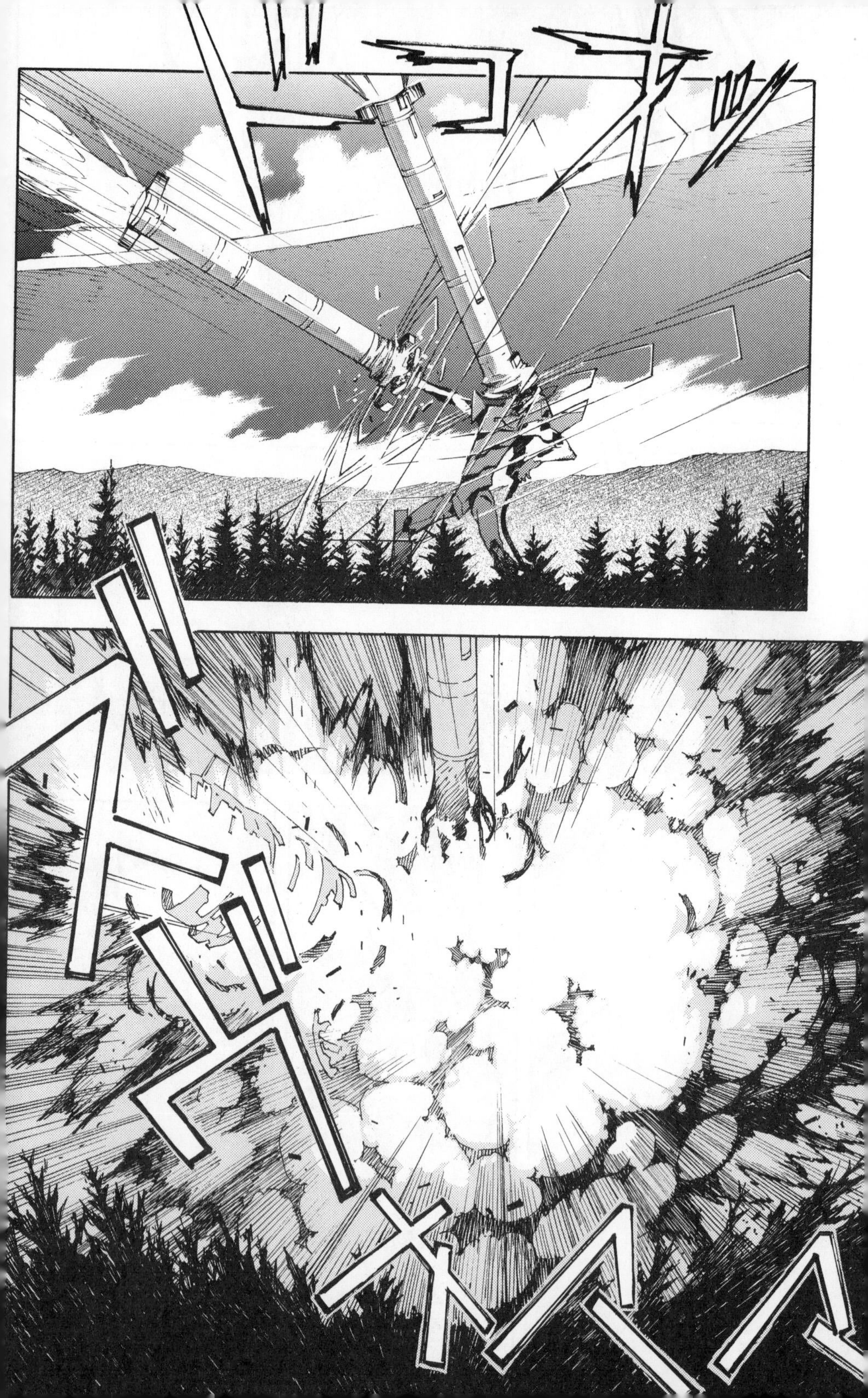
ドゴオッ

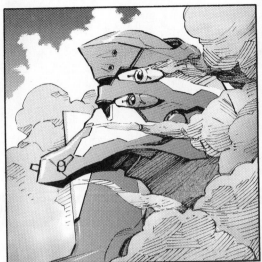

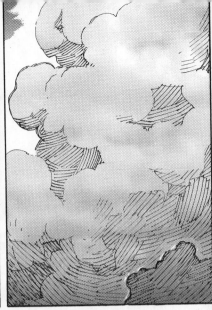

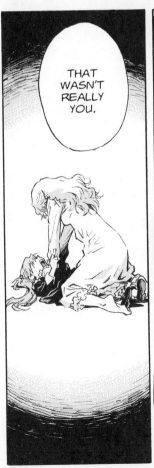

MAMA...
...NOW I UNDERSTAND...
...THE MEANING OF THE A.T. FIELD.
THAT WASN'T REALLY YOU.

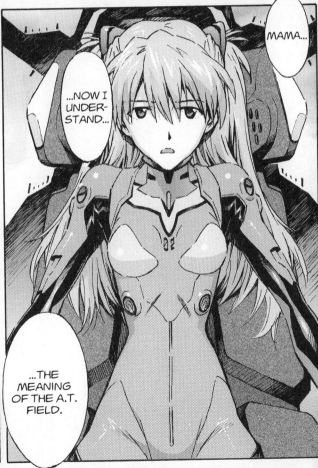

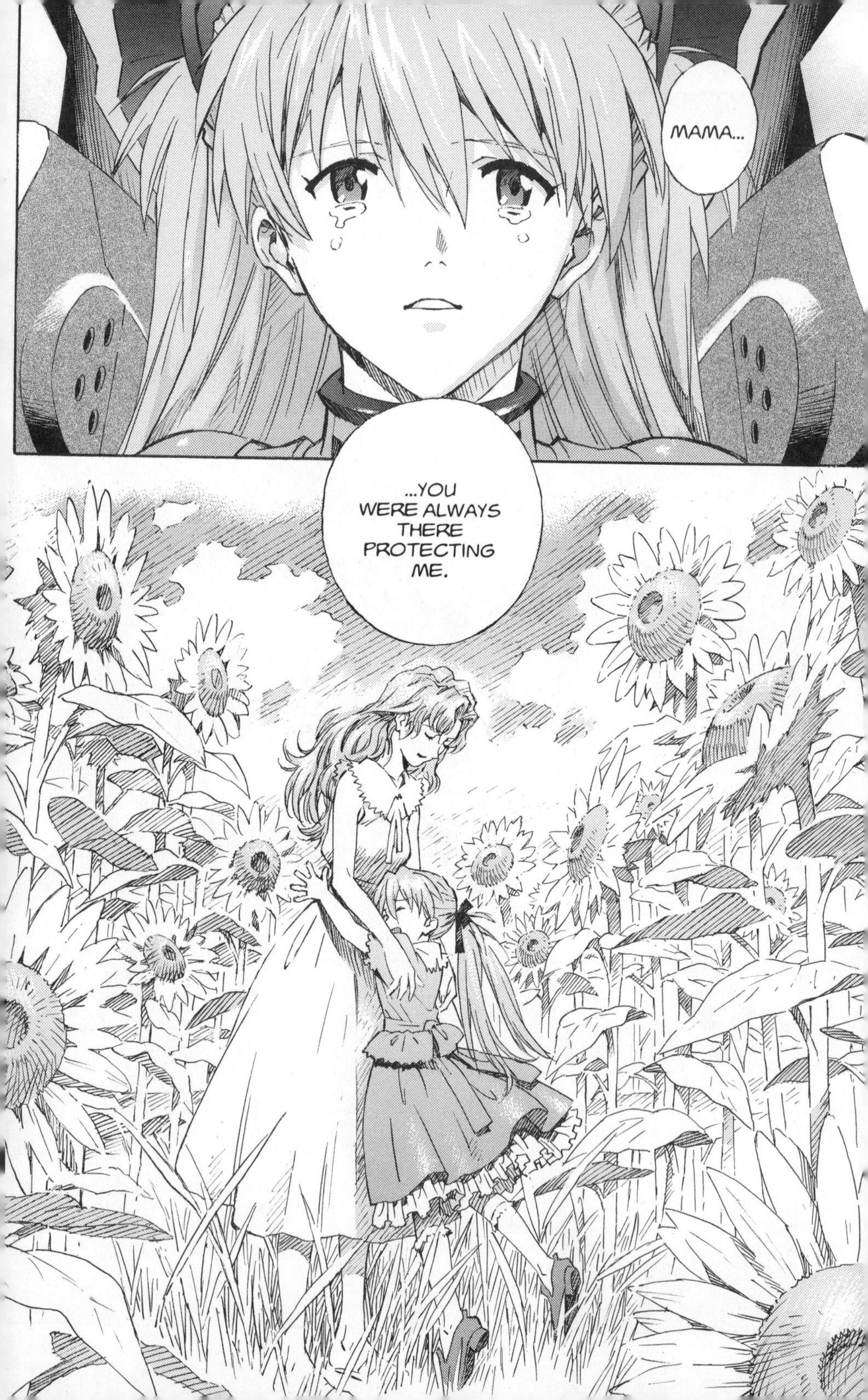
MAMA...
...YOU WERE ALWAYS THERE PROTECTING ME.

NEON GENESIS
EVANGELION
STAGE 81: ENEMY FROM THE SKY

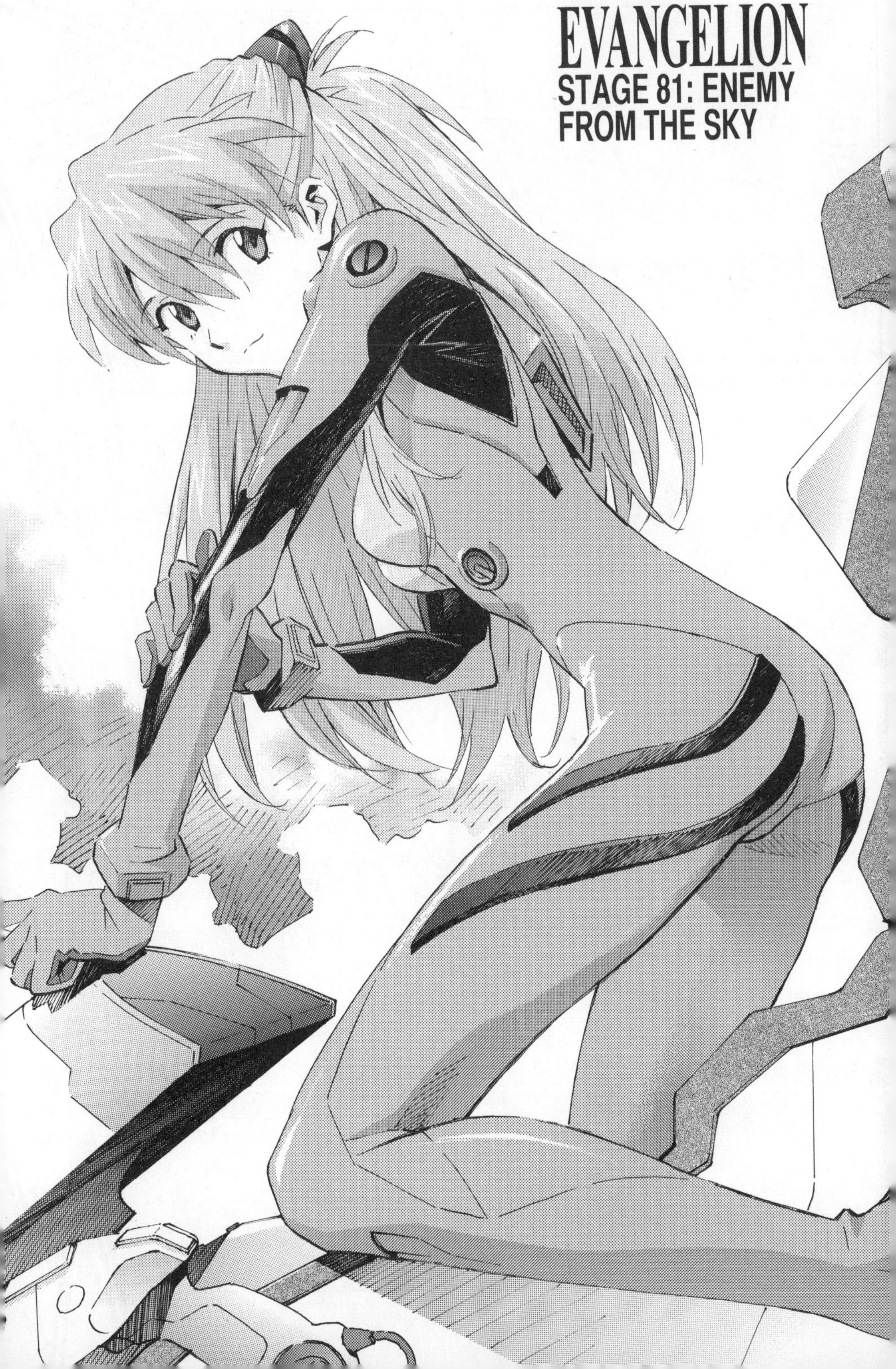

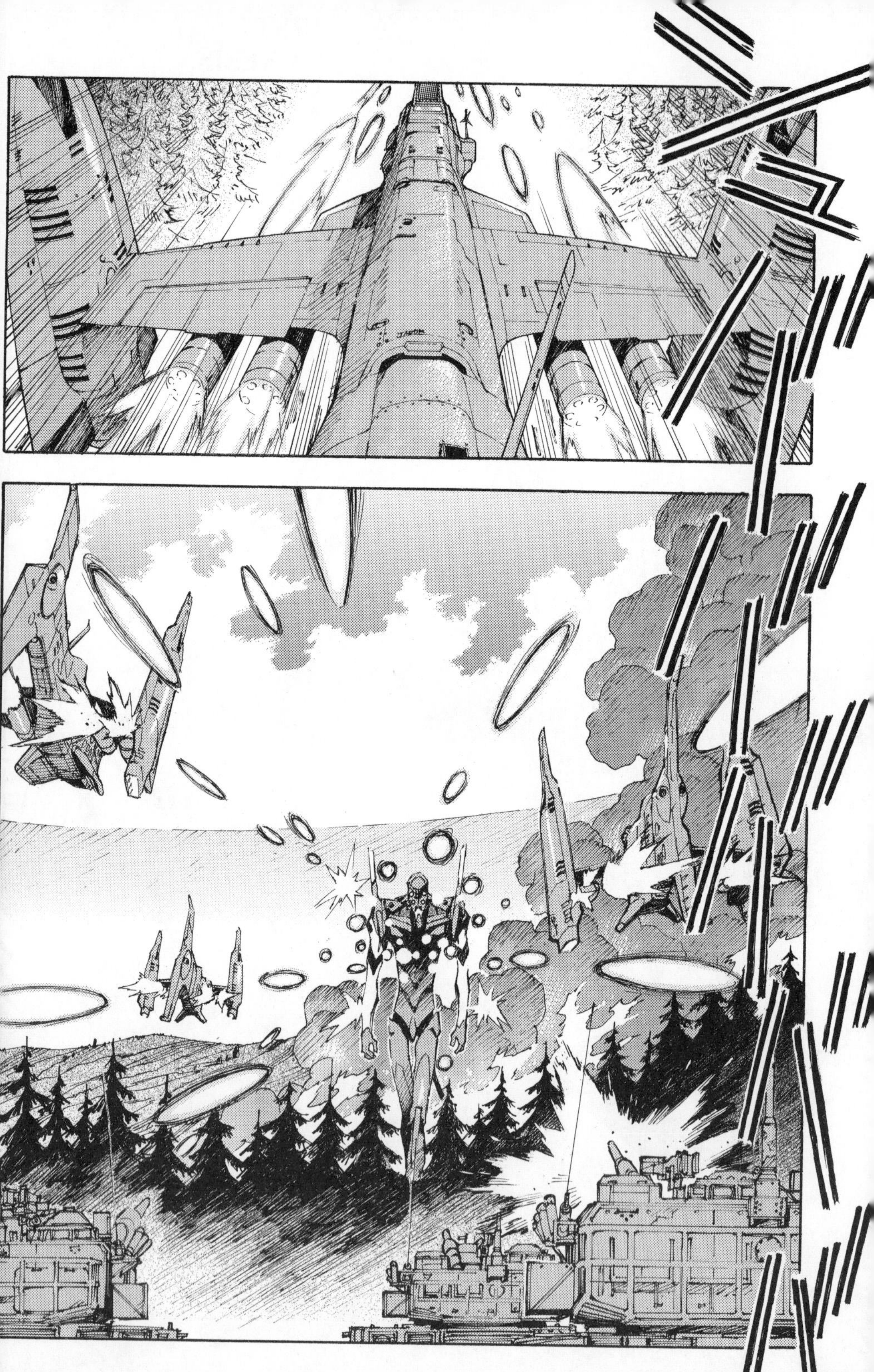

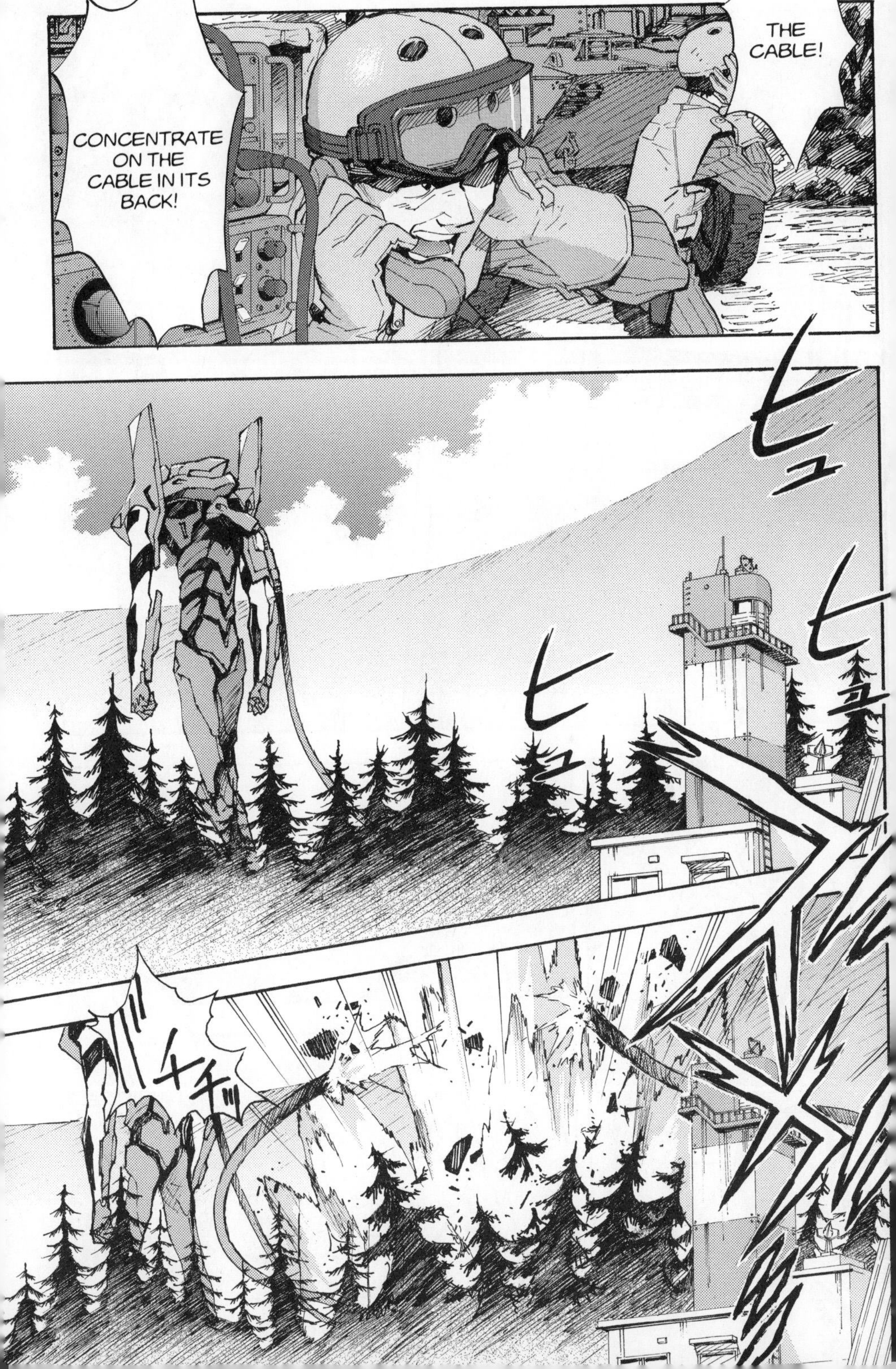
THE CABLE!
CONCENTRATE ON THE CABLE IN ITS BACK!
ヒュ
ヒュ
ヒュ
ブチッ

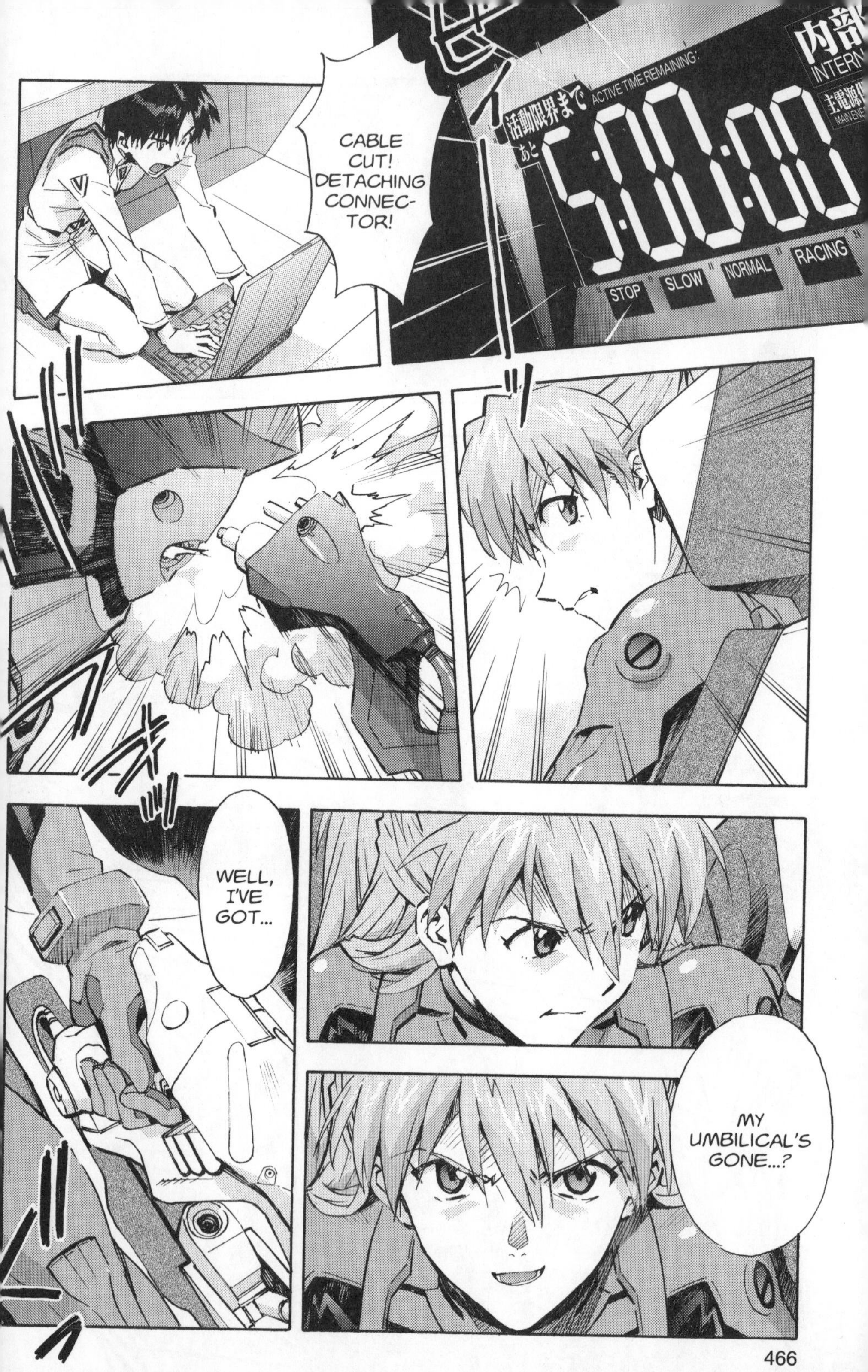
内部
INTERN
活動限界まで あと
ACTIVE TIME REMAINING:
5:00:00
主電源
MAIN ENE
RACING
NORMAL
SLOW
STOP
CABLE CUT! DETACHING CONNECTOR!
MY UMBILICAL'S GONE...?
WELL, I'VE GOT...

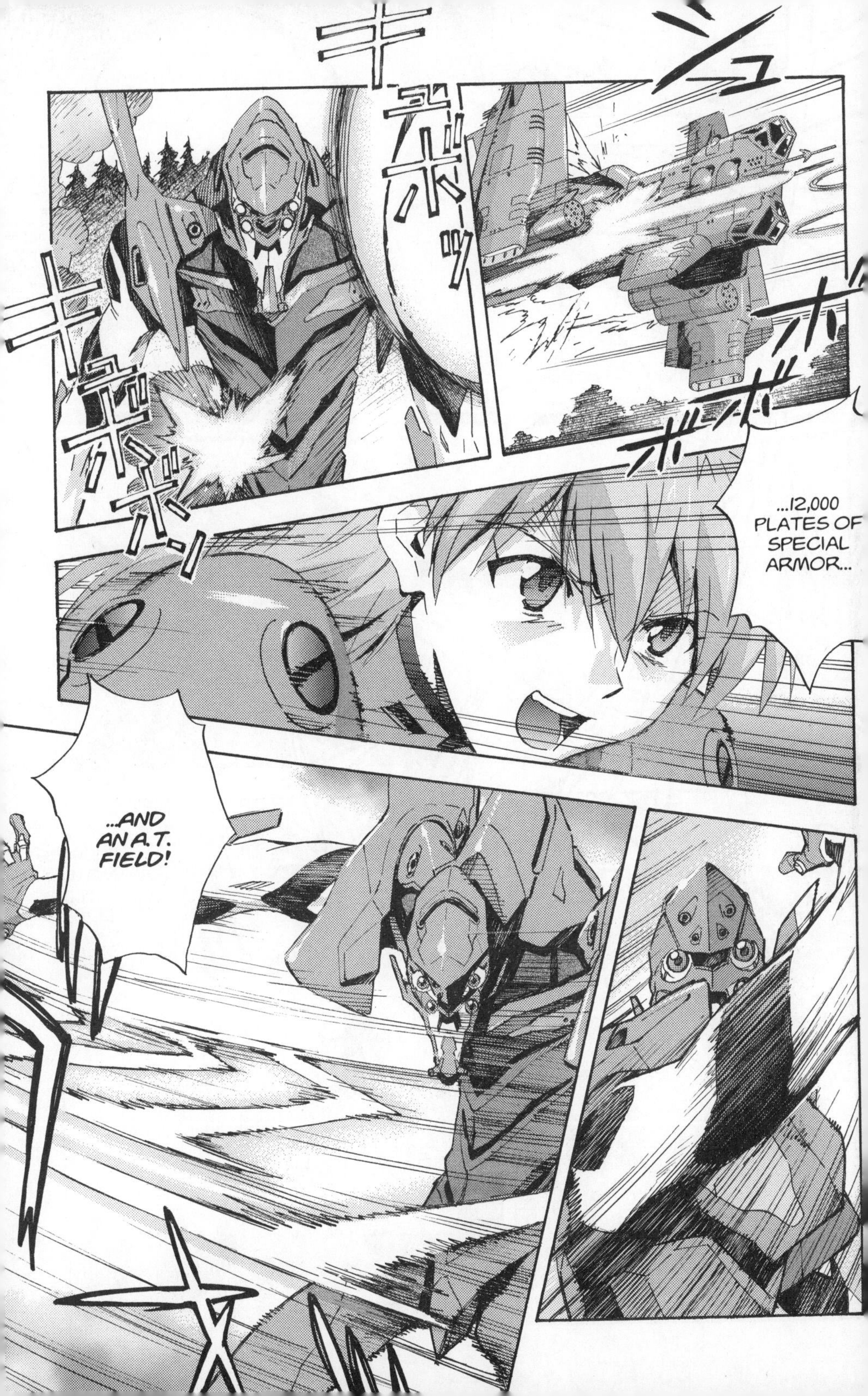
...12,000 PLATES OF SPECIAL ARMOR...
...AND AN A.T. FIELD!

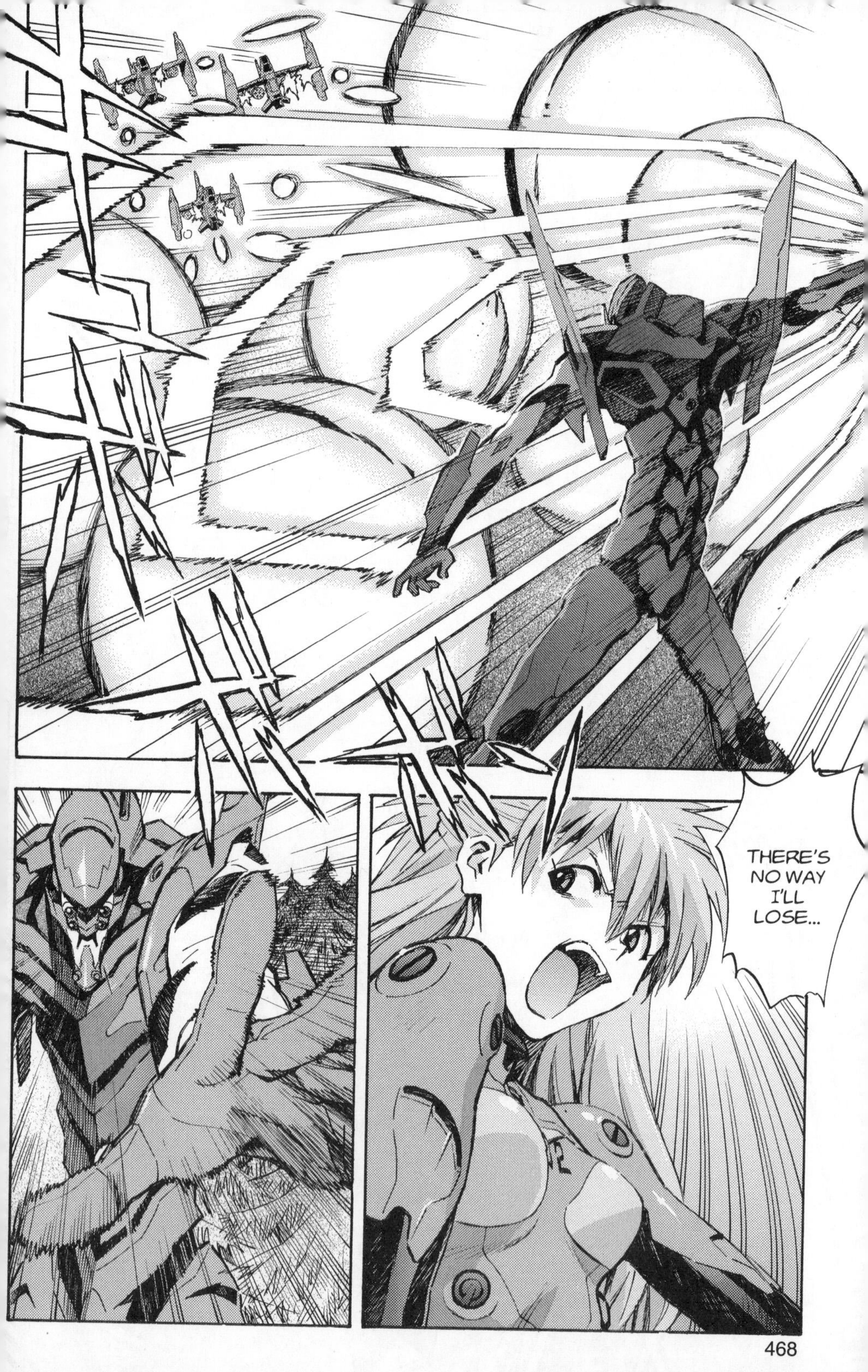
THERE'S NO WAY I'LL LOSE...

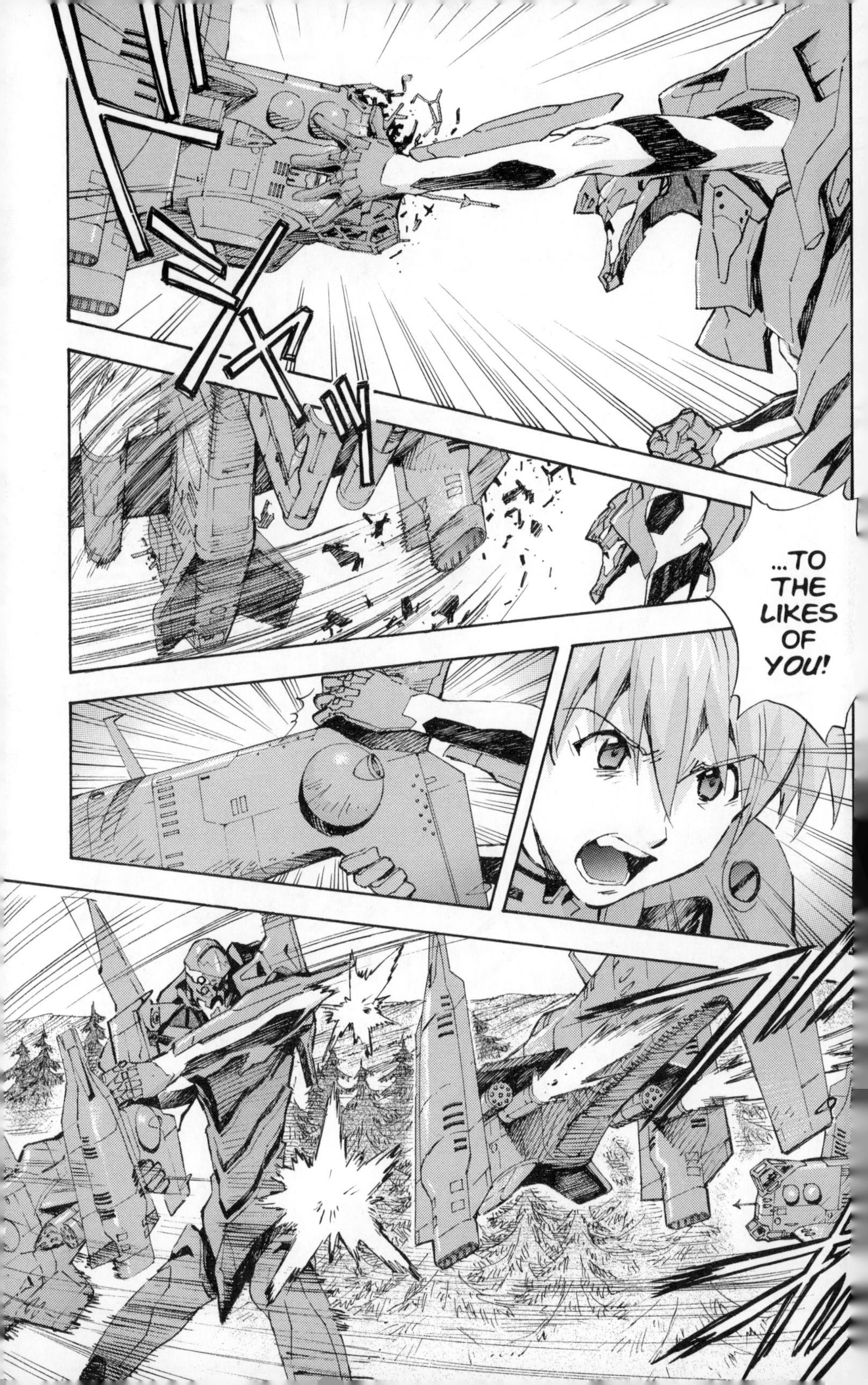
...TO THE LIKES OF YOU!

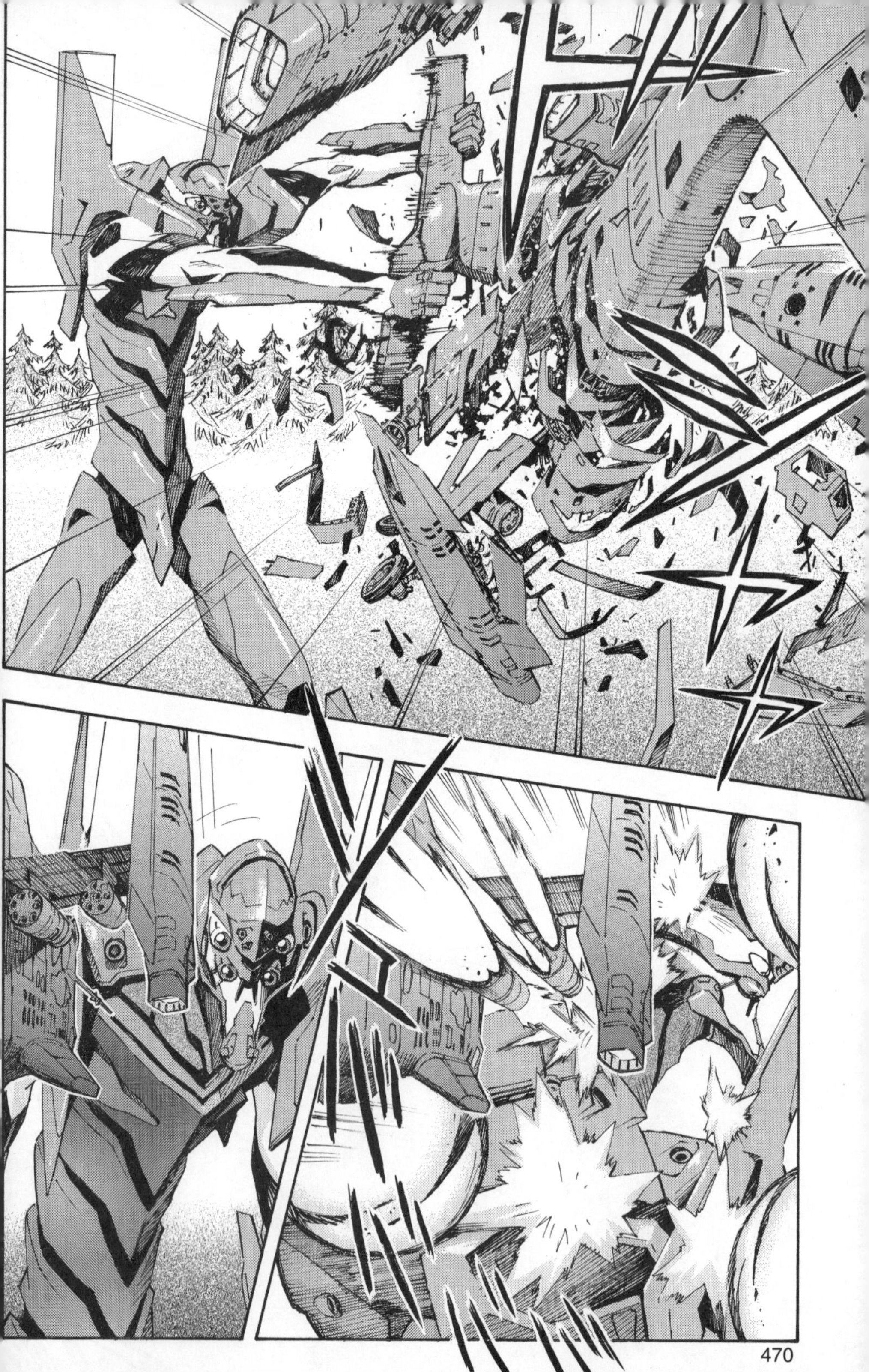

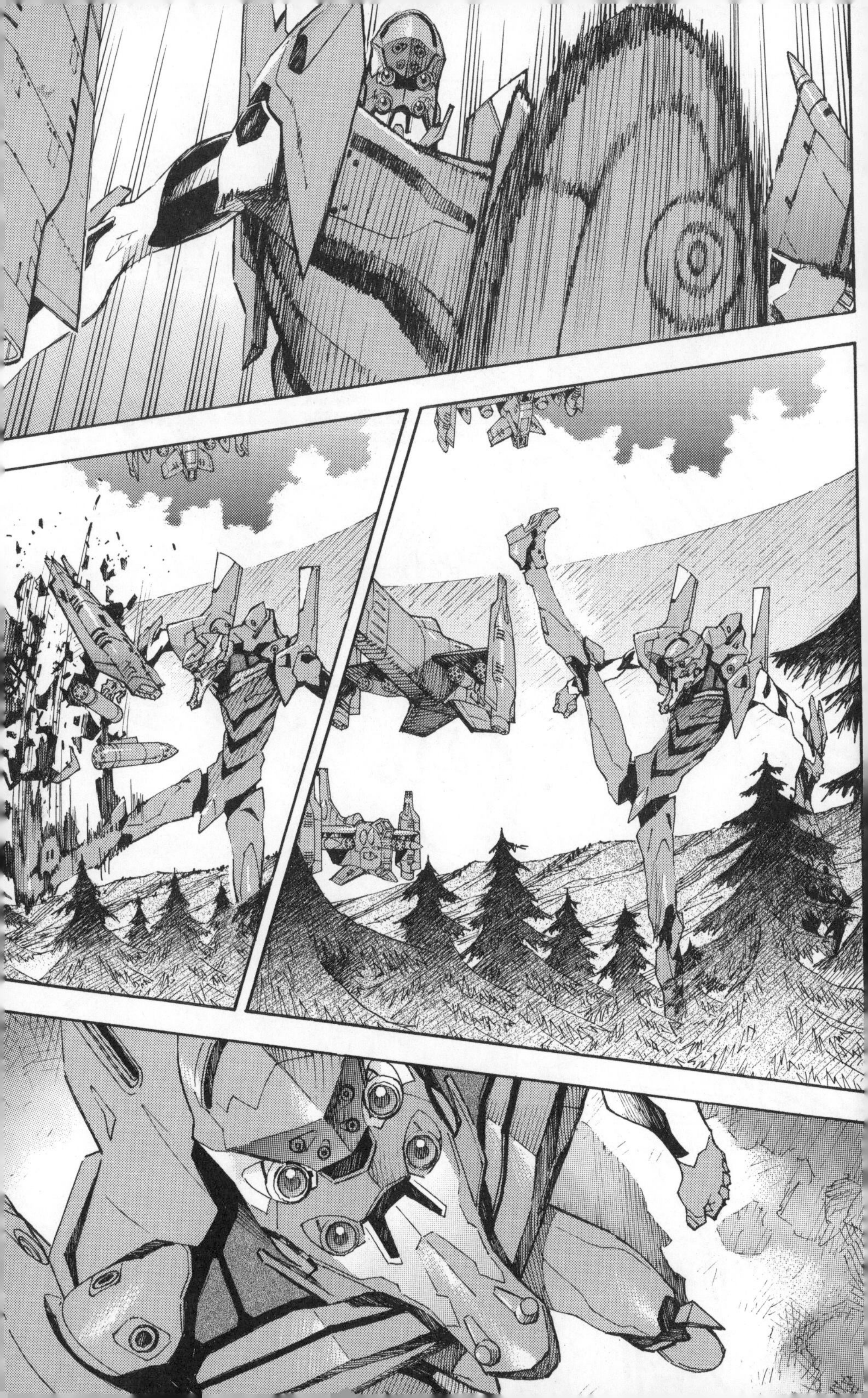

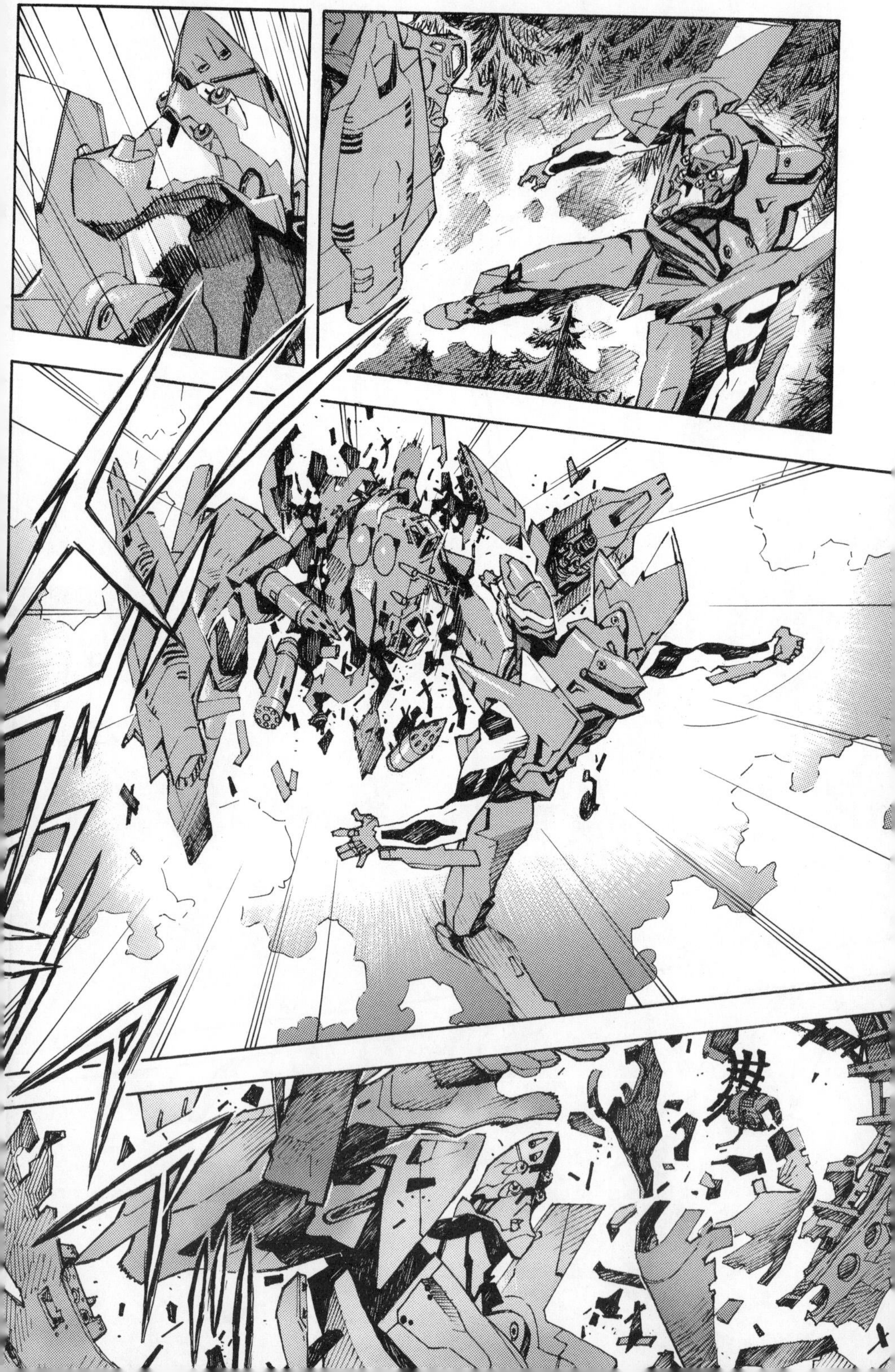

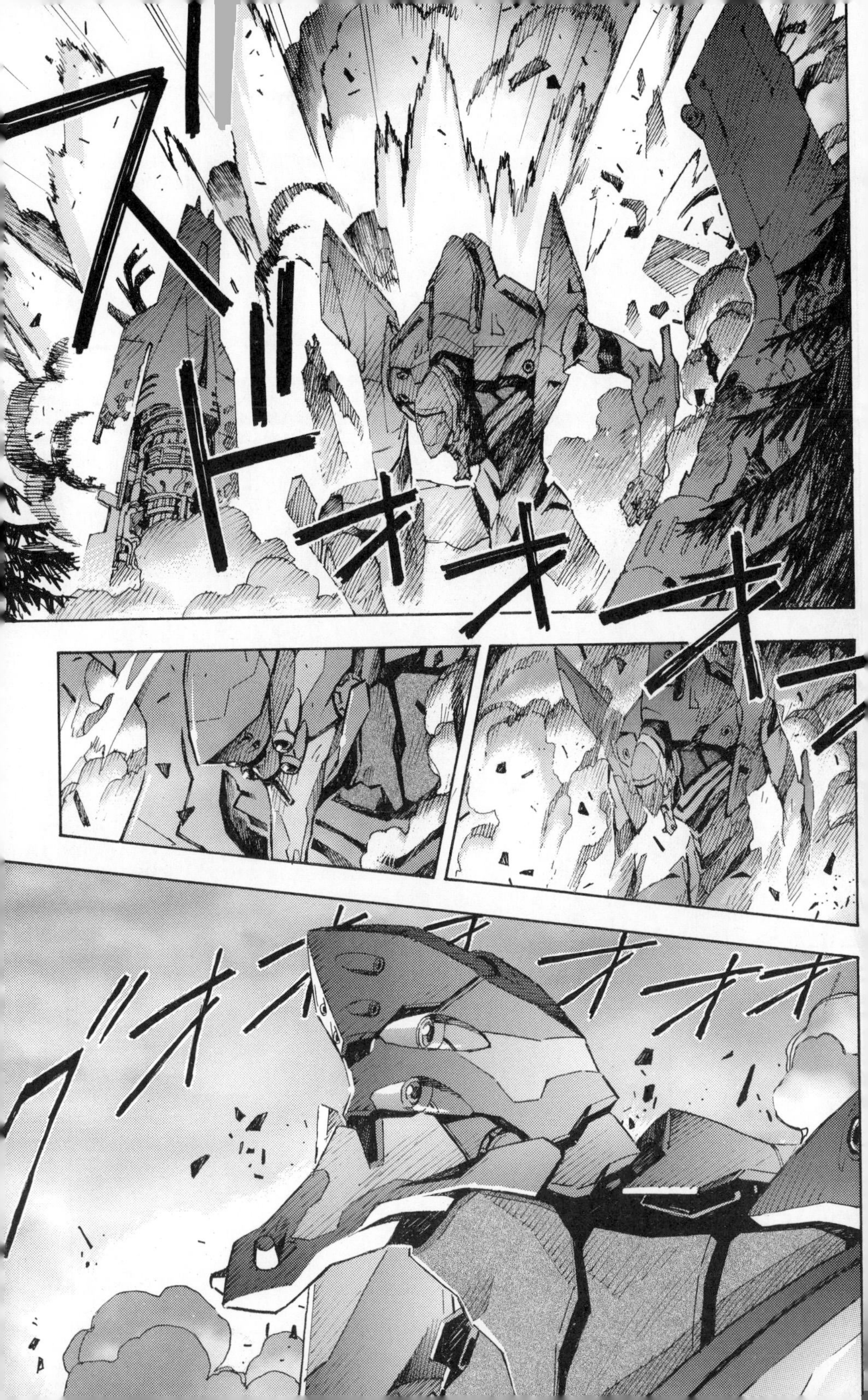
ズドオオオー
ヴオオオオオ

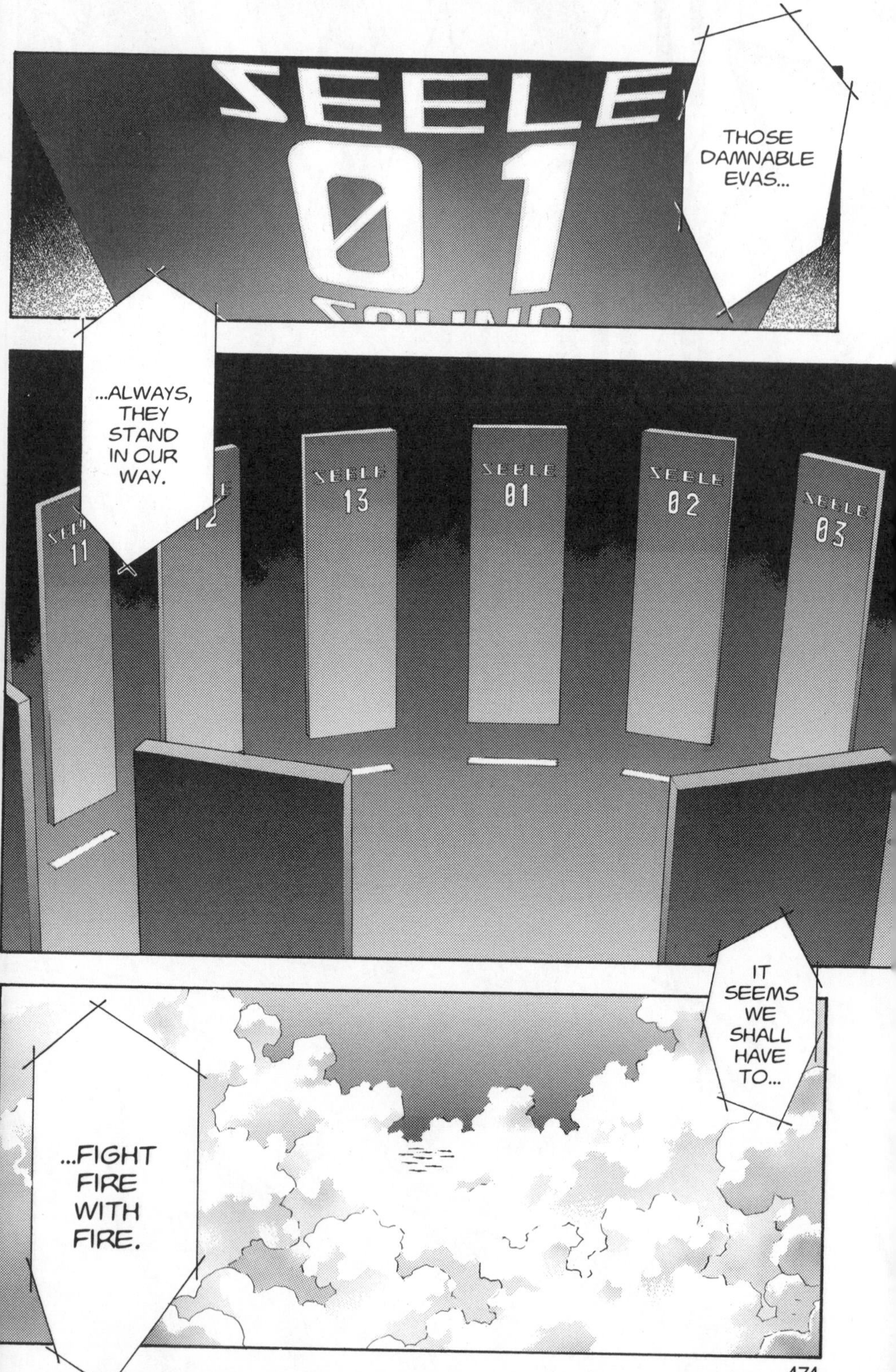
SEELE
01
THOSE DAMNABLE EVAS...
...ALWAYS, THEY STAND IN OUR WAY.
IT SEEMS WE SHALL HAVE TO...
...FIGHT FIRE WITH FIRE.

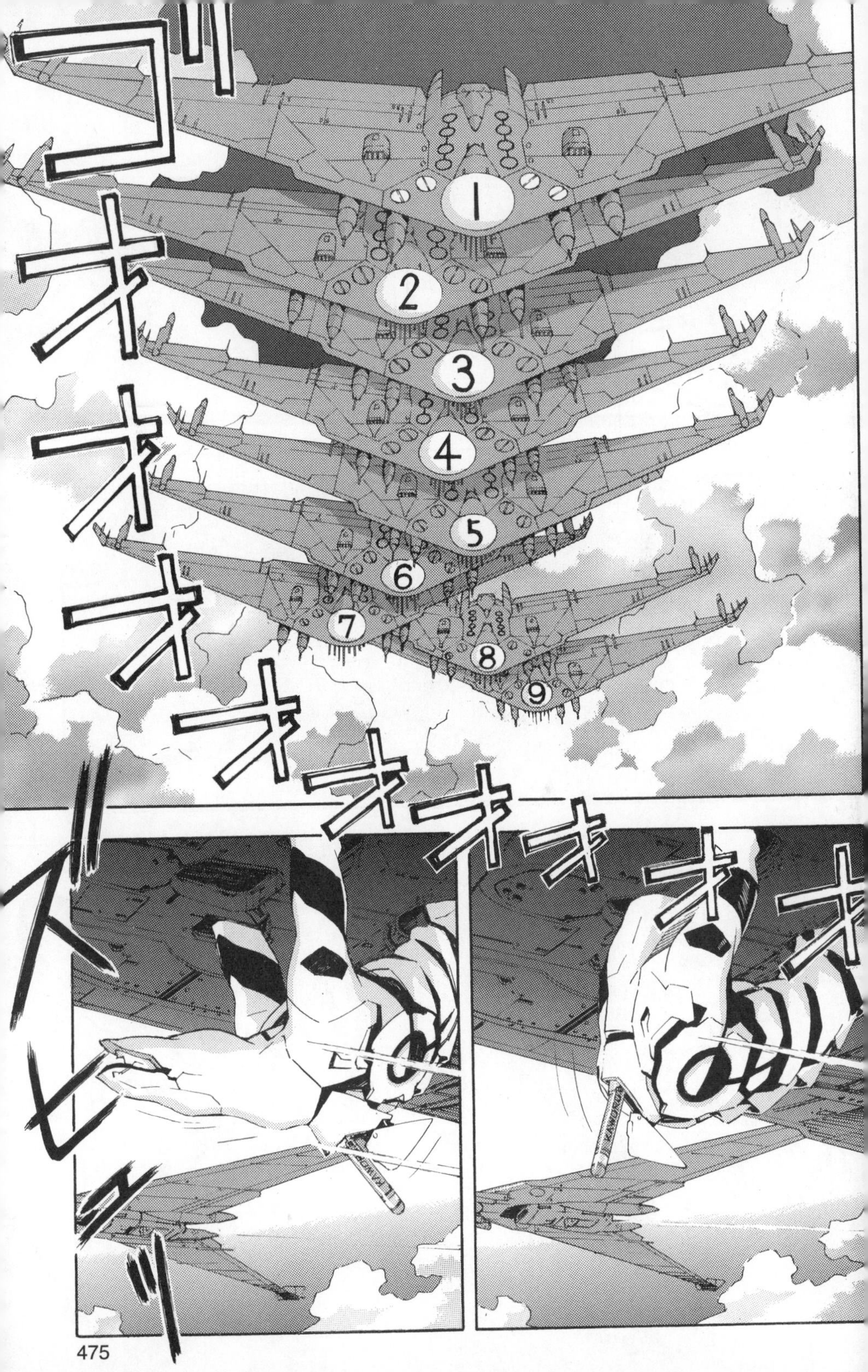
ゴオオオオオオオオオ
ズビュッ

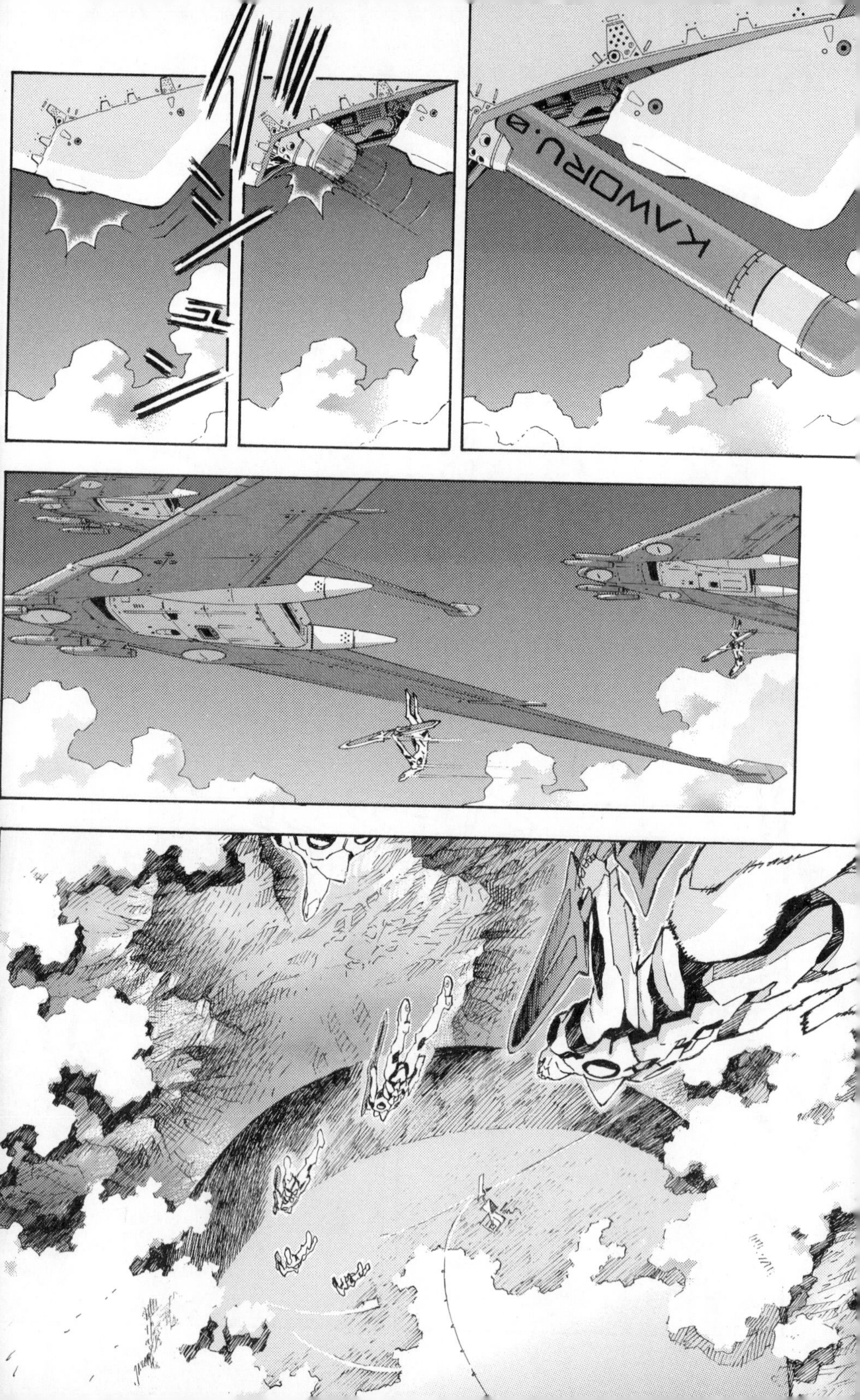
KAWORU.0

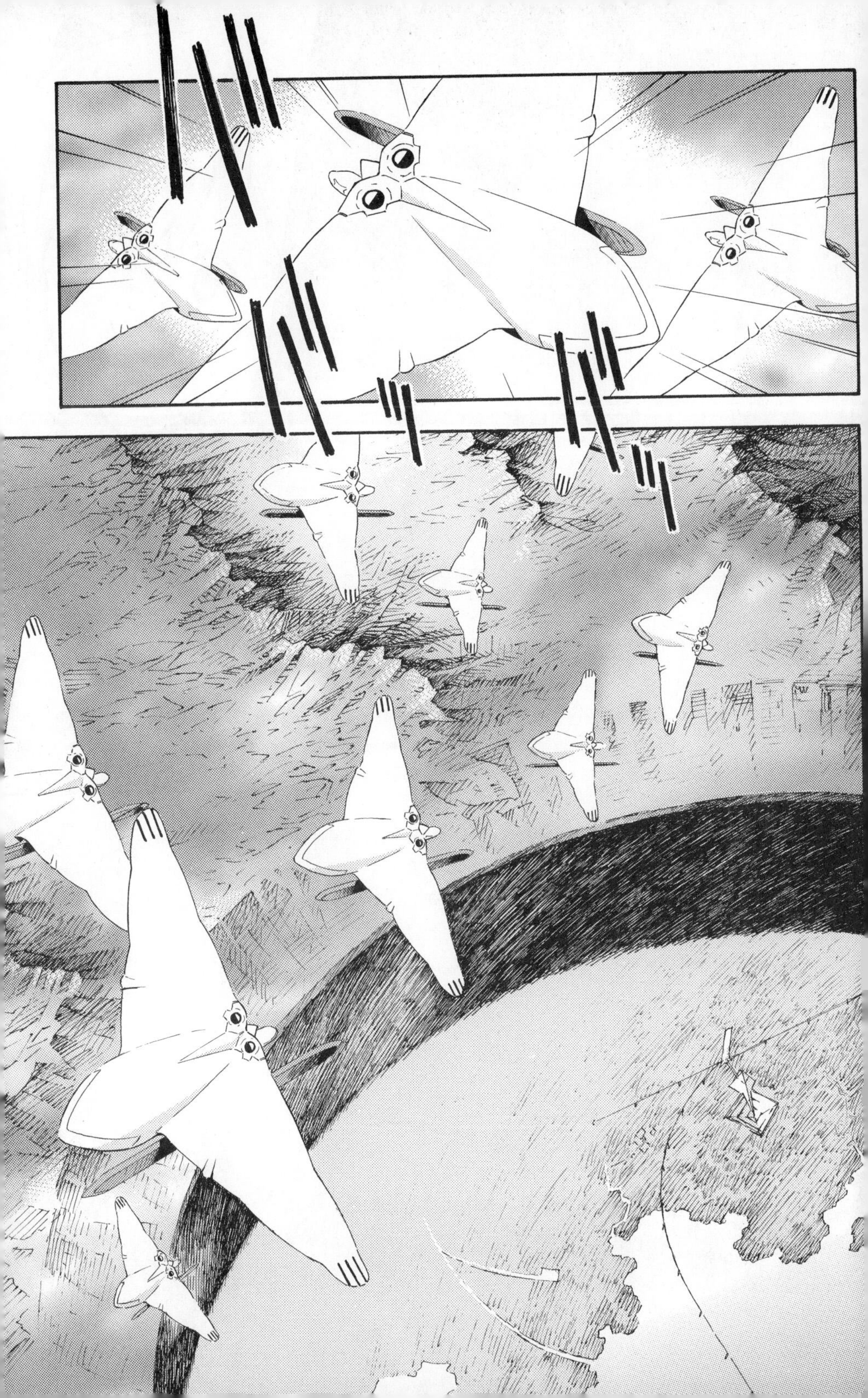

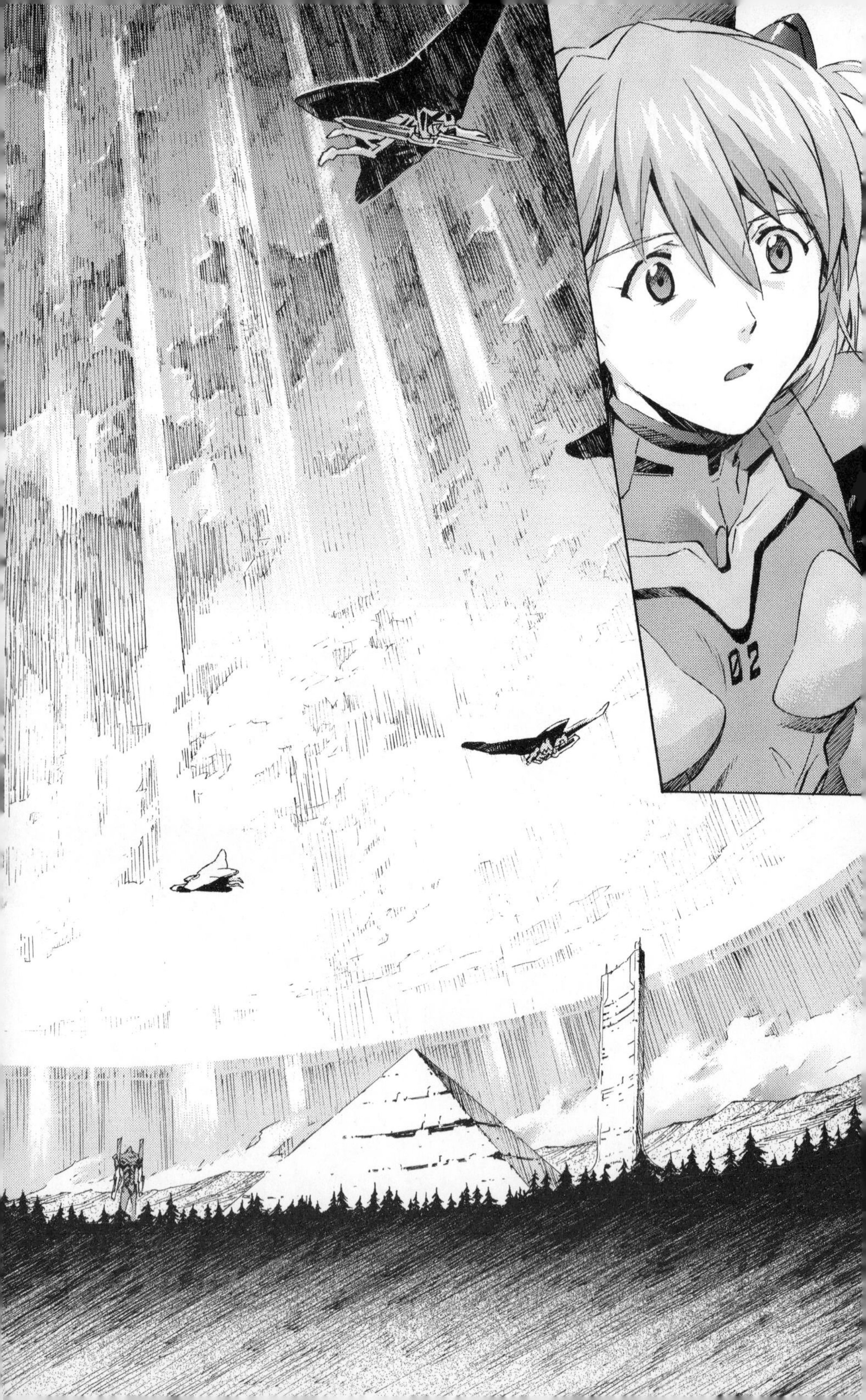

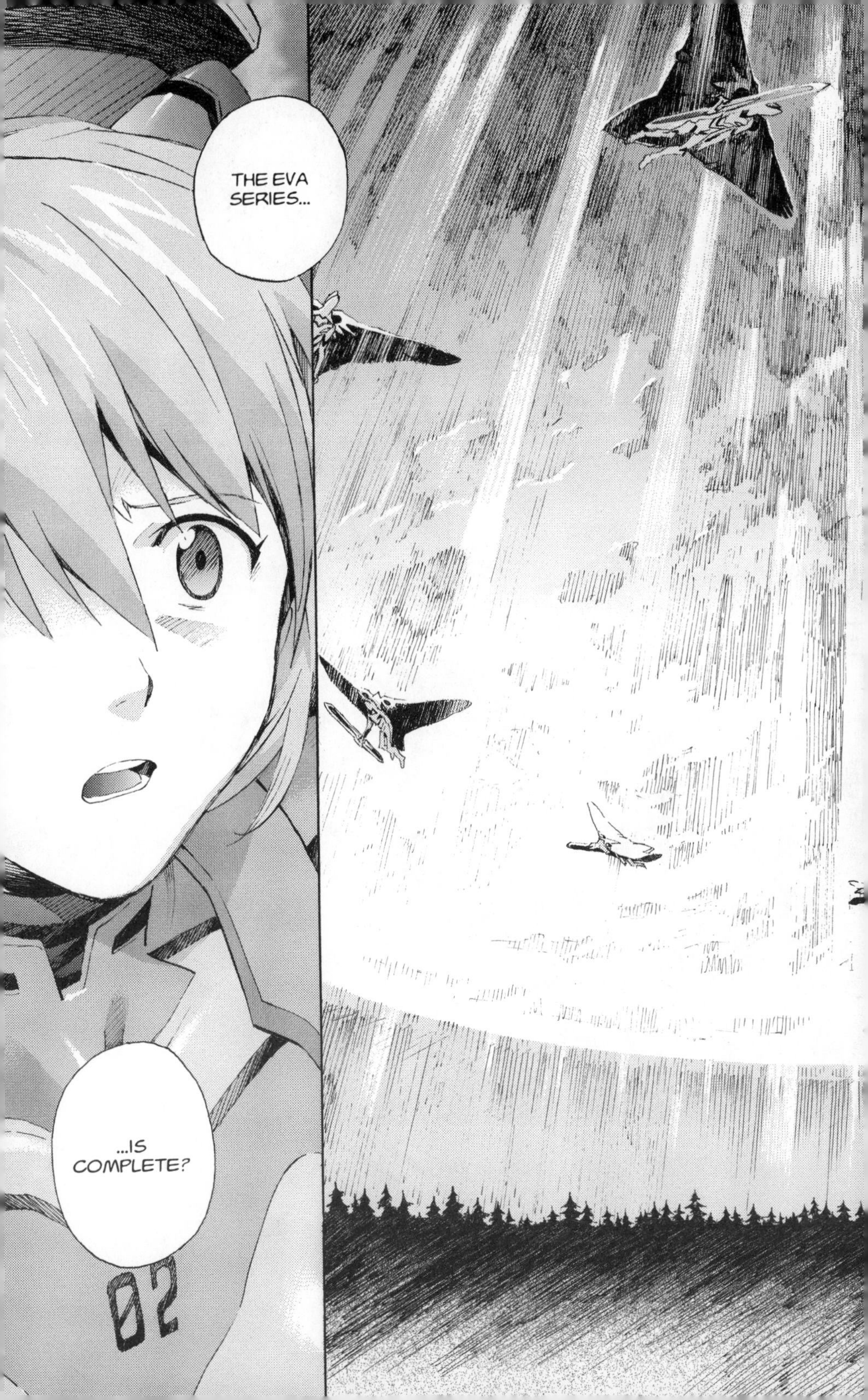
THE EVA SERIES...
...IS COMPLETE?

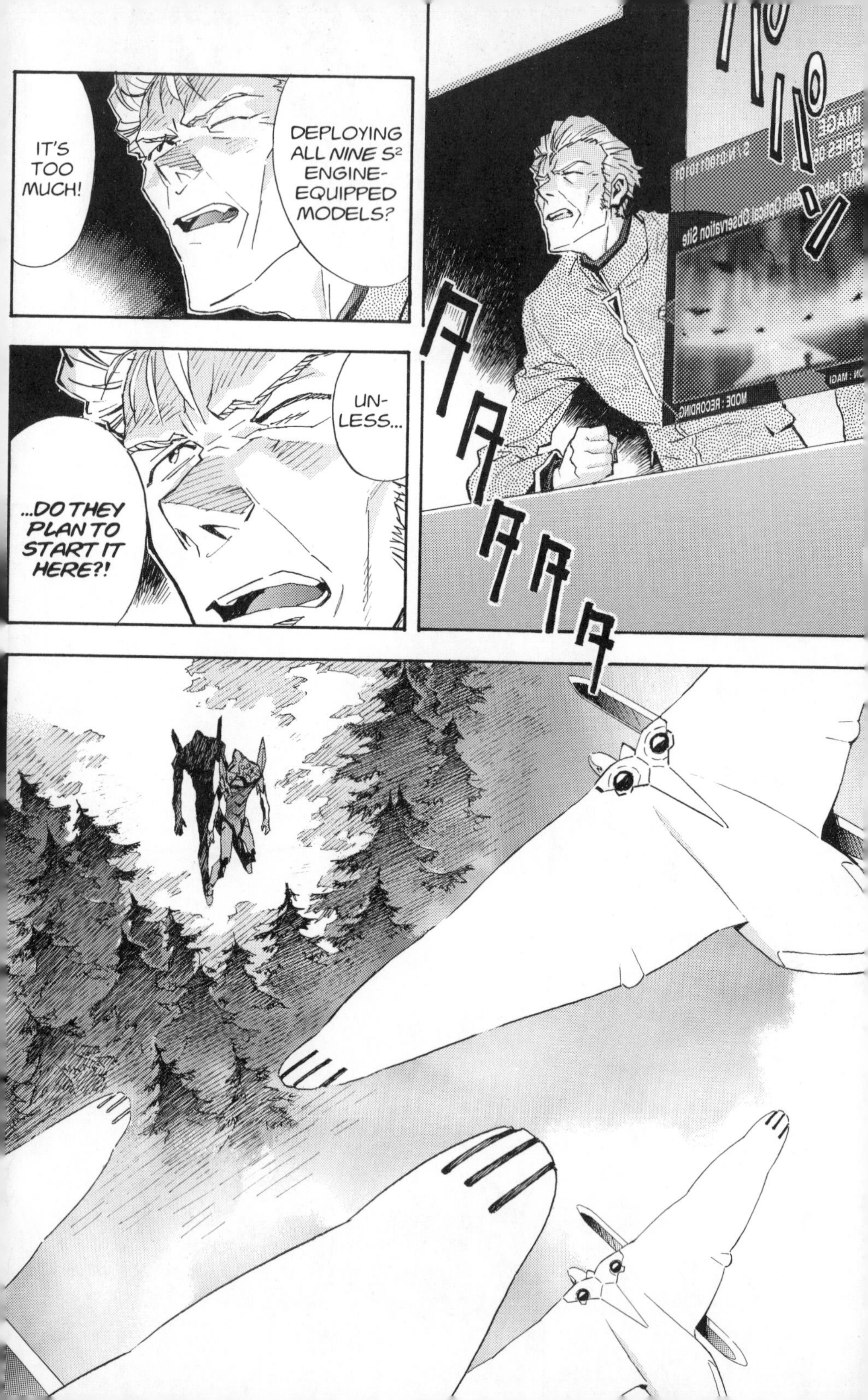
Optical Observation Site
MODE : RECORDING
DEPLOYING ALL NINE S^2 ENGINE-EQUIPPED MODELS?
IT'S TOO MUCH!
UN-LESS...
...DO THEY PLAN TO START IT HERE?!

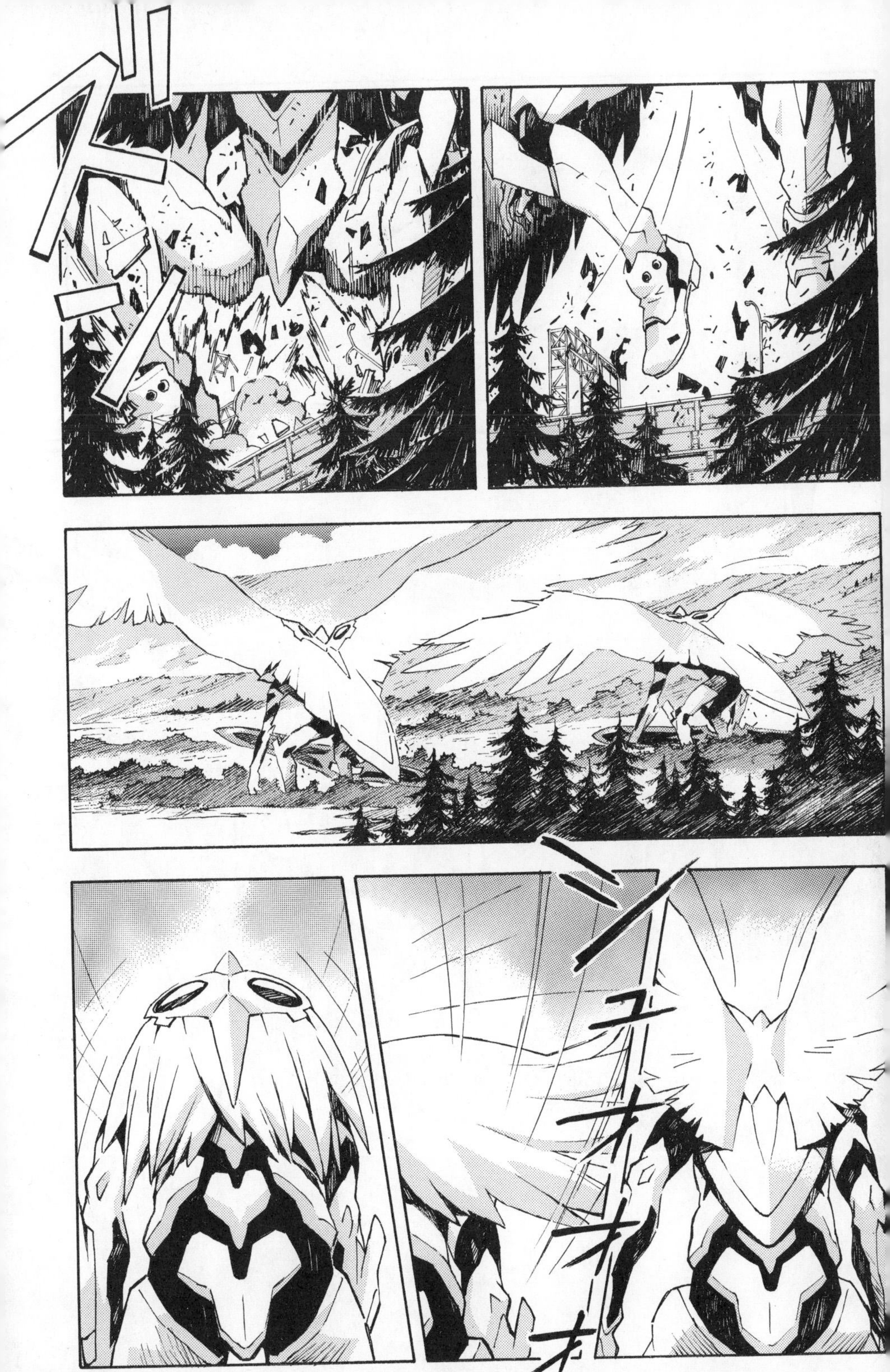
ズン
シュオオォ

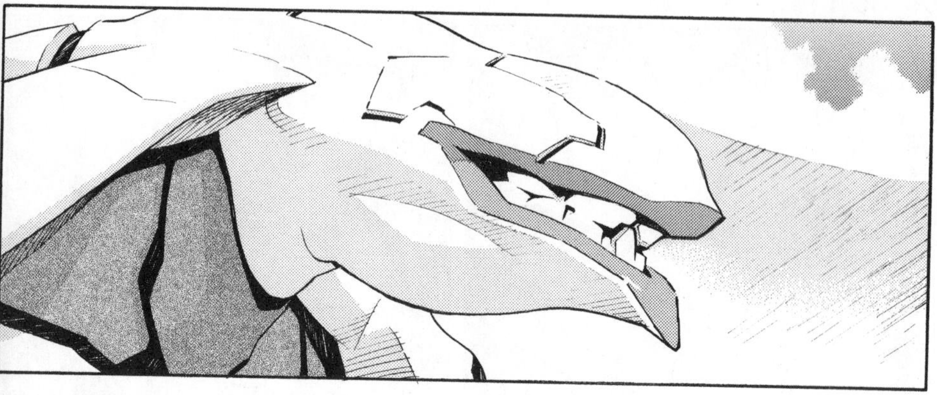

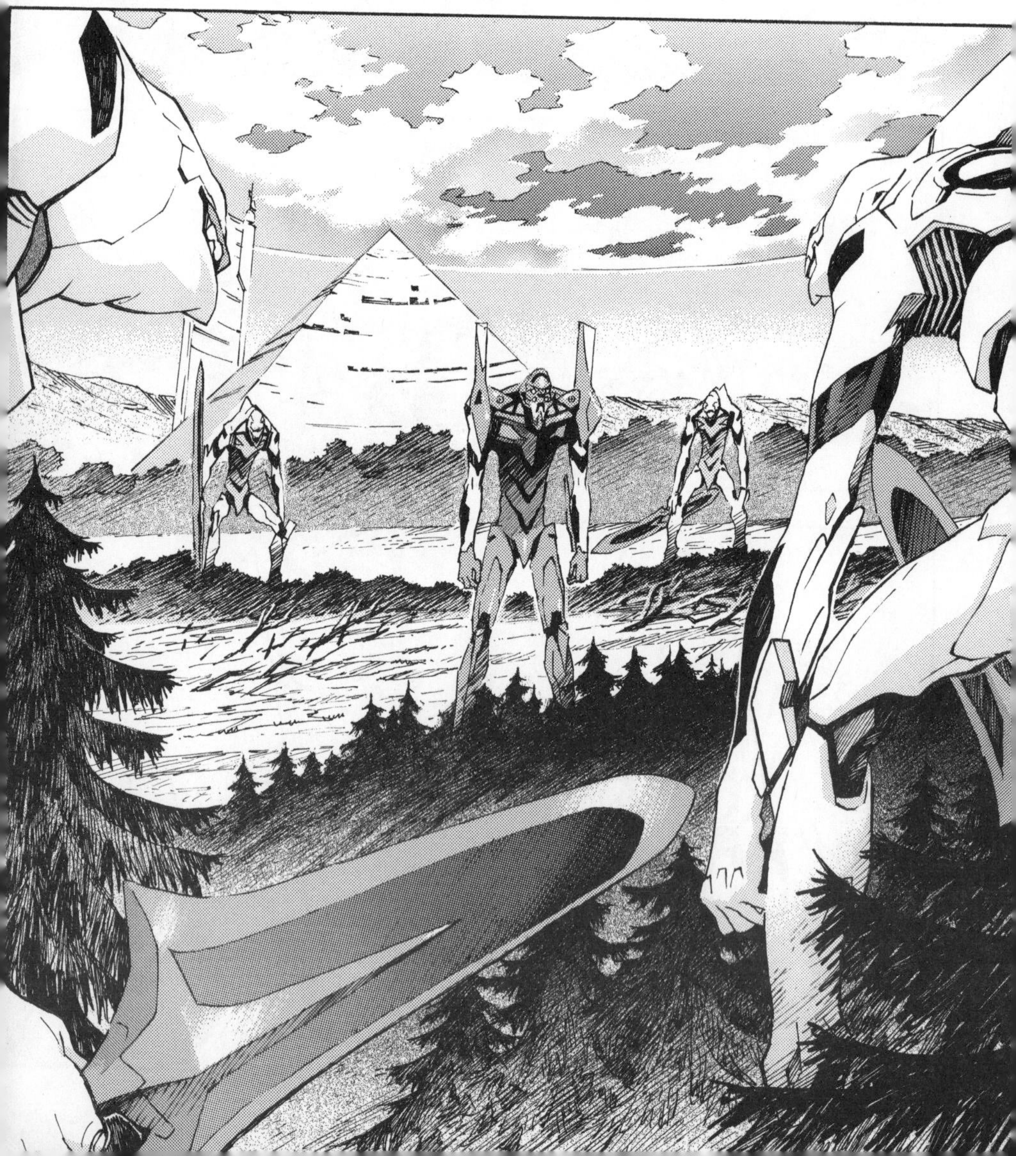

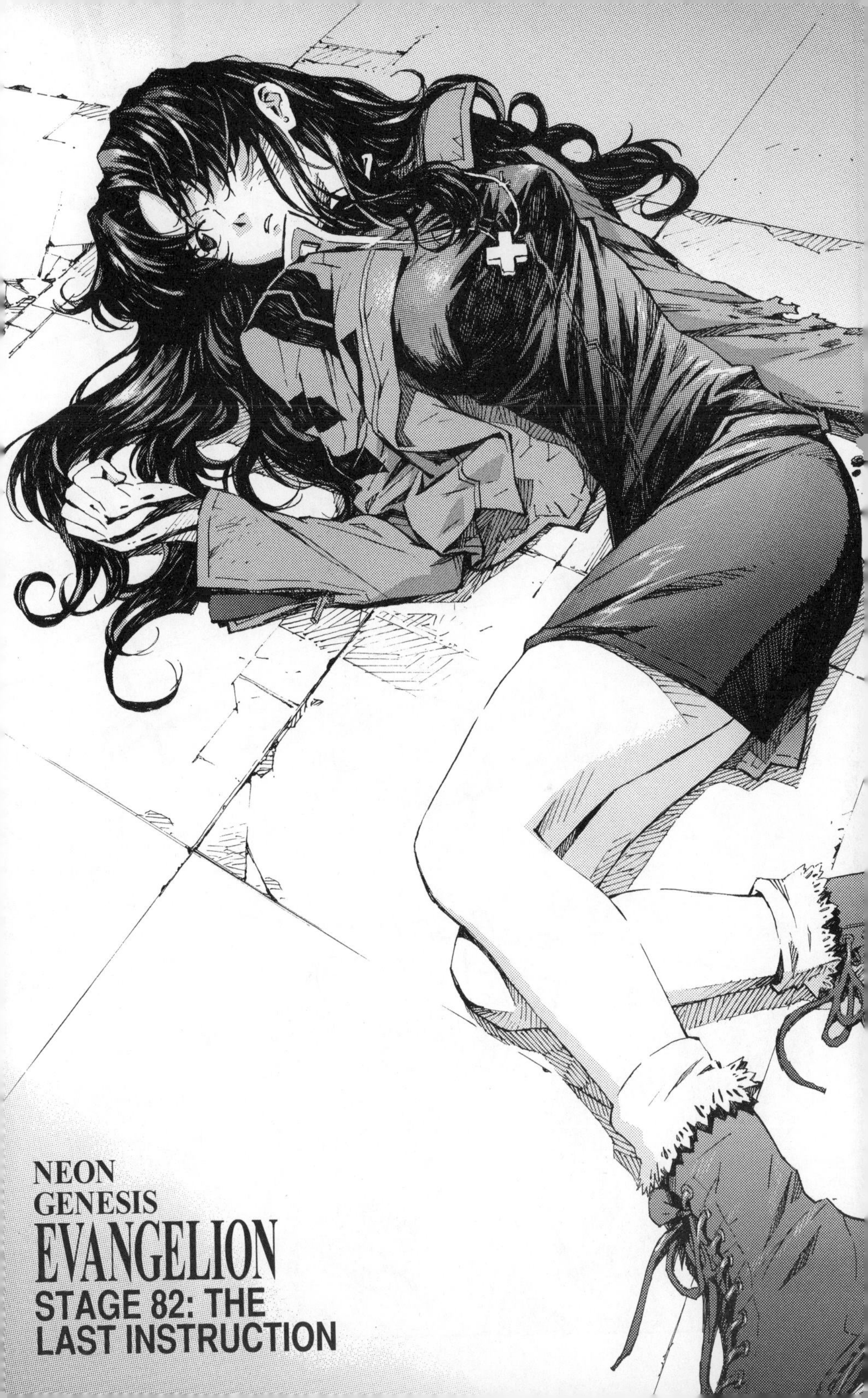

NEON GENESIS
EVANGELION
STAGE 82: THE LAST INSTRUCTION

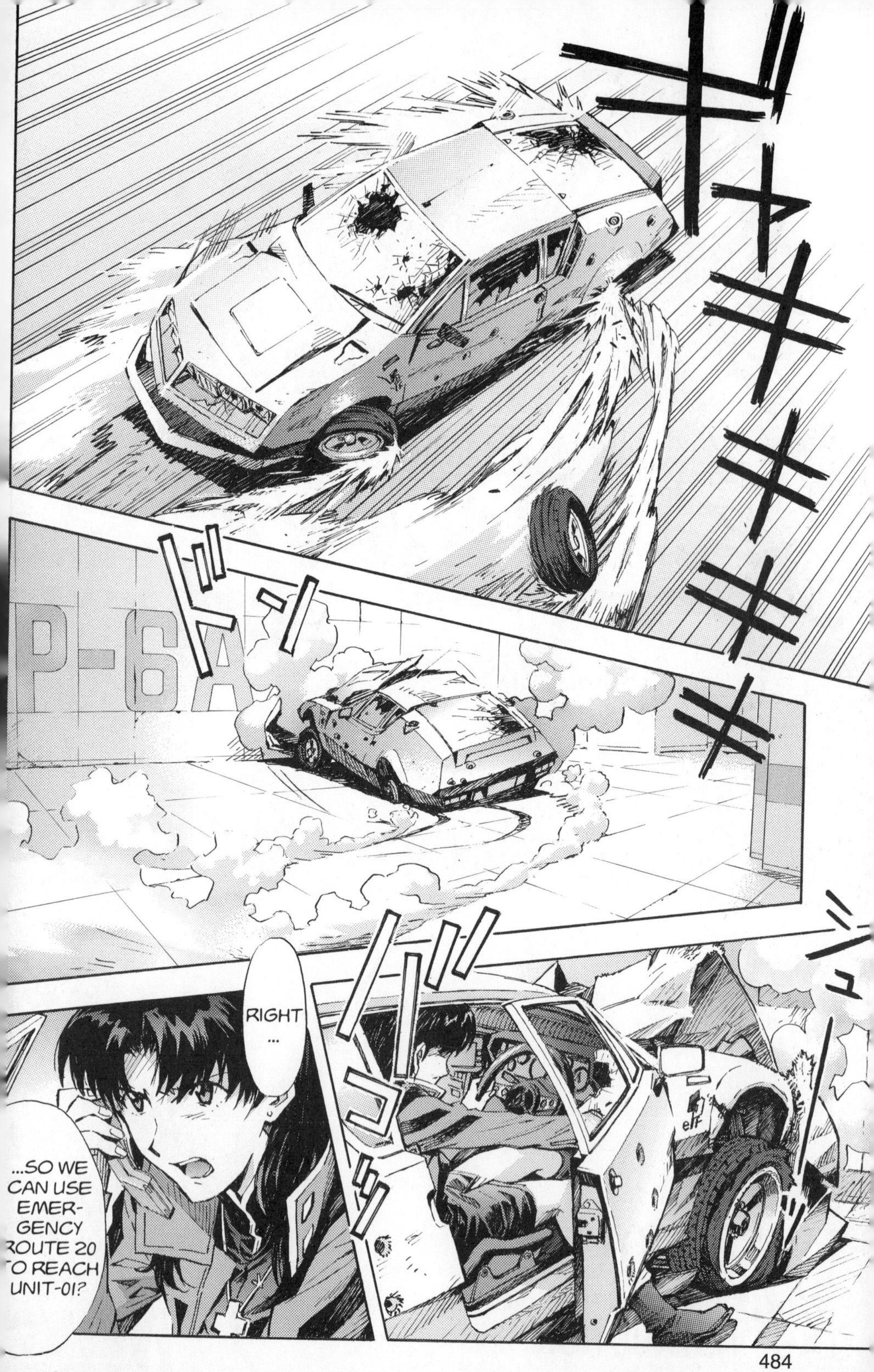
RIGHT ...
...SO WE CAN USE EMER-GENCY ROUTE 20 TO REACH UNIT-01?

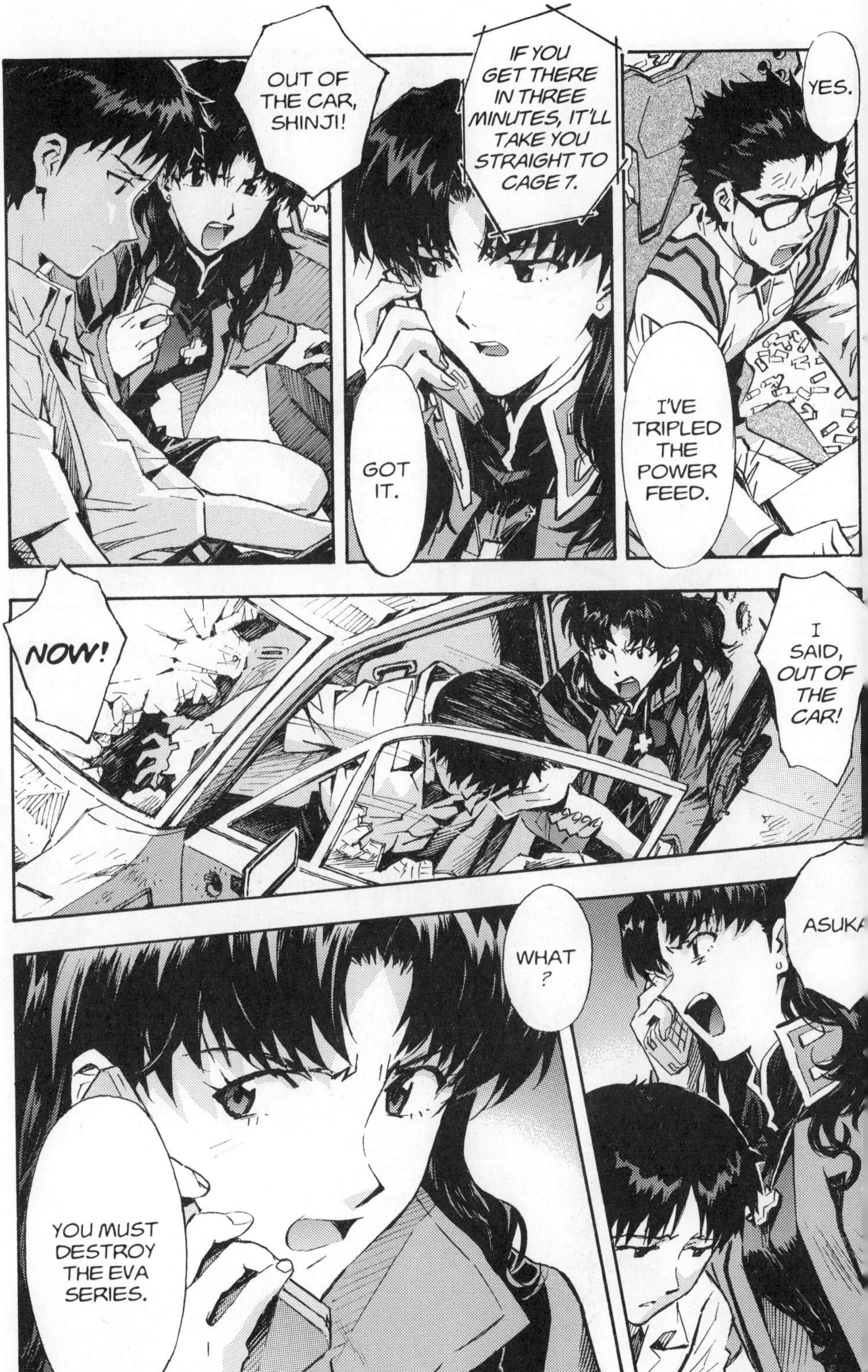
YES.
I'VE TRIPLED THE POWER FEED.
IF YOU GET THERE IN THREE MINUTES, IT'LL TAKE YOU STRAIGHT TO CAGE 7.
GOT IT.
OUT OF THE CAR, SHINJI!
I SAID, OUT OF THE CAR!
NOW!
ASUKA
WHAT?
YOU MUST DESTROY THE EVA SERIES.

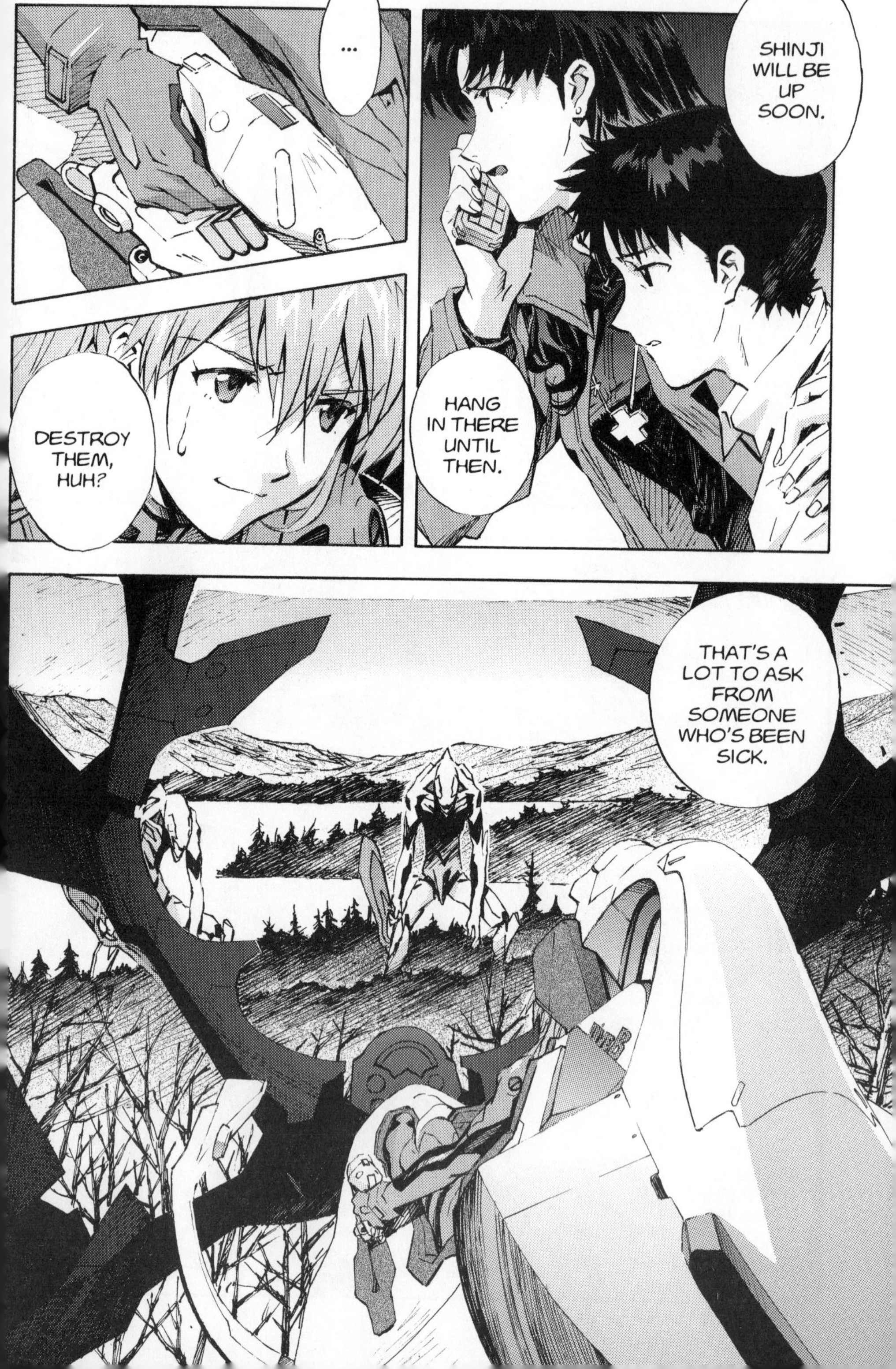
SHINJI WILL BE UP SOON.
HANG IN THERE UNTIL THEN.
...
DESTROY THEM, HUH?
THAT'S A LOT TO ASK FROM SOMEONE WHO'S BEEN SICK.

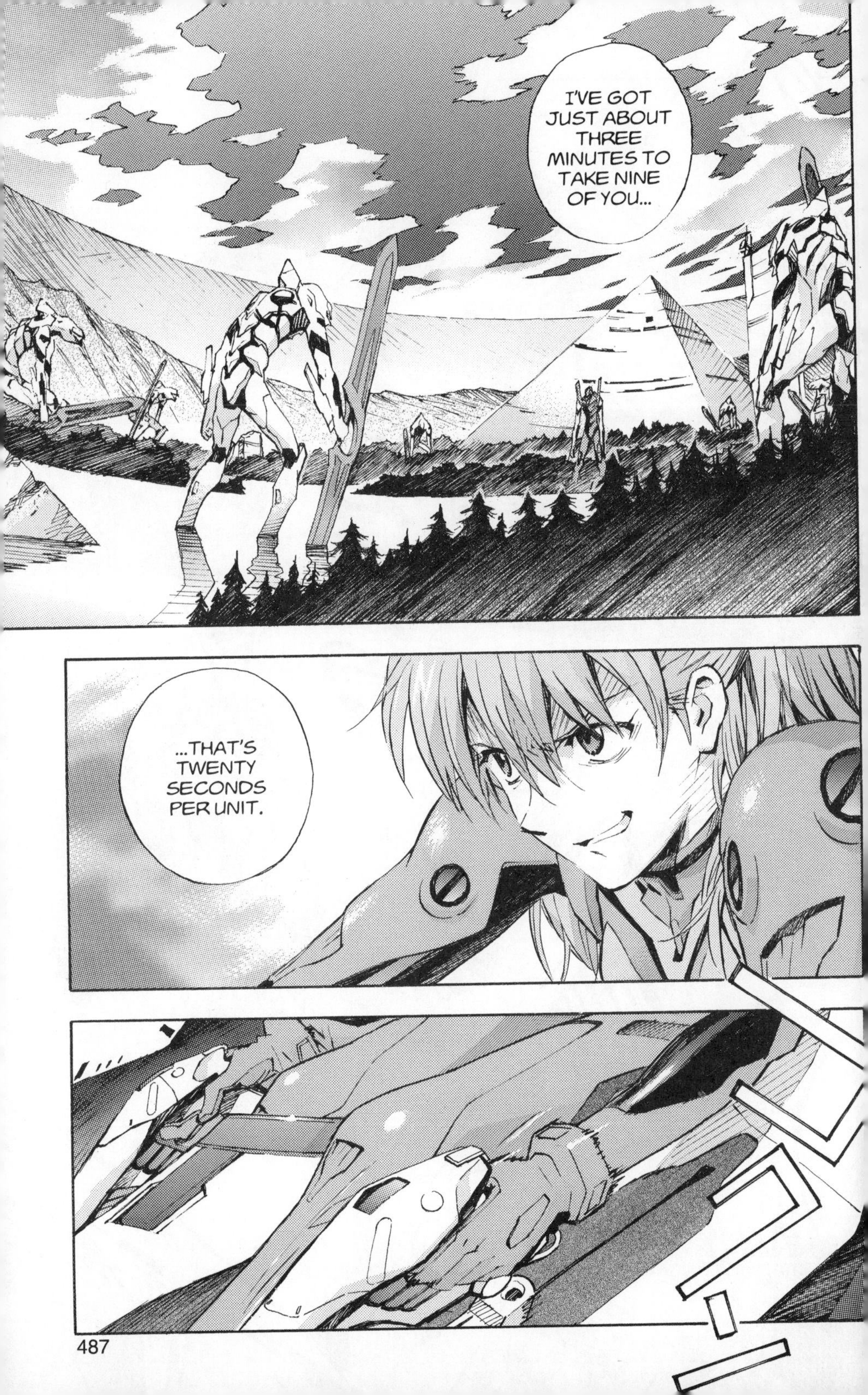
I'VE GOT JUST ABOUT THREE MINUTES TO TAKE NINE OF YOU...
...THAT'S TWENTY SECONDS PER UNIT.

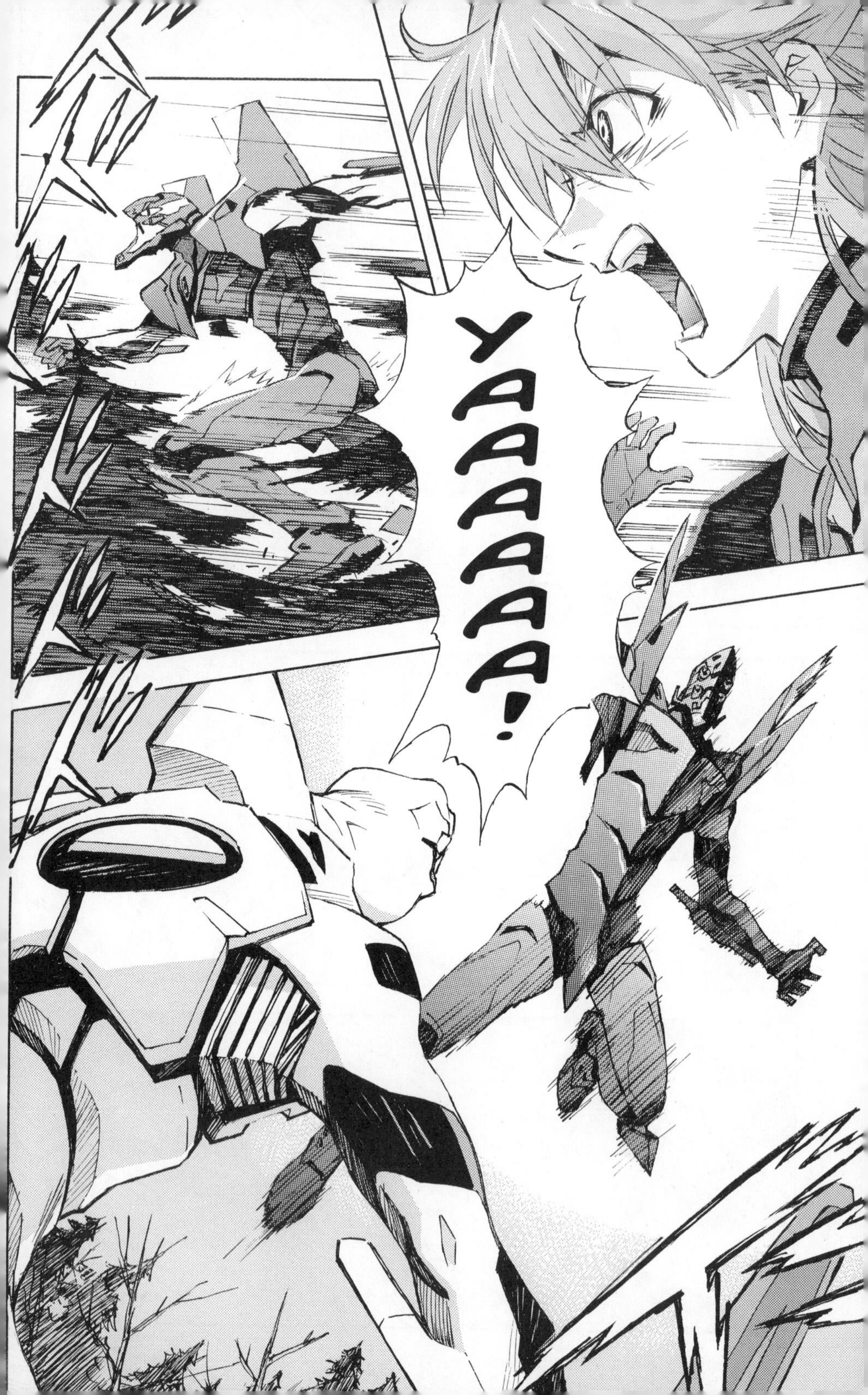
YAAAAAA!

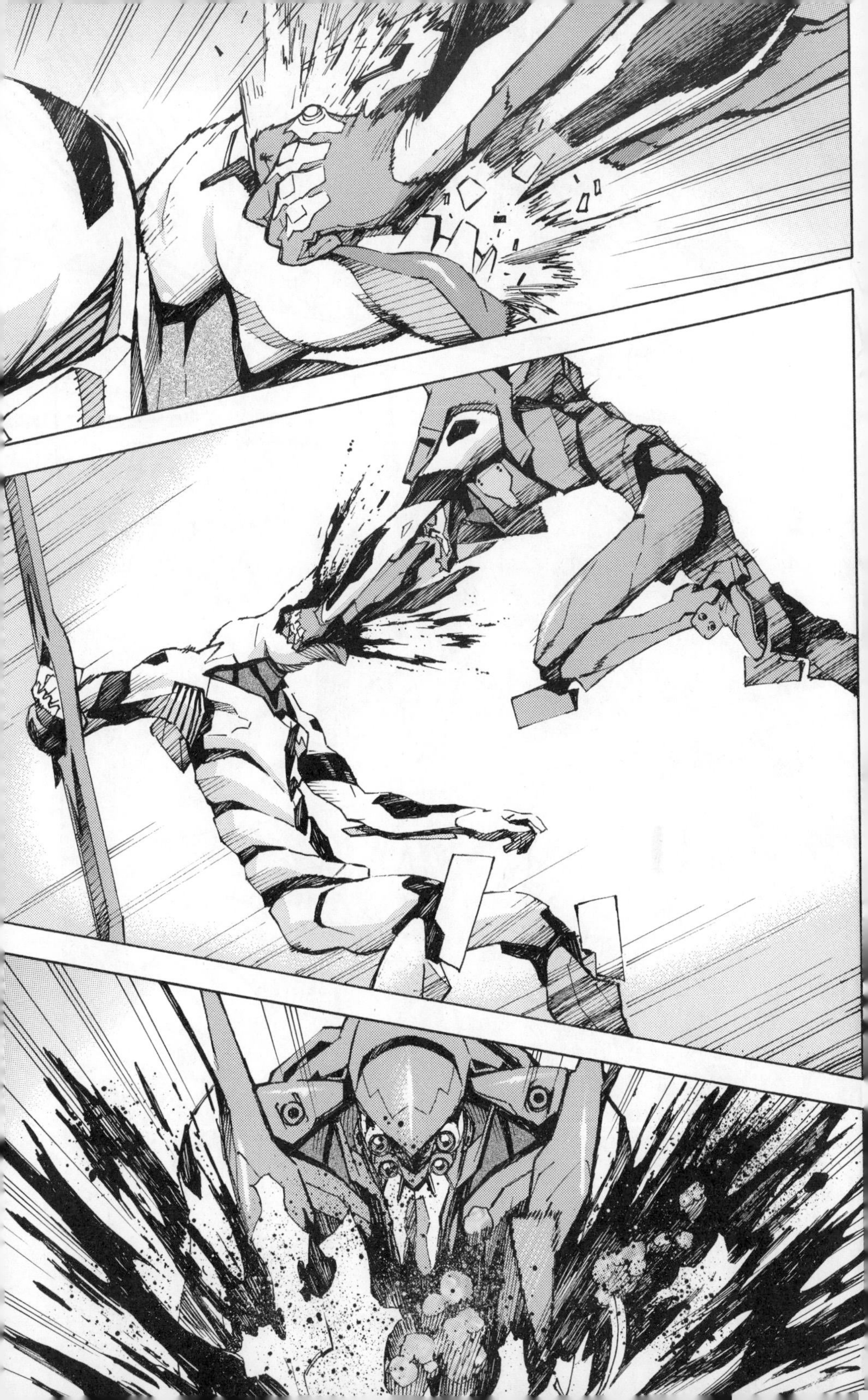

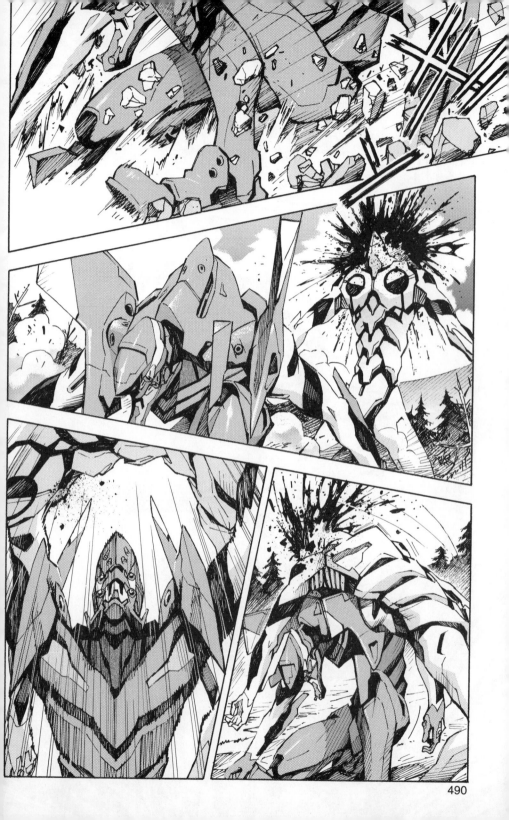

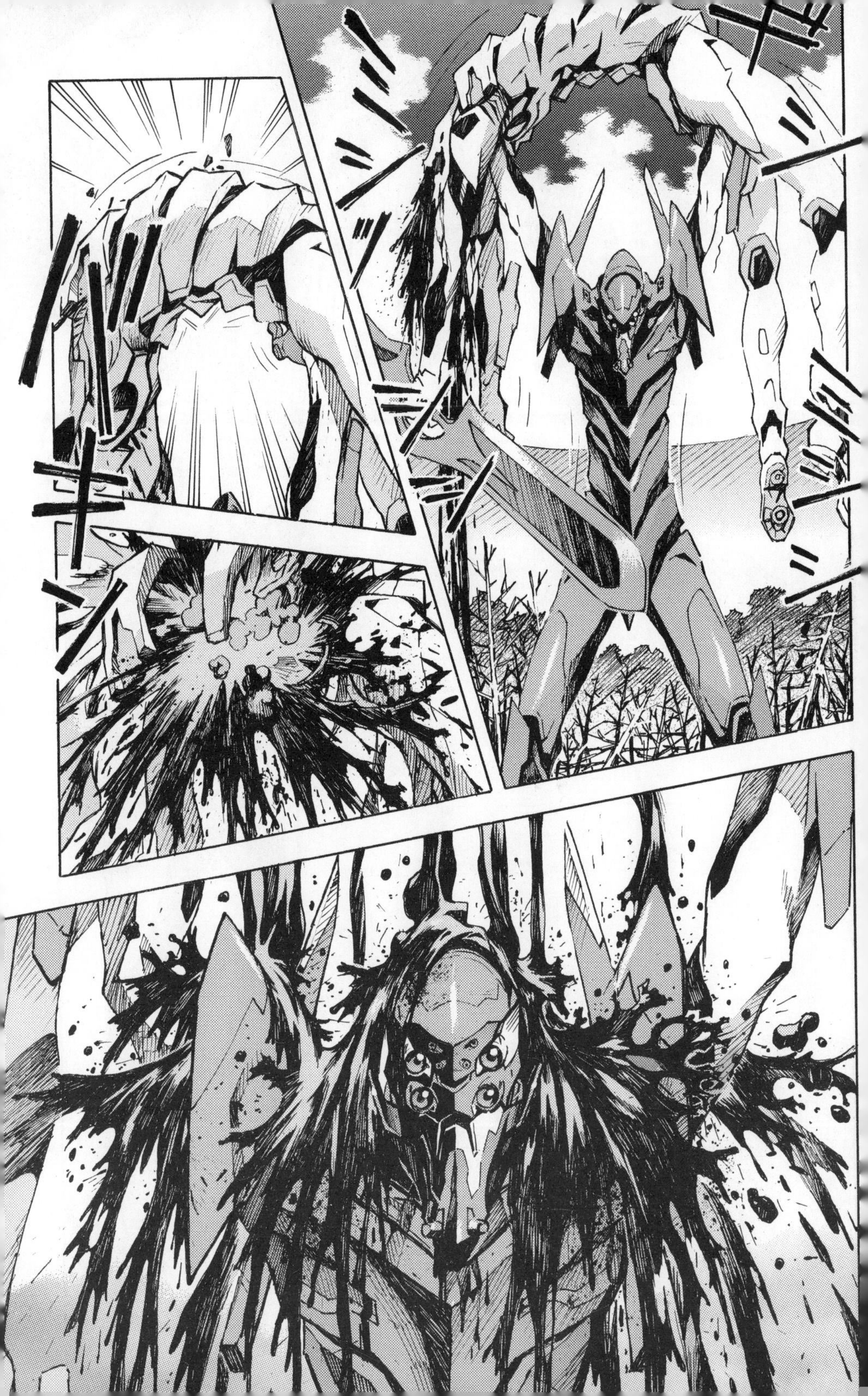

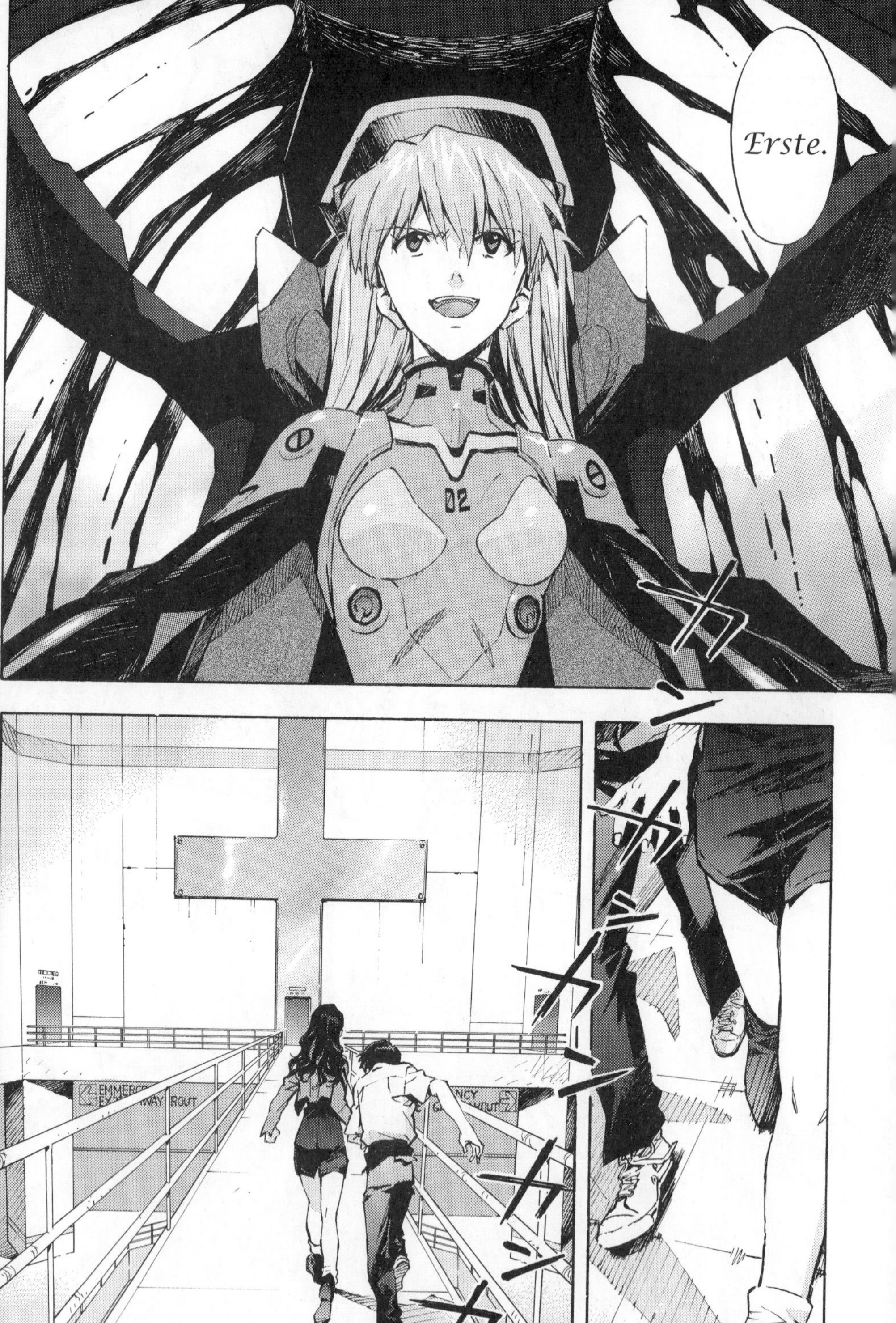
Erste.

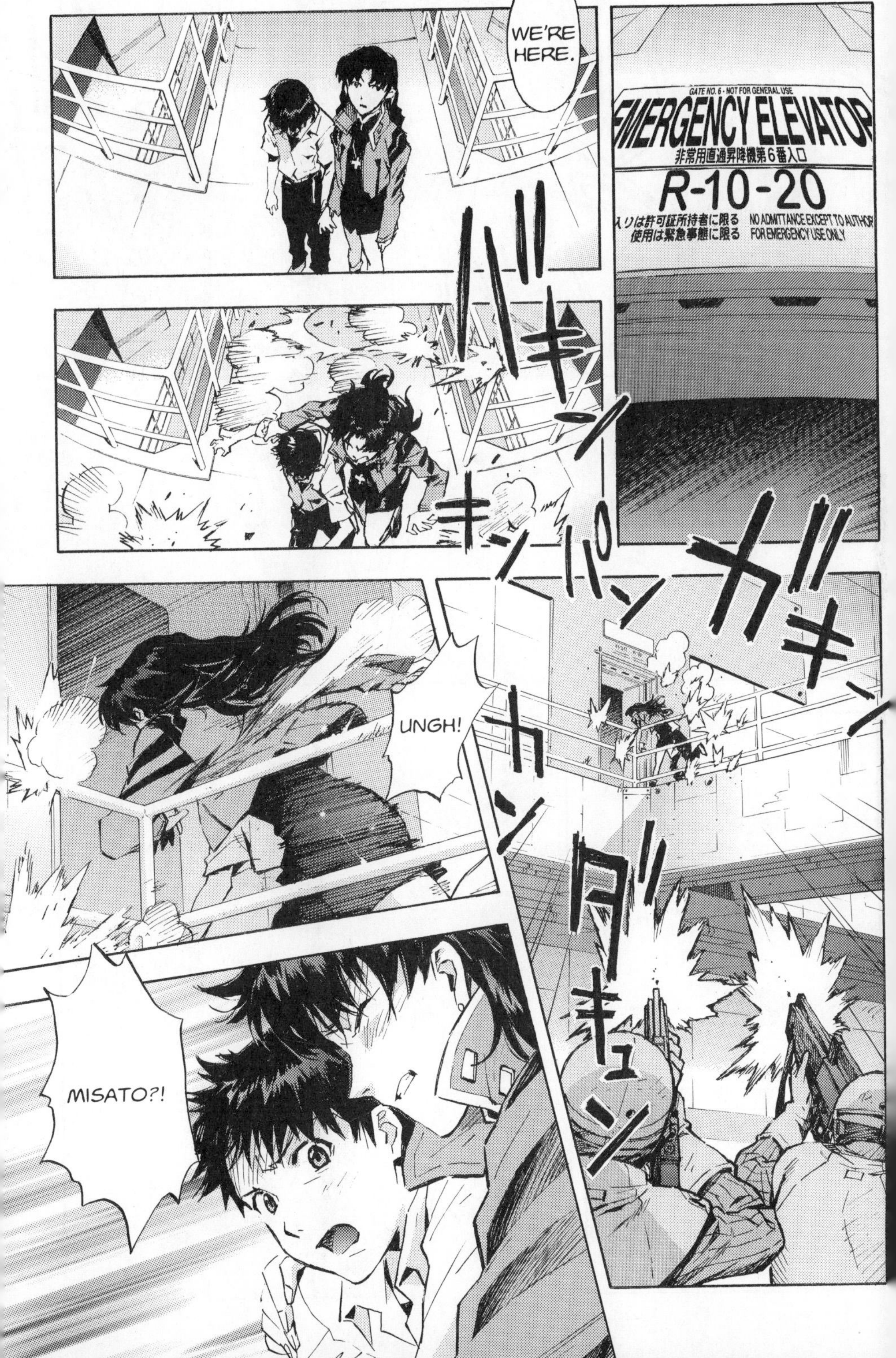
GATE NO. 6 - NOT FOR GENERAL USE
EMERGENCY ELEVATOR
非常用直通昇降機第6番入口
R-10-20
入りは許可証所持者に限る NO ADMITTANCE EXCEPT TO AUTHOR
使用は緊急事態に限る FOR EMERGENCY USE ONLY
WE'RE HERE.
バキーン
キン
パン
ガキーン
カン
ダキューン
UNGH!
MISATO?!

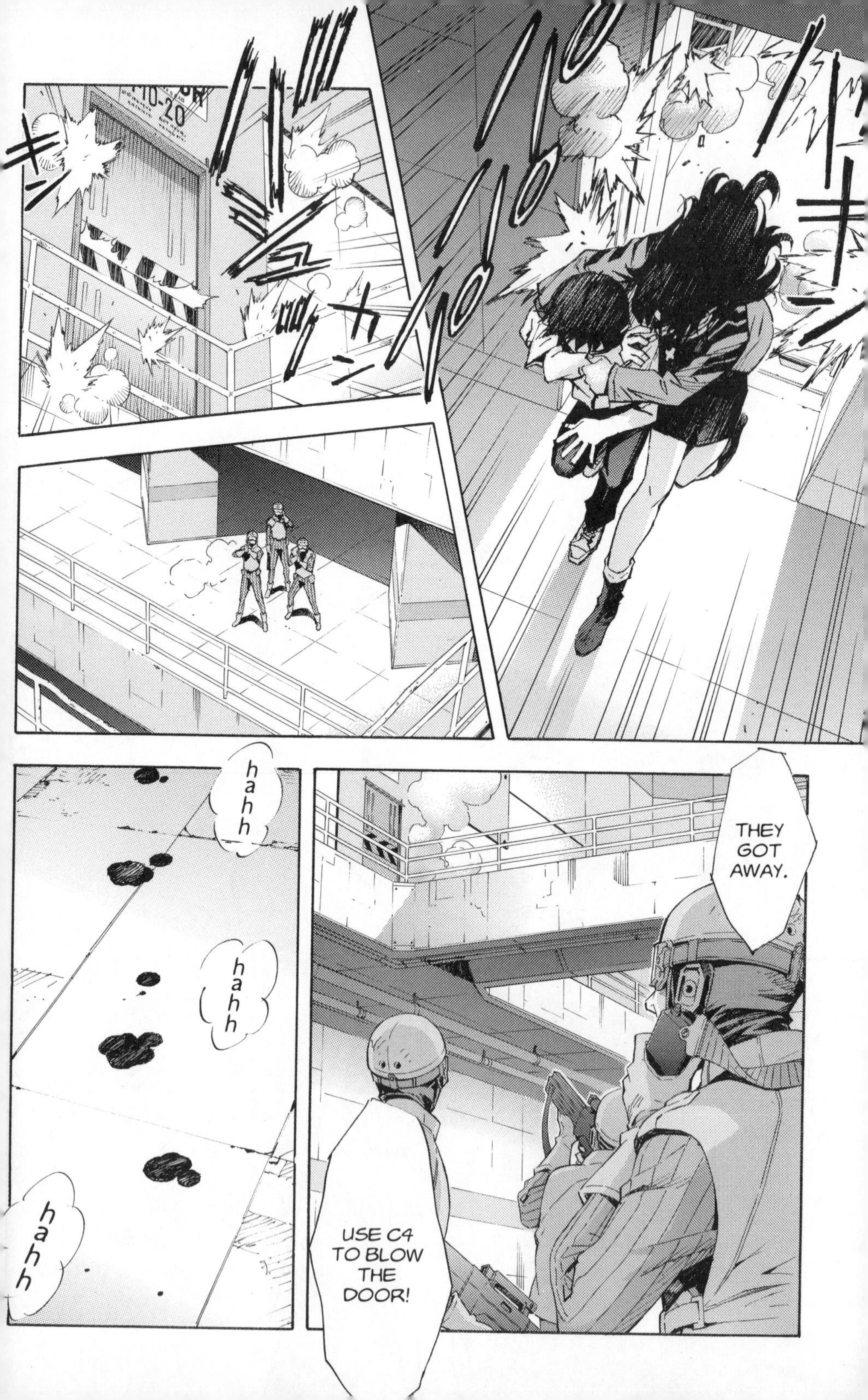
キン
THEY GOT AWAY.
USE C4 TO BLOW THE DOOR!
hahh
hahh
hahh

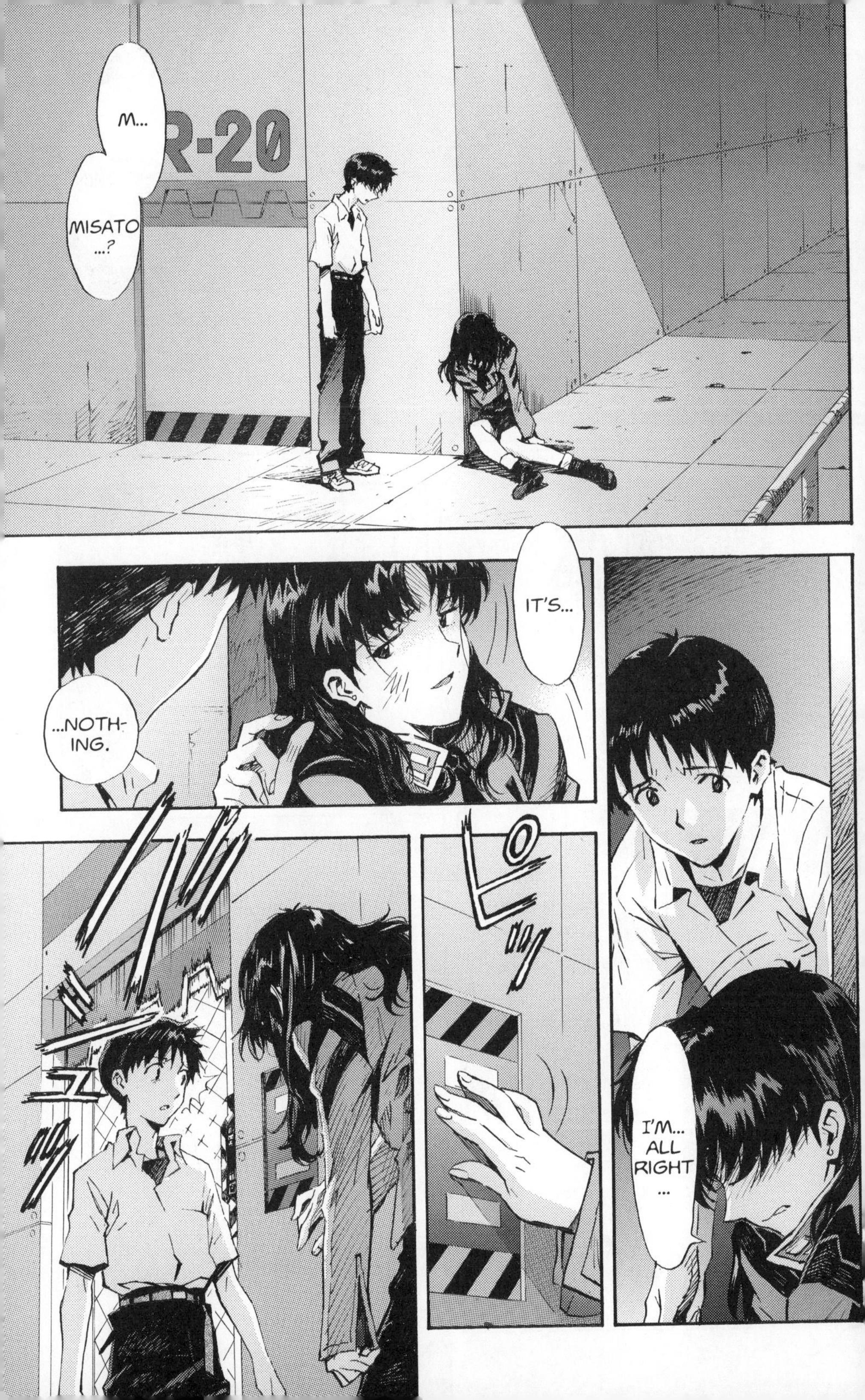
M...
MISATO ...?
I'M... ALL RIGHT ...
IT'S...
...NOTHING.

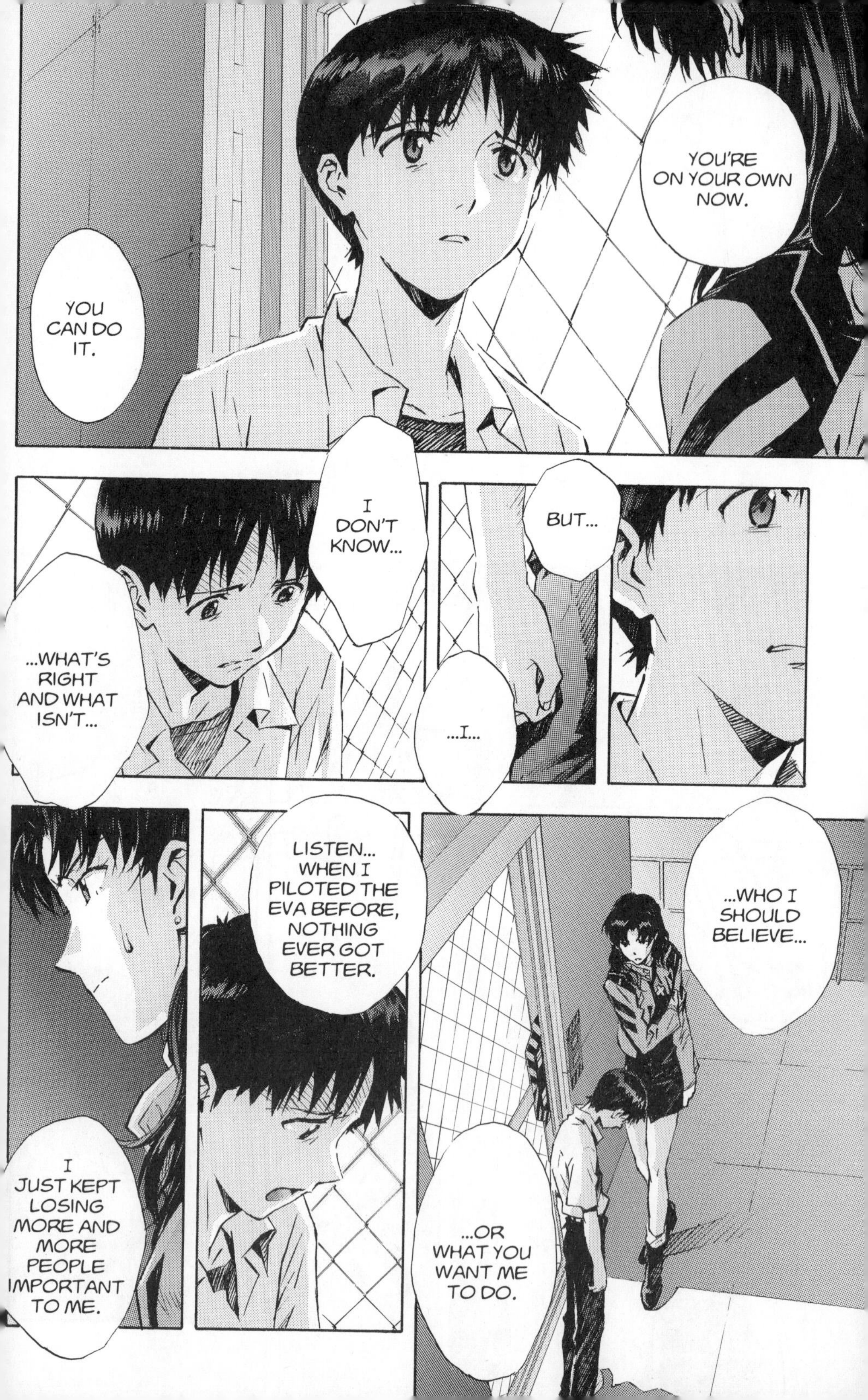
YOU'RE ON YOUR OWN NOW.
YOU CAN DO IT.
BUT...
...I...
I DON'T KNOW...
...WHAT'S RIGHT AND WHAT ISN'T...
...WHO I SHOULD BELIEVE...
...OR WHAT YOU WANT ME TO DO.
LISTEN... WHEN I PILOTED THE EVA BEFORE, NOTHING EVER GOT BETTER.
I JUST KEPT LOSING MORE AND MORE PEOPLE IMPORTANT TO ME.

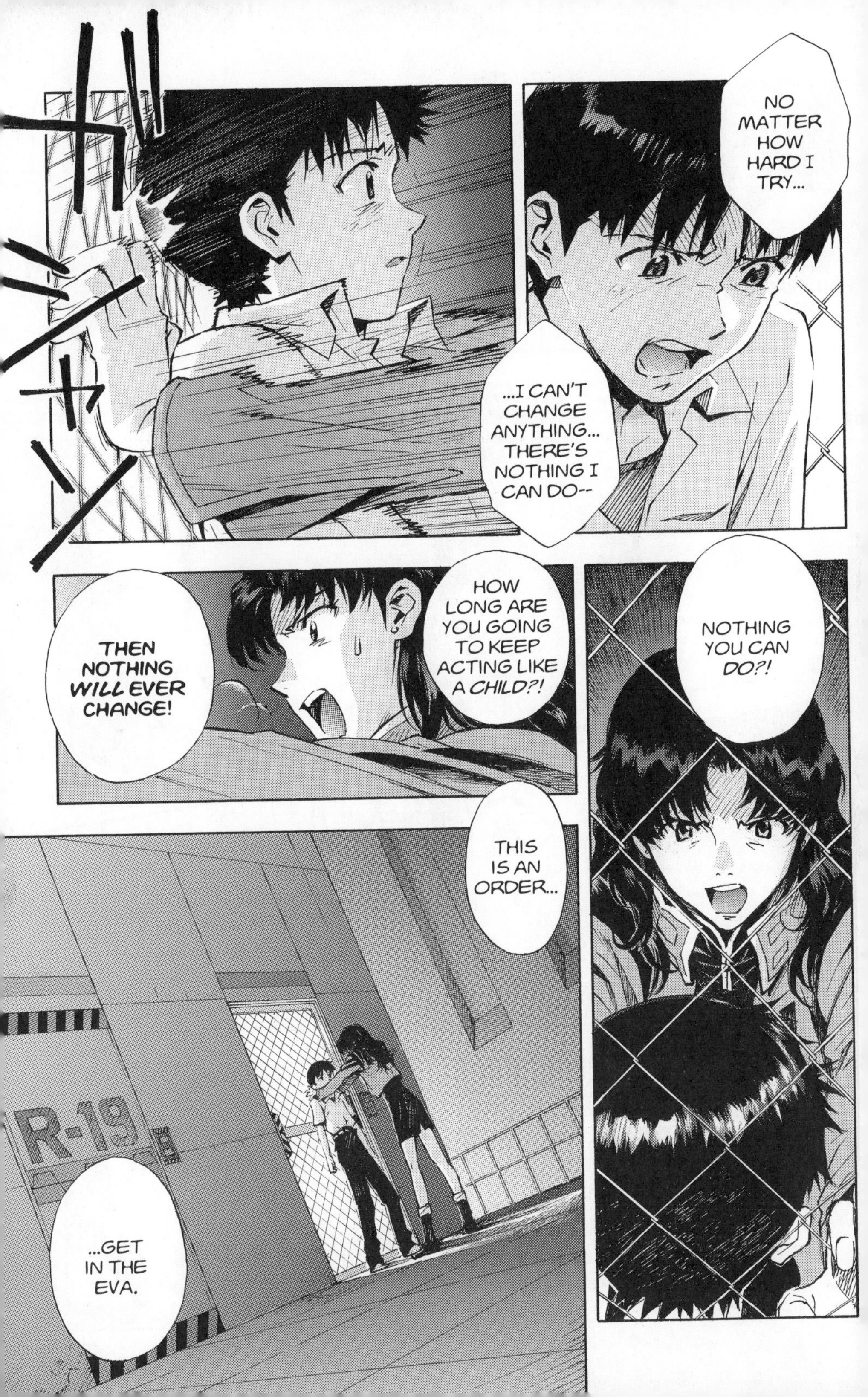
NO MATTER HOW HARD I TRY...
...I CAN'T CHANGE ANYTHING... THERE'S NOTHING I CAN DO--
ガシャン
NOTHING YOU CAN *DO?!*
HOW LONG ARE YOU GOING TO KEEP ACTING LIKE A *CHILD?!*
THEN NOTHING ***WILL*** EVER CHANGE!
THIS IS AN ORDER...
R-19
...GET IN THE EVA.

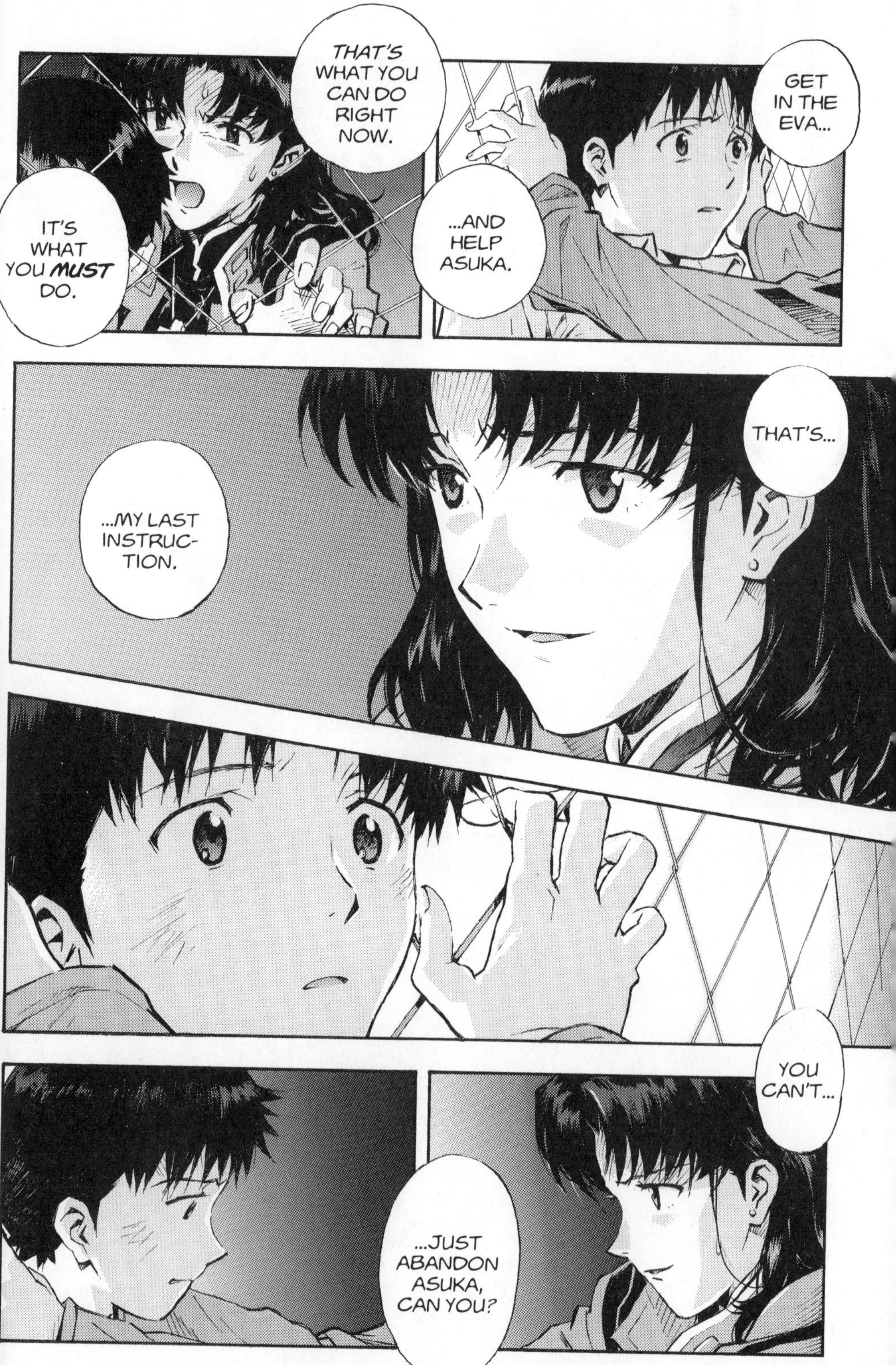
GET IN THE EVA...
...AND HELP ASUKA.
THAT'S WHAT YOU CAN DO RIGHT NOW.
IT'S WHAT YOU MUST DO.
THAT'S...
...MY LAST INSTRUCTION.
YOU CAN'T...
...JUST ABANDON ASUKA, CAN YOU?

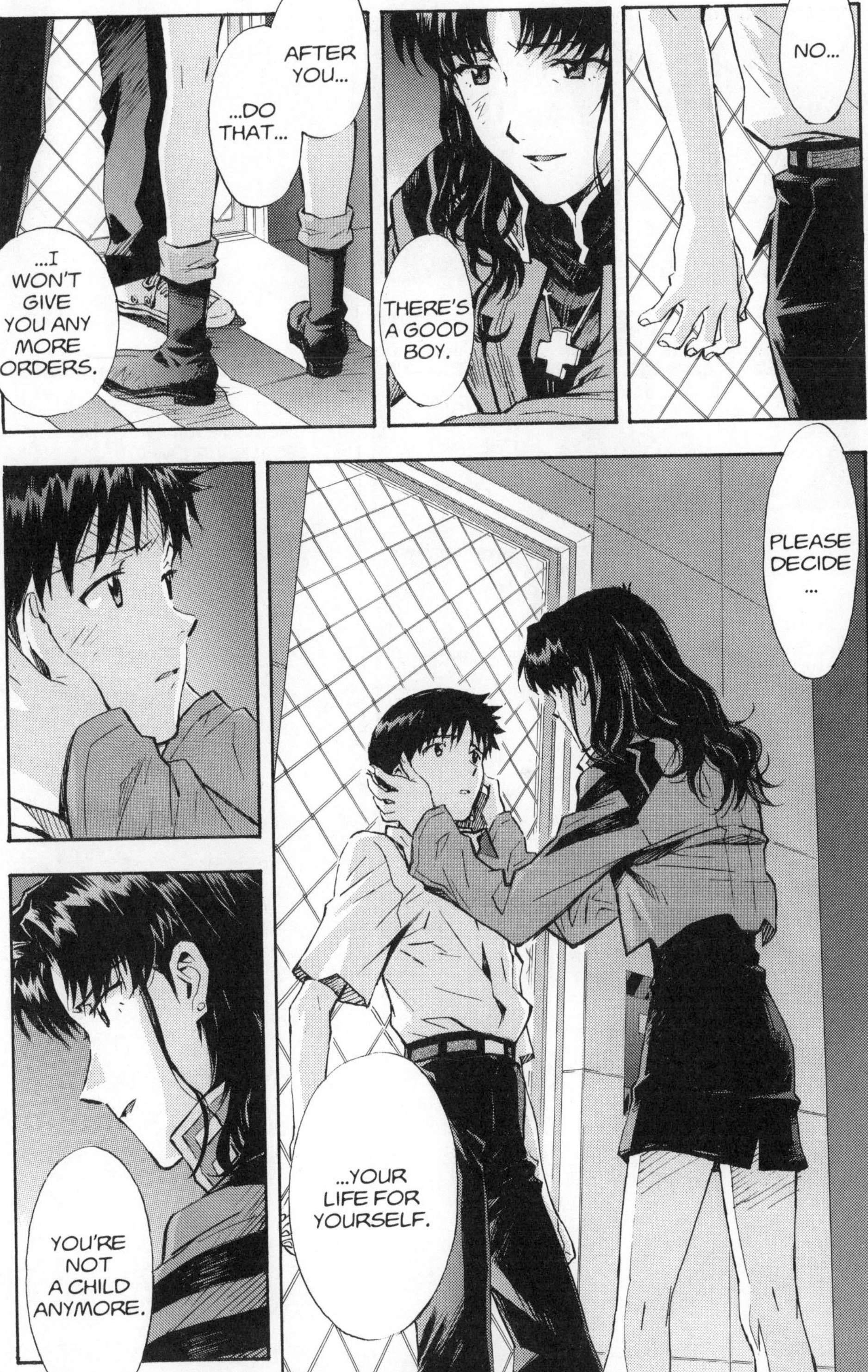
NO...
THERE'S A GOOD BOY.
AFTER YOU...
...DO THAT...
...I WON'T GIVE YOU ANY MORE ORDERS.
PLEASE DECIDE ...
...YOUR LIFE FOR YOURSELF.
YOU'RE NOT A CHILD ANYMORE.

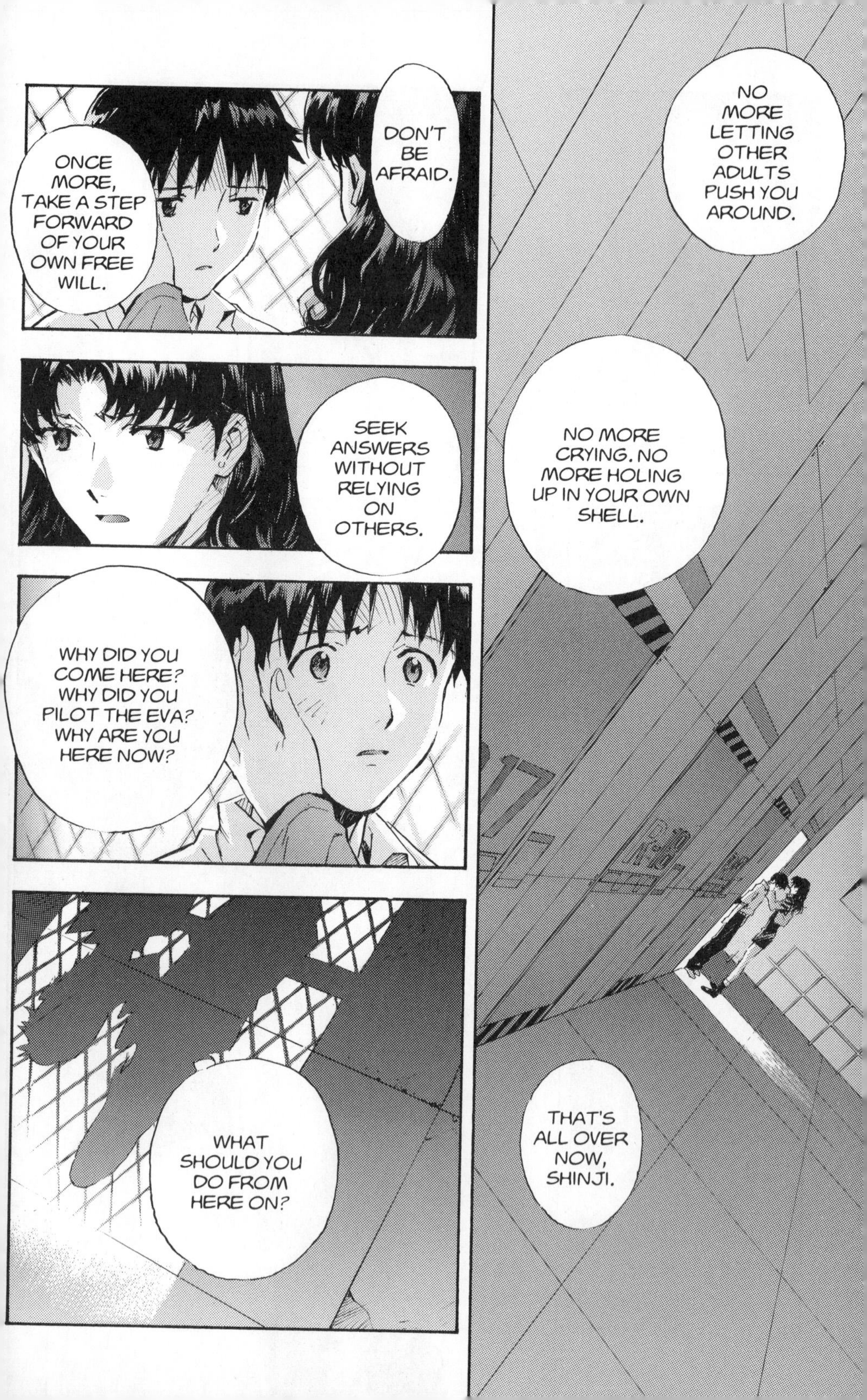
NO MORE LETTING OTHER ADULTS PUSH YOU AROUND.
NO MORE CRYING. NO MORE HOLING UP IN YOUR OWN SHELL.
THAT'S ALL OVER NOW, SHINJI.
DON'T BE AFRAID.
ONCE MORE, TAKE A STEP FORWARD OF YOUR OWN FREE WILL.
SEEK ANSWERS WITHOUT RELYING ON OTHERS.
WHY DID YOU COME HERE? WHY DID YOU PILOT THE EVA? WHY ARE YOU HERE NOW?
WHAT SHOULD YOU DO FROM HERE ON?

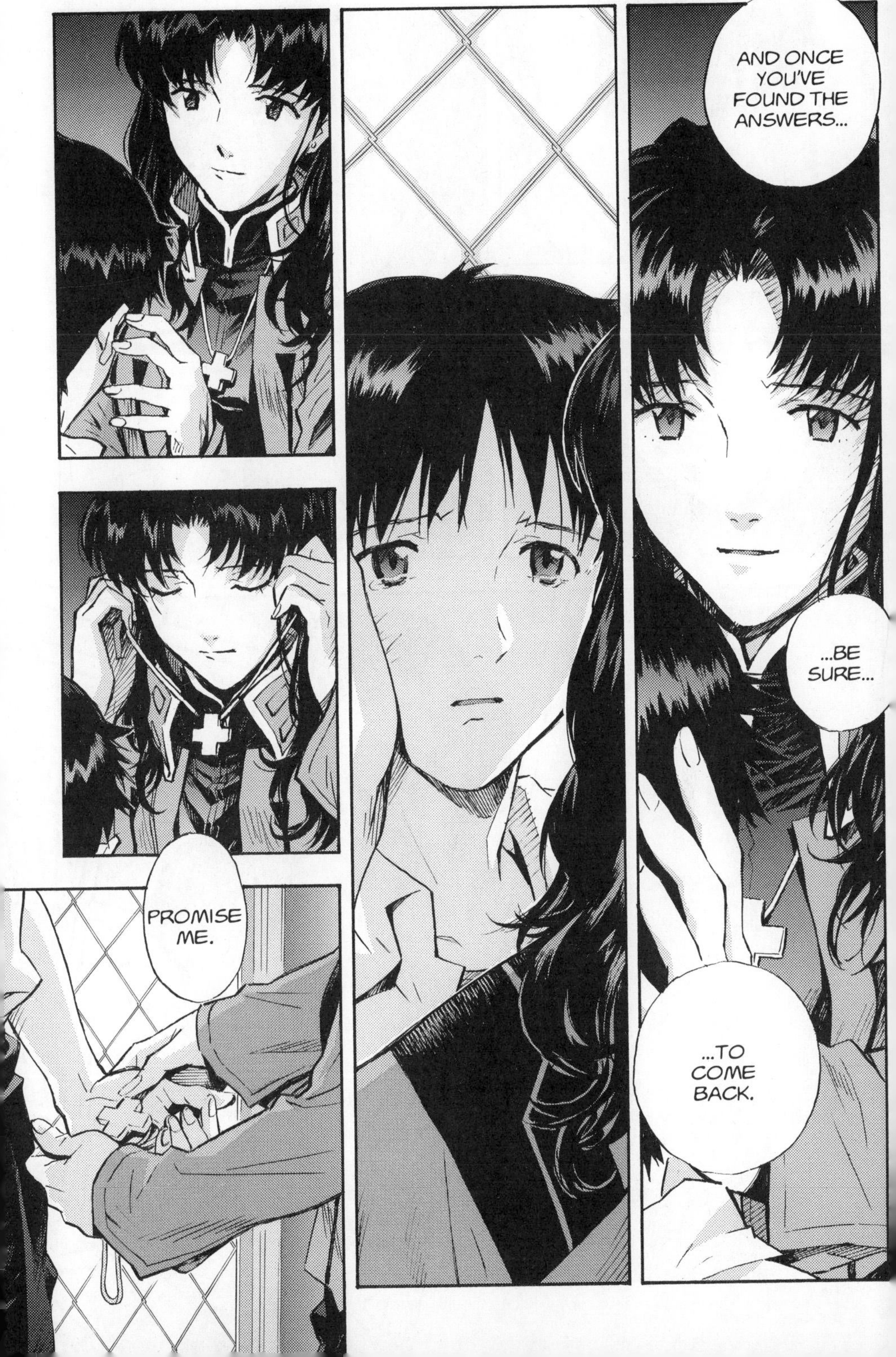
AND ONCE YOU'VE FOUND THE ANSWERS...
...BE SURE...
...TO COME BACK.
PROMISE ME.

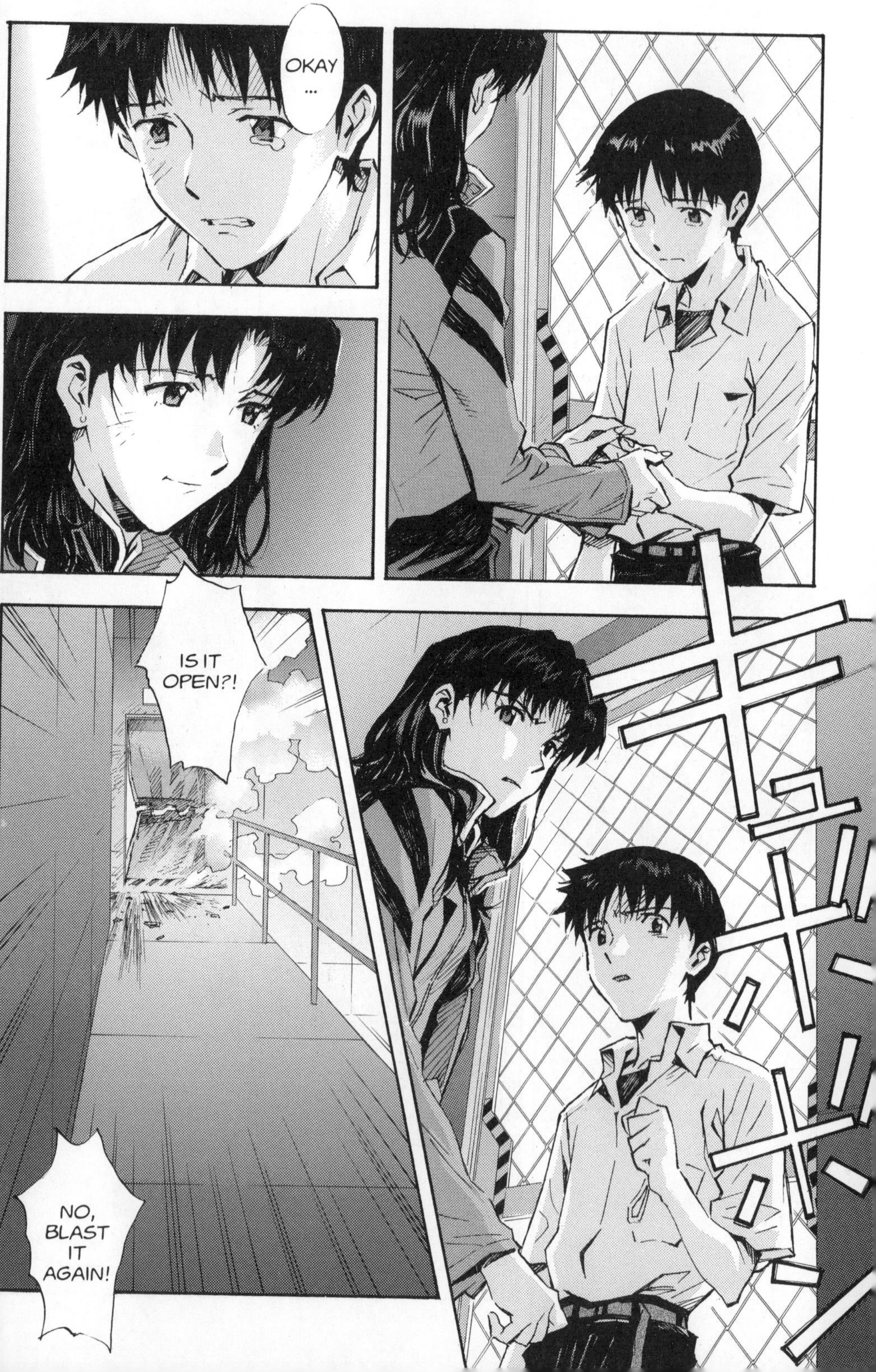
OKAY ...
IS IT OPEN?!
NO, BLAST IT AGAIN!

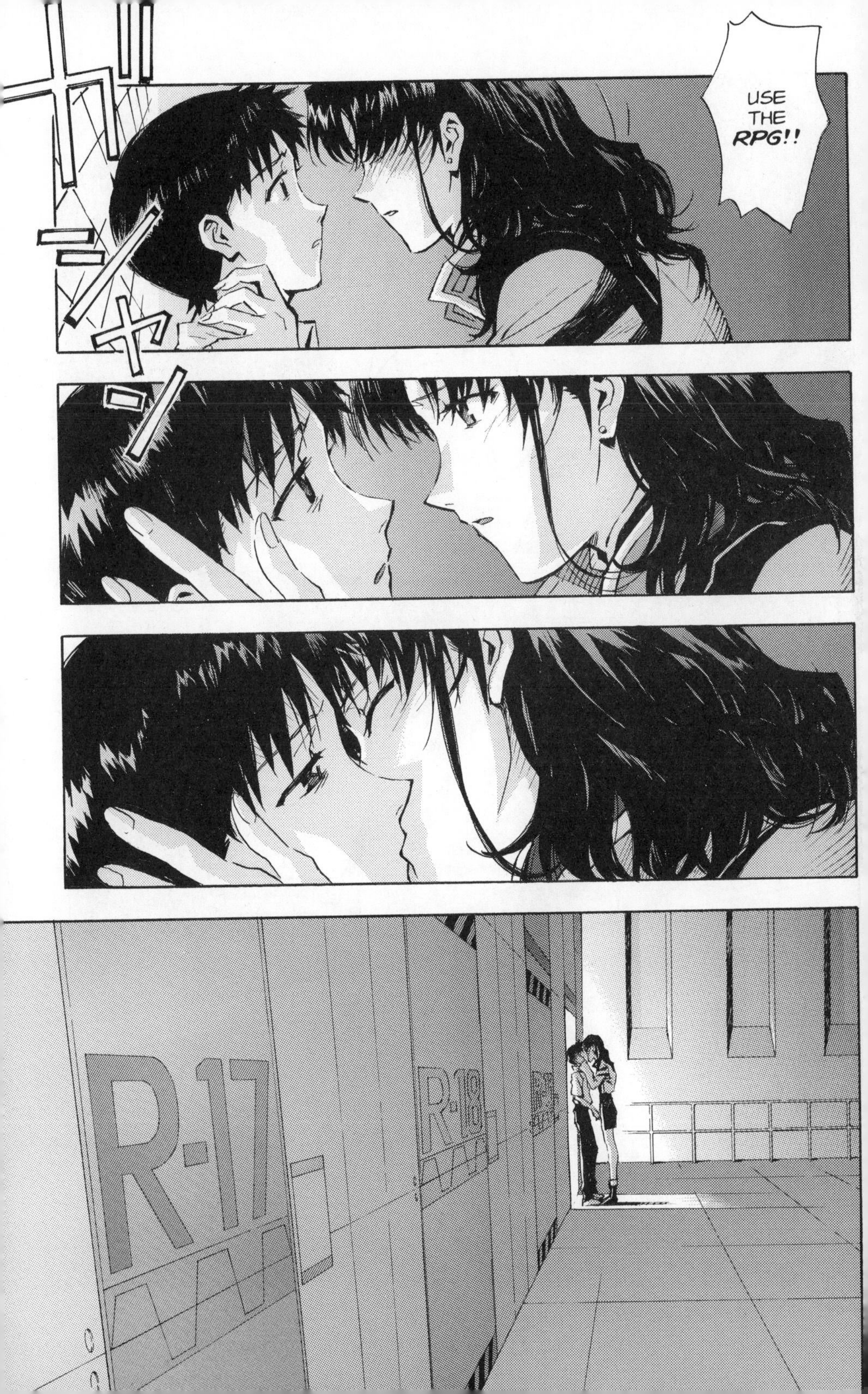
USE THE RPG!!

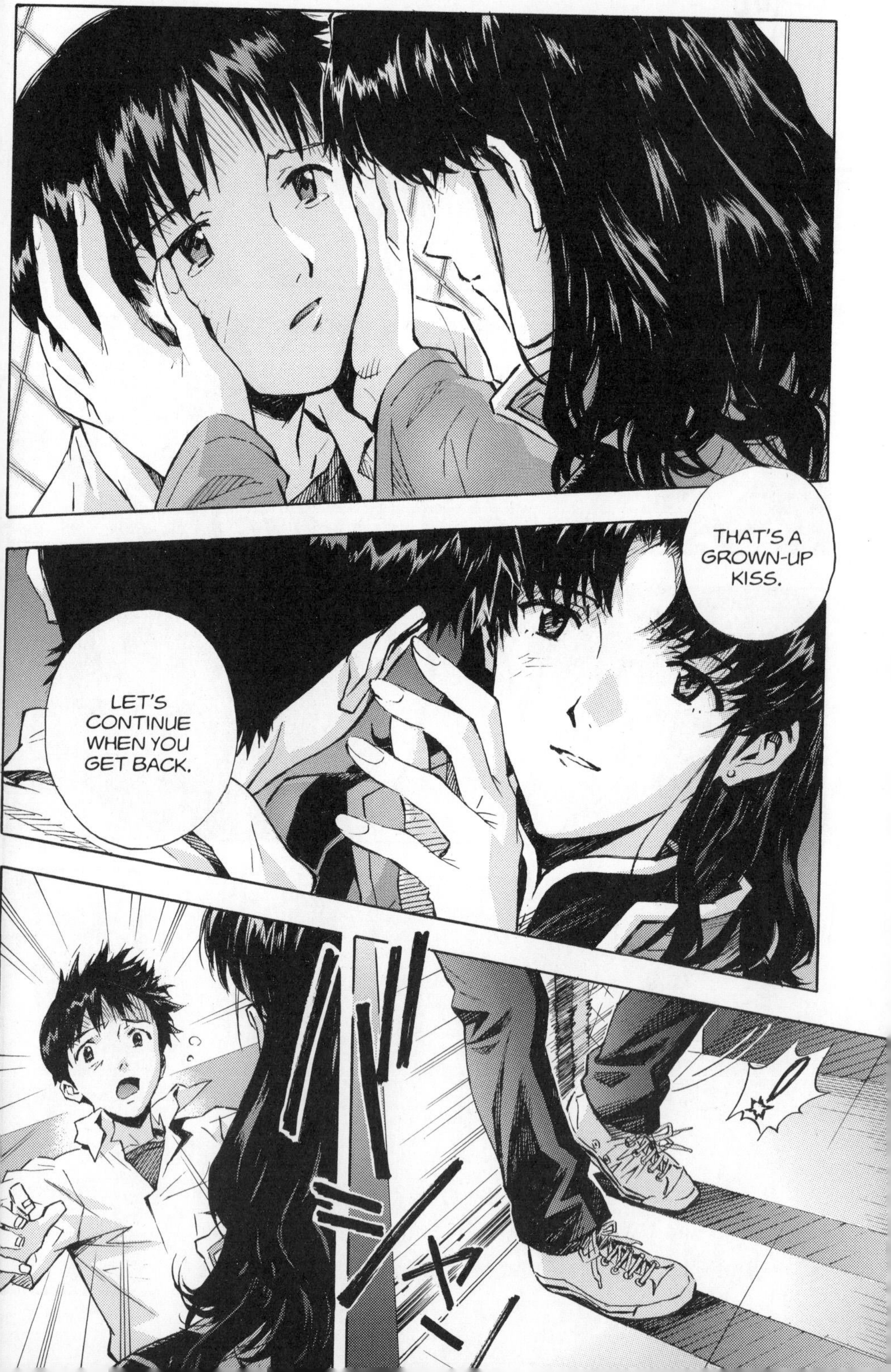
THAT'S A GROWN-UP KISS.
LET'S CONTINUE WHEN YOU GET BACK.

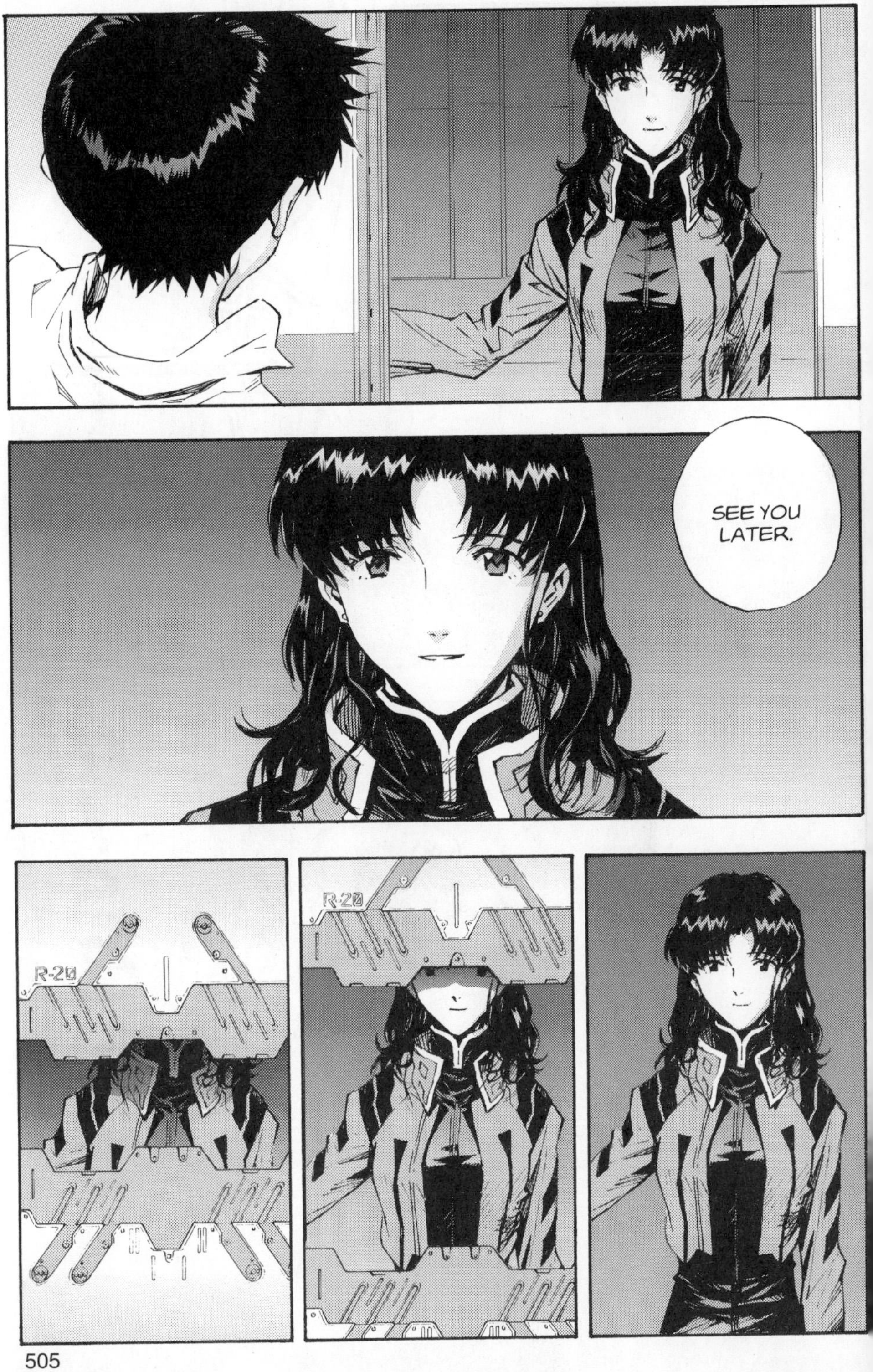
SEE YOU LATER.
R-20
R-20

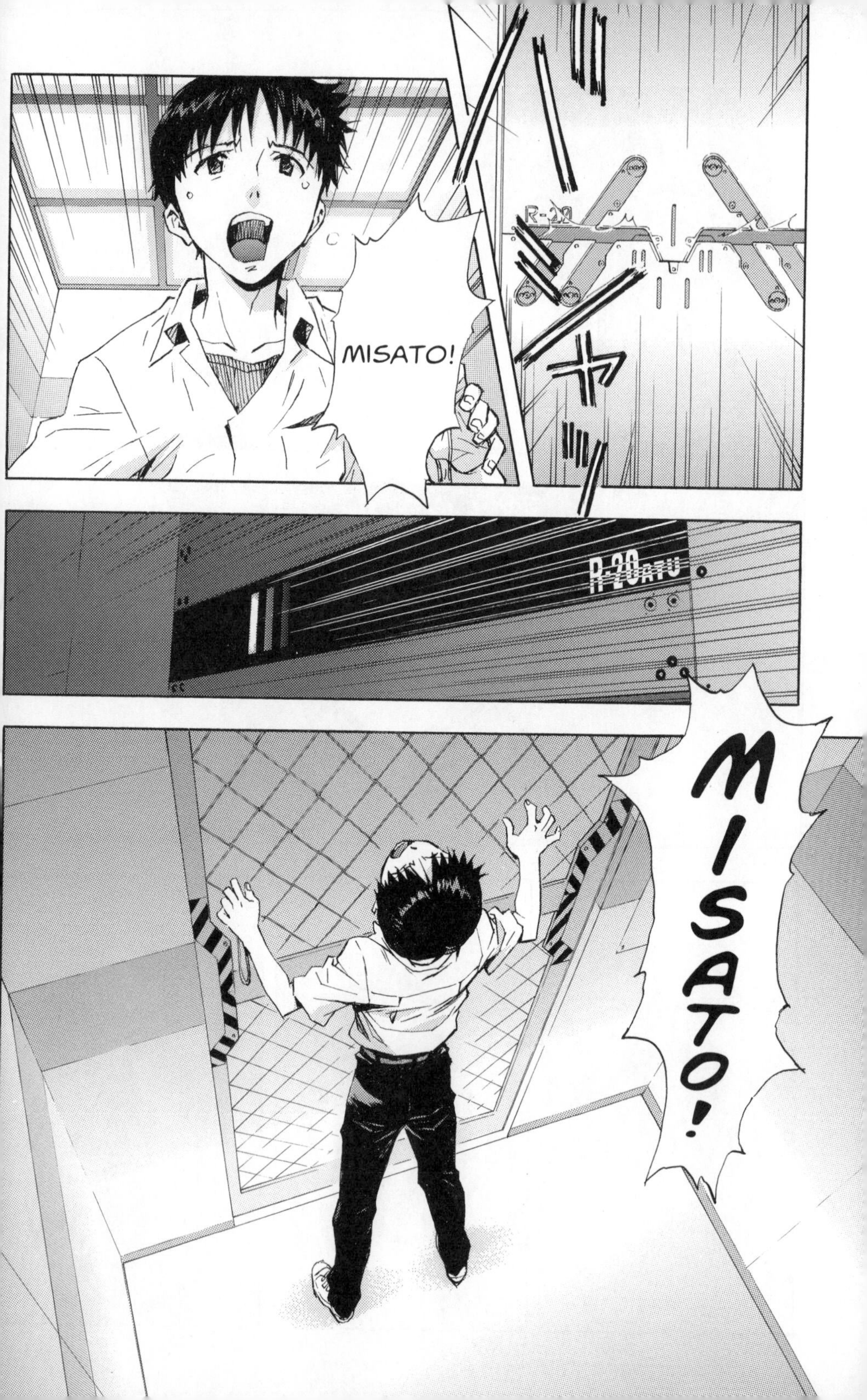
R-20
MISATO!
R-20ATU
MISATO!

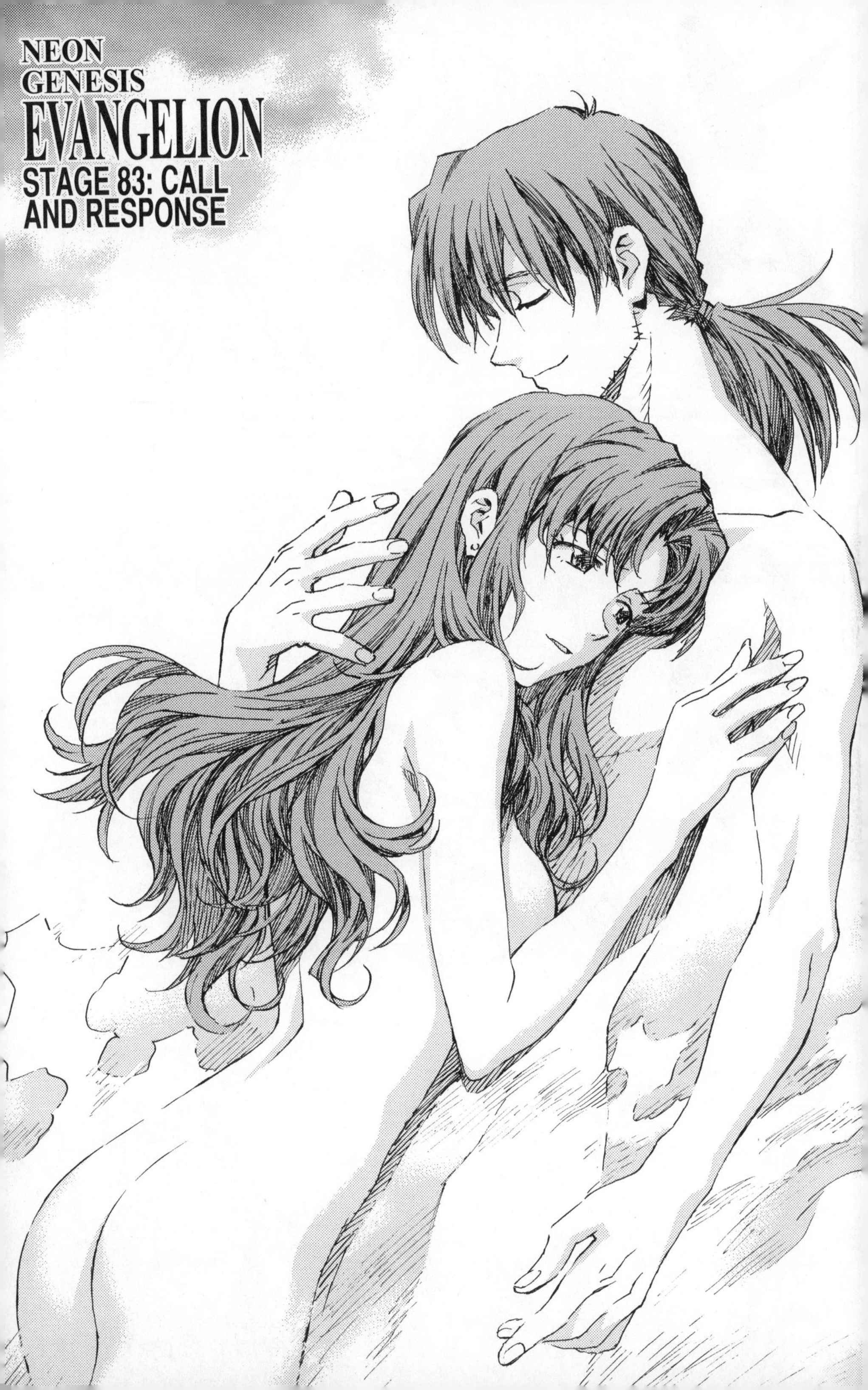
NEON
GENESIS
EVANGELION
STAGE 83: CALL
AND RESPONSE

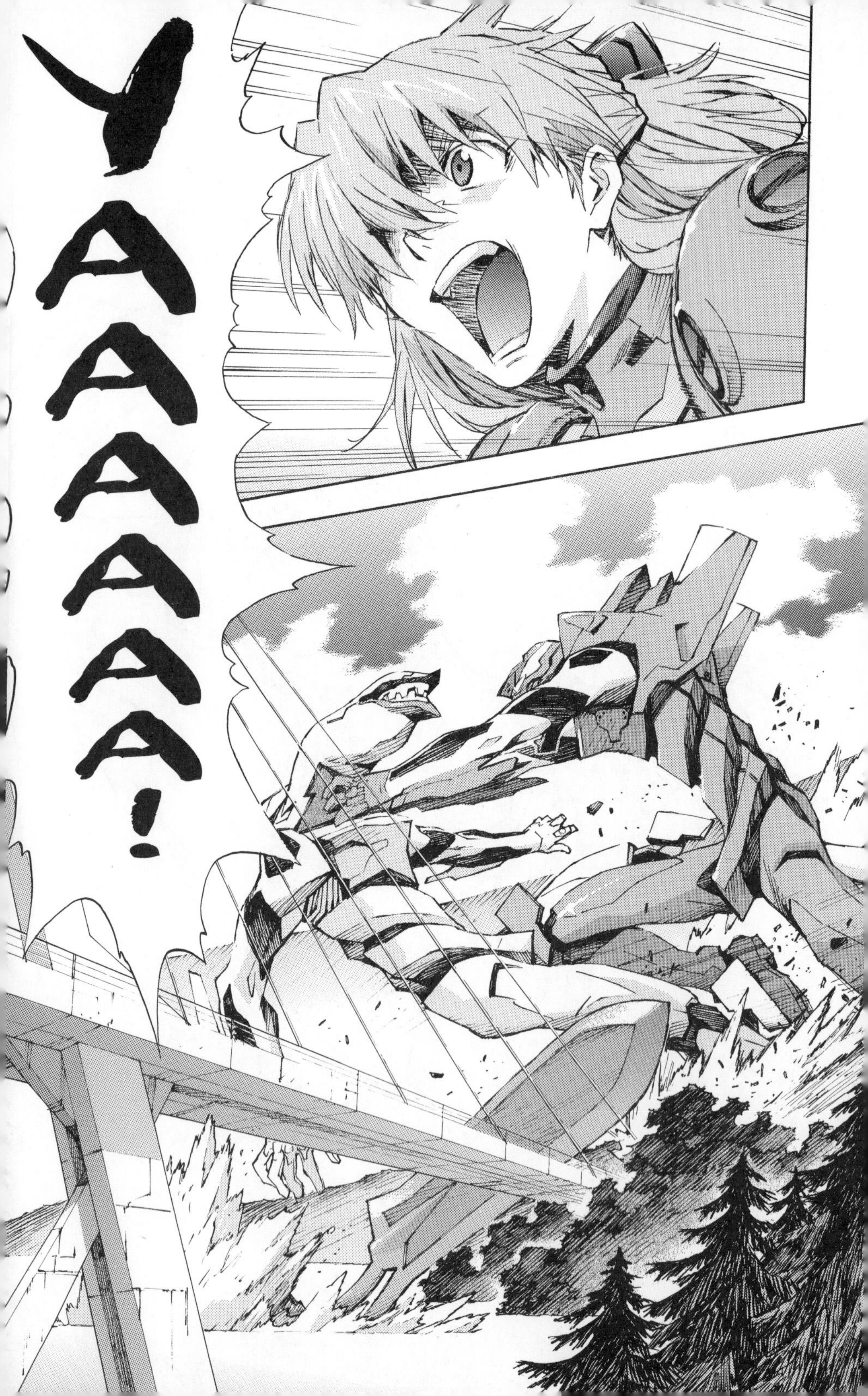
YAAAAAAAA!

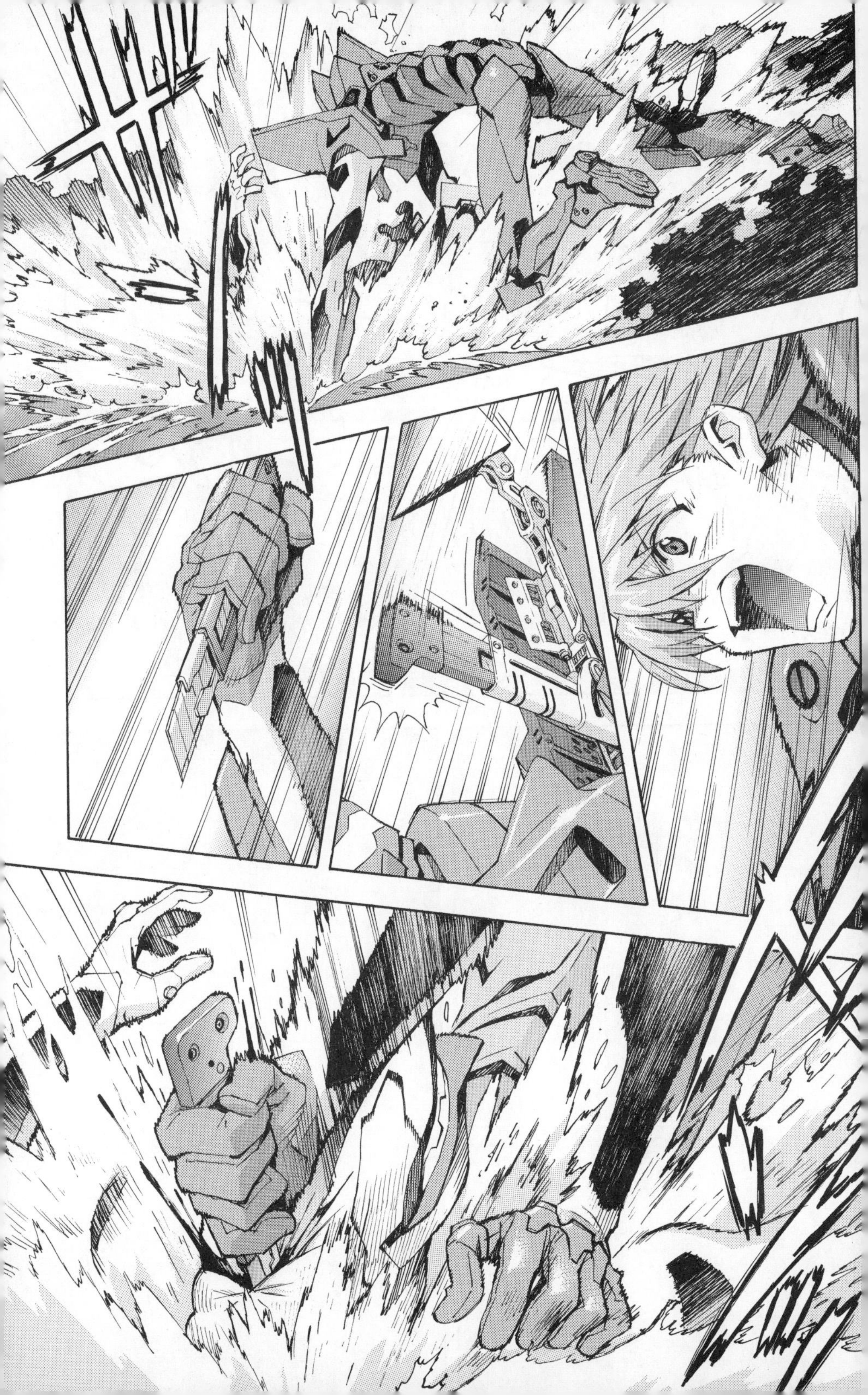

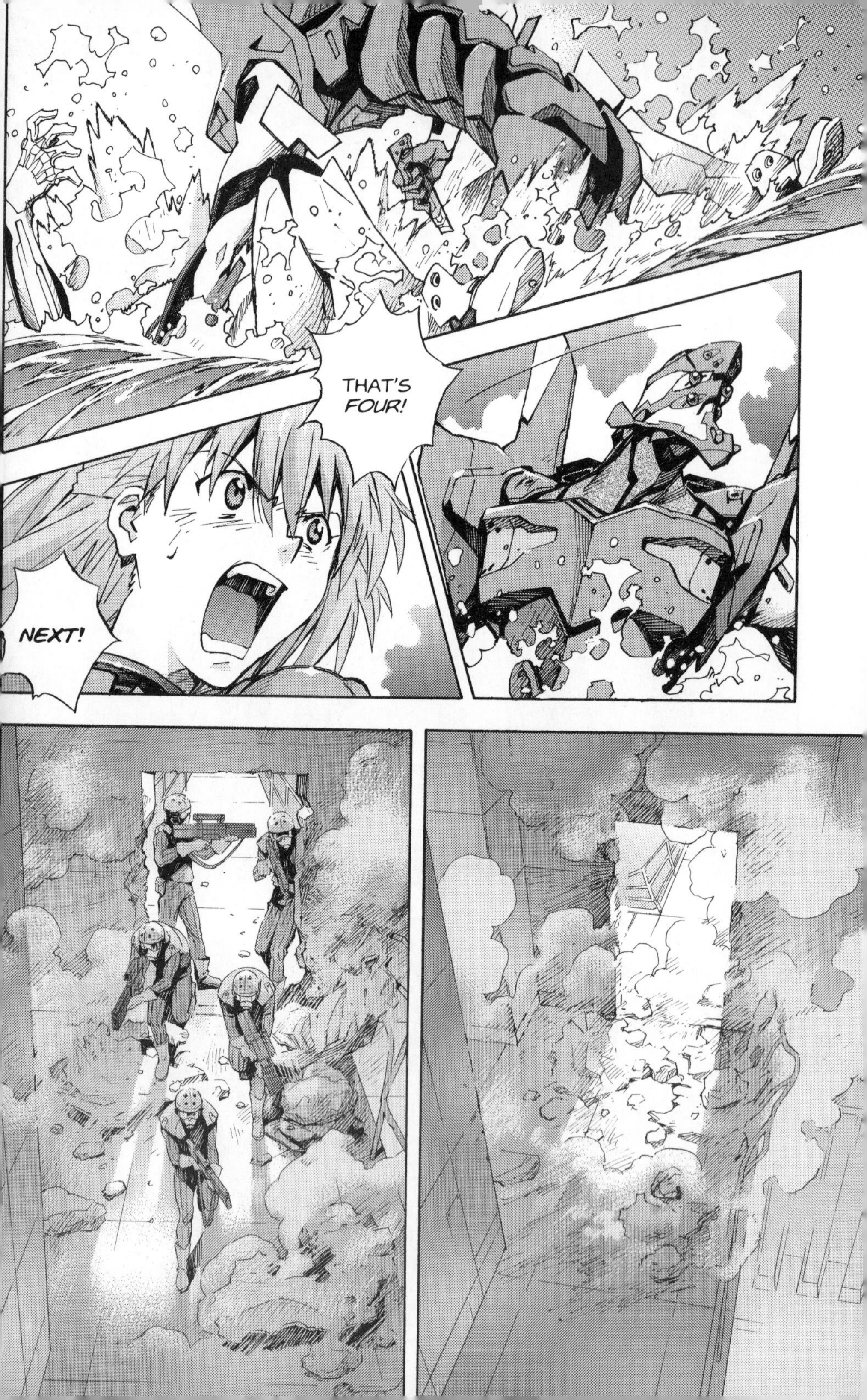
THAT'S FOUR!
NEXT!

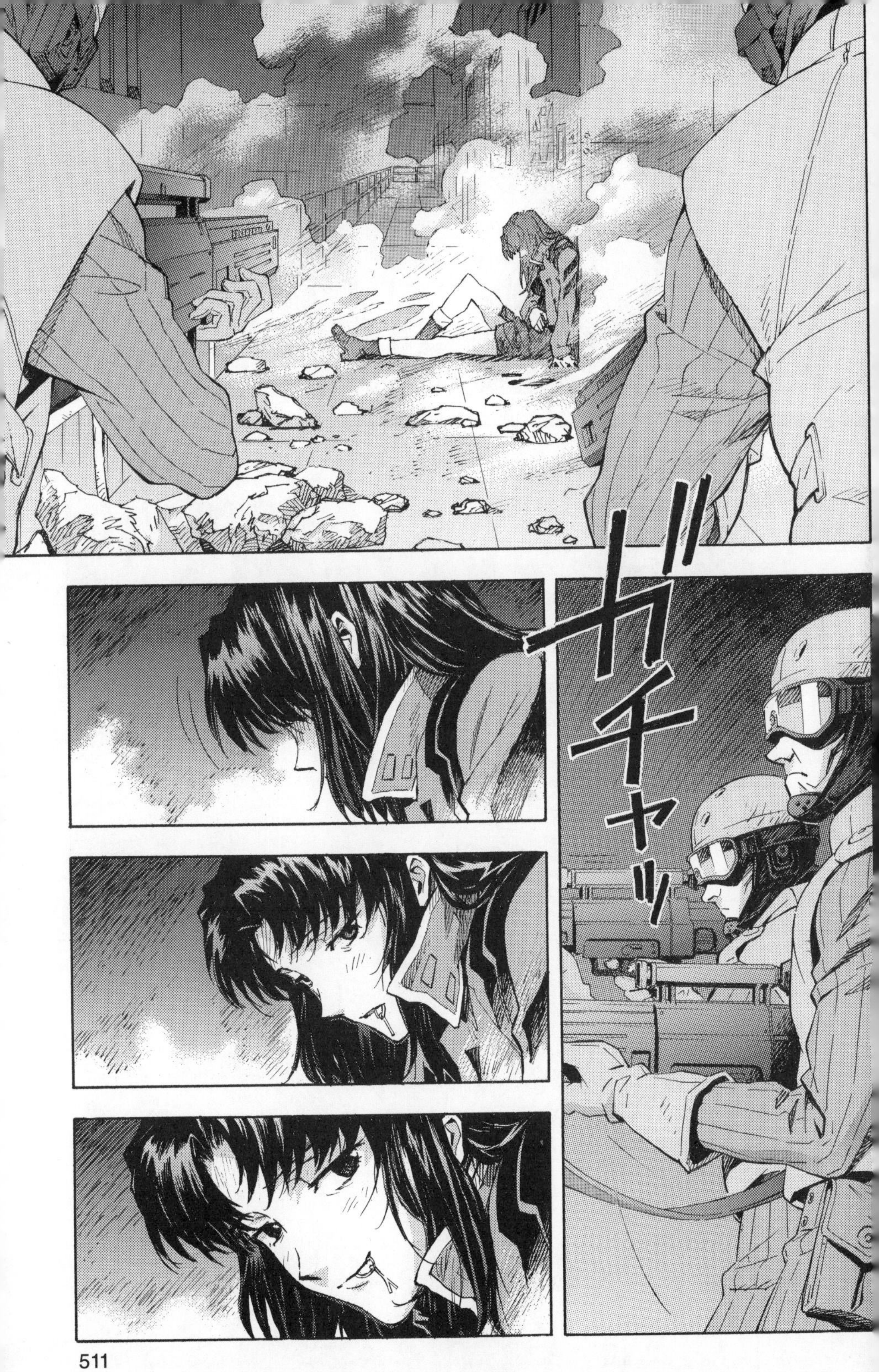
ガチャッ

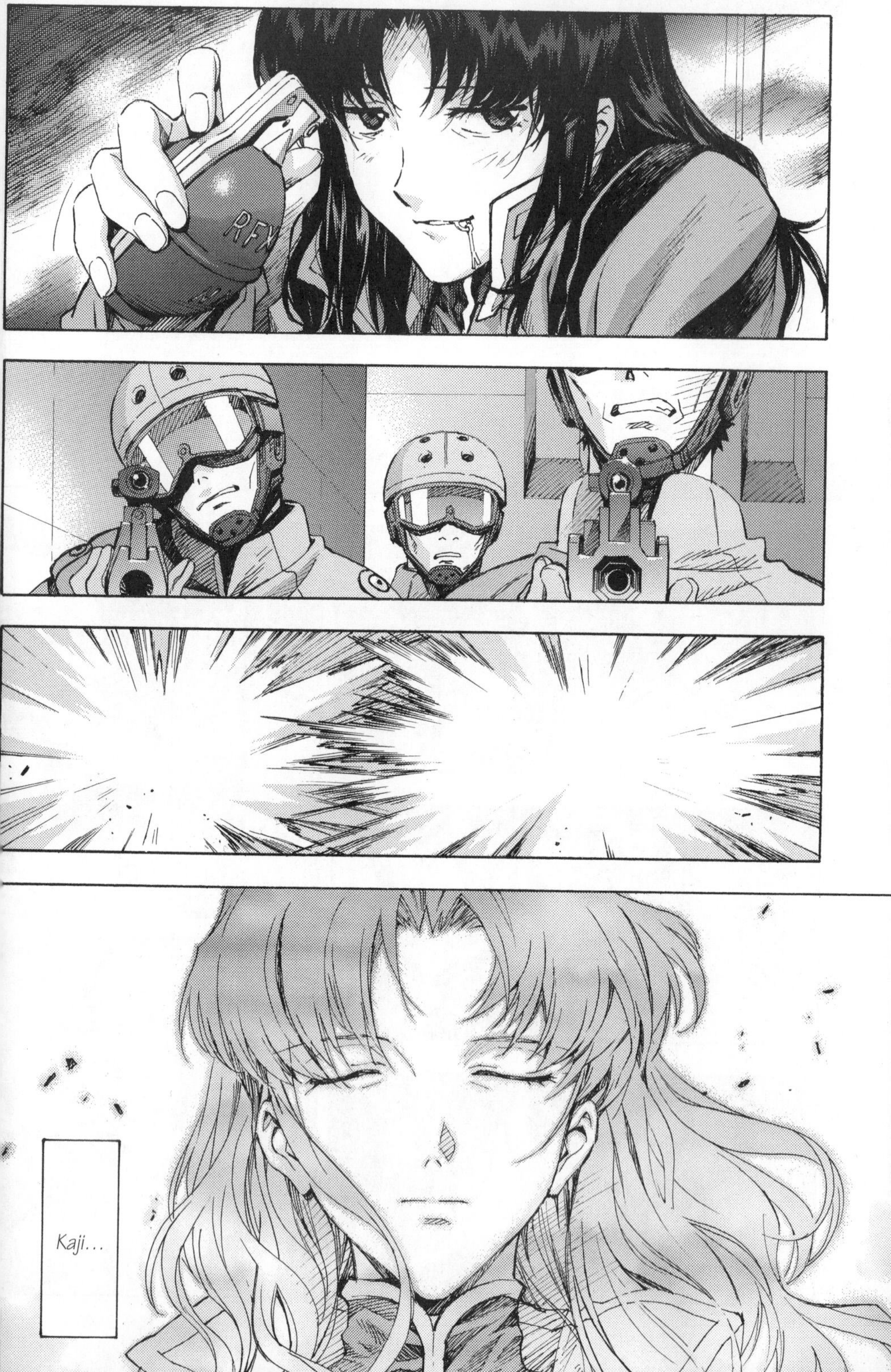
RFX
Kaji...

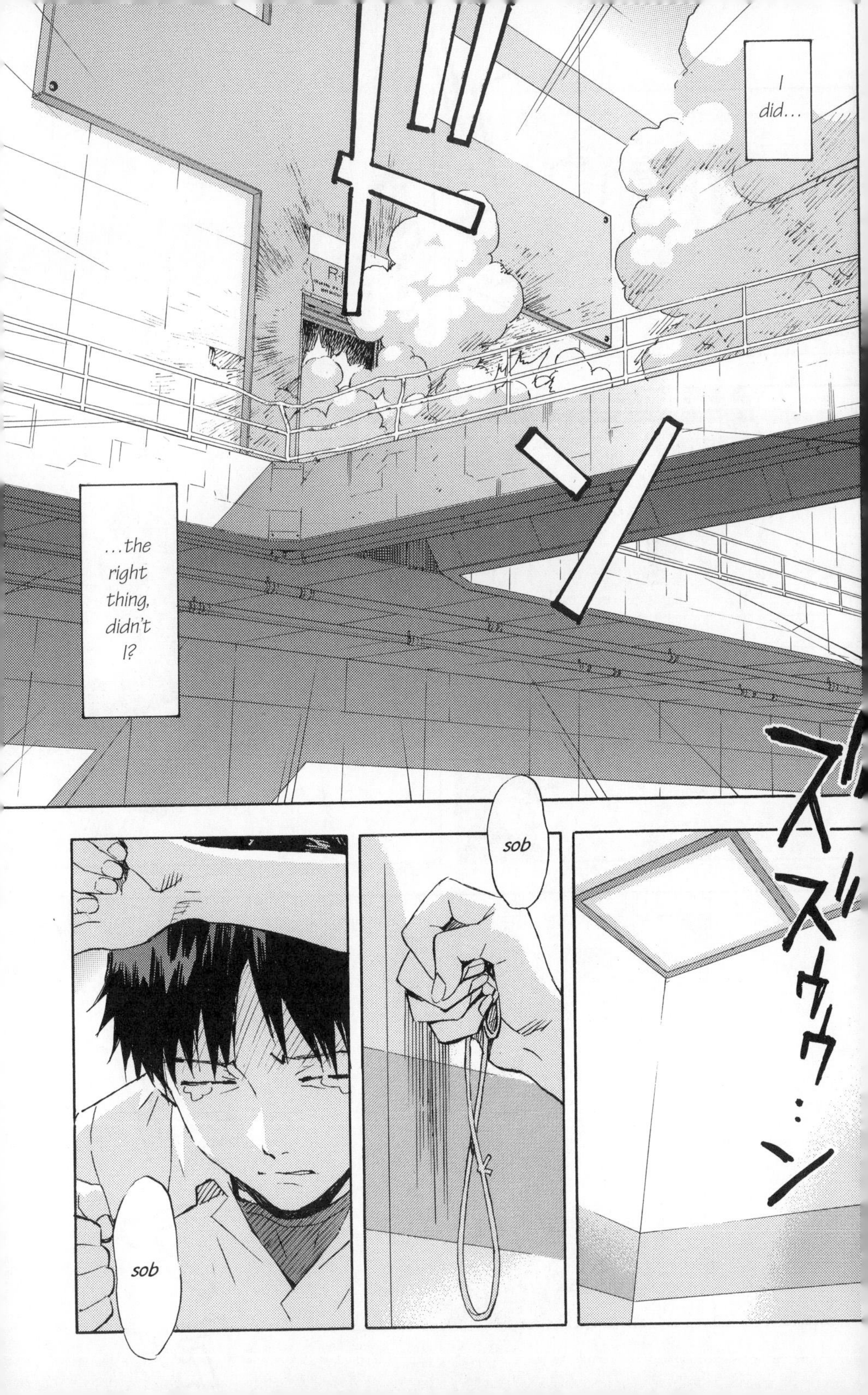
I did...
...the right thing, didn't I?
ドドーン
ズズズウウ…ン
sob
sob

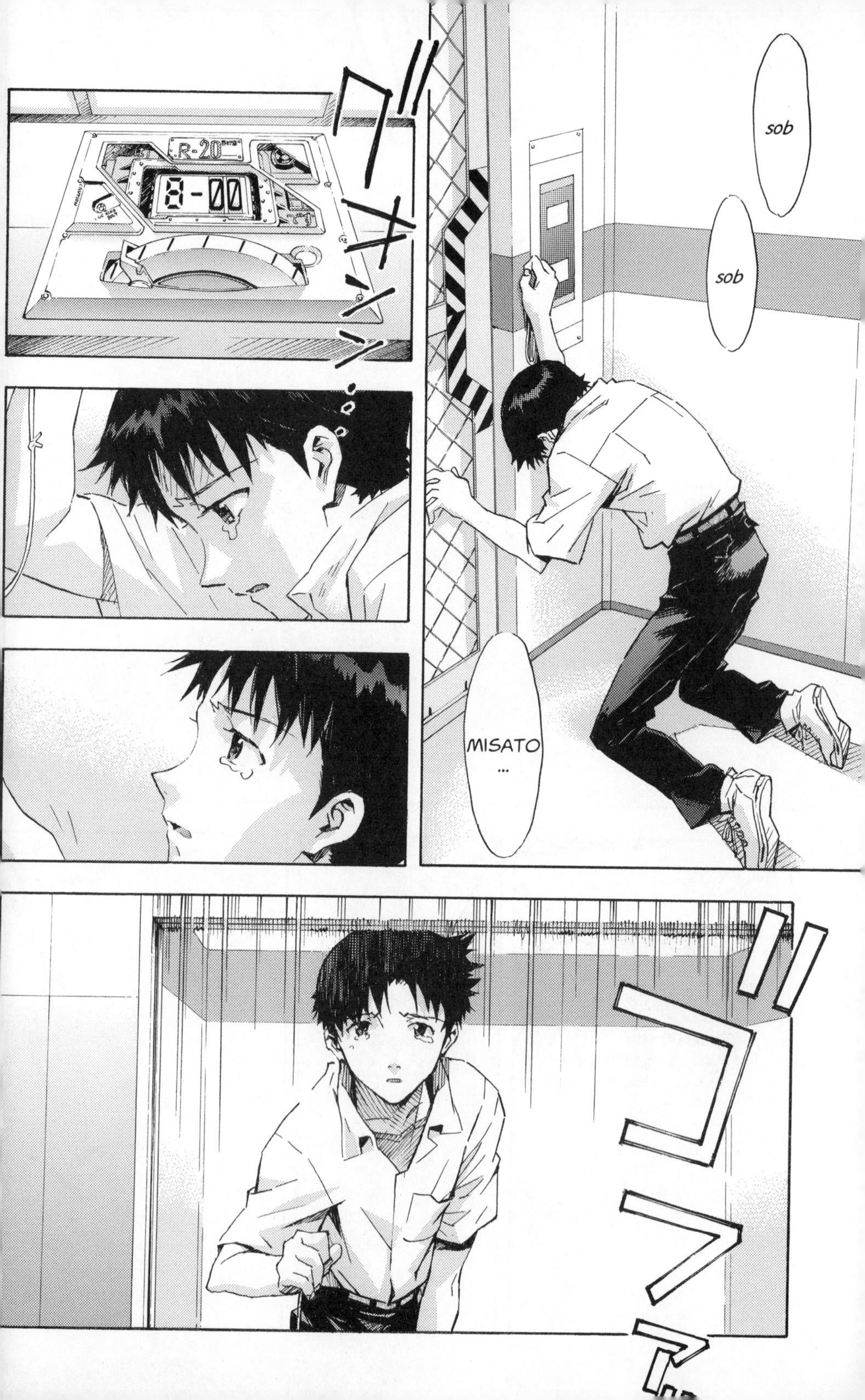
sob
sob
MISATO
...

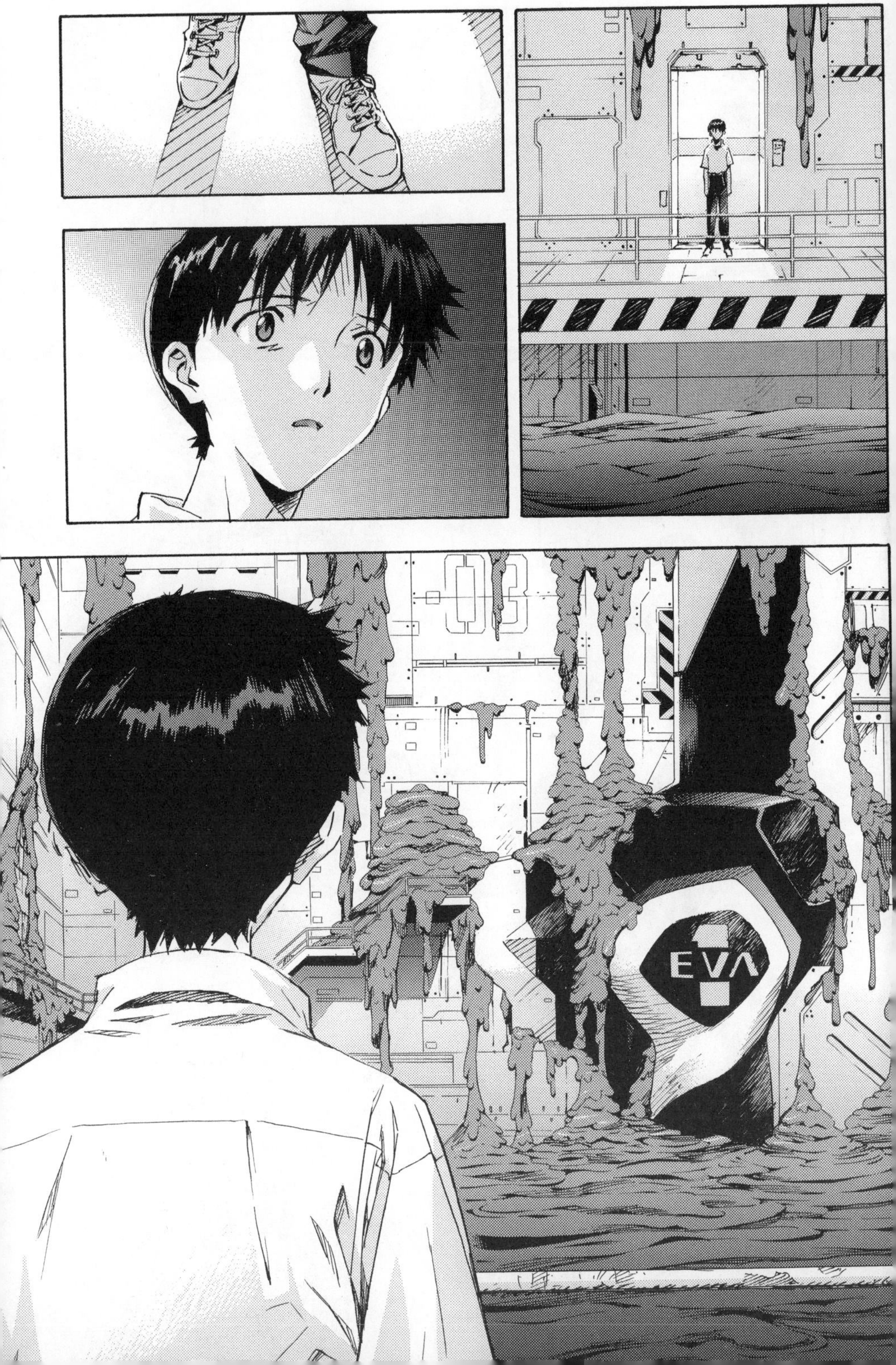
03
EVA

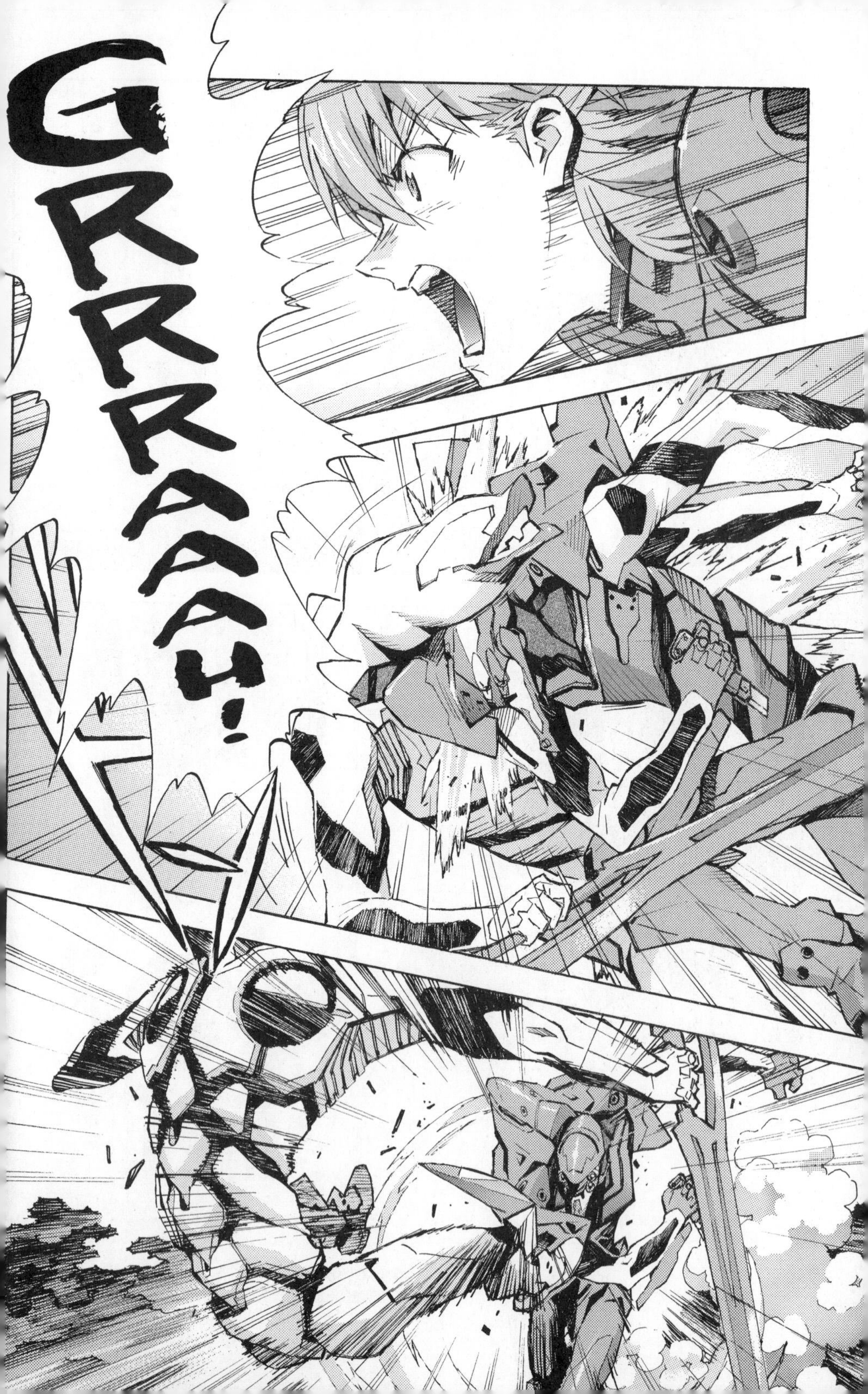
GRRRAAAAH!

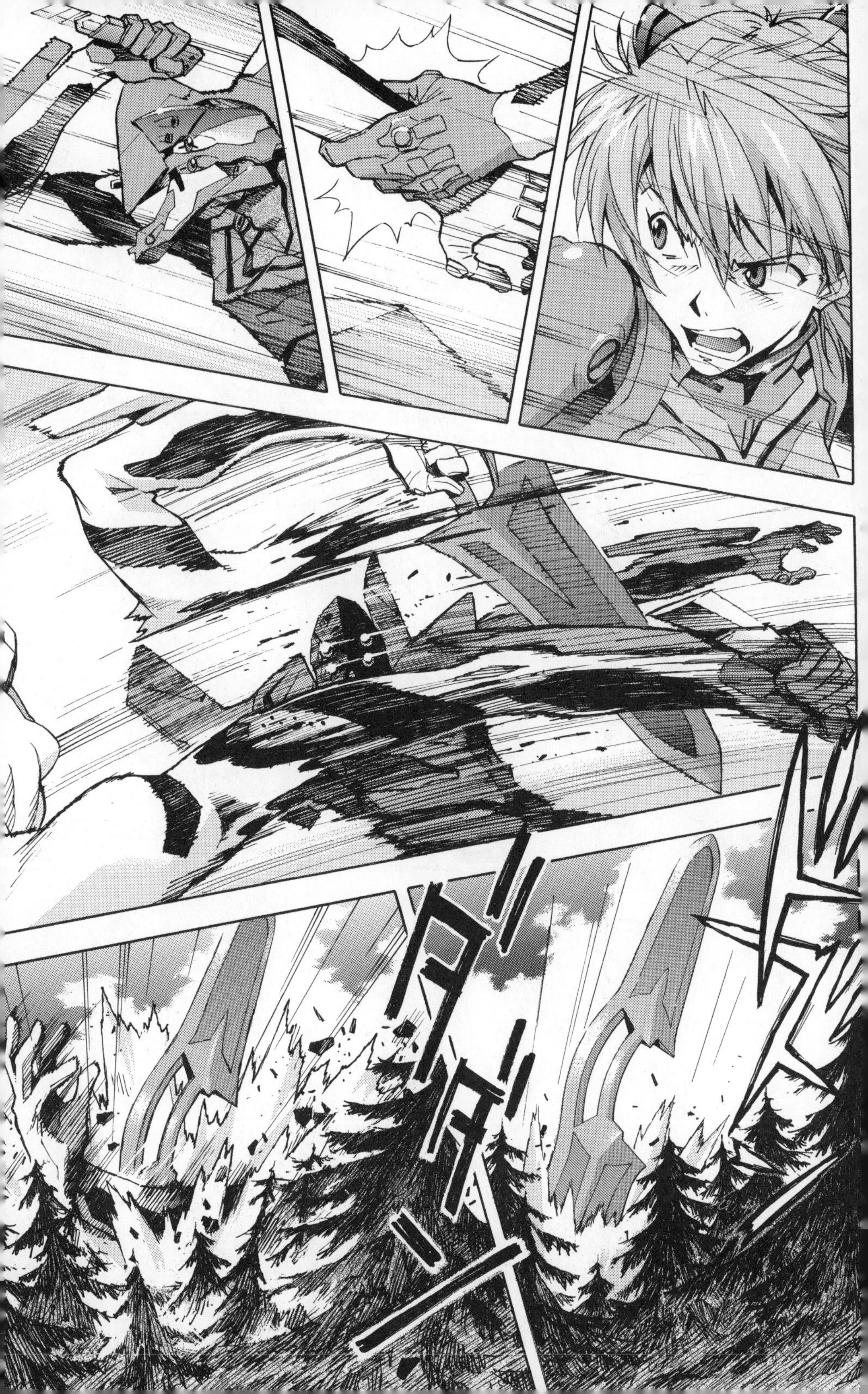

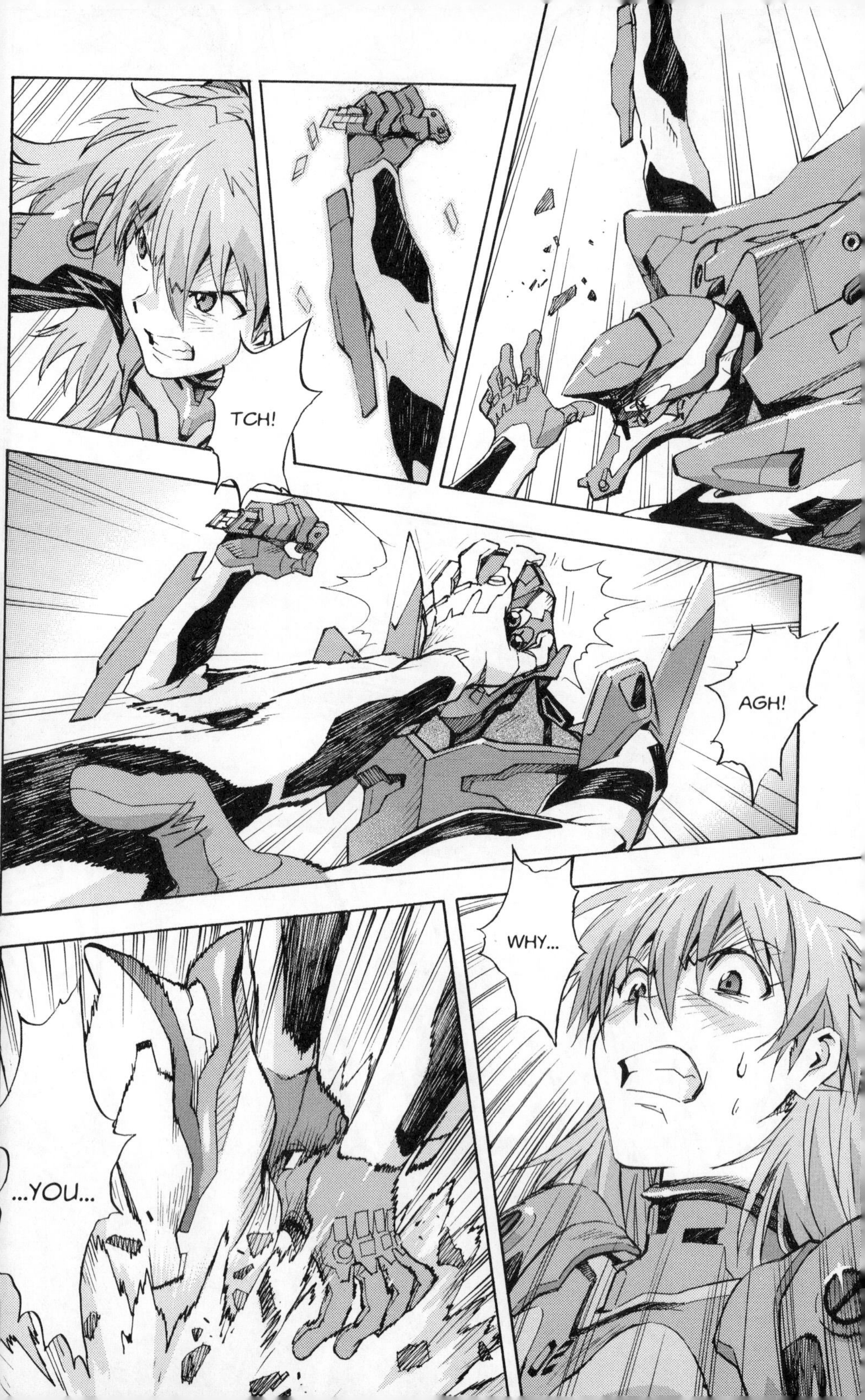
TCH!
AGH!
WHY...
...YOU...

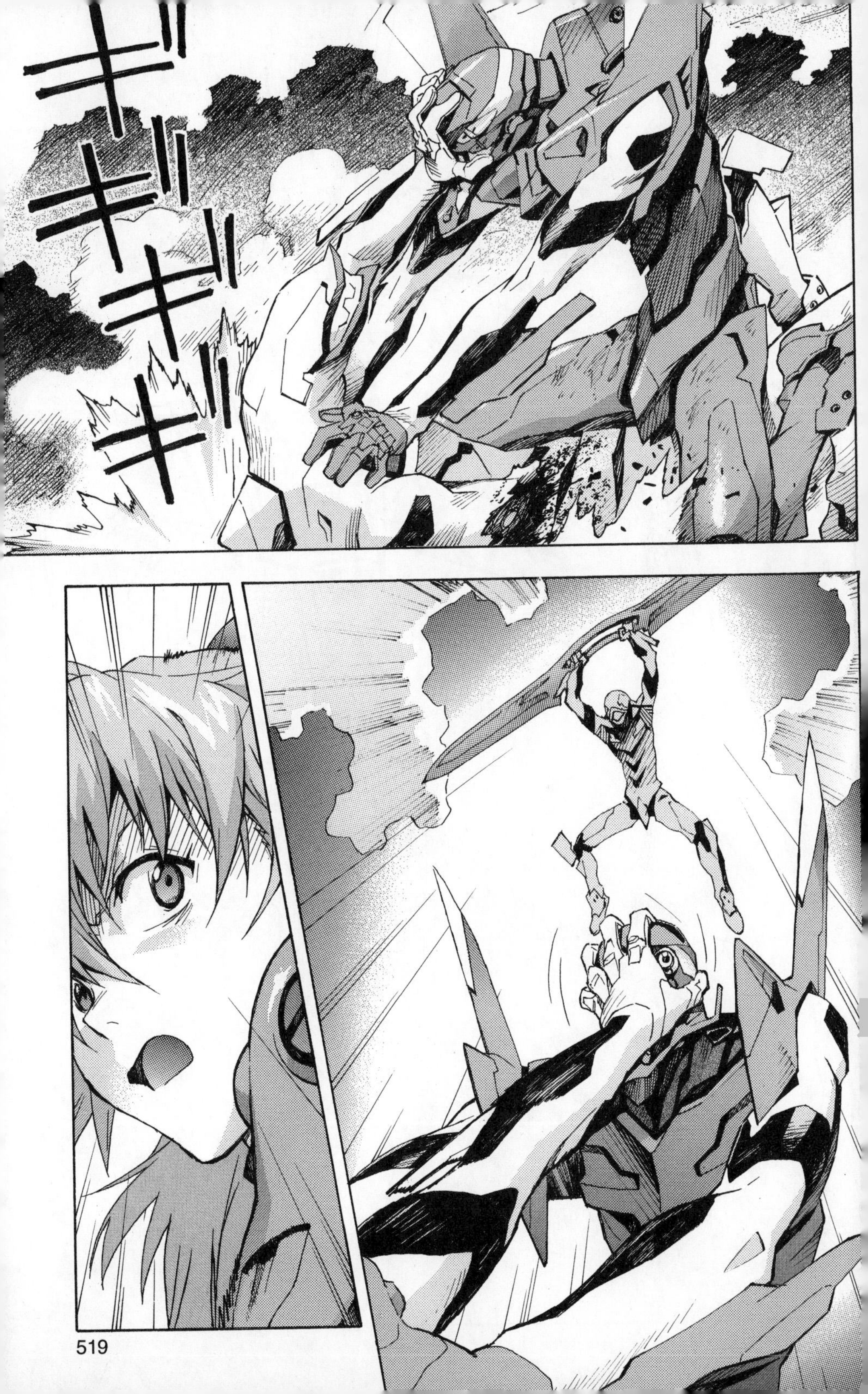
ギギギギ

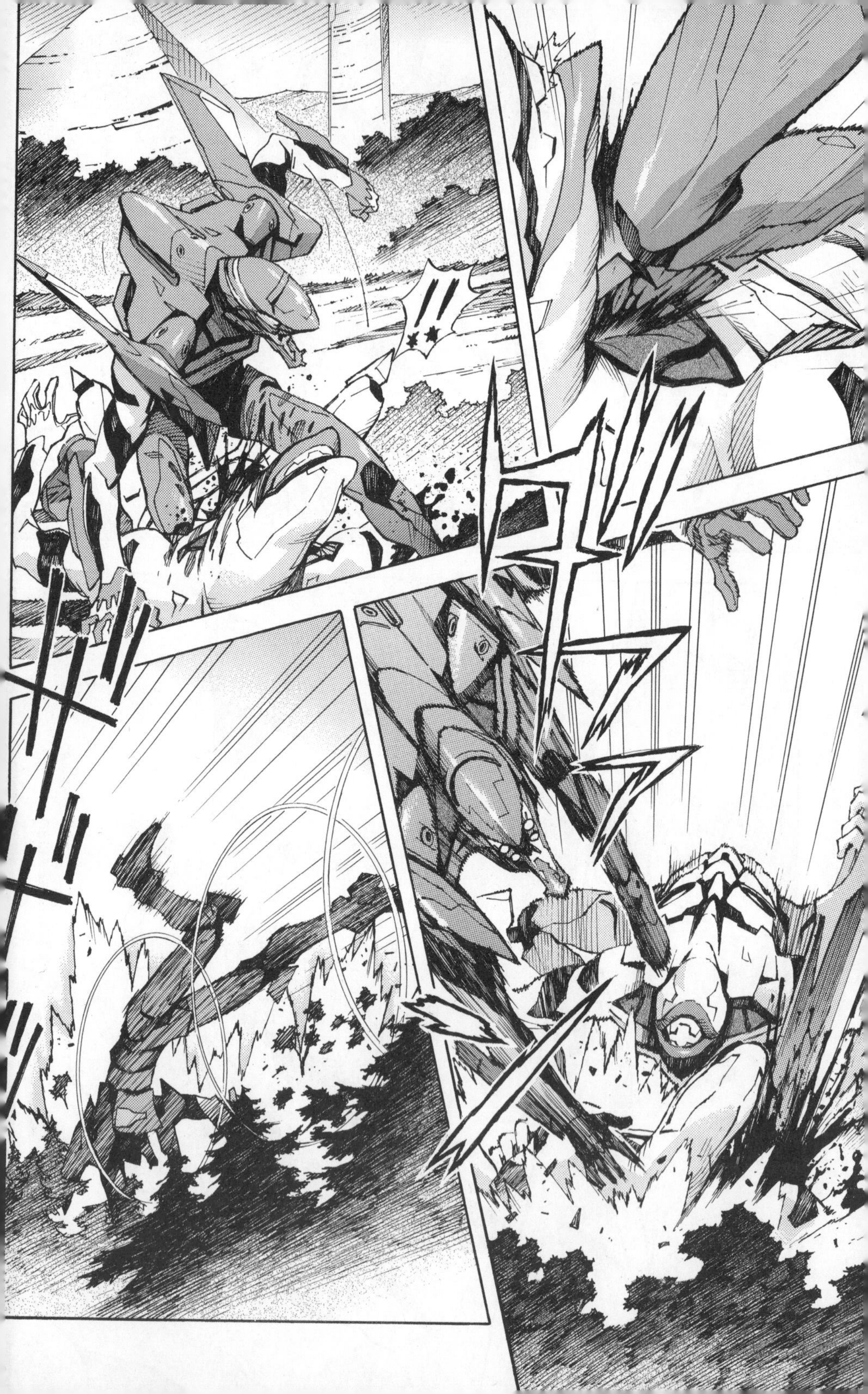
!!

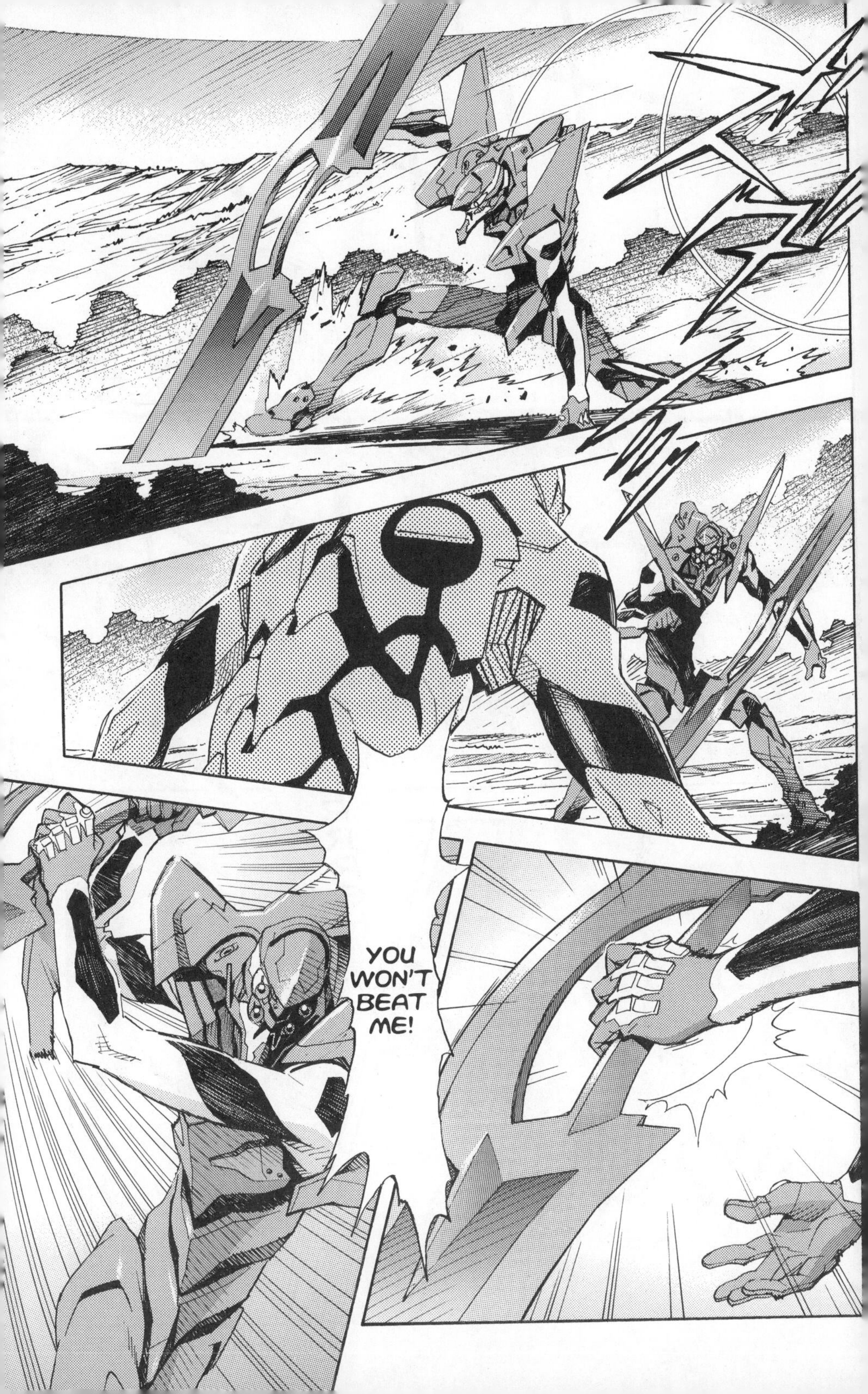
YOU WON'T BEAT ME!

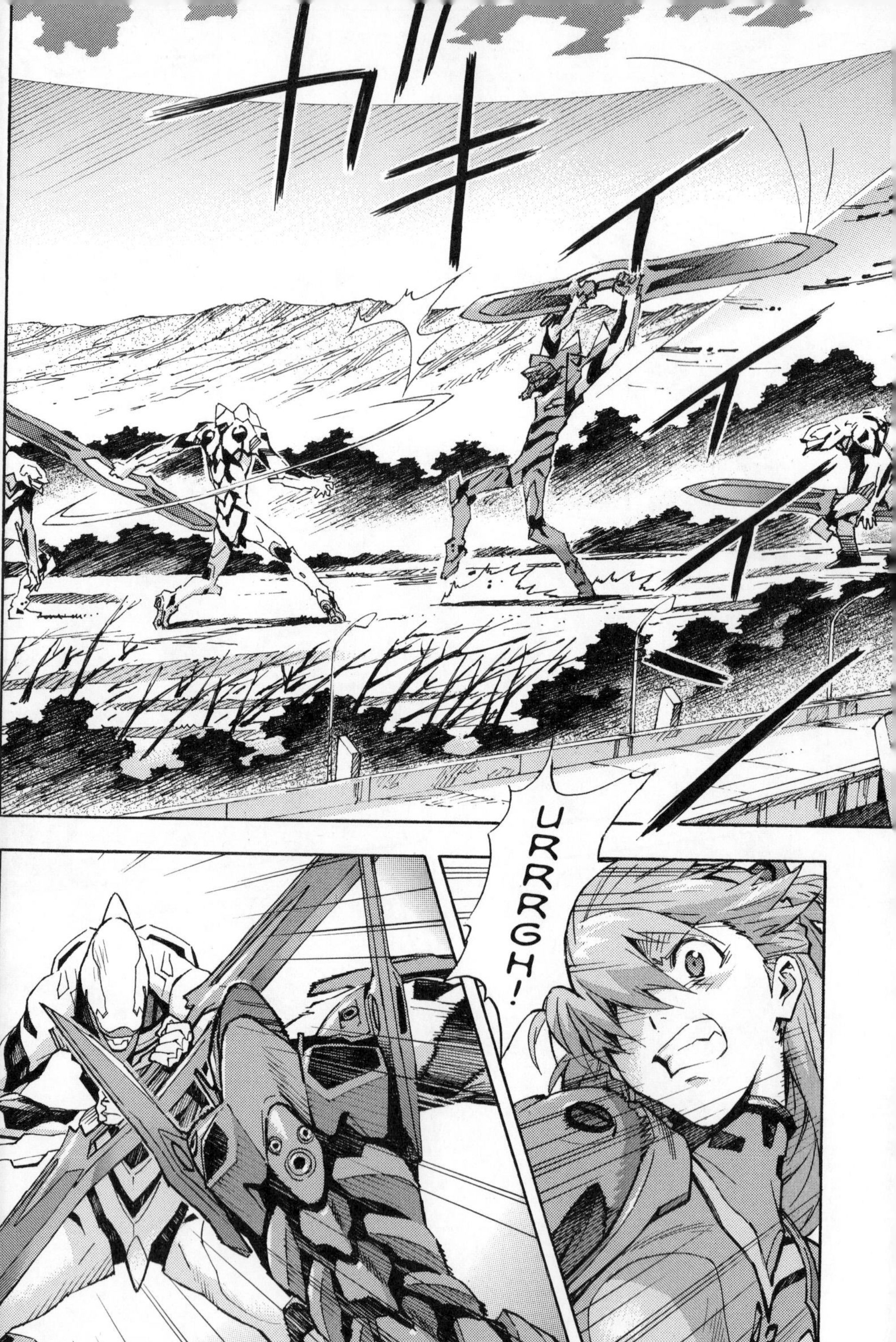

ガギィィン
URRRGH!

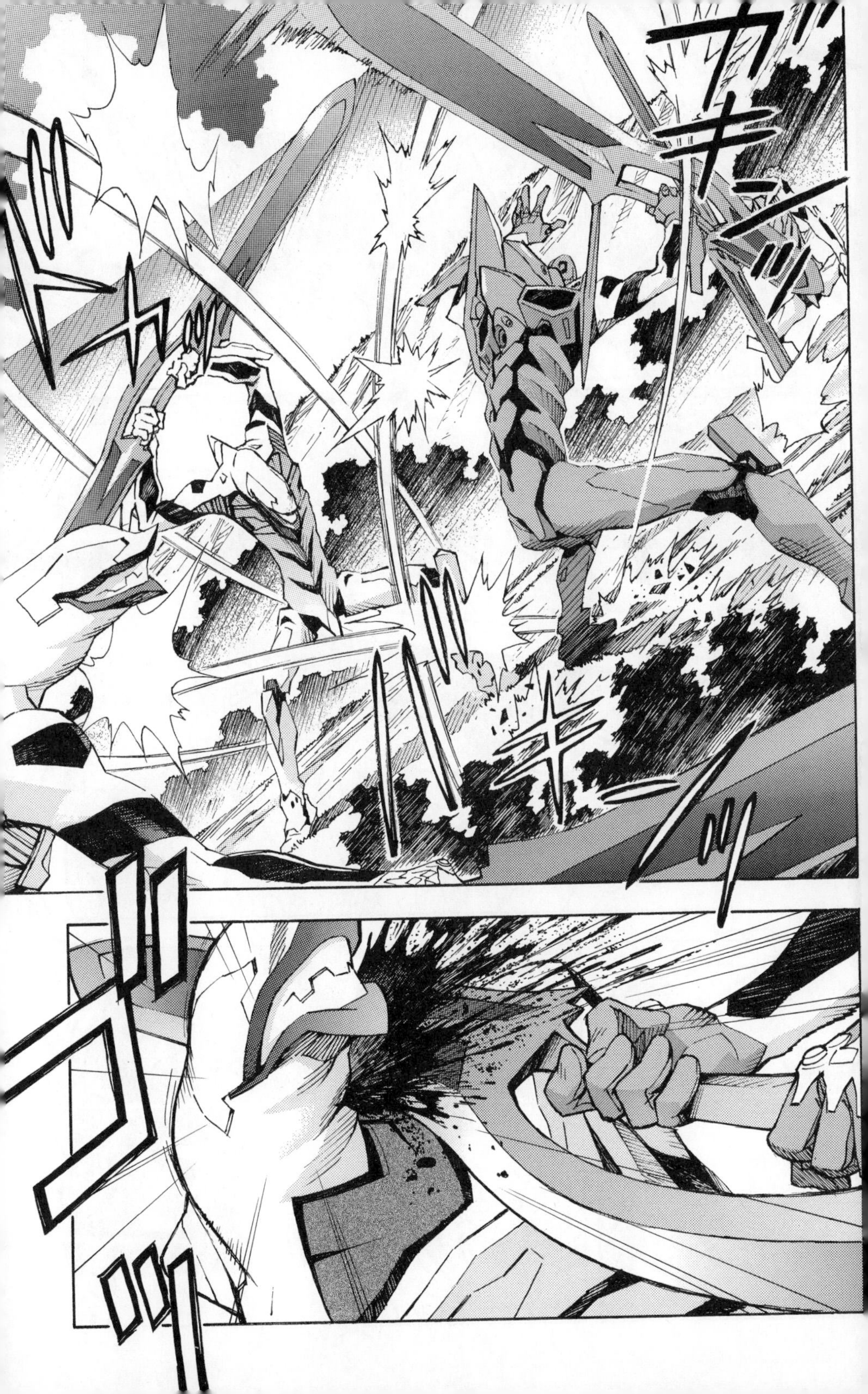
ガキンッ
ドカッ
ギンッ
ゴッ

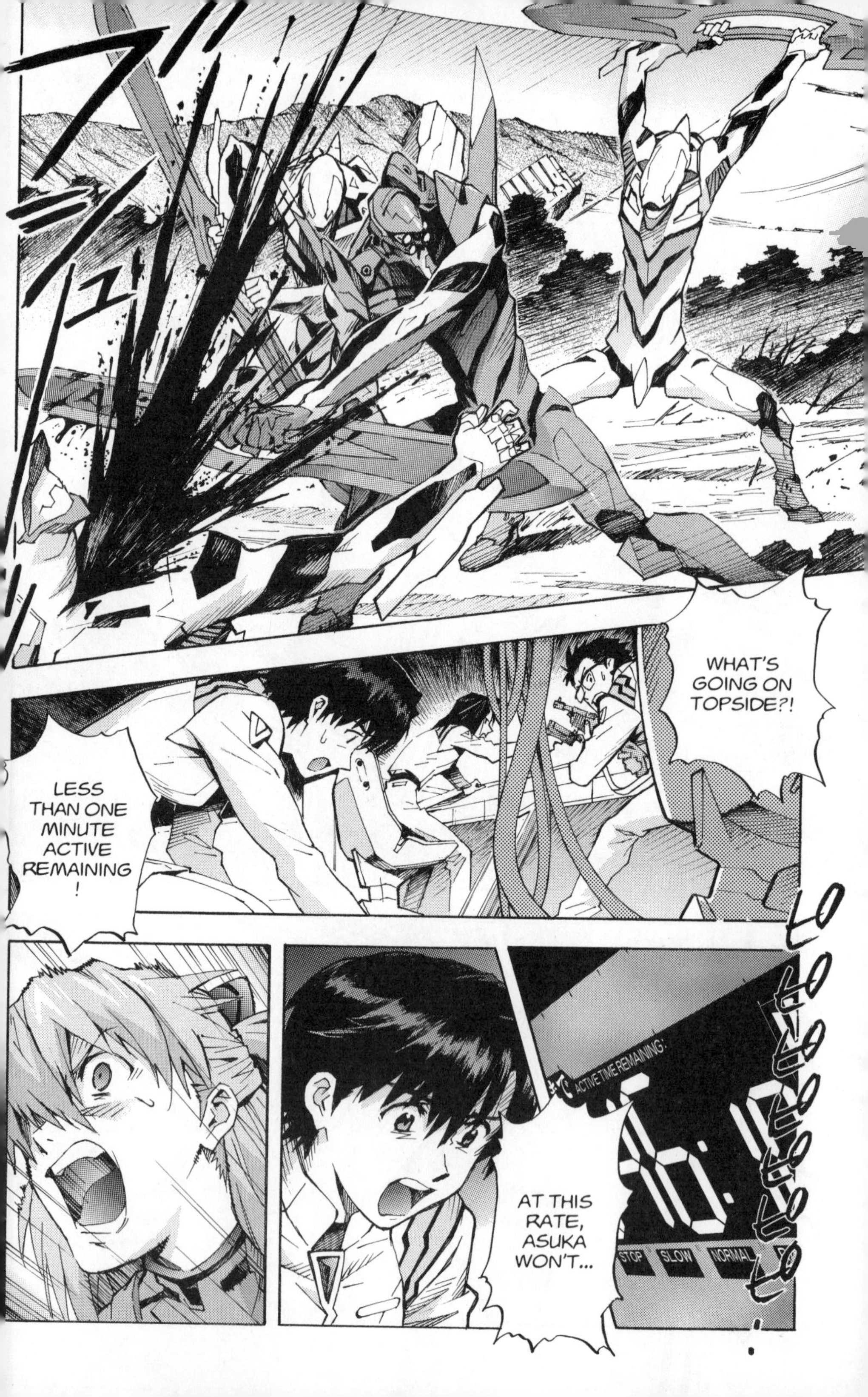
WHAT'S GOING ON TOPSIDE?!
LESS THAN ONE MINUTE ACTIVE REMAINING!
ACTIVE TIME REMAINING:
STOP
SLOW
NORMAL
AT THIS RATE, ASUKA WON'T...

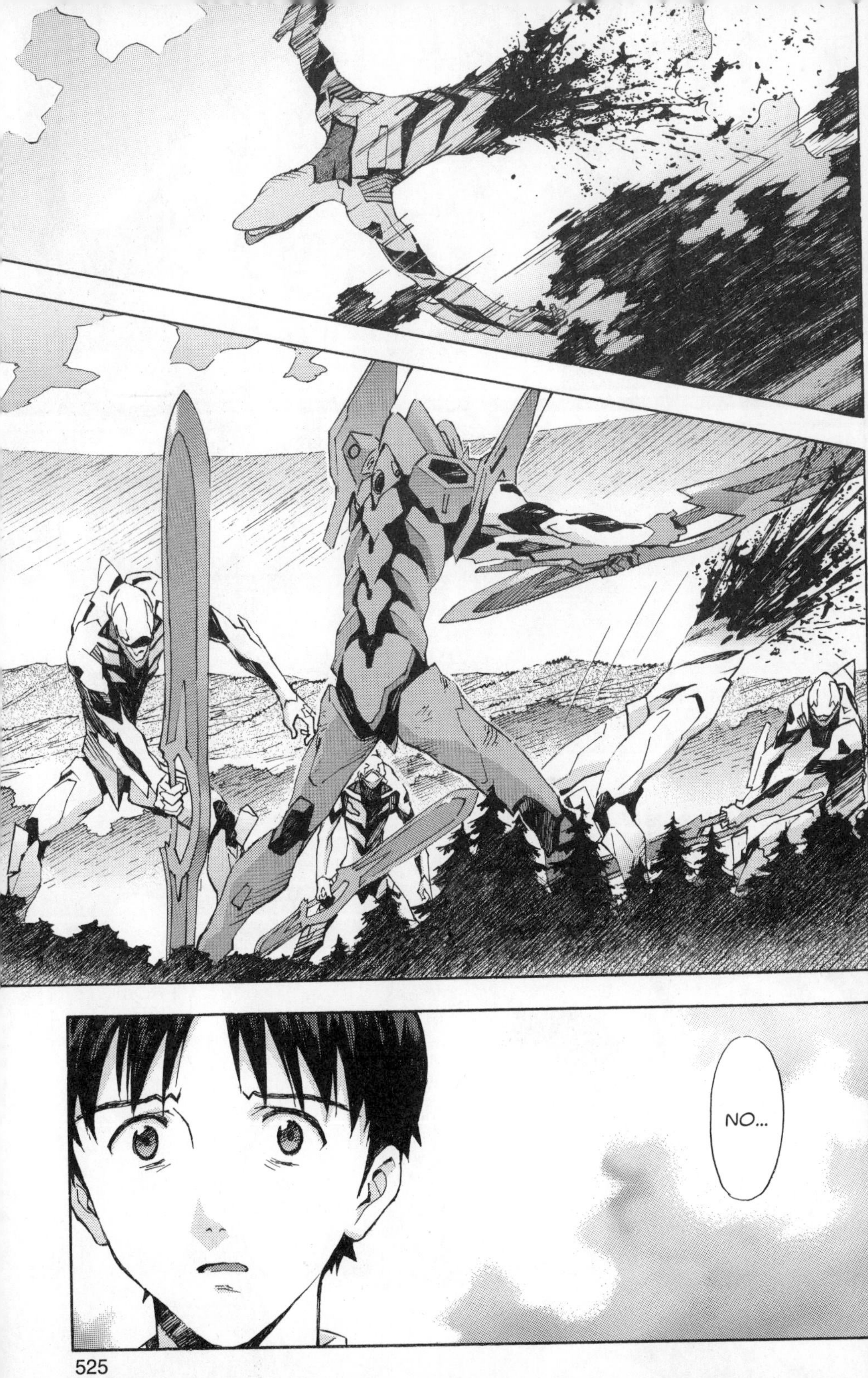
NO...

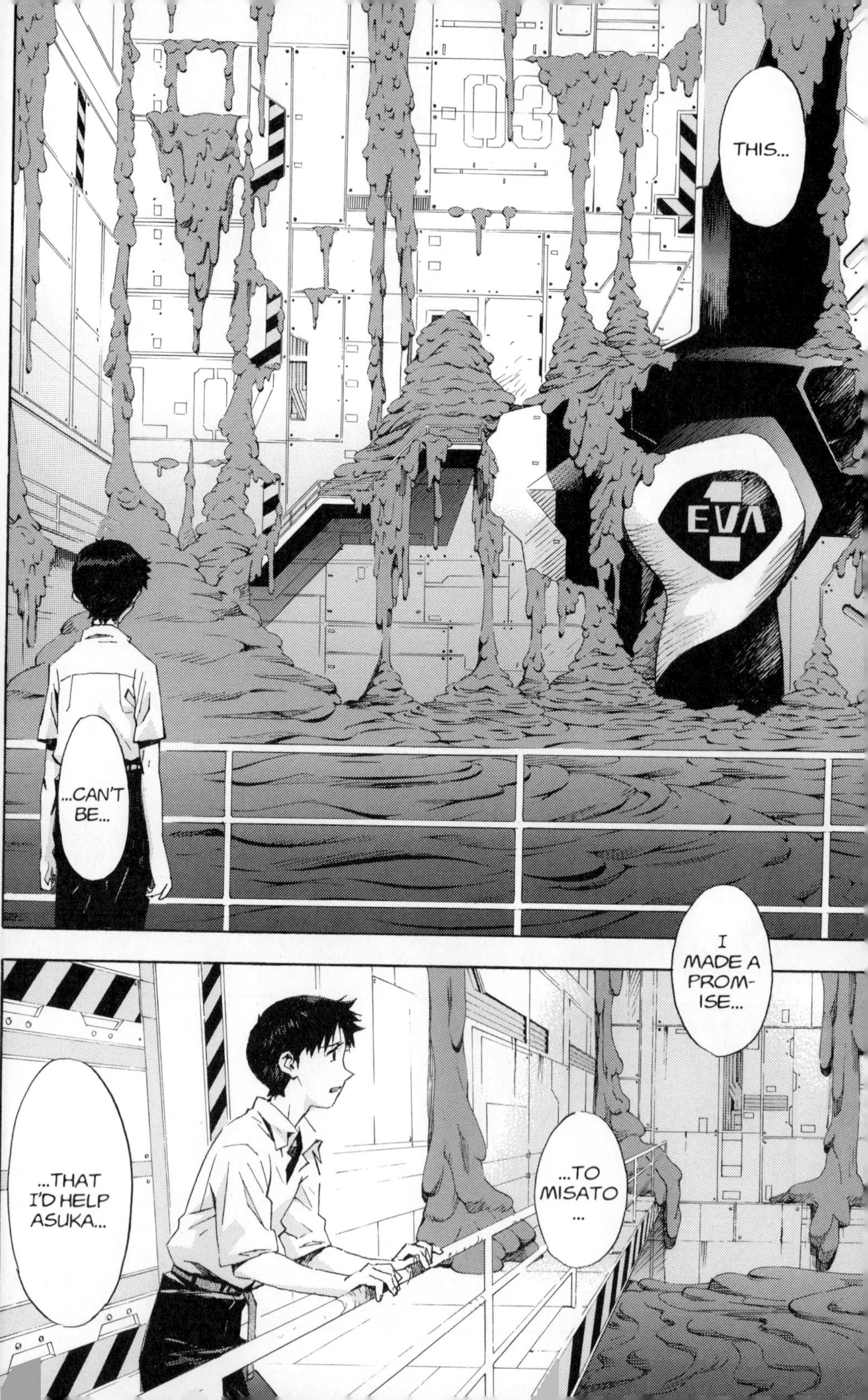

03
THIS...
EVA
...CAN'T BE...
I MADE A PROMISE...
...TO MISATO...
...THAT I'D HELP ASUKA...

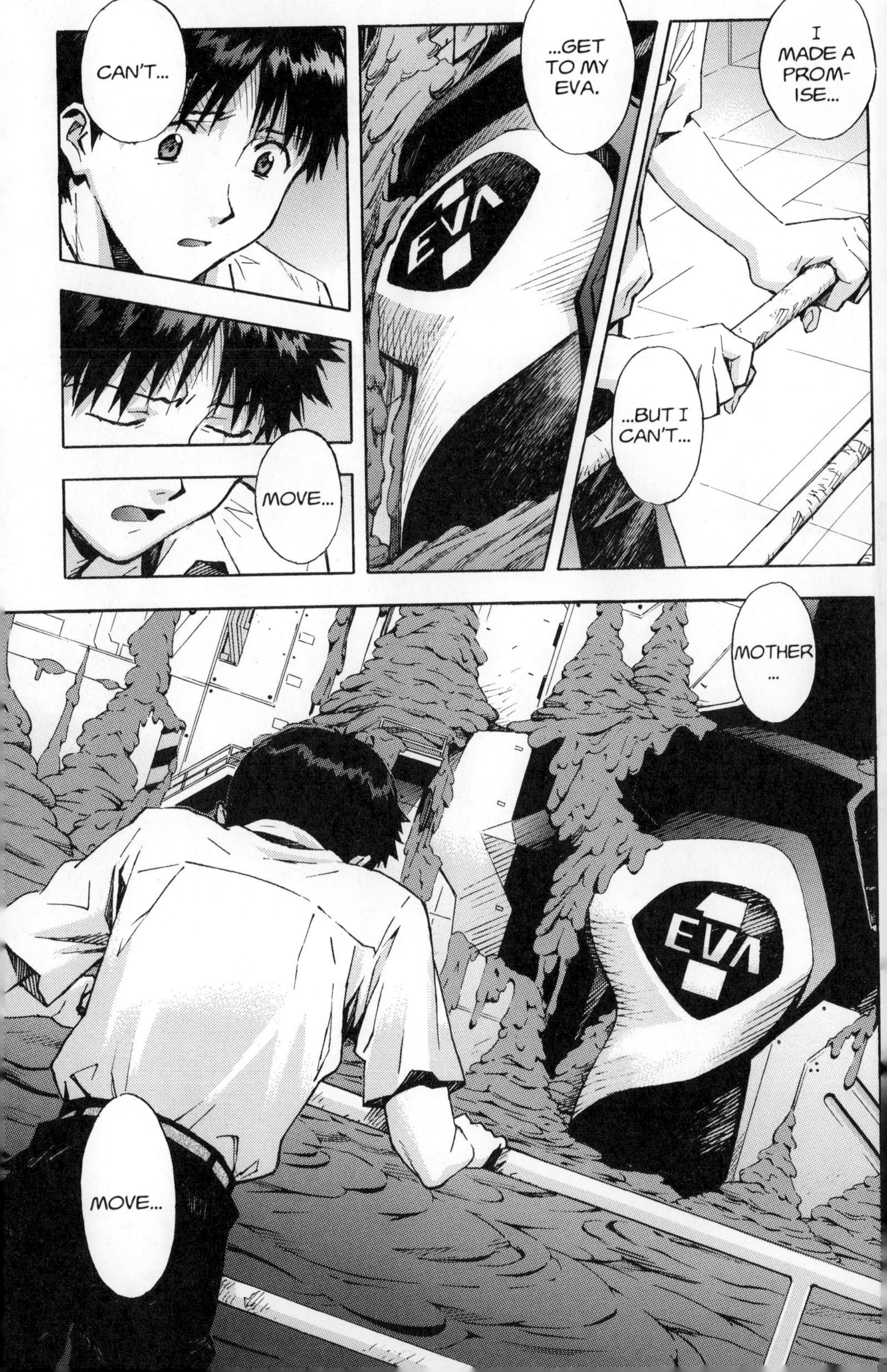
I MADE A PROMISE...
...BUT I CAN'T...
...GET TO MY EVA.
CAN'T...
MOVE...
MOTHER...
MOVE...

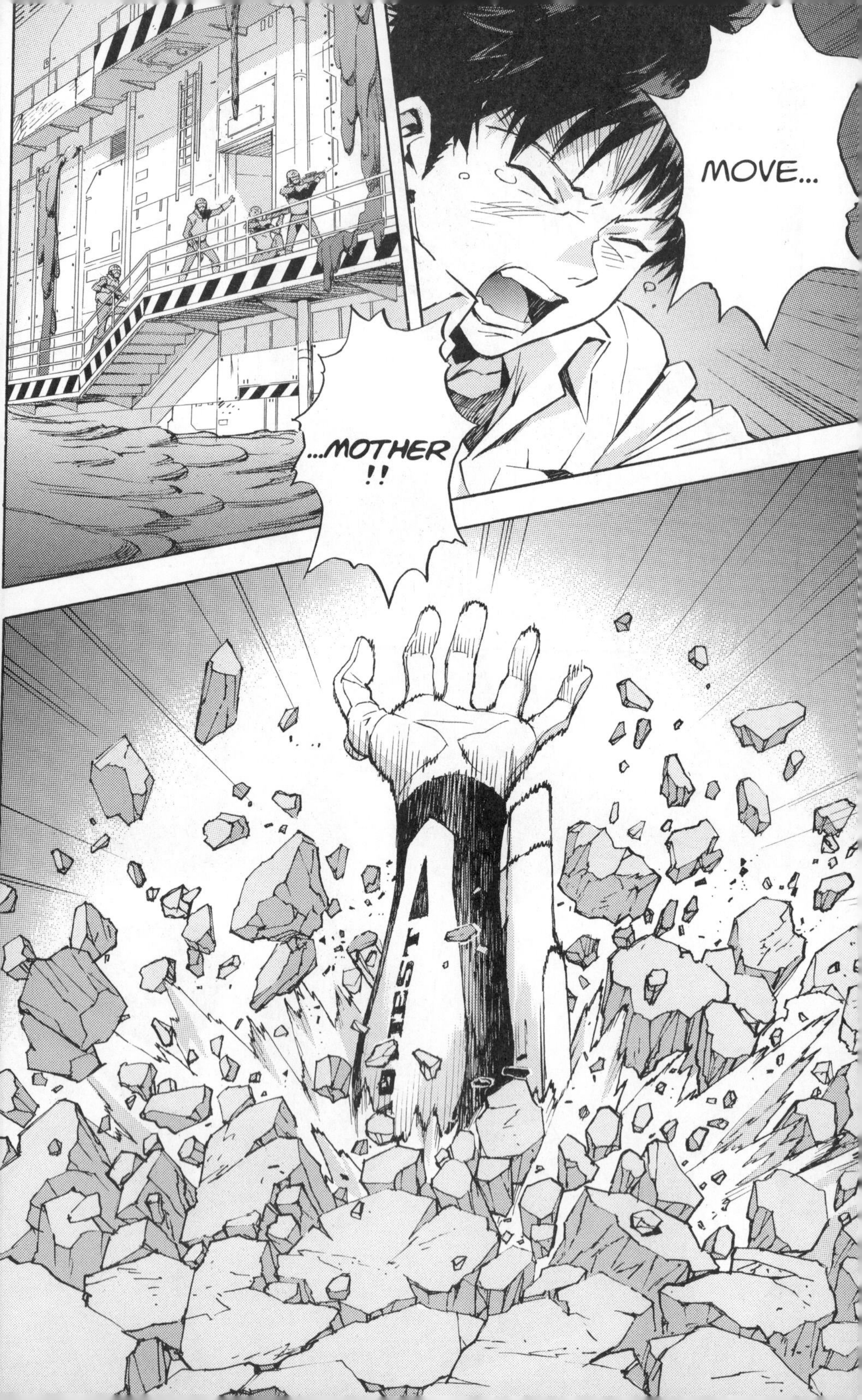
MOVE...
...MOTHER !!

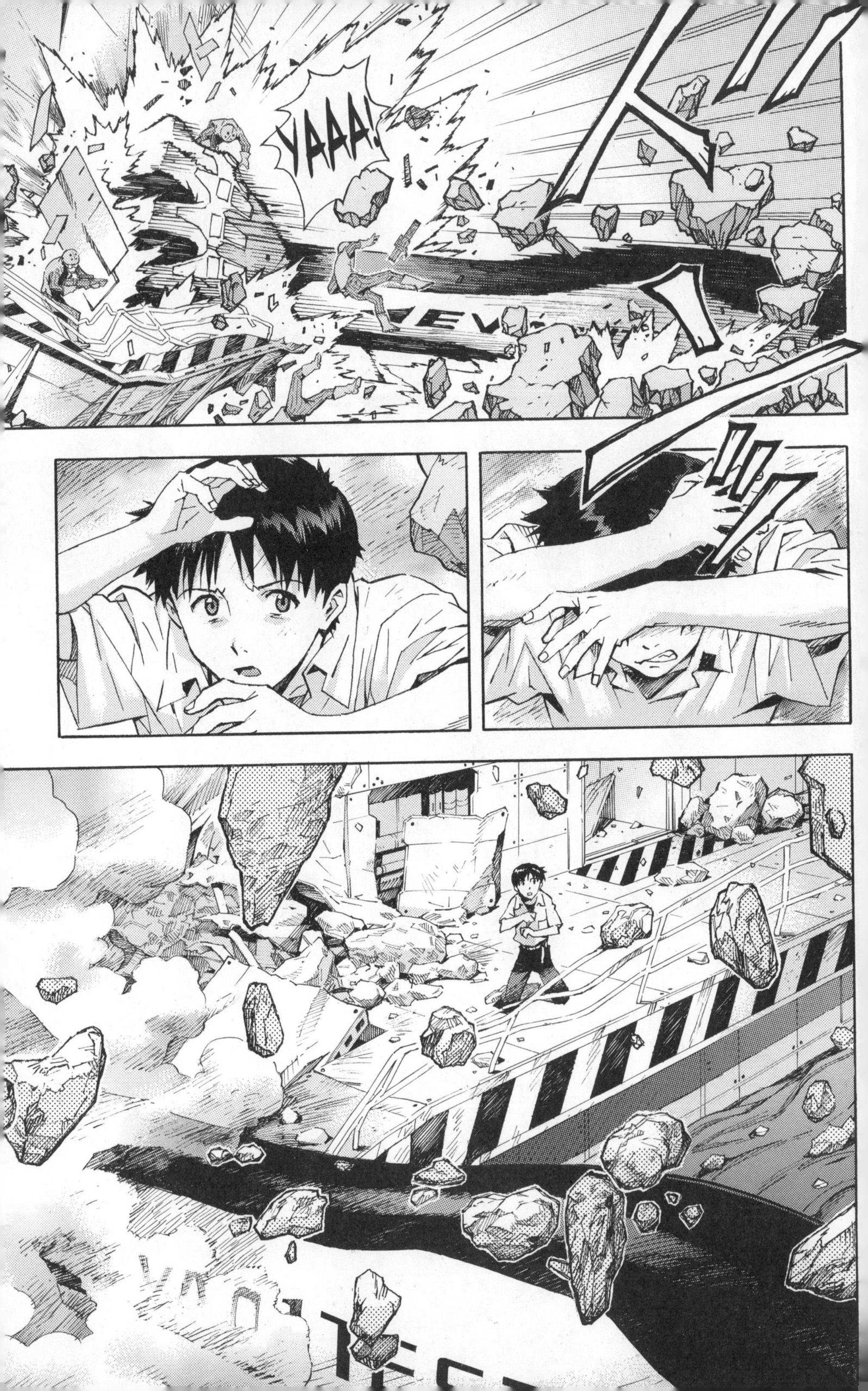
YAAA!

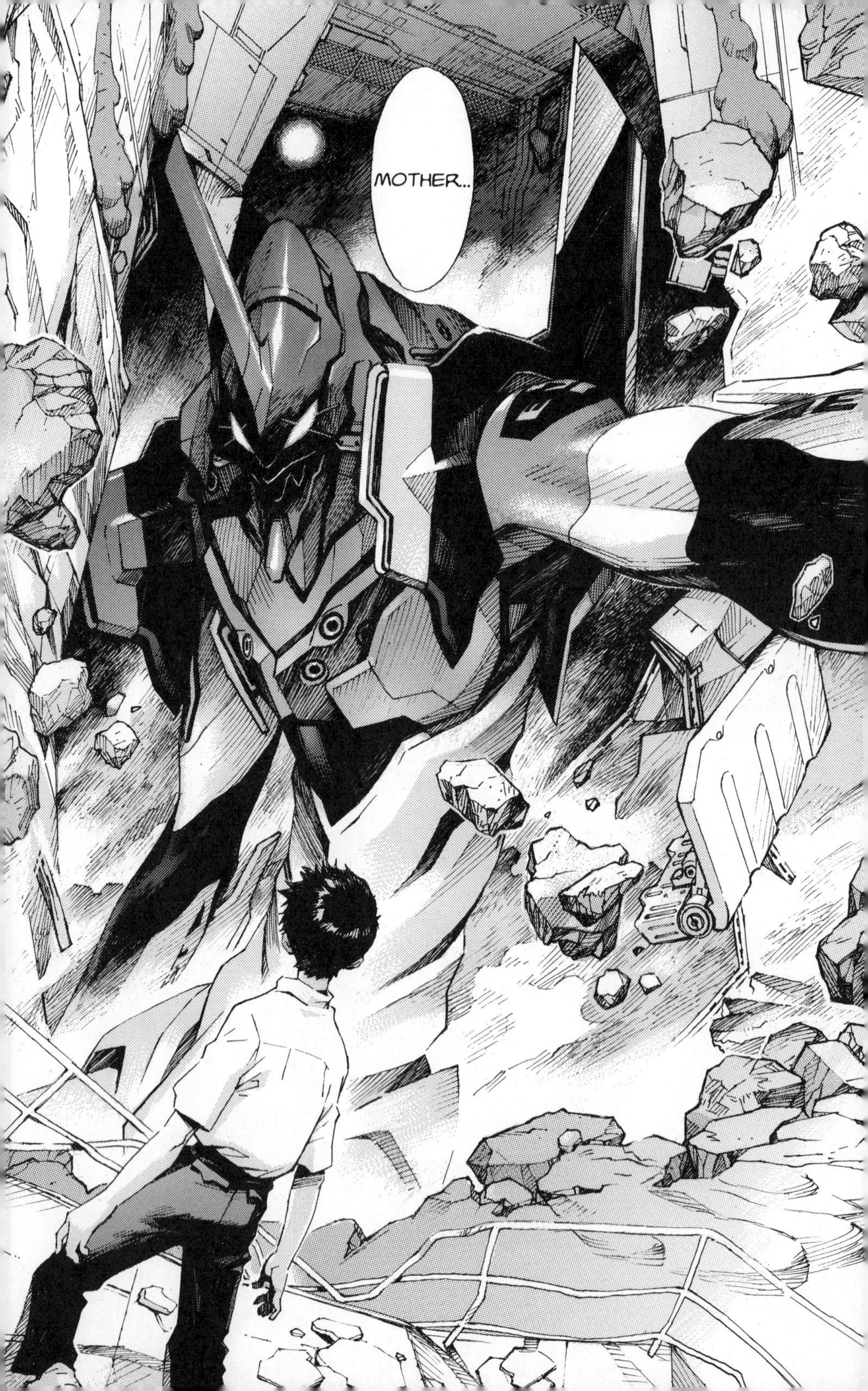
MOTHER...

YOSHIYUKI SADAMOTO

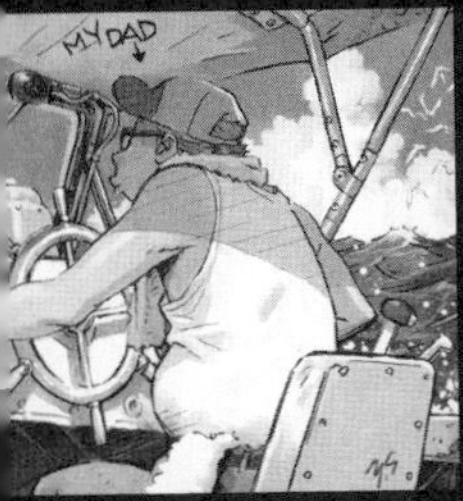
MY DAD

WRITER AND ARTIST

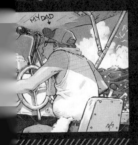

They say children don't choose their parents, but luckily my father was someone I respected. One minus, though, was that he died young and made my mother sad.

If I think about it, I always put myself in Shinji's emotional state when I draw the rough layouts, but I've got a son who's in high school, so I'm like Gendo. I can't emit an A.T. field, but when it comes to selfishness...(^_^)

VOICE ACTORS TIFFANY GRANT
AND
YUKO MIYAMURA

REFLECT ON THEIR MOST FAMOUS ROLES

Series Editor's note: This volume of the manga sees the return to action of Asuka; the second and most recent of the new Evangelion anime films, You Can (Not) Advance (2009) brings Asuka back as well.

Volume 4 of the manga featured an essay by Asuka's Japanese voice actress, Yuko Miyamura, written in 1997, when the Evangelion phenomenon was still young. But Asuka remains an iconic character even in the incredible future year of 2011 and, with her recent revival in both the anime and manga, I thought now might be an appropriate time to follow up—this time, with Asuka's English-language voice actor Tiffany Grant, as well.

It's not a common thing for the Japanese and English actors of an anime character to meet and to become good friends as well, but that's what happened in the case of Yuko and Tiffany, as you will see. My very sincere thanks go to Tiffany Grant, Yuko Miyamura and to Christine Busby, who translated Ms. Miyamura's remarks.

-Carl Gustav Horn

TIFFANY GRANT

Some time in early 1998, Matt Greenfield encouraged me to write an essay defending Asuka from her critics. I did, and you can read it on my website. At that point, as I recall, about half of the *Eva* TV series had been released on home video (two episodes per VHS about every other month for around $30).

Please keep in mind that I had only recently finished recording the TV series. There was as yet no English release of *Death & Rebirth*, *End of Evangelion*, *Director's Cut Platinum Edition*, and there most definitely were no proposed live-action or "Rebuild" films.

Back in 1998, I had not yet read any of Sadamoto's manga. Having now read all of it, I was very excited to be able to participate in this project. One especially impactful moment I experienced reading Sadamoto's books was Yuko Miyamura's own essay in volume 4, which touched me deeply. When we first met, I had her autograph it for me!

For this volume, Carl thought it might be interesting if I shared with you how my thoughts about Asuka have evolved over these many years.

First, my perspective on Asuka was changed dramatically by working on *EoE* and even more so by the Director's Cut footage. I said, "If these scenes had been in the TV show to begin with, people would've had a lot more sympathy for Asuka."

But the main thing that has happened since 1998 is that *Neon Genesis Evangelion* has become an international phenomenon. When I started recording this loud, assertive character that often swore in German, I knew I was having a great time with the role and that it was enjoyable for me as an actor. There was no way any of us could've known then what lay in store. *Eva* became cult phenomenon.

The enormous popularity of *Eva* is, I fully understand, the primary reason I get invited to conventions around the world. In this way alone, my association with Asuka has forever altered my life.

But I also feel something deeper than the obvious frequent flyer miles is at work here. For several years I actually denied that I was anything like Asuka—a period I refer to as my "I Am Not Spock" phase. I wrote "In Defense of Asuka" during that time.

Once I fully embraced my "inner Asuka," I realized the many ways that I related to this complex, flawed character. In the past twelve years, I feel I have become even closer to Asuka emotionally.

I think Shinji behaves in the way that most of us actually would react, but I believe we all wish we were a little more like Asuka—speak your mind, consequences be damned! I find that I don't just defend Asuka now, I actually admire her. I don't know how I'll feel in another twelve years, but if you don't like Asuka just a little bit, I have only one thing to say: What are you—stupid?

YUKO MIYAMURA

To be honest, a long time ago I used to hate Asuka and *Evangelion*.

If I were to comment using Asuka's words I would say,"I hate, I hate, I hate EVERYBODY!"

As to why I felt this way, well, I think the best way to describe it is to say that it was close to the feeling of being bullied. If a person has been bullied, would they want to remember it? I don't think they would.

Acting the part of Asuka was lots of fun at first. However, as Asuka started to mentally break down, acting her become quite tough.

The part that I disliked the most was during the scene when Asuka finally understood the meaning of the A.T. field. Just when she was able to mentally become strong and confident again, she was attacked by the mass-produced units and brutalized. That time in the film is really cool and there are lots of characters that I like in it. For Asuka on the other hand, it's the worst situation ever.

Furthermore, after that scene, she is strangled by Shinji with such apathy, and that's where the series ends. The mass-produced units, the Angels, their destiny; it just ends with all of them being defeated.

I closed the Asuka inside of me deep within my heart. While she was inside there, I didn't really like to bring her out. Remembering my complex feelings for Asuka and *Evangelion* was quite hard for me, and I didn't like it.

This all changed when I first met and talked to Asuka's English voice actor, Tiffany. Tiffany, as another person who acted as Asuka, was the only one who could understand the pain that I felt acting as Asuka. We both understood all the difficult emotions about Asuka and her complex personality, and we talked about many things. After this the feelings within me toward Asuka became more caring and understanding.

Even though at first I felt anger and dislike for Asuka, I now hold her close to my heart and I think of her like a daughter. Up until then Asuka had to deal with all the pain, sadness and sorrow by herself. Now it's different—I'm with her.

Today I'm a mother myself and I'm raising my own daughter. The feelings I have for my child are similar to what I feel for Asuka. Even though it's different from my own real-life situation, Asuka is an important existence to me and I feel that I am able to accept her into my life.

What destiny lies ahead for Asuka?

Furthermore, what choice will she make?

Whatever happens I will accept everything about Asuka. I will cheer her on because I feel I am close to her. No matter what, I will defend Asuka.

It has been about ten years since the time when the other units took Asuka and Shinji and tried to strangle her. Now, a new *Evangelion* has begun!

In the new movies, the once-complex Asuka is now happier. I'm excited to see how Asuka stands and faces her destiny in the new movies compared to Asuka's fate from ten years ago of being defeated.

If I were to say a comment in the new movie in Asuka's words it would be "You hurt my pride...I'LL GIVE IT BACK TO YOU TEN TIMES WORSE." I like this confident side of Asuka.

Whatever becomes of Asuka in the world of *Eva*, I will always love Asuka the most!

Once again, I would like to thank Tiffany, Yuko and Christine. Although it's great to see the friendship between these two voice actors just on a human level, I think it also sets a good example for our two (sometimes struggling) industries themselves—I wonder whether the Japanese and the Western sides wouldn't both benefit from more personal contacts and understanding.

Something Tiffany said took me back to 1998 when I was editing the early parts of this manga. But at the time I was also an editor writing about anime at VIZ Media's Animerica *magazine, and the $30 Tiffany mentions for two episodes was pretty standard for the whole U.S. anime industry, not just the Evangelion release. So that meant you'd have to pay $390 for the whole series (in late-'90s dollars; with inflation that'd be more like $500 today). And that was for VHS format, with all its built-in limitations compared to DVD—no special features, no chapter skipping, no separate audio or subtitle tracks (if you wanted dubbed or subtitled, you had to buy a whole different set of tapes) and of course, lesser video and audio quality. It's something to think about next time a U.S. anime DVD release seems expensive...^_^*

-Carl Gustav Horn

CRIPT

I remember the first time I saw episode 24 of the anime. It was the same way I saw all of the series; there used to be this place in the Kintetsu Building in San Francisco's Japantown, downstairs from Kinokuniya, that would rent of tapes of new shows recorded off Japanese TV. How it worked was, every fourth episode, someone in Japan would airmail off another tape to the store. Every fourth one, because four episodes were what you could fit on VHS at normal speed (this was 1996, an age when the Internet brought riches instead of ruin). And being airmail, it got there in a few days—meaning that if you rented it as soon as it came in, for a day or two you would be caught up with the Japanese audience. With *Neon Genesis Evangelion*, which seemed to raise the stakes not only for itself but for television anime with every fourth episode, you were watching it in real time. And 24 divided by six tapes is, of course, four—the number of death, as even a Japanese dropout such as myself knows. They teach you that the first week.

So there we all were, in the middle of March—just me, maybe a few dozen other *gaijin* with their own hook-ups, and several million Japanese, watching Kaworu's twelve-minute life and one-minute death. I remember my impressions during that one minute going something like this: the first twenty seconds: all right, this is the dramatic pause...the tension is building...any moment it will; the next twenty seconds: for God's sake, it's called animation... hey, I bet the storyboards for this didn't take too long to draw...I can practically see the budget savings adding up, it's like watching the meter on an idling taxi; and then, oddly enough, breaking through, once again, to admiration in the final twenty: wow, as usual, Anno's got a lot of guts. So presumably, did the hand of Unit-01, a moment later.

I laugh off the death, as no one is able to in *Evangelion's* fiction, where these deaths must be experienced for real. Yet in the manga, Sadamoto draws Shinji with at least a smile, the very narrowest of smiles, as the parting gift to him of Kaworu Nagisa; Tabris, the Angel of Free Will, a name more beautiful than its bearer, which was no mean feat. Stop following me, Shinji had told the stray kitten when they first met in volume 9, I can't take care of you. And then the boy who had

POSTS

not yet introduced himself, other than to say, I'm lost...I was never meant to be in a place like this, picked up the kitten, and with his hands showed what Shinji's choice meant.

This is the point where a certain shrill keening went up; not so much from Shinji, but from some segments of the readership, at Sadamoto's sudden and unprecedented use of shock value, a concept surely as foreign to *Neon Genesis Evangelion* as fan service. He had ruined sweet Kaworu—you know, the sweet Kaworu who came to wipe us out, but kindly offered Shinji the option to kill what he loved instead. But it was a kitten—a kitten, somewhere among the hundreds, thousands, millions, and billions of dead people of *Evangelion's* storyline. I'll bet if we could somehow convince the president to squash a goldfish during his next press conference—I don't know, tell him it's for rush week or something—America would suddenly come to the horrified realization that *oh my God, war means death!!!*

Well, okay, maybe I was a little shocked too, but for different reasons. Like almost every *Evangelion* fan, my own image of Kaworu was shaped by the anime. When Sadamoto has him make his first appearance at the end of volume 7, smiling in his tube to Kiel as Rei did to Gendo, it looks as if he's going to go along lines similar to how Kaworu was treated in the anime: as SEELE's secret child, much as Rei was NERV's, raised in darkness and obedience. Indeed in both versions, the two pilots encounter one another, to show they are very similar—but not the same. In the anime, Kaworu expresses the very interest in intimacy and connection that Rei as yet can barely articulate; yet both maintain an etherealness about them. Suddenly, Sadamoto gives us this *kichiku-zeme...*

You know, if I remember right, regardless of whether in the anime Kaworu liked Shinji or loved Shinji, at no point did Kaworu actually promise that whatever he felt for him would make Shinji happy. It was a natural thing for Shinji to assume (an ass out of you and me both, see, and there you've got your *doujishi* again) of course, from this evidently beautiful, apparently kind person who said he loved him and said he understood him. What Kaworu understood, though, was how fragile Shinji's heart was. It fascinated him, much as one might wonder at an object of fine crystal. And when you are enchanted by such a thing, your wish is not that it be transformed and made more able to endure, its latticework replaced by steel—or even the simple, tough fiber of a human heart, the kind Misato and Kaji had, surviving a childhood as bad as the Children's to find some kind of happiness, some kind of resilience.

There's nothing sadistic or callous about the way the anime Kaworu treats Shinji; it's just that, being an Angel, he has a little difficulty understanding the human perspective—and that it's not just about he viewed Shinji, but how Shinji viewed him. This is where the manga Kaworu, Sadamoto's Kaworu, shows his difference, and where Sadamoto confirms the value of his interpretation. For various crazy gaijin reasons—I dunno, maybe because his death takes place before a giant freaking cross to which a being is nailed and which previously had an artifact called the Spear of Longinus thrust into its side—many Eva fans around the world discussed the idea of Kaworu as a quasi-Christ figure. The orthodox image of Christ was that he was a sinless being, God become man, who permitted himself to suffer for the redemption of sinners. A sacrificial lamb—but that itself is an interesting image...after all, a lamb is something that humans understand much as Kaworu "understood" Shinji; that is, with an assigned significance...

But the suffering of mankind day to day is far more than just having to walk around donkey- and dateless (actually, fig-less; Matthew 21:19), let alone the scourge and the nail—it's the state of being impure, of sinning itself. When Christ was said to have been both divine and human, the theologians mean human like Adam was before he ate of the tree of knowledge of good and evil, as referenced in the ugly-ass new logos for NERV and SEELE seen in *Rebuild of Evangelion*. Adam before the fall, in other words. But that's not being a human, the way actual human beings are. What an actual human would experience, in even a short life, is the state of being a sinner, which at its least argumentative means harming the innocent. Killing a kitten would probably qualify. And knowing love, not in its divine, Platonic and soft vinyl form, but as something flowing...lukewarm, sticky, and heavy, as Kaworu describes it to Shinji after kissing him. How does it feel to have someone like that take an interest in you? he asks Shinji—because to him, it felt like it was slowly constricting my chest...like I couldn't breathe. It gave me the creeps.

The creeps? The anime Kaworu would have never gotten "the creeps." But then, the anime Kaworu doesn't partake of humanity the way Sadamoto's does. He is indeed SEELE's child, raised in secret, but his reflection in NERV is not Rei, but Shinji, from whom far more secrets were kept. I think one reason some anime Shinji x Kaworu shippers might not like Sadamoto's version is because it's almost as if he's making fun of fanfic: In this version of the story, Kaworu enters combat with Rei and Shinji before the events of Episode 24. Exposed to Rei's longing for Shinji during battle, Kaworu angers Shinji by calling her a fool, yet Shinji seeks sanctuary in Kaworu's room afterwards. Kaworu's confusion over his feelings leads to a new level of intimacy between them, but Shinji slaps Kaworu's caressing hand away: "Guys don't like guys!" "Why do you hate me so much?" demands the tousle-headed Angel...I mean, one expects the actual creator to keep a certain reserve...

And then. As you have read on page 171, Sadamoto, in the best traditions of *Evangelion*, flips over his trump card. Just as Anno once did with Misato and Shinji, it turns out he wasn't bluffing, and it wasn't fan service; he found that he was actually trying to feel something for Kaworu Nagisa as an artist. As he has done all along with *Neon Genesis Evangelion*, Sadamoto is making an effort to express the story in way that is convincing to him, as *Evangelion's* co-creator, an approach that is often the equal and opposite of Anno's. Whereas Anno gave of his persona in making the anime, Sadamoto is taking it into his person. Whereas the anime projected a 35-year-old's thoughts on a 14-year-old named Shinji Ikari. Go back and read his interview in volume 2, which isn't the thoughts of a guy whose involvement was simply sketching out the designs. "Unless I get into Shinji's head," said Sadamoto, "I can't draw the manga...I have to empathize with the character before I can draw."

And what his empathy ends up giving us is something more mutual than the anime did between Shinji and Kaworu. Just as Sadamoto had Shinji know ahead of time that Toji was in Eva Unit-03, he prepares an understanding between them—and when the tragedy comes, it is deeper for being complicit: Euangelion loudas.

In volume 10 I recommended that if you wanted to go from wtf to well-that's-fascinating on *Eva*, to check out the forums at evamonkey.com. Since then, it's doubled its registered users from 800 to 1,740 and now contains over 164,000 postings as of August 2008, including lengthy threads on such topics as the domestic political overtones of *Eva* in Japan, whether Rei is made of "particle wave matter," and careful documentation of all appearances of the characters' panties. In short, it seems very close to becoming the kind of collective super-consciousness Kaworu promises us we can evolve into, if we'll just sign that extinction work order. Before you punch your keyboard, however, this site has also undergone a name change from evamonkey.com to evageeks.org; although I wonder perhaps if that change truly symbolizes progress. I'm reminded of Paul Broca's comment that he'd rather be a transformed ape than a degenerate son of Adam.

Evageeks doesn't have too much on this manga (its discussion exists as a thread within the subforum "Everything Else *Evangelion*," sort of the way the Reverend Lovejoy once described Apu's religion as "miscellaneous") despite the fact Sadamoto's version was around before the

anime, and who knows, might still be unfinished when the new films receive the last of their re-release director's cuts. I sometimes feel that in spite of their different creative approaches, Sadamoto is staying closer to what Anno was trying to say than to the idea that *Eva* is a million-piece jigsaw. Even were it true, and you found a way to complete it, it doesn't take a Franz Kafka to point out that you've just spent years assembling a million-piece jigsaw. In case people didn't get it the first time, Anno literally turned the camera back on the theater, and then walked out into the street in *The End of Evangelion*; I remember seeing a fan version of the film that cut this part out as "boring." You've been told many times before, Anno's pointed to the door, but no one had the guts to leave the temple. Perhaps he too gave up after a while and just decided to rebuild it...

I'm not in such a good position to criticize, perhaps, as I, in my best otaku way, delighted in the five years that *Evangelion* was a monthly comic book (that's right, it used to be one—you know, like those things with the staples, color, and really small eyes) in writing its "Dossier" section, which detailed such Eva-soterica as SEELE, LCL, the Spear of Longinus, etc., combining what was known from "canonical" sources—as if this was some kind of church—with speculation couched in a grandiloquent vagueness worthy of that Clinton era (if the comic had arisen during the Bush era, the legal theory would have simply been that everything was canonical if the editor said so).

Most of these "Dossier" articles (the Spear of Longinus one mysteriously went missing, spawning its own mini-conspiracy theory) were reprinted in volumes 5 and 6 of the current graphic novel edition of *Eva*. Volume 7 continued the tradition with a remarkable word-count drawn forth from the mere handful of Biblical verses associated with *Evangelion* (I always sense a certain nervousness when the Bible gets brought up at *Eva* con panels, and it's probably because more than one attendee told their parents they were going to church camp that weekend). And in case the $9.99-a-semester (well, let's be honest, annual) tuition that is the *Evangelion* manga wasn't giving you enough gnosis, volume 8 absolutely dared you to seek out the best of its native criticism, never mind that it was in Japanese; it could hardly be less comprehensible than graduate semiotics.

But, again, go back, *tolle lege*—the most important truths that are likely to ever be revealed about *Evangelion* are in volumes 1 through 4: Anno's statement of attempt; Sadamoto's interview; Yoshitou Asari's statement of attempt; Sadamoto's interview; Yoshitou Asari's anticipation of the pattern the series' critique would take and Megumi Ogata's (who herself considered Sadamoto the co-creator of the character she portrayed), Yuko Miyamura's, and Megumi Hayashibara's confrontation of their roles. What distinguishes all these comments are not just who made them, but that they were within the making of *Evangelion* itself. They lack coolness, detachment, and hindsight, and thus have the kind of meaning for *Eva* you can't type, but which you can make for yourself, the only way it can ever mean anything: in real time, in reality.

-Carl Gustav Horn

P.S. It's interesting that among the events portrayed as part of human beings "hurting one another" on page 32 are the attacks of September 11, 2001, despite the fact that in *Evangelion's* timeline, that date was almost a year after the Second Impact. If I can go Evageeks on you for a moment, it seems somewhat implausible that the conspiracy to attack the World Trade Center would have gone ahead as planned, given that lower Manhattan, like the original Tokyo, would presumably already have been evacuated and underwater thanks to the rapid melting of the Antarctic ice cap. On the other hand, it's part of the official *Evangelion* timeline that the week following the Second Impact saw both the outbreak of an India-Pakistan conflict and the detonation of a nuclear bomb in Tokyo by unknown parties, showing that the human race was still able to take a little time out for war and terrorism despite the fact it was already facing the greatest catastrophe in recorded history. Failing that, one can always say the reference to 9/11 falls under the idea of many possible paths within the Instrumentality (although SEELE seems to favor one of destiny and control, rather than choice and freedom), or simply my favorite explanation for everything, lol editors.

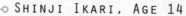

Shinji Ikari, Age 14

Shinji was the "Third Child" chosen to pilot the monstrous Evangelion series; biomechanical combat units developed by the secret UN paramilitary agency known as NERV. Resentful of his father and desperate for his approval, Shinji climbed into the entry plug of Eva Unit-01 to do battle with the enigmatic Angels.

Rei Ayanami, Age 14

Rei is the "First Child" to be chosen to pilot an Evangelion. While piloting Eva Unit-01, she was severely wounded fighting the Angel Sachiel during the same battle in which Shinji arrived at Tokyo-3.

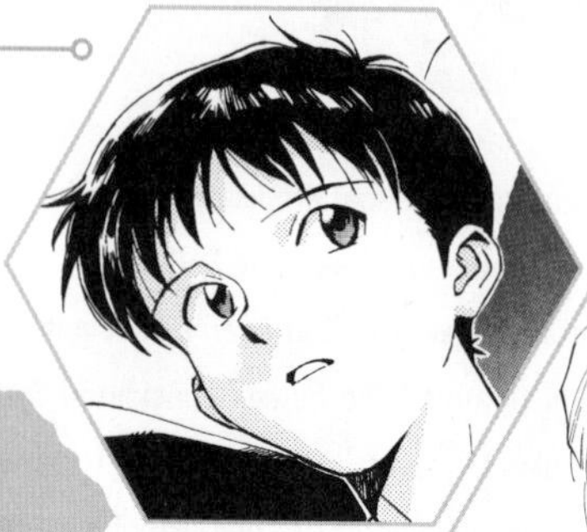

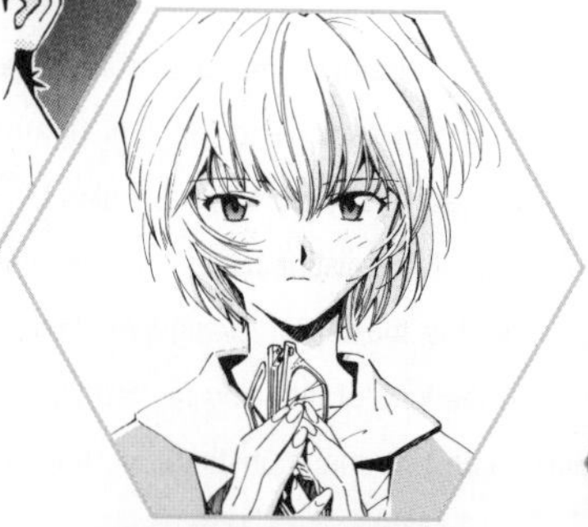

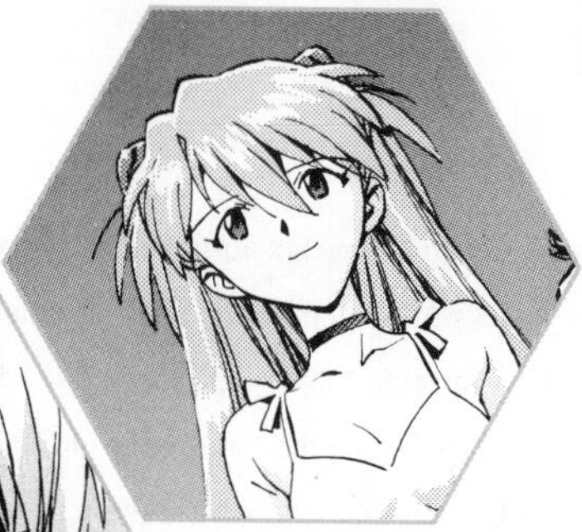

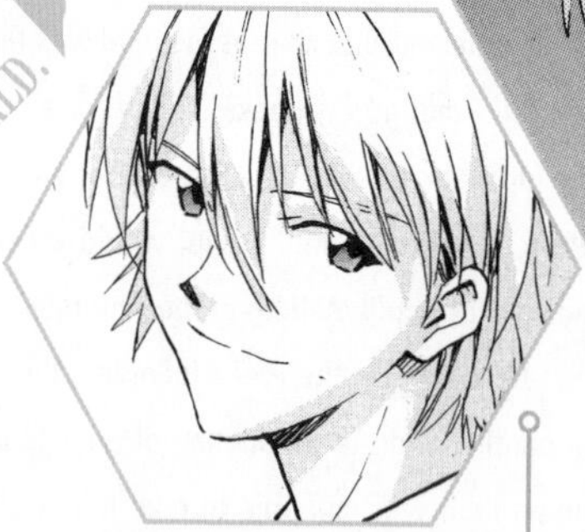

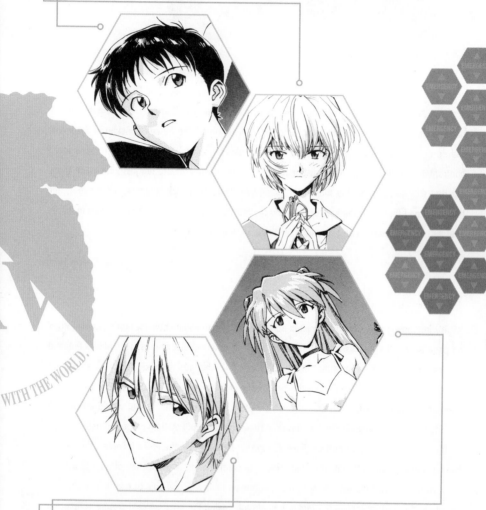

Asuka Langley Soryu, Age 14

A U.S. citizen of mixed Japanese and German ancestry, Asuka is a product of eugenic breeding. Selected to begin training as an Eva pilot from a very early age, Asuka is an excellent fighter, but she struggles with traumatic memories of her childhood.

Kaworu Nagisa, Age 14?

Kaworu introduces himself to NERV as the "Fifth Child." SEELE has sent him to NERV directly, not bothering to go through the Marduk Agency. But as NERV keeps the First Angel, Adam, so has SEELE kept the last, Tabris, the true name and identity of Kaworu Nagisa.

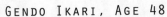

Gendo Ikari, Age 48

Shinji's father. This ruthless and enigmatic man is the guiding force behind the development of NERV's Evangelion system. He is also the man entrusted to carry out the even more secret Instrumentality Project. Gendo was an absent father, leaving Shinji's upbringing to the boy's aunt and uncle.

Misato Katsuragi, Age 29

Captain Katsuragi is the chief tactician for NERV, responsible for planning and guiding Evangelion missions against the Angels. She has forced Shinji to move into her apartment in an attempt to "fix" his "attitude"...

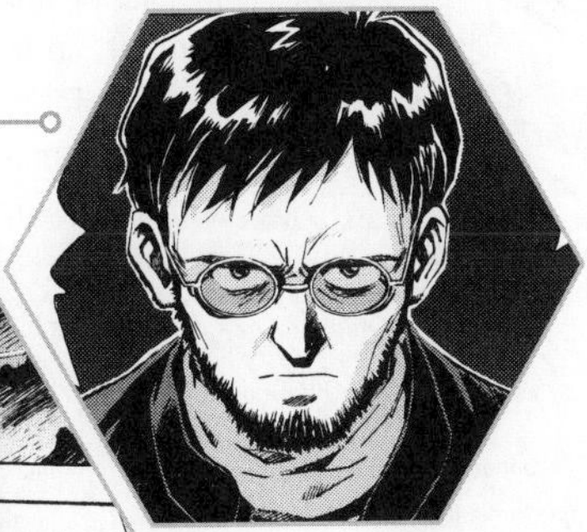

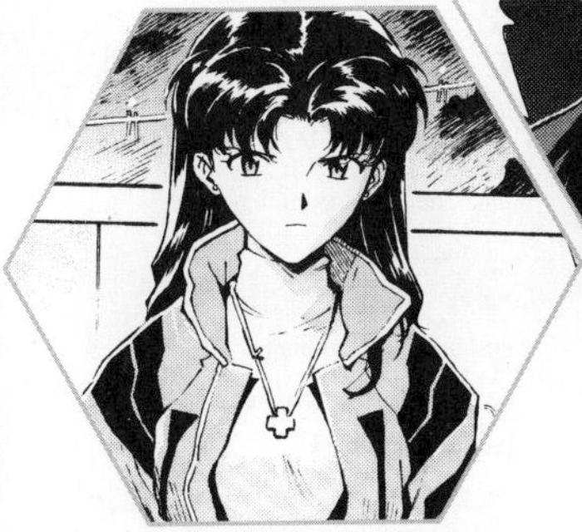

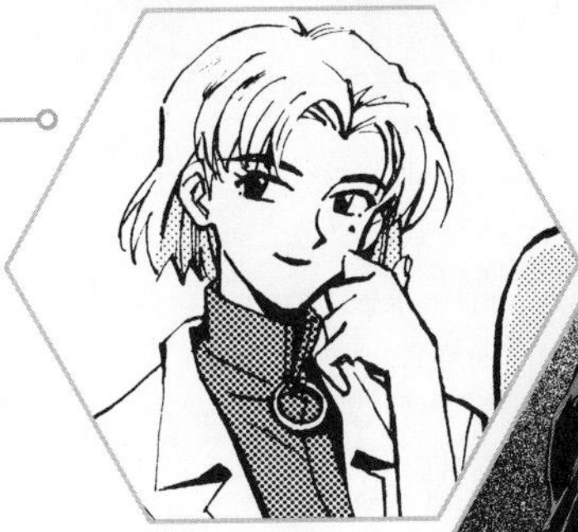

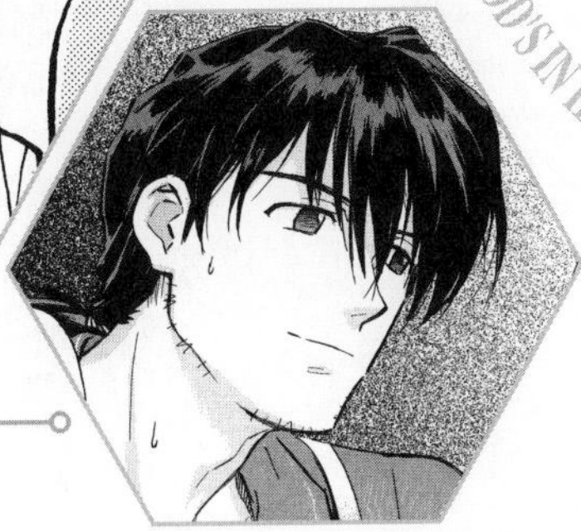

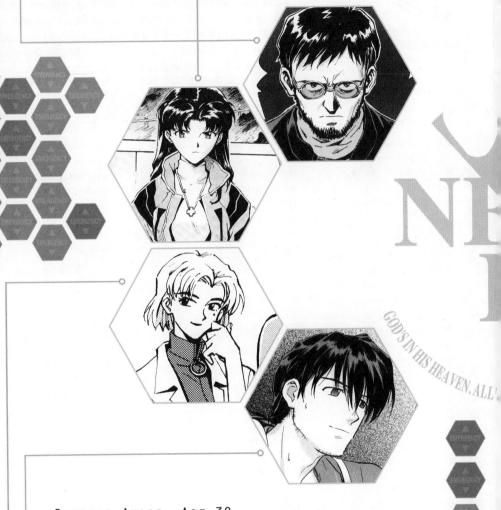

Ritsuko Akagi, Age 30

Technical supervisor for NERV's Project E (Evangelion). Dr. Akagi is a polymath genius who rode the wave of scientific revolution following the cracking of the human genetic code at the end of the twentieth century. Her disciplines include physics, biotechnology and computer science.

Ryoji Kaji, Age 29

Intelligence agent working for NERV, although its senior personnel know that he is also spying for the Japanese Interior Ministry. It has also been suggested that Kaji is secretly working for a third party, SEELE. Despite his handsome, cool exterior, Kaji regards himself as weak, his life haunted by a youthful betrayal.

SOUND EFFECTS GLOSSARY

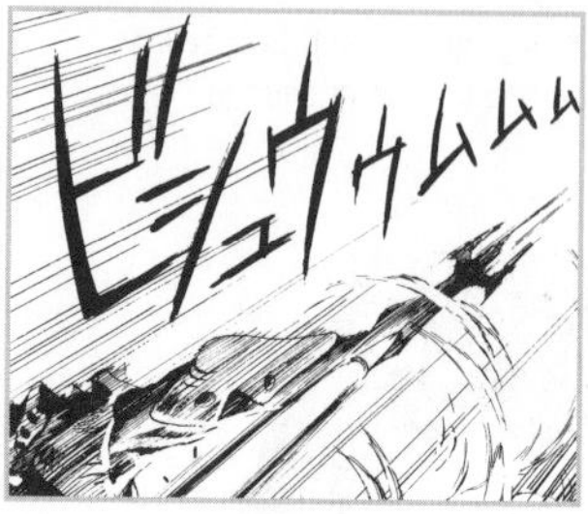
ビジュウウムムム

The sound effects in this 3-in-1 edition of *Neon Genesis Evangelion* have been preserved in their original Japanese format. To avoid additional lettering cluttering up the panels we have provided this list of sound effects (FX). Each FX is listed by page and panel number, so for example 6-5 would mean the FX is on page 6 in panel 5. If there is a third number, it means there is more than one FX in the panel—6-5-1 and 6-5-2 for example. The transliteration is given, followed by the English translation/approximation.

Part 1

8-1	vzuvzuvzuvzuvzuvzu [cracking]
8-3	bikibikibiki [creaking]
9-1	gakun [sudden jerking]
9-2	zudododon [rumbling]
11-1-1	zuvvvvvv [vibrating]
11-1-2	bikibikibikibikibiki [creaking]
11-3	ba [sudden movement]
11-4	dodon [loud thud]
11-5	guku [creaking]
12-1-1	shu [sliding]
12-1-2	bababa [hitting]
12-3	bashu [cutting]
13-2	bushuuu [cutting]
13-3	zudodon [rumbling]
14-2	dororo [thick substance dripping sound, like gloop]
14-4	gugu [fast turning]
14-6	byu [flying through air]
15-1	do [hitting]
15-3	zuvvvv [vibrating]
16-3-1	gugugugu [straining]
16-3-2	biki biki biki [creaking]
17-1	pipipipi [beeping]
17-3	gachagacha [rattling]
20-1	gugu... [straining]
20-3	biki biki [creaking]
20-4	gu... [feel lump in throat]
20-5	biki...[creaking]
22-3-1	biki biki biki [creaking]
22-3-2	zuzuzuzu [rumbling]
22-4-1	zuzuzu... [rumbling]
22-4-2	biki biki [creaking]
22-5-1	biki biki biki [creaking]
22-5-2	zuzuzu [rumbling]
27-2	pata pata [pitter pattering]
28-3	gigigigi [creaking]
28-4	zuhyu... [flying through air]
29-1	doshuuuuu [penetrating]
34-1	bachi [catch snapping open]
34-2	bashuuuuu [exhaust]
34-3	gogogogogogo [door cranking open]
34-4	zuo [rising sound, like whooomf]
35-1	gan [hitting]
35-4	gu [clenched fist]
36-1	gugugugu [straining]
37-1	gan gan gan [thudding footsteps]
37-2	zuhyuru [flying object]
37-3	doshururururu [flying object]
39-2	pau pau [shooting]
42-3	zuzu [rumbling]
42-5	zuzuzu [rumbling]
42-6	boko boko [clickling]
46-3	gashan [crashing]
47-4	doshuuuu [penetrating]
48-3	ga [gasping]
48-4	gugugugu [straining}
48-5	biki biki [creaking]
49-4	gu [groaning]
49-5	gugugugugu [straining]
51-2	byu byu [flying through the air]
52-2	pikyon [releasing lever]
52-3	ga shu... [pulling lever up]
52-4	fiiiiiii [spinning]
53-6	boko bokon [hitting]
54-1	bokon boko boko [hitting]
65-1	gooooooo [blasting]
71-1	gan [hitting]
73-1	dosa [falling]
73-4	hyuu [exhaling]
74-1	babababababababa [propeller]
77-2	pushu [door opening]
79-1	gako [hitting]
95-5-1	vvvvvvvv [phone on vibrate]
95-5-2	vvvvvvvv [phone on vibrate]
96-1-1	vvvvvvvv [phone on vibrate]
96-1-2	vvvvvvvv [phone on vibrate]
96-2	vvvvvvvv [phone on vibrate]
98-2	suuhaa [deep breathing]
101-5	gui [grabbing]
105-4-1	vvvvvvvv [phone on vibrate]
105-4-2	vvvvvvvv [phone on vibrate]
105-5-1	vvvvvvvv [phone on vibrate]
105-5-2	ba [quick grabbing]
116-2	shu [door closing]
116-3	ka ka [sound of footsteps]
116-4	dosa [falling into chair]
119-4	pushun [door closing shut]
120-2	basa [pages fanning out as it hits the floor]
121-1-1	ka [pecking]
121-1-2	ka [pecking]
126-3	shururu [twirling]
126-4	basa [falling to ground]
128-4	mishu [crushing]
128-5	mishu mishu [crushing]
150-3	pipi [beeping]
150-4	pii [beeping]
154-1	zuuuuuuun [door sliding closed]

154-2	gogon [door closing]
155-1	kashon [turning on lights]
161-1	pi [beeping]
165-5	fura [staggering]
169-2	gobobo [crumbling]
173-1	aaaaaa [screaming]

Part 2

195-2	pii [beeping]
196-3	pii [beeping]
205-5	kashan [door closing]
224-2	bii bii bii [beeping]
229-1	gagon [machine movement]
229-2	gagon [machine movement]
229-3	gagon [machine movement]
230-4/5	bagaaaaaaan [crashing through]
234-2	ga [hitting]
234-3	zugogogogogogogo [descending fast]
237-1	gashiiiin [clashing]
237-2-1	gigigi [creaking]
237-2-2	gigi [creaking]
238-2	jyakin [metal hitting]
238-5	ga [sudden draw]
239-1	bakin [piercing metal]
239-2	bachichiiiin [metal hitting and reverberating]
241-1	gyarin [snapping off metal]
242-1	bakiiiin [metal hitting A.T. Field]
246-2	do [stabbing chest]
247-3	doshu [stabbing neck]
247-4	bushuuuuu [hitting]
249-6	zuzun [heavy vibration]
250-1	zuzuzuzuzu [heavy vibration]
254-1	gakun [thrust forward]
255-4	kashan [door closing]
259-3	zuzun [slipping]
259-4	goba [falling against door]
260-1	bagaaaa [door battered down]
260-2	bashaaaa [falling into water]
264-4	gu [clenching fist]
265-1	zu [quickly sliding foot across void]
272-2	zuzuzuzun [vibration]
288-1	vun [power restored to monitor]
291-1	konkon [knocking]
294-2	kue [happy cooing]
303-6-1	gogon [heavy vibration]
303-6-2	gachan [parking lift locking into place]
305-1	gacha [car door closing]
305-4	gogon [double doors closing]
314-5	gui [grabbing]
316-4	kyaaaaaa [screaming]
319-1	gohon gohon [coughing]
320-3-1	bashu… [air moving from door swiftly closing]
320-3-2	ban [door slamming]
324-2	zuzu… [sliding]
326-1	gooooooooon [resonating hum]
326-2	kacha kacha [typing]
326-3	kacha kacha [typing]
328-1	pipipipipipipipipi [beeping]
328-3	ba [sudden reach for gun]
328-6	fu [exhaling in relief]
329-2	bi bi bi [beeping]
329-3	zawa zawa zawa [voices in control room]
332-2	basa [letting hair down]
333-4-1	bi [beeping]
333-4-2	gashan [arrival of lift]
336-5	Graffiti: Ikari no bakayaroo ["Ikari, you bastard"]
336-6	pipipipipi [beeping]
336-7	pii [beeping]
338-5	miin miin miin [cicadas chirping]
339-1	miin miin miin miin [cicadas chirping]
339-3	gacha [slamming down field phone]
339-5	kiiii [jet engines]
340-1	iiiiiiin [jet engines]
340-2	doshu doshu doshu [shooting missiles]
340-4	bonon bo [explosions]
341-1	gogogogogogogogogo [rumble of tanks]
341-2	gyari gyari gyari [rotation of turrets]
341-3	don don [guns firing]
341-4	shubababababa [rocket launcher firing]
342-1/2	kyuba [explosion]
342-2	bii bii bii [beeping]
342-3	bii bii [beeping]
344-4/5	hui hui hui [alarm]
346-1	dodoon [explosions]
346-2	zuzuuu…n [reverberation]
347-1	gogogogogogogogo [doors opening]
347-3	dadadadada [running]
348-3	gang on [shells hitting]
348-5	don [explosion]

Part 3

361-4	don dodon [explosions]
361-5	zudooon [heavy collision]
362-1	dodooon [explosion]
362-3	pan papa papapan [gunshots]
363-2	shuba [firing rocket launcher]
363-3	dogaan [explosion]
364-1	zuhyuuuuu [aircraft humming]
364-5	vu vooon [shooting]
365-1	gigigigi [doors sliding]
365-2	gashan gashan [doors closing]
365-3	dooon [explosions]
365-4	fii fii [alarms]
368-5	tapapapapapapapa [machinegun fire]
369-1	tatatatata [machinegun fire]
369-2	bufoooo [flamethrower]
369-3	dogoaan [explosion]
370-5	bashu [burst of energy]
370-6	go [lurching upward]
371-1	bashuuuu [shooting upward]
371-2	zuzuzuzuzuzu [sliding]
372-2	bun [image appearing]
373-2	gata [standing up]
374-6	zu zuzu [dragging]
375-4	papa [gunshots]
376-4	bashuuuu [injecting liquid]
376-5	dodododo [liquid pouring in]
377-1	dodododo [liquid pouring in]
377-2	kashon [ramming in clip]
377-3	basha [cocking pistol]
378-1-1	zudodododo [distant fighting]
378-1-2	tan tan [gunshots]
379-4	jaki [pointing weapon]
380-3	gu [pressing]
380-5	gugu [pulling trigger]
381-1	pan pan [gunshots]
381-5	dosa [falling]
386-4	papapapapa [machinegun fire]
388-2	pappan [gunshots]
388-3	pan [gunshot]
388-4	doza [falling]
389-5	gui [pulling]
393-4	gui [pulling]
399-2	dakyuun [bullet ricocheting]
401-4-1	papapapa [machinegun fire]

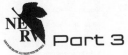

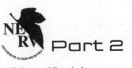

488-2/3	zudododododododo [running and jumping]	
490-1	zan [landing]	
491-1	gishi mishishi shin mishi [slowly breaking]	
491-2/3	bakin [snapping]	
492-2/3	kan kan kan kan kan [footsteps]	
493-3	bakin kin [bullets striking]	
493-3/4	pan [gunshot]	
493-4-1	gakin [bullet striking]	
493-4-2	kan [bullet striking]	
493-4-3	dakyun [shooting]	
494-1-1	bakin [bullet striking]	
494-1-2	papapa [machinegun fire]	
494-2-1	kan [bullet striking]	
494-2-2	bashu [door closing]	
494-2-3	kin [bullet striking]	
495-4	pi [beep]	
495-5	bashu [door opening]	
497-2	gashan [grabbing wire mesh]	
502-4	kyubobon [explosion]	
503-1	gashan [pushing Shinji against the wire]	
504-3/4	bashan [partition moving aside]	
506-1	basha [door closing]	
509-1	zan [slamming opponent down]	
509-5	don [stabbing]	
511-2	gacha [leveling weapons]	
513-1	don [explosion]	
513-2	zuzuuun [rumbling]	
514-2	guonn [elevator moving]	
514-5	gofa [door opening]	
516-2	don [hitting]	
517-5	dozun [falling]	
517-5/6	dadan [explosion]	
519-1	gigigigi [struggling]	
520-3	daaan [landing]	
520-4	zaza [rolling aside]	
521-1	zudan [getting up]	
522-1	gakiiiin [blades clashing]	
523-1-1	gakin [blades clashing]	
523-1-2	doka [blades clashing]	
523-1-3	bakin [blades clashing]	
523-2	go [hitting]	
524-1	bushuu [liquid squirting]	
524-3	pipipipipipipi [beeping]	
529-1	don [hitting]	

442-2	dun [blast]	
443-3/4	zabaaaaa [splash]	
445-3/4	bamu [closing door]	
445-5	kyurururu [starting engine]	
450-2-1	gaa [static]	
450-2-2	pii [beep]	
451-2	doshu doshu doshu [firing missiles]	
452-1	dodododon [explosions]	
453-1	dogaaaa [crashing]	
453-2	dovooa [explosion]	
455-2	hyururururu [missiles flying]	
456-1	dodododododo [explosions]	
457-4	zuka [landing]	
458-1	dododoon [smashing]	
458-2	shuoooo [missile flying]	
459-1	zuka [missile hitting]	
460-1	dokoo [hitting the missile]	
460-2	zuvooa [explosions]	
464-1/2	shubabababa [aircraft shooting]	
465-2	hyu hyu hyu [explosives flying toward cable]	
465-3-1	zuga [explosion]	
465-3-2	bachichi [energy crackling]	
466-1	bii [beep]	
466-4	bafo [cable separating]	
466-7	gu [gripping]	
467-1	shubobobo [shooting]	
467-2	kyubo kyubobon [explosions]	
467-5	buo [swinging arm]	
468-1	kyubobobon [explosions]	
469-1	dosha [hitting]	
469-5	buo [swinging aircraft]	
470-1	doshaa [hitting]	
470-2	shubababab a [firing missiles]	
472-3/4	doguwashaa [smashing]	
473-1/2	zudoooooo [explosion]	
473-4	guoooooo [roar overhead]	
475-1/2	goooooooooo [roar of aircraft]	
475-3	zuhyu [head appearing]	
476-2/3	bashun [retracting]	
477-1	ba ba ba [wings opening]	
480-1-1	papan [gunshots]	
480-1-2	tatatatata [machinegun fire]	
481-2	zun [landing]	
481-4/5	shuooo [retracting wings]	
484-1	gyakikikiki [tires screeching]	
484-2	don [hitting the wall]	
484-3-1	shuu [steam]	
484-3-2	bako [opening door]	
487-3	gokun [lurching forward]	

401-4-2	topapapa [machinegun fire]	
402-1	pan pa pan [gunshots]	
404-1-1	topapapaa [machinegun fire]	
404-1-2	tatata [machinegun fire]	
404-2	gacha [loading weapon]	
405-3	doka [kicking]	
406-1	su [pulling out pistol]	
406-3	tan [gunshot]	
406-6	pan pan pan [gunshots]	
407-1	zuzu [sliding]	
407-2	dosa [falling]	
410-1	gara [opening drawer]	
411-1	boooon [explosion]	
412-1	tapapapapa tapapapapapa [machinegun fire]	
412-2-1	bachun [bullet striking]	
412-2-2	kiiin [bullet striking]	
412-3-1	kyun [bullet striking]	
412-3-2	bachiin [bullet striking]	
412-4	chuiin [bullet striking]	
413-4	bachun [bullet striking]	
414-1-1	zaa [static]	
414-1-2	pii [beep]	
417-3	pashi [slapping]	
419-1-1	pa papa pa [gunshots]	
419-1-2	tatatatata [machinegun fire]	
419-2-1	tatata [machinegun fire]	
419-2-2	papapapa [machinegun fire]	
420-1	kyun kyun [bullets whizzing by]	
420-2	pappapa [gunshots]	
420-3	pa papa papan [gunshots]	
423-1/4	dobaaaaa [bomb blast]	
423-4/5	zuzuzuzuzu [rumbling]	
424-1/2	zudododododo [rumbling]	
426-1/2	zudododododododododododo [rumbling]	
427-1	dododo dododdo [blasts striking]	
428-1	zuzun [distant explosion]	
428-3	zuzun [distant explosion]	
429-3	gachi gachi [pulling trigger]	
436-2	bon bon bon [firing weapons]	
436-3	zuboboooon [explosions]	
437-2-1	kyuba [explosion]	
437-2-2	bobon [explosion]	
438-1-1	gogon [explosions gripping Unit-02]	
438-1-2	ga [explosions gripping Unit-02]	
438-1-3	gago [explosions gripping Unit-02]	
438-2	gogon [bomb hitting Unit-02]	
438-3	kyuba [explosion]	

GOD'S IN HIS HEAVEN. ALL'S RIGHT WITH THE WORLD.

Hey! You're Reading in the Wrong Direction!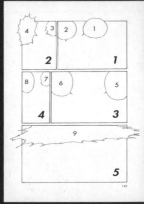

This is the **end** of this graphic novel!

To properly enjoy this VIZ graphic novel, please turn it around and begin reading from **right to left.** Unlike English, Japanese is read right to left, so Japanese comics are read in reverse order from the way English comics are typically read.

Follow the action this way

This book has been printed in the original Japanese format in order to preserve the orientation of the original artwork. Have fun with it!